Readings on Human Nature

Readings on Human Nature

edited by Peter Loptson

broadview press

Canadian Cataloguing in Publication Data

Readings on human nature

Includes bibliographical references.
ISBN 1-55111-156-X

1. Philosophical anthropology I. Loptson, Peter.

BD450.R34 1998   128   C98-930078-1

Broadview Press
Post Office Box 1243, Peterborough, Ontario, Canada K9J 7H5

in the United States of America:
3576 California Road, Orchard Park, NY 14127

in the United Kingdom:
B.R.A.D. Book Representation & Distribution Ltd.,
244A, London Road, Hadleigh, Essex SS7 2DE

Broadview Press gratefully acknowledges the support of the the Ontario Arts Council and the Ministry of Canadian Heritage.

Book design and composition by George Kirkpatrick

PRINTED IN CANADA

CONTENTS

Introduction

I ANCIENT AND EARLY MODERN VIEWS OF HUMAN NATURE

1. Plato, *Republic* [3]
2. Aristotle, *Nicomachean Ethics* [12]; *Politics* [18]
3. René Descartes, *Principles of Philosophy* [24]
4. François de La Rochefoucauld, *Maxims* [27]
5. Earl of Rochester, *A Satyre Against Mankind* [30]

II CHRISTIAN VIEWS OF HUMAN NATURE

6. St. Augustine, *Confessions* [35]; *On Free Choice of the Will* [51]
7. St. Thomas Aquinas, *On the Virtues in General* [56]; *On Free Choice* [60]
8. Martin Luther, *The Freedom of a Christian* [63]
9. John Locke, *The Reasonableness of Christianity* [77]; *The Second Treatise of* (civil) *Government* [78]; *A Letter Concerning Toleration* [79]
10. Joseph Butler, *Fifteen Sermons* [84]
11. Immanuel Kant, *Religion Within the Limits of Reason Alone* [99]
12. Dietrich Bonhoeffer, *A Testament to Freedom* [114]

III LIBERALISM

13. Immanuel Kant, *An Answer to the Question: What is Enlightenment?* [121]
14. Antoine-Nicolas de Condorcet, *Sketch for a Historical Picture of the Progress of the Human Mind* [125]
15. Wilhelm von Humboldt, *The Limits of State Action* [129]
16. J.S. Mill, *On Liberty* [139]; *Utilitarianism* [148]
17. L.T. Hobhouse, *Liberalism* [150]
18. John Rawls, *Political Liberalism* [161]

IV CONSERVATIVE INDIVIDUALISM

19. Niccolò Machiavelli, *The Prince* [169]
20. Thomas Hobbes, *Leviathan* [173]
21. James Boswell, The *Life of Dr. Johnson* [177]; Samuel Johnson, *The Rambler* [178]; *The Idler* [180]

22. Simone Weil, *The Need for Roots* [181]
23. Ayn Rand, *For the New Intellectual* [196]
24. Michael Oakeshott, *Rationalism in Politics* [202]

V DIALECTICAL THEORIES OF HUMAN NATURE

25. Jean-Jacques Rousseau, *Discourse on the Origins of Inequality* [219]
26. G.W.F. Hegel, *Phenomenology of Mind* [241]; *Philosophy of Right* [246]
27. Karl Marx, *Economic and Philosophic Manuscripts of 1844* [265]; *Thesis on Feuerbach* [269]; *The German Ideology* [270]
28. Friedrich Nietzsche, *On the Genealogy of Morals* [277]

VI BIOLOGICAL THEORIES

29. Charles Darwin, *The Descent of Man* [285]
30. Edward O. Wilson, *On Human Nature* [315]

VII FREUD

31 Sigmund Freud, *Character and Culture* [343]; *Civilization and its Discontents* [353]

VIII BEHAVIORISM AND NON-SELF THEORIES

32. David Hume, *A Treatise of Human Nature* [365]
33. Julien de La Mettrie, *Man a Machine* [378]
34. J.B. Watson, *The Ways of Behaviorism* [385]; *Behaviorism* [390]
35. Margaret A. Boden, *Artificial Intelligence in Psychology* [399]
36. Daniel C. Dennett, *Consciousness Explained* [407]

IX FEMINISM

37. Mary Wollstonecraft, *A Vindication of the Rights of Woman* [421]
38. Simone de Beauvoir, *The Second Sex* [445]
39. Juliet Mitchell, *Psychoanalysis and Feminism* [452]; *Women: the Longest Revolution* [460]
40. Carol Gilligan, *In a Different Voice* [466]
41. Katha Pollitt, "Marooned on Gilligan's Island: Are Women Morally Superior to Men?" [476]

X SOME CONTRARY VOICES

42. Jean-Paul Sartre, *Existentialism and Humanism* [487]
43. Camille Paglia, *Sexual Personae* [490]

XI TWENTIETH-CENTURY VIEWS IN SOCIOLOGY AND ANTHROPOLOGY

44. Ferdinand Tönnies, *Community and Society* [517]
45. Marvin Harris, *Cultural Materialism* [532]; *Our Kind* [549]

INTRODUCTION

The present volume of readings on human nature is intended as an accompaniment to my book *Theories of Human Nature*. But it is also intended to stand on its own by providing a diverse range of primary sources in human nature theory, or reactions to or critiques of them. One of the guiding ideas in *Theories of Human Nature* was that the views discussed there be living positions in the rather strong sense that considerable numbers of contemporary readers would identify themselves explicitly as sharing the view in question. This somewhat strict demand is abandoned here. All eleven of the theories of the earlier book are well represented, and are signalled as such. Other theories, also currently significantly subscribed to, are here. In addition, several major views of the past appear, which no one now living would claim for themselves without qualification. For the perspective of my earlier book four criteria seemed appropriate for appearance as a human nature theory deserving focused attention: the theory should be interesting, original, plausible, and have believers. Interest and plausibility are of course less matters of record than the other two: if not entirely items in the eye of the beholder, they depend on an angle of view, and require a case for others to share it. Again, these criteria are somewhat relaxed, or elasticized, for the present selection. I don't myself think that all the views to be met with here are particularly plausible conceptions to have of human beings, given much that we know (or think that we know) about the world in which we live. But every one of these theories, if not a persuasive take on humanity or a stance with a constituency of living adherents, has had immense influence, or is important as contributing a conceptually rich piece to the puzzle of unscrambling, sorting out, or assembling who or what we are, or why we behave as we do. And certainly, in any case, not all of the selections are the expression of original stances: some are synoptic summations of others' views or in some cases oppositional critiques of them.

In some cases a theory is of importance because it contributes to our understanding, or to our imaginations, a very distinctive view of human beings which, even if it may seem implausible, or outlandish, or bizarre, rings in memory as special, as an Idea. One may say, what a way to think people to be; or ask, what if we were like that? And add: isn't it amazing that someone came up with that clear, novel read of the human being? At any rate these theories, in these readings, are offered mostly as themselves, for their own sake, and some will appeal to the reader, or seem to have something going for them, and others not.

It must be stressed emphatically that the groupings provided for the selections that follow are, in varying degrees by case, arbitrary. The common denominator uniting all of them is the individuality of view that each manifests. This is how –

or more accurately, a little bit of how – this particular thinker sees human beings. And, quite secondarily usually, this view has certain affinities with *other* views; some of those others will be found here conjoined with the selection in question, but others will be elsewhere, sometimes quite some distance elsewhere, across a chasm of (rather often) committed ideological space. And sometimes, even when creatively original, a thinker appears here not only as proponent of his or her vision of humankind, but as critic of other visions, or as broad and autonomous contributor to the table of concerns and stances. Thus Freud is here not only as creative advocate of psychoanalysis, but also as both cultural analyst and critical analyst – one of the sharpest, in my view – of the religious impulse and stance. Both varieties of analysis are situated, certainly, within the broad psychoanalytic frame. Many, then, are here doing multiple duty. One passage will offer a classic presentation of a core or nugget concept, that has taken on an important life of its own, and which the creative original thinker, or his or her theory, may be said no longer to "own." Another will provide a succinct summation of the thinker's view at a time and in a place, for many of our authors had changes, or at least modifications, of heart.

In a rather straightforward way one may distinguish human nature theories developed by particular individual thinkers whose stamp they bear, and others constituting a perspective with diverse contributors. Both are represented in this volume. The second category requires the special comment that the *typical* situation is that a thinker of interest and substance will not be a representative of a broad impersonal position, but rather will speak in his or her own voice. So one is cautioned not to expect those labelled liberal, or conservative, or feminist, or Christian, to embody or exhibit a full repertoire of traits that a stereotype may connect to those labels. The reader should expect contributory strands or notes, and not, in any single case, something definitive.

Other cautionary remarks need to address those who may be disappointed that thinkers they regard as major human nature theorists (or critics) do not appear, or do not appear in the selections they would have chosen. Of course no anthology can include everyone, and everything, nor everyone and everything relevant, significant, and interesting. And concerns that this book not be still a great deal longer than it is have led me to deny space to some authors or passages that certainly seemed to me reasonable candidates for inclusion. (There were also two cases of readings originally intended to be included, whose copyright-holders' requirements for permission to reprint seemed to me excessive, and which were, as a result, and with regret, not included.)

One category of theory has led to particular kinds of exclusions. Just as moral theory and political theory typically rest upon human nature theory while the latter is something quite distinct from either, so too a theory about human nature is not the same as a theory about the *mind,* or *soul* (even if there will be connections of intimacy between both). For some theories of human nature, the central, most important and anchoring set of facts about us are facts about the individual mind (or soul). These are (more or less) individualist psychological views of what human beings are like, what makes them tick. For such theories – Freud's is an obvious case – the constituent theory of the mind and its workings is clearly, not merely relevant, but the heart and core of the theory. But someone who thinks, say, that human identity is primarily constructed out of social relations may also happen to have some distinctive views about minds or brains. Those views won't automatically comprise even a substantive part of a theory of human nature. A theory of the nature of mind (or soul) is not *as such* a theory of human nature. Because of considerations like these many of the classic philosophical theories of mind will not be found represented here.

The selections in this volume are discussions of human nature within a broadly Western perspective, and, understandably, some would wish that writings of non-Western thinkers appeared as well. I candidly acknowledge my own ignorance of systematic theoretical work on human nature from non-Western sources: that ignorance is by itself a sufficient reason for this exclusion. Still another kind of work is absent (except perhaps for the Rochester selection). Creative literature – the world's great novels, and some of its major poetry – unquestionably gives expression to deep insight about human nature; indeed, it offers some of the most acute and illuminating understandings of the human condition ever penned. A quite different sort of anthology than the present one could attractively and intelligently assemble some of the most significant of the literary analysis of humanity.

As this volume stands, it is large and its contents quite diverse. Instructors using it for a course may well want (or need) to assign and discuss less than the full set of readings. The extended length of many individual selections is intended to permit a closer or more thorough consideration of some of the major thinkers represented than many other anthologies would make possible. Indeed, a reasonable selection of readings for a one-semester course on human nature might limit itself to, say, the twenty or thirty *longest* individual selections.

Finally, a few remarks on the bibliographies following the selections. In some cases these are works cited in the selection itself. More usually they are books and articles that the reader may find helpful for coming to a more extensive understanding or assessment of the thinker or the theory concerned. The literature on all the theories in the volume is enormous. The works cited are by no means intended to be exhaustive, or definitive, or, in all cases, the very most recent secondary account. In some cases the bibliographies include non-standard interpretative work that I think has something accessible, and interesting or important, to offer the inquirer. At any rate, the aim throughout is to provide a small sample of secondary work that may be found useful.

I

ANCIENT AND EARLY MODERN VIEWS
OF HUMAN NATURE

CHAPTER ONE — PLATO

Except possibly for rather strict advocates of the central value of a "scientific philosophy," or those philosophers who think philosophy as a whole has mostly been a mistake, everyone surveying the course of western philosophy has accorded to Plato (428-348 B.C.) a position at the very pinnacle of creative achievement in the subject. If he is not the greatest philosopher of all time, he divides such honours with a tiny handful of other giants – Aristotle, Hume, Kant, possibly Hegel, and perhaps a twentieth-century figure or two (Russell, some would say, or, others, Wittgenstein; still others, Heidegger).

Plato was the pupil of Socrates, and the teacher of Aristotle. He founded a school, in a physical and institutional as well as a doctrinal sense – the Academy, in Athens, which was to last over eight hundred years, one of the shining cultural glories of the ancient Greco-Roman world. In his school Plato seems to have developed and taught a complex deductive systematic philosophy, deriving in considerable part from the ideas of the Presocratic philosopher Pythagoras (and also from other sources, the synthesis and much of the content wholly original with Plato himself). This "mathematical" philosophy makes somewhat veiled or incomplete appearances in Plato's *Dialogues* – 26 works in all but one of which his revered teacher Socrates is the central character and Plato's mouthpiece, arguing usually with skill and subtlety against what Plato sees as errors (often dangerous ones), and in favour of Plato's own views. These dialogues, together with some letters, are what survive of Plato's written legacy, and they have stirred, interested, and sometimes provoked humanity every since their first appearance.

Plato was an extremely gifted literary artist, as well as a profoundly important philosopher. His dialogues exhibit often a rich and vivid awareness of human psychology, and the portraiture of Socrates, his teacher and the voice for his own philosophical views in the dialogues, is a masterpiece of psychological artifice. The following selections from *The Republic*, Plato's longest and most famous work, aim primarily to display some of Plato's *theoretical* views about human beings. But many more of the Platonic texts may also be recommended for their literary depictions of human nature.

Plato. *The Republic.*

(Source: Plato. *The Republic*. Trans. Francis MacDonald Cornford. Oxford: Oxford University Press, 1941, 131-138, 148-155, 296-297.)

Well, but we decided that a society was just when each of the three types of human character it contained performed its own function; and again, it was temperate and brave and wise by virtue of certain other affections and states of mind of those same types.

True.

Accordingly, my friend, if we are to be justified in attributing those same virtues to the individual, we shall expect to find that the individual soul contains the same three elements and that they are affected in the same way as are the corresponding types in society.

That follows.

Here, then, we have stumbled upon another little problem: Does the soul contain these three elements or not?

Not such a very little one, I think. It may be a true

saying, Socrates, that what is worth while is seldom easy.

Apparently; and let me tell you, Glaucon, it is my belief that we shall never reach the exact truth in this matter by following our present methods of discussion; the road leading to that goal is longer and more laborious. However, perhaps we can find an answer that will be up to the standard we have so far maintained in our speculations.

Is not that enough? I should be satisfied for the moment.

Well, it will more than satisfy me, I replied.

Don't be disheartened, then, but go on.

Surely, I began, we must admit that the same elements and characters that appear in the state must exist in every one of us; where else could they have come from? It would be absurd to imagine that among peoples with a reputation for a high-spirited character, like the Thracians and Scythians and northerners generally, the states have not derived that character from their individual members; or that it is otherwise with the love of knowledge, which would be ascribed chiefly to our own part of the world, or with the love of money, which one would specially connect with Phoenicia and Egypt.

Certainly.

So far, then, we have a fact which is easily recognized. But here the difficulty begins. Are we using the same part of ourselves in all these three experiences, or a different part in each? Do we gain knowledge with one part, feel anger with another, and with yet a third desire the pleasures of food, sex, and so on? Or is the whole soul at work in every impulse and in all these forms of behaviour? The difficulty is to answer that question satisfactorily.

I quite agree.

Let us approach the problem whether these elements are distinct or identical in this way. It is clear that the same thing cannot act in two opposite ways or be in two opposite states at the same time, with respect to the same part of itself, and in relation to the same object. So if we find such contradictory actions or states among the elements concerned, we shall know that more than one must have been involved.

Very well.

Consider this proposition of mine, then. Can the same thing, at the same time and with respect to the same part of itself, be at rest and in motion?

Certainly not.

We had better state this principle in still more precise terms, to guard against misunderstanding later on. Suppose a man is standing still, but moving his head and arms. We should not allow anyone to say that the same man was both at rest and in motion at the same time, but only that part of him was at rest, part in motion. Isn't that so?

Yes.

An ingenious objector might refine still further and argue that a peg-top, spinning with its peg fixed at the same spot, or indeed any body that revolves in the same place, is both at rest and in motion as a whole. But we should not agree, because the parts in respect of which such a body is moving and at rest are not the same. It contains an axis and a circumference; and in respect of the axis it is at rest inasmuch as the axis is not inclined in any direction, while in respect of the circumference it revolves; and if, while it is spinning, the axis does lean out of the perpendicular in all directions, then it is in no way at rest.

That is true.

No objection of that sort, then, will disconcert us or make us believe that the same thing can ever act or be acted upon in two opposite ways, or be two opposite things, at the same time, in respect of the same part of itself, and in relation to the same object.

I can answer for myself at any rate.

Well, anyhow, as we do not want to spend time in reviewing all such objections to make sure that they are unsound, let us proceed on this assumption, with the understanding that, if we ever come to think otherwise, all the consequences based upon it will fall to the ground.

Yes, that is a good plan.

Now, would you class such things as assent and dissent, striving after something and refusing it, attraction and repulsion, as pairs of opposite actions or states of mind – no matter which?

Yes, they are opposites.

And would you not class all appetites such as hunger and thirst, and again willing and wishing, with the affirmative members of those pairs I have just mentioned? For instance, you would say that the soul of a man who desires something is striving after it, or trying to draw to itself the thing it wishes to possess, or again, in so far as it is willing to have its want satisfied, it is giving its assent to its own longing, as if to an inward question.

Yes.

And, on the other hand, disinclination, unwillingness, and dislike, we should class on the negative side with acts of rejection or repulsion.

Of course.

That being so, shall we say that appetites form one class, the most conspicuous being those we call thirst and hunger?

Yes.

Thirst being desire for drink, hunger for food?

Yes.

Now, is thirst, just in so far as it is thirst, a desire in the soul for anything more than simply drink? Is it, for instance, thirst for hot drink or for cold, for much drink or for little, or in a word for drink of any particular kind? Is it not rather true that you will have a desire for cold drink only if you are feeling hot as well as thirsty, and for hot drink only if you are feeling cold; and if you want much drink or little, that will be because your thirst is a great thirst or a little one? But, just in itself, thirst or hunger is a desire for nothing more than its natural object, drink or food, pure and simple.

Yes, he agreed, each desire, just in itself, is simply for its own natural object. When the object is of such and such a particular kind, the desire will be correspondingly qualified.[1]

We must be careful here, or we might be troubled by the objection that no one desires mere food and drink, but always wholesome food and drink. We shall be told that what we desire is always something that is good; so if thirst is a desire, its object must be, like that of any other desire, something – drink or whatever it may be – that will be good for one.[2]

Yes, there might seem to be something in that objection.

But surely, wherever you have two correlative terms, if one is qualified, the other must always be qualified too; whereas if one is unqualified, so is the other.

I don't understand.

Well, 'greater' is a relative term; and the greater is greater than the less; if it is much greater, then the less is much less; if it is greater at some moment, past or future, than the less is less at that same moment. The same principle applies to all such correlatives, like 'more' and 'fewer,' 'double' and 'half'; and again to terms like 'heavier' and 'lighter,' 'quicker' and 'slower,' and to things like hot and cold.

Yes.

Or take the various branches of knowledge: is it not the same there? The object of knowledge pure and simple is the knowable – if that is the right word – without any qualification; whereas a particular kind of knowledge has an object of a particular kind. For example, as soon as men learnt how to build houses, their craft was distinguished from others under the name of architecture, because it had a unique character, which was itself due to the character of its object; and all other branches of craft and knowledge were distinguished in the same way.

True.

This, then, if you understand me now, is what I meant by saying that, where there are two correlatives, the one is qualified if, and only if, the other is so. I am not saying that the one must have the same quality as the other – that the science of health and disease is itself healthy and diseased, or the knowledge of good and evil is itself good and evil – but only that, as soon as you have a knowledge that is restricted to a particular kind of object, namely health and disease, the knowledge itself becomes a particular kind of knowledge. Hence we no longer call it merely knowledge, which would have for its object whatever can be known, but we add the qualification and call it medical science.

I understand now and I agree.

Now, to go back to thirst: is not that one of these

---

1   The object of the following subtle argument about relative terms is to distinguish thirst as a mere blind craving for drink from a more complex desire whose object includes the pleasure or health expected to result from drinking. We thus forestall the objection that all desires have 'the good' (apparent or real) for their object and include an intellectual or rational element, so that the conflict of motives might be reduced to an intellectual debate, in the same 'part' of the soul, on the comparative values of two incompatible ends.

2   If this objection were admitted, it would follow that the desire would always be correspondingly qualified. It is necessary to insist that we do experience blind cravings which can be isolated from any judgement about the goodness of their object.

relative terms? It is essentially thirst for something.

Yes, for drink.

And if the drink desired is of a certain kind, the thirst will be correspondingly qualified. But thirst which is just simply thirst is not for drink of any particular sort – much or little, good or bad – but for drink pure and simple.

Quite so.

We conclude, then, that the soul of a thirsty man, just in so far as he is thirsty, has no other wish than to drink. That is the object of its craving, and towards that it is impelled.

That is clear.

Now if there is ever something which at the same time pulls it the opposite way, that something must be an element in the soul other than the one which is thirsting and driving it like a beast to drink; in accordance with our principle that the same thing cannot behave in two opposite ways at the same time and towards the same object with the same part of itself. It is like an archer drawing the bow: it is not accurate to say that his hands are at the same time both pushing and pulling it. One hand does the pushing, the other the pulling.

Exactly.

Now, is it sometimes true that people are thirsty and yet unwilling to drink?

Yes, often.

What, then, can one say of them, if not that their soul contains something which urges them to drink and something which holds them back, and that this latter is a distinct thing and overpowers the other?

I agree.

And is it not true that the intervention of this inhibiting principle in such cases always has its origin in reflection; whereas the impulses driving and dragging the soul are engendered by external influences and abnormal conditions?[3]

Evidently.

We shall have good reason, then, to assert that they arc two distinct principles. We may call that part of the soul whereby it reflects, rational; and the other, with which it feels hunger and thirst and is distracted by sexual passion and all the other desires, we will call irrational appetite, associated with pleasure in the replenishment of certain wants.

Yes, there is good ground for that view.

Let us take it, then, that we have now distinguished two elements in the soul. What of that passionate element which makes us feel angry and indignant? Is that a third, or identical in nature with one of those two?

It might perhaps be identified with appetite.

I am more inclined to put my faith in a story I once heard about Leontius, son of Aglaion. On his way up from the Piraeus outside the north wall, he noticed the bodies of some criminals lying on the ground, with the executioner standing by them. He wanted to go and look at them, but at the same time he was disgusted and tried to turn away. He struggled for some time and covered his eyes, but at last the desire was too much for him. Opening his eyes wide, he ran up to the bodies and cried, 'There you are, curse you; feast yourselves on this lovely sight!'

Yes, I have heard that story too.

The point of it surely is that anger is sometimes in conflict with appetite, as if they were two distinct principles. Do we not often find a man whose desires would force him to go against his reason, reviling himself and indignant with this part of his nature which is trying to put constraint on him? It is like a struggle between two factions, in which indignation takes the side of reason. But I believe you have never observed, in yourself or anyone else, indignation make common cause with appetite in behaviour which reason decides to be wrong.

No, I am sure I have not.

Again, take a man who feels he is in the wrong. The more generous his nature, the less can he be indignant at any suffering, such as hunger and cold, inflicted by the man he has injured. He recognizes such treatment as just, and, as I say, his spirit refuses to be roused against it.

That is true.

But now contrast one who thinks it is he that is being wronged. His spirit boils with resentment and sides with the right as he conceives it. Persevering all the more for the hunger and cold and other pains he suffers, it triumphs and will not

---

3   Some of the most intense bodily desires are due to morbid conditions, e.g. thirst in fever, and even milder desires are caused by a departure from the normal state, which demands 'replenishment' (*Philebus*, 45-46, and *Republic*, Chap. XXXIII).

give in until its gallant struggle has ended in success or death; or until the restraining voice of reason, like a shepherd calling off his dog, makes it relent.

An apt comparison, he said; and in fact it fits the relation of our Auxiliaries to the Rulers: they were to be like watch-dogs obeying the shepherds of the commonwealth.

Yes, you understand very well what I have in mind. But do you see how we have changed our view? A moment ago we were supposing this spirited element to be something of the nature of appetite; but now it appears that, when the soul is divided into factions, it is far more ready to be up in arms on the side of reason.

Quite true.

Is it, then, distinct from the rational element or only a particular form of it, so that the soul will contain no more than two elements, reason and appetite? Or is the soul like the state, which had three orders to hold it together, traders, Auxiliaries, and counsellors ? Does the spirited element make a third, the natural auxiliary of reason, when not corrupted by bad upbringing?

It must be a third.

Yes, I said, provided it can be shown to be distinct from reason, as we saw it was from appetite.

That is easily proved. You can see that much in children: they are full of passionate feelings from their very birth; but some, I should say, never become rational, and most of them only late in life.

A very sound observation, said I, the truth of which may also be seen in animals. And besides, there is the witness of Homer in that line I quoted before: 'He smote his breast and spoke, chiding his heart.' The poet is plainly thinking of the two elements as distinct, when he makes the one which has chosen the better course after reflection rebuke the other for its unreasoning passion.

I entirely agree.

...

We must go back, then, to a subject which ought, perhaps, to have been treated earlier in its proper place; though, after all, it may be suitable that the women should have their turn on the stage when the men have quite finished their performance, especially since you are so insistent. In my judgement, then, the question under what conditions people born and educated as we have described should possess wives and children, and how they should treat them, can be rightly settled only by keeping to the course on which we started them at the outset. We undertook to put these men in the position of watch-dogs guarding a flock. Suppose we follow up the analogy and imagine them bred and reared in the same sort of way. We can then see if that plan will suit our purpose.

How will that be?

In this way. Which do we think right for watch-dogs: should the females guard the flock and hunt with the males and take a share in all they do, or should they be kept within doors as fit for no more than bearing and feeding their puppies, while all the hard work of looking after the flock is left to the males?

They are expected to take their full share, except that we treat them as not quite so strong.

Can you employ any creature for the same work as another, if you do not give them both the same upbringing and education?

No.

Then, if we are to set women to the same tasks as men, we must teach them the same things. They must have the same two branches of training for mind and body and also be taught the art of war, and they must receive the same treatment.

That seems to follow.

Possibly, if these proposals were carried out, they might be ridiculed as involving a good many breaches of custom.

They might indeed.

The most ridiculous – don't you think? – being the notion of women exercising naked along with the men in the wrestling-schools; some of them elderly women too, like the old men who still have a passion for exercise when they are wrinkled and not very agreeable to look at.

Yes, that would be thought laughable, according to our present notions.

Now we have started on this subject, we must not be frightened of the many witticisms that might be aimed at such a revolution, not only in the matter of bodily exercise but in the training of women's minds, and not least when it comes to their bearing arms and riding on horseback. Having begun upon these rules, we must not draw back from the harsher provisions. The wits may be asked to stop being witty and try to be serious; and we may remind them that it is not so long since the Greeks, like most foreign nations of the present day, thought it ridiculous and shameful for men to be seen naked.

When gymnastic exercises were first introduced in Crete and later at Sparta, the humorists had their chance to make fun of them; but when experience had shown that nakedness is better uncovered than muffled up, the laughter died down and a practice which the reason approved ceased to look ridiculous to the eye. This shows how idle it is to think anything ludicrous but what is base. One who tries to raise a laugh at any spectacle save that of baseness and folly will also, in his serious moments, set before himself some other standard than goodness of what deserves to be held in honour.

Most assuredly.

The first thing to be settled, then, is whether these proposals are feasible; and it must be open to anyone, whether a humorist or serious-minded, to raise the question whether, in the case of mankind, the feminine nature is capable of taking part with the other sex in all occupations, or in none at all, or in some only; and in particular under which of these heads this business of military service falls. Well begun is half done, and would not this be the best way to begin?

Yes.

Shall we take the other side in this debate and argue against ourselves? We do not want the adversary's position to be taken by storm for lack of defenders.

I have no objection.

Let us state his case for him. 'Socrates and Glaucon,' he will say, 'there is no need for others to dispute your position; you yourselves, at the very outset of founding your commonwealth, agreed that everyone should do the one work for which nature fits him.' Yes, of course; I suppose we did. 'And isn't there a very great difference in nature between man and woman?' Yes, surely. 'Does not that natural difference imply a corresponding difference in the work to be given to each?' Yes. 'But if so, surely you must be mistaken now and contradicting yourselves when you say that men and women, having such widely divergent natures, should do the same things?' What is your answer to that, my ingenious friend?

It is not easy to find one at the moment. I can only appeal to you to state the case on our own side, whatever it may be.

This, Glaucon, is one of many alarming objections which I foresaw some time ago. That is why I shrank from touching upon these laws concerning the possession of wives and the rearing of children.

It looks like anything but an easy problem.

True, I said; but whether a man tumbles into a swimming-pool or into mid-ocean, he has to swim all the same. So must we, and try if we can reach the shore, hoping for some Arion's dolphin or other miraculous deliverance to bring us safe to land.[4]

I suppose so.

Come then, let us see if we can find the way out. We did agree that different natures should have different occupations, and that the natures of man and woman are different; and yet we are now saying that these different natures are to have the same occupations. Is that the charge against us?

Exactly.

It is extraordinary, Glaucon, what an effect the practice of debating has upon people.

Why do you say that?

Because they often seem to fall unconsciously into mere disputes which they mistake for reasonable argument, through being unable to draw the distinctions proper to their subject; and so, instead of a philosophical exchange of ideas, they go off in chase of contradictions which are purely verbal.

I know that happens to many people; but does it apply to us at this moment?

Absolutely. At least I am afraid we are slipping unconsciously into a dispute about words. We have been strenuously insisting on the letter of our principle that different natures should not have the same occupations, as if we were scoring a point in a debate; but we have altogether neglected to consider what sort of sameness or difference we meant and in what respect these natures and occupations were to be defined as different or the same. Consequently, we might very well be asking one another whether there is not an opposition in nature between bald and long-haired men, and, when that was admitted, forbid one set to be shoemakers, if the other were following that trade.

That would be absurd.

Yes, but only because we never meant any and

---

4   The musician Arion, to escape the treachery of Corinthian sailors, leapt into the sea and was carried ashore at Taenarum by a dolphin, Herod, i. 24.

every sort of sameness or difference in nature, but the sort that was relevant to the occupations in question. We meant, for instance, that a man and a woman have the same nature if both have a talent for medicine; whereas two men have different natures if one is a born physician, the other a born carpenter.

Yes, of course.

If, then, we find that either the male sex or the female is specially qualified for any particular form of occupation, then that occupation, we shall say, ought to be assigned to one sex or the other. But if the only difference appears to be that the male begets and the female brings forth, we shall conclude that no difference between man and woman has yet been produced that is relevant to our purpose. We shall continue to think it proper for our Guardians and their wives to share in the same pursuits.

And quite rightly.

The next thing will be to ask our opponent to name any profession or occupation in civic life for the purposes of which woman's nature is different from man's.

That is a fair question.

He might reply, as you did just now, that it is not easy to find a satisfactory answer on the spur of the moment, but that there would be no difficulty after a little reflection.

Perhaps.

Suppose, then, we invite him to follow us and see if we can convince him that there is no occupation concerned with the management of social affairs that is peculiar to women. We will confront him with a question: When you speak of a man having a natural talent for something, do you mean that he finds it easy to learn, and after a little instruction can find out much more for himself; whereas a man who is not so gifted learns with difficulty and no amount of instruction and practice will make him even remember what he has been taught? Is the talented man one whose bodily powers are readily at the service of his mind, instead of being a hindrance? Are not these the marks by which you distinguish the presence of a natural gift for any pursuit?

Yes, precisely.

Now do you know of any human occupation in which the male sex is not superior to the female in all these respects? Need I waste time over exceptions like weaving and watching over saucepans and batches of cakes, though women are supposed to be good at such things and get laughed at when a man does them better?

It is true, he replied, in almost everything one sex is easily beaten by the other. No doubt many women are better at many things than many men; but taking the sexes as a whole, it is as you say.

To conclude, then, there is no occupation concerned with the management of social affairs which belongs either to woman or to man, as such. Natural gifts are to be found here and there in both creatures alike; and every occupation is open to both, so far as their natures are concerned, though woman is for all purposes the weaker.

Certainly.

Is that a reason for making over all occupations to men only?

Of course not.

No, because one woman may have a natural gift for medicine or for music, another may not.

Surely.

Is it not also true that a woman may, or may not, be warlike or athletic ?

I think so.

And again, one may love knowledge, another hate it; one may be high-spirited, another spiritless?

True again.

It follows that one woman will be fitted by nature to be a Guardian, another will not; because these were the qualities for which we selected our men Guardians. So for the purpose of keeping watch over the commonwealth, woman has the same nature as man, save in so far as she is weaker.

So it appears.

It follows that women of this type must be selected to share the life and duties of Guardians with men of the same type, since they are competent and of a like nature, and the same natures must be allowed the same pursuits.

Yes.

We come round, then, to our former position, that there is nothing contrary to nature in giving our Guardians' wives the same training for mind and body. The practice we proposed to establish was not impossible or visionary, since it was in accordance with nature. Rather, the contrary practice which now prevails turns out to be unnatural.

So it appears.

Well, we set out to inquire whether the plan we

proposed was feasible and also the best. That it is feasible is now agreed; we must next settle whether it is the best.

Obviously.

Now, for the purpose of producing a woman fit to be a Guardian, we shall not have one education for men and another for women, precisely because the nature to be taken in hand is the same.

True.

What is your opinion on the question of one man being better than another? Do you think there is no such difference?

Certainly I do not.

And in this commonwealth of ours which will prove the better men – the Guardians who have received the education we described, or the shoe-makers who have been trained to make shoes?[6]

It is absurd to ask such a question.

Very well. So these Guardians will be the best of all the citizens?

By far.

And these women the best of all the women?

Yes.

Can anything be better for a commonwealth than to produce in it men and women of the best possible type?

No.

And that result will be brought about by such a system of mental and bodily training as we have described?

Surely.

We may conclude that the institution we proposed was not only practicable, but also the best for the commonwealth.

Yes.

The wives of our Guardians, then, must strip for exercise, since they will be clothed with virtue, and they must take their share in war and in the other social duties of guardianship. They are to have no other occupation; and in these duties the lighter part must fall to the women, because of the weakness of their sex. The man who laughs at naked women, exercising their bodies for the best of reasons, is like one that 'gathers fruit unripe,'[7] for he does not know what it is that he is laughing at or

what he is doing. There will never be a finer saying than the one which declares that whatever does good should be held in honour, and the only shame is in doing harm.

That is perfectly true.

...

Here I feel the need to define, more fully than we have so far done, the number and nature of the appetites. Otherwise it will not be so easy to see our way to a conclusion.

Well, it is not too late.

Quite so. Now, about the appetites, here is the point I want to make plain. Among the unnecessary pleasures and desires, some, I should say, are unlawful. Probably they are innate in everyone; but when they are disciplined by law and by the higher desires with the aid of reason, they can in some people be got rid of entirely, or at least left few and feeble, although in others they will be comparatively strong and numerous.

What kind of desires do you mean?

Those which bestir themselves in dreams, when the gentler part of the soul slumbers and the control of reason is withdrawn; then the wild beast in us, full-fed with meat or drink, becomes rampant and shakes off sleep to go in quest of what will gratify its own instincts. As you know, it will cast away all shame and prudence at such moments and stick at nothing. In phantasy it will not shrink from intercourse with a mother or anyone else, man, god, or brute, or from forbidden food or any deed of blood. In a word, it will go to any length of shamelessness and folly.

Quite true.

It is otherwise with a man sound in body and mind, who, before he goes to sleep, awakens the reason within him to feed on high thoughts and questionings in collected meditation. If he has neither starved nor surfeited his appetites, so that, lulled to rest, no delights or griefs of theirs may trouble that better part, but leave it free to reach out, in pure and independent thought, after some new knowledge of things past, present, or to come;

---

6   The elementary education of Chap. IX will be open to all citizens, but presumably carried further (to the age of 17 or 18,...) in the case of those who show special promise.

7   An adapted quotation from Pindar (frag. 209, Schr.).

if, likewise, he has soothed his passions so as not to fall asleep with his anger roused against any man; if, in fact, he does not take his rest until he has quieted two of the three elements in his soul and awakened the third wherein wisdom dwells, then he is in a fair way to grasp the truth of things, and the visions of his dreams will not be unlawful. However, we have been carried away from our point, which is that in every one of us, even those who seem most respectable, there exist desires, terrible in their untamed lawlessness, which reveal themselves in dreams. Do you agree?

I do.

Bibliography

Gosling, J.C.B. *Plato*. London and New York: Routledge, 1973.

Grube, G.M.A. *Plato's Thought*. Second edition. Indianapolis: Hackett, 1980.

Hackforth, R. *Plato's Examination of Pleasure*. New York: Liberal Arts Press, 1945.

Hare, R.M. *Plato*. Oxford and New York: Oxford University Press, 1982.

Irwin, T. *Plato's Moral Theory*. Oxford: Oxford University Press, 1977.

Vlastos, G., ed. *Plato: A Collection of Critical Essays*. 2 vols. New York: Anchor Books, 1970, 1971.

CHAPTER TWO — ARISTOTLE

In Dante's *Inferno* the poet visits the first circle of hell, where virtuous non-Christians reside. Among them are ten philosophers. All are named, except for one, the leader and greatest of them, the one who comes first: "'l maestro di color che sanno," Dante designated him – "the master of all those who know." No name is necessary. It is Aristotle (384-322 B.C.), as all of Dante's fourteenth-century audience would have realized. The same acknowledged pre-eminence in medieval thought, is also shown by St. Thomas Aquinas's usual term for referring to Aristotle. He calls him simply "philosophus" – "the philosopher" – without proper name; and often in Aquinas's work a matter is taken to be shown or confirmed by the fact that "philosophus dicit" – "the philosopher says it" – without need of inspecting what arguments the philosopher may have had. Aquinas's philosophy became in the course of time the official philosophy of the Roman Catholic Church. Since Aquinas's views rest heavily on those of Aristotle, the latter's ideas have had an impact far beyond those of perhaps any other philosopher in shaping the way the world is seen by the largest Christian community.

Aristotle's significance is by no means confined to the Middle Ages, or to Catholicism. Aristotle's work, covering virtually every area of philosophy and much of science – in some cases creating the basic disciplines of both (e.g., logic, biology, political theory) – was acknowledged and studied with intelligent respect in antiquity, and still is at the present time. Some of this interest now is, to be sure, historical only. But on many themes and topics Aristotle remains a fresh and contemporary voice. In ethics, on the foundations of political society, in the study of practical reason, on the metaphysical status of *natural kinds*, and other topics, there are still, or are again, many Aristotelians – many Aristotelians who are Catholic, and many who are not, indeed many of wholly secular orientation.

In different parts of his work Aristotle developed different facets of his distinctive view of human nature, only some of which is shown in the selections that follow. In general Aristotle sought what he conceived as a middle ground of view, between extremes. Thus he stresses both our animality and our rational capacities, our individuality and our sociability. Most deeply Aristotle speaks for the idea of a human *telos*, a mode of being and living to which we are most suited, in which we typically thrive, and for which we were designed by nature.

Aristotle. *Nicomachean Ethics.*

(Source: Aristotle. *Nicomachean Ethics*. Trans. Terence Irwin. Indianapolis, Cambridge: Hackett Publishing Company, 1985, 30-37, 280-287.)

1.92 A discussion of virtue requires a discussion of the soul

It is clear that the virtue we must examine is human virtue, since we are also seeking the human good and human happiness. And by human virtue we mean virtue of the soul, not of the body, since we also say that happiness is an activity of the soul. If this is so, then it is clear that the politician must acquire some knowledge about the soul, just as someone setting out to heal the eyes must acquire knowledge about the whole body as well. This is all the more true to the extent that political science is better and more honourable than medicine – and even among doctors the cultivated ones devote a lot of effort to acquiring knowledge about the body. Hence the politician as well [as the student of nature] must study the soul.

But he must study it for the purpose [of inquiring into virtue], as far as suffices for what he seeks; for a more exact treatment would presumably take more effort than his purpose requires. [We] have discussed the soul sufficiently [for our purposes] in [our] popular works as well [as our less popular], and we should use this discussion.

1. 93 The rational and nonrational parts of the soul

We have said, e.g., that one [part] of the soul is nonrational, while one has reason. Are these distinguished as parts of a body and everything divisible into parts are? Or are they two only in account, and inseparable by nature, as the convex and the concave are in a surface? It does not matter for present purposes.

The nonrational part: (a) One part of it is unresponsive to reason

Consider the nonrational [part]. One [part] of it, i.e. the cause of nutrition and growth, is seemingly plant-like and shared [with other living things]: for we can ascribe this capacity of the soul to everything that is nourished, including embryos, and the same one to complete living things, since this is more reasonable than to ascribe another capacity to them.

Hence the virtue of this capacity is apparently shared, not [specifically] human. For this part and capacity more than others seem to be active in sleep, and here the good and the bad person are least distinct, which is why happy people are said to be no better off than miserable people for half their lives.

And this lack of distinction is not surprising, since sleep is inactivity of the soul in so far as it is called excellent or base, unless to some small extent some movements penetrate [to our awareness], and in this way the decent person comes to have better images [in dreams] than just any random person has. Enough about this, however, and let us leave aside the nutritive part, since by nature it has no share in human virtue.

(b) Another part is also nonrational

Another nature in the soul would also seem to be nonrational, though in a way it shares in reason.

[Clearly it is nonrational.] For in the continent and the incontinent person we praise their reason,

i.e. the [part] of the soul that has reason, because it exhorts them correctly and towards what is best; but they evidently also have in them some other [part] that is by nature something besides reason, conflicting and struggling with reason.

For just as paralysed parts of a body, when we decide to move them to the right, do the contrary and move off to the left, the same is true of the soul; for incontinent people have impulses in contrary directions. In bodies, admittedly, we see the part go astray, whereas we do not see it in the soul; nonetheless, presumably, we should suppose that the soul also has a [part] besides reason, contrary to and countering reason. The [precise] way it is different does not matter.

But it is responsive to reason

However, this [part] as well [as the rational part] appears, as we said, to share in reason. At any rate, in the continent person it obeys reason; and in the temperate and the brave person it presumably listens still better to reason, since there it agrees with reason in everything.

Hence it differs both from the wholly unresponsive part. . .

The nonrational [part], then, as well [as the whole soul] apparently has two parts. For while the plant-like [part] shares in reason not at all, the [part] with appetites and in general desires shares in reason in a way, in so far as it both listens to reason and obeys it.

It listens in the way in which we are said to 'listen to reason' from father or friends, not in the way in which we ['give the reason'] in mathematics.

The nonrational part also [obeys and] is persuaded in some way by reason, as is shown by chastening, and by every sort of reproof and exhortation.

And from the wholly rational part

If we ought to say, then, that this [part] also has reason, then the [part] that has reason, as well [as the nonrational part] will have two parts, one that has reason to the full extent by having it within itself, and another [that has it] by listening to reason as to a father.

1.94 The division of the virtues corresponds to the parts of the soul

The distinction between virtues also reflects this difference. For some virtues are called virtues of thought, other virtues of character; wisdom, comprehension and intelligence are called virtues of thought, generosity and temperance virtues of character.

For when we speak of someone's character we do not say that he is wise or has good comprehension, but that he is gentle or temperate. [Hence these are the virtues of character.] And yet, we also praise the wise person for his state, and the states that are praiseworthy are the ones we call virtues. [Hence wisdom is also a virtue.]

2. Virtues of Character in General

2.1 How a Virtue of Character is Acquired

Virtue, then, is of two sorts, virtue of thought and virtue of character. Virtue of thought arises and grows mostly from teaching, and hence needs experience and time. Virtue of character [i.e. of *ethos*] results from habit [*ethos*]; hence its name 'ethical', slightly varied from '*ethos*'.

Virtue comes about, not by a process of nature, but by habituation

Hence it is also clear that none of the virtues of character arises in us naturally.

(1) What is natural cannot be changed by habituation

For if something is by nature [in one condition], habituation cannot bring it into another condition. A stone, e.g., by nature moves downwards, and habituation could not make it move upwards, not even if you threw it up ten thousand times to habituate it; nor could habituation make fire move downwards, or bring anything that is by nature in one condition into another condition.

Thus the virtues arise in us neither by nature nor against nature. Rather, we are by nature able to acquire them, and reach our complete perfection through habit.

(2) Natural capacities are not acquired by habituation

Further, if something arises in us by nature, we first have the capacity for it, and later display the activity. This is clear in the case of the senses; for we did not acquire them by frequent seeing or hearing, but already had them when we exercised them, and did not get them by exercising them.

Virtues, by contrast, we acquire, just as we acquire crafts, by having previously activated them.

For we learn a craft by producing the same product that we must produce when we have learned it, becoming builders, e.g., by building and harpists by playing the harp; so also, then, we become just by doing just actions, temperate by doing temperate actions, brave by doing brave actions.

(3) Legislators concentrate on habituation

What goes on in cities is evidence for this also. For the legislator makes the citizens good by habituating them, and this is the wish of every legislator; if he fails to do it well he misses his goal. [The right] habituation is what makes the difference between a good political system and a bad one.

(4) Virtue and vice are formed by good and bad actions

Further, just as in the case of a craft, the sources and means that develop each virtue also ruin it. For playing the harp makes both good and bad harpists, and it is analogous in the case of builders and all the rest; for building well makes good builders, building badly, bad ones. If it were not so, no teacher would be needed, but everyone would be born a good or a bad craftsman.

It is the same, then, with the virtues. For actions in dealings with [other] human beings make some people just, some unjust; actions in terrifying situations and the acquired habit of fear or confidence make some brave and others cowardly. The same is true of situations involving appetites and anger; for one or another sort of conduct in these situations makes some people temperate and gentle, others intemperate and irascible.

Conclusion: The importance of habituation

To sum up, then, in a single account: A state [of character] arises from [the repetition of] similar activities. Hence we must display the right activities, since differences in these imply corresponding differences in the states. It is not unimportant, then, to acquire one sort of habit or another, right from our youth; rather, it is very important, indeed all-important.

2.12 What is the right sort of habituation?

This is an appropriate question, for the aim of ethical theory is practical

Our present inquiry does not aim, as our others do, at study; for the purpose of our examination is not to know what virtue is, but to become good, since otherwise the inquiry would be of no benefit to us. Hence we must examine the right way to act, since, as we have said, the actions also control the character of the states we acquire.

First, then, actions should express correct reason. That is a common [belief], and let us assume it; later we will say what correct reason is and how it is related to the other virtues.

But let us take it as agreed in advance that every account of the actions we must do has to be stated in outline, not exactly. As we also said at the start, the type of accounts we demand should reflect the subject-matter; and questions about actions and expediency, like questions about health, have no fixed [and invariable answers].

And when our general account is so inexact, the account of particular cases is all the more inexact. For these fall under no craft or profession, and the agents themselves must consider in each case what the opportune action is, as doctors and navigators do.

The account we offer, then, in our present inquiry is of this inexact sort; still, we must try to offer help.

The right sort of habituation must avoid excess and deficiency

First, then, we should observe that these sorts of states naturally tend to be ruined by excess and deficiency. We see this happen with strength and health, which we mention because we must use what is evident as a witness to what is not. For both excessive and deficient exercises ruin strength; and likewise, too much or too little eating or drinking ruins health, while the proportionate amount produces, increases and preserves it.

The same is true, then, of temperance, bravery and the other virtues. For if, e.g., someone avoids and is afraid of everything, standing firm against nothing, he becomes cowardly, but if he is afraid of nothing at all and goes to face everything, he becomes rash. Similarly, if he gratifies himself with every pleasure and refrains from none, he becomes intemperate, but if he avoids them all, as boors do, he becomes some sort of insensible person. Temperance and bravery, then, are ruined by excess and deficiency but preserved by the mean.

The same actions, then, are the sources and causes both of the emergence and growth of virtues and of their ruin; but further, the activities of the virtues will be found in these same actions. For this is also true of more evident cases, e.g. strength, which arises from eating a lot and from withstanding much hard labour, and it is the strong person who is most able to do these very things. It is the same with the virtues. Refraining from pleasures makes us become temperate, and when we have become temperate we are most able to refrain from pleasures. And it is similar with bravery; habituation in disdaining what is fearful and in standing firm against it makes us become brave, and when we have become brave we shall be most able to stand firm.

....

Book X

12. 72 The function of each kind of animal determines its proper activity and its proper pleasure

Each kind of animal seems to have its own proper pleasure, just as it has its own proper function; for the proper pleasure will be the one that corresponds to its activity.

This is apparent if we also study each kind. For a horse, a dog and a human being have different pleasures; and, as Heracleitus says, an ass would choose chaff over gold, since asses find food pleasanter than gold. Hence animals that differ in species also have pleasures that differ in species; and it would be reasonable for animals of the same species to have the same pleasures also.

12. 73 The human function determines the proper human pleasure, as measured by the virtuous person

In fact, however, the pleasures differ quite a lot, in human beings at any rate. For the same things delight some people, and cause pain to others; and while some find them painful and hateful, others find them pleasant and lovable. The same is true of sweet things. For the same things do not seem sweet to a feverish and to a healthy person, or hot to an enfeebled and to a vigorous person; and the same is true of other things.

But in all such cases it seems that what is really so is what appears so to the excellent person. If this is correct, as it seems to be, and virtue, i.e. the good person in so far as he is good, is the measure of each thing, then what appear pleasures to him will also *be* pleasures, and what is pleasant will be what he enjoys.

And if what he finds objectionable appears pleasant to someone, that is nothing surprising, since human beings suffer many sorts of corruption and damage. It is not pleasant, however, except to these people in these conditions. Clearly, then, we should say that the pleasures agreed to be shameful are not pleasures at all, except to corrupted people.

But what about those pleasures that seem to be decent? Of these, which kind, or which particular pleasure, should we take to be the pleasure of a human being? Surely it will be clear from the activities, since the pleasures are consequences of these.

Hence the pleasures that complete the activities of the complete and blessedly happy man, whether he has one activity or more than one, will be called the human pleasures to the fullest extent. The other pleasures will be human in secondary and even more remote ways corresponding to the character of the activities.

13. Happiness: Further Discussion

13.1 Recapitulation: Happiness is an End in Itself, Consisting in Virtuous Action

We have now finished our discussion of the types of virtue; of friendship; and of pleasure. It remains for us to discuss happiness in outline, since we take this to be the end of human [aims]. Our discussion will be shorter if we first take up again what we said before.

We said, then, that happiness is not a state. For if it were, someone might have it and yet be asleep for his whole life, living the life of a plant, or suffer the greatest misfortunes. If we do not approve of this, we count happiness as an activity rather than a state, as we said before.

Some activities are necessary, i.e. choiceworthy for some other end, while others are choiceworthy in themselves. Clearly, then, we should count happiness as one of those activities that are choiceworthy in themselves, not as one of those choiceworthy for some other end. For happiness lacks nothing, but is self-sufficient; and an activity is choiceworthy in itself when nothing further beyond it is sought from it.

This seems to be the character of actions expressing virtue; for doing fine and excellent actions is choiceworthy for itself.

13.2 Happiness is Virtuous Action, not Amusement

13.21 Amusement is popularly regarded as happiness

But pleasant amusements also [seem to be choiceworthy in themselves]. For they are not chosen for other ends, since they actually cause more harm than benefit, by causing neglect of our bodies and possessions.

Moreover, most of those people congratulated for their happiness resort to these sorts of pastimes. Hence people who are witty participants in them have a good reputation with tyrants, since they offer themselves as pleasant [partners] in the tyrant's aims, and these are the sort of people the tyrant requires. And so these amusements seem to have the character of happiness because people in supreme power spend their leisure in them.

13.22 But popular reputation is inadequate evidence

However, these sorts of people are presumably no evidence. For virtue and understanding, the sources of excellent activities, do not depend on holding supreme power. Further, these powerful people have had no taste of pure and civilized pleasure, and so they resort to bodily pleasures. But that is no reason to think these pleasures are most choiceworthy, since boys also think that what they honour is best. Hence, just as different things appear honourable to boys and to men, it is reasonable that in the same way different things appear honourable to base and to decent people.

As we have often said, then, what is honourable and pleasant is what is so to the excellent person; and to each type of person the activity expressing his own proper state is most choiceworthy; hence the activity expressing virtue is most choiceworthy to the excellent person [and hence is most honourable and pleasant].

13.23 Happiness cannot be amusement

Happiness, then, is not found in amusement; for it would be absurd if the end were amusement, and our lifelong efforts and sufferings aimed at amusing ourselves. For we choose practically everything for some other end – except for happiness, since it is [the] end; but serious work and toil aimed [only] at amusement appears stupid and excessively childish. Rather, it seems correct to amuse ourselves so that we can do something serious, as Anacharsis says; for amusement would seem to be relaxation, and it is because we cannot toil continuously that we require relaxation. Relaxation, then, is not [the] end, since we pursue it [to prepare] for activity.

Further, the happy life seems to be a life expressing virtue, which is a life involving serious actions, and not consisting in amusement.

Besides, we say that things to be taken seriously are better than funny things that provide amusement, and that in each case the activity of the better part and the better person is more serious and excellent; and the activity of what is better is superior, and thereby has more the character of happiness.

Moreover, anyone at all, even a slave, no less than the best person, might enjoy bodily pleasures; but no one would allow that a slave shares in happiness, if one does not [also allow that the slave shares in the sort of] life [needed for happiness]. Happiness, then, is found not in these pastimes, but in the activities expressing virtue, as we also said previously.

13.3 Theoretical Study is the Supreme Element of Happiness

If happiness, then, is activity expressing virtue, it is reasonable for it to express the supreme virtue, which will be the virtue of the best thing.

The best is understanding, or whatever else seems to be the natural ruler and leader, and to understand what is fine and divine, by being itself either divine or the most divine element in us.

Hence complete happiness will be its activity expressing its proper virtue; and we have said that this activity is the activity of study. This seems to agree with what has been said before, and also with the truth.

13.31 The activity of theoretical study is best

For this activity is supreme, since understanding is the supreme element in us, and the objects of understanding are the supreme objects of knowledge.

13.32 It is most continuous

Besides, it is the most continuous activity, since we are more capable of continuous study than of any continuous action.

13.33 It is pleasantest

We think pleasure must be mixed into happiness; and it is agreed that the activity expressing wisdom is the pleasantest of the activities expressing virtue. At any rate, philosophy seems to have remarkably pure and firm pleasures; and it is reasonable for those who have knowledge to spend their lives more pleasantly than those who seek it.

13.34 It is most self-sufficient

Moreover, the self-sufficiency we spoke of will be found in study above all.

For admittedly the wise person, the just person and the other virtuous people all need the good things necessary for life. Still, when these are adequately supplied, the just person needs other people as partners and recipients of his just actions; and the same is true of the temperate person and the brave person and each of the others.

But the wise person is able, and more able the wiser he is, to study even by himself; and though he presumably does it better with colleagues, even so he is more self-sufficient than any other [virtuous person].

13.35 It aims at no end beyond itself

Besides, study seems to be liked because of itself alone, since it has no result beyond having studied. But from the virtues concerned with action we try to a greater or lesser extent to gain something beyond the action itself.

13.36 It involves leisure

Happiness seems to be found in leisure, since we accept trouble so that we can be at leisure, and fight wars so that we can be at peace. Now the virtues concerned with action have their activities in politics or war, and actions here seem to require trouble.

This seems completely true for actions in war, since no one chooses to fight a war, and no one continues it, for the sake of fighting a war; for someone would have to be a complete murderer if he made his friends his enemies so that there could be battles and killings.

But the actions of the politician require trouble also. Beyond political activities themselves these actions seek positions of power and honours; or at least they seek happiness for the politician himself and for his fellow-citizens, which is something different from political science itself, and clearly is sought on the assumption that it is different.

Hence among actions expressing the virtues those in politics and war are pre-eminently fine and great; but they require trouble, aim at some [further] end, and are choiceworthy for something other than themselves.

But the activity of understanding, it seems, is superior in excellence because it is the activity of study, aims at no end beyond itself and has its own proper pleasure, which increases the activity. Further, self-sufficiency, leisure, unwearied activity (as far as is possible for a human being), and any other features ascribed to the blessed person, are evidently features of this activity.

Hence a human being's complete happiness will be this activity, if it receives a complete span of life, since nothing incomplete is proper to happiness.

13.37 It is a god-like life

Such a life would be superior to the human level. For someone will live it not in so far as he is a human being, but in so far as he has some divine element in him. And the activity of this divine element is as much superior to the activity expressing the rest of virtue as this element is superior to the compound. Hence if understanding is something divine in comparison with a human being, so also will the life that expresses understanding be divine in comparison with human life.

We ought not to follow the proverb-writers, and 'think human, since you are human', or 'think mortal, since you are mortal'. Rather, as far as we can, we ought to be pro-immortal, and go to all lengths to live a life that expresses our supreme element; for however much this element may lack in bulk, by much more it surpasses everything in power and value.

13.38 It realizes the supreme element in human nature

Moreover, each person seems to be his understanding, if he is his controlling and better element; it would be absurd, then, if he were to choose not his own life, but something else's.

And what we have said previously will also apply now. For what is proper to each thing's nature is supremely best and pleasantest for it; and hence for a human being the life expressing understanding

will be supremely best and pleasantest, if understanding above all is the human being. This life, then, will also be happiest.

13.4 The Relation of Study to the Other Virtues in Happiness

13.41 The other virtues are human, not divine

The life expressing the other kind of virtue [i.e. the kind concerned with action] is [happiest] in a secondary way because the activities expressing this virtue are human.

For we do just and brave actions, and the others expressing the virtues, in relation to other people, by abiding by what fits each person in contracts, services, all types of actions, and also in feelings; and all these appear to be human conditions.

Indeed, some feelings actually seem to arise from the body; and in many ways virtue of character seems to be proper to feelings.

Besides, intelligence is yoked together with virtue of character, and so is this virtue with intelligence. For the origins of intelligence express the virtues of character; and correctness in virtues of character expresses intelligence. And since these virtues are also connected to feelings, they are concerned with the compound. Since the virtues of the compound are human virtues, the life and the happiness expressing these virtues is also human.

The virtue of understanding, however, is separated [from the compound]. Let us say no more about it, since an exact account would be too large a task for our present project.

Aristotle, *Politics*

(Source: *Aristotle's Politics*. Trans. Benjamin Jowett. Oxford: Clarendon Press, 1923, 26-30, 32-37, 50-53.)

In the first place there must be a union of those who cannot exist without each other; namely, of male and female, that the race may continue (and this is a union which is formed, not of deliberate purpose, but because, in common with other animals and with plants, mankind have a natural desire to leave behind them an image of themselves), and of natural ruler and subject, that both may be preserved. For that which can foresee by the exercise of mind is by nature intended to be lord and master, and that which can with its body give effect to such foresight is a subject, and by nature a slave; hence master and slave have the same interest. Now nature has distinguished between the female and the slave. For she is not niggardly, like the smith who fashions the Delphian knife for many uses; she makes each thing for a single use, and every instrument is best made when intended for one and not for many uses. But among barbarians no distinction is made between women and slaves, because there is no natural ruler among them: they are a community of slaves, male and female. Wherefore the poets say –

'It is meet that Hellenes should rule over barbarians';

as if they thought that the barbarian and the slave were by nature one.

Out of these two relationships between man and woman, master and slave, the first thing to arise is the family, and Hesiod is right when he says –

'First house and wife and an ox for the plough,'

for the ox is the poor man's slave. The family is the association established by nature for the supply of men's everyday wants, and the members of it are called by Charondas 'companions of the cupboard', and by Epimenides the Cretan, 'companions of the manger'. But when several families are united, and the association aims at something more than the supply of daily needs, the first society to be formed is the village. And the most natural form of the village appears to be that of a colony from the family, composed of the children and grandchildren, who are said to be 'suckled with the same milk'. And this is the reason why Hellenic states were originally governed by kings; because the Hellenes were under royal rule before they came together, as the barbarians still are. Every family is ruled by the eldest and therefore in the colonies of the family the kingly form of government prevailed because they were of the same blood. As Homer says:[1]

'Each one gives law to his children and to his wives.'

For they lived dispersedly, as was the manner in ancient times Wherefore men say that the Gods have a king, because they themselves either are or were in ancient times under the rule of a king. For they imagine, not only the forms of the Gods, but their ways of life to be like their own.

When several villages are united in a single complete community, large enough to be nearly or quite self-suffing, the state comes into existence, originating in the bare needs of life, and continuing in existence for the sake of a good life. And therefore, if the earlier forms of society are natural, so is the state, for it is the end of them, and the nature of a thing is its end. For what each thing is when fully developed, we call its nature, whether we are speaking of a man, a horse, or a family. Besides, the final cause and end of a thing is the best, and to be self-suffing is the end and the best.

Hence it is evident that the state is a creation of nature, and that man is by nature a political animal. And he who by nature and not by mere accident is without a state, is either a bad man or above humanity; he is like the

'Tribeless, lawless, hearthless one,'

whom Homer[2] denounces – the natural outcast is forthwith a lover of war; he may be compared to an isolated piece at draughts.

Now, that man is more of a political animal than bees or any other gregarious animals is evident. Nature, as we often say, makes nothing in vain, and man is the only animal whom she has endowed with the gift of speech. And whereas mere voice is but an indication of pleasure or pain, and is therefore found in other animals (for their nature attains to the perception of pleasure and pain and the intimation of them to one another, and no further) the power of speech is intended to set forth the expedient and inexpedient, and therefore likewise the just and the unjust. And it is a characteristic of man that he alone has any sense of good and evil, of just and unjust, and the like, and the association of living beings who have this sense makes a family and a state.

Further, the state is by nature clearly prior to the family and to the individual, since the whole is of

---

1   *Od.* ix. 114, quoted by Plato, *Laws, iii.* 680 B, and in *N. Eth.* x.1180[a 28.]

2   *Il.* ix 63

necessity prior to the part; for example, if the whole body be destroyed, there will be no foot or hand, except in an equivocal sense, as we might speak of a stone hand; for when destroyed the hand will be no better than that. But things are defined by their working and power; and we ought not to say that they are the same when they no longer have their proper quality, but only that they have the same name. The proof that the state is a creation of nature and prior to the individual is that the individual, when isolated, is not self-sufficing; and therefore he is like a part in relation to the whole. But he who is unable to live in society, or who has no need because he is sufficient for himself, must be either a beast or a god: he is no part of a state. A social instinct is implanted in all men by nature, and yet he who first founded the state was the greatest of benefactors. For man, when perfected, is the best of animals, but, when separated from law and justice, he is the worst of all, since armed injustice is the more dangerous, and he is equipped at birth with arms, meant to be used by intelligence and virtue, which he may use for the worst ends. Wherefore, if he have not virtue, he is the most unholy and the most savage of animals, and the most full of lust and gluttony. But justice is the bond of men in states for the administration of justice, which is the determination of what is just,[3] is the principle of order in political society.

....

But is there any one thus intended by nature to be a slave, and for whom such a condition is expedient and right, or rather is not all slavery a violation of nature?

There is no difficulty in answering this question, on grounds both of reason and of fact. For that some should rule and others be ruled is a thing not only necessary, but expedient; from the hour of their birth, some are marked out for subjection, others for rule.

And there are many kinds both of rulers and subjects (and that rule is the better which is exercised over better subjects – for example, to rule over men is better than to rule over wild beasts; for the work is better which is executed by better workmen, and where one man rules and another is ruled, they may

be said to have a work); for in all things which form a composite whole and which are made up of parts, whether continuous or discrete, a distinction between the ruling and the subject element comes to light. Such a duality exists in living creatures, but not in them only; it originates in the constitution of the universe: even in things which have no life there is a ruling principle, as in a musical mode. But we are wandering from the subject. We will therefore restrict ourselves to the living creature, which, in the first place, consists of soul and body: and of these two, the one is by nature the ruler, and the other the subject. But then we must look for the intentions of nature in things which retain their nature, and not in things which are corrupted. And therefore we must study the man who is in the most perfect state both of body and soul, for in him we shall see the true relation of the two; although in bad or corrupted natures the body will often appear to rule over the soul because they are in an evil and unnatural condition. At all events we may firstly observe in living creatures both a despotical and a constitutional rule: for the soul rules the body with a despotical rule, whereas the intellect rules the appetites with a constitutional and royal rule. And it is clear that the rule of the soul over the body and of the mind and the rational element over the passionate, is natural and expedient; whereas the equality of the two or the rule of the inferior is always hurtful. The same holds good of animals in relation to men; for tame animals have a better nature than wild, and all tame animals are better off when they are ruled by man; for then they are preserved. Again, the male is by nature superior, and the female inferior, and the one rules, and the other is ruled; this principle, of necessity, extends to all mankind. Where then there is such a difference as that between soul and body, or between men and animals (as in the case of those whose business is to use their body, and who can do nothing better), the lower sort are by nature slaves, and it is better for them as for all inferiors that they should be under the rule of a master. For he who can be, and therefore is, another's, and he who participates in rational principle enough to apprehend, but not to have, such a principle, is a slave by nature. Whereas the lower animals cannot even apprehend a principle; they obey their instincts.

---

3   Cp. N Eth. v. 1134ª 31

And indeed the use made of slaves and of tame animals is not very different, for both with their bodies minister to the needs of life. Nature would like to distinguish between the bodies of freemen and slaves, making the one strong for servile labour, the other upright, and although useless for such services, useful for political life in the arts both of war and peace. But the opposite often happens – that some have the souls and others have the bodies of freemen. And doubtless if men differed from one another in the mere forms of their bodies as much as the statues of the Gods do from men, all would acknowledge that the inferior class should be slaves of the superior. And if this is true of the body, how much more just that a similar distinction should exist in the soul? but the beauty of the body is seen, whereas the beauty of the soul is not seen. It is clear, then, that some men are by nature free, and others slaves, and that for these latter slavery is both expedient and right.

But that those who take the opposite view have in a certain way right on their side, may be easily seen. For the words slavery and slave are used in two senses. There is a slave or slavery by law as well as by nature. The law of which I speak is a sort of convention – the law by which whatever is taken in war is supposed to belong to the victors. But this right many jurists impeach, as they would an orator who brought forward an unconstitutional measure: they detest the notion that, because one man has the power of doing violence and is superior in brute strength, another shall be his slave and subject. Even among philosophers there is a difference of opinion. The origin of the dispute, and what makes the views invade each other's territory, is as follows: in some sense virtue, when furnished with means, has actually the greatest power of exercising force: and as superior power is only found where there is superior excellence of some kind, power seems to imply virtue, and the dispute to be simply one about justice (for it is due to one party identifying justice with goodwill,[4] while the other identifies it with the mere rule of the stronger) . If these views are thus set out separately, the other views[5] have no force or plausibility against the view that the superior in virtue ought to rule, or be master. Others, clinging, as they think, simply to a principle of justice (for law and custom are a sort of justice), assume that slavery in accordance with the custom of war is justified by law, but at the same moment they deny this. For what if the cause of the war be unjust? And again, no one would ever say that he is a slave who is unworthy to be a slave. Were this the case, men of the highest rank would be slaves and the children of slaves if they or their parents chance to have been taken captive and sold. Wherefore Hellenes do not like to call Hellenes slaves, but confine the term to barbarians. Yet, in using this language, they really mean the natural slave of whom we spoke at first; for it must be admitted that some are slaves everywhere, others nowhere. The same principle applies to nobility. Hellenes regard themselves as noble everywhere, and not only in their own country, but they deem the barbarians noble only when at home, thereby implying that there are two sorts of nobility and freedom, the one absolute, the other relative. The Helen of Theodectes says:

'Who would presume to call me servant who am on both sides sprung from the stem of the Gods?'

What does this mean but that they distinguish freedom and slavery, noble and humble birth, by the two principles of good and evil? They think that as men and animals beget men and animals, so from good men a good man springs. But this is what nature, though she may intend it, cannot always accomplish.

We see then that there is some foundation for this difference of opinion, and that all are not either slaves by nature or freemen by nature, and also that there is in some cases a marked distinction between the two classes, rendering it expedient and right for the one to be slaves and the others to be masters: the one practising obedience, the others exercising the authority and lordship which nature intended them to have. The abuse of this authority is injurious to both; for the interests of part and whole, of body and soul, are the same, and the slave is a part of the master, a living but separated part of his

---

4   i. e. mutual goodwill, which is held to be incompatible with the relation of master and slave.

5   i e. those stated in ll. 5-12, that the stronger always has, and that he never has, a right to enslave the weaker. Aristotle finds that these views cannot maintain themselves against his intermediate view, that the superior in *virtue* should rule.

bodily frame. Hence, where the relation of master and slave between them is natural they are friends and have a common interest, but where it rests merely on law and force the reverse is true.

....

Thus it is clear that household management attends more to men than to the acquisition of inanimate things, and to human excellence more than to the excellence of property which we call wealth, and to the virtue of freemen more than to the virtue of slaves. A question may indeed be raised, whether there is any excellence at all in a slave beyond and higher than merely instrumental and ministerial qualities – whether he can have the virtues of temperance, courage, justice, and the like; or whether slaves possess only bodily and ministerial qualities. And, whichever way we answer the question, a difficulty arises; for, if they have virtue, in what will they differ from freemen? On the other hand, since they are men and share in rational principle, it seems absurd to say that they have no virtue. A similar question may be raised about women and children, whether they too have virtues: ought a woman to be temperate and brave and just, and is a child to be called temperate, and intemperate, or not? So in general we may ask about the natural ruler, and the natural subject, whether they have the same or different virtues. For if a noble nature is equally required in both, why should one of them always rule, and the other always be ruled? Nor can we say that this is a question of degree, for the difference between ruler and subject is a difference of kind, which the difference of more and less never is. Yet how strange is the supposition that the one ought, and that the other ought not, to have virtue! For if the ruler is intemperate and unjust, how can he rule well? If the subject, how can he obey well? If he be licentious and cowardly, he will certainly not do his duty. It is evident, therefore, that both of them must have a share of virtue, but varying as natural subjects also vary among themselves. Here the very constitution of the soul has shown us the way; in it one part naturally rules, and the other is subject, and the virtue of the ruler we maintain to be different from that of the subject; – the one being the virtue of the rational, and the other of the irrational part. Now, it is obvious that the same principle applies generally, and therefore almost all things rule and are ruled according to nature. But the kind of rule differs;– the freeman rules over the slave after another manner from that in which the male rules over the female, or the man over the child; although the parts of the soul are present in all of them, they are present in different degrees. For the slave has no deliberative faculty at all; the woman has, but it is without authority, and the child has, but it is immature. So it must necessarily be supposed to be with the moral virtues also; all should partake of them, but only in such manner and degree as is required by each for the fulfillment of his duty. Hence the ruler ought to have moral virtue in perfection, for his function, taken absolutely, demands a master artificer, and rational principle is such an artificer; the subjects, on the other hand, require only that measure of virtue which is proper to each of them. Clearly, then, moral virtue belongs to all of them; but the temperance of a man and of a woman, or the courage and justice of a man and of a woman, are not, as Socrates maintained,[6] the same; the courage of a man is shown in commanding, of a woman in obeying. And this holds of all other virtues, as will be more clearly seen if we look at them in detail, for those who say generally that virtue consists in a good disposition of the soul, or in doing rightly, or the like, only deceive themselves. Far better than such definitions is their mode of speaking, who, like Gorgias,[7] enumerate the virtues. All classes must be deemed to have their special attributes; as the poet says of women,

'Silence is a woman's glory,'

but this is not equally the glory of man. The child is imperfect, and therefore obviously his virtue is not relative to himself alone, but to the perfect man and to his teacher, and in like manner the virtue of the slave is relative to a master. Now we determined that a slave is useful for the wants of life, and therefore he will obviously require only so much virtue as will prevent him from failing in his duty through cowardice or lack of self-control. Some one will ask whether if what we are saying is true, virtue will not be required also in the artisans, for they

---

6   Plato, *Meno*, 72 A-73C.
7   *Meno*, 71 E, 72 A.

often fail in their work through the lack of self-control? But is there not a great difference in the two cases? For the slave shares in his master's life; the artisan is less closely connected with him, and only attains excellence in proportion as he becomes a slave. The meaner sort of mechanic has a special and separate slavery; and whereas the slave exists by nature, not so the shoemaker or other artisan. It is manifest, then, that the master ought to be the source of such excellence in the slave, and not a mere possessor of the art of mastership which trains the slave in his duties. Wherefore they are mistaken who forbid us to converse with slaves and say that we should employ command only,[8] for slaves stand even more in need of admonition than children.

So much for this subject; the relations of husband and wife, parent and child, their several virtues, what in their intercourse with one another is good and what is evil, and how we may pursue the good and escape the evil, will have to be discussed when we speak of the different forms of government.[9] For, inasmuch as every family is a part of a state, and these relationships are the parts of a family, and the virtue of the part must have regard to the virtue of the whole, women and children must be trained by education with an eye to the constitution, if the virtues of either of them are supposed to make any difference in the virtues of the state. And they must have a difference: for the children grow up to be citizens, and half the free persons in a state are women.[10]

Bibliography

Barnes, Jonathan. *Aristotle*. Oxford and New York: Oxford University Press, 1982.

Barnes, Jonathan, ed. *The Cambridge Companion to Aristotle*. Cambridge: Cambridge University Press, 1995.

Jaeger, Werner. *Aristotle*. Oxford and New York: Oxford University Press, 1962. [originally published in German in 1923].

Moravcsik, J.M.E., ed. *Aristotle: A Collection of Critical Essays*. New York: Anchor Books, 1967.

Robinson, Timothy A. *Aristotle in Outline*. Indianapolis: Hackett Publishing Company, 1995.

Ross, Sir David. *Aristotle*. London: Methuen, 1964. [originally published 1923].

---

8   Plato, *Laws*, vi. 777E
9   The question is not actually discussed in the *Politics*.
10 Plato, *Laws*, vi. 781 A.

CHAPTER THREE— RENÉ DESCARTES

René Descartes (1596-1650) is generally styled "the father of modern philosophy," which may or may not help make intelligible from Freudian, feminist, and possibly other points of view, why he is so frequently attacked by twentieth-century thinkers. Seen as obsessively monomaniacally preoccupied with certainty, or as conceiving us along the most austerely abstractionist lines, as disembodied atoms of ratiocination, Descartes has been slammed by successive waves of critics – phenomenologist (Merleau-Ponty), ordinary-language analytic (Ryle), feminist, and postmodernist – as the author of most errors and wrong paths.

In fact much in these critiques seems to be caricature, or to miss Descartes's real aims and (putative) results. His goal and ambition was to be the grand synthesizing theorist of the newly emerging science, the successor (in such a role) of Aristotle. These aims notwithstanding, Descartes seems to have had one foot in modernity, and the other in the mediaeval world he supposed himself to have superseded. Most of the concern with certainty (appearing particularly dramatically in the first and second *Meditations*) seems actually to have been intended to foster rationalism, i.e., the conviction that the senses are inept and inadequate bases for theoretical knowledge, which must, Descartes held, rest on fundamental principles discerned in conceptual illumination. Descartes does not genuinely deny, or even neglect, bodily or social reality in favour of supposed disembodied atomism. The author of the *Meditations* and the "Replies" to the seven sets of "Objections" to them by diverse colleagues is aware of the cooperative, i.e., social character of the cognitive enterprise. And Descartes argues that the veracity of God ensures that we are substantially united to and in a physical body.

The dualism is real. Descartes, like many other thinkers before him, and to the present day, cannot see how freedom ("free will") can be reconciled with the closed causal structure of the physical world – which last Descartes sees in a particularly pronounced and mechanical form. Proclaiming our seamless "bodiness" does not obviously make this dilemma just go away.

Descartes has a remarkably egalitarian anti-elitist view of human nature. Our differences, for him are trivial; all of us are capable of philosophy, indeed, of coming to the (supposed) truths of Cartesian philosophy.

René Descartes, *Principles of Philosophy*

(Source: René Descartes. *Principles of Philosophy*. Trans. by Elizabeth S. Haldane and G.R.T. Ross. *The Philosophical Works of Descartes*. Cambridge: Cambridge University Press, 1931).

7. *That we cannot doubt our existence without existing while we doubt; and this is the first knowledge that we obtain when we philosophise in an orderly way.*

While we thus reject all that of which we can possibly doubt, and feign that it is false, it is easy to suppose that there is no God, nor heaven, nor bodies, and that we possess neither hands, nor feet, nor indeed any body; but we cannot in the same way conceive that we who doubt these things are not; for there is a contradiction in conceiving that what thinks does not at the same time as it thinks, exist. And hence this conclusion *I think, therefore I am,* is the first and most certain of all that occurs to one who philosophises in an orderly way.

8. This furnishes us with the distinction which exists between the soul and the body, or between that which thinks and that which is corporeal.

This, then, is the best way to discover the nature of mind and the distinction between it and the body. For, in considering what we are who suppose that all things apart from ourselves [our thought] are false, we observe very clearly that there is no extension, figure, local motion, or any such thing which may be attributed to body, which pertains to our nature, but only thought alone; and consequently this notion of thought precedes that of all corporeal things and is the most certain; since we still doubt whether there are any other things in the world, while we already perceive that we think.

9. What thought[1] is.

By the word thought I understand all that of which we are conscious as operating in us. And that is why not alone understanding, willing, imagining, but also feeling, are here the same thing as thought. For if I say I see, or I walk, I therefore am, and if by seeing and walking I mean the action of my eyes or my legs, which is the work of my body, my conclusion is not absolutely certain; because it may be that, as often happens in sleep, I think I see or I walk, although I never open my eyes or move from my place, and the same thing perhaps might occur if I had not a body at all. But if I mean only to talk of my sensation,[2] or my consciously seeming to see or to walk, it becomes quite true because my assertion now refers only to my mind, which alone is concerned with my feeling or thinking that I see or I walk.

32. That in us there are but two modes of thought, the perception of the understanding and the action of the will.

For all the modes of thinking that we observed in ourselves may be related to two general modes, the one of which consists in perception, or in the operation of the understanding, and the other in volition, or the operation of the will. Thus sense-perception,[3] imagining, and conceiving things that are purely intelligible, are just different methods of perceiving[4]; but desiring, holding in aversion, affirming, denying, doubting, all these are the different modes of willing.

37. That the principal perfection of man is to have the power of acting freely or by will, and that this is what renders him deserving of either praise or blame.

That will should extend widely is in accordance with its nature, and it is the greatest perfection in man to be able to act by its means, that is freely, and by so doing we are in a peculiar way masters of our actions, and thereby merit praise or blame. For we do not praise automatic machines although they respond exactly to the movements which they were destined to produce, since their actions are performed necessarily. We praise the workman who has made the machines because he has formed them with accuracy and has done so freely and not of necessity. And for the same reason when we choose what is true, much more credit is due to us when the choice is made freely, than when it is made of necessity.

39. That freedom of the will is self-evident.

Finally it is so evident that we are possessed of a free will that can give or withhold its assent, that this may be counted as one of the first and most ordinary notions that are found innately in us. We had before a very clear proof of this, for at the same time as we tried to doubt all things and even supposed that He who created us employed His unlimited powers in deceiving us in every way, we perceived in ourselves a liberty such that we were able to abstain from believing what was not perfectly certain and indubitable. But that of which we could not doubt at such a time is as self-evident and clear as anything we can ever know.

---

1   cogitatio.
2   sensu.
3   sentire.
4   percipiendi.

53. That each substance has a principal attribute, and that the attribute of the mind is thought, while that of body is extension.

But although any one attribute is sufficient to give us a knowledge of substance, there is always one principal property of substance which constitutes its nature and essence, and on which all the others depend. Thus extension in length, breadth and depth, constitutes the nature of corporeal substance; and thought constitutes the nature of thinking substance. For all else that may be attributed to body presupposes extension, and is but a mode of this extended thing; as everything that we find in mind is but so many diverse forms of thinking. Thus, for example, we cannot conceive figure but as an extended thing, nor movement but as in an extended space; so imagination, feeling, and will, only exist in a thinking thing. But, on the other hand, we can conceive extension without figure or action, and thinking without imagination or sensation, and so on with the rest; as is quite clear to anyone who attends to the matter.

66. That we also have a clear knowledge of our sensations, affections, and appetites, although we frequently err in the judgments we form of them.

There remain our sensations, affections and appetites, as to which we may likewise have a clear knowledge, if we take care to include in the judgments we form of them that only which we know to be precisely contained in our perception of them, and of which we are intimately conscious. It is, however, most difficult to observe this condition, in regard to our senses at least, because we, everyone of us, have judged from our youth up that all things of which we have been accustomed to have sensation have had an existence outside our thoughts, and that they have been entirely similar to the sensation, that is the idea which we have formed of them. Thus, when, for example, we perceived a certain colour, we thought that we saw something which existed outside of us and which clearly resembled the idea of colour which we then experienced in ourselves, and from the habit of judging in this way we seemed to see this so clearly and distinctly as to be convinced that it is certain and indubitable.

67. That we frequently deceive ourselves in judging of pain itself.

The same is true in regard to all our other sensations, even those which have to do with agreeable sensation and pain. For although we do not believe that these feelings exist outside of us, we are not wont to regard them as existing merely in our mind or our perception, but as being in our hands, feet, or some other part of our body. But there is no reason that we should be obliged to believe that the pain, for example, which we feel in our foot, is anything beyond our mind which exists in our foot, nor that the light which we imagine ourselves to see in the sun really is in the sun [as it is in us]; for both these are prejudices of our youth, as will clearly appear in what follows.

Bibliography

Cottingham, John. *A Descartes Dictionary.* Oxford: Blackwell, 1993.

Cottingham, John. *Descartes.* Oxford: Blackwell, 1986.

Garber, D. *Descartes' Metaphysical Physics.* Chicago: University of Chicago Press, 1992.

Moyal, J.D., ed. *René Descartes, Critical Assessments.* 4 vols. London and New York: Routledge, 1991.

Rosenfield, L.C. *From Beast-Machine to Man-Machine: The Theme of Animal Soul in French Letters from Descartes to La Mettrie.* New York: Oxford University Press, 1941.

Scott, J.F. *The Scientific Work of René Descartes.* London: Taylor and Francis, 1952.

CHAPTER FOUR — LA ROCHEFOUCAULD

François, 2nd duc de La Rochefoucauld (1613-1680) was a noble, a soldier, and a writer in the reigns of Kings Louis XIII and Louis XIV of France. From 1656 until his death he lived in Paris, and frequented the court and the literary salons of the capital. This led to his *Maximes*, short aphoristic observations of human nature. Published in successive editions, these have enjoyed a very considerable success ever since their first appearance. Too cynical or misanthropic for some sensibilities, La Rochefoucauld is seen by others as having captured fundamental facets of humanity's makeup.

La Rochefoucauld, *Maxims*

(Source: La Rochefoucauld. *Maxims*. Trans. Leonard Tancock. Harmondsworth: Penguin, 1959.)

11
Passions often engender their opposites. Avarice sometimes begets prodigality and prodigality avarice; a man is often resolute through weakness and bold through timidity.

12
Whatever care a man takes to veil his passions with appearances of piety and honour, they always show through.

13
Our self-esteem is more inclined to resent criticism of our tastes than of our opinions.

14
Not only do men tend to forget kindnesses and wrongs alike, but they even hate those who have done them kindnesses and give up hating those who have wronged them. The effort needed to reward goodness and take revenge upon evil seems to them a tyranny to which they are loth to submit.

17
The moderation of happy people comes from the tranquillity that good fortune gives to their disposition.

19
We all have strength enough to endure the troubles of others.

21
Condemned men sometimes affect a steadfastness and indifference to death which is really only fear of looking death in the face; thus it can be said that this steadfastness and indifference do for their spirit what the bandage does for their eyes.

22
Philosophy easily triumphs over past ills and ills to come, but present ills triumph over philosophy.

27
We often pride ourselves on even the most criminal passions, but envy is a timid and shamefaced passion we never dare acknowledge.

78
In most men love of justice is only fear of suffering injustice.

83
What men have called friendship is merely association, respect for each other's interests, and exchange of good offices, in fact nothing more than a business arrangement from which self-love is always out to draw some profit.

87
Social life would not last long if men were not taken in by each other.

88
Our self-esteem magnifies or minimizes the good qualities of our friends according to how pleased we are with them, and we measure their worth by the way they get on with us.

93

Old people are fond of giving good advice; it consoles them for no longer being capable of setting a bad example.

122

When we resist our passions it is more on account of their weakness than our strength.

135

At times we are as different from ourselves as we are from others.

136

Some people would never have fallen in love if they had never heard of love.

146

We seldom praise except to get praise back.

149

To refuse to accept praise is to want to be praised twice over.

173

There are various forms of curiosity: one, based on self-interest, makes us want to learn what may be useful, another, based on pride, comes from a desire to know what others don't.

178

What makes us like new acquaintances is not so much weariness of the old ones or the pleasure of making a change, as displeasure at not being sufficiently admired by those who know us too well, and the hope of being more admired by those who do not yet know us well enough.

184

We own up to our failings so that our honesty may repair the damage those failings do us in other men's eyes.

196

Our misdeeds are easily forgotten when they are known only to ourselves.

199

Desire to appear clever often prevents our becoming so.

207

Childishness follows us all the days of our life. If anybody seems wise it is only because his follies are in keeping with his age and circumstances.

223

Gratitude is like commercial good faith: it keeps trade going, and we pay up, not because it is right to settle our account but so that people will be more willing to extend us credit.

235

We easily find consolation for the misfortunes of our friends when these give us a chance to display our fondness for them.

254

Humility is often merely feigned submissiveness assumed in order to subject others, an artifice of pride which stoops to conquer, and although pride has a thousand ways of transforming itself it is never so well disguised and able to take people in as when masquerading as humility.

256

In every walk of life each man puts on a personality and outward appearance so as to look what he wants to be thought: in fact you might say that society is entirely made up of assumed personalities.

259

The pleasure of love is loving, and we get more happiness from the passion we feel than from the passion we inspire.

262

There is no passion in which love of self rules so despotically as love, and we are always more inclined to sacrifice the loved one's tranquillity than to lose our own.

263

What is called generosity is most often just the vanity of giving, which we like more than what we give.

264

Pity is often feeling our own sufferings in those of others, a shrewd precaution against misfortunes that may befall us. We give help to others so that they have to do the same for us on similar occasions, and these kindnesses we do them are, to put it plainly, gifts we bestow on ourselves in advance.

267

Readiness to believe the worst without adequate examination comes from pride and laziness: we want to find culprits but cannot be bothered to investigate the crimes.

296

It is difficult to love those we do not respect, but it is no less difficult to love those whom we respect far more than ourselves.

303

Whatever good we are told about ourselves, we learn nothing new.

304

We often forgive those who bore us, but we cannot forgive those who find us boring.

312

The reason lovers never tire of each other's company is that the conversation is always about themselves.

329

Sometimes we think we dislike flattery, but it is only the way it is done that we dislike.

372

Most young people think they are being natural when really they are just ill-mannered and crude.

386

No people are more often wrong than those who cannot bear to be.

473

Rare though true love may be, true friendship is rarer still.

475

Desire for sympathy or admiration is usually the main reason for our confiding in others.

623

We do not readily believe what is beyond our field of vision.

Bibliography

Lewis, Philip E. *La Rochefoucauld: The Art of Abstraction*. Ithaca, N.Y.: Cornell University Press, 1977.

Mourgues, Odette de. *Two French moralists: La Rochefoucauld and La Bruyère*. Cambridge: Cambridge University Press, 1978.

Thweatt, Vivien. *La Rochefoucauld and the seventeenth-century concept of the self*. Geneva: Droz, 1980.

CHAPTER FIVE — ROCHESTER

John Wilmot, 2nd Earl of Rochester (1647-1680) was a leading figure of the Restoration court of King Charles II of England. He was a brilliant poet, and an individual who definitely burned the candle at both ends, dying prematurely following a life of excess, with a conversion to Christianity in his final months. His verse is typically satirical, or obscene (and sometimes both). The title of the work that follows is evidently intended to pun: the poem is both a satire against mankind, and a satyr's perspective on our species. More than one theory that appears in the present volume comes within range of Rochester's verse.

Earl of Rochester, *A Satyre Against Mankind*

Were I (who to my cost already am)
One of those strange, prodigious creatures, man
A spirit free to choose for my own share
What case of flesh and blood I pleased to wear,
I'd be a dog, a monkey, or a bear,
Or anything but that vain animal
Who is so proud of being rational.
The senses are too gross, and he'll contrive
A sixth to contradict the other five,
And before certain instinct, will prefer
Reason, which fifty times for one does err;
Reason, an *ignis fatuus* in the mind,
Which leaves the light of nature, sense, behind,
Pathless and dangerous wandering ways it takes
Through error's fenny bogs and thorny brakes,
Whilst the misguided follower climbs with pain
Mountains of whimseys heaped in his own brain;
Tumbling from thought to thought, falls headlong
        down
Into doubt's boundless sea, where, like to drown,
Books bear him up awhile and make him try
To swim with bladders of philosophy.
In hope still to o'ertake th'escaping light,
The vapour dances in his dazzled sight
Till spent, it leaves him to eternal night.
Then Old Age and Experience, hand and hand,
Lead him to death and make him understand,
After a search so painful and so long,
That all his life he has been in the wrong.
Huddled in dirt, the reasoning engine lies,
Who was so proud, so witty, and so wise.
Pride drew him in, as cheats their bubbles catch,
And made him venture to be made a wretch.
His wisdom did his happiness destroy,
Aiming to know that world he should enjoy.

And wit was his vain, frivolous pretense
Of pleasing others at his own expense.
For wits are treated just like common whores;
First they're enjoyed and then kicked out of doors.
The pleasure past, a threatening doubt remains
That frights th'enjoyer with succeeding pains.
Women and men of wit are dangerous tools
And ever fatal to admiring fools.
Pleasure allures, and when the fops escape,
'Tis not that they're belov'd but fortunate,
And therefore what they fear, at heart they hate.
But now methinks some formal band and beard
Takes me to task. Come on, sir, I'm prepared.
  'Then, by your favour, anything that's writ
Against this gibing, jingling knack called wit
Likes me abundantly, but you'll take care
Upon this point, not to be too severe.
Perhaps my muse were fitter for this part,
For I profess I can be very smart
On wit, which I abhor with all my heart.
I long to lash it in some sharp essay,
But your grand indiscretion bids me stay
And turns my tide of ink another way.
What rage ferments in your degenerate mind
To make you rail at reason and mankind?
Blest, glorious man, to whom alone kind heaven
An everlasting soul hath freely given,
Whom his great maker took such care to make
That from himself he did the image take
And this fair frame in shining reason dressed
To dignify his nature above beast;
Reason, by whose aspiring influence
We take a flight beyond material sense,
Dive into mysteries, then soaring pierce
The flaming limits of the universe,
Search heaven and hell, find out what's acted
        there,

And give the world true grounds of hope and
    fear!'
 'Hold, mighty man,' I cry, 'all this we know
From the pathetic pen of Ingelo,
From Patrick's *Pilgrim*, Stillingfleet's replies,
And 'tis this very reason I despise
This supernatural gift that makes a mite
Think he's the image of the infinite,
Comparing his short life, void of all rest,
To the eternal and the ever blest,
This busy, puzzling stirrer up of doubt
That frames deep myst'ries and then finds them
    out,
Filling with frantic crowds of thinking fools
Those reverend bedlams, colleges and schools,
Borne on whose wings, each heavy sot can pierce
The limits of the boundless universe;
So charming ointments make an old witch fly
And bear a crippled carcass through the sky.
'Tis this exalted power, whose business lies
In nonsense and impossibilities,
This made a whimsical philosopher
Before the spacious world his tub prefer,
And we have modern, cloistered coxcombs who
Retire to think, 'cause they have nought to do.
But thoughts were given for action's government;
Where action ceases, thought's impertinent.
Our sphere of action is life's happiness,
And he who thinks beyond thinks like an ass.
Thus, whilst against false reasoning I inveigh,
I own right reason, which I would obey,
That reason which distinguishes by sense
And gives us rules of good and ill from thence,
That bounds desires with a reforming will
To keep them more in vigour, not to kill.
Your reason hinders, mine helps to enjoy,
Renewing appetites yours would destroy.
My reason is my friend, yours is a cheat:
Hunger calls out, my reason bids me eat,
Perversely, yours your appetites does mock;
This asks for food, that answers, "What's
    o'clock?"
This plain distinction, sir, your doubt secures:
'Tis not true reason I despise, but yours.'
 Thus I think reason righted, but for man
I'll ne'er recant; defend him if you can.
For all his pride and his philosophy,
'Tis evident beasts are in their degree
As wise at least and better far than he.
Those creatures are the wisest who attain

By surest means the ends at which they aim.
If therefore Jowler finds and kills his hares
Better than Meres supplies committee chairs,
Though one's a statesman, t'other but a hound,
Jowler in justice would be wiser found.
   You see how far man's wisdom here extends,
Look next if human nature makes amends.
Whose principles most gen'rous are and just,
And to whose morals you would sooner trust,
Be judge yourself, I'll bring it to the test
Which is the basest creature, man or beast?
Birds feed on birds, beasts on each other prey,
But savage man alone does man betray.
Pressed by necessity, they kill for food;
Man undoes man to do himself no good.
With teeth and claws by nature armed, they hunt
Nature's allowance to supply their want,
But man with smiles, embraces, friendship, praise,
Most humanly his fellow's life betrays,
With voluntary pains works his distress,
Not through necessity but wantonness.
For hunger or for love they bite and tear,
Whilst wretched man is still in arms for fear.
For fear he arms and is of arms afraid,
From fear to fear successively betrayed,
Base fear, the source whence his best actions
    came,
His boasted honour and his dear-bought fame,
The lust of power to which he's such a slave
And for the which alone he dares be brave,
To which his various projects are designed,
Which makes him generous, affable, and kind,
For which he takes such pains to be thought wise,
And screws his actions in a forced disguise,
Leads a most tedious life in misery
Under laborious, mean hypocrisy.
Look to the bottom of this vast design,
Wherein man's wisdom, power, and glory join:
The good he acts, the ill he does endure,
'Tis all from fear, to make himself secure.
Merely for safety, after fame they thirst,
For all men would be cowards if they durst,
And honesty's against all common sense:
Men must be knaves, 'tis in their own defence.
Mankind's dishonest; if you think it fair
Amongst known cheats to play upon the square,
You'll be undone.
Nor can weak truth your reputation save:
The knaves will all agree to call you knave.
Wronged shall he live, insulted o'er, oppressed,

Who dares be less a villain than the rest.
Thus here you see what human nature craves:
Most men are cowards, all men should be knaves.
The difference lies, as far as I can see,
Not in the thing itself, but the degree,
And all the subject matter of debate
Is only, Who's a knave of the first rate?
   All this with indignation have I hurled
At the pretending part of the proud world,
Who, swollen with selfish vanity, devise
False freedoms, holy cheats, and formal lies
Over their fellow slaves to tyrannize.
   But if in court so just a man there be
(In court, a just man, yet unknown to me)
Who does his needful flattery direct,
Not to oppress and ruin, but protect;
Since flattery, which way soever laid,
Is still a tax on that unhappy trade,
If so upright a statesman you can find,
Whose passions bend to his unbiased mind,
Who does his arts and policies apply
To raise his country, not his family,
Nor while his pride owned avarice withstands,
Receives close bribes from friends' corrupted
      hands;
Is there a churchman who on God relies,
Whose life, his faith and doctrine justifies;
Not one blown up with vain, prelatic pride,
Who for reproof of sins does man deride;
Whose envious heart makes preaching a pretense,
With his obstreperous, saucy eloquence,
Dares chide at kings and rail at men of sense;

Who from his pulpit vents more peevish lies,
More bitter railings, scandals, calumnies,
Than at a gossiping are thrown about
When the good wives get drunk and then fall out;
None of that sensual tribe whose talents lie
In avarice, pride, sloth, and gluttony,
Who hunt good livings but abhor good lives,
Whose lust exalted to that height arrives
They act adultery with their own wives,
And ere a score of years completed be,
Can from the lofty pulpit proudly see
Half a large parish their own progeny;
Nor doting bishop who would be adored
For domineering at the council board,
A greater fop in business at fourscore,
Fonder of serious toys, affected more
Than the gay, glittering fool at twenty proves
With all his noise, his tawdry clothes, and loves;
But a meek, humble man of modest sense,
Who, preaching peace, does practise continence,
Whose pious life's a proof he does believe
Mysterious truths which no man can conceive;
If upon earth there dwell such God-like men,
I'll here recant my paradox to them,
Adore those shrines of virtue, homage pay,
And with the rabble world their laws obey.
   If such there are, yet grant me this at least,
Man differs more from man than man from beast.

(Source: *Collected Works of John Wilmot, Earl of Rochester*. Ed. John Hayward. London: Nonesuch Press, 1926.)

II

CHRISTIAN VIEWS OF HUMAN NATURE

CHAPTER SIX — ST. AUGUSTINE

St. Augustine (354-411) was a giant of the Christian church and of Christian theology in their first half-millennium, and his influence continued to be extremely powerful thereafter. Augustine is responsible for the first fully crafted Christian view of the world and humanity's place within it, and its relation to the deity.

Part of the basis for the comprehensive success of this work was Augustine's clear talent for – indeed, brilliant originality in – philosophy. His writings often exhibit a resolve to contemplative piety which gets sidetracked into detailed investigation of themes like the nature of time, and what it is for a sign to be meaningful, or, as in the present primary selection, the nature of memory. Augustine seems to have been incapable of refraining from philosophizing, and the result is frequently a searching, innovative, still significant exploration of the topic that has preoccupied him.

A distinctive and importantly Christian account of human nature emerges in the course of his grappling with his own personal religious odyssey, and assembling a Christian scheme of things at large. Much of that account will be seen in the selections that follow. Augustine wrote what is often seen as the first autobiography ever produced, the *Confessions* (from which our lengthier selection derives). As a result, it is sometimes claimed that he is the discoverer of, or the first articulate vehicle for, full human self-consciousness – the self overhearing itself thinking, and reflecting on its actions and presence in the world. It is certainly possible to overstate this case. The Roman poet Ovid, especially in his poetry of exile, achieves a nearly comparable autobiographical note, as do other ancient poets and, occasionally, the Platonic character of Socrates in some of the dialogues; and the *Psalms* of the Old Testament sometimes express an impressive degree of self-consciousness. Still, there is something to the claim made for Augustine, and it has importance for what he contributes to the theory of human nature. This is very much the voice of the self in its self-apprehending subjectivity, trying to understand that self inwardly and in relation to other selves (especially a divine self) and the surrounding universe. Finally, Augustine develops an account of mind – and its special primary components and functions – and body that echoes Plato, yet has its own originality.

St. Augustine, *Confessions*

(Source: St. Augustine. *Confessions*. Trans. R.S. Pine-Coffin. Middlesex: Penguin Books, 1961, 207-252.)

Book X
2

So, O Lord, all that I am is laid bare before you. I have declared how it profits me to confess to you.

And I make my confession, not in words and sounds made by the tongue alone, but with the voice of my soul and in my thoughts which cry aloud to you. Your ear can hear them. For when I am sinful, if I am displeased with myself, this is a confession that I make to you; and when I am good, if I do not claim the merit for myself, this too is confession. For you, O Lord *give your benediction to the just,*[1] but first *you make a just man of the sinner.*[2] And so my confession is made both silently

---

1   Ps. 5 13 (5:12).
2   Rom. 4:5.

in your sight, my God, and aloud as well, because even though my tongue utters no sound, my heart cries to you. For whatever good I may speak to men you have heard it before in my heart, and whatever good you hear in my heart, you have first spoken to me yourself.

3

Why, then, does it matter to me whether men should hear what I have to confess, as though it were they who were to cure all the evil that is in me? They are an inquisitive race, always anxious to pry into other men's lives, but never ready to correct their own. Why do they wish to hear from me what sort of man I am, though they will not listen to you when you tell them what they are? When they hear me speak about myself, how do they know whether I am telling the truth, since no one *knows a man's thoughts, except the man's own spirit that is within him?*[3] But if they listen to what you tell them about themselves, they cannot say 'The Lord is lying,' for to heed what you tell them about themselves is simply to recognize themselves for what they are. And if a man recognises his true self, can he possibly say 'This is false,' unless he is himself a liar? But charity believes all things – all things, that is, which are spoken by those who are joined as one in charity – and for this reason I, too, O Lord, make my confession aloud in the hearing of men. For although I cannot prove to them that my confessions are true, at least I shall be believed by those whose ears are opened to me by charity.

Physician of my soul, make me see clearly how it profits me to do this. You have forgiven my past sins and drawn a veil over them, and in this way you have given me happiness in yourself, changing my life by faith and your sacrament. But when others read of those past sins of mine, or hear about them, their hearts are stirred so that they no longer lie listless in despair, crying 'I cannot.' Instead their hearts are roused by the love of your mercy and the joy of your grace, by which each one of us, weak though he be, is made strong, since by it he is made conscious of his own weakness. And the good are glad to hear of the past sins of others who are now free of them. They are glad, not because those sins are evil, but because what was evil is now evil no more.

What does it profit me, then, O Lord, to whom my conscience confesses daily, confident more in the hope of your mercy than in its own innocence, what does it profit me, I ask, also to make known to men in your sight, through this book, not what I once was, but what I am now? I know what profit I gain by confessing my past, and this I have declared. But many people who know me, and others who do not know me but have heard of me or read my books, wish to hear what I am now, at this moment, as I set down my confessions. They cannot lay their ears to my heart, and yet it is in my heart that I am whatever I am. So they wish to listen as I confess what I am in my heart, into which they cannot pry by eye or ear or mind. They wish to hear and they are ready to believe; but can they really know me? Charity, which makes them good, tells them that I do not lie about myself when I confess what I am, and it is this charity in them that believes me.

4
....

The good I do is done by you in me and by your grace: the evil is my fault; it is the punishment you send me. Let my brothers draw their breath in joy for the one and sigh with grief for the other. Let hymns of thanksgiving and cries of sorrow rise together from their hearts, as though they were vessels burning with incense before you. And I pray you, O Lord, to be pleased with the incense that rises in your holy temple and, for your name's sake, to *have mercy on me, as you are ever rich in mercy*.[4] Do not relinquish what you have begun, but make perfect what is still imperfect in me.

So, if I go on to confess, not what I was, but what I am, the good that comes of it is this. There is joy in my heart when I confess to you, yet there is fear as well; there is sorrow, and yet hope. But I confess not only to you but also to the believers among men, all who share my joy and all who, like me, are doomed to die; all who are my fellows in your kingdom and all who accompany me on this pilgrimage, whether they have gone before or are still to come or are with me as I make my way through life. They are your servants and my brothers. You have chosen them to be your sons. You have named them

---

3 I Cor. 2:11.
4 Ps. 50:3 (51:1)

as the masters whom I am to serve if I wish to live with you and in your grace. This is your bidding, but it would hold less meaning for me if it were made known to me in words alone and I had not the example of Christ, who has shown me the way by his deeds as well. I do your bidding in word and deed alike. I do it beneath the protection of your wings, for the peril would be too great if it were not that my soul has submitted to you and sought the shelter of your wings and that my weakness is known to you. I am no more than a child, but my Father lives for ever and I have a Protector great enough to save me. For he who begot me and he who watches over me are one and the same, and for me there is no good but you, the Almighty, who are with me even before I am with you. So to such as you command me to serve I will reveal, not what I have been, but what I have become and what I am. But, since I do not *scrutinize my own conduct*,[5] let my words be understood as they are meant.

5

It is you, O Lord, who judge me. For though no one *can know a man's thoughts, except the man's own spirit that is within him*,[6] there are some things in man which even his own spirit within him does not know. But you, O Lord, know all there is to know of him, because you made him. Yet though, in your sight, I despise myself and consider myself as mere dust and ashes, there is one thing that I know about you which I do not know about myself. I know that it is impossible for you to suffer harm, whereas I do not know which temptations I can resist and which I cannot. This much I know, although *at present I am looking at a confused reflection in a mirror, not yet face to face*,[7] and therefore, as long as I am away from you, during my pilgrimage, I am more aware of myself than of you. But my hope lies in the knowledge that *you do not play us false; you will not allow us to be tempted beyond our powers. With the temptation itself, you will ordain the issue of it, and enable us to hold our own.*[8]

I shall therefore confess both what I know of myself and what I do not know. For even what I know about myself I only know because your light shines upon me; and what I do not know about myself I shall continue not to know until I see you face to face and *my dusk is noonday*.[9]

6
....

. . . I turned to myself and asked, 'Who are you?' 'A man,' I replied. But it is clear that I have both body and soul, the one the outer, the other the inner part of me. Which of these two ought I to have asked to help me find my God? With my bodily powers I had already tried to find him in earth and sky, as far as the sight of my eyes could reach, like an envoy sent upon a search. But my inner self is the better of the two, for it was to the inner part of me that my bodily senses brought their messages. They delivered to their arbiter and judge the replies which they carried back from the sky and the earth and all that they contain, those replies which stated 'We are not God and God is he who made us.' The inner part of man knows these things through the agency of the outer part. I, the inner man know these things; I, the soul, know them through the senses of my God. I asked the whole mass of the universe about my God, and it replied, 'I am not God. God is he who made me.' Surely everyone whose senses are not impaired is aware of the universe around him? Why, then, does it not give the same message to us all? The animals, both great and small, are aware of it, but they cannot inquire into its meaning because they are not guided by reason, which can sift the evidence relayed to them by their senses. Man, on the other hand, can question nature. He is able to *catch sight of God's invisible nature through his creatures*,[10] but his love of these material things is too great. He becomes their slave, and slaves cannot be judges. Nor will the world supply an answer to those who question it, unless they also have the faculty to judge it. It does not answer in different language – that is, it does not change its aspect – according to whether a man merely looks at it or subjects it to inquiry while he looks. If it did, its appearance would be different in each case. Its

---

5   I Cor. 4:3.
6   I Cor. 2 11.
7   I Cor. 13:12.
8   I Cor. 10:13.
9   Is. 58:10.
10   Rom. I:20.

aspect is the same in both cases, but to the man who merely looks it says nothing, while to the other it gives an answer. It would be nearer the truth to say that it gives an answer to all, but it is only understood by those who compare the message it gives them through their senses with the truth that is in themselves. For truth says to me, 'Your God is not heaven or earth or any kind of bodily thing.' We can tell this from the very nature of such things, for those who have eyes to see know that their bulk is less in the part than in the whole. And I know that my soul is the better part of me, because it animates the whole of my body. It gives it life, and this is something that nobody can give to another body. But God is even more. He is the Life of the life of my soul.

7

What, then, do I love when I love God? Who is this Being who is so far above my soul? If I am to reach him, it must be through my soul. But I must go beyond the power by which I am joined to my body and by which I fill its frame with life. This is not the power by which I could find my God, for if it were, *the horse and the mule, senseless creatures*,[11] could find him too, because they also have this same power which gives life to their bodies. But there is another faculty in me besides this. By it I not only give life to my body but also give it the power of perceiving things by its senses. God gave me this faculty when he ordered my eyes not to hear but to see and my ears not to see but to hear. And to each of the other senses he assigned its own place and its own function. I, the soul, who am one alone, exercise all these different functions by means of my senses. But I must go beyond this faculty as well, for horses and mules also have it, since they too feel by means of their bodies.

8

So I must also go beyond this natural faculty of mine, as I rise by stages towards the God who made me. The next stage is memory which is like a great field or a spacious palace, a storehouse for countless images of all kinds which are conveyed to it by the senses. In it are stored away all the thoughts by which we enlarge upon or diminish or modify in any way the perceptions at which we arrive through the senses, and it also contains anything else that has been entrusted to it for safe keeping, until such time as these things are swallowed up and buried in forgetfulness. When I use my memory, I ask it to produce whatever it is that I wish to remember. Some things it produces immediately; some are forthcoming only after a delay, as though they were being brought out from some inner hiding place; others come spilling from the memory, thrusting themselves upon us when what we want is something quite different, as much as to say 'Perhaps we are what you want to remember?' These I brush aside from the picture which memory presents to me, allowing my mind to pick what it chooses, until finally that which I wish to see stands out clearly and emerges into sight from its hiding place. Some memories present themselves easily and in the correct order just as I require them. They come and give place in their turn to others that follow upon them, and as their place is taken they return to their place of storage, ready to emerge again when I want them. This is what happens when I recite something by heart.

In the memory everything is preserved separately, according to its category. Each is admitted through its own special entrance. For example, light, colour, and shape are admitted through the eyes; sound of all kinds through the ears; all sorts of smell through the nostrils; and every kind of taste through the mouth. The sense of touch, which is common to all parts of the body, enables us to distinguish between hard and soft, hot and cold, rough and smooth, heavy and light, and it can be applied to things which are inside the body as well as to those which are outside it. All these sensations are retained in the great storehouse of the memory, which in some indescribable way secretes them in its folds. They can be brought out and called back again when they are needed, but each enters the memory through its own gateway and is retained in it. The things which we sense do not enter the memory themselves, but their images are there ready to present themselves to our thoughts when we recall them.

We may know by which of the senses these images were recorded and laid up in the memory, but who can tell how the images themselves are formed? Even when I am in darkness and in silence I can, if

---

11   Ps. 31:9 (32:9).

I wish, picture colours in my memory. I can distinguish between black and white and any other colours that I wish. And while I reflect upon them, sounds do not break in and confuse the images of colour, which reached me through the eye. Yet my memory holds sounds as well, though it stores them separately. If I wish, I can summon them too. They come forward at once, so that I can sing as much as I want, even though my tongue does not move and my throat utters no sound. And when I recall into my mind this rich reserve of sound, which entered my memory through my ears, the images of colour, which are also there in my memory, do not interfere or intrude. In the same way I can recall at will all the other things which my other senses brought into my memory and deposited in it. I can distinguish the scent of lilies from that of violets, even though there is no scent at all in my nostrils, and simply by using my memory I recognize that I like honey better than wine and smooth things better than rough ones, although at that moment I neither taste nor touch anything.

All this goes on inside me, in the vast cloisters of my memory. In it are the sky, the earth, and the sea, ready at my summons, together with everything that I have ever perceived in them by my senses, except the things which I have forgotten. In it I meet myself as well. I remember myself and what I have done, when and where I did it, and the state of my mind at the time. In my memory, too, are all the events that I remember, whether they are things that have happened to me or things that I have heard from others. From the same source I can picture to myself all kinds of different images based either upon my own experience or upon what I find credible because it tallies with my own experience. I can fit them into the general picture of the past; from them I can make a surmise of actions and events and hopes for the future; and I can contemplate them all over again as if they were actually present. If I say to myself in the vast cache of my mind, where all those images of great things are stored, 'I shall do this or that,' the picture of this or that particular thing comes to my mind at once. Or I may say to myself 'If only this or that would happen!' or 'God forbid that this or that should be!' No sooner do I say this than the images of all the things of which I speak spring forward from the same great treasure-house of the memory. And, in fact, I could not even mention them at all if the images were lacking.

The power of the memory is prodigious, my God. It is a vast, immeasurable sanctuary. Who can plumb its depths? And yet it is a faculty of my soul. Although it is part of my nature, I cannot understand all that I am. This means, then, that the mind is too narrow to contain itself entirely. But where is that part of it which it does not itself contain? Is it somewhere outside itself and not within it? How then, can it be part of it, if it is not contained in it?

I am lost in wonder when I consider this problem. It bewilders me. Yet men go out and gaze in astonishment at high mountains, the huge waves of the sea, the broad reaches of rivers, the ocean that encircles the world, or the stars in their courses. But they pay no attention to themselves. They do not marvel at the thought that while I have been mentioning all these things, I have not been looking at them with my eyes, and that I could not even speak of mountains or waves, rivers or stars, which are things that I have seen, or of the ocean, which I know only on the evidence of others, unless I could see them in my mind's eye, in my memory, and with the same vast spaces between them that would be there if I were looking at them in the world outside myself. When I saw them with the sight of my eyes, I did not draw them bodily into myself. They are not inside me themselves, but only their images. And I know which of my senses imprinted each image on my mind.

9

But these are not the only treasures stored in the vast capacity of my memory. It also contains all that I have ever learnt of the liberal sciences, except what I have forgotten. This knowledge it keeps apart from the rest, in an inner place – though it is wrong to speak of it as a place – and in their case it does not retain mere images but the facts themselves. For any knowledge I may have of grammar, or of the art of debating, or of the different categories of questions, remains in my memory, but not as though I merely retained an image of it, leaving the facts outside myself, or as though it had sounded in my ear and then passed away. It is not like a voice which is imprinted on the mind through the ears, leaving a trace by which it can be recalled, as if its sound were still to be heard even after it has become silent. Nor is it like an odour which, even though it does not last and is carried away on the wind, affects the sense of smell and through it conveys to the memory an impression of itself, by which it can be remembered and reproduced. It is not like food, which certainly loses its taste once it reaches the belly, and yet can be said to retain its taste in the memory. Again, it is unlike anything which the body feels by the sense of touch and can still be sensed in the memory even after contact with it is lost. In these cases the things themselves do not penetrate into the memory. It is simply that the memory captures their images with astonishing speed and stores them away in its wonderful system of compartments, ready to produce them again in just as wonderful a way when we remember them.

10

When I am told that it is possible to ask three kinds of question – whether a thing is, what it is, and of what sort it is – I retain images of the sounds of which these words are composed. I know that these sounds have passed through the air and now are no more. But the facts which they represent have not reached me through any of my bodily senses. I could not see them at all except in my mind, and it is not their images that I store in my memory but the facts themselves. But they must themselves tell me, if they can, by what means they entered my mind. For I can run through all the organs of sense, which are the body's gateways to the mind, but I cannot find any by which these facts could have entered. My eyes tell me 'If they have colour we reported them.' My ears say 'If they have sound, it was we who gave notice of them.' My nose says 'If they have any smell, it was through me that they passed into the mind.' The sense of taste says 'If they have no taste, do not put your question to me.' The sense of touch says 'If it is not a body, I did not touch it, and if I did not touch it, I had no message to transmit.'

How, then, did these facts get into my memory? Where did they come from? I do not know. When I learned them, I did not believe them with another man's mind. It was my own mind which recognized them and admitted that they were true. I entrusted them to my own mind as though it were a place of storage from which I could produce them at will. Therefore they must have been in my mind even before I learned them, though not present to my memory. Then whereabouts in my mind were they? How was it that I recognized them when they were mentioned and agreed that they were true? It must have been that they were already in my memory, hidden away in its deeper recesses, in so remote a part of it that I might not have been able to think of them at all, if some other person had not brought them to the fore by teaching me about them.

11

From this we can conclude that learning these facts, which do not reach our minds as images by means of the senses but are recognised by us in our minds, without images, as they actually are, is simply a process of thought by which we gather together things which although they are muddled and confused, are already contained in the memory. When we give them our attention, we see to it that these facts, which have been lying scattered and unheeded, are placed ready to hand, so that they are easily forthcoming once we have grown used to them. My memory holds a great number of facts of this sort, things which I have already discovered and, as I have said, placed ready to hand. This is what is meant by saying that we have learnt them and know them. If, for a short space of time, I cease to give them my attention, they sink back and recede again into the more remote cells of my memory, so that I have to think them out again, like a fresh set of facts, if I am to know them. I have to shepherd them out again from their old lairs, because there is no other place where they can have gone. In other words, once they have been dispersed, I have to collect them again, and this is the derivation of the word *cogitare*, which means *to think* or *to collect one's thoughts*. For in Latin the word *cogo,* meaning *I assemble* or *I collect,* is related to *cogito,* which means *I think,* in the same way as *ago* is related to *agito* or *facio* to *factito*. But the word *cogito* is restricted to the function of the mind. It is correctly used only of what is assembled in the mind, not what is assembled elsewhere.

12

The memory also contains the innumerable principles and laws of numbers and dimensions. None of these can have been conveyed to it by means of the bodily senses, because they cannot be seen, heard, smelled, tasted, or touched. I have heard the sounds of the words by which their meaning is expressed when they are discussed, but the words are one thing and the principles another. The words may sometimes be spoken in Latin and at other times in Greek, but the principles are neither Greek nor Latin. They are not language at all. I have seen lines drawn by architects, and they are sometimes as fine as the thread spun by spiders. But these principles are different. They are not images of things which the eye of my body has reported to me. We know them simply by recognizing them inside ourselves without reference to any material object. With all the senses of my body I have become aware of numbers as they are used in counting things. But the principle of number, by which we count, is not the same. It is not an image of the things we count, but something which is there in its own right. If anyone is blind to it, he may laugh at my words: I shall pity him for his ridicule.

13

I carry all these facts in my memory, and I also remember how I learned them. I have also heard, and remember, many false arguments put forward to dispute them. Even if the arguments are false the fact that I remember them is not false. I also remember distinguishing between the true facts and the false theories advanced against them, and there is a difference between seeing myself make this distinction now and remembering that I have made it often in the past, every time that I have given the matter any thought. So I not only remember that I have often understood these facts in the past, but I also commit to memory the fact that I understand them and distinguish the truth from the falsehood at the present moment. By this means I ensure that later on I shall remember that I understood them at this time. And I remember that I have remembered, just as later on, if I remember that I have been able to remember these facts now, it will be by the power of my memory that I shall remember doing so.

14

My memory also contains my feelings, not in the same way as they are present to the mind when it experiences them, but in a quite different way that is in keeping with the special powers of the memory. For even when I am unhappy I can remember times when I was cheerful, and when I am cheerful I can remember past unhappiness. I can recall past fears and yet not feel afraid, and when I remember that I once wanted something, I can do so without wishing to have it now. Sometimes memory induces the opposite feeling, for I can be glad to remember sorrow that is over and done with and sorry to remember happiness that has come to an end. There would be nothing remarkable in this if memory recalled only our bodily sensations, for the mind is one thing and the body another, and it would not be strange if I were glad to remember some bygone bodily pain. But the mind and the memory are one and the same. We even call the memory the mind, for when we tell another person to remember something, we say 'See that you bear this in mind,' and when we forget something, we say 'It was not in my mind' or 'It slipped out of my mind.' This being so, how can it be that, when I am glad to remember sorrow that is past – that is, when there is joy in my mind and sadness in my memory – how can it be that my mind is happy because of the joy that is in it and yet my memory is not sad by reason of the sadness that is in it? No one could pretend that the memory does not belong to the mind. We might say that the memory is a sort of stomach for the mind, and that joy or sadness are like sweet or bitter food. When this food is committed to the memory, it is as though it had passed into the stomach where it can remain but also loses its taste. Of course it is absurd to suppose that the memory is like the stomach, but there is some similarity none the less.

But when I say that the mind can experience four kinds of emotion – desire, joy, fear, and sorrow – I call them to mind from my memory, and if I enlarge upon this by analysing and defining each of these emotions according to the different forms which each can take, I draw upon my memory and produce from it whatever I am going to say. Yet while I remember these feelings by drawing them from my memory, they do not produce any emotional effect in me. Before I recalled them and thought about them, they must have been present in my memory, because it was from there that I was able to summon them by the act of remembering. Perhaps these emotions are brought forward from the memory by the act of remembering in the same way as cattle bring up food from the stomach when they chew the cud. But if this is so, when a man discusses them – that is, when he recalls them to mind – why does he not experience the pleasure of joy or the pain of sorrow in his mind just as the animal tastes the food in its mouth? Perhaps the simile is unjustified, because the two processes are not alike in all points. For if we had to experience sorrow or fear every time that we mentioned these emotions, no one would be willing to speak of them. Yet we could not speak of them at all unless we could find in our memory not only the sounds of their names, which we retain as images imprinted on the memory by the senses of the body, but also the ideas of the emotions themselves. But we did not admit these ideas through any of the body's gateways to the mind. They were either committed to the memory by the mind itself, as a result of its own experience of emotion, or else the memory retained them even though they were not entrusted to it by the mind.

15

Whether this process takes place by means of images or not, it is not easy to say. I can mention a stone or the sun when these things are not actually present to my senses, but their images are present in my memory. I can speak of physical pain, but as long as I do not feel it, the pain itself is not present to me. Yet if an image of pain were not present in my memory, I should not know how to describe it nor could I distinguish it from pleasure when I spoke of it. I can talk of physical health when I am in good health. The condition of which I speak is present to me. But unless an image of it were also present in my memory, I could not possibly remember what the sound of the word meant, nor could sick people know what was meant when health was mentioned, unless an image of it were retained by the power of memory even when health itself is absent from the body. I can speak of the numbers which we use in counting, but it is the numbers themselves, not their images, which are present in my memory. I speak of the sun's image, and this too is in my memory but it is the image itself, not the image of an image, that I recall. It is the sun's image that presents itself to my mind when I perform the act of remembering. I can speak of memory and I recognize what I speak of. But where else do I recognize it except in my memory itself? Can it be that the memory is not present to itself in its own right but only by means of an image of itself?

16

I can mention forgetfulness and recognize what the word means, but how can I recognize the thing itself unless I remember it? I am not speaking of the sound of the word but of the thing which it signifies. If I had forgotten the thing itself, I should be utterly unable to recognize what the sound implied. When I remember memory, my memory is present to itself by its own power; but when I remember forgetfulness, two things are present, memory, by which I remember it, and forgetfulness, which is what I remember. Yet what is forgetfulness but absence of memory? When it is present, I cannot remember. Then how can it be present in such a way that I can remember it? If it is true that what we remember we retain in our memory, and if it is also true that unless we remembered forgetfulness, we could not possibly recognize the meaning of the word when we heard it, then it is true that forgetfulness is retained in the memory. It follows that the very thing which by its presence causes us to forget must be present if we are to remember it. Are we to understand from this that, when we remember it, it is not itself present in the memory, but is only there by means of its image? For if forgetfulness were itself present, would not its effect be to make us forget, not to remember?

Who is to carry the research beyond this point? Who can understand the truth of the matter? O Lord, I am working hard in this field, and the field of my labours is my own self. I have become a problem to myself, like land which a farmer works only with difficulty and at the cost of much sweat. For I am not now investigating the tracts of the heavens, or measuring the distance of the stars, or trying to discover how the earth hangs in space. I am investigating myself, my memory, my mind. There is nothing strange in the fact that whatever is not myself is far from me. But what could be nearer to me than myself? Yet I do not understand the power of memory that is in myself, although without it I could not even speak of myself. What am I to say, when I am quite certain that I can remember forgetfulness? Am I to say that what I remember is not in my memory? Or am I to say that the reason why forgetfulness is in my memory is to prevent me from forgetting? Both suggestions are utterly absurd. There is the third possibility, that I should say that when I remember forgetfulness, it is its image that is retained in my memory, not the thing itself. But how can I say this when, if the image of any thing is imprinted on the memory, the thing itself must first be present in order that the memory may receive the impression of its image? It is by this means that I remember Carthage and all the other places where I have been. By the same method I remember the faces of persons whom I have seen and everything that the other senses have reported to me. By it I remember the health and sickness of my own body. My memory captured images of these things when they were present, and the images remained so that I could see them and think about them by remembering them even when the things themselves were absent. Therefore, if forgetfulness is retained in the memory, not by itself, but by means of its image, it must have been present at some time in order that the memory could capture its image. But when it was present, how did it inscribe its image on the memory when its mere presence is enough to delete what is already noted there? Yet, however it may be, and in whatever inexplicable and incomprehensible way it happens, I am certain that I remember forgetfulness, even though forgetfulness obliterates all that we remember.

17

The power of the memory is great, O Lord. It is awe-inspiring in its profound and incalculable complexity. Yet it is my mind: it is my self. What, then, am I, my God? What is my nature? A life that is ever varying, full of change, and of immense power. The wide plains of my memory and its innumerable caverns and hollows are full beyond compute of countless things of all kinds. Material things are there by means of their images; knowledge is there of itself; emotions are there in the form of ideas or impressions of some kind, for the memory retains them even while the mind does not experience them, although whatever is in the memory must also be in the mind. My mind has the freedom of them all. I can glide from one to the other. I can probe deep into them and never find the end of them. This is the power of memory! This is the great force of life in living man, mortal though he is!

My God, my true Life, what, then, am I to do? I shall go beyond this force that is in me, this force which we call memory, so that I may come to you, my Sweetness and my Light. What have you to say to me? You are always there above me, and as I rise up towards you in my mind, I shall go beyond even this force which is in me, this force which we call memory, longing to reach out to you by the only possible means and to cling to you in the only way in which it is possible to cling to you. For beasts and birds also have memory: otherwise they could never find their lairs or nests or the many other things which are part of their habitual life. In fact they could have no habits at all if it were not for their memory. So I must go beyond memory too, if I am to reach the God who made me different from the beasts that walk on the earth and wiser than the birds that fly in the air. I must pass beyond memory to find you, my true Good, my sure Sweetness. But where will the search lead me? Where am I to find you? If I find you beyond my memory, it means that I have no memory of you. How, then, am I to find you, if I have no memory of you?

20

How, then, do I look for you, O Lord? For when I look for you, who are my God, I am looking for a life of blessed happiness. I shall look for you, so that my soul may live. For it is my soul that gives life to my body, and it is you who give life to my soul. How then, am I to search for this blessed life? For I do not possess it until I can rightly say, 'This is all that I want. Happiness is here.' Am I to seek it in memory, as though I had forgotten it but still remembered that I had forgotten it? Or am I to seek it through the desire to get to know it as if it were something unknown to me, either because I have never known it or because I have forgotten it so completely that I do not even remember having forgotten it? Surely happiness is what everyone wants, so much so that there can be none who do not want it. But if they desire it so much, where did they learn what it was? If they have learnt to love it, where did they see it? Certainly happiness is in us, though how it comes to be there I cannot tell. Some people are happy in the sense that they have actually achieved a state of happiness. Others are happy only in the hope of achieving it. They possess happiness in a lesser degree than those who have achieved it but even so they are better off than those who are happy neither in the achievement of this blessed state nor in the expectation of it. Yet even these others must possess happiness in a certain sense, otherwise they would not long for it as they do; and there can be no doubt that they do long for it. By some means or other they have learnt what it is. In some sense they have knowledge of it, and the problem before me is to discover whether or not this knowledge is in the memory. If it is, it means that at some time in the past we have been happy. It may be that we were all once happy individually, or it may be that we were all happy in Adam, the first sinner, in whom we all died and from whom we are all descended in a heritage of misery. But this is not the question which is now before me. The problem is whether happiness is in the memory. For we should not love happiness unless we knew what it was. We have heard it named and we all admit that it is our ambition to achieve it, for we do not take pleasure simply in the sound of the word. When a Greek hears it named in Latin, he derives no pleasure from it because he does not know what has been said. But we get pleasure from it, just as he would if he heard it spoken in Greek. This is because happiness is neither Greek nor Latin, but we are all eager to achieve it, whether we speak Greek or Latin or any other language. It must, then, be known to all, and there can be no doubt that if it were possible to put the question in a common language and ask all men whether they wished to be happy, all would reply that they did. But this could only happen if happiness itself, that is, the state which the word signifies, were to be found somewhere in their memories.

21

But is it to be found in the memory in the same way as Carthage, which I have seen, is present in my memory? This cannot be the case, because happiness cannot be seen by the eye, since it is not a material object. Is it in the memory in the same way as we remember numbers? Again this cannot be the case, because once we have the knowledge of numbers we cease trying to acquire it; but even though we have knowledge of happiness, and love it for that reason, we continue to wish to achieve it, so that we may be happy. Is it then in the memory in the same way as the art of public speaking is there? Here again the answer is no. People recognize what is meant by the word 'eloquence' even though they have not mastered the art themselves, and many of them would like to be eloquent. This shows that they have knowledge of what it is. But by means of their bodily senses they have been made aware of eloquence in others. It has given them pleasure and they desire the gift for themselves. Of course they would get no pleasure from it unless they had some deeper knowledge of it, and they would not wish to have it for themselves unless they enjoyed it. But in the case of happiness there is no bodily sense by which we can experience it in others.

Perhaps it is in the memory in the same way as we remember joy. Even when I am sad I can remember joy, just as I can visualize happiness when I am unhappy. Yet I have never been aware of joy through any of the bodily senses. I have not seen or heard it, smelled, tasted or touched it. It is something that I have experienced in my mind on occasions of joy, and the knowledge of it has remained firmly in my memory, so that I can always recall it, sometimes with disgust and sometimes with longing, according to the differences between things which I remember having enjoyed. For I have at times taken great joy in shameful things, and when I remember them now, I loathe and detest them. At other times I have enjoyed good and honourable things and I remember them with longing, although they may now be beyond my reach, so that the remembrance of past joy makes me sad.

Where and when, therefore, did I experience a state of blessed happiness, so that I am enabled to remember it and love it and long for it? I am not alone in this desire, nor are there only a few who share it with me: without exception we all long for happiness. Unless we had some sure knowledge of it, we should not desire it with such certainty. But if two men were asked whether they wanted to serve in the army, one might reply that he did and the other that he did not. If, on the other hand, they were asked whether they wanted to be happy, they would both reply at once and without hesitation that they did. The only reason why one of them should wish to serve in the army and the other not to serve would be that they wanted to be happy. Is it that different persons find joy in different things? All agree that they want to be happy, just as, if they were asked, they would all agree that they desired joy. In fact they think that joy is the same as happiness. They may all search for it in different ways, but all try their hardest to reach the same goal, that is, joy. No one can say that he has no experience of joy, and this is why he finds it in his memory and recognises it when he hears the phrase 'a state of happiness.'

22

O Lord, far be it from the heart of your servant who confesses to you, far be it from me to think that whatever joy I feel makes me truly happy. For there is a joy that is not given to those who do not love you, but only to those who love you for your own sake. You yourself are their joy. Happiness is to rejoice in you and for you and because of you. This is true happiness and there is no other. Those who think that there is another kind of happiness look for joy elsewhere, but theirs is not true joy. Yet their minds are set upon something akin to joy.

23

We cannot therefore be certain that all men desire true happiness, because there are some who do not look for joy in you; and since to rejoice in you is the only true happiness, we must conclude that they do not desire true happiness. It may be that all men do desire to be happy, but because *the impulses of nature and the impulses of the spirit are at war with one another,* so that *they cannot do all that their will approves,*[12] they fall back upon what they are able to do and find contentment in this way. For their will to do what they cannot do is not strong enough to enable them to do it. If I ask them whether they prefer truth or falsehood as the foundation of their joy, they all reply that they would choose truth, and they say this as unhesitatingly as they say that they wish to be happy. True happiness is to rejoice in the truth, for to rejoice in the truth is to rejoice in you, O God, who are the Truth, you, my God, my true Light, to whom I look for salvation. This is the happiness that all desire. All desire this, the only true state of happiness. All desire to rejoice in truth. I have known many men who wished to deceive, but none who wished to be deceived. Where did they learn the meaning of happiness unless it was when they learned the meaning of truth? For they love truth, since they do not like to be deceived, and when they love happiness – which is the same as to rejoice in truth – they must love truth also. But they could not love it unless they had some knowledge of it in their memory. Why, then, do they not take joy in it? Why are they not happy? It is because they attend far more close-ly to other things whose power to make them unhappy is greater than the power of their dim memory of truth to make them happy. There is still a faint glow of light in man.[13] Let him walk on, for fear that darkness may engulf him.

But why does truth engender hatred? Why does your servant meet with hostility when he preaches the truth, although men love happiness, which is simply the enjoyment of truth? It can only be that man's love of truth is such that when he loves something which is not the truth, he pretends to himself that what he loves is the truth, and because he hates to be proved wrong, he will not allow himself to be convinced that he is deceiving himself. So he hates the real truth for the sake of what he takes to his heart in its place. Men love truth when it bathes them in its light: they hate it when it proves them wrong. Because they hate to be deceived themselves, but are glad if they can deceive others, they love the truth when it is revealed to them but hate it when it reveals that they are wrong. They reap their just reward, for those who do not wish to stand condemned by the truth find themselves unmasked against their will and also find that truth is denied to them. This is precisely the behaviour of the human mind. In its blind inertia, in its abject shame, it loves to lie concealed, yet it wishes that nothing should be concealed from it. Its reward is just the opposite of its desire, for it cannot conceal itself from the truth, but truth remains hidden from it. Yet even in this wretched state it would still rather find joy in truth than in falsehood. One day, then, it shall be happy, if it learns to ignore all that distracts it and to rejoice in truth, the sole Truth by which all else is true.

28

When at last I cling to you with all my being, for me there will be no more sorrow, no more toil. Then at last I shall be alive with true life, for my life will be wholly filled by you. You raise up and sustain all whose lives you fill, but my life is not yet filled by you and I am a burden to myself. The pleasures I find in the world, which should be cause for tears, are at strife with its sorrows, in which I should rejoice, and I cannot tell to which the victory will

---

12 Gal. 5:17.
13 See John 12:35.

fall. Have pity on me, O Lord, in my misery! My sorrows are evil and they are at strife with joys that are good, and I cannot tell which will gain the victory. Have pity on me, O Lord, in my misery! I do not hide my wounds from you. I am sick, and you are the physician. You are merciful: I have need of your mercy. Is not our life on earth a period of trial? For who would wish for hardship and difficulty? You command us to endure these troubles, not to love them. No one loves what he endures, even though he may be glad to endure it. For though he may rejoice in his power of endurance, he would prefer that there should be nothing for him to endure. When I am in trouble I long for good fortune, but when I have good fortune I fear to lose it. Is there any middle state between prosperity and adversity, some state in which human life is not a trial? In prosperity as the world knows it there is twofold cause for grief, for there is grief in the fear of adversity and grief in joy that does not last. And in what the world knows as adversity the causes of grief are threefold, for not only is it hard to bear, but it also causes us to long for prosperous times and to fear that our powers of endurance may break. Is not man's life on earth a long, unbroken period of trial?

29

There can be no hope for me except in your great mercy. Give me the grace to do as you command, and command me to do what you will! You command us to control our bodily desires. And, as we are told, when I knew that no man can *be master of himself, except of God's bounty, I was wise enough already to know whence the gift came*.[14] Truly it is by continence that we are made as one and regain that unity of self which we lost by falling apart in the search for a variety of pleasures. For a man loves you so much the less if, besides you, he also loves something else which he does not love for your sake. O Love ever burning, never quenched! O Charity, my God, set me on fire with your love! You command me to be continent. Give me the grace to do as you command, and command me to do what you will!

30

It is truly your command that I should be continent

and restrain myself from *gratification of corrupt nature, gratification of the eye, the empty pomp of living*.[15] You commanded me not to commit fornication, and though you did not forbid me to marry, you counselled me to take a better course. You gave me the grace and I did your bidding, even before I became a minister of your sacrament. But in my memory, of which I have said much, the images of things imprinted upon it by my former habits still linger on. When I am awake they obtrude themselves upon me, though with little strength. But when I dream, they not only give me pleasure but are very much like acquiescence in the act. The power which these illusory images have over my soul and my body is so great that what is no more than a vision can influence me in sleep in a way that the reality cannot do when I am awake. Surely it cannot be that when I am asleep I am not myself, O Lord my God? And yet the moment when I pass from wakefulness to sleep, or return again from sleep to wakefulness, marks a great difference in me. During sleep where is my reason which, when I am awake, resists such suggestions and remains firm and undismayed even in face of the realities themselves? Is it sealed off when I close my eyes? Does it fall off when I close my eyes? Does it fall asleep with the senses of the body? And why is it that even in sleep I often resist the attractions of these images, for I remember my chaste resolutions and abide by them and give no consent to temptations of this sort? Yet the difference between waking and sleeping is so great that even when, during deep, it happens otherwise, I return to a clear conscience when I wake and realize that, because of this difference, I was not responsible for the act, although I am sorry that by some means or other it happened to me.

34
....

By every kind of art and the skill of their hands men make innumerable things – clothes, shoes, pottery, and other useful objects, besides pictures and various works which are the fruit of their imagination. They make them on a far more lavish scale than is required to satisfy their own modest needs or to express their devotion, and all these things are additional temptations to the eye, made by men

14   Wisdom 8:21.
15   I John 2:16.

who love the worldly things they make themselves but forget their own Maker and destroy what he made in them. But, O my God, my Glory, for these things too I offer you a hymn of thanksgiving. I make a sacrifice of praise to him who sanctifies me, for the beauty which flows through men's minds into their skilful hands comes from that Beauty which is above their souls and for which my soul sighs all day and night. And it is from the same supreme Beauty that men who make things of beauty and love it in its outward forms derive the principle by which they judge it: but they do not accept the same principle to guide them in the use they make of it. Yet it is there, and they do not see it. If only they could see it, they would not depart from it. They would preserve their strength for you,[16] not squander it on luxuries that make them weary.

Though I say this and see that it is true, my feet are still caught in the toils of this world's beauty. But you will free me, O Lord; I know that you will free me. For *ever I keep your mercies in mind*.[17] I am caught and need your mercy, and by your mercy you will save me from the snare. Sometimes, if I have not fallen deep into the trap, I shall feel nothing when you rescue me; but at other times, when I am fast ensnared, I shall suffer the pain of it.

35

I must now speak of a different kind of temptation, more dangerous than these because it is more complicated. For in addition to our bodily appetites, which make us long to gratify all our senses and our pleasures and lead to our ruin if we stay away from you by becoming their slaves, the mind is also subject to a certain propensity to use the sense of the body, not for self-indulgence of a physical kin, but for the satisfaction of its own inquisitiveness. This futile curiosity masquerades under the name of science and learning, and since it derives from our thirst for knowledge and sight is the principal sense by which knowledge is acquired, in the Scriptures it is called *gratification of the eye*.[18] For although, correctly speaking, to see is the proper function of the eyes, we use the word of the other senses too, when we employ them to acquire knowledge. We do not say 'Hear how it glows,'

'Smell how bright it is,' 'Taste how it shines,' or 'Feel how it glitters,' because these are all things which we say that we see. Yet we not only say 'See how it shines' when we are speaking of something which only the eyes can perceive, but we also say 'See how loud it is, 'See how it smells,' 'See how it tastes,' and 'See how hard it is' . So, as I said, sense-experience in general is called the lust of the eyes because, although the function of sight belongs primarily to the eyes, we apply it to the other organs of sense as well, by analogy, when they are used to discover any item of knowledge.

We can easily distinguish between the motives of pleasure and curiosity. When the senses demand pleasure, they look for objects of visual beauty, harmonious sounds, fragrant perfumes, and things that are pleasant to the taste or soft to the touch. But when their motive is curiosity, they may look for just the reverse of these things, simply to put it to the proof, not for the sake of an unpleasant experience, but from a relish for investigation and discovery. What pleasure can there be in the sight of a mangled corpse, which can only horrify? Yet people will flock to see one lying on the ground, simply for the sensation of sorrow and horror that it gives them. They are even afraid that it may bring them nightmares, as though it were something that they had been forced to look at while they were awake or something to which they had been attracted by rumours of its beauty. The same is true of the other senses, although it would be tedious to give further examples. It is to satisfy this unhealthy curiosity that freaks and prodigies are put on show in the theatre, and for the same reason men are led to investigate the secrets of nature which are irrelevant to our lives, although such knowledge is of no value to them and they wish to gain it merely for the sake of knowing. It is curiosity, too, which causes men to turn to sorcery in the effort to obtain knowledge for the same perverted purpose. And it even invades our religion, for we put God to the test when we demand signs and wonders from him, not in the hope of salvation, but simply for the love of the experience.

In this immense forest, so full of snares and dangers, I have pared away many sins and thrust them from my heart, for you have given me the grace to

---

16 See Ps. 58:10 (59:9).
17 Ps. 25:3 (26:3).
18 I John 2:16.

do this, O God, my Saviour. But as long as my daily life is passed in the midst of the clamour raised by so many temptations of this sort, when can I presume to say that nothing of this kind can hold my attention or tempt me into idle speculation? It is true that the theatres no longer attract me; the study of astrology does not interest me; I have never dealt in necromancy; and I detest all sacrilegious rites. But how often has not the enemy used his wiles upon me to suggest that I should ask for some sign from you, Lord my God, to whom I owe my humble, undivided service? I beseech you, by Christ our King and by Jerusalem the chaste, our only homeland, that just as I now withhold my consent from these suggestions, I may always continue to ward them off and keep them still farther from me. But when I pray to you for the salvation of another, the purpose and intention of my prayer is far different. For you do what you will and you grant me, as you always will, the grace to follow you gladly.

Yet who can tell how many times each day our curiosity is tempted by the most trivial and insignificant matters? Who can tell how often we give way? So often it happens that, when others tell foolish tales, at first we bear with them for fear of offending the weak, and then little by little we begin to listen willingly. I no longer go to watch a dog chasing a hare at the games in the circus. But if I should happen to see the same thing in the country as I pass by, the chase might easily hold my attention and distract me from whatever serious thoughts occupied my mind. It might not actually compel me to turn my horse from the path, but such would be the inclination of my heart; and unless you made me realize my weakness and quickly reminded me, either to turn my eyes from the sight and raise my thoughts to you in contemplation, or to despise it utterly and continue on my way, I should simply stop and gloat. What excuse can I make for myself when often, as I sit at home, I cannot turn my eyes from the sight of a lizard catching flies or a spider entangling them as they fly into her web? Does it make any difference that these are only small animals? It is true that the sight of them inspires me to praise you for the wonders of your creation and the order in which you have disposed

all things, but I am not intent upon your praises when I first begin to watch. It is one thing to rise quickly from a fall, another not to fall at all.

My life is full of such faults, and my only hope is in your boundless mercy. For when our hearts become repositories piled high with such worthless stock as this, it is the cause of interruption and distraction from our prayers. And although, in your presence, the voices of our hearts are raised to your ear, all kinds of trivial thoughts break in and cut us off from the great act of prayer.

36

Must I not consider this too as one of the faults which I ought to despise? Can anything restore me to hope except your mercy? That you are merciful I know, for you have begun to change me. You know how great a change you have worked in me, for first of all you have cured me of the desire to assert my claim to liberty, so that you may also pardon me all my other sins, *heal all my mortal ills, rescue my life from deadly peril, crown me with the blessings of your mercy, content all my desire for good.*[19] You know how great a change you have worked in me, for you have curbed my pride by teaching me to fear you and you have tamed my neck to your yoke. And now that I bear your yoke, I find its burden light, for this was your promise and you have kept your word. In truth, though I did not know it, it was light even in the days when I was afraid to bend my neck to it.

But, O Lord, you who alone rule without pride since you are the only true Lord and no other lord rules over you, there is a third kind of temptation which, I fear, has not passed from me. Can it ever pass from me in all this life? It is the desire to be feared or loved by other men, simply for the pleasure that it gives me, though in such pleasure there is no true joy. It means only a life of misery and despicable vainglory. It is for this reason more than any other that men neither love you nor fear you in purity of heart. It is for this reason that you thwart the proud and keep your grace for the humble.[20] This is why, with a voice of thunder, you condemn the ambitions of this world, so that *the very foundations of the hills quail and quake.*[21] This is why the enemy of our true happiness persists in his

---

19   Ps. 102:3-5 (103:2-5).
20   I Pet. 5:5.
21   Ps. 17:8 (18:7).

attacks upon me, for he knows that when men hold certain offices in human society, it is necessary that they should be loved and feared by other men. He sets his traps about me, baiting them with tributes of applause, in the hope that in my eagerness to listen I may be caught off my guard. He wants me to divorce my joy from the truth and place it in man's duplicity. He wants me to enjoy being loved and feared by others, not for your sake, but in your place, so that in this way he may make me like himself and keep me to share with him, not the true fellowship of charity, but the bonds of common punishment. For he determined to set his throne in the north,[22] where, chilled, and benighted, men might serve him as he imitates you in his perverse, distorted way.

But we, O Lord, are your *little flock*.[23] Keep us as your own. Spread your wings and let us shelter beneath them. Let us glory in you alone. If we are loved or feared by others, let it be for your sake. No man who seeks the praise of other men can be defended by men when you call him to account. Men cannot save him when you condemn. But it happens too, not that praise is given to the man who is *proud of his wicked end achieved*[24] or that the evildoer wins applause, but that a man is praised for some gift which you have given him. And if he takes greater joy in the praise which he receives than in the possession of the gift for which men praise him, then the price he pays for their applause is the loss of your favour and he, the receiver of praise, is worse off than the giver. For the one finds pleasure in God's gift in man, while the other finds less pleasure in God's gift than in the gift of men.

37

Day after day without ceasing these temptations put us to the test, O Lord. The human tongue is a furnace in which the temper of our souls is daily tried. And in this matter too you command us to be continent. Give me the grace to do as you command, and command me to do what you will! You know how I have cried to you from the depths of my heart, and how I have wept floods of tears because of this difficulty. For I cannot easily deduce

how far I am cured of this disease, and I have great fear of offending you unawares by sins to which I am blind, though to your eyes they are manifest. In other kinds of temptation I have some means of examining myself, but in this I have almost none. For I can see what progress I have made in the ability to restrain my mind from giving in to sensual pleasures or idle curiosity. It becomes plain when I do without these things, either voluntarily or for lack of the occasion, because I then ask myself how much, or how little, it troubles me to be without them. The same is true of wealth, which men grasp because they want the means of satisfying one or another of these three kinds of temptation, or perhaps two or even all three of them. If the soul, when it has riches, cannot tell whether it despises them, it can put itself to the proof by discarding them. But if we are to do without praise in order to test our powers, are we to live such outrageously wicked and abandoned lives that all who know us will detest us? Is it possible to imagine a more insane proposal than this? If praise is normally associated with a good life and good works, and rightly so, we ought neither to cease living good lives nor to abandon the rightful consequence. But I cannot tell whether or not I have the forbearance to do without anything, unless it is taken away from me.

What, then, is my attitude to temptation of this kind? What am I to confess to you, O Lord? I can only say that I am gratified by praise, but less by praise than by the truth. For if I were asked whether I would prefer to be commended by all my fellow men for wild delusions and errors on all counts, or to be stigmatized by them for constancy and assurance in the truth, it is clear which I would choose. But I wish that words of praise from other men did not increase the joy I feel for any good qualities that I may have. Yet I confess that it does increase my joy. What is more, their censure detracts from it. And when I am worried by this wretched failing, an excuse occurs to me, though how good an excuse it is only you know, O God: it leaves me in doubt. For you have commanded us not only to be continent, but also to be just, that is, to withhold our love from certain things and to bestow it on

---

22   The allusion is to Is. 14:13, 14.
23   Luke 12:32.
24   Ps. 9:24 (10:3).

others. You want us not only to love you, but also to love our neighbour. For this reason I tell myself that when I am gratified by the praise of a man who well understands what it is that he praises, the true reason for my pleasure is that my neighbour has made good progress and shows promise for the future. Similarly, when I hear him cast a slur upon something which he does not understand or something which in fact is good, I am sorry that he should have this failing. I am sometimes sorry, too, to hear my own praises, either when others commend me for qualities which I am not glad to possess, or when they value in me, more highly than their due, qualities which may be good, but are of little importance. But here again I cannot tell whether this feeling comes from reluctance to allow the man who praises me to disagree with me about my own qualities, not because I am concerned for his welfare, but because the good qualities which please me in myself please me still more when they please others as well. For in a certain sense it is no compliment to me when my own opinion of myself is not upheld, in other words either when qualities which displease me are commended, or when those which please me least are most applauded.

Am I not right, then, to say that I am in doubt about this problem? My God, in the light of your truth I see that if my feelings are stirred by the praise which I receive, it should not be for my own sake but for the good of my neighbour. But whether this is so with me I do not know, for in this matter I know less about myself than I know of you. I beg you, my God, to reveal me to my own eyes, so that I may confess to my brothers in Christ what wounds I find in myself, for they will pray for me. Let me examine myself again, more closely. If it is the good of my neighbour that touches my heart when I hear my own praises, why am I less aggrieved when blame is unjustly laid at another's door than when it is laid at mine? Why do insults sting me more when they are offered to me than when I hear them offered to others with equal injustice? Can I plead ignorance in this case too? Or is the truth of the matter that I deceive myself and that in heart and tongue alike I am guilty of falsehood in your presence? O Lord, keep such folly far from me, for fear that my lips should sin, *sleeking my head with the oil of their flattery.*[25]

38

I am poor and needy and I am better only when in sorrow of heart I detest myself and seek your mercy, until what is faulty in me is repaired and made whole and finally I come to that state of peace which the eye of the proud cannot see. Yet in what others say about us and in what they know of our deeds there is grave danger of temptation. For our love of praise leads us to court the good opinion of others and hoard it for our personal glorification. And even when I reproach myself for it, the love of praise tempts me. There is temptation in the very process of self-reproach, for often, by priding himself on his contempt for vainglory, a man is guilty of even emptier pride; and for this reason his contempt of vainglory is an empty boast, because he cannot really hold it in contempt as long as he prides himself on doing so.

39

Deep in our inner selves there is another evil, the outcome of the same kind of temptation. This is self-complacency, the vanity of those who are pleased with themselves, although they either fail to please others or have no wish to do so and even actively displease them. But though they are pleasing to themselves, they are gravely displeasing to you, because they congratulate themselves not only upon qualities which are not good, as though they were good, but also upon good qualities received from you, as though they were their own gifts to themselves; or else they recognize them as yours but claim them for their own merits, or, again, they know that they have received them by your grace alone, but still they grudge your grace to others and will not rejoice in it with them.

You see how my heart trembles and strains in the midst of all these perils and others of a like kind. It is not as though I do not suffer wounds, but I feel rather that you heal them over and over again.

40

You have walked everywhere at my side, O Truth, teaching me what to seek and what to avoid, whenever I laid before you the things that I was able to see in this world below and asked you to counsel me. As far as my senses enabled me to do so, I surveyed the world about me and explored both the

---

25   Ps. 140:5 (141:5).

life which my body has from me and the senses themselves. Next I probed the depths of my memory, so vast in its ramifications and filled in so wonderful a way with riches beyond number. I scrutinized all these things and stood back in awe, for without you I could see none of them, and I found that none of them was you. Nor was I myself the truth, I who found them, I who explored them all and tried to distinguish and appraise each according to its worth. Some of them were conveyed to me by means of my physical senses, and I subjected them to question. Others, which closely concerned my own self, I encountered in my feelings. I enumerated the various means by which their messages were brought to me and distinguished between them. And in the great treasury of my memory there were yet other things that I examined. Some of them I returned to the keeping of my memory, others I picked out for study. But when I was doing all this, I was not myself the truth; that is, the power by which I did it was not the truth; for you, the Truth, are the unfailing Light from which I sought counsel upon all these things, asking whether they were, what they were, and how they were to be valued. But I heard you teaching me and I heard the commands you gave.

Often I do this. I find pleasure in it, and whenever I can relax from my necessary duties, I take refuge in this pleasure. But in all the regions where I thread my way, seeking your guidance, only in you do I find a safe haven for my mind, a gathering-place for my scattered parts, where no portion of me can depart from you. And sometimes you allow me to experience a feeling quite unlike my normal state, an inward sense of delight which, if it were to reach perfection in me, would be something not encountered in this life, though what it is I cannot tell. But my heavy burden of distress drags me down again to earth. Again I become a prey to my habits, which hold me fast. My tears flow, but still I am held fast. Such is the price we pay for the burden of custom! In this state I am fit to stay, unwilling though I am; in that other state, where I wish to stay, I am not fit to be. I have double cause for sorrow.

43

But there is a true Mediator, whom in your secret mercy you have shown to men. You sent him so that by his example they too might learn humility. He is *the Mediator between God and men, Jesus Christ, who is a man,*[26] and he appeared on earth between men, who are sinful and mortal, and God, who is immortal and just. Like men he was mortal: like God, he was just. And because the reward of the just is life and peace, he came so that by his own justness, which is his in union with God, he might make null the death of the wicked whom he justified, by choosing to share their death. He was made known to holy men in ancient times, so that they might be saved through faith in his passion to come, just as we are saved through faith in the passion he suffered long ago. For as man, he is our Mediator; but as the Word of God, he is not an intermediary between God and man because he is equal with God, and God with God, and together with him one God.

St. Augustine, *On Free Choice of the Will*

(Source: St. Augustine. *On Free Choice of the Will.* Trans. Anna S. Benjamin & L. H. Hackstaff. New York: The Bobbs-Merrill Company, Inc. 1964, 18-20; 28-30; 32-33; 44-45; 48-49; 104-106.)

BOOK ONE

VIII.

Reason should be master in human life.

61.A.This is what I mean: whatever it is that sets man above beast – whether it is called mind or spirit [*spiritus*] (or, more correctly, both, since we find both in the Holy Scriptures) – if it controls and commands whatever else man consists of, then man is ordered in the highest degree. We see that we have many things in common not only with beasts, but even with trees and plants. Trees, though they are on the lowest plane of life, take nourishment, grow, reproduce, and become strong. Furthermore, beasts see, hear, and can perceive corporeal things by touch, taste, and smell more keenly than we. Add to this energy, power, strength of limb, speed, and agility of bodily motion. In all of these faculties we excel some, equal others, and to some are inferior.

Things of this sort we clearly share with beasts. Indeed, to seek the pleasures of the body and to avoid harm constitute the entire activity of a beast's

26 I Tim. 2:5.

life. There are other things which do not seem to fall to the lot of beasts, but which nevertheless are not the highest attributes of man: jesting and laughing, for example, which anyone who judges human nature correctly judges to be human, though he rates them low. Again, there are the love of praise and glory and the desire for power; while beasts do not have these, nevertheless we are not to be judged better than beasts because of them. For this craving, when not subject to reason, makes men wretched, and no one has ever thought himself superior to another because of his own wretchedness. When reason is master of these emotions [*motus animae*], a man may be said to be well ordered [*ordinatus*]. No order in which the better are subject to the worse can be called right, or can even be called order at all. Do you agree?

E.It is obvious.

A.Therefore, when reason, whether mind or spirit, rules the irrational emotions, then there exists in man the very mastery which the law that we know to be eternal prescribes.

E.I understand and follow.

IX.

What distinguishes the wise from the foolish?

A.When a man is so constituted and ordered, do you not consider him wise?

E.No one could be considered wise except such a man.

A.I imagine too that you realize that many men are fools.

E.This is quite certain.

A.If a fool is the opposite of a wise man, and we know what a wise man is, you surely know what a fool is.

E.Who could not see that a fool is a man in whom the mind does not have full mastery?

A.What are we to say of a fool? That he lacks a mind? Or that the mind, though it exists in him, does not have mastery?

E.The latter.

A.I would like to hear from you on what basis you feel that there is a mind in a man when it does not exert its authority.

E.I wish you would take over the argument, for it is not easy for me to maintain my position in the face of your attack.

A. At least it is easy for you to remember what we have just said, how beasts are tamed by men and obey men; the reverse could happen, as the argument showed, were it not for the fact that man is superior in some way. We found that the superiority was not in the body. Since the superiority plainly lay in the spirit, we know nothing else to call it except reason [*ratio*]. Then we recalled that reason can be called mind or spirit [*spiritus*]. If reason is one thing and mind another, surely we agree that only mind can use reason, so that we have proved that he who has reason cannot be without mind.

E.I remember this well, and I accept it.

A.Do you believe that the masters of beasts cannot be masters unless they are wise? I call those men wise whom the truth commands to be called wise, that is, those who are at peace because they have made lust subject to the rule of the mind.

E.It is absurd to think those men wise who are commonly called animal trainers, or even shepherds, plowmen, or charioteers. We see that animals obey these men, and that by their work the wild animals are tamed.

A.You have the clearest evidence to show that mind can be present in man, and yet not have control. Indeed it is present in man, for men do things that could not be done without mind; yet the mind does not have control, for they are foolish. Rule by the human mind, it has been acknowledged, belongs only to wise men.

E.I am amazed that, though all this was proved by earlier arguments, I could not think what I should answer.

....

XIV.

Why are so few men happy when all want to be?

A.Good. But do you think that every man does not in every way want and desire the happy life?

E.Who doubts that every man wants a happy life?

A.Why then do not all men achieve it? For we have said and agreed between us that it is by the will that men merit a happy life, and by the will that they merit an unhappy one. Thus they merit what they receive. But now arises some sort of conflict, and unless we watch carefully, it will upset our previous reasoning, which was so careful and certain. For how, by will, does anyone suffer an unhappy life when no one by any means wants to live unhappily? Or how does a man gain a happy life through his will, when although all want to be happy, there are so many unhappy men? Is this the result of the fact that it is one thing to wish rightly or wrongly, and another thing to merit something through a good or evil will? Those who are happy, who also ought to be good, are not happy because they desire to live happily, which even evil men desire, but rather because they will to live rightly – which evil men do not. Thus it is no wonder that unhappy men do not attain what they want, that is, a happy life, for they do not also will to live rightly – a thing which accompanies the happy life, and without which a happy life can be neither merited nor attained by anyone. The eternal law, to which it is time now to turn our attention, established with immutable firmness the point that merit lies in the will, while happiness and unhappiness are a matter of reward and punishment.

Thus when we say that men are unhappy because of their will, we do not mean that they wish to be unhappy, but that they are in that state of will where unhappiness must result even if they do not want it. So it is not inconsistent with our previous reasoning to say that all men wish to be happy, but all men cannot be, since not all possess that will to live rightly to which the happy life is due. Do you have any objections to raise?

E. I have none.

XV.

The love of temporal things and the love of eternal things. Unhappiness stems from lust after temporal things.

E. But let us see how these points are related to our question about the two laws.

A. Yes. First tell me whether the man who loves to live rightly and is so delighted by the righteous life that he finds it not only right, but even sweet and pleasing – tell me whether that man loves and holds most precious the law according to which a happy life is allotted to the good will, and an unhappy one to the evil will?

E. He loves it completely and utterly, for it is by following that very law that he lives thus.

A. When he loves this law, does he love something changeable and temporal, or unchanging and eternal?

E. Eternal, surely, and immutable.

A. Can those who persist in an evil will, but who still desire to be happy, love the very law by which unhappiness is justly meted out to them?

E. No, not by any means.

A. Do they love nothing else?

E. On the contrary, they love many things – the

very things, in fact, that the evil will persists in obtaining and in clinging to.

A. I think you mean riches, honors, pleasures, bodily beauty, and all the other things which their will alone cannot obtain for them, and which they can lose, although they are unwilling to.

E. These are the things.

A. You do not think, do you, that these things are eternal, since you see that they are liable to the vicissitudes of time?

E. Who but a madman would think so?

A. Since it is clear that some men love eternal things while others love temporal ones, and since we have agreed that there exist two laws, the eternal and the temporal – if you know anything about equity, who do you judge ought to be subject to eternal law, and who to temporal?

E. I think that what you ask is obvious. It is apparent that happy men, because they love eternal things, act under the eternal law, while unhappy men are subject to the temporal law.

....

A. Therefore, you also understand that if men did not love what can be taken away from them against their will, there would be no punishment, either through wrong done to them or through retribution exacted from them for some wrong.

E. I understand this also.

A. Thus some men make evil use of these things, and others make good use. And the man who makes evil use clings to them with love and is entangled by them (that is, he becomes subject to those things which ought to be subject to him, and creates for himself goods whose right and proper use require that he himself be good); but the man who uses these rightly proves that they are indeed goods, though not for him (for they do not make him good or better, but become better because of him). Therefore he is not attached to them by love, lest he make them limbs, as it were, of his spirit (which happens if he loves them), and lest they weaken him with pain and wasting when they begin to be cut off from him. Instead, let him be above temporal things completely. He must be ready to possess and control them, and even more ready to lose and not to possess them. Since this is so, you do not think, do you, that silver or gold should be blamed because of greedy men, or food and wine because of gluttons and drunkards, or womanly beauty because of adulterers and fornicators? And so on with other things, especially since you may see a doctor use fire well, and the poisoner using bread for his crime.

E.This is most true. The things themselves are not to be blamed, but rather the men who make evil use of them.

....

BOOK TWO

IV.

The inner sense perceives that it perceives; the bodily senses do not.

A.It is also clear, I think, not only that the inner sense perceives what is presented by the five senses of the body, but also that it perceives the bodily senses themselves. Otherwise, a beast would not move either to seek or to avoid something, unless the beast were aware that it perceived – a thing not perceived by any of the five senses. It is not so that it may know (which is the function of reason) that a beast perceives that it perceives, but only so that it may move. If this is still obscure, it will become clearer if you turn your attention to one sense, like sight, which will furnish a quite sufficient example. A beast could not open its eyes and move it to look at what it wanted to see unless when the eye was closed, or when it was not moved, the beast perceived that its eye did not see. Moreover, if a beast is aware that it does not see when it does not see, it is also aware that it sees when it sees; for when the beast sees, it does not move its eye because of the same impulse which causes it to move its eye when it does not see; and it notes that it perceives both of these conditions. Whether this life which is aware that it perceives corporeal objects also perceives itself is not so obvious, unless we consider the fact that everyone, when he seeks within himself, finds that every living thing avoids death. Since death is the opposite to life, necessarily life, which avoids its opposite, perceives itself. But if this is not yet clear, let us omit it, so that we may work toward what we want only by clear, proven evidence. This much is proven: corporeal objects are perceived by the senses of the body; a sense cannot perceive itself; moreover, by means of the inner sense, corporeal objects are perceived through the senses of the body, and the senses of the body themselves are also perceived by the inner sense; but by means of reason, all these things, and reason itself, become

known and are included in knowledge. Do you not think so?

E.I do indeed.

....

VI.

Reason is the highest and most excellent faculty of man. God and that which is more excellent than reason.

A.Now see if reason makes any judgement about the inner sense. I am not asking whether you doubt that reason is better than the inner sense, since I am sure you think it is. I think that now we do not need to question whether reason makes judgements about the inner sense. For, of the things that are under reason – bodies, bodily senses, and the inner sense – how would one be better than another and reason more excellent than all, unless reason itself told us so? Certainly this is possible only if reason makes judgements concerning them.

E.That is evident.

A.Therefore, since the nature which merely exists and does not live or understand (for example, the inanimate body) is inferior to the nature that not only exists, but also lives, though it does not understand (for example, the soul of beasts); and since this in turn is inferior to that which at once exists, lives, and understands (for example, the rational mind in man) – you do not think then, do you, that anything can be found in us more excellent (that is, among those things by which our nature is perfected so that we are men) than this which we put in the third place? Clearly we have a body, and a kind of life that makes the body live and grow. We recognize these two conditions in beasts as well. We have also a third thing: a head or eye of our soul, as it were, or whatever term can be more aptly applied to our reason and understanding. This is what the nature of a beast does not have. Please see whether you can find anything in man's nature which is more noble than reason.

E.I see absolutely nothing more noble.

....

VIII.

No one, not even the suicide, freely chooses not to exist.

A.See how foolish and inconsistent it is to say, 'I would prefer not to be, than to be unhappy.' The man who says, 'I prefer this to that,' chooses something; but 'not to be' is not something, but nothing. Therefore, you cannot in any way choose rightly when you choose something that does not exist. You say that you wish to exist although you are unhappy, but that you ought not to wish this. What, then, ought you to have willed? You answer, 'Not to exist.' But if you ought to have willed not to exist, then 'not to exist' is better. However, what does not exist cannot be better; therefore, you should not have willed this. The feeling through which you do not will not to exist is truer than the opinion by which you think that you ought to will not to exist.

Furthermore, a man necessarily becomes better when he achieves what he rightly chose to seek. He who does not exist, however, cannot be better. No one, therefore, can rightly choose not to exist. We should not be impressed by the judgement of the men who, in their unhappiness, committed suicide. They escaped to where they thought they would be better. But whatever they thought, this is no refutation of our reasoning. If they believed that they would not exist at all, the fallacious choice of men who choose nothing at all is even less disturbing. How can I follow a man who, when I ask him what he chooses, answers that he chooses nothing? The man who chooses not to be, surely chooses to be nothing. Even if he will not give this answer, he is refuted.

Let me summarize, if I can, what I think of this matter: I think that when a man takes his life or somehow wishes to die, he does not have the feeling that he will have life after death, although he may have this opinion. Opinion, whether maintained by reason or by faith, is either true or false, while a feeling prevails either by custom or by nature. That one thing can appeal to opinion and another to feeling is readily seen from the fact that we believe that we ought to do one thing, but we delight in doing another. Sometimes the feeling is closer to the truth than opinion, especially if the feeling is natural and the opinion false, as in the case of a sick man who often wants cold water which would do him good, but nevertheless believes that it will be harmful if he drinks it. Sometimes opinion is closer to the truth than feeling, as in the case of the man who believes the word of doctors that cold water is harmful and neverthe-

less chooses to drink it in spite of the fact that it is harmful. Sometimes both are true. This occurs when a man not only believes but also desires what is beneficial to him. Sometimes both are wrong, as when what is harmful is believed to be beneficial and does not cease to be desirable.

It is often the case, however, that a right opinion corrects a wrong habit, or that a wrong opinion ruins what is right by nature. So strong is the force of opinion in the dominion and realm of reason! When someone who believes that at his death he will cease to exist is driven by unendurable troubles to yearn for death, he makes his decision and takes his life. He has the false opinion that he will be totally annihilated, but his natural feeling is a longing for peace. What is at peace, however, is not nothing; on the contrary, it exists to a greater degree than something that is not at peace. Restlessness changes a man's emotions so that one feeling destroys another. Peace, however, is constant, and because of this constancy it is said of peace that it exists. Every willful desire for death is directed toward peace, not toward nonexistence. Although a man erroneously believes that he will not exist after death, nevertheless by nature, he desires to be at peace; that is, he desires to *be* in a higher degree. Therefore, just as no one can will in any way not to exist, so no one who exists should be ungrateful for the goodness of the Creator.

Bibliography

Brown, P. *Augustine of Hippo: A Biography*. London: Faber and Faber, 1967.

Cahill, Thomas. *How The Irish Saved Civilization*. New York: Anchor Books, 1995 (ch. II).

Chadwick, Henry. *Augustine*. Oxford: Oxford University Press, 1986.

Clark, Mary T. *Augustine*. London: Geoffrey Chapman, 1994.

Copleston, Frederick. *A History of Philosophy*. Vol. 2 (chs. III & VIII). New York: Image Books, 1962.

Gilson, E. *The Christian Philosophy of Saint Augustine*. Trans. L.E.M. Lynch. London: Victor Gollancz, 1961.

Kirwan, C.A. *Augustine*. London: Routledge, 1989.

St. Thomas Aquinas (1225-1274) was the supreme systematic Christian philosopher of the Middle Ages. The system he developed, usually called Thomism, is often seen as a sort of union or amalgam of the philosophy of Aristotle and Christian theology. Though this characterization is not without a certain degree of validity, it is overly simple. Much of Thomas's philosophical work is importantly original, and highly creative. Particular discussions of problems posed by motion, and by existence and essence, are among a number of metaphysical topics to which he brings significant original focus.

Thomas was a member of the Dominican order of priests and was canonized in 1323. For a protracted period in the later Middle Ages the Thomists and the Scotists – associated specially with the Dominicans and Franciscans, respectively – vied for philosophical preponderance in the Latin Christian west. In the nineteenth century, Thomism was revived within the Catholic church, and in 1879 Pope Leo XIII issued a "rescript" commending Aquinas's system as official representation of Catholic philosophical thought. The system of the "Angelic Doctor," as Aquinas was honorifically styled, was given a central role in Catholic educational institutions, which it has enjoyed ever since. "Official status" is not necessarily a particularly enviable status for a philosophy to have, at any rate from a philosopher's point of view. Philosophy is unendingly anarchically variable and authority-challenging. A consequence of the special status Thomism has been accorded has been its identification by Catholics and non-Catholics alike as "the Catholic philosophy." This has resulted in Aquinas's work being defended, sometimes with a resolve that may owe more to piety than to disinterested rational conviction; and it has certainly had the result that non-Catholic philosophers have tended to ignore even genuinely insightful and subtly argued constituents of the system.

With special reference to human nature, the particular challenges that combining Aristotle with Christian theology poses should be noted. Among them is the fact that for Aristotle humans are parts of the animal world, while Christianity sees a marked contradistinction between humanity and all other parts of terrestrial nature.

St. Thomas Aquinas, *On The Virtues in General*

(Source: St. Thomas Aquinas. *Selected Writings of St. Thomas Aquinas*. Trans. Robert P. Goodwin. The Library of Liberal Arts, New York: The Bobbs-Merrill Co., 1965, 92-99; 121-125.)

....

Similarly, with respect to the sciences and virtues,

some claim that they are in us by nature, and that study only removes the impediments to science and virtue. This appears to be what Plato held, for he claimed that the sciences and virtues are caused in us by a participation in the separated forms, but the soul is impeded from using them through union with the body.[1] This impediment had to be removed through study of the sciences and the exercise of the virtues.

---

1   St. Thomas' knowledge of Plato was largely based on Aristotelian accounts. Aristotle quotes Plato frequently on this point, e.g., *Prior Analytics* II. 21, 67a22; *Metaphysics* I. 9, 991b3 and XIII. 5, 1080a2. Relevant passages from Plato are *Meno* 81c-86c and *Phaedo* 96a-100e.

Others, indeed, said that the sciences and virtues are in us through the influence of the agent intellect, for the reception of whose influence man is disposed through study and practice. The third is the intermediate opinion: sciences and virtues are in us by nature according to aptitude, but their perfection is not in us by nature. This opinion is better because just as the virtue of natural agents takes away nothing with respect to natural forms, so study and practice maintain its efficacy with respect to the attainment of science and virtue.

It should be understood, however, that an aptitude for a perfection and a form can exist in a subject in two ways: in one way according to passive potency only, like the aptitude in the matter of air for the form of fire; in another way according to passive and active potency at once, like the aptitude in a diseased body for health, inasmuch as the body is receptive to health. It is in this latter fashion that man has a natural aptitude for virtue – partly because of the nature of his species, insofar as the aptitude for virtue is common to all men, and partly because of the makeup of an individual, insofar as certain men are more apt for virtue than others.

As evidence for this it must be known that there can be a threefold subject of virtue in man,... namely, the intellect, the will, and the inferior appetite, which is divided into the concupiscible and the irascible. In any one we must consider in some way both the susceptibility to virtue and the active principle of virtue.

It is clear that in the intellective part there is a possible intellect[2] which is in potency to all intelligibles, in the cognition of which consists intellectual virtue. There is also the agent intellect, by whose light the intelligibles come to be in act, some of which are from the beginning immediately and naturally known by man without study or inquiry. These are first principles, not only in speculative matters, such as "every whole is greater than any one of its parts," and similar ones, but also in practical matters, such as "evil is to be avoided" and the like. Known naturally, these are the principles of all subsequent cognition acquired by study, be it practical or speculative.

Similarly, it is clear that the will is a certain natural, active principle, since it is naturally inclined to the ultimate end. The end, however, in practical matters has the character of a natural principle. Therefore, the inclination of the will is a certain active principle with respect to every disposition that is acquired through practice in the affective part.[3] Moreover, it is clear that the will itself, insofar as it is a potency undetermined to any means to an end, is susceptible of an habitual inclination to this one or that one.

The irascible and concupiscible appetites, however, are naturally subject to reason. Hence, they are naturally receptive to virtue, which is perfected in them according as they are disposed to follow the good of reason.

All the aforementioned beginnings of virtues are consequent upon the nature of the human species and, hence, are common to all men.

There is, however, a certain beginning of virtue which is consequent upon the nature of the individual, according as a man, from his natural makeup or from a celestial impression,[4] is inclined to the act of some virtue. This inclination is indeed a certain beginning of virtue. It is not, however, perfect virtue, because perfect virtue requires the moderation of reason. Hence, the definition of virtue includes the choice of a means according to right reason. For if someone follows an inclination of this sort without the discretion of reason, he frequently sins. And just as the beginning of virtue without the operation of reason lacks the character of perfect virtue, so also do some of the things which precede virtue.

For one proceeds through the investigation of reason from universal principles to special cases. Through the function of reason, man is led from the desire for the ultimate end to those things which are conducive to that end. Reason itself in directing the irascible and concupiscible appetites makes them subject to itself. Accordingly it is evident that complete virtue requires the work of reason,

---

2   *Possible intellect*: the power of intellectual cognition, usually referred to simply as the intellect..

3   *Affective part*: a term embracing will and the irascible and concupisciple powers. It is usually used in opposition to *cognitive part*. Cf. St. Thomas, *De Veritate*, q. X, a. 9 ad 7.

4   St. Thomas refers here to some outmoded astronomical theories of Aristotle. Aristotle believed that heavenly bodies affect and change things on earth. See Aristotle, *On Generation and Corruption* II. 10, 336b16-20. Cf. Sir David Ross, *Aristotle* (London: Methuen and Co., 1960), pp. 95-99, 107-108; St. Thomas, *De Potentia*, q. 6, a. 3c.

whether the virtue be in the intellect, in the will, or in the concupiscible or the irascible appetite.

In summary, the beginning of virtue in the superior part is ordered to the virtue of the inferior part. Thus a man is prepared for virtue in his will by the beginning of virtue in his will and intellect. Man is prepared for virtue in the irascible and concupiscible appetites by the beginning of virtue in them, and by the beginning of virtue which is in the superior parts but not vice versa. Hence, it is also clear that reason, which is superior, operates for the completion of all virtue.

Moreover, the operative principle is divided in two: one is reason, as opposed to the other, which is nature, as is evident in the second book of the *Physics*.[5] Their difference lies in this: the rational power is ordered to opposites, while nature is ordered to one. Hence it is clear that the completion of virtue is not by nature but by reason.

Article IX
Whether Virtues Are Acquired by Actions

REPLY: It must be said that since a virtue is the ultimate perfection of a potency to which any potency extends itself so that it operate, that is, so that the operation be good, it is clear that the virtue of anything is that through which it produces a good operation. Because everything exists for the sake of its operation[6] and, moreover, because everything is good insofar as it is properly related to its end,[7] each thing must be good and must operate well through a virtue proper to it.

Moreover, the proper good of one thing is not the same as the proper good of another, for there are diverse perfections corresponding to the diverse capacities for perfections. Accordingly man's good is other than a horse's or a rock's good. In addition, man's good is taken in various ways, according to the diverse viewpoints which can be adopted toward him. The good of man, as a man, is different from his good as a citizen.

The good of a man as man consists in the perfection of his reason in the cognition of truth and in the regulation of his inferior appetites according to the rule of reason, for a man is man by his rationality. However, the good of man as a citizen lies in his being ordered to the good of all within a commonwealth. Because of this the Philosopher says in Book Three of the *Politics*[8] that the virtue by which a man is a good man is not the same as the virtue by which a man is a good citizen. Man, however, is not only a terrestrial citizen but a participant in the heavenly city, Jerusalem,[9] whose governor is the Lord and whose citizens comprise the angels and all the saints, whether they reign in glory and are at peace in Heaven, or are travellers on earth. This accords with the words of the Apostle in Ephesians 2:19: "You are citizens with the saints and members of God's family," etc. To be a participant in this city, man's nature does not suffice. It must be elevated to this by the grace of God.[10] For it is evident that those virtues which are in man as a participant in this city cannot be acquired by him by his own natural powers. Hence, they are not caused by our actions, but are infused in us by divine favor.

The virtues, however, which are in a man as man, or in him as a citizen of an earthly commonwealth, do not exceed the faculty of human nature. Hence, man can acquire them by actions proper to him through his natural powers. This is evident by what follows.

Anything with the natural aptitude for some perfection can acquire it. But if this aptitude arises from a passive principle alone, then it cannot be acquired by an action proper to the thing, but only by the action of some natural exterior agent, just as the air receives light from the sun. If, however, something has the natural aptitude for a certain perfection arising out of a principle that is active and passive at once, then it can acquire the perfection through an action proper to itself, as the body

---

5   Aristotle, *Physics* II. 6, 198a11-12.

6   On the notion of perfection through action, see St. Thomas, *Summa Theologiae*, I-II, 3, 2c; 32, 1c.

7   On the relation of good and end, see St. Thomas, *Summa Contra Gentiles*, III, 3 and 24; *Summa Theologiae*, I, 5, 1c.

8   Aristotle, *Politics* III. 4, 1276b35 and 1277a1.

9   Jerusalem, often under the name Zion, figures familiarly in both Jewish and Christian literature as a symbol for the capital of the Messiah and the prototype of the heavenly city.

10   On grace, see St. Thomas, *De Veritate*, XXVII, aa. 1-7; *Summa Theologiae*, I-II, 110, 1c; *Summa Contra Gentiles*, III, 150.

of a sick man which has a natural aptitude for health. And because a subject is naturally receptive of health through a natural, active virtue oriented to healing, it follows that a sick man is sometimes cured without the action of an exterior agent.

It was shown, however, in the preceding question that the natural aptitude for virtue that man possesses arises out of principles which are both active and passive. The very order of potencies makes this clear. In the intellective part there is a quasi-passive principle, the possible intellect, which is reduced to its perfection by the agent intellect. The intellect in act, moreover, moves the will, since the known good is the end which moves an appetite. The will, however, moved by reason, is meant to move the sensitive appetite,[11] namely, the irascible and concupiscible powers, which in turn are meant to obey reason. Accordingly, it is also evident that any virtue which makes a human operation good has a proper act in man, who, by his action, can reduce the virtue to act, be it in the intellect, the will, or the irascible or concupiscible appetite.

Virtues in the intellective part and in the appetitive part, however, are actualized in different ways. The action of the intellect and of the cognitive virtue of the intellect consists in its assimilation[12] of the knowable object in a certain way. Hence, intellectual virtue comes about in the intellective part by means of the intellectual species[13] being made present in it, either actually or habitually, by the agent intellect. The action of the appetitive virtue, however, consists in a certain inclination to the appetitive object. Hence, in order for virtue to come about in the appetitive part an inclination to some determinate thing must be given to it.

It should be known, moreover, that the inclination of natural things follows their form and is therefore an inclination to one through the exigency of the form. As long as this form remains, such inclination cannot be taken away nor can the contrary inclination be induced. Because of this, natural things do not become accustomed or unaccustomed to something. For however often a rock is raised, it never becomes accustomed to this raised position, but always is inclined to descend. Those things, however, which are related to both do not have a form through which they are turned aside to one determinately. Rather, they are determined to some one by the proper mover. By being determined to it, they are disposed in a certain way to the same thing. Since they are inclined on many different occasions, they are determined to the same thing by the proper mover, and the determinate inclination to that thing grows firm. This superadded disposition is something like a form which tends in the way nature does to one thing. It is on account of this that custom is said to be another nature.

Therefore, since the appetitive power is related to a number of objects, it does not tend to one of them unless it is determined to it by reason. Therefore, when reason repeatedly inclines the appetitive power to some one object, a certain firm disposition becomes established in the appetitive power, through which it is inclined to the one thing to which it is accustomed. This disposition thus established is a habit of virtue.

Therefore, if it be rightly considered, a virtue of the appetitive part is nothing other than a certain disposition or form marked and impressed upon the appetitive power by reason. Because of this, however strong the disposition to something be in the appetitive power, it cannot have the character of virtue unless reason is involved. Accordingly, reason is put in the definition of virtue, for the Philosopher states in Book Two of the *Ethics*[14] that virtue is a chosen habit in the mind consisting of a determinate species insofar as a man of wisdom will determine it.

....

---

11   On the will's relation to inferior powers, see St. Thomas, *Summa Theologiae*, I, 81, 3c; I-II, 17, 7c; *De Veritate*, q. 25, a. 4.

12   In order to know, the knower must possess in a cognitive way the object known. See St. Thomas, *In De An.*, Bk. II, lect. 12, no. 377.

13   The species of the intellect is produced by the agent intellect using the phantasm. See ... St. Thomas, *Quodlibet*, VIII, q. 2, a. 1.

14   Aristotle, *Nicomachean Ethics* II. 6, 1107a1-3.

St. Thomas Aquinas, *On Free Choice*

Trans. Robert P. Goodwin (1965)

Article I
Whether Man Possesses Free Choice

REPLY: Without doubt it must be said that man has free choice. Faith demands that we hold this position, since without free choice one could not merit or demerit, or be justly rewarded or punished. There are clear indications of this if one considers the occasions when man appears to choose one thing freely and reject another. Finally, reason, too, demands that we hold this position, and following its dictates we examine the origin of free choice, proceeding in the following manner.[15]

In things that are moved or that move another, there is found this difference: some have within themselves the principle of their motion or operation, whereas others, such as things which are moved by violence have it outside themselves. In these, "the principle of motion is extrinsic to them, so that in receiving the force they contribute nothing," as the Philosopher states in the third book of the *Ethics*.[16] We cannot posit free choice in these, since they are not the cause of their motion. But that is free "which is its own cause," according to the Philosopher in the beginning of his *Metaphysics*.[17]

Among those whose principle of motion and operation is within themselves, some, such as animals, move themselves. Others, such as heavy and light things, do not move themselves even though they do have a certain interior principle of their motion. They do not move themselves since they cannot be distinguished into two parts, one of which would be the mover, the other the moved, as is found in animals. Although their movement follows a principle intrinsic to them, namely, the form,

yet since they receive this form from that which generated them, they are said to be moved essentially by that which generated them, according to the Philosopher in the seventh book of the *Physics*.[18] They are said to be moved accidentally, however, by what removes the impediment to their motion. They are moved in themselves, but not by themselves. Hence, they do not possess free choice, since they themselves cause neither motion nor their action. Rather, they are bound to acting and moving through what they receive from another.

Among those things which are moved by themselves, the motion of some proceeds from a judgment of reason, whereas the motion of others proceeds from a natural judgment.

Men act and are moved by a judgment of reason, for they deliberate about courses of action. All brute animals, however, act and are moved by natural judgment. This is evident when you consider that all the members of a species act in a similar way, as, for example, swallows all build their nests in the same way. It is also evident from the fact that their judgment is determined to one course of action and not open to all, as bees are skilled in producing nothing but honeycombs. The case is similar for other animals.

Hence, it is clear to anyone who considers the matter rightly that the way in which motion and action are attributed to inanimate things of nature is the same as the way in which the judging of actions is attributed to brute animals. Just as heavy and light things do not move themselves such that they would be the causes of their own motion, so too brutes do not judge of their own judgments,[19] but follow the judgment imprinted upon them by God. And since they do not cause their choice, they do not have freedom of choice.

Man, however, judging about his actions through his power of reason, can judge concerning his choice insofar as he can know the nature of the end

---

15   It should be noted that St. Thomas' approach to the question of free choice is not the usual introspective one, wherein one notes the occasions when it is apparent that a man selects one alternative rather than another. In this paragraph he does mention such occasions, but his procedure is to analyze the genesis of internal movement, especially that of men, from which he develops his theory of freedom. Technically such an argument is a *propter quid* demonstration, or a demonstration by cause.

16   Aristotle, *Nicomachean Ethics* III. 1, 110a1-4.

17   Aristotle, *Metaphysics* I. 2, 982b26-26.

18   Aristotle, *Physics* VIII. 4. 2555b24-256a3.

19   Aquinas is referring here to the operation of the estimative power by which brutes are aware, without any learning, that certain things are good or bad for them. See his *Summa Theologiae,* I, 78, 4c; *De An.*, q. *unica.* a. 13c; *De Veritate*, q. 14, a. 1 ad 9.

and of the means to the end, and, likewise, the relation and order of the one to the other. Man, therefore, is his own cause, not only in moving but also in judging. Hence he has free choice, as one is speaking of the free judgments as to whether to act or not.

Article II
Whether Brute Animals Possess Free Choice

REPLY: We must say that brute animals in no way possess free choice.

In support of this contention, one must realize that since three things are involved in our operation – namely, knowledge, appetite, and the operation itself – the whole nature of liberty depends upon the mode of knowledge.

Appetite follows knowledge, since appetite seeks only the good, which is proposed to it by a cognitive power. Sometimes, though, an appetite appears not to follow cognition. This happens because the judgment of cognition and the appetite are not taken with respect to the same thing. For appetite is concerned with a particular thing to be done, while a judgment of reason is sometimes concerned with something universal, which occasionally is contrary to the appetite. But a judgment about this particular thing to be done now can never be contrary to the appetite. Whoever wishes to fornicate, although he knows in general that fornication is evil, nevertheless judges that an act of fornication for him now is good, and chooses it under the aspect of being good. For no one acts intending to do evil, as Dionysius says.[20]

If nothing interferes, however, motion or operation follow the appetite. Therefore, if the judgment of the cognitive power is not in someone's power, but is determined by another, then neither will his appetite be in his power. Consequently, neither will

its motion nor operation be in his power absolutely.

Moreover, judgment is within the power of one judging insofar as he can judge of his own judgment. For we can judge of whatever is in our power. Indeed to judge of one's own judgment belongs only to reason, which reflects upon its own act and knows the relations of things of which it judges and through which it judges. The root of all liberty, therefore, is found in reason. Hence, according as something is related to reason, so is it related to free choice.

Now reason is found fully and perfectly only in man, and so free choice is found fully in him alone.

Brutes, however, have a certain semblance of reason, insofar as they participate in a certain natural prudence, in accordance with the way an inferior nature in some way attains what belongs to a superior one. This similitude consists in their having an orderly judgment about certain things. This judgment, however, arises out of a natural estimation, and not from any deliberation, since they are ignorant of the rationale of their judgments.[21] Because their judgment is of this kind, it does not extend to all things as does the judgment of reason, but only to certain determinate things.

Likewise, they possess something similar to free choice inasmuch as they are able to do or not do one and the same thing in accordance with their judgment. Therefore they possess something close to a certain conditioned liberty. If they judge that they should act, they can act; if they do not so judge, they can abstain from acting.

Since their judgment is determined to one thing, it follows that their appetite and action are likewise determined to one thing. Accordingly, as Augustine holds in *De Genesi ad Litteram*,[22] they are moved by what they see; or, as Damascene contends,[23] they are affected by their passions, because they naturally judge according to such sights or passions. By

---

20   St. Thomas thought, as did all the scholars of his day, that they were in possession of a work composed by the Dionysius converted by St. Paul in Athens (Acts of the Apostles 17:34). More recent scholarship has shown that this work was composed in the late fifth or early sixth century. Reference is to *On Divine Names, IV, 20*, in *Dionysius the Areopagite on the Divine Names and the Mystical Theology*, trans. C.E. Rolt (London: Macmillan, 1940), pp. 115 and 127.

21   See above, note 19

22   St. Augustine, *De Genesi as Litteram*, Bk. IX, Pt. 14 in *Corpus Scriptorum Ecclesiasticorum Latinorum*, Vol. XXVI-II, p. 284.

23   St. John Damascene (ca. 675-749), a Syrian theologian who spent his first fifty years in active secular life, but joined a monastery for the remainder of his life, devoting himself to theological speculation and writing. Reference here is to his *The Orthodox Faith*, in *The Fathers of the Church*, 41 vols. to date, R.J. Deferrari *et al.*, eds. (New York: Fathers of the Church, Inc., 1958), Bk. III, chap. 18 (Vol. XXXVII, pp. 320-321)

necessity they are moved by the sight of something or by an aroused passion toward it to flee or pursue that thing, as a sheep necessarily becomes afraid and flees at the sight of a wolf, or as a dog, because of an aroused passion of anger, must bark and pursue something in order to do it harm.

Man, however, is not moved necessarily by things appearing to him or by aroused passions, since he can either accept or reject them. Therefore, man has free choice, but brutes do not.

Bibliography

Davies, Brian. *The Thought of Thomas Aquinas.* Oxford: Clarendon Press, 1992.

Kenny, Anthony. *Aquinas.* Oxford and New York: Oxford University Press, 1980.

Kenny, Anthony, ed. *Aquinas: A Collection of Critical Essays.* New York: Anchor, 1969.

Kretzmann, Norman, and Eleonore Stump, eds. *The Cambridge Companion to Aquinas.* Cambridge: Cambridge University Press, 1993.

CHAPTER EIGHT — MARTIN LUTHER

The life of Martin Luther (1483-1546) almost exactly coincides with that of Hernandes Cortés (1485-1547), the Spanish adventurer and conqueror of Mexico. This is significant, because between them they symbolize in a fundamental way the inception of the early modern European world, its break from its earlier patterns and ambit, and the hegemonic character of the place of European civilization in the fortunes of our planet over the past half-millennium.

Luther, of course, is the single most important individual in the creation of the Protestant Reformation, which critically and irreversibly sundered Western or Latin Catholic Christianity, and brought into the world a significant new dimension of Christian thought. For these reasons Hegel identifies Luther as a "world-historical individual," one of the handful of individual human beings who, in Hegelian philosophical history, stamp the course of world history with their personalities and turn its trajectory of movement in profound world-altering ways. Most of the other world-historical individuals Hegel names explicitly are military conquerors – Alexander the Great, Julius Caesar, and Napoleon, most notably – so this adds to Luther's stature in the Hegelian picture.

Luther was not a systematic philosopher. On the other hand his published writings amount to some dozens of volumes. Long treatises, short occasion-focused tracts, Biblical commentary, letters, and other work, theological, practical, polemical, fill these volumes. In the course of them notions of the nature and place of humanity in the divine scheme of things emerge repeatedly. It is not easy to see all of his views as consistent. One notable work – "the Bondage of the Will" – argues, with some vehemence, that the freedom of the human will is an illusion, while the treatise from which the present selection derives speaks for "the freedom of a Christian." There is perhaps a higher synthesis that reconciles both, but there are certainly challenges to finding or formulating it.

The single most important note in Luther's conception of human nature may be said to be its stress on the *inwardness* of conscience and self-scrutiny. It is the chief base of the Christian philosophies of human nature of Butler and Kant.

Martin Luther, *The Freedom of a Christian*

(Source: Martin Luther. *Luther's Works*. Vol. 31. Trans. W.A. Lambert. Rev. Harold J. Grim. Philadelphia: Muhlenberg Press, 1957, 343-377.)

Many people have considered Christian faith an easy thing, and not a few have given it a place among the virtues. They do this because they have not experienced it and have never tasted the great strength there is in faith. It is impossible to write well about it or to understand what has been written about it unless one has at one time or another experienced the courage which faith gives a man when trials oppress him. But he who has had even a taste of it can never write, speak, meditate, or hear enough concerning it. It is a living "spring of water welling up to eternal life," as Christ calls it in John 4[:14].

As for me, although I have no wealth of faith to boast of and know how scant my supply is, I nevertheless hope that I have attained to a little faith, even though I have been assailed by great and various temptations; and I hope that I can discuss it, if not more elegantly, certainly more to the point, than those literalists and subtle disputants have previously done, who have not even understood what they have written.

To make the way smoother for the unlearned – for only them do I serve – I shall set down the following two propositions concerning the freedom and the bondage of the spirit:

A Christian is a perfectly free lord of all, subject to none.
A Christian is a perfectly dutiful servant of all, subject to all.

These two theses seem to contradict each other. If, however, they should be found to fit together they would serve our purpose beautifully. Both are Paul's own statements, who says in I Cor. 9[:19], "For though I am free from all men, I have made myself a slave to all," and in Rom. 13 [:8], "Owe no one anything, except to love one another." Love by its very nature is ready to serve and be subject to him who is loved. So Christ, although he was Lord of all, was "born of woman, born under the law" [Gal. 4:4], and therefore was at the same time a free man and a servant, "in the form of God" and "of a servant" [Phil. 2:6-7].

Let us start, however, with something more remote from our subject, but more obvious. Man has a twofold nature, a spiritual and a bodily one. According to the spiritual nature, which men refer to as the soul, he is called a spiritual, inner, or new man. According to the bodily nature, which men refer to as flesh, he is called a carnal, outward, or old man, of whom the Apostle writes in II Cor. 4 [:16], "Though our outer nature is wasting away, our inner nature is being renewed every day." Because of this diversity of nature the Scriptures assert contradictory things concerning the same man, since these two men in the same man contradict each other, "for the desires of the flesh are against the Spirit, and the desires of the Spirit are against the flesh," according to Gal. 5 [:17].

First, let us consider the inner man to see how a righteous, free, and pious Christian, that is, a spiritual, new, and inner man, becomes what he is. It is evident that no external thing has any influence in producing Christian righteousness or freedom, or in producing unrighteousness or servitude. A simple argument will furnish the proof of this statement. What can it profit the soul if the body is well, free, and active, and eats, drinks, and does as it pleases? For in these respects even the most godless slaves of vice may prosper. On the other hand, how will poor health or imprisonment or hunger or thirst or any other external misfortune harm the soul? Even the most godly men, and those who are free because of clear consciences, are afflicted with these things. None of these things touch either the freedom or the servitude of the soul. It does not help the soul if the body is adorned with the sacred robes of priests or dwells in sacred places or is occupied with sacred duties or prays, fasts, abstains from certain kinds of food, or does any work that can be done by the body and in the body. The righteousness and the freedom of the soul require something far different since the things which have been mentioned could be done by any wicked person. Such works produce nothing but hypocrites. On the other hand, it will not harm the soul if the body is clothed in secular dress, dwells in unconsecrated places, eats and drinks as others do, does not pray aloud, and neglects to do all the above-mentioned things which hypocrites can do.

Furthermore, to put aside all kinds of works, even contemplation, meditation, and all that the soul can do, does not help. One thing, and only one thing, is necessary for Christian life, righteousness, and freedom. That one thing is the most holy Word of God, the gospel of Christ, as Christ says, John 11 [:25], "I am the resurrection and the life; he who believes in me, though he die, yet shall he live"; and John 8 [:36], "So if the Son makes you free, you will be free indeed"; and Matt. 4 [:4], "Man shall not live by bread alone, but by every word that proceeds from the mouth of God." Let us then consider it certain and firmly established that the soul can do without anything except the Word of God and that where the Word of God is missing there is no help at all for the soul. If it has the Word of God it is rich and lacks nothing since it is the Word of life, truth, light, peace, righteousness, salvation, joy, liberty, wisdom, power, grace, glory, and of every incalculable blessing.

....

The Word of God cannot be received and cherished by any works whatever but only by faith. Therefore it is clear that, as the soul needs only the Word of God for its life and righteousness, so it is justified by faith alone and not any works; for if it could be justified by anything else, it would not need the Word, and consequently it would not need faith.

This faith cannot exist in connection with works – that is to say, if you at the same time claim to be justified by works, whatever their character – for that would be the same as "limping with two different opinions" [I Kings 18:21], as worshipping Baal and kissing one's own hand [Job 31:27-28], which, as Job says, is a very great iniquity. Therefore the moment you begin to have faith you learn that all things in you are altogether blameworthy, sinful, and damnable, as the Apostle says in Rom. 3[:23], "Since all have sinned and fall short of the glory of God," and, "None is righteous, no, not one; ... all have turned aside, together they have gone wrong" (Rom. 3:10-12). When you have learned this you will know that you need Christ, who suffered and rose again for you so that, if you believe in him, you may through this faith become a new man in so far as your sins are forgiven and you are justified by the merits of another, namely, of Christ alone.

Since, therefore, this faith can rule only in the inner man, as Rom. 10 [:10] says, "For man believes with his heart and so is justified," and since faith alone justifies, it is clear that the inner man cannot be justified, freed, or saved by any outer work or action at all, and that these works, whatever their character, have nothing to do with this inner man. On the other hand, only ungodliness and unbelief of heart, and no outer work, make him guilty and a damnable servant of sin. Wherefore it ought to be the first concern of every Christian to lay aside all confidence in works and increasingly to strengthen faith alone and through faith to grow in the knowledge, not of works, but of Christ Jesus, who suffered and rose for him, as Peter teaches in the last chapter of his first Epistle (I Pet. 5:10). No other work makes a Christian.

....

[T]he entire Scripture of God is divided into two parts: commandments and promises. Although the commandments teach things that are good, the things taught are not done as soon as they are taught, for the commandments show us what we ought to do but do not give us the power to do it. They are intended to teach man to know himself, that through them he may recognize his inability to do good and may despair of his own ability. That is

why they are called the Old Testament and constitute the Old Testament. For example, the commandment, "You shall not covet" [Exod. 20:17], is a command which proves us all to be sinners, for no one can avoid coveting no matter how much he may struggle against it. Therefore, in order not to covet and to fulfil the commandment, a man is compelled to despair of himself, to seek the help which he does not find in himself elsewhere and from someone else, as stated in Hosea [13:9]: "Destruction is your own, O Israel: your help is only in me." As we fare with respect to one commandment, so we fare with all, for it is equally impossible for us to keep any one of them.

Now when a man has learned through the commandments to recognize his helplessness and is distressed about how he might satisfy the law – since the law must be fulfilled so that not a jot or tittle shall be lost, otherwise man will be condemned without hope – then, being truly humbled and reduced to nothing in his own eyes, he finds in himself nothing whereby he may be justified and saved. Here the second part of Scripture comes to our aid, namely, the promises of God which declare the glory of God, saying, "If you wish to fulfil the law and not covet, as the law demands, come, believe in Christ in whom grace, righteousness, peace, liberty, and all things are promised you. If you believe, you shall have all things; if you do not believe, you shall lack all things." That which is impossible for you to accomplish by trying to fulfil all the works of the law – many and useless as they all are – you will accomplish quickly and easily through faith. God our Father has made all things depend on faith so that whoever has faith will have everything, and whoever does not have faith will have nothing. "For God has consigned all men to disobedience, that he may have mercy upon all," as it is stated in Rom. 11 [:32]. Thus the promises of God give what the commandments of God demand and fulfil what the law prescribes so that all things may be God's alone, both the commandments and the fulfilling of the commandments. He alone commands, he alone fulfils. Therefore the promises of God belong to the New Testament. Indeed, they are the New Testament.

Since these promises of God are holy, true, righteous, free, and peaceful words, full of goodness, the soul which clings to them with a firm faith will be so closely united with them and altogether absorbed by them that it not only will share in all their power but will be saturated and intoxicated by them. If a touch of Christ healed, how much more will this most tender spiritual touch, this absorbing of the Word, communicate to the soul all things that belong to the Word. This, then, is how through faith alone without works the soul is justified by the Word of God, sanctified, made true, peaceful, and free, filled with every blessing and truly made a child of God, as John I [:12] says: "But to all who ... believed in his name, he gave power to become children of God."

From what has been said it is easy to see from what source faith derives such great power and why a good work or all good works together cannot equal it. No good work can rely upon the Word of God or live in the soul, for faith alone and the Word of God rule in the soul. Just as the heated iron glows like fire because of the union of fire with it, so the Word imparts its qualities to the soul. It is clear, then, that a Christian has all that he needs in faith and needs no works to justify him; and if he has no need of works, he has no need of the law; and if he has no need of the law, surely he is free from the law. It is true that "the law is not laid down for the just" [I Tim. 1:9]. This is that Christian liberty, our faith, which does not induce us to live in idleness or wickedness but makes the law and works unnecessary for any man's righteousness and salvation.

This is the first power of faith. Let us now examine also the second. It is a further function of faith that it honors him whom it trusts with the most reverent and highest regard since it considers him truthful and trustworthy. There is no other honor equal to the estimate of truthfulness and righteousness with which we honor him whom we trust. Could we ascribe to a man anything greater than truthfulness and righteousness and perfect goodness? On the other hand, there is no way in which we can show greater contempt for a man than to regard him as false and wicked and to be suspicious of him, as we do when we do not trust him. So when the soul firmly trusts God's promises, it regards him as truthful and righteous. Nothing more excellent than this can be ascribed to God. The very highest worship of God is this that we ascribe to him truthfulness, righteousness, and whatever else should be ascribed to one who is trusted. When this is done, the soul consents to his

will. Then it hallows his name and allows itself to be treated according to God's good pleasure for, clinging to God's promises, it does not doubt that he who is true, just, and wise will do, dispose, and provide all things well.

Is not such a soul most obedient to God in all things by this faith? What commandment is there that such obedience has not completely fulfilled? What more complete fulfilment is there than obedience in all things? This obedience, however, is not rendered by works, but by faith alone. On the other hand, what greater rebellion against God, what greater wickedness, what greater contempt of God is there than not believing his promise? For what is this but to make God a liar or to doubt that he is truthful? – that is, to ascribe truthfulness to one's self but lying and vanity to God? Does not a man who does this deny God and set himself up as an idol in his heart? Then of what good are works done in such wickedness, even if they were the works of angels and apostles? Therefore God has rightly included all things, not under anger or lust, but under unbelief, so that they who imagine that they are fulfilling the law by doing the works of chastity and mercy required by the law (the civil and human virtues) might not be saved. They are included under the sin of unbelief and must either seek mercy or be justly condemned.

....

That we may examine more profoundly that grace which our inner man has in Christ, we must realize that in the Old Testament God consecrated to himself all the first-born males. The birthright was highly prized for it involved a twofold honor, that of priesthood and that of kingship. The first-born brother was priest and lord over all the others and a type of Christ, the true and only first-born of God the Father and the Virgin Mary and true king and priest, but not after the fashion of the flesh and the world, for his kingdom is not of this world [John 18:36]. He reigns in heavenly and spiritual things and consecrates them – things such as righteousness, truth, wisdom, peace, salvation, etc. This does not mean that all things on earth and in hell are not also subject to him – otherwise how could he protect and save us from them? – but that his kingdom consists neither in them nor of them. Nor does his priesthood consist in the outer splendor of robes and postures like those of the human priesthood of Aaron and our present-day church; but it consists of spiritual things through which he by an invisible service intercedes for us in heaven before God, there offers himself as a sacrifice, and does all things a priest should do, as Paul describes him under the type of Melchizedek in the Epistle to the Hebrews [Heb. 6-7]. Nor does he only pray and intercede for us but he teaches us inwardly through the living instruction of his Spirit, thus performing the two real functions of a priest, of which the prayers and the preaching of human priests are visible types.

Now just as Christ by his birthright obtained these two prerogatives, so he imparts them to and shares them with everyone who believes in him according to the law of the above-mentioned marriage, according to which the wife owns whatever belongs to the husband. Hence all of us who believe in Christ are priests and kings in Christ, as I Pet. 2 [:9] says: "You are a chosen race, God's own people, a royal priesthood, a priestly kingdom, that you may declare the wonderful deeds of him who called you out of darkness into his marvelous light."

The nature of this priesthood and kingship is something like this: First, with respect to the kingship, every Christian is by faith so exalted above all things that, by virtue of a spiritual power, he is lord of all things without exception, so that nothing can do him any harm. As a matter of fact, all things are made subject to him and are compelled to serve him in obtaining salvation. Accordingly Paul says in Rom. 8 [:28], "All things work together for good for the elect," and in I Cor. 3 [:21-23], "All things are yours whether…life or death or the present or the future, all are yours; and you are Christ's…." This is not say that every Christian is placed over all things to have and control them by physical power – a madness with which some churchmen are afflicted – for such power belongs to kings, princes, and other men on earth. Our ordinary experience in life shows us that we are subjected to all, suffer many things, and even die. As a matter of fact, the more Christian a man is, the more evils, sufferings, and deaths he must endure, as we see in Christ the first-born prince himself, and in all his brethren, the saints. The power of which we speak is spiritual. It rules in the midst of enemies and is powerful in the midst of oppression. This means nothing else than that "power is made perfect in weakness" [II

Cor. 12:9] and that in all things I can find profit toward salvation [Rom. 8:28], so that the cross and death itself are compelled to serve me and to work together with me for my salvation. This is a splendid privilege and hard to attain, a truly omnipotent power, a spiritual dominion in which there is nothing so good and nothing so evil but that it shall work together for good to me, if only I believe. Yes, since faith alone suffices for salvation, I need nothing except faith exercising the power and dominion of its own liberty. Lo, this is the inestimable power and liberty of Christians.

Not only are we the freest of kings, we are also priests forever, which is far more excellent than being kings, for as priests we are worthy to appear before God to pray for others and to teach one another divine things. These are the functions of priests, and they cannot be granted to any unbeliever. Thus Christ has made it possible for us, provided we believe in him, to be not only his brethren, co-heirs, and fellow-kings, but also his fellow priests. Therefore we may boldly come into the presence of God in the spirit of faith [Heb. 10:19, 22] and cry "Abba, Father!" pray for one another, and do all things which we see done and foreshadowed in the outer and visible works of priests.

He, however, who does not believe is not served by anything. On the contrary, nothing works for his good, but he himself is a servant of all, and all things turn out badly for him because he wickedly uses them to his own advantage and not to the glory of God. So he is no priest but a wicked man whose prayer becomes sin and who never comes into the presence of God because God does not hear sinners [John 9:31]. Who then can comprehend the lofty dignity of the Christian? By virtue of his royal power he rules over all things, death, life, and sin, and through his priestly glory is omnipotent with God because he does the things which God asks and desires, as it is written, "He will fulfil the desire of those who fear him; he also will hear their cry and save them" [cf. Phil. 4:13]. To this glory a man attains, certainly not by any works of his, but by faith alone.

….

You will ask, "If all who are in the church are priests, how do these whom we now call priests differ from laymen?" I answer: Injustice is done those words "priest," "cleric," "spiritual," "ecclesiastic," when they are transferred from all Christians to those few who are now by a mischievous usage called "ecclesiastics." Holy Scripture makes no distinction between them, although it gives the name "ministers," "servants," "stewards" to those who are now proudly called popes, bishops, and lords and who should according to the ministry of the Word serve others and teach them the faith of Christ and the freedom of believers. Although we are all equally priests, we cannot all publicly minister and teach. We ought not do so even if we could. Paul writes accordingly in I Cor. 4 [1], "This is how one should regard us, as servants of Christ and stewards of the mysteries of God."

....

What man is there whose heart, upon hearing these things, will not rejoice to its depth, and when receiving such comfort will not grow tender so that he will love Christ as he never could by means of any laws or works? Who would have the power to harm or frighten such a heart? If the knowledge of sin or the fear of death should break in upon it, it is ready to hope in the Lord. It does not grow afraid when it hears tidings of evil. It is not disturbed when it sees its enemies. This is so because it believes that the righteousness of Christ is its own and that its sin is not its own, but Christ's, and that all sin is swallowed up by the righteousness of Christ. This, as has been said above,[1] is a necessary consequence on account of faith in Christ. So the heart learns to scoff at death and sin and to say with the Apostle, "O death, where is thy victory? O death, where is thy sting? The sting of death is sin, and the power of sin is the law. But thanks be to God, who gives us the victory through our Lord Jesus Christ" [I Cor.-15:55-57]. Death is swallowed up not only in the victory of Christ but also by our victory, because through faith his victory has become ours and in that faith we also are conquerors.

Let this suffice concerning the inner man, his liberty, and the source of his liberty, the righteousness of faith. He needs neither laws nor good works but, on the contrary, is injured by them if he believes that he is justified by them.

Now let us turn to the second part, the outer man. Here we shall answer all those who, offended by the word "faith" and by all that has been said, now ask, "If faith does all things and is alone sufficient unto righteousness, why then are good works commanded? We will take our ease and do no works and be content with faith." I answer: not so, you wicked men, not so. That would indeed be proper if we were wholly inner and perfectly spiritual men. But such we shall be only at the last day, the day of the resurrection of the dead. As long as we live in the flesh we only begin to make some progress in that which shall be perfected in the future life. For this reason the Apostle in Rom. 8 [:23] calls all that we attain in this life "the first fruits of the Spirit" because we shall indeed receive the greater portion, even the fulness of the Spirit, in the future. This is the place to assert that which was said above, namely, that a Christian is the servant of all and made subject to all. Insofar as he is free he does no works, but insofar as he is a servant he does all kinds of works. How this is possible we shall see.

Although, as I have said, a man is abundantly and sufficiently justified by faith inwardly, in his spirit, and so has all that he needs, except insofar as this faith and these riches must grow from day to day even to the future life; yet he remains in this mortal life on earth. In this life he must control his own body and have dealings with men. Here the works begin; here a man cannot enjoy leisure; here he must indeed take care to discipline his body by fastings, watchings, labors, and other reasonable discipline and to subject it to the Spirit so that it will obey and conform to the inner man and faith and not revolt against faith and hinder the inner man, as it is the nature of the body to do if it is not held in check. The inner man, who by faith is created in the image of God, is both joyful and happy because of Christ in whom so many benefits are conferred upon him; and therefore it is his one occupation to serve God joyfully and without thought of gain, in love that is not constrained.

While he is doing this, behold, he meets a contrary will in his own flesh which strives to serve the world and seeks its own advantage. This the spirit of faith cannot tolerate, but with joyful zeal it attempts to put the body under control and hold it in check, as Paul says in Rom. 7 [:22-23], "For I delight in the law of God, in my inmost self, but I

---

1   Cf. p. 67

see in my members another law at war with the law of my mind and making me captive to the law of sin," and in another place, "But I pommel my body and subdue it, lest after preaching to others I myself should be disqualified" [I Cor. 9:27], and in Galatians [5:24], "And those who belong to Christ Jesus have crucified the flesh with its passions and desires."

In doing these works, however, we must not think that a man is justified before God by them, for faith, which alone is righteousness before God, cannot endure that erroneous opinion. We must, however, realize that these works reduce the body to subjection and purify it of its evil lusts, and our whole purpose is to be directed only toward the driving out of lusts. Since by faith the soul is cleansed and made to love God, it desires that all things, and especially its own body, shall be purified so that all things may join with it in loving and praising God. Hence a man cannot be idle, for the need of his body drives him and he is compelled to do many good works to reduce it to subjection. Nevertheless the works themselves do not justify him before God, but he does the works out of spontaneous love in obedience to God and considers nothing except the approval of God, whom he would most scrupulously obey in all things.

In this way everyone will easily be able to learn for himself the limit and discretion, as they say, of his bodily castigations, for he will fast, watch, and labor as much as he finds sufficient to repress the lasciviousness and lust of his body. But those who presume to be justified by works do not regard the mortifying of the lusts, but only the works themselves, and think that if only they have done as many and as great works as are possible, they have done well and have become righteous. At times they even addle their brains and destroy, or at least render useless, their natural strength with their works. This is the height of folly and utter ignorance of Christian life and faith, that a man should seek to be justified and saved by works and without faith.

In order to make that which we have said more easily understood, we shall explain by analogies. We should think of the works of a Christian who is justified and saved by faith because of the pure and free mercy of God, just as we would think of the works which Adam and Eve did in Paradise, and all their children would have done if they had not sinned. We read in Gen. 2 [:15] that "The Lord God took the man and put him in the garden of Eden to till it and keep it." Now Adam was created righteous and upright and without sin by God so that he had no need of being justified and made upright through his tilling and keeping the garden; but, that he might not be idle, the Lord gave him a task to do, to cultivate and protect the garden. This task would truly have been the freest of works, done only to please God and not to obtain righteousness, which Adam already had in full measure and which would have been the birthright of us all.

The works of a believer are like this. Through his faith he has been restored to Paradise and created anew, has no need of works that he may become or be righteous; but that he may not be idle and may provide for and keep his body, he must do such works freely only to please God. Since, however, we are not wholly recreated, and our faith and love are not yet perfect, these are to be increased, not by external works, however, but of themselves.

....

A good or a bad house does not make a good or bad builder; but a good or a bad builder makes a good or a bad house. And in general, the work never makes the workman like itself, but the workman makes the work like himself. So it is with the works of man. As the man is, whether believer or unbeliever, so also is his work – good if it was done in faith, wicked if it was done in unbelief. But the converse is not true, that the work makes the man either a believer or unbeliever. As works do not make a man a believer, so also they do not make him righteous. But as faith makes a man a believer and righteous, so faith does good works. Since, then, works justify no one, and a man must be righteous before he does a good work, it is very evident that it is faith alone which, because of the pure mercy of God through Christ and in his Word, worthily and sufficiently justifies and saves the person. A Christian has no need of any work or law in order to be saved since through faith he is free from every law and does everything out of pure liberty and freely. He seeks neither benefit nor salvation since he already abounds in all things and is saved through the grace of God because in his faith he now seeks only to please God.

Furthermore, no good work helps justify or save an unbeliever. On the other hand, no evil work makes him wicked or damns him; but the unbelief which makes the person and the tree evil does the evil and damnable works. Hence when a man is good or evil, this is effected not by works, but by faith or unbelief, as the Wise Man says, "This is the beginning of sin, that a man falls away from God" [cf. Sirach 10:14-15], which happens when he does not believe. And Paul says in Heb. 11[:6], "For whoever would draw near to God must believe..." And Christ says the same: "Either make the tree good, and its fruit good; or make the tree bad, and its fruit bad" [Matt. 12:33], as if he would say, "Let him who wishes to have good fruit begin by planting a good tree." So let him who wishes to do good works begin not with the doing of works, but with believing, which makes the person good, for nothing makes a man good except faith, or evil except unbelief.

....

Christ, like his forerunner John, not only said, "Repent" [Matt. 3:2; 4:17], but added the word of faith, saying, "The kingdom of heaven is at hand." We are not to preach only one of these words of God, but both; we are to bring forth out of our treasure things new and old, the voice of the law as well as the word of grace [Matt. 13:52]. We must bring forth the voice of the law that men may be made to fear and come to a knowledge of their sins and so be converted to repentance and a better life. But we must not stop with that, for that would only amount to wounding and not binding up, smiting and not healing, killing and not making alive, leading down into hell and not bringing back again, humbling and not exalting. Therefore we must also preach the word of grace and the promise of forgiveness by which faith is taught and aroused. Without this word of grace the works of the law, contrition, penitence, and all the rest are done and taught in vain.

Preachers of repentance and grace remain even to our day, but they do not explain God's law and promise that a man might learn from them the source of repentance and grace. Repentance proceeds from the law of God, but faith or grace from the promise of God, as Rom. 10 [:17] says, "So faith comes from what is heard, and what is heard comes by the preaching of Christ." Accordingly man is consoled and exalted by faith in the divine promise after he has been humbled and led to a knowledge of himself by the threats and the fear of the divine law. So we read in Psalm 30 [:5], "Weeping may tarry for the night, but joy comes with the morning."

Let this suffice concerning works in general and at the same time concerning the works which a Christian does for himself. Lastly, we shall also speak of the things which he does toward his neighbor. A man does not live for himself alone in this mortal body to work for it alone, but he lives also for all men on earth; rather, he lives only for others and not for himself. To this end he brings his body into subjection that he may the more sincerely and freely serve others, as Paul says in Rom. 14 [:7-8], "None of us lives to himself, and none of us dies to himself. If we live, we live to the Lord, and if we die, we die to the Lord." He cannot ever in this life be idle and without works toward his neighbors, for he will necessarily speak, deal with, and exchange views with men, as Christ also, being made in the likeness of men [Phil. 2:7], was found in form as a man and conversed with men, as Baruch 3 [:38] says.

Man, however, needs none of these things for his righteousness and salvation. Therefore he should be guided in all his works by this thought and contemplate this one thing alone, that he may serve and benefit others in all that he does, considering nothing except the need and the advantage of his neighbor. Accordingly the Apostle commands us to work with our hands so that we may give to the needy, although he might have said that we should work to support ourselves. He says, however, "that he may be able to give to those in need" [Eph. 4:28]. This is what makes caring for the body a Christian work, that through its health and comfort we may be able to work, to acquire, and lay by funds with which to aid those who are in need, that in this way the strong member may serve the weaker, and we may be sons of God, each caring for and working for the other, bearing one another's burdens and so fulfilling the law of Christ [Gal. 6:2]. This is a truly Christian life. Here faith is truly active through love [Gal. 5:6], that is, it finds expression in works of the freest service, cheerfully and lovingly done, with which a man willingly serves another without hope of reward; and for himself he is satisfied with the fullness and wealth of his faith.

Accordingly Paul, after teaching the Philippians how rich they were made through faith in Christ, in which they obtained all things, thereafter teaches them, saying, "So if there is any encouragement in

Christ, any incentive of love, any participation in the Spirit, any affection and sympathy, complete my joy by being of the same mind, having the same love, being in full accord and of one mind. Do nothing from selfishness or conceit, but in humility count others better than yourselves. Let each of you look not only to his own interests, but also to the interests of others" [Phil. 2:1-4]. Here we see clearly that the Apostle has prescribed this rule for the life of Christians, namely, that we should devote all our works to the welfare of others, since each has such abundant riches in his faith that all his other works and his whole life are a surplus with which he can by voluntary benevolence serve and do good to his neighbor.

As an example of such life the Apostle cites Christ, saying, "Have this mind among yourselves, which you have in Christ Jesus, who, though he was in the form of God, did not count equality with God a thing to be grasped, but emptied himself, taking the form of a servant, being born in the likeness of men. And being found in human form he humbled himself and became obedient unto death" [Phil, 2:5-8]. This salutary word of the Apostle has been obscured for us by those who have not at all understood his words, "form of God," "form of a servant," "human form," "likeness of men," and have applied them to the divine and the human nature. Paul means this: Although Christ was filled with the form of God and rich in all good things, so that he needed no work and no suffering to make him righteous and saved (for he had all this eternally), yet he was not puffed up by them and did not exalt himself above us and assume power over us, although he could rightly have done so; but, on the contrary, he so lived, labored, worked, suffered, and died that he might be like other men and in fashion and in actions be nothing else than a man, just as if he had need of all these things and had nothing of the form of God. But he did all this for our sake, that he might serve us and that all things which he accomplished in this form of a servant might become ours.

So a Christian, like Christ his head, is filled and made rich by faith and should be content with this form of God which he has obtained by faith; only, as I have said, he should increase this faith until it is made perfect. For this faith is his life, his righteousness, and his salvation: it saves him and makes him acceptable, and bestows upon him all things that are Christ's, as has been said above, and as

Paul asserts in Gal. 2[:20] when he says, "And the life I now live in the flesh I live by faith in the Son of God." Although the Christian is thus free from all works, he ought in this liberty to empty himself, take upon himself the form of a servant, be made in the likeness of men, be found in human form, and to serve, help, and in every way deal with his neighbor as he sees that God through Christ has dealt and still deals with him. This he should do freely, having regard for nothing but divine approval.

He ought to think: "Although I am an unworthy and condemned man, my God has given me in Christ all the riches of righteousness and salvation without any merit on my part, out of pure, free mercy, so that from now on I need nothing except faith which believes that this is true. Why should I not therefore freely, joyfully, with all my heart, and with an eager will do all things which I know are pleasing and acceptable to such a Father who has overwhelmed me with his inestimable riches? I will therefore give myself as a Christ to my neighbor, just as Christ offered himself to me; I will do nothing in this life except what I see is necessary, profitable, and salutary to my neighbor, since through faith I have an abundance of all good things in Christ."

Behold, from faith thus flow forth love and joy in the Lord, and from love a joyful, willing, and free mind that serves one's neighbor willingly and takes no account of gratitude or ingratitude, of praise or blame, of gain or loss. For a man does not serve that he may put men under obligations. He does not distinguish between friends and enemies or anticipate their thankfulness or unthankfulness, but he most freely and most willingly spends himself and all that he has, whether he wastes all on the thankless or whether he gains a reward. As his Father does, distributing all things to all men richly and freely, making "his sun rise on the evil and on the good" [Matt. 5:45], so also the son does all things and suffers all things with that freely bestowing joy which is his delight when through Christ he sees it in God, the dispenser of such great benefits.

Therefore, if we recognize the great and precious things which are given us, as Paul says [Rom. 5:5], our hearts will be filled by the Holy Spirit with the love which makes us free, joyful, almighty workers and conquerors over all tribulations, servants of our neighbors, and yet lords of all. For those who do not recognize the gifts bestowed upon them through Christ, however, Christ has been born in vain; they go their way with their works and shall never come to taste or feel those things. Just as our neighbor is in need and lacks that in which we abound, so we were in need before God and lacked his mercy. Hence, as our heavenly Father has in Christ freely come to our aid, we also ought freely to help our neighbor through our body and its works, and each one should become as it were a Christ to the other that we may be Christs to one another and Christ may be the same in all, that is, that we may be truly Christians.

Who then can comprehend the riches and the glory of the Christian life? It can do all things and has all things and lacks nothing. It is lord over sin, death, and hell, and yet at the same time it serves, ministers to, and benefits all men. But alas in our day this life is unknown throughout the world; it is neither preached about nor sought after; we are altogether ignorant of our own name and do not know why we are Christians or bear the name of Christians. Surely we are named after Christ, not because he is absent from us, but because he dwells in us, that is, because we believe in him and are Christs one to another and do to our neighbors as Christ does to us. But in our day we are taught by the doctrine of men to seek nothing but merits, rewards, and the things that are ours; of Christ we have made only a taskmaster far harsher than Moses.

We have a pre-eminent example of such a faith in the blessed Virgin. As is written in Luke 2 [:22], she was purified according to the law of Moses according to the custom of all women, although she was not bound by that law and did not need to be purified. Out of free and willing love, however, she submitted to the law like other women that she might not offend or despise them. She was not justified by this work, but being righteous she did it freely and willingly. So also our works should be done, not that we may be justified by them, since, being justified beforehand by faith, we ought to do all things freely and joyfully for the sake of others.

St. Paul also circumcised his disciple Timothy, not because circumcision was necessary for his righteousness, but that he might not offend or despise the Jews who were weak in the faith and could not

yet grasp the liberty of faith. But, on the other hand, when they despised the liberty of faith and insisted that circumcision was necessary for righteousness, he resisted them and did not allow Titus to be circumcised Gal. 2 [:3]. Just as he was unwilling to offend or despise any man's weak faith and yielded to their will for a time, so he was also unwilling that the liberty of faith should be offended against or despised by stubborn, work-righteous men. He chose a middle way, sparing the weak for a time, but always withstanding the stubborn, that he might convert all to the liberty of faith. What we do should be done with the same zeal to sustain the weak in faith, as in Rom. 14 [:1], but we should firmly resist the stubborn teachers of works. Of this we shall say more later.

Christ also, in Matt. 17 [:24-27], when the tax money was demanded of his disciples, discussed with St. Peter whether the sons of the king were not free from the payment of tribute, and Peter affirmed that they were. Nonetheless, Christ commanded Peter to go to the sea and said, "Not to give offense to them, go to the sea and cast a hook, and take the first fish that comes up, and when you open its mouth you will find a shekel; take that and give it to them for me and for yourself." This incident fits our subject beautifully for Christ here calls himself and those who are his children sons of the king, who need nothing; and yet he freely submits and pays the tribute. Just as necessary and helpful as this work was to Christ's righteousness or salvation, just so much do all other works of his or his followers avail for righteousness, since they all follow after righteousness and are free and are done only to serve others and to give them an example of good works.

Of the same nature are the precepts which Paul gives in Rom. 13 [:1-7], namely, that Christians should be subject to the governing authorities and be ready to do every good work, not that they shall in this way be justified, since they already are righteous through faith, but that in the liberty of the Spirit they shall by so doing serve others and the authorities themselves and obey their will freely and out of love. The works of all colleges,[2] monasteries, and priests should be of this nature. Each one should do the works of his profession and station, not that by them he may strive after right-

2   The word "college" here denotes a corporation of clergy supported by a foundation and performing certain religious services.

eousness, but that through them he may keep his body under control, be an example to others who also need to keep their bodies under control, and finally that by such works he may submit his will to that of others in the freedom of love. But very great care must always be exercised so that no man in a false confidence imagines that by such works he will be justified or acquire merit or be saved; for this is the work of faith alone, as I have repeatedly said.

Anyone knowing this could easily and without danger find his way through those numberless mandates and precepts of pope, bishops, monasteries, churches, princes, and magistrates upon which some ignorant pastors insist as if they were necessary to righteousness and salvation, calling them "precepts of the church," although they are nothing of the kind. For a Christian, as a free man, will say, "I will fast, pray, do this and that as men command, not because it is necessary to my righteousness or salvation; but that I may show due respect to the pope, the bishop, the community, a magistrate, or my neighbor, and give them an example. I will do and suffer all things, just as Christ did and suffered far more for me, although he needed nothing of it all for himself, and was made under the law for my sake, although he was not under the law." Although tyrants do violence or injustice in making their demands, yet it will do no harm as long as they demand nothing contrary to God.

From what has been said, everyone can pass a safe judgement on all works and laws and make a trustworthy distinction between them and know who are the blind and ignorant pastors and who are the good and true. Any work that is not done solely for the purpose of keeping the body under control or of serving one's neighbor, as long as he asks nothing contrary to God, is not good or Christian. For this reason I greatly fear that few or no colleges, monasteries, altars, and offices of the church are really Christian in our day – nor the special fasts and prayers on certain saints' days. I fear, I say, that in all these we seek only our profit, thinking that through them our sins are purged away and that we find salvation in them. In this way Christian liberty perishes altogether. This is a consequence of our ignorance of Christian faith and liberty.

This ignorance and suppression of liberty very many blind pastors take pains to encourage. They stir up and urge on their people in these practices by praising such works, puffing them up with their indulgences, and never teaching faith. If, however, you wish to pray, fast, or establish a foundation in the church, I advise you to be careful not to do it in order to obtain some benefit, whether temporal or eternal, for you would do injury to your faith which alone offers you all things. Your one care should be that faith may grow, whether it is trained by works or sufferings. Make your gifts freely and for no consideration, so that others may profit by them and fare well because of you and your goodness. In this way you shall be truly good and Christian. Of what benefit to you are the good works which you do not need for keeping your body under control? Your faith is sufficient for you, through which God has given you all things.

See, according to this rule the good things we have from God should flow from one to the other and be common to all, so that everyone should "put on" his neighbor and so conduct himself toward him as if he himself were in the other's place. From Christ the good things have flowed and are flowing into us. He has so "put on" us and acted for us as if he had been what we are. From us they flow on to those who have need of them so that I should lay before God my faith and my righteousness that they may cover and intercede for the sins of my neighbor which I take upon myself and so labor and serve in them as if they were my very own. That is what Christ did for us. This is true love and the genuine rule of a Christian life. Love is true and genuine where there is true and genuine faith. Hence the Apostle says of love in I Cor. 13 [:5] that "it does not seek its own."

We conclude, therefore, that a Christian lives not in himself but in Christ and in his neighbor. Otherwise he is not a Christian. He lives in Christ through faith, in his neighbor through love. By faith he is caught up beyond himself into God. By love he descends beneath himself into his neighbor. Yet he always remains in God and in his love, as Christ says in John 1 [:51], "Truly, truly, I say to you, you will see heaven opened, and the angels of God ascending and descending upon the Son of man."

Enough now of freedom. As you see, it is a spiritual and true freedom and makes our hearts free from all sins, laws, and commands, as Paul says, I Tim. 1 [:9], "The law is not laid down for the just."

It is more excellent than all other liberty, which is external, as heaven is more excellent than earth. May Christ give us this liberty both to understand and to preserve. Amen.

Finally, something must be added for the sake of those for whom nothing can be said so well that they will not spoil it by misunderstanding it. It is questionable whether they will understand even what will be said here. There are very many who, when they hear of this freedom of faith, immediately turn it into occasion for the flesh and think that now all things are allowed them. They want to show that they are free men and Christians only by despising and finding fault with ceremonies, traditions, and human laws; as if they were Christians because on stated days they do not fast or eat meat when others fast, or because they do not use the accustomed prayers, and with upturned nose scoff at the precepts of men, although they utterly disregard all else that pertains to the Christian religion. The extreme opposite of these are those who rely for their salvation solely on their reverent observance of ceremonies, as if they would be saved because on certain days they fast or abstain from meats, or pray certain prayers; these make a boast of the precepts of the church and of the fathers, and do not care a fig for the things which are of the essence of our faith. Plainly, both are in error because they neglect the weightier things which are necessary to salvation, and quarrel so noisily about trifling and unnecessary matters.

How much better is the teaching of the Apostle Paul who bids us take a middle course and condemns both sides when he says, "Let not him who eats despise him who abstains, and let not him who abstains pass judgement on him who eats" [Rom. 14:3]. Here you see that they who neglect and disparage ceremonies, not out of piety, but out of mere contempt, are reproved, since the Apostle teaches us not to despise them. Such men are puffed up by knowledge. On the other hand, he teaches those who insist on the ceremonies not to judge the others, for neither party acts toward the other according to the love that edifies. Wherefore we ought to listen to Scripture which teaches that we should follow the statutes of the Lord which are right, "rejoicing the heart" [Ps. 19:8]. As a man is not righteous because he keeps and clings to the works and forms of the ceremonies, so also will a man not be counted righteous merely because he neglects and despises them.

Our faith in Christ does not free us from works but from false opinions concerning works, that is, from the foolish presumption that justification is acquired by works. Faith redeems, corrects, and preserves our consciences so that we know that righteousness does not consist in works, although works neither can nor ought to be wanting; just as we cannot be without food and drink and all the works of this mortal body, yet our righteousness is not in them, but in faith; and yet those works of the body are not to be despised or neglected on that account. In this world we are bound by the needs of our bodily life, but we are not righteous because of them. "My kingship is not of this world" [John 18:36], says Christ. He does not, however, say, "My kingship is not here, that is, in this world." And Paul says, "Through we live in the world we are not carrying on a worldly war" [II Cor. 10:3], and in Gal. 2 [:20], "The life I now live in the flesh I live by faith in the Son of God." Thus what we do, live, and are in works and ceremonies, we do because of the necessities of this life and of the effort to rule our body. Nevertheless we are righteous, not in these, but in the faith of the Son of God.

Hence the Christian must take a middle course and face those two classes of men. He will meet first the unyielding, stubborn ceremonialists who like deaf adders are not willing to hear the truth of liberty [Ps. 58:4] but, having no faith, boast of, prescribe, and insist upon their ceremonies as means of justification. Such were the Jews of old, who were unwilling to learn how to do good. These he must resist, do the very opposite, and offend them boldly lest by their impious views they drag many with them into error. In the presence of such men it is good to eat meat, break the fasts, and for the sake of the liberty of faith do other things which they regard as the greatest of sins. Of them we must say, "Let them alone; they are blind guides." According to this principle Paul would not circumcise Titus when the Jews insisted that he should [Gal. 2:3], and Christ excused the apostles when they plucked ears of grain on the Sabbath [Matt. 12:1-8]. There are many similar instances. The other class of men whom a Christian will meet are the simple-minded, ignorant men, weak in the faith, as the Apostle calls them, who cannot yet grasp the liberty of faith, even if they were willing to do so [Rom. 14:1]. These he must take care not to offend. He must yield to their weakness until they are more fully instructed. Since they do and think as they do, not because they are stubbornly wicked, but only because their faith is weak, the fasts and other things which they consider necessary must be observed to avoid giving them offense. This is the command of love which would harm no one but would serve all men. It is not by their fault that they are weak, but by that of their pastors who have taken them captive with the snares of their traditions and have wickedly used these traditions as rods with which to beat them. They should have been delivered from these pastors by the teachings of faith and freedom. So the Apostle teaches us in Romans 14: "If food is a cause of my brother's falling, I will never eat meat" [cf. Rom. 14:21 and I Cor. 8:13]; and again, "I know and am persuaded in the Lord Jesus that nothing is unclean in itself; but it is unclean for any one who thinks it unclean" [Rom. 14:14].

For this reason, although we should boldly resist those teachers of traditions and sharply censure the laws of the popes by means of which they plunder the people of God, yet we must spare the timid multitude whom those impious tyrants hold captive by means of these laws until they are set free. Therefore fight strenuously against the wolves, but for the sheep and not also against the sheep. This you will do if you inveigh against the laws and the lawgivers and at the same time observe the laws with the weak so that they will not be offended, until they also recognize tyranny and understand their freedom. If you wish to use your freedom, do so in secret, as Paul says, Rom. 14 [:22], "The faith that you have, keep between yourself and God"; but take care not to use your freedom in the sight of the weak. On the other hand, use your freedom constantly and consistently in the sight of and despite the tyrants and the stubborn so that they also may learn that they are impious, that their laws are of no avail for righteousness, and that they had no right to set them up.

Since we cannot live our lives without ceremonies and works, and the perverse and untrained youth need to be restrained and saved from harm by such bonds; and since each one should keep his body under control by means of such works, there is need that the minister of Christ be far-seeing and faithful. He ought so to govern and teach Christians in all these matters that their conscience

and faith will not be offended and that there will not spring up in them a suspicion and a root of bitterness and many will thereby be defiled, as Paul admonishes the Hebrews [Heb. 12:15]; that is, that they may not lose faith and become defiled by the false estimate of the value of works and think that they must be justified by works. Unless faith is at the same time constantly taught, this happens easily and defiles a great many, as has been done until now through the pestilent, impious, soul-destroying traditions of our popes and the opinions of our theologians. By these snares numberless souls have been dragged down to hell, so that you might see in this the work of Antichrist.

In brief, as wealth is the test of poverty, business the test of faithfulness, honors the test of humility, feasts the test of temperance, pleasures the test of chastity, so ceremonies are the test of the righteousness of faith. "Can a man," asks Solomon, "carry fire in his bosom and his clothes and not be burned?" [Prov. 6:27]. Yet as a man must live in the midst of wealth, business, honors, pleasures, and feasts, so also must he live in the midst of ceremonies, that is, in the midst of dangers. Indeed, as infant boys need beyond all else to be cherished in the bosoms and by the hands of maidens to keep them from perishing, yet when they are grown up their salvation is endangered if they associate with maidens, so the inexperienced and perverse youth need to be restrained and trained by the iron bars of ceremonies lest their unchecked ardor rush headlong into vice after vice. On the other hand, it would be death for them always to be held in bondage to ceremonies, thinking that these justify them. They are rather to be taught that they have been so imprisoned in ceremonies, not that they should be made righteous or gain great merit by them, but that they might thus be kept from doing evil and might more easily be instructed to the righteousness of faith. Such instruction they would not endure if the impulsiveness of their youth were not restrained.

Hence ceremonies are to be given the same place in the life of a Christian as models and plans have among builders and artisans. They are prepared, not as a permanent structure, but because without them nothing could be built or made. When the structure is complete the models and plans are laid aside. You see, they are not despised, rather they are greatly sought after; but what we despise is the false estimate of them since no one holds them to be the real and permanent structure.

If any man were so flagrantly foolish as to care for nothing all his life long except the most costly, careful, and persistent preparation of plans and models and never think of the structure itself, and were satisfied with his work in producing such plans and mere aids to work, and boasted of it, would not all men pity his insanity and think that something great might have been built with what he has wasted? Thus we do not despise ceremonies and works, but we set great store by them; but we despise the false estimate placed upon works in order that no one may think that they are true righteousness, as those hypocrites believe who spend and lose their whole lives in zeal for works and never reach that goal for the sake of which the works are to be done, who, as the Apostle says, "will listen to anybody and can never arrive at a knowledge of the truth" [II Tim. 3:7]. They seem to wish to build, they make their preparations, and yet they never build. Thus they remain caught in the form of religion and do not attain unto its power [II Tim. 3:5]. Meanwhile they are pleased with their efforts and even dare to judge all others whom they do not see shining with like show of works. Yet with the gifts of God which they have spent and abused in vain they might, if they had been filled with faith, have accomplished great things to their own salvation and that of others.

Since human nature and natural reason, as it is called, are by nature superstitious and ready to imagine, when laws and works are prescribed, that righteousness must be obtained through laws and works; and further, since they are trained and confirmed in this opinion by the practice of all earthly lawgivers, it is impossible that they should of themselves escape from the slavery of works and come to a knowledge of the freedom of faith. Therefore there is need of the prayer that the Lord may give us and make us *theodidacti*, that is, those taught by God [John 6:45], and himself, as he has promised, write his law in our hearts; otherwise there is no hope for us. If he himself does not teach our hearts this wisdom hidden in mystery [I Cor. 2:7], nature can only condemn it and judge it to be heretical because nature is offended by it and regards it as foolishness. So we see that it happened in the old days in the case of the apostles and prophets, and so godless and blind popes and their flatterers do to me and to those who are like me. May God at last be merciful to them and to us and cause his face to shine upon us that we may know his way upon earth [Ps. 67:1-2], his salvation among all nations, God, who is blessed forever [II Cor. 11:13]. Amen.

Bibliography

Atkinson, J. *Martin Luther and the Birth of Protestantism*. 2nd ed. London: Marshall, Morgan & Scott, 1982.

Cargill Thompson, W.D.J. *The Political Thought of Martin Luther*. Brighton, Sussex: Harvester, 1984.

Gerrish, B.A. *Grace and Reason: A Study in the Theology of Luther*. Oxford: Oxford University Press, 1962.

CHAPTER NINE — JOHN LOCKE

John Locke (1632-1704) is best known as a leading empiricist in epistemology and as a liberal in political theory. His two great works, both published in 1690, the *Essay Concerning Human Understanding* and *Two Treatises of Government*, were profoundly influential in their respective spheres. Locke was a fellow of the Royal Society (from 1668), and part of a circle of Englishmen concerned with the development of "the new science," the most prominent figures of which were Sir Isaac Newton and Robert Boyle. In the *Essay*, Locke seeks to study in a fresh and empirically grounded way the "equipment" with which we experience the world – that part of ourselves whereby we *understand*. We would now call the enterprise to which Locke sought to contribute *cognitive psychology*. Together with a theory of the formation of thought through *ideas* that we derive from inner and outer sensation and reflection, Locke considers and contributes to a wide range of fundamental topics in epistemology and metaphysics.

In the *Treatises*, especially the second one, Locke sets out an account of the formation and justification of political society. This work is much less developed than the *Essay*: it is considerably shorter, and it was written and published as part of a process of explaining and consolidating the "Glorious Revolution" of 1688. Locke was part of the political movement that overthrew King James II and established William III on the British throne. Part of Locke's task was to provide a public rationale for having unseated the heir of a line of kings going back to the eleventh century, and for the idea of popular sovereignty. In the course of doing so Locke produced a theory of private property and of social formation, which constitute much of the core of classical liberal theory.

Locke would have a reasonable and justified place among the liberal theorists and thinkers of this volume. But Locke also belongs, as he is placed here, among the Christian philosophers of human nature. For Locke was a sincere and devout Anglican Christian, and his religious commitments are not mere adjuncts or constituents of his views of cognizers and social individuals; they are, in an important sense, their foundation. Locke is of virtually the last generation of western European thinkers for whom God's existence and his goodness constitute wholly certain data and basic explanatory principles of the world and the place of humanity within it, regarded as more or less universally shared public knowledge.

John Locke, *The Reasonableness of Christianity*

(Source: John Locke. *The Works of John Locke*. Vol. VII. London: Thomas Tegg *et al.*, [1823], 132-133.)

There is another difficulty often to be met with, which seems to have something of more weight in it: and that is, that "though the faith of those before Christ, (believing that God would send the Messiah, to be a Prince and a Saviour to his people, as he had promised) and the faith of those since his time, (believing Jesus to be that Messiah, promised and sent by God) shall be accounted to them for righteousness; yet what shall become of all the rest of mankind, who, having never heard of the promise or news of a Saviour; nor a word of a Messiah to be sent, or that was come; have had no thought or belief concerning him?"

To this I answer, that God will require of every man, "according to what a man hath, and not according to what he hath not." He will not expect the improvement of ten talents, where he gave but one; nor require any one should believe a promise of which he has never heard. The apostle's reasoning, Rom. x. 14, is very just: "How shall they believe in him of whom they have not heard?" But though there be many, who being strangers to the commonwealth of Israel, were also strangers to the oracles of God, committed to that people; many, to whom the promise of the Messiah never came, and so were never in a capacity to believe or reject that revelation; yet God had, by the light of reason, revealed to all mankind, who would make use of that light, that he was good and merciful. The same spark of the divine nature and knowledge in man, which, making him a man, showed him the law he was under, as a man; showed him also the way of atoning the merciful, kind, compassionate Author and Father of him and his being, when he had transgressed that law. He that made use of this candle of the Lord, so far as to find what was his duty, could not miss to find also the way to reconciliation and forgiveness, when he had failed of his duty: though, if he used not his reason this way, if he put out or neglected this light, he might, perhaps, see neither.

John Locke, *The Second Treatise of (Civil) Government*

(Source: John Locke. *The Second Treatise of (Civil) Government. The Works of John Locke.* Vol. V. London: Thomas Tegg *et al.*, [1823], 325-354.)

Whether we consider natural reason, which tells us that men, being once born, have a right to their preservation, and consequently to meat and drink and such other things as nature affords for their subsistence; or revelation, which gives us an account of those grants God made of the world to Adam, and to Noah and his sons; it is very clear that God, as King David says (Psalm cxv. 16), "has given the earth to the children of men," given it to mankind in common. But this being supposed, it seems to some a very great difficulty how any one should ever come to have a property in anything. I will not content myself to answer that if it be difficult to make out property upon a supposition that God gave the world to Adam and his posterity in common, it is impossible that any man but one universal monarch should have any property upon a supposition that God gave the world to Adam and his heirs in succession, exclusive of all the rest of his posterity. But I shall endeavor to show how men might come to have a property in several parts of that which God gave to mankind in common, and that without any express compact of all the commoners.

God, who has given the world to men in common, has also given them reason to make use of it to the best advantage of life and convenience. The earth and all that is therein is given to men for the support and comfort of their being. And though all the fruits it naturally produces and beasts it feeds belong to mankind in common, as they are produced by the spontaneous hand of nature; and nobody has originally a private dominion exclusive of the rest of mankind in any of them, as they are thus in their natural state; yet, being given for the use of men, there must of necessity be a means to appropriate them some way or other before they can be of any use or at all beneficial to any particular man. The fruit or venison which nourishes the wild Indian, who knows no enclosure and is still a tenant in common, must be his, and so his, i. e., a part of him, that another can no longer have any right to it before it can do him any good for the support of his life.

Though the earth and all inferior creatures be common to all men, yet every man has a property in his own person; this nobody has any right to but himself. The labor of his body and the work of his hands, we may say, are properly his. Whatsoever then he removes out of the state that nature has provided and left it in, he has mixed his labor with, and joined to it something that is his own, and thereby makes it his property. It being by him removed from the common state nature has placed it in, it has by this labor something annexed to it that excludes the common right of other men. For this labor being the unquestionable property of the laborer, no man but he can have a right to what that is once joined to, at least where there is enough and as good left in common for others.

John Locke, *A Letter Concerning Toleration*

(Source: John Locke. *A Letter Concerning Toleration. The Works of John Locke* Vol. VI. London: Thomas Tegg *et al*, [1823], 5-13, 20, 41-43.)

Since you are pleased to inquire what are my thoughts about the mutual toleration of Christians in their different professions of religion, I must needs answer you freely that I esteem that toleration to be the chief characteristic mark of the true church. For whatsoever some people boast of the antiquity of places and names, or of the pomp of their outward worship; others, of the reformation of their discipline; all, of the orthodoxy of their faith – for everyone is orthodox to himself – these things, and all others of this nature, are much rather marks of men striving for power and empire over one another than of the church of Christ. Let anyone have never so true a claim to all these things, yet if he be destitute of charity, meekness, and goodwill in general toward all mankind, even to those that are not Christians, he is certainly yet short of being a true Christian himself. "The kings of the Gentiles exercise lordship over them," said our Saviour to His disciples, "but ye shall not be so" [Luke 22:25]. The business of true religion is quite another thing. It is not instituted in order to the erecting of an external pomp, nor to the obtaining of ecclesiastical dominion, nor to the exercising of compulsive force, but to the regulating of men's lives, according to the rules of virtue and piety. Whosoever will list himself under the banner of Christ must in the first place, and above all things, make war upon his own lusts and vices. It is in vain for any man to usurp the name of Christian without holiness of life, purity of manners, benignity and meekness of spirit. "Let everyone that nameth the name of Christ, depart from iniquity" [2 Tim. 2:19]. "Thou, when thou art converted, strengthen thy brethren," said our Lord to Peter [Luke 22:32]. It would, indeed, be very hard for one that appears careless about his own salvation to persuade me that he were extremely concerned for mine. For it is impossible that those should sincerely and heartily apply themselves to make other people Christians who have not really embraced the Christian religion in their own hearts. If the Gospel and the apostles may be credited, no man can be a Christian without charity, and without that faith which works, not by force, but by love. Now I appeal to the consciences of those that persecute, torment, destroy, and kill other men upon pretense of religion, whether they do it out of friendship and kindness toward them or no? And I shall then indeed, and not until then, believe they do so, when I shall see those fiery zealots correcting, in the same manner, their friends and familiar acquaintance for the manifest sins they commit against the precepts of the Gospel; when I shall see them persecute with fire and sword the members of their own communion that are tainted with enormous vices, and without amendment are in danger of eternal perdition; and when I shall see them thus express their love and desire of the salvation of their souls by the infliction of torments and exercise of all manner of cruelties. For if it be out of a principle of charity, as they pretend, and love to men's souls, that they deprive them of their estates, maim them with corporal punishments, starve and torment them in noisome prisons, and in the end even take away their lives – I say, if all this be done merely to make men Christians and procure their salvation, why then do they suffer whoredom, fraud, malice, and suchlike enormities, which (according to the apostle [Rom. I]) manifestly relish of heathenish corruption, to predominate so much and abound amongst their flocks and people? These, and suchlike things, are certainly more contrary to the glory of God, to the purity of the church, and to the salvation of souls, than any conscientious dissent from ecclesiastical decisions, or separation from public worship, whilst accompanied with innocence of life. Why then does this burning zeal for God, for the church, and for the salvation of souls – burning I say, literally, with fire and faggot – pass by those moral vices and wickednesses, without any chastisement, which are acknowledged by all men to be diametrically opposite to the profession of Christianity, and bend all its nerves either to the introducing of ceremonies, or to the establishment of opinions, which for the most part are about nice and intricate matters that exceed the capacity of ordinary understandings? Which of the parties contending about these things is in the right, which of them is guilty of schism or heresy, whether those that domineer or those that suffer, will then at last be manifest when the causes of their separation comes to be judged of. He, certainly, that follows Christ embraces His doctrine and bears His yoke, though he forsake both father and mother, separate from the public assemblies and ceremonies of his country, or whomsoever or whatsoever else he relinquishes, will not then be judged a heretic.

Now, though the divisions that are amongst sects should be allowed to be never so obstructive of the salvation of souls; yet, nevertheless, adultery, fornication, uncleanliness, lasciviousness, idolatry, and suchlike things, cannot be denied to be works of the flesh, concerning which the apostle has expressly declared [Gal. 5] that "they who do them shall not inherit the kingdom of God." Whosoever, therefore, is sincerely solicitous about the kingdom of God, and thinks it his duty to endeavor the enlargement of it amongst men, ought to apply himself with no less care and industry to the rooting out of these immoralities than to the extirpation of sects. But if anyone do otherwise, and whilst he is cruel and implacable toward those that differ from him in opinion, he be indulgent to such iniquities and immoralities as are unbecoming the name of a Christian, let such a one talk never so much of the church, he plainly demonstrates by his actions that it is another kingdom he aims at, and not the advancement of the kingdom of God.

That any man should think fit to cause another man – whose salvation he heartily desires – to expire in torments, and that even in an unconverted state, would, I confess, seem very strange to me and I think to any other also. But nobody, surely, will ever believe that such a carriage can proceed from charity, love, or goodwill. If anyone maintain that men ought to be compelled by fire and sword to profess certain doctrines, and conform to this or that exterior that they do not believe and allowing them to practice things that the Gospel does not permit, it cannot be doubted indeed but such a one is desirous to have a numerous assembly joined in the same profession with himself; but that he principally intends by those means to compose a truly Christian church is altogether incredible. It is not, therefore, to be wondered at if those who do not really contend for the advancement of the true religion, and of the church of Christ, make use of arms that do not belong to the Christian warfare. If, like the Captain of our salvation, they sincerely desired the good of souls, they would tread in the steps and follow the perfect example of that Prince

of Peace, who sent out His soldiers to the subduing of nations, and gathering them into His church, not armed with the sword or other instruments of force, but prepared with the Gospel of peace and with the exemplary holiness of their conversation. This was His method. Though if infidels were to be converted by force, if those that are either blind or obstinate were to be drawn off from their errors by armed soldiers, we know very well that it was much more easy for Him to do it with armies of heavenly legions than for any son of the church, how potent soever, with all his dragoons.

The toleration of those that differ from others in matters of religion is so agreeable to the Gospel of Jesus Christ, and to the genuine reason of mankind, that it seems monstrous for men to be so blind as not to perceive the necessity and advantage of it in so clear a light. I will not here tax the pride and ambition of some, the passion and uncharitable zeal of others. These are faults from which human affairs can perhaps scarce ever be perfectly freed; but yet such as nobody will bear the plain imputation of, without covering them with some specious color; and so pretend to commendation, whilst they are carried away by their own irregular passions. But, however, that some may not color their spirit of persecution and un-Christian cruelty with a pretense of care of the public weal and observation of the laws; and that others, under pretense of religion, may not seek impunity for their libertinism and licentiousness – in a word, that none may impose either upon himself or others by the pretenses of loyalty and obedience to the prince, or of tenderness and sincerity in the worship of God; I esteem it above all things necessary to distinguish exactly the business of civil government from that of religion, and to settle the just bounds that lie between the one and the other. If this be not done, there can be no end put to the controversies that will be always arising between those that have, or at least pretend to have on the one side, a concernment for the interest of men's souls, and, on the other side, a care of the commonwealth.

The commonwealth seems to me to be a society of men constituted only for the procuring, preserving, and advancing their own civil interests.

Civil interests I call life, liberty, health, and indolency of body; and the possession of outward things, such as money, lands, houses, furniture, and the like.

It is the duty of the civil magistrate, by the impartial execution of equal laws, to secure unto all the people in general, and to every one of his subjects in particular, the just possession of these things belonging to this life. If anyone presume to violate the laws of public justice and equity, established for the preservation of those things, his presumption is to be checked by the fear of punishment consisting of the deprivation or diminution of those civil interests or goods which otherwise he might and ought to enjoy. But seeing no man does willingly suffer himself to be punished by the deprivation of any part of his goods, and much less of his liberty or life, therefore is the magistrate armed with the force and strength of all his subjects, in order to the punishment of those that violate any other man's rights.

Now that the whole jurisdiction of the magistrate reaches only to these civil concernments; and that all civil power, right and dominion is bounded and confined to the only care of promoting these things; and that it neither can nor ought in any manner to be extended to the salvation of souls, these following considerations seem unto me abundantly to demonstrate.

First, because the care of souls is not committed to the civil magistrate any more than to other men. It is not committed unto him, I say, by God; because it appears not that God has ever given any such authority to one man over another, as to compel anyone to his religion. Nor can any such power be vested in the magistrate by the consent of the people, because no man can so far abandon the care of his own salvation as blindly to leave to the choice of any other, whether prince or subject, to prescribe to him what faith or worship he shall embrace. For no man can, if he would, conform his faith to the dictates of another. All the life and power of true religion consist in the inward and full persuasion of the mind; and faith is not faith without believing. Whatever profession we make to whatever outward worship we conform, if we are not fully satisfied in our own mind that the one is true, and the other well pleasing unto God, such profession and such practice, far from being any

furtherance, are indeed great obstacles to our salvation. For in this manner, instead of expiating other sins by the exercise of religion, I say, in offering thus unto God Almighty such a worship as we esteem to be displeasing unto Him, we add unto the number of our other sins those also of hypocrisy and contempt of His Divine Majesty.

In the second place, the care of souls cannot belong to the civil magistrate because his power consists only in outward force; but true and saving religion consists in the inward persuasion of the mind, without which nothing can be acceptable to God. And such is the nature of the understanding that it cannot be compelled to the belief of anything by outward force. Confiscation of estate, imprisonment, torments, nothing of that nature can have any such efficacy as to make men change the inward judgment that they have framed of things.

It may indeed be alleged that the magistrate may make use of arguments, and thereby draw the heterodox into the way of truth and procure their salvation. I grant it; but this is common to him with other men. In teaching, instructing, and redressing the erroneous by reason, he may certainly do what becomes any good man to do. Magistracy does not oblige him to put off either humanity or Christianity; but it is one thing to persuade, another to command; one thing to press with arguments, another with penalties. This civil power alone has a right to do; to the other, goodwill is authority enough. Every man has commission to admonish, exhort, convince another of error, and, by reasoning, to draw him into truth; but to give laws, receive obedience, and compel with the sword, belongs to none but the magistrate. And upon this ground I affirm that the magistrate's power extends not to the establishing of any articles of faith or forms of worship by the force of his laws. For laws are of no force at all without penalties, and penalties in this case are absolutely impertinent, because they are not proper to convince the mind. Neither the profession of any articles of faith, nor the conformity to any outward form of worship (as has been already said), can be available to the salvation of souls unless the truth of the one, and the acceptableness of the other unto God, be thoroughly believed by those that so profess and practice. But penalties are no way capable to produce such belief. It is only light and evidence that can work a change in men's opinions; which light can in no manner proceed from corporal sufferings or any other outward penalties.

In the third place, the care of the salvation of men's souls cannot belong to the magistrate; because, though the rigor of laws and the force of penalties were capable to convince and change men's minds, yet would not that help at all to the salvation of their souls. For there being but one truth, one way to heaven, what hope is there that more men would be led into it if they had no rule but the religion of the court, and were put under the necessity to quit the light of their own reason, and oppose the dictates of their own consciences, and blindly to resign themselves up to the will of their governors and to the religion which either ignorance, ambition, or superstition had chanced to establish in the countries where they were born? In the variety and contradiction of opinions in religion, wherein the princes of the world are as much divided as in their secular interests, the narrow way would be much straitened; one country alone would be in the right, and all the rest of the world put under an obligation of following their princes in the ways that lead to destruction; and that which heightens the absurdity, and very ill suits the notion of a Deity, men would owe their eternal happiness or misery to the places of their nativity.

These considerations, to omit many others that might have been urged to the same purpose, seem unto me sufficient to conclude that all the power of civil government relates only to men's civil interests, is confined to the care of the things of this world, and hath nothing to do with the world to come.

Let us now consider what a church is. A church, then, I take to be a voluntary society of men, joining themselves together of their own accord in order to the public worshiping of God in such manner as they judge acceptable to Him, and effectual to the salvation of their souls.

I say it is a free and voluntary society. Nobody is born a member of any church; otherwise the religion of parents would descend unto children by the same right of inheritance as their temporal estates, and everyone would hold his faith by the same tenure he does his lands, than which nothing can be imagined more absurd. Thus, therefore, that matter stands. No man by nature is bound unto any particular church or sect, but everyone joins himself voluntarily to that society in which he believes he has found that profession and worship which is truly acceptable to God. The hope of salvation, as it was the only cause of his entrance into that communion, so it can be the only reason of his stay there. For if afterwards he discover anything either erroneous in the doctrine or incongruous in the worship of that society to which he has joined himself, why should it not be as free for him to go out as it was to enter? No member of a religious society can be tied with any other bonds but what proceed from the certain expectation of eternal life. A church, then, is a society of members voluntarily uniting to that end.

....

Nobody, therefore, in fine, neither single persons nor churches, nay, nor even commonwealths, have any just title to invade the civil rights and worldly goods of each other upon pretense of religion. Those that are of another opinion would do well to consider with themselves how pernicious a seed of discord and war, how powerful a provocation to endless hatreds, rapines, and slaughters they thereby furnish unto mankind. No peace and security, no, not so much as common friendship, can ever be established or preserved amongst men so long as this opinion prevails that dominion is founded in grace and that religion is to be propagated by force of arms.

....

Every man has an immortal soul, capable of eternal happiness or misery, whose happiness depending upon his believing and doing those things in this life which are necessary to the obtaining of God's favor, and are prescribed by God to that end: it follows from thence, first, that the observance of these things is the highest obligation that lies upon mankind, and that our utmost care, application, and diligence ought to be exercised in the search and performance of them; because there is nothing in this world that is of any consideration in comparison with eternity. Secondly, that seeing one man does not violate the right of another by his erroneous opinions and undue manner of worship, nor is his perdition any prejudice to another man's affairs, therefore, the care of each man's salvation belongs only to himself. But I would not have this understood as if I meant hereby to condemn all charitable admonitions and affectionate endeavors to reduce men from errors, which are indeed the greatest duty of a Christian. Anyone may employ as many exhortations and arguments as he pleases, toward the promoting of another man's salvation. But all force and compulsion are to be forborne. Nothing is to be done imperiously. Nobody is obliged in that manner to yield obedience unto the admonitions or injunctions of another, further than he himself is persuaded. Every man in that has the supreme and absolute authority of judging for himself. And the reason is because nobody else is concerned in it, nor can receive any prejudice from his conduct therein.

But besides their souls, which are immortal, men have also their temporal lives here upon earth; the state whereof being frail and fleeting, and the duration uncertain, they have need of several outward conveniences to the support thereof, which are to be procured or preserved by pains and industry. For those things that are necessary to the comfortable support of our lives are not the spontaneous products of nature, nor do offer themselves fit and prepared for our use. This part therefore draws on another care, and necessarily gives another employment. But the pravity of mankind being such that they had rather injuriously prey upon the fruits of other men's labors than take pains to provide for themselves, the necessity of preserving men in the possession of what honest industry has already acquired, and also of preserving their liberty and strength, whereby they may acquire what they further want, obliges men to enter into society with one another, that by mutual assistance and joint force they may secure unto each other their properties, in the things that contribute to the comfort and happiness of this life, leaving in the meanwhile to every man the care of his own eternal happiness, the attainment whereof can neither be facilitated

by another man's industry, nor can the loss of it turn to another man's prejudice, nor the hope of it be forced from him by any external violence. But, forasmuch as men thus entering into societies, grounded upon their mutual compacts of assistance for the defense of their temporal goods, may, nevertheless, be deprived of them, either by the rapine and fraud of their fellow citizens or by the hostile violence of foreigners, the remedy of this evil consists in arms, riches, and multitude of citizens; the remedy of the other in laws; and the care of all things relating both to one and the other is committed by the society to the civil magistrate. This is the original, this is the use, and these are the bounds of the legislative (which is the supreme) power in every commonwealth. I mean that provision may be made for the security of each man's private possessions, for the peace, riches, and public commodities of the whole people, and, as much as possible, for the increase of their inward strength against foreign invasions.

Bibliography

Grant, Ruth W. *John Locke's Liberalism*. Chicago and London: University of Chicago Press, 1987.

Passmore, John. "Locke and the Ethics of Belief." The Dawes Hicks Lecture for 1978. *Proceedings of the British Academy*, 74 (1978), 185-208.

Seliger, M. *The Liberal Politics of John Locke*. London: George Allen and Unwin, 1968.

Tully, James. *A Discourse on Property: John Locke and His Adversaries*. Cambridge: Cambridge Univesity Press, 1980.

Yolton, John W. *John Locke and the Way of Ideas*. Oxford Classical and Philosophical Monographs. London: Oxford University Press, 1956; reps. Oxford: Clarendon Press, 1968.

Yolton, John W. *A Locke Dictionary*. Oxford: Blackwell, 1993.

CHAPTER TEN — JOSEPH BUTLER

Joseph Butler (1692-1752) was an English clergyman, of very considerable philosophical gift. Originally of Presbyterian background, he was ordained in the Church of England, rising successively to being bishop of Bristol, dean of St. Paul's (as the great poet John Donne had been), and bishop of Durham. Butler's two great works were the *Fifteen Sermons preached at Rolls Chapel* (1726), from which the selection that follows is drawn, and *The Analogy of Religion* (1736), which argues for revealed religion against deism.

Butler is one of the major moral theorists of the eighteenth century. Although his ethical views rest ultimately on Christian convictions, and were regarded by Butler as providing support for a Christian view of the world, they are offered secularly and with appeal to the experience and judgment of common sense and reflective humanity. Butler's outlook is not at odds with modernity; he is cheerful, sensible, and psychologically acute.

It bears reminder, in the face of the predominant "paganism" of the Enlightenment overall, how considerable and continuous a Christian voice remained throughout the eighteenth century, and beyond. There is indeed a "Christian Enlightenment," the unity of whose culture has not perhaps adequately been explored.

Joseph Butler, *Fifteen Sermons Preached at the Rolls Chapel and A Dissertation Upon the Nature of Virtue*

(Source: Joseph Butler. *Fifteen Sermons Preached at the Rolls Chapel and A Dissertation Upon the Nature of Virtue*. Reprinted in W.L. Gladstone, ed., *The Works of Joseph Butler* [Oxford: Clarendon Press, 1896], vol. ii, 31-76.)

SERMON I
UPON HUMAN NATURE

For as we have many members in one body, and all members have not the same office: so we, being many, are one body in Christ, and every one members one of another (Romans XII: 4, 5).

[1.] The epistles in the New Testament have all of them a particular reference to the condition and usages of the Christian world at the time they were written. Therefore, as they cannot be thoroughly understood unless that condition and those usages are known and attended to, so further, though they be known, yet if they be discontinued or changed, exhortations, precepts, and illustrations of things, which refer to such circumstances now ceased or altered, cannot at this time be urged in that manner and with that force which they were to the primitive Christians. Thus the text now before us, in its first intent and design, relates to the decent management of those extraordinary gifts which were then in the church,[1] but which are now totally ceased. And even as to the allusion that "we are one body in Christ," though what the apostle here intends is equally true of Christians in all circumstances – and the consideration of it is plainly still an additional motive, over and above moral considerations, to the discharge of the several duties and offices of a Christian – yet it is manifest this allusion must have appeared with much greater force to those who, by the many difficulties they went through for the sake of their religion, were led to keep always in view the relation they stood in to their Saviour, who had undergone the same; to those who, from the idolatries of all around them and their ill treatment, were taught to consider themselves as not of the world in which they lived, but as a distinct society of themselves, with laws and ends, and principles of life and action, quite

1   I Cor. XII

contrary to those which the world professed themselves at that time influenced by. Hence the relation of a Christian was by them considered as nearer than that of affinity and blood; and they almost literally esteemed themselves as members one of another.

[2] It cannot indeed possibly be denied that our being God's creatures, and virtue being the natural law we are born under, and the whole constitution of man being plainly adapted to it, are prior obligations to piety and virtue than the consideration that God sent his Son into the world to save it, and the motives which arise from the peculiar relations of Christians, as members one of another under Christ our Head. However, though all this be allowed, as it expressly is by the inspired writers, yet it is manifest that Christians at the time of the revelation, and immediately after, could not but insist mostly upon considerations of this latter kind.

[3.] These observations show the original particular reference of the text; and the peculiar force with which the thing intended by the allusion in it, must have been felt by the primitive Christian world. They likewise afford a reason for treating it at this time in a more general way.

[4.] The relation which the several parts or members of the natural body have to each other and to the whole body is here compared to the relation which each particular person in society has to other particular persons and to the whole society; and the latter is intended to be illustrated by the former. And if there be a likeness between these two relations, the consequence is obvious: that the latter shows us [we were intended][2] to do good to others, as the former shows us that [the several members of the natural body were intended to be instruments of good to each other and the whole body].[3] But as there is scarce any ground for a comparison between society and the mere material body, this without the mind being a dead unactive thing, much less can the comparison be carried to any length. And since the apostle speaks of the several members as having distinct offices, which implies the mind, it cannot be thought an unallowable liberty, instead of the *body* and *its members,* to substitute the *whole nature of man* and *all the variety of internal principles which belong to it.* And then the comparison will be between the nature of man as respecting self and tending to private good, his own preservation and happiness, and the nature of man as having respect to society and tending to promote public good, the happiness of that society. These ends do indeed perfectly coincide; and to aim at public and private good are so far from being inconsistent that they mutually promote each other; yet in the following discourse they must be considered as entirely distinct, otherwise the nature of man as tending to one, or as tending to the other, cannot be compared. There can no comparison be made without considering the things compared as distinct and different.

[5.] From this review and comparison of the nature of man as respecting self and as respecting society, it will plainly appear that there are as real and the same kind of indications in human nature that we were made for society and to do good to our fellow creatures, as that we were intended to take care of our own life and health and private good; and that the same objections lie against one of these assertions as against the other. For,

[6.] First, there is a natural principle of *benevolence*[4] in man, which is in some degree to *society* what *self-love* is to the *individual.* And if there be in mankind any disposition to friendship; if there

---

2   [Ed. I.: "it is our duty."]

3   [Ed. I.: "we are to take care of our own private interest."]

4   Suppose a man of learning to be writing a grave book upon *human nature,* and to show in several parts of it that he had an insight into the subject he was considering; amongst other things, the following one would require to be accounted for: the appearance of benevolence or goodwill in men toward each other in the instances of natural relation, and in others (Hobbes, *Of Human Nature, c. ix.* 7). Cautious of being deceived with outward show, he retires within himself to see exactly what that is in the mind of man from whence this appearance proceeds; and, upon deep reflection, asserts the principle in the mind to be only the love of power, and delight in the exercise of it. Would not everybody think here was a mistake of one word for another; that the philosopher was contemplating and accounting for some other human actions, some other behavior of man to man? And could anyone be thoroughly satisfied that what is commonly called benevolence or goodwill was really the affection meant, but only by being

be any such thing as compassion, for compassion is momentary love; if there be any such thing as the paternal or filial affections; if there be any affection in human nature the object and end of which is the good of another – this is itself benevolence or the love of another. Be it ever so short, be it in ever so low a degree, or ever so unhappily confined, it proves the assertion and points out what we were designed for, as really as though it were in a higher degree and more extensive. I must however remind you that though benevolence and self-love are different, though the former tends most directly to public good, and the latter to private, yet they are so perfectly coincident that the greatest satisfactions to ourselves depend upon our having benevolence in a due degree, and that self-love is one chief security of our right behavior toward society. It may be added that their mutual coinciding, so that we can scarce promote one without the other, is equally a proof that we were made for both.

[7.] Secondly, this will further appear, from observing that the *several passions and affections,* which are distinct[5] both from benevolence and self-love,

---

made to understand that this learned person had a general hypothesis to which the appearance of goodwill could no otherwise be reconciled? That what has this appearance is often nothing but ambition; that delight in superiority often (suppose always) mixes itself with benevolence, only makes it more specious to call it ambition than hunger, of the two: but in reality that passion does no more account for the whole appearances of goodwill than this appetite does. Is there not often the appearance of one man's wishing that good to another which he knows himself unable to procure him; and rejoicing in it, though bestowed by a third person? And can love of power anyway possibly come in to account for this desire or delight? Is there not often the appearance of men's distinguishing between two or more persons, preferring one before another, to do good to, in cases where love of power cannot in the least account for the distinction and preference? For this principle can no otherwise distinguish between objects than as it is a greater instance and exertion of power to do good to one rather than to another. Again, suppose goodwill in the mind of man to be nothing but delight in the exercise of power; men might indeed be restrained by distant and accidental considerations; but these restraints being removed, they would have a disposition to, and delight in, mischief as an exercise and proof of power: and this disposition and delight would arise from or be the same principle in the mind, as a disposition to, and delight in, charity. Thus cruelty, as distinct from envy and resentment, would be exactly the same in the mind of man as goodwill – that one tends to the happiness, the other to the misery of our fellow creatures, is, it seems, merely an accidental circumstance, which the mind has not the least regard to. These are the absurdities which even men of capacity run into when they have occasion to belie their nature, and will perversely disclaim that image of God which was originally stamped upon it, the traces of which, however faint, are plainly discernible upon the mind of man.

If any person can in earnest doubt whether there be such a thing as goodwill in one man toward another (for the question is not concerning either the degree or extensiveness of it, but concerning the affection itself), let it be observed that whether man be thus or otherwise constituted, what is the inward frame in this particular, is a mere question of fact or natural history, not provable immediately by reason. It is therefore to be judged of and determined in the same way other facts or matters of natural history are: by appealing to the external senses or inward perceptions respectively, as the matter under consideration is cognizable by one or the other; by arguing from acknowledged facts and actions; for a great number of actions in the same kind, in different circumstances, and respecting different objects, will prove, to a certainty, what principles they do not, and, to the greatest probability, what principles they do proceed from; and lastly, by the testimony of mankind. Now that there is some degree of benevolence amongst men may be as strongly and plainly proved in all these ways, as it could possibly be proved, supposing there was this affection in our nature. And should anyone think fit to assert that resentment in the mind of man was absolutely nothing but reasonable concern for our own safety, the falsity of this, and what is the real nature of that passion, could be shown in no other ways than those in which it may be shown, that there is such a thing in some degree as real goodwill in man toward man. It is sufficient that the seeds of it be implanted in our nature by God. There is, it is owned, much left for us to do upon our own heart and temper; to cultivate, to improve, to call it forth, to exercise it in a steady, uniform manner. This is our work; this is virtue and religion.

5   Everybody makes a distinction between self-love and the several particular passions, appetites, and affections; and yet they are often confounded again. That they are totally different, will be seen by any one who will distinguish between the passions and appetites themselves, and endeavoring after the means of their gratification. Consider the appetite of hunger, and the desire of esteem; these being the occasion both of pleasure and pain, the coolest self-love, as well as the appetites and passions themselves, may put us upon making use of the proper methods of

do in general contribute and lead us to *public* good as really as to *private*. It might be thought too minute and particular, and would carry us too great a length, to distinguish between and compare together the several passions or appetites distinct from benevolence, whose primary use and intention is the security and good of society; and the passions distinct from self-love, whose primary intention and design is the security and good of the individual.[6] It is enough to the present argument that desire of esteem from others, contempt and esteem of them, love of society as distinct from affection to the good of it, indignation against successful vice – that these are public affections or passions, have an immediate respect to others, naturally lead us to regulate our behavior in such a manner as will be of service to our fellow creatures. If any or all of these may be considered likewise as private affections, as tending to private good, this does not hinder them from being public affections, too, or destroy the good influence of them upon society, and their tendency to public good. It may be added that as persons without any conviction from reason of the desirableness of life would yet of course preserve it merely from the appetite of hunger, so by acting merely from regard (suppose) to reputation, without any consideration of the

good of others, men often contribute to public good. In both these instances they are plainly instruments in the hands of another, in the hands of Providence, to carry on ends, the preservation of the individual and good of society, which they themselves have not in their view or intention. The sum is, men have various appetites, passions, and particular affections, quite distinct both from self-love and from benevolence – all of these have a tendency to promote both public and private good, and may be considered as respecting others and ourselves equally and in common; but some of them seem most immediately to respect others, or tend to public good, others of them most immediately to respect self, or tend to private good; as the former are not benevolence, so the latter are not self-love; neither sort are instances of our love either to ourselves or others, but only instances of our Maker's care and love both of the individual and the species, and proofs that He intended we should be instruments of good to each other, as well as that we should be so to ourselves.

[8.] Thirdly, there is a principle of reflection in men by which they distinguish between, approve and disapprove, their own actions. We are plainly constituted such sort of creatures as to reflect upon our

---

obtaining that pleasure, and avoiding that pain; but the feelings themselves, the pain of hunger and shame, and the delight from esteem, are no more self-love than they are anything in the world. Though a man hated himself, he would as much feel the pain of hunger as he would that of the gout; and it is plainly supposable there may be creatures with self-love in them to the highest degree, who may be quite insensible and indifferent (as men in some cases are) to the contempt and esteem of those upon whom their happiness does not in some further respects depend. And as self-love and the several particular passions and appetites are in themselves totally different, so that some actions proceed from one, and some from the other, will be manifest to any who will observe the two following very supposable cases. One man rushes upon certain ruin for the gratification of a present desire; nobody will call the principle of this action self-love. Suppose another man to go through some laborious work upon promise of a great reward, without any distinct knowledge what the reward will be; this course of action cannot be ascribed to any particular passion. The former of these actions is plainly to be imputed to some particular passion or affection, the latter as plainly to the general affection or principle of self-love. That there are some particular pursuits or actions concerning which we cannot determine how far they are owing to one, and how far to the other, proceeds from this that the two principles are frequently mixed together, and run up into each other. This distinction is further explained in the eleventh sermon.

6   If any desire to see this distinction and comparison made in a particular instance, the appetite and passion now mentioned may serve for one. Hunger is to be considered as a private appetite; because the end for which it was given us is the preservation of the individual. Desire of esteem is a public passion; because the end for which it was given us is to regulate our behavior toward society. The respect which this has to private good is as remote as the respect that has to public good: and the appetite is no more self-love than the passion is benevolence. The object and end of the former is merely food; the object and end of the latter is merely esteem; but the latter can no more be gratified without contributing to the good of society, than the former can be gratified without contributing to the preservation of the individual.

own nature. The mind can take a view of what passes within itself, its propensions, aversions, passions, affections, as respecting such objects and in such degrees, and of the several actions consequent thereupon. In this survey it approves of one, disapproves of another, and toward a third is affected in neither of these ways, but is quite indifferent. This principle in man by which he approves or disapproves his heart, temper, and actions, is conscience [for this is the strict sense of the word, though sometimes it is used so as to take in more].[7] And that this faculty tends to restrain men from doing mischief to each other, and leads them to do good, is too manifest to need being insisted upon. Thus a parent has the affection of love to his children; this leads him to take care of, to educate, to make due provision for them; the natural affection leads to this, but the reflection that it is his proper business, what belongs to him, that it is right and commendable so to do – this added to the affection becomes a much more settled principle and carries him on through more labor and difficulties for the sake of his children than he would undergo from that affection alone, if he thought it, and the course of action it led to, either indifferent or criminal. This indeed is impossible, to do that which is good and not to approve of it; for which reason they are frequently not considered as distinct, though they really are, for men often approve of the actions of others which they will not imitate, and likewise do that which they approve not. It cannot possibly be denied that there is this principle of reflection or conscience in human nature. Suppose a man to relieve an innocent person in great distress, suppose the same man afterwards, in the fury of anger, to do the greatest mischief to a person who had given no just cause of offense; to aggravate the injury, add the circumstances of former friendship and obligation from the injured person, let the man who is supposed to have done these two different actions coolly reflect upon them afterwards, without regard to their consequences to himself; to assert that any common man would be affected in the same way toward these different actions, that he would make no distinction between them, but approve or disapprove them equally, is too glaring a falsity to need being confuted. There is therefore this principle of reflection or conscience in

mankind. It is needless to compare the respect it has to private good with the respect it has to public, since it plainly tends as much to the latter as to the former, and is commonly thought to tend chiefly to the latter. This faculty is now mentioned merely as another part in the inward frame of man, pointing out to us in some degree what we are intended for, and as what will naturally and of course have some influence. The particular place assigned to it by nature, what authority it has, and how great influence it ought to have, shall be hereafter considered.

[9.] From this comparison of benevolence and self-love, of our public and private affections, of the courses of life they lead to, and of the principle of reflection or conscience as respecting each of them, it is as manifest that we were made for society and to promote the happiness of it, as that we were intended to take care of our own life and health and private good.

[10.] And from this whole review must be given a different draught of human nature from what we are often presented with. Mankind are by nature so closely united, there is such a correspondence between the inward sensations of one man and those of another that disgrace is as much avoided as bodily pain, and to be the object of esteem and love as much desired as any external goods; and in many particular cases, persons are carried on to do good to others, as the end their affection tends to and rests in, and manifest that they find real satisfaction and enjoyment in this course of behavior. There is such a natural principle of attraction in man toward man that having trod the same tract of land, having breathed in the same climate, barely having been born in the same artificial district or division, becomes the occasion of contracting acquaintances and familiarities many years after; for anything may serve the purpose. Thus relations merely nominal are sought and invented, not by governors, but by the lowest of the people; which are found sufficient to hold mankind together in little fraternities and copartnerships – weak ties indeed, and what may afford fund enough for ridicule if they are absurdly considered as the real principles of that union; but they are in truth

---

7 [Ed. I.: "which word is used in different senses, but often in this."]

merely the occasions, as anything may be of anything, upon which our nature carries us on according to its own previous bent and bias; which occasions therefore would be nothing at all were there not this prior disposition and bias of nature. Men are so much one body that in a peculiar manner they feel for each other; shame, sudden danger, resentment, honor, prosperity, distress; one or another, or all of these, from the social nature in general, from benevolence, upon the occasion of natural relation, acquaintance, protection, dependence – each of these being distinct cements of society. And therefore to have no restraint from, no regard to, others in our behavior is the speculative absurdity of considering ourselves as single and independent, as having nothing in our nature which has respect to our fellow creatures, reduced to action and practice. And this is the same absurdity as to suppose a hand or any part to have no natural respect to any other or to the whole body.

[11.] But allowing all this, it may be asked, "Has not man dispositions and principles within, which lead him to do evil to others as well as to do good? Whence come the many miseries else, which men are the authors and instruments of to each other?" These questions, so far as they relate to the foregoing discourse, may be answered by asking, Has not man also dispositions and principles within, which lead him to do evil to himself as well as good? Whence come the many miseries else, sickness, pain, and death, which men are instruments and authors of to themselves?

[12.] It may be thought more easy to answer one of these questions than the other, but the answer to both is really the same – that mankind have ungoverned passions which they will gratify at any rate, as well to the injury of others as in contradiction to known private interest, but that as there is no such thing as self-hatred, so neither is there any such thing as ill-will in one man toward another,

emulation and resentment being away, whereas there is plainly benevolence or good-will; there is no such thing as love of injustice, oppression, treachery, ingratitude, but only eager desires after such and such external goods, which, according to a very ancient observation, the most abandoned would choose to obtain by innocent means if they were as easy and as effectual to their end that even emulation and resentment, by any one who will consider what these passions really are in nature,[8] will be found nothing to the purpose of this objection; and that the principles and passions in the mind of man, which are distinct both from self-love and benevolence, primarily and most directly lead to right behavior with regard to others as well as himself, and only secondarily and accidentally to what is evil. Thus, though men, to avoid the shame of one villainy, are sometimes guilty of a greater, yet it is easy to see that the original tendency of shame is to prevent the doing of shameful actions; and its leading men to conceal such actions when done is only in consequence of their being done, that is, of the passion's not having answered its first end.

[13.] If it be said that there are persons in the world who are in great measure without the natural affections toward their fellow creatures, there are likewise instances of persons without the common natural affections to themselves; but the nature of man is not to be judged of by either of these, but by what appears in the common world, in the bulk of mankind.

[14.] I am afraid it would be thought very strange if to confirm the truth of this account of human nature and make out the justness of the foregoing comparison, it should be added that, from what appears, men in fact as much and as often contradict that *part* of their nature which respects *self* and which leads them to their *own private* good and happiness, as they contradict that *part* of it

---

8   Emulation is merely the desire and hope of equality with, or superiority over, others with whom we compare ourselves. There does not appear to be any other grief in the natural passion, but only that want which is implied in desire. However, this may be so strong as to be the occasion of great grief. To desire the attainment of this equality or superiority by the particular means of others being brought down to our own level, or below it, is, I think, the distinct notion of envy. From whence it is easy to see that the real end, which the natural passion, emulation, and which the unlawful one, envy, aims at, is exactly the same – namely, that equality or superiority and consequently that to do mischief is not the end of envy, but merely the means it makes use of to attain its end. As to resentment, see the eighth sermon.

which respects *society* and tends to *public* good; that there are as few persons who attain the greatest satisfaction and enjoyment which they might attain in the present world, as who do the greatest good to others which they might do – nay, that there are as few who can be said really and in earnest to aim at one as at the other. Take a survey of mankind: the world in general, the good and bad, almost without exception, equally are agreed that were religion out of the case, the happiness of the present life would consist in a manner wholly in riches, honors, sensual gratifications, insomuch that one scarce hears a reflection made upon prudence, life, conduct, but upon this supposition. Yet on the contrary, that persons in the greatest affluence of fortune are no happier than such as have only a competency; that the cares and disappointments of ambition for the most part far exceed the satisfactions of it; as also the miserable intervals of intemperance and excess, and the many untimely deaths occasioned by a dissolute course of life – these things are all seen, acknowledged, by every one acknowledged, but are thought no objections against, though they expressly contradict this universal principle that the happiness of the present life consists in one or other of them. Whence is all this absurdity and contradiction? Is not the middle way obvious? Can anything be more manifest than that the happiness of life consists in these possessed and enjoyed only to a certain degree, that to pursue them beyond this degree is always attended with more inconvenience than advantage to a man's self, and often with extreme misery and unhappiness? Whence then, I say, is all this absurdity and contradiction? Is it really the result of consideration in mankind how they may become most easy to themselves, most free from care, and enjoy the chief happiness attainable in this world? Or is it not manifestly owing either to this that they have not cool and reasonable concern enough for themselves to consider wherein their chief happiness in the present life consists, or else, if they do consider it, that they will not act conformably to what is the result of that consideration; that is, reasonable concern for themselves, or cool self-love, is prevailed over by passion and appetite. So that, from what appears, there is no ground to assert [that those principles in

the nature of man which most directly lead to promote the good of our fellow creatures are more generally or in a greater degree violated than those which most directly lead us to promote our own private good and happiness.][9]

[15.] The sum of the whole is plainly this. The nature of man considered in his single capacity, and with respect only to the present world, is adapted and leads him to attain the greatest happiness he can for himself in the present world. The nature of man considered in his public or social capacity leads him to a right behavior in society, to that course of life which we call virtue. Men follow or obey their nature in both these capacities and respects to a certain degree, but not entirely; their actions do not come up to the whole of what their nature leads them to in either of these capacities or respects; and they often violate their nature in both. That is, as they neglect the duties they owe to their fellow creatures, to which their nature leads them, and are injurious, to which their nature is abhorrent, so there is a manifest negligence in men of their real happiness or interest in the present world when that interest is inconsistent with a present gratification, for the sake of which they negligently, nay, even knowingly, are the authors and instruments of their own misery and ruin. Thus they are as often unjust to themselves as to others, and for the most part are equally so to both by the same actions.

SERMON II
UPON HUMAN NATURE

For when the Gentiles, which have not the law, do by nature the thing contained in the law, these, having not the law, are a law unto themselves (Romans II: 14).

[1.] As speculative truth admits of different kinds of proof, so likewise moral obligations may be shown by different methods. If the real nature of any creature leads him and is adapted to such and such purposes only, or more than to any other, this is a reason to believe the Author of that nature intended it for those purposes. Thus there is no

---

9 [Ed. I.: "that cool self-love has any more influence upon the actions of men than the principles of virtue and benevolence have."]

doubt the eye was intended for us to see with. And the more complex any constitution is, and the greater variety of parts there are which thus tend to some one end, the stronger is the proof that such end was designed. However, when the inward frame of man is considered as any guide in morals, the utmost caution must be used that none make peculiarities in their own temper, or anything which is the effect of particular customs, though observable in several, the standard of what is common to the species; and above all, that the highest principle be not forgotten or excluded, that to which belongs the adjustment and correction of all other inward movements and affections; which principle will of course have some influence, but which being in nature supreme, as shall now be shown, ought to preside over and govern all the rest. The difficulty of rightly observing the two former cautions, the appearance there is of some small diversity amongst mankind with respect to this faculty, with respect to their natural sense of moral good and evil, and the attention necessary to survey with any exactness what passes within, have occasioned that it is not so much agreed what is the standard of the internal nature of man as of his external form. Neither is this last exactly settled. Yet we understand one another when we speak of the shape of a human body; so likewise we do when we speak of the heart and inward principles, how far soever the standard is from being exact or precisely fixed. There is therefore ground for an attempt of showing men to themselves, of showing them what course of life and behavior their real nature points out and would lead them to. Now obligations of virtue shown, and motives to the practice of it enforced, from a review of the nature of man, are to be considered as an appeal to each particular person's heart and natural conscience, as the external senses are appealed to for the proof of things cognizable by them. Since then our inward feelings, and the perceptions we receive from our external senses, are equally real; to argue from the former to life and conduct is as little liable to exception as to argue from the latter to absolute speculative truth. A man can as little doubt whether his eyes were given him to see with, as he can doubt of the truth of the science of *optics* deduced from ocular experiments. And allowing the inward feeling, shame, a man can as little doubt whether it was given him to prevent his doing shameful actions, as he can doubt

whether his eyes were given him to guide his steps. And as to these inward feelings themselves – that they are real, that man has in his nature passions and affections, can no more be questioned than that he has external senses. Neither can the former be wholly mistaken, though to a certain degree liable to greater mistakes than the latter.

[2.] There can be no doubt but that several propensions or instincts, several principles in the heart of man, carry him to society, and to contribute to the happiness of it, in a sense and a manner in which no inward principle leads him to evil. These principles, propensions, or instincts which lead him to do good are approved of by a certain faculty within, quite distinct from these propensions themselves. All this hath been fully made out in the foregoing discourse.

[3.] But it may be said, "What is all this, though true, to the purpose of virtue and religion? These require not only that we do good to others, when we are led this way by benevolence or reflection happening to be stronger than other principles, passions, or appetites, but likewise that the *whole* character be formed upon thought and reflection, that *every* action be directed by some determinate rule, some other rule than the strength and prevalency of any principle or passion. What sign is there in our nature (for the inquiry is only about what is to be collected from thence) that this was intended by its Author? Or how does so various and fickle a temper as that of man appear adapted thereto? It may indeed be absurd and unnatural for men to act without any reflection, nay, without regard to that particular kind of reflection which you call conscience; because this does belong to our nature. For as there never was a man but who approved one place, prospect, building, before another, so it does not appear that there ever was a man who would not have approved an action of humanity rather than of cruelty, interest and passion being quite out of the case. But interest and passion do come in, and are often too strong for and prevail over reflection and conscience. Now as brutes have various instincts by which they are carried on to the end the Author of their nature intended them for, is not man in the same condition, with this difference only that to his instincts (that is, appetites and passions) is added the principle of reflection or conscience? And as brutes act agreeably to their nature, in following that principle or particular instinct which for the present is strongest in them, does not man likewise act agreeably to his nature or obey the law of his creation by following that principle, be it passion or conscience, which for the present happens to be strongest in him? Thus different men are by their particular nature hurried on to pursue honor or riches or pleasure; there are also persons whose temper leads them in an uncommon degree to kindness, compassion, doing good to their fellow creatures, as there are others who are given to suspend their judgment, to weigh and consider things, and to act upon thought and reflection. Let everyone then quietly follow his nature, as passion, reflection, appetite, the several parts of it, happen to be strongest; but let not the man of virtue take upon him to blame the ambitious, the covetous, the dissolute, since these equally with him obey and follow their nature. Thus, as in some cases we follow our nature in doing the works contained in the law, so in other cases we follow nature in doing contrary."

[4.] Now all this licentious talk entirely goes upon a supposition that men follow their nature in the same sense, in violating the known rules of justice and honesty for the sake of a present gratification, as they do in following those rules when they have no temptation to the contrary. And if this were true, that could not be so which St. Paul asserts, that men are "by nature a law to themselves." If by following nature were meant only acting as we please, it would indeed be ridiculous to speak of nature as any guide in morals, nay, the very mention of deviating from nature would be absurd; and the mention of following it, when spoken by way of distinction, would absolutely have no meaning. For did ever any one act otherwise than as he pleased? And yet the ancients speak of deviating from nature as vice, and of following nature so much as a distinction, that according to them the perfection of virtue consists therein. So that language itself should teach people another sense of the words "following nature" than barely acting as we please. Let it however be observed that though the words "human nature" are to be explained, yet the real

question of this discourse is not concerning the meaning of words – any other than as the explanation of them may be needful to make out and explain the assertion that every man is naturally a law to himself, that everyone may find within himself the rule of right, and obligations to follow it. This St. Paul affirms in the words of the text, and this the foregoing objection really denies by seeming to allow it. And the objection will be fully answered and the text before us explained, by observing that "nature" is considered in different views, and the words used in different senses; and by showing in what view it is considered, and in what sense the word is used, when intended to express and signify that which is the guide of life, that by which men are a law to themselves. I say the explanation of the term will be sufficient, because from thence it will appear that in some senses of the word "nature" cannot be, but that in another sense it manifestly is, a law to us.

[5.] I. By nature is often meant no more than some principle in man, without regard either to the kind or degree of it. Thus the passion of anger and the affection of parents to their children would be called equally "natural." And as the same person hath often contrary principles, which at the same time draw contrary ways, he may by the same action both follow and contradict his nature in this sense of the word; he may follow one passion and contradict another.

[6.] II. *Nature is* frequently spoken of as consisting in those passions which are strongest and most influence the actions; which being vicious ones, mankind is in this sense naturally vicious, or vicious by nature. Thus St. Paul says of the Gentiles, "who were dead in trespasses and sins, and walked according to the spirit of disobedience, that they were by nature the children of wrath."[10] They could be no otherwise "children of wrath" by nature than they were vicious by nature.

[7.] Here then are two different senses of the word "nature," in neither of which men can at all be said to be a law to themselves. They are mentioned only to be excluded, to prevent their being confounded, as the latter is in the objection, with another sense

10   Ephes. II: 3

of it which is now to be inquired after and explained.

[8.] III. The apostle asserts that the Gentiles "do by *nature* the things contained in the law." Nature is indeed here put by way of distinction from revelation, but yet it is not a mere negative. He intends to express more than that by which they *did not,* that by which they *did* the works of the law, namely, by *nature.* It is plain the meaning of the word is not the same in this passage as in the former, where it is spoken of as evil; for in this latter it is spoken of as good, as that by which they acted or might have acted virtuously. What that is in man by which he is "naturally a law to himself," is explained in the following words: "which show the work of the law written in their hearts, their conscience also bearing witness, and their thoughts the meanwhile accusing or else excusing one another."[11] If there be a distinction to be made between the *works written in their hearts* and the *witness of conscience,* by the former must be meant the natural disposition to kindness and compassion, to do what is of good report, to which this apostle often refers; that part of the nature of man, treated of in the foregoing discourse, which with very little reflection and of course leads him to society, and by means of which he naturally acts a just and good part in it unless other passions or interest lead him astray. Yet since other passions and regards to private interest, which lead us (though indirectly, yet they lead us) astray, are themselves in a degree equally natural and often most prevalent; and since we have no method of seeing the particular degrees in which one or the other is placed in us by nature, it is plain the former, considered merely as natural, good and right as they are, can no more be a law to us than the latter. But there is a superior principle of reflection or conscience in every man which distinguishes between the internal principles of his heart as well as his external actions, which passes judgment upon himself and them, pronounces determinately some actions to be in themselves just, right, good; others to be in themselves evil, wrong, unjust, which, without being consulted, without being advised with, magisterially exerts itself, and approves or condemns him the doer of them accordingly; and which, if not forcibly stopped,

naturally and always of course goes on to anticipate a higher and more effectual sentence which shall hereafter second and affirm its own. But this part of the office of conscience is beyond my present design explicitly to consider. It is by this faculty, natural to man, that he is a moral agent, that he is a law to himself; by this faculty, I say, not to be considered merely as a principle in his heart, which is to have some influence as well as others, but considered as a faculty in kind and in nature supreme over all others, and which bears its own authority of being so.

[9.] This *prerogative,* this *natural supremacy* of the faculty which surveys, approves or disapproves, the several affections of our mind and actions of our lives, being that by which men "are a law to themselves" – their conformity or disobedience to which law of our nature renders their actions, in the highest and most proper sense, natural or unnatural – it is fit it be further explained to you, and I hope it will be so if you will attend to the following reflections.

[10.] Man may act according to that principle or inclination which for the present happens to be strongest, and yet act in a way disproportionate to, and violate, his real proper nature. Suppose a brute creature by any bait to be allured into a snare by which he is destroyed. He plainly followed the bent of his nature, leading him to gratify his appetite; there is an entire correspondence between his whole nature and such an action – such action therefore is natural. But suppose a man, foreseeing the same danger of certain ruin, should rush into it for the sake of a present gratification; he in this instance would follow his strongest desire, as did the brute creature, but there would be as manifest a disproportion between the nature of a man and such an action as between the meanest work of art and the skill of the greatest master in that art; which disproportion arises, not from considering the action singly in *itself* or in its *consequences,* but from comparison of it with the nature of the agent. And since such an action is utterly disproportionate to the nature of man, it is in the strictest and most proper sense unnatural, this word expressing that disproportion. Therefore, instead of the words "disproportionate to his nature," the word

11   [Rom. II: 15]

"unnatural" may now be put, this being more familiar to us; but let it be observed that it stands for the same thing precisely.

[11.] Now what is it which renders such a rash action unnatural? Is it that he went against the principle of reasonable and cool self-love considered *merely* as a part of his nature? No; for if he had acted the contrary way, he would equally have gone against a principle or part of his nature, namely, passion or appetite. But to deny a present appetite, from foresight that the gratification of it would end in immediate ruin or extreme misery, is by no means an unnatural action, whereas to contradict or go against cool self-love for the sake of such gratification is so in the instance before us. Such an action then being unnatural, and its being so not arising from a man's going against a principle or desire barely, nor in going against that principle or desire which happens for the present to be strongest, it necessarily follows that there must be some other difference or distinction to be made between these two principles, passion and cool self-love, than what I have yet taken notice of. And this difference, not being a difference in strength or degree, I call a difference in *nature* and in *kind*. And since, in the instance still before us, if passion prevails over self-love, the consequent action is unnatural; but if self-love prevails over passion, the action is natural; it is manifest that self-love is in human nature a superior principle to passion. This may be contradicted without violating that nature, but the former cannot. So that, if we will act conformably to the economy of man's nature, reasonable self-love must govern. Thus, without particular consideration of conscience, we may have a clear conception of the *superior nature* of one inward principle to another, and see that there really is this natural superiority, quite distinct from degrees of strength and prevalency.

[12.] Let us now take a view of the nature of man as consisting partly of various appetites, passions, affections and partly of the principle of reflection or conscience, leaving quite out all consideration of the different degrees of strength in which either of them prevail, [and it will further appear that there is this natural superiority of one inward principle to another, and that it is even part of the idea of

reflection or conscience.][12]

[13.] Passion or appetite implies a direct simple tendency toward such and such objects, without distinction of the means by which they are to be obtained. Consequently, it will often happen there will be a desire of particular objects in cases where they cannot be obtained without manifest injury to others. Reflection or conscience comes in, and disapproves the pursuit of them in these circumstances; but the desire remains. Which is to be obeyed, appetite or reflection? Cannot this question be answered, from the economy and constitution of human nature, without saying which is strongest? Or need this at all come into consideration? Would not the question be intelligibly and fully answered by saying that the principle of reflection or conscience being compared with the various appetites, passions, and affections in men, the former is manifestly superior and chief, without regard to strength? And how often soever the latter happens to prevail, it is mere usurpation; the former remains in nature and in kind its superior, and every instance of such prevalence of the latter is an instance of breaking in upon and violation of the constitution of man.

[14.] All this is no more than the distinction which everybody is acquainted with, between *mere power* and *authority;* only instead of being intended to express the difference between what is possible and what is lawful in civil government, here it has been shown applicable to the several principles in the mind of man. Thus that principle by which we survey and either approve or disapprove our own heart, temper, and actions, is not only to be considered as what is in its turn to have some influence, which may be said of every passion, of the lowest appetites, but likewise as being superior; as from its very nature manifestly claiming superiority over all others, insomuch that you cannot form a notion of this faculty, conscience, without taking in judgment, direction, superintendency. This is a constituent part of the idea, that is, of the faculty itself; and to preside and govern, from the very economy and constitution of man, belongs to it. Had it strength, as it has right; had it power, as it has manifest authority, it would absolutely govern the world.

---

12 [missing in Ed.I.]

[15.] This gives us a further view of the nature of man, shows us what course of life we were made for; not only that our real nature leads us to be influenced in some degree by reflection and conscience, but likewise in what degree we are to be influenced by it if we will fall in with and act agreeably to the constitution of our nature; that this faculty was placed within to be our proper governor, to direct and regulate all under principles, passions, and motives of action. This is its right and office; thus sacred is its authority. And how often soever men violate and rebelliously refuse to submit to it, for supposed interest which they cannot otherwise obtain, or for the sake of passion which they cannot otherwise gratify, this makes no alteration as to the *natural right* and *office* of conscience.

[16.] Let us now turn this whole matter another way and suppose there was no such thing at all as this natural supremacy of conscience, that there was no distinction to be made between one inward principle and another but only that of strength; and see what would be the consequence.

[17.] Consider then what is the latitude and compass of the actions of man with regard to himself, his fellow creatures, and the Supreme Being? What are their bounds, besides that of our natural power? With respect to the two first, they are plainly no other than these: no man seeks misery as such for himself, and no one unprovoked does mischief to another for its own sake. For in every degree within these bounds, mankind knowingly from passion or wantonness bring ruin and misery upon themselves and others. [And impiety and profaneness, I mean what everyone would call so who believes the being of God, have absolutely no bounds at all.]¹³ Men blaspheme the Author of nature, formally and in words renounce their allegiance to their Creator. Put an instance then with respect to any one of these three. [Though we should suppose profane swearing, and in general that kind of impiety now mentioned, to mean nothing, yet it implies wanton disregard and irreverence toward an infinite Being, our Creator; and is this as suitable to the nature of man as reverence and dutiful submission of heart toward that Almighty Being? Or]¹⁴ suppose a man guilty of parricide, with all the circumstances of cruelty which such an action can admit of. This action is done in consequence of its principle being for the present strongest; and if there be no difference between inward principles but only that of strength, the strength being given, you have the whole nature of the man given, so far as it relates to this matter. The action plainly corresponds to the principle, the principle being in that degree of strength it was; it therefore corresponds to the whole nature of the man. Upon comparing the action and the whole nature, there arises no disproportion, there appears no unsuitableness between them. Thus the murder of a father and the nature of man correspond to each other, as the same nature and an act of filial duty. If there be no difference between inward principles but only that of strength, we can make no distinction between these two actions, considered as the actions of such a creature; but in our coolest hours must approve or disapprove them equally; than which nothing can be reduced to a greater absurdity.

SERMON III
UPON HUMAN NATURE

For when the Gentiles, which have not the law, do by nature the things contained in the law, these, having not the law, are a law unto themselves (Romans II: 14).

[1.] The natural supremacy of reflection or conscience being thus established, we may from it form a distinct notion of what is meant by "human nature," when virtue is said to consist in following it, and vice in deviating from it.

[2.] As the idea of a civil constitution implies in it united strength, various subordinations under one direction, that of the supreme authority, the different strength of each particular member of the society not coming into the idea; whereas, if you leave out the subordination, the union, and the one direction, you destroy and lose it; so reason, several appetites, passions, and affections, prevailing in different degrees of strength, is not *that* idea or

---

13 [In Ed. I.: "And with respect to the Supreme Being there is absolutely no bound at all to profaneness; I mean, that every one would call so who believeth the Being of God."]

14 [missing in Ed. I.]

notion of *human nature,* but *that nature* consists in these several principles considered as having a natural respect to each other, in the several passions being naturally subordinate to the one superior principle of reflection or conscience. Every bias, instinct, propension within is a real part of our nature, but not the whole; add to these the superior faculty, whose office it is to adjust, manage, and preside over them and take in this its natural superiority, and you complete the idea of human nature. And as in civil government the constitution is broken in upon and violated by power and strength prevailing over authority, so the constitution of man is broken in upon and violated by the lower faculties or principles within prevailing over that which is in its nature supreme over them all. Thus, when it is said by ancient writers that tortures and death are not so contrary to human nature as injustice – by this, to be sure, is not meant that the aversion to the former in mankind is less strong and prevalent than their aversion to the latter, but that the former is only contrary to our nature considered in a partial view, and which takes in only the lowest part of it, that which we have in common with the brutes; whereas the latter is contrary to our nature considered, in a higher sense, as a system and constitution contrary to the whole economy of man.[15]

[3.] And from all these things put together, nothing can be more evident than that, exclusive of revelation, man cannot be considered as a creature left by his Maker to act at random and live at large up to the extent of his natural power, as passion, humor, wilfulness happen to carry him, which is the condition brute creatures are in; but that from his make, constitution, or nature, he is in the strictest and most proper sense a law to himself. He hath the rule of right within; what is wanting is only that he honestly attend to it.

[4.] The inquiries which have been made by men of leisure, after some general rule the conformity to, or disagreement from, which should denominate our actions good or evil, are in many respects of great service. Yet let any plain honest man, before he engages in any course of action, ask himself, Is this I am going about right, or is it wrong? Is it good, or is it evil? I do not in the least doubt but that this question would be answered agreeably to truth and virtue, by almost any fair man in almost any circumstance. Neither do there appear any cases which look like exceptions to this, but those of superstition and of partiality to ourselves. Superstition may perhaps be somewhat of an exception; but partiality to ourselves is not, this being itself dishonesty. For a man to judge that to be the equitable, the moderate, the right part for him to act which he would see to be hard, unjust, oppressive in another – this is plain vice, and can

---

15 Every man in his physical nature is one individual single agent. He has likewise properties and principles, each of which may be considered separately and without regard to the respects which they have to each other. Neither of these are the nature we are taking a view of. But it is the inward frame of man considered as a *system* or *constitution*–whose several parts are united, not by a physical principle of individuation, but by the respects they have to each other; the chief of which is the subjection which the appetites, passions, and particular affections have to the one supreme principle of reflection or conscience. The system or constitution is formed by and consists in these respects and this subjection. Thus the body is a *system* or *constitution;* so is a tree; so is every machine. Consider all the several parts of a tree without the natural respects they have to each other, and you have not at all the idea of a tree; but add these respects, and this gives you the idea. The body may be impaired by sickness, a tree may decay, a machine may be out of order, and yet the system and constitution of them not totally dissolved. There is plainly somewhat which answers to all this in the moral constitution of man. Whoever will consider his own nature, will see that the several appetites, passions, and particular affections have different respects amongst themselves. They are restraints upon, and are in a proportion to, each other [cp. Serm. V, 13]. This proportion is just and perfect when all those under principles are perfectly coincident with conscience, so far as their nature permits, and in all cases under its absolute and entire direction. The least excess or defect, the least alteration of the due proportions amongst themselves, or of their coincidence with conscience, though not proceeding into action, is some degree of disorder in the moral constitution. But perfection, though plainly intelligible and supposable, was never attained by any man. If the higher principle of reflection maintains its place, and as much as it can corrects that disorder, and hinders it from breaking out into action, this is all that can be expected in such a creature as man. And though the appetites and passions have not their exact due proportion to each other; though they often strive for mastery with judgment and reflection; yet, since the superiority of this principle to all others is the chief respect which forms the constitution, so far as this superiority is maintained, the character, the man, is good, worthy, virtuous.

proceed only from great unfairness of mind.

[5.] But allowing that mankind hath the rule of right within himself, yet it may be asked, "What obligations are we under to attend to and follow it?" I answer, It has been proved that man by his nature is a law to himself, without the particular distinct consideration of the positive sanctions of that law; the rewards and punishments which we feel, and those which from the light of reason we have ground to believe are annexed to it. The question then carries its own answer along with it. Your obligation to obey this law is its being the law of your nature. That your conscience approves of and attests to such a course of action is itself alone an obligation. Conscience does not only offer itself to show us the way we should walk in, but it likewise carries its own authority with it; that it is our natural guide, the guide assigned us by the Author of our nature; it therefore belongs to our condition of being, it is our duty to walk in that path and follow this guide, without looking about to see whether we may not possibly forsake them with impunity.

[6.] However, let us hear what is to be said against obeying this law of our nature. And the sum is no more than this: "Why should we be concerned about anything out of and beyond ourselves? If we do find within ourselves regards to others, and restraints of we know not how many different kinds, yet these being embarrassments and hindering us from going the nearest way to our own good, why should we not endeavor to suppress and get over them?"

[7.] Thus people go on with words which, when applied to human nature and the condition in which it is placed in this world, have really no meaning. For does not all this kind of talk go upon supposition that our happiness in this world consists in somewhat quite distinct from regards to others, and that it is the privilege of vice to be without restraint or confinement? Whereas, on the contrary, the enjoyments, in a manner, all the common enjoyments of life, even the pleasures of vice, depend upon these regards of one kind or another to our fellow creatures. Throw off all regards to others, and we should be quite indifferent to infamy and to honor; there could be no such thing at all as ambition, and scarce any such thing as covetousness, for we should likewise be equally indifferent to the disgrace of poverty, the several neglects and kinds of contempt which accompany this state, and to the reputation of riches, the regard and respect they usually procure. Neither is restraint by any means peculiar to one course of life, but our very nature, exclusive of conscience and our condition, lays us under an absolute necessity of it. We cannot gain any end whatever without being confined to the proper means, which is often the most painful and uneasy confinement. And in numberless instances a present appetite cannot be gratified without such apparent and immediate ruin and misery that the most dissolute man in the world chooses to forego the pleasure rather than endure the pain.

[8.] Is the meaning then to indulge those regards to our fellow creatures, and submit to those restraints which upon the whole are attended with more satisfaction than uneasiness, and get over only those which bring more uneasiness and inconvenience than satisfaction? "Doubtless this was our meaning." You have changed sides then. Keep to this; be consistent with yourselves; and you and the men of virtue are *in general* perfectly agreed. But let us take care and avoid mistakes. Let it not be taken for granted that the temper of envy, rage, resentment yields greater delight than meekness, forgiveness, compassion, and goodwill; especially when it is acknowledged that rage, envy, resentment are in themselves mere misery; and the satisfaction arising from the indulgence of them is little more than relief from that misery, whereas the temper of compassion and benevolence is itself delightful; and the indulgence of it, by doing good, affords new positive delight and enjoyment. Let it not be taken for granted that the satisfaction arising from the reputation of riches and power, however obtained, and from the respect paid to them, is greater than the satisfaction arising from the reputation of justice, honesty, charity, and the esteem which is universally acknowledged to be their due. And if it be doubtful which of these satisfactions is the greatest, as there are persons who think neither of them very considerable, yet there can be no doubt concerning ambition and covetousness, virtue and a good mind, considered in themselves and as leading to different courses of life – there can, I say, be no doubt which temper and which course is attended with most peace and tranquility of mind, which with most perplexity, vexation, and inconvenience. And both the virtues and vices which have been now mentioned do in a manner equally imply in them regards of one kind or another to our fellow creatures. And with respect to restraint and confinement: whoever will consider the restraints from fear and shame, the dissimulation, mean arts of concealment, servile compliances – one or other of which belong to almost every course of vice – will soon be convinced that the man of virtue is by no means upon a disadvantage in this respect. How many instances are there in which men feel and own and cry aloud under the chains of vice with which they are enthralled, and which yet they will not shake off? How many instances in which persons manifestly go through more pains and self-denial to gratify a vicious passion than would have been necessary to the conquest of it? To this is to be added that when virtue is become habitual, when the temper of it is acquired, what was before "confinement" ceases to be so, by becoming choice and delight. Whatever restraint and guard upon ourselves may be needful to unlearn any unnatural distortion or odd gesture, yet, in all propriety of speech, natural behavior must be the most easy and unrestrained. It is manifest that, in the common course of life, there is seldom any inconsistency between our duty and what is *called* interest; it is much seldomer that there is any inconsistency between duty and what is really our present interest – meaning by "interest" happiness and satisfaction. Self-love then, though confined to the interest of the present world, does in general perfectly coincide with virtue, and leads us to one and the same course of life. But, whatever exceptions there are to this, which are much fewer than they are commonly thought, all shall be set right at the final distribution of things. It is a manifest absurdity to suppose evil prevailing finally over good, under the conduct and administration of a perfect Mind.

[9.] The whole argument which I have been now insisting upon, may be thus summed up and given you in one view: The Nature of man is adapted to some course of action or other. Upon comparing some actions with this nature, they appear suitable and correspondent to it; from comparison of other actions with the same nature, there arises to our view some unsuitableness or disproportion. The correspondence of actions to the nature of the agent renders them natural; their disproportion to it, unnatural. That an action is correspondent to the nature of the agent does not arise from its being agreeable to the principle which happens to be the strongest, for it may be so, and yet be quite disproportionate to the nature of the agent. The correspondence, therefore, or disproportion arises from somewhat else. This can be nothing but a difference in nature and kind, altogether distinct from strength, between the inward principles. Some then are in nature and kind superior to others. And the correspondence arises from the action being conformable to the higher principle, and the unsuitableness from its being contrary to it. Reasonable self-love and conscience are the chief or superior principles in the nature of man, because an action may be suitable to this nature, though all other principles be violated; but becomes unsuitable, if either of those are. Conscience and self-love, if we understand our true happiness, always lead us the same way. Duty and interest are perfectly coincident, for the most part in this world, but entirely and in every instance if we take in the future and the whole, this being implied in the notion of a good and perfect administration of things. Thus they who have been so wise in their generation as to regard only their own supposed interest, at the expense and to the injury of others, shall at last find that he who has given up all the advantages of the present world rather than violate his conscience and the relations of life, has infinitely better provided for himself and secured his own interest and happiness.

Bibliography

Cunliffe, Christopher, ed. *Joseph Butler's Moral and Religious Thought*. Oxford: Clarendon Press, 1992.

Duncan-Jones, Austin. *Butler's Moral Philosophy*. Harmondsworth: Penguin, 1952.

Frey, R.G. *Joseph Butler*. Oxford and New York: Oxford University Press, 1996.

Gay, Peter. *The Enlightenment: An Interpretation*. New York: Vintage Books, 1968. [originally published 1966].

Penelhum, Terence. *Butler*. London and New York: Routledge, 1985.

CHAPTER ELEVEN — IMMANUEL KANT

Immanuel Kant (1724-1804) is without question one of the very greatest philosophers. Some have seen him in fact as the supreme creative philosophical mind since the ancient Greeks. Even those who would dispute so elevated a ranking – and there are many – acknowledge that Kant is deeply original and extremely influential. Kant's primary contributions were in a series of "critiques" (the *Critique of Pure Reason*, the *Critique of Practical Reason*, and the *Critique of Judgment*) concerned with knowledge, morality, and aesthetics. But in the course of his many writings Kant engaged almost every topic that has occupied philosophers.

Kant had a good deal to say about human nature, and other interesting and important selections from his work could have been chosen in addition to the readings included here and in Chapter 13. Kant was a political liberal in the early years of liberal political philosophy, and he receives representation in Part III as an advocate of a liberal view of humanity. At the same time, Kant thought our best selves united with a darker, more intractable, quarrelsome, animal nature – what he called the "crooked timber of humanity" – and a case might be made for including him as a certain sort of conservative individualist.

These plausible options notwithstanding, Kant is encountered here especially as a representative of Christian philosophy of human nature. This might seem problematic in light of Kant's full commitment to *scientific modernism* – to the idea that we know our world to be one of natural lawful regularity, whose fundamental features (at any rate as they are known by us) the sciences are actively, and generally successfully, engaged in disclosing. It might also seem problematic because of the highly complicated conception Kant developed of the prospect of having genuine knowledge of the world as a whole, or its governance. Kant is a Christian thinker nonetheless, and one of great importance. The "pagan" freethinking European Enlightenment had already come to occupancy of a kind of centre of intellectual gravity; Kant represents self-conscious intelligence, mindful of a secular cultural reality and imbued with respect for science's achievements and conscious of its unrestricted writ in the world we know, but who nonetheless opts for Christian theism. Of equal or greater importance, Kant is the most developed embodiment of the Lutheran Protestant ideal of a foundation of human possibility in the inner moral life.

Immanuel Kant, *Religion Within The Limits Of Reason Alone*

(Source: Immanuel Kant. *Religion Within The Limits Of Reason Alone*. Trans. Theodore M. Greene & Hoyt H. Hudson. New York: Harper Torchbooks, 1934, 3-6, 21-39, 170-173.

Preface to the First Edition

So far as morality is based upon the conception of man as a free agent who, just because he is free, binds himself through his reason to unconditioned laws, it stands in need neither of the idea of another Being over him, for him to apprehend his duty, nor of an incentive other than the law itself, for him to do his duty. At least it is man's own fault if he is subject to such a need; and if he is, this need can be relieved through nothing outside himself: for whatever does not originate in himself and his own freedom in no way compensates for the deficiency of his morality. Hence for its own sake morality does not need religion at all (whether objectively, as regards willing, or subjectively, as regards ability [to act]); by virtue of pure practical reason it is self-sufficient. For since its laws are binding, as the highest condition (itself unconditioned) of all ends, through the bare form of universal legality of the maxims, which must be chosen accordingly, morality requires absolutely no material determining ground of free choice,[1] that is, no end, in order either to know what duty is or to impel the performance of duty. On the contrary, when it is a question of duty, morality is perfectly able to ignore all ends, and it ought to do so. Thus, for example, in order to know whether I should (or indeed can) be truthful in my testimony before a court, or whether I should be faithful in accounting for another man's property entrusted to me, it is not at all necessary for me to search for an end which I might perhaps propose to achieve with my declaration, since it matters not at all what sort of end this is; indeed, the man who finds it needful, when his avowal is lawfully demanded, to look about him for some kind of [ulterior] end, is, by this very fact, already contemptible.

But although for its own sake morality needs no representation of an end which must precede the determining of the will, it is quite possible that it is necessarily related to such an end, taken not as the ground but at the [sum of] inevitable consequences of maxims adopted as conformable to that end. For in the absence of all reference to an end no determination of the will can take place in man, since such determination cannot be followed by no effect whatever; and the representation of the effect must be capable of being accepted, not, indeed, as the basis for the determination of the will and as an end antecedently aimed at, but yet as an end conceived of as the result ensuing from the will's determination through the law (*finis in consequentiam veniens*). Without an end of this sort a will, envisaging to itself no definite goal for a contemplated act, either objective or subjective (which it has, or ought to have, in view), is indeed informed as to *how* it ought to act, but not *whither*, and so can achieve no satisfaction. It is true, therefore, that morality requires no end for right conduct; the law, which contains the formal condition of the use of freedom in general, suffices. Yet an end does arise out of morality; for how the question, *What is to result from this right conduct of ours?* is to be answered, and towards what, as an end – even granted it may not be wholly subject to our control – we might direct our actions and abstentions so as at least to be in harmony with that end: these cannot possibly be matters of indifference to reason. Hence the end is no more than an idea of an object which takes the formal condition of all such ends as we *ought* to have (duty) and combines it with whatever is conditioned, and in harmony with duty, in all the ends which we *do* have (happiness proportioned to obedience to duty) – that is to say, the idea of a highest good in the world for whose possibility we must postulate a higher, moral, most holy, and omnipotent Being which alone can unite the two elements of this highest good. Yet (viewed practically) this idea is not an empty one, for it

---

1   Those who, in the conception of duty, are not satisfied with the merely formal determining ground as such (conformity to law) as the basis of determination, do indeed admit that such a basis cannot be discovered in *self-love* directed to one's own *comfort*. Hence there remain but two determining grounds: one, which is rational, namely, one's own *perfection*, and another, which is empirical, the *happiness* of others. Now if they do not conceive of the first of these as the moral determining ground (a will, namely, unconditionally obedient to the law) which is necessarily unique–and if they so interpreted it they would be expounding in a circle–they would have to have in mind man's natural perfection, so far as it is capable of enhancement, and this can be of many kinds, such as skill in the arts and sciences, taste, bodily adroitness, etc. But these are always good only on the condition that their use does not conflict with the moral law (which alone commands unconditionally); set up as an end, therefore, perfection cannot be the principle of concepts of duty. The same holds for the end which aims at the happiness of other men. For an act must, first of all, itself be weighed according to the moral law before it is directed to the happiness of others. The requirement laid down by this end, therefore, is a duty only conditionally and cannot serve as the supreme principle of moral maxims.

does meet our natural need to conceive of some sort of final end for all our actions and abstentions, taken as a whole, an end which can be justified by reason and the absence of which would be a hindrance to moral decision. Most important of all, however, this idea arises out of morality and is not its basis; it is an end the adoption of which as one's own presupposes basic ethical principles. Therefore it cannot be a matter of unconcern to morality as to whether or not it forms for itself the concept of a final end of all things (harmony with which, while not multiplying men's duties, yet provides them with a special point of focus for the unification of all ends); for only thereby can objective, practical reality be given to the union of the purposiveness arising from freedom with the purposiveness of nature, a union with which we cannot possibly dispense. Take a man who, honouring the moral law, allows the thought to occur to him (he can scarcely avoid doing so) of what sort of world he would create, under the guidance of practical reason, were such a thing in his power, a world into which, moreover, he would place himself as a member. He would not merely make the very choice which is determined by that moral idea of the highest good, were he vouchsafed solely the right to choose; he would also will that [such] a world should by all means come into existence (because the moral law demands that the highest good possible through our agency should be realized) and he would so will even though, in accordance with this idea, he saw himself in danger of paying in his own person a heavy price in happiness – it being possible that he might not be adequate to the [moral] demands of the idea, demands which reason lays down as conditioning happiness. Accordingly he would feel compelled by reason to avow this judgement with complete impartiality, as though it were rendered by another and yet, at the same time, as his own; whereby man gives evidence of the need, morally effected in him, of also conceiving a final end for his duties, as their consequence.

Morality thus leads ineluctably to religion, through which it extends itself[2] to the idea of a

---

2   If the proposition, There is a God, hence there is a highest good in the world, is to arise (as a dogma) from morality alone, it is a synthetic *a priori* proposition: for even though accepted only for practical reference, it does yet pass beyond the concept of duty which morality contains (and which presupposes merely the formal laws, and not the matter, of choice), and hence cannot analytically be evolved out of morality. *But how is such a proposition* a priori *possible?* Agreement with the bare idea of a moral Lawgiver for all men is, indeed, identical with the general moral concept of duty, and so far the proposition commanding this agreement would be analytic. But acknowledgement of His existence asserts more than the bare possibility of such a thing. The key to the solution of this problem, so far as I believe myself to understand it, I can only indicate here and not develop.

An *end* is always the object of an *inclination*, that is, of an immediate craving for possession of a thing through one's action, just as the *law* (which commands practically) is an object of *respect*. An objective end (i.e., the end which we ought to have) is that which is proposed to us as such by reason alone. The end which embraces the unavoidable and at the same time sufficient condition of all other ends is the *final end*. The subjective final end of rational worldly beings is their own happiness (each of them *has* this end by virtue of having a nature dependent upon sensuous objects, and hence it would be absurd to say that anyone *ought* to have it) and all the practical propositions which are based on this final end are synthetic, and at the same time empirical. But that everyone ought to make the highest *good* possible in the world a *final end* is a synthetic practical proposition a priori (and indeed objectively practical) given by pure reason; for it is a proposition which goes beyond the concept of duties in this world and adds a consequence (an effect) thereof which is not contained in the moral laws and therefore cannot be evolved out of them analytically. For these laws command absolutely, be the consequence what it will; indeed, they even require that the consideration of such consequence be completely waived when a particular act is concerned; and thereby they make duty an object of highest respect without offering or proposing to us an end (or a final end) such as would have to constitute duty's recommendation and the incentive to the fulfilment of our duty. All men could have sufficient incentive if (as they should) they adhere solely to the dictation of pure reason in the law. What need have they to know the outcome of their moral actions and abstentions, an outcome which the world's course will bring about? It suffices for them that they do their duty; even though all things end with earthly life and though, in this life, happiness and desert may never meet. And yet it is one of the inescapable limitations of man and of his faculty of practical reason (a limitation, perhaps, of all other worldly beings as well) to have regard, in every action, to the consequence thereof, in order to discover therein what could serve him as an end and also prove the purity of his intention – which consequence, though last in practice (*nexu effectivo*) is yet first in representation and intention powerful moral Lawgiver, outside of mankind, for Whose will that is the final end (of creation) which at the same time can and ought to be man's final end.

....

I. Concerning the Original Predisposition to Good in Human Nature

We may conveniently divide this predisposition, with respect to function, into three divisions, to be considered as elements in the fixed character and destiny of man:

(1) The predisposition to *animality* in man, taken as a *living* being;

(2) The predisposition to *humanity* in man, taken as a living and at the same time a *rational* being;

(3) The predisposition to *personality* in man, taken as a rational and at the same time an *accountable* being.[3]

1. The predisposition to *animality* in mankind may be brought under the general title of physical and purely *mechanical* self-love, wherein no reason is demanded. It is threefold: first, for self-preservation; second, for the propagation of the species, through the sexual impulse, and for the care of off-spring so begotten; and third, for community with other men, *i.e.*, the social impulse. On these three stems can be grafted all kinds of vices (which, however, do not spring from this predisposition itself as a root). They may be termed vices of the coarseness of nature, and in their greatest deviation from natural purposes are called the *beastly* vices of *gluttony* and *drunkenness, lasciviousness,* and *wild lawlessness* (in relation to other men).

2. The predisposition to humanity can be brought under the general title of a self-love which is physical and yet *compares* (for which reason is required); that is to say, we judge ourselves happy or unhappy only by making comparison with others. Out of this self-love springs the inclination *to acquire worth in the opinion of others*. This is originally a desire merely for *equality*, to allow no one superiority above oneself, bound up with a constant care lest others strive to attain such superiority; but from this arises gradually the unjustifiable craving to win it for oneself over others. Upon this twin stem of *jealousy* and *rivalry* may be grafted the very great vices of secret and open animosity against all whom we look upon as not belonging to us – vices, however, which really do not sprout of

---

(*nexu finali*). In this end, if directly presented to him by reason alone, man seeks something that he can *love;* therefore the law, which merely arouses his *respect,* even though it does not acknowledge this object of love as a necessity does yet extend itself on its behalf by including the moral goal of reason among its determining grounds. That is, the proposition: Make the highest good possible in the world your own final end! is a synthetic proposition *a priori,* which is introduced by the moral law itself, although practical reason does, indeed, extend itself therein beyond the law. This extension is possible because of the moral law's being taken in relation to the natural characteristic of man, that for all his actions he must conceive of an end over and above the law (a characteristic which makes man an object of experience). And further, this extension (as with theoretical propositions *a priori* which are synthetic) is possible only because this end embraces the *a priori* principle of the knowledge of the determining grounds in experience of a free will, so far as this experience, by exhibiting the effects of morality in its ends, gives objective though merely practical reality to the concept of morality as causal in the world. But if, now, the strictest obedience to moral laws is to be considered the cause of the ushering in of the highest good (as end), then, since human capacity does not suffice for bringing about happiness in the world proportionate to worthiness to be happy, an omnipotent moral Being must be postulated as ruler of the world, under whose care this [balance] occurs. That is, morality leads inevitably to religion.

3 We cannot regard this as included in the concept of the preceding, but necessarily must treat it as a special predisposition. For from the fact that a being has reason it by no means follows that this reason, by the mere representing of the fitness of its maxims to be laid down as universal laws, is thereby rendered capable of determining the will unconditionally, so as to be "practical" of itself; at least, not so far as we can see. The most rational mortal being in the world might still stand in need of certain incentives, originating in objects of desire, to determine his choice. He might, indeed, bestow the most rational reflection on all that concerns not only the greatest sum of these incentives in him but also the means of attaining the end thereby determined, without ever suspecting the possibility of such a thing as the absolutely imperative moral law which proclaims that it is itself an incentive, and, indeed, the highest. Were it not given us from within, we should never by any ratiocination subtilize it into existence or win over our will to it; yet this law is the only law which informs us of the independence of our will from determination by all other incentives (of our freedom) and at the same time of the accountability of all our actions.

themselves from nature as their root; rather are they inclinations, aroused in us by the anxious endeavours of others to attain a hated superiority over us, to attain for ourselves as a measure of precaution and for the sake of safety such a position over others. For nature, indeed, wanted to use the idea of such rivalry (which in itself does not exclude mutual love) only as a spur to culture. Hence the vices which are grafted upon this inclination might be their termed vices of *culture*; in highest degree of malignancy, as, for example, in *envy, ingratitude, spitefulness*, etc. (where they are simply the idea of a maximum of evil going, beyond what is human), they can be called the *diabolical vices*.

3. The predisposition to *personality* is the capacity for respect for the moral law as *in itself a sufficient incentive of the will*. This capacity for simple respect for the moral law within us would thus be moral feeling, which in and through itself does not constitute an end of the natural predisposition except so far as it is the motivating force of the will. Since this is possible only when the free will incorporates such moral feeling into its maxim, the property of such a will is good character. The latter, like every character of the free will, is something which can only be acquired; its possibility, however, demands the presence in our nature of a predisposition on which it is absolutely impossible to graft anything evil. We cannot rightly call the idea of the moral law, with the respect which is inseparable from it, *a predisposition* to *personality*; it is personality itself (the idea of humanity considered quite intellectually). But the subjective ground for the adoption into our maxims of this respect as a motivating force seems to be an adjunct to our personality, and thus to deserve the name of a predisposition to its furtherance.

If we consider the three predispositions named, in terms of the conditions of their possibility, we find that the first requires no reason, the second is based on practical reason, but a reason thereby subservient to other incentives, while the third alone is rooted in reason which is practical of itself, that is, reason which dictates laws unconditionally. All of these predispositions are not only *good* in negative fashion (in that they do not contradict the moral law); they are also predispositions *toward good* (they enjoin the observance of the law). They are *original*, for they are bound up with the possibility of human nature. Man can indeed use the first two contrary to their ends, but he can extirpate none of them. By the predispositions of a being we understand not only its constituent elements which are necessary to it, but also the forms of their combination, by which the being is what it is. They are *original* if they are involved necessarily in the possibility of such a being, but *contingent* if it is possible for the being to exist of itself without them. Finally, let it be noted that here we treat only those predispositions which have immediate reference to the faculty of desire and the exercise of the will.

II. Concerning the Propensity to Evil in Human Nature

By *propensity (propensio)* I understand the subjective ground of the possibility of an inclination (habitual craving, *concupiscentia*)[4] so far as mankind in general is liable to it.[5] A propensity is distinguished from a predisposition by the fact that although it can indeed be innate, it *ought* not to be represented merely thus; for it can be regarded as having been *acquired* (if it is good), or *brought* by man *upon himself* (if it is evil). Here, however, we are speaking only of the propensity to genuine, that is, moral evil; for since such evil is possible only as a determination of the free will, and since the will

---

4   [*Concupiscentia* added in the Second Edition.] [Notes in square brackets have been added by editor of this edition.]

5   A *propensity* (*Hang*) is really only the *predisposition* to crave a delight which, when once experienced, arouses in the subject an *inclination* to it. Thus all savage peoples have a propensity for intoxicants; for though many of them are wholly ignorant of intoxication and in consequence have absolutely no craving for an intoxicant, let them but once sample it and there is aroused in them an almost inextinguishable craving for it.

Between inclination, which presupposes acquaintance with the object of desire, and propensity there still is *instinct*, which is a felt want to do or to enjoy something of which one has as yet no conception (such as the constructive impulse in animals, or the sexual impulse). Beyond inclination there is finally a further stage in the faculty of desire, *passion* (not *emotion*, for this has to do with the feeling of pleasure and pain), which is an inclination that excludes the mastery over oneself.

can be appraised as good or evil only by means of its maxims, this propensity to evil must consist in the subjective ground of the possibility of the deviation of the maxims from the moral law. If, then, this propensity can be considered as belonging universally to mankind (and hence as part of the character of the race), it may be called a *natural* propensity in man to evil. We may add further that the will's capacity or incapacity, arising from this natural propensity, to adopt or not to adopt the moral law into its maxim, may be called *a good or an evil heart*.

In this capacity for evil there can be distinguished three distinct degrees. First, there is the weakness of the human heart in the general observance of adopted maxims, or in other words, the *frailty* of human nature; second, the propensity for mixing unmoral with moral motivating causes (even when it is done with good intent and under maxims of the good), that is, impurity; third, the propensity to adopt evil maxims, that is, the *wickedness* of human nature or of the human heart.

First: the frailty (*fragilitas*) of human nature expressed even in the complaint of an Apostle, "What I would, that I do not!"[6]. In other words, I adopt the good (the law) into the maxim of my will, but this good, which objectively, in its ideal conception (*in thesi*), in an irresistible incentive, is subjectively (*in hypothesi*), when the maxim is to be followed, the weaker (in comparison with inclination).

Second: the impurity (*impuritas, improbitas*) of the human heart consists in this, that although the maxim is indeed good in respect of its object (the intended observance of the law) and perhaps even strong enough for practice, it is yet not purely moral; that is, it has not, as it should have, adopted the law *alone* as its *all-sufficient* incentive: instead, it usually (perhaps, every time) stands in need of other incentives beyond this, in determining the will to do what duty demands; in other words, actions called for by duty are done not purely for duty's sake.

Third: the wickedness (*vitiositas, pravitas*) or, if you like, the *corruption* (*corruptio*) of the human heart is the propensity of the will to maxims which neglect the incentives springing from the moral law

in favor of others which are not moral. It may also be called the *perversity* (*perversitas*) of the human heart, for it reverses the ethical order [of priority] among the incentives of a *free* will; and although conduct which is lawfully good (*i.e.*, legal) may be found with it, yet the cast of mind is thereby corrupted at its root (so far as the moral disposition is concerned), and the man is hence designated as evil.

It will be remarked that this propensity to evil is here ascribed (as regards conduct) to men in general, even to the best of them; this must be the case if it is to be proved that the propensity to evil in mankind is universal, or, what here comes to the same thing, that it is woven into human nature.

There is no difference, however, as regards conformity of conduct to the moral law, between a man of good morals (*bene moratus*) and a morally good man (*moraliter bonus*) – at least there ought to be no difference, save that the conduct of the one has not always, perhaps never, the law as its sole and supreme incentive while the conduct of the other has it *always*. Of the former it can be said: He obeys the law according to the *letter* (that is, his conduct conforms to what the law conmmands); but of the second: He obeys the law according to the *spirit* (the spirit of the moral law consisting in this, that the law is sufficient in itself as an incentive). *Whatever is not of this faith is sin*[7] (as regards cast of mind). For when incentives other than the law itself (such as ambition, self-love in general, yes, even a kindly instinct such as sympathy) are necessary to determine the will to conduct *conformable to the law*, it is merely accidental that these causes coincide with the law, for they could equally well incite its violation. The maxim, then, in terms of whose goodness all moral worth of the individual must be appraised, is thus contrary to the law, and the man, despite all his good deeds, is nevertheless evil.

The following explanation is also necessary in order to define the concept of this propensity. Every propensity is either physical, *i.e.*, pertaining to the will of man as a natural being, or moral, *i.e.*, pertaining to his will as a moral being. In the first sense there is no propensity to moral evil, for such a propensity must spring from freedom; and a

---

6   [Cf. Romans, VII, 15]
7   [Cf. *Romans* XIV, 23]

physical propensity (grounded in sensuous impulses) towards any use of freedom whatsoever – whether for good or bad – is a contradiction. Hence a propensity to evil can inhere only in the moral capacity of the will. But nothing is morally evil (*i.e.*, capable of being imputed) but that which is our own *act*. On the other hand, by the concept of a propensity we understand a subjective determining ground of the will which *precedes all acts* and which, therefore, is itself not an act. Hence in the concept of a simple propensity to evil there would be a contradiction were it not possible to take the word "act" in two meanings, both of which are reconcilable with the concept of freedom. The term "act" can apply in general to that exercise of freedom whereby the supreme maxim (in harmony with the law or contrary to it) it is adopted by the will, but also to the exercise of freedom whereby the actions themselves (considered materially, *i.e.*, with reference to the objects of volition) are performed in accordance with that maxim. The propensity to evil, then, is an act in the first sense (*peccatum originarium*), and at the same time the formal ground of all unlawful conduct in the second sense, which latter, considered materially, violates the law and is termed vice (*peccatum derivatum*); and the first offense remains, even though the second (from incentives which do not subsist in the law itself) may be repeatedly avoided. The former is intelligible action, cognizable by means of pure reason alone, apart from every temporal condition; the latter is sensible action, empirical, given in time (*factum phaenomenon*). The former, particularly when compared with the latter, is entitled a simple propensity and innate, [first] because it cannot be eradicated (since for such eradication the highest maxim would have to be that of the good – whereas in this propensity it already has been postulated as evil), but chiefly because we can no more assign a further cause for the corruption in us by evil of just this highest maxim, although this is our own action, than we can assign a cause for any fundamental attribute belonging to our nature. Now it can be understood, from what has just been said, why it was that in this section we sought, at the very first, the three sources of the morally evil solely in what, according to laws of freedom, touches the ultimate ground of the adoption or the observance of our maxims, and not in what touches sensibility (regarded as receptivity).

III. Man is Evil by Nature

Vitiis nemo sine nascitur. – Horace[8]

In view of what has been said above, the proposition, Man is *evil*, can mean only, He is conscious of the moral law but has nevertheless adopted into his maxim the (occasional) deviation therefrom. He is evil *by nature*, means but this, that evil can be predicated of man as a species; not that such a quality can be inferred from the concept of his species (that is, of man in general) – for then it would be necessary; but rather that from what we know of man through experience we cannot judge otherwise of him, or, that we may presuppose evil to be subjectively necessary to every man, even to the best. Now this propensity must itself be considered as morally evil, yet not as a natural predisposition but rather as something that can be imputed to man, and consequently it must consist in maxims of the will which are contrary to the law. Further, for the sake of freedom, these maxims must in themselves be considered contingent, a circumstance which, on the other hand, will not tally with the universality of this evil *unless* the ultimate subjective ground of all maxims somehow or other is entwined with and, as it were, rooted in humanity itself. Hence we can call this a natural propensity to evil, and as we must, after all, ever hold man himself responsible for it, we can further call it a *radical* innate *evil* in human nature (yet none the less brought upon us by ourselves).

That such a corrupt propensity must indeed be rooted in man need not be formally proved in view of the multitude of crying examples which experience *of the actions* of men puts before our eyes. If we wish to draw our examples from that state in which various philosophers hoped preeminently to discover the natural goodliness of human nature, namely, from the so-called *state of nature*, we need but compare with this hypothesis the scenes of unprovoked cruelty in the murder-dramas enacted

---

8   [*Satires*, I,iii, 68: "No one is born free from vices."]

in Tofoa, New Zealand, and in the Navigator Islands, and the unending cruelty (of which Captain Hearne[9] tells) in the wide wastes of north-western America, cruelty from which, indeed, not a soul reaps the smallest benefit;[10] and we have vices of barbarity more than sufficient to draw us from such an opinion. If, however, we incline to the opinion that human nature can better be known in the civilized state (in which its predispositions can more completely develop), we must listen to a long melancholy litany of indictments against humanity: of secret falsity even in the closest friendship, so that a limit upon trust in the mutual confidences of even the best friends is reckoned a universal maxim of prudence in intercourse; of a propensity to hate him to whom one is indebted, for which a benefactor must always be prepared; of a hearty well-wishing which yet allows of the remark that "in the misfortunes of our best friends there is something which is not altogether displeasing to us";[11] and of many other vices still concealed under the appearance of virtue, to say nothing of the vices of those who do not conceal them, for we are content to call him good who is *a man bad in a way common to all*; and we shall have enough of the vices of *culture*

and civilization (which are the most offensive of all) to make us rather turn away our eyes from the conduct of men lest we ourselves contract another vice, misanthropy. But if we are not yet content, we need but contemplate a state which is compounded in strange fashion of both the others, that is, the international situation, where civilized nations stand towards each other in the relation obtaining in the barbarous state of nature (a state of continuous readiness for war), a state, moreover, from which they have taken fixedly into their heads never to depart. We then become aware of the fundamental principles of the great societies called states[12] – principles which flatly contradict their public pronouncements but can never be laid aside, and which no philosopher has yet been able to bring into agreement with morality. Nor (sad to say) has any philosopher been able to propose better principles which at the same time can be brought into harmony with human nature. The result is that the *philosophical millennium*, which hopes for a state of perpetual peace based on a league of peoples, a world-republic, even as the *theological millennium*, which tarries for the completed moral improvement of the entire

---

9   [Samuel Hearne (1745-1792), an English traveller, in the service of the Hudson Bay Company. His *Account of a Journey from Prince of Wales's Fort in Hudson's Bay to the Northwest* was published in 1795. Kant evidently had read the brief account of Hearne's travels in Douglas's Introduction to *Cook's Third Voyage*, London, 1784.]

10   Thus the war ceaselessly waged between the Arathapescaw Indians and the Dog Rib Indians has no other object than mere slaughter. Bravery in war is, in the opinion of savages, the highest virtue. Even in a civilized state it is an object of admiration and a basis for the special regard commanded by that profession in which bravery is the sole merit; and this is not without rational cause. For that man should be able to possess a thing (*i.e.*, honor) and make it an end to be valued more than life itself, and because of it renounce all self-interest, surely bespeaks a certain nobility in his natural disposition. Yet we recognize in the complacency with which victors boast their mighty deeds (massacres, butchery without quarter, and the like) that it is merely their own superiority and the destruction they can wreak, without any other objective, in which they really take satisfaction.

11   [La Rochefoucauld, *Maximes,* No. 583: "Dans l'adversité de nos meilleurs amis, nous trouvons toujours quelque chose qui ne nous déplaît pas."]

12   When we survey the history of these, merely as the phenomenon of the inner predispositions of mankind which are for the most part concealed from us, we become aware of a certain machine-like movement of nature toward ends which are nature's own rather than those of the nations. Each separate state, so long as it has a neighboring state which it dares hope to conquer, strives to aggrandize itself through such a conquest, and thus to attain a world-monarchy, a polity wherein all freedom, and with it (as a consequence) virtue, taste, and learning, would necessarily expire. Yet this monster (in which laws gradually lose their force), after it has swallowed all its neighbors, finally dissolves of itself, and through rebellion and disunion breaks up into many smaller states. These, instead of striving toward a league of nations (a republic of federated free nations), begin the same game over again, each for itself, so that war (that scourge of humankind) may not be allowed to cease. Although war is not so incurably evil as that tomb, a universal autocracy (or even as a confederacy which exists to hasten the weakening of a despotism in any single state), yet, as one of the ancients put it, war creates more evil men than it destroys. ["This is also cited by Kant in the first Appendix to Section II of *Zum ewigen Frieden.* The quotation is termed 'a saying of that Greek'; unfortunately, its source has not been found." (Note in Berlin Edition.)]

human race, is universally ridiculed as a wild fantasy.

Now the ground of this evil (1) cannot be placed, as is so commonly done, in man's *sensuous nature* and the natural inclinations arising therefrom. For not only are these not directly related to evil (rather do they afford the occasion for what the moral disposition in its power can manifest, namely, virtue); we must not even be considered responsible for their existence (we cannot be, for since they are implanted in us we are not their authors). We are accountable, however, for the propensity to evil, which, as it affects the morality of the subject, is to be found in him as a free-acting being and for which it must be possible to hold him accountable as the offender – this, too, despite the fact that this propensity is so deeply rooted in the will that we are forced to say that it is to be found in man by nature. Neither can the ground of this evil (2) be placed in a *corruption* of the morally legislative reason – as if reason could destroy the authority of the very law which is its own, or deny the obligation arising therefrom; this is absolutely impossible. To conceive of oneself as a freely acting being and yet as exempt from the law which is appropriate to such a being (the moral law) would be tantamount to conceiving a cause operating without any laws whatsoever (for determination according to natural laws is excluded by the fact of freedom); this is a self-contradiction. In seeking, therefore, a ground of the morally-evil in man, [we find that] *sensuous nature* comprises too little, for when the incentives which can spring from freedom are taken away, man is reduced to a merely *animal* being. On the other hand, a reason exempt from the moral law, a *malignant reason* as it were (a thoroughly evil will), comprises too much, for thereby opposition to the law would itself be set up as an incentive (since in the absence of all incentives the will cannot be determined), and thus the subject would be made a *devilish* being. Neither of these designations is applicable to man.

But even if the existence of this propensity to evil in human nature can be demonstrated by experiential proofs of the real opposition, in time, of man's will to the law, such proofs do not teach us the essential character of that propensity or the ground of this opposition. Rather, because this character concerns a relation of the will, which is free (and the concept of which is therefore not empirical), to

the moral law as an incentive (the concept of which, likewise, is purely intellectual), it must be apprehended *a priori* through the concept of evil, so far as evil is possible under the laws of freedom (of obligation and accountability). This concept may be developed in the following manner.

Man (even the most wicked) does not, under any maxim whatsoever, repudiate the moral law in the manner of a rebel (renouncing obedience to it). The law, rather, forces itself upon him irresistibly by virtue of his moral predisposition; and were no other incentive working in opposition, he would adopt the law into his supreme maxim as the sufficient determining ground of his will; that is, he would be morally good. But by virtue of an equally innocent natural predisposition he depends upon the incentives of his sensuous nature and adopts them also (in accordance with the subjective principle of self-love) into his maxim. If he took the latter into his maxim *as in themselves wholly adequate* to the determination of the will, without troubling himself about the moral law (which, after all, he does have in him), he would be morally evil. Now, since he naturally adopts *both* into his maxim, and since, further, he would find either, if it were alone, adequate in itself for the determining of the will, it follows that if the difference between the maxims amounted merely to the difference between the two incentives (the content of the maxims), that is, if it were merely a question as to whether the law or the sensuous impulse were to furnish the incentive, man would be at once good and evil: this, however, (as we saw in the Introduction) is a contradiction. Hence the distinction between a good man and one who is evil cannot lie in the difference between the incentives which they adopt into their maxim (not in the content of the maxim), but rather must depend upon *subordination* (the form of the maxim), *i.e., which of the two incentives he makes the condition of the other.* Consequently man (even the best) is evil only in that he reverses the moral order of the incentives when he adopts them into his maxim. He adopts, indeed, the moral law along with the law of self-love; yet when he becomes aware that they cannot remain on a par with each other but that one must be subordinated to the other as its supreme condition, he makes the incentive of self-love and its inclinations the condition of obedience to the moral law; whereas, on the contrary, the latter, as the *supreme condition* of the satisfaction of the former, ought to have been adopted into the universal maxim of the will as the sole incentive.

Yet, even with this reversal of the ethical order of the incentives in and through his maxim, a man's actions still may prove to be as much in conformity to the law as if they sprang from true basic principles. This happens when reason employs the unity of the maxims in general, a unity which is inherent in the moral law, merely to bestow upon the incentives of inclination, under the name of *happiness*, a unity of maxims which otherwise they cannot have. (For example, truthfulness, if adopted as a basic principle, delivers us from the anxiety of making our lies agree with one another and of not being entangled by their serpent coils.) The empirical character is then good, but the intelligible character is still evil.

Now if a propensity to this[13] does lie in human nature, there is in man a natural propensity to evil; and since this very propensity must in the end be sought in a will which is free, and can therefore be imputed, it is morally evil. This evil is *radical*, because it corrupts the ground of all maxims; it is, moreover, as a natural propensity, *inextirpable* by human powers, since extirpation could occur only through good maxims, and cannot take place when the ultimate subjective ground of all maxims is postulated as corrupt; yet at the same time it must be possible to *overcome* it, since it is found in man, a being whose actions are free.

We are not, then, to call the depravity of human nature *wickedness* taking the word in its strict sense as a disposition (the subjective *principle* of the maxims) to adopt evil *as evil* into our maxim as our incentives (for that is diabolical); we should rather term it the *perversity* of the heart, which, then, because of what follows from it, is also called an *evil heart*. Such a heart may coexist with a will which in general is good: it arises from the frailty of human nature, the lack of sufficient strength to follow out the principles it has chosen for itself, joined with its impurity, the failure to distinguish the incentives (even of well-intentioned actions) from each other by the gauge of morality; and so at last, if the extreme is reached, [it results] from looking only to the squaring of these actions with the law and not to the derivation of them from the law as

the sole motivating spring. Now even though there does not always follow therefrom an unlawful act and a propensity thereto, namely, *vice*, yet the mode of thought which sets down the absence of such vice as being conformity of the *disposition* to the law of duty (as being virtue) – since in this case no attention whatever is paid to the motivating forces in the maxim but only to the observance of the letter of the law – itself deserves to be called a radical perversity in the human heart.

This *innate* guilt (*reatus*), which is so denominated because it may be discerned in man as early as the first manifestations of the exercise of freedom, but which, none the less, must have originated in freedom and hence can be imputed, – this guilt may be judged in its first two stages (those of frailty and impurity) to be unintentional guilt (*culpa*), but in the third to be deliberate guilt (*dolus*) and to display in its character a certain *insidiousness* of the human heart (*dolus malus*), which deceives itself in regard to its own good and evil dispositions, and, if only its conduct has not evil consequences – which it might well have, with such maxims – does not trouble itself about its disposition but rather considers itself justified before the law. Thence arises the peace of conscience of so many men (conscientious in their own esteem) when, in the course of conduct concerning which they did not take the law into their counsel, or at least in which the law was not the supreme consideration, they merely elude evil consequences by good fortune. They may even picture themselves as meritorious, feeling themselves guilty of no such offenses as they see others burdened with; nor do they ever inquire whether good luck should not have the credit, or whether by reason of the cast of mind which they could discover, if they only would, in their own inmost nature, they would not have practised similar vices, had not inability, temperament, training, and circumstances of time and place which serve to tempt one (matters which are not imputable), kept them out of the way of those vices. This dishonesty, by which we humbug ourselves and which thwarts the establishing of a true moral disposition in us, extends itself outwardly also to falsehood and deception of others. If this is not to be termed wickedness, it at least deserves the name of worthlessness, and is an element in the radical evil of human nature, which (inasmuch as it puts out of

---

13   [*i.e.*, to the inversion of the ethical order of the incentives.]

tune the moral capacity to judge what a man is to be taken for, and renders wholly uncertain both internal and external attribution of responsibility) constitutes the foul taint in our race. So long as we do not eradicate it, it prevents the seed of goodness from developing as it otherwise would.

A member of the British Parliament[14] once exclaimed, in the heat of debate, "Every man has his price, for which he sells himself." If this is true (a question to which each must make his own answer), if there is no virtue for which some temptation cannot be found capable of overthrowing it, and if whether the good or evil spirit wins us over to his party depends merely on which bids the most and pays us most promptly, then certainly it holds true of men universally as the apostle said:[15] "They are all under sin, – there is none righteous (in the spirit of the law), no, not one."[16]

IV. Concerning the Origin of Evil in Human Nature

An origin (a first origin) is the derivation of an effect from its first cause, that is, from that cause which is not in turn the effect of another cause of the same kind. It can be considered either as an *origin in reason* or as an *origin in time*. In the former sense, regard is had only to the *existence* of the effect; in the latter, to its *occurrence*, and hence it is related as an event to its *first cause in time*. If an effect is referred to a cause to which it is bound under the laws of freedom, as is true in the case of moral evil, then the determination of the will to the production of this effect is conceived of as bound up with its determining ground not in time but merely in rational representation; such an effect cannot be derived from any *preceding* state whatsoever. Yet derivation of this sort is always necessary when an evil action, as an *event* in the world, is referred to its natural cause. To seek the temporal origin of free acts as such (as though they were natural effects) is thus a contradiction. Hence it is also a contradiction to seek the temporal origin of man's moral character, so far as it is considered as contingent, since this character signifies the ground of the *exercise* of freedom; this ground (like the determining ground of the free will generally) must be sought in purely rational representations.

However the origin of moral evil in man is constituted, surely of all the explanations of the spread and propagation of this evil through all members and generations of our race, the most inept is that which describes it as descending to us as an *inheritance* from our first parents; for one can say of moral evil precisely what the poet said of good:[17] *genus et proavos, et* quae non fecimus ipsi, *vix ea nostra puto.*[18] Yet we should note that, in our search for the origin of this evil, we do not deal first

---

14 [Sir Robert Walpole. What he said, however, was not so universal: "All those men" (referring to certain "patriots") "have their price."]

15 [Cf. Romans III, 9-10]

16 The special proof of this sentence of condemnation by morally judging reason is to be found in the preceding section rather than in this one, which contains only the confirmation of it by experience. Experience, however, never can reveal the root of evil in the supreme maxim of the free will relating to the law, a maxim which. as *intelligible act,* precedes all experience. Hence from the singleness of the supreme maxim, together with the singleness of the law to which it relates itself, we can also understand why, for the pure intellectual judgment of mankind, the rule of excluding a mean between good and evil must remain fundamental; yet for the empirical judgment based on *sensible conduct* (actual performance and neglect) the rule may be laid down that there is a mean between these extremes – on the one hand a negative mean of indifference prior to all education, on the other hand a positive, a mixture, partly good and partly evil. However, this latter is merely a judgment upon the morality of mankind as appearance, and must give place to the former in a final judgment.

17 [Ovid, *Metamorphoses,* XIII, 140-141: "Race and ancestors, and those things *which we ourselves have not made,* I scarcely account our own."]

18 The three so-called "higher faculties" (in the universities) would explain this transmission of evil each in terms of its own specialty, as *inherited disease, inherited debt,* or *inherited sin.* (1) The *faculty of medicine* would represent this hereditary evil somewhat as it represents the tapeworm, concerning which several naturalists actually believe that, since no specimens have been met with anywhere but in us, not even (of this particular type) in other animals, it must have existed in our first parents. (2) The *faculty of law* would regard this evil as the legitimate consequence of succeeding to the *patrimony* bequeathed us by our first parents, [an inheritance] encumbered, however, with heavy forfeitures (for to be born is no other than to inherit the use of earthly goods so far as they are necessary to

of all with the propensity thereto (as *peccatum in potentia*); rather do we direct our attention to the actual evil of given actions with respect to its inner possibility – to what must take place within the will if evil is to be performed.

In the search for the rational origin of evil actions, every such action must be regarded as though the individual had fallen into it directly from a state of innocence. For whatever his previous deportment may have been, whatever natural causes may have been influencing him, and whether these causes were to be found within him or outside him, his action is yet free and determined by none of these causes; hence it can and must always be judged as an *original* use of his will. He should have refrained from that action whatever his temporal circumstances and entanglements; for through no cause in the world can he cease to be a freely acting being. Rightly is it said that to a man's account are set down the *consequences* arising from his former free acts which were contrary to the law; but this merely amounts to saying that man need not involve himself in the evasion of seeking to establish whether or not these consequences are free, since there exists in the admittedly free action, which was their cause, ground sufficient for holding him accountable. However evil a man has been up to the very moment of an impending free act (so that evil has actually become custom or second nature) it was not only his duty to have been better [in the past], it is *now* still his duty to better himself. To do so must be within his power, and if he does not do so, he is susceptible of, and subjected to, imputability in the very moment of that action, just as much as though, endowed with a predisposition to good (which is inseparable from freedom), he had stepped out of a state of innocence into evil. Hence we cannot inquire into

the temporal origin of this deed, but solely into its rational origin, if we are thereby to determine and, wherever possible, to elucidate the propensity, if it exists, *i.e.*, the general subjective ground of the adoption of transgression into our maxim.

The foregoing agrees well with that manner of presentation which the Scriptures use, whereby the origin of evil in the human race is depicted as having a [temporal] *beginning*, this beginning being presented in a narrative, wherein what in its essence must be considered as primary (without regard to the element of time) appears as coming first in time. According to this account, evil does not start from a propensity thereto as its underlying basis, for otherwise the beginning of evil would not have its source in freedom; rather does it start from *sin* (by which is meant the transgressing of the moral law as a *divine command*). The state of man prior to all propensity to evil is called the state of *innocence*. The moral law became known to mankind, as it must to any being not pure but tempted by desires, in the form of a *prohibition* (Genesis II, 16-17). Now instead of straightway following this law as an adequate incentive (the only incentive which is unconditionally good and regarding which there is no further doubt), man looked about for other incentives (Genesis III, 6) such as can be good only conditionally (namely, so far as they involve no infringement of the law). He then made it his maxim – if one thinks of his action as consciously springing from freedom – to follow the law of duty, not as duty, but, if need be, with regard to other aims. Thereupon he began to call in question the severity of the commandment which excludes the influence of all other incentives; then by sophistry he reduced[19] obedience to the law to the merely conditional character of a means (subject to the principle of self-love); and finally he adopted into

---

our continued existence). Thus we must fulfil payment (atone) and at the end still be dispossessed (by death) of the property. How just is legal justice! (3) The *theological faculty* would regard this evil as the personal participation by our first parents in the *fall* of a condemned rebel, maintaining either that we ourselves then participated (although now unconscious of having done so), or that even now, born under the rule of the rebel (as prince of this world), we prefer his favors to the supreme command of the heavenly Ruler, and do not possess enough faith to free ourselves; wherefore we must also eventually share his doom.

19   All homage paid to the moral law is an act of hypocrisy, if, in one's maxim, ascendancy is not at the same time granted to the law as an incentive sufficient in itself and higher than all other determining grounds of the will. The propensity to do this is inward deceit, i.e., a tendency to deceive oneself in the interpretation of the moral law, to its detriment (Genesis III, 5). Accordingly, the Bible (the Christian portion of it) denominates the author of evil (who is within us) as the liar from the beginning, and thus characterizes man with respect to what seems to be the chief ground of evil in him.

his maxim of conduct the ascendancy of the sensuous impulse over the incentive which springs from the law – and thus occurred sin (Genesis III, 6). *Mutato nomine de te fabula narratur.*[20] From all this it is clear that we daily act in the same way, and that therefore "in Adam all have sinned"[21] and still sin; except that in us there is presupposed an innate propensity to transgression, whereas in the first man, from the point of view of time, there is presupposed no such propensity but rather innocence; hence transgression on his part is called *a fall into sin*; but with us sin is represented as resulting from an already innate wickedness in our nature. This propensity, however, signifies no more than this, that if we wish to address ourselves to the explanation of evil in terms of its *beginning in time*, we must search for the causes of each deliberate transgression in a previous period of our lives, far back to that period wherein the use of reason had not yet developed, and thus back to a propensity to evil (as a natural ground) which is therefore called innate – the source of evil. But to trace the causes of evil in the instance of the first man, who is depicted as already in full command of the use of his reason, is neither necessary nor feasible, since otherwise this basis (the evil propensity) would have had to be created in him; therefore his sin is set forth as engendered directly from innocence. We must not, however, look for an origin in time of a moral character for which we are to be held responsible; though to do so is inevitable if we wish to *explain* the contingent existence of this character (and perhaps it is for this reason that Scripture, in conformity with this weakness of ours, has thus pictured the temporal origin of evil).

But the rational origin of this perversion of our will whereby it makes lower incentives supreme among its maxims, that is, of the propensity to evil, remains inscrutable to us, because this propensity itself must be set down to our account and because, as a result, that ultimate ground of all maxims would in turn involve the adoption of an evil maxim [as its basis]. Evil could have sprung only from the morally-evil (not from mere limitations in our nature); and yet the original predisposition (which no one other than man himself could have corrupted, if he is to be held responsible for this corruption) is a predisposition to good; there is then for us no conceivable ground from which the moral evil in us could originally have come. This inconceivability, together with a more accurate specification of the wickedness of our race, the Bible expresses in the historical narrative as follows.[22] It finds a place for evil at the creation of the world, yet not in man, but in a *spirit* of an originally loftier destiny. Thus is the *first* beginning of all evil represented as inconceivable by us (for whence came evil to that spirit?); but man is represented as having fallen into evil only *through seduction*, and hence as being *not basically* corrupt (even as regards his original predisposition to good) but rather as still capable of an improvement, in contrast to a seducing *spirit*, that is, a being for whom temptation of the flesh cannot be accounted as an alleviation of guilt. For man, therefore, who despite a corrupted heart yet possesses a good will, there remains hope of a return to the good from which he has strayed.

....

Godliness comprises two determinations of the moral disposition in relation to God: *fear* of God is this disposition in obedience to His commands from *bounden* duty (the duty of a subject), *i.e.,* from respect for the law; *love* of God, on the other hand, is the disposition to obedience from one's own *free choice* and from approval of the law (the duty of a son). Both involve, therefore, over and above morality, the concept of a supersensible

---

20   [Horace, *Satires* I, I. "Change but the name, of you the tale is told" (Conington).]

21   [Cf. Romans V, 12]

22   What is written here must not be read as though intended for Scriptural exegesis, which lies beyond the limits of the domain of bare reason. It is possible to explain how an historical account is to be put to a moral use without deciding whether this is the intention of the author or merely our interpretation, provided this meaning is true in itself, apart from all historical proof, and is moreover the only one whereby we can derive something conducive to our betterment from a passage which otherwise would be only an unfruitful addition to our historical knowledge. We must not quarrel unnecessarily over a question or over its historical aspect, when, however it is understood, it in no way helps us to be better men, and when that which can afford such help is discovered without historical proof, and indeed must be apprehended without it. That historical knowledge which has no inner bearing valid for all men belongs to the class of *adiaphora,* which each man is free to hold as he finds edifying.

Being provided with the attributes which are requisite to the carrying out of that highest good which is aimed at by morality but which transcends our powers. Now if we go beyond the moral relation of the idea of this Being to us, to a concept of His *nature*, there is always a danger that we shall think of it anthropomorphically and hence in a manner directly hurtful to our basic moral principles. Thus the idea of such a Being cannot subsist of itself in speculative reason; even its origin, and still more its power, are wholly grounded in its relation to our self-subsistent determination to duty. Which, now, is the more natural in the first instruction of youth and even in discourses from the pulpit: to expound the doctrine of virtue before the doctrine of godliness, or that of godliness before that of virtue (without perhaps even mentioning the doctrine of virtue at all)? Both obviously stand in necessary connection with one another. But, since they are not *of a kind*, this is possible only if one of them is conceived of and explained as end, the other merely as means. The doctrine of virtue, however, subsists of itself (even without the concept of God), whereas the doctrine of godliness involves the concept of an object which we represent to ourselves, in relation to our morality, as the cause supplementing our incapacity with respect to the final moral end. Hence the doctrine of godliness cannot of itself constitute the final goal of moral endeavor but can merely serve as a means of strengthening that which in itself goes to make a better man, to wit, the virtuous disposition, since it reassures and guarantees this endeavor (as a striving for goodness, and even for holiness) in its expectation of the final goal with respect to which it is impotent. The doctrine of virtue, in contrast, derives from the soul of man. He is already in full possession of it, undeveloped, no doubt, but not needing, like the religious concept, to be rationalized into being by means of logistics. In the purity of this concept of virtue, in the awakening of consciousness to a capacity which otherwise we would never surmise (a capacity of becoming able to master the greatest obstacles within ourselves), in the dignity of humanity which man must respect in his own person and human destiny, toward which he strives, if he is to attain it – in all this there is something which so exalts the soul, and so leads it to the very Deity, who is worthy of adoration only because of His holiness and as Legislator for virtue, that man, even when he is still far from allowing to this concept the power of influencing his maxims, is yet not unwillingly sustained by it because he feels himself to a certain extent ennobled by this idea already, even while the concept of a World-Ruler who transforms this duty into a command to us, still lies far from him. But to commence with this latter concept would incur the danger of dashing man's courage (which goes to constitute the essence of virtue) and transforming godliness into a fawning slavish subjection to a despotically commanding might. The courage to stand on one's own feet is itself strengthened by the doctrine of atonement, when it follows the ethical doctrine, in that this doctrine portrays as wiped out what cannot be altered, and opens up to man the path to a new mode of life; whereas, when this doctrine is made to come first, the futile endeavor to render undone what has been done (expiation), the fear regarding appropriation of this atonement, the idea of his complete incapacity for goodness, and the anxiety lest he slip back into evil must rob[23] a man of his

---

23   The various kinds of belief among peoples seem to give them, after a time, a character, revealing itself outwardly in civil relations, which is later attributed to them as though it were universally a temperamental trait. Thus Judaism in its original economy, under which a people was to separate itself from all other peoples by means of every conceivable, and some arduous, observances and was to refrain from all intermingling with them, drew down upon itself the charge of *misanthropy*. Mohammedanism is characterized by *arrogant pride* because it finds confirmation of its faith not in miracles but in victories and the subjugation of many peoples, and because its devotional practices are all of the spirited sort. (This remarkable phenomenon (of the pride of an ignorant though intelligent people in its faith) may also originate from the fancy of its founder that he alone had once again renewed on earth the concept of God's unity and of His supersensible nature. He would indeed have ennobled his people by release from image-worship and the anarchy of polytheism could he with justice have credited himself with this achievement. As regards the characteristic of the third type of religious fellowship [the Christian], which is based upon a misconceived humility, the depreciation of self-conceit in the evaluation of one's own moral worth, through consideration of the holiness of the law, should bring about not contempt for oneself but rather the resolution, conformable to this noble predisposition in us, to approach ever nearer to agreement with this law. Instead of this, however, virtue,

courage and reduce him to a state of sighing moral passivity in which nothing great or good is undertaken and everything is expected from the mere wishing for it. In that which concerns the moral disposition everything depends upon the highest concept under which one subsumes one's duties. When reverence for God is put first, with virtue therefore subordinated to it, this object [of reverence] becomes an *idol*, that is, He is thought of as a Being whom we may hope to please not through morally upright conduct on earth but through adoration and ingratiation; and religion is then idolatry. But godliness is not a surrogate for virtue, whereby we may dispense with the latter; rather is it virtue's consummation, enabling us to be crowned with the hope of the ultimate achievement of all our good ends.

Bibliography

Cassirer, Ernst. *The Philosophy of the Enlightenment*. Princeton, N. J.: Princeton University Press, 1951.

Caygill, Howard. *A Kant Dictionary*. Oxford: Blackwell, 1995.

Guyer, P., ed. *The Cambridge Companion to Kant*. Cambridge: Cambridge University Press, 1992.

Kant, Immanuel. *Perpetual Peace and Other Essays*. Trans. T. Humphrey. Indianapolis: Hackett Publishing Company, 1983.

McFarland, J.D. *Kant's Concept of Teleology*. Edinburgh: University of Edinburgh Press, 1970.

Paton, H.J. *The Categorical Imperative*. New York: Harper Torchbooks, 1967.

Scruton, Roger. *Kant*. Oxford and New York: Oxford University Press, 1982.

Walker, Ralph C.S. *Kant*. London and New York: Routledge, 1978.

Wolff, Robert Paul, ed. *Kant: A Collection of Critical Essays*. New York: Anchor Books, 1967.

which really consists in the courage for this improvement, has, as a name already suspected of self-conceit, been exiled into paganism, and sycophantic courting of favor is extolled in its place.

Devotional hypocrisy (bigotry, *devotia spuria*) consists in the habit of identifying the practice of piety not with well-pleasing actions (in the performance of all human duties) but with direct commerce with God through manifestations of awe. This practice must then be classed as *compulsory service (opus operatum)*, except that it adds to this superstition the fanatical illusion of imagined supersensible (heavenly) feelings.) The Hindu faith gives its adherents the character of *pusillanimity* for reasons which are directly opposed to those productive of the temper just mentioned [the Mohammedan].

Now surely it is not because of the inner nature of the Christian faith but because of the manner in which it is presented to the heart and mind, that a similar charge can be brought against it with respect to those who have the most heartfelt intentions toward it but who, starting with human corruption, and despairing of all virtue, place their religious principle solely in *piety* (whereby is meant the principle of a passive attitude toward a godliness which is to be awaited from a power above). Such men never place any reliance in themselves, but look about them, in perpetual anxiety, for a supernatural assistance, and in this very self-abnegation (which is not humility) fancy themselves to possess a means of obtaining favor. The outward expression of this (in pietism or in spurious devotion) signalizes a *slavish* cast of mind.

CHAPTER TWELVE — DIETRICH BONHOEFFER

Dietrich Bonhoeffer (1906-1945) was a leading Lutheran Protestant theologian, in whose writings a distinctive (and distinctively modern) rendering of Christian analysis of humanity's place in the world appears. He was also an activist leader of his church, in Germany, and an opponent of the Nazi regime. Twice Bonhoeffer left Germany, with the open possibility of securing refuge in exile, in England in 1933, and in the United States in 1939. In both cases he chose to return to his homeland and engage in the struggle there. He was eventually arrested and imprisoned, and implicated in the resistance to Hitler (and the network of opponents linked to the assassination attempt on Hitler's life in 1944), he was executed in 1945. A public leader, and a hero and martyr, Bonhoeffer also brought a fresh and intellectually well-grounded (and philosophically and scientifically well-educated) perspective to the attempt to unite Christianity with modernity.

Much of Bonhoeffer's work was published posthumously; both his influence and the discussion of his ideas have been greater in the decades since his death than during his lifetime.

Dietrich Bonhoeffer, *A Testament to Freedom*

(Source: Geffrey B. Kelly and Burton F. Nelson. *A Testament to Freedom: The Essential Writings of Dietrich Bonhoeffer*. Trans. Geffrey B. Kelly *et al*. San Francisco: Harper, 1995, 106-109, 349, 368-371)

Then God said, "Let us make humankind in our image, according to our likeness." Human beings are to proceed from God as the ultimate, the new, and as the image of God in God's works. There is no transition here from somewhere or other; here there is new creation. This has nothing at all to do with Darwinism. Quite independently of this, the human person remains the new, free, and unconstricted work of God. We certainly have no wish to deny our connection with the animal world: rather it is just the opposite. But we are very anxious not to lose the unique relationship of humans and God in the process. In our concern with the origin and nature of human beings, it would be a hopeless effort for us to attempt to make a gigantic leap back into the world of the lost beginning. It is hopeless for us to want to know for ourselves what the original human being was like, to identify one's own ideal of the human with the creational reality of God. Such attempts fail to understand that we can know about the original human beings only if

we start from Christ. This hopeless, though understandable, attempt has again and again delivered the church up to unbridled speculation on this dangerous point. Only in the middle, as those who live from Christ, do we know of the beginning.

God creates God's image on earth in the human. This means that humans are like the Creator in that they are free. Actually one is free only through God's creation, by means of the Word of God; one is free for the worship of the Creator. In the language of the Bible, freedom is not something persons have for themselves but something they have for others. No one enjoys freedom "in itself," that is, in a vacuum, the same way that one may be musical, intelligent, or blind as such. Freedom is not a quality of the human person. Nor is it an ability, a disposition, a kind of being that somehow deeply germinates in a person. Whoever scrutinizes the human to discover freedom will find nothing of it. Why? Because freedom is not a quality that can be discovered. It is not a possession, a presence, or an object. Nor is it a pattern for existence. Rather, it is a relationship; otherwise, it is nothing. Indeed it is a relationship between two persons. Being free means "being free for the other," because the other has bound me to himself or herself. Only in relationship with the other am I free.

No substantial or individualistic concept of freedom has the ability to encompass freedom.

Freedom is something over which I have no control as a possession. It is simply the event, the experience, that happens to me through the other. If we ask how we know this, or whether this is not just another speculation about the beginning that results from being in the middle, we can answer that it is the message of the gospel itself, that God's freedom has bound us to the divine self, that God's free grace becomes real only in this relationship with us, and that God does not will to be free for the divine self but for man and woman. Because God in Christ is free for us humans, because God does not hoard freedom for the divine self we can envision freedom only as a "being free for." For us who live in the middle through Christ and know our humanity in his resurrection, that God is free means nothing more than that we are free for God. The freedom of the Creator is confirmed by the fact that God allows us to be free for God and that means nothing other than that God creates God's image on earth. The paradox of created freedom is not eliminated. Indeed, it ought even to be made the primary focal point. Here created *freedom* means – and this is what surpasses all the previous deeds of God, deeds which are unique for their excellence – that God enters into God's creation.

Now God not only commands and God's word becomes deed, but God enters into creation and thus creates freedom. In this, human beings differ from the other creatures in that God is in them, in that they are God's very image in whom the free Creator views the divine self. The old dogmatists meant this when they spoke of the "indwelling" of the Trinity in Adam. In the free creature the Holy Spirit worships the Creator, the uncreated freedom is praised in created freedom. The creature loves the Creator, because the Creator loves the creature. Created *freedom* is freedom in the Holy Spirit, but as *created* freedom, it is the freedom of *humans* themselves. How does the created being of the free person express itself? In what way does the freedom of the Creator differ from the freedom of the creature? How is the created one free?

Those who are created are free in that they are in relationship with other creatures; the human person is free for others. And God created them a man and a woman. The man is not alone; he exists in duality and it is in this dependence on the other that his creatureliness consists. The creatureliness of humans, no more than their freedom, is neither a quality, nor a disposition to be encountered, nor is it a mode of being. It is to be defined, rather, as absolutely nothing other than the relations of human beings with one another, over against one another, in dependence on one another. The "image ... after God's likeness" is, consequently, not an *analogia entis* (analogy of being) by which humans, in their existence in and for themselves, would in their being live in the likeness to God's being. Indeed, there is no such analogy between God and the human. This is because God, who in underived being (*aseität*) is the only one existing in and for the self and at the same time existing for creatures, binding and giving God's freedom to human beings, must not be thought of as only "being," since God is the one who in Christ witnesses to "being for people." The likeness, the analogy of the human to God, is not *analogia entis* but *analogia relationis* (analogy of relationship). This means, first of all, that the relationship is not a capacity, possibility, or structure proper to the human. It is rather a relationship that is given as a gift and decreed as passive justice. *Justitia passiva!* And in this decreed relationship, freedom is established. From this it follows, secondly, that this analogy must not be understood as though humans somehow have this likeness in their possession, or at their disposal. On the contrary, the analogy, the likeness, must be understood so very strictly, that the likeness in question derives its resemblance from the original image *alone*. Thus it always refers us *only* to the original exemplar the divine self and is "likeness" *only* in reference to this. *Analogia relationis* is, therefore, the relationship established by God and is an analogy only in this relationship decreed by God. The relationship of creature with creature is a God-given relationship because it exists in freedom and freedom originates from God.

Human beings in their duality – husband and wife – are brought into this world of the stars and of living things in their likeness to God. And just as one's freedom over/against people consisted in the fact that one was to be free *for* them, one's freedom over/against the rest of the created world is to be freedom *from* it. This means that they are its master; they have command over it; they rule it. And here is precisely the other side of their created likeness to God. Humans are to rule; indeed, to rule over God's creation, to rule like one who as such receives the mission and power of dominion from God. Being free from what is created is not the ideal freedom of the spirit from nature. Rather, this freedom of the one who has dominion includes one's being directly bound to the creatures who are ruled. The soil and the animals, over which I have dominion, are the world in which I live, without which I cease to be. It is my world, my earth, over which I rule. I am not free from it in the sense that my own being, my spirit, has no need of that nature, which is foreign to my spirit. On the contrary, in my entire being, in my creatureliness, I belong completely to this world. It bears me, nurtures me, and holds me. But my freedom from it consists in the fact that this world, to which I am bound like master to his servant, like the peasant to his earth, is subjected to me, and I am supposed to be *master* over the earth which is and remains my earth. Because it is *my* earth, all the more strongly do I rule over it. It is nothing other than the authority conferred by God's word on human beings that so uniquely binds them to and sets them over/against other creatures.

This much has been told to us. We are those who live in the middle and who know nothing more about all this and to whom all this is pious myth or a lost world. Indeed, we also attempt to dominate, but the same thing happens here as on Walpurgis Night. We think that we are the ones doing the moving, but we are the ones being moved. We do not rule; rather, we are being ruled. The thing, the world, rules the human. Human beings are made prisoners, slaves of the world. Their rule is an illusion. Technology is the power with which the earth grips people and subdues them. And because we no longer are in command, we lose ground. The earth is, therefore, no longer *our* earth, and thus we become strangers to the earth. But we do not rule over it, since we do not know the world as God's creation and because we do not receive our dominion as God-given but seize hold of it for ourselves. Here there is no "being-free-from" without the "being-free-for." There is no dominion without serving God. With the one, people necessarily lose the other. Without God, without our brother or sister, we lose the earth. In the sentimental aversion to exercising dominion over the earth, however, one has so far always lost God and one's brother and sister. God, brother and sister, and the earth belong together. But for those who have once lost the

earth, for us in the middle, there is no way back to the earth except the way to God and to one's brother and sister. From the very beginning the way of human beings to the earth has only been possible as God's way to people. Only where God and brother and sister come to us can we find our way back to the earth. Our being-free-for God and other people and our being-free-from the creature in our dominion over it is the likeness to God of the first human beings. [*Schöpfung und Fall*, pp. 40-45.]

....

For Christians there is no other law than the law of freedom, as the New Testament paradoxically puts it. There is no generally valid law which could be expounded to them by others, or even by themselves. Those who surrender freedom surrender their very nature as Christians. Christians stand free, without any protection, before God and before the world, and they alone are wholly responsible for what they do with the gift of freedom. Now through this freedom Christians becomes creative in ethical action. Acting in accordance with principles is unproductive, imitating the law, copying. Acting from freedom is creative. Christians choose the forms of their ethical action as it were from eternity, they put them sovereign in the world, as their act, their creation from the freedom of a child of God. Christians even create their standards of good and evil for themselves. Only they can justify their own actions, just as only they can bear the responsibility. The Christian creates new tables, a new Decalogue, as Nietzsche said of the Superman. Nietzsche's Superman is not really, as he supposed, the opposite of the Christian; without knowing it, Nietzsche has here introduced many traits of the Christian made free, as Paul and Luther describe him. Time-honored morals – even if they are given out to be the consensus of Christian opinion – can never for Christians become the standard of their actions. They act, because the will of God seems to bid them to, without a glance at the others, at what is usually called morals, and no one but themselves and God can know whether they have acted well or badly. In ethical decision we are brought into the deepest solitude, the solitude in which they stand before the living God. No one can stand beside us there, no one can take anything from us, because God lays on us a burden which we alone must bear.

Our "I" awakes only in the consciousness of being called, of being claimed by God. Only through the call of God does this "I" become isolated from all the others, drawn into responsibility by God, knowing myself to confront eternity alone. And because in the solitude I come face to face with God, I can only know for myself, completely personally, what is good and what is evil. There are no actions which are bad in themselves – even murder can be justified – there is only faithfulness to God's will or deviation from it; there is similarly no law in the sense of a law containing precepts, but only the law of freedom, i.e., of our bearing our responsibility alone before God and ourselves. But because the law remains superseded once for all and because it follows from the Christian idea of God that there can be no more law, the ethical commandments, the apparent laws of the New Testament must also be understood from this standpoint.

....

The world, like all created things, is created through Christ and with Christ as its end, and consists in Christ alone (John 1:10; Col. 1:16). To speak of the world without speaking of Christ is empty and abstract. The world is relative to Christ, no matter whether it knows it or not. This relativeness of the world to Christ assumes concrete form in certain mandates of God in the world. The Scriptures name four such mandates: labor, marriage, government, and the church. We speak of divine mandates rather than of divine orders because the word mandate refers more clearly to a divinely imposed task rather than to a determination of being. It is God's will that there shall be labor, marriage, government, and church in the world; and it is God's will that all these, each in its own way, shall be through Christ, directed toward Christ, and in Christ. God has imposed all these mandates on all people. God has not merely imposed one of these mandates on each individual, but has imposed all four on all people. This means that there can be no retreating from a "secular" into a "spiritual" sphere. There can be only the practice, the learning of the Christian life under these four mandates of God. And it will not do to regard the first three mandates as "secular," in contradistinction to the fourth. For even in the midst of

the world these are divine mandates, no matter whether their topic be labor, marriage, government, or the church. These mandates are, indeed, divine only by virtue of their original and final relation to Christ. [*Ethics*, p. 207]

....

In the course of historical life there comes a point where the exact observance of the formal law of a state, of a commercial undertaking, of a family, or for that matter of a scientific discovery, suddenly finds itself in violent conflict with the ineluctable necessities of the lives of humans; at this point responsible and pertinent action leaves behind it the domain of principle and convention, the domain of the normal and regular, and is confronted by the extraordinary situation of ultimate necessities, a situation which no law can control. It was for this situation that Machiavelli in his political theory coined the term *necessità*. In the field of politics this means that the technique of statecraft has now been supplanted by the necessity of state. There can be no doubt that such necessities exist; to deny their existence is to abandon the attempt to act in accordance with reality. But it is equally certain that these necessities are a primary fact of life itself and cannot, therefore, be governed by any law or themselves constitute a law. They appeal directly to the free responsibility of the agent, a responsibility which is bound by no law. They create a situation which is extraordinary; they are by nature peripheral and abnormal events. They no longer leave a multiplicity of courses open to human reason but they confront it with the question of the *ultima ratio*.... The extraordinary necessity appeals to the freedom of the person who is responsible. There is now no law behind which the responsible person can seek cover, and there is, therefore, also no law which can compel the responsible person to take any particular decision in the face of such necessities. In this situation there can only be a complete renunciation of every law, together with the knowledge that here one must make one's decision as a free venture, together also with the open admission that here the law is being infringed and violated and that necessity obeys no commandment. Precisely in this breaking of the law, the validity of the law is acknowledged, and in this renunciation of all law, and in this alone, one's own decision and deed are entrusted unreservedly to the divine governance of history. [*Ethics*, pp. 238-40]

Bibliography

Bethge, Eberhard. "The Challenge of Dietrich Bonhoeffer's Life and Theology." *The Chicago Theological Seminary Register*. Vol. 51 (Feb 1961), 1-38.

Feil, Ernst. *The Theology of Dietrich Bonhoeffer*. Philadelphia: Fortress Press, 1985.

Marty, Martin E., ed. *The Place of Bonhoeffer*. New York: Holt, Rinehart and Winston, 1962.

III

LIBERALISM

For introductory comments on Kant, see p. 99 above.

Immanuel Kant, *An Answer to the Question: What is Enlightenment?*[1]

(Source: Immanuel Kant. *Perceptual Peace and Other Essays*. Trans. Ted Humphrey. Indianapolis and Cambridge: Hackett Publishing Company, 1983, 41-48.)

Enlightenment is man's emergence from his self-imposed immaturity. Immaturity *is* the inability to use one's understanding without guidance from another. This immaturity is *self-imposed* when its cause lies not in lack of understanding, but in lack of resolve and courage to use it without guidance from another. *Sapere Aude!*[2] "Have courage to use your own understanding!" – that is the motto of enlightenment.

Laziness and cowardice are the reasons why so great a proportion of men, long after nature has released them from alien guidance *(naturaliter maiorennes)*,[3] nonetheless gladly remain in lifelong immaturity, and why it is so easy for others to establish themselves as their guardians. It is so easy to be immature. If I have a book to serve as my understanding, a pastor to serve as my conscience, a physician to determine my diet for me, and so on, I need not exert myself at all. I need not think, if only I can pay: others will readily undertake the irksome work for me. The guardians who have so benevolently taken over the supervision of men have carefully seen to it that the far greatest part of them (including the entire fair sex) regard taking the step to maturity as very dangerous, not to mention difficult. Having first made their domestic livestock dumb, and having carefully made sure that these docile creatures will not take a single step without the go-cart to which they are harnessed, these guardians then show them the danger that threatens them, should they attempt to walk alone.

Now this danger is not actually so great, for after falling a few times they would in the end certainly learn to walk; but an example of this kind makes men timid and usually frightens them out of all further attempts.

Thus, it is difficult for any individual man to work himself out of the immaturity that has all but become his nature. He has even become fond of this state and for the time being is actually incapable of using his own understanding, for no one has ever allowed him to attempt it. Rules and formulas, those mechanical aids to the rational use, or rather misuse, of his natural gifts, are the shackles of a permanent immaturity. Whoever threw them off would still make only an uncertain leap over the smallest ditch, since he is unaccustomed to this kind of free movement. Consequently, only a few have succeeded, by cultivating their own minds, in freeing themselves from immaturity and pursuing a secure course.

But that the public should enlighten itself is more likely; indeed, if it is only allowed freedom, enlightenment is almost inevitable. For even among the entrenched guardians of the great masses a few will always think for themselves, a few who, after having themselves thrown off the yoke of immaturity, will spread the spirit of a rational appreciation for both their own worth and for each person's calling to think for himself. But it should be particularly noted that if a public that was first placed in this yoke by the guardians is suitably aroused by some of those who are altogether incapable of enlightenment, it may force the guardians themselves to remain under the yoke – so pernicious is it to instill prejudices, for they finally take revenge upon their originators, or on their descendants. Thus a public can only attain enlightenment slowly. Perhaps a revolution can overthrow autocratic despotism and profiteering or power-grabbing oppression, but it

---

1   A. A., VIII, 33-42. This essay first appeared in the *Berlinische Monatsschrift,* December, 1784.
2   "Dare to know!" (Horace, *Epodes*, 1,2,40.) This motto was adopted by the Society of the Friends of Truth, an important circle of the German Enlightenment.
3   "Those who have come of age by virtue of nature."

can never truly reform a manner of thinking; instead, new prejudices, just like the old ones they replace, will serve as a leash for the great unthinking mass.

Nothing is required for this enlightenment, however, except *freedom*; and the freedom in question is the least harmful of all, namely, the freedom to use reason *publicly* in all matters. But on all sides I hear: *"Do not argue!"* The officer says, "Do not argue, drill!" The taxman says, "Do not argue, pay!" The pastor says, "Do not argue, believe!" (Only one ruler in the world[4] says, *"Argue as much as you want and about what you want, but obey!")* In this we have [examples of] pervasive restrictions on freedom. But which restriction hinders enlightenment and which does not, but instead actually advances it? I reply: The *public* use of one's reason must always be free, and it alone can bring about enlightenment among mankind; the *private use* of reason may, however, often be very narrowly restricted, without otherwise hindering the progress of enlightenment. By the public use of one's own reason I understand the use that anyone as a *scholar* makes of reason before the entire *literate world*. I call the private use of reason that which a person may make in a *civic post* or office that has been entrusted to him. Now in many affairs conducted in the interests of a community, a certain mechanism is required by means of which some of its members must conduct themselves in an entirely passive manner so that through an artificial unanimity the government may guide them toward public ends, or at least prevent them from destroying such ends. Here one certainly must not argue, instead one must obey. However, insofar as this part of the machine also regards himself as a member of the community as a whole, or even of the world community, and as a consequence addresses the public in the role of a scholar, in the proper sense of that term, he can most certainly argue, without thereby harming the affairs for which as a passive member he is partly responsible. Thus it would be disastrous if an officer on duty who was given a command by his superior were to question the appropriateness or utility of the order. He must obey. But as a scholar he cannot be justly constrained from making comments about errors in military service, or from placing them before the public for its judgment. The citizen cannot refuse to pay the taxes imposed on him; indeed, impertinent criticism of such levies, when they should be paid by him, can be punished as a scandal (since it can lead to widespread insubordination). But the same person does not act contrary to civic duty when, as a scholar, he publicly expresses his thoughts regarding the impropriety or even injustice of such taxes. Likewise a pastor is bound to instruct his catecumens and congregation in accordance with the symbol of the church he serves, for he was appointed on that condition. But as a scholar he has complete freedom, indeed even the calling, to impart to the public all of his carefully considered and well-intentioned thoughts concerning mistaken aspects of that symbol, as well as his suggestions for the better arrangement of religious and church matters. Nothing in this can weigh on his conscience. What he teaches in consequence of his office as a servant of the church he sets out as something with regard to which he has no discretion to teach in accord with his own lights; rather, he offers it under the direction and in the name of another. He will say, "Our church teaches this or that and these are the demonstrations it uses." He thereby extracts for his congregation all practical uses from precepts to which he would not himself subscribe with complete conviction, but whose presentation he can nonetheless undertake, since it is not entirely impossible that truth lies hidden in them, and, in any case, nothing contrary to the very nature of religion is to be found in them. If he believed he could find anything of the latter sort in them, he could not in good conscience serve in his position; he would have to resign. Thus an appointed teacher's use of his reason for the sake of his congregation is merely *private,* because, however large the congregation is, this use is always only domestic; in this regard, as a priest, he is not free and cannot be such because he is acting under instructions from someone else. By contrast, the cleric – as a scholar who speaks through his writings to the public as such, i.e., the world – enjoys in this *public use* of reason an unrestricted freedom to use his own rational capacities and to speak his own mind. For that the (spiritual) guardians of a people should themselves be immature is an absurdity that would insure the perpetuation of absurdities.

---

4   Frederick II (the Great) of Prussia.

But would a society of pastors, perhaps a church assembly or venerable presbytery (as those among the Dutch call themselves), not be justified in binding itself by oath to a certain unalterable symbol in order to secure a constant guardianship over each of its members and through them over the people, and this for all time: I say that this is wholly impossible. Such a contract, whose intention is to preclude forever all further enlightenment of the human race, is absolutely null and void, even if it should be ratified by the supreme power, by parliaments, and by the most solemn peace treaties. One age cannot bind itself, and thus conspire, to place a succeeding one in a condition whereby it would be impossible for the later age to expand its knowledge (particularly where it is so very important), to rid itself of errors,and generally to increase its enlightenment. That would be a crime against human nature, whose essential destiny lies precisely in such progress; subsequent generations are thus completely justified in dismissing such agreements as unauthorized and criminal. The criterion of everything that can be agreed upon as a law by a people lies in this question: Can a people impose such a law on itself? Now it might be possible, in anticipation of a better state of affairs, to introduce a provisional order for a specific, short time, all the while giving all citizens, especially clergy, in their role as scholars, the freedom to comment publicly, i.e., in writing, on the present institution's shortcomings. The provisional order might last until insight into the nature of these matters had become so widespread and obvious that the combined (if not unanimous) voices of the populace could propose to the crown that it take under its protection those congregations that, in accord with their newly gained insight, had organized themselves under altered religious institutions, but without interfering with those wishing to allow matters to remain as before. However, it is absolutely forbidden that they unite into a religious organization that nobody may for the duration of a man's lifetime publicly question, for so doing would deny, render fruitless, and make detrimental to succeeding generations an era in man's progress toward improvement. A man may put off enlightenment with regard to what he ought to know, though only

for a short time and for his own person; but to renounce it for himself, or, even more, for subsequent generations, is to violate and trample man's divine rights underfoot. And what a people may not decree for itself may still less be imposed on it by a monarch, for his lawgiving authority rests on his unification of the people's collective will in his own. If he only sees to it that all genuine or purported improvement is consonant with civil order, he can allow his subjects to do what they find necessary to their spiritual well-being, which is not his affair. However, he must prevent anyone from forcibly interfering with another's working as best he can to determine and promote his well-being. It detracts from his own majesty when he interferes in these matters, since the writings in which his subjects attempt to clarify their insights lend value to his conception of governance. This holds whether he acts from his own highest insight – whereby he calls upon himself the reproach, "Caesar non est supra grammaticos."[5] as well as, indeed even more, when he despoils his highest authority by supporting the spiritual despotism of some tyrants in his state over his other subjects.

If it is now asked, "Do we presently live in an enlightened age?" the answer is, "No, but we do live in an age of enlightenment." As matters now stand, a great deal is still lacking in order for men as a whole to be, or even to put themselves into a position to be able without external guidance to apply understanding confidently to religious issues. But we do have clear indications that the way is now being opened for men to proceed freely in this direction and that the obstacles to general enlightenment – to their release from their self-imposed immaturity – are gradually diminishing. In this regard, this age is the age of enlightenment, the century of Frederick.[6]

A prince who does not find it beneath him to say that he takes it to be his duty to prescribe nothing, but rather to allow men complete freedom in religious matters – who thereby renounces the arrogant title of tolerance – is himself enlightened and deserves to be praised by a grateful present and by posterity as the first, at least where the government is concerned, to release the human race from immaturity and to leave everyone free to use his

---

5   "Caesar is not above the grammarians." See *Perpetual Peace*, 368f.
6   Frederick II (the Great), King of Prussia.

own reason in all matters of conscience. Under his rule, venerable pastors, in their role as scholars and without prejudice to their official duties, may freely and openly set out for the world's scrutiny their judgments and views, even where these occasionally differ from the accepted symbol. Still greater freedom is afforded to those who are not restricted by an official post. This spirit of freedom is expanding even where it must struggle against the external obstacles of governments that misunderstand their own function. Such governments are illuminated by the example that the existence of freedom need not give cause for the least concern regarding public order and harmony in the commonwealth. If only they refrain from inventing artifices to keep themselves in it, men will gradually raise themselves from barbarism.

I have focused on religious matters in setting out my main point concerning enlightenment, i.e., man's emergence from self-imposed immaturity, first because our rulers have no interest in assuming the role of their subjects' guardians with respect to the arts and sciences, and secondly because that form of immaturity is both the most pernicious and disgraceful of all. But the manner of thinking of a head of state who favors religious enlightenment goes even further, for he realizes that there is no danger to his *legislation* in allowing his subjects to use reason *publicly* and to set before the world their thoughts concerning better formulations of his laws, even if this involves frank criticism of legislation currently in effect. We have before us a shining example, with respect to which no monarch surpasses the one whom we honor.

But only a ruler who is himself enlightened and has no dread of shadows, yet who likewise has a well-disciplined, numerous army to guarantee public peace, can say what no republic may dare, namely: *"Argue as much as you want and about what you want, but obey!"* Here as elsewhere, when things are considered in broad perspective, a strange, unexpected pattern in human affairs reveals itself, one in which almost everything is paradoxical. A greater degree of civil freedom seems advantageous to a people's *spiritual* freedom; yet the former establishes impassable boundaries for the latter; conversely, a lesser degree of civil freedom provides enough room for all fully to expand their abilities. Thus, once nature has removed the hard shell from this kernel for which she has most fondly cared, namely, the inclination to and vocation for free *thinking,* the kernel gradually reacts on a people's mentality (whereby they become increasingly able to *act freely*), and it finally even influences the principles of *government,* which finds that it can profit by treating men, *who are now more than machines,* in accord with their dignity.*

Königsberg in Prussia, 30 September 1784
I. Kant

---

* Today I read in Büsching's *Wöchentliche Nachtrichten* for September 13th a notice concerning this month's *Berlinischen Monatsschift* that mentions *Mendelssohn's* answer to this same question. I have not yet seen this journal, otherwise I would have withheld the foregoing reflections, which I now set out in order to see to what extent two person's thoughts may coincidentally agree.

CHAPTER FOURTEEN – CONDORCET

The Spirit of the Enlightenment was preponderantly anti-clerical, rationalist, and progressivist. It was also hedonic. Ideals of sexual liberation – often, simply the practice without any particular ideals – accompanied ideals of cognitive and political liberation. Casanova is as central and characteristic a figure of eighteenth-century Europe as is Diderot or Montesquieu; all three are of course not average or typical, but super-abundant exemplars of patterns that were not uncommon. Many leading Enlightenment thinkers were sexual libertines; some – like La Mettrie – with theories to inform (or accommodate) lifestyle.

These thinkers were, of course, primarily men. Although the conceptions of the areas of life upon which the light of Enlightenment should shine were wide, they did not for the most part include the condition of women. Law, economic life, and education were to be made freer and more rational; development in the arts, the sciences, and technology was strongly promoted; and the study of human nature, and the realization of a social and political condition of broad equality, were pursued. It is unsurprising that many facets of life would inevitably be neglected, including aspects of personal and social reality where the beacon of progress might seem most naturally to appear. In fact, though, many of the eighteenth-century thinkers – by no means only Rousseau – viewed the female half of humanity as of lesser rational capacity than the male half, and as meant by nature essentially and primarily for domestic or sexual purposes.

The great exception to this pattern was Condorcet. Marie-Jean-Antoine-Nicolas Caritat, Marquis de Condorcet (1743-1794) is a figure of the later Enlightenment – he was just eight when the first volume of the *Encyclopédie* appeared, and eleven when Montesquieu died. A mathematician of talent and originality (like d'Alembert), Condorcet published an essay on the integral calculus and contributed significantly to the later volumes of the *Encyclopédie* (the 35th and last of which appeared in 1776). Condorcet developed social views that encompassed a theory of human history as a graduated progressive evolution toward a condition of enlightenment and equality, which Condorcet explicitly envisaged as including both sexes. He denounced what he saw as the condition of servitude and educational neglect in which women had hitherto mostly lived, and appears as an original early modern liberal and feminist. His private life paralleled his theoretical views. A strong supporter of the French Revolution, Condorcet fell a victim to the Terror, suffering the fate usual for the liberal moderate in revolutionary times.

Marie-Jean Antoine-Nicolas de Caritat, Marquis de Condorcet, *Sketch for a Historical Picture of The Progress of The Human Mind*

(Source: Antoine-Nicolas de Condorcet. *Sketch for a Historical Picture of the Progress of the Human Mind*. Trans. June Barraclough. Intr. Stuart Hampshire. London: Weidenfeld and Nicolson, 1955, 173, 176-179, 191-195.)

The future progress of the human mind

If man can, with almost complete assurance, predict phenomena when he knows their laws, and if, even when he does not, he can still, with great expectation of success, forecast the future on the basis of his experience of the past, why, then, should it be regarded as a fantastic undertaking to sketch, with some pretence to truth, the future destiny of man on the basis of his history? The sole foundation for belief in the natural sciences is this idea, that the general laws directing the phenomena of the universe, known or unknown, are necessary and constant. Why should this principle be any less true for the development of the intellectual and moral faculties of man than for the other operations of nature? Since beliefs founded on past experience of like conditions provide the only rule of conduct for the wisest of men, why should the philosopher be forbidden to base his conjectures on these same foundations, so long as he does not attribute to them a certainty superior to that warranted by the number, the constancy, and the accuracy of his observations?

....

The sugar industry, establishing itself throughout the immense continent of Africa, will destroy the shameful exploitation which has corrupted and depopulated that continent for the last two centuries.

Already in Great Britain, friends of humanity have set us an example; and if the Machiavellian government of that country has been restrained by public opinion from offering any opposition, what may we not expect of this same spirit, once the reform of a servile and venal constitution has led to a government worthy of a humane and generous nation? Will not France hasten to imitate such undertakings dictated by philanthropy and the true self-interest of Europe alike? Trading stations have been set up in the French islands, in Guiana and in some English possessions, and soon we shall see the downfall of the monopoly that the Dutch have sustained with so much treachery, persecution and crime. The nations of Europe will finally learn that monopolistic companies are nothing more than a tax imposed upon them in order to provide their governments with a new instrument of tyranny.

So the peoples of Europe, confining themselves to free trade, understanding their own rights too well to show contempt for those of other peoples, will respect this independence, which until now they have so insolently violated. Their settlements, no longer filled with government hirelings hastening, under the cloak of place or privilege, to amass treasure by brigandry and deceit, so as to be able to return to Europe and purchase titles and honour, will now be peopled with men of industrious habit, seeking in these propitious climates the wealth that eluded them at home. The love of freedom will retain them there, ambition will no longer recall them, and what have been no better than the counting-houses of brigands will become colonies of citizens propagating throughout Africa and Asia the principles and the practice of liberty, knowledge and reason, that they have brought from Europe. We shall see the monks who brought only shameful superstition to these peoples and aroused their antagonism by the threat of yet another tyranny, replaced by men occupied in propagating amongst them the truths that will promote their happiness and in teaching them about their interests and their rights. Zeal for the truth is also one of the passions, and it will turn its efforts to distant lands, once there are no longer at home any crass prejudices to combat, any shameful errors to dissipate.

These vast lands are inhabited partly by large tribes who need only assistance from us to become civilized, who wait only to find brothers amongst the European nations to become their friends and pupils; partly by races oppressed by sacred despots or dull-witted conquerors, and who for so many centuries have cried out to be liberated; partly by tribes living in a condition of almost total savagery in a climate whose harshness repels the sweet blessings of civilization and deters those who would teach them its benefits; and finally, by conquering hordes who know no other law but force, no other profession but piracy. The progress of these two last classes of people will be slower and stormier; and perhaps it will even be that, reduced in number as they are driven back by civilized nations, they will finally disappear imperceptibly before them or merge into them.

We shall point out how these events will be the inevitable result not merely of the progress of Europe but also of the freedom that the French and the North American Republics can, and in their own real interest should, grant to the trade of Africa and Asia; and how they must of necessity be born either of a new-found wisdom on the part of the European nations, or of their obstinate attachment to mercantilist prejudices.

We shall show that there is only one event, a new invasion of Asia by the Tartars, that could prevent this revolution, and that this event is now impossible. Meanwhile everything forecasts the imminent decadence of the great religions of the East, which in most countries have been made over to the people, and, not uncontaminated by the corruption of their ministers, are in some already regarded by the ruling classes as mere political inventions; in consequence of which they are now powerless to retain human reason in hopeless bondage, in eternal infancy.

The progress of these peoples is likely to be more rapid and certain than our own because they can receive from us everything that we have had to find out for ourselves, and in order to understand those simple truths and infallible methods which we have acquired only after long error, all that they need to do is to follow the expositions and proofs that appear in our speeches and writings. If the progress of the Greeks was lost to later nations, this was because of the absence of any form of communication between the different peoples, and for this we must blame the tyrannical domination of the Romans. But when mutual needs have brought all men together, and the great powers have established equality between societies as well as between individuals and have raised respect for the independence of weak states and sympathy for ignorance and misery to the rank of political principles, when maxims that favour action and energy have ousted those which would compress the province of human faculties, will it then be possible to fear that there are still places in the world inaccessible to enlightenment, or that despotism in its pride can raise barriers against truth that are insurmountable for long?

....

Until men progress in the practice as well as in the science of morality, it will be impossible for them to attain any insight into either the nature and development of the moral sentiments, the principles of morality, the natural motives that prompt their actions, or their own true interests either as individuals or as members of society. Is not a mistaken sense of interest the most common cause of actions contrary to the general welfare? Is not the violence of our passions often the result either of habits that we have adopted through miscalculation, or of our ignorance how to restrain them, tame them, deflect them, rule them?

Is not the habit of reflection upon conduct, of listening to the deliverances of reason and conscience upon it, of exercising those gentle feelings which identify our happiness with that of others, the necessary consequence of a well planned study of morality and of a greater equality in the conditions of the social pact? Will not the free man's sense of his own dignity and a system of education built upon a deeper knowledge of our moral constitution, render common to almost every man those principles of strict and unsullied justice, those habits of an active and enlightened benevolence, of a fine and generous sensibility which nature has implanted in the hearts of all and whose flowering waits only upon the favourable influences of enlightenment and freedom? Just as the mathematical and physical sciences tend to improve the arts that we use to satisfy our simplest needs, is it not also part of the necessary order of nature that the moral and political sciences should exercise a similar influence upon the motives that direct our feelings and our actions?

What are we to expect from the perfection of laws and public institutions, consequent upon the progress of those sciences, but the reconciliation, the identification of the interests of each with the interests of all? Has the social art any other aim save that of destroying their apparent opposition? Will not a country's constitution and laws accord best with the rights of reason and nature when the path of virtue is no longer arduous and when the temptations that lead men from it are few and feeble?

Is there any vicious habit, any practice contrary to good faith, any crime, whose origin and first cause cannot be traced back to the legislation, the institutions, the prejudices of the country wherein this habit, this practice, this crime can be observed? In short will not the general welfare that results from the progress of the useful arts once they are grounded on solid theory, or from the progress of legislation once it is rooted in the truths of political science, incline mankind to humanity, benevolence and justice? In other words, do not all these observations which I propose to develop further in my book, show that the moral goodness of man, the necessary consequence of his constitution, is capable of indefinite perfection like all his other faculties, and that nature has linked together in an unbreakable chain truth, happiness and virtue?

Among the causes of the progress of the human mind that are of the utmost importance to the general happiness, we must number the complete anni-hilation of the prejudices that have brought about an inequality of rights between the sexes, an inequality fatal even to the party in whose favour it works. It is vain for us to look for a justification of this principle in any differences of physical organi-zation, intellect or moral sensibility between men and women. This inequality has its origin solely in an abuse of strength, and all the later sophistical attempts that have been made to excuse it are vain.

We shall show how the abolition of customs authorized, laws dictated by this prejudice, would add to the happiness of family life, would encour-age the practice of the domestic virtues on which all other virtues are based, how it would favour the progress of education, and how, above all, it would bring about its wider diffusion; for not only would education be extended to women as well as to men, but it can only really be taken proper advantage of when it has the support and encouragement of the mothers of the family. Would not this belated trib-ute to equity and good sense, put an end to a prin-ciple only too fecund of injustice, cruelty and crime, by removing the dangerous conflict between the strongest and most irrepressible of all natural inclinations and man's duty or the interests of soci-ety? Would it not produce what has until now been no more than a dream, national manners of a mild-ness and purity, formed not by proud asceticism, not by hypocrisy, not by the fear of shame or reli-gious terrors but by freely contracted habits that are inspired by nature and acknowledged by rea-son?

Once people are enlightened they will know that they have the right to dispose of their own life and wealth as they choose; they will gradually learn to regard war as the most dreadful of scourges, the most terrible of crimes. The first wars to disappear will be those into which usurpers have forced their subjects in defence of their pretended hereditary rights.

Nations will learn that they cannot conquer other nations without losing their own liberty; that per-manent confederations are their only means of pre-serving their independence; and that they should seek not power but security. Gradually mercantile prejudices will fade away: and a false sense of com-mercial interest will lose the fearful power it once had of drenching the earth in blood and of ruining nations under pretext of enriching them. When at last the nations come to agree on the principles of politics and morality, when in their own better interests they invite foreigners to share equally in all the benefits men enjoy either through the boun-ty of nature or by their own industry, then all the causes that produce and perpetuate national ani-mosities and poison national relations will disap-pear one by one; and nothing will remain to encourage or even to arouse the fury of war.

Organizations more intelligently conceived than those projects of eternal peace which have filled the leisure and consoled the hearts of certain philoso-phers, will hasten the progress of the brotherhood of nations, and wars between countries will rank with assassinations as freakish atrocities, humiliat-ing and vile in the eyes of nature and staining with indelible opprobrium the country or the age whose annals record them.

Bibliography

Martin, Kingsley. *French Liberal Thought in the Eighteenth Century*. Rev. 2nd. ed. London: Turnstile Press, 1954.

Schapiro, J. Salwyn. *Condorcet and the Rise of Liberalism*. New York: Harcourt, Brace and Company, 1934.

CHAPTER FIFTEEN — VON HUMBOLDT

Because of historical patterns and developments over the past two hundred years it is common, and natural, to think of German and French – broadly, "continental" European – intellectual trends as contrasting sharply with those of the English-speaking world. Continental Europe, in terms of such archetypal structures, is a domain of polar extremes of political stance, from right to left, and of positions of high abstraction (and great obscurity) philosophically, almost all of them some kind or other of celebration of the Subject. Britain, and its overseas extensions in the New Worlds of North America and the south Pacific, by contrast are supposed to be the steady repository of empiricism and naturalism, a middle ground of at least relatively plain speech, liberal politics, and friendship – or at least non-hostility – to the natural sciences.

It bears reminder and reassertion, therefore, that such cultural and philosophical divisions as there have been, of which the English Channel is the symbolic boundary, were superimposed upon a much deeper and older commonality, in the Enlightenment, and to a very significant degree well beyond the Enlightenment into the nineteenth century. In the eighteenth century a common tide, and bond, of liberal naturalist progressivism united the leading thinkers of at any rate northern Europe. In fact the first voices of many "extra-continental" movements are to be found in France or Germany, not the British Isles. These include feminism, perfectionist liberalism, psycho-physiological mechanism, materialist social science, and universal citizen-democracy.

Our attention here is primarily on the second of the developments just named. Wilhelm von Humboldt (1767-1835) is the leading and the earliest articulator of what eventually becomes the "reform" or "welfare" or "perfectionist" liberal political philosophy and liberal philosophy of human nature, of major significance from the 1880s through to the present day. He shares much with Condorcet in this; and both are part of a broad cultural and intellectual movement of the late Enlightenment, centred in immediately pre-revolutionary France, then in the France of the revolutionary and Napoleonic period, which encompasses also Germany. Humboldt was a linguistic scholar and theorist, university reformer, and statesman; and elder brother of the scientist and geographer Alexander von Humboldt.

Wilhelm von Humboldt, *The Limits of State Action*

(Source: Wilhelm von Humboldt. *The Limits of State Action*. Edited with an introduction and notes by J.W.Burrow. Trans. J.W. Burrow (1969), based on Joseph Coulthand (1854). Cambridge: Cambridge University Press, 1969, 16-21, 71-81.)

CHAPTER II
Of the individual man, and the highest ends of his existence

The true end of Man, or that which is prescribed by the eternal and immutable dictates of reason, and not suggested by vague and transient desires, is the highest and most harmonious development of his powers to a complete and consistent whole. Freedom is the first and indispensable condition which the possibility of such a development presupposes; but there is besides another essential – intimately connected with freedom, it is true – a variety of situations. Even the most free and self-reliant of men is hindered in his development, when set in a monotonous situation. But as it is evident, on the one hand, that such a diversity is a constant result of freedom, and on the other hand, that there is a species of oppression which, without imposing restrictions on man himself, gives a peculiar impress of its own to surrounding circumstances; these two conditions, of freedom and variety of situation, may be regarded, in a certain sense, as one and the same. Still, it may contribute to clarity to point out the distinction between them.

Every human being, then, can act with only one dominant faculty at a time; or rather, our whole nature disposes us at any given time to some single form of spontaneous activity. It would therefore seem to follow from this, that man is inevitably destined to a partial cultivation, since he only enfeebles his energies by directing them to a multiplicity of objects. But man has it in his power to avoid this one-sidedness, by attempting to unite the distinct and generally separately exercised faculties of his nature, by bringing into spontaneous cooperation, at each period of his life, the dying sparks of one activity, and those which the future will kindle, and endeavouring to increase and diversify the powers with which he works, by harmoniously combining them, instead of looking for a mere variety of objects for their separate exercise. What is achieved, in the case of the individual, by the union of the past and future with the present, is produced in society by the mutual cooperation of its different members; for, in all the stages of his life, each individual can achieve only one of those perfections, which represent the possible features of human character. It is through a social union, therefore, based on the internal wants and capacities of its members, that each is enabled to participate in the rich collective resources of all the others. The experience of all, even the rudest, nations, furnishes us an example of a union formative of individual character, in the union of the sexes. And, although in this case the difference as well as the longing for union, appears more marked and striking, it is still no less active in other kinds of association where there is actually no difference of sex; it is only more difficult to discover in these, and may perhaps be more powerful for that very reason. If we were to follow out this idea, it might perhaps lead us to a clearer insight into those relations so much in vogue among the ancients, and more especially the Greeks, among whom we find them engaged in even by the legislators themselves: I mean those so frequently, but unworthily, given the name of ordinary love, and sometimes, but always erroneously, that of mere friendship. The effectiveness of all such relations as instruments of cultivation, entirely depends on the extent to which the members can succeed in combining their personal independence with the intimacy of the association; for whilst, without this intimacy, one individual cannot sufficiently possess, as it were, the nature of the others, independence is no less essential, in order that each, in being possessed, may be transformed in his own unique way. On the one hand, individual energy is essential to both parties and, on the other hand, a difference between them, neither so great as to prevent one from comprehending the other, nor so small as to exclude admiration for what the other possesses, and the desire to assimilate it into one's own character.

This individual vigour, then, and manifold diversity, combine themselves in originality; and hence, that on which the whole greatness of mankind ultimately depends – towards which every human being must ceaselessly direct his efforts, and of which especially those who wish to influence their fellow-men must never lose sight: individuality of energy and self-development. Just as this individuality springs naturally from freedom of action, and the greatest diversity in the agents, it tends in turn directly to produce them. Even inanimate nature, which, proceeding according to unchangeable laws, advances by regular steps, appears more individual to the man who has been developed in his individuality. He transports himself, as it were, into nature itself; and it is in the highest sense true that each man perceives the beauty and abundance of the outer world, in the same degree as he is conscious of them in his own soul. How much closer must this correspondence become between effect and cause – this reaction between internal feeling and outward perception – when man is not only passively open to external sensations and impressions, but is himself also an agent?

If we attempt to test these principles by a closer application of them to the nature of the individual man, we find that everything in the latter, reduces itself to the two elements of form and substance. The purest form beneath the most delicate veil, we call idea; the crudest substance, with the most imperfect form, we call sensuous perception. Form springs from the combinations of substance. The richer and more various the substance that is combined, the more sublime is the resulting form. A child of the gods is the offspring only of immortal parents: and as the blossom ripens into fruit, and from the seed of the fruit the new stalk shoots with newly clustering buds; so does the form become in turn the substance of a still more exquisite form. The intensity of power, moreover, increases in proportion to the greater variety and delicacy of the substance; since the internal cohesion increases with them. The substance seems as if blended in the form, and the form merged in the substance. Or, to speak without metaphor, the richer a man's feelings become in ideas, and his ideas in feelings, the more transcendent his nobility, for upon this constant intermingling of form and substance, or of diversity with the individual unity, depends the perfect fusion of the two natures which co-exist in man, and upon this, his greatness. But the intensity of the fusion depends upon the energy of the generating forces. The highest point of human existence is this flowering. In the vegetable world, the simple and less graceful form seems to prefigure the more perfect bloom and symmetry of the flower which it precedes, and into which it gradually expands. Everything hastens towards the moment of blossoming. What first springs from the seed is not nearly so attractive. The full thick trunk, the broad leaves rapidly detaching themselves from each other, seem to require some fuller development; as the eye glances up the ascending stem, it marks the grades of this development; more tender leaves seem longing to unite themselves, and draw closer and closer together, until the central calyx of the flower seems to satisfy this desire.[1] But destiny has not blessed the tribe of plants in this respect. The flower fades and dies, and the germ of the fruit reproduces the stem, as rude and unfinished as the former, to ascend slowly through the same stages of development as before. But when, in man, the blossom fades away, it is only to give place to another still more beautiful; and the charm of the most

beautiful is only hidden from our view in the endlessly receding vistas of an inscrutable eternity. Now, whatever man receives externally, is only like the seed. It is his own active energy alone that can turn the most promising seed into a full and precious blessing for himself. It is beneficial only to the extent that it is full of vital power and essentially individual. The highest ideal, therefore, of the co-existence of human beings, seems to me to consist in a union in which each strives to develop himself from his own inmost nature, and for his own sake. The requirements of our physical and moral being would, doubtless, bring men together into communities; and as the conflicts of warfare are more honourable than the fights of the arena, and the struggles of exasperated citizens more glorious than the hired efforts of mercenaries, so the exertions of such spontaneous agents succeed in exciting the highest energies.

And is it not exactly this which so inexpressibly captivates us in contemplating the age of Greece and Rome, and which in general captivates any age in contemplating a remoter one? Is it not that these men had harder struggles with fate to endure, and harder struggles with their fellow-men? that greater and more original energy and individuality constantly encountered each other, and created wonderful new forms of life? Every later epoch – and how rapidly must this decline now proceed! – is necessarily inferior in variety to that which it succeeded: in variety of nature – the vast forests have been cleared, the morasses dried up and so on; in variety of human life, by ever-increasing intercommunication and agglomeration.[2] This is one of the chief reasons why the idea of the new, the uncommon, the marvellous, is so much more rare, so that affright or astonishment are almost a disgrace, while the discovery of fresh and, till now, unknown expedients, and also all sudden, unpremeditated and urgent decisions are far less necessary. For, partly, the pressure of outward circumstances is less, while man is provided with more means for opposing them; partly, this resistance is no longer possible with the simple forces which nature gives to all alike for immediate use. Again, it is partly that a higher and more extended knowledge renders expedients less necessary, and the very increase of learning blunts the energy necessary to it. It is,

---

1   Goethe, *Über die Metamorphose der Pflanzen.*
2   Rousseau has also noticed this in his *Emile.* [*Emile*, bk. v.]

on the other hand, undeniable that, whereas physical variety has declined, it has been succeeded by an infinitely richer and more satisfying intellectual and moral variety, and that our superior refinement can recognize more delicate distinctions and gradations, and our cultivated and sensitive character, if not so strongly developed, as that of the ancients, can transfer them into the practical conduct of life – distinctions and gradations which might have escaped the notice of the sages of antiquity, or at least would have been discernible by them alone. To the human race as a whole, the same has happened as to the individual: the ruder features have faded away, the finer only have remained. And in view of this sacrifice of energy from generation to generation, we might regard it as a blessed dispensation if the whole species were as one man; or the living force of one age could be transmitted to the succeeding one, along with its books and inventions. But this is far from being the case. It is true that our refinement possesses a peculiar force of its own, perhaps even surpassing the former in strength, according to the measure of its refinement; but the question is whether the earlier development, through the more robust and vigorous stages, must not always be the prior transition. Still, it is certain that the sensuous element in our nature, as it is the first germ, is also the most vivid expression of the spiritual.

Whilst this is not the place, however, to enter on a discussion of this point, we are justified in concluding, from the other considerations we have urged, that we must at least preserve, with the most eager concern, all the energy and individuality we may yet possess, and cherish anything that can in any way promote them.

I therefore deduce, as the natural inference from what has been argued, *that reason cannot desire for man any other condition than that in which each individual not only enjoys the most absolute freedom of developing himself by his own energies, in his perfect individuality, but in which external nature itself is left unfashioned by any human agency, but only receives the impress given to it by each individual by himself and of his own free will, according to the measure of his wants and instincts, and restricted only by the limits of his powers and his rights.*

From this principle it seems to me, that reason must never retract anything except what is absolutely necessary. It must therefore be the basis of every political system, and must especially constitute the starting-point of the inquiry which at present claims our attention.

CHAPTER VIII
Amelioration of morals
....

Still, to remain faithful to the principle which has guided us so far, and first of all to regard any means the State may use in the light of man's true and unmistakable interests – it becomes necessary to look into the influence of sensualism on human life, culture, activity, and happiness – an inquiry which, in that it attempts to show the inner significance of human activity and enjoyment, will at the same time illustrate more graphically the harmful or beneficial consequences which flow in general from restrictions imposed on freedom. Only after doing this can we consider in all its implications the State's competence to act positively on morals, and so arrive at the solution of this part of the general question we have proposed.

The impression, inclinations, and passions which have their immediate source in the senses, are those which first and most violently show themselves in human nature. Wherever, before the refining influences of culture have given a new direction to the soul's energies, these sensuous impressions, etc., are not apparent, all energy is dead, and nothing good or great can flourish. They constitute the original source of all spontaneous activity, and all living warmth in the soul. They bring life and vigour to the soul: when not satisfied, they make it active, ingenious in the invention of schemes, and courageous in their execution; when satisfied, they promote an easy and unhindered play of ideas. In general, they animate and quicken all concepts and images with a greater and more varied activity, suggest new views, point out hitherto unnoticed aspects, and, according to the manner in which they are satisfied, they react on the physical organization, which in its turn acts upon the soul in a manner which we only observe from the results.

The influence, however, of these impressions and inclinations differs, not only in its intensity, but in the manner of its operation. This is, to a certain extent, owing to their strength or weakness; but it is also partly to be attributed to their degree of affinity with the spiritual element in human nature, or from the ease or difficulty of raising them from animal gratifications to human pleasures. Thus, for instance, the eye imparts to the substance of its impressions that outline of form which is so full of enjoyment and suggestive of ideas; while the ear lends to sound the proportionate succession of tones in the order of time. Much that is new and highly interesting could perhaps be said of the diverse nature of these impressions and their manner of operation, if this were the proper place for such a topic, but I will only pause to notice their different uses in the culture of the soul.

The eye supplies the reason, so to speak, with a more prepared substance; and our inner nature, in association with the other things with which it is always connected in our imagination, is presented to us in a definite form and in a particular situation. If we conceive of the ear merely as an organ of sense, and in so far as it does not receive and communicate words, it conveys far less distinctness of impression. And it is for this reason that Kant gives the preference to the plastic arts when compared with music. But he notices very rightly that this presupposes as a standard a culture in which the arts minister, and I would add, minister directly, to the spirit,

The question, however, presents itself whether this is the correct standard. Energy appears to me to be the first and unique virtue of mankind. Whatever raises his energies to a higher pitch is worth more than what merely puts materials into our hands for its exercise. Now, as it is characteristic of man's nature to perceive only one thing at a time, it will be most affected by what presents only one object to him at a time, and in which the relation in which the parts stand to each other being a relation of sequence, each is given a certain ranking by virtue of what has preceded it, and in turn influences what follows. Now all this is true of music. The sequence of time, moreover, is its peculiar and essential property; this is all that is specified in it. The series which it presents hardly impels us to any definite sensation. It gives us a theme, to which we can supply an endless number of texts; and what the soul of the hearer contributes, in so far as he is, in general, in a receptive mood, springs up freely and naturally from his own resources, and so is more warmly embraced than what is received passively, which is more often observed than truly grasped. As it is not my province to examine the nature and properties of music, I will not consider its other striking characteristics, such as that it evokes tones from natural objects, and therein keeps closer to nature than painting, sculpture, or poetry. I only wished, in introducing it, to illustrate more clearly the varied character of sensuous impressions.

But the manner of influence just described, is not peculiar to music alone. Kant observes it to be possible with shifting patterns of colour, and it characterizes still more remarkably the impressions we receive from the sense of touch. Even in taste it is unmistakable. In taste, also, there are different gradations of satisfaction, which, as it were, yearn towards a resolution, and when it is achieved, vanish in a series of diminishing reverberations. This influence may be least noticeable, perhaps, in the sense of smell. Now, as it is the course of sensation, its degree, its increase and decrease, its pure and perfect harmony, which attract attention more than the stuff of sensation itself, we forget that the nature of the sensations mainly determines the progression, and still more, the harmony, of the sequence; and further, as sensitive man, like the image of blossoming spring, is the most interesting of all spectacles, so also, in the fine arts, it is this visible image of his sensations which man especially looks for. Painting and sculpture make this their province. The eye of Guido Reni's Madonna is not limited to a single, fleeting glance. The tense and straining muscles of the Borghese Gladiator foretell the blow he is about deal. In a still higher degree poetry makes use of the same means. And, to make my idea clearer, without wishing to give special attention to the comparative excellence of the fine arts, I would observe that they exercise their influence in two ways, and while these are shared by each, we find them combined in very different manner. They immediately convey ideas, or they excite sensations; thus they bring harmony to the soul, and, if the expression is not too affected, enrich or exalt its powers. Now the more one of these sources of influence borrows aid from the other, the more it weakens its own peculiar force. Poetry unites both in the highest degree, and it is therefore, in this respect, the most perfect of all the fine arts; but when we regard it in another light, it is also the most weak and imperfect. While it represents its objects less vividly than painting and sculpture, it does not speak so forcibly to the senses as song and music. But, not to speak of that many-sidedness which so especially characterises poetry, we are ready to overlook this imperfection when we see that it is nearest to the true inner nature of man, since it clothes not only thought, but sensation, with the most delicate veil.

The stimulation of sensuous impressions (for I only refer to the arts by way of illustrating these) acts in different ways; partly as they are more or less harmoniously related to each other, partly as the elements of stuff of which the impressions are composed fasten more or less strongly on the soul. Thus, the human voice, of equal melodiousness and quality, affects us more powerfully than a lifeless instrument. For nothing is ever so near to us as the personal, physical feeling; and where this feeling is called into play, the effect produced is the greatest. But here, as always, the disproportionate power of the substance suppresses, as it were, the delicacy of the form, and there must always exist a just relation between them. Wherever there is such a disproportion, the proper equilibrium can be restored by strengthening one or weakening the other. But it is always wrong to cultivate anything by weakening, unless the energy reduced is not natural, but artificial; only when this is the case should any limitation be imposed. It is better that it should destroy itself than slowly die away. But I cannot dwell longer on this subject. I hope I have sufficiently explained my idea, although I would like to take the opportunity of acknowledging the difficulties in this inquiry; on the one hand the interest of the subject, and the impossibility of borrowing the necessary conclusions from other writers, for I know of none who proceed from precisely my present point of view, led me to enlarge on this theme; on the other, the reflection that these considerations do not strictly belong to this subject, but are only subsidiary, recalled me to my proper task. I must make the same excuse for what follows.

Although it is impossible to isolate the subject completely, I have hitherto tried to speak only of sensuous impressions as such. But the sensual and spiritual are linked together by a mysterious bond, sensed by our emotions, though hidden from our eyes. To this double nature of the visible and invisible world – to the profound longing for the latter, coupled with the feeling of the sweet necessity of the former, we owe all sound and logical systems of philosophy, truly based on the immutable principles of our nature, just as from the same source arise the most senseless enthusiasms. A constant endeavour to combine these two elements, so that each may deprive the other as little as possible has always seemed to me the true end of wisdom. The aesthetic feeling, in virtue of which the sensuous is to us a veil of the spiritual, and the spiritual the living principle of the world of sense, is everywhere unmistakable. The continual contemplation of this physiognomy of nature forms the true man. For nothing exercises such a widely diffused influence on the whole character, as the expression of the spiritual in the sensuous – of the sublime, the simple, the beautiful in all the works of nature and products of art which surround us. Here, too, we find the difference apparent between the sense impressions which stimulate human energy and those which do not. If the ultimate object of all our mortal striving is solely to discover, nourish, and recreate what truly exists in ourselves and others, although in its original form for ever invisible – if it is the intuitive anticipation of this which endears and consecrates each of its symbols in our eyes, then the nearer we approach this original essence in contemplating the image of its endlessly animating energy. We commune with it in a language which is indeed difficult, and often misinterpreted, but which often startles us with the surest premonitions of truth, whilst the form and representation, so to speak, of that energy are further from the truth.

This is the soil, moreover, on which the beautiful flourishes, and even more especially the sublime, which brings us still nearer to the divine. The need for some purer satisfaction, without any specific goal, and not to be grasped intellectually, apprises man of his origin in the invisible and his kinship with it; and the feeling of his utter inadequateness to the transcendental object, blends together, in the most human and divine way, infinite greatness with the most devoted humility. Were it not for his feeling for the beautiful, man would cease to love things for their own sake; were it not for the sublime, he would lose that sense of dutiful submission which disdains rewards and ignores unworthy fear. The study of the beautiful bestows taste; that of the sublime (if it also may be studied and the feeling and representation of it is not the fruit of genius alone) brings a balanced greatness. But taste alone, which must always rest on greatness as its basis (since only the great needs moderation, and only the powerful, composure), blends all the tones of a perfectly adjusted being into exquisite harmony. It induces in all our impressions, and impulses, even those which are purely spiritual, something measured, composed, concentrated into one focal point. Where taste is lacking, sensual desire is rude and unrestrained; and although without it, scientific inquiries may be both acute and profound, there is no refinement, no polish, nothing fruitful in their application. In general, where there is no taste, the greatest depth of thought and the treasures of wisdom are barren and lifeless, and even the sublime strength of the moral will is rough and without a warm beneficence.

To inquire and to create – these are the centres around which all human pursuits more or less directly revolve. Before inquiry can get to the root of things, or to the limits of reason, it presupposes, in addition to profundity, a rich diversity and an inner warmth of soul – the harmonious exertion of all the human faculties combined. It is the analytical philosopher alone, perhaps, who is able to arrive at his results through the calm, but cold processes of reason. But real depth of thought and a mind which has found means to cultivate all its powers to an equal degree of perfection, are essential to discover the links which unite synthetic propositions. Thus Kant, who, it may be truly said, has never been surpassed in profundity, will often be charged with enthusiasm when treating of morals or aesthetics, and has indeed been so accused; but while I am willing to confess that there are passages (as, for example, his interpretation of the prismatic colours) which, though rare, appear to indicate something of this nature, I am only led to deplore my own want of intellectual depth. To follow these ideas out, would naturally lead us to the difficult but interesting inquiry into the essential difference between the metaphysician and the poet. And were it not that a thorough re-investigation of this might perhaps invalidate my previous conclusions, I would limit my definition of the difference to this, that the philosopher concerns himself with perceptions alone, and the poet, on the contrary, with sensations; while both require the same degree and cultivation of mental power. But to establish this would lead me too far astray from

my immediate subject and I trust I have shown already, by my previous arguments, that, even to form the calmest thinker, the pleasures of sense and fancy must have often played around the soul. But to pass from transcendental to psychological inquiries (where man as he appears is the object of our studies) would not the man to explore most deeply this most richly creative species, and represent it most truly and vividly, be the one whose own sensibility is most comprehensive in its sympathies. Hence the man whose sensibility is thus cultivated and developed, displays the full beauty of his character when he enters into practical life when, externally and internally, he creatively enriches what he receives. The analogy between the laws of plastic nature and those of intellectual creation, has been already noticed by a mind[3] of singular power of penetration, and established by proofs. But perhaps his exposition would have been still more interesting, and psychology enriched with the results of a more extended knowledge, if, instead of inquiring into the inscrutable laws of biological development, the process of intellectual creation had been shown to be, as it were, a more refined offspring of the physical.

To speak first of the moral life, which seems to be the special province of cold reason; it is only the idea of the sublime which enables us to obey absolute and unconditional laws, both humanly, through the medium of feeling, and with godlike disinterestedness, through the utter absence of all ulterior reference to happiness or misfortune. The feeling of the inadequacy of human strength to the full performance of the moral law, the profound consciousness that the most virtuous man is he who feels most conscious of how unattainably high the law is exalted above him, inspires awe – a sensation which seems to be no more shrouded in a corporeal veil than is necessary not to dazzle mortal eyes by the full splendour. Now, when the moral law obliges us to regard every man as an end in himself, it becomes fused with that feeling for the beautiful which loves to animate the merest clay, so that even in it, it may rejoice in an individual existence, and which receives and embraces man all the more completely and beautifully in that it is independent of intellectual concepts and is not therefore limited to considering the few isolated charac-

---

3   F.v Dalberg. *Vom Bilden und Erfinden.*

teristics which are all that intellectual concepts can comprehend.

The union with the feeling for the beautiful seems as if it would impair the purity of the moral will, and it might, and indeed would, have this effect, if this feeling were to become the sole motive to morality. But it will only claim the duty of discovering those more varied applications of the moral law which would otherwise escape the cold, and hence in such cases, coarser processes of reason; and since we are not forbidden to receive happiness in such intimate connection with virtue, but only to barter virtue for this happiness, it will also enjoy the privilege of bestowing on human nature its sweetest feelings. In general, the more I reflect on this subject, the less does this difference to which I refer appear to be either subtle or fanciful. However eagerly man may strive to grasp at enjoyment – however he may try to represent to himself a constant union between happiness and virtue, even under the most unfavourable circumstances, his soul still remains alive to the grandeur of the moral law. He cannot screen himself from the influence and authority of this imposing grandeur over his actions, and it is only from being penetrated with a sense of it, that he acts without reference to enjoyment; for he never loses the consciousness that no misfortune whatever would compel him to adopt another course of behaviour.

It is, however, true that the soul only acquires this strength in a way similar to that which I described earlier – only by a mighty internal pressure, and a complex external struggle. But all strength springs from man's sensuous nature; and however seemingly remote, still depends on it. Now the man who ceaselessly tries to heighten his powers, and to rejuvenate them by frequent enjoyment; who often calls in his strength of character to aid him in asserting his independence of sensualism, while he tries to combine this independence with the most exquisite susceptibility; whose honest and profound intelligence tirelessly searches after the truth; whose just and delicate feeling for the beautiful notices every charming form; whose impulse to assimilate his external perceptions, and to make them bear new fruit, to infuse his own individuality into all forms of beauty and to shape it creatively anew – such a man may cherish the consoling consciousness that he is on the right path to approach the ideal which the boldest flight of fancy has ventured to indicate.

I have in this brief sketch tried to show how intimately sensualism, with all its beneficial consequences, is interwoven with the whole tissue of human life and pursuits. Although such a topic is in itself somewhat foreign to a political essay, it was appropriate and even necessary in the order of ideas adopted in this inquiry; and in these remarks on sensualism, I intended to win for it greater freedom and esteem. Still, I must not forget that sensualism is also the immediate source of innumerable physical and moral evils. Even morally speaking, it is only beneficial in a proper relationship with the exercise of the mental faculties; it easily acquires a harmful preponderance. When once the equilibrium is destroyed, human pleasure becomes degraded to mere animal gratification, and taste disappears, or becomes distorted into unnatural directions. At the same time I would make the reservation with regard to this last expression, and chiefly with reference to certain one-sided opinions, that we are not to condemn anything as unnatural which does not exactly fulfil this or that purpose of nature, but only whatever frustrates its general ultimate design with regard to man. Now this is, that his nature should always be developing itself to higher degrees of perfection, and hence, especially, that his powers of thought and sensibility should always be indissolubly linked in the proper proportions. But again, lack of relation may arise between the manner in which a man develops and manifests his powers, and the means of activity and enjoyment afforded by his position; and this is a fresh source of evil. Now, according to our former principles, the State may not attempt to act upon the situation of the citizen with any positive ends in view. Therefore, the citizen's situation would not have stamped upon it such a specific and prescribed form, and this greater freedom would ensure that it would be chiefly shaped by the citizen's own ways of thinking and acting, which would diminish the disproportion between self-cultivation and the means available to it. Still, the fact that, even so, the original danger would remain – a danger which is far from being unimportant – might suggest the necessity of checking and opposing the corruption of morals by laws and State institutions.

But even if such laws and institutions were effectual, the harm they did would be proportionate to their effectiveness. A State, in which the citizens were compelled or moved by such means to obey even the best of laws, might be a tranquil, peaceable, prosperous State; but it would always seem to me a multitude of well-cared-for slaves, rather than a nation of free and independent men, with no restraint save such as was required to prevent any infringement of rights. There are, doubtless, many methods of producing given actions and sentiments; but none of these lead to true moral perfection. Sensual impulses to certain actions, or the continuing necessity of refraining from them, gradually come to create a habit; through the force of habit the satisfaction which was at first connected with these impulses alone, is transferred to the action itself; the inclination, which was at first only suppressed by necessity, becomes wholly stifled; and thus man may be led to keep his actions within the limits of virtue, and to a certain extent to entertain virtuous sentiments. But his spiritual energy is not heightened by such a process, nor are his views of his vocation and his own worth made clearer, nor does his will gain greater power to conquer his rebellious desires; and hence, he does not advance a single step towards true, intrinsic perfection. Those, therefore, who look to the cultivation of man rather than to external ends will never make use of such inadequate means. For, setting aside the fact that coercion and guidance can never succeed in producing virtue, they manifestly tend to weaken energy; and what is outward morality without true moral strength and virtue? Moreover, however great an evil immorality may be, we must not forget that it is not without its beneficial consequences. It is only through extremes that men can arrive at the middle path of wisdom and virtue. Extremes, like large masses shining far off, must operate at a distance. In order that blood may be supplied to the narrowest veins in the body, there must be a considerable amount in the larger ones. To wish to disturb the order of nature in these respects, is to acquiesce in a moral, in order to prevent a physical evil.

Moreover, I think we err in supposing that the danger of immorality is either so great or so urgent; and while much that I have said tends more or less to establish this, the following conclusions may serve to give it additional confirmation –

1. Man is naturally more disposed to beneficent than selfish actions. This we learn even from the history of savages. The domestic virtues have something in them so inviting, and the public virtues of the citizen something so grand and inspiring, that even the man who has only just escaped being corrupted, is seldom able to resist their charm.

2. Freedom heightens energy, and, as the natural consequence, promotes all kinds of liberality. Coercion stifles energy, and engenders all selfish desires, and all the mean artifices of weakness. Coercion may prevent many transgressions; but it robs even actions which are legal of a part of their beauty. Freedom may lead to many transgressions, but it lends even to vices a less ignoble form.

3. The man who is left to himself arrives with greater difficulty at just principles, but they show themselves ineffaceably in his actions. The man who is led by some preconcerted design, receives such principles with greater facility; but they still give way before his natural energies, however weakened they may be.

4. All political arrangements, in that they have to bring a variety of widely discordant interests into unity and harmony, necessarily produce various clashes. From these clashes spring a disproportion between men's desires and their powers; and from these, transgressions. The more active the State is, the greater is the number of these. If it were possible to make an accurate calculation of the evils which police regulations occasion, and of those which they prevent, the number of the former would, in all cases, exceed that of the latter.

5. How far the strictest search into crimes actually committed, the infliction of just, carefully calculated, but irrevocable punishment, and the consequent rarity of impunity, are really practicable, has never yet been tried.

I have now sufficiently shown, according to my views, how questionable is every effort of the State to oppose or even to prevent any dissoluteness of morals (in so far as it does not imply injury to individual rights); how few the beneficial results to morality to be expected from such attempts; and how the exercise of such an influence on the character of a nation, is not even necessary for the preservation of security.

If now, in addition to this, we bring forward the principles already developed, which disapprove of all State agency directed to positive aims, and which apply here with particular force, since it is precisely the moral man who feels every restriction most deeply; reflecting, further, that if there is one aspect of development more than any other which owes its highest beauty to freedom, it is precisely the cultivation of character and morals; then the justice of the following principle will be sufficiently obvious: *that the State must wholly refrain from every attempt to operate directly or indirectly on the morals and character of the nation, except in so far as such a policy may become inevitable as a natural consequence of its other absolutely necessary measures; and that everything calculated to promote such a design, and particularly all special supervision of education, religion, sumptuary laws, etc., lies wholly outside the limits of its legitimate activity.*

Bibliography

Krieger, L. *The German Idea of Freedom*. Chicago: University of Chicago Press, 1957.

Sweet, P.R. *Wilhelm von Humboldt: a biography*. 2 vols. Columbus: Ohio State University Press, 1978-80.

Vogel, U. "Liberty is beautiful: von Humboldt's gift to liberalism." *History of Political Thought* 3 (1982), 77-101.

CHAPTER SIXTEEN — JOHN STUART MILL

John Stuart Mill (1806-1873) was a polymath of very wide talents and interests. Subjected to a famous educational experiment in childhood, Mill was given instruction at home by his father, James Mill, a leading social progressive, utilitarian, and economist of his time. Taught Greek at three, Latin and arithmetic at eight, logic at twelve, and political economy at thirteen – it was fortunate that the boy was of prodigious natural ability – Mill was denied association with other children his own age, and given minimal contact with literature or the emotional sphere of life. From fourteen the educational system his father had devised expanded to history, law, and philosophy. It will occasion little surprise that Mill had a sort of nervous breakdown in early adulthood, which took him a few years to recover from.

But recover he did. In 1823 he became an employee of the East India Co., a private corporation with a Crown charter to govern most of British India, where his father also was employed. Mill remained with the East India Co. until it was dissolved and the British government assumed direct control of the British possessions in India in 1858. Mill served one term as a member of Parliament. He agreed to stand for election on the condition that he would do no electoral campaigning. This secured him victory in 1865, but not in the subsequent election.

Mill worked in virtually every area of philosophy, most originally and creatively in philosophy of science and ethics. He was a highly prolific writer of primary academic work in philosophy and economics, and of essays, tracts, letters, and editorial contributions in journals of his time. Mill was a "public intellectual" and a social activist, in the forefront of efforts to implement utilitarian and ameliorist innovations. He was arrested at the age of eighteen for distributing birth control literature to the London poor. A strong feminist, Mill campaigned for female suffrage in Parliament and throughout his career. His essay *The Subjection of Women* is arguably the most important piece of feminist writing between Wollstonecraft and De Beauvoir.

Mill is primarily represented here as a perfectionist liberal. Drawing on the ideas of Wilhelm von Humboldt, as he acknowledges, Mill formulated a particularly clear and vivid account of the liberal philosophy of human nature in his classic works *On Liberty* and *Utilitarianism*, from which the following selections are taken.

J.S. Mill, *On Liberty*

(Source: John Stuart Mill. *On Liberty*. London: Watts & Co., 1929, 11-13, 67-87. *On Liberty* was originally published in 1859; the last (fourth) edition published in Mill's lifetime appeared in 1869.)

Chapter I

The object of this essay is to assert one very simple principle, as entitled to govern absolutely the dealings of society with the individual in the way of compulsion and control, whether the means used be physical force in the form of legal penalties or the moral coercion of public opinion. That principle is that the sole end for which mankind are warranted, individually or collectively, in interfering with the liberty of action of any of their number is self-protection. That the only purpose for which power can be rightfully exercised over any member of a civilized community, against his will, is to prevent harm to others. His own good, either physical or moral, is not a sufficient warrant. He cannot rightfully be compelled to do or forbear because it will be better for him to do so, because it will make him happier, because, in the opinions of others, to do so would be wise or even right. These are good reasons for remonstrating with him, or reasoning with him, or persuading him, or entreating him, but not for compelling him or visiting him with any evil in case he do otherwise. To justify that, the conduct from which it is desired to deter him must be calculated to produce evil to someone else. The only part of the conduct of anyone for which he is amenable to society is that which concerns others. In the part which merely concerns himself, his independence is, of right, absolute. Over himself, over his own body and mind, the individual is sovereign.

It is, perhaps, hardly necessary to say that this doctrine is meant to apply only to human beings in the maturity of their faculties. We are not speaking of children or of young persons below the age which the law may fix as that of manhood or womanhood. Those who are still in a state to require being taken care of by others must be protected against their own actions as well as against external injury. For the same reason we may leave out of consideration those backward states of society in which the race itself may be considered as in its nonage. The early difficulties in the way of spontaneous progress are so great that there is seldom any choice of means for overcoming them; and a ruler full of the spirit of improvement is warranted in the use of any expedients that will attain an end perhaps unattainable. Despotism is a legitimate mode of government in dealing with barbarians, provided the end be their improvement and the means justified by actually effecting that end. Liberty, as a principle, has no application to any state of things anterior to the time when mankind have become capable of being improved by free and equal discussion. Until then, there is nothing for them but implicit obedience to an Akbar or a Charlemagne if they are so fortunate as to find one. But as soon as mankind have attained the capacity of being guided to their own improvement by conviction or persuasion (a period long since reached in all nations with whom we need here concern ourselves), compulsion, either in the direct form or in that of pains and penalties for noncompliance, is no longer admissible as a means to their own good, and justifiable only for the security of others.

....

Chapter III
OF INDIVIDUALITY, AS ONE OF THE ELEMENTS OF WELL-BEING

....

.... No one pretends that actions should be as free as opinions. On the contrary, even opinions lose their immunity when the circumstances in which they are expressed are such as to constitute their expression a positive instigation to some mischievous act. An opinion that corn dealers are starvers of the poor, or that private property is robbery, ought to be unmolested when simply circulated through the press, but may justly incur punishment when delivered orally to an excited mob assembled before the house of a corn dealer, or when handed about among the same mob in the form of a placard. Acts, of whatever kind, which without justifiable cause do harm to others may be, and in the more important cases absolutely require to be, controlled by the unfavourable sentiments, and, when needful, by the active interference of mankind. The liberty of the individual must be thus far limited; he must not make himself a nuisance to other people. But if he refrains from molesting others in what concerns them, and merely acts according to his own inclination and judgment in things which concern himself, the same reasons which show that opinion should be free prove also that he should be allowed, without molestation, to carry his opinions into practice at his own cost. That mankind are not infallible; that their truths, for the most part, are only half-truths; that unity of opinion, unless resulting from the fullest and freest comparison of opposite opinions, is not desirable, and diversity not an evil, but a good, until mankind are much more capable than at present of recognizing all sides of the truth, are principles applicable to men's modes of action not less than to their opinions. As it is useful that while mankind are imperfect there should be different opinions, so it is that there should be different experiments of living; that free scope should be given to varieties of character, short of injury to others; and that the worth of different modes of life should be proved practically, when anyone thinks fit to try them. It is desirable, in short, that in things which do not primarily concern others individuality should assert itself. Where not the person's own character but the traditions or customs of other people are the rule of conduct, there is wanting one of the principal ingredients of human happiness, and quite the chief ingredient of individual and social progress.

In maintaining this principle, the greatest difficulty to be encountered does not lie in the appreciation of means toward an acknowledged end, but in the indifference of persons in general to the end itself. If it were felt that the free development of individuality is one of the leading essentials of well-being; that it is not only a co-ordinate element with all that is designated by the terms civilization, instruction, education, culture, but itself a necessary part and condition of all those things, there would be no danger that liberty should be undervalued, and the adjustment of the boundaries between it and social control would present no extraordinary difficulty. But the evil is that individual spontaneity is hardly recognized by the common modes of thinking as having any intrinsic worth, or deserving any regard on its own account. The majority, being satisfied with the ways of mankind as they now are (for it is they who make them what they are), cannot comprehend why those ways should not be good enough for everybody; and what is more, spontaneity forms no part of the ideal of the majority of moral and social reformers, but is rather looked on with jealousy, as a troublesome and perhaps rebellious obstruction to the general acceptance of what these reformers in their own judgement, think would be best for mankind. Few persons, out of Germany, even comprehend the meaning of the doctrine which Wilhelm von Humboldt, so eminent both as a savant and as a politician, made the text of a treatise – that "the end of man, or that which is prescribed by the eternal or immutable dictates of reason, and not suggested by vague and transient desires, is the highest and most harmonious development of his powers to a complete and consistent whole"; that, therefore, the object "toward which

every human being must ceaselessly direct his efforts, and on which especially those who design to influence their fellow men must ever keep their eyes, is the individuality of power and development"; that for this there are two requisites, "freedom, and variety of situations"; and that from the union of these arise "individual vigour and manifold diversity," which combine themselves in "originality."[1]

Little, however, as people are accustomed to a doctrine like that of von Humboldt, and surprising as it may be to them to find so high a value attached to individuality, the question, one must nevertheless think, can only be one of degree. No one's idea of excellence in conduct is that people should do absolutely nothing but copy one another. No one would assert that people ought not to put into their mode of life, and into the conduct of their concerns, any impress whatever of their own judgement or of their own individual character. On the other hand, it would be absurd to pretend that people ought to live as if nothing whatever had been known in the world before they came into it; as if experience had as yet done nothing toward showing that one mode of existence, or of conduct, is preferable to another. Nobody denies that people should be so taught and trained in youth as to know and benefit by the ascertained results of human experience. But it is the privilege and proper condition of a human being, arrived at the maturity of his faculties, to use and interpret experience in his own way. It is for him to find out what part of recorded experience is properly applicable to his own circumstances and character. The traditions and customs of other people are, to a certain extent, evidence of what their experience has taught *them* – presumptive evidence, and as such, have a claim to his deference: but, in the first place, their experience may be too narrow, or they may have not interpreted it rightly. Secondly, their interpretation of experience may be correct, but unsuitable to him. Customs are made for customary circumstances and customary characters; and his circumstances or his character may be uncustomary. Thirdly, though the customs be both good as customs and suitable to him, yet to conform to custom merely as custom does not educate or develop in him any of the qualities which are the distinctive

1 *The Sphere and Duties of Government*, from the German of Baron Wilhelm von Humboldt, pp. 11-13.

endowment of a human being. The human faculties of perception, judgment, discriminative feeling, mental activity, and even moral preference are exercised only in making a choice. He gains no practice either in discerning or in desiring what is best. The mental and moral, like the muscular, powers are improved only by being used. The faculties are called into no exercise by doing a thing merely because others do it, no more than by believing a thing merely because others believe it. If the grounds of an opinion are not conclusive to the person's own reason, his reason cannot be strengthened, but is likely to be weakened, by his adopting it: and if the inducements to an act are not such as are consentaneous to his own feelings and character (where affection, or the rights of others are not concerned), it is so much done toward rendering his feelings and character inert and torpid instead of active and energetic.

He who lets the world, or his own portion of it, choose his plan of life for him has no need of any other faculty than the ape-like one of imitation. He who chooses his plan for himself employs all his faculties. He must use observation to see, reasoning and judgment to foresee, activity to gather materials for decision, discrimination to decide, and when he has decided, firmness and self-control to hold to his deliberate decision. And these qualities he requires and exercises exactly in proportion as the part of his conduct which he determines according to his own judgment and feelings is a large one. It is possible that he might be guided in some good path, and kept out of harm's way, without any of these things. But what will be his comparative worth as a human being? It really is of importance, not only what men do, but also what manner of men they are that do it. Among the works of man which human life is rightly employed in perfecting and beautifying, the first in importance surely is man himself. Supposing it were possible to get houses built, corn grown, battles fought, causes tried, and even churches erected and prayers said by machinery – by automatons in human form – it would be a considerable loss to exchange for these automatons even the men and women who at present inhabit the more civilized parts of the world, and who assuredly are but starved specimens of what nature can and will produce. Human nature is not a machine to be built after a model and set to do exactly the work prescribed for it, but a tree, which requires to grow and develop itself on all sides, according to the tendency of the inward forces which make it a living thing.

It will probably be conceded that it is desirable people should exercise their understandings, and that an intelligent following of custom, or even occasionally an intelligent deviation from custom, is better than a blind and simply mechanical adhesion to it. To a certain extent it is admitted that our understanding should be our own; but there is not the same willingness to admit that our desires and impulses should be our own likewise, or that to possess impulses of our own, and of any strength, is anything but a peril and a snare. Yet desires and impulses are as much a part of a perfect human being as beliefs and restraints; and strong impulses are only perilous when not properly balanced, when one set of aims and inclinations is developed into strength, while others, which ought to coexist with them, remain weak and inactive. It is not because men's desires are strong that they act ill; it is because their consciences are weak. There is no natural connection between strong impulses and a weak conscience. The natural connection is the other way. To say that one person's desires and feelings are stronger and more various than those of another is merely to say that he has more of the raw material of human nature and is therefore capable, perhaps of more evil, but certainly of more good. Strong impulses are but another name for energy. Energy may be turned to bad uses; but more good may always be made of an energetic nature than of an indolent and impassive one. Those who have most natural feeling are always those whose cultivated feelings may be made the strongest. The same strong susceptibilities which make the personal impulses vivid and powerful are also the source from whence are generated the most passionate love of virtue and the sternest self-control. It is through the cultivation of these that society both does it duty and protects its interests, not by rejecting the stuff of which heroes are made, because it knows not how to make them. A person whose desires and impulses are his own – are the expression of his own nature, as it has been developed and modified by his own culture – is said to have a character. One whose desires and impulses are not his own has no character, no more than a steam engine has a character. If, in addition to being his own, his impulses are strong and are under the government of a strong will, he has an energetic character. Whoever thinks that individuality of desires and impulses should not be encouraged to unfold itself must maintain that society has no need of strong natures – is not the better for containing many persons who have much character – and that a high general average of energy is not desirable.

In some early states of society, these forces might be, and were, too much ahead of the power which society then possessed of disciplining and controlling them. There has been a time when the element of spontaneity and individuality was in excess, and the social principle had a hard struggle with it. The difficulty then was to induce men of strong bodies or minds to pay obedience to any rules which required them to control their impulses. To overcome this difficulty, law and discipline, like the Popes struggling against the Emperors, asserted a power over the whole man, claiming to control all his life in order to control his character – which society has not found any other sufficient means of binding. But society has now fairly got the better of individuality; and the danger which threatens human nature is not the excess, but the deficiency, of personal impulses and preferences. Things are vastly changed since the passions of those who were strong by station or by personal endowment were in a state of habitual rebellion against laws and ordinances, and required to be rigorously chained up to enable the persons within their reach to enjoy any particle of security. In our times, from the highest class of society down to the lowest, everyone lives as under the eye of a hostile and dreaded censorship. Not only in what concerns others, but in what concerns only themselves, the individual or the family do not ask themselves, what do I prefer? or, what would suit my character and disposition? or, what would allow the best and highest in me to have fair play and enable it to grow and thrive? They ask themselves, what is suitable to my position? what is usually done by persons of my station and pecuniary circumstances? or (worse still) what is usually done by persons of a station and circumstances superior to mine? I do not mean that they choose what is customary in preference to what suits their own inclination. It does not occur to them to have any inclination except for what is customary. Thus the mind itself is bowed to the yoke: even in what people do for pleasure, confor-mity is the first thing thought of; they like in crowds; they exercise choice only among things commonly done; peculiarity of taste, eccentricity of conduct are shunned equally with crimes, until by dint of not following their own nature they have no nature to follow: their human capacities are withered and starved; they become incapable of any strong wishes or native pleasures, and are generally without either opinions or feelings of home growth, or properly their own. Now is this, or is it not, the desirable condition of human nature?

It is so, on the Calvinistic theory. According to that, the one great offense of man is self-will. All the good of which humanity is capable is comprised in obedience. You have no choice; thus you must do, and no otherwise: "Whatever is not a duty is a sin." Human nature being radically corrupt, there is no redemption for anyone until human nature is killed within him. To one holding this theory of life, crushing out any of the human faculties, capacities, and susceptibilities is no evil: man needs no capacity but that of surrendering himself to the will of God; and if he uses any of his faculties for any other purpose but to do that supposed will more effectually, he is better without them. This is the theory of Calvinism; and it is held, in a mitigated form, by many who do not consider themselves Calvinists; the mitigation consisting in giving a less ascetic interpretation to the alleged will of God, asserting it to be his will that mankind should gratify some of their inclinations, of course not in the manner they themselves prefer, but in the way of obedience, that is, in a way prescribed to them by authority, and, therefore, by the necessary condition of the case, the same for all.

In some such insidious form there is at present a strong tendency to this narrow theory of life, and to the pinched and hidebound type of human character which it patronizes. Many persons, no doubt, sincerely think that human beings thus cramped and dwarfed are as their Maker designed them to be, just as many have thought that trees are a much finer thing when clipped into pollards, or cut into figures of animals, than as nature made them. But if it be any part of religion to believe that man was made by a good Being, it is more consistent with that faith to believe that this Being gave all human faculties that they might be cultivated and unfolded, not rooted out and consumed, and that he takes delight in every nearer approach made by his creatures to the ideal conception embodied in them, every increase in any of their capabilities of comprehension, of action, or of enjoyment. There is a different type of human excellence from the Calvinistic: a conception of humanity as having its nature bestowed on it for other purposes than merely to be abnegated. "Pagan self-assertion" is one of the elements of human worth, as well as "Christian self-denial."[2] There is a Greek ideal of self-development, which the Platonic and Christian ideal of self-government blends with, but does not supersede. It may be better to be a John Knox than an Alcibiades, but it is better to be a Pericles than either; nor would a Pericles, if we had one in these days, be without anything good which belonged to John Knox.

It is not by wearing down into uniformity all that is individual in themselves, but by cultivating it and calling it forth, within the limits imposed by the rights and interests of others, that human beings become a noble and beautiful object of contemplation; and as the works partake the character of those who do them, by the same process human life also becomes rich, diversified, and animating, furnishing more abundant aliment to high thoughts and elevating feelings, and strengthening the tie which binds every individual to the race, by making the race infinitely better worth belonging to. In proportion to the development of his individuality, each person becomes more valuable to himself, and is, therefore, capable of being more valuable to others. There is a greater fullness of life about his own existence, and when there is more life in the units there is more in the mass which is composed of them. As much compression as is necessary to prevent the stronger specimens of human nature from encroaching on the rights of others cannot be dispensed with; but for this there is ample compensation even in the point of view of human development. The means of development which the individual loses by being prevented from gratifying his inclinations to the injury of others are chiefly obtained at the expense of the development of other people. And even to himself there is a full equivalent in the better development of the social part of his nature, rendered possible by the restraint put upon the selfish part. To be held to rigid rules of justice for the sake of others develops

the feelings and capacities which have the good of others for their object. But to be restrained in things not affecting their good, by their mere displeasure, develops nothing valuable except such force of character as may unfold itself in resisting the restraint. If acquiesced in, it dulls and blunts the whole nature. To give any fair play to the nature of each, it is essential that different persons should be allowed to lead different lives. In proportion as this latitude has been exercised in any age has that age been noteworthy to posterity. Even despotism does not produce its worst effects so long as individuality exists under it; and whatever crushes individuality is despotism, by whatever name it may be called and whether it professes to be enforcing the will of God or the injunctions of men.

Having said that the individuality is the same thing with development, and that it is only the cultivation of individuality which produces, or can produce, well-developed human beings, I might here close the argument; for what more or better can be said of any condition of human affairs than that it brings human beings themselves nearer to the best thing they can be? Or what worse can be said of any obstruction to good than that it prevents this? Doubtless, however, these considerations will not suffice to convince those who most need convincing; and it is necessary further to show that these developed human beings are of some use to the undeveloped – to point out to those who do not desire liberty, and would not avail themselves of it, that they may be in some intelligible manner rewarded for allowing other people to make use of it without hindrance.

In the first place, then, I would suggest that they might possibly learn something from them. It will not be denied by anybody that originality is a valuable element in human affairs. There is always need of persons not only to discover new truths and point out when what were once truths are true no longer, but also to commence new practices and set the example of more enlightened conduct and better taste and sense in human life. This cannot well be gainsaid by anybody who does not believe that the world has already attained perfection in all its ways and practices. But these few are the salt of the earth; without them, human life would become a stagnant pool. Not only is it they who introduce

2   Sterling's *Essays*.

good things which did not before exist; it is they who keep the life in those which already exist. If there were nothing new to be done, would human intellect cease to be necessary? Would it be a reason why those who do the old things should forget why they are done, and do them like cattle, not like human beings? There is only too great a tendency in the best beliefs and practices to degenerate into the mechanical; and unless there were a succession of persons whose ever-recurring originality prevents the grounds of those beliefs and practices from becoming merely traditional, such dead matter would not resist the smallest shock from anything really alive, and there would be no reason why civilization should not die out, as in the Byzantine Empire. Persons of genius, it is true, are, and are always likely to be, a small minority; but in order to have them, it is necessary to preserve the soil in which they grow. Genius can only breathe freely in an *atmosphere* of freedom. Persons of genius are, *ex vi termini*,[3] more individual than any other people – less capable, consequently, of fitting themselves, without hurtful compression, into any of the small number of molds which society provides in order to save its members the trouble of forming their own character. If from timidity they consent to be forced into one of these molds, and to let all that part of themselves which cannot expand under the pressure remain unexpanded, society will be little the better for their genius. If they are of a strong character and break their fetters, they become a mark for the society which has not succeeded in reducing them to commonplace, to point out with solemn warnings as "wild," "erratic," and the like – much as if one should complain of the Niagara river for not flowing smoothly between its banks like a Dutch canal.

I insist thus emphatically on the importance of genius and the necessity of allowing it to unfold itself freely both in thought and in practice, being well aware that no one will deny the position in theory, but knowing also that almost everyone, in reality, is totally indifferent to it. People think a genius a fine thing if it enables a man to write an exciting poem or paint a picture. But in its true sense, that of originality in thought and action, though no one says that it is not a thing to be admired, nearly all, at heart, think that they can do very well without

it. Unhappily this is too natural to be wondered at. Originality is the one thing which unoriginal minds cannot feel the use of. They cannot see what it is to do for them: how should they? If they could see what it is to do for them, it would not be originality. The first service which originality has to render them is that of opening their eyes: which being once fully done, they would have a chance of being themselves original. Meanwhile, recollecting that nothing was ever done which someone was not the first to do, and that all good things which exist are the fruits of originality, let them be modest enough to believe that there is something still left for it to accomplish, and assure themselves that they are more in need of originality, the less they are conscious of the want.

In sober truth, whatever homage may be professed, or even paid, to real or supposed mental superiority, the general tendency of things throughout the world is to render mediocrity the ascendant power among mankind. In ancient history, in the Middle Ages, and in a diminishing degree through the long transition from feudality to the present time, the individual was a power in himself; and if he had either great talents or a high social position, he was a considerable power. At present individuals are lost in a crowd. In politics it is almost a triviality to say that public opinion now rules the world. The only power deserving the name is that of masses, and of governments while they make themselves the organ of the tendencies and instincts of masses. This is as true in the moral and social relations of private life as in public transactions. Those whose opinions go by the name of public opinion are not always the same sort of public: in America, they are the whole white population; in England, chiefly the middle class. But they are always a mass, that is to say, collective mediocrity. And what is a still greater novelty, the mass do not now take their opinions from dignitaries in Church or State, from ostensible leaders, or from books. Their thinking is done for them by men much like themselves, addressing them or speaking in their name, on the spur of the moment, through the newspapers. I am not complaining of all this. I do not assert that anything better is compatible, as a general rule, with the present low state of the human mind. But that does not hinder the government of mediocrity from

---

3   By definition.

being mediocre government. No government by a democracy or a numerous aristocracy, either in its political acts or in the opinions, qualities, and tone of mind which it fosters, ever did or could rise above mediocrity except in so far as the sovereign Many have let themselves be guided (which in their best times they always have done) by the counsels and influence of a more highly gifted and instructed *one* or *few*. The initiation of all wise or noble things comes and must come from individuals; generally at first from some one individual. The honor and glory of the average man is that he is capable of following that initiative; that he can respond internally to wise and noble things, and be led to them with eyes open. I am not countenancing the sort of "hero-worship" which applauds the strong man of genius for forcibly seizing on the government of the world and making it do his bidding in spite of itself. All he can claim is freedom to point out the way. The power of compelling others into it is not only inconsistent with the freedom and development of all the rest, but corrupting to the strong man himself. It does seem, however, that when the opinions of masses of merely average men are everywhere become or becoming the dominant power, the counterpoise and corrective to that tendency would be the more and more pronounced individuality of those who stand on the higher eminences of thought. It is in these circumstances most especially that exceptional individuals, instead of being deterred, should be encouraged in acting differently from the mass. In other times there was no advantage in their doing so, unless they acted not only differently but better. In this age, the mere example of nonconformity, the mere refusal to bend the knee to custom, is itself a service. Precisely because the tyranny of opinion is such as to make eccentricity a reproach, it is desirable, in order to break through that tyranny, that people should be eccentric. Eccentricity has always abounded when and where strength of character has abounded; and the amount of eccentricity in a society has generally been proportional to the amount of genius, mental vigor, and moral courage it contained. That so few now dare to be eccentric marks the chief danger of the time.

I have said that it is important to give the freest scope possible to uncustomary things, in order that it may in time appear which of these are fit to be converted into customs. But independence of action and disregard of custom are not solely deserving of encouragement for the chance they afford that better modes of action, and customs more worthy of general adoption, may be struck out; nor is it only persons of decided mental superiority who have a just claim to carry on their lives in their own way. There is no reason that all human existence should be constructed on some one or some small number of patterns. If a person possesses any tolerable amount of common sense and experience, his own mode of laying out his existence is the best, not because it is the best in itself, but because it is his own mode. Humans beings are not like sheep; and even sheep are not undistinguishably alike. A man cannot get a coat or a pair of boots to fit him unless they are either made to his measure or he has a whole warehouseful to choose from; and is it easier to fit him with a life than with a coat, or are human beings more like one another in their whole physical and spiritual conformation than in the shape of their feet? If it were only that people have diversities of taste, that is reason enough for not attempting to shape them all after one model. But different persons also require different conditions for their spiritual development; and can no more exist healthily in the same moral than all the variety of plants can in the same physical, atmosphere and climate. The same things which are helps to one person toward the cultivation of his higher nature are hindrances to another. The same mode of life is a healthy excitement to one, keeping all his faculties of action and enjoyment in their best order, while to another it is a distracting burden which suspends or crushes all internal life. Such are the differences among human beings in their sources of pleasure, their susceptibilities of pain, and the operation on them of different physical and moral agencies that, unless there is a corresponding diversity in their modes of life, they neither obtain their fair share of happiness, nor grow up to the mental, moral, and aesthetic stature of which their nature is capable. Why then should tolerance, as far as the public sentiment is concerned, extend only to tastes and modes of public life which extort acquiescence by the multitude of their adherents? Nowhere (except in some monastic institutions) is diversity of taste entirely unrecognized; a person may, without blame, either like or dislike rowing, or smoking, or music, or athletic exercises, or chess, or cards, or study, because both those who like each of these things and those who dislike them are too numerous to be put down. But the man, and still more the woman, who can be accused either of doing "what nobody does," or of not doing "what everybody does," is the subject of as much depreciatory remark as if he or she had committed some grave moral delinquency. Persons require to possess a title, or some other badge of rank, or of the consideration of people of rank, to be able to indulge somewhat in the luxury of doing as they like without detriment to their estimation. To indulge somewhat, I repeat: for whoever allow themselves much of that indulgence incur the risk of something worse than disparaging speeches – they are in peril of a commission *de lunatico* and of having their property taken from them and given to their relations.[4]

There is one characteristic of the present direction of public opinion peculiarly calculated to make it intolerant of any marked demonstrations of individuality. The general average of mankind are not only moderate in intellect, but also moderate in inclinations; they have no tastes or wishes strong enough to incline them to do anything unusual, and they consequently do not understand those who have, and class all such with the wild and intemperate whom they are accustomed to look down upon. Now, in addition to this fact which is general, we have only to suppose that a strong movement has set in toward the improvement of morals, and it is evident what we have to expect. In these days such a movement has set in; much has actually been effected in the way of increased regularity of conduct and discouragement of excesses; and there is a philanthropic spirit abroad for the exercise of which there is no more inviting field than the moral and prudential improvement of our fellow creatures. These tendencies of the times cause the public to be more disposed than at most former periods to prescribe general rules of conduct and endeavour to make everyone conform to the approved standard. And that standard, express or tacit, is to desire nothing strongly. Its ideal of character is to be without any marked character – to maim by compression, like a Chinese lady's foot, every part of human nature which stands out prominently and tends to make the person markedly dissimilar in outline to commonplace humanity.

As is usually the case with ideals which exclude one-half of what is desirable, the present standard of approbation produces only an inferior imitation of the other half. Instead of great energies guided by vigorous reason and strong feelings strongly controlled by a conscientious will, its result is weak feelings and weak energies, which therefore can be kept in outward conformity to rule without any strength either of will or of reason. Already energetic characters on any large scale are becoming merely traditional. There is now scarcely any outlet for energy in this country except business. The energy expended in this may still be regarded as considerable. What little is left from that employment is expended on some hobby, which may be a useful, even a philanthropic, hobby, but is always some one thing, and generally a thing of small dimensions. The greatness of England is now all collective; individually small, we only appear capable of anything great by our habit of combining; and with this our moral and religious philanthropists are perfectly contented. But it was men of another stamp than this that made England what it

---

4   There is something both contemptible and frightful in the sort of evidence on which, of late years, any person can be judicially declared unfit for the management of his affairs; and after his death, his disposal of his property can be set aside if there is enough of it to pay the expenses of litigation – which are charged on the property itself. All the minute details of his daily life are pried into, and whatever is found which, seen through the medium of the perceiving and describing faculties of the lowest of the low, bears an appearance unlike absolute commonplace, is laid before the jury as evidence of insanity, and often with success; the jurors being little, if at all, less vulgar and ignorant than the witnesses, while the judges, with that extraordinary want of knowledge of human nature and life which continually astonishes us in English lawyers, often help to mislead them. These trials speak volumes as to the state of feeling and opinion among the vulgar with regard to human liberty. So far from setting any value on individuality – so far from respecting the right of each individual to act, in things indifferent, as seems good to his own judgement and inclinations, judges and juries cannot even conceive that a person in a state of sanity can desire such freedom. In former days, when it was proposed to burn atheists, charitable people used to suggest putting them in a madhouse instead; it would be nothing surprising nowadays were we to see this done, and the doers applauding themselves because, instead of persecuting for religion, they had adopted so humane and Christian a mode of treating these unfortunates, not without a silent satisfaction at their having thereby obtained their deserts.

has been; and men of another stamp will be need-ed to prevent its decline.

The despotism of custom is everywhere the stand-ing hindrance to human advancement, being in unceasing antagonism to that disposition to aim at something better than customary, which is called, according to circumstances, the spirit of liberty, or that of progress or improvement. The spirit of improvement is not always a spirit of liberty, for it may aim at forcing improvements on an unwilling people; and the spirit of liberty, in so far as it resists such attempts, may ally itself locally and tem-porarily with the opponents of improvement; but the only unfailing and permanent source of improvement is liberty, since by it there are as many possible independent centers of improvement as there are individuals. The progressive principle, however, in either shape, whether as the love of lib-erty or of improvement, is antagonistic to the sway of custom, involving at least emancipation from that yoke; and the contest between the two consti-tutes the chief interest of the history of mankind. The greater part of the world has, properly speak-ing, no history, because the despotism of Custom is complete....

.....

J.S. Mill, *Utilitarianism*

(Source: John Stuart Mill. *Utilitarianism*. London: J. M. Dent, n.d. [original edition 1863], 15-19.)

.... When, however, it is thus positively asserted to be impossible that human life should be happy, the assertion, if not something like a verbal quibble, is at least an exaggeration. If by happiness be meant a continuity of highly pleasurable excitement, it is evident enough that this is impossible. A state of exalted pleasure lasts only moments or in some cases, and with some intermissions, hours or days, and is the occasional brilliant flash of enjoyment, not its permanent and steady flame. Of this the philosophers who taught that happiness is the end of life were as fully aware as those who taunt them. The happiness which they meant was not a life of rapture, but moments of such, in an existence made up of few and transitory pains, many and various pleasures, with a decided predominance of the active over the passive, and having as the founda-tion of the whole not to expect more from life than

it is capable of bestowing. A life thus composed, to those who have been fortunate enough to obtain it, has always appeared worthy of the name of happi-ness. And such an existence is even now the lot of many during some considerable portion of their lives. The present wretched education and wretched social arrangements are the only real hin-drance to its being attainable by almost all.

The objectors perhaps may doubt whether human beings, if taught to consider happiness as the end of life, would be satisfied with such a mod-erate share of it. But great numbers of mankind have been satisfied with much less. The main con-stituents of a satisfied life appear to be two, either of which by itself is often found sufficient for the purpose: tranquillity and excitement. With much tranquillity, many find that they can be content with very little pleasure; with much excitement, many can reconcile themselves to a considerable quantity of pain. There is assuredly no inherent impossibility of enabling even the mass of mankind to unite both, since the two are so far from being incompatible that they are in natural alliance, the prolongation of either being a preparation for, and exciting a wish for, the other. It is only those in whom indolence amounts to a vice that do not desire excitement after an interval of repose; it is only those in whom the need of excitement is a dis-ease that feel the tranquillity which follows excite-ment dull and insipid, instead of pleasurable in direct proportion to the excitement which preceded it. When people who are tolerably fortunate in their outward lot do not find in life sufficient enjoyment to make it valuable to them, the cause generally is caring for nobody but themselves. To those who have neither public nor private affections, the excitements of life are much curtailed, and in any case dwindle in value as the time approaches when all selfish interests must be terminated by death; while those who leave after them objects of person-al affection, and especially those who have also cul-tivated a fellow-feeling with the collective interests of mankind, retain as lively an interest in life on the eve of death as in the vigor of youth and health. Next to selfishness, the principal cause which makes life unsatisfactory is want of mental cultiva-tion. A cultivated mind – I do not mean that of a philosopher, but any mind to which the fountains of knowledge have been opened, and which has been taught, in any tolerable degree, to exercise its faculties – finds sources of inexhaustible interest in all that surrounds it: in the objects of nature, the achievements of art, the imaginations of poetry, the incidents of history, the ways of mankind, past and present, and their prospects in the future. It is possible, indeed, to become indifferent to all this, and that too without having exhausted a thousandth part of it, but only when one has had from the beginning no moral or human interest in these things and has sought in them only the gratification of curiosity.

Now there is absolutely no reason in the nature of things why an amount of mental culture sufficient to give an intelligent interest in these objects of contemplation should not be the inheritance of everyone born in a civilized country. As little is there an inherent necessity that any human being should be a selfish egotist, devoid of every feeling or care but those which center in his own miserable individuality. Something far superior to this is sufficiently common even now, to give ample earnest of what the human species may be made. Genuine private affections and a sincere interest in the public good are possible, though in unequal degrees, to every rightly brought up human being. In a world in which there is so much to interest, so much to enjoy, and so much also to correct and improve, everyone who has this moderate amount of moral and intellectual requisites is capable of an existence which may be called enviable; and unless such a person, through bad laws or subjection to the will of others, is denied the liberty to use the sources of happiness within his reach, he will not fail to find this enviable existence, if he escapes the positive evils of life, the great sources of physical and mental suffering – such as indigence, disease, and the unkindness, worthlessness, or premature loss of objects of affection. The main stress of the problem lies, therefore, in the contest with these calamities from which it is a rare good fortune entirely to escape; which, as things now are, cannot be obviated, and often cannot be in any material degree mitigated. Yet no one whose opinion deserves a moment's consideration can doubt that most of the great positive evils of the world are in themselves removable, and will, if human affairs continue to improve, be in the end reduced within narrow limits. Poverty, in any sense implying suffering, may be completely extinguished by the wisdom of society combined with the good sense and providence of individuals. Even that most intractable of enemies, disease, may be indefinitely reduced in dimensions by good physical and moral education and proper control of noxious influences, while the progress of science holds out a promise for the future of still more direct conquests over this detestable foe. And every advance in that direction relieves us from some, not only of the chances which cut short our own lives, but, what concerns us still more, which deprive us of those in whom out happiness is wrapt up. As for vicissitudes of fortune and other disappointments connected with worldly circumstances, these are principally the effect of gross imprudence, of ill-regulated desires, or of bad or imperfect social institutions. All the grand sources, in short, of human suffering are in a great degree, many of them almost entirely, conquerable by human care and effort; and though their removal is grievously slow – though a long succession of generations will perish in the breach before the conquest is completed, and this world becomes all that, if will and knowledge were not wanting, it might easily be made – yet every mind sufficiently intelligent and generous to bear a part, however small and inconspicuous, in the endeavor will draw a noble enjoyment from the contest itself, which he would not for any bribe in the form of selfish indulgence consent to be without.

Bibliography

Britton, Karl. *John Stuart Mill*. Melbourne, London, and Baltimore: Penguin Books, 1953.

Donner, Wendy. *The Liberal Self: John Stuart Mill's Moral and Political Philosophy*. Ithaca, N.Y.: Cornell University Press, 1991.

McCloskey, H.J. *John Stuart Mill: A Critical Study*. London: Macmillan, 1971.

Skorupski, John. *John Stuart Mill*. London and New York: Routledge, 1989.

Spitz, David, ed. *John Stuart Mill: On Liberty*. New York and London: W.W. Norton and Company, 1975.

Ten, C. L. *Mill on Liberty*. Oxford: Oxford University Press, 1980.

Thomas, William. *Mill*. Oxford and New York: Oxford University Press, 1985.

CHAPTER SEVENTEEN — L.T. HOBHOUSE

L.T. (Leonard Trelawney) Hobhouse (1864-1929) was a journalist, journal editor, and trade unionist in the earlier part of his career, then an academic for the later – he was professor of sociology at the University of London from 1907 until his death. He wrote several books on a diversity of subjects (ethics and epistemology, as well as sociological studies, theoretical and practical). He is a leading figure, and a foremost public advocate, of the second great phase of liberalism, the "reform" or "welfare" or "perfectionist" liberalism developed in the later stages of John Stuart Mill's work and, more fully and (perhaps) coherently, in the thinking and writings of T.H. Green and other reformers within the British Liberal Party in and after the 1880s. Hobhouse's little book *Liberalism* (1911), from which the following selection is drawn, is possibly the most eloquent articulation of reform liberalism – the liberalism of Lloyd George's policies and Roosevelt's New Deal – ever penned. Hobhouse gave greater attention to liberal ideals of personal development, and to the roles of education and social mutuality, than most later political programs did.

L.T. Hobhouse, *Liberalism*

(Source: L.T. Hobhouse. *Liberalism*. London: Thornton Butterworth Limited, 1911, 110-154.)

The foundation of liberty on this side, then, is the conception of thought as a growth dependent on spiritual laws, flourishing in the movement of ideas as guided by experience, reflection and feeling, corrupted by the intrusion of material considerations, slain by the guillotine of finality. The same conception is broadened out to cover the whole idea of personality. Social well-being cannot be incompatible with individual well-being. But individual well-being has as its foundation the responsible life of the rational creature. Manhood, and Mill would emphatically add womanhood too, rests on the spontaneous development of faculty. To find vent for the capacities of feeling, of emotion, of thought, of action, is to find oneself. The result is no anarchy. The self so found has as the pivot of its life the power of control. To introduce some unity into life, some harmony into thought, action and feeling, is its central achievement, and to realize its relation to others and guide its own life thereby, its noblest rule. But the essential of control is that it should be self-control. Compulsion may be necessary for the purposes of external order, but it adds nothing to the inward life that is the true being of man. It even threatens it with loss of authority and infringes the sphere of its responsibility. It is a means and not an end, and a means that readily becomes a danger to ends that are very vital. Under self-guidance individuals will diverge widely, and some of their eccentricities will be futile, others wasteful, others even painful and abhorrent to witness. But, upon the whole, it is good that they should differ. Individuality is an element of well-being, and that not only because it is the necessary consequence of self-government, but because, after all allowances for waste, the common life is fuller and richer for the multiplicity of types that it includes, and that go to enlarge the area of collective experience. The larger wrong done by the repression of women is not the loss to women themselves who constitute one half of the community, but the impoverishment of the community as a whole, the loss of all the elements in the common stock which the free play of the woman's mind would contribute.

Similar principles underlie Mill's treatment of representative government. If the adult citizen, male or female, has a right to vote, it is not so much as a means to the enforcement of his claims upon society, but rather as a means of enforcing his personal responsibility for the actions of the community. The problem of character is the determining issue in the question of government. If men could be spoon-fed with happiness, a benevolent despotism would be the ideal system. If they are to take a part in working out their own salvation, they must be summoned to their share in the task of directing the common life. Carrying this principle further, Mill turned the edge of the common objection to the extension of the suffrage based on the ignorance and the irresponsibility of the voters. To learn anything men must practise. They must be trusted with more responsibility if they are to acquire the sense of responsibility. There were dangers in the process, but there were greater dangers and there were fewer elements of hope as long as the mass of the population was left outside the circle of civic rights and duties. The greatest danger that Mill saw in democracy was that of the tyranny of the majority. He emphasized, perhaps more than any Liberal teacher before him, the difference between the desire of the majority and the good of the community. He recognized that the different rights for which the Liberal was wont to plead might turn out in practice hard to reconcile with one another, that if personal liberty were fundamental it might only be imperilled by a so-called political liberty which would give to the majority unlimited powers of coercion. He was, therefore, for many years anxiously concerned with the means of securing a fair hearing and fair representation to minorities, and as a pioneer of the movement for Proportional Representation he sought to make Parliament the reflection not of a portion of the people, however preponderant numerically, but of the whole.

On the economic side of social life Mill recognized in principle the necessity of controlling contract where the parties were not on equal terms, but his insistence on personal responsibility made him chary in extending the principle to grown-up persons, and his especial attachment to the cause of feminine emancipation led him to resist the tide of feeling which was, in fact, securing the first elements of emancipation for the woman worker. He trusted at the outset of his career to the elevation of the standard of comfort as the best means of improving the position of the wage-earner, and in this elevation he regarded the limitation of the family as an essential condition. As he advanced in life, however, he became more and more dissatisfied with the whole structure of a system which left the mass of the population in the position of wage-earners, while the minority lived on rents, profits, and the interest on invested capital. He came to look forward to a co-operative organization of society in which a man would learn to "dig and weave for his country," as he now is prepared to fight for it, and in which the surplus products of industry would be distributed among the producers. In middle life voluntary co-operation appeared to him the best means to this end, but towards the close he recognized that his change of views was such as, on the whole, to rank him with the Socialists, and the brief exposition of the Socialist ideal given in his Autobiography remains perhaps the best summary statement of Liberal Socialism that we possess.

VI
THE HEART OF LIBERALISM

The teaching of Mill brings us close to the heart of Liberalism. We learn from him, in the first place, that liberty is no mere formula of law, or of the restriction of law. There may be a tyranny of custom, a tyranny of opinion, even a tyranny of circumstance, as real as any tyranny of government and more pervasive. Nor does liberty rest on the self-assertion of the individual. There is scope abundant for Liberalism and illiberalism in personal conduct. Nor is liberty opposed to discipline, to organization, to strenuous conviction as to what is true and just. Nor is it to be identified with tolerance of opposed opinions. The Liberal does not meet opinions which he conceives to be false with toleration, as though they did not matter. He meets them with justice, and exacts for them a fair hearing as though they mattered just as much as his own. He is always ready to put his own convictions to the proof, not because he doubts them, but because he believes in them. For, both as to that which he holds for true and as to that which he holds for false, he believes that one final test applies. Let error have free play, and one of two things will happen. Either as it develops, as its implications and consequences become clear, some elements of truth will appear within it. They will separate themselves out; they will go to enrich the stock of human ideas; they will add something to the truth which he himself mistakenly took as final; they will serve to explain the root of the error; for error itself is generally a truth misconceived, and it is only when it is explained that it is finally and satisfactorily confuted. Or, in the alternative, no element of truth will appear. In that case the more fully the error is understood, the more patiently it is followed up in all the windings of its implications and consequences, the more thoroughly will it refute itself. The cancerous growth cannot be extirpated by the knife. The root is always left, and it is only the evolution of the self-protecting anti-toxin that works the final cure. Exactly parallel is the logic of truth. The more the truth is developed in all its implications, the greater is the opportunity of detecting any element of error that it may contain; and, conversely, if no error appears, the more completely does it establish itself as the whole truth and nothing but the truth. Liberalism applies the wisdom of Gamaliel in no spirit of indifference, but in the full conviction of the potency of truth. If this thing be of man, i.e. if it is not rooted in actual verity, it will come to nought. If it be of God, let us take care that we be not found fighting against God.

Divergences of opinion, of character, of conduct are not unimportant matters. They may be most serious matters, and no one is called on in the name of Liberalism to overlook their seriousness. There are, for example, certain disqualifications inherent in the profession of certain opinions. It is not illiberal to recognize such disqualifications. It is not illiberal for a Protestant in choosing a tutor for his son to reject a conscientious Roman Catholic who avows that all his teaching is centred on the doctrine of his Church. It would be illiberal to reject the same man for the specific purpose of teaching arithmetic, if he avowed that he had no intention of using his position for the purpose of religious propagandism. For the former purpose the divergence of religious opinion is an inherent disqualification. It negates the object propounded, which is the general education of the boy on lines in which the father believes. For the latter purpose the opinion is no disqualification. The devout Catholic accepts the multiplication table, and can impart his knowledge without reference to the infallibility of the Pope. To refuse to employ him is to impose an extraneous penalty on his convictions. It is not illiberal for an editor to decline the services of a member of the opposite party as a leader writer, or even as a political reviewer or in any capacity in which his opinions would affect his work. It is illiberal to reject him as a compositor or as a clerk, or

in any capacity in which his opinions would not affect his work for the paper. It is not illiberal to refuse a position of trust to the man whose record shows that he is likely to abuse such a trust. It is illiberal – and this the "moralist" has yet to learn – to punish a man who has done a wrong in one relation by excluding him from the performance of useful social functions for which he is perfectly fitted, by which he could at once serve society and reestablish his own self-respect. There may, however, yet come a time when Liberalism, already recognized as a duty in religion and in politics, will take its true place at the centre of our ethical conceptions, and will be seen to have its application not only to him whom we conceive to be the teacher of false opinions, but to the man whom we hold a sinner.

The ground of Liberalism so understood is certainly not the view that a man's personal opinions are socially indifferent, nor that his personal morality matters nothing to others. So far as Mill rested his case on the distinction between selfregarding actions and actions that affect others, he was still dominated by the older individualism. We should frankly recognize that there is no side of a man's life which is unimportant to society, for whatever he is, does, or thinks may affect his own well-being, which is and ought to be matter of common concern, and may also directly or indirectly affect the thought, action, and character of those with whom he comes in contact. The underlying principle may be put in two ways. In the first place, the man is much more than his opinions and his actions. Carlyle and Sterling did not differ "except in opinion." To most of us that is just what difference means. Carlyle was aware that there was something much deeper, something that opinion just crassly formulates, and for the most part formulates inadequately, that is the real man. The real man is something more than is ever adequately expressed in terms which his fellows can understand; and just as his essential humanity lies deeper than all distinctions of rank, and class, and colour, and even, though in a different sense, of sex, so also it goes far below those comparatively external events which make one man figure as a saint and another as a criminal. This sense of ultimate oneness is the real meaning of equality, as it is the foundation of social solidarity and the bond which, if genuinely experienced, resists the disruptive force of all conflict, intellectual, religious, and ethical.

But, further, while personal opinions and social institutions are like crystallized results, achievements that have been won by certain definite processes of individual or collective effort, human personality is that within which lives and grows, which can be destroyed but cannot be made, which cannot be taken to pieces and repaired, but can be placed under conditions in which it will flourish and expand, or, if it is diseased, under conditions in which it will heal itself by its own recuperative powers. The foundation of liberty is the idea of growth. Life is learning, but whether in theory or practice what a man genuinely learns is what he absorbs, and what he absorbs depends on the energy which he himself puts forth in response to his surroundings. Thus, to come at once to the real crux, the question of moral discipline, it is of course possible to reduce a man to order and prevent him from being a nuisance to his neighbours by arbitrary control and harsh punishment. This may be to the comfort of the neighbours, as is admitted, but regarded as a moral discipline it is a contradiction in terms. It is doing less than nothing for the character of the man himself. It is merely crushing him, and unless his will is killed the effect will be seen if ever the superincumbent pressure is by chance removed. It is also possible, though it takes a much higher skill, to teach the same man to discipline himself, and this is to foster the development of will, of personality, of self control, or whatever we please to call that central harmonizing power which makes us capable of directing our own lives. Liberalism is the belief that society can safely be founded on this self-directing power of personality, that it is only on this foundation that a true community can be built, and that so established its foundations are so deep and so wide that there is no limit that we can place to the extent of the building. Liberty then becomes not so much a right of the individual as a necessity of society. It rests not on the claim of A to be let alone by B, but on the duty of B to treat A as a rational being. It is not right to let crime alone or to let error alone, but it is imperative to treat the criminal or the mistaken or the ignorant as beings capable of right and truth, and to lead them on instead of merely beating them down. The rule of liberty is just the application of rational method. It is the opening of the door to the appeal of reason, of imagination, of social feeling; and except through the response to this appeal there is no assured progress of society.

Now, I am not contending that these principles are free from difficulty in application. At many points they suggest difficulties both in theory and in practice, with some of which I shall try to deal later on. Nor, again, am I contending that freedom is the universal solvent, or the idea of liberty the sole foundation on which a true social philosophy can be based. On the contrary, freedom is only one side of social life. Mutual aid is not less important than mutual forbearance, the theory of collective action no less fundamental than the theory of personal freedom. But, in an inquiry where all the elements are so closely interwoven as they are in the field of social life, the point of departure becomes almost indifferent. Wherever we start we shall, if we are quite frank and consistent, be led on to look at the whole from some central point, and this, I think, has happened to us in working with the conception of 'liberty.' For, beginning with the right of the individual, and the antithesis between personal freedom and social control, we have been led on to a point at which we regard liberty as primarily a matter of social interest, as something flowing from the necessities of continuous advance in those regions of truth and of ethics which constitute the matters of highest social concern. At the same time, we have come to look for the effect of liberty in the firmer establishment of social solidarity, as the only foundation on which such solidarity can securely rest. We have, in fact, arrived by a path of our own at that which is ordinarily described as the organic conception of the relation between the individual and society – a conception towards which Mill worked through his career, and which forms the starting-point of T. H. Green's philosophy alike in ethics and in politics.

The term organic is so much used and abused that it is best to state simply what it means. A thing is called organic when it is made up of parts which are quite distinct from one another, but which are destroyed or vitally altered when they are removed from the whole. Thus, the human body is organic because its life depends on the functions performed by many organs, while each of these organs depends in turn on the life of the body, perishing and decomposing if removed therefrom. Now, the organic view of society is equally simple. It means that, while the life of society is nothing but the life of individuals as they act one upon another, the life of the individual in turn would be something utterly different if he could be separated from society. A great deal of him would not exist at all. Even if he himself could maintain physical existence by the luck and skill of a Robinson Crusoe, his mental and moral being would, if it existed at all, be something quite different from anything that we know. By language, by training, by simply living with others, each of us absorbs into his system the social atmosphere that surrounds us. In particular, in the matter of rights and duties which is cardinal for Liberal theory, the relation of the individual to the community is everything. His rights and his duties are alike defined by the common good. What, for example, is my right? On the face of it, it is something that I claim. But a mere claim is nothing. I might claim anything and everything. If my claim is of right it is because it is sound, well grounded, in the judgment of an impartial observer. But an impartial observer will not consider me alone. He will equally weigh the opposed claims of others. He will take us in relation to one another, that is to say, as individuals involved in a social relationship. Further, if his decision is in any sense a rational one, it must rest on a principle of some kind; and again, as a rational man, any principle which he asserts he must found on some good result which it serves or embodies, and as an impartial man he must take the good of every one affected into account. That is to say, he must found his judgment on the common good. An individual right, then, cannot conflict with the common good, nor could any right exist apart from the common good.

The argument might seem to make the individual too subservient to society. But this is to forget the other side of the original supposition. Society consists wholly of persons. It has no distinct personality separate from and superior to those of its members. It has, indeed, a certain collective life and character. The British nation is a unity with a life of its own. But the unity is constituted by certain ties that bind together all British subjects, which ties are in the last resort feelings and ideas, sentiments of patriotism, of kinship, a common pride, and a thousand more subtle sentiments that bind together men who speak a common language, have behind them a common history, and understand one another as they can understand no one else.

The British nation is not a mysterious entity over and above the forty odd millions of living souls who dwell together under a common law. Its life is their life, its well-being or ill-fortune their well-being or ill-fortune. Thus, the common good to which each man's rights are subordinate is a good in which each man has a share. This share consists in realizing his capacities of feeling, of loving, of mental and physical energy, and in realizing these he plays his part in the social life, or, in Green's phrase, he finds his own good in the common good.

Now, this phrase, it must be admitted, involves a certain assumption, which may be regarded as the fundamental postulate of the organic view of society. It implies that such a fulfillment or full development of personality is practically possible not for one man only but for all members of a community. There must be a line of development open along which each can move in harmony with others. Harmony in the full sense would involve not merely absence of conflict but actual support. There must be for each, then, possibilities of development such as not merely to permit but actively to further the development of others. Now, the older economists conceived a natural harmony, such that the interests of each would, if properly understood and unchecked by outside interference, inevitably lead him in courses profitable to others and to society at large. We saw that this assumption was too optimistic. The conception which we have now reached does not assume so much. It postulates, not that there is an actually existing harmony requiring nothing but prudence and coolness of judgment for its effective operation, but only that there is a possible ethical harmony, to which, partly by discipline, partly by the improvement of the conditions of life, men might attain, and that in such attainment lies the social ideal. To attempt the systematic proof of this postulate would take us into the field of philosophical first principles. It is the point at which the philosophy of politics comes into contact with that of ethics. It must suffice to say here that, just as the endeavour to establish coherent system in the world of thought is the characteristic of the rational impulse which lies at the root of science and philosophy, so the impulse to establish harmony in the world of feeling and action – a harmony which must include all those who think and feel – is of the essence of the rational impulse in the world of practice. To move towards harmony is the persistent impulse of the rational being, even if the goal lies always beyond the reach of accomplished effort.

These principles may appear very abstract, remote from practical life, and valueless for concrete teaching. But this remoteness is of the nature of first principles when taken without the connecting links that bind them to the details of experience. To find some of these links let us take up again our old Liberal principles, and see how they look in the light of the organic, or, as we may now call it, the harmonic conception. We shall readily see, to begin with, that the old idea of equality has its place. For the common good includes every individual. It is founded on personality, and postulates free scope for the development of personality in each member of the community. This is the foundation not only of equal rights before the law, but also of what is called equality of opportunity. It does not necessarily imply actual equality of treatment for all persons any more than it implies original equality of powers.[1] It does, I think, imply that whatever inequality of actual treatment, of income, rank, office, consideration, there be in a good social system, it would rest, not on the interest of the favoured individual as such, but on the common good. If the existence of millionaires on the one hand and of paupers on the other is just, it must be because such contrasts are the result of an economic system which upon the whole works out for the common good, the good of the pauper being included therein as well as the good of the millionaire; that is to say, that when we have well weighed the good and the evil of all parties concerned we can find no alternative open to us which could do better for the good of all. I am not for the moment either attacking or defending any economic system. I point out only that this is the position which according to the organic or harmonic view of society must be made good by any rational defence of grave inequality in the distribution of wealth. In relation to equality, indeed, it appears, oddly enough, that the harmonic principle can adopt wholesale and even expand, one of the "Rights of Man" as formulated in 1789 – "Social distinctions can only be founded upon common utility." If it is really just that A should be superior to B in wealth or power or position, it is only because when the good of all concerned is considered, among whom B is one, it turns out that there is a net gain in the arrangement as compared with any alternative that we can devise.

If we turn from equality to liberty, the general lines of argument have already been indicated, and the discussion of difficulties in detail must be left for the next chapter. It need only be repeated here that on the harmonic principle the fundamental importance of liberty rests on the nature of the "good" itself, and that whether we are thinking of the good of society or the good of the individual. The good is something attained by the development of the basal factors of personality, a development proceeding by the widening of ideas, the awakening of the imagination, the play of affection and passion, the strengthening and extension of rational control. As it is the development of these factors in each human being that makes his life worth having, so it is their harmonious interaction, the response of each to each, that makes of society a living whole. Liberty so interpreted cannot, as we have seen, dispense with restraint; restraint, however, is not an end but a means to an end, and one of the principal elements in that end is the enlargement of liberty.

But the collective activity of the community does not necessarily proceed by coercion or restraint. The more securely it is founded on freedom and general willing assent, the more it is free to work out all the achievements in which the individual is feeble or powerless while combined action is strong. Human progress, on whatever side we consider it, is found to be in the main social progress, the work of conscious or unconscious co-operation. In this work voluntary association plays a large and increasing part. But the State is one form of association among others, distinguished by its use of coercive power, by its supremacy, and by its claim to control all who dwell within its geographical limits. What the functions of such a form of association are to be we shall have to consider a little further in connection with the other questions which we have already raised. But that, in general, we are justified in regarding the State as one among many forms of human association for the maintenance and improvement of life is the general principle that we have to point out here, and this is the

---

1   An absurd misconception fostered principally by opponents of equality for controversial purposes.

point at which we stand furthest from the older Liberalism. We have, however, already seen some reason for thinking that the older doctrines led, when carefully examined, to a more enlarged conception of State action than appeared on the surface; and we shall see more fully before we have done that the "positive" conception of the State which we have now reached not only involves no conflict with the true principle of personal liberty, but is necessary to its effective realization.

There is, in addition, one principle of historic Liberalism with which our present conception of the State is in full sympathy. The conception of the common good as it has been explained can be realized in its fullness only through the common will. There are, of course, elements of value in the good government of a benevolent despot or of a fatherly aristocracy. Within any peaceful order there is room for many good things to flourish. But the full fruit of social progress is only to be reaped by a society in which the generality of men and women are not only passive recipients but practical contributors. To make the rights and responsibilities of citizens real and living, and to extend them as widely as the conditions of society allow, is thus an integral part of the organic conception of society, and the justification of the democratic principle. It is, at the same time, the justification of nationalism so far as nationalism is founded on a true interpretation of history. For inasmuch as the true social harmony rests on feeling and makes use of all the natural ties of kinship, of neighbourliness, of congruity of character and belief, and of language and mode of life, the best, healthiest, and most vigorous political unit is that to which men are by their own feelings strongly drawn. Any breach of such unity, whether by forcible disruption or by compulsory inclusion in a larger society of alien sentiments and laws, tends to mutilate – or, at lowest, to cramp – the spontaneous development of social life. National and personal freedom are growths of the same root, and their historic connection rests on no accident, but on ultimate identity of idea.

Thus in the organic conception of society each of the leading ideas of historic Liberalism has its part to play. The ideal society is conceived as a whole which lives and flourishes by the harmonious growth of its parts, each of which in developing on its own lines and in accordance with its own nature tends on the whole to further the development of others. There is some elementary trace of such harmony in every form of social life that can maintain itself, for if the conflicting impulses predominated society would break up, and when they do predominate society does break up. At the other extreme, true harmony is an ideal which is perhaps beyond the power of man to realize, but which serves to indicate the line of advance. But to admit this is to admit that the lines of possible development for each individual or, to use a more general phrase, for each constituent of the social order are not limited and fixed. There are many possibilities, and the course that will in the end make for social harmony is only one among them, while the possibilities of disharmony and conflict are many. The progress of society like that of the individual depends, then, ultimately on choice. It is not "natural," in the sense in which a physical law is natural, that is, in the sense of going forward automatically from stage to stage without backward turnings, deflections to the left, or fallings away on the right. It is natural only in this sense, that it is the expression of deep-seated forces of human nature which come to their own only by an infinitely slow and cumbersome process of mutual adjustment. Every constructive social doctrine rests on the conception of human progress. The heart of Liberalism is the understanding that progress is not a matter of mechanical contrivance, but of the liberation of living spiritual energy. Good mechanism is that which provides the channels wherein such energy can flow unimpeded, unobstructed by its own exuberance of output, vivifying the social structure, expanding and ennobling the life of mind.

VII
THE STATE AND THE INDIVIDUAL

We have seen something of the principle underlying the Liberal idea and of its various applications. We have now to put the test question. Are these different applications compatible? Will they work together to make that harmonious whole of which it is easy enough to talk in abstract terms? Are they themselves really harmonious in theory and in practice? Does scope for individual development, for example, consort with the idea of equality? Is popular sovereignty a practicable basis of personal freedom, or does it open an avenue to the tyranny of the mob? Will the sentiment of nationality dwell in unison with the ideal of peace? Is the love of liberty compatible with the full realization of the common will? If reconcilable in theory, may not these ideals collide in practice? Are there not clearly occasions demonstrable in history when development in one direction involves retrogression in another? If so, how are we to strike the balance of gain and loss? Does political progress offer us nothing but a choice of evils, or may we have some confidence that, in solving the most pressing problem of the moment, we shall in the end be in a better position for grappling with the obstacles that come next in turn?

I shall deal with these questions as far as limits of space allow, and I will take first the question of liberty and the common will upon which everything turns. Enough has already been said on this topic to enable us to shorten the discussion. We have seen that social liberty rests on restraint. A man can be free to direct his own life only in so far as others are prevented from molesting and interfering with him. So far there is no real departure from the strictest tenets of individualism. We have, indeed, had occasion to examine the application of the doctrine to freedom of contract on the one hand, and to the action of combinations on the other, and have seen reason to think that in either case nominal freedom, that is to say, the absence of legal restraint, might have the effect of impairing real freedom, that is to say, would allow the stronger party to coerce the weaker. We have also seen that the effect of combination may be double edged, that it may restrict freedom on one side and enlarge it on the other. In all these cases our contention has been simply that we should be guided by real and not by verbal considerations, – that we should ask in every case what policy will yield effective freedom – and we have found a close connection in each instance between freedom and equality. In these cases, however, we were dealing with the relations of one man with another, or of one body of men with another, and we could regard the community as an arbiter between them whose business it was to see justice done and prevent the abuse of coercive power. Hence we could treat a very large part of the modern development of social control as motived by the desire for a more effective liberty. The case is not so clear when we find the will of the individual in conflict with the will of the community as a whole. When such conflict occurs, it would seem that we

must be prepared for one of two things. Either we must admit the legitimacy of coercion, avowedly not in the interests of freedom but in furtherance, without regard to freedom, of other ends which the community deems good. Or we must admit limitations which may cramp the development of the general will, and perchance prove a serious obstacle to collective progress. Is there any means of avoiding this conflict? Must we leave the question to be fought out in each case by a balance of advantages and disadvantages, or are there any general considerations which help us to determine the true sphere of collective and of private action?

Let us first observe that, as Mill pointed out long ago, there are many forms of collective action which do not involve coercion. The State may provide for certain objects which it deems good without compelling any one to make use of them. Thus it may maintain hospitals, though any one who can pay for them remains free to employ his own doctors and nurses. It may and does maintain a great educational system, while leaving every one free to maintain or to attend a private school. It maintains parks and picture galleries without driving any one into them. There is a municipal tramway service, which does not prevent private people from running motor 'buses along the same streets, and so on. It is true that for the support of these objects rates and taxes are compulsorily levied, but this form of compulsion raises a set of questions of which we shall have to speak in another connection, and does not concern us here. For the moment we have to deal only with those actions of State which compel all citizens, or all whom they concern, to fall in with them and allow of no divergence. This kind of coercion tends to increase. Is its extension necessarily an encroachment upon liberty, or are the elements of value secured by collective control distinct from the elements of value secured by individual choice, so that within due limits each may develop side by side?

We have already declined to solve the problem by applying Mill's distinction between self-regarding and other-regarding actions, first because there are no actions which may not directly or indirectly affect others, secondly because even if there were they would not cease to be matter of concern to others. The common good includes the good of every member of the community, and the injury which a man inflicts upon himself is matter of common concern, even apart from any ulterior effect upon others. If we refrain from coercing a man for his own good, it is not because his good is indifferent to us, but because it cannot be furthered by coercion. The difficulty is founded on the nature of the good itself, which on its personal side depends on the spontaneous flow of feeling checked and guided not by external restraint but by rational self-control. To try to form character by coercion is to destroy it in the making. Personality is not built up from without but grows from within, and the function of the outer order is not to create it, but to provide for it the most suitable conditions of growth. Thus, to the common question whether it is possible to make men good by Act of Parliament, the reply is that it is not possible to compel morality because morality is the act or character of a free agent, but that it is possible to create the conditions under which morality can develop, and among these not the least important is freedom from compulsion by others.

The argument suggests that compulsion is limited not by indifference – how could the character of its members be matter of indifference to the community? – but by its own incapacity to achieve its ends. The spirit cannot be forced. Nor, conversely, can it prevail by force. It may require social expression. It may build up an association, a church for example, to carry out the common objects and maintain the common life of all who are like-minded. But the association must be free, because spiritually everything depends not on what is done but on the will with which it is done. The limit to the value of coercion thus lies not in the restriction of social purpose, but in the conditions of personal life. No force can compel growth. Whatever elements of social value depend on the accord of feeling, on comprehension of meaning, on the assent of will, must come through liberty. Here is the sphere and function of liberty in the social harmony.

Where, then, is the sphere of compulsion, and what is its value? The reply is that compulsion is of value where outward conformity is of value, and this may be in any case where the nonconformity of one wrecks the purpose of others. We have already remarked that liberty itself only rests upon restraint. Thus a religious body is not, properly speaking, free to march in procession through the streets unless people of a different religion are restrained from pelting the procession with stones

and pursuing it with insolence. We restrain them from disorder not to teach them the genuine spirit of religion, which they will not learn in the police court, but to secure to the other party the right of worship unmolested. The enforced restraint has its value in the action that it sets free. But we may not only restrain one man from obstructing another – and the extent to which we do this is the measure of the freedom that we maintain – but we may also restrain him from obstructing the general will; and this we have to do whenever uniformity is necessary to the end which the general will has in view. The majority of employers in a trade we may suppose would be willing to adopt certain precautions for the health or safety of their workers, to lower hours or to raise the rate of wages. They are unable to do so, however, as long as a minority, perhaps as long as a single employer, stands out. He would beat them in competition if they were voluntarily to undertake expenses from which he is free. In this case, the will of a minority, possibly the will of one man, thwarts that of the remainder. It coerces them, indirectly, but quite as effectively as if he were their master. If they, by combination, can coerce him no principle of liberty is violated. It is coercion against coercion, differing possibly in form and method, but not in principle or in spirit. Further, if the community as a whole sympathizes with the one side rather than the other, it can reasonably bring the law into play. Its object is not the moral education of the recusant individuals. Its object is to secure certain conditions which it believes necessary for the welfare of its members, and which can only be secured by an enforced uniformity.

It appears, then, that the true distinction is not between self-regarding and other-regarding actions, but between coercive and non-coercive actions. The function of State coercion is to override individual coercion, and, of course, coercion exercised by any association of individuals within the State. It is by this means that it maintains liberty of expression, security of person and property, genuine freedom of contract, the rights of public meeting and association, and finally its own power to carry out common objects undefeated by the recalcitrance of individual members. Undoubtedly it endows both individuals and associations with powers as well as with rights. But over these powers it must exercise supervision in the interests of equal justice. Just as compulsion failed in the sphere of liberty, the sphere of spiritual growth, so liberty fails in the external order wherever, by the mere absence of supervisory restriction, men are able directly or indirectly to put constraint on one another. This is why there is no intrinsic and inevitable conflict between liberty and compulsion, but at bottom a mutual need. The object of compulsion is to secure the most favourable external conditions of inward growth and happiness so far as these conditions depend on combined action and uniform observance. The sphere of liberty is the sphere of growth itself. There is no true opposition between liberty as such and control as such, for every liberty rests on a corresponding act of control. The true opposition is between the control that cramps the personal life and the spiritual order, and the control that is aimed at securing the external and material conditions of their free and unimpeded development.

I do not pretend that this delimitation solves all problems. The "inward" life will seek to express itself in outward acts. A religious ordinance may bid the devout refuse military service, or withhold the payment of a tax, or decline to submit a building to inspection. Here are external matters where conscience and the State come into direct conflict, and where is the court of appeal that is to decide between them? In any given case the right, as judged by the ultimate effect on human welfare, may, of course, be on the one side, or on the other, or between the two. But is there anything to guide the two parties as long as each believes itself to be in the right and sees no ground for waiving its opinion? To begin with, clearly the State does well to avoid such conflicts by substituting alternatives. Other duties than that of military service may be found for a follower of Tolstoy, and as long as he is willing to take his full share of burdens the difficulty is fairly met. Again, the mere convenience of the majority cannot be fairly weighed against the religious convictions of the few. It might be convenient that certain public work should be done on Saturday, but mere convenience would be an insufficient ground for compelling Jews to participate in it. Religious and ethical conviction must be weighed against religious and ethical conviction. It is not number that counts morally, but the belief that is reasoned out according to the best of one's lights as to the necessities of the common good.

But the conscience of the community has its rights just as much as the conscience of the individual. If we are convinced that the inspection of a convent laundry is required in the interest, not of mere official routine, but of justice and humanity, we can do nothing but insist upon it, and when all has been done that can be done to save the individual conscience the common conviction of the common good must have its way. In the end the external order belongs to the community, and the right of protest to the individual.

On the other side, the individual owes more to the community than is always recognized. Under modern conditions he is too much inclined to take for granted what the State does for him and to use the personal security and liberty of speech which it affords him as a vantage ground from which he can in safety denounce its works and repudiate its authority. He assumes the right to be in or out of the social system as he chooses. He relies on the general law which protects him, and emancipates himself from some particular law which he finds oppressive to his conscience. He forgets or does not take the trouble to reflect that, if every one were to act as he does, the social machine would come to a stop. He certainly fails to make it clear how a society would subsist in which every man should claim the right of unrestricted disobedience to a law which he happens to think wrong. In fact, it is possible for an over-tender conscience to consort with an insufficient sense of social responsibility. The combination is unfortunate; and we may fairly say that, if the State owes the utmost consideration to the conscience, its owner owes a corresponding debt to the State. With such mutual consideration, and with the development of the civic sense, conflicts between law and conscience are capable of being brought within very narrow limits, though their complete reconciliation will always remain a problem until men are generally agreed as to the fundamental conditions of the social harmony.

It may be asked, on the other hand, whether in insisting on the free development of personality we have not understated the duty of society to its members. We all admit a collective responsibility for children. Are there not grown-up people who stand just as much in need of care? What of the idiot, the imbecile, the feebleminded or the drunkard? What does rational self-determination mean for these classes? They may injure no one but themselves except by the contagion of bad example. But have we no duty towards them, having in view their own good alone and leaving every other consideration aside? Have we not the right to take the feeble-minded under our care and to keep the drunkard from drink, purely for their own good and apart from every ulterior consideration? And, if so, must we not extend the whole sphere of permissible coercion, and admit that a man may for his own sake and with no ulterior object, be compelled to do what we think right and avoid what we think wrong?

The reply is that the argument is weak just where it seeks to generalize. We are compelled to put the insane under restraint for social reasons apart from their own benefit. But their own benefit would be a fully sufficient reason if no other existed. To them, by their misfortune, liberty, as we understand the term, has no application, because they are incapable of rational choice and therefore of the kind of growth for the sake of which freedom is valuable. The same thing is true of the feebleminded, and if they are not yet treated on the same principle it is merely because the recognition of their type as a type is relatively modern. But the same thing is also in its degree true of the drunkard, so far as he is the victim of an impulse which he has allowed to grow beyond his own control; and the question whether he should be regarded as a fit object for tutelage or not is to be decided in each case by asking whether such capacity of self-control as he retains would be impaired or repaired by a period of tutelar restraint. There is nothing in all this to touch the essential of liberty which is the value of the power of self-governance where it exists. All that is proved is that where it does not exist it is right to save men from suffering, and if the case admits to put them under conditions in which the normal balance of impulse is most likely to be restored. It may be added that, in the case of the drunkard – and I think the argument applies to all cases where overwhelming impulse is apt to master the will – it is a still more obvious and elementary duty to remove the sources of temptation, and to treat as anti-social in the highest degree every attempt to make profit out of human weakness, misery, and wrong-doing. The case is not unlike that of a very unequal contract. The tempter is coolly seeking his profit, and the sufferer is beset with a fiend within. There is a form of coercion here which the genuine spirit of liberty will not fail to recognize as its enemy, and a form of injury to another which is not the less real because its weapon is an impulse which forces that other to the consent which he yields.

I conclude that there is nothing in the doctrine of liberty to hinder the movement of general will in the sphere in which it is really efficient, and nothing in a just conception of the objects and methods of the general will to curtail liberty in the performance of the functions, social and personal, in which its value lies. Liberty and compulsion have complementary functions, and the self-governing State is at once the product and the condition of the self-governing individual.

Bibliography

Elshtain, Jean Bethke. *Public Man, Private Woman.* 2nd ed. Princeton, N.J.: Princeton University Press, 1993.

Gray, John. *Liberalism.* 2nd. ed. Minneapolis: University of Minnesota Press, 1995.

Lasch, Christopher. *The Culture of Narcissism.* Rev. ed. New York: W.W. Norton, 1991.

Manning, D.J. *Liberalism.* New York: St. Martin's Press, 1976.

CHAPTER EIGHTEEN — JOHN RAWLS

John Rawls (b. 1921) is one of the most significant and influential moral theorists of the second half of the twentieth century. This impact was principally achieved through one book, *A Theory of Justice*, published in 1971. In it Rawls argues for liberal political conclusions on a basis in social contract theory. The principles of justice are held to be those which a set of rational human beings would choose for a social order they were instituting if they were in a position of ignorance about their own individual traits, including their natural advantages and disadvantages.

A more recent book articulates more fully a portrait of human nature as Rawls sees it. It is from this work that the following selection comes.

John Rawls, *Political Liberalism*

(Source: John Rawls. *Political Liberalism*. New York: Columbia University Press, 1993, 18-28; 29-35.)

3. Now consider the fundamental idea of the person.[1] There are, of course, many aspects of human nature that can be singled out as especially significant, depending on our point of view. This is witnessed by such expressions as "homo politicus" and "homo economicus," "homo ludens" and "homo faber." Since our account of justice as fairness begins with the idea that society is to be conceived as a fair system of cooperation over time between generations, we adopt a conception of the person to go with this idea. Beginning with the ancient world, the concept of the person has been understood, in both philosophy and law, as the concept of someone who can take part in, or who can play a role in, social life, and hence exercise and respect its various rights and duties. Thus, we say that a person is someone who can be a citizen, that is, a normal and fully cooperating member of society over a complete life. We add the phrase "over a complete life" because society is viewed not only as

closed (§2.1) but as a more or less complete and self-sufficient scheme of cooperation, making room within itself for all the necessities and activities of life, from birth until death. A society is also conceived as existing in perpetuity: it produces and reproduces itself and its institutions and culture over generations and there is no time at which it is expected to wind up its affairs.

Since we start within the tradition of democratic thought, we also think of citizens as free and equal persons. The basic idea is that in virtue of their two moral powers (a capacity for a sense of justice and for a conception of the good) and the powers of reason (of judgment, thought, and inference connected with these powers), persons are free. Their having these powers to the requisite minimum degree to be fully cooperating members of society makes persons equal.[2]

To elaborate: since persons can be full participants in a fair system of social cooperation, we ascribe to them the two moral powers connected with the elements in the idea of social cooperation noted above: namely, a capacity for a sense of justice and a capacity for a conception of the good. A sense of justice is the capacity to understand, to apply, and to act from the public conception of jus-

---

1   It should be emphasized that a conception of the person, as I understand it here, is a normative conception, whether legal, political, or moral, or indeed also philosophical or religious, depending on the overall view to which it belongs. In the present case the conception of the person is a moral conception, one that begins from our everyday conception of persons as the basic units of thought, deliberation, and responsibility, and adapted to a political conception of justice and not to a comprehensive doctrine. It is in effect a political conception of the person, and given the aims of justice as fairness, a conception suitable for the basis of democratic citizenship. As a normative conception, it is to be distinguished from an account of human nature given by natural science and social theory and it has a different role in justice as fairness. On this last, see II:8.

2   See [A] *Theory* [of *Justice*], §77, where this basis of equality is discussed.

tice which characterizes the fair terms of social cooperation. Given the nature of the political conception as specifying a public basis of justification, a sense of justice also expresses a willingness, if not the desire, to act in relation to others on terms that they also can publicly endorse (II:1). The capacity for a conception of the good is the capacity to form, to revise, and rationally to pursue a conception of one's rational advantage or good.

In addition to having these two moral powers, persons also have at any given time a determinate conception of the good that they try to achieve. Such a conception must not be understood narrowly but rather as including a conception of what is valuable in human life. Thus, a conception of the good normally consists of a more or less determinate scheme of final ends, that is, ends we want to realize for their own sake, as well as attachments to other persons and loyalties to various groups and associations. These attachments and loyalties give rise to devotions and affections, and so the flourishing of the persons and associations who are objects of these sentiments is also part of our conception of the good. We also connect with such a conception a view of our relation to the world – religious, philosophical, and moral – by reference to which the value and significance of our ends and attachments are understood. Finally, persons' conceptions of the good are not fixed but form and develop as they mature, and may change more or less radically over the course of life.

4. Since we begin from the idea of society as a fair system of cooperation, we assume that persons as citizens have all the capacities that enable them to be cooperating members of society. This is done to achieve a clear and uncluttered view of what, for us, is the fundamental question of political justice: namely, what is the most appropriate conception of justice for specifying the terms of social cooperation between citizens regarded as free and equal, and as normal and fully cooperating members of society over a complete life?

By taking this as the fundamental question we do not mean to say, of course, that no one ever suffers from illness and accident; such misfortunes are to be expected in the ordinary course of life, and provision for these contingencies must be made. But given our aim, I put aside for the time being these temporary disabilities and also permanent disabilities or mental disorders so severe as to prevent peo-

ple from being cooperating members of society in the usual sense. Thus, while we begin with an idea of the person implicit in the public political culture, we idealize and simplify this idea in various ways in order to focus first on the main question.

....

.... To understand what is meant by describing a conception of the person as political, consider how citizens are represented in that position as free persons. The representation of their freedom seems to be one source of the idea that a metaphysical doctrine is presupposed. Now citizens are conceived as thinking of themselves as free in three respects, so I survey each of these and indicate the way in which the conception of the person is political.

2. First, citizens are free in that they conceive of themselves and of one another as having the moral power to have a conception of the good. This is not to say that, as part of their political conception, they view themselves as inevitably tied to the pursuit of the particular conception of the good that they affirm at any given time. Rather, as citizens, they are seen as capable of revising and changing this conception on reasonable and rational grounds, and they may do this if they so desire. As free persons, citizens claim the right to view their persons as independent from and not identified with any particular such conception with its scheme of final ends. Given their moral power to form, revise, and rationally pursue a conception of the good, their public identity as free persons is not affected by changes over time in their determinate conception of it.

For example, when citizens convert from one religion to another, or no longer affirm an established religious faith, they do not cease to be, for questions of political justice, the same persons they were before. There is no loss of what we may call their public, or institutional, identity, or their identity as a matter of basic law. In general, they still have the same basic rights and duties, they own the same property and can make the same claims as before, except insofar as these claims were connected with their previous religious affiliation. We can imagine a society (history offers many examples) in which basic rights and recognized claims depend on religious affiliation and social class. Such a society has a different political conception of the person. It lacks a conception of equal citizenship, for this conception goes with that of a democratic society of free and equal citizens.

There is a second sense of identity specified by reference to citizens' deeper aims and commitments. Let's call it their noninstitutional or moral identity.[3] Citizens usually have both political and nonpolitical aims and commitments. They affirm the values of political justice and want to see them embodied in political institutions and social policies. They also work for the other values in nonpublic life and for the ends of the associations to which they belong. These two aspects of their moral identity citizens must adjust and reconcile. It can happen that in their personal affairs, or in the internal life of associations, citizens may regard their final ends and attachments very differently from the way the political conception supposes. They may have, and often do have at any given time, affections, devotions, and loyalties that they believe they would not, indeed could and should not, stand apart from and evaluate objectively. They may regard it as simply unthinkable to view themselves apart from certain religious, philosophical, and moral convictions, or from certain enduring attachments and loyalties.

These two kinds of commitments and attachments – political and nonpolitical – specify moral identity and give shape to a person's way of life, what one sees oneself as doing and trying to accomplish in the social world. If we suddenly lost them, we would be disoriented and unable to carry on.[4] But our conceptions of the good may and often do change over time, usually slowly but sometimes rather suddenly. When these changes are sudden, we are likely to say that we are no longer the same person. We know what this means: we refer to a profound and pervasive shift, or reversal, in our final ends and commitments; we refer to our different moral (which includes our religious) identity. On the road to Damascus Saul of Tarsus becomes Paul the Apostle. Yet such a conversion implies no change in our public or institutional identity, nor in our personal identity as this concept is understood by some writers in the philosophy of mind.[5] Moreover, in a well-ordered society supported by an overlapping consensus, citizens' (more general) political values and commitments, as part of their noninstitutional or moral identity, are roughly the same.

3. A second respect in which citizens view themselves as free is that they regard themselves as self-authenticating sources of valid claims. That is, they regard themselves as being entitled to make claims

---

3   I am indebted to Erin Kelly for the distinction between the two kinds of aims that characterizes people's moral identity as described in this and the next paragraph.

4   This role of commitments is often emphasized by Bernard Williams, for example, in "Persons, Character and Morality," in *Moral Luck* (Cambridge: Cambridge University Press, 1981), pp. 10-14.

5   Though I have used the term *identity* in the text, it would, I think, cause less misunderstanding to use the phrase "our conception of ourselves," or "the kind of person we want to be." Doing so would distinguish the question with important moral elements from the question of the sameness, or identity, of a substance, continuant, or thing, through different changes in time and space. In saying this I assume that an answer to the problem of personal identity tries to specify the various criteria (for example, psychological criteria of memories and physical continuity of body, or some part thereof) in accordance with which two different psychological states or actions, say, which occur at two different times may be said to be states or actions of the same person who endures over time; and it also tries to specify how this enduring person is to be conceived, whether as a Cartesian or a Leibnizian substance, or a Kantian transcendental ego, or as a continuant of some kind, for example, bodily and physical. See the collection of essays edited by John Perry, *Personal Identity* (Berkeley: University of California Press, 1975), especially Perry's introduction, pp. 1-30; and Sydney Shoemaker's essay in *Personal Identity* (Oxford: Basil Blackwell, 1984), both of which consider a number of views. Sometimes in discussions of this problem, continuity of fundamental aims is largely ignored, for example in views like H.P. Grice's (in Perry's collection), which emphasizes continuity of memory. However, once the continuity of these aims is counted as also basic, as in Derek Parfit's *Reasons and Persons* (Oxford: Clarendon Press, 1984), pt. III, there is no sharp distinction between the problem of a person's nonpublic or moral identity and the problem of their personal identity. The latter problem raises profound questions on which past and current philosophical views widely differ and surely will continue to differ. For this reason it is important to try to develop a political conception of justice that avoids this problem as far as possible. Even so, to refer to the example in the text, all agree, I assume, that for the purposes of public life, Saul of Tarsus and St. Paul the Apostle are the same person. Conversion is irrelevant to our public, or institutional, identity.

on their institutions so as to advance their conceptions of the good (provided these conceptions fall within the range permitted by the public conception of justice). These claims citizens regard as having weight of their own apart from being derived from duties and obligations specified by a political conception of justice, for example, from duties and obligations owed to society. Claims that citizens regard as founded on duties and obligations based on their conception of the good and the moral doctrine they affirm in their own life are also, for our purposes here, to be counted as self-authenticating. Doing this is reasonable in a political conception of justice for a constitutional democracy, for provided the conceptions of the good and the moral doctrines citizens affirm are compatible with the public conception of justice, these duties and obligations are self-authenticating from a political point of view.

When we describe the way in which citizens regard themselves as free, we describe how citizens think of themselves in a democratic society when questions of political justice arise. That this aspect belongs to a particular political conception is clear from the contrast with a different political conception in which people are not viewed as self-authenticating sources of valid claims. Rather, their claims have no weight except insofar as they can be derived from the duties and obligations owed to society, or from their ascribed roles in a social hierarchy justified by religious or aristocratic values.

To take an extreme case, slaves are human beings who are not counted as sources of claims, not even claims based on social duties or obligations, for slaves are not counted as capable of having duties or obligations. Laws that prohibit the maltreatment of slaves are not based on claims made by slaves, but on claims originating from slaveholders, or from the general interests of society (which do not include the interests of slaves). Slaves are, so to speak, socially dead: they are not recognized as persons at all.[6] This contrast with slavery makes clear why conceiving of citizens as free persons in virtue of their moral powers and their having a conception of the good goes with a particular political conception of justice.

4. The third respect in which citizens are viewed as free is that they are viewed as capable of taking responsibility for their ends and this affects how their various claims are assessed.[7] Very roughly, given just background institutions and given for each person a fair index of primary goods (as required by the principles of justice), citizens are thought to be capable of adjusting their aims and aspirations in the light of what they can reasonably expect to provide for. Moreover, they are viewed as capable of restricting their claims in matters of justice to the kinds of things the principles of justice allow.

Citizens are to recognize, then, that the weight of their claims is not given by the strength and psychological intensity of their wants and desires (as opposed to their needs as citizens), even when their wants and desires are rational from their point of view. The procedure is as before: we start with the basic idea of society as a fair system of cooperation. When this idea is developed into a conception of political justice, it implies that, viewing citizens as persons who can engage in social cooperation over a complete life, they can also take responsibility for their ends: that is, they can adjust their ends so that those ends can be pursued by the means they can reasonably expect to acquire in return for what they can reasonably expect to contribute. The idea of responsibility for ends is implicit in the public political culture and discernible in its practice. A political conception of the person articulates this idea and fits it into the idea of society as a fair system of cooperation.

5. To sum up, I recapitulate three main points of this and the preceding two sections:

First, in §3 persons were regarded as free and equal persons in virtue of their possessing to the requisite degree the two powers of moral personality, namely, the capacity for a sense of justice and the capacity for a conception of the good. These powers we associated with the two main elements of the idea of cooperation , the idea of the fair terms of cooperation, and the idea of each participant's rational advantage, or good.

Second, in this section (§5), we surveyed three respects in which persons are regarded as free, and

---

6   For the idea of social death, see Orlando Patterson's *Slavery and Social Death* (Cambridge, Mass.: Harvard University Press, 1982), esp. pp. 5-9, 38-45, 337.

7   See further V:3-4, esp. 3.6.

have noted that in the public political culture of a constitutional democratic regime citizens conceive of themselves as free in these ways.

Third, since the question of which conception of political justice is most appropriate for realizing in basic institutions the values of liberty and equality has long been deeply controversial within the very tradition in which citizens are regarded as free and equal, the aim of justice as fairness is to resolve this question by starting from the idea of society as a fair system of cooperation in which the fair terms of cooperation are agreed upon by citizens so conceived. In §4, we saw why this approach, once the basic structure of society is taken as the primary subject of justice, leads to the idea of the original position as a device of representation.

Bibliography

Daniels, Norman, ed. *Reading Rawls*. New York: Basic Books, 1975.

Gray, John. *Liberalism*. 2nd. ed. Minneapolis: University of Minnesota Press, 1995.

Pogge, Thomas. *Realizing Rawls*. Ithaca, N.Y.: Cornell University Press, 1989.

IV

CONSERVATIVE INDIVIDUALISM

CHAPTER NINETEEN — NICCOLÒ MACHIAVELLI

Niccolò Machiavelli (1469-1527) has had what may be the most radically contrasting of reputations of any thinker in the western tradition. Seen by some essentially as a hack apologist for the unprincipled rule of an armed thug, by others as the author of a practical guidebook – a "how-to" study – for acquiring and keeping nondemocratic state power, Machiavelli has been viewed by some interpreters as the first modern political philosopher, and (by no means necessarily implied by the latter) as a deeply moral and principled analyst of the human condition and its prospects in an uncertain and dangerous world. These diversities of assessment spring chiefly from the divergent reactions that have been evoked by Machiavelli's most famous book, *The Prince*, from which the following selections are drawn. Published posthumously in 1532, this short study of statecraft quickly drew upon itself reproach and condemnation for what was seen as its cynical amoralism. It also drew large numbers of fascinated readers, some of them individuals aspiring to state power and sometimes finding success in their endeavours. The word "Machiavellian" conveys still the notion of cunning dissimulation for self-interested advantage.

Machiavelli is of significance for human nature theory as someone who is trying to see human beings as they are, without wishful thinking or a model or vision of a human ideal state or *telos*, to the realization of which social and educational forces should be directed. Although developed within a Christian society, and against a formally Christian intellectual backdrop, Machiavelli's view is of humans on their own, who must strive for their good – sometimes their bare survival – as they are able to do, with special opportunities for some to special degrees of pre-eminence, or power, or security.

Machiavelli was born during the later Italian Renaissance in 1469 – exactly 300 years before Napoleon, who was often seen as having exemplified "Machiavellian ideas" (in both negative and positive senses of the phrase) in particularly striking ways. It is important to note that that brilliant and remarkable civilization, which inaugurates the modern world, had the models both of ancient Athenian republicanism in the texts it celebrated and of Christian universal human brotherhood and sisterhood in its religious ideology. It was itself wholly undemocratic, its political regimes uniformly despotic in nature.

Niccolò Machiavelli, *The Prince*

(Source: Nicolò Machiavelli. *The Prince*. Intr. Christian Gauss. Trans. Luigi Ricci (1903), rev. E.R P. Vincent. Oxford: Oxford University Press, 1935, 89-94)

17

....

From this arises the question whether it is better to be loved more than feared, or feared more than loved. The reply is, that one ought to be both feared and loved, but as it is difficult for the two to go together,it is much safer to be feared than loved, if one of the two has to be wanting. For it may be said of men in general that they are ungrateful, voluble, dissemblers, anxious to avoid danger, and covetous of gain; as long as you benefit them, they are entirely yours; they offer you their blood, their goods, their life, and their children, as I have before said, when the necessity is remote; but when it approaches, they revolt. And the prince who has relied solely on their words, without making other preparations, is ruined; for the friendship which is gained by purchase and not through grandeur and nobility of spirit is bought but not secured, and at a pinch is not to be expended in your service. And men have less scruple in offending one who makes himself loved than one who makes himself feared; for love is held by a chain of obligation which, men being selfish, is broken whenever it serves their purpose; but fear is maintained by a dread of punishment which never fails.

Still, a prince should make himself feared in such a way that if he does not gain love, he at any rate avoids hatred; for fear and the absence of hatred may well go together, and will be always attained by one who abstains from interfering with the property of his citizens and subjects or with their women. And when he is obliged to take the life of any one, let him do so when there is a proper justification and manifest reason for it; but above all he must abstain from taking the property of others, for men forget more easily the death of their father than the loss of their patrimony. Then also pretexts for seizing property are never wanting, and one who begins to live by rapine will always find some reason for taking the goods of others, whereas causes for taking life are rarer and more fleeting.

But when the prince is with his army and has a large number of soldiers under his control, then it is extremely necessary that he should not mind being thought cruel; for without this reputation he could not keep an army united or disposed to any duty. Among the noteworthy actions of Hannibal is numbered this that although he had an enormous army, composed of men of all nations and fighting in foreign countries, there never arose any dissension either among them or against the prince, either in good fortune or in bad. This could not be due to anything but his inhuman cruelty, which together with his infinite other virtues, made him always venerated and terrible in the sight of his soldiers, and without it his other virtues would not have sufficed to produce that effect. Thoughtless writers admire on the one hand his actions, and on the other blame the principal cause of them.

And that it is true that his other virtues would not have sufficed may be seen from the case of Scipio (famous not only in regard to his own times, but all times of which memory remains), whose armies rebelled against him in Spain, which arose from

nothing but his excessive kindness, which allowed more licence to the soldier than was consonant with military discipline. He was reproached with this in the senate by Fabius Maximus, who called him a corrupter of the Roman militia. Locri having been destroyed by one of Scipio's officers was not revenged by him, nor was the insolence of that officer punished, simply by reason of his easy nature; so much so, that some one wishing to excuse him in the senate said that there were many men who knew rather how not to err, than how to correct the errors of others. This disposition would in time have tarnished the fame and glory of Scipio had he persevered in it under the empire, but living under the rule of the senate this harmful quality was not only concealed but became a glory to him.

I conclude, therefore, with regard to being feared and loved, that men love at their own free will, but fear at the will of the prince, and that a wise prince must rely on what is in his power and not on what is in the power of others, and he must only contrive to avoid incurring hatred, as has been explained.

18
In What Way Princes Must Keep Faith

How laudable it is for a prince to keep good faith and live with integrity, and not with astuteness, every one knows. Still the experience of our times shows those princes to have done great things who have had little regard for good faith, and have been able by astuteness to confuse men's brains, and who have ultimately overcome those who have made loyalty their foundation.

You must know, then, that there are two methods of fighting, the one by law, the other by force: the first method is that of men, the second of beasts; but as the first method is often insufficient, one must have recourse to the second. It is therefore necessary for a prince to know well how to use both the beast and the man. This was covertly taught to rulers by ancient writers, who relate how Achilles and many others of those ancient princes were given to Chiron the centaur to be brought up and educated under his discipline. The parable of this semi-animal, semi-human teacher is meant to indicate that a prince must know how to use both natures, and that the one without the other is not durable.

A prince being thus obliged to know well how to

act as a beast must imitate the fox and the lion, for the lion cannot protect himself from traps, and the fox cannot defend himself from wolves. One must therefore be a fox to recognise traps, and a lion to frighten wolves. Those that wish to be only lions do not understand this. Therefore, a prudent ruler ought not to keep faith when by so doing it would be against his interest, and when the reasons which made him bind himself no longer exist. If men were all good, this precept would not be a good one; but as they are bad, and would not observe their faith with you, so you are not bound to keep faith with them. Nor have legitimate grounds ever failed a prince who wished to show colourable excuse for the non-fulfilment of his promise. Of this one could furnish an infinite number of modern examples, and show how many times peace has been broken, and how many promises rendered worthless, by the faithlessness of princes, and those that have been best able to imitate the fox have succeeded best. But it is necessary to be able to disguise this character well, and to be a great feigner and dissembler; and men are so simple and so ready to obey present necessities, that one who deceives will always find those who allow themselves to be deceived.

I will only mention one modern instance. Alexander VI did nothing else but deceive men, he thought of nothing else, and found the occasion for it; no man was ever more able to give assurances, or affirmed things with stronger oaths, and no man observed them less; however, he always succeeded in his deceptions, as he well knew this aspect of things.

It is not, therefore, necessary for a prince to have all the above-named qualities, but it is very necessary to seem to have them. I would even be bold to say that to possess them and always to observe them is dangerous but to appear to possess them is useful. Thus it is well to seem merciful, faithful, humane, sincere, religious, and also to be so; but you must have the mind so disposed that when it is needful to be otherwise you may be able to change to the opposite qualities. And it must be understood that a prince, and especially a new prince

cannot observe all those things which are considered good in men, being often obliged, in order to maintain the state, to act against faith, against charity, against humanity, and against religion. And, therefore, he must have a mind disposed to adapt itself according to the wind, and as the variations of fortune dictate, and, as I said before, not deviate from what is good, if possible, but be able to do evil if constrained.

A prince must take great care that nothing goes out of his mouth which is not full of the above-named five qualities, and, to see and hear him, he should seem to be all mercy, faith, integrity, humanity, and religion. And nothing is more necessary than to seem to have this last quality, for men in general judge more by the eyes than by the hands, for every one can see, but very few have to feel. Everybody sees what you appear to be, few feel what you are, and those few will not dare to oppose themselves to the many, who have the majesty of the state to defend them; and in the actions of men, and especially of princes, from which there is no appeal, the end justifies the means. Let a prince therefore aim at conquering and maintaining the state, and the means will always be judged honourable and praised by every one, for the vulgar is always taken by appearances and the issue of the event; and the world consists only of the vulgar, and the few who are not vulgar are isolated when the many have a rallying point in the prince.

Bibliography

Burckhardt, Jacob. *The Civilization of the Renaissance in Italy*. New York: Random House, 1954.

Parel, Anthony, ed. *The Political Calculus: Essays on Machiavelli's Philosophy*. Toronto: University of Toronto Press, 1972.

Rebhorn, Wayne A. *Foxes and Lions: Machiavelli's Confidence Men*. Ithaca, N.Y.: Cornell University Press, 1988.

Skinner, Quentin. *Machiavelli*. Oxford: Oxford University Press, 1981.

CHAPTER TWENTY — THOMAS HOBBES

Intellectual work requires the sheltering and nurturing tree of patronage. One of the indices of changing socio-economic and cultural reality in the western world is the successive forms such patronage has taken. From the early medieval period the patron of intellectual endeavour was almost exclusively the church, typically operating through the university, and most philosophers and theorists were, at least formally and nominally, priests, usually members of religious orders. The Renaissance witnessed a mixture of ecclesiastical and state patronage. The "age of reason" – the scientific revolution of the seventeenth century and the Enlightenment that followed – was supremely an aristocratic age. Probably a majority of the significant philosophers and scientists between 1600 and 1800 were members of armigerous landed families, or were directly sponsored and supported by people who were. Thus, Hobbes was a client and employee of the Cavendish family, as was Locke of the Ashley-Coopers, and Leibniz of the ruling family of Hanover; and members of the first two of these families (Henry Cavendish, and the third Earl of Shaftesbury) were themselves prominent intellectual workers. The age that follows is the contemporary period, a time, like the medieval period, chiefly of institutional patronage. In its earlier phase we may identify a preponderant role for the private economic institution: thus both James Mill and his more famous son were employees of the East India Company and did their intellectual work within an umbrella it afforded. Since the 1850s, an institution which has been a sometime patron since western emergence from the Dark Ages has become overwhelmingly predominant: the (now mostly secularized) university. There have always been exceptions to these patterns, and patrons of major stature in one age appearing also in times when they are generally minor.

These general remarks apply to most of the thinkers represented in this volume. Yet they are attached especially to introductory comments about Thomas Hobbes (1588-1679) because his ideas about the human condition are relatively well-known, and in any case fairly clearly explained in his prose; and because it may be especially appropriate to locate Hobbes *materially* within the long sweep of western intellectual history of the past millennium.

Hobbes had keen interests in the classics and in mathematics, as well as in accounting for and analyzing the formation and the nature of political society. He had a long life, much of it spent in turbulent times. *Leviathan*, his primary classic work, was published in 1651, just after the violent conclusion of the bitter English civil war; Hobbes himself was nearly lynched in 1666, the superstitious London mob having concluded that this might best appease divine wrath following the great fire of London. Hobbes was infamous in his time: he and Spinoza were regarded as possibly the wickedest men in Europe. His public reputation as a thinker with notoriously unsettling dangerous ideas may be compared with that of Darwin three centuries later, or of Marx, Nietzsche, Freud, and others thereafter.

Thomas Hobbes, *Leviathan*

(Source: Thomas Hobbes. *Leviathan or the Matter, Forme and Power of a Commonwealth Ecclesiasticall and Civil*. Sir William Molesworth, ed., *The English Works of Thomas Hobbes*. London: Bohn, 1839, vol iii, 85-90, 110-114.)

Chapter XI
OF THE DIFFERENCE OF MANNERS

What is here meant by manners. BY MANNERS, I mean not here, decency of behaviour; as how one should salute another, or how a man should wash his mouth, or pick his teeth before company, and such other points of the *small morals*; but those qualities of mankind, that concern their living together in peace, and unity. To which end we are to consider, that the felicity of this life, consisteth not in the repose of a mind satisfied. For there is no such *finis ultimus*, utmost aim, nor *summum bonum*, greatest good, as is spoken of in the books of the old moral philosophers. Nor can a man any more live, whose desires are at an end, than he, whose sense and imaginations are at a stand. Felicity is a continual progress of the desire, from one object to another; the attaining of the former, being still but the way to the latter. The cause whereof is, that the object of man's desire, is not to enjoy once only, and for one instant of time; but to assure for ever, the way of his future desire. And therefore the voluntary actions, and inclinations of all men, tend, not only to the procuring, but also to the assuring of a contented life; and differ only in the way: which ariseth partly from the diversity of passions, in divers men; and partly from the difference of the knowledge, or opinion each one has of the causes, which produce the effect desired.

A restless desire of power in all men. So that in the first place, I put for a general inclination of all mankind, a perpetual and restless desire of power after power, that ceaseth only in death. And the cause of this, is not always that a man hopes for a more intensive delight, than he has already attained to; or that he cannot be content with a moderate power: but because he cannot assure the power and means to live well, which he hath present, without the acquisition of more. And from hence it is, that kings, whose power is greatest, turn their endeavours to the assuring it at home by laws, or abroad by wars: and when that is done, there succeedeth a new desire; in some, of fame from new conquest; in others, of ease and sensual pleasure; in others, of admiration, or being flattered for excellence in some art, or other ability of the mind.

Love of contention from competition. Competition of riches, honour, command, or other power, inclineth to contention, enmity, and war: because the way of one competitor, to the attaining of his desire, is to kill, subdue, supplant, or repel the other. Particularly, competition of praise, inclineth to a reverence of antiquity. For men contend with the living, not with the dead; to these ascribing more than due, that they may obscure the glory of the other.

Civil obedience from love of ease. From fear of death, or wounds. Desire of ease, and sensual delight, disposeth men to obey a common power: because by such desires, a man doth abandon the protection that might be hoped for from his own industry, and labour. Fear of death, and wounds, disposeth to the same; and for the same reason. On the contrary, needy men, and hardy, not contented with their present condition; as also, all men that are ambitious of military command, are inclined to continue the causes of war; and to stir up trouble and sedition: for there is no honour military but by war; nor any such hope to mend an ill game, as by causing a new shuffle.

And from love of arts. Desire of knowledge, and arts of peace, inclineth men to obey a common power: for such desire, containeth a desire of leisure; and consequently protection from some other power than their own.

Love of virtue from love of praise. Desire of praise, disposeth to laudable actions, such as please them whose judgment they value; for of those men whom we contemn, we contemn also the praises. Desire of fame after death does the same. And though after death, there be no sense of the praise given us on earth, as being joys, that are either swallowed up in the unspeakable joys of Heaven, or extinguished in the extreme torments of hell: yet is not such fame vain; because men have a present delight therein, from the foresight of it, and of the benefit that may redound thereby to their posterity; which though they now see not, yet they imagine; and any thing that is pleasure to the sense, the same also is pleasure in the imagination.

Hate, from difficulty of requiting great benefits.

To have received from one, to whom we think ourselves equal, greater benefits than there is hope to requite, disposeth to counterfeit love; but really secret hatred; and puts a man into the estate of a desperate debtor, that in declining the sight of his creditor, tacitly wishes him there, where he might never see him more. For benefits oblige, and obligation is thraldom; and unrequitable obligation perpetual thraldom; which is to one's equal, hateful. But to have received benefits from one, whom we acknowledge for superior, inclines to love; because the obligation is no new depression: and cheerful acceptation, which men call *gratitude*, is such an honour done to the obliger, as is taken generally for retribution. Also to receive benefits, though from an equal, or inferior, as long as there is hope of requital, disposeth to love: for in the intention of the receiver, the obligation is of aid and service mutual; from whence proceedeth an emulation of who shall exceed in benefiting; the most noble and profitable contention possible; wherein the victor is pleased with his victory, and the other revenged by confessing it.

And from conscience of deserving to be hated. To have done more hurt to a man, than he can, or is willing to expiate, inclineth the doer to hate the sufferer. For he must expect revenge, or forgiveness; both which are hateful.

Promptness to hurt, from fear. Fear of oppression, disposeth a man to anticipate, or to seek aid by society: for there is no other way by which a man can secure his life and liberty.

And from distrust of their own wit. Men that distrust their own subtlety, are, in tumult and sedition, better disposed for victory, than they that suppose themselves wise, or crafty. For these love to consult, the other, fearing to be circumvented, to strike first. And in sedition, men being always in the precincts of battle, to hold together, and use all advantages of force, is a better stratagem, than any that can proceed from subtlety of wit.

Vain undertaking from vain-glory. Vain-glorious men, such as without being conscious to themselves of great sufficiency, delight in supposing themselves gallant men, are inclined only to ostentation; but not to attempt: because when danger or difficulty appears, they look for nothing but to have their insufficiency discovered.

Vain-glorious men, such as estimate their suffi-

ciency by the flattery of other men, or the fortune of some precedent action, without assured ground of hope from the true knowledge of themselves, are inclined to rash engaging; and in the approach of danger, or difficulty, to retire if they can: because not seeing the way of safety, they will rather hazard their honour, which may be salved with an excuse; than their lives, for which no salve is sufficient.

Ambition, from opinion of sufficiency. Men that have a strong opinion of their own wisdom in matter of government, are disposed to ambition. Because without public employment in council or magistracy, the honour of their wisdom is lost. And therefore eloquent speakers are inclined to ambition; for eloquence seemeth wisdom, both to themselves and others.

Irresolution, from too great valuing of small matters. Pusillanimity disposeth men to irresolution, and consequently to lose the occasions, and fittest opportunities of action. For after men have been in deliberation till the time of action approach, if it be not then manifest what is best to be done, it is a sign, the difference of motives, the one way and the other, are not great: therefore not to resolve then, is to lose the occasion by weighing of trifles; which is pusillanimity.

Frugality, though in poor men a virtue, maketh a man unapt to achieve such actions, as require the strength of many men at once: for it weakeneth their endeavour, which is to be nourished and kept in vigour by reward.

Confidence in others, from ignorance of the marks of wisdom and kindness. Eloquence, with flattery, disposeth men to confide in them that have it; because the former is seeming wisdom, the latter seeming kindness. Add to them military reputation, and it disposeth men to adhere, and subject themselves to those men that have them. The two former having given them caution against danger from him; the latter gives them caution against danger from others.

And from ignorance of natural causes. Want of science, that is, ignorance of causes, disposeth, or rather constraineth a man to rely on the advice, and authority of others. For all men whom the truth concerns, if they rely not on their own, must rely on the opinion of some other, whom they think wiser than themselves, and see not why he should deceive them.

....

Chapter XIII
OF THE NATURAL CONDITION OF MANKIND AS CONCERNING THEIR FELICITY, AND MISERY

Men by nature equal. NATURE hath made men so equal, in the faculties of the body, and mind; as that though there be found one man sometimes manifestly stronger in body, or of quicker mind than another; yet when all is reckoned together, the difference between man, and man, is not so considerable, as that one man can thereupon claim to himself any benefit, to which another may not pretend, as well as he. For as to the strength of body, the weakest has strength enough to kill the strongest, either by secret machination, or by confederacy with others, that are in the same danger with himself.

And as to the faculties of the mind, setting aside the arts grounded upon words, and especially that skill of proceeding upon general, and infallible rules, called science; which very few have, and but in few things; as being not a native faculty, born with us; nor attained, as prudence, while we look after somewhat else, I find yet a greater equality amongst men, than that of strength. For prudence, is but experience; which equal time, equally bestows on all men, in those things they equally apply themselves unto. That which may perhaps make such equality incredible, is but a vain conceit of one's own wisdom, which almost all men think they have in a greater degree, than the vulgar; that is, than all men but themselves, and a few others, whom by fame, or for concurring with themselves, they approve. For such is the nature of men, that howsoever they may acknowledge many others to be more witty, or more eloquent, or more learned; yet they will hardly believe there be many so wise as themselves; for they see their own wit at hand, and other men's at a distance. But this proveth rather that men are in that point equal, than unequal. For there is not ordinarily a greater sign of the equal distribution of any thing, than that every man is contented with his share.

From equality proceeds diffidence. From this equality of ability, ariseth equality of hope in the attaining of our ends. And therefore if any two men desire the same thing, which nevertheless they cannot both enjoy, they become enemies; and in the way to their end, which is principally their own conservation, and sometimes their delectation only, endeavour to destroy, or subdue one another. And from hence it comes to pass, that where an invader hath no more to fear, than another man's single power; if one plant, sow, build, or possess a convenient seat, others may probably be expected to come prepared with forces united, to dispossess, and deprive him, not only of the fruit of his labour, but also of his life, or liberty. And the invader again is in the like danger of another.

From diffidence war. And from this diffidence of one another, there is no way for any man to secure himself, so reasonable, as anticipation; that is, by force, or wiles, to master the persons of all men he can, so long, till he see no other power great enough to endanger him: and this is no more than his own conservation requireth, and is generally allowed. Also because there be some, that taking pleasure in contemplating their own power in the acts of conquest, which they pursue farther than their security requires; if others, that otherwise would be glad to be at ease within modest bounds, should not by invasion increase their power, they would not be able, long time, by standing only on their defence, to subsist. And by consequence, such augmentation of dominion over men being necessary to a man's conservation, it ought to be allowed him.

Again, men have no pleasure, but on the contrary a great deal of grief, in keeping company, where there is no power able to over-awe them all. For every man looketh that his companion should value him, at the same rate he sets upon himself: and upon all signs of contempt, or undervaluing, naturally endeavours, as far as he dares, (which amongst them that have no common power to keep them in quiet, is far enough to make them destroy each other), to extort a greater value from his contemners, by damage; and from others, by the example.

So that in the nature of man, we find three principal causes of quarrel. First, competion; secondly, diffidence; thirdly, glory.

The first, maketh men invade for gain; the second, for safety; and the third, for reputation. The first use violence, to make themselves masters of other men's persons, wives, children, and cattle; the second, to defend them; the third, for trifles, as a word, a smile, a different opinion, and any other sign of undervalue, either direct in their persons, or by reflection in their kindred, their friends, their nation, their profession, or their name.

Out of civil states, there is always war of every one against every one. Hereby it is manifest, that during the time men live without a power to keep them all in awe, they are in that condition which is called war; and such a war, as is of every man, against every man. For WAR, consisteth not in battle only, or the act of fighting; but in a tract of time, wherein the will to contend by battle is sufficiently known: and therefore the notion of *time*, is to be considered in the nature of war; as it is in the nature of weather. For as the nature of foul weather, lieth not in a shower or two of rain; but in an inclination thereto of many days together: so the nature of war, consisteth not in actual fighting; but in the known disposition thereto, during all the time there is no assurance to the contrary. All other time is PEACE.

The incommodities of such a war. Whatsoever therefore is consequent to a time of war, where every man is enemy to every man; the same is consequent to the time, wherein men live without other security, than what their own strength, and their own invention shall furnish them withal. In such condition, there is no place for industry; because the fruit thereof is uncertain: and consequently no culture of the earth; no navigation, nor use of the commodities that may be imported by sea; no commodious building; no instruments of moving, and removing, such things as require much force; no knowledge of the face of the earth; no account of time; no arts; no letters; no society; and which is worst of all, continual fear, and danger of violent death; and the life of man, solitary, poor, nasty, brutish, and short.

It may seem strange to some man, that has not well weighed these things; that nature should thus dissociate, and render men apt to invade, and destroy one another: and he may therefore, not trusting to this inference, made from the passions, desire perhaps to have the same confirmed by experience. Let him therefore consider with himself, when taking a journey, he arms himself, and seeks to go well accompanied; when going to sleep, he locks his doors; when even in his house he locks his chests; and this when he knows there be laws, and public officers, armed, to revenge all injuries shall be done him; what opinion he has of his fellow-subjects, when he rides armed; of his fellow citizens, when he locks his doors; and of his children, and servants, when he locks his chests. Does he not there as much accuse mankind by his actions, as I do by my words? But neither of us accuse man's nature in it. The desires, and other passions of man, are in themselves no sin. No more are the actions, that proceed from those passions, till they know a law that forbids them: which till laws be made they cannot know: nor can any law be made, till they have agreed upon the person that shall make it.

Bibliography

Cranston, Maurice, and Richard S. Peters, eds. *Hobbes and Rousseau.* New York: Anchor, 1972.

Gauthier, David P. *The Logic of Leviathan.* Oxford: Oxford University Press, 1969.

Sorell, Tom. *Hobbes.* London and New York: Routledge and Kegan Paul, 1986.

Sorell, Tom, ed. *The Cambridge Companion to Hobbes.* Cambridge: Cambridge University Press, 1996.

CHAPTER TWENTY-ONE — JAMES BOSWELL AND SAMUEL JOHNSON

Boswell's *Life of Johnson* is one of the classics of the English language and of human psychological portraiture. Samuel Johnson (1709-1784) was a literary critic, essayist, poet, biographer, and the compiler of an important dictionary of English. He was, in short, what came to be called a man of letters. Almost all of his adult activity was set in London, among a circle of friends and acquaintances. Johnson's conversation was legendary: his remarks on topics and individuals of his time and place, and of all times and places, were distinctive, often witty, and constitute a special perspective on the world. Johnson bears some comparison to Socrates, even if he was not (nor aspired to be) a philosopher of Socrates' depth or range.

Socrates, of course, had Plato to record (and augment) his conversations. He also had Xenophon, less well known, but another of the Socratic circle. More like the latter than the former, James Boswell (1740-1795) undertook to record Johnson's comments and remarks as faithfully to the syllable of utterance as he could, and set them within a biography of his revered friend.

A mere excerpt of the result is offered here, although additional passages would also have been interesting to include. Johnson is important as a human nature theorist, as a conservative individualist, and as a Christian. Johnson is the plain man of honest and moral discernment, who sees a human world that is all too often occupied by rogues, or by other varieties of very fallible human clay. He takes people as he sees them, and describes them as found.

Johnson's own essays in the periodicals *The Idler* and *The Rambler* also offer much of a Johnsonian portrait of human nature. Two short selections are provided that add to the conservative individualist view of humanity.

James Boswell, *The Life of Dr. Johnson*   ....

(Source: James Boswell. *The Life of Dr. Johnson*, Vol. I. New York: E.P. Dutton & Co. Inc., 1906, 392, 458, 548.)

He used frequently to observe, that there was more to be endured than enjoyed, in the general condition of human life; and frequently quoted those lines of Dryden:

'Strange cozenage! none would live past years again, Yet all hope pleasure from what still remain.'

For his part, he said, he never passed that week in his life which he would wish to repeat, were an angel to make the proposal to him.

I told him that Mrs. Macaulay said, she wondered how he could reconcile his political principles with his moral: his notions of inequality and subordination with wishing well to the happiness of all mankind who might live so agreeably, had they all their portions of land, and none to domineer over another.

JOHNSON. "Why, Sir, I reconcile my principles very well, because mankind are happier in a state of inequality and subordination. Were they to be in this pretty state of equality, they would soon degenerate into brutes; – they would become Monboddo's nation; – their tails would grow. Sir, all would become losers, were all to work for all: –

they would have no intellectual improvement. All intellectual improvement arises from leisure; all leisure arises from one working for another."

....

He this day enlarged upon Pope's melancholy remark,

"Man never *is*, but always *to be* blest."

He asserted, that *the present* was never a happy state state to any human being; but that, as every part of life, of which we are conscious, was at some point of time a period yet to come, in which felicity was expected, there was some happiness produced by hope. Being pressed upon this subject, and asked if he really was of opinion, that though, in general, happiness was very rare in human life, a man was not sometimes happy in the moment that was present, he answered, "Never, but when he is drunk."

....

Samuel Johnson, *The Rambler* (No. 6. Saturday, 7 April 1750)

That man should never suffer his happiness to depend upon external circumstances, is one of the chief precepts of the Stoical philosophy; a precept, indeed, which that lofty sect has extended beyond the condition of human life, and in which some of them seem to have comprised an utter exclusion of all corporal pain and pleasure, from the regard or attention of a wise man.

Such *sapientia insaniens*, as Horace calls the doctrine of another sect, such extravagance of philosophy, can want neither authority nor argument for its confutation; it is overthrown by the experience of every hour, and the powers of nature rise up against it. But we may very properly enquire, how near to this exalted state it is in our power to approach, how far we can exempt ourselves from outward influences, and secure to our minds a state of tranquillity: For, though the boast of absolute independence is ridiculous and vain, yet a mean flexibility to every impulse, and a patient submission to the tyranny of casual troubles, is below the dignity of that mind, which, however depraved or weakened, boasts its derivation from a celestial original, and hopes for an union with infinite goodness, and invariable felicity.

Ni vitiis pejora fovens
Proprium deserat ortum.
Boethius, CONSOLATIO, III. metr. 6.9.

Unless the soul, to vice a thrall,
Desert her own original.

The necessity of erecting ourselves to some degree of intellectual dignity, and of preserving resources of pleasure, which may not be wholly at the mercy of accident, is never more apparent than when we turn our eyes upon those whom fortune has let loose to their own conduct; who not being chained down by their condition to a regular and stated allotment of their hours, are obliged to find themselves business or diversion, and having nothing within that can entertain or employ them, are compelled to try all the arts of destroying time.

The numberless expedients practised by this class of mortals to alleviate the burthen of life, is not less shameful, nor, perhaps, much less pitiable, than those to which a trader on the edge of bankruptcy is reduced. I have seen melancholy overspread a whole family at the disappointment of a party for cards; and when, after the proposal of a thousand schemes, and the dispatch of the footman upon a hundred messages, they have submitted, with gloomy resignation, to the misfortune of passing one evening in conversation with each other, on a sudden, such are the revolutions of the world, an unexpected visitor has brought them relief, acceptable as provision to a starving city, and enabled them to hold out till the next day.

The general remedy of those, who are uneasy without knowing the cause, is change of place; they are willing to imagine that their pain is the consequence of some local inconvenience, and endeavour to fly from it, as children from their shadows; always hoping for more satisfactory delight from every new scene, and always returning home with disappointment and complaints.

Who can look upon this kind of infatuation, without reflecting on those that suffer under the dreadful symptom of canine madness, termed by physicians the hydrophobia, or "dread of water"? These miserable wretches, unable to drink, though burning with thirst, are sometimes known to try various contortions, or inclinations of the body, flattering themselves that they can swallow in one posture that liquor, which they find in another to repel their lips.

Yet such folly is not peculiar to the thoughtless or ignorant, but sometimes seizes those minds which seem most exempted from it, by the variety of attainments, quickness of penetration, or severity of judgment; and, indeed, the pride of wit and knowledge is often mortified by finding, that they confer no security against the common errors, which mislead the weakest and meanest of mankind.

These reflexions arose in my mind upon the remembrance of a passage in Cowley's preface to his poems, where, however exalted by genius, and enlarged by study, he informs us of a scheme of happiness to which the imagination of a girl, upon the loss of her first lover, could have scarcely given way; but which he seems to have indulged till he had totally forgotten its absurdity, and would probably have put in execution, had he been hindered only by his reason.

"My desire," says he, "has been for some years past, though the execution has been accidentally diverted, and does still vehemently continue, to retire myself to some of our American plantations, not to seek for gold, or enrich myself with the traffic of those parts, which is the end of most men that travel thither; but to forsake this world for ever, with all the vanities and vexations of it, and to bury myself there in some obscure retreat, but not without the consolation of letters and philosophy."

Such was the chimerical provision which Cowley had made, in his own mind, for the quiet of his remaining life, and which he seems to recommend to posterity, since there is no other reason for disclosing it. Surely no stronger instance can be given of a persuasion that content was the inhabitant of particular regions, and that a man might set sail with a fair wind, and leave behind him all his cares, incumbrances, and calamities.

If he travelled so far with no other purpose than to "bury himself in some obscure retreat," he might have found, in his own country, innumerable coverts sufficiently dark to have concealed the genius of Cowley; for, whatever might be his opinion of the importunity with which he should be summoned back into publick life, a short experience would have convinced him, that privation is easier than acquisition, and that it would require little continuance to free himself from the intrusion

of the world. There is pride enough in the human heart to prevent much desire of acquaintance with a man by whom we are sure to be neglected, however his reputation for science or virtue may excite our curiosity or esteem; so that the lover of retirement needs not be afraid lest the respect of strangers should overwhelm him with visits. Even those to whom he has formerly been known will very patiently support his absence, when they have tried a little to live without him, and found new diversions for those moments which his company contributed to exhilarate.

It was, perhaps, ordained by providence, to hinder us from tyrannising over one another, that no individual should be of such importance, as to cause, by his retirement or death, any chasm in the world. And Cowley had conversed to little purpose with mankind, if he had never remarked, how soon the useful friend, the gay companion, and the favoured lover, when once they are removed from before the sight, give way to the succession of new objects.

The privacy, therefore, of his hermitage might have been safe enough from violation, though he had chosen it within the limits of his native island; he might have found here preservatives against the "vanities" and "vexations" of the world, not less efficacious than those which the woods or fields of America could afford him: but having once his mind imbittered with disgust, he conceived it impossible to be far enough from the cause of his uneasiness; and was posting away with the expedition of a coward, who, for want of venturing to look behind him, thinks the enemy perpetually at his heels.

When he was interrupted by company, or fatigued with business, he so strongly imaged to himself the happiness of leisure and retreat, that he determined to enjoy them for the future without interruption, and to exclude for ever all that could deprive him of his darling satisfaction. He forgot, in the vehemence of desire, that solitude and quiet owe their pleasures to those miseries, which he was so studious to obviate; for such are the vicissitudes of the world, through all its parts, that day and night, labour and rest, hurry and retirement, endear each other; such are the changes that keep the mind in action; we desire, we pursue, we obtain, we are satiated; we desire something else, and begin a new persuit.

If he had proceeded in his project, and fixed his habitation in the most delightful part of the new world, it may be doubted, whether his distance from the "vanities" of life would have enabled him to keep away the "vexations." It is common for a man, who feels pain, to fancy that he could bear it better in any other part. Cowley having known the troubles and perplexities of a particular condition, readily persuaded himself that nothing worse was to be found, and that every alteration would bring some improvement; he never suspected that the cause of his unhappiness was within, that his own passions were not sufficiently regulated, and that he was harrassed by his own impatience, which could never be without something to awaken it, would accompany him over the sea, and find its way to his American elysium. He would, upon the tryal, have been soon convinced, that the fountain of content must spring up in the mind; and that he, who has so little knowledge of human nature, as to seek happiness by changing any thing, but his own dispositions, will waste his life in fruitless efforts, and multiply the griefs which he purposes to remove.

Samuel Johnson, *The Idler* (No. 92, Saturday, 19 January 1760)

Whatever is useful or honourable will be desired by many who never can obtain it, and that which cannot be obtained when it is desired, artifice or folly will be diligent to counterfeit. Those to whom fortune has denied gold and diamonds decorate themselves with stones and metals which have something of the show but little of the value; and every moral excellence or intellectual faculty has some vice or folly which imitates its appearance.

Every man wishes to be wise, and they who cannot be wise are almost always cunning. The less is the real discernment of those whom business or conversation brings together, the more illusions are practised; nor is caution ever so necessary as with associates or opponents of feeble minds.

Cunning differs from wisdom as twilight from open day. He that walks in the sunshine goes boldly forward by the nearest way; he sees that where the path is streight and even he may proceed in security, and where it is rough and crooked he easily complies with the turns and avoids the obstructions. But the traveller in the dusk fears more as he sees less; he knows there may be danger, and therefore suspects that he is never safe, tries every step before he fixes his foot, and shrinks at every noise lest violence should approach him. Wisdom comprehends at once the end and the means, estimates easiness or difficulty, and is cautious or confident in due proportion. Cunning discovers little at a time, and has no other means of certainty than multiplication of stratagems and superfluity of suspicion. The man of cunning always considers that he can never be too safe, and therefore always keeps himself enveloped in a mist, impenetrable, as he hopes to the eye of rivalry or curiosity.

....

It is remarked by Bacon that many men try to procure reputation only by objections, of which if they are once admitted the nullity never appears, because the design is laid aside. "This false feint of wisdom," says he, "is the ruin of business." The whole power of cunning is privative; to say nothing, and to do nothing, is the utmost of its reach. Yet men thus narrow by nature, and mean by art, are sometimes able to rise by the miscarriages of bravery and the openness of integrity, and by watching failures and snatching opportunities, obtain advantages which belong properly to higher characters.

CHAPTER TWENTY-TWO — SIMONE WEIL

Simone Weil (1909-1943) was singular, both in her thought and her life, and not altogether assimilable to any general stance or theory. Yet something like this is true of many writers represented in the present volume, and one can see after all that Weil is primarily a proponent, if an idiosyncratic one, of what we are calling conservative individualism. This may be seen reasonably well in the selection that follows. Like some other conservative individualists, Weil has (and advocates) strong moral commitments to the community, and above all to its weaker members.

It will also be discernible that Weil's view of human nature is unsystematic, and that it is not so much argued for as stated, with appeals to the reader's experience. The view is interspersed, sometimes inextricably, with reflections on politics, economic life, French history from the eighteenth century to the Vichy régime, and with simple moralizing. Nonetheless, it is plain, Weil is a marked individualist, for whom humanity has a higher calling – she is a Catholic of passionate intensity and pronounced commitments to free will – which the species falls short of all too often. The influence of Rousseau, as well as of Catholicism, may be observed in Weil's portrait of human nature and its catalogue of human needs, and in her doubts about democracy and a fully open market place of ideational advocacy. At the same time, Weil's conception is peculiarly her own.

Simone Weil, *The Need for Roots*

(Source: Simone Weil. *The Need for Roots*. Trans. A.F. Wills, 1952. Boston: Beacon Press, 1955, 3-40.)

THE NEEDS OF THE SOUL

The notion of obligations comes before that of rights, which is subordinate and relative to the former. A right is not effectual by itself, but only in relation to the obligation to which it corresponds, the effective exercise of a right springing not from the individual who possesses it, but from other men who consider themselves as being under a certain obligation toward him. Recognition of an obligation makes it effectual. An obligation which goes unrecognized by anybody loses none of the full force of its existence. A right which goes unrecognized by anybody is not worth very much.

It makes nonsense to say that men have, on the one hand, rights, and on the other hand, obligations. Such words only express differences in point of view. The actual relationship between the two is as between object and subject. A man, considered in isolation, only has duties, among which are certain duties toward himself. Other men, seen from his point of view, only have rights. He, in his turn, has rights, when seen from the point of view of other men, who recognize that they have obligations toward him. A man left alone in the universe would have no rights whatever, but he would have obligations.

The notion of rights, being of an objective order, is inseparable from the notions of existence and reality. This becomes apparent when the obligation descends to the realm of fact; consequently, it always involves to a certain extent the taking into account of actual given states and particular situations. Rights are always found to be related to certain conditions. Obligations alone remain independent of conditions. They belong to a realm situated above all conditions, because it is situated above this world.

The men of 1789 did not recognize the existence of such a realm. All they recognized was the one on the human plane. That is why they started off with the idea of rights. But at the same time they wanted to postulate absolute principles. This contradiction caused them to tumble into a confusion of language and ideas which is largely responsible for the present political and social confusion. The realm of what is eternal, universal, unconditioned is other than the one conditioned by facts, and different ideas hold sway there, ones which are related to the most secret recesses of the human soul.

Obligations are only binding on human beings. There are no obligations for collectivities, as such. But they exist for all human beings who constitute, serve, command, or represent a collectivity, in that part of their existence which is related to the collectivity as in that part which is independent of it.

All human beings are bound by identical obligations, although these are performed in different ways according to particular circumstances. No human being, whoever he may be, under whatever circumstances, can escape them without being guilty of crime; save where there are two genuine obligations which are in fact incompatible, and a man is forced to sacrifice one of them.

The imperfections of a social order can be measured by the number of situations of this kind it harbors within itself.

But even in such a case, a crime is committed if the obligation so sacrificed is not merely sacrificed in fact, but its existence denied into the bargain.

The object of any obligation, in the realm of human affairs, is always the human being as such. There exists an obligation toward every human being for the sole reason that he or she is a human being, without any other condition requiring to be fulfilled, and even without any recognition of such obligation on the part of the individual concerned.

This obligation is not based upon any *de facto* situation, nor upon jurisprudence, customs, social structure, relative state of forces, historical heritage, or presumed historical orientation; for no *de facto* situation is able to create an obligation.

This obligation is not based upon any convention; for all conventions are liable to be modified according to the wishes of the contracting parties, whereas in this case no change in the mind and will of Man can modify anything whatsoever.

This obligation is an eternal one. It is coextensive with the eternal destiny of human beings. Only human beings have an eternal destiny. Human collectives have not got one. Nor are there, in regard to the latter, any direct obligations of an eternal nature. Duty toward the human being as such –

that alone is eternal.

This obligation is an unconditional one. If it is founded on something, that something, whatever it is, does not form part of our world. In our world, it is not founded on anything at all. It is the one and only obligation in connection with human affairs that is not subject to any condition.

This obligation has no foundation, but only a verification in the common consent accorded by the universal conscience. It finds expression in some of the oldest written texts which have come down to us. It is recognized by everybody without exception in every single case where it is not attacked as a result of interest or passion. And it is in relation to it that we measure our progress.

The recognition of this obligation is expressed in a confused and imperfect form, that is, more or less imperfect according to the particular case, by what are called positive rights. To the extent to which positive rights are in contradiction with it, to that precise extent is their origin an illegitimate one.

Although this eternal obligation is coextensive with the eternal destiny of the human being, this destiny is not its direct motive. A human being's eternal destiny cannot be the motive of any obligation, for it is not subordinate to external actions.

The fact that a human being possesses an eternal destiny imposes only one obligation: respect. The obligation is only performed if the respect is effectively expressed in a real, not a fictitious, way; and this can only be done through the medium of Man's earthly needs.

On this point, the human conscience has never varied. Thousands of years ago, the Egyptians believed that no soul could justify itself after death unless it could say, "I have never let any one suffer from hunger." All Christians know they are liable to hear Christ Himself say to them one day, "I was an hungered, and ye gave me no meat." Every one looks on progress as being, in the first place, a transition to a state of human society in which people will not suffer from hunger. To no matter whom the question may be put in general terms, nobody is of the opinion that any man is innocent if, possessing food himself in abundance and finding someone on his doorstep three parts dead from hunger, he brushes past without giving him anything.

So it is an eternal obligation toward the human being not to let him suffer from hunger when one has the chance of coming to his assistance. This obligation being the most obvious of all, it can serve as a model on which to draw up the list of eternal duties toward each human being. In order to be absolutely correctly made out, this list ought to proceed from the example just given by way of analogy.

Consequently, the list of obligations toward the human being should correspond to the list of such human needs as are vital, analogous to hunger.

Among such needs, there are some which are physical, like hunger itself. They are fairly easy to enumerate. They are concerned with protection against violence, housing, clothing, heating, hygiene and medical attention in case of illness. There are others which have no connection with the physical side of life, but are concerned with its moral side. Like the former, however, they are earthly, and are not directly related, so far as our intelligence is able to perceive, to the eternal destiny of Man. They form, like our physical needs, a necessary condition of our life on this earth. Which means to say that if they are not satisfied, we fall little by little into a state more or less resembling death, more or less akin to a purely vegetative existence.

They are much more difficult to recognize and to enumerate than are the needs of the body. But every one recognizes that they exist. All the different forms of cruelty that a conqueror can exercise over a subject population, such as massacre, mutilation, organized famine, enslavement, or large-scale deportation, are generally considered to be measures of a like description, even though a man's liberty or his native land are not physical necessities. Every one knows that there are forms of cruelty that can injure a man's life without injuring his body. They are such as deprive him of a certain form of food necessary to the life of the soul.

Obligations, whether unconditional or relative, eternal or changing, direct or indirect with regard to human affairs, all stem, without exception, from the vital needs of the human being. Those which do not directly concern this, that, or the other specific human being all exist to serve requirements which, with respect to Man, play a role analogous to food.

We owe a cornfield respect, not because of itself, but because it is food for mankind.

In the same way, we owe our respect to a collectivity, of whatever kind – country, family, or any other – not for itself, but because it is food for a certain number of human souls.

Actually, this obligation makes different attitudes, actions necessary according to different situations. But, taken by itself, it is absolutely identical for everybody. More particularly is this so for all those outside such a collectivity.

The degree of respect owing to human collectivities is a very high one, for several reasons.

To start with, each is unique, and, if destroyed, cannot be replaced. One sack of corn can always be substituted for another sack of corn. The food that collectivity supplies, for the souls of those who form part of it has no equivalent in the entire universe.

Secondly, because of its continuity, a collectivity is already moving forward into the future. It contains food, not only for the souls of the living, but also for the souls of beings yet unborn which are to come into the world during the immediately succeeding centuries.

Lastly, due to this same continuity, a collectivity has its roots in the past. It constitutes the sole agency for preserving the spiritual treasures accumulated by the dead, the sole transmitting agency by means of which the dead can speak to the living. And the sole earthly reality which is directly connected with the eternal destiny of Man is the irradiating light of those who have managed to become fully conscious of this destiny, transmitted from generation to generation.

Because of all this, it may happen that the obligation toward a collectivity which is in danger reaches the point of entailing a total sacrifice. But it does not follow from this that collectivities are superior to human beings. It sometimes happens, too, that the obligation to go to the help of a human being in distress makes a total sacrifice necessary, without that implying any superiority on the part of the individual so helped.

A peasant may, under certain circumstances, be under the necessity, in order to cultivate his land, of risking exhaustion, illness, or even death. But all the time he will be conscious of the fact that it is solely a matter of bread.

Similarly, even when a total sacrifice is required, no more is owed to any collectivity whatever than a respect analogous to the one owed to food.

It very often happens that the roles are reversed. There are collectivities which, instead of serving as food, do just the opposite: they devour souls. In such cases, the social body is diseased, and the first duty is to attempt a cure; in certain circumstances, it may be necessary to have recourse to surgical methods.

With regard to this matter, too, the obligation for those inside as for those outside the collectivity is an identical one.

It also happens that a collectivity supplies insufficient food for the souls of those forming part of it. In that case, it has to be improved.

Finally, there are dead collectivities which, without devouring souls, don't nourish them either. If it is absolutely certain that they are well and truly dead, that it isn't just a question of a temporary lethargy, then and only then should they be destroyed.

The first thing to be investigated is what are those needs which are for the life of the soul, what the needs in the way of food, sleep, and warmth are for the life of the body. We must try to enumerate and define them.

They must never be confused with desires, whims, fancies, and vices. We must also distinguish between what is fundamental and what is fortuitous. Man requires, not rice or potatoes, but food; not wood or coal, but heating. In the same way, for the needs of the soul, we must recognize the different, but equivalent, sorts of satisfaction which cater for the same requirements. We must also distinguish between the soul's foods and poisons which, for a time, can give the impression of occupying the place of the former.

The lack of any such investigation forces governments, even when their intentions are honest, to act sporadically and at random.

Below are offered a few indications.

ORDER

The first of the soul's needs, the one which touches most nearly its eternal destiny, is order; that is to say, a texture of social relationships such that no one is compelled to violate imperative obligations in order to carry out other ones. It is only where this, in fact, occurs that external circumstances have any power to inflict spiritual violence on the soul. For he for whom the threat of death or suffering is the one thing standing in the way of the performance of an obligation, can overcome this dis-

ability, and will only suffer in his body. But he who finds that circumstances, in fact, render the various acts necessitated by a series of strict obligations incompatible with one another is, without being able to offer any resistance thereto, made to suffer in his love of good.

At the present time, a very considerable amount of confusion and incompatibility exists between obligations.

Whoever acts in such a way as to increase this incompatibility is a troublemaker. Whoever acts in such a way as to diminish it is an agent of order. Whoever, so as to simplify problems, denies the existence of certain obligations has, in his heart, made a compact with crime.

Unfortunately, we possess no method for diminishing this incompatibility. We cannot even be sure that the idea of an order in which all obligations would be compatible with one another isn't itself a fiction. When duty descends to the level of facts, so many independent relationships are brought into play that incompatibility seems far more likely than compatibility.

Nevertheless, we have every day before us the example of a universe in which an infinite number of independent mechanical actions concur so as to produce an order that, in the midst of variations, remains fixed. Furthermore, we love the beauty of the world, because we sense behind it the presence of something akin to that wisdom we should like to possess to slake our thirst for good.

In a minor degree, really beautiful works of art are examples of ensembles in which independent factors concur, in a manner impossible to understand, so as to form a unique thing of beauty.

Finally, a consciousness of the various obligations always proceeds from a desire for good which is unique, unchanging, and identical with itself for every man, from the cradle to the grave. This desire, perpetually stirring in the depths of our being, makes it impossible for us ever to resign ourselves to situations in which obligations are incompatible with one another. Either we have recourse to lying in order to forget their existence, or we struggle blindly to extricate ourselves from them.

The contemplation of veritable works of art, and much more still that of the beauty of the world, and again much more that of the unrealized good to which we aspire, can sustain us in our efforts to think continually about that human order which should be the subject uppermost in our minds.

The great instigators of violence have encouraged themselves with the thought of how blind, mechanical force is sovereign throughout the whole universe.

By looking at the world with keener senses than theirs, we shall find a more powerful encouragement in the thought of how these innumerable blind forces are limited, made to balance one against the other, brought to form a united whole by something which we do not understand, but which we call beauty.

If we keep ever present in our minds the idea of a veritable human order, if we think of it as of something to which a total sacrifice is due should the need arise, we shall be in a similar position to that of a man traveling, without a guide, through the night, but continually thinking of the direction he wishes to follow. Such a traveler's way is lit by a great hope.

Order is the first need of all, it even stands above all needs properly so-called. To be able to conceive it, we must know what the other needs are.

The first characteristic which distinguishes needs from desires, fancies, or vices, and foods from gluttonous repasts or poisons is that needs are limited, in exactly the same way as are the foods corresponding to them. A miser never has enough gold, but the time comes when any man provided with an unlimited supply of bread finds he has had enough. Food brings satiety. The same applies to the soul's foods.

The second characteristic, closely connected with the first, is that needs are arranged in antithetical pairs and have to combine together to form a balance. Man requires food, but also an interval between his meals; he requires warmth and coolness, rest and exercise. Likewise in the case of the soul's needs.

What is called the golden mean actually consists in satisfying neither the one nor the other of two contrary needs. It is a caricature of the genuinely balanced state in which contrary needs are each fully satisfied in turn.

LIBERTY

One of the indispensable foods of the human soul is liberty. Liberty, taking the word in its concrete sense, consists in the ability to choose. We must understand by that, of course, a real ability. Wherever men are living in community, rules imposed in the common interest must necessarily limit the possibilities of choice.

But a greater or lesser degree of liberty does not depend on whether the limits set are wider or narrower. Liberty attains its plenitude under conditions which are less easily gauged.

Rules should be sufficiently sensible and sufficiently straightforward so that any one who so desires and is blessed with average powers of application may be able to understand, on the one hand the useful ends they serve, and on the other hand the actual necessities which have brought about their institution. They should emanate from a source of authority which is not looked upon as strange or hostile, but loved as something belonging to those placed under its direction. They should be sufficiently stable, general and limited in number for the mind to be able to grasp them once and for all, and not find itself brought up against them every time a decision has to be made.

Under these conditions, the liberty of men of good will, though limited in the sphere of action, is complete in that of conscience. For, having incorporated the rules into their own being, the prohibited possibilities no longer present themselves to the mind, and have not to be rejected. Just as the habit, formed by education, of not eating disgusting or dangerous things is not felt by the normal man to be any limitation of his liberty in the domain of food. Only a child feels such a limitation.

Those who are lacking in good will or who remain adolescent are never free under any form of society.

When the possibilities of choice are so wide as to injure the commonweal, men cease to enjoy liberty. For they must either seek refuge in irresponsibility, puerility, and indifference – a refuge where the most they can find is boredom – or feel themselves weighed down by responsibility at all times for fear of causing harm to others. Under such circumstances, men, believing, wrongly, that they are in possession of liberty, and feeling that they get no enjoyment out of it, end up by thinking that liberty is not a good thing.

OBEDIENCE

Obedience is a vital need of the human soul. It is of two kinds: obedience to established rules and obedience to human beings looked upon as leaders. It presupposes consent, not in regard to every single order received, but the kind of consent that is given once and for all, with the sole reservation, in case of need, that the demands of conscience be satisfied.

It requires to be generally recognized, and above all by leaders themselves, that consent and not fear of punishment or hope of reward constitutes, in fact, the mainspring of obedience, so that submission may never be mistaken for servility. It should also be realized that those who command, obey in their turn, and the whole hierarchy should have its face set in the direction of a goal whose importance and even grandeur can be felt by all, from the highest to the lowest.

Obedience being a necessary food of the soul, whoever is definitely deprived of it is ill. Thus, any body politic governed by a sovereign ruler accountable to nobody is in the hands of a sick man.

That is why wherever a man is placed for life at the head of the social organism, he ought to be a symbol and not a ruler, as is the case with the king of England; etiquette ought also to restrict his freedom more narrowly than that of any single man of the people. In this way, the effective rulers, rulers though they be, have somebody over them; on the other hand, they are able to replace each other in unbroken continuity, and consequently to receive, each in his turn, that indispensable amount of obedience due to him.

Those who keep masses of men in subjection by exercising force and cruelty deprive them at once of two vital foods, liberty and obedience; for it is no longer within the power of such masses to accord their inner consent to the authority to which they are subjected. Those who encourage a state of things in which the hope of gain is the principal motive take away from men their obedience, for consent, which is its essence, is not something which can be sold.

There are any number of signs showing that the men of our age have now for a long time been starved of obedience. But advantage has been taken of the fact to give them slavery.

RESPONSIBILITY

Initiative and responsibility, to feel one is useful and even indispensable, are vital needs of the human soul.

Complete privation from this point of view is the case of the unemployed person, even if he receives assistance to the extent of being able to feed, clothe, and house himself. For he represents nothing at all in the economic life of his country, and the voting paper, which represents his share in its political life, doesn't hold any meaning for him.

The manual laborer is in a scarcely better position.

For this need to be satisfied it is necessary that a man should often have to take decisions in matters great or small affecting interests that are distinct from his own, but in regard to which he feels a personal concern. He also requires to be continually called upon to supply fresh efforts. Finally, he requires to be able to encompass in thought the entire range of activity of the social organism to which he belongs, including branches in connection with which he has never to take a decision or offer any advice. For that, he must be made acquainted with it, be asked to interest himself in it, be brought to feel its value, its utility, and, where necessary, its greatness, and be made fully aware of the part he plays in it.

Every social organism, of whatever kind it may be, which does not provide its members with these satisfactions, is diseased and must be restored to health.

In the case of every person of fairly strong character, the need to show initiative goes so far as the need to take command. A flourishing local and regional life, a host of educational activities and youth movements ought to furnish whoever is able to take advantage of it with the opportunity to command at certain periods of his life.

EQUALITY

Equality is a vital need of the human soul. It consists in a recognition, at once public, general, effective, and genuinely expressed in institutions and customs, that the same amount of respect and consideration is due to every human being because this respect is due to the human being as such and is not a matter of degree.

It follows that the inevitable differences among men ought never to imply any difference in the degree of respect. And so that these differences may not be felt to bear such an implication, a certain balance is necessary between equality and inequality.

A certain combination of equality and inequality is formed by equality of opportunity. If no matter who can attain the social rank corresponding to the function he is capable of filling, and if education is sufficiently generalized so that no one is prevented from developing any capacity simply on account of his birth, the prospects are the same for every child. In this way, the prospects for each man are the same as for any other man, both as regards himself when young, and as regards his children later on.

But when such a combination acts alone, and not as one factor among other factors, it ceases to constitute a balance and contains great dangers.

To begin with, for a man who occupies an inferior position and suffers from it to know that his position is a result of his incapacity and that everybody is aware of the fact is not any consolation, but an additional motive of bitterness; according to the individual character, some men can thereby be thrown into a state of depression, while others can be encouraged to commit crime.

Then, in social life, a sort of aspirator toward the top is inevitably created. If a descending movement does not come to balance this ascending movement, the social body becomes sick. To the extent to which it is really possible for the son of a farm laborer to become one day a minister, to the same extent should it really be possible for the son of a minister to become one day a farm laborer. This second possibility could never assume any noticeable proportions without a very dangerous degree of social constraint.

This sort of equality, if allowed full play by itself, can make social life fluid to the point of decomposing it.

There are less clumsy methods of combining equality with differentiation. The first is by using proportion. Proportion can be defined as the combination of equality with inequality, and everywhere throughout the universe it is the sole factor making for balance.

Applied to the maintenance of social equilibrium, it would impose on each man burdens corresponding to the power and well being he enjoys, and corresponding risks in cases of incapacity or neglect. For instance, an employer who is incapable or guilty of an offense against his workmen ought to be made to suffer far more, both in the spirit and in the flesh, than a workman who is incapable or guilty of an offense against his employer. Furthermore, all workmen ought to know that this is so. It would imply, on the one hand, a certain rearrangement with regard to risks, on the other hand, in criminal law, a conception of punishment in which social rank, as an aggravating circumstance, would necessarily play an important part in deciding what the penalty was to be. All the more reason, therefore, why the exercise of important public functions should carry with it serious personal risks.

Another way of rendering equality compatible with differentiation would be to take away as far as possible all quantitative character from differences. Where there is only a difference in kind, not in degree, there is no inequality at all.

But making money the sole, or almost the sole, motive of all actions, the sole, or almost the sole, measure of all things, the poison of inequality has been introduced everywhere. It is true that this inequality is mobile; it is not attached to persons, for money is made and lost; it is none the less real.

There are two sorts of inequality, each with its corresponding stimulant. A more or less stable inequality, like that of ancient France, produces an idolizing of superiors – not without a mixture of repressed hatred – and a submission to their commands. A mobile, fluid inequality produces a desire to better oneself. It is no nearer to equality than is stable inequality, and is every bit as unwholesome. The Revolution of 1789, in putting forward equality, only succeeded in reality in sanctioning the substitution of one form of inequality for another.

The more equality there is in a society, the smaller is the action of the two stimulants connected with the two forms of inequality, and hence other stimulants are necessary.

Equality is all the greater in proportion as different human conditions are regarded as being, not more nor less than one another, but simply as other. Let us look on the professions of miner and minister simply as two different vocations, like those of poet and mathematician. And let the material hardships attaching to the miner's condition be counted in honor of those who undergo them.

In wartime, if an army is filled with the right spirit, a soldier is proud and happy to be under fire instead of at headquarters; a general is proud and happy to think that the successful outcome of the battle depends on his forethought; and at the same time the soldier admires the general and the general the soldier.

Such a balance constitutes an equality. There would be equality in social conditions if this balance could be found therein. It would mean honoring each human condition with those marks of respect which are proper to it, and are not just a hollow pretense.

HIERARCHISM

Hierarchism is a vital need of the human soul. It is composed of a certain veneration, a certain devotion toward superiors, considered not as individuals, nor in relation to the powers they exercise, but as symbols. What they symbolize is that realm situated high above all men and whose expression in this world is made up of the obligations owed by each man to his fellow men. A veritable hierarchy presupposes a consciousness on the part of the superiors of this symbolic function and a realization that it forms the only legitimate object of devotion among their subordinates. The effect of true hierarchism is to bring each one to fit himself morally into the place he occupies.

HONOR

Honor is a vital need of the human soul. The respect due to every human being as such, even if effectively accorded, is not sufficient to satisfy this need, for it is identical for every one and unchanging; whereas honor has to do with a human being considered not simply as such, but from the point of view of his social surroundings. This need is fully satisfied where each of the social organisms to which a human being belongs allows him to share in a noble tradition enshrined in its past history and given public acknowledgment.

For example, for the need of honor to be satisfied in professional life, every profession requires to have some association really capable of keeping alive the memory of all the store of nobility, heroism, probity, generosity, and genius spent in the exercise of that profession.

All oppression creates a famine in regard to the need of honor, for the noble traditions possessed by those suffering oppression go unrecognized, through lack of social prestige.

Conquest always has that effect. Vercingetorix was no hero to the Romans. Had France been conquered by the English in the fifteenth century, Joan of Arc would be well and truly forgotten, even to a great extent by us. We now talk about her to the Annamites and the Arabs; but they know very well that here in France we don't allow their heroes and saints to be talked about; therefore the state in which we keep them is an affront to their honor.

Social oppression has the same effects. Guynemer and Mermoz have become part of the public consciousness, thanks to the social prestige of aviation; the sometimes incredible heroism displayed by miners or fishermen barely awakes an echo among miners or fishermen themselves.

Deprivation of honor attains its extreme degree with that total deprivation of respect reserved for certain categories of human beings. In France, this affects, under various forms, prostitutes, ex-convicts, police agents, and the subproletariat composed of colonial immigrants and natives. Categories of this kind ought not to exist.

Crime alone should place the individual who has committed it outside the social pale, and punishment should bring him back again inside it.

PUNISHMENT

Punishment is a vital need of the human soul. There are two kinds of punishment, disciplinary and penal. The former offers security against failings with which it would be too exhausting to struggle if there were no exterior support. But the most indispensable punishment for the soul is that inflicted for crime. By committing crime, a man places himself, of his own accord, outside the chain of eternal obligations that bind every human being to every other one. Punishment alone can weld him back again; fully so, if accompanied by consent on his part; otherwise only partially so. Just as the only way of showing respect for somebody suffering from hunger is to give him something to eat, so the only way of showing respect for somebody who has placed himself outside the law is to reinstate him inside the law by subjecting him to the punishment ordained by the law.

The need of punishment is not satisfied where, as is generally the case, the penal code is merely a method of exercising pressure through fear.

So that this need may be satisfied, it is above all necessary that everything connected with the penal law should wear a solemn and consecrated aspect; that the majesty of the law should make its presence felt by the court, the police, the accused, the guilty man – even when the case dealt with is of minor importance, provided it entails a possible loss of liberty. Punishment must be an honor. It must not only wipe out the stigma of the crime, but must be regarded as a supplementary form of education, compelling a higher devotion to the public good. The severity of the punishment must also be in keeping with the kind of obligation which has been violated, and not with the interests of public security.

The discredit attaching to the police, the irresponsible conduct of the judiciary, the prison system, the permanent social stigma cast upon ex-convicts, the scale of penalties, which provides a much harsher punishment for ten acts of petty larceny than for one rape or certain types of murder, and which even provides punishments for ordinary misfortune – all this makes it impossible for there to exist among us, in France, anything that deserves the name of punishment.

For offenses, as for crimes, the relative degree of immunity should increase, not as you go up, but as you go down the social scale. Otherwise the hardships inflicted will be felt to be in the nature of constraints or even abuses of power, and will no longer constitute punishments. Punishment only takes place where the hardship is accompanied at some time or another, even after it is over, and in retrospect, by a feeling of justice. Just as the musician awakens the sense of beauty in us by sounds, so the penal system should know how to awaken the sense of justice in the criminal by the infliction of pain, or even, if need be, of death. And in the same way as we can say of the apprentice who injures himself at his trade, that it is the trade which is getting into *him,* so punishment is a method for getting justice into the soul of the criminal by bodily suffering.

The question of the best means to employ to prevent a conspiracy from arising in high places with the object of obtaining immunity from the law, is one of the most difficult political problems to solve. It can only be solved if there are men whose duty it is to prevent such a conspiracy, and whose situation in life is such that they are not tempted to enter it themselves.

FREEDOM OF OPINION

Freedom of opinion and freedom of association are usually classed together. It is a mistake. Save in the case of natural groupings, association is not a need, but an expedient employed in the practical affairs of life.

On the other hand, complete, unlimited freedom of expression for every sort of opinion, without the least restriction or reserve, is an absolute need on the part of the intelligence. It follows from this that it is a need of the soul, for when the intelligence is ill-at-ease the whole soul is sick. The nature and limits of the satisfaction corresponding to this need are inscribed in the very structure of the various faculties of the soul. For the same thing can be at once limited and unlimited, just as one can produce the length of a rectangle indefinitely without it ceasing to be limited in width.

In the case of a human being, the intelligence can be exercised in three ways. It can work on technical problems, that is to say, discover means to achieve an already given objective. It can provide light when a choice lies before the will concerning the path to be followed. Finally, it can operate alone, separately from the other faculties, in a purely theoretical speculation where all question of action has been provisionally set aside.

When the soul is in a healthy condition, it is exercised in these three ways in turn, with different degrees of freedom. In the first function, it acts as a servant. In the second function, it acts destructively and requires to be reduced to silence immediately it begins to supply arguments to that part of the soul which, in the case of any one not in a state of perfection, always places itself on the side of evil. But when it operates alone and separately, it must be in possession of sovereign liberty; otherwise something essential is wanting to the human being.

The same applies in a healthy society. That is why it would be desirable to create an absolutely free reserve in the field of publication, but in such a way as for it to be understood that the works found therein did not pledge their authors in any way and contained no direct advice for readers. There it would be possible to find, set out in their full force, all the arguments in favor of bad causes. It would be an excellent and salutary thing for them to be so displayed. Anybody could there sing the praises of what he most condemns. It would be publicly recognized that the object of such works was not to define their authors' attitudes vis-à-vis the problems of life, but to contribute, by preliminary researches, toward a complete and correct tabulation of data concerning each problem. The law would see to it that their publication did not involve any risk of whatever kind for the author.

On the other hand, publications destined to influence what is called opinion, that is to say, in effect, the conduct of life, constitute acts and ought to be subjected to the same restrictions as are all acts. In other words, they should not cause unlawful harm of any kind to any human being, and above all, should never contain any denial, explicit or implicit, of the eternal obligations toward the human being, once these obligations have been solemnly recognized by law.

The distinction between the two fields, the one which is outside action and the one which forms part of action, is impossible to express on paper in juridical terminology. But that doesn't prevent it from being a perfectly clear one. The separate existence of these two fields is not difficult to establish in fact, if only the will to do so is sufficiently strong.

It is obvious, for example, that the entire daily and weekly press comes within the second field; reviews also, for they all constitute, individually, a focus of radiation in regard to a particular way of thinking; only those that were to renounce this function would be able to lay claim to total liberty.

The same applies to literature. It would solve the argument which arose not long ago on the subject of literature and morals, and which was clouded over by the fact that all the talented people, through professional solidarity, were found on one side, and only fools and cowards on the other.

But the attitude of the fools and cowards was none the less, to a large extent, consistent with the demands of reason. Writers have an outrageous habit of playing a double game. Never so much as

in our age have they claimed the role of directors of conscience and exercised it. Actually, during the years immediately preceding the war, no one challenged their right to it except the savants. The position formerly occupied by priests in the moral life of the country was held by physicists and novelists, which is sufficient to gauge the value of our progress. But if somebody called upon writers to render an account of the orientation set by their influence, they barricaded themselves indignantly behind the sacred privilege of art for art's sake.

There is not the least doubt, for example, that André Gide has always known that books like the *Nourritures Terrestres* and the *Caves du Vatican* have exercised an influence on the practical conduct of life of hundreds of young people, and he has been proud of the fact. There is, then, no reason for placing such books behind the inviolable barrier of art for art's sake, and sending to prison a young fellow who pushes somebody off a train in motion.[1] One might just as well claim the privileges of art for art's sake in support of crime. At one time the Surrealists came pretty close to doing so. All that has been repeated by so many idiots *ad nauseam* about the responsibility of our writers in the defeat of France in 1940 is, unfortunately, only too true.

If a writer, thanks to the complete freedom of expression accorded to pure intelligence, publishes written matter that goes contrary to the moral principles recognized by law, and if later on he becomes a notorious focus of influence, it is simple enough to ask him if he is prepared to state publicly that his writings do not express his personal attitude. If he is not prepared to do so, it is simple enough to punish him. If he lies, it is simple enough to discredit him. Moreover, it ought to be recognized that the moment a writer fills a role among the influences directing public opinion, he cannot claim to exercise unlimited freedom. Here again, a juridical definition is impossible; but the facts are not really difficult to discern. There is no reason at all why the sovereignty of the law should be limited to the field of what can be expressed in legal formulas, since that sovereignty is exercised just as well by judgments in equity.

Besides, the need of freedom itself, so essential to the intellect, calls for a corresponding protection

---

1   *"D'emprisonner un garçon qui jette quelqu'un hors d'un train en marche"*: a reference to a gratuitous act performed by Lafcadio, hero of André Gide's *Caves du Vatican*, who pushes somebody off a train in Italy to prove to himself that he *is* capable of committing any act whatever, however motiveless, unrelated to preceding events. [Translator.]

against suggestion, propaganda, influence by means of obsession. These are methods of constraint, a special kind of constraint, not accompanied by fear or physical distress, but which is none the less a form of violence. Modern technique places extremely potent instruments at its service. This constraint is, by its very nature, collective, and human souls are its victims.

Naturally, the State is guilty of crime if it makes use of such methods itself, save in cases where the public safety is absolutely at stake. But it should, furthermore, prevent their use. Publicity, for example, should be rigorously controlled by law and its volume very considerably reduced; it should also be severely prohibited from ever dealing with subjects which belong to the domain of thought.

Likewise, repression could be exercised against the press, radio broadcasts, or anything else of a similar kind, not only for offenses against moral principles publicly recognized, but also for baseness of tone and thought, bad taste, vulgarity, or a subtly corrupting moral atmosphere. This sort of repression could take place without in any way infringing on freedom of opinion. For instance, a newspaper could be suppressed without the members of its editorial staff losing the right to go on publishing wherever they liked, or even, in the less serious cases, remain associated to carry on the same paper under another name. Only, it would have been publicly branded with infamy and would run the risk of being so again. Freedom of opinion can be claimed solely – and even then with certain reservations – by the journalist, not by the paper; for it is only the journalist who is capable of forming an opinion.

Generally speaking, all problems to do with freedom of expression are clarified if it is posited that this freedom is a need of the intelligence, and that intelligence resides solely in the human being, individually considered. There is no such thing as a collective exercise of the intelligence. It follows that no group can legitimately claim freedom of expression, because no group has the slightest need of it.

In fact the opposite applies. Protection of freedom of thought requires that no group should be permitted by law to express an opinion. For when a group starts having opinions, it inevitably tends to impose them on its members. Sooner or later, these individuals find themselves debarred, with a greater or lesser degree of severity, and on a number of problems of greater or lesser importance, from expressing opinions opposed to those of the group, unless they care to leave it. But a break with any group to which one belongs always involves suffering – at any rate of a sentimental kind. And just as danger, exposure to suffering are healthy and necessary elements in the sphere of action, so are they unhealthy influences in the exercise of the intelligence. A fear, even a passing one, always provokes either a weakening or a tautening, depending on the degree of courage, and that is all that is required to damage the extremely delicate and fragile instrument of precision that constitutes our intelligence. Even friendship is, from this point of view, a great danger. The intelligence is defeated as soon as the expression of one's thoughts is preceded, explicitly or implicitly, by the little word "we." And when the light of the intelligence grows dim, it is not very long before the love of good becomes lost.

The immediate, practical solution would be the abolition of political parties. Party strife, as it existed under the Third Republic, is intolerable. The single party, which is, moreover, its inevitable outcome, is the worst evil of all. The only remaining possibility is a public life without parties. Nowadays, such an idea strikes us as a novel and daring proposition. All the better, since something novel is what is wanted. But, in point of fact, it is only going back to the tradition of 1789. In the eyes of the people of 1789, there was literally no other possibility. A public life like ours has been over the course of the last half century would have seemed to them a hideous nightmare. They would never have believed it possible that a representative of the people should so divest himself of all personal dignity as to allow himself to become the docile member of a party.

Moreover, Rousseau had clearly demonstrated how party strife automatically destroys the Republic. He had foretold its effects. It would be a good thing just now to encourage the reading of the *Contrat Social*. Actually, at the present time, wherever there were political parties, democracy is dead. We all know that the parties in England have a certain tradition, spirit, and function making it impossible to compare them to anything else. We all know, besides, that the rival teams in the United States are not political parties. A democracy where public life is made up of strife between political parties is incapable of preventing the formation of a party whose avowed aim is the overthrow of that democracy. If such a democracy brings in discriminatory laws, it cuts its own throat. If it doesn't, it is just as safe as a little bird in front of a snake.

A distinction ought to be drawn between two sorts of associations: those concerned with interests, where organization and discipline would be countenanced up to a certain point, and those concerned with ideas, where such things would be strictly forbidden. Under present conditions, it is a good thing to allow people to group themselves together to defend their interests, in other words, their wage receipts and so forth, and to leave these associations to act within very narrow limits and under the constant supervision of the authorities. But such associations should not be allowed to have anything to do with ideas. Associations in which ideas are being canvassed should be not so much associations as more or less fluid social mediums. When some action is contemplated within them, there is no reason why it need be put into execution by any persons other than those who approve of it.

In the working-class movement, for example, such a distinction would put an end to the present inextricable confusion. In the period before the war, the workingman's attention was being continually pulled in three directions at once. In the first place, by the struggle for higher wages; secondly, by what remained – growing ever feebler, but still showing some signs of life – of the old trade-union spirit of former days, idealist and more or less libertarian in character; and, lastly, by the political parties. Very often, when a strike was on, the workmen who struggled and suffered would have been quite incapable of deciding for themselves whether it was all a matter of wages, a revival of the old trade-union spirit, or a political maneuver conducted by a party; and nobody looking on from the outside was in any better position to judge.

That is an impossible state of affairs. When the war broke out, the French trade-unions were dead or moribund, in spite of their millions of members – or because of them. They again took on some semblance of life, after a prolonged lethargy, when the Resistance against the invader got under way. That doesn't prove that they are viable. It is perfectly clear that they had been all but destroyed by two sorts of poison, each of which by itself is deadly.

Trade-unions cannot flourish if at their meetings the workmen are obsessed by their earnings to the same extent as they are in the factory, when engaged in piecework. To begin with, because the result is that sort of moral death always brought about by an obsession in regard to money. Next, because the trade-union, having become, under present social conditions, a factor continually acting upon the economic life of the country, ends up inevitably by being transformed into a single, compulsory, professional organization, obliged to toe the line in public affairs. It has then been changed into the semblance of a corpse.

Besides, it is no less evident that trade-unions cannot live in intimate contact with political parties. There is something resulting from the normal play of mechanical forces that makes such a thing quite impossible. For an analogous reason, moreover, the Socialist party cannot live side by side with the Communist party, because the latter's party character is, as it were, marked to a so much greater degree.

Furthermore, the obsession about wages strengthens Communist influence, because questions to do with money, however closely they may affect the majority of men, produce at the same time in all men a sensation of such deadly boredom that it requires to be compensated by the apocalyptic prospect of the Revolution, according to Communist tenets. If the middle classes haven't the same need of an apocalypse, it is because long rows of figures have a poetry, a prestige which tempers in some sort the boredom associated with money; whereas, when money is counted in sixpences, we have boredom in its pure, unadulterated state. Nevertheless, that taste shown by bourgeois, both great and small, for Fascism, indicates that, in spite of everything, they too can feel bored.

Under the Vichy Government, single and compulsory professional organizations for workmen have been created. It is a pity that they have been given, according to the modern fashion, the name of corporation, which denotes, in reality, something so very different and so beautiful. But it is a good thing that such dead organizations should be there to take over the dead part of trade union activity. It would be dangerous to do away with them. It is far better to charge them with the day-to-day business of dealing with wages and what are called immediate demands. As for the political parties, if they were all strictly prohibited in a general atmosphere of liberty, it is to be hoped their underground existence would at any rate be made difficult for them.

In that event, the workmen's trade-unions, if they still retain a spark of any real life, could become again, little by little, the expression of working-class thought, the instrument of working-class integrity. According to the traditions of the French working-class movement, which has always looked upon itself as responsible for the whole world, they would concern themselves with everything to do with justice – including, where necessary, questions about wages; but only at long intervals and to rescue human beings from poverty.

Naturally, they would have to be able to exert an influence on professional organizations, according to methods of procedure defined by law.

There would, perhaps, only be advantages to be gained by making it illegal for professional organizations to launch a strike, and allowing trade-unions – with certain restrictions – to do so, while at the same time attaching risks to this responsibility, prohibiting any sort of coercion, and safeguarding the continuity of economic life.

As for the lockout, there is no reason why it should not be entirely suppressed.

The authorized existence of associations for promoting ideas could be subject to two conditions. First, that excommunication may not be applied. Recruitment would be voluntary and as a result of personal affinity, without, however, making anybody liable to be invited to subscribe to a collection of assertions crystallized in written form. But once a member had been admitted, he could not be expelled except for some breach of integrity or undermining activities; which latter offense would, moreover, imply the existence of an illegal organization, and consequently expose the offender to a more severe punishment.

This would, in fact, amount to a measure of public safety, experience having shown that totalitarian states are set up by totalitarian parties, and that these totalitarian parties are formed by dint of expulsions for the crime of having an opinion of one's own.

The second condition could be that ideas must really be put into circulation, and tangible proof of such circulation given in the shape of pamphlets, reviews, or typed bulletins in which problems of general interest were discussed. Too great a uniformity of opinion would render any such association suspect.

For the rest, all associations for promoting ideas would be authorized to act according as they thought fit, on condition that they didn't break the law or exert any sort of disciplinary pressure on their members.

As regards associations for promoting interests, their control would, in the first place, involve the making of a distinction, namely, that the word "interest" sometimes expresses a need and at other times something quite different. In the case of a poor workingman, interest means food, lodging, and heating. For an employer, it means something of a different kind. When the word is taken in its first sense, the action of the authorities should be mainly to stimulate, uphold, and defend the interests concerned. When used in its second sense, the action of the authorities should be continually to supervise, limit, and, whenever possible, curb the activities of the associations representing such interests. It goes without saying that the severest restrictions and the hardest punishments should be reserved for those which are, by their nature, the most powerful.

What has been called freedom of association has been, in fact, up to now, freedom for associations. But associations have not got to be free; they are instruments, they must be held in bondage. Only the human being is fit to be free.

As regards freedom of thought, it is very nearly true to say that without freedom there is no thought. But it is truer still to say that when thought is nonexistent, it is nonfree into the bargain. There has been a lot of freedom of thought over the past few years, but no thought. Rather like the case of a child who, not having any meat, asks for salt with which to season it.

SECURITY

Security is an essential need of the soul. Security means that the soul is not under the weight of fear or terror, except as the result of an accidental conjunction of circumstances and for brief and exceptional periods. Fear and terror, as permanent states of the soul, are well-nigh mortal poisons, whether they be caused by the threat of unemployment, police persecution, the presence of a foreign conqueror, the probability of invasion, or any other calamity which seems too much for human strength to bear.

The Roman masters used to place a whip in the hall within sight of their slaves, knowing that this spectacle reduced their hearts to that half-dead condition indispensable for slavery. On the other hand, according to the Egyptians, the just man should be able to say after death, "I never caused any one any fear." Even if permanent fear constitutes a latent state only, so that its painful effects are only rarely experienced directly, it remains always a disease. It is a semiparalysis of the soul.

RISK

Risk is an essential need of the soul. The absence of risk produces a type of boredom which paralyzes in a different way from fear, but almost as much. Moreover, there are certain situations which, involving as they do a diffused anguish without any clearly defined risks, spread the two kinds of disease at once.

Risk is a form of danger which provokes a deliberate reaction; that is to say, it doesn't go beyond the soul's resources to the point of crushing the soul beneath a load of fear. In some cases, there is a gambling aspect to it; in others, where some definite obligation forces a man to face it, it represents the finest possible stimulant.

The protection of mankind from fear and terror doesn't imply the abolition of risk; it implies, on the contrary, the permanent presence of a certain amount of risk in all aspects of social life; for the absence of risk weakens courage to the point of leaving the soul, if the need should arise, without the slightest inner protection against fear. All that is wanted is for risk to offer itself under such conditions that it is not transformed into a sensation of fatality.

PRIVATE PROPERTY

Private property is a vital need of the soul. The soul feels isolated, lost, if it is not surrounded by objects which seem to it like an extension of the bodily members. All men have an invincible inclination to appropriate in their own minds anything which over a long, uninterrupted period they have used for their work, pleasure, or the necessities of life. Thus, a gardener, after a certain time, feels that the

garden belongs to him. But where the feeling of appropriation doesn't coincide with any legally recognized proprietorship, men are continually exposed to extremely painful spiritual wrenches.

Once we recognize private property to be a need, this implies for everyone the possibility of possessing something more than the articles of ordinary consumption. The forms this need takes can vary considerably, depending on circumstances; but it is desirable that the majority of people should own their house and a little piece of land round it, and, whenever not technically impossible, the tools of their trade. Land and livestock figure among the tools necessary to the peasant's trade.

The principle of private property is violated where the land is worked by agricultural laborers and farm hands under the orders of an estate manager, and owned by townsmen who receive the profits. For of all those who are connected with that land, there is not one who, in one way or another, is not a stranger to it. It is wasted, not from the point of view of corn production, but from that of the satisfaction of the property need which it could procure. Between this extreme case and that other one of the peasant who cultivates with his family the land he owns, there are a number of intermediate states where Man's need of appropriation is more or less unrecognized.

COLLECTIVE PROPERTY

Participation in collective possessions – a participation consisting not in any material enjoyment, but in a feeling of ownership – is a no less important need. It is more a question of a state of mind than of any legal formula. Where a real civic life exists, each one feels he has a personal ownership in the public monuments, gardens, ceremonial pomp and circumstance; and a display of sumptuousness, in which nearly all human beings seek fulfillment, is in this way placed within the reach of even the poorest. But it isn't just the State which ought to provide this satisfaction; it is every sort of collectivity in turn.

A great modern factory is a waste from the point of view of the need of property; for it is unable to provide either the workers, or the manager who is paid his salary by the board of directors, or the members of the board who never visit it, or the shareholders who are unaware of its existence with the least satisfaction in connection with this need.

When methods of exchange and acquisition are such as to involve a waste of material and moral foods, it is time they were transformed.

There is no natural connection between property and money. The connection established nowadays is merely the result of a system which has made money the focus of all other possible motives. This system being an unhealthy one, we must bring about a dissociation in inverse order.

The true criterion in regard to property is that it is legitimate so long as it is real. Or, to be more precise, the laws concerning property are so much the better the more advantages they draw from the opportunities offered by the possessions of this world for the satisfaction of the property need common to all men.

Consequently, the present modes of acquisition and possession require to be transformed in the name of the principle of property. Any form of possession which doesn't satisfy somebody's need of private or collective property can reasonably be regarded as useless.

That does not mean that it is necessary to transfer it to the State; but rather to try and turn it into some genuine form of property.

TRUTH

The need of truth is more sacred than any other need. Yet it is never mentioned. One feels afraid to read when once one has realized the quantity and the monstrousness of the material falsehoods shamelessly paraded, even in the books of the most reputable authors. Thereafter one reads as though one were drinking from a contaminated well.

There are men who work eight hours a day and make the immense effort of reading in the evenings so as to acquire knowledge. It is impossible for them to go and verify their sources in the big libraries. They have to take the book on trust. One has no right to give them spurious provender. What sense is there in pleading that authors act in good faith? *They* don't have to do physical labor for eight hours a day. Society provides for their sustenance so that they may have the leisure and give themselves the trouble to avoid error. A switchman responsible for a train accident and pleading good faith would hardly be given a sympathetic hearing.

All the more reason why it is disgraceful to tolerate the existence of newspapers on which, as everybody knows, not one of the collaborators would be able to stop, unless he were prepared from time to time to tamper knowingly with the truth.

The public is suspicious of newspapers, but its suspicions don't save it. Knowing, in a general way, that a newspaper contains both true and false statements, it divides the news up into these two categories, but in a rough-and-ready fashion, in accordance with its own predilections. It is thus delivered over to error.

We all know that when journalism becomes indistinguishable from organized lying, it constitutes a crime. But we think it is a crime impossible to punish. What is there to stop the punishment of activities once they are recognized to be criminal ones? Where does this strange notion of nonpunishable crimes come from? It constitutes one of the most monstrous deformations of the judicial spirit.

Isn't it high time it were proclaimed that every discernible crime is a punishable one, and that we are resolved, if given the opportunity, to punish all crimes?

Bibliography

McLellan, David. *Simone Weil: Utopian Pessimist.* Houndmills, Basingstoke: Macmillan, 1989.

CHAPTER TWENTY-THREE — AYN RAND

Ayn Rand (1905-1982) was a Russian writer who settled in the United States, becoming an American citizen in 1931. A screenwriter, playwright, essayist, and philosopher, her greatest success was as a novelist. In her work she celebrates creative individualism, and ethical realism. She founded a philosophical school which she named objectivism, and whose essential tenets are the advocacy of reason, self-interest, and capitalism. She dissociated her views from the principal conservative and libertarian positions in recent American political life; and certainly the only philosophical influence and model she acknowledged was Aristotle.

Sometimes there will be striking commonalities between thinkers who are otherwise quite different, even oppositional. Rand wrote scathingly of the ideas of Friedrich Nietzsche and Jean-Paul Sartre, for example, and indisputably there is much in both thinkers' work which is quite alien in spirit and letter to her views. At the same time many will see a common ground of similarity in a shared emphasis on the creative, indeed heroic individual, and humanity's inability to avoid its marked metaphysical and ethical liberty, the result of whose exercise is, too often according to all three philosophers, inauthenticity and parasitism. Sartre, in fact, was Rand's exact contemporary, also born in 1905. He became in his later decades a Marxist, which could hardly be more antithetical to Rand's high valuation of capitalist entrepreneurialism. (Sartre's critics often see profound inconsistency between his Marxism and the radical freedom of the self-determining individual in his existentialism, it should be noted.) Other affinities or similarities for Rand, for example, with the nineteenth-century philosopher Herbert Spencer (often regarded as the originator of "Social Darwinism"), and the twentieth-century economist and philosopher F.A. Hayek, will come to mind – though in these cases too there are important differences.

Ayn Rand, *For The New Intellectual*

(Source: Ayn Rand. *For The New Intellectual*. Toronto: Signet, 1963, 13-22.)

"The tragic joke of human history" – I am quoting John Galt in *Atlas Shrugged* – "is that on any of the altars men erected, it was always man whom they immolated and the animal whom they enshrined. It was always the animal's attributes, not man's, that humanity worshipped: the idol of instinct and the idol of force – the mystics and the kings – the mystics, who longed for an irresponsible consciousness and ruled by means of the claim that their dark emotions were superior to reason, that knowledge came in blind, causeless fits, blindly to be followed, not doubted – and the kings, who ruled by means of claws and muscles, with conquest as their method and looting as their aim, with a club or a gun as sole sanction of their power. The defenders of man's soul were concerned with his feelings, and the defenders of man's body were concerned with his stomach – but both were united against his mind."

These two figures – the man of faith and the man of force – are philosophical archetypes, psychological symbols and historical reality. As philosophical archetypes, they embody two variants of a certain view of man and of existence. As psychological symbols, they represent the basic motivation of a great many men who exist in any era, culture or society. As historical reality, they are the actual rulers of most of mankind's societies, who rise to power whenever men abandon reason.[1]

---

1   I am indebted to Nathaniel Branden for many valuable observations on this subject and for his eloquent designation of the two archetypes, which I shall use hereafter: *Attila and the Witch Doctor*.

The essential characteristics of these two remain the same in all ages: *Attila*, the man who rules by brute force, acts on the range of the moment, is concerned with nothing but the physical reality immediately before him, respects nothing but man's muscles, and regards a fist, a club or a gun as the only answer to any problem – and *the Witch Doctor*, the man who dreads physical reality, dreads the necessity of practical action, and escapes into his emotions, into visions of some mystic realm where his wishes enjoy a supernatural power unlimited by the absolute of nature.

Superficially, these two may appear to be opposites, but observe what they have in common: a consciousness held down to the *perceptual* method of functioning, an awareness that does not choose to extend beyond the automatic, the immediate, the given, the involuntary, which means: an animal's "epistemology" or as near to it as a human consciousness can come.

Man's consciousness shares with animals the first two stages of its development: sensations and perceptions; but it is the third state, *conceptions*, that makes him man. Sensations are integrated into perceptions automatically, by the brain of a man or of an animal. But to integrate perceptions into conceptions by a process of abstraction, is a feat that man alone has the power to perform – and he has to perform it *by choice*. The process of abstraction, and of concept-formation is a process of reason, of *thought*; it is not automatic nor instinctive nor involuntary nor infallible. Man has to initiate it, to sustain it and to bear responsibility for its results. The pre-conceptual level of consciousness is non-volitional; volition begins with the first syllogism. Man has the choice to think or to evade – to maintain a state of full awareness or to drift from moment to moment, in a semi-conscious daze, at the mercy of whatever associational whims the unfocused mechanism of his consciousness produces.

But the living organisms that possess the faculty of consciousness need to exercise it in order to survive. An animal's consciousness functions automatically; an animal perceives what it is able to perceive and survives accordingly, no further than the perceptual level permits and no better. Man cannot survive on the perceptual level of *his* consciousness; his senses do not provide him the knowledge he needs, only the *material* of knowledge, which his mind has to integrate. Man is the only living species who has to perceive reality – which means: to be *conscious* – by choice. But he shares with other species the penalty of unconsciousness: destruction. For an animal, the question of survival is primarily physical; for man, primarily epistemological.

Man's unique reward, however, is that while animals survive by adjusting themselves to their background, man survives by adjusting his background to himself. If a drought strikes them, animals perish – man builds irrigation canals; if a flood strikes them, animals perish – man builds dams; if a carnivorous pack attacks them animals perish – man writes the Constitution of the United States. But one does not obtain food, safety or freedom – by instinct.

It is against this faculty, the faculty of *reason*, that Attila and the Witch Doctor rebel. The key to both their souls is their longing for the effortless, irresponsible, automatic consciousness of an animal. Both dread the necessity, the risk and the responsibility of rational cognition. Both dread the fact that "nature, to be commanded, must be obeyed." Both seek to exist, not by conquering nature, but by adjusting to the given, the immediate, the known. There is only one means of survival for those who do not choose to conquer nature: to conquer those who do.

The *physical* conquest of men is Attila's method of survival. He regards men as others regard fruit trees or farm animals: as objects in nature, his for the seizing. But while a good farmer knows, at least, that fruit trees and animals have a specific nature and require a specific kind of handling, the *perceptual* mentality of Attila does not extend to so abstract a level: men, to him, are natural phenomena and an irreducible primary, as all natural phenomena are irreducible primaries to an animal. Attila feels no need to understand, to explain, nor even to wonder, *how* men manage to produce the things he covets – "*somehow*" is a fully satisfactory answer inside his skull, which refuses to consider such questions as "how?" and "why?" or such concepts as identity and causality. All he needs, his "urges" tell him, is bigger muscles, bigger clubs or a bigger gang than theirs in order to seize their bodies and their products, after which their bodies will obey his commands and will provide him, somehow, with the satisfaction of any whim. He approaches men as a beast of prey, and the consequences of his actions or the possibility of exhausting his victims never enters his consciousness, which does not choose to extend beyond the given moment. His view of the universe does not include the power of production. The power of destruction, of brute force, is, to him, metaphysically omnipotent.

An Attila never thinks of creating, only of *taking over*. Whether he conquers a neighbouring tribe or overruns a continent, material looting is his only goal and it ends with the act of seizure: he has no other purpose, no plan, no system to impose on the conquered, no values. His pleasures are closer to the level of sensations than of perceptions: food, drink, palatial shelter, rich clothing, indiscriminate sex, contests of physical prowess, gambling – all those activities which do not demand or involve the use of the conceptual level of consciousness. He does not originate his pleasures: he desires and pursues whatever those around him seem to find desirable. Even in the realm of desires, he does not create, he merely takes over.

But a human being cannot live his life moment by moment; a human consciousness preserves a certain continuity and demands a certain degree of integration, whether a man seeks it or not. A human being needs a frame of reference, a comprehensive view of existence, no matter how rudimentary, and, since his consciousness *is* volitional, a sense of being *right*, a moral justification of his actions, which means: a philosophical code of values. Who, then, provides Attila with values? The Witch Doctor.

If Attila's method of survival is the conquest of those who conquer nature, the Witch Doctor's method of survival is safer, he believes, and spares him the risks of physical conflict. *His* method is the conquest of those who conquer those who conquer nature. It is not men's bodies that he seeks to rule, but men's souls.

To Attila, as to an animal, the phenomena of nature are an irreducible primary. To the Witch Doctor, as to an animal, the irreducible primary is the automatic phenomena of his own consciousness.

An animal has no critical faculty; he has no control over the function of his brain and no power to question its content. To an animal, whatever strikes his awareness is an absolute that corresponds to reality – or rather, it is a distinction he is incapable of making: reality, to him, is whatever he senses or

feels. And *this* is the Witch Doctor's epistemological ideal, the mode of consciousness he strives to induce in himself. To the Witch Doctor, emotions are tools of cognition, and wishes take precedence over facts. He seeks to escape the risks of a quest for knowledge by obliterating the distinction between consciousness and reality, between the perceiver and the perceived, hoping that an automatic certainty and an infallible knowledge of the universe will be granted to him by the blind, unfocused stare of his eyes turned inward, contemplating the sensations, the feelings, the urgings, the muggy associational twistings projected by the rudderless mechanism of his undirected consciousness. Whatever his mechanism produces is an absolute not to be questioned; and whenever it clashes with reality, it is reality that he ignores.

Since the clash is constant, the Witch Doctor's solution is to believe that what he perceives is another, "higher" reality – where his wishes are omnipotent, where contradictions are possible and A is non-A, where his assertions, which are false on earth, become true and acquire the status of a "superior" truth which *he* perceives by means of a special faculty denied to other, "inferior" beings. The only validation of his consciousness he can obtain on earth is the belief and the obedience of others, when they accept his "truth" as superior to their own perception of reality. While Attila exorts their obedience by means of a club, the Witch Doctor obtains it by means of a much more powerful weapon: he pre-empts the field of *morality*.

There is no way to turn morality into a weapon of enslavement except by divorcing it from man's reason and from the goals of his own existence. There is no way to degrade man's life on earth except by the lethal opposition of the *moral* and the *practical*. Morality is a code of values to guide man's choices and actions; when it is set to oppose his own life and mind, it makes him turn against himself and blindly act as the tool of his own destruction. There is no way to make a human being accept the role of a sacrificial animal except by destroying his self-esteem. There is no way to destroy his self-esteem except by making him reject his own consciousness. There is no way to make him reject his own consciousness except by convincing him of its impotence.

The damnation of this earth as a realm where nothing is possible to man but pain, disaster and defeat, a realm inferior to another, "higher" reality; the damnation of all values, enjoyment, achievement and success on earth as a proof of depravity; the damnation of man's mind as a source of *pride*, and the damnation of reason as a "limited," deceptive, unreliable, impotent faculty, incapable of perceiving the "real" reason and the "true" truth; the split of man in two, setting his consciousness (his soul) against his body, and his moral values against his own interests; the damnation of man's nature, body and *self* as evil; the commandment of self-sacrifice, renunciation, suffering, obedience, humility and faith, as the good; the damnation of life and the worship of death, with the promise of rewards beyond the grave – *these* are the necessary tenets of the Witch Doctor's view of existence, as they have been in every variant of Witch Doctor philosophy throughout the course of mankind's history.

The secret of the Witch Doctor's power lies in the fact that man needs an integrated view of life, a *philosophy*, whether he is aware of his need or not – and whenever, through ignorance, cowardice or mental sloth, men choose not to be aware of it, their chronic sense of guilt, uncertainty and terror makes them feel that the Witch Doctor's philosophy is true.

The first to feel it is Attila.

The man who lives by brute force, at the whim and mercy of the moment, lives on a narrow island suspended in a fog of the unknown, where invisible threats and unpredictable disasters can descend upon him any morning. He is willing to surrender his consciousness to the man who offers him protection against those intangible questions which he does not wish to consider, yet dreads.

Attila's fear of reality is as great as the Witch Doctor's. Both hold their consciousness on a subhuman level and method of functioning: Attila's brain is a jumble of concretes unintegrated by abstractions; the Witch Doctor's brain is a miasma of floating abstractions unrelated to concretes. Both are guided and motivated – ultimately – not by thoughts, but by feelings and whims. Both cling to their whims as to their only certainty. Both feel secretly inadequate to the task of dealing with existence.

Thus they come to need each other. Attila feels that the Witch Doctor can give him what he lacks: a long-range view, an insurance against the dark unknown of tomorrow or next week or next year, a code of moral values to sanction his actions and to disarm his victims. The Witch Doctor feels that Attila can give him the material means of survival, can protect him from physical reality, can spare him the necessity of practical action, and can enforce his mystic edicts on any recalcitrant who may choose to challenge his authority. Both of them are incomplete parts of a human being, who seek completion in each other: the man of muscle and the man of feelings, seeking to exist without *mind*.

Since no man can fully escape the conceptual level of consciousness, it is not the case that Attila and the Witch Doctor cannot or do not think; they can and do – but thinking, to them, is not a means of perceiving reality, it is a means of justifying their escape from the necessity of rational perception. Reason, to them, is a means of defeating their victims, a menial servant charged with the task of rationalizing the metaphysical validity and power of their whims. Just as a bank robber will spend years of planning, ingenuity and effort in order to prove to himself that he can exist without effort, so both Attila and the Witch Doctor will go to any length of cunning, calculation and thought in order to demonstrate the impotence of thought and preserve the image of a pliable universe where miracles are possible and whims are efficacious. The power of *ideas* has no reality for either of them, and neither cares to learn that the proof of that power lies in his own chronic sense of guilt and terror.

Thus Attila and the Witch Doctor form an alliance and divide their respective domains. Attila rules the realm of men's consciousness. Attila herds men into armies – the Witch Doctor sets the armies' goals. Attila conquers empires – the Witch Doctor writes their laws. Attila loots and plunders – the Witch Doctor exhorts the victims to surpass their selfish concern with material property. Attila slaughters – the Witch Doctor proclaims to the survivors that scourges are a retribution for their sins. Attila rules by means of *fear*, by keeping men under a constant threat of destruction – the Witch Doctor rules by means of *guilt*, by keeping men convinced of their innate depravity, impotence and insignificance. Attila turns men's life on earth into a living hell – the Witch Doctor tells them that it could not be otherwise.

But the alliance of the two rulers is precarious: it is based on mutual fear and mutual contempt.

Attila is an extrovert, resentful of any concern with consciousness – the Witch Doctor is an introvert, resentful of any concern with physical existence. Attila professes scorn for values, ideals, principles, theories, abstractions – the Witch Doctor professes scorn for material property, for wealth, for man's body, for this earth. Attila considers the Witch Doctor impractical – the Witch Doctor considers Attila immoral. But, secretly, each of them believes that the other possesses a mysterious faculty *he* lacks, that the other is the true master of reality, the true exponent of the power to deal with existence. In terms, not of thought, but of chronic anxiety, it is the Witch Doctor who believes that brute force rules the world – and it is Attila who believes in the supernatural; his name for it is "fate" or "luck".

Against whom is this alliance formed? Against those men whose existence and character both Attila and the Witch Doctor refuse to admit into their view of the universe: the men who produce. In any age or society, there are men who *think* and work, who discover how to deal with existence, how to produce the intellectual and the material values it requires. These are the men whose effort is the only means of survival for the parasites of all varieties: the Attilas, the Witch Doctors and the human ballast. The ballast consists of those who go through life in a state of unfocused stupor, merely repeating the words and the motions they learned from others. But the men from whom they learn, the men who are first to discover any scrap of new knowledge, are the men who deal with reality, with the task of conquering nature, and who, to that extent, assume the responsibility of cognition: of exercising their rational faculty.

A producer is any man who works and knows what he is doing. He may function on a fully human, conceptual level of awareness only some part of his time, but, to that extent, he is the Atlas who supports the existence of mankind; he may spend the rest of his time in an unthinking daze, like the others, and, to that extent, he is the exploited, drained, tortured, self-destroying victim of their schemes.

Men's epistemology – or, more precisely, their *psycho-epistemology*, their method of awareness – is the most fundamental standard by which they can be classified. Few men are consistent in that respect; most men keep switching from one level of awareness to another, according to the circum-stances or the issues involved, ranging from moments of full rationality to an almost somnam-bulistic stupor. But the battle of human history is fought and determined by those who are predomi-nantly consistent, those who, for good or evil, are committed to and motivated by their chosen psy-cho-epistemology and its corollary view of exis-tence – with echoes responding to them, in support or opposition, in the switching, flickering souls of the others.

A man's method of using his consciousness deter-mines his method of survival. The three contestants are Attila, the Witch Doctor and the Producer – or the man of force, the man of feelings, the man of reason – or the brute, the mystic, the thinker. The rest of mankind calls it expedient to be tossed by the current of events from one of those roles to another, not choosing to identify the fact that those three are the source which determines the current's direction.

The producers, so far, have been the forgotten men of history. With the exception of a few brief periods, the producers have not been the leaders or the term-setters of men's societies, although the degree of their influence and freedom was the degree of a society's welfare and progress. Most societies have been ruled by Attila and the Witch Doctor. The cause is not some innate tendency to evil in human nature, but the fact that reason is a volitional faculty which man has to choose to dis-cover, employ and preserve. Irrationality is a state of default, the state of an unachieved human stature. When men do not choose to reach the con-ceptual level, their consciousness has no recourse but to its automatic, perceptual, semi-animal func-tions. If a missing link between the human and the animal species is to be found, Attila and the Witch Doctor are that missing link – the profiteers on men's default.

Bibliography

Baker, James T. *Ayn Rand*. Boston: Twayne Publishers, 1987.

Den Uyl, Douglas J., and Douglas B. Rasmussen, eds. *The Philosophic Thought of Ayn Rand*. Urbana, Ill.: University of Illinois Press, 1984.

Peikoff, Leonard. *Objectivism: The Philosophy of Ayn Rand*. New York: Dutton, 1991.

CHAPTER TWENTY-FOUR — OAKESHOTT

Three conservative philosophies may be discerned in our age. They share significant commonalities, but are also importantly distinct. The three may be called, respectively, traditionalist conservatism, corporatist conservatism, and conservative individualism. The first is a stance which values old ways because they are old. It makes investments of sentiment and ideology in what has gone on, and is regarded – by this kind of conservative – as of proven utility and validity, through long experience. Characteristically this stance is patriotic and religious. Edmund Burke is perhaps its supreme theorist (though he has also other views of arguably greater substance).

Corporatist conservatism is more abstract and more grandly philosophical. It grounds human identity, and teleology, in a shared cultural or community life, which might or might not have religious foundations, or celebrate ancestral ways because they are ancestral. A spectrum of views and political affiliations fall under this conception. Although this will be protested, formal and theoretical fascist ideology occupies one location on this spectrum, as does Heideggerian ideology, whatever its relation is (this is disputed) to fascism. So do some Hegelian positions, with their stress on *Sittlichkeit* (shared ethical life, familial, social and political), and civil society, as a subrational social glue. Likewise contemporary communitarian positions are typically of corporatist conservative stamp, although they are milder, vaguer, and "pinker" (i.e., moral left-liberal in orientation) than the others named. Although many corporatist conservatives are convinced and committed democrats, many also are not; and for none is democracy a primary or unqualified good. Roger Scruton identifies conservatism – mistakenly, I think – with corporatist conservatism. He was a communitarian *avant la lettre*, but of a robust and not particularly democratic type.

Conservative individualism is more properly a theory of human nature than are the previous two, although both of the latter involve claims of human fundamentals. Conservative individualism sees people as (metaphysically) free, yet with predispositions to selfishness and to sloth and to malice, both in attitudes and actions. Conservative individualism, then, believes in what we may call original sin; even though many conservative individualists are not religious believers, and almost all of them also believe in individual cases of heroism and virtue.

Michael Oakeshott (1901-1995) has a primarily conservative individualist view, though he underplays the predisposition to sin that conservatives usually affirm. Further, Oakeshott may be seen as describing a conservatve human type (compatible with quite distinct kinds of people), which may not seem quite the same thing as a conservative theory of what human beings in general are like. Oakeshott's conservativism is a cast of mind and temperament which prefers the familiar to the new. Yet he neglects to recognize that a social democratic order – a welfare state, with activist social redistributive practices – can itself become an established order, of sufficiently continued duration that *it* is the familiar. Those who want it to continue so will nonetheless not be called conservatives. The latter, rather, will want a generally socio-economically inactive government, where people will rise or fall as they may, with chiefly private and individual succour if they fall.

These qualifications noted, Oakeshott is a particularly vivid and eloquent spokesperson for conservative moral, political, and human nature views.

Michael Oakeshott, *Rationalism in Politics*

(Source: Michael Oakeshott. *Rationalism in Politics*. London: Methuen and Co. Ltd, 1962, 168-196.)

ON BEING CONSERVATIVE

The common belief that it is impossible (or, if not impossible, then so unpromising as to be not worth while attempting) to elicit explanatory general principles from what is recognized to be conservative conduct is not one that I share. It may be true that conservative conduct does not readily provoke articulation in the idiom of general ideas, and that consequently there has been a certain reluctance to undertake this kind of elucidation; but it is not to be presumed that conservative conduct is less eligible than any other for this sort of interpretation, for what it is worth. Nevertheless, this is not the enterprise I propose to engage in here. My theme is not a creed or a doctrine, but a disposition. To be conservative is to be disposed to think and behave in certain manners; it is to prefer certain kinds of conduct and certain conditions of human circumstances to others; it is to be disposed to make certain kinds of choices. And my design here is to construe this disposition as it appears in contemporary character, rather than to transpose it into the idiom of general principles.

The general characteristics of this disposition are not difficult to discern, although they have often been mistaken. They centre upon a propensity to use and to enjoy what is available rather than to wish for or to look for something else; to delight in what is present rather than what was or what may be. Reflection may bring to light an appropriate gratefulness for what is available, and consequently the acknowledgment of a gift or an inheritance from the past; but there is no mere idolizing of what is past and gone. What is esteemed is the present; and it is esteemed not on account of its connections with a remote antiquity, nor because it is recognized to be more admirable than any possible alternative, but on account of its familiarity: not, *Verweile doch, du bist so schön,* but, *Stay with me because I am attached to you.*

If the present is arid, offering little or nothing to be used or enjoyed, then this inclination will be weak or absent; if the present is remarkably unsettled, it will display itself in a search for a firmer foothold and consequently in a recourse to and an exploration of the past; but it asserts itself characteristically when there is much to be enjoyed, and it will be strongest when this is combined with evident risk of loss. In short, it is a disposition appropriate to a man who is acutely aware of having something to lose which he has learned to care for; a man in some degree rich in opportunities for enjoyment, but not so rich that he can afford to be indifferent to loss. It will appear more naturally in the old than in the young, not because the old are more sensitive to loss but because they are apt to be more fully aware of the resources of their world and therefore less likely to find them inadequate. In some people this disposition is weak merely because they are ignorant of what their world has to offer them: the present appears to them only as a residue of inopportunities.

To be conservative, then, is to prefer the familiar to the unknown, to prefer the tried to the untried, fact to mystery, the actual to the possible, the limited to the unbounded, the near to the distant, the sufficient to the superabundant, the convenient to the perfect, present laughter to utopian bliss. Familiar relationships and loyalties will be preferred to the allure of more profitable attachments; to acquire and to enlarge will be less important than to keep, to cultivate and to enjoy; the grief of loss will be more acute than the excitement of novelty or promise. It is to be equal to one's own fortune, to live at the level of one's own means, to be content with the want of greater perfection which belongs alike to oneself and one's circumstances.

With some people this is itself a choice; in others it is a disposition which appears, frequently or less frequently, in their preferences and aversions, and is not itself chosen or specifically cultivated.

Now, all this is represented in a certain attitude towards change and innovation; change denoting alterations we have to suffer and innovation those we design and execute.

Changes are circumstances to which we have to accommodate ourselves, and the disposition to be conservative is both the emblem of our difficulty in doing so and our resort in the attempts we make to do so. Changes are without effect only upon those who notice nothing, who are ignorant of what they possess and apathetic to their circumstances; and they can be welcomed indiscriminately only by those who esteem nothing, whose attachments are fleeting and who are strangers to love and affection. The conservative disposition provokes neither of these conditions: the inclination to enjoy what is present and available is the opposite of ignorance and apathy and it breeds attachment and affection. Consequently, it is averse from change, which appears always, in the first place, as deprivation. A storm which sweeps away a copse and transforms a favourite view, the death of friends, the sleep of friendship, the desuetude of customs of behaviour, the retirement of a favourite clown, involuntary exile, reversals of fortune, the loss of abilities enjoyed and their replacement by others – these are changes, none perhaps without its compensations, which the man of conservative temperament unavoidably regrets. But he has difficulty in reconciling himself to them, not because what he has lost in them was intrinsically better than any alternative might have been or was incapable of improvement, nor because what takes its place is inherently incapable of being enjoyed, but because what he has lost was something he actually enjoyed and had learned how to enjoy and what takes its place is something to which he has acquired no attachment. Consequently, he will find small and slow changes more tolerable than large and sudden; and he will value highly every appearance of continuity. Some changes, indeed, will present no difficulty; but, again, this is not because they are manifest improvements but merely because they are easily assimilated: the changes of the seasons are mediated by their recurrence and the growing up of children by its continuousness. And, in general, he will accommodate himself more readily to changes which do not offend expectation than to the destruction of what seems to have no ground of dissolution within itself.

Moreover, to be conservative is not merely to be averse from change (which may be an idiosyncrasy); it is also a manner of accommodating ourselves to changes, an activity imposed upon all men. For, change is a threat to identity, and every change is an emblem of extinction. But a man's identity (or that of a community) is nothing more than an unbroken rehearsal of contingencies, each at the mercy of circumstance and each significant in proportion to its familiarity. It is not a fortress into which we may retire, and the only means we have of defending it (that is, ourselves) against the hostile forces of change is in the open field of our experience; by throwing our weight upon the foot which for the time being is most firmly placed, by cleaving to whatever familiarities are not immediately threatened and thus assimilating what is new without becoming unrecognizable to ourselves. The Masai, when they were moved from their old country to the present Masai reserve in Kenya, took with them the names of their hills and plains and rivers and gave them to the hills and plains and rivers of the new country. And it is by some such subterfuge of conservatism that every man or people compelled to suffer a notable change avoids the shame of extinction.

Changes, then, have to be suffered; and a man of conservative temperament (that is, one strongly disposed to preserve his identity) cannot be indifferent to them. In the main, he judges them by the disturbance they entail and, like everyone else, deploys his resources to meet them. The idea of innovation, on the other hand, is improvement. Nevertheless, a man of this temperament will not himself be an ardent innovator. In the first place, he is not inclined to think that nothing is happening unless great changes are afoot and therefore he is not worried by the absence of innovation: the use and enjoyment of things as they are occupies most of his attention. Further, he is aware that not all innovation is, in fact, improvement; and he will think that to innovate without improving is either designed or inadvertent folly. Moreover, even when an innovation commends itself as a convincing improvement, he will look twice at its claims before accepting them. From his point of view, because every improvement involves change, the disruption entailed has always to be set against the benefit anticipated. But when he has satisfied himself about this, there will be other considerations to be taken into the account. Innovating is always an equivocal enterprise, in which gain and loss (even excluding the loss of familiarity) are so closely interwoven that it is exceedingly difficult to forecast the final up-shot: there is no such thing as an unqualified improvement. For, innovating is an activity which generates not only the 'improvement' sought, but a new and complex situation of which this is only one of the components. The total change is always more extensive than the change designed; and the whole of what is entailed can neither be foreseen nor circumscribed. Thus, whenever there is innovation there is the certainty that the change will be greater than was intended, that there will be loss as well as gain and that the loss and the gain will not be equally distributed among the people affected; there is the chance that the benefits derived will be greater than those which were designed; and there is the risk that they will be offset by changes for the worse.

From all this the man of conservative temperament draws some appropriate conclusions. First, innovation entails certain loss and possible gain, therefore, the onus of proof, to show that the proposed change may be expected to be on the whole beneficial, rests with the would-be innovator. Secondly, he believes that the more closely an innovation resembles growth (that is, the more clearly it is intimated in and not merely imposed upon the situation) the less likely it is to result in a preponderance of loss. Thirdly, he thinks that an innovation which is a response to some specific defect, one designed to redress some specific disequilibrium, is more desirable than one which springs from a notion of a generally improved condition of human circumstances, and is far more desirable than one generated by a vision of perfection. Consequently, he prefers small and limited innovations to large and indefinite. Fourthly, he favours a slow rather than a rapid pace, and pauses to observe current consequences and make appropriate adjustments. And lastly, he believes the occasion to be important; and, other things being equal, he considers the most favourable occasion for innovation to be when the projected change is most likely to be limited to what is intended and least likely to be corrupted by undesired and unmanageable consequences.

The disposition to be conservative is, then, warm and positive in respect of enjoyment, and correspondingly cool and critical in respect of change and innovation: these two inclinations support and elucidate one another. The man of conservative temperament believes that a known good is not lightly to be surrendered for an unknown better. He is not in love with what is dangerous and difficult; he is unadventurous; he has no impulse to sail uncharted seas; for him there is no magic in being lost, bewildered or shipwrecked. If he is forced to navigate the unknown, he sees virtue in heaving the lead every inch of the way. What others plausibly identify as timidity, he recognizes in himself as rational prudence; what others interpret as inactivity, he recognizes as a disposition to enjoy rather than to exploit. He is cautious, and he is disposed to indicate his assent or dissent, not in absolute, but in graduated terms. He eyes the situation in terms of its propensity to disrupt the familiarity of the features of his world.

2

It is commonly believed that this conservative disposition is pretty deeply rooted in what is called 'human nature'. Change is tiring, innovation calls for effort, and human beings (it is said) are more apt to be lazy than energetic. If they have found a not unsatisfactory way of getting along in the world, they are not disposed to go looking for trouble. They are naturally apprehensive of the unknown and prefer safety to danger. They are reluctant innovators, and they accept change not because they like it but (as Rochefoucauld says they accept death) because it is inescapable. Change generates sadness rather than exhilaration: heaven is the dream of a changeless no less than of a perfect world. Of course, those who read 'human nature' in this way agree that this disposition does not stand alone; they merely contend that it is an exceedingly strong, perhaps the strongest, of human propensities. And, so far as it goes, there is something to be said for this belief: human circumstances would certainly be very different from what they are if there were not a large ingredient of conservatism in human preferences. Primitive peoples are said to cling to what is familiar and to be averse from change; ancient myth is full of warnings against innovation; our folklore and proverbial wisdom about the conduct of life abounds in conservative precepts; and how many tears are shed by children in their unwilling accommodation to change.

Indeed, wherever a firm identity has been achieved, and wherever identity is felt to be precariously balanced, a conservative disposition is likely to prevail. On the other hand, the disposition of adolescence is often predominantly adventurous and experimental: when we are young, nothing seems more desirable than to take a chance; *pas de risque, pas de plaisir.* And while some peoples, over long stretches of time, appear successfully to have avoided change, the history of others displays periods of intense and intrepid innovation. There is, indeed, not much profit to be had from general speculation about 'human nature', which is no steadier than anything else in our acquaintance. What is more to the point is to consider current human nature, to consider ourselves.

With us, I think, the disposition to be conservative is far from being notably strong. Indeed, if he were to judge by our conduct during the last five centuries or so, an unprejudiced stranger might plausibly suppose us to be in love with change, to have an appetite only for innovation and to be either so out of sympathy with ourselves or so careless of our identity as not to be disposed to give it any consideration. In general, the fascination of what is new is felt far more keenly than the comfort of what is familiar. We are disposed to think that nothing important is happening unless great innovations are afoot, and that what is not being improved must be deteriorating. There is a positive prejudice in favour of the yet untried. We readily presume that all change is, somehow, for the better, and we are easily persuaded that all the consequences of our innovating activity are either themselves improvements or at least a reasonable price to pay for getting what we want. While the conservative, if he were forced to gamble, would bet on the field, we are disposed to back our individual fancies with little calculation and no apprehension of loss. We are acquisitive to the point of greed; ready to drop the bone we have for its reflection magnified in the mirror of the future. Nothing is made to outlast probable improvement in a world where everything is undergoing incessant improvement: the expectation of life of everything except human beings themselves continuously declines. Pieties are fleeting, loyalties evanescent, and the pace of change warns us against too deep attach-

ments. We are willing to try anything once, regardless of the consequences. One activity vies with another in being 'up-to-date': discarded motor-cars and television sets have their counterparts in discarded moral and religious beliefs: the eye is ever on the new model. To see is to imagine what might be in the place of what is; to touch is to transform. Whatever the shape or quality of the world, it is not for long as we want it. And those in the van of movement infect those behind with their energy and enterprise. *Omnes eodem cogemur:* when we are no longer light-footed we find a place for ourselves in the band.[1]

Of course, our character has other ingredients besides this lust for change (we are not devoid of the impulse to cherish and preserve), but there can be little doubt about its pre-eminence. And, in these circumstances, it seems appropriate that a conservative disposition should appear, not as an intelligible (or even plausible) alternative to our mainly 'progressive' habit of mind, but either as an unfortunate hindrance to the movement afoot, or as the custodian of the museum in which quaint examples of superseded achievement are preserved for children to gape at, and as the guardian of what from time to time is considered not yet ripe for destruction, which we call (ironically enough) the amenities of life.

Here our account of the disposition to be conservative and its current fortunes might be expected to end, with the man in whom this disposition is strong last seen swimming against the tide, disregarded not because what he has to say is necessarily false but because it has become irrelevant; outmanoeuvred, not on account of any intrinsic demerit but merely by the flow of circumstance; a faded, timid, nostalgic character, provoking pity as an outcast and contempt as a reactionary. Nevertheless, I think there is something more to be said. Even in these circumstances, when a conservative disposition in respect of things in general is unmistakably at a discount, there are occasions when this disposition remains not only appropriate, but supremely so; and there are connections in which we are unavoidably disposed in a conservative direction.

In the first place, there is a certain kind of activity (not yet extinct) which can be engaged in only in

---

1   'Which of us,' asks a contemporary (not without some equivocation), 'would not settle, at whatever cost in nervous anxiety, for a febrile and creative rather than a static society?'

virtue of a disposition to be conservative, namely, activities where what is sought is present enjoyment and not a profit, a reward, a prize or a result in addition to the experience itself. And when these activities are recognized as the emblems of this disposition, to be conservative is disclosed, not as prejudiced hostility to a 'progressive' attitude capable of embracing the whole range of human conduct, but as a disposition exclusively appropriate in a large and significant field of human activity. And the man in whom this disposition is pre-eminent appears as one who prefers to engage in activities where to be conservative is uniquely appropriate, and not as a man inclined to impose his conservatism indiscriminately upon all human activity. In short, if we find ourselves (as most of us do) inclined to reject conservatism as a disposition appropriate in respect of human conduct in general, there still remains a certain kind of human conduct for which this disposition is not merely appropriate but a necessary condition.

There are, of course, numerous human relationships in which a disposition to be conservative, a disposition merely to enjoy what they offer for its own sake, is not particularly appropriate: master and servant, owner and bailiff, buyer and seller, principal and agent. In these, each participant seeks some service or some recompense for service. A customer who finds a shopkeeper unable to supply his wants either persuades him to enlarge his stock or goes elsewhere; and a shopkeeper unable to meet the desires of a customer tries to impose upon him others which he can satisfy. A principal ill-served by his agent, looks for another. A servant ill-recompensed for his service, asks for a rise; and one dissatisfied with his conditions of work, seeks a change. In short, these are all relationships in which some result is sought; each party is concerned with the ability of the other to provide it. If what is sought is lacking, it is to be expected that the relationship will lapse or be terminated. To be conservative in such relationships, to enjoy what is present and available regardless of its failure to satisfy any want and merely because it has struck our fancy and become familiar, is conduct which discloses a *jusqu'aubuiste* conservatism, an irrational inclination to refuse all relationships which call for the exercise of any other disposition. Though even these relationships seem to lack something appropriate to them when they are confined to a nexus of

supply and demand and allow no room for the intrusion of the loyalties and attachments which spring from familiarity.

But there are relationships of another kind in which no result is sought and which are engaged in for their own sake and enjoyed for what they are and not for what they provide. This is so of friendship. Here, attachment springs from an intimation of familiarity and subsists in a mutual sharing of personalities. To go on changing one's butcher until one gets the meat one likes, to go on educating one's agent until he does what is required of him, is conduct not inappropriate to the relationship concerned; but to discard friends because they do not behave as we expected and refuse to be educated to our requirements is the conduct of a man who has altogether mistaken the character of friendship. Friends are not concerned with what might be made of one another, but only with the enjoyment of one another; and the condition of this enjoyment is a ready acceptance of what is and the absence of any desire to change or to improve. A friend is not somebody one trusts to behave in a certain manner, who supplies certain wants, who has certain useful abilities, who possesses certain merely agreeable qualities, or who holds certain acceptable opinions; he is somebody who engages the imagination, who excites contemplation, who provokes interest, sympathy, delight and loyalty simply on account of the relationship entered into. One friend cannot replace another; there is all the difference in the world between the death of a friend and the retirement of one's tailor from business. The relationship of friend to friend is dramatic, not utilitarian; the tie is one of familiarity, not usefulness; the disposition engaged is conservative, not 'progressive'. And what is true of friendship is not less true of other experiences – of patriotism, for example, and of conversation – each of which demands a conservative disposition as a condition of its enjoyment.

But further, there are activities, not involving human relationships, that may be engaged in, not for a prize, but for the enjoyment they generate, and for which the only appropriate disposition is the disposition to be conservative. Consider fishing. If your project is merely to catch fish it would be foolish to be unduly conservative. You will seek out the best tackle, you will discard practices which prove unsuccessful, you will not be bound by unprofitable attachments to particular localities, pieties will be fleeting, loyalties evanescent; you may even be wise to try anything once in the hope of improvement. But fishing is an activity that may be engaged in, not for the profit of a catch, but for its own sake; and the fisherman may return home in the evening not less content for being empty-handed. Where this is so, the activity has become a ritual and a conservative disposition is appropriate. Why worry about the best gear if you do not care whether or not you make a catch? What matters is the enjoyment of exercising skill (or, perhaps, merely passing the time),[2] and this is to be had with any tackle, so long as it is familiar and is not grotesquely inappropriate.

All activities, then, where what is sought is enjoyment springing, not from the success of the enterprise but from the familiarity of the engagement, are emblems of the disposition to be conservative. And there are many of them. Fox placed gambling among them when he said that it gave two supreme pleasures, the pleasure of winning and the pleasure of losing. Indeed, I can think of only one activity of this kind which seems to call for a disposition other than conservative: the love of fashion, that is, wanton delight in change for its own sake no matter what it generates.

But, besides the not inconsiderable class of activities which we can engage in only in virtue of a disposition to be conservative, there are occasions in the conduct of other activities when this is the most appropriate disposition; indeed there are few activities which do not, at some point or other, make a call upon it. Whenever stability is more profitable than improvement, whenever certainty is more valuable than speculation, whenever familiarity is more desirable than perfection, whenever agreed error is superior to controversial truth, whenever the disease is more sufferable than the cure, whenever the satisfaction of expectations is more important than the 'justice' of the expectations themselves, whenever a rule of some sort is better than the risk of having no rule at all, a disposition to be conservative will be more appropriate than any other; and on any reading of human conduct these cover a not negligible range of circumstances.

Those who see the man of conservative disposition (even in what is vulgarly called a 'progressive' society) as a lonely swimmer battling against the overwhelming current of circumstance must be thought to have adjusted their binoculars to exclude a large field of human occasion.

In most activities not engaged in for their own sake a distinction appears, at a certain level of observation, between the project undertaken and the means employed, between the enterprise and the tools used for its achievement. This is not, of course, an absolute distinction; projects are often provoked and governed by the tools available, and on rarer occasions the tools are designed to fit a particular project. And what on one occasion is a project, on another is a tool. Moreover there is at least one significant exception: the activity of being a poet. It is, however, a relative distinction of some usefulness because it calls our attention to an appropriate difference of attitude towards the two components of the situation.

In general, it may be said that our disposition in respect of tools is appropriately more conservative than our attitude towards projects; or, in other words, tools are less subject to innovation than projects because, except on rare occasions, tools are not designed to fit a particular project and then thrown aside, they are designed to fit a whole class of projects. And this is intelligible because most tools call for skill in use and skill is inseparable from practice and familiarity: a skilled man, whether he is a sailor, a cook or an accountant, is a man familiar with a certain stock of tools. Indeed, a carpenter is usually more skilful in handling his own tools than in handling other examples of the kind of tools commonly used by carpenters; and the solicitor can use his own (annotated) copy of Pollock on *Partnership* or Jarman on *Wills* more readily than any other. Familiarity is the essence of tool using; and in so far as man is a tool using animal he is disposed to be conservative.

Many of the tools in common use have remained unchanged for generations; the design of others has undergone considerable modification; and our stock of tools is always being enlarged by new inventions and improved by new designs. Kitchens,

---

2   When Prince Wen Wang was on a tour of inspection in Tsang, he saw an old man fishing. But his fishing was not real fishing, for he did not fish in order to catch fish, but to amuse himself. So Wen Wang wished to employ him in the administration of government, but he feared his own ministers, uncles and brothers might object. On the other hand, if he let the old man go, he could not bear to think of the people being deprived of his influence. *Chuang Tzu*.

factories, workshops, building sites and offices disclose a characteristic mixture of long tried and newly invented equipment. But, be that how it may, when business of any kind is afoot, when a particular project has been engaged in – whether it is baking a pie or shoeing a horse, floating a loan or a company, selling fish or insurance to a customer, building a ship or a suit of clothes, sowing wheat or lifting potatoes, laying down port or putting up a barrage – we recognize it to be an occasion when it is particularly appropriate to be conservative about the tools we employ. If it is a large project, we put it in charge of a man who has the requisite knowledge, and we expect him to engage subordinates who know their own business and are skilled in the use of certain stocks of tools. At some point in this hierarchy of tool-users the suggestion may be made that in order to do this particular job an addition or modification is required in the available stock of tools. Such a suggestion is likely to come from somewhere about the middle of the hierarchy: we do not expect a designer to say 'I must go away and do some fundamental research which will take me five years before I can go on with the job' (his bag of tools is a body of knowledge and we expect him to have it handy and to know his way about it); and we do not expect the man at the bottom to have a stock of tools inadequate for the needs of his particular part. But even if such a suggestion is made and is followed up, it will not disrupt the appropriateness of a conservative disposition in respect of the whole stock of tools being used. Indeed, it is clear enough that no job would ever get done, no piece of business could ever be transacted if, on the occasion, our disposition in respect of our tools were not, generally speaking, conservative. And since doing business of one sort or another occupies most of our time and little can be done without tools of some kind, the disposition to be conservative occupies an unavoidably large place in our character.

The carpenter comes to do a job, perhaps one the exact like of which he has never before tackled; but he comes with his bag of familiar tools and his only chance of doing the job lies in the skill with which he uses what he has at his disposal. When the plumber goes to fetch his tools he would be away even longer than is usually the case if his purpose were to invent new or to improve old ones. Nobody questions the value of money in the market place. No business would ever get done if, before a pound of cheese were weighed or a pint of beer drawn, the relative usefulness of these particular scales of weight and measurement as compared with others were threshed out. The surgeon does not pause in the middle of an operation to redesign his instruments. The MCC does not authorize a new width of bat, a new weight of ball or a new length of wicket in the middle of a Test Match, or even in the middle of a cricket season. When your house is on fire you do not get in touch with a fire-prevention research station to design a new appliance; as Disraeli pointed out, unless you are a lunatic, you send for the parish fire-engine. A musician may improvise music, but he would think himself hardly done-by if, at the same time, he were expected to improvise an instrument. Indeed, when a particularly tricky job is to be done, the workman will often prefer to use a tool that he is thoroughly familiar with rather than another he has in his bag, of new design, but which he has not yet mastered the use of. No doubt there is a time and a place to be radical about such things, for promoting innovation and carrying out improvements in the tools we employ, but these are clearly occasions for the exercise of a conservative disposition.

Now, what is true about tools in general, as distinct from projects, is even more obviously true about a certain kind of tool in common use, namely, general rules of conduct. If the familiarity that springs from relative immunity from change is appropriate to hammers and pincers and to bats and balls, it is supremely appropriate, for example, to an office routine. Routines, no doubt, are susceptible of improvement; but the more familiar they become, the more useful they are. Not to have a conservative disposition in respect of a routine is obvious folly. Of course, exceptional occasions occur which may call for a dispensation; but an inclination to be conservative rather than reformist about a routine is unquestionably appropriate. Consider the conduct of a public meeting, the rules of debate in the House of Commons or the procedure of a court of law. The chief virtue of these arrangements is that they are fixed and familiar; they establish and satisfy certain expectations, they allow to be said in a convenient order whatever is relevant, they prevent extraneous collisions and they conserve human energy. They are typical tools-instruments eligible for use in a variety of different but similar jobs. They are the product of reflection and choice, there is nothing sacrosanct about them, they are susceptible of change and improvement; but if our disposition in respect of them were not, generally speaking, conservative, if we were disposed to argue about them and change them on every occasion, they would rapidly lose their value. And while there may be rare occasions when it is useful to suspend them, it is pre-eminently appropriate that they should not be innovated upon or improved while they are in operation. Or again, consider the rules of a game. These, also, are the product of reflection and choice, and there are occasions when it is appropriate to reconsider them in the light of current experience; but it is inappropriate to have anything but a conservative disposition towards them or to consider putting them all together at one time into the melting-pot; and it is supremely inappropriate to change or improve upon them in the heat and confusion of play. Indeed, the more eager each side is to win, the more valuable is an inflexible set of rules. Players in the course of play may devise new tactics, they may improvise new methods of attack and defence, they may do anything they choose to defeat the expectations of their opponents, except invent new rules. That is an activity to be indulged sparingly and then only in the off-season.

There is much more that might be said about the relevance of the disposition to be conservative and its appropriateness even in a character, such as ours, chiefly disposed in the opposite direction. I have said nothing of morals, nothing of religion; but perhaps I have said enough to show that, even if to be conservative on all occasions and in all connections is so remote from our habit of thought as to be almost unintelligible, there are, nevertheless, few of our activities which do not on all occasions call into partnership a disposition to be conservative and on some occasions recognize it as the senior partner; and there are some activities where it is properly master.

3

How, then, are we to construe the disposition to be conservative in respect of politics? And in making this inquiry what I am interested in is not merely the intelligibility of this disposition in any set of circumstances, but its intelligibility in our own contemporary circumstances.

Writers who have considered this question commonly direct our attention to beliefs about the world in general, about human beings in general, about associations in general and even about the universe; and they tell us that a conservative disposition in politics can be correctly construed only when we understand it as a reflection of certain beliefs of these kinds. It is said, for example, that conservatism in politics is the appropriate counterpart of a generally conservative disposition in respect of human conduct: to be reformist in business, in morals or in religion and to be conservative in politics is represented as being inconsistent. It is said that the conservative in politics is so by virtue of holding certain religious beliefs; a belief, for example, in a natural law to be gathered from human experience, and in a providential order reflecting a divine purpose in nature and in human history to which it is the duty of mankind to conform its conduct and departure from which spells injustice and calamity. Further, it is said that a disposition to be conservative in politics reflects what is called an 'organic' theory of human society; that it is tied up with a belief in the absolute value of human personality, and with a belief in a primordial propensity of human beings to sin. And the 'conservatism' of an Englishman has even been connected with Royalism and Anglicanism.

Now, setting aside the minor complaints one might be moved to make about this account of the situation, it seems to me to suffer from one large defect. It is true that many of these beliefs have been held by people disposed to be conservative in political activity, and it may be true that these people have also believed their disposition to be in some way confirmed by them, or even to be founded upon them; but, as I understand it, a disposition to be conservative in politics does not entail either that we should hold these beliefs to be true or even that we should suppose them to be true. Indeed, I do not think it is necessarily connected with any particular beliefs about the universe, about the world in general or about human conduct in general. What it is tied to is certain beliefs about the activity of governing and the instruments of government, and it is in terms of beliefs on these topics, and not on others, that it can be made to appear intelligible. And, to state my view briefly before elaborating it, what makes a conservative disposition in politics intelligible is nothing to do with a natural law or a providential order, nothing to do with morals or religion; it is the observation of our current manner of living combined with the belief (which from our point of view need be regarded as no more than an hypothesis) that governing is a specific and limited activity, namely the provision and custody of general rules of conduct, which are understood, not as plans for imposing substantive activities, but as instruments enabling people to pursue the activities of their own choice with the minimum frustration, and therefore something which it is appropriate to be conservative about.

Let us begin at what I believe to be the proper starting-place; not in the empyrean, but with ourselves as we have come to be. I and my neighbours, my associates, my compatriots, my friends, my enemies and those who I am indifferent about, are people engaged in a great variety of activities. We are apt to entertain a multiplicity of opinions on every conceivable subject and are disposed to change these beliefs as we grow tired of them or as they prove unserviceable. Each of us is pursuing a course of his own; and there is no project so unlikely that somebody will not be found to engage in it, no enterprise so foolish that somebody will not undertake it. There are those who spend their lives trying to sell copies of the Anglican Catechism to the Jews. And one half of the world is engaged in trying to make the other half want what it has hitherto never felt the lack of. We are all inclined to be passionate about our own concerns, whether it is making things or selling them, whether it is business or sport, religion or learning, poetry, drink or drugs. Each of us has preferences of his own. For some, the opportunities of making choices (which are numerous) are invitations readily accepted; others welcome them less eagerly or even find them burdensome. Some dream dreams of new and better worlds: others are more inclined to move in familiar paths or even to be idle. Some are apt to deplore the rapidity of change, others delight in it; all recognize it. At times we grow tired and fall asleep: it is a blessed relief to gaze in a shop window and see nothing we want; we are grateful for ugliness merely because it repels attention. But, for the most part, we pursue happiness by seeking the satisfaction of desires which spring from one another inexhaustably. We enter into relationships of interest and of competition, partnership, guardianship, love, friendship, jealousy and hatred, some of which are more durable than others. We make agreements with one another; we have expectations about one another's conduct; we approve,

we are indifferent and we disapprove. This multiplicity of activity and variety of opinion is apt to produce collisions: we pursue courses which cut across those of others, and we do not all approve the same sort of conduct. But, in the main, we get along with one another, sometimes by giving way, sometimes by standing fast, sometimes in a compromise. Our conduct consists of activity assimilated to that of others in small, and for the most part unconsidered and unobtrusive, adjustments.

Why all this should be so, does not matter. It is not necessarily so. A different condition of human circumstance can easily be imagined, and we know that elsewhere and at other times activity is, or has been, far less multifarious and changeful and opinion far less diverse and far less likely to provoke collision; but, by and large, we recognize this to be our condition. It is an acquired condition, though nobody designed or specifically chose it in preference to all others. It is the product, not of 'human nature' let loose, but of human beings impelled by an acquired love of making choices for themselves. And we know as little and as much about where it is leading us as we know about the fashion in hats of twenty years' time or the design of motor-cars.

Surveying the scene, some people are provoked by the absence of order and coherence which appears to them to be its dominant feature; its wastefulness, its frustration, its dissipation of human energy, its lack not merely of a premeditated destination but even of any discernible direction of movement. It provides an excitement similar to that of a stock-car race; but it has none of the satisfaction of a well-conducted business enterprise. Such people are apt to exaggerate the current disorder; the absence of plan is so conspicuous that the small adjustments, and even the more massive arrangements, which restrain the chaos seem to them nugatory; they have no feeling for the warmth of untidiness but only for its inconvenience. But what is significant is not the limitations of their powers of observation, but the turn of their thoughts. They feel that there ought to be something that ought to be done to convert this so-called chaos into order, for this is no way for rational human beings to be spending their lives. Like Apollo when he saw Daphne with her hair hung carelessly about her neck, they sigh and say to themselves: 'What if it were properly arranged.' Moreover, they tell us that they have seen in a dream the glorious, collisionless manner of living proper to all mankind, and this dream they understand as their warrant for seeking to remove the diversities and occasions of conflict which distinguish our current manner of living. Of course, their dreams are not all exactly alike; but they have this in common: each is a vision of a condition of human circumstance from which the occasion of conflict has been removed, a vision of human activity co-ordinated and set going in a single direction and of every resource being used to the full. And such people appropriately understand the office of government to be the imposition upon its subjects of the condition of human circumstances of their dream. To govern is to turn a private dream into a public and compulsory manner of living. Thus, politics becomes an encounter of dreams and the activity in which government is held to this understanding of its office and provided with the appropriate instruments.

I do not propose to criticize this jump to glory style of politics in which governing is understood as a perpetual take-over bid for the purchase of the resources of human energy in order to concentrate them in a single direction; it is not at all unintelligible, and there is much in our circumstances to provoke it. My purpose is merely to point out that there is another quite different understanding of government, and that it is no less intelligible and in some respects perhaps more appropriate to our circumstances.

The spring of this other disposition in respect of governing and the instruments of government – a conservative disposition – is to be found in the acceptance of the current condition of human circumstances as I have described it: the propensity to make our own choices and to find happiness in doing so, the variety of enterprises each pursued with passion, the diversity of beliefs each held with the conviction of its exclusive truth; the inventiveness, the changefulness and the absence of any large design; the excess, the over-activity and the informal compromise. And the office of government is not to impose other beliefs and activities upon its subjects, not to tutor or to educate them, not to make them better or happier in another way, not to direct them, to galvanize them into action, to lead them or to coordinate their activities so that no occasion of conflict shall occur; the office of government is merely to rule. This is a specific and limited activity, easily corrupted when it is combined with any other, and, in the circumstances, indispensable. The image of the ruler is the umpire whose business is to administer the rules of the game, or the chairman who governs the debate according to known rules but does not himself participate in it.

Now people of this disposition commonly defend their belief that the proper attitude of government towards the current condition of human circumstance is one of acceptance by appealing to certain general ideas. They contend that there is absolute value in the free play of human choice, that private property (the emblem of choice) is a natural right, that it is only in the enjoyment of diversity of opinion and activity that true belief and good conduct can be expected to disclose themselves. But I do not think that this disposition requires these or any similar beliefs in order to make it intelligible. Something much smaller and less pretentious will do: the observation that this condition of human circumstance is, in fact, current, and that we have learned to enjoy it and how to manage it; that we are not children *in statu pupillari* but adults who do not consider themselves under any obligation to justify their preference for making their own choices; and that it is beyond human experience to suppose that those who rule are endowed with a superior wisdom which discloses to them a better range of beliefs and activities and which gives them authority to impose upon their subjects a quite different manner of life. In short, if the man of this disposition is asked: Why ought governments to accept the current diversity of opinion and activity in preference to imposing upon their subjects a dream of their own? it is enough for him to reply: Why not? Their dreams are no different from those of anyone else; and if it is boring to have to listen to dreams of others being recounted, it is insufferable to be forced to re-enact them. We tolerate monomaniacs, it is our habit to do so; but why should we be *ruled* by them? Is it not (the man of conservative disposition asks) an intelligible task for a government to protect its subjects against the nuisance of those who spend their energy and their wealth in the service of some pet indignation, endeavouring to impose it upon everybody, not by suppressing their activities in favour of others of a similar kind, but by setting a limit to the amount of noise anyone may emit?

Nevertheless, if this acceptance is the spring of the conservative's disposition in respect of government, he does not suppose that the office of government is to do nothing. As he understands it, there is work to be done which can be done only in virtue of a genuine acceptance of current beliefs simply because they are current and current activities simply because they are afoot. And, briefly, the office he attributes to government is to resolve some of the collisions which this variety of beliefs and activities generates; to preserve peace, not by placing an interdict upon choice and upon the diversity that springs from the exercise of preference, not by imposing substantive uniformity, but by enforcing general rules of procedure upon all subjects alike.

Government, then, as the conservative in this matter understands it, does not begin with a vision of another, different and better world, but with the observation of the self-government practised even by men of passion in the conduct of their enterprises; it begins in the informal adjustments of interests to one another which are designed to release those who are apt to collide from the mutual frustration of a collision. Sometimes these adjustments are no more than agreements between two parties to keep out of each other's way; sometimes they are of wider application and more durable character, such as the International Rules for the prevention of collisions at sea. In short, the intimations of government are to be found in ritual, not in religion or philosophy; in the enjoyment of orderly and peaceable behaviour, not in the search for truth or perfection.

But the self-government of men of passionate belief and enterprise is apt to break down when it is most needed. It often suffices to resolve minor collisions of interest, but beyond these it is not to be relied upon. A more precise and a less easily corrupted ritual is required to resolve the massive collisions which our manner of living is apt to generate and to release us from the massive frustrations in which we are apt to become locked. The custodian of this ritual is 'the government', and the rules it imposes are 'the law'. One may imagine a government engaged in the activity of an arbiter in cases of collisions of interest but doing its business without the aid of laws, just as one may imagine a game without rules and an umpire who was appealed to in cases of dispute and who on each occasion merely used his judgment to devise *ad hoc* a way of releasing the disputants from their mutual frustration. But the diseconomy of such an arrangement is so obvious that it could only be expected to occur to those inclined to believe the ruler to be super-

naturally inspired and to those disposed to attribute to him a quite different office, – that of leader, or tutor, or manager. At all events the disposition to be conservative in respect of government is rooted in the belief that where government rests upon the acceptance of the current activities and beliefs of its subjects, the only appropriate manner of ruling is by making and enforcing rules of conduct. In short, to be conservative about government is a reflection of the conservatism we have recognized to be appropriate in respect of rules of conduct.

To govern, then, as the conservative understands it, is to provide a *vinculum juris* for those manners of conduct which, in the circumstances, are least likely to result in a frustrating collision of interests; to provide redress and means of compensation for those who suffer from others behaving in a contrary manner; sometimes to provide punishment for those who pursue their own interests regardless of the rules; and, of course, to provide a sufficient force to maintain the authority of an arbiter of this kind. Thus, governing is recognized as a specific and limited activity; not the management of an enterprise, but the rule of those engaged in a great diversity of self-chosen enterprises. It is not concerned with concrete persons, but with activities; and with activities only in respect of their propensity to collide with one another. It is not concerned with moral right and wrong, it is not designed to make men good or even better; it is not indispensable on account of 'the natural depravity of mankind' but merely because of their current disposition to be extravagant: its business is to keep its subjects at peace with one another in the activities in which they have chosen to seek their happiness. And if there is any general idea entailed in this view, it is, perhaps that a government which does not sustain the loyalty of its subjects is worthless; and that while one which (in the old puritan phrase) 'commands for truth' is incapable of doing so (because some of its subjects will believe its 'truth' to be error), one which is indifferent to 'truth' and 'error' alike, and merely pursues peace, presents no obstacle to the necessary loyalty.

Now, it is intelligible enough that any man who thinks in this manner about government should be averse from innovation: government is providing rules of conduct, and familiarity is a supremely important virtue in a rule. Nevertheless, he has room for other thoughts. The current condition of human circumstances is one in which new activities (often springing from new inventions) are constantly appearing and rapidly extend themselves, and in which beliefs are perpetually being modified or discarded; and for the rules to be inappropriate to the current activities and beliefs is as unprofitable as for them to be unfamiliar. For example, a variety of inventions and considerable changes in the conduct of business, seem now to have made the current law of copyright inadequate. And it may be thought that neither the newspaper nor the motor-car nor the aeroplane have yet received proper recognition in the law of England; they have all created nuisances that call out to be abated. Or again, at the end of the last century our governments engaged in an extensive codification of large parts of our law and in this manner both brought it into closer relationship with current beliefs and manners of activity and insulated it from the small adjustments to circumstances which are characteristic of the operation of our common law. But many of these Statutes are now hopelessly out of date. And there are older Acts of Parliament (such as the Merchant Shipping Act), governing large and important departments of activity, which are even more inappropriate to current circumstances. Innovation, then, is called for if the rules are to remain appropriate to the activities they govern. But, as the conservative understands it, modification of the rules should always reflect, and never impose, a change in the activities and beliefs of those who are subject to them, and should never on any occasion be so great as to destroy the *ensemble*. Consequently, the conservative will have nothing to do with innovations designed to meet merely hypothetical situations; he will prefer to enforce a rule he has got rather than invent a new one; he will think it appropriate to delay a modification of the rules until it is clear that the change of circumstance it is designed to reflect has come to stay for a while; he will be suspicious of proposals for change in excess of what the situation calls for, of rulers who demand extra-ordinary powers in order to make great changes and whose utterances are tied to generalities like 'the public good' or 'social justice', and of Saviours of Society who buckle on armour and seek dragons to slay; he will think it proper to consider the occasion of the innovation with care; in short, he will be disposed to regard politics as an activity in which a valuable set of tools is renovated from time to time and kept in trim rather than as an opportunity for perpetual re-equipment.

All this may help to make intelligible the disposition to be conservative in respect of government; and the detail might be elaborated to show, for example, how a man of this disposition understands the other great business of a government, the conduct of a foreign policy; to show why he places so high a value upon the complicated set of arrangements we call 'the institution of private property'; to show the appropriateness of his rejection of the view that politics is a shadow thrown by economics; to show why he believes that the main (perhaps the only) specifically economic activity appropriate to government is the maintenance of a stable currency. But, on this occasion, I think there is something else to be said.

To some people, 'government' appears as a vast reservoir of power which inspires them to dream of what use might be made of it. They have favourite projects of various dimensions, which they sincerely believe are for the benefit of mankind, and to capture this source of power, if necessary to increase it, and to use it for imposing their favourite projects upon their fellows is what they understand as the adventure of governing men. They are, thus, disposed to recognize government as an instrument of passion; the art of politics is to inflame and direct desire. In short, governing is understood to be just like any other activity – making and selling a brand of soap, exploiting the resources of a locality, or developing a housing estate – only the power here is (for the most part) already mobilized, and the enterprise is remarkable only because it aims at monopoly and because of its promise of success once the source of power has been captured. Of course a private enterprise politician of this sort would get nowhere in these days unless there were people with wants so vague that they can be prompted to ask for what he has to offer, or with wants so servile that they prefer the promise of a provided abundance to the opportunity of choice and activity on their own account. And it is not all as plain sailing as it might appear: often a politician of this sort misjudges the situation; and then, briefly, even in democratic politics, we become aware of what the camel thinks of the camel driver.

Now, the disposition to be conservative in respect of politics reflects a quite different view of the activity of governing. The man of this disposition understands it to be the business of a government not to inflame passion and give it new objects to feed upon, but to inject into the activities of already too passionate men an ingredient of moderation; to restrain, to deflate, to pacify and to reconcile; not to stoke the fires of desire, but to damp them down. And all this, not because passion is vice and moderation virtue, but because moderation is indispensable if passionate men are to escape being locked in an encounter of mutual frustration. A government of this sort does not need to be regarded as the agent of a benign providence, as the custodian of a moral law, or as the emblem of a divine order. What it provides is something that its subjects (if they are such people as we are) can easily recognize to be valuable; indeed, it is something that, to some extent, they do for themselves in the ordinary course of business or pleasure. They scarcely need to be reminded of its indispensability, as Sextus Empiricus tells us the ancient Persians were accustomed periodically to remind themselves by setting aside all laws for five hair-raising days on the death of a king. Generally speaking, they are not averse from paying the modest cost of this service; and they recognize that the appropriate attitude to a government of this sort is loyalty (sometimes a confident loyalty, at others perhaps the heavy-hearted loyalty of Sidney Godolphin), respect and some suspicion, not love or devotion or affection. Thus, governing is understood to be a secondary activity; but it is recognized also to be a specific activity, not easily to be combined with any other, because all other activities (except the mere contemplation of the scene) entail taking sides and the surrender of the indifference appropriate (on this view of things) not only to the judge but also to the legislator, who is understood to occupy a judicial office. The subjects of such a government require that it shall be strong, alert, resolute, economical and neither capricious nor over-active: they have no use for a referee who does not govern the game according to the rules, who takes sides, who plays a game of his own, or who is always blowing his whistle; after all, the game's the thing, and in playing the game we neither need to be, nor at present are disposed to be, conservative.

But there is something more to be observed in this style of governing than merely the restraint imposed by familiar and appropriate rules. Of course, it will not countenance government by suggestion or cajolery or by any other means than by law; an avuncular Home Secretary or a threatening Chancellor of the Exchequer. But the spectacle of its indifference to the beliefs and substantive activities of its subjects may itself be expected to provoke a habit of restraint. Into the heat of our engagements, into the passionate clash of beliefs, into our enthusiasm for saving the souls of our neighbours or of all mankind, a government of this sort injects an ingredient, not of reason (how should we expect that?) but of the irony that is prepared to counteract one vice by another, of the raillery that deflates extravagance without itself pretending to wisdom, of the mockery that disperses tension, of inertia and of scepticism: indeed, it might be said that we keep a government of this sort to do for us the scepticism we have neither the time nor the inclination to do for ourselves. It is like the cool touch of the mountain that one feels in the plain even on the hottest summer day. Or, to leave metaphor behind, it is like the 'governor' which, by controlling the speed at which its parts move, keeps an engine from racketing itself to pieces.

It is not, then, mere stupid prejudice which disposes a conservative to take this view of the activity of governing; nor are any highfalutin metaphysical beliefs necessary to provoke it or make it intelligible. It is connected merely with the observation that where activity is bent upon enterprise the indispensable counterpart is another order of activity, bent upon restraint, which is unavoidably corrupted (indeed, altogether abrogated) when the power assigned to it is used for advancing favourite projects. An 'umpire' who at the same time is one of the players is no umpire; 'rules' about which we are not disposed to be conservative are not rules but incitements to disorder; the conjunction of dreaming and ruling generates tyranny.

4

Political conservatism is, then, not at all unintelligible in a people disposed to be adventurous and enterprising, a people in love with change and apt to rationalize their affections in terms of 'progress.'[3] And one does not need to think that the

---

3   I have not forgotten to ask myself the question: Why, then, have we so neglected what is appropriate to our circumstances as to make the activist dreamer the stereotype of the modern politician? And I have tried to answer it elsewhere.

belief in 'progress' is the most cruel and unprofitable of all beliefs, arousing cupidity without satisfying it, in order to think it inappropriate for a government to be conspicuously 'progressive'. Indeed, a disposition to be conservative in respect of government would seem to be pre-eminently appropriate to men who have something to do and something to think about on their own account, who have a skill to practise or an intellectual fortune to make, to people whose passions do not need to be inflamed, whose desires do not need to be provoked and whose dreams of a better world need no prompting. Such people know the value of a rule which imposes orderliness without directing enterprise, a rule which concentrates duty so that room is left for delight. They might even be prepared to suffer a legally established ecclesiastical order; but it would not be because they believed it to represent some unassailable religious truth, but merely because it restrained the indecent competition of sects and (as Hume said) moderated 'the plague of a too diligent clergy'.

Now, whether or not these beliefs recommend themselves as reasonable and appropriate to our circumstances and to the abilities we are likely to find in those who rule us, they and their like are in my view what make intelligible a conservative disposition in respect of politics. What would be the appropriateness of this disposition in circumstances other than our own, whether to be conservative in respect of government would have the same relevance in the circumstances of an unadventurous, a slothful or a spiritless people, is a question we need not try to answer: we are concerned with ourselves as we are. I myself think that it would occupy an important place in any set of circumstances. But what I hope I have made clear is that it is not at all inconsistent to be conservative in respect of government and radical in respect of almost every other activity. And, in my opinion, there is more to be learnt about this disposition from Montaigne, Pascal, Hobbes and Hume than from Burke or Bentham.

Of the many entailments of this view of things that might be pointed to, I will notice one, namely, that politics is an activity unsuited to the young, not on account of their vices but on account of what I at least consider to be their virtues.

Nobody pretends that it is easy to acquire or to sustain the mood of indifference which this manner of politics calls for. To rein-in one's own beliefs and desires, to acknowledge the current shape of things, to feel the balance of things in one's hand, to tolerate what is abominable, to distinguish between crime and sin, to respect formality even when it appears to be leading to error, these are difficult achievements; and they are achievements not to be looked for in the young.

Everybody's young days are a dream, a delightful insanity, a sweet solipsism. Nothing in them has a fixed shape, nothing a fixed price; everything is a possibility, and we live happily on credit. There are no obligations to be observed; there are no accounts to be kept. Nothing is specified in advance; everything is what can be made of it. The world is a mirror in which we seek the reflection of our own desires. The allure of violent emotions is irresistible. When we are young we are not disposed to make concessions to the world; we never feel the balance of a thing in our hands - unless it be a cricket bat. We are not apt to distinguish between our liking and our esteem; urgency is our criterion of importance; and we do not easily understand that what is humdrum need not be despicable. We are impatient of restraint; and we readily believe, like Shelley, that to have contracted a habit is to have failed. These, in my opinion, are among our virtues when we are young; but how remote they are from the disposition appropriate for participating in the style of government I have been describing. Since life is a dream, we argue (with plausible but erroneous logic) that politics must be an encounter of dreams, in which we hope to impose our own. Some unfortunate people, like Pitt (laughably called 'the Younger'), are born old, and are eligible to engage in politics almost in their cradles; others, perhaps more fortunate, belie the saying that one is young only once, they never grow up. But these are exceptions. For most there is what Conrad called the 'shadow line' which, when we pass it, discloses a solid world of things, each with its fixed shape, each with its own point of balance, each with its price; a world of fact, not poetic image, in which what we have spent on one thing we cannot spend on another; a world inhabited by others besides ourselves who cannot be reduced to mere reflections of our own emotions. And coming to be at home in this commonplace world qualifies us (as no knowledge of 'political science' can ever qualify us), if we are so inclined and have nothing better to think about, to engage in what the man of conservative disposition understands to be political activity.

1956

Bibliography

Grant, Robert. *Oakeshott*. London: Claridge Press, 1990.

Hayek, F.A. *The Fatal Conceit*. Chicago: University of Chicago Press, 1988. [*The Collected Works of F. A. Hayek,* Vol. I].

Honderich, J. *Conservatism*. Boulder: Westview Press, 1991.

Mandeville, Bernard. *The Fable of the Bees*. 2 vols. Indianapolis: Liberty Classics, 1988. [originally published in several editions 1714-1732.]

Minogue, Kenneth, ed. *Conservative Realism: New Essays on Conservatism*. New York: Harper Collins/Centre for Policy Studies, 1996.

O'Sullivan, Noël. *Conservatism*. New York: St. Martin's Press, 1976.

Scruton, Roger. *The Meaning of Conservatism*. Totowa, NJ: Barnes and Noble Books, 1980.

Scruton, Roger, ed. *Conservative Texts*. New York: St. Martin's Press, 1991.

V

DIALECTICAL THEORIES OF HUMAN NATURE

CHAPTER TWENTY-FIVE — JEAN-JACQUES ROUSSEAU

The philosophical merits of the ideas and work of Jean-Jacques Rousseau (1712-1778) have been debated since their first appearance, but about their originality and historical importance and influence there has never been any doubt. Rousseau was originally from Switzerland – from Protestant (Calvinist) French-speaking Geneva. He came to Paris in 1741, and quickly became part of the cultural and intellectual world of the French capital.

Rousseau wrote plays, essays, treatises, and novels. Their style is informal, frequently personal; moral judgment is interspersed with analysis in ways not always easily disentangled. Rousseau was a "public intellectual," a writer holding up a certain kind of moral mirror to the age he lived in and the society of which he was a part. Those undertaking that role had previously more usually adopted the vehicle of *satire*, but Rousseau writes instead with a kind of disarmed candour. His topics are the origins of society, and of the modern state; what is recoverable as an original and underlying human nature; what is amiss with the modern social and political order, and what prospects there may be for putting it right; what system and method of education might be best, and what it should aim at; what are the respective natures of the sexes, and how the world might better work in their regard. Throughout, Rousseau's concerns are with what is the case (and how it got to be that way), and what ought to be the case. Sometimes he does not seem to differentiate between or among them. In part, or in some instances, this seems due to a kind of classical *teleologism* in Rousseau's work: he is taking an idea (the idea of the state, for example, in *The Social Contract*) and exploring what it *is*, i.e., what ideal profile it should have, what, in thriving realization of what is inherent in the idea, will be found in its (ideal) exemplification.

Rousseau had a great deal of influence on changing the course of Enlightenment culture, from the valorization of reason and civilization to that of the "natural," of pre-civilized rural simplicities expressive of the heart rather than the head. Rousseau also played a profoundly important iconic role in the background of the French Revolution, and in the attendant struggles for human rights, and democracy. Much of his theory of human nature will be found in the following selection.

Jean-Jacques Rousseau, *Discourse on the Origins of Inequality*

(Source: Jean-Jacques Rousseau. *Discourse on the Origins of Inequality (Second Discourse): Polemics, and Political Economy.* Eds. Roger D. Masters and Christopher Kelly. Trans. Judith R. Bush, Roger D. Masters, Christopher Kelly, and Terence Marshall. Hanover and London: University Press of New England, 1992, 18-67.)

Discourse on the Origin and Foundations of Inequality among Men

It is of man that I am to speak; and the question I examine informs me that I am going to speak to men; for such questions are not proposed by those who are afraid of honoring the truth. Therefore I shall defend with confidence the cause of humanity before the wise men who invite me to do so, and I shall not be discontent with myself if I prove myself worthy of my subject and my judges.

I conceive of two sorts of inequality in the human Species: one, which I call natural or Physical, because it is established by Nature and consists in the difference of ages, health, Bodily strengths, and qualities of Mind or Soul; the other, which may be called moral or Political inequality, because it depends upon a sort of convention and is established, or at least authorized, by the consent of Men. The latter consists in the different Privileges that some men enjoy to the prejudice of others, such as to be richer, more honored, more Powerful than they, or even to make themselves obeyed by them.

One cannot ask what the source of Natural inequality is, because the answer would be found enunciated in the simple definition of the word. Still less can one inquire if there would not be some essential link between the two inequalities; for that would be asking, in other terms, whether those who command are necessarily worth more than those who obey, and whether strength of Body or Mind, wisdom or virtue, are always found in the same individuals in proportion to Power or Wealth: a question perhaps good for Slaves to discuss in the hearing of their Masters, but not suitable for reasonable and free Men who seek the truth.

Precisely what, then, is at issue in this Discourse? To indicate in the progress of things the moment when, Right taking the place of Violence, Nature was subjected to Law; to explain by what sequence of marvels the strong could resolve to serve the weak, and the People to buy a repose in ideas at the price of a real felicity.

The Philosophers who have examined the foundations of society have all felt the necessity of going back to the state of Nature, but none of them has reached it. Some have not hesitated to attribute to Man in that state the notion of the Just and Unjust, without troubling themselves to show that he had to have that notion or even that it was useful to him. Others have spoken of the Natural Right that everyone has to preserve what belongs to him, without explaining what they meant by belong. Still others, giving the stronger authority over the weaker from the first, have forthwith made Government arise, without thinking of the time that must have elapsed before the meaning of the words "authority" and "government" could exist among Men. All of them, finally, speaking contin-

ually of need, avarice, oppression, desires, and pride, have carried over to the state of Nature ideas they had acquired in society: they spoke about savage man and they described Civil man. It did not even enter the minds of most of our philosophers to doubt that the state of Nature had existed, even though it is evident from reading the Holy Scriptures that the first Man, having received enlightenment and precepts directly from God, was not himself in that state; and that giving the Writings of Moses the credence that any Christian Philosopher owes them, it must be denied that even before the Flood Men were ever in the pure state of Nature, unless they fell back into it because of some extraordinary Event: a Paradox that is very embarrassing to defend and altogether impossible to prove.

Let us therefore begin by setting all the facts aside, for they do not affect the question. The Researches which can be undertaken concerning this Subject must not be taken for historical truths, but only for hypothetical and conditional reasonings better suited to clarify the Nature of things than to show their genuine origin, like those our Physicists make every day concerning the formation of the World. Religion commands us to believe that since God Himself took Men out of the state of Nature immediately after the creation, they are unequal because He wanted them to be so; but it does not forbid us to form conjectures, drawn solely from the nature of man and the Beings surrounding him, about what the human Race might have become if it had remained abandoned to itself. That is what I am asked, and what I propose to examine in this Discourse. As my subject concerns man in general, I shall try to use a language that suits all Nations, or rather, forgetting times and Places in order to think only of the Men to whom I speak, I shall imagine myself in the Lyceum of Athens, repeating the Lessons of my Masters, with Plato and Xenocrates for judges, and the human Race for an Audience.

O Man, whatever Country you may come from, whatever your opinions may be, listen: here is your history as I believed it to read, not in the Books of your Fellow-men, who are liars, but in Nature, which never lies. Everything that comes from Nature will be true; there will be nothing false except what I have involuntarily put in of my own. The times of which I am going to speak are very far off: how you have changed from what you were! It is, so to speak, the life of your species that I am going to describe to you according to the qualities you received, which your education and habits have been able to corrupt but have not been able to destroy. There is, I feel, an age at which the individual man would want to stop: you will seek the age at which you would desire your Species had stopped. Discontented with your present state for reasons that foretell even greater discontents for your unhappy Posterity, perhaps you would want to be able to go backward in time. This sentiment must be the Eulogy of your first ancestors, the criticism of your contemporaries, and the dread of those who will have the unhappiness to live after you.

First Part

Important as it may be, in order to judge the natural state of Man correctly, to consider him from his origin and examine him, so to speak, in the first Embryo of the species, I shall not follow his organic structure through its successive developments. I shall not stop to investigate in the animal System what he could have been at the beginning in order to become at length what he is. I shall not examine whether, as Aristotle thinks, man's elongated nails were not at first hooked claws; whether he was not hairy like a bear; and whether, if he walked on all fours his gaze, directed toward the Earth and confined to a horizon of several paces, did not indicate both the character and the limits of his ideas. On this subject I could form only vague and almost imaginary conjectures. Comparative Anatomy has as yet made too little progress and the observations of Naturalists are as yet too uncertain for one to be able to establish the basis of solid reasoning upon such foundations. Thus, without having recourse to the supernatural knowledge we have on this point, and without regard to the changes that must have come about in the internal as well as external conformation of man as he applied his limbs to new uses and as he nourished himself on new foods, I shall suppose him to have been formed from all time as I see him today: walking on two feet, using his hands as we do ours, directing his gaze on all of Nature, and measuring the vast expanse of Heaven with his eyes.

Stripping this Being, so constituted, of all the supernatural gifts he could have received and of all the artificial faculties he could only have acquired by long progress – considering him, in a word, as he must have come from the hands of Nature – I see an animal less strong than some, less agile than others, but all things considered, the most advantageously organized of all. I see him satisfying his hunger under an oak, quenching his thirst at the first Stream, finding his bed at the foot of the same tree that furnished his meal: and therewith his needs are satisfied.

The Earth, abandoned to its natural fertility and covered by immense forests never mutilated by the Axe, offers at every step Storehouses and shelters to animals of all species. Men, dispersed among the animals, observe and imitate their industry, and thereby develop in themselves the instinct of the Beasts; with the advantage that whereas each species has only its own proper instinct, man – perhaps having none that belongs to him – appropriates them all to himself, feeds himself equally well with most of the diverse foods which the other animals share, and consequently finds his subsistence more easily than any of them can.

Accustomed from infancy to inclemencies of the weather and the rigor of the seasons, trained in fatigue, and forced, naked and without weapons, to defend their lives and their Prey against other wild Beasts, or to escape by outrunning them, men develop a robust and almost unalterable physique. Children, bringing into the world the excellent constitution of their Fathers and fortifying it with the same training that produced it, thus acquire all the vigor of which the human species is capable. Nature treats them precisely as the Law of Sparta treated the Children of Citizens: it renders strong and robust those who are well constituted and makes all the others perish, thereby differing from our societies, in which the State, by making Children burdensome to their Fathers, kills them indiscriminately before their birth.

The savage man's body being the only implement he knows, he employs it for various uses of which, through lack of training, our bodies are incapable; our industry deprives us of the strength and agility that necessity obliges him to acquire. If he had an axe, would his wrist break such strong branches? If he had a sling, would he throw a stone so hard? If he had a ladder, would he climb a tree so nimbly? If he had a Horse, would he run so fast? Give

Civilized man time to assemble all his machines around him and there can be no doubt that he will easily overcome Savage man. But if you want to see an even more unequal fight, put them, naked and disarmed, face to face, and you will soon recognize the advantage of constantly having all of one's strength at one's disposal, of always being ready for any event, and of always carrying oneself, so to speak, entirely with one.

Hobbes claims that man is naturally intrepid and seeks only to attack and fight. An illustrious Philosopher thinks, on the contrary, and Cumberland and Pufendorf also affirm, that nothing is so timid as man in the state of Nature, and that he is always trembling and ready to flee at the slightest noise he hears, at the slightest movement he perceives. That may be so with respect to objects he does not know; and I do not doubt that he is frightened by all the new Spectacles that present themselves to him every time he can neither discern the Physical good and evil to be expected nor compare his strength with the dangers he must run: rare circumstances in the state of Nature, where all things move in such a uniform manner, and where the face of the Earth is not subject to those brusque and continual changes caused by the passions and inconstancy of united Peoples. But Savage man, living dispersed among the animals and early finding himself in a position to measure himself against them, soon makes the comparison; and sensing that he surpasses them in skill more than they surpass him in strength, he learns not to fear them any more. Pit a bear or a wolf against a Savage who is robust, agile, courageous, as they all are, armed with stones and a good stick, and you will see that the danger will be reciprocal at the very least, and that after several similar experiences wild Beasts, which do not like to attack each other, will hardly attack man willingly, having found him to be just as wild as they. With regard to animals that actually have more strength than man has skill, he is in the position of the other weaker species, which nevertheless subsist. But man has the advantage that, no less adept at running than they and finding almost certain refuge in trees, he always has the option of accepting or leaving the encounter and the choice of flight or combat. Let us add that it does not appear that any animal naturally makes war upon man except in case of self-defense or extreme hunger, or gives evidence of those violent antipathies toward him that seem to announce that one species is destined by Nature to serve as food for the other.

These are, without doubt, the reasons why Negroes and Savages trouble themselves so little about the wild beasts they may encounter in the woods. In this respect the Caribs of Venezuela, among others, live in the most profound security and without the slightest inconvenience. Although they go nearly naked, says François Corréal, they nevertheless expose themselves boldly in the woods armed only with bow and arrow, but no one has ever heard that any of them were devoured by beasts.

Other more formidable enemies, against which man does not have the same means of defense, are natural infirmities: infancy, old age, and illnesses of all kinds, sad signs of our weakness, of which the first two are common to all animals and the last belongs principally to man living in Society. I even observe on the subject of Infancy that the Mother, since she carries her child with her everywhere, can nourish it with more facility than the females of several animals, which are forced to come and go incessantly with great fatigue, in one direction to seek their food and in the other to suckle or nourish their young. It is true that if the woman should die, the child greatly risks dying with her; but this danger is common to a hundred other species, whose young are for a long time unable to go and seek their nourishment themselves. And if Infancy is longer among us, so also is life; everything remains approximately equal in this respect, although there are, concerning the duration of the first age and the number of young, other rules which are not within my Subject. Among the Aged, who act and perspire little, the need for food diminishes with the faculty of providing for it; and since Savage life keeps gout and rheumatism away from them and since old age is, of all ills, the one that human assistance can least relieve, they finally die without it being perceived that they cease to be, and almost without perceiving it themselves.

With regard to illnesses, I shall not repeat the vain and false declamations against Medicine made by most People in good health; rather, I shall ask whether there is any solid observation from which one might conclude that in Countries where this art is most neglected, the average life of man is shorter than in those where it is cultivated with the greatest care. And how could that be, if we give ourselves more ills than Medicine can furnish Remedies? The extreme inequality in our way of life: excess of idleness in some, excess of labor in others; the ease of stimulating and satisfying our appetites and our sensuality; the overly refined foods of the rich, which nourish them with binding juices and overwhelm them with indigestion; the bad food of the Poor, which they do not even have most of the time, so that their want inclines them to overburden their stomachs greedily when the occasion permits; late nights, excesses of all kinds, immoderate ecstasies of all the Passions, fatigues and exhaustion of Mind; numberless sorrows and afflictions which are felt in all conditions and by which souls are perpetually tormented: these are the fatal proofs that most of our ills are our own work, and that we would have avoided almost all of them by preserving the simple, uniform, and solitary way of life prescribed to us by Nature. If she destined us to be healthy, I almost dare affirm that the state of reflection is a state contrary to Nature and that the man who meditates is a depraved animal. When one thinks of the good constitution of Savages, at least of those whom we have not ruined with our strong liquors; when one learns that they know almost no illnesses except wounds and old age, one is strongly inclined to believe that the history of human illnesses could easily be written by following that of civil Societies. This at least is the opinion of Plato, who judges, from certain Remedies used or approved by Podalirius and Machaon at the siege of Troy, that various illnesses that should have been caused by those remedies were not yet known at that time among men; and Paracelsus reports that the diet, so necessary today, was invented only by Hippocrates.

With so few sources of illness, man in the state of Nature hardly has need of remedies, still less of Doctors. In this respect the human species is not in any worse condition than all the others; and it is easy to learn from Hunters whether in their chases they find many sick animals. They find many that have received extensive but very well healed wounds, that have had bones and even limbs broken and set again with no other Surgeon than time, no other regimen than their ordinary life, and that are no less perfectly cured for not having been tormented with incisions, poisoned with Drugs, or weakened with fasting. Finally, however useful

well-administered medicine may be among us, it is still certain that if a sick Savage abandoned to himself has nothing to hope for except from Nature, in return he has nothing to fear except from his illness, which often renders his situation preferable to ours.

Let us therefore take care not to confuse Savage man with the men we have before our eyes. Nature treats all the animals abandoned to its care with a partiality that seems to show how jealous it is of this right. The Horse, the Cat, the Bull, even the Ass, are mostly taller, and all have a more robust constitution, more vigor, more strength and courage in the forest than in our houses. They lose half of these advantages in becoming Domesticated, and it might be said that all our cares to treat and feed these animals well end only in their degeneration. It is the same even for man. In becoming sociable and a Slave he becomes weak, fearful, servile; and his soft and effeminate way of life completes the enervation of both his strength and his courage. Let us add that between Savage and Domesticated conditions the difference from man to man must be still greater than that from beast to beast; for animal and man having been treated equally by Nature, all the commodities of which man gives himself more than the animals he tames are so many particular causes that make him degenerate more noticeably.

Nakedness, lack of habitation, and deprivation of all those useless things we believe so necessary are not, then, such a great misfortune for these first men; nor, above all, are they such a great obstacle to their preservation. If they do not have hairy skin, they have no need of it in warm Countries, and in cold Countries they soon know how to appropriate the skins of Beasts they have overcome. If they have only two feet to run with, they have two arms to provide for their defense and their needs. Perhaps their Children walk late and with difficulty, but Mothers carry them with ease: an advantage lacking in other species in which the mother, being pursued, finds herself forced to abandon her young or to regulate her speed by theirs. Finally, unless we suppose those singular and fortuitous combinations of circumstances of which I shall speak hereafter and which could very well never happen, it is clear in any case that the first man who made himself clothing or a Dwelling, in doing so gave himself things that were hardly necessary, since he had done without them until then and since it is hard to see why he could not endure, as a grown man, a kind of life he had endured from his infancy.

Alone, idle, and always near danger, Savage man must like to sleep, and be a light sleeper like animals which, thinking little, sleep so to speak all the time they do not think. His self-preservation being almost his only care, his best-trained faculties must be those having as principal object attack and defense, either to subjugate his prey or to save himself from being the prey of another animal. On the contrary, the organs that are perfected only by softness and sensuality must remain in a state of crudeness which excludes any kind of delicacy in him; and his senses being divided in this regard, he will have extremely crude touch and taste, and sight, hearing, and smell of the greatest subtlety. Such is the animal state in general; and according to reports of Travelers, such also is that of most Savage Peoples. Thus one must not be surprised that the Hottentots of the Cape of Good Hope sight Vessels on the high sea with their naked eyes as far away as do the Dutch with Spyglasses; nor that American Savages could smell Spaniards on the trail as the best Dogs could have done; nor that all these Barbarous Nations endure their nakedness without discomfort, sharpen their taste by means of Peppers, and drink European Liquors like water.

I have to this point considered only Physical Man; let us now try to look at him from the Metaphysical and Moral side.

In every animal I see only an ingenious machine to which nature has given senses in order to revitalize itself and guarantee itself, to a certain point, from all that tends to destroy or upset it. I perceive precisely the same things in the human machine, with the difference that Nature alone does everything in the operations of a Beast, whereas man contributes to his operations by being a free agent. The former chooses or rejects by instinct and the latter by an act of freedom, so that a Beast cannot deviate from the Rule that is prescribed to it even when it would be advantageous for it to do so, and a man deviates from it often to his detriment. Thus a Pigeon would die of hunger near a Basin filled with the best meats, and a Cat upon heaps of fruits or grain, although each could very well nourish itself on the food it disdains if it made up its mind to try some. Thus dissolute men abandon themselves to excesses which cause them fever and

death, because the Mind depraves the senses and because the will still speaks when Nature is silent.

Every animal has ideas, since it has senses; it even combines its ideas up to a certain point, and in this regard man differs from a Beast only in degree. Some Philosophers have even suggested that there is more difference between a given man and another than between a given man and a given beast. Therefore it is not so much understanding which constitutes the distinction of man among the animals as it is his being a free agent. Nature commands every animal, and the Beast obeys. Man feels the same impetus, but he realizes that he is free to acquiesce or resist; and it is above all in the consciousness of this freedom that the spirituality of his soul is shown. For Physics explains in some way the mechanism of the senses and the formation of ideas; but in the power of willing, or rather of choosing, and in the sentiment of this power are found only purely spiritual acts about which the Laws of Mechanics explain nothing.

But if the difficulties surrounding all these questions should leave some room for dispute on this difference between man and animal, there is another very specific quality that distinguishes them and about which there can be no dispute: the faculty of self-perfection, a faculty which, with the aid of circumstances, successively develops all the others, and resides among us as much in the species as in the individual. By contrast an animal is at the end of a few months what it will be all its life; and its species is at the end of a thousand years what it was the first year of that thousand. Why is man alone subject to becoming imbecile? Is it not that he thereby returns to his primitive state; and that – while the Beast, which has acquired nothing and which has, moreover, nothing to lose, always retains its instinct – man, losing again by old age or other accidents all that his *perfectibility* had made him acquire, thus falls back lower than the Beast itself? It would be sad for us to be forced to agree that this distinctive and almost unlimited faculty is the source of all man's misfortunes; that it is this faculty which, by dint of time, draws him out of that original condition in which he would pass tranquil and innocent days; that it is this faculty which, bringing to flower over the centuries his enlightenment and his errors, his vices and his virtues, in the long run makes him the tyrant of himself and of Nature. It would be horrible to be obliged to praise as a beneficent being the one who first suggested to the inhabitant of the banks of the Orinoco the use of those Pieces of wood which he binds on the temples of his Children, and which assure them at least a part of their imbecility and original happiness.

Savage Man, by Nature committed to instinct alone, or rather compensated for the instinct he perhaps lacks by faculties capable of substituting for it at first, and then of raising him far above Nature, will therefore begin with purely animal functions. To perceive and feel will be his first state, which he will have in common with all animals. To will and not will, to desire and fear, will be the first and almost the only operations of his soul until new circumstances cause new developments in it.

Whatever the Moralists may say about it, human understanding owes much to the Passions, which by common agreement also owe much to it. It is by their activity that our reason is perfected; we seek to know only because we desire to have pleasure; and it is impossible to conceive why one who had neither desires nor fears would go to the trouble of reasoning. The Passions in turn derive their origin from our needs and their progress from our knowledge. For one can desire or fear things only through the ideas one can have of them or by the simple impulsion of Nature; and Savage man, deprived of every kind of enlightenment, feels only the Passions of this last kind. His desires do not exceed his Physical needs, the only goods he knows in the Universe are nourishment, a female, and repose; the only evils he fears are pain and hunger. I say pain and not death because an animal will never know what it is to die; and knowledge of death and its terrors is one of the first acquisitions that man has made in moving away from the animal condition.

It would be easy for me, were it necessary, to support this sentiment by facts and to demonstrate that in all Nations of the world progress of the Mind has been precisely proportioned to the needs that Peoples had received from Nature or to those to which circumstances had subjected them, and consequently to the passions which inclined them to provide for those needs. I would show the arts coming into existence in Egypt and spreading with the flooding of the Nile. I would follow their progress among the Greeks, where they were seen to spring up, grow, and rise to the Heavens among the Sands and Rocks of Attica though they could not take root on the fertile Banks of the Eurotas. I would note that, in general, the Peoples of the North are more industrious than those of the south because they can less afford not to be, as if Nature thereby wanted to equalize things by giving to Minds the fertility it refuses the Earth.

But without having recourse to the uncertain testimonies of History, who does not see that everything seems to remove Savage man from the temptation and means of ceasing to be savage? His imagination portrays nothing to him; his heart asks nothing of him. His modest needs are so easily found at hand, and he is so far from the degree of knowledge necessary for desiring to acquire greater knowledge, that he can have neither foresight nor curiosity. The spectacle of Nature becomes indifferent to him by dint of becoming familiar. There is always the same order, there are always the same revolutions; he does not have the mind to wonder at the greatest marvels; and one must not seek in him the Philosophy that man needs in order to know how to observe once what he has seen every day. His soul, agitated by nothing, is given over to the sole sentiment of its present existence without any idea of the future, however near it may be, and his projects, as limited as his views, barely extend to the end of the day. Such is, even today, the degree of foresight of the Carib: in the morning he sells his bed of Cotton and in the evening he comes weeping to buy it back, for want of having foreseen that he would need it for the coming night.

The more one meditates on this subject, the more the distance from pure sensations to the simplest knowledge increases in our eyes; and it is impossible to conceive how a man, by his strength alone, without the aid of communication and without the stimulus of necessity, could have bridged so great a gap. How many centuries perhaps elapsed before men were capable of seeing another fire than that from Heaven? How many different risks did they have to run to learn the most common uses of that element? How many times did they let it die out before they had acquired the art of reproducing it? And how many times, perhaps, did each of these secrets die with the ones who had discovered it? What shall we say of agriculture, an art which demands so much labor and foresight, which depends on so many other arts, which very clearly is practicable only in a society that has at least been started, and which does not serve so much to bring from the Earth foods it would easily provide without agriculture as to force from it those preferences most to our taste? But let us suppose that men had multiplied so greatly that the natural productions no longer sufficed to nourish them: a supposition which, it may be added in passing, would show a great advantage for the human Species in that way of life. Let us suppose that without forges and Workshops, the implements for Farming had fallen from Heaven into the hands of the Savages; that these men had conquered the mortal hatred they all have for continuous labor; that they had learned to foresee their needs so long in advance; that they had guessed how Land must be cultivated, grains sown, and Trees planted; that they had discovered the art of grinding Wheat and fermenting grapes – all things they would have had to be taught by the Gods, as it is impossible to conceive how they could have learned them by themselves. After that, what man would be insane enough to torment himself cultivating a Field that will be plundered by the first comer, whether man or beast, for whom the crop is suitable? And how could each man resolve to spend his life in hard labor, when the more he will need its reward, the more certain he will be of not reaping it? In a word, how could this situation incline men to cultivate the Earth as long as it is not divided among them: that is to say, as long as the state of Nature is not annihilated?

Should we want to suppose a Savage man as skillful in the art of thinking as our Philosophers make him; should we, following their example, make him a Philosopher himself, discovering alone the most sublime truths and making for himself, by chains of very abstract reasoning, maxims of justice, and reason drawn from love of order in general or from the known will of his Creator; in a word, should we suppose his mind to have as much intelligence and enlightenment as he must and is in fact found to have dullness and stupidity, what utility would the Species draw from all this Metaphysics, which could not be communicated and which would perish with the individual who would have invented it? What progress could the human Race make, scattered in the Woods among the Animals? And to what point could men mutually perfect and enlighten one another, who, having neither fixed Domicile nor any need of one another, would perhaps meet hardly twice in their lives, without knowing each other and without talking to each other.

Let us consider how many ideas we owe to the use of speech; how much Grammar trains and facilitates the operations of the Mind; and let us think of the inconceivable difficulties and the infinite time which the first invention of Languages must have cost. Join these reflections to the preceding ones, and we shall judge how many thousands of Centuries would have been necessary to develop successively in the human Mind the Operations of which it was capable.

May I be allowed to consider for an instant the obstacles to the origin of Languages. I could be satisfied to cite or repeat here the researches that the Abbé de Condillac has made on this matter, which all fully confirm my sentiment, and which perhaps gave me the first idea of it. But since the way this Philosopher resolves the difficulties he himself raises concerning the origin of instituted signs shows that he assumed what I question – namely, a kind of society already established among the inventors of language – I believe, in referring to his reflections, that I ought to add to them my own, in order to present the same difficulties in the way that suits my subject. The first that comes up is to imagine how languages could have become necessary; for since Men had no communication among themselves nor any need of it, one can conceive neither the necessity of this invention nor its possibility were it not indispensable. I might well say, as many others do, that Languages were born in the domestic intercourse of Fathers, Mothers, and Children. But not only would that fail to resolve the objections, it would be committing the error of those who, reasoning about the state of Nature, carry over to it ideas taken from Society, and always see the family gathered in the same habitation and its members maintaining among themselves a union as intimate and permanent as among us, where so many common interests unite them. Instead, in the primitive state, having neither Houses, nor Huts, nor property of any kind, everyone took up his lodging by chance and often for only one night. Males and females united fortuitously, depending on encounter, occasion, and desire, without speech being a very necessary interpreter of the things they had to say to each other; they left each other with the same ease. The mother nursed her Children at first for her own need; then, habit having endeared them to her, she nourished them afterward for their need. As soon as they had the strength to seek their food, they did not delay in leaving the Mother herself; and as there was practically no other way to find one another again than not to lose sight of each other, they were soon at a point of not even recognizing one another. Note also that the Child having all his needs to explain and consequently more things to say to the Mother than the Mother to the Child, it is the child who must make the greatest efforts of invention, and that the language he uses must be in great part his own work, which multiplies Languages as many times as there are individuals to speak them. A wandering and vagabond life contributes further to this, since it does not give any idiom the time to gain consistency. For to say that the Mother teaches the Child the words he ought to use to ask her for one thing or another shows well how one teaches already formed Languages, but it does not teach us how they are formed.

Let us suppose this first difficulty conquered; let us skip over for a moment the immense distance there must have been between the pure state of Nature and the need for Languages; and let us seek, assuming them to be necessary, how they could begin to be established. New difficulty, worse still than the preceding one. For if Men needed speech in order to learn to think, they had even greater need of knowing how to think in order to discover the art of speech; and even should we understand how the sounds of the voice were taken for the conventional interpreters of our ideas, it would still remain to be seen what could have been the specific interpreters of this convention for ideas that, having no perceptible object, could be indicated neither by gesture nor by voice. So that one can hardly form tenable conjectures about the birth of this Art of communicating thoughts and establishing intercourse between Minds: a sublime Art which is now very far from its Origin, but which the Philosopher still sees at so prodigious a distance from its perfection that no man is bold enough to guarantee it will ever achieve it, even should the revolutions time necessarily brings be suspended in its favor, should prejudices quit the academies or be silent before them, and should they be able to attend to that thorny matter for whole Centuries without interruption.

Man's first language, the most universal, most energetic, and only language he needed before it was necessary to persuade assembled men, is the cry of Nature. As this cry was elicited only by a kind of instinct in pressing emergencies, to beg for help in great dangers, or for relief in violent ills, it was not of much use in the ordinary course of life, where more moderate sentiments prevail. When the ideas of men began to spread and multiply, and when closer communication was established among them, they sought more numerous signs and a more extensive language; they multiplied the inflections of the voice, and joined to it gestures which are more expressive by their Nature, and whose meaning is less dependent on prior determination. They therefore expressed visible and mobile objects by gestures, and audible ones by imitative sounds. But because gesture indicates hardly anything except present or easily described objects and visible actions; because its usage is not universal since darkness or the interposition of a body render it useless; and since it requires attention rather than stimulates it, men finally thought to substitute articulations of the voice which, without having the same relation to certain ideas, are better suited to represent all ideas as instituted signs: a substitution which cannot be made except by a common consent, and in a way rather difficult to practice for men whose crude organs as yet had no training, and even more difficult to conceive in itself, since that unanimous agreement must have had a motive, and since speech seems to have been highly necessary in order to establish the use of speech.

....

Whatever these origins may be, from the little care taken by Nature to bring Men together through mutual needs and to facilitate their use of speech, one at least sees how little it prepared their Sociability, and how little it contributed to everything men have done to establish Social bonds. In fact, it is impossible to imagine why, in that primitive state, a man would sooner have need of another man than a monkey or a Wolf of its Fellow creature; nor, supposing this need, what motive could induce the other to provide for it, nor even, in this last case, how they could agree between them on the conditions. I know we are repeatedly told that nothing would have been so miserable as man in that state; and if it is true, as I believe I have proved, that only after many Centuries could man have had the desire and opportunity to leave that state, it would be a Fault to find with Nature and not with him who would have been so constituted by Nature. But if I understand properly this term *miserable,* it is a word that has no meaning or only signifies a painful privation and the suffering of the Body or soul. Now I would really like someone to explain to me what type of misery there can be for a free being whose heart is at peace and whose body is healthy? I ask which, Civil or natural life, is most liable to become unbearable to those who enjoy it? We see around us practically no People who do not complain of their existence, even many who deprive themselves of it insofar as they have the capacity; and the combination of divine and human Laws hardly suffices to stop this disorder. I ask if anyone has ever heard it said that a Savage in freedom even dreamed of complaining about life and killing himself. Let it then be judged with less pride on which side genuine misery lies. Nothing, on the contrary, would have been so miserable as Savage man dazzled by enlightenment, tormented by Passions, and reasoning about a state different from his own. It was by a very wise Providence that his potential faculties were to develop only with the opportunities to exercise them, so that they were neither superfluous and burdensome to him beforehand, nor tardy and useless when needed. He had, in instinct alone, everything necessary for him to live in the state of Nature: he has, in a cultivated reason, only what is necessary for him to live in society.

It seems at first that men in that state, not having among themselves any kind of moral relationship or known duties, could be neither good nor evil, and had neither vices nor virtues: unless, taking these words in a physical sense, one calls vices in the individual the qualities that can harm his own preservation, and virtues those that can contribute to it; in which case, it would be necessary to call the most virtuous the one who least resists the simple impulses of Nature. But without departing from the ordinary meaning, it is appropriate to suspend the judgment we could make of such a situation and to beware of our Prejudices, until one has examined with Scale in hand whether there are more virtues than vices among civilized men; or whether their virtues are more advantageous than their vices are deadly; or whether the progress of their knowledge is a sufficient compensation for the harms they do one another as they learn of the

good they ought to do; or whether all things considered, they would not be in a happier situation having neither harm to fear nor good to hope for from anyone, rather than subjecting themselves to a universal dependence and obliging themselves to receive everything from those who do not obligate themselves to give them anything.

Above all, let us not conclude with Hobbes that because man has no idea of goodness he is naturally evil; that he is vicious because he does not know virtue; that he always refuses his fellows services he does not believe he owes them; nor that, by virtue of the right he reasonably claims to things he needs, he foolishly imagines himself to be the sole proprietor of the whole Universe. Hobbes saw very clearly the defect of all modern definitions of Natural right; but the consequences he draws from his own definition show that he takes it in a sense which is no less false. Reasoning upon the principles he establishes, this Author ought to have said that since the state of Nature is that in which care of our self-preservation is the least prejudicial to the self-preservation of others, that state was consequently the best suited to Peace and the most appropriate for the Human Race. He says precisely the opposite, because of having improperly included in the Savage man's care of self-preservation the need to satisfy a multitude of passions which are the product of Society and which have made Laws necessary. The evil man, he says, is a robust Child. It remains to be seen whether Savage Man is a robust Child. Should we grant this to him, what would he conclude from it? That if, when he is robust, this man were as dependent on others as when he is weak, there is no kind of excess to which he would not be inclined: that he would beat his Mother when she would be too slow in giving him her breast; that he would strangle one of his young brothers when he would be inconvenienced by him; that he would bite another's leg when he was hit or annoyed by it. But to be robust and to be dependent are two contradictory suppositions in the state of Nature. Man is weak when he is dependent, and he is emancipated before he is robust. Hobbes did not see that the same cause that prevents Savages from using their reason, as our Jurists claim, prevents them at the same time from abusing their faculties, as he himself claims. Thus one could say that Savages are not evil precisely because they do not know what it is to be good; for it is neither the growth of enlightenment nor the restraint of Law, but the calm of passions and the ignorance of vice which prevent them from doing evil: *Tanto plus in illis proficit vitiorum ignoratio, quam in his cognitio virtutis*[1]. There is, besides, another Principle which Hobbes did not notice, and which – having been given to man in order to soften, under certain circumstances, the ferocity of his amour-propre or the desire for self-preservation before the birth of this love – tempers the ardor he has for his own well-being by an innate repugnance to see his fellow suffer. I do not believe I have any contradiction to fear in granting man the sole Natural virtue that the most excessive Detractor of human virtues was forced to recognize. I speak of Pity, a disposition that is appropriate to beings as weak and subject to as many ills as we are; a virtue all the more universal and useful to man because it precedes in him the use of all reflection; and so Natural that even Beasts sometimes give perceptible signs of it. Without speaking of the tenderness of Mothers for their young and of the perils they brave to guard them, one observes daily the repugnance of Horses to trample a living Body underfoot. An animal does not pass near a dead animal of its Species without uneasiness. There are even some animals that give them a kind of sepulcher; and the sad lowing of Cattle entering a Slaughterhouse announces the impression they receive from the horrible sight that strikes them. One sees with pleasure the author of the *Fable of the Bees,* forced to recognize man as a compassionate and sensitive Being, departing from his cold and subtle style in the example he gives in order to offer us the pathetic image of an imprisoned man who sees outside a wild Beast tearing a Child from his Mother's breast, breaking his weak limbs in its murderous teeth, and ripping apart with its claws the palpitating entrails of this Child. What horrible agitation must be felt by this witness of an event in which he takes no personal interest! What anguish must he suffer at this sight, unable to bring help to the fainting Mother or to the dying Child.

Such is the pure movement of Nature prior to all reflection. Such is the force of natural pity, which

the most depraved morals still have difficulty destroying, since daily in our theaters one sees, moved and crying for the troubles of an unfortunate person, a man who, if he were in the Tyrant's place, would aggravate his enemy's torments even more-like bloodthirsty Sulla, so sensitive to ills he had not caused, or like Alexander of Pherae, who did not dare attend the performance of any tragedy lest he be seen moaning with Andromache and Priam, whereas he listened without emotion to the cries of so many citizens murdered daily on his orders.

> *Mollissima corda*
> *Humano generi dare se natura fatetur,*
> *Quae lacrimas dedit.*[2]

Mandeville sensed very well that even with all their morality men would never have been anything but monsters if Nature had not given them pity in support of reason; but he did not see that from this quality alone flow all the social virtues he wants to question in men. In fact, what are generosity, Clemency, Humanity, if not Pity applied to the weak, to the guilty, or to the human species in general? Benevolence and even friendship are, rightly understood, the products of a constant pity fixed on a particular object: for is desiring that someone not suffer anything but desiring that he be happy? Even should it be true that commiseration is only a feeling that puts us in the position of him who suffers – a feeling that is obscure and lively in Savage man, developed but weak in Civilized man – what would this idea matter to the truth of what I say, except to give it more force? In fact, commiseration will be all the more energetic as the Observing animal identifies himself more intimately with the suffering animal. Now it is evident that this identification must have been infinitely closer in the state of Nature than in the state of reasoning. Reason engenders amour-propre and reflection fortifies it; reason turns man back upon himself, it separates him from all that bothers and afflicts him. Philosophy isolates him; because of it he says in secret, at the sight of a suffering man: perish if you

---

1   "To such an extent has ignorance of vices been more profitable to them [the Scythians] than the understanding of virtue to these [the Greeks]," Justin, *Histories*, II,ii.

2   Translated freely: "Nature, who gave men tears, confesses she gives the human race most tender hearts." Juvenal, *Satires*, XV, 131-133.

will, I am safe. No longer can anything except dangers to the entire society trouble the tranquil sleep of the Philosopher and tear him from his bed. His fellow can be murdered with impunity right under his window; he has only to put his hands over his ears and argue with himself a bit to prevent Nature, which revolts within him, from identifying him with the man who is being assassinated. Savage man does not have this admirable talent, and for want of wisdom and reason he is always seen heedlessly yielding to the first feeling of humanity. In Riots or Street fights the Populace assembles, the prudent man moves away; it is the rabble, the Marketwomen, who separate the combatants and prevent honest people from murdering each other.

It is very certain, therefore, that pity is a natural feeling which, moderating in each individual the activity of love of oneself, contributes to the mutual preservation of the entire species. It carries us without reflection to the aid of those whom we see suffer; in the state of Nature, it takes the place of Laws, morals, and virtue, with the advantage that no one is tempted to disobey its gentle voice; it will deter every robust Savage from robbing a weak child or an infirm old man of his hard-won subsistence if he himself hopes to be able to find his own elsewhere. Instead of that sublime maxim of reasoned justice, *Do unto others as you would have them do unto you,* it inspires all Men with this other maxim of natural goodness, much less perfect but perhaps more useful than the preceding one: *Do what is good for you with the least possible harm to others.* In a word, it is in this Natural feeling, rather than in subtle arguments, that we must seek the cause of the repugnance every man would feel in doing evil, even independently of the maxims of education. Although it may behoove Socrates and Minds of his stamp to acquire virtue through reason, the human Race would have perished long ago if its preservation had depended only on the reasonings of its members.

With such inactive passions and such a salutary restraint, men – more untamed than evil, and more attentive to protecting themselves from harm they could receive than tempted to harm others – were not subject to very dangerous quarrels. Since they had no kind of commerce among themselves; since they consequently knew neither vanity, nor consideration, nor esteem, nor contempt; since they did not have the slightest notion of thine and mine, nor any genuine idea of justice; since they regarded the violences they might suffer as harm easy to redress and not as an insult which must be punished, and since they did not even dream of vengeance, except perhaps mechanically and on the spot, like the dog that bites the stone thrown at him, their disputes would rarely have had bloody consequences had there been no more sensitive subject than Food. But I see a more dangerous subject left for me to discuss.

Among the passions that agitate the heart of man, there is an ardent, impetuous one that makes one sex necessary to the other; a terrible passion which braves all dangers, overcomes all obstacles, and which, in its fury, seems fitted to destroy the human Race it is destined to preserve. What would become of men, tormented by this unrestrained and brutal rage, without chastity, without modesty, daily fighting over their loves at the price of their blood?

It must first be agreed that the more violent the passions, the more necessary Laws are to contain them. But besides the fact that the disorders and crimes these passions cause every day among us show well enough the inadequacy of Laws in this regard, it would still be good to examine whether these disorders did not arise with the Laws themselves; for then, even should they be capable of repressing these disorders, the very least that ought to be required of the laws is to stop an evil which would not exist without them.

Let us begin by distinguishing between the moral and the Physical in the feeling of love. The Physical is that general desire which inclines one sex to unite with the other. The moral is that which determines this desire and fixes it exclusively on a single object, or which at least gives it a greater degree of energy for this preferred object. Now it is easy to see that the moral element of love is an artificial feeling born of the usage of society, and extolled with much skill and care by women in order to establish their empire and make dominant the sex that ought to obey. This feeling, founded on certain notions of merit or beauty that a Savage is not capable of having, and on comparisons he is not capable of making, must be almost null for him. For as his mind could not form abstract ideas of regularity and proportion, so his heart is not susceptible to the feelings of admiration and love that, even without its being noticed, arise from the application of these ideas. He heeds solely the temperament he received from Nature, and not the taste he has not been able to acquire; any woman is good for him.

Limited solely to that which is Physical in love, and fortunate enough to be ignorant of those preferences that irritate its feeling and augment its difficulties, men must feel the ardors of their temperament less frequently and less vividly, and consequently have fewer and less cruel disputes among themselves. Imagination, which causes so much havoc among us, does not speak to Savage hearts. Everyone peaceably waits for the impulsion of Nature, yields to it without choice with more pleasure than frenzy; and the need satisfied, all desire is extinguished.

It is therefore incontestable that love itself, like all the other passions, has acquired only in society that impetuous ardor which so often makes it fatal for men; and it is all the more ridiculous to portray Savages continually murdering each other to satisfy their brutality as this opinion is directly contrary to experience, and as the Caribs, that of all existing Peoples which until now has departed least from the state of Nature, are precisely the most peaceful in their loves and the least subject to jealousy, even though they live in a burning hot Climate, which always seems to give greater activity to these passions.

Regarding inferences that one could draw, in some species of animals, from the fights of Males which bloody our farmyards in all seasons or which make our forests resound with their cries in Spring as they contend for a female, it is necessary to begin by excluding all species in which Nature has manifestly established, in the relative power of the Sexes, other relations than among us: thus Cockfights do not provide an inference for the human species. In species where the Proportion is better observed, these fights can have for causes only the scarcity of females with reference to the number of Males, or the exclusive intervals during which the female constantly refuses to let the male approach her, which amounts to the first cause; for if each female tolerates the male during only two months of the year, in this respect it is the same as if the number of females were reduced by five-sixths. Now neither of these two cases is applicable to the human species, in which the number of females generally surpasses the number of males, and in which it has never been observed that, even among Savages, females,

like those of other species, have times of heat and exclusion. Moreover, among some of these animals, since the entire species enters a state of heat at the same time, there comes a terrible moment of general ardor, tumult, disorder, and fighting: a moment that does not take place in the human species, in which love is never periodic. Therefore one cannot conclude from the fights of certain animals for the possession of females that the same thing would happen to man in the state of Nature. And even if one could draw that conclusion, as these dissensions do not destroy the other species, one must consider at least that they would not be more fatal to ours; and it is very apparent that they would cause still less havoc in the state of Nature than they do in Society, particularly in Countries where, Morals still counting for something, the jealousy of Lovers and the vengeance of Husbands are a daily cause of Duels, Murders, and worse things; where the obligation to eternal fidelity serves only to create adulterers; and where even the Laws of continence and honor necessarily spread debauchery and multiply abortions.

Let us conclude that wandering in the forests, without industry, without speech, without domicile, without war and without liaisons, with no need of his fellows, likewise with no desire to harm them, perhaps never even recognizing anyone individually, Savage man, subject to few passions and self-sufficient, had only the feelings and intellect suited to that state; he felt only his true needs, saw only what he believed he had an interest to see; and his intelligence made no more progress than his vanity. If by chance he made some discovery, he was all the less able to communicate it because he did not recognize even his Children. Art perished with the inventor. There was neither education nor progress; the generations multiplied uselessly; and everyone always starting from the same point, Centuries passed in all the crudeness of the first ages; the species was already old, and man remained ever a child.

If I have spent so much time on the supposition of this primitive condition, it is because, having ancient errors and inveterate prejudices to destroy, I thought I ought to dig down to the root and show, in the panorama of the genuine state of Nature, how far even natural inequality is from having as much reality and influence in that state as our Writers claim.

In fact, it is easy to see that, among the differences that distinguish men, some pass for natural that are uniquely the work of habit and the various types of life men adopt in Society. Thus a robust or delicate temperament, and the strength or weakness that depend on it, often come more from the harsh or effeminate way in which one has been raised than from the primitive constitution of bodies. The same is true of strength of Mind; and not only does education establish a difference between cultivated Minds and those which are not, but it augments the difference among the former in proportion to their culture; for should a Giant and a Dwarf walk on the same road, every step they both take will give fresh advantage to the Giant. Now if one compares the prodigious diversity of educations and types of life that prevails in the different orders of the civil state with the simplicity and uniformity of animal and savage life, in which all nourish themselves on the same foods, live in the same manner, and do exactly the same things, it will be understood how much less the difference between one man and another must be in the state of 'Nature than in society, and how much natural inequality must increase in the human species through instituted inequality.

But even should Nature assign as many preferences in the distribution of its gifts as is claimed, what advantage would the most favored draw from them to the prejudice of others in a state of things which permitted almost no sort of relationship among them? Where there is no love, of what use is beauty? What is the use of wit for people who do not speak, and ruse for those who have no dealings? I hear it always repeated that the stronger will oppress the weak. But let someone explain to me what is meant by this word oppression. Some will dominate by violence, the others will groan, enslaved to all their whims. That is precisely what I observe among us; but I do not see how that could be said of Savage men, to whom one would even have much trouble explaining what servitude and domination are. A man might well seize the fruits another has gathered, the game he has killed, the cave that served as his shelter; but how will he ever succeed in making himself obeyed? And what can be the chains of dependence among men who possess nothing? If someone chases me from one tree, I am at liberty to go to another; if someone torments me in one place, who will prevent me from going elsewhere? Is there a man whose strength is sufficiently superior to mine and who is, in addition, depraved enough, lazy enough, and wild enough to force me to provide for his subsistence while he remains idle? He must resolve not to lose sight of me for a single moment and to keep me very carefully tied up during his sleep, for fear that I should escape or kill him – that is to say, he is obliged to expose himself voluntarily to much greater trouble than he wants to avoid and gives to me. After all that, should his vigilance relax for a moment, should an unforseen noise make him turn his head, I take twenty steps in the forest, my chains are broken, and he never in his life sees me again.

Without uselessly prolonging these details, everyone must see that, since the bonds of servitude are formed only from the mutual dependence of men and the reciprocal needs that unite them, it is impossible to enslave a man without first putting him in the position of being unable to do without another; a situation which, as it did not exist in the state of Nature, leaves each man there free of the yoke, and renders vain the Law of the stronger.

After having proved that Inequality is barely perceptible in the state of Nature, and that its influence there is almost null, it remains for me to show its origin and progress in the successive developments of the human Mind. After having shown that *perfectibility,* social virtues, and the other faculties that Natural man had received in potentiality could never develop by themselves, that in order to develop they needed the chance combination of several foreign causes which might never have arisen and without which he would have remained eternally in his primitive constitution, it remains for me to consider and bring together the different accidents that were able to perfect human reason while deteriorating the species, make a being evil while making him sociable, and from such a distant origin finally bring man and the world to the point where we see them.

I admit that as the events I have to describe could have happened in several ways, I can make a choice only by conjectures. But besides the fact that these conjectures become reasons when they are the most probable that one can draw from the nature of things, and the sole means that one can have to discover the truth, the conclusions I want to deduce from mine will not thereby be conjectural, since, on the principles I have established, one could not conceive of any other system that would not provide me with the same results, and from which I could not draw the same conclusions...

Second Part

The first person who, having fenced off a plot of ground, took it into his head to say *this is mine* and found people simple enough to believe him, was the true founder of civil society. What crimes, wars, murders, what miseries and horrors would the human Race have been spared by someone who, uprooting the stakes or filling in the ditch, had shouted to his fellows: Beware of listening to this impostor; you are lost if you forget that the fruits belong to all and the Earth to no one! But it is very likely that by then things had already come to the point where they could no longer remain as they were. For this idea of property, depending on many prior ideas which could only have arisen successively, was not conceived all at once in the human mind. It was necessary to make much progress, to acquire much industry and enlightenment, and to transmit and augment them from age to age, before arriving at this last stage of the state of Nature. Therefore let us start further back in time and attempt to assemble from a single point of view this slow succession of events and knowledge in their most natural order.

Man's first sentiment was that of his existence, his first care that of his preservation. The products of the Earth furnished him with all the necessary help; instinct led him to make use of them. Hunger and other appetites making him experience by turns various manners of existing, there was one appetite that invited him to perpetuate his species; and this blind inclination, devoid of any sentiment of the heart, produced only a purely animal act. This need satisfied, the two sexes no longer recognized each other, and even the child no longer meant anything to his mother as soon as he could do without her.

Such was the condition of nascent man; such was the life of an animal limited at first to pure sensations and scarcely profiting from the gifts Nature offered him, far from dreaming of wresting anything from it. But difficulties soon arose; it was necessary to learn to conquer them. The height of Trees, which prevented him from reaching their fruits, the competition of animals that sought to nourish themselves with these fruits, the ferocity of those animals that wanted to take his very life, all obliged him to apply himself to bodily exercises. It was necessary to become agile, fleet in running, vigorous in combat. Natural arms, which are branches of trees and stones were soon discovered at hand. He learned to surmount Nature's obstacles, combat other animals when necessary, fight for his subsistence even with men, or make up for what had to be yielded to the stronger.

In proportion as the human Race spread, difficulties multiplied along with men. Differences of soil, Climate, and season could force them to admit differences in their ways of life. Barren years, long and hard winters, and scorching Summers which consume everything required of them new industry. Along the sea and Rivers they invented the fishing line and hook, and became fishermen and eaters of Fish. In forests they made bows and arrows, and became Hunters and Warriors. In cold Countries they covered themselves with the skins of beasts they had killed. Lightning, a Volcano, or some happy accident introduced them to fire, a new resource against the rigor of winter. They learned to preserve this element, then to reproduce it, and finally to prepare with it meats they previously devoured raw.

This repeated utilization of various beings in relation to himself, and of some beings in relation to others, must naturally have engendered in man's mind perceptions of certain relations. Those relationships that we express by the words large, small, strong, weak, fast, slow, fearful, bold, and other similar ideas, compared when necessary and almost without thinking about it, finally produced in him some sort of reflection, or rather a mechanical prudence that indicated to him the precautions most necessary for his safety.

The new enlightenment that resulted from this development increased his superiority over the other animals by making him aware of his superiority. He practiced setting traps for them; he tricked them in a thousand ways; and although several surpassed him in strength at fighting, or in speed at running, of those which might serve him or hurt him he became with time the master of the former, and the scourge of the latter. Thus the first glance he directed upon himself produced in him the first stirring of pride; thus, as yet scarcely knowing how to distinguish ranks, and considering himself in the first rank as a species, he prepared himself from afar to claim first rank as an individual.

Although his fellows were not for him what they are for us, and although he scarcely had more intercourse with them than with other animals, they were not forgotten in his observations. The conformities that time could make him perceive among them, his female, and himself led him to judge of those which he did not perceive; and seeing that they all behaved as he would have done under similar circumstances, he concluded that their way of thinking and feeling conformed entirely to his own. And this important truth, well established in his mind, made him follow, by a premonition as sure as Dialectic and more prompt, the best rules of conduct that it was suitable to observe toward them for his advantage and safety.

Taught by experience that love of well-being is the sole motive of human actions, he found himself able to distinguish the rare occasions when common interest should make him count on the assistance of his fellows, and those even rarer occasions when competition should make him distrust them. In the first case he united with them in a herd; or at most by some kind of free association that obligated no one and lasted only as long as the passing need that had formed it. In the second case, everyone sought to obtain his own advantage, either by naked force if he believed he could, or by cleverness and cunning if he felt himself to be the weaker.

That is how men could imperceptibly acquire some crude idea of mutual engagements and of the advantages of fulfilling them, but only insofar as present and perceptible interest could require; for foresight meant nothing to them, and far from being concerned about a distant future, they did not even think of the next day. Was it a matter of catching a Deer, everyone clearly felt that for this purpose he ought faithfully to keep his post; but if a hare happened to pass within reach of one of them, there can be no doubt that he pursued it without scruple, and that having obtained his prey, he cared very little about having caused his Companions to miss theirs.

It is easy to understand that such intercourse did not require a language much more refined than that of Crows or Monkeys, which group together in approximately the same way. For a long time inarticulate cries, many gestures, and some imitative noises must have composed the universal Language; by joining to this in each Country a few articulated and conventional sounds – the institution of which, as I have already said, is not too easy to explain – there were particular languages, but crude imperfect ones, approximately like those which various Savage Nations still have today.

I cover multitudes of centuries like a flash, forced by the time that elapses, the abundance of things I have to say, and the almost imperceptible progress of the beginnings; for the more slowly events followed upon one another, the more quickly they can be described.

These first advances finally put man in a position to make more rapid ones. The more the mind was enlightened, the more industry was perfected. Soon, ceasing to fall asleep under the first tree or to withdraw into Caves, they discovered some kinds of hatchets of hard, sharp stones, which served to cut wood, scoop out earth, and make huts from branches they later decided to coat with clay and mud. This was the epoch of a first revolution, which produced the establishment and differentiation of families, and which introduced a sort of property – from which perhaps many quarrels and Fights already arose. However, as the stronger were probably the first to make themselves lodgings they felt capable of defending, it is to be presumed that the weak found it quicker and safer to imitate them than to try to dislodge them; and as for those who already had Huts, each man must seldom have sought to appropriate his neighbor's, less because it did not belong to him than because it was of no use to him, and because he could not seize it without exposing himself to a lively fight with the family occupying it.

The first developments of the heart were the effect of a new situation, which united husbands and Wives, Fathers and Children in a common habitation. The habit of living together gave rise to the sweetest sentiments known to men: conjugal love and Paternal love. Each family became a little Society all the better united because reciprocal affection and freedom were its only bonds; and it was then that the first difference was established in the way of life of the two Sexes, which until this time had had but one. Women became more sedentary and grew accustomed to tend the Hut and the Children, while the man went to seek their common subsistence. The two Sexes also began, by their slightly softer life, to lose something of their ferocity and vigor. But if each one separately became less suited to combat savage beasts, on the contrary it was easier to assemble in order to resist them jointly.

In this new state, with a simple and solitary life, very limited needs, and the implements they had invented to provide for them, since men enjoyed very great leisure, they used it to procure many kinds of commodities unknown to their Fathers; and that was the first yoke they imposed on themselves without thinking about it, and the first source of the evils they prepared for their Descendants. For, besides their continuing thus to soften body and mind, as these commodities had lost almost all their pleasantness through habit, and as they had at the same time degenerated into true needs, being deprived of them became much more cruel than possessing them was sweet; and people were unhappy to lose them without being happy to possess them.

At this point one catches a slightly better glimpse of how the use of speech was established or perfected imperceptibly in the bosom of each family; and one can conjecture further how particular causes could have spread language and accelerated its progress by making it more necessary. Great floods or earthquakes surrounded inhabited Cantons with water or precipices; Revolutions of the Globe detached and broke up portions of the Continent into Islands. One conceives that among men thus brought together and forced to live together, a common Idiom must have been formed sooner than among those who wandered freely in the forests on solid Ground. Thus it is very possible that after their first attempts at Navigation, Islanders brought the use of speech to us; and it is at least very probable that Society and languages came into being on Islands and were perfected there before they were known on the Continent.

Everything begins to change its appearance. Men who until this time wandered in the Woods, having adopted a more fixed settlement, slowly come together, unite into different bands, and finally form in each country a particular Nation, unified by morals and character, not by Regulations and Laws but by the same kind of life and foods and by the common influence of Climate. A permanent proximity cannot fail to engender at length some contact between different families. Young people of

different sexes live in neighboring Huts; the passing intercourse demanded by Nature soon leads to another kind no less sweet and more permanent through mutual frequentation. People grow accustomed to consider different objects and to make comparisons; imperceptibly they acquire ideas of merit and beauty which produce sentiments of preference. By dint of seeing one another, they can no longer do without seeing one another again. A tender and gentle sentiment is gradually introduced into the soul and at the least obstacle becomes an impetuous fury. Jealousy awakens with love; Discord triumphs, and the gentlest of the passions receives sacrifices of human blood.

In proportion as ideas and sentiments follow upon one another and as mind and heart are trained, the human Race continues to be tamed, contacts spread, and bonds are tightened. People grew accustomed to assembling in front of the Huts or around a large Tree; song and dance, true children of love and leisure, became the amusement or rather the occupation of idle and assembled men and women. Each one began to look at the others and to want to be looked at himself, and public esteem had a value. The one who sang or danced the best, the handsomest, the strongest, the most adroit, or the most eloquent became the most highly considered; and that was the first step toward inequality and, at the same time, toward vice. From these first preferences were born on one hand vanity and contempt, on the other shame and envy; and the fermentation caused by these new leavens eventually produced compounds fatal to happiness and innocence.

As soon as men had begun to appreciate one another, and the idea of consideration was formed in their minds, each one claimed a right to it, and it was no longer possible to be disrespectful toward anyone with impunity. From this came the first duties of civility, even among Savages; and from this any voluntary wrong became an outrage, because along with the harm that resulted from the injury, the offended man saw in it contempt for his person which was often more unbearable than the harm itself. Thus, everyone punishing the contempt shown him by another in a manner proportionate to the importance he accorded himself, vengeances became terrible, and men bloodthirsty and cruel. This is precisely the point reached by most of the Savage Peoples known to us, and it is for want of having sufficiently distinguished between ideas and noticed how far these Peoples already were from the first state of Nature that many have hastened to conclude that man is naturally cruel, and that he needs Civilization in order to make him gentler. On the contrary, nothing is so gentle as man in his primitive state when, placed by Nature at equal distances from the stupidity of brutes and the fatal enlightenment of Civil man, and limited equally by instinct and reason to protecting himself from the harm that threatens him, he is restrained by Natural pity from harming anyone himself, and nothing leads him to do so even after he has received harm. For, according to the axiom of the wise Locke, *where there is no property, there is no injury.*

But it must be noted that the beginnings of Society and the relations already established among men required in them qualities different from those they derived from their primitive constitution; that, morality beginning to be introduced into human Actions, and each man, prior to Laws, being sole judge and avenger of the offenses he had received, the goodness suitable for the pure state of Nature was no longer that which suited nascent Society; that it was necessary for punishments to become more severe as the occasions for offense became more frequent; and that it was up to the terror of revenge to take the place of the restraint of Laws. Thus although men had come to have less endurance and although natural pity had already undergone some alteration, this period of the development of human faculties, maintaining a golden mean between the indolence of the primitive state and the petulant activity of our amour-propre, must have been the happiest and most durable epoch. The more one thinks about it, the more one finds that this state was the least subject to revolutions, the best for man, and that he must have come out of it only by some fatal accident, which for the common utility ought never to have happened. The example of Savages, who have almost all been found at this point, seems to confirm that the human Race was made to remain in it always; that this state is the veritable youth of the World; and that all subsequent progress has been in appearance so many steps toward the perfection of the individual, and in fact toward the decrepitude of the species.

As long as men were content with their rustic huts, as long as they were limited to sewing their clothing of skins with thorns or fish bones, adorning themselves with feathers and shells, painting their bodies with various colors, perfecting or embellishing their bows and arrows, carving with sharp stones a few fishing Canoes or a few crude Musical instruments; in a word, as long as they applied themselves only to tasks that a single person could do and to arts that did not require the cooperation of several hands, they lived free, healthy, good, and happy insofar as they could be according to their Nature, and they continued to enjoy among themselves the sweetness of independent intercourse. But from the moment one man needed the help of another, as soon as they observed that it was useful for a single person to have provisions for two, equality disappeared, property was introduced, labor became necessary; and vast forests were changed into smiling Fields which had to be watered with the sweat of men, and in which slavery and misery were soon seen to germinate and grow with the crops.

Metallurgy and agriculture were the two arts whose invention produced this great revolution. For the Poet it is gold and silver, but for the Philosopher it is iron and wheat which have Civilized men and ruined the human Race. Accordingly, both of these were unknown to the Savages of America, who therefore have always remained Savage; other Peoples even seem to have remained Barbarous as long as they practiced one of these arts without the other. And perhaps one of the best reasons why Europe has been, if not earlier, at least more constantly and better Civilized than the other parts of the world is that it is at the same time the most abundant in iron and the most fertile in wheat...

The invention of the other arts was therefore necessary to force the human Race to apply itself to that of agriculture. As soon as some men were needed to smelt and forge iron, other men were needed to feed them. The more the number of workers was multiplied, the fewer hands were engaged in furnishing the common subsistence, without there being fewer mouths to consume it; and since some needed foodstuffs in exchange for their iron, the others finally found the secret of using iron in order to multiply foodstuffs. From this arose husbandry and agriculture on the one hand, and on the other the art of working metals and multiplying their uses.

From the cultivation of land, its division necessarily followed; and from property once recognized, the first rules of justice. For in order to give everyone what is his, it is necessary that everyone can have something; moreover, as men began to look to the future and as they all saw themselves with some goods to lose, there was not one of them who did not have to fear reprisals against himself for wrongs he might do to another. This origin is all the more natural as it is impossible to conceive of the idea of property arising from anything except manual labor; because one cannot see what man can add, other than his own labor, in order to appropriate things he has not made. It is labor alone which, giving the Cultivator a right to the product of the land he has tilled, gives him a right to the soil as a consequence, at least until the harvest, and thus from year to year; which, creating continuous possession, is easily transformed into property. When the Ancients, says Grotius, gave Ceres the epithet of legislatrix, and gave the name of Thesmaphories to a festival celebrated in her honor, they thereby made it clear that the division of lands produced a new kind of right: that is, the right of property, different from the one which results from natural Law.

Things in this state could have remained equal if talents had been equal, and if, for example, the use of iron and the consumption of foodstuffs had always been exactly balanced. But this proportion, which nothing maintained, was soon broken; the stronger did more work; the cleverer turned his to better advantage; the more ingenious found ways to shorten his labor; the Farmer had greater need of iron or the blacksmith greater need of wheat; and working equally, the one, earned a great deal while the other barely had enough to live. Thus does natural inequality imperceptibly manifest itself along with contrived inequality; and thus do the differences among men, developed by those of circumstances, become more perceptible, more permanent in their effects, and begin to have a proportionate influence over the fate of individuals.

Things having reached this point, it is easy to imagine the rest. I shall not stop to describe the successive invention of the other arts, the progress of languages, the testing and use of talents, the inequality of fortunes, the use or abuse of Wealth, nor all the details that follow these, and that everyone can easily fill in. I shall simply limit myself to casting a glance at the human Race placed in this new order of things.

Behold all our faculties developed, memory and imagination in play, amour-propre aroused, reason rendered active, and the mind having almost reached the limit of the perfection of which it is susceptible. Behold all the natural qualities put into action, the rank and fate of each man established, not only upon the quantity of goods and the power to serve or harm, but also upon the mind, beauty, strength, or skill, upon merit or talents. And these qualities being the only ones which could attract consideration, it was soon necessary to have them or affect them; for one's own advantage, it was necessary to appear to be other than what one in fact was. To be and to seem to be became two altogether different things; and from this distinction came conspicuous ostentation, deceptive cunning, and all the vices that follow from them. From another point of view, having formerly been free and independent, behold man, due to a multitude of new needs, subjected so to speak to all of Nature and especially to his fellows, whose slave he becomes in a sense even in becoming their master; rich, he needs their services; poor, he needs their help; and mediocrity cannot enable him to do without them. He must therefore incessantly seek to interest them in his fate, and to make them find their own profit, in fact or in appearance, in working for his. This makes him deceitful and sly with some, imperious and harsh with others, and makes it necessary for him to abuse all those whom he needs when he cannot make them fear him and does not find his interest in serving them usefully. Finally, consuming ambition, the fervor to raise one's relative fortune less out of genuine need than in order to place oneself above others, inspires in all men a base inclination to harm each other, a secret jealousy all the more dangerous because, in order to strike its blow in greater safety, it often assumes the mask of benevolence: in a word, competition and rivalry on one hand, opposition of interest on the other; and always the hidden desire to profit at the expense of others. All these evils are the first effect of property and the inseparable consequence of nascent inequality.

Before representative signs of wealth had been invented, it could hardly consist of anything except land and livestock, the only real goods men can possess. Now when inheritances had increased in number and extent to the point of covering the entire earth and of all bordering on each other, some of them could no longer be enlarged except at the expense of others; and the supernumeraries, whom weakness or indolence had prevented from acquiring an inheritance in their turn, having become poor without having lost anything – because while everything around them changed they alone had not changed at all – were obliged to receive or steal their subsistence from the hand of the rich; and from that began to arise, according to the diverse characters of the rich and the poor, domination and servitude or violence and rapine. The rich, for their part, had scarcely known the pleasure of domination when they soon disdained all others, and using their old Slaves to subdue new ones, they thought only of subjugating and enslaving their neighbors: like those famished wolves which, having once tasted human flesh, refuse all other food and thenceforth want only to devour men.

Thus, as the most powerful or most miserable made of their force or their needs a sort of right to the goods of others, equivalent according to them to the right of property, the destruction of equality was followed by the most frightful disorder; thus the usurpations of the rich, the brigandage of the Poor, the unbridled passions of all, stifling natural pity and the as yet weak voice of justice, made man avaricious, ambitious, and evil. Between the right of the stronger and the right of the first occupant there arose a perpetual conflict which ended only in fights and murder.

Nascent Society gave way to the most horrible state of war: the human Race, debased and desolated, no longer able to turn back or renounce the unhappy acquisitions it had made, and working only toward its shame by abusing the faculties that honor it, brought itself to the brink of its ruin.

Attonitus novitate mali, divesque, miserque,
Effugere optat opes, et quae modo voverat, odit.[3]

It is not possible that men should not at last have reflected upon such a miserable situation and upon the calamities overwhelming them. The rich above all must have soon felt how disadvantageous to

them was a perpetual war in which they alone paid all the costs, and in which the risk of life was common to all while the risk of goods was theirs alone. Moreover, whatever pretext they might give for their usurpations, they were well aware that these were established only on a precarious and abusive right, and that having been acquired only by force, force could take them away without their having grounds for complaint. Even those enriched by industry alone could hardly base their property upon better titles. In vain might they say: But I built this wall; I earned this field by my labor. Who gave you its dimensions, they might be answered, and by virtue of what do you presume to be paid at our expense for work we did not impose on you? Do you not know that a multitude of your brethren die or suffer from need of what you have in excess, and that you needed express and unanimous consent of the human Race to appropriate for yourself anything from common subsistence that exceeded your own? Destitute of valid reasons to justify himself and of sufficient forces to defend himself; easily crushing an individual, but himself crushed by groups of bandits; alone against all, and unable because of mutual jealousies to unite with his equals against enemies united by the common hope of plunder, the rich, pressed by necessity, finally conceived the most deliberate project that ever entered the human mind. It was to use in his favor the very forces of those who attacked him, to make his defenders out of his adversaries, inspire them with other maxims, and give them other institutions which were as favorable to him as natural Right was adverse.

To this end, after having shown his neighbors the horror of a situation that made them all take up arms against one another, that made their possessions as burdensome as their needs, and in which no one found security in either poverty or wealth, he easily invented specious reasons to lead them to his goal. "Let us unite," he says to them, "to protect the weak from oppression, restrain the ambitious, and secure for everyone the possession of what belongs to him. Let us institute regulations of Justice and peace to which all are obliged to conform, which make an exception of no one, and which compensate in some way for the caprices of

---

3 "Shocked by the newness of the ill, rich and yet wretched, he seeks to run away from his wealth and hates what he once prayed for." Ovid, *Metamorphoses*, XV, 127-128.

fortune by equally subjecting the powerful and the weak to mutual duties. In a word, instead of turning our forces against ourselves, let us gather them into one supreme power which governs us according to wise Laws, protects and defends all the members of the association, repulses common enemies, and maintains us in an eternal concord."

Far less than the equivalent of this Discourse was necessary to win over crude, easily seduced men, who in addition had too many disputes to straighten out among themselves to be able to do without arbiters, and too much avarice and ambition to be able to do without Masters for long. All ran to meet their chains believing they ensured their freedom, for although they had enough reason to feel the advantages of a Political establishment, they did not have enough experience to forsee its dangers. Those most capable of anticipating the abuses were precisely those who counted on profiting from them; and even the wise saw the necessity of resolving to sacrifice one part of their freedom for the preservation of the other, just as a wounded man has his arm cut off to save the rest of his Body.

Such was, or must have been, the origin of Society and Laws, which gave new fetters to the weak and new forces to the rich, destroyed natural freedom for all time, established forever the Law of property and inequality, changed a clever usurpation into an irrevocable right, and for the profit of a few ambitious men henceforth subjected the whole human Race to work, servitude, and misery.

....

In discovering and following thus the forgotten and lost routes that must have led man from the Natural state to the Civil state; in re-establishing, along with the intermediary positions I have just noted, those that the pressure of time has made me suppress or that imagination has not suggested to me, every attentive Reader cannot fail to be struck by the immense space that separates these two states. It is in this slow succession of things that he will see the solution to an infinite number of problems of morality and Politics which the Philosophers cannot resolve. He will sense that, the human Race of one age not being the human Race of another, the reason Diogenes did not find a man was that he sought among his contemporaries the man of a time that no longer existed. Cato, he will say, perished with Rome and freedom because he

was out of place in his century; and the greatest of men only astonished the world, which he would have governed five hundred years earlier. In a word, he will explain how the soul and human passions, altering imperceptibly, change their Nature so to speak; why our needs and our pleasures change their objects in the long run; why, original man vanishing by degrees, Society no longer offers to the eyes of the wise man anything except an assemblage of artificial men and factitious passions which are the work of all these new relations and have no true foundation in Nature. What reflection teaches us on this subject, observation confirms perfectly: Savage man and Civilized man differ so much in the bottom of their Hearts and inclinations that what constitutes the supreme happiness of one would reduce the other to despair. The former breathes only repose and freedom; he wants only to live and remain idle; and even the perfect quietude of the Stoic does not approach his profound indifference for all other objects. On the contrary, the Citizen, always active, sweats, agitates himself, torments himself incessantly in order to seek still more laborious occupations; he works to death, he even rushes to it in order to get in condition to live, or renounces life in order to acquire immortality. He pays court to the great whom he hates, and to the rich whom he scorns. He spares nothing in order to obtain the honor of serving them; he proudly boasts of his baseness and their protection; and proud of his slavery, he speaks with disdain of those who do not have the honor of sharing it. What a Sight the difficult and envied labors of a European Minister are for a Carib! How many cruel deaths would that indolent Savage not prefer to the horror of such a life, which often is not even sweetened by the pleasure of doing good. But in order to see the goal of so many cares, the words *power* and *reputation* would have to have a meaning in his mind; he would have to learn that there is a kind of men who count for something the consideration of the rest of the universe and who know how to be happy and content with themselves on the testimony of others rather than on their own. Such is, in fact, the genuine cause of all these differences: the Savage lives within himself; the sociable man, always outside of himself, knows how to live only in the opinion of others; and it is, so to speak, from their judgment alone that he draws the sentiment of his own existence. It is not part of my subject to show how, from such a disposition, so much indifference for good and evil arises along with such fine discourses on morality; how, everything being reduced to appearances, everything becomes artificial and deceptive: honor, friendship, virtue, and often even vices themselves, about which men finally discover the secret of boasting; how, in a word, always asking others what we are and never daring to question ourselves on this subject in the midst of so much Philosophy, humanity, politeness, and Sublime maxims, we have only a deceitful and frivolous exterior, honor without virtue, reason without wisdom, and pleasure without happiness. It is sufficient for me to have proved that this is not the original state of man; and that it is the spirit of Society alone, and the inequality it engenders, which thus change and alter all our natural inclinations.

I have tried to set forth the origin and progress of inequality, the establishment and abuse of political Societies, insofar as these things can be deduced from the Nature of man by the light of reason alone, and independently of the sacred Dogmas which give to Sovereign authority the Sanction of Divine Right. It follows from this exposition that inequality, being almost null in the state of Nature, draws its force and growth from the development of our faculties and the progress of the human Mind, and finally becomes stable and legitimate by the establishment of property and Laws. It follows, further, that moral inequality, authorized by positive right alone, is contrary to Natural Right whenever it is not combined in the same proportion with Physical inequality: a distinction which sufficiently determines what one ought to think in this regard of the sort of inequality that reigns among all civilized Peoples; since it is manifestly against the Law of Nature, in whatever manner it is defined, that a child command an old man, an imbecile lead a wise man, and a handful of men be glutted with superfluities while the starving multitude lacks necessities.

Bibliography

Dent, N.J.H. *A Rousseau Dictionary*. Oxford: Blackwell, 1992.

Dent, N.J.H. *Rousseau: Introduction to his Psychological, Social, and Political Theory*. Oxford and New York: Blackwell, 1988.

Grimsley, Ronald. *The Philosophy of Rousseau*. London and New York: Oxford University Press, 1973.

Horowitz, Asher. *Rousseau, Nature, and History*. Toronto: University of Toronto Press, 1987.

Keeley, Lawrence H. *War Before Civilization*. New York and Oxford: Oxford University Press, 1996.

Wokler, Robert. *Rousseau*. Oxford: Oxford University Press, 1995.

CHAPTER TWENTY-SIX — G.W.F. HEGEL

Georg Wilhelm Friedrich Hegel (1770-1831) is one of the most wide-ranging, ambitious, creative – and varyingly assessed – philosophers in the "canon." Hegel developed a system and a methodology, and both are set out in books that are often densely challenging; indeed they seem sometimes almost to be in a *code* requiring multi-faceted keys to unlock. Yet also much of Hegel's work is accessible and reasonably straightforward, including much (not all) of the *Philosophy of Right* (1821), from which most of the selection here is drawn. (There is also a selection from Hegel's earlier classic presentation of his system, the *Phenomenology of Spirit* [1807].)

Hegel is deeply similar to Aristotle in quite a number of respects (and Aristotle is one of many important influences on his ideas). Like Aristotle, Hegel is widely acquainted with the knowledge of his culture, and seeks both to coordinate it synoptically and to go beyond it. In a similar manner, Hegel seeks to draw the considerable truth that he sees in his predecessors and to distil and transcend it. Many other features of his thought may be reminiscent of Aristotle.

Hegel sees a fundamental contrast between freedom (self-consciousness) and necessity (nature). Yet he opposes disembodied, over-abstract conceptions of human subjectivity. We are in and of a natural world, even as we create ourselves through conscious activity and self-understanding, through history. Hegel is an historical *idealist*. For him, ideas importantly shape and determine the historical destiny of the species. That destiny is directional, and intelligible, and leads us in evolutionary stages to a condition of fully articulated self-understanding. Key to our development – indeed, what initiates and sustains history – is a fundamental need for *recognition*, of ourselves as free rational agents, with *worth* and the capacity of morality. Humanity for Hegel, as for Aristotle, is a species being, necessarily incomplete, indeed unintelligible, without location in a nexus of community, that if rational – fulfilling of our *telos* – affirms both our individuality and our interlocked corporate unity.

G.W.F. Hegel, *Phenomenology of Mind*

(Source: G.W.F. Hegel. *The Phenomenology of Mind*. Trans. and Intr. J.B. Baillie. London: George Allen and Unwin Ltd, 1931, 228-241.)

INDEPENDENCE AND DEPENDENCE OF SELF-CONSCIOUSNESS LORDSHIP AND BONDAGE

Self-consciousness exists in itself and for itself, in that, and by the fact that it exists for another self-consciousness; that is to say, it *is* only by being acknowledged or "recognized." The conception of this its unity in its duplication, of infinitude realizing itself in self-consciousness, has many sides to it and encloses within it elements of varied significance. Thus its moments must on the one hand be strictly kept apart in detailed distinctiveness, and, on the other, in this distinction must, at the same time, also be taken as not distinguished, or must always be accepted and understood in their opposite sense. This double meaning of what is distinguished lies in the nature of self-consciousness: – of its being infinite, or directly the opposite of the determinateness in which it is fixed. The detailed exposition of the notion of this spiritual unity in its duplication will bring before us the process of Recognition.

Self-consciousness has before it another self-consciousness; it has come outside itself. This has a double significance. First it has lost its own self, since it finds itself as an *other* being; secondly, it has thereby sublated that other, for it does not regard the other as essentially real, but sees its own self in the other.

It must cancel this its other. To do so is the sublation of that first double meaning, and is therefore a second double meaning. First, it must set itself to sublate the other independent being, in order thereby to become certain of itself as true being, secondly, it thereupon proceeds to sublate its own self, for this other is itself.

This sublation in a double sense of its otherness in a double sense is at the same time a return in a double sense into its self. For, firstly, through sublation, it gets back itself, because it becomes one with itself again through the cancelling of *its* otherness; but secondly, it likewise gives otherness back again to the other self-consciousness, for it was aware of being in the other, it cancels this its own being in the other and thus lets the other again go free.

This process of self-consciousness in relation to another self-consciousness has in this manner been represented as the action of one alone. But this action on the part of the one has itself the double significance of being at once its own action and the action of that other as well. For the other is likewise independent, shut up within itself, and there is nothing in it which is not there through itself. The first does not have the object before it only in the passive form characteristic primarily of the object of desire, but as an object existing independently for itself, over which therefore it has no power to do anything for its own behoof, if that object does not *per se* do what the first does to it. The process then is absolutely the double process of both self-consciousnesses. Each sees the other do the same as itself; each itself does what it demands on the part of the other, and for that reason does what it does, only so far as the other does the same. Action from one side only would be useless, because what is to happen can only be brought about by means of both.

The action has then a *double entente* not only in the sense that it is an act done to itself as well as to the other, but also in the sense that the act *simpliciter* is the act of the one as well as of the other regardless of their distinction.

In this movement we see the process repeated which came before us as the play of forces; in the present case, however, it is found in consciousness. What in the former had effect only for us [contemplating experience], holds here for the terms themselves. The middle term is self-consciousness which breaks itself up into the extremes; and each extreme is this interchange of its own determinateness, and complete transition into the opposite. While *qua* consciousness, it no doubt comes outside itself, still, in being outside itself, it is at the same time restrained within itself, it exists for itself, and its self-externalization is for consciousness. *Consciousness* finds that it immediately is and is not another consciousness, as also that this other is for itself only when it cancels itself as existing for itself, and has self-existence only in the self-existence of the other. Each is the mediating term to the other, through which each mediates and unites itself with itself; and each is to itself and to the other an immediate self-existing reality, which, at the same time, exists thus for itself only through this mediation. They recognize themselves as mutually recognizing one another.

This pure conception of recognition, of duplication of self-consciousness within its unity, we must now consider in the way its process appears for self-consciousness. It will, in the first place, present the aspect of the disparity of the two, or the break-up of the middle term into the extremes, which, *qua* extremes, are opposed to one another, and of which one is merely recognized, while the other only recognizes.

Self-consciousness is primarily simple existence for self, self-identity by exclusion of every other from itself. It takes its essential nature and absolute object to be Ego; and in this immediacy, in this bare fact of its self-existence, it is individual. That which for it is other stands as unessential object, as object with the impress and character of negation. But the other is also a self-consciousness; an individual makes its appearance in antithesis to an individual. Appearing thus in their immediacy, they are for each other in the manner of ordinary objects. They are independent individual forms, modes of consciousness that have not risen above the bare level of life (for the existent object here has been determined as life). They are, moreover, forms of consciousness which have not yet accomplished for one another the process of absolute abstraction, of uprooting all immediate existence, and of being merely the bare, negative fact of self-identical consciousness; or, in other words, have not yet revealed themselves to each other as existing purely for themselves, i.e., as self-consciousness. Each is indeed certain of its own self, but not of the other, and hence its own certainty of itself is still without truth. For its truth would be merely that its own individual existence for itself would be shown to it to be an independent object, or, which is the same thing, that the object would be exhibited as this pure certainty of itself. By the notion of recognition, however, this is not possible, except in the form that as the other is for it, so it is for the other; each in its self through its own action and again through the action of the other achieves this pure abstraction of existence for self.

The presentation of itself, however, as pure abstraction of self-consciousness consists in showing itself as a pure negation of its objective form, or in showing that it is fettered to no determinate existence, that it is not bound at all by the particularity everywhere characteristic of existence as such, and is not tied up with life. The process of bringing all this out involves a twofold action – action on the part of the other and action on the part of itself. In so far as it is the other's action, each aims at the destruction and death of the other. But in this there is implicated also the second kind of action, self-activity; for the former implies that it risks its own life. The relation of both self-consciousnesses is in this way so constituted that they prove themselves and each other through a life-and-death struggle. They must enter into this struggle, for they must bring their certainty of themselves, the certainty of being for themselves, to the level of objective truth, and make this a fact both in the case of the other and in their own case as well. And it is solely by risking life that freedom is obtained; only thus is it tried and proved that the essential nature of self-consciousness is not bare existence, is not the merely immediate form in which it at first makes its appearance, is not its mere absorption in the expanse of life. Rather it is thereby guaranteed that there is nothing present but what might be taken as a vanishing moment – that self-consciousness is merely pure self-existence, being-for-self. The indi-

vidual, who has not staked his life, may, no doubt, be recognized as a Person; but he has not attained the truth of this recognition as an independent self-consciousness. In the same way each must aim at the death of the other, as it risks its own life thereby; for that other is to it of no more worth than itself; the other's reality is presented to the former as an external other, as outside itself; it must cancel that externality. The other is a purely existent consciousness and entangled in manifold ways; it must view its otherness as pure existence for itself or as absolute negation.

This trial by death, however, cancels both the truth which was to result from it, and therewith the certainty of self altogether. For just as life is the natural "position" of consciousness, independence without absolute negativity, so death is the natural "negation" of consciousness, negation without independence, which thus remains without the requisite significance of actual recognition. Through death, doubtless, there has arisen the certainty that both did stake their life, and held it lightly both in their own case and in the case of the other; but that is not for those who underwent this struggle. They cancel their consciousness which had its place in this alien element of natural existence; in other words, they cancel themselves and are sublated as terms or extremes seeking to have existence on their own account. But along with this there vanishes from the play of change the essential moment, viz. that of breaking up into extremes with opposite characteristics; and the middle term collapses into a lifeless unity which is broken up into lifeless extremes, merely existent and not opposed. And the two do not mutually give and receive one another back from each other through consciousness; they let one another go quite indifferently, like things. Their act is abstract negation, not the negation characteristic of consciousness, which cancels in such a way that it preserves and maintains what is sublated, and thereby survives its being sublated.

In this experience self-consciousness becomes aware that *life* is as essential to it as pure self-consciousness. In immediate self-consciousness the simple ego is absolute object, which, however, is for us or in itself absolute mediation, and has as its essential moment substantial and solid independence. The dissolution of that simple unity is the result of the first experience; through this there is posited a pure self-consciousness, and a consciousness which is not purely for itself, but for another, i.e. as an existent consciousness, consciousness in the form and shape of thinghood. Both moments are essential, since, in the first instance, they are unlike and opposed, and their reflexion into unity has not yet come to light, they stand as two opposed forms or modes of consciousness. The one is independent, and its essential nature is to be for itself; the other is dependent, and its essence is life or existence for another. The former is the Master, or Lord, the latter the Bondsman.

The master is the consciousness that exists *for itself;* but no longer merely the general notion of existence for self. Rather, it is a consciousness existing on its own account which is mediated with itself through an other consciousness, i.e. through an other whose very nature implies that it is bound up with an independent being or with thinghood in general. The master brings himself into relation to both these moments, to a thing as such, the object of desire, and to the consciousness whose essential character is thinghood. And since the master is *(a) qua* notion of self-consciousness, an immediate relation of self-existence, but *(b)* is now moreover at the same time mediation, or a being-for-self which is for itself only through an other – he [the master] stands in relation *(a)* immediately to both *(b)* mediately to each through the other. The master relates himself to the bondsman mediately through independent existence, for that is precisely what keeps the bondsman in thrall; it is his chain, from which he could not in the struggle get away, and for that reason he proved himself to be dependent, to have his independence in the shape of thinghood. The master, however, is the power controlling this state of existence, for he has shown in the struggle that he holds it to be merely something negative. Since he is the power dominating existence, while this existence again is the power controlling the other [the bondsman], the master holds, *par consequence,* this other in subordination. In the same way the master relates himself to the thing mediately through the bondsman. The bondsman being a self-consciousness in the broad sense, also takes up a negative attitude to things and cancels them; but the thing is, at the same time, independent for him, and, in consequence, he cannot, with all his negating, get so far as to annihilate it outright and be done with it; that is to say, he merely works on it. To the master, on the other hand, by means of this mediating process, belongs the immediate relation, in the sense of the pure negation of it, in other words he gets the enjoyment. What mere desire did not attain, he now succeeds in attaining, viz. to have done with the thing, and find satisfaction in enjoyment. Desire alone did not get the length of this, because of the independence of the thing. The master, however, who has interposed the bondsman between it and himself, thereby relates himself merely to the dependence of the thing, and enjoys it without qualification and without reserve. The aspect of its independence he leaves to the bondsman, who labours upon it.

In these two moments, the master gets his recognition through an other consciousness, for in them the latter affirms itself as unessential, both by working upon the thing, and, on the other hand, by the fact of being dependent on a determinate existence; in neither case can this other get the mastery over existence, and succeed in absolutely negating it. We have thus here this moment of recognition, viz. that the other consciousness cancels itself as self-existent, and, *ipso facto,* itself does what the first does to it. In the same way we have the other moment, that this action on the part of the second is the action proper of the first; for what is done by the bondsman is properly an action on the part of the master. The latter exists only for himself, that is his essential nature; he is the negative power without qualification, a power to which the thing is naught. And he is thus the absolutely essential act in this situation, while the bondsman is not so, he is an unessential activity. But for recognition proper there is needed the moment that what the master does to the other he should also do to himself, and what the bondsman does to himself, he should do to the other also. On that account a form of recognition has arisen that is one-sided and unequal.

In all this, the unessential consciousness is, for the master, the object which embodies the truth of his certainty of himself. But it is evident that this object does not correspond to its notion; for, just where the master has effectively achieved lordship, he really finds that something has come about quite different from an independent consciousness. It is not an independent, but rather a dependent consciousness that he has achieved. He is thus not assured of self-existence as his truth; he finds that his truth is rather the unessential consciousness, and the fortuitous unessential action of that consciousness.

The truth of the independent consciousness is accordingly the consciousness of the bondsman. This doubtless appears in the first instance outside itself, and not as the truth of self-consciousness. But just as lordship showed its essential nature to be the reverse of what it wants to be, so, too, bondage will, when completed, pass into the opposite of what it immediately is: being a consciousness repressed within itself, it will enter into itself, and change round into real and true independence.

We have seen what bondage is only in relation to lordship. But it is a self-consciousness, and we have now to consider what it is, in this regard, in and for itself. In the first instance, the master is taken to be the essential reality for the state of bondage; hence, for it, the truth is the independent consciousness existing for itself, although this truth is not taken yet as inherent in bondage itself. Still, it does in fact contain within itself this truth of pure negativity and self-existence, because it has experienced this reality within it. For this consciousness was not in peril and fear for this element or that, nor for this or that moment of time, it was afraid for its entire being; it felt the fear of death, the sovereign master. It has been in that experience melted to its inmost soul, has trembled throughout its every fibre, and all that was fixed and steadfast has quaked within it. This complete perturbation of its entire substance, this absolute dissolution of all its stability into fluent continuity, is, however, the simple, ultimate nature of self-consciousness, absolute negativity, pure self-referent existence, which consequently is involved in this type of consciousness. This moment of pure self-existence is moreover a fact for it; for in the master it finds this as its object. Further, this bondsman's consciousness is not only this total dissolution in a general way; in serving and toiling the bondsman actually carries this out. By serving he cancels in every particular aspect his dependence on and attachment to natural existence, and by his work removes this existence away.

The feeling of absolute power, however, realized both in general and in the particular form of service, is only dissolution implicitly; and albeit the fear of the lord is the beginning of wisdom, consciousness is not therein aware of being self-existent. Through work and labour, however, this consciousness of the bondsman comes to itself. In the moment which corresponds to desire in the case of the master's consciousness, the aspect of the non-essential relation to the thing seemed to fall to the lot of the servant, since the thing there retained its independence. Desire has reserved to itself the pure negating of the object and thereby unalloyed feeling of self. This satisfaction, however, just for that reason is itself only a state of evanescence, for it lacks objectivity or subsistence. Labour, on the other hand, is desire restrained and checked, evanescence delayed and postponed; in other words, labour shapes and fashions the thing. The negative relation to the object passes into the *form* of the object, into something that is permanent and remains; because it is just for the labourer that the object has independence. This negative mediating agency, this activity giving shape and form, is at the same time the individual existence, the pure self-existence of that consciousness, which now in the work it does is externalized and passes into the condition of permanence. The consciousness that toils and serves accordingly attains by this means the direct apprehension of that independent being as its self.

But again, shaping or forming the object has not only the positive significance that the bondsman becomes thereby aware of himself as factually and objectively self-existent; this type of consciousness has also a negative import, in contrast with its first moment, the element of fear. For in shaping the thing it only becomes aware of its own proper negativity, its existence on its own account, as an object, through the fact that it cancels the actual form confronting it. But this objective negative element is precisely the alien, external reality, before which it trembled. Now, however, it destroys this extraneous alien negative, affirms and sets itself up as a negative in the element of permanence, and thereby becomes for itself a self-existent being. In the master, the bondsman feels self-existence to be something external, an objective fact; in fear self-existence is present within himself; in fashioning the thing, self-existence comes to be felt explicitly as his own proper being, and he attains the consciousness that he himself exists in its own right and on its own account (*an und für sich*). By the fact that the form is objectified, it does not become something other than the consciousness moulding the thing through work; for just that form is his pure self-existence, which therein becomes truly realized. Thus precisely in labour where there seemed to be merely some outsider's mind and ideas involved, the bondsman becomes aware, through this re-discovery of himself by himself, of having and being a "mind of his own."

For this reflexion of self into self the two moments, fear and service in general, as also that of formative activity, are necessary: and at the same time both must exist in a universal manner. Without the discipline of service and obedience, fear remains formal and does not spread over the whole known reality of existence. Without the formative activity shaping the thing, fear remains inward and mute, and consciousness does not become objective for itself. Should consciousness shape and form the thing without the initial state of absolute fear, then it has a merely vain and futile "mind of its own"; for its form or negativity is not negativity *per se,* and hence its formative activity cannot furnish the consciousness of itself as essentially real. If it has endured not absolute fear, but merely some slight anxiety, the negative reality has remained external to it, its substance has not been through and through infected thereby. Since the entire content of its natural consciousness has not tottered and shaken, it is still inherently a determinate mode of being; having a "mind of its own" *(der eigene Sinn)* is simply stubbornness *(Eigensinn),* a type of freedom which does not get beyond the attitude of bondage. As little as the pure form can become its essential nature, so little is that form, considered as extending over particulars, a universal formative activity, an absolute notion; it is rather a piece of cleverness which has mastery within a certain range, but not over the universal power nor over the entire objective reality.

G.W.F. Hegel, *Philosophy of Right*

(Source: *Hegel's Philosophy of Right.* Trans. T.M. Knox, 1952. London: Oxford University Press, 1967, 105-151.

142. Ethical life is the Idea of freedom in that on the one hand it is the good become alive – the good endowed in self-consciousness with knowing and willing and actualized by self-conscious action – while on the other hand self-consciousness has in the ethical realm its absolute foundation and the end which actuates its effort. Thus ethical life is the

concept of freedom developed into the existing world and the nature of self-consciousness.

143. Since this unity of the concept of the will with its embodiment – i.e. the particular will – is knowing, consciousness of the distinction between these two moments of the Idea is present, but present in such a way that now each of these moments is in its own eyes the totality of the Idea and has that totality as its foundation and content.

144. (α) The objective ethical order, which comes on the scene in place of good in the abstract, is substance made concrete by subjectivity as infinite form. Hence it posits within itself distinctions whose specific character is thereby determined by the concept, and which endow the ethical order with a stable content independently necessary and subsistent in exaltation above subjective opinion and caprice. These distinctions are absolutely valid laws and institutions.

145. It is the fact that the ethical order is the system of these specific determinations of the Idea which constitutes its rationality. Hence the ethical order is freedom or the absolute will as what is objective, a circle of necessity whose moments are the ethical powers which regulate the life of individuals. To these powers individuals are related as accidents to substance, and it is in individuals that these powers are represented, have the shape of appearance, and become actualized.

146. (β) The substantial order, in the self-consciousness which it has thus actually attained in individuals, knows itself and so is an object of knowledge. This ethical substance and its laws and powers are on the one hand an object over against the subject, and from his point of view they *are* – 'are' in the highest sense of self-subsistent being. This is an absolute authority and power infinitely more firmly established than the being of nature.

The sun, the moon, mountains, rivers, and the natural objects of all kinds by which we are surrounded, *are.* For consciousness they have the authority not only of mere being but also of possessing a particular nature which it accepts and to which it adjusts itself in dealing with them, using them, or in being otherwise concerned with them. The authority of ethical laws is infinitely higher, because natural objects conceal rationality under the cloak of contingency and exhibit it only in their utterly external and disconnected way.

147. On the other hand, they are not something alien to the subject. On the contrary, his spirit bears witness to them as to its own essence, the essence in which he has a feeling of his self-hood, and in which he lives as in his own element which is not distinguished from himself. The subject is thus directly linked to the ethical order by a relation which is more like an identity than even the relation of faith or trust.

Faith and trust emerge along with reflection; they presuppose the power of forming ideas and making distinctions. For example, it is one thing to be a pagan, a different thing to believe in a pagan religion. This relation or rather this absence of relation, this identity in which the ethical order is the actual living soul of self-consciousness, can no doubt pass over into a relation of faith and conviction and into a relation produced by means of further reflection, i.e. into an *insight* due to reasoning starting perhaps from some particular purposes, interests, and considerations, from fear or hope, or from historical conditions. But adequate *knowledge* of this identity depends on thinking in terms of the concept.

148. As substantive in character, these laws and institutions are duties binding on the will of the individual, because as subjective, as inherently undetermined, or determined as particular, he distinguishes himself from them and hence stands related to them as to the substance of his own being.

The 'doctrine of duties' in moral philosophy (I mean the objective doctrine, not that which is supposed to be contained in the empty principle of moral subjectivity, because that principle determines nothing...) is therefore comprised in the systematic development of the circle of ethical necessity which follows in this Third Part. The difference between the exposition in this book and the form of a 'doctrine of duties' lies solely in the fact that, in what follows, the specific types of ethical life turn up as necessary relationships; there the exposition ends, without being supplemented in each case by the addition that 'therefore men have a duty to conform to this institution.'

A 'doctrine of duties' which is other than a philosophical science takes its material from existing relationships and shows its connexion with the moralist's personal notions or with principles and thoughts, purposes, impulses, feelings, &c., that are forthcoming everywhere; and as reasons for accepting each duty in turn, it may tack on its further consequences in their bearing on the other ethical relationships or on welfare and opinion. But an immanent and logical 'doctrine of duties' can be nothing except the serial exposition of the relationships which are necessitated by the Idea of freedom and are therefore actual in their entirety, to wit in the state.

149. The bond of duty can appear as a restriction only on indeterminate subjectivity or abstract freedom, and on the impulses either of the natural will or of the moral will which determines its indeterminate good arbitrarily. The truth is, however, that in duty the individual finds his liberation; first, liberation from dependence on mere natural impulse and from the depression which as a particular subject he cannot escape in his moral reflections on what ought to be and what might be; secondly, liberation from the indeterminate subjectivity which, never reaching reality or the objective determinacy of action, remains self-enclosed and devoid of actuality. In duty the individual acquires his substantive freedom.

150. Virtue is the ethical order reflected in the individual character so far as that character is determined by its natural endowment. When virtue displays itself solely as the individual's simple conformity with the duties of the station to which he belongs, it is rectitude.

In an *ethical* community, it is easy to say what man must do, what are the duties he has to fulfil in order to be virtuous: he has simply to follow the well-known and explicit rules of his own situation. Rectitude is the general character which may be demanded of him by law or custom. But from the standpoint of *morality,* rectitude often seems to be something comparatively inferior, something beyond which still higher demands must be made on oneself and others, because the craving to be something special is not satisfied with what is absolute and universal; it finds consciousness of peculiarity only in what is exceptional.

The various facets of rectitude may equally well be called virtues, since they are also properties of the individual, although not specially of him in contrast with others. Talk about virtue, however, readily borders on empty rhetoric, because it is only about something abstract and indeterminate; and furthermore, argumentative and expository talk of the sort is addressed to the individual as to a being of caprice and subjective inclination. In an existing ethical order in which a complete system of ethical relations has been developed and actualized, virtue in the strict sense of the word is in place and actually appears only in exceptional circumstances or when one obligation clashes with another. The clash, however, must be a genuine one, because moral reflection can manufacture clashes of all sorts to suit its purpose and give itself a consciousness of being something special and having made sacrifices. It is for this reason that the phenomenon of virtue proper is commoner when societies and communities are uncivilized, since in those circumstances ethical conditions and their actualization are more a matter of private choice or the natural genius of an exceptional individual. For instance, it was especially to Hercules that the ancients ascribed virtue. In the states of antiquity, ethical life had not grown into this free system of an objective order self-subsistently developed, and consequently it was by the personal genius of individuals that this defect had to be made good. It follows that if a 'doctrine of virtues' is not a mere 'doctrine of duties,' and if therefore it embraces the particular facet of character, the facet grounded in natural endowment, it will be a natural history of mind.

Since virtues are ethical principles applied to the particular, and since in this their subjective aspect they are something indeterminate, there turns up here for determining them the quantitative principle of more or less. The result is that consideration of them introduces their corresponding defects or vices, as in Aristotle, who defined each particular virtue as strictly a mean between an excess and a deficiency.

The content which assumes the form of duties and then virtues is the same as that which also has the form of impulses .... Impulses have the same basic content as duties and virtues, but in impulses this content still belongs to the immediate will and to instinctive feeling; it has not been developed to the point of becoming ethical. Consequently impulses have in common with the content of duties and virtues only the abstract object on which they are directed, an object indeterminate in itself, and so devoid of anything to discriminate them as good or evil. Or in other words, impulses, considered abstractly in their positive aspect alone, are good, while, considered abstractly in their negative aspect alone, they are evil ....

151. But when individuals are simply identified with the actual order, ethical life (*das Sittliche*) appears as their general mode of conduct, i.e. as custom (*Sitte*), while the habitual practice of ethical living appears as a second nature which, put in the place of the initial, purely natural will, is the soul of custom permeating it through and through, the significance and the actuality of its existence. It is mind living and present as a world, and the substance of mind thus exists now for the first time as mind.

152. In this way the ethical substantial order has attained its right, and its right its validity. That is to say, the self-will of the individual has vanished together with his private conscience which had claimed independence and opposed itself to the ethical substance, For, when his character is ethical, he recognizes as the end which moves him to act the universal which is itself unmoved but is disclosed in its specific determinations as rationality actualized. He knows that his own dignity and the whole stability of his particular ends are grounded in this same universal, and it is therein that he actually attains these. Subjectivity is itself the absolute form and existent actuality of the substantial order, and the distinction between subject on the one hand and substance on the other, as the object, end, and controlling power of the subject, is the same as, and has vanished directly along with, the distinction between them in form.

Subjectivity is the ground wherein the concept of freedom is realized.... At the level of morality, subjectivity is still distinct from freedom, the concept of subjectivity; but at the level of ethical life it is the realization of the concept in a way adequate to the concept itself.

153. The right of individuals to be subjectively destined to freedom is fulfilled when they belong to an actual ethical order, because their conviction of their freedom finds its truth in such an objective

order, and it is in an ethical order that they are actually in possession of their own essence or their own inner universality....

When a father inquired about the best method of educating his son in ethical conduct, a Pythagorean replied: 'Make him a citizen of a state with good laws.' (The phrase has also been attributed to others.)

154. The right of individuals to their *particular* satisfaction is also contained in the ethical substantial order, since particularity is the outward appearance of the ethical order – a mode in which that order is existent.

155. Hence in this identity of the universal will with the particular will, right and duty coalesce, and by being in the ethical order a man has rights in so far as he has duties, and duties in so far as he has rights. In the sphere of abstract right, I have the right and another has the corresponding duty. In the moral sphere, the right of my private judgement and will, as well as of my happiness, has not, but only ought to have, coalesced with duties and become objective.

156. The ethical substance, as containing independent self-consciousness united with its concept, is the actual mind of a family and a nation.

157. The concept of this Idea has being only as mind, as something knowing itself and actual, because it is the objectification of itself, the movement running through the form of its moments. It is therefore

(A) ethical mind in its natural or immediate phase – the *Family*. This substantiality loses its unity, passes over into division, and into the phase of relation, i.e. into

(B) *Civil Society* – an association of members as self-subsistent individuals in a universality which, because of their self-subsistence, is only abstract. Their association is brought about by their needs, by the legal system – the means to security of person and property – and by an external organization for attaining their particular and common interests. This external state

(C) is brought back to and welded into unity in

the *Constitution of the State* which is the end and actuality of both the substantial universal order and the public life devoted thereto.

SUB-SECTION I
THE FAMILY

158. The family, as the immediate substantiality of mind, is specifically characterized by love, which is mind's feeling of its own unity. Hence in a family, one's frame of mind is to have self-consciousness of one's individuality within this unity as the absolute essence of oneself, with the result that one is in it not as an independent person but as a member.

159. The right which the individual enjoys on the strength of the family unity and which is in the first place simply the individual's life within this unity, takes on the *form* of right (as the abstract moment of determinate individuality) only when the family begins to dissolve. At that point those who should be family-members both in their inclination and in actuality begin to be self-subsistent persons, and whereas they formerly constituted one specific moment within the whole, they now receive their share separately and so only in an external fashion by way of money, food, educational expenses, and the like.

160. The family is completed in these three phases:
 (a) Marriage, the form assumed by the concept of the family in its immediate phase;
 (b) Family Property and Capital (the external embodiment of the concept) and attention to these;
 (c) The Education of Children and the Dissolution of the Family.

A. *Marriage*

161. Marriage, as the immediate type of ethical relationship, contains first, the moment of physical life; and since marriage is a *substantial* tie, the life involved in it is life in its totality, i.e. as the actuality of the race and its life-process. But, secondly, in self-consciousness the natural sexual union – a union purely inward or implicit and for that very reason *existent* as purely external – is changed into a union on the level of mind, into self-conscious love.

162. On the subjective side, marriage may have a

more obvious source in the particular inclination of the two persons who are entering upon the marriage tie, or in the foresight and contrivance of the parents, and so forth. But its objective source lies in the free consent of the persons, especially in their consent to make themselves one person, to renounce their natural and individual personality to this unity of one with the other. From this point of view, their union is a self-restriction, but in fact it is their liberation, because in it they attain their substantive self-consciousness.

Our objectively appointed end and so our ethical duty is to enter the married state. The external origin of any *particular* marriage is in the nature of the case contingent, and it depends principally on the extent to which reflective thought has been developed. At one extreme, the first step is that the marriage is arranged by the contrivance of benevolent parents; the appointed end of the parties is a union of mutual love, and their inclination to marry arises from the fact that each grows acquainted with the other from the first as a destined partner. At the other extreme, it is the inclination of the parties which comes first, appearing in them as *these* two infinitely particularized individuals. The more ethical way to matrimony may be taken to be the former extreme or any way at all whereby the decision to marry comes first and the inclination to do so follows, so that in the actual wedding both decision and inclination coalesce. In the latter extreme, it is the uniqueness of the infinitely particularized which makes good its claims in accordance with the subjective principle of the modern world ....

But those works of modern art, dramatic and other, in which the love of the sexes is the main interest, are pervaded by a chill despite the heat of passion they portray, for they associate the passion with accident throughout and represent the entire dramatic interest as if it rested solely on the characters as *these individuals;* what rests on them may indeed be of infinite importance to *them,* but is of none whatever in itself.

163. The ethical aspect of marriage consists in the parties' consciousness of this unity as their substantive aim, and so in their love, trust, and common sharing of their entire existence as individuals.

When the parties are in this frame of mind and their union is actual, their physical passion sinks to the level of a physical moment, destined to vanish in its very satisfaction. On the other hand, the spiritual bond of union secures its rights as the substance of marriage and thus rises, inherently indissoluble, to a plane above the contingency of passion and the transience of particular caprice.

... [M]arriage, so far as its essential basis is concerned, is not a contractual relation. On the contrary, though marriage begins in contract, it is precisely a contract to transcend the standpoint of contract, the standpoint from which persons are regarded in their individuality as self-subsistent units. The identification of personalities, whereby the family becomes one person and its members become its accidents (though substance is in essence the relation of accidents to itself), is the ethical mind. Taken by itself and stripped of the manifold externals of which it is possessed owing to its embodiment in *these* individuals and the interests of the phenomenal realm, interests limited in time and numerous other ways, this mind emerges in a shape for representative thinking and has been revered as *Penates,* &c.; and in general it is in this mind that the religious character of marriage and the family, or *pietas,* is grounded. It is a further abstraction still to separate the divine, or the substantive, from its body, and then to stamp it, together with the feeling and consciousness of mental unity, as what is falsely called 'Platonic' love. This separation is in keeping with the monastic doctrine which characterizes the moment of physical life as purely negative and which, precisely by thus separating the physical from the mental, endows the former by itself with infinite importance.

164. Mere agreement to the stipulated terms of a contract in itself involves the genuine transfer of the property in question .... Similarly, the solemn declaration by the parties of their consent to enter the ethical bond of marriage, and its corresponding recognition and confirmation by their family and community,[1] constitutes the formal completion and actuality of marriage. The knot is tied and made ethical only after this ceremony, whereby through the use of signs, i.e. of language (the most mental

---

1   The fact that the church comes in in this connexion is a further point, but not one for discussion here.

embodiment of mind...), the substantial thing in the marriage is brought completely into being. As a result, the sensuous moment, the one proper to physical life, is put into its ethical place as something only consequential and accidental, belonging to the external embodiment of the ethical bond, which indeed can subsist exclusively in reciprocal love and support.

If with a view to framing or criticizing legal enactments, the question is asked: what should be regarded as the chief end of marriage?, the question may be taken to mean: which single facet of marriage in its actuality is to be regarded as the most essential one? No one facet by itself, however, makes up the whole range of its implicit and explicit content, i.e. of its ethical character, and one or other of its facets may be lacking in an existing marriage without detriment to the essence of marriage itself.

It is in the actual conclusion of a marriage, i.e. in the wedding, that the essence of the tie is expressed and established beyond dispute as something ethical, raised above the contingency of feeling and private inclination. If this ceremony is taken as an external formality, a mere so-called 'civil requirement', it is thereby stripped of all significance except perhaps that of serving the purpose of edification and attesting the civil relation of the parties. It is reduced indeed to a mere *fiat* of a civil or ecclesiastical authority. As such it appears as something not merely indifferent to the true nature of marriage, but actually alien to it. The heart is constrained by the law to attach a value to the formal ceremony and the latter is looked upon merely as a condition which must precede the complete mutual surrender of the parties to one another. As such it appears to bring disunion into their loving disposition and, like an alien intruder, to thwart the inwardness of their union. Such a doctrine pretentiously claims to afford the highest conception of the freedom, inwardness, and perfection of love; but in fact it is a travesty of the ethical aspect of love, the higher aspect which restrains purely sensual impulse and puts it in the background. Such restraint is already present at the instinctive level in shame, and it rises to chastity and modesty as consciousness becomes more specifically intelligent. In particular, the view just criticized casts aside marriage's specifically ethical character, which consists in this, that the consciousness of the parties is crystallized out of its physical and subjective mode and lifted to the thought of what is substantive; instead of continually reserving to itself the contingency and caprice of bodily desire, it removes the marriage bond from the province of this caprice, surrenders to the substantive, and swears allegiance to the *Penates;* the physical moment it subordinates until it becomes something wholly conditioned by the true and ethical character of the marriage relation and by the recognition of the bond as an ethical one. It is effrontery and its buttress, the Understanding, which cannot apprehend the speculative character of the substantial tie; nevertheless, with this speculative character there correspond both ethical purity of heart and the legislation of Christian peoples.

165. The difference in the physical characteristics of the two sexes has a rational basis and consequently acquires an intellectual and ethical significance. This significance is determined by the difference into which the ethical substantiality, as the concept, internally sunders itself in order that its vitality may become a concrete unity consequent upon this difference.

166. Thus one sex is mind in its self-diremption into explicit personal self-subsistence and the knowledge and volition of free universality, i.e. the self-consciousness of conceptual thought and the volition of the objective final end. The other sex is mind maintaining itself in unity as knowledge and volition of the substantive, but knowledge and volition in the form of concrete individuality and feeling. In relation to externality, the former is powerful and active, the latter passive and subjective. It follows that man has his actual substantive life in the state, in learning, and so forth, as well as in labour and struggle with the external world and with himself so that it is only out of his diremption that he fights his way to self-subsistent unity with himself. In the family he has a tranquil intuition of this unity, and there he lives a subjective ethical life on the plane of feeling. Woman, on the other hand, has her substantive destiny in the family, and to be imbued with family piety is her ethical frame of mind.

For this reason, family piety is expounded in Sophocles' *Antigone* – one of the most sublime presentations of this virtue – as principally the law of woman, and as the law of a substantiality at once subjective and on the plane of feeling, the law of the inward life, a life which has not yet attained its full actualization; as the law of the ancient gods, 'the gods of the underworld'; as 'an everlasting lady, and no man knows at what time it was first put forth'.[2] This law is there displayed as a law opposed to public law, to the law of the land. This is the supreme opposition in ethics and therefore in tragedy; and it is individualized in the same play in the opposing natures of man and woman.[3]

167. In essence marriage is monogamy because it is personality – immediate exclusive individuality – which enters into this tie and surrenders itself to it; and hence the tie's truth and inwardness (i.e. the subjective form of its substantiality) proceeds only from the mutual, wholehearted, surrender of this personality. Personality attains its right of being conscious of itself in another only in so far as the other is in this identical relationship as a person, i.e. as an atomic individual.

Marriage, and especially monogamy, is one of the absolute principles on which the ethical life of a community depends. Hence marriage comes to be recorded as one of the moments in the founding of states by gods or heroes.

168. Further, marriage results from the free surrender by both sexes of their personality – a personality in every possible way unique in each of the parties. Consequently, it ought not to be entered by two people identical in stock who are already acquainted and perfectly known to one another; for individuals in the same circle of relationship have no special personality of their own in contrast with that of others in the same circle. On the contrary, the parties should be drawn from separate families and their personalities should be different in origin. Since the very conception of marriage is that it is a freely undertaken ethical transaction, not a tie directly grounded in the physical organism and its desires, it follows that the marriage of blood-relations runs counter to this conception and so also to genuine natural feeling.

Marriage itself is sometimes said to be grounded not in natural rights but simply in instinctive sexual impulses; or again it is treated as a contract with an arbitrary basis. External arguments in support of monogamy have been drawn from physical considerations such as the number of men and women. Dark feelings of repulsion are advanced as the sole ground for prohibiting consanguineous marriage. The basis of all these views is the fashionable idea of a state of nature and a natural origin for rights, and the lack of the concept of rationality and freedom.

169. The family, as person, has its real external existence in property; and it is only when this property takes the form of capital that it becomes the embodiment of the substantial personality of the family.

B. *The Family Capital*

170. It is not merely property which a family possesses; as a universal and enduring person, it requires possessions specifically determined as permanent and secure, i.e. it requires capital. The arbitrariness of a single owner's particular needs is one moment in property taken abstractly; but this moment, together with the selfishness of desire, is here transformed into something ethical, into labour and care for a common possession.

In the sagas of the founding of states, or at least of a social and orderly life, the introduction of permanent property is linked with the introduction of marriage. The nature of this capital, however, and the proper means of its consolidation will appear in the section on civil society.

171. The family as a legal entity in relation to others must be represented by the husband as its head. Further, it is his prerogative to go out and work for its living, to attend to its needs, and to control and administer its capital. This capital is common property so that, while no member of the family has property of his own, each has his right in the common stock. This right, however, may come into collision with the head of the family's right of administration owing to the fact that the ethical temper of the family is still only at the level of immediacy (see Paragraph 158) and so is exposed to partition and contingency.

---

2   *Antigone*, 11. 450-7.
3   Cf. *Phenomenology*, [1st ed.], pp. 383ff., 417 ff. [Eng. Tr. Pp. 466 ff., 495 ff.].

172. A marriage brings into being a new family which is self-subsistent and independent of the clans or 'houses' from which its members have been drawn. The tie between these and the new family has a natural basis – consanguinity, but the new family is based on love of an ethical type. Thus an individual's property too has an essential connexion with his conjugal relationship and only a comparatively remote one with his relation to his clan or 'house'.

The significance of marriage settlements which impose a restriction on the couple's common ownership of their goods, of arrangements to secure continued legal assistance for the woman, and so forth, lies in their being provisions in case of the dissolution of the marriage, either naturally by death, or by divorce, &c. They are also safeguards for securing that in such an eventuality the different members of the family shall secure their share of the common stock.

C. The Education of Children and the Dissolution of the Family

173. In substance marriage is a unity, though only a unity of inwardness or disposition; in outward existence, however, the unity is sundered in the two parties. It is only in the children that the unity itself exists externally, objectively, and explicitly as a unity, because the parents love the children as their love, as the embodiment of their own substance. From the physical point of view, the presupposition – persons immediately existent (as parents) – here becomes a result, a process which runs away into the infinite series of generations, each producing the next and presupposing the one before. This is the mode in which the single mind of the Penates reveals its existence in the finite sphere of nature as a race.

174. Children have the right to maintenance and education at the expense of the family's common capital. The right of the parents to the service as service of their children is based upon and is restricted by the common task of looking after the family generally. Similarly, the right of the parents over the wishes of their children is determined by the object in view – discipline and education. The punishment of children does not aim at justice as such; the aim is more subjective and moral in char-

acter, i.e. to deter them from exercising a freedom still in the toils of nature and to lift the universal into their consciousness and will.

175. Children are potentially free and their life directly embodies nothing save potential freedom. Consequently they are not things and cannot be the property either of their parents or others. In respect of his relation to the family, the child's education has the positive aim of instilling ethical principles into him in the form of an immediate feeling for which differences are not yet explicit, so that thus equipped with the foundation of an ethical life, his heart may live its early years in love, trust, and obedience. In respect of the same relation, this education has the negative aim of raising children out of the instinctive, physical, level on which they are originally, to self-subsistence and freedom of personality and so to the level on which they have power to leave the natural unity of the family.

One of the blackest marks against Roman legislation is the law whereby children were treated by their fathers as slaves. This gangrene of the ethical order at the tenderest point of its innermost life is one of the most important clues for understanding the place of the Romans in the history of the world and their tendency towards legal formalism.

The necessity for education is present in children as their own feeling of dissatisfaction with themselves as they are, as the desire to belong to the adult world whose superiority they divine, as the longing to grow up. The play theory of education assumes that what is childish is itself already something of inherent worth and presents it as such to the children; in their eyes it lowers serious pursuits, and education itself, to a form of childishness for which the children themselves have scant respect. The advocates of this method represent the child, in the immaturity in which he feels himself to be, as really mature and they struggle to make him satisfied with himself as he is. But they corrupt and distort his genuine and proper need for something better, and create in him a blind indifference to the substantial ties of the intellectual world, a contempt of his elders because they have thus posed before him, a child, in a contemptible and childish fashion, and finally a vanity and conceit which feeds on the notion of its own superiority.

176. Marriage is but the ethical Idea in its *immediacy* and so has its objective actuality only in the inwardness of subjective feeling and disposition. In this fact is rooted the fundamental contingency of marriage in the world of existence. There can be no compulsion on people to marry; and, on the other hand, there is no merely legal or positive bond which can hold the parties together once their dispositions and actions have become hostile and contrary. A third ethical authority, however, is called for to maintain the right of marriage – an ethical substantiality – against the mere whims of hostile disposition or the accident of a purely passing mood, and so forth. Such an authority distinguishes these from the total estrangement of the two parties and may not grant divorce until it is satisfied that the estrangement is total.

177. The ethical dissolution of the family consists in this, that once the children have been educated to freedom of personality, and have come of age, they become recognized as persons in the eyes of the law and as capable of holding free property of their own and founding families of their own, the sons as heads of new families, the daughters as wives. They now have their substantive destiny in the new family; the old family on the other hand falls into the background as merely their ultimate basis and origin, while *a fortiori* the clan is an abstraction, devoid of rights.

....

Transition of the Family into Civil Society

181. The family disintegrates (both essentially, through the working of the principle of personality, and also in the course of nature) into a plurality of families, each of which conducts itself as in principle a self-subsistent concrete person and therefore as externally related to its neighbours. In other words, the moments bound together in the unity of the family, since the family is the ethical Idea still in its concept, must be released from the concept to self-subsistent objective reality. This is the stage of difference. This gives us, to use abstract language in the first place, the determination of particularity which is related to universality but in such a way

that universality is its basic principle, though still only an inward principle; for that reason, the universal merely shows in the particular as its form. Hence this relation of reflection prima facie portrays the disappearance of ethical life or, since this life as the essence necessarily shows itself,[4] this relation constitutes the world of ethical appearance – civil society.

The expansion of the family, as its transition into a new principle, is in the external world sometimes its peaceful expansion until it becomes a people, i.e. a nation, which thus has a common natural origin, or sometimes the federation of scattered groups of families under the influence of an overlord's power or as a result of a voluntary association produced by the tie of needs and the reciprocity of their satisfaction.

SUB-SECTION 2
CIVIL SOCIETY

182. The concrete person, who is himself the object of his particular aims, is, as a totality of wants and a mixture of caprice and physical necessity, one principle of civil society. But the particular person is essentially so related to other particular persons that each establishes himself and finds satisfaction by means of the others, and at the same time purely and simply by means of the form of universality, the second principle here.

183. In the course of the actual attainment of selfish ends – an attainment conditioned in this way by universality – there is formed a system of complete interdependence, wherein the livelihood, happiness, and legal status of one man is interwoven with the livelihood, happiness, and rights of all. On this system, individual happiness, &c., depend, and only in this connected system are they actualized and secured. This system may be prima facie regarded as the external state, the state based on need, the state as the Understanding envisages it.

184. The Idea in this its stage of division imparts to each of its moments a characteristic embodiment; to particularity it gives the right to develop and launch forth in all directions; and to universality the right to prove itself not only the ground and

---

4   Cf. [Hegel's] *Encyclopaedia*. [1st edn.] 64ff., 81 ff. [3rd edn. 115 ff., 131 ff.].

necessary form of particularity, but also the authority standing over it and its final end. It is the system of the ethical order, split into its extremes and lost, which constitutes the Idea's abstract moment, its moment of reality. Here the Idea is present only as a relative totality and as the inner necessity behind this outward appearance.

185. Particularity by itself, given free rein in every direction to satisfy its needs, accidental caprices, and subjective desires, destroys itself and its substantive concept in this process of gratification. At the same time, the satisfaction of need, necessary and accidental alike, is accidental because it breeds new desires without end, is in thoroughgoing dependence on caprice and external accident, and is held in check by the power of universality. In these contrasts and their complexity, civil society affords a spectacle of extravagance and want as well as of the physical and ethical degeneration common to them both.

The development of particularity to self-subsistence... is the moment which appeared in the ancient world as an invasion of ethical corruption and as the ultimate cause of that world's downfall. Some of these ancient states were built on the patriarchal and religious principle, others on the principle of an ethical order which was more explicitly intellectual, though still comparatively simple; in either case they rested on primitive unsophisticated intuition. Hence they could not withstand the disruption of this state of mind when self-consciousness was infinitely reflected into itself; when this reflection began to emerge, they succumbed to it, first in spirit and then in substance, because the simple principle underlying them lacked the truly infinite power to be found only in that unity which allows both sides of the antithesis of reason to develop themselves separately in all their strength and which has so overcome the antithesis that it maintains itself in it and integrates it in itself.

In his *Republic,* Plato displays the substance of ethical life in its ideal beauty and truth; but he could only cope with the principle of self-subsistent particularity, which in his day had forced its way into Greek ethical life, by setting up in opposition to it his purely substantial state. He absolutely excluded it from his state, even in its very beginnings in private property... and the family, as well as in its more mature form as the subjective will, the

choice of a social position, and so forth. It is this defect which is responsible both for the misunderstanding of the deep and substantial truth of Plato's state and also for the usual view of it as a dream of abstract thinking, as what is often called a 'mere ideal'. The principle of the self-subsistent inherently infinite personality of the individual, the principle of subjective freedom, is denied its right in the purely substantial form which Plato gave to mind in its actuality. This principle dawned in an inward form in the Christian religion and in an external form (and therefore in one linked with abstract universality) in the Roman world. It is historically subsequent to the Greek world, and the philosophic reflection which descends to its depth is likewise subsequent to the substantial Idea of Greek philosophy.

186. But in developing itself independently to totality, the principle of particularity passes over into universality, and only there does it attain its truth and the right to which its positive actuality is entitled. This unity is not the identity which the ethical order requires, because at this level, that of division (see Paragraph 184), both principles are self-subsistent. It follows that this unity is present here not as freedom but as necessity, since it is by compulsion that the particular rises to the form of universality and seeks and gains its stability in that form.

187. Individuals in their capacity as burghers in this state are private persons whose end is their own interest. This end is *mediated* through the universal which thus *appears* as a *means* to its realization. Consequently, individuals can attain their ends only in so far as they themselves determine their knowing, willing, and acting in a universal way and make themselves links in this chain of social connexions. In these circumstances, the interest of the Idea – an interest of which these members of civil society are as such unconscious – lies in the process whereby their singularity and their natural condition are raised, as a result of the necessities imposed by nature as well as of arbitrary needs, to formal freedom and formal universality of knowing and willing – the process whereby their particularity is educated up to subjectivity.

The idea that the state of nature is one of innocence and that there is a simplicity of manners in uncivilized (*ungebildeter*) peoples, implies treating education *(Bildung)* as something purely external, the ally of corruption. Similarly, the feeling that needs, their satisfaction, the pleasures and comforts of private life, and so forth, are absolute ends, implies treating education as a mere means to these ends. Both these views display lack of acquaintance with the nature of mind and the end of reason. Mind attains its actuality only by creating a dualism within itself, by submitting itself to physical needs and the chain of these external necessities, and so imposing on itself this barrier and this finitude, and finally by maturing *(bildet)* itself inwardly even when under this barrier until it overcomes it and attains its objective reality in the finite. The end of reason, therefore, is neither the manners of an unsophisticated state of nature, nor, as particularity develops, the pleasure for pleasure's sake which education procures. On the contrary, its end is to banish natural simplicity, whether the passivity which is the absence of the self, or the crude type of knowing and willing, i.e. immediacy and singularity, in which mind is absorbed. It aims in the first instance at securing for this, its external condition, the rationality of which it is capable, i.e. the form of universality or the Understanding *(Verständigkeit)*. By this means alone does mind become at home with itself within this pure externality. There, then, mind's freedom is existent and mind becomes objective to itself in this element which is implicitly inimical to mind's appointed end, freedom; it has to do there only with what it has itself produced and stamped with its seal. It is in this way then that the form of universality comes explicitly into existence in thought, and this form is the only worthy element for the existence of the Idea. The final purpose of education, therefore, is liberation and the struggle for a higher liberation still; education is the absolute transition from an ethical substantiality which is immediate and natural to the one which is intellectual and so both infinitely subjective and lofty enough to have attained universality of form. In the individual subject, this liberation is the hard struggle against pure subjectivity of demeanour, against the immediacy of desire, against the empty subjectivity of feeling and the caprice of inclination. The disfavour showered on education is due in part to its being this hard struggle; but it is through this educational struggle that the subjective will itself attains objectivity within, an objectivity in which alone it is for its part capable and worthy of being the actuality of the Idea. Moreover, this form of universality – the Understanding, to which particularity has worked its way and developed itself, brings it about at the same time that particularity becomes individuality genuinely existent in its own eyes. And since it is from this particularity that the universal derives the content which fills it as well as its character as infinite self-determination, particularity itself is present in ethical life as infinitely independent free subjectivity. This is the position which reveals education as a moment immanent in the Absolute and which makes plain its infinite value.

188. Civil society contains three moments:

(A) The mediation of need and one man's satisfaction through his work and the satisfaction of the needs of all others – the *System of Needs*.

(B) The actuality of the universal principle of freedom therein contained – the protection of property through the *Administration of Justice*.

(C) Provision against contingencies still lurking in systems (A) and (B), and care for particular interests as a common interest, by means of the *Police* and the *Corporation*.

A. *The System of Needs*

189. Particularity is in the first instance characterized in general by its contrast with the universal principle of the will and thus is subjective need.... This attains its objectivity, i.e. its satisfaction, by means of (α) external things, which at this stage are likewise the property and product of the needs and wills of others, and (β) work and effort, the middle term between the subjective and the objective. The aim here is the satisfaction of subjective particularity, but the universal asserts itself in the bearing which this satisfaction has on the needs of others and their free arbitrary wills. The show of rationality thus produced in this sphere of finitude is the Understanding, and this is the aspect which is of most importance in considering this sphere and which itself constitutes the reconciling element within it.

Political economy is the science which starts from this view of needs and labour but then has the task of explaining mass-relationships and mass-movements in their complexity and their qualitative and quantitative character. This is one of the sciences which have arisen out of the conditions of the modern world. Its development affords the interesting spectacle (as in Smith, Say, and Ricardo) of thought working upon the endless mass of details which confront it at the outset and extracting therefrom the simple principles of the thing, the Understanding effective in the thing and directing it. It is to find reconciliation here to discover in the sphere of needs this show of rationality lying in the thing, and effective there; but if we look at it from the opposite point of view, this is the field in which the Understanding with its subjective aims and moral fancies vents its discontent and moral frustration.

(a) The Kind of Need and Satisfaction [typical of civil society]

190. An animal's needs and its ways and means of satisfying them are both alike restricted in scope. Though man is subject to this restriction too, yet at the same time he evinces his transcendence of it and his universality, first by the multiplication of needs and means of satisfying them, and secondly by the differentiation and division of concrete need into single parts and aspects which in turn become different needs, particularized and so more abstract.

In [abstract] right, what we had before us was the person; in the sphere of morality, the subject; in the family, the family-member; in civil society as a whole, the burgher or *bourgeois*. Here at the standpoint of needs... what we have before us is the composite idea which we call *man*. Thus this is the first time, and indeed properly the only time, to speak of *man* in this sense.

191. Similarly, the means to particularized needs and all the various ways of satisfying these are themselves divided and multiplied and so in turn become proximate ends and abstract needs. This multiplication goes on *ad infinitum*; taken as a whole, it is refinement, i.e. a discrimination between these multiplied needs, and judgement on the suitability of means to their ends.

192. Needs and means, as things existent *realiter,* become something which has being for others by whose needs and work satisfaction for all alike is conditioned. When needs and means become abstract in quality (see Paragraph 191), abstraction is also a character of the reciprocal relation of individuals to one another. This abstract character, universality, is the character of being recognized and is the moment which makes concrete, i.e. social, the isolated and abstract needs and their ways and means of satisfaction.

193. This social moment thus becomes a particular end-determinant for means in themselves and their acquisition, as well as for the manner in which needs are satisfied. Further, it directly involves the demand for equality of satisfaction with others. The need for this equality and for emulation, which is the equalizing of oneself with others, as well as the other need also present here, the need of the particular to assert itself in some distinctive way, become themselves a fruitful source of the multiplication of needs and their expansion.

194. Since in social needs, as the conjunction of immediate or natural needs with mental needs arising from ideas, it is needs of the latter type which because of their universality make themselves preponderant, this social moment has in it the aspect of liberation, i.e. the strict natural necessity of need is obscured and man is concerned with his own opinion, indeed with an opinion which is universal, and with a necessity of his own making alone, instead of with an external necessity, an inner contingency, and mere caprice.

The idea has been advanced that in respect of his needs man lived in freedom in the so-called 'state of nature' when his needs were supposed to be confined to what are known as the simple necessities of nature, and when he required for their satisfaction only the means which the accidents of nature directly assured to him. This view takes no account of the moment of liberation intrinsic to work, on which see the following Paragraphs. And apart from this, it is false, because to be confined to mere physical needs as such and their direct satisfaction would simply be the condition in which the mental is plunged in the natural and so would be one of savagery and unfreedom, while freedom itself is to be found only in the reflection of mind into itself, in mind's distinction from nature, and in the reflex of mind in nature.

195. This liberation is abstract since the particular-

ity of the ends remains their basic content. When social conditions tend to multiply and subdivide needs, means, and enjoyments indefinitely – a process which, like the distinction between natural and refined needs, has no qualitative limits – this is luxury. In this same process, however, dependence and want increase *ad infinitum,* and the material to meet these is permanently barred to the needy man because it consists of external objects with the special character of being property, the embodiment of the free will of others, and hence from his point of view its recalcitrance is absolute.

(b) The Kind of Work [typical of civil society]

196. The means of acquiring and preparing the particularized means appropriate to our similarly particularized needs is work. Through work the raw material directly supplied by nature is specifically adapted to these numerous ends by all sorts of different processes. Now this formative change confers value on means and gives them their utility, and hence man in what he consumes is mainly concerned with the products of men. It is the products of human effort which man consumes.

197. The multiplicity of objects and situations which excite interest is the stage on which theoretical education develops. This education consists in possessing not simply a multiplicity of ideas and facts, but also a flexibility and rapidity of mind, ability to pass from one idea to another, to grasp complex and general relations, and so on. It is the education of the understanding in every way, and so also the building up of language. Practical education, acquired through working, consists first in the automatically recurrent need for something to do and the habit of simply being busy; next, in the strict adaptation of one's activity according not only to the nature of the material worked on, but also, and especially, to the pleasure of other workers; and finally, in a habit, produced by this discipline, of objective activity and universally recognized aptitudes.

198. The universal and objective element in work, on the other hand, lies in the abstracting process which effects the subdivision of needs and means and thereby *eo ipso* subdivides production and brings about the division of labour. By this division,

the work of the individual becomes less complex, and consequently his skill at his section of the job increases, like his output. At the same time, this abstraction of one man's skill and means of production from another's completes and makes necessary everywhere the dependence of men on one another and their reciprocal relation in the satisfaction of their other needs. Further, the abstraction of one man's production from another's makes work more and more mechanical, until finally man is able to step aside and install machines in his place.

(c) Capital [and class-divisions]

199. When men are thus dependent on one another and reciprocally related to one another in their work and the satisfaction of their needs, subjective self-seeking turns into a contribution to the satisfaction of the needs of everyone else. That is to say, by a dialectical advance, subjective self-seeking turns into the mediation of the particular through the universal, with the result that each man in earning, producing, and enjoying on his own account is *eo ipso* producing and earning for the enjoyment of everyone else. The compulsion which brings this about is rooted in the complex interdependence of each on all, and it now presents itself to each as the universal permanent capital (see Paragraph 170) which gives each the opportunity, by the exercise of his education and skill, to draw a share from it and so be assured of his livelihood, while what he thus earns by means of his work maintains and increases the general capital.

200. A particular man's resources, or in other words his opportunity of sharing in the general resources, are conditioned, however, partly by his own unearned principal (his capital), and partly by his skill; this in turn is itself dependent not only on his capital, but also on accidental circumstances whose multiplicity introduces differences in the development of natural, bodily, and mental characteristics, which were already in themselves dissimilar. In this sphere of particularity, these differences are conspicuous in every direction and on every level, and, together with the arbitrariness and accident which this sphere contains as well, they have as their inevitable consequence disparities of individual resources and ability.

The objective right of the particularity of mind is

contained in the Idea. Men are made unequal by nature, where inequality is in its element, and in civil society the right of particularity is so far from annulling this natural inequality that it produces it out of mind and raises it to an inequality of skill and resources, and even to one of moral and intellectual attainment. To oppose to this right a demand for equality is a folly of the Understanding which takes as real and rational its abstract equality and its 'ought-to-be'.

This sphere of particularity, which fancies itself the universal, is still only relatively identical with the universal, and consequently it still retains in itself the particularity of nature, i.e. arbitrariness, or in other words the relics of the state of nature. Further, it is reason, immanent in the restless system of human needs, which articulates it into an organic whole with different members (see the following Paragraph).

201. The infinitely complex, crisscross, movements of reciprocal production and exchange, and the equally infinite multiplicity of means therein employed, become crystallized, owing to the universality inherent in their content, and distinguished into general groups. As a result, the entire complex is built up into particular systems of needs, means, and types of work relative to these needs, modes of satisfaction and of theoretical and practical education, i.e. into systems, to one or other of which individuals are assigned – in other words, into class-divisions.

202. The classes are specifically determined in accordance with the concept as (a) the *substantial* or immediate [or agricultural] class; (b) the reflecting or *formal* [or business] class; and finally, *(c)* the *universal* class [the class of civil servants].

....

206. It is in accordance with the concept that class-organization, as particularity become objective to itself, is split in this way into its general divisions. But the question of the particular class to which an individual is to belong is one on which natural capacity, birth, and other circumstances have their influence, though the essential and final determin-

ing factors are subjective opinion and the individual's arbitrary will, which win in this sphere their right, their merit, and their dignity. Hence what happens here by inner necessity occurs at the same time by the mediation of the arbitrary will, and to the conscious subject it has the shape of being the work of his own will.

In this respect too there is a conspicuous difference, in relation to the principle of particularity and the subject's arbitrary will, between the political life of the east and the west, and also between that of the ancient and the modern world. In the former, the division of the whole into classes came about objectively of itself, because it is inherently rational; but the principle of subjective particularity was at the same time denied its rights, in that, for example, the allotment of individuals to classes was left to the ruling class, as in Plato's *Republic*,[5] or to the accident of birth, as in the Indian caste-system. Thus subjective particularity was not incorporated into the organization of society as a whole; it was not reconciled in the whole, and therefore – since as an essential moment it emerges there in any event – it shows itself there as something hostile, as a corruption of the social order (see Remark to Paragraph 185). Either it overthrows society, as happened in the Greek states and in the Roman Republic; or else, should society preserve itself in being as a force or as a religious authority, for instance, it appears as inner corruption and complete degeneration, as was the case to some extent in Sparta and is now altogether the case in India.

But when subjective particularity is upheld by the objective order in conformity with it and is at the same time allowed its rights, then it becomes the animating principle of the entire civil society, of the development alike of mental activity, merit, and dignity. The recognition and the right that what is brought about by reason of necessity in civil society and the state shall at the same time be effected by the mediation of the arbitrary will is the more precise definition of what is primarily meant by freedom in common parlance....

207. A man actualizes himself only in becoming something definite, i.e. something specifically particularized; this means restricting himself

5   Book iii [415 a-d].

exclusively to one of the particular spheres of need. In this class-system, the ethical frame of mind therefore is rectitude and *esprit de corps*, i.e. the disposition to make oneself a member of one of the moments of civil society by one's own act, through one's energy, industry, and skill, to maintain oneself in this position, and to fend for oneself only through this process of mediating oneself with the universal, while in this way gaining recognition both in one's own eyes and in the eyes of others. Morality has its proper place in this sphere where the paramount thing is reflection on one's doings, and the quest of happiness and private wants, and where the contingency in satisfying these makes into a duty even a single and contingent act of assistance.

At first (i.e. especially in youth) a man chafes at the idea of resolving on a particular social position, and looks upon this as a restriction on his universal character and as a necessity imposed on him purely *ab extra*. This is because his thinking is still of that abstract kind which refuses to move beyond the universal and so never reaches the actual. It does not realize that if the concept is to be determinate, it must first of all advance into the distinction between the concept and its real existence and thereby into determinacy and particularity .... It is only thus that the concept can win actuality and ethical objectivity.

208. As the private particularity of knowing and willing, the principle of this system of needs contains absolute universality, the universality of freedom, only abstractly and therefore as the right of property. At this point, however, this right is no longer merely implicit but has attained its recognized actuality as the protection of property through the administration of justice.

B. *The Administration of Justice*

209. The relatedness arising from the reciprocal bearing on one another of needs and work to satisfy these is first of all reflected into itself as infinite personality, as abstract right. But it is this very sphere of relatedness – a sphere of education – which gives abstract right the determinate existence of being something universally recognized, known, and willed, and having a validity and an objective actuality mediated by this known and willed character.

It is part of education, of thinking as the consciousness of the single in the form of universality, that the ego comes to be apprehended as a universal person in which all are identical. A man counts as a man in virtue of his manhood alone, not because he is a Jew, Catholic, Protestant, German, Italian, &c. This is an assertion which thinking ratifies and to be conscious of it is of infinite importance. It is defective only when it is crystallized, e.g. as a cosmopolitanism in opposition to the concrete life of the state.

210. The objective actuality of the right consists, first, in its existence for consciousness, in its being known in some way or other; secondly, in its possessing the power which the actual possesses, in its being valid, and so also in its becoming known as universally valid.

(a) Right as Law

211. The principle of rightness becomes the law *(Gesetz)* when, in its objective existence, it is posited *(gesetzt)*, i.e. when thinking makes it determinate for consciousness and makes it known as what is right and valid; and in acquiring this determinate character, the right becomes positive law in general.

To posit something as universal, i.e. to bring it before consciousness as universal, is, I need hardly say, to think.... Thereby its content is reduced to its simplest form and so is given its final determinacy. In becoming law, what is right acquires for the first time not only the form proper to its universality, but also its true determinacy. Hence making a law is not to be represented as merely the expression of a rule of behaviour valid for everyone, though that is one moment in legislation; the more important moment, the inner essence of the matter, is knowledge of the content of the law in its determinate universality.

Since it is only animals which have their law as instinct, while it is man alone who has law as custom, even systems of customary law contain the moment of being thoughts and being known. Their difference from positive law consists solely in this, that they are known only in a subjective and accidental way, with the result that in themselves they are less determinate and the universality of thought is less clear in them. (And apart from this, knowledge of a system of law either in general or in its details, is the accidental possession of a few.) The supposition that it is customary law, on the strength of its character as custom, which possesses the privilege of having become part of life is a delusion, since the valid laws of a nation do not cease to be its customs by being written and codified – and besides, it is as a rule precisely those versed in the deadest of topics and the deadest of thoughts who talk nowadays of 'life' and of 'becoming part of life'. When a nation begins to acquire even a little culture, its customary law must soon come to be collected and put together. Such a collection is a legal code, but one which, as a mere collection, is markedly formless, indeterminate, and fragmentary. The main difference between it and a code properly so-called is that in the latter the principles of jurisprudence in their universality, and so in their determinacy, have been apprehended in terms of thought and expressed. English national law or municipal law is contained, as is well known, in statutes (written laws) and in so-called 'unwritten' laws. This unwritten law, however, is as good as written, and knowledge of it may, and indeed must, be acquired simply by reading the numerous quartos which it fills. The monstrous confusion, however, which prevails both in English law and its administration is graphically portrayed by those acquainted with the matter. In particular, they comment on the fact that, since this unwritten law is contained in court verdicts and judgements, the judges are continually legislators. The authority of precedent is binding on them, since their predecessors have done nothing but give expression to the unwritten law; and yet they are just as much exempt from its authority, because they are themselves repositories of the unwritten law and so have the right to criticize previous judgements and pronounce whether they accorded with the unwritten law or not....

No greater insult could be offered to a civilized people or to its lawyers than to deny them ability to codify their law; for such ability cannot be that of constructing a legal system with a novel content, but only that of apprehending, i.e. grasping in thought, the content of existing laws in its determinate universality and then applying them to particular cases.

....

217. The principle of rightness passes over in civil society into law. My individual right, whose embodiment has hitherto been immediate and abstract, now similarly becomes embodied in the existent will and knowledge of everyone, in the sense that it becomes recognized. Hence property acquisitions and transfers must now be undertaken and concluded only in the form which that embodiment gives to them. In civil society, property rests on contract and on the formalities which make ownership capable of proof and valid in law.

Original, i.e. direct, titles and means of acquisition... are simply discarded in civil society and appear only as isolated accidents or as subordinated factors of property transactions. It is either feeling, refusing to move beyond the subjective, or reflection, clinging to its abstract essences, which casts formalities aside, while the dry-as-dust Understanding may for its part cling to formalities instead of the real thing and multiply them indefinitely.

Apart from this, however, the march of mental development is the long and hard struggle to free a content from its sensuous and immediate form, endow it with its appropriate form of thought, and thereby give it simple and adequate expression. It is because this is the case that when the development of law is just beginning, ceremonies and formalities are more circumstantial and count rather as the thing itself than as its symbol....

218. Since property and personality have legal recognition and validity in civil society, wrongdoing now becomes an infringement, not merely of what is subjectively infinite, but of the universal thing which is existent with inherent stability and strength. Hence a new attitude arises: the action is seen as a danger to society and thereby the magnitude of the wrongdoing is increased. On the other hand, however, the fact that society has become strong and sure of itself diminishes the external importance of the injury and so leads to a mitigation of its punishment.

The fact that an injury to one member of society is an injury to all others does not alter the conception of wrongdoing, but it does alter it in respect of its outward existence as an injury done, an injury which now affects the mind and consciousness of civil society as a whole, not merely the external embodiment of the person directly injured. In heroic times, as we see in the tragedy of the ancients, the citizens did not feel themselves injured by wrongs which members of the royal houses did to one another.

Implicitly, crime is an infinite injury; but as an existent fact it must be measured in quantity and quality..., and since its field of existence here has the essential character of affecting an idea and consciousness of the validity of the laws, its danger to civil society is a determinant of the magnitude of a crime, or even *one* of its qualitative characteristics.

Now this quality or magnitude varies with the state of civil society; and this is the justification for sometimes attaching the penalty of death to a theft of a few pence or a turnip, and at other times a light penalty to a theft of a hundred or more times that amount. If we consider its danger to society, this seems at first sight to aggravate the crime; but in fact it is just this which has been the prime cause of the mitigation of its punishment. A penal code, then, is primarily the child of its age and the state of civil society at the time.

(c) The Court of Justice

219. By taking the form of law, right steps into a determinate mode of being. It is then something on its own account, and in contrast with particular willing and opining of the right, it is self-subsistent and has to vindicate itself as something universal. This is achieved by recognizing it and making it actual in a particular case without the subjective feeling of private interest; and this is the business of a public authority – the court of justice.

The historical origin of the judge and his court may have had the form of a patriarch's gift to his people or of force or free choice; but this makes no difference to the concept of the thing. To regard the introduction of a legal system as no more than an optional act of grace or favour on the part of monarchs and governments... is a piece of the mere thoughtlessness which has no inkling of the point at issue in a discussion of law and the state. The point is that legal and political institutions are rational in principle and therefore absolutely necessary, and the question of the form in which they arose or were introduced is entirely irrelevant to a consideration of their rational basis....

....

236. The differing interests of producers and consumers may come into collision with each other; and although a fair balance between them on the whole may be brought about automatically, still their adjustment also requires a control which stands above both and is consciously undertaken. The right to the exercise of such control in a single case (e.g. in the fixing of the prices of the commonest necessaries of life) depends on the fact that, by being publicly exposed for sale, goods in absolutely universal daily demand are offered not so much to an individual as such but rather to a universal purchaser, the public; and thus both the defence of the public's right not to be defrauded, and also the management of goods inspection, may lie, as a common concern, with a public authority. But public care and direction are most of all necessary in the case of the larger branches of industry, because these are dependent on conditions abroad and on combinations of distant circumstances which cannot be grasped as a whole by the individuals tied to these industries for their living.

At the other extreme to freedom of trade and commerce in civil society is public organization to provide for everything and determine everyone's labour – take for example in ancient times the labour on the pyramids and the other huge monuments in Egypt and Asia which were constructed for public ends, and the worker's task was not mediated through his private choice and particular interest. This interest invokes freedom of trade and commerce against control from above; but the more blindly it sinks into self-seeking aims, the more it requires such control to bring it back to the universal. Control is also necessary to diminish the danger of upheavals arising from clashing interests and to abbreviate the period in which their tension should be eased through the working of a necessity of which they themselves know nothing.

237. Now while the possibility of sharing in the general wealth is open to individuals and is assured to them by the public authority, still it is subject to contingencies on the subjective side (quite apart from the fact that this assurance must remain incomplete), and the more it presupposes skill, health, capital, and so forth as its conditions, the more is it so subject.

238. Originally the family is the substantive whole whose function it is to provide for the individual on his particular side by giving him either the means and the skill necessary to enable him to earn his living out of the resources of society, or else subsistence and maintenance in the event of his suffering a disability. But civil society tears the individual from his family ties, estranges the members of the family from one another, and recognizes them as self-subsistent persons. Further, for the paternal soil and the external inorganic resources of nature from which the individual formerly derived his livelihood, it substitutes its own soil and subjects the permanent existence of even the entire family to dependence on itself and to contingency. Thus the individual becomes a son of civil society which has as many claims upon him as he has rights against it.

239. In its character as a universal family, civil society has the right and duty of superintending and influencing education, inasmuch as education bears upon the child's capacity to become a member of society. Society's right here is paramount over the arbitrary and contingent preferences of parents, particularly in cases where education is to be completed not by the parents but by others. To the same end, society must provide public educational facilities so far as is practicable.

240. Similarly, society has the right and duty of acting as trustee to those whose extravagance destroys the security of their own subsistence or their families'. It must substitute for extravagance the pursuit of the ends of society and the individuals concerned.

241. Not only caprice, however, but also contingencies, physical conditions, and factors grounded in external circumstances (see Paragraph 200) may reduce men to poverty. The poor still have the needs common to civil society, and yet since society has withdrawn from them the natural means of acquisition (see Paragraph 217) and broken the bond of the family – in the wider sense of the clan (see Paragraph 181) – their poverty leaves them more or less deprived of all the advantages of society, of the opportunity of acquiring skill or education of any kind, as well as of the administration of justice, the public health services, and often even of the conso-

lations of religion, and so forth. The public authority takes the place of the family where the poor are concerned in respect not only of their immediate want but also of laziness of disposition, malignity, and the other vices which arise out of their plight and their sense of wrong.

242. Poverty and, in general, the distress of every kind to which every individual is exposed from the start in the cycle of his natural life has a subjective side which demands similarly subjective aid, arising both from the special circumstances of a particular case and also from love and sympathy. This is the place where morality finds plenty to do despite all public organization. Subjective aid, however, both in itself and in its operation, is dependent on contingency and consequently society struggles to make it less necessary, by discovering the general causes of penury and general means of its relief, and by organizing relief accordingly.

Casual almsgiving and casual endowments, e.g. for the burning of lamps before holy images, &c., are supplemented by public almshouses, hospitals, street-lighting, and so forth. There is still quite enough left over and above these things for charity to do on its own account. A false view is implied both when charity insists on having this poor relief reserved solely to private sympathy and the accidental occurrence of knowledge and a charitable disposition, and also when it feels injured or mortified by universal regulations and ordinances which are *obligatory*. Public social conditions are on the contrary to be regarded as all the more perfect the less (in comparison with what is arranged publicly) is left for an individual to do by himself as his private inclination directs.

243. When civil society is in a state of unimpeded activity, it is engaged in expanding internally in population and industry. The amassing of wealth is intensified by generalizing (a) the linkage of men by their needs, and (b) the methods of preparing and distributing the means to satisfy these needs, because it is from this double process of generalization that the largest profits are derived. That is one side of the picture. The other side is the subdivision and restriction of particular jobs. This results in the dependence and distress of the class tied to work of that sort, and these again entail inability to feel and enjoy the broader freedoms

and especially the intellectual benefits of civil society.

244. When the standard of living of a large mass of people falls below a certain subsistence level – a level regulated automatically as the one necessary for a member of the society – and when there is a consequent loss of the sense of right and wrong, of honesty and the self-respect which makes a man insist on maintaining himself by his own work and effort, the result is the creation of a rabble of paupers. At the same time this brings with it, at the other end of the social scale, conditions which greatly facilitate the concentration of disproportionate wealth in a few hands.

245. When the masses begin to decline into poverty, (a) the burden of maintaining them at their ordinary standard of living might be directly laid on the wealthier classes, or they might receive the means of livelihood directly from other public sources of wealth (e.g. from the endowments of rich hospitals, monasteries, and other foundations). In either case, however, the needy would receive subsistence directly, not by means of their work, and this would violate the principle of civil society and the feeling of individual independence and self-respect in its individual members. (b) As an alternative, they might be given subsistence indirectly through being given work, i.e. the opportunity to work. In this event the volume of production would be increased, but the evil consists precisely in an excess of production and in the lack of a proportionate number of consumers who are themselves also producers, and thus it is simply intensified by both of the methods (a) and (b) by which it is sought to alleviate it. It hence becomes apparent that despite an excess of wealth civil society is not rich enough, i.e. its own resources are insufficient to check excessive poverty and the creation of a penurious rabble.

In the example of England we may study these phenomena on a large scale and also in particular the results of poor-rates, immense foundations, unlimited private beneficence, and above all the abolition of the Guild Corporations. In Britain, particularly in Scotland, the most direct measure against poverty and especially against the loss of shame and self-respect – the subjective bases of society – as well as against laziness and extravagance, &c., the begetters of the rabble, has turned out to be to leave the poor to their fate and instruct them to beg in the streets.

246. This inner dialectic of civil society thus drives it – or at any rate drives a specific civil society – to push beyond its own limits and seek markets, and so its necessary means of subsistence, in other lands which are either deficient in the goods it has overproduced, or else generally backward in industry, &c....

Bibliography

Harris, H.S. *Hegel: Phenomenology and System*. Indianapolis: Hackett Publishing Company, 1995.

Inwood, Michael. *A Hegel Dictionary*. Oxford: Blackwell Publishers, 1992.

Kaufmann, Walter, ed. *Hegel's Political Philosophy*. New York: Atherton Press, 1970.

MacIntyre, Alasdair, ed. *Hegel: A Collection of Critical Essays*. New York: Anchor Books, 1972.

Singer, Peter. *Hegel*. Oxford: Oxford University Press, 1983.

Stewart, Jon, ed. *The Hegel Myths and Legends*. Evanston, Ill.: Northwestern University Press, 1996.

Taylor, Charles. *Hegel*. Cambridge: Cambridge University Press, 1975.

Taylor, Charles. *Hegel and Modern Society*. Cambridge: Cambridge University Press, 1979.

CHAPTER TWENTY-SEVEN — KARL MARX

Very, very few individuals, men or women of action or theorists, technological innovators or military conquerors, have had the degree of impact on the world that Karl Marx (1818-1883) has had. Marx famously complained that philosophers sought only to understand the world, where the essential point was to *change* it; and Marx undoubtedly did that. Beginning with Russia in 1917, approximately a third of the earth's societies came to be fashioned explicitly in Marx's name, and with aspiration to implement and realize his analyses and his visions of an ideal long-term future for human life. There seemed reasonable possibility that most or all human societies would come eventually to versions, at least, of Marxian models and blueprints. The course of geopolitical transformation aside, wide sectors of the thinking classes, in some societies of the "first world" as well as the "second" and the "third," came in the course of the twentieth century to embrace deeply Marxian perspectives on social, historical, moral, and human reality.

Fortune is famously fickle, and in the space of less than a decade most of this tide of imprint and influence has crumbled and largely fallen away. Only possibly excepting Cuba, there are no seriously or authentically Marxist societies left in the world today, and many see the leading "post-Marxist" intellectual movement currently – namely, what is commonly called postmodernism – as merely an academic travesty of its progenitor.

What the stature of Marx's views of human beings will be in another quarter-century, or beyond, is extremely difficult to say. The fact is that Marx (in many of the writings Marx and his colleague Friedrich Engels [1820-1895]), assembled a remarkably comprehensive and wide-ranging – it is problematic whether it is also altogether self-consistent – understanding of human history and the principles of historical change, of the relations between individuals and the social groupings within which they are found, of fundamental human motivation, of the role and significance of ethical and other symbolic or normative structures of ideas for human life, and of many other topics of human concern. Part of this same legacy are proposals for and exhortation to dramatic social and economic transformation, of making the world over in directions discernible threads of development point to. Themes of historical inevitability, dispassionately laid out through the analysis of large patterns and trends, sit alongside disclosures of the extent of the world's wickednesses – its avoidable, ultimately annullable wickednesses. It remains a fascinating and important picture of our predicament and prospects.

Karl Marx, *The Economic and Philosophic Manuscripts of 1844*

(Source: Karl Marx. *The Economic and Philosophic Manuscripts of 1844*. Ed. and intr. Dirk J. Struik. Trans. Martin Milligan, 1964. New York: International Publishers, 1964, 112-114, 142-146, 155-156.)

Man is a species being, not only because in practice and in theory he adopts the species as his object (his own as well as those of other things), but – and this is only another way of expressing it – also because he treats himself as the actual, living species; because he treats himself as a *universal* and therefore a free being.

The life of the species, both in man and in animals, consists physically in the fact that man (like the animal) lives on inorganic nature; and the more universal man is compared with an animal, the more universal is the sphere of inorganic nature on which he lives. Just as plants, animals, stones, air, light, etc., constitute theoretically a part of human consciousness, partly as objects of natural science, partly as objects of art – his spiritual inorganic nature, spiritual nourishment which he must first prepare to make palatable and digestible – so also in the realm of practice they constitute a part of human life and human activity. Physically man lives only on these products of nature, whether they appear in the form of food, heating, clothes, a dwelling, etc The universality of man appears in practice precisely in the universality which makes all nature his *inorganic* body – both inasmuch as nature is (1) his direct means of life, and (2) the material, the object, and the instrument of his life activity. Nature is man's *inorganic body* – nature, that is, in so far as it is not itself the human body. Man *lives* on nature – means that nature is his *body,* with which he must remain in continuous interchange if he is not to die. That man's physical and spiritual life is linked to nature means simply that nature is linked to itself, for man is a part of nature.

In estranging from man (1) nature, and (2) himself, his own active functions, his life activity, estranged labor estranges the *species* from man. It changes for him the *life of the species* into a means of individual life. First it estranges the life of the species and individual life, and secondly it makes individual life in its abstract form the purpose of the life of the species, likewise in its abstract and estranged form.

Indeed, labor, *life-activity, productive life* itself, appears in the first place merely as a *means* of satisfying a need – the need to maintain physical existence. Yet the productive life is the life of the species. It is life-engendering life. The whole character of a species – its species character – is contained in the character of its life activity; and free, conscious activity is man's species character. Life itself appears only as a *means to life.*

The animal is immediately one with its life activity. It does not distinguish itself from it. It is *its life activity*. Man makes his life activity itself the object of his will and of his consciousness. He has conscious life activity. It is not a determination with which he directly merges. Conscious life activity distinguishes man immediately from animal life activity. It is just because of this that he is a species being. Or rather, it is only because he is a species being that he is a conscious being, i.e., that his own life is an object for him. Only because of that is his activity free activity. Estranged labor reverses this relationship, so that it is just because man is a conscious being that he makes his life activity, his *essential* being, a mere means to his *existence.*

In creating a *world of objects* by his practical activity, in *his work upon* inorganic nature, man proves himself a conscious species being, i.e., as a being that treats the species as its own essential being, or that treats itself as a species being. Admittedly animals also produce. They build themselves nests, dwellings, like the bees, beavers, ants, etc. But an animal only produces what it immediately needs for itself or its young. It produces one-sidedly, whilst man produces universally. It produces only under the dominion of immediate physical need, whilst man produces even when he is free from physical need and only truly produces in freedom therefrom. An animal produces only itself, whilst man reproduces the whole of nature. An animal's product belongs immediately to its physical body, whilst man freely confronts his product. An animal forms things in accordance with the standard and the need of the species to which it belongs, whilst man knows how to produce in accordance with the standard of every species, and knows how to apply everywhere the inherent standard to the object. Man therefore also forms things in accordance with the laws of beauty.

It is just in his work upon the objective world, therefore, that man first really proves himself to be a *species being*. This production is his active species life. Through and because of this production, nature appears as *his* work and his reality. The object of labor is, therefore, the *objectification of man's species life:* for he duplicates himself not only, as in consciousness, intellectually, but also actively, in reality, and therefore he contemplates himself in a world that he has created. In tearing away from man the object of his production, therefore, estranged labor tears from him his *species life,* his real objectivity as a member of the species and transforms his advantage over animals into the disadvantage that his inorganic body, nature, is taken away from him.

Similarly, in degrading spontaneous, free activity, to a means, estranged labor makes man's species life a means to his physical existence.

The consciousness which man has of his species is thus transformed by estrangement in such a way that species life becomes for him a means.

Estranged labor turns thus:

(3) *Man's species being,* both nature and his spiritual species property, into a being *alien* to him, into a *means* to his *individual existence.* It estranges from man his own body, as well as external nature and his spiritual essence, his *human* being.

(4) An immediate consequence of the fact that man is estranged from the product of his labor, from his life activity, from his species being is the *estrangement of man* from *man.* When man confronts himself, he confronts the *other* man. What applies to a man's relation to his work, to the product of his labor and to himself, also holds of a man's relation to the other man, and to the other man's labor and object of labor.

In fact, the proposition that man's species nature is estranged from him means that one man is estranged from the other, as each of them is from man's essential nature.

....

The *natural sciences* have developed an enormous activity and have accumulated an ever-growing mass of material. Philosophy, however, has remained just as alien to them as they remain to philosophy. Their momentary unity was only a *chimerical illusion.* The will was there, but the means were lacking. Even historiography pays regard to natural science only occasionally, as a factor of enlightenment, utility, and of some special great discoveries. But natural science has invaded and transformed human life all the more *practically* through the medium of industry; and has prepared human emancipation, although its immediate effect had to be the furthering of the dehumanization of man. *Industry* is the *actual,* historical relationship of nature, and therefore of natural science, to man. If, therefore, industry is conceived as

the *exoteric* revelation of man's *essential powers,* we also gain an understanding of the *human* essence of nature or the *natural* essence of man. In consequence, natural science will lose its abstractly material – or rather, its idealistic – tendency, and will become the basis of *human* science, as it has already become the basis of actual human life, albeit in an estranged form. *One* basis for life and another basis for *science* is *a priori* a lie. The nature which develops in human history – the genesis of human society – is man's *real* nature; hence nature as it develops through industry, even though in an *estranged* form, is true *anthropological* nature.

Sense-perception (see Feuerbach) must be the basis of all science. Only when it proceeds from sense-perception in the twofold form both of *sensuous* consciousness and of *sensuous* need – that is, only when science proceeds from nature – is it *true* science. All history is the preparation for *"man"* to become the object of *sensuous* consciousness, and for the needs of "man as man" to become [natural, sensuous] needs. History itself is a *real* part of *natural history* – of nature developing into man. Natural science will in time incorporate into itself the science of man, just as the science of man will incorporate into itself natural science: there will be *one* science.

Man is the immediate object of natural science; for immediate, *sensuous nature* for man is, immediately, human sensuousness (the expressions are identical) – presented immediately in the form of the *other* man sensuously present for him. Indeed, his own sensuousness first exists as human sensuousness for himself through the *other* man. But *nature* is the immediate object of the *science of man:* the first object of man – man – is nature, sensuousness; and the particular sensuous human essential powers can only find their self-understanding in the science of the natural world in general, since they can find their objective realization in *natural* objects only. The element of thought itself – the element of thought's living expression – *language* – is of a sensuous nature. The *social* reality of nature, and *human* natural science, or the *natural science about man,* are identical terms.

It will be seen how in place of the *wealth* and *poverty* of political economy comes the *rich human being* and the rich *human* need. The *rich* human being is simultaneously the human being *in need of* a totality of human manifestations of life – the man in whom his own realization exists as an inner necessity, as *need*. Not only *wealth*, but likewise the *poverty* of man – under the assumption of socialism – receives in equal measure a *human* and therefore social significance. Poverty is the passive bond which causes the human being to experience the need of the greatest wealth – the *other* human being. The dominion of the objective being in me, the sensuous outburst of my life activity, is *passion*, which thus becomes here the *activity* of my being.

(5) A *being* only considers himself independent when he stands on his own feet; and he only stands on his own feet when he owes his *existence* to himself. A man who lives by the grace of another regards himself as a dependent being. But I live completely by the grace of another if I owe him not only the maintenance of my life, but if he has, moreover, *created* my *life* – if he is the *source* of my life. When it is not of my own creation, my life has necessarily a source of this kind outside of it. The *Creation* is therefore an idea very difficult to dislodge from popular consciousness. The fact that nature and man exist in their own account is *incomprehensible* to it, because it contradicts everything *tangible* in practical life.

The creation of the *earth* has received a mighty blow from geogeny – i.e., from the science which presents the formation of the earth, the further development of the earth, as a process, as a self-generation. *Generatio aequivoca* is the only practical refutation of the theory of creation.

Now it is certainly easy to say to the single individual what Aristotle has already said: You have been begotten by your father and your mother; therefore in you the mating of two human beings – a species-act of human beings – has produced the human being. You see, therefore, that even physically, man owes his existence to man. Therefore you must not only keep sight of the *one* aspect – the *infinite* progression which leads you further to enquire: "Who begot my father? Who his grandfather?," etc. You must also hold on to the *circular movement* sensuously perceptible in that progression, by which man repeats himself in procreation, *man* thus always remaining the subject. You will reply, however: I grant you this circular movement; now grant me the progression which drives me ever further until I ask: Who begot the first man, and nature as a whole? I can only answer you: Your question is itself a product of abstraction. Ask yourself how you arrived at that question. Ask yourself whether your question is not posed from a standpoint to which I cannot reply, because it is wrongly put. Ask yourself whether that progression as such exists for a reasonable mind. When you ask about the creation of nature and man, you are abstracting, in so doing, from man and nature. You postulate them as *non-existent*, and yet you want me to prove them to you as *existing*. Now I say to you: Give up your abstraction and you will also give up your question. Or if you want to hold on to your abstraction, then be consistent, and if you think of man and nature as *non-existent*, then think of yourself as non-existent, for you too are surely nature and man. Don't think, don't ask me, for as soon as you think and ask, your *abstraction* from the existence of nature and man has no meaning. Or are you such an egotist that you conceive everything as nothing, and yet want yourself to exist?

You can reply: I do not want to conceive the nothingness of nature, etc. I ask you about *its genesis*, just as I ask the anatomist about the formation of bones, etc.

But since for the socialist man the *entire so-called history of the world* is nothing but the creation of man through human labor, nothing but the emergence of nature for man, so he has the visible, irrefutable proof of his *birth* through himself, of the *process of his creation*. Since the *real existence* of man and nature – since man has become for man as the being of nature, and nature for man as the being of man has become practical, sensuous, perceptible – the question about an *alien* being, about a being above nature and man – a question which implies the admission of the unreality of nature and of man – has become impossible in practice. *Atheism*, as the denial of this unreality, has no longer any meaning, for atheism is a *negation of God*, and postulates the *existence of man* through this negation; but socialism as socialism no longer stands in any need of such a mediation. It proceeds from the *practically and theoretically sensuous consciousness* of man and of nature as the *essence*. Socialism is man's *positive self-consciousness*, no longer mediated through the annulment of religion, just as *real life* is man's positive reality, no longer mediated through the annulment of private property, through *communism*. Communism is the position as the negation of the negation, and is hence the *actual* phase necessary for the next stage of historical development in the process of human emancipation and rehabilitation. *Communism* is the necessary pattern and the dynamic principle of the immediate future, but communism as such is not the goal of human development – which goal is the structure of human society.

....

We have said above that man is regressing to the *cave dwelling*, etc., – but that he is regressing to it in an estranged, malignant form. The savage in his cave – a natural element which freely offers itself for his use and protection – feels himself no more a stranger, or rather feels himself to be just as much at home as a *fish* in water. But the cellar dwelling of the poor man is a hostile, dwelling, "an alien, restraining power which only gives itself up to him in so far as he gives up to it his blood and sweat" – a dwelling which he cannot regard as his own home where he might at last exclaim, "Here I am at home," but where instead he finds himself in *someone else's* house, in the house of a *stranger* who daily lies in wait for him and throws him out if he does not pay his rent. He is also aware of the contrast in quality between his dwelling and a human dwelling – a residence in that *other* world, the heaven of wealth.

Estrangement is manifested not only in the fact that *my* means of life belong to *someone else*, that *my* desire is the inaccessible possession of *another*, but also in the fact that everything is itself something *different* from itself – that my activity is *something else* and that, finally (and this applies also to the capitalist), all is under the sway of *inhuman* power. There is a form of inactive, extravagant wealth given over wholly to pleasure, the enjoyer of which on the one hand *behaves* as a mere *ephemeral* individual frantically spending himself to no purpose, knows the slave-labor of others (human *sweat and blood)* as the prey of his cupidity, and therefore knows man himself, and hence also his own self, as a sacrificed and empty being. With such wealth contempt of man makes its appearance, partly as arrogance and as squandering of what can give sustenance to a hundred human lives, and partly as the infamous illusion that his own unbridled extravagance and ceaseless, unproductive consumption is the condition of the other's *labor* and therefore of his *subsistence*. He knows the realization of the *essential powers* of many only as the realization of his own excesses, his whims and capricious, bizarre notions. This wealth which, on the other hand, again knows wealth as a mere means, as something that is good for nothing but to be annihilated and which is therefore at once slave and master, at once generous and mean, capricious, presumptuous, conceited, refined, cultured and witty – this wealth has not yet experienced *wealth* as an utterly *alien power* over itself: it sees in it, rather, only its own power, and not wealth but *gratification* [is its] final aim and end.

Karl Marx, *Thesis on Feuerbach*

(Source: Lewis S. Feuer, ed. *Marx and Engels: Basic Writings on Politics and Philosophy*. New York: Anchor Books, 1959, 243-245.)

I

The chief defect of all hitherto existing materialism – that of Feuerbach included – is that the thing [*Gegenstand*], reality, sensuousness, is conceived only in the form of the *object [Objekt]* or of *contemplation [Anschauung]*, but not as *human sensuous activity, practice,* not subjectively. Hence it happened that the *active* side, in contradistinction to materialism, was developed by idealism – but only abstractly, since, of course, idealism does not know real, sensuous activity as such. Feuerbach wants sensuous objects really differentiated from the thought objects, but he does not conceive human activity itself as *objective [gegenständliche]* activity. Hence, in the *Essence of Christianity,* he regards the theoretical attitude as the only genuinely human attitude, while practice is conceived and fixed only in its dirty-judaical form of appearance. Hence he does not grasp the significance of "revolutionary," of "practical-critical," activity.

II

The question whether objective *[gegenständliche]* truth can be attributed to human thinking is not a question of theory, but is a *practical* question. In practice man must prove the truth, that is, the reality and power, the this-sidedness *[Diesseitigkeit]* of his thinking. The dispute over the reality or non-reality of thinking which is isolated from practice is a purely *scholastic* question.

III

The materialist doctrine that men are products of circumstances and upbringing, and that, therefore, changed men are products of other circumstances and changed upbringing, forgets that it is men that change circumstances, and that the educator himself needs educating. Hence this doctrine necessarily arrives at dividing society into two parts, of which one is superior to society (in Robert Owen, for example).

The coincidence of the changing of circumstances and of human activity can be conceived and rationally understood only as *revolutionizing practice.*

IV

Feuerbach starts out from the fact of religious self-alienation, the duplication of the world into a religious, imaginary world and a real one. His work consists in the dissolution of the religious world into its secular basis. He overlooks the fact that after completing this work, the chief thing still remains to be done. For the fact that the secular foundation detaches itself from itself and establishes itself in the clouds as an independent realm is really to be explained only by the self-cleavage and self-contradictoriness of this secular basis. The latter must itself, therefore, first be understood in its contradiction and then, by the removal of the contradiction, revolutionized in practice. Thus, for instance, once the earthly family is discovered to be the secret of the holy family, the former must then itself be criticized in theory and revolutionized in practice.

V

Feuerbach, not satisfied with *abstract thinking,* appeals to *sensuous contemplation,* but he does not conceive sensuousness as *practical,* human-sensuous activity.

VI

Feuerbach resolves the religious essence into the *human* essence. But the human essence is no abstraction inherent in each single individual. In its reality it is the ensemble of the social relations.

Feuerbach, who does not enter upon a criticism of this real essence, is consequently compelled:

1. To abstract from the historical process and to fix the religious sentiment *[Gemüt]* as something by itself, and to presuppose an abstract – *isolated* – human individual.

2. The human essence, therefore, can with him be comprehended only as "genus," as an internal, dumb generality which merely *naturally* unites the many individuals.

VII

Feuerbach, consequently, does not see that the "religious sentiment" is itself a *social product,* and that the abstract individual whom he analyzes belongs in reality to a particular form of society.

VIII

Social life is essentially *practical.* All mysteries which mislead theory to mysticism find their rational solution in human practice and in the comprehension of this practice.

IX

The highest point attained by *contemplative* materialism, that is, materialism which does not understand sensuousness as practical activity, is the contemplation of single individuals in "civil society."

X

The standpoint of the old materialism is *"civil"* society; the standpoint of the new is *human* society, or socialized humanity.

XI

The philosophers have only *interpreted* the world, in various ways; the point, however, is to *change* it.

....

Karl Marx and Friedrich Engels, *The German Ideology*

(Source: Lewis S. Feuer, ed. *Marx and Engels: Basic Writings on Politics and Philosophy.* New York: Anchor Books, 1959, 246-259.)

.... The fact is, therefore, that definite individuals

who are productively active in a definite way enter into these definite social and political relations. Empirical observation must in each separate instance bring out empirically, and without any mystification and speculation, the connection of the social and political structure with production. The social structure and the state are continually evolving out of the life process of definite individuals, but of individuals not as they may appear in their own or other people's imagination, but as they really are, i.e., as they are effective, produce materially, and are active under definite material limits, presuppositions, and conditions independent of their will.

The production of ideas, of conceptions, of consciousness is at first directly interwoven with the material activity and the material intercourse of men, the language of real life. Conceiving, thinking, the mental intercourse of men appear at this stage as the direct efflux of their material behavior. The same applies to mental production as expressed in the language of the politics, laws, morality, religion, metaphysics of a people. Men are the producers of their conceptions, ideas, etc. – real, active men, as they are conditioned by a definite development of their productive forces and of the intercourse corresponding to these, up to its furthest forms. Consciousness can never be anything else than conscious existence, and the existence of men is their actual life process. If in all ideology men and their circumstances appear upside down, as in a *camera obscura*, this phenomenon arises just as much from their historical life process as the inversion of objects on the retina does from their physical life process.

In direct contrast to German philosophy, which descends from heaven to earth, here we ascend from earth to heaven. That is to say, we do not set out from what men say, imagine, conceive, nor from men as narrated, thought of, imagined, conceived, in order to arrive at men in the flesh. We set out from real, active men, and on the basis of their real life process we demonstrate the development of the ideological reflexes and echoes of this life process. The phantoms formed in the human brain are also, necessarily, sublimates of their material life process, which is empirically verifiable and bound to material premises. Morality, religion, metaphysics, all the rest of ideology and their corresponding forms of consciousness, thus no longer retain the semblance of independence. They have

no history, no development; but men, developing their material production and their material intercourse, alter, along with this, their real existence, their thinking, and the products of their thinking. Life is not determined by consciousness, but consciousness by life. In the first method of approach the starting point is consciousness taken as the living individual; in the second it is the real, living individuals themselves, as they are in actual life, and consciousness is considered solely as *their* consciousness.

This method of approach is not devoid of premises. It starts out from the real premises, and does not abandon them for a moment. Its premises are men, not in any fantastic isolation or abstract definition, but in their actual, empirically perceptible process of development under definite conditions. As soon as this active life process is described, history ceases to be a collection of dead facts, as it is with the empiricists (themselves still abstract), or an imagined activity of imagined subjects, as with the idealists.

Where speculation ends – in real life – there real, positive science begins: the representation of the practical activity, of the practical process of development of men. Empty talk about consciousness ceases, and real knowledge has to take its place. When reality is depicted, philosophy as an independent branch of activity loses its medium of existence. At best, its place can be taken only by a summing up of the most general results, abstractions which arise from the observation of the historical development of men. Viewed apart from real history, these abstractions have in themselves no value whatsoever. They can only serve to facilitate the arrangement of historical material, to indicate the sequence of its separate strata. But they by no means afford a recipe or schema, as does philosophy, for neatly trimming the epochs of history. On the contrary, our difficulties begin only when we set about the observation and the arrangement – the real depiction – of our historical material, whether of a past epoch or of the present. The removal of these difficulties is governed by premises which it is quite impossible to state here, but which only the study of the actual life process and the activity of the individuals of each epoch will make evident. We shall select here some of these abstractions, which we use to refute the ideologists, and shall illustrate them by historical examples.

(a) History

Since we are dealing with the Germans, who do not postulate anything, we must begin by stating the first premise of all human existence, and therefore of all history, the premise, namely, that men must be in a position to live in order to be able to "make history." But life involves, before everything else, eating and drinking, a habitation, clothing, and many other things. The first historical act is thus the production of the means to satisfy these needs, the production of material life itself. And indeed this is a historical act, a fundamental condition of all history, which today, as thousands of years ago, must daily and hourly be fulfilled merely in order to sustain human life.... The first necessity therefore in any theory of history is to observe this fundamental fact in all its significance and all its implications, and to accord it its due importance. This, as is notorious, the Germans have never done, and they have never, therefore, had an earthly basis for history and consequently never a historian. The French and the English, even if they have conceived the relation of this fact with so-called history only in an extremely one-sided fashion, particularly as long as they remained in the toils of political ideology, have nevertheless made the first attempts to give the writing of history a materialistic basis by being the first to write histories of civil society, of commerce and industry....

The second fundamental point is that as soon as a need is satisfied (which implies the action of satisfying, and the acquisition of an instrument), new needs are made; and this production of new needs is the first historical act. Here we recognize immediately the spiritual ancestry of the great historical wisdom of the Germans, who, when they run out of positive material and when they can serve up neither theological, nor political nor literary rubbish, do not write history at all but invent the "prehistoric era." They do not, however, enlighten us as to how we proceed from this nonsensical "prehistory" to history proper; although, on the other hand, in their historical speculation they seize upon this "prehistory" with especial eagerness because they imagine themselves safe there from interference on the part of "crude facts," and, at the same time, because there they can give full rein to their speculative impulse and set up and knock down hypotheses by the thousand.

The third circumstance which, from the very first, enters into historical development is that men, who daily remake their own life, begin to make other men, to propagate their kind: the relation between man and wife, parents and children, the *family*. The family, which to begin with is the only social relationship, becomes later, when increased needs create new social relations and the increased population new needs, a subordinate one (except in Germany) and must then be treated and analyzed according to the existing empirical data,[1] not according to "the concept of the family," as is the custom in Germany. These three aspects of social activity are not of course to be taken as three different stages, but just, as I have said, as three aspects or, to make it clear to the Germans, three "moments," which have existed simultaneously since the dawn of history and the first men, and still assert themselves in history today.

The production of life, both of one's own in labor and of fresh life in procreation, now appears as a double relationship: on the one hand as a natural, on the other as a social relationship. By social we understand the cooperation of several individuals,

---

1   The building of houses. With savages each family has of course its own cave or hut like the separate family tent of the nomads. This separate domestic economy is made only the more necessary by the further development of private property. With the agricultural peoples a communal domestic economy is just as impossible as a communal cultivation of the soil. A great advance was the building of towns. In all previous periods, however, the abolition of individual economy, which is inseparable from the abolition of private property, was impossible for the simple reason that the material conditions governing it were not present. The setting up of a communal domestic economy presupposes the development of machinery, of the use of natural forces and of many other productive forces-e.g., of water supplies, of gas lighting, steam heating, etc., the removal of the antagonism of town and country. Without these conditions a communal economy would not in itself form a new productive force; lacking any material basis and resting on a purely theoretical foundation, it would be a mere freak and would end in nothing more than a monastic economy. What was possible can be seen in the formation of towns and the erection of communal buildings for various definite purposes (prisons, barracks, etc.). That the abolition of individual economy is inseparable from the abolition of the family is self-evident.

no matter under what conditions, in what manner, and to what end. It follows from this that a certain mode of production or industrial stage is always combined with a certain mode of co-operation, or social stage, and this mode of co-operation is itself a "productive force." Further, that the multitude of productive forces accessible to men determines the nature of society, hence that the "history of humanity" must always be studied and treated in relation to the history of industry and exchange. But it is also clear how in Germany it is impossible to write this sort of history, because the Germans lack not only the necessary power of comprehension and the material but also the "evidence of their senses," for across the Rhine you cannot have any experience of these things since history has stopped happening. Thus it is quite obvious from the start that there exists a materialistic connection of men with one another, which is determined by their needs and their mode of production and which is as old as men themselves. This connection is ever taking on new forms and thus presents a "history" independently of the existence of any political or religious nonsense which would hold men together on its own.

Only now, after having considered four moments, four aspects of the fundamental historical relationships, do we find that man also possesses "consciousness"; but, even so, not inherent, not "pure" consciousness. From the start the "spirit" is afflicted with the curse of being "burdened" with matter, which here makes its appearance in the form of agitated layers of air, sounds – in short, of language. Language is as old as consciousness; language is practical consciousness, as it exists for other men, and for that reason is really beginning to exist for me personally as well; for language, like consciousness, arises only from the need, the necessity, of intercourse with other men. Where there exists a relationship, it exists for me: the animal has no "relations" with anything, cannot have any. For the animal, its relation to others does not exist as a relation. Consciousness is therefore from the very beginning a social product and remains so as long as men exist at all. Consciousness is at first, of course, merely consciousness concerning the immediate sensuous environment and consciousness of the limited connection with other persons and things outside the individual who is growing self-conscious. At the same time it is consciousness of

nature, which first appears to men as a completely alien, all-powerful, and unassailable force, with which men's relations are purely animal and by which they are overawed like beasts; it is thus a purely animal consciousness of nature (natural religion).

We see here immediately: this natural religion or animal behavior toward nature is determined by the form of society and vice versa. Here, as everywhere, the identity of nature and man appears in such a way that the restricted relation of men to nature determines their restricted relation to one another, and their restricted relation to one another determines men's restricted relation to nature, just because nature is as yet hardly modified historically; and, on the other hand, man's consciousness of the necessity of associating with the individuals around him is the beginning of the consciousness that he is living in society at all. This beginning is as animal as social life itself at this stage. It is mere herd-consciousness, and at this point man is only distinguished from sheep by the fact that with him consciousness takes the place of instinct or that his instinct is a conscious one.

This sheeplike or tribal consciousness receives its further development and extension through increased productivity, the increase of needs, and, what is fundamental to both of these, the increase of population. With these there develops the division of labor, which was originally nothing but the division of labor in the sexual act, then that division of labor which develops spontaneously or "naturally" by virtue of natural predisposition (e.g., physical strength), needs, accidents, etc., etc. Division of labor becomes truly such only from the moment when a division of material and mental labor appears. From this moment onward consciousness *can* really flatter itself that it is something other than consciousness of existing practice, that it is *really* conceiving something without conceiving something *real*; from now on consciousness is in a position to emancipate itself from the world and to proceed to the formation of "pure" theory, theology, philosophy, ethics, etc. But even if this theory, theology, philosophy, ethics, etc., comes into contradiction with the existing relations, this can occur only as a result of the fact that existing social relations have come into contradiction with existing forces of production; this, moreover, can also occur in a particular national sphere of relations through the appearance of the contradiction, not within the national orbit, but between this national consciousness and the practice of other nations; i.e., between the national and the general consciousness of a nation.

Moreover, it is quite immaterial what consciousness starts to do on its own: out of all such muck we get only the one inference that these three moments, the forces of production, the state of society, and consciousness, can and must come into contradiction with one another, because the division of labor implies the possibility – nay, the fact – that intellectual and material activity – enjoyment and labor, production and consumption – devolve on different individuals and that the only possibility of their not coming into contradiction lies in the negation in its turn of the division of labor. It is self-evident, moreover, that "specters," "bonds," "the higher being," "concept," "scruple" are merely the idealistic, spiritual expression, the conception apparently of the isolated individual, the image of very empirical fetters and limitations, within which the mode of production of life and the form of intercourse coupled with it move.

With the division of labor, in which all these contradictions are implicit and which in its turn is based on the natural division of labor in the family and the separation of society into individual families opposed to one another, is given simultaneously the distribution, and indeed the unequal distribution (both quantitative and qualitative), of labor and its products, hence property: the nucleus, the first form, of which lies in the family, where wife and children are the slaves of the husband. This latent slavery in the family, though still very crude, is the first property, but even at this early stage it corresponds perfectly to the definition of modern economists who call it the power of disposing of the labor power of others. Division of labor and private property are, moreover, identical expressions: in the one the same thing is affirmed with reference to activity as is affirmed in the other with reference to the product of the activity.

Further, the division of labor implies the contradiction between the interest of the separate individual or the individual family and the communal interest of all individuals who have intercourse with one another. And indeed, this communal interest does not exist merely in the imagination, as "the general good," but first of all in reality, as the mutual interdependence of the individuals among whom the labor is divided. And finally, the division of labor offers us the first example of how, as long as man remains in natural society – that is, as long as a cleavage exists between the particular and the common interest – as long, therefore, as activity is not voluntarily but naturally divided, man's own deed becomes an alien power opposed to him, which enslaves him instead of being controlled by him. For as soon as labor is distributed, each man has a particular, exclusive sphere of activity which is forced upon him and from which he cannot escape. He is a hunter, a fisherman, a shepherd, or a critical critic, and must remain so if he does not want to lose his means of livelihood; while in communist society, where nobody has one exclusive sphere of activity but each can become accomplished in any branch he wishes, society regulates the general production and thus makes it possible for me to do one thing today and another tomorrow, to hunt in the morning, fish in the afternoon, rear cattle in the evening, criticize after dinner, just as I have a mind, without ever becoming hunter, fisherman, shepherd, or critic.

This crystallization of social activity, this consolidation of what we ourselves produce into an objective power above us, growing out of our control, thwarting our expectations, bringing to naught our calculations, is one of the chief factors in historical development up till now. And out of this very contradiction between the interest of the individual and that of the community the latter takes an independent form as the state, divorced from the real interests of individual and community, and at the same time as an illusory communal life, always based, however, on the real ties existing in every family and tribal conglomeration (such as flesh and blood, language, division of labor on a larger scale, and other interests) and especially, as we shall enlarge upon later, on the classes, already determined by the division of labor, which in every such mass of men separate out, and of which one dominates all the others. It follows from this that all struggles within the state, the struggle between democracy, aristocracy, and monarchy, the struggle for the franchise, etc., etc., are merely the illusory forms in which the real struggles of the different classes are fought out among one another (of this the German theoreticians have not the faintest inkling, although they have received a sufficient introduction to the subject in *The German-French Annals* and *The Holy Family*).

Further, it follows that every class which is struggling for mastery, even when its domination, as is the case with the proletariat, postulates the abolition of the old form of society in its entirety and of mastery itself, must first conquer for itself political power in order to represent its interest in turn as the general interest, a step to which in the first moment it is forced. Just because individuals seek *only* their particular interest, i.e., that not coinciding with their communal interest (for the "general good" is the illusory form of communal life), the latter will be imposed on them as an interest "alien" to them, and "independent" of them, as in its turn a particular, peculiar "general interest"; or they must meet face to face in this antagonism, as in democracy. On the other hand, too, the *practical* struggle of these particular interests, which constantly *really* run counter to the communal and illusory communal interests, makes *practical* intervention and control necessary through the illusory "general interest" in the form of the state. The social power, i.e., the multiplied productive force, which arises through the co-operation of different individuals as it is determined within the division of labor, appears to these individuals, since their co-operation is not voluntary but natural, not as their own united power, but as an alien force existing outside them, of the origin and end of which they are ignorant, which they thus cannot control, which, on the contrary, passes through a peculiar series of phases and stages independent of the will and the action of man, nay even being the prime governor of these.

This "estrangement" (to use a term which will be comprehensible to the philosophers) can, of course, be abolished given only two *practical* premises. For it to become an "intolerable" power, i.e., a power against which men make a revolution, it must necessarily have rendered the great mass of humanity "propertyless" and produced, at the same time, the contradiction of an existing world of wealth and culture, both of which conditions presuppose a great increase in productive power, a high degree of its development. And, on the other hand, this development of productive forces (which itself implies the actual empirical existence of men in their *world-historical,* instead of local, being) is absolutely necessary as a practical premise: first,

for the reason that without it only *want* is made general, and with want the struggle for necessities and all the old filthy business would necessarily be reproduced, and second, because only with this universal development of productive forces is a *universal* intercourse between men established which produces in all nations simultaneously the phenomenon of the "propertyless" mass (universal competition), makes each nation dependent on the revolutions of the others, and finally has put *world-historical,* empirically universal individuals in place of local ones. Without this, (1) communism could exist only as a local event, (2) the forces of intercourse themselves could not have developed as universal, hence intolerable powers – they would have remained home-bred superstitious conditions, and (3) each extension of intercourse would abolish local communism. Empirically communism is possible only as the act of the dominant peoples "all at once" or simultaneously, which presupposes the universal development of productive forces and the world intercourse bound up with them. How otherwise could property have had a history at all, have taken on different forms, and landed property, for instance, according to the different premises given, have proceeded in France from parcellation to centralization in the hands of a few, in England from centralization in the hands of a few to parcellation, as is actually the case today? Or how does it happen that trade, which after all is nothing more than the exchange of products of various individuals and countries, rules the whole world through the relation of supply and demand – a relation which, as an English economist says, hovers over the earth like the Fate of the ancients, and with invisible hand allots fortune and misfortune to men, sets up empires and overthrows empires, causes nations to rise and to disappear – while with the abolition of the basis of private property, with the communistic regulation of production (and, implicit in this, the destruction of the alien relation between men and what they themselves produce), the power of the relation of supply and demand is dissolved into nothing, and men get exchange, production, the mode of their mutual relation, under their own control again?

Communism is for us not a stable state which is to be established, an *ideal* to which reality will have to adjust itself. We call communism the *real* movement which abolishes the present state of things.

The conditions of this movement result from the premises now in existence. Besides, the world market is presupposed by the mass of propertyless workers – labor power cut off as a mass from capital or from even a limited satisfaction – and therefore no longer by the mere precariousness of labor, which, not giving an assured livelihood, is often lost through competition. The proletariat can thus exist only *world historically,* just as communism, its movement, can only have a "world-historical" existence. World-historical existence of individuals, i.e., existence of individuals which is directly linked up with world history....

Our conception of history depends on our ability to expound the real process of production, starting out from the simple material production of life, and to comprehend the form of intercourse connected with this and created by this (i.e., civil society in its various stages), as the basis of all history; further, to show it in its action as state, and so, from this starting point, to explain the whole mass of different theoretical products and forms of consciousness, religion, philosophy, ethics, etc., and trace their origins and growth, by which means, of course, the whole thing can be shown in its totality (and therefore, too, the reciprocal action of these various sides on one another). It has not, like the idealistic view of history, in every period to look for a category, but remains constantly on the real ground of history; it does not explain practice from the idea, but explains the formation of ideas from material practice, and accordingly it comes to the conclusion that all forms and products of consciousness cannot be dissolved by mental criticism, by resolution into "self-consciousness" or transformation into "apparitions," "specters," "fancies," etc., but only by the practical overthrow of the actual social relations which gave rise to this idealistic humbug; that not criticism but revolution is the driving force of history, also of religion, of philosophy, and all other types of theory. It shows that history does not end by being resolved into "self-consciousness" as "spirit of the spirit," but that in it at each stage there is found a material result: a sum of productive forces, a historically created relation of individuals to nature and to one another, which is handed down to each generation from its predecessor; a mass of productive forces, different forms of capital, and conditions, which, indeed, is modified by the new generation on the one hand, but also on the other prescribes for it its conditions

of life and gives it a definite development, a special character. It shows that circumstances make men just as much as men make circumstances.

This sum of productive forces, forms of capital, and social forms of intercourse, which every individual and generation finds in existence as something given, is the real basis of what the philosophers have conceived as "substance" and "essence of man," and what they have deified and attacked: a real basis which is not in the least disturbed, in its effect and influence on the development of men, by the fact that these philosophers revolt against it as "self-consciousness" and "the unique." These conditions of life, which different generations find in existence, decide also whether or not the periodically recurring revolutionary convulsion will be strong enough to overthrow the basis of all existing forms. And if these material elements of a complete revolution are not present (namely, on the one hand the existence of productive forces, on the other the formation of a revolutionary mass, which revolts not only against separate conditions of society up till then, but against the very "production of life" till then, the "total activity" on which it was based), then, as far as practical development is concerned, it is absolutely immaterial whether the "idea" of this revolution has been expressed a hundred times already, as the history of communism proves.

Bibliography

Berlin, Isaiah. *Karl Marx.* 4th ed. Oxford and New York: Oxford University Press, 1978.

Bottomore, Tom, ed. *A Dictionary of Marxist Thought.* Cambridge, Mass.: Harvard University Press, 1978.

Cohen, G.A. *Karl Marx's Theory of History.* Princeton, N.J.: Princeton University Press, 1978.

Miller, Richard W. *Analyzing Marx.* Princeton, N.J.: Princeton University Press, 1984.

Plamenatz, John. *Karl Marx's Philosophy of Man.* Oxford: Clarendon Press, 1975.

Singer, Peter. *Marx.* Oxford and New York: Oxford University Press, 1980.

Tucker, Robert. *Philosophy and Myth in Karl Marx.* Cambridge: Cambridge University Press, 1961.

Ware, Robert, and Kai Nielsen, eds. *Analyzing Marxism.* Calgary: University of Calgary Press, 1989.

CHAPTER TWENTY-EIGHT — FRIEDRICH NIETZSCHE

Friedrich Nietzsche (1844-1900) was the son of a German Lutheran pastor. He became a classical philologist – a professor of Greek and Latin – then, due to ill-health, left academic life for a career as a writer. After an extended series of books, Nietzsche suffered a total mental collapse in 1889, and spent the remainder of his life institutionalized.

Nietzsche's work, as will be seen in the selection that follows, is highly personal, not systematically or theoretically structured, emotive, aphoristic, and moralistic. Nietzsche writes above all as a commentator on European civilization. He is a severe critic of much of the nineteenth-century world he was part of, and offers insight into what he sees as spiritual malady.

Nietzsche was and remains controversial. He was a vehement opponent of Christianity and of democracy, celebrating creative individualism and the drive of the self-directed masterful hero-artist. Scattered remarks in his writings, which may or may not constitute facets of a single underlying conception of human reality, lent themselves to various currents in social, cultural, and political life over the course of the twentieth century – among them fascism.

There seems little doubt that Nietzsche was a Lamarckian – a believer that acquired characteristics, e.g., practices or habits of a few or several generations, can be hereditarily transmitted, and a "social Darwinist" – a believer in the tonic value for individuals and peoples of aggressive competitive struggle. Nietzsche was certainly an inegalitarian, factually and normatively, and his inegalitarianism extended to the sexes: the male for him was and ought to be ruler of the female. On the other hand, Nietzsche was an anti-nationalist, and was opposed to the growing anti-Semitism of his society.

His view of human nature is distinctive; his ideas and his writings continue to attract many readers. Like Plato, Nietzsche is a remarkably astute literary psychologist.

Fredrich Nietzsche, *On the Genealogy of Morals*

(Source: Friedrich Nietzsche. *On the Genealogy of Morals* and *Ecce Homo*. Ed. Walter Kaufmann. Trans. Walter Kaufmann & R. J. Hollingdale. New York: Random House, 1967, 36-39, 120-125.)

10

The slave revolt in morality begins when *ressentiment*[1] itself becomes creative and gives birth to values: the *ressentiment* of natures that are denied the true reaction, that of deeds, and compensate themselves with an imaginary revenge. While every noble morality develops from a triumphant affirmation of itself, slave morality from the outset says No to what is "outside," what is "different," what is "not itself"; and *this* No is its creative deed. This inversion of the value-positing eye – this *need* to direct one's view outward instead of back to oneself – is of the essence of *ressentiment*: in order to exist, slave morality always first needs a hostile external world; it needs, physiologically speaking, external stimuli in order to act at all – its action is fundamentally reaction.

The reverse is the case with the noble mode of valuation: it acts and grows spontaneously, it seeks its opposite only so as to affirm itself more

---

1   Resentment.

gratefully and triumphantly – its negative concept "low," "common," "bad" is only a subsequently-invented pale, contrasting image in relation to its positive basic concept – filled with life and passion through and through – "we noble ones, we good, beautiful, happy ones!" When the noble mode of valuation blunders and sins against reality, it does so in respect to the sphere with which it is *not* sufficiently familiar, against a real knowledge of which it has indeed inflexibly guarded itself: in some circumstances it misunderstands the sphere it despises, that of the common man, of the lower orders; on the other hand, one should remember that, even supposing that the affect of contempt, of looking down from a superior height, *falsifies* the image of that which it despises, it will at any rate still be a much less serious falsification than that perpetrated on its opponent – *in effigie* of course – by the submerged hatred, the vengefulness of the impotent. There is indeed too much carelessness, too much taking lightly, too much looking away and impatience involved in contempt, even too much joyfulness, for it to be able to transform its object into a real caricature and monster.

One should not overlook the almost benevolent nuances that the Greek nobility, for example, bestows on all the words it employs to distinguish the lower orders from itself; how they are continuously mingled and sweetened with a kind of pity, consideration, and forbearance, so that finally almost all the words referring to the common man have remained as expressions signifying "unhappy," "pitiable" (compare *deilos*,[2] *deilaios*,[3] *poneros*,[4] *mochtheros*,[5] the last two of which properly designate the common man as work-slave and beast of burden) – and how on the other hand "bad," "low," "unhappy" have never ceased to sound to the Greek ear as one note with a tone-color in which "unhap-py" preponderates: this as an inheritance from the ancient nobler aristocratic mode of evaluation, which does not belie itself even in its contempt (philologists should recall the sense in which *oïzyros*,[6] *anolbos*,[7] *tlēmon*,[8] *dystychein*,[9] *xymphora*[10] are employed). The "well-born" *felt* themselves to be the "happy"; they did not have to establish their happiness artificially by examining their enemies, or to persuade themselves, *deceive* themselves, that they were happy (as all men of *ressentiment* are in the habit of doing); and they likewise knew, as rounded men replete with energy and therefore *necessarily* active, that happiness should not be sundered from action – being active was with them necessarily a part of happiness (whence *eu prattein*[11] takes its origin) – all very much the opposite of "happiness" at the level of the impotent, the oppressed, and those in whom poisonous and inimical feelings are festering, with whom it appears as essentially narcotic, drug, rest, peace, "sabbath," slackening of tension and relaxing of limbs, in short *passively*.

While the noble man lives in trust and openness with himself (*gennaios*[12] "of noble descent" underlines the nuance "upright" and probably also "naïve"), the man of *ressentiment* is neither upright nor naïve nor honest and straightforward with himself. His soul *squints*; his spirit loves hiding places, secret paths and back doors, everything covert entices him as *his* world, *his* security, *his* refreshment; he understands how to keep silent, how not to forget, how to wait, how to be provisionally self-deprecating and humble. A race of such men of *ressentiment* is bound to become eventually *cleverer* than any noble race; it will also honor cleverness to a far greater degree: namely, as a condition of existence of the first importance; while with noble men cleverness can easily acquire

---

2 All of the footnoted words in this section are Greek. The first four mean *wretched*, but each has a separate note to suggest some of its other connotations. *Deilos*: cowardly, worthless, vile.
3 Paltry.
4 Oppressed by toils, good for nothing, worthless, knavish, base, cowardly.
5 Suffering hardship, knavish.
6 Woeful, miserable, toilsome; wretch.
7 Unblest, wretched, luckless, poor.
8 Wretched, miserable.
9 To be unlucky, unfortunate.
10 Misfortune.
11 To do well in the sense of faring well.
12 High-born, noble, high-minded.

a subtle flavor of luxury and subtlety – for here it is far less essential than the perfect functioning of the regulating *unconscious* instincts or even than a certain imprudence, perhaps a bold recklessness whether in the face of danger or of the enemy, or that enthusiastic impulsiveness in anger, love, reverence, gratitude, and revenge by which noble souls have at all times recognized one another. *Ressentiment* itself, if it should appear in the noble man, consummates and exhausts itself in an immediate reaction, and therefore does not *poison*: on the other hand, it fails to appear at all on countless occasions on which it inevitably appears in the weak and impotent.

To be incapable of taking one's enemies, one's accidents, even one's misdeeds seriously for very long – that is the sign of strong full natures in whom there is an excess of the power to form, to mold, to recuperate and to forget (a good example of this in modern times is Mirabeau,[13] who had no memory for insults and vile actions done to him and was unable to forgive simply because he forgot). Such a man shakes off with a *single* shrug much vermin that eats deep into others; here alone genuine "love of one's enemies" is possible – supposing it to be possible at all on earth. How much reverence has a noble man for his enemies! – and such reverence is a bridge to love. For he desires his enemy for himself, as his mark of distinction; he can endure no other enemy than one in whom there is nothing to despise and *very much* to honor! In contrast to this, picture "the enemy" as the man of *ressentiment* conceives him – and here precisely is his deed, his creation: he has conceived "the evil enemy," "*the Evil One*," and this in fact is his basic concept, from which he then evolves, as an afterthought and pendant, a "good one" – himself!

....

13

... It will be immediately obvious that such a self-contradiction as the ascetic appears to represent, "life *against* life," is, physiologically considered and not merely psychologically, a simple absurdity.

It can only be *apparent*; it must be a kind of provisional formulation, an interpretation and psychological misunderstanding of something whose real nature could not for a long time be understood or described *as it really was* – a mere word inserted into an old *gap* in human knowledge. Let us replace it with a brief formulation of the facts of the matter: *the ascetic ideal springs from the protective instinct of a degenerating life* which tries by all means to sustain itself and to fight for its existence; it indicates a partial physiological obstruction and exhaustion against which the deepest instincts of life, which have remained intact, continually struggle with new expedients and devices. The ascetic ideal is such an expedient; the case is therefore the opposite of what those who reverence this ideal believe: life wrestles in it and through it with death and *against* death; the ascetic ideal is an artifice for the *preservation* of life.

That this ideal acquired such power and ruled over men as imperiously as we find in history, especially wherever the civilization and taming of man has been carried through, expresses a great fact: the *sickliness* of the type of man we have had hitherto, or at least of the tamed man, and the physiological struggle of man against death (more precisely: against disgust with life, against exhaustion, against the desire for the "end"). The ascetic priest is the incarnate desire to be different, to be in a different place, and indeed this desire at its greatest extreme, its distinctive fervor and passion; but precisely this power of his desire is the chain that holds him captive so that he becomes a tool for the creation of more favourable conditions for being here and being man – it is precisely this *power* that enables him to persuade to existence the whole herd of the ill-constituted, disgruntled, underprivileged, unfortunate, and all who suffer of themselves, by instinctively going before them as their shepherd. You will see my point: this ascetic priest, this apparent enemy of life, this *denier* – precisely he is among the greatest *conserving* and yes-creating[14] forces of life.

Where does it come from, this sickliness? For man

---

13   Honoré Gabriel Riqueti, Comte de Mirabeau (1749-1791), was a celebrated French Revolutionary statesman and writer.

14   *Dieser Verneinende ... und Ja-schaffende:* cf. Goethe, *Faust*, lines 1335 ff., where Mephistopheles calls himself: "The spirit that negates [*verneint*]" and "part of that force which would / Do evil evermore, and yet creates the good." In the next paragraph, the portrait of "the great experimenter" brings to mind Goethe's Faust.

is more sick, uncertain, changeable, indeterminate than any other animal, there is no doubt of that – he is the *sick* animal: how has that come about? Certainly he has dared more, done more new things, braved more and challenged fate more than all the other animals put together: he, the great experimenter with himself, discontented and insatiable, wrestling with animals, nature, and gods for ultimate dominion – he, still unvanquished, eternally directed toward the future, whose own restless energies never leave him in peace, so that his future digs like a spur into the flesh of every present – how should such a courageous and richly endowed animal not also be the most imperiled, the most chronically and profoundly sick of all sick animals?

Man has often had enough: there are actual epidemics of having had enough (as around 1348, at the time of the dance of death); but even this nausea, this weariness, this disgust with himself – all this bursts from him with such violence that it at once becomes a new fetter. The No he says to life brings to light, as if by magic, an abundance of tender Yeses; even when he *wounds* himself, this master of destruction, of self-destruction – the very wound itself afterward compels him to *live*.

14

The more normal sickliness becomes among men – and we cannot deny its normality – the higher should be the honor accorded the rare cases of great power of soul and body, man's *lucky hits*; the more we should protect the well-constituted from the worst kind of air, the air of the sickroom. Is this done?

The sick represent the greatest danger for the healthy; it is *not* the strongest but the weakest who spell disaster for the strong. Is this known?

Broadly speaking, it is not fear of man that we should desire to see diminished; for this fear compels the strong to be strong, and occasionally terrible – it *maintains* the well-constituted type of man. What is to be feared, what has a more calamitous effect than any other calamity, is that man should inspire not profound fear but profound *nausea*; also not great fear but great *pity*. Suppose these two were one day to unite, they would inevitably beget one of the uncanniest monsters: the "last will" of

man, his will to nothingness, nihilism. And indeed a great deal points to this union. Whoever can smell not only with his nose but also with his eyes and ears, scents almost everywhere he goes today something like the air of madhouses and hospitals – I am speaking, of course, of the cultural domain, of every kind of "Europe" on this earth. The *sick* are man's greatest danger; *not* the evil, *not* the "beasts of prey." Those who are failures from the start, downtrodden, crushed – it is they, the *weakest,* who must undermine life among men, who call into question and poison most dangerously our trust in life, in man, and in ourselves. Where does one not encounter that veiled glance which burdens one with a profound sadness, that inward-turned glance of the born failure which betrays how such a man speaks to himself – that glance which is a sigh! "If only I were someone else," sighs the glance: "but there is no hope of that. I am who I am: how could I ever get free of myself? And yet – I *am sick of myself!*"

It is on such soil, on swampy ground, that every weed, every poisonous plant grows, always so small, so hidden, so false, so saccharine. Here the worms of vengefulness and rancor swarm; here the air stinks of secrets and concealment; here the web of the most malicious of all conspiracies is being spun constantly – the conspiracy of the suffering against the well-constituted and victorious, here the aspect of the victorious is *hated*. And what mendaciousness is employed to disguise that this hatred is hatred! What a display of grand words and postures, what an art of "honest" calumny! These failures: what noble eloquence flows from their lips! How much sugary, slimy, humble, submissiveness swims in their eyes! What do they really want? At least to *represent* justice, love, wisdom, superiority – that is the ambition of the "lowest," the sick. And how skillful such an ambition makes them! Admire above all the forger's skill with which the stamp of virtue, even the ring, the golden-sounding ring of virtue, is here counterfeited. They monopolize virtue, these weak, hopelessly sick people, there is no doubt of it: "we alone are the good and just," they say "we alone are *homines bonae voluntatis*."[15] They walk among us as embodied reproaches, as warnings to us – as if health, well-constitutedness, strength, pride, and

---

15   Men of good will.

the sense of power were in themselves necessarily vicious things for which one must pay some day, and pay bitterly: how ready they themselves are at bottom to *make* one pay; how they crave to be *hangmen*. There is among them an abundance of the vengeful disguised as judges, who constantly bear the word "justice" in their mouths like poisonous spittle, always with pursed lips, always ready to spit upon all who are not discontented but go their way in good spirits. Nor is there lacking among them that most disgusting species of the vain, the mendacious failures whose aim is to appear as "beautiful souls" and who bring to market their deformed sensuality, wrapped up in verses and other swaddling clothes, as "purity of heart": the species of moral masturbators and "self-gratifiers." The will of the weak to represent *some* form of superiority, their instinct for devious paths to tyranny over the healthy – where can it not be discovered, this will to power of the weakest!

The sick woman especially: no one can excel her in the wiles to dominate, oppress, and tyrannize. The sick woman spares nothing, living or dead; she will dig up the most deeply buried things (the Bogos say: "woman is a hyena").

Examine the background of every family, every organization, every commonwealth: everywhere the struggle of the sick against the healthy – a silent struggle as a rule, with petty poisons, with pinpricks, with sly long-suffering expressions, but occasionally also with that invalid's Phariseeism of *loud* gestures that likes best to pose as "noble indignation." This hoarse, indignant barking of sick dogs, this rabid mendaciousness and rage of "noble" Pharisees, penetrates even the hallowed halls of science (I again remind readers who have ears for such things of that Berlin apostle of revenge, Eugen Dühring, who employs moral mumbo-jumbo more indecently and repulsively than anyone else in Germany today: Dühring, the foremost moral bigmouth today – unexcelled even among his own ilk, the anti-Semites).

They are all men of *ressentiment*, physiologically unfortunate and worm-eaten, a whole tremulous realm of subterranean revenge, inexhaustible and insatiable in outbursts against the fortunate and happy[16] and in masquerades of revenge and pretexts for revenge: when would they achieve the ultimate, subtlest, sublimest triumph of revenge? Undoubtedly if they succeeded in *poisoning the consciences* of the fortunate with their own misery, with all misery, so that one day the fortunate began to be ashamed of their good fortune and perhaps said one to another: "it is disgraceful to be fortunate: *there is too much misery!*"

But no greater or more calamitous misunderstanding is possible than for the happy, well-constituted, powerful in soul and body, to begin to doubt their *right to happiness* in this fashion. Away with this "inverted world"! Away with this shameful emasculation of feeling! That the sick should *not* make the healthy sick – and this is what such an emasculation would involve – should surely be our supreme concern on earth; but this requires above all that the healthy should be *segregated* from the sick, guarded even from the sight of the sick, that they may not confound themselves with the sick. Or is it their task, perhaps, to be nurses or physicians?[17]

But no worse misunderstanding and denial of *their* task can be imagined: the higher *ought* not to degrade itself to the status of an instrument of the lower, the pathos of distance *ought* to keep their tasks eternally separate! Their right to exist, the privilege of the full-toned bell over the false and cracked, is a thousand times greater: they alone are our *warranty* for the future, they alone are *liable* for the future of man. The sick can never have the ability or obligation to do what *they* can do, what *they* ought to do: but if they are to be able to do what *they* alone ought to do, how can they at the same time be physicians, consolers, and "saviors" of the sick?

And therefore let us have fresh air! fresh air! and keep clear of the madhouses and hospitals of culture! And therefore let us have good company, *our* company! Or solitude, if it must be! But away from the sickening fumes of inner corruption and the

16 "Fortunate and happy": *die Glücklichen*. In the next sentence the word is rendered "the fortunate," and *Glück* as "good fortune"; but in the next paragraph "happy" and "happiness" have been used, as Nietzsche evidently means both.

17 Cf. Goethe's letter to Frau von Stein, June 8, 1787: "Also, I must say myself, I think it true that humanity will triumph eventually, only I fear that at the same time the world will become a large hospital and each will become the other's human nurse." In a letter to Rée, April 17, 1877, Nietzsche writes, "each the other's 'humane nurse'.".

hidden rot of disease! ... So that we may, at least for a while yet, guard ourselves, my friends, against the two worst contagions that may be reserved just for us – against the *great nausea at man!* against *great pity for man!*[18]

Bibliography

Kaufmann, Walter. *Nietzsche: Philosopher, Psychologist, Antichrist.* Princeton: Princeton University Press, 1950.

Nahamas, Alexander. *Nietzsche: Life as Literature.* Cambridge, Mass.: Harvard University Press, 1985.

Patton, Paul, ed. *Nietzsche, Feminism and Political Theory.* London and New York: Routledge, 1993.

Schacht, Richard. *Nietzsche.* London and New York: Routledge, 1983.

Solomon, Robert, ed. *Nietzsche: A Collection of Critical Essays.* New York: Anchor Books, 1973.

Young, Julian. *Nietzsche's Philosophy of Art.* Cambridge: Cambridge University Press, 1992.

---

18   The dangers of the great nausea and the great pity are among the central motifs of *Thus Spoke Zarathustra*. The theme of nausea is introduced in the chapter "On the Rabble" in Part Two and is encountered again and again in later chapters. Another chapter in Part Two bears the title "On the Pitying," and the whole of Part Four, which bears a motto from that chapter, is cast in the form of a story: having overcome his nausea at the end of Part Three, Zarathustra's final temptation is pity.

VI

BIOLOGICAL THEORIES

CHAPTER TWENTY-NINE — CHARLES DARWIN

Charles Darwin (1809-1882) is by general consent the greatest creative biologist of modern times, perhaps of all times, and since he had a variety of things to say about human nature, for this reason alone it is appropriate that he is represented in this volume. In fact, the significance of Darwin's work directly or indirectly connected to conceptions of human identity in and since the nineteenth century is still greater than this. As well as having developed his own original and distinctive views about humans, Darwin is claimed as the guiding thinker for several subsequent theories, some of which go in very different, indeed incompatible directions. Accordingly, in assessing claimants to the mantle of continuity with Darwin's ground-breaking work, it is good to have the explicit record of Darwin's text at hand.

The chief Darwinian text for human nature theory is *The Descent of Man* (1871), from which the selections that follow are drawn. This is Darwin's second major book on evolutionary theory; the first is of course *The Origin of Species* (1859).

More than some other thinkers encountered in this book, Darwin is well left to speak in his own voice. As well as being a brilliant scientist Darwin is a fine Victorian English writer. It is to be noted that he developed his views wholly independently of the formation of genetic theory. Twentieth-century evolutionary theory is a kind of union of Darwin's work, and its subsequent modifications, with genetics. The pioneer of the latter science was Gregor Mendel (1822-1884), an Austrian priest and botanist. Darwin knew nothing of Mendel's work, and it is clear that the British scientist thinks always of the individual animal or plant as the unit of evolutionary significance.

It may seem at first odd to find, as the reader will, so much of the selection that follows, intended to set out Darwin's view of human beings, devoted to the behaviour of *other* species of animals. Its point, as will be seen, is that Darwin is seeking to establish how few of the characteristics usually heralded as uniquely human aren't also found in one form or degree or other among the other animals. Even the one major trait that Darwin does view as the hallmark of the human – morality – he accounts for in terms of capacities of sympathetic projection (as do Hume, Schopenhauer, and other philosophers), which itself has analogs in other animals' behaviour.

Charles Darwin, *The Descent of Man*

(Source: Charles Darwin. *The Descent of Man and Selection in Relation to Sex*. Vol. I. London: John Murray, 1871, 34-106, 158-167.)

CHAPTER II.
COMPARISON OF THE MENTAL POWERS OF MAN AND THE LOWER ANIMALS.

The difference in mental power between the highest ape and the lowest savage, immense – Certain instincts in common – The emotions – Curiosity – Imitation – Attention – Memory – Imagination –

Reason – Progressive improvement – Tools and weapons used by animals – Language – Self-consciousness – Sense of beauty – Belief in God, spiritual agencies, superstitions.

We have seen in the last chapter that man bears in his bodily structure clear traces of his descent from some lower form; but it may be urged that, as man differs so greatly in his mental power from all other animals, there must be some error in this conclusion. No doubt the difference in this respect is enormous, even if we compare the mind of one of the lowest savages, who has no words to express any number higher than four, and who uses no abstract terms for the commonest objects or affections,[1] with that of the most highly organised ape. The difference would, no doubt, still remain immense, even if one of the higher apes had been improved or civilised as much as a dog has been in comparison with its parent-form, the wolf or jackal. The Fuegians rank amongst the lowest barbarians; but I was continually struck with surprise how closely the three natives on board H.M.S. "Beagle," who had lived some years in England and could talk a little English, resembled us in disposition and in most of our mental faculties. If no organic being excepting man had possessed any mental power, or if his powers had been of a wholly different nature from those of the lower animals, then we should never have been able to convince ourselves that our high faculties had been gradually developed. But it can be clearly shewn that there is no fundamental difference of this kind. We must also admit that there is a much wider interval in mental power between one of the lowest fishes, as a lamprey or lancelet, and one of the higher apes, than between an ape and man; yet this immense interval is filled up by numberless gradations.

Nor is the difference slight in moral disposition between a barbarian, such as the man described by the old navigator Byron, who dashed his child on the rocks for dropping a basket of sea-urchins, and a Howard or Clarkson; and in intellect, between a savage who does not use any abstract terms, and a Newton or Shakspeare. Differences of this kind between the highest men of the highest races and the lowest savages, are connected by the finest gradations. Therefore it is possible that they might pass and be developed into each other.

My object in this chapter is solely to shew that there is no fundamental difference between man and the higher mammals in their mental faculties.... The variability of the faculties in the individuals of the same species is an important point for us, and some few illustrations will here be given. But it would be superfluous to enter into many details on this head, for I have found on frequent enquiry, that it is the unanimous opinion of all those who have long attended to animals of many kinds, including birds, that the individuals differ greatly in every mental characteristic. In what manner the mental powers were first developed in the lowest organisms, is as hopeless an enquiry as how life first originated. These are problems for the distant future, if they are ever to be solved by man.

As man possesses the same senses with the lower animals, his fundamental intuitions must be the same. Man has also some few instincts in common, as that of self-preservation, sexual love, the love of the mother for her new-born offspring, the power possessed by the latter of sucking, and so forth. But man, perhaps, has somewhat fewer instincts than those possessed by the animals which come next to him in the series. The orang in the Eastern islands, and the chimpanzee in Africa, build platforms on which they sleep; and, as both species follow the same habit, it might be argued that this was due to instinct, but we cannot feel sure that it is not the result of both animals having similar wants and possessing similar powers of reasoning. These apes, as we may assume, avoid the many poisonous fruits of the tropics, and man has no such knowledge; but as our domestic animals, when taken to foreign lands and when first turned out in the spring, often eat poisonous herbs, which they afterwards avoid, we cannot feel sure that the apes do not learn from their own experience or from that of their parents what fruits to select. It is however certain, as we shall presently see, that apes have an instinctive dread of serpents, and probably of other dangerous animals.

The fewness and the comparative simplicity of the instincts in the higher animals are remarkable in contrast with those of the lower animals. Cuvier

---

1   See the evidence on these points, as given by Lubbock, 'Prehistoric Times,' p. 354, &c.

maintained that instinct and intelligence stand in an inverse ratio to each other; and some have thought that the intellectual faculties of the higher animals have been gradually developed from their instincts. But Pouchet in an interesting essay,[2] has shewn that no such inverse ratio really exists. Those insects which possess the most wonderful instincts are certainly the most intelligent. In the vertebrate series, the least intelligent members, namely fishes and amphibians, do not possess complex instincts; and amongst mammals the animal most remarkable for its instincts, namely the beaver, is highly intelligent, as will be admitted by every one who has read Mr. Morgan's excellent account of this animal.[3]

Although the first dawnings of intelligence, according to Mr. Herbert Spencer,[4] have been developed through the multiplication and co-ordination of reflex actions, and although many of the simpler instincts graduate into actions of this kind and can hardly be distinguished from them, as in the case of young animals sucking, yet the more complex instincts seem to have originated independently of intelligence. I am, however, far from wishing to deny that instinctive actions may lose their fixed and untaught character, and be replaced by others performed by the aid of the free will. On the other hand, some intelligent actions – as when birds on oceanic islands first learn to avoid man – after being performed during many generations, become converted into instincts and are inherited. They may then be said to be degraded in character, for they are no longer performed through reason or from experience. But the greater number of the more complex instincts appear to have been gained in a wholly different manner, through the natural selection of variations of simpler instinctive actions. Such variations appear to arise from the same unknown causes acting on the cerebral organisation, which induce slight variations or individual differences in other parts of the body; and these variations, owing to our ignorance, are often said to arise spontaneously. We can, I think, come to no other conclusion with respect to the origin of the more complex instincts, when we reflect on the marvellous instincts of sterile worker-ants and bees, which leave no offspring to inherit the effects of experience and of modified habits.

Although a high degree of intelligence is certainly compatible with the existence of complex instincts, as we see in the insects just named and in the beaver, it is not improbable that they may to a certain extent interfere with each other's development. Little is known about the functions of the brain, but we can perceive that as the intellectual powers become highly developed, the various parts of the brain must be connected by the most intricate channels of intercommunication; and as a consequence each separate part would perhaps tend to become less well fitted to answer in a definite and uniform, that is instinctive, manner to particular sensations or associations.

I have thought this digression worth giving, because we may easily underrate the mental powers of the higher animals, and especially of man, when we compare their actions founded on the memory of past events. on foresight, reason, and imagination, with exactly similar actions instinctively performed by the lower animals; in this latter case the capacity of performing such actions having been gained, step by step, through the variability of the mental organs and natural selection, without any conscious intelligence on the part of the animal during each successive generation. No doubt, as Mr. Wallace has argued,[5] much of the intelligent work done by man is due to imitation and not to reason; but there is this great difference between his actions and many of those performed by the lower animals, namely, that man cannot, on his first trial, make, for instance, a stone hatchet or a canoe, through his power of imitation. He has to learn his work by practice; a beaver, on the other hand, can make its dam or canal, and a bird its nest, as well, or nearly as well, the first time it tries, as when old and experienced.

To return to our immediate subject: the lower animals, like man, manifestly feel pleasure and pain, happiness and misery. Happiness is never better

---

2   'L'Instinct chez les Insectes. Revue des Deux Mondes,' Feb. 1870, p. 690.
3   'The American Beaver and his Works,' 1868.
4   'The Principles of Psychology,' 2nd edit. 1870, pp. 418-443.
5   'Contributions to the Theory of Natural Selection,' 1870, p. 212.

exhibited than by young animals, such as puppies, kittens, lambs, &c., when playing together, like our own children. Even insects play together, as has been described by that excellent observer, P. Huber,[6] who saw ants chasing and pretending to bite each other, like so many puppies.

The fact that the lower animals are excited by the same emotions as ourselves is so well established, that it will not be necessary to weary the reader by many details. Terror acts in the same manner on them as on us, causing the muscles to tremble, the heart to palpitate, the sphincters to be relaxed, and the hair to stand on end. Suspicion, the offspring of fear, is eminently characteristic of most wild animals. Courage and timidity are extremely variable qualities in the individuals of the same species, as is plainly seen in our dogs. Some dogs and horses are ill-tempered and easily turn sulky; others are good-tempered; and these qualities are certainly inherited. Every one knows how liable animals are to furious rage, and how plainly they show it. Many anecdotes, probably true, have been published on the long-delayed and artful revenge of various animals. The accurate Rengger and Brehm[7] state that the American and African monkeys which they kept tame, certainly revenged themselves. The love of a dog for his master is notorious; in the agony of death he has been known to caress his master, and every one has heard of the dog suffering under vivisection, who licked the hand of the operator; this man, unless he had a heart of stone, must have felt remorse to the last hour of his life. As Whewell[8] has remarked, "who that reads the touching instances of maternal affection, related so often of the women of all nations, and of the females of all animals, can doubt that the principle of action is the same in the two cases?"

We see maternal affection exhibited in the most trifling details; thus Rengger observed an American monkey (a Cebus) carefully driving away the flies which plagued her infant; and Duvaucel saw a Hylobates washing the faces of her young ones in a stream. So intense is the grief of female monkeys for the loss of their young, that it invariably caused the death of certain kinds kept under confinement by Brehm in N. Africa. Orphan-monkeys were always adopted and carefully guarded by the other monkeys, both males and females. One female baboon had so capacious a heart that she not only adopted young monkeys of other species, but stole young dogs and cats, which she continually carried about. Her kindness, however, did not go so far as to share her food with her adopted offspring, at which Brehm was surprised, as his monkeys always divided everything quite fairly with their own young ones.... Some of Brehm's monkeys took much delight in teasing, in various ingenious ways, a certain old dog whom they disliked, as well as other animals.

Most of the more complex emotions are common to the higher animals and ourselves. Every one has seen how jealous a dog is of his master's affection, if lavished on any other creature; and I have observed the same fact with monkeys. This shews that animals not only love, but have the desire to be loved. Animals manifestly feel emulation. They love approbation or praise; and a dog carrying a basket for his master exhibits in a high degree self-complacency or pride. There can, I think, be no doubt that a dog feels shame, as distinct from fear, and something very like modesty when begging too often for food. A great dog scorns the snarling of a little dog, and this may be called magnanimity. Several observers have stated that monkeys certainly dislike being laughed at; and they sometimes invent imaginary offences. In the Zoological Gardens I saw a baboon who always got into a furious rage when his keeper took out a letter or book and read it aloud to him; and his rage was so violent that, as I witnessed on one occasion, he bit his own leg till the blood flowed.

We will now turn to the more intellectual emotions and faculties, which are very important, as forming the basis for the development of the higher mental powers. Animals manifestly enjoy excitement and suffer from ennui, as may be seen with dogs, and, according to Rengger, with monkeys. All animals feel Wonder, and many exhibit Curiosity.

---

6   'Recherches sur les Moeurs des Fourmis.' 1810, p. 173.

7   All the following statements, given on the authority of these two naturalists, are taken from Rengger's 'Naturges der Saugethiere von Paraguay,' 1830, s. 41-57, and from Brehm's 'Thierleben,' B i. s.10-87.

8   'Bridgewater Treatise,' p. 263.

They sometimes suffer from this latter quality, as when the hunter plays antics and thus attracts them; I have witnessed this with deer, and so it is with the wary chamois, and with some kinds of wild-ducks. Brehm gives a curious account of the instinctive dread which his monkeys exhibited towards snakes; but their curiosity was so great that they could not desist from occasionally satiating their horror in a most human fashion, by lifting up the lid of the box in which the snakes were kept...

The principle of *Imitation* is strong in man, and especially in man in a barbarous state. Desor[9] has remarked that no animal voluntarily imitates an action performed by man, until in the ascending scale we come to monkeys, which are well-known to be ridiculous mockers. Animals, however, sometimes imitate each others' actions: thus two species of wolves, which had been reared by dogs, learned to bark, as does sometimes the jackal,[10] but whether this can be called voluntary imitation is another question. From one account which I have read, there is reason to believe that puppies nursed by cats sometimes learn to lick their feet and thus to clean their faces: it is at least certain, as I hear from a perfectly trustworthy friend, that some dogs behave in this manner. Birds imitate the songs of their parents, and sometimes those of other birds; and parrots are notorious imitators of any sound which they often hear.

Hardly any faculty is more important for the intellectual progress of man than the power of *Attention*. Animals clearly manifest this power, as when a cat watches by a hole and prepares to spring on its prey. Wild animals sometimes become so absorbed when thus engaged, that they may be easily approached...

It is almost superfluous to state that animals have excellent *Memories* for persons and places. A baboon at the Cape of Good Hope, as I have been informed by Sir Andrew Smith, recognised him with joy after an absence of nine months. I had a dog who was savage and averse to all strangers, and I purposely tried his memory after an absence of five years and two days. I went near the stable where he lived, and shouted to him in my old manner; he showed no joy, but instantly followed me out walking and obeyed me, exactly as if I had parted with him only half-an-hour before. A train of old associations, dormant during five years, had thus been instantaneously awakened in his mind...

The *Imagination,* is one of the highest prerogatives of man. By this faculty he unites, independently of the will, former images and ideas, and thus creates brilliant and novel results. A poet, as Jean Paul Richter remarks,[11] "who must reflect whether he shall make a character say yes or no – to the devil with him; he is only a stupid corpse." Dreaming gives us the best notion of this power; as Jean Paul again says, "The dream is an involuntary art of poetry." The value of the products of our imagination depends of course on the number, accuracy, and clearness of our impressions; on our judgment and taste in selecting or rejecting the involuntary combinations, and to a certain extent on our power of voluntarily combining them. As dogs, cats, horses, and probably all the higher animals, even birds, as is stated on good authority,[12] have vivid dreams, and this is shewn by their movements and voice, we must admit that they possess some power of imagination.

Of all the faculties of the human mind, it will, I presume, be admitted that *Reason* stands at the summit. Few persons any longer dispute that animals possess some power of reasoning. Animals may constantly be seen to pause, deliberate, and resolve. It is a significant fact, that the more the habits of any particular animal are studied by a naturalist, the more he attributes to reason and the less to unlearnt instincts.[13] In future chapters we shall see that some animals extremely low in the scale apparently display a certain amount of reason. No doubt it is often difficult to distinguish between the power of reason and that of instinct...

So many facts have been recorded in various

---

9 Quoted by Vogt, 'Mémoire sur les Microcéphales,' 1867, p. 168.

10 'The Variation of Animals and Plants under Domestication,' vol. i. p. 27.

11 Quoted in Dr. Maudsley's 'Physiology and Pathology of Mind,' 1868, pp. 19, 220.

12 Dr. Jerdon, 'Birds of India,' vol. i. 1862, p. xxi.

13 Mr. L. H. Morgan's work on 'The American Beaver,' 1868, offers a good illustration of this remark. I cannot, however, avoid thinking that he goes too far in underrating the power of Instinct.

works shewing that animals possess some degree of reason, that I will here give only two or three instances, authenticated by Rengger, and relating to American monkeys, which stand low in their order. He states that when he first gave eggs to his monkeys, they smashed them and thus lost much of their contents; afterwards they gently hit one end against some hard body, and picked off the bits of shell with their fingers. After cutting themselves only once with any sharp tool, they would not touch it again, or would handle it with the greatest care. Lumps of sugar were often given them wrapped up in paper; and Rengger sometimes put a live wasp in the paper, so that in hastily unfolding it they got stung; after this had once happened, they always first held the packet to their ears to detect any movement within. Any one who is not convinced by such facts as these, and by what he may observe with his own dogs, that animals can reason, would not be convinced by anything that I could add. Nevertheless I will give one case with respect to dogs, as it rests on two distinct observers, and can hardly depend on the modification of any instinct. Mr. Colquhoun[14] winged two wild-ducks, which fell on the opposite side of a stream; his retriever tried to bring over both at once, but could not succeed; she then, though never before known to ruffle a feather, deliberately killed one, brought over the other, and returned for the dead bird. Col. Hutchinson relates that two partridges were shot at once, one being killed, the other wounded; the latter ran away, and was caught by the retriever, who on her return came across the dead bird; "she stopped, evidently greatly puzzled, and after one or two trials, finding she could not take it up without permitting the escape of the winged bird, she considered a moment, then deliberately murdered it by giving it a severe crunch, and afterwards brought away both together. This was the only known instance of her ever having wilfully injured any game." Here we have reason, though not quite perfect, for the retriever might have brought the wounded bird first and then returned for the dead one, as in the case of the two wild-ducks.

The muleteers in S. America say, " I will not give you the mule whose step is easiest, but *la mas racional,* – the one that reasons best;" and Humboldt[15] adds, "this popular expression, dictated by long experience, combats the system of animated machines, better perhaps than all the arguments of speculative philosophy."

It has, I think, now been shewn that man and the higher animals, especially the Primates, have some few instincts in common. All have the same senses, intuitions and sensations – similar passions, affections, and emotions, even the more complete ones; they feel wonder and curiosity; they possess the same faculties of imitation, attention, memory, imagination, and reason though in very different degrees. Nevertheless many authors have insisted that man is separated through his mental faculties by an impassable barrier from all the lower animals. I formerly made a collection of above a score of such aphorisms, but they are not worth giving, as their wide difference and number prove the difficulty, if not the impossibility, of the attempt. It has been asserted that man alone is capable of progressive improvement; that he alone makes use of tools or fire, domesticates other animals, possesses property, or employs language; that no other animal is self-conscious, comprehends itself, has the power of abstraction, or possesses general ideas; that man alone has a sense of beauty, is liable to caprice, has the feeling of gratitude, mystery, &c.; believes in God, or is endowed with a conscience. I will hazard a few remarks on the more important and interesting of these points.

Archbishop Sumner formerly maintained[16] that man alone is capable of progressive improvement. With animals, looking first to the individual, every one who has had any experience in setting traps knows that young animals can be caught much more easily than old ones; and they can be much more easily approached by an enemy. Even with respect to old animals, it is impossible to catch many in the same place and in the same kind of trap, or to destroy them by the same kind of poison; yet it is improbable that all should have partaken of the poison, and impossible that all should

---

14   'The Moor and the Loch,' p.45. Col. Hutchinson on 'Dog Breaking,' 1850, p. 46.
15   'Personal Narrative,' Eng. translat. vol. iii. p. 106.
16   Quoted by Sir C. Lyell, 'Antiquity of Man,' p. 497. Vol. I.

have been caught in the trap. They must learn caution by seeing their brethren caught or poisoned. In North America, where the fur-bearing animals have long been pursued, they exhibit, according to the unanimous testimony of all observers, an almost incredible amount of sagacity, caution, and cunning; but trapping has been there so long carried on that inheritance may have come into play.

If we look to successive generations, or to the race, there is no doubt that birds and other animals gradually both acquire and lose caution in relation to man or other enemies;[17] and this caution is certainly in chief part an inherited habit or instinct, but in part the result of individual experience. A good observer, Leroy,[18] states that in districts where foxes are much hunted, the young when they first leave their burrows are incontestably much more wary than the old ones in districts where they are not much disturbed...

It has often been said that no animal uses any tool; but the chimpanzee in a state of nature cracks a native fruit, somewhat like a walnut, with a stone.[19] Rengger[20] easily taught an American monkey thus to break open hard palm-nuts, and afterwards of its own accord it used stones to open other kinds of nuts, as well as boxes. It thus also removed the soft rind of fruit that had a disagreeable flavour. Another monkey was taught to open the lid of a large box with a stick, and afterwards it used the stick as a lever to move heavy bodies; and I have myself seen a young orang put a stick into a crevice, slip his hand to the other end, and use it in the proper manner as a lever. In the cases just mentioned stones and sticks were employed as implements; but they are likewise used as weapons...

The Duke of Argyll[21] remarks, that the fashioning of an implement for a special purpose is absolutely peculiar to man; and he considers that this forms an immeasurable gulf between him and the brutes. It is no doubt a very important distinction, but there appears to me much truth in Sir J. Lubbock's suggestion,[22] that when primeval man first used flint-stones for any purpose, he would have accidentally splintered them, and would then have used the sharp fragments. From this step it would be a small one to intentionally break the flints, and not a very wide step to rudely fashion them. This latter advance, however, may have taken long ages, if we may judge by the immense interval of time which elapsed before the men of the neolithic period took to grinding and polishing their stone tools. In breaking the flints, as Sir J. Lubbock likewise remarks, sparks would have been emitted, and in grinding them heat would have been evolved: "thus the two usual methods of obtaining fire may have originated." The nature of fire would have been known in the many volcanic regions where lava occasionally flows through forests. The anthropomorphous apes, guided probably by instinct, build for themselves temporary platforms; but as many instincts are largely controlled by reason, the simpler ones, such as this of building a platform, might readily pass into a voluntary and conscious act. The orang is known to cover itself at night with the leaves of the Pandanus; and Brehm states that one of his baboons used to protect itself from the heat of the sun by throwing a straw-mat over its head. In these latter habits, we probably see the first steps towards some of the simpler arts; namely rude architecture and dress, as they arose amongst the early progenitors of man.

Language.– This faculty has justly been considered as one of the chief distinctions between man and the lower animals. But man, as a highly competent judge, Archbishop Whately remarks, "is not the only animal that can make use of language to express what is passing in his mind, and can understand, more or less, what is so expressed by another."[23] In Paraguay the *Cebus azarae* when excited utters at least six distinct sounds, which excite in other monkeys similar emotions.[24] The movements of the features and gestures of monkeys are understood by us, and they partly understand ours, as

---

17   'Journal of Researches during the Voyage of the "Beagle,"' 1845, p.398. 'Origin of Species,' 5th edit. p. 260.
18   'Lettres Phil. sur l'Intelligence des Animaux,' nouvelle edit. 1802, p. 86.
19   Savage and Wyman in 'Boston Journal of Nat. Hist.' vol. iv. 1843-44, p. 383.
20   'Säugethiere von Paraguay,' 1830, s.51-56.
21   'Primeval Man,' 1869, pp. 145, 147.
22   'Pre-historic Times,' 1865, p. 473, &c.
23   Quoted in 'Anthropological Review,' 1864, p. 158.
24   Rengger, ibid. s.45.

Rengger and others declare. It is a more remarkable fact that the dog, since being domesticated, has learnt to bark[25] in at least four or five distinct tones. Although barking is a new art, no doubt the wild species, the parents of the dog, expressed their feelings by cries of various kinds. With the domesticated dog we have the bark of eagerness, as in the chase; that of anger; the yelping or howling bark of despair, as when shut up; that of joy, as when starting on a walk with his master; and the very distinct one of demand or supplication, as when wishing for a door or window to be opened.

Articulate language is, however, peculiar to man; but he uses in common with the lower animals inarticulate cries to express his meaning, aided by gestures and the movements of the muscles of the face.[26] This especially holds good with the more simple and vivid feelings, which are but little connected with our higher intelligence. Our cries of pain, fear, surprise, anger, together with their appropriate actions, and the murmur of a mother to her beloved child, are more expressive than any words. It is not the mere power of articulation that distinguishes man from other animals, for as every one knows, parrots can talk; but it is his large power of connecting definite sounds with definite ideas; and this obviously depends on the development of the mental faculties.

As Horne Tooke, one of the founders of the noble science of philology, observes, language is an art, like brewing or baking; but writing would have been a much more appropriate simile. It certainly is not a true instinct, as every language has to be learnt. It differs, however, widely from all ordinary arts, for man has an instinctive tendency to speak, as we see in the babble of our young children; whilst no child has an instinctive tendency to brew, bake, or write. Moreover, no philologist now supposes that any language has been deliberately invented; each has been slowly and unconsciously developed by many steps. The sounds uttered by birds offer in several respects the nearest analogy to language, for all the members of the same species utter the same instinctive cries expressive of their emotions; and all the kinds that have the power of singing exert this power instinctively; but the actual song, and even the call-notes, are learnt from their parents or foster-parents. These sounds, as Daines Barrington[27] has proved, "are no more innate than language is in man. The first attempts to sing may be compared to the imperfect endeavour in a child to babble." The young males continue practising, or, as the bird-catchers say, recording, for ten or eleven months. Their first essays show hardly a rudiment of the future song; but as they grow older we can perceive what they are aiming at; and at last they are said "to sing their song round."...

With respect to the origin of articulate language, after having read on the one side the highly interesting works of Mr. Hensleigh Wedgwood, the Rev. F. Farrar, and Prof. Schleicher,[28] and the celebrated lectures of Prof. Max Müller on the other side, I cannot doubt that language owes its origin to the imitation and modification, aided by signs and gestures, of various natural sounds, the voices of other animals, and man's own instinctive cries. When we treat of sexual selection we shall see that primeval man, or rather some early progenitor of man, probably used his voice largely, as does one of the gibbon-apes at the present day, in producing true musical cadences, that is in singing; we may conclude from a widely-spread analogy that this power would have been especially exerted during the courtship of the sexes, serving to express various emotions, as love, jealousy, triumph, and serving as a challenge to their rivals. The imitation by articulate sounds of musical cries might have given rise to words expressive of various complex emotions. As bearing on the subject of imitation, the strong ten-

---

25   See my 'Variation of Animals and Plants under Domestication,' vol. i. p. 27.

26   See a discussion on this subject in Mr. E.B. Tylor's very interesting work, 'Researches into the Early History of Mankind,' 1865, chaps. ii. to iv.

27   Hon. Daines Barrington in 'Philosoph. Transactions,' 1773, p. 262. See also Dureau de la Malle, in 'Ann. des Sc. Nat.' 3rd series, Zoolog. tom. x.p. 119.

28   'On the Origin of Language,' by H. Wedgwood, 1866. 'Chapters on Language,' by the Rev. F. W. Farrar, 1865. These works are most interesting. See also 'De la Phys. et de Parole,' par Albert Lemoine, 1865, p. 190. The work on this subject, by the late Prof. Aug. Schleicher, has been translated by Dr. Bikkers into English under the title cf 'Darwinism tested by the Science of Language,' 1869.

dency in our nearest allies, the monkeys, in micro-cephalous idiots,[29] and in the barbarous races of mankind, to imitate whatever they hear deserves notice. As monkeys certainly understand much that is said to them by man, and as in a state of nature they utter signal-cries of danger to their fellows,[30] it does not appear altogether incredible, that some unusually wise ape-like animal should have thought of imitating the growl of a beast of prey, so as to indicate to his fellow monkeys the nature of the expected danger. And this would have been a first step in the formation of a language.

As the voice was used more and more, the vocal organs would have been strengthened and perfect-ed through the principle of the inherited effects of use and this would have reacted on the power of speech. But the relation between the continued use of language and the development of the brain has no doubt been far more important. The mental powers in some early progenitor of man must have been more highly developed than in any existing ape, before even the most imperfect form of speech could have come into use; but we may confidently believe that the continued use and advancement of this power would have reacted on the mind by enabling and encouraging it to carry on long trains of thought. A long and complex train of thought can no more be carried on without the aid of words, whether spoken or silent, than a long calcu-lation without the use of figures or algebra. It appears, also, that even ordinary trains of thought almost require some form of language, for the dumb, deaf, and blind girl, Laura Bridgman, was observed to use her fingers whilst dreaming.[31] Nevertheless a long succession of vivid and con-nected ideas, may pass through the mind without the aid of any form of language, as we may infer from the prolonged dreams of dogs. We have, also, seen that retriever-dogs are able to reason to a cer-tain extent; and this they manifestly do without the aid of language. The intimate connection between the brain, as it is now developed in us, and the fac-ulty of speech, is well shewn by those curious cases of brain-disease, in which speech is specially affect-ed, as when the power to remember substantives is lost, whilst other words can be correctly used.[32] There is no more improbability in the effects of the continued use of the vocal and mental organs being inherited, than in the case of handwriting, which depends partly on the structure of the hand and partly on the disposition of the mind; and hand-writing is certainly inherited.[33]

Why the organs now used for speech should have been originally perfected for this purpose, rather than any other organs, it is not difficult to see. Ants have considerable powers of intercommunication by means of their antennae, as shewn by Huber, who devotes a whole chapter to their language. We might have used our fingers as efficient instru-ments, for a person with practice can report to a deaf man every word of a speech rapidly delivered at a public meeting; but the loss of our hands, whilst thus employed, would have been a serious inconvenience. As all the higher mammals possess vocal organs constructed on the same general plan with ours, and which are used as a means of com-munication, it was obviously probable, if the power of communication had to be improved, that these same organs would have been still further devel-oped; and this has been effected by the aid of adjoining and well-adapted parts, namely the tongue and lips.[34] The fact of the higher apes not using their vocal organs for speech, no doubt depends on their intelligence not having been suffi-ciently advanced. The possession by them of organs, which with long-continued practice might have been used for speech, although not thus used, is paralleled by the case of many birds which pos-sess organs fitted for singing, though they never sing...

The formation of different languages and of dis-tinct species, and the proofs that both have been

---

29   Vogt, 'Mémoire sur les Microcéphales,' 1867, p. 169. With respect to savages, I have given some facts in my 'Journal of Researches,' &c., 1845, p. 206.

30   See clear evidence on this head in the two works so often quoted by Brehm and Rengger.

31   See remarks on this head by Dr. Maudsley, 'The Physiology and Pathology of Mind,' 2nd edit. 1868, p. 199.

32   Many curious cases have been recorded. See, for instance, 'Inquiries Concerning the Intellectual Powers,' by Dr. Abercrombie, 1838, p. 150.

33   'The Variation of Animals and Plants under Domestication,' vol. ii. p. 6.

34   See some good remarks to this effect by Dr. Maudsley, 'The Physiology and Pathology of Mind,' 1868, p. 199.

developed through a gradual process, are curiously the same...[35] Languages, like organic beings, can be classed in groups under groups; and they can be classed either naturally according to descent, or artificially by other characters. Dominant languages and dialects spread widely and lead to the gradual extinction of other tongues. A language, like a species, when once extinct, never, as Sir C. Lyell remarks, reappears. The same language never has two birth-places. Distinct languages may be crossed or blended together.[36] We see variability in every tongue, and new words are continually cropping up; but as there is a limit to the powers of the memory, single words, like whole languages, gradually become extinct. As Max Müller[37] has well remarked: – "A struggle for life is constantly going on amongst the words and grammatical forms in each language. The better, the shorter, the easier forms are constantly gaining the upper hand, and they owe their success to their own inherent virtue." To these more important causes of the survival of certain words, mere novelty may, I think, be added; for there is in the mind of man a strong love for slight changes in all things. The survival or preservation of certain favoured words in the struggle for existence is natural selection...

Self-consciousness, Individuality, Abstraction, General Ideas, &c. – It would be useless to attempt discussing these high faculties, which, according to several recent writers, make the sole and complete distinction between man and the brutes, for hardly two authors agree in their definitions. Such faculties could not have been fully developed in man until his mental powers had advanced to a high standard, and this implies the use of a perfect language. No one supposes that one of the lower animals reflects whence he comes or whither he goes, – what is death or what is life, and so forth. But can we feel sure that an old dog with an excellent memory and some power of imagination, as shewn by his dreams, never reflects on his past pleasures in the chase? and this would be a form of self-consciousness. On the other hand, as Büchner[38] has remarked, how little can the hard-worked wife of a degraded Australian savage, who uses hardly any abstract words and cannot count above four, exert her self-consciousness, or reflect on the nature of her own existence.

That animals retain their mental individuality is unquestionable. When my voice awakened a train of old associations in the mind of the above-mentioned dog, he must have retained his mental individuality, although every atom of his brain had probably undergone change more than once during the interval of five years. This dog might have brought forward the argument lately advanced to crush all evolutionists, and said, "I abide amid all mental moods and all material changes.... The teaching that atoms leave their impressions as legacies to other atoms falling into the places they have vacated is contradictory of the utterance of consciousness, and is therefore false but it is the teaching necessitated by evolutionism, consequently the hypothesis is a false one."[39]

Sense of Beauty. This sense has been declared to be peculiar to man. But when we behold male birds elaborately displaying their plumes and splendid colours before the females, whilst other birds not thus decorated make no such display, it is impossible to doubt that the females admire the beauty of their male partners. As women everywhere deck themselves with these plumes, the beauty of such ornaments cannot be disputed. The Bower-birds by tastefully ornamenting their playing-passages with gaily-coloured objects, as do certain humming-birds their nests, offer additional evidence that they possess a sense of beauty. So with the song of birds, the sweet strains poured forth by the males during the season of love are certainly admired by the females, of which fact evidence will hereafter be given. If female birds had been incapable of appreciating the beautiful colours, the ornaments, and

---

35 See the very interesting parallelism between the development of speech and languages, given by Sir C. Lyell in 'The Geolog. Evidences of the Antiquity of Man,' 1863. chap. xxiii.

36 See remarks to this effect by the Rev. F.W. Farrar, in an interesting article, entitled "Philology and Darwinism" in 'Nature,' March 24th, 1870, p. 528.

37 'Nature,' Jan. 6th, 1870, p. 257.

38 'Conférences sur la Théorie Darwinienne,' French translat., 1869, p. 132.

39 The Rev. Dr. J.M. Cann, 'Anti-Darwinism,' 1869, p. 13.

voices of their male partners, all the labour and anxiety exhibited by them in displaying their charms before the females would have been thrown away; and this it is impossible to admit. Why certain bright colours and certain sounds should excite pleasure, when in harmony, cannot, I presume, be explained any more than why certain flavours and scents are agreeable; but assuredly the same colours and the same sounds are admired by us and by many of the lower animals.

The taste for the beautiful, at least as far as female beauty is concerned, is not of a special nature in the human mind; for it differs widely in the different races of man, as will hereafter be shewn, and is not quite the same even in the different nations of the same race. Judging from the hideous ornaments and the equally hideous music admired by most savages, it might be urged that their aesthetic faculty was not so highly developed as in certain animals, for instance, in birds. Obviously no animal would be capable of admiring such scenes as the heavens at night, a beautiful landscape, or refined music; but such high tastes, depending as they do on culture and complex associations, are not enjoyed by barbarians or by uneducated persons.

Many of the faculties, which have been of inestimable service to man for his progressive advancement, such as the powers of the imagination, wonder, curiosity, an undefined sense of beauty, a tendency to imitation, and the love of excitement or novelty, could not fail to have led to the most capricious changes of customs and fashions. I have alluded to this point, because a recent writer[40] has oddly fixed on Caprice "as one of the most remarkable and typical differences between savages and brutes." But not only can we perceive how it is that man is capricious, but the lower animals are, as we shall hereafter see, capricious in their affections, aversions, and sense of beauty. There is also good reason to suspect that they love novelty, for its own sake.

Belief in God – Religion. – There is no evidence that man was aboriginally endowed with the ennobling belief in the existence of an Omnipotent God. On the contrary there is ample evidence, derived not from hasty travellers, but from men who have long resided with savages, that numerous races have existed and still exist, who have no idea of one or more gods, and who have no words in their languages to express such an idea.[41] The question is of course wholly distinct from that higher one, whether there exists a Creator and Ruler of the universe; and this has been answered in the affirmative by the highest intellects that have ever lived.

If, however, we include under the term "religion" the belief in unseen or spiritual agencies, the case is wholly different; for this belief seems to be almost universal with the less civilised races. Nor is it difficult to comprehend how it arose. As soon as the important faculties of the imagination, wonder, and curiosity, together with some power of reasoning, had become partially developed, man would naturally have craved to understand what was passing around him, and have vaguely speculated on his own existence. As Mr. M'Lennan[42] has remarked, "Some explanation of the phenomena of life, a man must feign for himself; and to judge from the universality of it, the simplest hypothesis, and the first to occur to men, seems to have been that natural phenomena are ascribable to the presence in animals, plants, and things, and in the forces of nature, of such spirits prompting to action as men are conscious they themselves possess." It is probable, as Mr. Tylor has clearly shewn, that dreams may have first given rise to the notion of spirits; for savages do not readily distinguish between subjective and objective impressions. When a savage dreams, the figures which appear before him are believed to have come from a distance and to stand over him; or "the soul of the dreamer goes out on its travels, and comes home with a remembrance of what it has seen."[43] But until the above-named faculties of imagination, curiosity, reason, &c., had

---

40 'The Spectator,' Dec. 4th, 1869, p. 1430.

41 See an excellent article on this subject by the Rev. F. W. Farrar in the 'Anthropological Review,' Aug. 1864, p. ccxvii. For further facts see Sir J. Lubbock, 'Prehistoric Times,' 2nd edit. 1869, p. 564; and especially the chapters on Religion in his 'Origin of Civilisation,' 1870.

42 The Worship of Animals and Plants, in the 'Fortnightly Review,' Oct. 1, 1869, p. 422.

43 Tylor, 'Early History of Mankind,' 1865, p. 6. See also the three striking chapters on the Development of Religion, in Lubbock's 'Origin of Civilisation,' 1870. In a like manner Mr. Herbert Spencer, in his ingenious essay in the 'Fortnightly Review' (May 1st, 1870, p. 535), accounts for the earliest forms of religious belief throughout the world,

been fairly well developed in the mind of man, his dreams would not have led him to believe in spirits, any more than in the case of a dog.

The tendency in savages to imagine that natural objects and agencies are animated by spiritual or living essences, is perhaps illustrated by a little fact which I once noticed: my dog, a full-grown and very sensible animal, was lying on the lawn during a hot and still day; but at a little distance a slight breeze occasionally moved an open parasol, which would have been wholly disregarded by the dog, had any one stood near it. As it was, every time that the parasol slightly moved, the dog growled fiercely and barked. He must, I think, have reasoned to himself in a rapid and unconscious manner, that movement without any apparent cause indicated the presence of some strange living agent, and no stranger had a right to be on his territory.

The belief in spiritual agencies would easily pass into the belief in the existence of one or more gods. For savages would naturally attribute to spirits the same passions, the same love of vengeance or simplest form of justice, and the same affections which they themselves experienced. The Fuegians appear to be in this respect in an intermediate condition, for when the surgeon on board the "Beagle" shot some young ducklings as specimens, York Minster declared in the most solemn manner, " Oh! Mr. Bynoe, much rain, much snow, blow much;" and this was evidently a retributive punishment for wasting human food. So again he related how, when his brother killed a " wild man," storms long raged, much rain and snow fell. Yet we could never discover that the Fuegians believed in what we should call a God, or practised any religious rites; and Jemmy Button, with justifiable pride, stoutly maintained that there was no devil in his land. This latter assertion is the more remarkable, as with savages the belief in bad spirits is far more common than the belief in good spirits.

The feeling of religious devotion is a highly complex one, consisting of love, complete submission to an exalted and mysterious superior, a strong sense of dependence,[44] fear, reverence, gratitude, hope for the future, and perhaps other elements. No being could experience so complex an emotion until advanced in his intellectual and moral faculties to at least a moderately high level. Nevertheless we see some distant approach to this state of mind, in the deep love of a dog for his master, associated with complete submission, some fear, and perhaps other feelings. The behaviour of a dog when returning to his master after an absence, and, as I may add, of a monkey to his beloved keeper, is widely different from that towards their fellows. In the latter case the transports of joy appear to be somewhat less, and the sense of equality is shewn in every action. Professor Braubach[45] goes so far as to maintain that a dog looks on his master as on a god.

The same high mental faculties which first led man to believe in unseen spiritual agencies, then in fetishism, polytheism, and ultimately in monotheism, would infallibly lead him, as long as his reasoning powers remained poorly developed, to various strange superstitions and customs. Many of these are terrible to think of – such as the sacrifice of human beings to a blood-loving god; the trial of innocent persons by the ordeal of poison or fire; witchcraft, &c. yet it is well occasionally to reflect on these superstitions, for they shew us what an infinite debt of gratitude we owe to the improvement of our reason, to science, and our accumulated knowledge.[46] As Sir J. Lubbock has well

---

by man being led through dreams, shadows, and other causes, to look at himself as a double essence, corporeal and spiritual. As the spiritual being is supposed to exist after death and to be powerful, it is propitiated by various gifts and ceremonies, and its aid invoked. He then further shews that names or nicknames given from some animal or other object to the early progenitors or founders of a tribe, are supposed after a long interval to represent the real progenitor of the tribe; and such animal or object is then naturally believed still to exist as a spirit, is held sacred, and worshipped as a god. Nevertheless I cannot but suspect that there is a still earlier and ruder stage, when anything which manifests power or movement is thought to be endowed with some form of life, and with mental faculties analogous to our own.

44   See an able article on the Psychical Elements of Religion, by Mr. L. Owen Pike, in 'Anthropolog. Review,' April, 1870, p. lxiii

45   'Religion, Moral, &c., der Darwin'schen Art-Lehre,' 1869, s.53.

46   'Prehistoric Times,' 2nd edit. p.571. In this work (at p. 553) there will be found an excellent account of the many strange and capricious customs of savages.

observed, "it is not too much to say that the horrible dread of unknown evil hangs like a thick cloud over savage life, and embitters every pleasure." These miserable and indirect consequences of our highest faculties may be compared with the incidental and occasional mistakes of the instincts of the lower animals.

CHAPTER III
COMPARISON OF THE MENTAL POWERS OF MAN AND THE LOWER ANIMALS –
continued

The moral sense – Fundamental proposition – The qualities of social animals – Origin of sociability – Struggle between opposed instincts – Man a social animal – The more enduring social instincts conquer other less persistent instincts – The social virtues alone rewarded by savages – The self-regarding virtues acquired at a later stage of development – The importance of the judgment of the members of the same community on conduct – Transmission of moral tendencies – Summary.

I fully subscribe to the judgment of those writers[47] who maintain that of all the differences between man and the lower animals, the moral sense or conscience is by far the most important. This sense, as Mackintosh[48] remarks, "has a rightful supremacy over every other principle of human action;" it is summed up in that short but imperious word *ought,* so full of high significance. It is the most noble of all the attributes of man, leading him without a moment's hesitation to risk his life for that of a fellow-creature; or after due deliberation, impelled simply by the deep feeling of right or duty, to sacrifice it in some great cause. Immanuel Kant exclaims, "Duty! Wondrous thought, that workest neither by fond insinuation, flattery, nor by any threat, but merely by holding up thy naked law in the soul, and so extorting for thyself always reverence, if not always obedience; before whom all appetites are dumb, however secretly they rebel; whence thy original?"[49]

This great question has been discussed by many writers[50] of consummate ability; and my sole excuse for touching on it is the impossibility of here passing it over, and because, as far as I know, no one has approached it exclusively from the side of natural history. The investigation possesses, also, some independent interest, as an attempt to see how far the study of the lower animals can throw light on one of the highest psychical faculties of man.

The following proposition seems to me in a high degree probable – namely, that any animal whatever, endowed with well-marked social instincts,[51] would inevitably acquire a moral sense or conscience, as soon as its intellectual powers had become as well developed, or nearly as well developed, as in man. For, *firstly,* the social instincts lead an animal to take pleasure in the society of its fellows, to feel a certain amount of sympathy with them, and to perform various services for them. The services may be of a definite and evidently instinctive nature; or there may be only a wish and

---

47   See, for instance, on this subject, Quatrefages, 'Unité de l'Espèce Humaine,' 1861, p. 21, &c.

48   'Dissertation on ethical Philosophy,' 1837, p. 231, &c.

49   'Metaphysics of Ethics,' translated by J. W. Semple, Edinburgh, 1836, p.21, &c.

50   'Mr. Bain gives a list ('Mental and Moral Science,' 1868, p. 543-725) of twenty-six British authors who have written on this subject, and whose names are familiar to every reader; to these, Mr. Bain's own name, and those of Mr. Lecky, Mr. Shadworth Hodgson, and Sir J. Lubbock, as well as of others, may be added.

51   Sir B. Brodie, after observing that man is a social animal ('Psychological Enquiries,' 1854, p. 192), asks the pregnant question "ought not this to settle the disputed question as to the existence of a moral sense?" Similar ideas have probably occurred to many persons, as they did long ago to Marcus Aurelius. Mr. J. S. Mill speaks, in his celebrated work, 'Utilitarianism,' (1864, p. 46), of the social feelings as a "powerful natural sentiment," and as "the natural basis of sentiment for utilitarian morality;" but on the previous page he says, "if, as is my own belief, the moral feelings are not innate, but acquired, they are not for that reason less natural." It is with hesitation that I venture to differ from so profound a thinker, but it can hardly be disputed that the social feelings are instinctive or innate in the lower animals; and why should they not be so in man? Mr. Bain (see, for instance, 'The Emotions and the Will,' 1865, p. 481) and others believe that the moral sense is acquired by each individual during his lifetime. On the general theory of evolution this is at least extremely improbable.

readiness, as with most of the higher social animals, to aid their fellows in certain general ways. But these feelings and services are by no means extended to all the individuals of the same species, only to those of the same association. *Secondly,* as soon as the mental faculties had become highly developed, images of all past actions and motives would be incessantly passing through the brain of each individual; and that feeling of dissatisfaction which invariably results, as we shall hereafter see, from any unsatisfied instinct, would arise, as often as it was perceived that the enduring and always present social instinct had yielded to some other instinct, at the time stronger, but neither enduring in its nature, nor leaving behind it a very vivid impression. It is clear that many instinctive desires, such as that of hunger, are in their nature of short duration; and after being satisfied are not readily or vividly recalled. *Thirdly,* after the power of language had been acquired and the wishes of the members of the same community could be distinctly expressed, the common opinion how each member ought to act for the public good, would naturally become to a large extent the guide to action. But the social instincts would still give the impulse to act for the good of the community, this impulse being strengthened, directed, and sometimes even deflected by public opinion, the power of which rests, as we shall presently see, on instinctive sympathy. *Lastly,* habit in the individual would ultimately play a very important part in guiding the conduct of each member; for the social instincts and impulses, like all other instincts, would be greatly strengthened by habit, as would obedience to the wishes and judgment of the community. These several subordinate propositions must now be discussed; and some of them at considerable length.

It may be well first to premise that I do not wish to maintain that any strictly social animal, if its intellectual faculties were to become as active and as highly developed as in man, would acquire exactly the same moral sense as ours. In the same manner as various animals have some sense of beauty, though they admire widely different objects, so they might have a sense of right and wrong, though led by it to follow widely different lines of conduct. If, for instance, to take an extreme case, men were reared under precisely the same conditions as hive-bees, there can hardly be a doubt that our unmarried females would, like the worker-bees, think it a sacred duty to kill their brothers, and mothers would strive to kill their fertile daughters; and no one would think of interfering. Nevertheless the bee, or any other social animal, would in our supposed case gain, as it appears to me, some feeling of right and wrong, or a conscience. For each individual would have an inward sense of possessing certain stronger or more enduring instincts, and others less strong or enduring; so that there would often be a struggle which impulse should be followed; and satisfaction or dissatisfaction would be felt, as past impressions were compared during their incessant passage through the mind. In this case an inward monitor would tell the animal that it would have been better to have followed the one impulse rather than the other. The one course ought to have been followed: the one would have been right and the other wrong; but to these terms I shall have to recur.

Sociability. – Animals of many kinds are social; we find even distinct species living together, as with some American monkeys, and with the united flocks of rooks, jackdaws, and starlings. Man shows the same feeling in his strong love for the dog, which the dog returns with interest. Every one must have noticed how miserable horses, dogs, sheep, &c. are when separated from their companions; and what affection at least the two former kinds show on their reunion. It is curious to speculate on the feelings of a dog, who will rest peacefully for hours in a room with his master or any of the family, without the least notice being taken of him; but if left for a short time by himself, barks or howls dismally. We will confine our attention to the higher social animals, excluding insects, although these aid each other in many important ways. The most common service which the higher animals perform for each other, is the warning each other of danger by means of the united senses of all. Every sportsman knows, as Dr. Jaeger remarks,[52] how difficult it is to approach animals in a herd or troop. Wild horses and cattle do not, I believe, make any danger-signal; but the attitude of any one who first

---

52 'Die Darwin'sche Theorie,' s.101.

discovers an enemy, warns the others. Rabbits stamp loudly on the ground with their hind-feet as a signal: sheep and chamois do the same, but with their fore-feet, uttering likewise a whistle. Many birds and some mammals post sentinels, which in the case of seals are said[53] generally to be the females. The leader of a troop of monkeys acts as the sentinel, and utters cries, expressive both of danger and of safety.[54] Social animals perform many little services for each other: horses nibble, and cows lick each other, on any spot which itches: monkeys search for each other's external parasites; and Brehm states that after a troop of the *Cercopithecus griseo-viridis* has rushed through a thorny brake, each monkey stretches itself on a branch, and another monkey sitting by "conscientiously" examines its fur and extracts every thorn or burr.

Animals also render more important services to each other: thus wolves and some other beasts of prey hunt in packs, and aid each other in attacking their victims. Pelicans fish in concert. The Hamadryas baboons turn over stones to find insects, &c.; and when they come to a large one, as many as can stand round, turn it over together and share the booty. Social animals mutually defend each other. The males of some ruminants come to the front when there is danger and defend the herd with their horns...

It is certain that associated animals have a feeling of love for each other which is not felt by adult and nonsocial animals. How far in most cases they actually sympathise with each other's pains and pleasures is more doubtful, especially with respect to the latter. Mr. Buxton, however, who had excellent means of observation[55] states that his macaws, which lived free in Norfolk, took "an extravagant interest" in a pair with a nest, and whenever the female left it, she was surrounded by a troop "screaming horrible acclamations in her honour." It is often difficult to judge whether animals have any feeling for each other's sufferings. Who can say what cows feel, when they surround and stare intently on a dying or dead companion? That animals sometimes are far from feeling any sympathy is too certain; for they will expel a wounded animal from the herd, or gore or worry it to death. This is almost the blackest fact in natural history, unless indeed the explanation which has been suggested is true, that their instinct or reason leads them to expel an injured companion, lest beasts of prey, including man, should be tempted to follow the troop. In this case their conduct is not much worse than that of the North American Indians who leave their feeble comrades to perish on the plains, or the Feegeans, who, when their parents get old or fall ill, bury them alive.[56]

Many animals, however, certainly sympathise with each other's distress or danger. This is the case even with birds; Capt. Stansbury[57] found on a salt lake in Utah an old and completely blind pelican, which was very fat, and must have been long and well fed by his companions. Mr. Blyth, as he informs me, saw Indian crows feeding two or three of their companions which were blind; and I have heard of an analogous case with the domestic cock. We may, if we choose, call these actions instinctive; but such cases are much too rare for the development of any special instinct.[58] I have myself seen a dog, who never passed a great friend of his, a cat which lay sick in a basket, without giving her a few licks with his tongue, the surest sign of kind feeling in a dog.

It must be called sympathy that leads a coura-

53 Mr. R. Browne in 'Proc. Zoolog. Soc.' 1868, p. 409.
54 Brehm, 'Thierleben.' B. i. 1864, s. 52, 79. For the case of the monkeys extracting thorns from each other, see s. 54. With respect to the Hamadryas turning over stones, the fact is given (s. 76) on the evidence of Alvarez, whose observations Brehm thinks quite trustworthy. For the case of the old male baboons attacking the dogs, see s. 79; and with respect to the eagle, s. 56.
55 'Annals and Mag. of Nat. Hist.' November, 1868, p. 382.
56 Sir J. Lubbock, 'Prehistoric Times,' 2nd edit. p. 446.
57 As quoted by Mr. L. H. Morgan, 'The American Beaver,' 1868, p. 272. Capt. Stansbury also gives an interesting account of the manner in which a very young pelican, carried away by a strong stream, was guided and encouraged in its attempts to reach the shore by half a dozen old birds.
58 As Mr. Bain states, "effective aid to a sufferer springs from sympathy proper:" 'Mental and Moral Science,' 1868, p. 245.

geous dog to fly at any one who strikes his master, as he certainly will. I saw a person pretending to beat a lady who had a very timid little dog on her lap, and the trial had never before been made. The little creature instantly jumped away, but after the pretended beating was over, it was really pathetic to see how perseveringly he tried to lick his mistress's face and comfort her. Brehm[59] states that when a baboon in confinement was pursued to be punished, the others tried to protect him. It must have been sympathy in the cases above given which led the baboons and Cercopitheci to defend their young comrades from the dogs and the eagle. I will give only one other instance of sympathetic and heroic conduct in a little American monkey. Several years ago a keeper at the Zoological Gardens, showed me some deep and scarcely healed wounds on the nape of his neck, inflicted on him whilst kneeling on the floor by a fierce baboon. The little American monkey, who was a warm friend of this keeper, lived in the same large compartment, and was dreadfully afraid of the great baboon. Nevertheless, as soon as he saw his friend the keeper in peril, he rushed to the rescue, and by screams and bites so distracted the baboon that the man was able to escape, after running great risk, as the surgeon who attended him thought, of his life.

Besides love and sympathy, animals exhibit other qualities which in us would be called moral; and I agree with Agassiz[60] that dogs possess something very like a conscience. They certainly possess some power of self-command, and this does not appear to be wholly the result of fear. As Braubach[61] remarks, a dog will refrain from stealing food in the absence of his master. Dogs have long been accepted as the very type of fidelity and obedience. All animals living in a body which defend each other or attack their enemies in concert, must be in some degree faithful to each other; and those that follow a leader must be in some degree obedient. When the baboons in Abyssinia[62] plunder a garden, they silently follow their leader; and if an imprudent young animal makes a noise, he receives a slap from the others to teach him silence and obedience; but as soon as they are sure that there is no danger, all

show their joy by much clamour.

With respect to the impulse which leads certain animals to associate together, and to aid each other in many ways, we may infer that in most cases they are impelled by the same sense of satisfaction or pleasure which they experience in performing other instinctive actions; or by the same sense of dissatisfaction, as in other cases of prevented instinctive actions. We see this in innumerable instances, and it is illustrated in a striking manner by the acquired instincts of our domesticated animals; thus a young shepherd-dog delights in driving and running round a flock of sheep, but not in worrying them; a young foxhound delights in hunting a fox, whilst some other kinds of dogs as I have witnessed, utterly disregard foxes. What a strong feeling of inward satisfaction must impel a bird, so full of activity, to brood day after day over her eggs. Migratory birds are miserable if prevented from migrating, and perhaps they enjoy starting on their long flight. Some few instincts are determined solely by painful feelings, as by fear, which leads to self-preservation, or is specially directed against certain enemies. No one, I presume, can analyse the sensations of pleasure or pain. In many cases, however, it is probable that instincts are persistently followed from the mere force of inheritance, without the stimulus of either pleasure or pain. A young pointer, when it first scents game, apparently cannot help pointing. A squirrel in a cage who pats the nuts which it cannot eat, as if to bury them in the ground, can hardly be thought to act thus either from pleasure or pain. Hence the common assumption that men must be impelled to every action by experiencing some pleasure or pain may be erroneous. Although a habit may be blindly and implicitly followed, independently of any pleasure or pain felt at the moment, yet if it be forcibly and abruptly checked, a vague sense of dissatisfaction is generally experienced; and this is especially true in regard to persons of feeble intellect.

It has often been assumed that animals were in the first place rendered social, and that they feel as a consequence uncomfortable when separated from each other, and comfortable whilst together; but it

---

59   'Thierleben,' B. i. s. 85.
60   'De l'Espèce et de la Class.' 1869, p. 97.
61   'Der Darwin'schen Art-Lehre,' 1869, s. 54.
62   Brehm, 'Thierleben,' B.i.s.76.

is a more probable view that these sensations were first developed, in order that those animals which would profit by living in society, should be induced to live together. In the same manner as the sense of hunger and the pleasure of eating were, no doubt, first acquired in order to induce animals to eat. The feeling of pleasure from society is probably an extension of the parental or filial affections; and this extension may be in chief part attributed to natural selection, but perhaps in part to mere habit. For with those animals which were benefited by living in close association, the individuals which took the greatest pleasure in society would best escape various dangers; whilst those that cared least for their comrades and lived solitary would perish in greater numbers. With respect to the origin of the parental and filial affections, which apparently lie at the basis of the social affections, it is hopeless to speculate; but we may infer that they have been to a large extent gained through natural selection. So it has almost certainly been with the unusual and opposite feeling of hatred between the nearest relations, as with the worker-bees which kill their brother-drones, and with the queen-bees which kill their daughter-queens; the desire to destroy instead of loving, their nearest relations having been here of service to the community.

The all-important emotion of sympathy is distinct from that of love. A mother may passionately love her sleeping and passive infant, but she can then hardly be said to feel sympathy for it. The love of a man for his dog is distinct from sympathy, and so is that of a dog for his master. Adam Smith formerly argued, as has Mr. Bain recently, that the basis of sympathy lies in our strong retentiveness of former states of pain or pleasure. Hence, "the sight of another person enduring hunger, cold, fatigue, revives in us some recollection of these states, which are painful even in idea." We are thus impelled to relieve the sufferings of another, in order that our own painful feelings may be at the same time relieved. In like manner we are led to participate in the pleasures of others.[63] But I cannot see how this view explains the fact that sympathy is

excited in an immeasurably stronger degree by a beloved than by an indifferent person. The mere sight of suffering, independently of love, would suffice to call up in us vivid recollections and associations. Sympathy may at first have originated in the manner above suggested; but it seems now to have become an instinct, which is especially directed towards beloved objects, in the same manner as fear with animals is especially directed against certain enemies. As sympathy is thus directed, the mutual love of the members of the same community will extend its limits. No doubt a tiger or lion feels sympathy for the sufferings of its own young, but not for any other animal. With strictly social animals the feeling will be more or less extended to all the associated members, as we know to be the case. With mankind selfishness, experience, and imitation probably add, as Mr. Bain has shewn, to the power of sympathy; for we are led by the hope of receiving good in return to perform acts of sympathetic kindness to others; and there can be no doubt that the feeling of sympathy is much strengthened by habit. In however complex a manner this feeling may have originated, as it is one of high importance to all those animals which aid and defend each other, it will have been increased, through natural selection; for those communities, which included the greatest number of the most sympathetic members, would flourish best and rear the greatest number of offspring.

In many cases it is impossible to decide whether certain social instincts have been acquired through natural selection, or are the indirect result of other instincts and faculties, such as sympathy, reason, experience, and a tendency to imitation; or again, whether they are simply the result of long-continued habit. So remarkable an instinct as the placing sentinels to warn the community of danger, can hardly have been the indirect result of any other faculty; it must therefore have been directly acquired. On the other hand, the habit followed by the males of some social animals, of defending the community and of attacking their enemies or their prey in concert, may perhaps have originated from

---

63   See the first and striking chapter in Adam Smith's 'Theory of Moral Sentiments.' Also Mr. Bain's 'Mental and Moral Science,' 1868, p. 244, and 275-282. Mr. Bain states, that "sympathy is, indirectly, a source of pleasure to the sympathiser;" and he accounts for this through reciprocity. He remarks that "the person benefited, or others in his stead, may make up, by sympathy and good offices returned, for all the sacrifice." But if, as appears to be the case, sympathy is strictly an instinct, its exercise would give direct pleasure, in the same manner as the exercise, as before remarked, of almost every other instinct.

mutual sympathy; but courage, and in most cases strength, must have been previously acquired, probably through natural selection.

Man a social animal. – Most persons admit that man is a social being. We see this in his dislike of solitude, and in his wish for society beyond that of his own family. Solitary confinement is one of the severest punishments which can be inflicted. Some authors suppose that man primevally lived in single families; but at the present day, though single families, or only two or three together, roam the solitudes of some savage lands, they are always, as far as I can discover, friendly with other families inhabiting the same district. Such families occasionally meet in council, and they unite for their common defence. It is no argument against savage man being a social animal, that the tribes inhabiting adjacent districts are almost always at war with each other; for the social instincts never extend to all the individuals of the same species. Judging from the analogy of the greater number of the Quadrumana, it is probable that the early ape-like progenitors of man were likewise social; but this is not of much importance for us. Although man, as he now exists, has few special instincts, having lost any which his early progenitors may have possessed, this is no reason why he should not have retained from an extremely remote period some degree of instinctive love and sympathy for his fellows. We are indeed all conscious that we do possess such sympathetic feelings;[64] but our consciousness does not tell us whether they are instinctive, having originated long ago in the same manner as with the lower animals, or whether they have been acquired by each of us during our early years As man is a social animal, it is also probable that he would inherit a tendency to be faithful to his comrades, for this quality is common to most social animals. He would in like manner possess some capacity for self-command, and perhaps of obedience to the leader of the community. He would from an inherited tendency still be willing to defend, in concert with others, his fellow-men, and would be ready to aid them in any way which did not too greatly interfere with his own welfare or his own strong desires.

The social animals which stand at the bottom of the scale are guided almost exclusively, and those which stand higher in the scale are largely guided, in the aid which they give to the members of the same community, by special instincts; but they are likewise in part impelled by mutual love and sympathy, assisted apparently by some amount of reason. Although man, as just remarked, has no special instincts to tell him how to aid his fellow-men, he still has the impulse, and with his improved intellectual faculties would naturally be much guided in this respect by reason and experience. Instinctive sympathy would, also, cause him to value highly the approbation of his fellow-men; for, as Mr. Bain has clearly shewn,[65] the love of praise and the strong feeling of glory, and the still stronger horror of scorn and infamy, "are due to the workings of sympathy." Consequently man would be greatly influenced by the wishes, approbation, and blame of his fellow-men, as expressed by their gestures and language. Thus the social instincts, which must have been acquired by man in a very rude state, and probably even by his early ape-like progenitors, still give the impulse to many of his best actions; but his actions are largely determined by the expressed wishes and judgment of his fellow-men, and unfortunately still oftener by his own strong, selfish desires. But as the feelings of love and sympathy and the power of self-command become strengthened by habit, and as the power of reasoning becomes clearer so that man can appreciate the justice of the judgments of his fellow-men, he will feel himself impelled, independently of any pleasure or pain felt at the moment, to certain lines of conduct. He may then say, I am the supreme judge of my own conduct, and in the words of Kant, I will not in my own person violate the dignity of humanity.

The more enduring Social Instincts conquer the less Persistent Instinct. – We have, however, not as yet considered the main point, on which the whole

---

64   Hume remarks ('An Enquiry Concerning the Principles of Morals,' edit. of 1751, p. 132), "there seems a necessity for confessing that the happiness and misery of others are not spectacles altogether indifferent to us, but that the view of the former . . . communicates a secret joy; the appearance of the latter . . . throws a melancholy damp over the imagination."

65   'Mental and Moral science,' 1868, p. 254.

question of the moral sense hinges. Why should a man feel that he ought to obey one instinctive desire rather than another? Why does he bitterly regret if he has yielded to the strong sense of self-preservation, and has not risked his life to save that of a fellow-creature; or why does he regret having stolen food from severe hunger?

It is evident in the first place, that with mankind the instinctive impulses have different degrees of strength; a young and timid mother urged by the maternal instinct will, without a moment's hesitation, run the greatest danger for her infant, but not for a mere fellow-creature. Many a man, or even boy, who never before risked his life for another, but in whom courage and sympathy were well developed, has, disregarding the instinct of self-preservation, instantaneously plunged into a torrent to save a drowning fellow-creature. In this case man is impelled by the same instinctive motive, which caused the heroic little American monkey, formerly described, to attack the great and dreaded baboon, to save his keeper. Such actions as the above appear to be the simple result of the greater strength of the social or maternal instincts than of any other instinct or motive; for they are performed too instantaneously for reflection, or for the sensation of pleasure or pain; though if prevented distress would be caused.

I am aware that some persons maintain that actions performed impulsively, as in the above cases, do not come under the dominion of the moral sense, and cannot be called moral. They confine this term to actions done deliberately, after a victory over opposing desires, or to actions prompted by some lofty motive. But it appears scarcely possible to draw any clear line of distinction of this kind; though the distinction may be real. As far as exalted motives are concerned, many instances have been recorded of barbarians, destitute of any feeling of general benevolence towards mankind, and not guided by any religious motive, who have deliberately as prisoners sacrificed their lives,[66] rather than betray their comrades; and surely their conduct ought to be considered as moral. As far as deliberation and the victory over opposing motives are concerned, animals may be seen doubting between opposed instincts, as in rescuing their offspring or comrades from danger; yet their actions, though done for the good of others, are not called moral. Moreover, an action repeatedly performed by us, will at last be done without deliberation or hesitation, and can then hardly be distinguished from an instinct; yet surely no one will pretend that an action thus done ceases to be moral. On the contrary, we all feel that an act cannot be considered as perfect, or as performed in the most noble manner, unless it be done impulsively, without deliberation or effort, in the same manner as by a man in whom the requisite qualities are innate. He who is forced to overcome his fear or want of sympathy before he acts, deserves, however, in one way higher credit than the man whose innate disposition leads him to a good act without effort. As we cannot distinguish between motives, we rank all actions of a certain class as moral, when they are performed by a moral being. A moral being is one who is capable of comparing his past and future actions or motives, and of approving or disapproving of them. We have no reason to suppose that any of the lower animals have this capacity; therefore when a monkey faces danger to rescue its comrade, or takes charge of an orphan-monkey, we do not call its conduct moral. But in the case of man, who alone can with certainty be ranked as a moral being, actions of a certain class are called moral, whether performed deliberately after a struggle with opposing motives, or from the effects of slowly-gained habit, or impulsively through instinct.

But to return to our more immediate subject; although some instincts are more powerful than others, thus leading to corresponding actions, yet it cannot be maintained that the social instincts are ordinarily stronger in man, or have become stronger through long-continued habit, than the instincts, for instance, of self-preservation, hunger, lust, vengeance, &c. Why then does man regret, even though he may endeavour to banish any such regret, that he has followed the one natural impulse, rather than the other; and why does he further feel that he ought to regret his conduct? Man in this respect differs profoundly from the

---

66   I have given one such case, namely of three Patagonian Indians who preferred being shot, one after the other, to
      betraying the plans of their companions in war ('Journal of Researches,' 1845, p. 103).

lower animals. Nevertheless we can, I think, see with some degree of clearness the reason of this difference.

Man, from the activity of his mental faculties, cannot avoid reflection: past impressions and images are incessantly passing through his mind with distinctness. Now with those animals which live permanently in a body, the social instincts are ever present and persistent. Such animals are always ready to utter the danger-signal, to defend the community, and to give aid to their fellows in accordance with their habits; they feel at all times, without the stimulus of any special passion or desire, some degree of love and sympathy for them; they are unhappy if long separated from them, and always happy to be in their company. So it is with ourselves. A man who possessed no trace of such feelings would be an unnatural monster. On the other hand, the desire to satisfy hunger, or any passion, such as vengeance, is in its nature temporary, and can for a time be fully satisfied. Nor is it easy, perhaps hardly possible, to call up with complete vividness the feeling, for instance, of hunger; nor indeed, as has often been remarked, of any suffering. The instinct of self-preservation is not felt except in the presence of danger; and many a coward has thought himself brave until he has met his enemy face to face. The wish for another man's property is perhaps as persistent a desire as any that can be named; but even in this case the satisfaction of actual possession is generally a weaker feeling than the desire: many a thief, if not an habitual one, after success has wondered why he stole some article.

Thus, as man cannot prevent old impressions continually repassing through his mind, he will be compelled to compare the weaker impressions of, for instance, past hunger, or of vengeance satisfied or danger avoided at the cost of other men, with the instinct of sympathy and good-will to his fellows, which is still present and ever in some degree active in his mind. He will then feel in his imagination that a stronger instinct has yielded to one which now seems comparatively weak; and then that sense of dissatisfaction will inevitably be felt with which man is endowed, like every other animal, in order that his instincts may be obeyed...

At the moment of action, man will no doubt be apt to follow the stronger impulse; and though this may occasionally prompt him to the noblest deeds, it will far more commonly lead him to gratify his own desires at the expense of other men. But after their gratification, when past and weaker impressions are contrasted with the ever-enduring social instincts, retribution will surely come. Man will then feel dissatisfied with himself, and will resolve with more or less force to act differently for the future. This is conscience; for conscience looks backwards and judges past actions, inducing that kind of dissatisfaction, which if weak we call regret, and if severe remorse.

These sensations are, no doubt, different from those experienced when other instincts or desires are left unsatisfied; but every unsatisfied instinct has its own proper prompting sensation, as we recognise with hunger, thirst, &c. Man thus prompted, will through long habit acquire such perfect self-command, that his desires and passions will at last instantly yield to his social sympathies, and there will no longer be a struggle between them. The still hungry, or the still revengeful man will not think of stealing food, or of wreaking his vengeance. It is possible, or, as we shall hereafter see, even probable, that the habit of self-command may, like other habits, be inherited. Thus at last man comes to feel, through acquired and perhaps inherited habit, that it is best for him to obey his more persistent instincts. The imperious word *ought* seems merely to imply the consciousness of the existence of a persistent instinct, either innate or partly acquired, serving him as a guide, though liable to be disobeyed. We hardly use the word *ought* in a metaphorical sense, when we say hounds ought to hunt, pointers to point, and retrievers to retrieve their game. If they fail thus to act, they fail in their duty and act wrongly.

If any desire or instinct, leading to an action opposed to the good of others, still appears to a man, when recalled to mind, as strong as, or stronger than, his social instinct, he will feel no keen regret at having followed it; but he will be conscious that if his conduct were known to his fellows, it would meet with their disapprobation; and few are so destitute of sympathy as not to feel discomfort when this is realised. If he has no such sympathy, and if his desires leading to bad actions are at the time strong, and when recalled are not overmastered by the persistent social instincts, then he is essentially a bad man;[67] and the sole restraining motive left is the fear of punishment, and the conviction that in the long run it would be best for his own selfish interests to regard the good of others rather than his own.

It is obvious that every one may with an easy conscience gratify his own desires, if they do not interfere with his social instincts, that is with the good of others; but in order to be quite free from self-reproach, or at least of anxiety, it is almost necessary for him to avoid the disapprobation, whether reasonable or not, of his fellow men. Nor must he break through the fixed habits of his life, especially if these are supported by reason; for if he does, he will assuredly feel dissatisfaction. He must likewise avoid the reprobation of the one God or gods, in whom according to his knowledge or superstition he may believe; but in this case the additional fear of divine punishment often supervenes.

The strictly Social Virtues at first alone regarded. – The above view of the first origin and nature of the moral sense, which tells us what we ought to do, and of the conscience which reproves us if we disobey it accords well with what we see of the early and undeveloped condition of this faculty in mankind. The virtues which must be practised, at least generally, by rude men, so that they may associate in a body, are those which are still recognised as the most important But they are practised almost exclusively in relation to the men of the same tribe; and their opposites are not rewarded as crimes in relation to the men of other tribes. No tribe could hold together if murder, robbery, treachery, &c., were common; consequently such crimes within the limits of the same tribe "are branded with everlasting infamy;"[68] but excite no such sentiment beyond these limits. A North-American Indian is well pleased with himself, and

is honoured by others, when he scalps a man of another tribe; and a Dyak cuts off the head of an unoffending person and dries it as a trophy. The murder of infants has prevailed on the largest scale throughout the world,[69] and has met with no reproach; but infanticide, especially of females, has been thought to be good for the tribe, or at least not injurious. Suicide during former times was not generally considered as a crime,[70] but rather from the courage displayed as an honourable act; and it is still largely practised by some semi-civilised nations without reproach, for the loss to a nation of a single individual is not felt: whatever the explanation may be, suicide, as I hear from Sir J. Lubbock, is rarely practised by the lowest barbarians. It has been recorded that an Indian Thug conscientiously regretted that he had not strangled and robbed as many travellers as did his father before him. In a rude state of civilisation the robbery of strangers is, indeed, generally considered as honourable.

The great sin of Slavery has been almost universal, and slaves have often been treated in an infamous manner. As barbarians do not regard the opinion of their women, wives are commonly treated like slaves. Most savages are utterly indifferent to the sufferings of strangers, or even delight in witnessing them. It is well known that the women and children of the North-American Indians aided in torturing their enemies. Some savages take a horrid pleasure in cruelty to animals,[71] and humanity with them is an unknown virtue. Nevertheless, feelings of sympathy and kindness are common, especially during sickness, between the members of the same tribe, and are sometimes extended beyond the limits of the tribe. Mungo Park's touching account of the kindness of the negro women of the interior to him is well known. Many instances could be given of the noble fidelity of savages towards each other, but not to strangers; common experience justifies the maxim of the Spaniard, "Never, never trust an

---

67 Dr. Prosper Despine, in his 'Psychologie Naturelle,' 1868 (tom. i. p. 243; tom ii. p. 169) gives many curious cases of the worst criminals, who apparently have been entirely destitute of conscience.

68 See an able article in the 'North British Review,' 1867, p. 395. See also Mr. W. Bagehot's article on the Importance of Obedience and Coherence to Primitive Man, in the 'Fortnightly Review,' 1867 p. 529, and 1868, p. 457,&c.

69 The fullest account which I have met with is by Dr. Gerland, in his 'Ueber der Aussterben der Naturvölker,' 1868; but I shall have to recur to the subject of infanticide in a future chapter.

70 See the very interesting discussion on Suicide in Lecky's 'History of European Morals,' vol. i. 1869, p.223.

71 See, for instance, Mr. Hamilton's account of the Kaffirs, 'Anthropological Review,' 1870, p. xv.

Indian." There cannot be fidelity without truth; and this fundamental virtue is not rare between the members of the same tribe: thus Mungo Park heard the negro women teaching their young children to love the truth. This, again, is one of the virtues which becomes so deeply rooted in the mind that it is sometimes practised by savages even at a high cost, towards strangers; but to lie to your enemy has rarely been thought a sin, as the history of modern diplomacy too plainly shews. As soon as a tribe has a recognised leader, disobedience becomes a crime, and even abject submission is looked at as a sacred virtue.

As during rude times no man can be useful or faithful to his tribe without courage, this quality has universally been placed in the highest rank; and although, in civilised countries, a good, yet timid, man may be far more useful to the community than a brave one, we cannot help instinctively honouring the latter above a coward, however benevolent. Prudence, on the other hand, which does not concern the welfare of others, though a very useful virtue, has never been highly esteemed. As no man can practise the virtues necessary for the welfare of his tribe without self-sacrifice, self-command, and the power of endurance, these qualities have been at all times highly and most justly valued. The American savage voluntarily submits without a groan to the most horrid tortures to prove and strengthen his fortitude and courage; and we cannot help admiring him, or even an Indian Fakir, who, from a foolish religious motive, swings suspended by a hook buried in his flesh.

The other self-regarding virtues, which do not obviously, though they may really, affect the welfare of the tribe, have never been esteemed by savages, though now highly appreciated by civilised nations. The greatest intemperance with savages is no reproach. Their utter licentiousness, not to mention unnatural crimes, is something astounding.[72] As soon, however, as marriage, whether polygamous or monogamous, becomes common, jealousy will lead to the inculcation of female virtue; and this being honoured will tend to spread to the unmarried females. How slowly it spreads to the male sex we see at the present day. Chastity eminently requires self-command; therefore it has been honoured from a very early period in the moral history of civilised man. As a consequence of this, the senseless practice of celibacy has been ranked from a remote period as a virtue.[73] The hatred of indecency, which appears to us so natural as to be thought innate, and which is so valuable an aid to chastity, is a modern virtue, appertaining exclusively, as Sir G. Staunton remarks,[74] to civilised life. This is shewn by the ancient religious rites of various nations, by the drawings on the walls of Pompeii, and by the practices of many savages.

We have now seen that actions are regarded by savages, and were probably so regarded by primeval man, as good or bad, solely as they affect in an obvious manner the welfare of the tribe, – not that of the species, nor that of man as an individual member of the tribe. This conclusion agrees well with the belief that the so-called moral sense is aboriginally derived from the social instincts, for both relate at first exclusively to the community. The chief causes of the low morality of savages, as judged by our standard, are, firstly, the confinement of sympathy to the same tribe. Secondly, insufficient powers of reasoning, so that the bearing of many virtues, especially of the self-regarding virtues, on the general welfare of the tribe is not recognised. Savages, for instance, fail to trace the multiplied evils consequent on a want of temperance, chastity, &c. And, thirdly, weak power of self-command; for this power has not been strengthened through long-continued, perhaps inherited, habit, instruction and religion.

I have entered into the above details on the immorality of savages,[75] because some authors have recently taken a high view of their moral nature, or have attributed most of their crimes to mistaken benevolence.[76] These authors appear to rest their conclusion on savages possessing, as they undoubtedly do possess, and often in a high degree, those virtues which are serviceable, or even necessary, for the existence of a tribal community.

---

72   Mr. McLennan has given ('Primitive Marriage,' 1865, p. 176) a good collection of facts on this head.
73   Lecky, 'History of European Morals,' vol. i 1869, p. 109.
74   'Embassy to China,' vol. ii. p. 348.
75   See on this subject copious evidence in Chap. vii. of Sir J. Lubbock, 'Origin of Civilisation,' 1870.
76   For instance Lecky, 'Hist. European Morals,' vol. i. p. 124.

Concluding Remarks. – Philosophers of the derivative[77] school of morals formerly assumed that the foundation of morality lay in a form of Selfishness; but more recently in the "Greatest Happiness principle." According to the view given above, the moral sense is fundamentally identical with the social instincts; and in the case of the lower animals it would be absurd to speak of these instincts as having been developed from selfishness, or for the happiness of the community. They have, however, certainly been developed for the general good of the community. The term, general good, may be defined as the means by which the greatest possible number of individuals can be reared in full vigour and health, with all their faculties perfect, under the conditions to which they are exposed. As the social instincts both of man and the lower animals have no doubt been developed by the same steps, it would be advisable, if found practicable, to use the same definition in both cases, and to take as the test of morality, the general good or welfare of the community, rather than the general happiness; but this definition would perhaps require some limitation on account of political ethics.

When a man risks his life to save that of a fellow creature, it seems more appropriate to say that he acts for the general good or welfare, rather than for the general happiness of mankind. No doubt the welfare and the happiness of the individual usually coincide; and a contented, happy tribe will flourish better than one that is discontented and unhappy. We have seen that at an early period in the history of man, the expressed wishes of the community will have naturally influenced to a large extent the conduct of each member; and as all wish for happiness, the "greatest happiness principle" will have become a most important secondary guide and object; the social instincts, including sympathy, always serving as the primary impulse and guide. Thus the reproach of laying the foundation of the most noble part of our nature in the base principle of selfishness is removed; unless indeed the satisfaction which every animal feels when it follows its proper instincts, and the dissatisfaction felt when prevented, be called selfish.

The expression of the wishes and judgment of the members of the same community, at first by oral and afterwards by written language, serves, as just remarked, as a most important secondary guide of conduct, in aid of the social instincts, but sometimes in opposition to them. This latter fact is well exemplified by the *Law of Honour,* that is the law of the opinion of our equals, and not of all our countrymen. The breach of this law, even when the breach is known to be strictly accordant with true morality, has caused many a man more agony than a real crime. We recognise the same influence in the burning sense of shame which most of us have felt even after the interval of years, when calling to mind some accidental breach of a trifling though fixed rule of etiquette. The judgment of the community will generally be guided by some rude experience of what is best in the long run for all the members; but this judgment will not rarely err from ignorance and from weak powers of reasoning. Hence the strangest customs and superstitions, in complete opposition to the true welfare and happiness of mankind, have become all-powerful throughout the world. We see this in the horror felt by a Hindoo who breaks his caste, in the shame of a Mahometan woman who exposes her face, and in innumerable other instances. It would be difficult to distinguish between the remorse felt by a Hindoo who has eaten unclean food, from that felt after committing a theft; but the former would probably be the more severe.

How so many absurd rules of conduct, as well as so many absurd religious beliefs, have originated we do not know; nor how it is that they have become, in all quarters of the world, so deeply impressed on the mind of men; but it is worthy of remark that a belief constantly inculcated during the early years of life, whilst the brain is impressible, appears to acquire almost the nature of an instinct; and the very essence of an instinct is that it is followed independently of reason. Neither can we say why certain admirable virtues, such as the love of truth, are much more highly appreciated by some savage tribes than by others;[78] nor, again, why

---

77   This term is used in an able article in the 'Westminister Review,' Oct. 1869, p. 498. For the Greatest Happiness principle, see J. S. Mill, 'Utilitarianism,' p. 17.

78   Good instances are given by Mr. Wallace in 'Scientific Opinion,' Sept. 15, 1869; and more fully in his 'Contributions to the Theory of Natural Selection,' 1870, p. 353.

similar differences prevail even amongst civilised nations. Knowing how firmly fixed many strange customs and superstitions have become, we need feel no surprise that the self-regarding virtues should now appear to us so natural, supported as they are by reason, as to be thought innate, although they were not valued by man in his early condition.

Notwithstanding many sources of doubt, man can generally and readily distinguish between the higher and lower moral rules. The higher are founded on the social instincts, and relate to the welfare of others. They are supported by the approbation of our fellow-men and by reason. The lower rules, though some of them when implying self-sacrifice hardly deserve to be called lower, relate chiefly to self, and owe their origin to public opinion, when matured by experience and cultivated; for they are not practised by rude tribes.

As man advances in civilisation, and small tribes are united into larger communities, the simplest reason would tell each individual that he ought to extend his social instincts and sympathies to all the members of the same nation, though personally unknown to him. This point being once reached, there is only an artificial barrier to prevent his sympathies extending to the men of all nations and races. If, indeed, such men are separated from him by great differences in appearance or habits, experience unfortunately shews us how long it is before we look at them as our fellow-creatures. Sympathy beyond the confines of man, that is humanity to the lower animals, seems to be one of the latest moral acquisitions. It is apparently unfelt by savages, except towards their pets. How little the old Romans knew of it is shewn by their abhorrent gladiatorial exhibitions. The very idea of humanity, as far as I could observe, was new to most of the Gauchos of the Pampas. This virtue, one of the noblest with which man is endowed, seems to arise incidentally from our sympathies becoming more tender and more widely diffused, until they are extended to all sentient beings. As soon as this virtue is honoured and practised by some few men, it spreads through instruction and example to the young, and eventually through public opinion.

The highest stage in moral culture at which we can arrive, is when we recognise that we ought to control our thoughts, and "not even in inmost thought to think again the sins that made the past so pleasant to us."[79] Whatever makes any bad action familiar to the mind, renders its performance by so much the easier. As Marcus Aurelius long ago said, "Such as are thy habitual thoughts, such also will be the character of thy mind; for the soul is dyed by the thoughts."[80]

Our great philosopher, Herbert Spencer, has recently explained his views on the moral sense. He says,[81] "I believe that the experiences of utility organised and consolidated through all past generations of the human race, have been producing corresponding modifications, which, by continued transmission and accumulation, have become in us certain faculties of moral intuition – certain emotions responding to right and wrong conduct, which have no apparent basis in the individual experiences of utility." There is not the least inherent improbability, as it seems to me, in virtuous tendencies being more or less strongly inherited; for, not to mention the various dispositions and habits transmitted by many of our domestic animals, I have heard of cases in which a desire to steal and a tendency to lie appeared to run in families of the upper ranks; and as stealing is so rare a crime in the wealthy classes, we can hardly account by accidental coincidence for the tendency occurring in two or three members of the same family. If bad tendencies are transmitted, it is probable that good ones are likewise transmitted. Excepting through the principle of the transmission of moral tendencies, we cannot understand the differences believed to exist in this respect between the various races of mankind. We have, however, as yet, hardly sufficient evidence on this head.

Even the partial transmission of virtuous tendencies would be an immense assistance to the primary impulse derived directly from the social instincts, and indirectly from the approbation of our fellow-men. Admitting for the moment that virtuous tendencies are inherited, it appears proba-

---

79   Tennyson, 'Idylls of the King,' p. 244.

80   'The Thoughts of the Emperor M. Aurelius Antoninus,' Eng. translat., 2nd edit., 1869, p. 112. Marcus Aurelius was born A.D. 121.

81   Letter to Mr. Mill in Bain's 'Mental and Moral Science,' 1868, p. 722.

ble, at least in such cases as chastity, temperance, humanity to animals, &c., that they become first impressed on the mental organisation through habit, instruction, and example, continued during several generations in the same family, and in a quite subordinate degree, or not at all, by the individuals possessing such virtues, having succeeded best in the struggle for life. My chief source of doubt with respect to any such inheritance, is that senseless customs, superstitions, and tastes, such as the horror of a Hindoo for unclean food, ought on the same principle to be transmitted. Although this in itself is perhaps not less probable than that animals should acquire inherited tastes for certain kinds of food or fear of certain foes, I have not met with any evidence in support of the transmission of superstitious customs or senseless habits.

Finally, the social instincts which no doubt were acquired by man, as by the lower animals, for the good of the community, will from the first have given to him some wish to aid his fellows, and some feeling of sympathy. Such impulses will have served him at a very early period as a rude rule of right and wrong. But as man gradually advanced in intellectual power and was enabled to trace the more remote consequences of his actions; as he acquired sufficient knowledge to reject baneful customs and superstitions; as he regarded more and more not only the welfare but the happiness of his fellow-men; as from habit, following on beneficial experience, instruction, and example, his sympathies became more tender and widely diffused, so as to extend to the men of all races, to the imbecile, the maimed, and other useless members of society, and finally to the lower animals, – so would the standard of his morality rise higher and higher. And it is admitted by moralists of the derivative school and by some intuitionists, that the standard of morality has risen since an early period in the history of man.[82]

As a struggle may sometimes be seen going on between the various instincts of the lower animals, it is not surprising that there should be a struggle in man between his social instincts, with their derived virtues, and his lower, though at the moment, stronger impulses or desires. This, as Mr. Galton[83] has remarked, is all the less surprising, as man has emerged from a state of barbarism within a comparatively recent period. After having yielded to some temptation we feel a sense of dissatisfaction, analogous to that felt from other unsatisfied instincts, called in this case conscience; for we cannot prevent past images and impressions continually passing through our minds, and these in their weakened state we compare with the ever-present social instincts, or with habits gained in early youth and strengthened during our whole lives, perhaps inherited, so that they are at last rendered almost as strong as instincts. Looking to future generations, there is no cause to fear that the social instincts will grow weaker, and we may expect that virtuous habits will grow stronger, becoming perhaps fixed by inheritance. In this case the struggle between our higher and lower impulses will be less severe, and virtue will be triumphant.

Summary of the two last Chapters. – There can be no doubt that the difference between the mind of the lowest man and that of the highest animal is immense. An anthropomorphous ape, if he could take a dispassionate view of his own case, would admit that though he could form an artful plan to plunder a garden – though he could use stones for fighting or for breaking open nuts, yet that the thought of fashioning a stone into a tool was quite beyond his scope. Still less, as he would admit, could he follow out a train of metaphysical reasoning, or solve a mathematical problem, or reflect on God, or admire a grand natural scene. Some apes, however, would probably declare that they could and did admire the beauty of the coloured skin and fur of their partners in marriage. They would admit, that though they could make other apes understand by cries some of their perceptions and simpler wants, the notion of expressing definite ideas by definite sounds had never crossed their minds. They might insist that they were ready to aid their fellow-apes of the same troop in many ways, to risk their lives for them, and to take charge

---

82 A writer in the 'North British Review' (July, 1869, p. 531), well capable of forming a sound judgment, expresses himself strongly to this effect. Mr. Lecky ('Hist. of Morals,' vol. i. p. 143) seems to a certain extent to coincide.

83 See his remarkable work on 'Hereditary Genius,' 1869, p.349. The Duke of Argyll ('Primeval Man,' 1869, p. 188) has some good remarks on the contest in man's nature between right and wrong.

of their orphans; but they would be forced to acknowledge that disinterested love for all living creatures, the most noble attribute of man, was quite beyond their comprehension.

Nevertheless the difference in mind between man and the higher animals, great as it is, is certainly one of degree and not of kind. We have seen that the senses and intuitions, the various emotions and faculties, such as love, memory, attention, curiosity, imitation, reason, &c., of which man boasts, may be found in an incipient, or even sometimes in a well-developed condition, in the lower animals. They are also capable of some inherited improvement, as we see in the domestic dog compared with the wolf or jackal. If it be maintained that certain powers, such as self-consciousness, abstraction, &c., are peculiar to man, it may well be that these are the incidental results of other highly advanced intellectual faculties; and these again are mainly the result of the continued use of a highly developed language. At what age does the new-born infant possess the power of abstraction, or become self-conscious and reflect on its own existence? We cannot answer; nor can we answer in regard to the ascending organic scale. The half-art and half-instinct of language still bears the stamp of its gradual evolution. The ennobling belief in God is not universal with man; and the belief in active spiritual agencies naturally follows from his other mental powers. The moral sense perhaps affords the best and highest distinction between man and the lower animals; but I need not say anything on this head, as I have so lately endeavoured to shew that the social instincts, – the prime principle of man's moral constitution[84] – with the aid of active intellectual powers and the effects of habit, naturally lead to the golden rule, "As ye would that men should do to you, do ye to them likewise;" and this lies at the foundation of morality.

In a future chapter I shall make some few remarks on the probable steps and means by which the several mental and moral faculties of man have been gradually evolved. That this at least is possible ought not to be denied, when we daily see their development in every infant; and when we may trace a perfect gradation from the mind of an utter idiot, lower than that of the lowest animal, to the mind of a Newton.

CHAPTER V
ON THE DEVELOPMENT OF THE INTELLECTUAL AND MORAL FACULTIES DURING PRIMEVAL AND CIVILISED TIMES.

The advancement of the intellectual powers through natural selection – Importance of imitation-Social and moral faculties – Their development within the limits of the same tribe – Natural selection as affecting civilised nations – Evidence that civilised nations were once barbarous.

The subjects to be discussed in this chapter are of the highest interest, but are treated by me in a most imperfect and fragmentary manner. Mr. Wallace,[85] in an admirable paper before referred to, argues that man after he had partially acquired those intellectual and moral faculties which distinguish him from the lower animals, would have been but little liable to have had his bodily structure modified through natural selection or any other means. For man is enabled through his mental faculties "to keep with an unchanged body in harmony with the changing universe." He has great power of adapting his habits to new conditions of life. He invents weapons, tools and various stratagems, by which he procures food and defends himself. When he migrates into a colder climate he uses clothes, builds sheds, and makes fires; and, by the aid of fire, cooks food otherwise indigestible. He aids his fellow-men in many ways, and anticipates future events. Even at a remote period he practised some subdivision of labour.

The lower animals, on the other hand, must have their bodily structure modified in order to survive under greatly changed conditions. They must be rendered stronger, or acquire more effective teeth or claws, in order to defend themselves from new enemies; or they must be reduced in size so as to escape detection and danger. When they migrate into a colder climate they must become clothed with thicker fur, or have their constitutions altered. If they fail to be thus modified, they will cease to exist.

The case, however, is widely different, as Mr. Wallace has with justice insisted, in relation to the

---

84   'The Thoughts of Marcus Aurelius,' &c., p. 139.
85   'Anthropological Review,' May, 1864, p. clviii.

intellectual and moral faculties of man. These faculties are variable; and we have every reason to believe that the variations tend to be inherited. Therefore, if they were formerly of high importance to primeval man and to his ape-like progenitors, they would have been perfected or advanced through natural selection. Of the high importance of the intellectual faculties there can be no doubt, for man mainly owes to them his pre-eminent position in the world. We can see that, in the rudest state of society, the individuals who were the most sagacious, who invented and used the best weapons or traps, and who were best able to defend themselves, would rear the greatest number of offspring. The tribes which included the largest number of men thus endowed would increase in number and supplant other tribes. Numbers depend primarily on the means of subsistence, and this, partly on the physical nature of the country, but in a much higher degree on the arts which are there practised. As a tribe increases and is victorious, it is often still further increased by the absorption of other tribes.[86] The stature and strength of the men of a tribe are likewise of some importance for its success, and these depend in part on the nature and amount of the food which can be obtained. In Europe the men of the Bronze period were supplanted by a more powerful and, judging from their sword-handles, larger-handed race;[87] but their success was probably due in a much higher degree to their superiority in the arts.

All that we know about savages, or may infer from their traditions and from old monuments, the history of which is quite forgotten by the present inhabitants, shew that from the remotest times successful tribes have supplanted other tribes. Relics of extinct or forgotten tribes have been discovered throughout the civilised regions of the earth, on the wild plains of America, and on the isolated islands in the Pacific Ocean. At the present day civilised nations are everywhere supplanting barbarous nations, excepting where the climate opposes a deadly barrier; and they succeed mainly, though not exclusively, through their arts, which are the products of the intellect. It is, therefore, highly probable that with mankind the intellectual faculties have been gradually perfected through natural selection; and this conclusion is sufficient for our purpose. Undoubtedly it would have been very interesting to have traced the development of each separate faculty from the state in which it exists in the lower animals to that in which it exists in man; but neither my ability nor knowledge permit the attempt.

It deserves notice that as soon as the progenitors of man became social (and this probably occurred at a very early period), the advancement of the intellectual faculties will have been aided and modified in an important manner, of which we see only traces in the lower animals, namely, through the principle of imitation, together with reason and experience. Apes are much given to imitation, as are the lowest savages; and the simple fact previously referred to, that after a time no animal can be caught in the same place by the same sort of trap, shews that animals learn by experience, and imitate each others' caution. Now, if some one man in a tribe, more sagacious than the others, invented a new snare or weapon, or other means of attack or defence, the plainest self-interest, without the assistance of much reasoning power, would prompt the other members to imitate him; and all would thus profit. The habitual practice of each new art must likewise in some slight degree strengthen the intellect. If the new invention were an important one, the tribe would increase in number, spread, and supplant other tribes. In a tribe thus rendered more numerous there would always be a rather better chance of the birth of other superior and inventive members. If such men left children to inherit their mental superiority, the chance of the birth of still more ingenious members would be somewhat better, and in a very small tribe decidedly better. Even if they left no children, the tribe would still include their blood-relations; and it has been ascertained by agriculturists[88] that by preserving and breeding from the family of an animal, which when slaughtered was found to be valuable, the desired character has been obtained.

Turning now to the social and moral faculties. In

---

86   After a time the members or tribes which are absorbed into another tribe assume, as Mr. Maine remarks ('Ancient Law,' 1861, p. 131), that they are the co-descendants of the same ancestors.

87   Morlot, 'Soc. Vaud. Sc. Nat.' 1860, p 294.

88   I have given instances in my 'Variation of Animals under Domestication,' vol. ii. p. 196.

order that primeval men, or the ape-like progenitors of man, should have become social, they must have acquired the same instinctive feelings which impel other animals to live in a body; and they no doubt exhibited the same general disposition. They would have felt uneasy when separated from their comrades, for whom they would have felt some degree of love; they would have warned each other of danger, and have given mutual aid in attack or defence. All this implies some degree of sympathy, fidelity, and courage. Such social qualities, the paramount importance of which to the lower animals is disputed by no one, were no doubt acquired by the progenitors of man in a similar manner, namely, through natural selection, aided by inherited habit. When two tribes of primeval man, living in the same country, came into competition, if the one tribe included (other circumstances being equal) a greater number of courageous, sympathetic, and faithful members, who were always ready to warn each other of danger, to aid and defend each other, this tribe would without doubt succeed best and conquer the other. Let it be borne in mind how all-important, in the never-ceasing wars of savages, fidelity and courage must be. The advantage which disciplined soldiers have over undisciplined hordes follows chiefly from the confidence which each man feels in his comrades. Obedience, as Mr. Bagehot has well shewn,[89] is of the highest value, for any form of government is better than none. Selfish and contentious people will not cohere, and without coherence nothing can be effected. A tribe possessing the above qualities in a high degree would spread and be victorious over other tribes; but in the course of time it would, judging from all past history, be in its turn overcome by some other and still more highly endowed tribe. Thus the social and moral qualities would tend slowly to advance and be diffused throughout the world.

But it may be asked, how within the limits of the same tribe did a large number of members first become endowed with these social and moral qualities, and how was the standard of excellence raised? It is extremely doubtful whether the offspring of the more sympathetic and benevolent parents, or of those which were the most faithful to their comrades, would be reared in greater number than the children of selfish and treacherous parents of the same tribe. He who was ready to sacrifice his life, as many a savage has been, rather than betray his comrades, would often leave no offspring to inherit his noble nature. The bravest men, who were always willing to come to the front in war, and who freely risked their lives for others, would on an average perish in larger number than other men. Therefore it seems scarcely possible (bearing in mind that we are not here speaking of one tribe being victorious over another) that the number of men gifted with such virtues, or that the standard of their excellence, could be increased through natural selection, that is, by the survival of the fittest.

Although the circumstances which lead to an increase in the number of men thus endowed within the same tribe are too complex to be clearly followed out, we can trace some of the probable steps. In the first place, as the reasoning powers and foresight of the members became improved, each man would soon learn from experience that if he aided his fellow-men, he would commonly receive aid in return. From this low motive he might acquire the habit of aiding his fellows; and the habit of performing benevolent actions certainly strengthens the feeling of sympathy, which gives the first impulse to benevolent actions. Habits, moreover, followed during many generations probably tend to be inherited.

But there is another and much more powerful stimulus to the development of the social virtues, namely, the praise and the blame of our fellowmen. The love of approbation and the dread of infamy, as well as the bestowal of praise or blame, are primarily due, as we have seen in the third chapter, to the instinct of sympathy; and this instinct no doubt was originally acquired, like all the other social instincts, through natural selection. At how early a period the progenitors of man, in the course of their development, became capable of feeling and being impelled by the praise or blame of their fellow-creatures, we cannot, of course, say. But it appears that even dogs appreciate encouragement, praise, and blame. The rudest savages feel the sentiment of glory, as they clearly show by preserving

---

89   See a remarkable series of articles on Physics and Politics in the 'Fortnightly Review,' Nov. 1867; April 1, 1868; July 1, 1869.

the trophies of their prowess, by their habit of excessive boasting, and even by the extreme care which they take of their personal appearance and decorations; for unless they regarded the opinion of their comrades, such habits would be senseless.

They certainly feel shame at the breach of some of their lesser rules; but how far they experience remorse is doubtful. I was at first surprised that I could not recollect any recorded instances of this feeling in savages; and Sir J. Lubbock[90] states that he knows of none. But if we banish from our minds all cases given in novels and plays and in death-bed confessions made to priests, I doubt whether many of us have actually witnessed remorse; though we may have often seen shame and contrition for smaller offences. Remorse is a deeply hidden feeling. It is incredible that a savage, who will sacrifice his life rather than betray his tribe, or one who will deliver himself up as a prisoner rather than break his parole,[91] would not feel remorse in his inmost soul, though he might conceal it, if he had failed in a duty which he held sacred.

We may therefore conclude that primeval man, at a very remote period, would have been influenced by the praise and blame of his fellows. It is obvious, that the members of the same tribe would approve of conduct which appeared to them to be for the general good, and would reprobate that which appeared evil. To do good unto others – to do unto others as ye would they should do unto you, – is the foundation-stone of morality. It is, therefore, hardly possible to exaggerate the importance during rude times of the love of praise and the dread of blame. A man who was not impelled by any deep, instinctive feeling, to sacrifice his life for the good of others, yet was roused to such actions by a sense of glory, would by his example excite the same wish for glory in other men, and would strengthen by exercise the noble feeling of admiration. He might thus do far more good to his tribe than by begetting offspring with a tendency to inherit his own high character.

With increased experience and reason, man perceives the more remote consequences of his actions, and the self-regarding virtues, such as temperance,

chastity, &c., which during early times are, as we have before seen, utterly disregarded, come to be highly esteemed or even held sacred. I need not, however, repeat what I have said on this head in the third chapter. Ultimately a highly complex sentiment, having its first origin in the social instincts, largely guided by the approbation of our fellow-men, ruled by reason, self-interest, and in later times by deep religious feelings, confirmed by instruction and habit, all combined, constitute our moral sense or conscience.

It must not be forgotten that although a high standard of morality gives but a slight or no advantage to each individual man and his children over the other men of the same tribe, yet that an advancement in the standard of morality and an increase in the number of well-endowed men will certainly give an immense advantage to one tribe over another. There can be no doubt that a tribe including many members who, from possessing in a high degree the spirit of patriotism, fidelity, obedience, courage, and sympathy, were always ready to give aid to each other and to sacrifice themselves for the common good, would be victorious over most other tribes; and this would be natural selection. At all times throughout the world tribes have supplanted other tribes; and as morality is one element in their success, the standard of morality and the number of well-endowed men will thus everywhere tend to rise and increase.

It is, however, very difficult to form any judgment why one particular tribe and not another has been successful and has risen in the scale of civilisation. Many savages are in the same condition as when first discovered several centuries ago. As Mr. Bagehot has remarked, we are apt to look at progress as the normal rule in human society; but history refutes this. The ancients did not even entertain the idea; nor do the oriental nations at the present day. According to another high authority, Mr. Maine,[92] "the greatest part of mankind has never shewn a particle of desire that its civil institutions should be improved." Progress seems to depend on many concurrent favourable conditions, far too complex to be followed out. But it has often

---

90   'Origin of Civilisation,' 1870, p. 265.
91   Mr. Wallace gives cases in his 'Contributions to the Theory of Natural Selection,' 1870, p. 354.
92   'Ancient Law,' 1861, p. 22. For Mr. Bagehot's remarks, 'Fortnightly Review,' April 1, 1868, p. 452.

been remarked, that a cool climate from leading to industry and the various arts has been highly favourable, or even indispensable for this end. The Esquimaux, pressed by hard necessity, have succeeded in many ingenious inventions, but their climate has been too severe for continued progress. Nomadic habits, whether over wide plains, or through the dense forests of the tropics, or along the shores of the sea, have in every case been highly detrimental. Whilst observing the barbarous inhabitants of Tierra del Fuego, it struck me that the possession of some property, a fixed abode, and the union of many families under a chief, were the indispensable requisites for civilisation. Such habits almost necessitate the cultivation of the ground; and the first steps in cultivation would probably result, as I have elsewhere shewn,[93] from some such accident as the seeds of a fruit-tree falling on a heap of refuse and producing an unusually fine variety. The problem, however, of the first advance of savages towards civilisation is at present much too difficult to be solved....

Bibliography

Alland, Alexander, Jr., ed. *Human Nature: Darwin's View.* New York: Columbia University Press, 1985.

Appleman, Philip, ed. *Darwin: A Norton Critical Edition.* 2nd ed. New York: W. W. Norton, 1979.

Darwin, Charles. *The Origin of Species.* Harmondsworth: Penguin, 1968. [originally published 1859].

Dawkins, Richard. *The Blind Watchmaker.* New York: W. W. Norton, 1987.

Dennett, Daniel C. *Darwin's Dangerous Idea.* New York: Simon and Schuster, 1995.

---

93   'The Variation of Animals and Plants under Domestication,' vol. i. p. 309.

CHAPTER THIRTY — EDWARD O. WILSON

Edward O. (Osborne) Wilson (b. 1929) is Frank B. Baird, Jr., Professor of Science and Curator of Entomology at the Museum of Comparative Zoology, Harvard University. He is a leading entomologist, a prominent Darwinian evolutionary biologist; and extending from the latter base, Wilson is the founder of sociobiology.

Sociobiology and its more recent cousin, evolutionary psychology, are attempts to create sciences of human nature based on Darwinian theory. They claim to be achieved sciences with a beachhead of results that the future will substantively augment. And they – especially sociobiology, the older and more famous of the two – are controversial, and their claims to genuinely scientific status contested.

The reader will see how some of the fundamentals of sociobiology are conceived and set out by Wilson. It may be said that the selection chosen shows sociobiology in its most orthodoxly Darwinian best-dress. Other passages display a bolder, more conceptually, or more empirically, challenging (and, critics say, challenged) body of claims and speculations. But these are the foundations for the science, or philosophy – whichever it is – and these will be, arguably, the fairest and conceptually best grounded of introductions to it.

Edward O. Wilson, *On Human Nature*

(Source: Edward O. Wilson. *Sociobiology: The New Synthesi*. Cambridge, Mass., and London: The Belknap Press of Harvard University Press, 1975, Ch. 27, pp. 547-555, 559-564, 567-569, 572-575.)

Man: From Sociobiology to Sociology

Let us now consider man in the free spirit of natural history, as though we were zoologists from another planet completing a catalog of social species on Earth. In this macroscopic view the humanities and social sciences shrink to specialized branches of biology; history, biography, and fiction are the research protocols of human ethology; and anthropology and sociology together constitute the sociobiology of a single primate species.

Homo sapiens is ecologically a very peculiar species. It occupies the widest geographical range and maintains the highest local densities of any of the primates. An astute ecologist from another planet would not be surprised to find that only one species of Homo exists. Modern man has preempted all the conceivable hominid niches. Two or more species of hominids did coexist in the past, when the *Australopithecus* man-apes and possibly an early Homo lived in Africa. But only one evolving line survived into late Pleistocene times to participate in the emergence of the most advanced human social traits.

Modern man is anatomically unique. His erect posture and wholly bipedal locomotion are not even approached in other primates that occasionally walk on their hind legs, including the gorilla and chimpanzee. The skeleton has been profoundly modified to accommodate the change: the spine is curved to distribute the weight of the trunk more evenly down its length; the chest is flattened to move the center of gravity back toward the spine; the pelvis is broadened to serve as an attachment for the powerful striding muscles of the upper legs and reshaped into a basin to hold the viscera; the tail is eliminated, its vertebrae (now called the coccyx) curved inward to form part of the floor of the pelvic basin; the occipital condyles have rotated far beneath the skull so that the weight of the head is balanced on them; the face is shortened to assist this shift in gravity; the thumb is enlarged to give power to the hand; the leg is lengthened; and the foot is drastically narrowed and lengthened to facilitate striding. Other changes have taken place. Hair has been lost from most of the body. It is still not known why modern man is a "naked ape." One plausible explanation is that nakedness served as a device to cool the body during the strenuous pursuit of prey in the heat of the African plains. It is associated with man's exceptional reliance on sweating to reduce body heat; the human body contains from two to five million sweat glands, far more than in any other primate species.

The reproductive physiology and behavior of *Homo sapiens* have also undergone extraordinary evolution. In particular, the estrous cycle of the female has changed in two ways that affect sexual and social behavior. Menstruation has been intensified. The females of some other primate species experience slight bleeding, but only in women is there a heavy sloughing of the wall of the "disappointed womb" with consequent heavy bleeding. The estrus, or period of female "heat," has been replaced by virtually continuous sexual activity. Copulation is initiated not by response to the conventional primate signals of estrus, such as changes in color of the skin around the female sexual organs and the release of pheromones, but by extended foreplay entailing mutual stimulation by the partners. The traits of physical attraction are, moreover, fixed in nature. They include the pubic hair of both sexes and the protuberant breasts and buttocks of women. The flattened sexual cycle and continuous female attractiveness cement the close marriage bonds that are basic to human social life.

At a distance a perceptive Martian zoologist would regard the globular head as a most significant clue to human biology. The cerebrum of *Homo* was expanded enormously during a relatively short span of evolutionary time.... Three million years ago *Australopithecus* had an adult cranial capacity of 400-500 cubic centimeters, comparable to that of the chimpanzee and gorilla. Two million years later its presumptive descendant *Homo erectus* had a capacity of about 1000 cubic centimeters. The next million years saw an increase to 1400-1700 cubic centimeters in Neanderthal man and 900-2000 cubic centimeters in modern *Homo sapiens*. The growth in intelligence that accompanied this enlargement was so great that it cannot yet be measured in any meaningful way. Human beings can be compared among themselves in terms of a few of the basic components of intelligence and creativity. But no scale has been invented that can objectively compare man with chimpanzees and other living primates.

We have leaped forward in mental evolution in a way that continues to defy self-analysis. The mental hypertrophy has distorted even the most basic primate social qualities into nearly unrecognizable forms. Individual species of Old World monkeys and apes have notably plastic social organizations; man has extended the trend into a protean ethnicity. Monkeys and apes utilize behavioral scaling to adjust aggressive and sexual interactions; in man the scales have become multidimensional, culturally adjustable, and almost endlessly subtle. Bonding and the practices of reciprocal altruism are rudimentary in other primates; man has expanded them into great networks where individuals consciously alter roles from hour to hour as if changing masks.

It is the task of comparative sociobiology to trace these and other human qualities as closely as possible back through time. Besides adding perspective and perhaps offering some sense of philosophical ease, the exercise will help to identify the behaviors and rules by which individual human beings increase their Darwinian fitness through the manipulation of society. In a phrase, we are searching for the human biogram (Count, 1958; Tiger and Fox, 1971). One of the key questions, never far from the thinking of anthropologists and biologists who pursue real theory, is to what extent the biogram represents an adaptation to modern cultural life and to what extent it is a phylogenetic vestige. Our civilizations were jerrybuilt around the biogram. How have they been influenced by it? Conversely, how much flexibility is there in the biogram, and in which parameters particularly? Experience with other animals indicates that when organs are hypertrophied, phylogeny is hard to reconstruct. This is the crux of the problem of the evolutionary analysis of human behavior. In the remainder of the chapter, human qualities will be discussed insofar as they appear to be general traits of the species. Then current knowledge of the evolution of the biogram will be reviewed, and finally some implications for the planning of future societies will be considered.

Plasticity of Social Organization

The first and most easily verifiable diagnostic trait is statistical in nature. The parameters of social organization, including group size, properties of hierarchies, and rates of gene exchange, vary far more among human populations than among those of any other primate species. The variation exceeds even that occurring between the remaining primate species. Some increase in plasticity is to be expected. It represents the extrapolation of a trend toward variability already apparent in the baboons, chimpanzees, and other cercopithecoids. What is truly surprising, however, is the extreme to which it has been carried.

Why are human societies this flexible? Part of the reason is that the members themselves vary so much in behavior and achievement. Even in the simplest societies individuals differ greatly. Within a small tribe of !Kung Bushmen can be found individuals who are acknowledged as the "best people" – the leaders and outstanding specialists among the hunters and healers. Even with an emphasis on sharing goods, some are exceptionally able entrepreneurs and unostentatiously acquire a certain amount of wealth. !Kung men, no less than men in advanced industrial societies, generally establish themselves by their mid-thirties or else accept a lesser status for life. There are some who never try to make it, live in run-down huts, and show little pride in themselves or their work (Pfeiffer, 1969). The ability to slip into such roles, shaping one's personality to fit, may itself be adaptive. Human societies are organized by high intelligence, and each member is faced by a mixture of social challenges that taxes all of his ingenuity. This baseline variation is amplified at the group level by other qualities exceptionally pronounced in human societies: the long, close period of socialization; the loose connectedness of the communication networks; the multiplicity of bonds; the capacity, especially within literate cultures, to communicate over long distances and periods of history; and from all these traits, the capacity to dissemble, to manipulate, and to exploit. Each parameter can be altered easily, and each has a marked effect on the final social structure. The result could be the observed variation among societies.

The hypothesis to consider, then, is that genes promoting flexibility in social behavior are strongly selected at the individual level. But note that variation in social organization is only a possible, not a necessary consequence of this process. In order to generate the amount of variation actually observed to occur, it is necessary for there to be multiple adaptive peaks. In other words, different forms of society within the same species must be nearly enough alike in survival ability for many to enjoy long tenure. The result would be a statistical ensemble of kinds of societies which, if not equilibrial, is at least not shifting rapidly toward one particular mode or another. The alternative, found in some social insects, is flexibility in individual behavior and caste development, which nevertheless results in an approach toward uniformity in the statistical distribution of the kinds of individuals when all individuals within a colony are taken together. In honeybees and in ants of the genera *Formica* and *Pogonomyrmex*, "personality" differences are strongly marked even within single castes. Some individuals, referred to by entomologists as the elites, are unusually active, perform more than their share of lifetime work, and incite others to work through facilitation. Other colony members are consistently sluggish. Although they are seemingly healthy and live long lives, their per-individual output is only a small fraction of that of the elites. Specialization also occurs. Certain individuals remain with the brood as nurses far longer than the average, while others concentrate on nest building or foraging. Yet somehow the total pattern of behavior in the colony converges on the species average. When one colony with its hundreds or thousands of members is compared with another of the same species, the statistical patterns of activity are about the same. We know that some of this consistency is due to negative feedback. As one requirement such as brood care or nest repair intensifies, workers shift their activities to compensate until the need is met, then change back again. Experiments have shown that disruption of the feedback loops, and thence deviation by the colony from the statistical norms, can be disastrous. It is therefore not surprising to find that the loops are both precise and powerful (Wilson, 1971).

The controls governing human societies are not nearly so strong, and the effects of deviation are not so dangerous. The anthropological literature abounds with examples of societies that contain obvious inefficiencies and even pathological flaws – yet endure. The slave society of Jamaica, compellingly described by Orlando Patterson (1967), was unquestionably pathological by the moral canons of civilized life. "What marks it out is the astonishing neglect and distortion of almost every one of the basic prerequisites of normal human living. This was a society in which clergymen were the 'most finished debauchees' in the land; in which the institution of marriage was officially condemned among both masters and slaves; in which the family was unthinkable to the vast majority of the population and promiscuity the norm; in which education was seen as an absolute waste of time and teachers shunned like the plague; in which the legal system was quite deliberately a travesty of anything that could be called justice; and in which all forms of refinements, of art, of folkways, were either absent or in a state of total disintegration. Only a small proportion of whites, who monopolized almost all of the fertile land in the island, benefited from the system. And these, no sooner had they secured their fortunes, abandoned the land which the production of their own wealth had made unbearable to live in, for the comforts of the mother country." Yet this Hobbesian world lasted for nearly two centuries. The people multiplied while the economy flourished.

The Ik of Uganda are an equally instructive case (Turnbull, 1972) They are former hunters who have made a disastrous shift to cultivation. Always on the brink of starvation, they have seen their culture reduced to a vestige. Their only stated value is *ngag*, or food; their basic notion of goodness (*marangik*) is the individual possession of food in the stomach; and their definition of a good man is *yakw ana marang*, "a man who has a full belly." Villages are still built, but the nuclear family has ceased to function as an institution. Children are kept with reluctance and from about three years of age are made to find their own way of life. Marriage ordinarily occurs only when there is a specific need for cooperation. Because of the lack of energy, sexual activity is minimal and its pleasures are considered to be about on the same level as those of defecation. Death is treated with relief or amusement, since it means more *ngag* for survivors. Because the unfortunate Ik are at the lowest sustainable level, there is a temptation to conclude that they are doomed. Yet somehow their society has remained intact and more or less stable for at least 30 years, and it could endure indefinitely.

How can such variation in social structure persist? The explanation may be lack of competition from other species, resulting in what biologists call ecological release. During the past ten thousand years or longer, man as a whole has been so successful in dominating his environment that almost

any kind of culture can succeed for a while, so long as it has a modest degree of internal consistency and does not shut off reproduction altogether. No species of ant or termite enjoys this freedom. The slightest inefficiency in constructing nests, in establishing odor trails, or in conducting nuptial flights could result in the quick extinction of the species by predation and competition from other social insects. To a scarcely lesser extent the same is true for social carnivores and primates. In short, animal species tend to be tightly packed in the ecosystem with little room for experimentation or play. Man has temporarily escaped the constraint of interspecific competition. Although cultures replace one another, the process is much less effective than interspecific competition in reducing variance.

It is part of the conventional wisdom that virtually all cultural variation is phenotypic rather than genetic in origin. This view has gained support from the ease with which certain aspects of culture can be altered in the space of a single generation, too quickly to be evolutionary in nature. The drastic alteration in Irish society in the first two years of the potato blight (1846-1848) is a case in point. Another is the shift in the Japanese authority structure during the American occupation following World War II. Such examples can be multiplied endlessly – they are the substance of history. It is also true that human populations are not very different from one another genetically. When Lewontin (1972) analyzed existing data on nine blood-type systems, he found that 85 percent of the variance was composed of diversity within populations and only 15 percent was due to diversity between populations. There is no a priori reason for supposing that this sample of genes possesses a distribution much different from those of other, less accessible systems affecting behavior.

The extreme orthodox view of environmentalism goes further, holding that in effect there is no genetic variance in the transmission of culture. In other words, the capacity for culture is transmitted by a single human genotype. Dobzhansky (1963) stated this hypothesis as follows: "Culture is not inherited through genes, it is acquired by learning from other human beings . . . In a sense, human genes have surrendered their primacy in human evolution to an entirely new, nonbiological or superorganic agent, culture. However, it should not be forgotten that this agent is entirely dependent on the human genotype." Although the genes have given away most of their sovereignty, they maintain a certain amount of influence in at least the behavioral qualities that underlie variations between cultures. Moderately high heritability has been documented in introversion-extroversion measures, personal tempo, psychomotor and sports activities, neuroticism, dominance, depression, and the tendency toward certain forms of mental illness such as schizophrenia (Parsons, 1967; Lerner, 1968). Even a small portion of this variance invested in population differences might predispose societies toward cultural differences. At the very least, we should try to measure this amount. It is not valid to point to the absence of a behavioral trait in one or a few societies as conclusive evidence that the trait is environmentally induced and has no genetic disposition in man. The very opposite could be true.

In short, there is a need for a discipline of anthropological genetics. In the interval before we acquire it, it should be possible to characterize the human biogram by two indirect methods. First, models can be constructed from the most elementary rules of human behavior. Insofar as they can be tested, the rules will characterize the biogram in much the same way that ethograms drawn by zoologists identify the "typical" behavioral repertoires of animal species. The rules can be legitimately compared with the ethograms of other primate species. Variation in the rules among human cultures, however slight, might provide clues to underlying genetic differences, particularly when it is correlated with variation in behavioral traits known to be heritable. Social scientists have in fact begun to take this first approach, although in a different context from the one suggested here. Abraham Maslow (1954, 1972) postulated that human beings respond to a hierarchy of needs, such that the lower levels must be satisfied before much attention is devoted to the higher ones. The most basic needs are hunger and sleep. When these are met, safety becomes the primary consideration, then the need to belong to a group and receive love, next self-esteem, and finally self-actualization and creativity. The ideal society in Maslow's dream is one which "fosters the fullest development of human potentials, of the fullest degree of humanness." When the biogram is freely expressed, its center of gravity should come to rest in the higher levels. A second social scientist, George C. Homans (1961), has adopted a Skinnerian approach in an attempt to reduce human behavior to the basic processes of associative learning. The rules he postulates are the following:

1. If in the past the occurrence of a particular stimulus-situation has been the occasion on which a man's activity has been rewarded, then the more similar the present stimulus-situation is to the past one, the more likely the man is at the present time to emit this activity or one similar to it.

2. The more often within a given period of time a man's activity rewards the behavior of another, the more often the other will perform the behavior.

3. The more valuable to a man a unit of the activity another gives him, the more often he behaves in the manner rewarded by the activity of the other.

4. The more often a man has in the recent past received a rewarding activity from another, the less valuable any further unit of that activity becomes to him.

Maslow the ethologist and visionary seems a world apart from Homans the behaviorist and reductionist. Yet their approaches are reconcilable. Homans' rules can be viewed as comprising some of the enabling devices by which the human biogram is expressed. His operational word is *reward,* which is in fact the set of all interactions defined by the emotive centers of the brain as desirable. According to evolutionary theory, desirability is measured in units of genetic fitness, and the emotive centers have been programmed accordingly. Maslow's hierarchy is simply the order of priority in the goals toward which the rules are directed.

The other indirect approach to anthropological genetics is through phylogenetic analysis. By comparing man with other primate species, it might be possible to identify basic primate traits that lie beneath the surface and help to determine the configuration of man's higher social behavior. This approach has been taken with great style and vigor in a series of popular books by Konrad Lorenz *(On Aggression),* Robert Ardrey *(The Social Contract),* Desmond Morris *(The Naked Ape),* and Lionel Tiger and Robin Fox *(The Imperial Animal).* Their efforts were salutary in calling attention to man's status as a biological species adapted to particular environments. The wide attention they received broke the stifling grip of the extreme behaviorists, whose view of the mind of man as a virtually equipotent response machine was neither correct nor heuristic. But their particular handling of the problem tended to be inefficient and misleading. They selected one plausible hypothesis or another based on a review of a small sample of animal species, then advocated the explanation to the limit. The weakness of this method was discussed earlier in a more general context (Chapter 2) and does not need repetition here.

The correct approach using comparative ethology is to base a rigorous phylogeny of closely related species on many biological traits. Then social behavior is treated as the dependent variable and its evolution deduced from it. When this cannot be done with confidence (and it cannot in man) the next best procedure is the one outlined in Chapter 7: establish the lowest taxonomic level at which each character shows significant intertaxon variation. Characters that shift from species to species or genus to genus are the most labile. We cannot safely extrapolate them from the cercopithecoid monkeys and apes to man. In the primates these labile qualities include group size, group cohesiveness, openness of the group to others, involvement of the male in parental care, attention structure, and the intensity and form of territorial defense. Characters are considered conservative if they remain constant at the level of the taxonomic family or throughout the order Primates, and they are the ones most likely to have persisted in relatively unaltered form into the evolution of *Homo*. These conservative traits include aggressive dominance systems, with males generally dominant over females; scaling in the intensity of responses, especially during aggressive interactions; intensive and prolonged maternal care, with a pronounced degree of socialization in the young; and matrilineal social organization. This classification of behavioral traits offers an appropriate basis for hypothesis formation. It allows a qualitative assessment of the probabilities that various behavioral traits have persisted into modern *Homo sapiens*. The possibility of course remains that some labile traits are homologous between man and, say, the chimpanzee. And conversely, some traits conservative throughout the rest of the primates might nevertheless have changed during the origin of man. Furthermore, the assessment is not meant to imply that conservative traits are more genetic – that is, have higher heritability – than labile ones. Lability can be based wholly on genetic differences between species or populations within species. Returning finally to the matter of cultural evolution, we can heuristically conjecture that the traits proven to be labile are also the ones most likely to differ from one human society to another on the basis of genetic differences. The evidence, reviewed in Table 27-1, is not inconsistent with this basic conception. Finally, it is worth special note that the comparative ethological approach does not in any way predict man's unique traits. It is a general rule of evolutionary studies that the direction of quantum jumps is not easily read by phylogenetic extrapolation.

Barter and Reciprocal Altruism

Sharing is rare among the nonhuman primates. It occurs in rudimentary form only in the chimpanzee and perhaps a few other Old World monkeys and apes. But in man it is one of the strongest social traits, reaching levels that match the intense trophallactic exchanges of termites and ants. As a result only man has an economy. His high intelligence and symbolizing ability make true barter possible. Intelligence also permits the exchanges to be stretched out in time, converting them into acts of reciprocal altruism (Trivers, 1971). The conventions of this mode of behavior are expressed in the familiar utterances of everyday life:

"Give me some now; I'll repay you later."

"Come to my aid this time, and I'll be your friend when you need me."

"I really didn't think of the rescue as heroism; it was only what I would expect others to do for me or my family in the same situation."

Money, as Talcott Parsons has been fond of pointing out, has no value in itself. It consists only of bits of metal and scraps of paper by which men pledge to surrender varying amounts of property and services upon demand; in other words it is a quantification of reciprocal altruism.

Perhaps the earliest form of barter in early human societies was the exchange of meat captured by the males for plant food gathered by the females. If living hunter-gatherer societies reflect the primitive state, this exchange formed an important element in a distinctive kind of sexual bond.

Fox (1972), following Lévi-Strauss (1949), has

Table 27-1 General social traits in human beings, classified according to whether they are unique, belong to a class of behaviors that are variable at the level of the species or genus in the remainder of the primates (labile), or belong to a class of behaviors that are uniform through the remainder of the primates (conservative).

Evolutionarily labile primate traits	Evolutionarily conservative primate traits	Human traits
		SHARED WITH SOME OTHER PRIMATES
Group size		Highly variable
Group cohesiveness		Highly variable
Openness of group to others		Highly variable
Involvement of male in parental care		Strong
Attention structure		Centripetal on leading males
Intensity and form of territorial defense		Highly variable, but territoriality is general
		SHARED WITH ALL OR ALMOST ALL OTHER PRIMATES
	Aggressive dominance systems, with males dominant over females	Consistent with other primates, although variable
	Scaling of responses especially in aggressive interactions	Consistent with other primates
	Prolonged maternal care; pronounced socialization of young	Consistent with other primates
	Matrilineal organization	Mostly consistent with other primates
		UNIQUE
		True language, elaborate culture
		Sexual activity continuous through menstrual cycle
		Formalized incest taboos and marriage exchange rules with recognition of kinship networks
		Cooperative division of labor between adult males and females

argued from ethnographic evidence that a key early step in human social evolution was the use of women in barter. As males acquired status through the control of females, they used them as objects of exchange to cement alliances and bolster kinship networks. Preliterate societies are characterized by complex rules of marriage that can often be interpreted directly as power brokerage. This is particularly the case where the elementary negative marriage rules, proscribing certain types of unions, are supplemented by positive rules that direct which exchanges must be made. Within individual Australian aboriginal societies two moieties exist between which marriages are permitted. The men of each moiety trade nieces, or more specifically their sisters' daughters. Power accumulates with age, because a man can control the descendants of nieces as remote as the daughter of his sister's daughter. Combined with polygyny, the system insures both political and genetic advantage to the old men of the tribe.

For all its intricacy, the formalization of marital exchanges between tribes has the same approximate genetic effect as the haphazard wandering of male monkeys from one troop to another or the exchange of young mature females between chimpanzee populations. Approximately 7.5 percent of marriages contracted among Australian aborigines prior to European influence were intertribal, and similar rates have been reported in Brazilian Indians and other preliterate societies (Morton, 1969). It will be recalled (Chapter 4) that gene flow of the order of 10 percent per generation is more than enough to counteract fairly intensive natural pressures that tend to differentiate populations. Thus intertribal marital exchanges are a major factor in creating the observed high degree of genetic similarity among populations. The ultimate adaptive basis of exogamy is not gene flow per se but rather the avoidance of inbreeding. Again, a 10 percent gene flow is adequate for the purpose.

The microstructure of human social organization is based on sophisticated mutual assessments that lead to the making of contracts. As Erving Goffman correctly perceived, a stranger is rapidly but politely explored to determine his socioeconomic status, intelligence and education, self-perception, social attitudes, competence, trust-worthiness, and emotional stability. The information, much of it subconsciously given and absorbed, has

an eminently practical value. The probe must be deep, for the individual tries to create the impression that will gain him the maximum advantage. At the very least he maneuvers to avoid revealing information that will imperil his status. The presentation of self can be expected to contain deceptive elements:

> Many crucial facts lie beyond the time and place of interaction or lie concealed within it. For example, the "true" or "real" attitudes, beliefs, and emotions of the individual can be ascertained only indirectly, through his avowals or through what appears to be involuntary expressive behavior. Similarly, if the individual offers the others a product or service, they will often find that during the interaction there will be no time or place immediately available for eating the pudding that the proof can be found in. They will be forced to accept some events as conventional or natural signs of something not directly available to the senses. (Goffman, 1959)

Deception and hypocrisy are neither absolute evils that virtuous men suppress to a minimum level nor residual animal traits waiting to be erased by further social evolution. They are very human devices for conducting the complex daily business of social life. The level in each particular society may represent a compromise that reflects the size and complexity of the society. If the level is too low, others will seize the advantage and win. If it is too high, ostracism is the result. Complete honesty on all sides is not the answer. The old primate frankness would destroy the delicate fabric of social life that has built up in human populations beyond the limits of the immediate clan. As Louis J. Halle correctly observed, good manners have become a substitute for love.

Bonding, Sex, and Division of Labor

The building block of nearly all human societies is the nuclear family (Reynolds, 1968; Leibowitz, 1968). The populace of an American industrial city, no less than a band of hunter-gatherers in the Australian desert, is organized around this unit. In both cases the family moves between regional communities, maintaining complex ties with primary kin by means of visits (or telephone calls and letters) and the exchange of gifts. During the day the women and children remain in the residential area while the men forage for game or its symbolic equivalent in the form of barter and money. The males cooperate in bands to hunt or deal with neighboring groups. If not actually blood relations, they tend at least to act as "bands of brothers." Sexual bonds are carefully contracted in observance with tribal customs and are intended to be permanent. Polygamy, either covert or explicitly sanctioned by custom, is practiced predominantly by the males. Sexual behavior is nearly continuous through the menstrual cycle and marked by extended foreplay. Morris (1967), drawing on the data of Masters and Johnson (1966) and others, has enumerated the unique features of human sexuality that he considers to be associated with the loss of body hair: the rounded and protuberant breasts of the young woman, the flushing of areas of skin during coition, the vaso-dilation and increased erogenous sensitivity of the lips, soft portions of the nose, ear, nipples, areolae, and genitals, and the large size of the male penis, especially during erection. As Darwin himself noted in 1871, even the naked skin of the woman is used as a sexual releaser. All of these alterations serve to cement the permanent bonds, which are unrelated in time to the moment of ovulation. Estrus has been reduced to a vestige, to the consternation of those who attempt to practice birth control by the rhythm method. Sexual behavior has been largely dissociated from the act of fertilization. It is ironic that religionists who forbid sexual activity except for purposes of procreation should do so on the basis of "natural law." Theirs is a misguided effort in comparative ethology, based on the incorrect assumption that in reproduction man is essentially like other animals.

The extent and formalization of kinship prevailing in almost all human societies are also unique features of the biology of our species. Kinship systems provide at least three distinct advantages. First, they bind alliances between tribes and subtribal units and provide a conduit for the conflict-free emigration of young members. Second, they are an important part of the bartering system by which certain males achieve dominance and leadership. Finally, they serve as a homeostatic device for seeing groups through hard times. When food grows scarce, tribal units can call on their allies for altruistic assistance in a way unknown in other social primates. The Athapaskan Dogrib Indians, a hunter-gatherer people of the nonwestern Canadian arctic, provide one example. The Athapaskans are organized loosely by the bilateral primary linkage principle (June Helm, 1968). Local bands wander through a common territory, making intermittent contacts and exchanging members by intermarriage. When famine strikes, the endangered bands can coalesce with those temporarily better off. A second example is the Yanomami of South America, who rely on kin when their crops are destroyed by enemies. (Chagnon, 1968).

As societies evolved from bands through tribes into chiefdoms and states, some of the modes of bonding were extended beyond kinship networks to include other kinds of alliances and economic agreements. Because the networks were then larger, the lines of communication longer, and the interactions more diverse, the total systems became vastly more complex. But the moralistic rules underlying these arrangements appear not to have been altered a great deal. The average individual still operates under a formalized code no more elaborate than that governing the members of hunter-gatherer societies.

Role Playing and Polyethism

The superman, like the super-ant or super-wolf, can never be an individual; it is the society, whose members diversify and cooperate to create a composite well beyond the capacity of any conceivable organism. Human societies have effloresced to levels of extreme complexity because their members have the intelligence and flexibility to play roles of virtually any degree of specification, and to switch them as the occasion demands. Modern man is an actor of many parts who may well be stretched to his limit by the constantly shifting demands of his environment. As Goffman (1961) observed, "Perhaps there are times when an individual does march up and down like a wooden soldier, tightly rolled up in a particular role. It is true that here and there we can pounce on a moment when an individual sits fully astride a single role, head erect, eyes front, but the next moment the picture is shattered into many pieces and the individual divides into different persons holding the ties of different spheres of life by his hands, by his teeth, and by his grimaces. When seen up close, the individual, bringing together in various ways all the connections he has in life, becomes a blur." Little wonder that the most acute inner problem of modern man is identity.

Roles in human societies are fundamentally different from the castes of social insects. The members of human societies sometimes cooperate closely in insectan fashion, but more frequently they compete for the limited resources allocated to their role-sector. The best and most entrepreneurial of the role-actors usually gain a disproportionate share of the rewards, while the least successful are displaced to other, less desirable positions. In addition, individuals attempt to move to higher socioeconomic positions by changing roles. Competition between classes also occurs, and in great moments of history it has proved to be a determinant of societal change.

A key question of human biology is whether there exists a genetic predisposition to enter certain classes and to play certain roles. Circumstances can be easily conceived in which such genetic differentiation might occur. The heritability of at least some parameters of intelligence and emotive traits is sufficient to respond to a moderate amount of disruptive selection. Dahlberg (1947) showed that if a single gene appears that is responsible for success and an upward shift in status, it can be rapidly concentrated in the uppermost socioeconomic classes. Suppose, for example, there are two classes, each beginning with only a 1 percent frequency of the homozygotes of the upward-mobile gene. Suppose further that 50 percent of the homozygotes in the lower class are transferred upward in each generation. Then in only ten generations, depending on the relative sizes of the groups, the upper class will be comprised of as many as 20 percent homozygotes or more and the lower class of as few as 0.5 percent or less. Using a similar argument, Herrnstein (1971) proposed that as environmental opportunities become more nearly equal within societies, socioeconomic groups will be defined increasingly by genetically based differences in intelligence.

A strong initial bias toward such stratification is created when one human population conquers and subjugates another, a common enough event in human history. Genetic differences in mental traits, however slight, tend to be preserved by the raising of class barriers, racial and cultural discrimination,

and physical ghettos. The geneticist C. D. Darlington (1969), among others, postulated this process to be a prime source of genetic diversity within human societies.

Yet despite the plausibility of the general argument, there is little evidence of any hereditary solidification of status. The castes of India have been in existence for 2000 years, more than enough time for evolutionary divergence, but they differ only slightly in blood type and other measurable anatomical and physiological traits. Powerful forces can be identified that work against the genetic fixation of caste differences. First, cultural evolution is too fluid. Over a period of decades or at most centuries ghettos are replaced, races and subject people are liberated, the conquerors are conquered. Even within relatively stable societies the pathways of upward mobility are numerous. The daughters of lower classes tend to marry upward. Success in commerce or political life can launch a family from virtually any socioeconomic group into the ruling class in a single generation. Furthermore, there are many Dahlberg genes, not just the one postulated for argument in the simplest model. The hereditary factors of human success are strongly polygenic and form a long list, only a few of which have been measured. IQ constitutes only one subset of the components of intelligence. Less tangible but equally important qualities are creativity, entrepreneurship, drive, and mental stamina. Let us assume that the genes contributing to these qualities are scattered over many chromosomes. Assume further that some of the traits are uncorrelated or even negatively correlated. Under these circumstances only the most intense forms of disruptive selection could result in the formation of stable ensembles of genes. A much more likely circumstance is the one that apparently prevails: the maintenance of a large amount of genetic diversity within societies and the loose correlation of some of the genetically determined traits with success. This scrambling process is accelerated by the continuous shift in the fortunes of individual families from one generation to the next

Even so, the influence of genetic factors toward the assumption of certain *broad* roles cannot be discounted. Consider male homosexuality. The surveys of Kinsey and his coworkers showed that in the 1940's approximately 10 percent of the sexually mature males in the United States were mainly or exclusively homosexual for at least three years prior to being interviewed. Homosexuality is also exhibited by comparably high fractions of the male populations in many if not most other cultures. Kallmann's twin data indicate the probable existence of a genetic predisposition toward the condition. Accordingly, Hutchinson (1959) suggested that the homosexual genes may possess superior fitness in heterozygous conditions. His reasoning followed lines now standard in the thinking of population genetics. The homosexual state itself results in inferior genetic fitness, because of course homosexual men marry much less frequently and have far fewer children than their unambiguously heterosexual counterparts. The simplest way genes producing such a condition can be maintained in evolution is if they are superior in the heterozygous state, that is, if heterozygotes survive into maturity better, produce more offspring, or both. An interesting alternative hypothesis has been suggested to me by Herman T. Spieth (personal communication) and independently developed by Robert L. Trivers (1974). The homosexual members of primitive societies may have functioned as helpers, either while hunting in company with other men or in more domestic occupations at the dwelling sites. Freed from the special obligations of parental duties, they could have operated with special efficiency in assisting close relatives. Genes favoring homosexuality could then be sustained at a high equilibrium level by kin selection alone. It remains to be said that if such genes really exist they are almost certainly incomplete in penetrance and variable in expressivity, meaning that which bearers of the genes develop the behavioral trait and to what degree depend on the presence or absence of modifier genes and the influence of the environment.

Other basic types might exist, and perhaps the clues lie in full sight. In his study of British nursery children Blurton Jones (1969) distinguished two apparently basic behavioral types. "Verbalists," a small minority, often remained alone, seldom moved about, and almost never joined in rough-and-tumble play. They talked a great deal and spent much of their time looking at books. The other children were "doers." They joined groups, moved around a great deal, and spent much of their time painting and making objects instead of talking. Blurton Jones speculated that the dichotomy results from an early divergence in behavioral development persisting into maturity. Should it prove general it might contribute fundamentally to diversity within cultures. There is no way of knowing whether the divergence is ultimately genetic in origin or triggered entirely by experiential events at an early age.

....

Culture, Ritual, and Religion

The rudiments of culture are possessed by higher primates other than man, including the Japanese monkey and chimpanzee (Chapter 7), but only in man has culture thoroughly infiltrated virtually every aspect of life. Ethnographic detail is genetically underprescribed, resulting in great amounts of diversity among societies. Underprescription does not mean that culture has been freed from the genes. What has evolved is the capacity for culture, indeed the overwhelming tendency to develop one culture or another. Robin Fox (1971) put the argument in the following form. If the proverbial experiments of the pharaoh Psammetichos and James IV of Scotland had worked, and children reared in isolation somehow survived in good health,

I do not doubt that they could speak and that theoretically, given time, they or their offspring would invent and develop a language despite their never having been taught one. Furthermore, this language, although totally different from any known to us, would be analyzable by linguists on the same basis as other languages and translatable into all known languages. But I would push this further. If our new Adam and Eve could survive and breed – still in total isolation from any cultural influences – then eventually they would produce a society which would have laws about property, rules about incest and marriage, customs of taboo and avoidance, methods of settling disputes with a minimum of bloodshed, beliefs about the supernatural and practices relating to it, a system of social status and methods of indicating it, initiation ceremonies for young men, courtship practices including the adornment of females, systems of symbolic body adornment generally, certain activities and associations set aside for men from which women were excluded, gambling of some kind, a tool- and weapon-making industry, myths and legends, dancing, adultery, and various doses of homicide, suicide, homosexuality, schizophrenia, psychosis and neuroses, and various practitioners to take advantage of or cure these, depending on how they are viewed.

Culture, including the more resplendent manifestations of ritual and religion, can be interpreted as a hierarchical system of environmental tracking devices. In Chapter 7 the totality of biological responses, from millisecond-quick biochemical reactions to gene substitutions requiring generations, was described as such a system. At that time culture was placed within the scheme at the slow end of the time scale. Now this conception can be extended. To the extent that the specific details of culture are nongenetic, they can be decoupled from the biological system and arrayed beside it as an auxiliary system. The span of the purely cultural tracking system parallels much of the slower segment of the biological tracking system, ranging from days to generations. Among the fastest cultural responses in industrial civilizations are fashions in dress and speech. Somewhat slower are political ideology and social attitudes toward other nations, while the slowest of all include incest taboos and the belief or disbelief in particular high gods. It is useful to hypothesize that cultural details are for the most part adaptive in a Darwinian sense, even though some may operate indirectly through enhanced group survival (Washburn and Howell, 1960; Masters, 1970). A second proposition worth considering, to make the biological analogy complete, is that the rate of change in a particular set of cultural behaviors reflects the rate of change in the environmental features to which the behaviors are keyed.

Slowly changing forms of culture tend to be encapsulated in ritual. Some social scientists have drawn an analogy between human ceremonies and the displays of animal communication. This is not correct. Most animal displays are discrete signals conveying limited meaning. They are commensurate with the postures, facial expressions, and elementary sounds of human paralanguage. A few animal displays, such as the most complex forms of sexual advertisement and nest changing in birds, are so impressively elaborate that they have occasionally been termed ceremonies by zoologists. But even here the comparison is misleading. Most

human rituals have more than just an immediate signal value. As Durkheim stressed, they not only label but reaffirm and rejuvenate the moral values of the community.

The sacred rituals are the most distinctively human. Their most elementary forms are concerned with magic, the active attempt to manipulate nature and the gods. Upper Paleolithic art from the caves of Western Europe shows a preoccupation with game animals. There are many scenes showing spears and arrows embedded in the bodies of the prey. Other drawings depict men dancing in animal disguises or standing with heads bowed in front of animals. Probably the function of the drawings was sympathetic magic, based on the quite logical notion that what is done with an image will come to pass with the real thing. This anticipatory action is comparable to the intention movements of animals, which in the course of evolution have often been ritualized into communicative signals. The waggle dance of the honeybee, it will be recalled, is a miniaturized rehearsal of the flight from the nest to the food. Primitive man might have understood the meaning of such complex animal behavior easily. Magic was, and still is in some societies, practiced by special people variously called shamans, sorcerers, or medicine men. They alone were believed to have the secret knowledge and power to deal effectively with the supernatural, and as such their influence sometimes exceeded that of the tribal headmen.

Formal religion *sensu stricto* has many elements of magic but is focused on deeper, more tribally oriented beliefs. Its rites celebrate the creation myths, propitiate the gods, and resanctify the tribal moral codes. Instead of a shaman controlling physical power, there is a priest who communes with the gods and curries their favor through obeisance, sacrifice, and the proffered evidences of tribal good behavior. In more complex societies, polity and religion have always blended naturally. Power belonged to kings by divine right, but high priests often ruled over kings by virtue of the higher rank of the gods.

It is a reasonable hypothesis that magic and totemism constituted direct adaptations to the environment and preceded formal religion in social evolution. Sacred traditions occur almost universally in human societies. So do myths that explain the origin of man or at the very least the relation of the

Table 27-3 The religious beliefs of 66 agrarian societies, partitioned according to the percentage of subsistence derived from herding. (From *Human Societies* by C. and Jean Lenski. Copyright 1970 by McGraw-Hill Book Company. Used with permission.)

Percentage of subsistence from herding	Percentage of societies believing in an active, moral creator God	Number of societies
36-45	92	13
26-35	82	28
16-25	40	20
6-15	20	5

tribe to the rest of the world. But belief in high gods is not universal. Among 81 hunter-gatherer societies surveyed by Whiting (1968), only 28, or 35 percent, included high gods in their sacred traditions. The concept of an active, moral God who created the world is even less widespread. Furthermore, this concept most commonly arises with a pastoral way of life. The greater the dependence on herding, the more likely the belief in a shepherd god of the Judaeo-Christian model (see Table 27-3). In other kinds of societies the belief occurs in 10 percent or less of the cases. Also, the God of monotheistic religions is always male. This strong patriarchal tendency has several cultural sources (Lenski, 1970). Pastoral societies are highly mobile, tightly organized, and often militant, all features that tip the balance toward male authority. It is also significant that herding, the main economic base, is primarily the responsibility of men. Because the Hebrews were originally a herding people, the Bible describes God as a shepherd and the chosen people as his sheep. Islam, one of the strictest of all monotheistic faiths, grew to early power among the herding people of the Arabian peninsula. The intimate relation of the shepherd to his flock apparently provides a microcosm which stimulates deeper questioning about the relation of man to the powers that control him.

An increasingly sophisticated anthropology has not given reason to doubt that Max Weber's conclusion that more elementary religions seek the supernatural for the purely mundane rewards of long life, abundant land and food, the avoidance of physical catastrophes, and the defeat of enemies. A form of group selection also operates in the competition between sects. Those that gain adherents

survive; those that cannot, fail. Consequently, religions, like other human institutions, evolve so as to further the welfare of their practitioners. Because this demographic benefit applies to the group as a whole, it can be gained in part by altruism and exploitation, with certain segments profiting at the expense of others. Alternatively, it can arise as the sum of generally increased individual fitnesses. The resulting distinction in social terms is between the more oppressive and the more beneficent religions. All religions are probably oppressive to some degree, especially when they are promoted by chiefdoms and states. The tendency is intensified when societies compete, since religion can be effectively harnessed to the purposes of warfare and economic exploitation.

The enduring paradox of religion is that so much of its substance is demonstrably false, yet it remains a driving force in all societies. Men would rather believe than know, have the void as purpose, as Nietzsche said, than be void of purpose. At the turn of the century Durkheim rejected the notion that such force could really be extracted from "a tissue of illusions." And since that time social scientists have sought the psychological Rosetta stone that might clarify the deeper truths of religious reasoning. In a penetrating analysis of this subject, Rappaport (1971) proposed that virtually all forms of sacred rites serve the purposes of communication. In addition to institutionalizing the moral values of the community, the ceremonies can offer information on the strength and wealth of tribes and families. Among the Maring of New Guinea there are no chiefs or other leaders who command allegiance in war. A group gives a ritual dance, and individual men indicate their willingness to give military support by whether they attend the dance or not. The strength of the consortium can then be precisely determined by a head count. In more advanced societies military parades, embellished by the paraphernalia and rituals of the state religion, serve the same purpose. The famous potlatch ceremonies of the Northwest Coast Indians enable individuals to advertise their wealth by the amount of goods they give away. Rituals also regularize relationships in which there would otherwise be ambiguity and wasteful imprecision. The best examples of this mode of communication are the *rites de passage*. As a boy matures his transition from child to man is very gradual in a biological and psychological sense. There will be times when he behaves like a child when an adult response would have been more appropriate, and vice versa. The society has difficulty in classifying him one way or the other. The *rite de passage* eliminates this ambiguity by arbitrarily changing the classification from a continuous gradient into a dichotomy. It also serves to cement the ties of the young person to the adult group that accepts him.

To sanctify a procedure or a statement is to certify it as beyond question and imply punishment for anyone who dares to contradict it. So removed is the sacred from the profane in everyday life that simply to repeat it in the wrong circumstance is a transgression. This extreme form of certification, the heart of all religions, is granted to the practices and dogmas that serve the most vital interests of the group. The individual is prepared by the sacred rituals for supreme effort and self-sacrifice. Overwhelmed by shibboleths, special costumes, and the sacred dancing and music so accurately keyed to his emotive centers he has a "religious experience." He is ready to reassert allegiance to his tribe and family, perform charities, consecrate his life, leave for the hunt, join the battle, die for God and country. *Deus vult* was the rallying cry of the First Crusade. God wills it, but the summed Darwinian fitness of the tribe was the ultimate if unrecognized beneficiary.

It was Henri Bergson who first identified a second force leading to the formalization of morality and religion. The extreme plasticity of human social behavior is both a great strength and a real danger. If each family worked out rules of behavior on its own, the result would be an intolerable amount of tradition drift and growing chaos. To counteract

selfish behavior and the "dissolving power" of high intelligence, each society must codify itself. Within broad limits virtually any set of conventions works better than none at all. Because arbitrary codes work, organizations tend to be inefficient and marred by unnecessary inequities. As Rappaport succinctly expressed it, "Sanctification transforms the arbitrary into the necessary, and regulatory mechanisms which are arbitrary are likely to be sanctified." The process engenders criticism, and in the more literate and self-conscious societies visionaries and revolutionaries set out to change the system. Reform meets repression, because to the extent that the rules have been sanctified and mythologized, the majority of the people regard them as beyond question, and disagreement is defined as blasphemy.

This leads us to the essentially biological question of the evolution of indoctrinability (Campbell, 1972). Human beings are absurdly easy to indoctrinate – they *seek* it. If we assume for argument that indoctrinability evolves, at what level does natural selection take place? One extreme possibility is that the group is the unit of selection. When conformity becomes too weak, groups become extinct. In this version selfish, individualistic members gain the upper hand and multiply at the expense of others. But their rising prevalence accelerates the vulnerability of the society and hastens its extinction. Societies containing higher frequencies of conformer genes replace those that disappear, thus raising the overall frequency of the genes in the metapopulation of societies. The spread of the genes will occur more rapidly if the metapopulation (for example, a tribal complex) is simultaneously enlarging its range. Formal models of the process, presented in Chapter 5, show that if the rate of societal extinction is high enough relative to the intensity of the counteracting individual selection, the altruistic genes can rise to moderately high levels. The genes might be of the kind that favors indoctrinability even at the expense of the individuals who submit. For example, the willingness to risk death in battle can favor group survival at the expense of the genes that permitted the fatal military discipline. The group-selection hypothesis is sufficient to account for the evolution of indoctrinability.

The competing, individual-level hypothesis is equally sufficient. It states that the ability of individuals to conform permits them to enjoy the benefits of membership with a minimum of energy expenditure and risk. Although their selfish rivals may gain a momentary advantage, it is lost in the long run through ostracism and repression. The conformists perform altruistic acts, perhaps even to the extent of risking their lives, not because of self-denying genes selected at the group level but because the group is occasionally able to take advantage of the indoctrinability which on other occasions is favorable to the individual.

The two hypotheses are not mutually exclusive. Group and individual selection can be reinforcing. If war requires spartan virtues and eliminates some of the warriors, victory can more than adequately compensate the survivors in land, power, and the opportunity to reproduce. The average individual will win the inclusive fitness game, making the gamble profitable, because the summed efforts of the participants give the average member a more than compensatory edge.

Ethics

Scientists and humanists should consider together the possibility that the time has come for ethics to be removed temporarily from the hands of the philosophers and biologicized. The subject at present consists of several oddly disjunct conceptualizations. The first is *ethical intuitionism*, the belief that the mind has a direct awareness of true right and wrong that it can formalize by logic and translate into rules of social action. The purest guiding precept of secular Western thought has been the theory of the social contract as formulated by Locke, Rousseau, and Kant. In our time the precept has been rewoven into a solid philosophical system by John Rawls (1971). His imperative is that justice should be not merely integral to a system of government but rather the object of the original contract. The principles called by Rawls "justice as fairness" are those which free and rational persons would choose if they were beginning an association from a position of equal advantage and wished to define the fundamental rules of the association. In judging the appropriateness of subsequent laws and behavior, it would be necessary to test their conformity to the unchallengeable starting position.

The Achilles heel of the intuitionist position is that it relies on the emotive judgment of the brain as though that organ must be treated as a black box. While few will disagree that justice as fairness is an ideal state for disembodied spirits, the conception is in no way explanatory or predictive with reference to human beings. Consequently, it does not consider the ultimate ecological or genetic consequences of the rigorous prosecution of its conclusions. Perhaps explanation and prediction will not be needed for the millennium. But this is unlikely – the human genotype and the ecosystem in which it evolved were fashioned out of extreme unfairness. In either case the full exploration of the neural machinery of ethical judgment is desirable and already in progress. One such effort, constituting the second mode of conceptualization, can be called *ethical behaviorism*. Its basic proposition, which has been expanded most fully by J. F. Scott (1971), holds that moral commitment is entirely learned, with operant conditioning being the dominant mechanism. In other words, children simply internalize the behavioral norms of the society. Opposing this theory is the *developmental-genetic conception* of ethical behavior. The best-documented version has been provided by Lawrence Kohlberg (1969). Kohlberg's viewpoint is structuralist and specifically Piagetian, and therefore not yet related to the remainder of biology. Piaget has used the expression "genetic epistemology" and Kohlberg "cognitive-developmental" to label the general concept. However, the results will eventually become incorporated into a broadened developmental biology and genetics. Kohlberg's method is to record and classify the verbal responses of children to moral problems. He has delineated six sequential stages of ethical reasoning through which an individual may progress as part of his mental maturation. The child moves from a primary dependence on external controls and sanctions to an increasingly sophisticated set of internalized standards (see Table 27-4). The analysis has not yet been directed to the question of plasticity in the basic rules. Intracultural variance has not been measured, and heritability therefore not assessed. The difference between ethical behaviorism and the current version of developmental-genetic analysis is that the former postulates a mechanism (operant conditioning) without evidence and the latter presents evidence without postulating a mechanism. No great conceptual difficulty underlies this dis-

Table 27-4 The classification of moral judgment into levels and stages of development. (Based on Kohlberg, 1969.)

Level	Basis of moral judgment	Stage of Development
I	Moral value is defined by punishment and reward	1. Obedience to rules and authority to avoid punishment 2. Conformity to obtain rewards and to exchange favors
II	Moral value resides in filling the correct roles, in maintaining order and meeting the expectations of others	3. Good-boy orientation: conformity to avoid dislike and rejection by others 4. Duty orientation: conformity to avoid censure by authority, disruption of order, and resulting guilt
III	Moral value resides in conformity to shared standards, rights, and duties	5. Legalistic orientation: recognition of the value of contracts, some arbitrariness in rule formation to maintain the common good. 6. Conscience or principle orientation: primary allegiance to principles of choice, which can over-rule law in cases where the law is judged to do more harm than good.

parity. The study of moral development is only a more complicated and less tractable version of the genetic variance problem (see Chapters 2 and 7). With the accretion of data the two approaches can be expected to merge to form a recognizable exercise in behavioral genetics.

Even if the problem were solved tomorrow, however, an important piece would still be missing. This is the *genetic evolution of ethics.* In the first chapter of this book I argued that ethical philosophers intuit the deontological canons of morality by consulting the emotive centers of their own hypothalamic-limbic system. This is also true of the developmentalists, even when they are being their most severely objective. Only by interpreting the activity of the emotive centers as a biological adaptation can the meaning of the canons be deciphered. Some of the activity is likely to be outdated, a relic of adjustment to the most primitive form of tribal organization. Some of it may prove to be *in statu nascendi,* constituting new and quickly changing adaptations to agrarian and urban life.

The resulting confusion will be reinforced by other factors. To the extent that unilaterally altruistic genes have been established in the population by group selection, they will be opposed by allelomorphs favored by individual selection. The conflict of impulses under their various controls is likely to be widespread in the population, since current theory predicts that the genes will be at best maintained in a state of balanced polymorphism (Chapter 5). Moral ambivalency will be further intensified by the circumstance that a schedule of sex- and age-dependent ethics can impart higher genetic fitness than a single moral code which is applied uniformly to all sex-age groups. The argument for this statement is the special case of the Gadgil-Bossert distribution in which the contributions of social interactions to survivorship and fertility schedules are specified (see Chapter 4). Some of the differences in the Kohlberg stages could be explained in this manner. For example, it should be of selective advantage for young children to be self-centered and relatively disinclined to perform altruistic acts based on personal principle. Similarly, adolescents should be more tightly bound by age-peer bonds within their own sex and hence unusually sensitive to peer approval. The reason is that at this time greater advantage accrues to the formation of alliances and rise in status than later, when sexual and parental morality become the paramount determinants of fitness. Genetically programmed sexual and parent-offspring conflict of the kind predicted by the Trivers models (Chapters 15 and 16) are also likely to promote age differences in the kinds and degrees of moral commitment. Finally, the moral standards of individuals during early phases of colony growth should differ in many details from those of individuals at demographic equilibrium or during episodes of overpopulation. Metapopulations subject to high levels of r extinction will tend to diverge genetically from other kinds of populations in ethical behavior (Chapter 5).

If there is any truth to this theory of innate moral pluralism, the requirement for an evolutionary approach to ethics is self-evident. It should also be clear that no single set of moral standards can be applied to all human populations, let alone all sex-age classes within each population. To impose a uniform code is therefore to create complex, intractable moral dilemmas – these, of course, are the current condition of mankind.

Esthetics

Artistic impulses are by no means limited to man. In 1962, when Desmond Morris reviewed the subject in *The Biology of Art,* 32 individual nonhuman primates had produced drawings and paintings in captivity. Twenty-three were chimpanzees, 2 were gorillas, 3 were orangutans, and 4 were capuchin monkeys. None received special training or anything more than access to the necessary equipment. In fact, attempts to guide the efforts of the animals by inducing imitation were always unsuccessful. The drive to use the painting and drawing equipment was powerful, requiring no reinforcement from the human observers. Both young and old animals became so engrossed with the activity that they preferred it to being fed and sometimes threw temper tantrums when stopped. Two of the chimpanzees studied extensively were highly productive. "Alpha" produced over 200 pictures, while the

famous "Congo," who deserves to be called the Picasso of the great apes, was responsible for nearly 400. Although most of the efforts consisted of scribbling, the patterns were far from random. Lines and smudges were spread over a blank page outward from a centrally located figure. When a drawing was started on one side of a blank page the chimpanzee usually shifted to the opposite side to offset it. With time the calligraphy became bolder, starting with simple lines and progressing to more complicated multiple scribbles. Congo's patterns progressed along approximately the same developmental path as those of very young human children, yielding fan-shaped diagrams and even complete circles. Other chimpanzees drew crosses.

The artistic activity of chimpanzees may well be a special manifestation of their tool-using behavior. Members of the species display a total of about ten techniques, all of which require manual skill. Probably all are improved through practice, while at least a few are passed as traditions from one generation to the next. The chimpanzees have a considerable facility for inventing new techniques, such as the use of sticks to pull objects through cage bars and to pry open boxes. Thus the tendency to manipulate objects and to explore their uses appears to have an adaptive advantage for chimpanzees.

The same reasoning applies a fortiori to the origin of art in man. As Washburn (1970) pointed out, human beings have been hunter-gatherers for over 99 percent of their history, during which time each man made his own tools. The appraisal of form and skill in execution were necessary for survival, and they probably brought social approval as well. Both forms of success paid off in greater genetic fitness. If the chimpanzee Congo could reach the stage of elementary diagrams, it is not too hard to imagine primitive man progressing to representational figures. Once that stage was reached, the transition to the use of art in sympathetic magic and ritual must have followed quickly. Art might then have played a reciprocally reinforcing role in the development of culture and mental capacity. In the end, writing emerged as the idiographic representation of language.

Music of a kind is also produced by some animals. Human beings consider the elaborate courtship and territorial songs of birds to be beautiful, and probably ultimately for the same reasons they are of use to the birds. With clarity and precision they identify the species, the physiological condition, and the mental set of the singer. Richness of information and precise transmission of mood are no less the standards of excellence in human music. Singing and dancing serve to draw groups together, direct the emotions of the people, and prepare them for joint action. The carnival displays of chimpanzees described in earlier chapters are remarkably like human celebrations in this respect. The apes run, leap, pound the trunks of trees in drumming motions, and call loudly back and forth. These actions serve at least in part to assemble groups at common feeding grounds. They may resemble the ceremonies of earliest man. Nevertheless, fundamental differences appeared in subsequent human evolution. Human music has been liberated from iconic representation in the same way that true language has departed from the elementary ritualization characterizing the communication of animals. Music has the capacity for unlimited and arbitrary symbolization, and it employs rules of phrasing and order that serve the same function as syntax.

....

The best procedure to follow, and one which I believe is relied on implicitly by most students of the subject, is to extrapolate backward from living hunter-gatherer societies. In Table 27-5 this technique is made explicit. Utilizing the synthesis edited by Lee and Devore (1968; see especially J. W. M. Whiting, pp.336-339), I have listed the most general traits of hunter-gatherer peoples. Then I have evaluated the lability of each behavioral category by noting the amount of variation in the category that occurs among the nonhuman primate species. The less labile the category, the more likely that the trait displayed by the living hunter-gatherers was also displayed by early man.

What we can conclude with some degree of confidence is that primitive men lived in small territorial groups, within which males were dominant over females. The intensity of aggressive behavior and the nature of its scaling remain unknown. Maternal care was prolonged, and the relationships were at least to some extent matrilineal. Speculation on remaining aspects of social life is not supported either way by the lability data and is therefore more tenuous. It is likely that the early

hominids foraged in groups. To judge from the behavior of baboons and geladas, such behavior would have conferred some protection from large predators. By the time *Australopithecus* and early *Homo* had begun to feed on large mammals, group hunting almost certainly had become advantageous and even necessary, as in the African wild dog. But there is no compelling reason to conclude that men did the hunting while women stayed at home. This occurs today in hunter-gatherer societies, but comparisons with other primates offer no clue as to *when* the trait appeared. It is certainly not essential to conclude a priori that males must be a specialized hunter class. In chimpanzees males do the hunting, which may be suggestive. But in lions, it will be recalled, the females are the providers, often working in groups and with cubs in tow, while the males usually hold back. In the African wild dog both sexes participate. This is not to suggest that male group hunting was not an early trait of hominids, only that there is no strong independent evidence to support the hypothesis.

This brings us to the prevailing theory of the origin of human sociality. It consists of a series of interlocking models that have been fashioned from bits of fossil evidence, extrapolations back from extant hunter-gatherer societies, and comparisons with other living primate species. The core of the theory can be appropriately termed the *autocatalysis model*. It holds that when the earliest hominids became bipedal as part of their terrestrial adaptation, their hands were freed, the manufacture and handling of artifacts was made easier, and intelligence grew as part of the improvement of the tool-using habit. With mental capacity and the tendency to use artifacts increasing through mutual reinforcement, the entire materials-based culture expanded. Cooperation during hunting was perfected, providing a new impetus for the evolution of intelligence, which in turn permitted still more sophistication in tool using, and so on through cycles of causation. At some point, probably during the late *Australopithecus* period or the transition from *Australopithecus* to *Homo*, this autocatalysis carried the evolving populations to a certain threshold of competence, at which the hominids were able to exploit the antelopes, elephants, and other large herbivorous mammals teeming around them on the African plains. Quite possibly the process began when the hominids

Table 27-5 Social traits of living hunter-gatherer groups and the likelihood that they were also possessed by early man.

Traits that occur generally in living hunter-gatherer societies	Variability of trait category among nonhuman primates	Reliability of concluding early man had the same trait through homology
Local group size: Mostly 100 or less	Highly variable but within range of 3-100	Very probably 100 or less but otherwise not reliable
Family as the nuclear unit	Highly variable	Not reliable
Sexual division of labor: Women gather, men hunt	Limited to man among living primates	Not reliable
Males dominant over females	Widespread although not universal	Reliable
Long-term sexual bonding (marriage) nearly universal; polygyny general	Highly variable	Not reliable
Exogamy universal, abetted by marriage rules	Limited to man among living primates	Not reliable
Subgroup composition changes often (fission-fusion principle)	Highly variable	Not reliable
Territoriality general, especially marked in rich gathering areas	Occurs widely, but variable in pattern	Probably occurred; pattern unknown
Game playing, especially games that entail physical skill but not strategy	Occurs generally, at least in elementary form	Very reliable
Prolonged maternal care; pronounced socialization of young; extended relationships between mother and children, especially mothers and daughters	Occurs generally in higher cercopithecoids	Very reliable

learned to drive big cats, hyenas, and other carnivores from their kills.... In time they became the primary hunters themselves and were forced to protect their prey from other predators and scavengers. The autocatalysis model usually includes the proposition that the shift to big game accelerated the process of mental evolution. The shift could even have been the impetus that led to the origin of early *Homo* from their australopithecine ancestors approximately two million years ago. Another proposition is that males became specialized for hunting. Child care was facilitated by close social bonding between the males, who left the domiciles to hunt, and the females, who kept the children and conducted most of the foraging for vegetable food. Many of the peculiar details of human sexual behavior and domestic life flow easily from this basic division of labor. But these details are not essential to the autocatalysis model. They are added because they are displayed by modern hunter-gatherer societies.

....

Later Social Evolution

Autocatalytic reactions in living systems never expand to infinity. Biological parameters normally change in a rate-dependent manner to slow growth and eventually bring it to a halt. But almost miraculously, this has not yet happened in human evolution. The increase in brain size and the refinement of stone artifacts indicate a gradual improvement in mental capacity throughout the Pleistocene. With the appearance of the Mousterian tool culture of *Homo sapiens neanderthalensis* some 75,000 years ago, the trend gathered momentum, giving way in Europe to the Upper Paleolithic culture of *Homo s. sapiens* about 40,000 years B.P. Starting about 10,000 years ago agriculture was invented and spread, populations increased enormously in density, and the primitive hunter-gatherer bands gave way locally to the relentless growth of tribes, chiefdoms, and states. Finally, after A.D. 1400 European-based civilization shifted gears again, and knowledge and technology grew not just exponentially but superexponentially ....

There is no reason to believe that during this final sprint there has been a cessation in the evolution of either mental capacity or the predilection toward special social behaviors. The theory of population genetics and experiments on other organisms show that substantial changes can occur in the span of less than 100 generations which for man reaches back only to the time of the Roman Empire. Two thousand generations, roughly the period since typical *Homo sapiens* invaded Europe, is enough time to create new species and to mold them in major ways. Although we do not know how much mental evolution has actually occurred, it would be false to assume that modern civilizations have been built entirely on capital accumulated during the long haul of the Pleistocene.

Since genetic and cultural tracking systems operate on parallel tracks, we can bypass their distinction for the moment and return to the question of the prime movers in later human social evolution in its broadest sense. Seed eating is a plausible explanation to account for the movement of hominids onto the savanna, and the shift to big-game hunting might account for their advance to the *Homo erectus* grade. But was the adaptation to group predation enough to carry evolution all the way to the *Homo sapiens* grade and farther, to agriculture and civilization? Anthropologists and biologists do not consider the impetus to have been sufficient. They have advocated the following series of additional factors, which can act singly or in combination.

Sexual Selection

Fox (1972), following a suggestion by Chance (1962), has argued that sexual selection was the auxiliary motor that drove human evolution all the way to the *Homo* grade. His reasoning proceeds as follows. Polygyny is a general trait in hunter-gatherer bands and may also have been the rule in the early hominid societies. If so, a premium would have been placed on sexual selection involving both epigamic display toward the females and intrasexual competition among the males. The selection would be enhanced by the constant mating provocation that arises from the female's nearly continuous sexual receptivity. Because of the existence of a high level of cooperation within the band, a legacy of the original *Australopithecus* adaptation, sexual selection would tend to be linked with hunting prowess, leadership, skill at tool making, and other visible attributes that contribute to the success of the family and the male band. Aggressiveness was constrained and the old forms of overt primate dominance replaced by complex social skills. Young males found it profitable to fit into the group, controlling their sexuality and aggression and awaiting their turn at leadership. As a result the dominant male in hominid societies was most likely to possess a mosaic of qualities that reflect the necessities of compromise: "controlled, cunning, cooperative, attractive to the ladies, good with the children, relaxed, tough, eloquent, skillful, knowledgeable and proficient in self-defense and hunting." Since positive feedback occurs between these more sophisticated social traits and breeding success, social evolution can proceed indefinitely without additional selective pressures from the environment.

Multiplier Effects in Cultural Innovation and in Network Expansion

Whatever its prime mover, evolution in cultural capacity was implemented by a growing power and readiness to learn. The network of contacts among individuals and bands must also have grown. We can postulate a critical mass of cultural capacity and network size in which it became advantageous for bands actively to enlarge both. In other words, the feedback became positive. This mechanism, like sexual selection, requires no additional input beyond the limits of social behavior itself. But unlike sexual selection, it probably reached the autocatalytic threshold level very late in human prehistory.

Increased Population Density and Agriculture

The conventional view of the development of civilization used to be that innovations in farming led to population growth, the securing of leisure time, the rise of a leisure class, and the contrivance of civilized, less immediately functional pursuits. The hypothesis has been considerably weakened by the discovery that !Kung and other hunter-gatherer peoples work less and enjoy more leisure time than most farmers. Primitive agricultural people generally do not produce surpluses unless compelled to do so by political or religious authorities (Carneiro, 1970). Ester Boserup (1965) has gone so far as to suggest the reverse causation: population growth induces societies to deepen their involvement and expertise in agriculture. However, this explanation does not account for the population growth in the first place. Hunter-gatherer societies remained in approximate demographic equilibrium for hundreds of thousands of years. Something else tipped a few of them into becoming the first farmers. Quite possibly the crucial events were nothing more than the attainment of a certain level of intelligence and lucky encounters with wild-growing food plants. Once launched, agricultural economies permitted higher population densities which in turn encouraged wider networks of social contact, technological advance, and further dependence on farming. A few innovations, such as irrigation and the wheel, intensified the process to the point of no return.

Warfare

Throughout recorded history the conduct of war has been common among tribes and nearly universal among chiefdoms and states. When Sorokin analyzed the histories of 11 European countries over periods of 275 to 1,025 years, he found that on the average they were engaged in some kind of military action 47 percent of the time, or about one year out of every two. The range was from 28 percent of the years in the case of Germany to 67 percent in the case of Spain. The early chiefdoms and

states of Europe and the Middle East turned over with great rapidity, and much of the conquest was genocidal in nature. The spread of genes has always been of paramount importance. For example, after the conquest of the Midianites Moses gave instructions identical in result to the aggression and genetic usurpation by male langur monkeys:

> Now kill every male dependent, and kill every woman who has had intercourse with a man, but spare for yourselves every woman among them who has not had intercourse. (Numbers 31)

And centuries later, von Clausewitz conveyed to his pupil the Prussian crown prince a sense of the true, biological joy of warfare:

> Be audacious and cunning in your plans, firm and persevering in their execution, determined to find a glorious end, and fate will crown your youthful brow with a shining glory, which is the ornament of princes, and engrave your image in the hearts of your last descendants.

The possibility that endemic warfare and genetic usurpation could be an effective force in group selection was clearly recognized by Charles Darwin. In *The Descent of Man* he proposed a remarkable model that foreshadowed many of the elements of modern group selection theory:

> Now, if some one man in a tribe, more sagacious than the others, invented a new snare or weapon, or other means of attack or defence, the plainest self-interest, without the assistance of much reasoning power, would prompt the other members to imitate him; and all would thus profit. The habitual practice of each new art must likewise in some slight degree strengthen the intellect. If the invention were an important one, the tribe would increase in number, spread, and supplant other tribes. In a tribe thus rendered more numerous there would always be a rather greater chance of the birth of other superior and inventive members. If such men left children to inherit their mental superiority, the chance of the birth of still more ingenious members would be somewhat better, and in a

very small tribe decidedly better. Even if they left no children, the tribe would still include their blood-relations, and it has been ascertained by agriculturists that by preserving and breeding from the family of an animal, which when slaughtered was found to be valuable, the desired character has been obtained.

Darwin saw that not only can group selection reinforce individual selection, but it can oppose it – and sometimes prevail, especially if the size of the breeding unit is small and average kinship correspondingly close. Essentially the same theme was later developed in increasing depth by Keith (1949), Bigelow (1969), and Alexander (1971). These authors envision some of the "noblest" traits of mankind, including team play, altruism, patriotism, bravery on the field of battle, and so forth, as the genetic product of warfare.

By adding the additional postulate of a threshold effect, it is possible to explain why the process has operated exclusively in human evolution (Wilson, 1972). If any social predatory mammal attains a certain level of intelligence, as the early hominids, being large primates, were especially predisposed to do, one band would have the capacity to consciously ponder the significance of adjacent social groups and to deal with them in an intelligent, organized fashion. A band might then dispose of a neighboring band, appropriate its territory, and increase its own genetic representation in the metapopulation, retaining the tribal memory of this successful episode, repeating it, increasing the geographic range of its occurrence, and quickly spreading its influence still further in the metapopulation. Such primitive cultural capacity would be permitted by the possession of certain genes. Reciprocally, the cultural capacity might propel the spread of the genes through the genetic constitution of the metapopulation. Once begun, such a mutual reinforcement could be irreversible. The only combinations of genes able to confer superior fitness in contention with genocidal aggressors would be those that produce either a more effective technique of aggression or else the capacity to preempt genocide by some form of pacific maneuvering. Either probably entails mental and cultural advance. In addition to being autocatalytic, such evolution has the interesting property of requiring a selection episode only very occasionally in order

to proceed as swiftly as individual level selection. By current theory, genocide or genosorption strongly favoring the aggressor need take place only once every few generations to direct evolution. This alone could push truly altruistic genes to a high frequency within the bands (see Chapter 5). The turnover of tribes and chiefdoms estimated from atlases of early European and Mideastern history (for example, the atlas by McEvedy, 1967) suggests a sufficient magnitude of differential group fitness to have achieved this effect. Furthermore, it is to be expected that some isolated cultures will escape the process for generations at a time, in effect reverting temporarily to what ethnographers classify as a pacific state.

Multifactorial Systems

Each of the foregoing mechanisms could conceivably stand alone as a sufficient prime mover of social evolution. But it is much more likely that they contributed jointly, in different strengths and with complex interaction effects. Hence the most realistic model may be fully cybernetic, with cause and effect reciprocating through sub-cycles that possess high degrees of connectivity with one another....

In both the unifactorial and multifactorial models of social evolution, an increasing internalization of the controls is postulated. This shift is considered to be the basis of the two-stage acceleration cited earlier. At the beginning of hominid evolution, the prime movers were external environmental pressures no different from those that have guided the social evolution of other animal species. For the moment, it seems reasonable to suppose that the hominids underwent two adaptive shifts in succession: first, to open-country living and seed eating, and second, after being preadapted by the anatomical and mental changes associated with seed eating, to the capture of large mammals. Big-game hunting induced further growth in mentality and social organization that brought the hominids across the threshold into the autocatalytic, more nearly internalized phase of evolution. This second stage is the one in which the most distinctive human qualities emerged. In stressing this distinction, however, I do not wish to imply that social evolution became independent of the environment. The iron laws of demography still clamped down on the spreading hominid populations, and the most spectacular cultural advances were impelled by the invention of new ways to control the environment. What happened was that mental and social change came to depend more on internal reorganization and less on direct responses to features in the surrounding environment. Social evolution, in short, had acquired its own motor.

The Future

When mankind has achieved an ecological steady state, probably by the end of the twenty-first century, the internalization of social evolution will be nearly complete. About this time biology should be at its peak, with the social sciences maturing rapidly. Some historians of science will take issue with this projection, arguing that the accelerating pace of discoveries in these fields implies a more rapid development. But historical precedents have misled us before: the subjects we are talking about are more difficult than physics or chemistry by at least two orders of magnitude.

Consider the prospects for sociology. This science is now in the natural history stage of its development. There have been attempts at system building but, just as in psychology, they were premature and came to little. Much of what passes for theory in sociology today is really labeling of phenomena and concepts, in the expected manner of natural history. Process is difficult to analyze because the fundamental units are elusive, perhaps nonexistent. Syntheses commonly consist of the tedious cross-referencing of differing sets of definitions and metaphors erected by the more imaginative thinkers (see for example Inkeles, 1964, and Friedrichs, 1970). That, too, is typical of the natural history phase.

With an increase in the richness of descriptions and experiments, sociology is drawing closer each day to cultural anthropology, social psychology, and economics, and will soon merge with them. These disciplines are fundamental to sociology *sensu lato* and are most likely to yield its first phenomenological laws. In fact, some viable qualitative laws probably already exist. They include tested statements about the following relationships: the effects of hostility and stress upon ethnocentrism and xenophobia (LeVine and Campbell, 1972); the positive correlation between and within

cultures of war and combative sports, resulting in the elimination of the hydraulic model of aggressive drive (Sipes, 1973); precise but still specialized models of promotion and opportunity within professional guilds (White, 1970); and, far from least, the most general models of economics.

The transition from purely phenomenological to fundamental theory in sociology must await a full, neuronal explanation of the human brain. Only when the machinery can be torn down on paper at the level of the cell and put together again will the properties of emotion and ethical judgment come clear. Simulations can then be employed to estimate the full range of behavioral responses and the precision of their homeostatic controls. Stress will be evaluated in terms of the neurophysiological perturbations and their relaxation times. Cognition will be translated into circuitry. Learning and creativeness will be defined as the alteration of specific portions of the cognitive machinery regulated by input from the emotive centers. Having cannibalized psychology, the new neurobiology will yield an enduring set of first principles for sociology.

The role of evolutionary sociobiology in this enterprise will be twofold. It will attempt to reconstruct the history of the machinery and to identify the adaptive significance of each of its functions. Some of the functions are almost certainly obsolete, being directed toward such Pleistocene exigencies as hunting and gathering and intertribal warfare. Others may prove currently adaptive at the level of the individual and family but maladaptive at the level of the group – or the reverse. If the decision is taken to mold cultures to fit the requirements of the ecological steady state, some behaviors can be altered experientially without emotional damage or loss in creativity. Others cannot. Uncertainty in this matter means that Skinner's dream of a culture predesigned for happiness will surely have to wait for the new neurobiology. A genetically accurate and hence completely fair code of ethics must also wait.

The second contribution of evolutionary sociobiology will be to monitor the genetic basis of social behavior. Optimum socioeconomic systems can never be perfect, because of Arrow's impossibility theorem and probably also because ethical standards are innately pluralistic. Moreover, the genetic foundation on which any such normative system is built can be expected to shift continuously.

Mankind has never stopped evolving, but in a sense his populations are drifting. The effects over a period of a few generations could change the identity of the socioeconomic optima. In particular, the rate of gene flow around the world has risen to dramatic levels and is accelerating, and the mean coefficients of relationship within local communities are correspondingly diminishing. The result could be an eventual lessening of altruistic behavior through the maladaption and loss of group-selected genes (Haldane, 1932; Eshel, 1972). It was shown earlier that behavioral traits tend to be selected out by the principle of metabolic conservation when they are suppressed or when their original function becomes neutral in adaptive value. Such traits can largely disappear from populations in as few as ten generations, only two or three centuries in the case of human beings. With our present inadequate understanding of the human brain, we do not know how many of the most valued qualities are linked genetically to more obsolete, destructive ones. Cooperativeness toward groupmates might be coupled with aggressivity toward strangers, creativeness with a desire to own and dominate, athletic zeal with a tendency to violent response, and so on. In extreme cases such pairings could stem from pleiotropism, the control of more than one phenotypic character by the same set of genes. If the planned society — the creation of which seems inevitable in the coming century — were to deliberately steer its members past those stresses and conflicts that once gave the destructive phenotypes their Darwinian edge, the other phenotypes might dwindle with them. In this, the ultimate genetic sense, social control would rob man of his humanity.

It seems that our autocatalytic social evolution has locked us onto a particular course which the early hominids still within us may not welcome. To maintain the species indefinitely we are compelled to drive toward total knowledge, right down to the levels of the neuron and gene. When we have progressed enough to explain ourselves in these mechanistic terms, and the social sciences come to full flower, the result might be hard to accept. It seems appropriate therefore to close this book as it began, with the foreboding insight of Albert Camus:

A world that can be explained even with bad reasons is a familiar world. But, on the other hand, in a universe divested of illusions and lights, man feels an alien, a stranger. His exile is without remedy since he is deprived of the memory of a lost home or the hope of a promised land.

This, unfortunately, is true. But we still have another hundred years.

Bibliography

Adams, R. McC. *The evolution of urban society: Early Mesopotamia and prehispanic Mexico.* Chicago: Aldine Publishing Co., 1966, xii + 191.

Alexander, R. D. "The search for an evolutionary philosophy of man." *Proceedings of the Royal Society of Victoria.* 84(1), 1971, 99-120.

Bergson, H. *The two sources of morality and religion.* Trans. R. A. Audra, C. Brereton, and W.H. Carter. New York: Henry Holt, 1935, viii + 308.

Bigelow, R. *The dawn warriors: man's evolution toward peace.* Boston: Atlantic Monthly Press, Little, Brown, 1969, xi + 277.

Blurton Jones, N. G. "An ethological study of some aspects of social behaviour of children in nursery school." In D. Morris, ed. (*q.v.*), *Primate ethology: essays on the socio-sexual behavior of apes and monkeys*, 1969, 437- 463.

Boserup, Ester. *The conditions of agricultural growth.* Chicago: Aldine Publishing Co., 1965, 124.

Campbell, D. T. "On the genetics of altruism and the counter-hedonic components in human culture." *Journal of Social Issues*, 28(3), 1972, 21-37.

Carneiro, R. L. "A theory of the origin of the state." *Science*, 169, 1970, 733-738.

Chagnon, N. A. *Yanomamö: the fierce people.* New York: Holt, Rinehart and Winston, 1968, xviii + 142.

Chance, M. R. A. "Social behaviour and primate evolution." In M. F. Ashley Montagu, ed., *Culture and the evolution of man*, 84-130. New York: Oxford University Press, 1962, xiii + 376.

Clausewitz, C. von. *Principles of war.* Trans. H. W. Gatzke from the Appendix of *Vom Kriege*, 1832. Harrisburg Pa: Stackpole Co., 1960, iv + 82.

Count, E. W. "The biological basis of human sociality." *American Anthropologist*, 60(6), 1958, 1049-1085.

Dahlberg, G. *Mathematical methods for popula-*

tion genetics. New York: S. Karger, 1947, 182.

Darlington, C. D. *The evolution of man and society.* New York: Simon and Schuster, 1969, 753.

Darwin, C. *The descent of man, and selection in relation to sex,* 2 vols. New York: Appleton, 1871, Vol. 1: vi + 409; Vol. 2: viii + 436.

Dobzhansky, T. "Anthropology and the natural sciences – the problem of human evolution." *Current Anthropology,* 4, 1963, 183, 146-148.

Eshel, I. "On the neighbor effect and the evolution of altruistic traits." *Theoretical Population Biology,* 3(3), 1972, 258- 277.

Fox, M. W. "Socio-ecological implications of individual differences in wolf litters: a developmental and evolutionary perspective." *Behaviour,* 46(3,4), 1972, 298-313.

Fox, R. "The cultural animal." In J. F. Eisenberg and W.S. Dillon, eds. (*q.v.*), *Man and beast: comparative social behavior,* 1971, 263-296.

Fox, R. "Alliance and constraint: sexual selection in the evolution of human kinship systems." In B. G. Campbell, ed. (*q.v.*) *Sexual selection and the descent of man 1871-1971,* 1972, 282-331.

Freidrichs. R. W. *A sociology of sociology.* New York: Free Press, Collier-Macmillan, 1970, xxxiv + 429.

Goffman, E. *The presentation of self in everyday life.* N.Y.: Doubleday Anchor Books, Doubleday, Garden City, 1959, xvi + 259.

Goffman, E. *Encounters: two studies in the sociology of interaction.* Indianapolis: Bobbs-Merrill, 1961, 152.

Haldane, J. B. S. *The causes of evolution.* London: Longmans, Green, 1932, vii + 234. (Reprinted as a paperback, Cornell University Press, Ithaca, N.Y., 1966. vi + 235 pp.)

Halle, L. J. "International behavior and the prospects for human survival." In J. F. Eisenberg and W. S. Dillon, eds. (*q.v.*) *Man and beast: comparative social behavior,* 1971, 353-368.

Helm, June. "The nature of Dogrib socioterritorial groups." In R. B. Lee and I. DeVore, eds. (*q.v.*) *Man the hunter,* 1968, 118-125.

Herrnstein, R. J. "I.Q." *Atlantic Monthly,* 228(3) (September), 1971, 43-64.

Homans, G. C. *Social behavior: its elementary forms.* New York: Harcourt, Brace & World, 1961, xii + 404.

Hutchinson, G. E. "A speculative consideration of certain possible forms of sexual selection in man." *American Naturalist,* 93(869), 1959, 81-91.

Inkeles, A. *What is sociology? An introduction to the discipline and profession.* Englewood Cliffs, N.J.: Prentice-Hall, 1964, viii + 120.

Jolly, C. J. "The seed-eaters: a new model of hominid differentiation based on a baboon analogy." *Man,* 5(1), 1970, 5- 26.

Kallmann, F. J. "Twin and sibship study of overt male homosexuality." *American Journal of Human Genetics,* 4(2), 1952, 136-146.

Keith, A. *A new theory of human evolution.* New York: Philosophical Library, 1949, x + 451.

Kohlberg, L. "Stage and sequence: the cognitive-developmental approach to socialization." In D. A. Goslin, ed., *Handbook of socialization theory and research,* 347-480. Chicago: Rand McNally Co., 1969, xii + 1182.

Lee, R. B., and I. DeVore, eds. *Man the hunter.* Chicago: Aldine Publishing Co., 1968, xvi + 415.

Leibowitz, Lila. "Founding families." *Journal of Theoretical Biology,* 21(2), 1968, 153-169.

Lenski, G. *Human societies: a macrolevel introduction to sociology.* New York: McGraw-Hill Book Co., 1970, xvi + 525.

Lerner, I. M. *Heredity, evolution, and society.* San Francisco: W. H. Freeman, 1968, xviii + 307.

LeVine, R. A., and D. T. Campbell. *Ethnocentrism: theories of conflict, ethnic attitudes, and group behavior.* New York: John Wiley & Sons, 1972, x + 310.

Lévi-Strauss, C. *Les structures élémentaires de la parenté.* Paris: Presses Universitaires de France, 1949, xiv + 639. (*The elementary structures of kinship,* rev. ed., trans. by J. H. Bell and J. R. von Sturmer and ed. by R. Needham, Boston: Beacon Press, 1969, xlii + 541.)

Lewontin, R. "The apportionment of human diversity." *Evolutionary Biology,* 6, 1972, 381-398.

Maslow, A. H. *Motivation and personality.* New York: Harper, 1954, 411.

Maslow, A. H. *The farther reaches of human nature.* New York: Viking Press, 1972, xxii + 423.

Masters, R. D. "Genes, language, and evolution." *Semiotica,* 2(4), 1970, 295-320.

Masters, W. H., and Virginia E. Johnson. *Human sexual response.* Boston: Little, Brown, 1966, xiii + 366.

McEvedy, D. *The Penguin atlas of ancient history.* Baltimore, Md.: Penguin Books, 1967, 96.

Moreton, N. E. "Human population structure."

Annual Review of Genetics, 3, 1969, 53-74.

Morris, D. *The biology of art.* New York: Alfred Knopf, 1962, 176.

Morris, D. *The naked ape: a zoologist's study of the human animal.* New York: McGraw-Hill Book Co., 1967, 252.

Parsons, P. A. *The genetic analysis of behaviour.* London: Methuen, 1967, x + 174.

Patterson, O. *The sociology of slavery: an analysis of the origins, development and structure of Negro slave society in Jamaica.* Cranbury, N.J.: Fairleigh Dickinson University Press, 1967, 310.

Pfeiffer, J. E. *The emergence of man.* New York: Harper & Row, 1969, xxiv + 477.

Rappaport, R. A. "The sacred in human evolution." *Annual Review of Ecology and Systematics*, 2, 1971, 23-44.

Rawls, J. *A theory of justice.* Cambridge: Belknap Press of Harvard University Press, 1971, xvi + 607.

Reynolds, V. "Kinship and the family in monkeys, apes and man." *Man*, 3(2), 1968, 209-233.

Scott, J. F. *Internalization of norms: a sociological theory of moral commitment.* Englewood Cliffs, N.J.: Prentice-Hall, 1971, xviii + 237.

Sipes, R. G. "War, sports and aggression: an empirical test of two rival theories." *American Anthropologist*, 75(1), 1973, 64-86.

Skinner, B. F. "The phylogeny and ontogeny of behavior." *Science*, 153, 1966, 1205-1213.

Sorokin, P. *Social and cultural dynamics.* Boston: Porter Sargent, 1957, 719.

Tiger, L., and R. Fox. *The imperial animal.* New York: Holt, Rinehart and Winston, 1971, xi + 308.

Trivers, R. L. "The evolution of reciprocal altruism." *Quarterly Review of Biology*, 46(4), 1971, 35-57.

Trivers, R. L. "Parent-offspring conflict." *American Zoologist*, 14(1), 1974, 249-264.

Turnbull, C. M. *The mountain people.* New York: Touchstone Books, Simon and Schuster, 1972, 309.

Washburn, S. L., Comment on: "A possible evolutionary basis for aesthetic appreciation in men and apes." *Evolution*, 24(4), 1970, 824-825.

Washburn, S. L., and F. C. Howell. "Human evolution and culture." In S. Tax, ed., *Evolution after Darwin*, vol. 2, *Evolution of man*, 33-56. Chicago: University of Chicago Press, 1960, viii + 473.

Weber, M. *The sociology of religion,* Ttrans. E. Fischoff, with an introduction by T. Parsons. Boston: Beacon Press, 1964, lxx + 304.

White, H. C. *Chains of opportunity: system models of mobility in organizations.* Cambridge: Harvard University Press, 1970, xvi + 418.

Whiting, J. W. M. Discussion, "Are the hunter-gatherers a cultural type?" In R. B. Lee and I. DeVore, eds. (*q.v.*) *Man the hunter*, 1965, 336-339.

Wilson, E. O. *The insect societies.* Cambridge: Belknap Press of Harvard University Press, 1971, x + 548.

Wilson, E. O. "On the queerness of social evolution." *Bulletin of the Entomological Society of America*, 19(1), 1972, 20-22.

VII

FREUD

CHAPTER THIRTY-ONE — SIGMUND FREUD

Like a number of other thinkers represented in this volume, Sigmund Freud (1856-1939) is a theorist whose ideas and work have been very divergently and incompatibly received and assessed. More than perhaps any other it is difficult in Freud's case to find, or defend, a middle ground of interpretation and evaluation. Freud developed – created, some would think the apter verb – psychoanalysis. Himself a physician – a neurologist – with classical nineteenth-century philosophical conceptions of science, Freud saw his work as the primary foundations of a biologically grounded science of mind. His many followers in the psychoanalytic movement, from the first decade of the twentieth century to the present, have shared this view, as for a time did wide sectors of the general public, especially in German-speaking Europe and the United States.

From its inception, psychoanalysis met also with hostility and rejection – and quite often as well, it must be said, with bemused indifference, or contemptuous dismissal. Quackery and pseudo-science have been epithets leveled at Freud's system. The scientific objectivity of psychoanalytic methodology – drawn almost entirely from impressionistic clinical practice, or else from speculative essays of Freud himself, or some of his followers – has been seen as problematic, and has also been defended.

What seems reasonably neutral, and accurate, to say is that Freud was an interesting and engaging writer, whose published work conveys a distinctive view of human nature; that Freud's aim that psychoanalysis should secure an accepted place among the sciences has not been realized; and that – in spite of repeated pronouncements of its moral turpitude, or its definitive refutation, or its having passed into the dustbin of history, a failed and now quite old-fashioned system of thought – psychoanalysis continues to be revisited, and to win some manner or other of qualified but deeply sympathetic support. The reader will find in Freud's own words what psychoanalysis is about; and must then decide for himself or herself what plausibility the theory may have.

Sigmund Freud, *Character and Culture*

(Source: Sigmund Freud. "Two Encyclopaedia Articles," in *The Standard Edition of the Complete Psychological Works of Sigmund Freud*. London: Hogarth Press, 1966-1974, vol. xviii, 235-256. Trans. James Strachey, 1942.)

Psychoanalysis[1] (1922)

Psychoanalysis is the name (1) of a procedure for the investigation of mental processes which are almost inaccessible in any other way, (2) of a method (based upon that investigation) for the treatment of neurotic disorders and (3) of a collec-

1 ["Psychoanalyse" and "Libidotheorie" (see volume on metapsychology, *General Psychological Theory*, Collier Books edition AS 58lV) were two articles designed for Max Marcuse's *Handwörterbuch für Sexualwissenschaft*, which was first published in 1923, and were reprinted *Ges. Schr.*, 11, 201, and *Ges. W.*, 13, 211. They were actually written during the summer of 1922, that is to say before Freud's final re-casting of his views upon the topography of the mind in *The Ego and the Id* (1923). But the new views though unexpressed in these articles, must already have been clearly present in his thoughts while he was writing them, for it was in September, 1922, at the Berlin Psychoanalytical Congress (which is actually mentioned in one of the articles) that he first made public his newly defined conceptions of ego, super-ego and id. Translation, reprinted from *Int. J. Psycho-Anal.*, 23 (1942), 97, by James Strachey.]

tion of psychological information obtained along those lines, which is gradually being accumulated into a new scientific discipline.

History. – The best way of understanding psychoanalysis is still tracing its origin and development. In 1880 and 1881 Dr. Josef Breuer of Vienna, a well-known physician and experimental physiologist, was occupied in the treatment of a girl who had fallen ill of a severe hysteria while she was nursing her sick father. The clinical picture was made up of motor paralyses, inhibitions and disturbances of consciousness. Following a hint given him by the patient herself, who was a person of great intelligence, he put her into a state of hypnosis and contrived that, by describing to him the moods and thoughts that were uppermost in her mind, she returned on each particular occasion to a normal mental condition. By consistently repeating the same wearisome process, he succeeded in freeing her from all her inhibitions and paralyses, so that in the end he found his trouble rewarded by a great therapeutic success as well as by an unexpected insight into the nature of the puzzling neurosis. Nevertheless, Breuer refrained from following up his discovery or from publishing anything about the case until some ten years later, when the personal influence of the present writer (Freud, who had returned to Vienna in 1886 after studying in the school of Charcot) prevailed upon him to take up the subject afresh and embark upon a joint study of it. These two, Breuer and Freud, published a preliminary paper "On the Psychical Mechanism of Hysterical Phenomena" in 1893, and in 1895 a volume entitled *Studien über Hysterie* (which reached its fourth edition in 1922), in which they described their therapeutic procedure as *"cathartic."*

Catharsis. – The investigations which lay at the root of Breuer and Freud's studies led above all to two results, and these have not been shaken by subsequent experience: first, that hysterical symptoms have sense and meaning, being substitutes for normal mental acts; and secondly, that the uncovering of this unknown meaning is accompanied by the removal of the symptoms – so that in this case scientific research and therapeutic effort coincide. The observations were carried out upon a series of patients who were treated in the same manner as Breuer's first patient, that is to say, put into a state of deep hypnosis; and the results seemed brilliant,

until later their weak side became evident. The theoretical ideas put forward at that time by Breuer and Freud were influenced by Charcot's theories upon traumatic hysteria and could find support in the findings of his pupil Pierre Janet, which, though they were published earlier than the *Studien,* were in fact subsequent to Breuer's first case. From the very beginning the factor of *affect* was brought into the foreground: hysterical symptoms, the authors maintained, came into existence when a mental process with a heavy charge of affect was in any way prevented from equalizing that charge by passing along the normal paths leading to consciousness and movement (*i.e.* from being *"abreacted"*), as a result of which the affect, which was in a sense *"strangulated,"* was diverted on to the wrong paths and found its discharge into the somatic innervation (a process named *"conversion"*). The occasions upon which "pathogenic ideas" of this kind arose were described by Breuer and Freud as *"psychical traumas,"* and, since these often dated back to the very remote past, it was possible for the authors to say that hysterics suffered to a large extent from reminiscences (which had not been dealt with). Under the treatment, therefore, *"catharsis"* came about when the path to consciousness was opened and there was a normal discharge of affect. It will be seen that an essential part of this theory was the assumption of the existence of *unconscious* mental processes. Janet too had made use of unconscious acts in mental life; but, as he insisted in his later polemics against psychoanalysis, to him the phrase was no more than a makeshift expression, *"une manière de parler,"* and he intended to suggest no new point of view by it.

In a theoretical section of the *Studien* Breuer brought forward some speculative ideas upon the processes of excitation in the mind. These ideas determined the direction of future lines of thought and even to-day have not received sufficient appreciation. But they brought his contributions to this branch of science to an end, and soon afterwards he withdrew from the common work.

The Transition to Psychoanalysis. – Contrasts between the views of the two authors had been visible even in the *Studien.* Breuer supposed that the pathogenic ideas produced their traumatic effect because they arose during *"hypnoid states,"* in which mental functioning was subject to special limitations. The present writer rejected this explanation and inclined to the belief that an idea became pathogenic if its content was in opposition to the predominant trend of the subject's mental life so that it provoked him into *"defence."* (Janet had attributed to hysterical patients a constitutional incapacity for holding together the contents of their minds; and it was at this point that his path diverged from that of Breuer and Freud.) Moreover, both of the innovations which led the present writer to move away from the cathartic method had already been mentioned in the *Studien.* After Breuer's withdrawal they became the starting-point of fresh developments.

Abandonment of Hypnosis. – The first of these innovations was based upon practical experience and led to a change in technique. The second consisted in an advance in the clinical understanding of neuroses. It soon appeared that the therapeutic hopes which had been placed upon cathartic treatment in hypnosis were to some extent unfulfilled. It was true that the disappearance of the symptoms went hand-in-hand with the catharsis, but total success turned out to be entirely dependent upon the patient's relation to the physician and thus resembled the effect of "suggestion." If that relation was disturbed, all the symptoms reappeared, just as though they had never been cleared up. In addition to this, the small number of people who could be put into a deep state of hypnosis involved a very considerable limitation, from the medical standpoint, of the applicability of the cathartic procedure. For these reasons the present writer decided to give up the use of hypnosis. But at the same time the impressions he had derived from hypnosis afforded him the means of replacing it.

Free Association. – The effect of the hypnotic condition upon the patient had been so greatly to increase his ability to make associations that he was able to find straightaway the path – inaccessible to his conscious reflection – which led from the symptom to the thoughts and memories connected with it. The abandonment of hypnosis seemed to make the situation hopeless, until the writer recalled a remark of Bernheim's to the effect that things that had been experienced in a state of somnambulism were only *apparently* forgotten and that they could be brought into recollection at any time if the physician insisted forcibly enough that

the patient knew them. The writer therefore endeavoured to press his *unhypnotized* patients into giving him their associations, so that from the material thus provided he might find the path leading to what had been forgotten or warded off. He noticed later that such pressure was unnecessary and that copious ideas almost always arose in the patient's mind, but that they were held back from being communicated and even from becoming conscious by certain objections put by the patient in his own way. It was to be expected – though this was still unproved and not until later confirmed by wide experience – that everything that occurred to a patient setting out from a particular starting-point must also stand in an internal connection with that starting-point; hence arose the technique of educating the patient to give up the whole of his critical attitude and of making use of the material which was brought to light for the purpose of uncovering the connections that were being sought. A strong belief in the strict determination of mental events certainly played a part in the choice of this technique as a substitute for hypnosis.

The "Fundamental Technical Rule" of this procedure of "free association" has from that time on been maintained in psychoanalytic work. The treatment is begun by the patient being required to put himself in the position of an attentive and dispassionate self-observer, merely to read off all the time the surface of his consciousness, and on the one hand to make a duty of the most complete candour while on the other not holding back any idea from communication, even if (1) he feels that it is too disagreeable or if (2) he judges that it is nonsensical or (3) too unimportant or (4) irrelevant to what is being looked for. It is uniformly found that precisely those ideas which provoke these last-mentioned reactions are of particular value in discovering the forgotten material.

Psychoanalysis as an Interpretative Art. – The new technique altered the picture of the treatment so greatly, brought the physician into such a new relation to the patient and produced so many surprising results that it seemed justifiable to distinguish the procedure from the cathartic method by giving it a new name. The present writer gave this method of treatment, which could now be extended to many other forms of neurotic disorder, the name of *psychoanalysis.* Now, in the first resort, this psychoanalysis was an art of *interpretation* and it set itself the task of carrying deeper the first of Breuer's great discoveries – namely, that neurotic symptoms are significant substitutes for other mental acts which have been omitted. It was now a matter of regarding the material produced by the patients' associations as though it hinted at a hidden meaning and of discovering that meaning from it. Experience soon showed that the attitude which the analytical physician could most advantageously adopt was to surrender himself to his own unconscious mental activity, in a state of *easy and impartial attention,* to avoid so far as possible reflection and the construction of conscious expectations, not to try to fix anything that he heard particularly in his memory, and by these means to catch the drift of the patient's unconscious with his own unconscious. It was then found that, except under conditions that were too unfavourable, the patient's associations emerged like allusions, as it were, to one particular theme and that it was only necessary for the physician to go a step further in order to guess the material which was concealed from the patient himself and to be able to communicate it to him. It is true that this work of interpretation was not to be brought under strict rules and left a great deal of play to the physician's tact and skill; but, with impartiality and practice, it was usually possible to obtain trustworthy results – that is to say, results which were confirmed by being repeated in similar cases. At a time when so little was yet known of the unconscious, the structure of the neuroses and the pathological processes underlying them, it was a matter for satisfaction that a technique of this kind should be available, even if it had no better theoretical basis. Moreover it is still employed in analyses at the present day in the same manner, though with a sense of greater assurance and with a better understanding of its limitations.

The Interpretation of Parapraxes and Chance Actions. – It was a triumph for the interpretative art of psychoanalysis when it succeeded in demonstrating that certain common mental acts of normal people, for which no one had hitherto attempted to put forward a psychological explanation, were to be regarded in the same light as the symptoms of neurotics: that is to say, they had a *meaning,* which was unknown to the subject but which could easily be discovered by analytic means. The phenomena in question were such events as the temporary forgetting of familiar words and names, forgetting to carry out prescribed tasks, everyday slips of the tongue and of the pen, misreadings, losses and mislayings of objects, certain mistakes, instances of apparently accidental self-injury, and finally habitual movements carried out seemingly without intention or in play, tunes hummed "thoughtlessly," and so on. All of these were shorn of their physiological explanation, if any such had ever been attempted, and were shown to be strictly determined and were revealed as an expression of the subject's suppressed intentions or as a result of a clash between two intentions one of which was permanently or temporarily unconscious. The importance of this contribution to psychology was of many kinds. The range of mental determinism was extended by it in an unforeseen manner; the supposed gulf between normal and pathological mental events was narrowed; in many cases a useful insight was afforded into the play of mental forces that must be suspected to lie behind the phenomena. Finally, a class of material was brought to light which is calculated better than any other to stimulate a belief in the existence of unconscious mental acts even in people to whom the hypothesis of something at once mental and unconscious seems strange and even absurd. The study of one's own parapraxes and chance actions, for which most people have ample opportunities, is even to-day the best preparation for an approach to psychoanalysis. In analytic treatment, the interpretation of parapraxes retains a place as a means of uncovering the unconscious, alongside the immeasurably more important interpretation of associations.

The Interpretation of Dreams. – A new approach to the depths of mental life was opened when the technique of free association was applied to dreams, whether one's own or those of patients in analysis. In fact, the greater and better part of what we know of the processes in the unconscious levels of the mind is derived from the interpretation of dreams. Psychoanalysis has restored to dreams the importance which was generally ascribed to them in ancient times, but it treats them differently. It does not rely upon the cleverness of the dream-interpreter but for the most part hands the task over to the dreamer himself by asking him for his associations to the separate elements of the dream. By pursuing these associations further we obtain knowledge of thoughts which coincide entirely with the dream but which can be recognized – up to a certain point – as genuine and completely intelligible portions of waking mental activity. Thus the recollected dream emerges as the *manifest dream-content,* in contrast to the *latent dream-thoughts* discovered by interpretation. The process which has transformed the latter into the former, that is to say into "the dream," and which is undone by the work of interpretation, may be called *"dream-work."*

We also describe the latent dream-thoughts, on account of their connection with waking life, as *"residues of the [previous] day."* By the operation of the dream-work (to which it would be quite incorrect to ascribe any "creative" character) the latent dream-thoughts are *condensed* in a remarkable way, they are *distorted* by the *displacement* of psychical intensities, they are arranged with a view to being *represented in visual pictures;* and, besides all this, before the manifest dream is arrived at, they are submitted to a process of *secondary elaboration* which seeks to give the new product something in the nature of sense and coherence. But, strictly speaking, this last process does not form a part of dream-work.

The Dynamic Theory of Dream-Formation. – An understanding of the dynamics of dream-formation did not involve any great difficulties. The motive power for the formation of dreams is not provided by the latent dream-thoughts or day's residues, but by an unconscious impulse, repressed during the day, with which the day's residues have been able to establish contact and which contrives to make a *wish-fulfilment* for itself out of the material of the latent thoughts. Thus every dream is on the one hand the fulfilment of a wish on the part of the unconscious and on the other hand (in so far as it succeeds in guarding the state of sleep against being disturbed) the fulfilment of the normal wish to sleep which set the sleep going. If we disregard the unconscious contribution to the formation of the dream and limit the dream to its latent thoughts, it can represent anything with which waking life has been concerned – a reflection, a warning, an intention, a preparation for the immediate future or, once again, the satisfaction of an unfulfilled wish. The unrecognizability, strangeness and absurdity of the manifest dream are partly the result of the translation of the thoughts into a different, so to say *archaic,* method of expression,

but partly the effect of a restrictive, critically disapproving agency in the mind, which does not entirely cease to function during sleep. It is plausible to suppose that the *"dream-censorship,"* which we regard as being responsible in the first instance for the distortion of the dream-thoughts into the manifest dream, is a manifestation of the same mental forces which during the day-time had held back or *repressed* the unconscious wishful impulse.

It has been worth while to enter in some detail into the explanation of dreams, since analytical work has shown that the dynamics of the formation of dreams are the same as those of the formation of symptoms. In both cases we find a struggle between two trends, of which one is unconscious and ordinarily repressed and strives towards satisfaction – that is, wish-fulfilment – while the other, belonging probably to the conscious ego, is disapproving and repressive. The outcome of this conflict is a *compromise-formation* (the dream or the symptom) in which both trends have found an incomplete expression. The theoretical importance of this conformity between dreams and symptoms is illuminating. Since dreams are not pathological phenomena, the fact shows that the mental mechanisms which produce the symptoms of illness are equally present in normal mental life, that the same uniform law embraces both the normal and the abnormal and that the findings of research into neurotics or psychotics cannot be without significance for our understanding of the healthy mind.

Symbolism. – In the course of investigating the form of expression brought about by dream-work, the surprising fact emerged that certain objects, arrangements and relations are represented, in a sense indirectly, by "symbols," which are used by the dreamer without his understanding them and to which as a rule he offers no associations. Their translation has to be provided by the analyst, who can himself only discover it empirically by experimentally fitting it into the context. It was later found that linguistic usage, mythology and folklore afford the most ample analogies to dream-symbols. Symbols, which raise the most interesting and hitherto unsolved problems, seem to be a fragment of extremely ancient inherited mental equipment. The use of a common symbolism extends far beyond the use of a common language.

The Aetiological Significance of Sexual Life. – The second novelty which emerged after the hypnotic technique had been replaced by free associations was of a clinical nature. It was discovered in the course of the prolonged search for the traumatic experiences from which hysterical symptoms appeared to be derived. The more carefully the search was pursued the more extensive seemed to be the network of aetiologically significant impressions, but the further back, too, did they reach into the patient's puberty or childhood. At the same time they assumed a uniform character and eventually it became inevitable to bow before the evidence and recognize that at the root of the formation of every symptom there were to be found traumatic experiences from early sexual life. Thus a sexual trauma stepped into the place of an ordinary trauma and the latter was seen to owe its aetiological significance to an associative or symbolic connection with the former, which had preceded it. An investigation of cases of common nervousness (falling into the two classes of *neurasthenia* and *anxiety neurosis)* which was simultaneously undertaken led to the conclusion that these disorders could be traced to *contemporary* abuses in the patients' sexual life and could be removed if these were brought to an end. It was thus easy to infer that neuroses in general are an expression of disturbances in sexual life, the so-called *actual-neuroses* being the consequences (by chemical agency) of *contemporary* injuries and the psycho-neuroses the consequences (by psychical modification) of *bygone* injuries to a biological function which had hitherto been gravely neglected by science. None of the theses of psychoanalysis has met with such tenacious scepticism or such embittered resistance as this assertion of the preponderating aetiological significance of sexual life in the neuroses. It should, however, be expressly remarked that, in its development up to the present day, psychoanalysis has found no reason to retreat from this opinion.

Infantile Sexuality. – As a result of its aetiological researches, psychoanalysis found itself in the position of dealing with a subject the very existence of which had scarcely been suspected previously. Science had become accustomed to consider sexual life as beginning with puberty and regarded manifestations of sexuality in children as rare signs of abnormal precocity and degeneracy. But now psychoanalysis revealed a wealth of phenomena, remarkable, yet of regular occurrence, which made it necessary to date back the beginning of the sex-

ual function in children almost to the commencement of extra-uterine existence; and it was asked with astonishment how all this could have come to be overlooked. The first glimpses of sexuality in children had indeed been obtained through the analytic examination of adults and were consequently saddled with all the doubts and sources of error that could be attributed to such a belated retrospect; but subsequently (from 1908 onwards) a beginning was made with the analysis of children themselves and with the unembarrassed observation of their behaviour, and in this way direct confirmation was reached for the whole factual basis of the new view.

Sexuality in children showed a different picture in many respects from that in adults, and, surprisingly enough, it exhibited numerous traces of what, in adults, were condemned as *"perversions."* It became necessary to enlarge the concept of what was sexual, till it covered more than the impulsion towards the union of the two sexes in the sexual act or towards provoking particular pleasurable sensations in the genitals. But this enlargement was rewarded by the new possibility of grasping infantile, normal and perverse sexual life as a single whole.

The analytic researches carried out by the writer fell, to begin with, into the error of greatly overestimating the importance of *seduction* as a source of sexual manifestations in children and as a root for the formation of neurotic symptoms. This misapprehension was corrected when it became possible to appreciate the extraordinarily large part played in the mental life of neurotics by the activities of *phantasy,* which clearly carried more weight in neurosis than did the external world. Behind these phantasies there came to light the material which allows us to draw the picture which follows of the development of the sexual function.

The Development of the Libido. – The sexual instinct, the dynamic manifestation of which in mental life we shall call *"libido,"* is made up of component instincts into which it may once more break up and which are only gradually united into well-defined organizations. The sources of these component instincts are the organs of the body and in particular certain specially marked *erotogenic zones;* but contributions are made to libido from every important functional process in the body. At first the individual component instincts strive for satisfaction independently of one another, but in the course of development they become more and more convergent and concentrated. The first (pre-genital) stage of organization to be discerned is the *oral* one, in which – in conformity with the suck-ling's predominant interest – the oral zone plays the leading part. This is followed by the *sadistic-anal* organization, in which the *anal* zone and the com-ponent instinct of *sadism* are particularly promi-nent; at this stage the difference between the sexes is represented by the contrast between active and passive. The third and final stage of organization is that in which the majority of the component instincts converge under the *primacy of the genital zones.* As a rule this development is passed through swiftly and unobtrusively; but some individual por-tions of the instincts remain behind at the prodro-mal stages of the process and thus give rise to *fixa-tions* of libido, which are important as constituting predispositions for subsequent irruptions of repressed impulses and which stand in a definite relation to the later development of neuroses and perversions. (See the article upon the Libido Theory [*General Psychological Theory,* Collier Books edition AS 582V].)

The Process of Finding an Object and the Oedipus Complex. – In the first instance the oral component instinct finds satisfaction by attaching itself to the sating of the desire for nourishment; and its object is the mother's breast. It then detach-es itself, becomes independent and at the same time *auto-erotic,* that is, it finds an object in the child's own body. Others of the component instincts also start by being auto-erotic and are not until later diverted on to an external object. It is a particular-ly important fact that the component instincts belonging to the genital zone habitually pass through a period of intense auto-erotic satisfac-tion. The component instincts are not all equally serviceable in the final genital organization of libido; some of them (for instance, the anal com-ponents) are consequently left aside and sup-pressed, or undergo complicated transformations.

In the very earliest years of childhood (approxi-mately between the ages of two and five) a conver-gence of the sexual impulses occurs of which, in the case of boys, the object is the mother. This choice of an object, in conjunction with a corre-sponding attitude of rivalry and hostility towards the father, provides the content of what is known as the *Oedipus complex,* which in every human being is of the greatest importance in determining the final shape of his erotic life. It has been found to be characteristic of a normal individual that he has learnt how to master his Oedipus complex, where-as the neurotic subject remains involved in it.

The Diphasic Onset of Sexual Development. – Towards the end of the fifth year this early period of sexual life normally comes to an end. It is suc-ceeded by a period of more or less complete *laten-cy,* during which ethical restraints are built up, to act as defences against the desires of the Oedipus complex. In the subsequent period of *puberty,* the Oedipus complex is revivified in the unconscious and embarks upon further modifications. It is only at puberty that the sexual instincts develop to their full intensity; but the direction of that develop-ment, as well as all the predispositions for it, have already been determined by the early efflorescence of sexuality during childhood which preceded it. This diphasic development of the sexual function – in two stages, interrupted by the latency period – appears to be a biological peculiarity of the human species and to contain the determining factor for the origin of neuroses.

The Theory of Repression. – These theoretical considerations, taken together with the immediate impressions derived from analytic work, lead to a view of the neuroses which may be described in the roughest outline as follows. The neuroses are the expression of conflicts between the ego and such of the sexual impulses as seem to the ego incompati-ble with its integrity or with its ethical standards. Since these impulses are not *ego-syntonic,* the ego has *repressed* them: that is to say, it has withdrawn its interest from them and has shut them off from becoming conscious as well as from obtaining sat-isfaction by motor discharge. If in the course of analytic work one attempts to make these repressed impulses conscious, one becomes aware of the repressive forces in the form of *resistance.* But the achievement of repression fails particularly easily in the case of the sexual instincts. Their dammed-up libido finds other ways out from the uncon-scious: for it *regresses* to earlier phases of develop-ment and earlier attitudes towards objects, and, at weak points in the libidinal development where there are infantile fixations, it breaks through into consciousness and obtains discharge. What results is a *symptom* and consequently in its essence a substitutive sexual satisfaction. Nevertheless the symptom cannot entirely escape from the repressive forces of the ego and must therefore submit to modification and displacements – exactly as happens with dreams by means of which its characteristic of being a sexual satisfaction becomes unrecognizable. Thus symptoms are in the nature of compromise-formations between the repressed sexual instincts and the repressive ego instincts; they represent a wish-fulfilment for both partners to the conflict simultaneously, but one which is incomplete for each of them. This is quite strictly true of the symptoms of hysteria, while in the symptoms of obsessional neurosis there is often a stronger emphasis upon the side of the repressive function owing to the erection of reaction-formations, which are assurances against sexual satisfaction.

Transference. – If further proof were needed of the truth that the motive forces behind the formation of neurotic symptoms are of a sexual nature, it would be found in the fact that in the course of analytic treatment a special emotional relation is regularly formed between the patient and the physician. This goes far beyond rational limits. It varies between the most affectionate devotion and the most obstinate enmity and derives all of its characteristics from earlier emotional erotic attitudes of the patient's which have become unconscious. This *transference* alike in its positive and in its negative form is used as a weapon by the resistance; but in the hands of the physician it becomes the most powerful therapeutic instrument and it plays a part that can scarcely be overestimated in the dynamics of the process of cure.

The Corner-stones of Psychoanalytic Theory. – The assumption that there are unconscious mental processes, the recognition of the theory of resistance and repression, the appreciation of the importance of sexuality and of the Oedipus complex – these constitute the principal subject-matter of psychoanalysis and the foundations of its theory. No one who cannot accept them all should count himself a psychoanalyst.

Later History of Psychoanalysis. – Psychoanalysis was carried approximately thus far by the work of the writer of this article, who for more than ten years was its sole representative. In 1906 the Swiss psychiatrist Bleuler and C. G. Jung began to play a lively part in analysis; in 1907 a first conference of its supporters took place at Salzburg; and the young science soon found itself the centre of interest both among psychiatrists and laymen. Its reception in Germany, with her morbid craving for authority, was not precisely to the credit of German science and moved even so cool a partisan as Bleuler to an energetic protest. Yet no condemnation or dismissal at official congresses served to hold up the internal growth or external expansion of psychoanalysis. In the course of the next ten years it extended far beyond the frontiers of Europe and became especially popular in the United States of America, and this was due in no small degree to the advocacy and collaboration of Putnam (Boston), Ernest Jones (Toronto; later London), Flournoy (Geneva), Ferenczi (Budapest), Abraham (Berlin), and many others besides. The anathema which was imposed upon psychoanalysis led its supporters to combine in an international organization which in the present year (1922) is holding its eighth private Congress in Berlin and now includes local groups in Vienna, Budapest, Berlin, Holland, Zurich, London, New York, Calcutta and Moscow. This development was not interrupted even by the World War. In 1918-19 Dr. Anton v. Freund of Budapest founded the Internationaler Psychoanalytischer Verlag, which publishes journals and books concerned with psychoanalysis, and in 1920 Dr. M. Eitingon opened in Berlin the first psychoanalytic clinic for the treatment of neurotics without private means. Translations of the writer's principal works, which are now in preparation, into French, Italian and Spanish, testify to a growing interest in psychoanalysis in the Latin world as well.

Between 1911 and 1913 two movements of divergence from psychoanalysis took place, evidently with the object of mitigating its repellent features. One of these (sponsored by C. G. Jung), in an endeavour to conform to ethical standards, divested the Oedipus complex of its real significance by giving it only a *symbolic* value, and in practice neglected the uncovering of the forgotten and, as we may call it, "prehistoric" period of childhood. The other (originated by Alfred Adler in Vienna) reproduced many factors from psychoanalysis under other names – repression, for instance, appeared in a sexualized version as the "masculine protest." But in other respects it turned away from the unconscious and the sexual instincts, and endeavoured to trace back the development of character and of the neuroses to the "will to power," which by means of over-compensations strives to check the dangers arising from "organ inferiority." Neither of these movements, with their systematic structures, had any permanent influence on psychoanalysis. In the case of Adler's theories it soon became clear that they had very little in common with psychoanalysis, which they were designed to replace.

More Recent Advances in Psychoanalysis. – Since psychoanalysis has become the field of work for such a large number of observers it has made advances, both in extent and depth; but unfortunately these can receive only the briefest mention in the present article.

Narcissism. – The most important theoretical advance has certainly been the application of the libido theory to the repressing ego. The ego itself came to be regarded as a reservoir of what was described as narcissistic libido, from which the libidinal cathexes of objects flowed out and into which they could be once more withdrawn. By the help of this conception it became possible to embark upon the analysis of the ego and to make a clinical distinction of the psychoneuroses into *transference neuroses* and *narcissistic* disorders. In the former the subject has at his disposal a quantity of libido striving to be transferred on to external objects, and use is made of this in carrying out analytic treatment; on the other hand, the narcissistic disorders (dementia praecox, paranoia, melancholia) are characterized by a withdrawal of the libido from objects and they are therefore scarcely accessible to analytic therapy. But their therapeutic inaccessibility has not prevented analysis from making the most fruitful beginnings in the deeper study of these illnesses, which are counted among the psychoses.

Development of Technique. – After the analyst's curiosity had, as it were, been gratified by the elaboration of the technique of interpretation, it was inevitable that interest should turn to the problem of discovering the most effective way of influencing the patient. It soon became evident that the physician's immediate task was to assist the patient in getting to know, and afterwards in overcoming, the resistances which emerged in him during treatment and of which, to begin with, he himself was unaware. And it was found at the same time that the essential part of the process of cure lay in the overcoming of these resistances and that unless this was achieved no permanent mental change could be brought about in the patient. Since the analyst's

efforts have in this way been directed upon the patient's resistance, analytic technique has attained a certainty and delicacy rivalling that of surgery. Consequently, everyone is strongly advised against undertaking psychoanalytic treatments without a strict training, and a physician who ventures upon them on the strength of his medical qualification is in no respect better than a layman.

Psychoanalysis as a Therapeutic Procedure. – Psychoanalysis has never set itself up as a panacea and has never claimed to perform miracles. In one of the most difficult spheres of medical activity it is the only possible method of treatment for certain illnesses and for others it is the method which yields the best or the most permanent results – though never without a corresponding expenditure of time and trouble. A physician who is not wholly absorbed in the work of giving help will find his labours amply repaid by obtaining an unhoped-for insight into the complications of mental life and the interrelations between the mental and the physical. Where at present it cannot offer help but only theoretical understanding, it may perhaps be preparing the way for some later, more direct means of influencing neurotic disorders. Its province is above all the two transference neuroses, hysteria and obsessional neurosis, in which it has contributed to the discovery of their internal structure and operative mechanisms; and, beyond them, all kinds of phobias, inhibitions, deformities of character, sexual perversions and difficulties in erotic life. Some analysts (Jelliffe, Groddeck, Felix Deutsch) have reported too that the analytic treatment of gross organic diseases is not unpromising, since a mental factor not infrequently contributes to the origin and continuance of such illnesses. Since psychoanalysis demands a certain amount of psychical plasticity from its patients, some kind of age limit must be laid down in their selection; and since it necessitates the devotion of long and intense attention to the individual patient, it would be uneconomical to squander such expenditure upon completely worthless persons who happen to be neurotic. Experience upon material in clinics can alone show what modifications may be necessary in order to make psychoanalytic treatment accessible to wider strata of the population or to adapt it to weaker intelligences.

Comparison between Psychoanalysis and Hypnotic and Suggestive Methods. – Psychoanalytic procedure differs from all methods making use of suggestion, persuasion, etc., in that it does not seek to suppress by means of authority any mental phenomenon that may occur in the patient. It endeavours to trace the causation of the phenomenon and to remove it by bringing about permanent modification in the conditions that led to it. In psychoanalysis the suggestive influence which is inevitably exercised by the physician is diverted on to the task assigned to the patient of overcoming his resistances, that is, of carrying forward the curative process. Any danger of falsifying the products of a patient's memory by suggestion can be avoided by prudent handling of the technique; but in general the arousing of resistances is a guarantee against the misleading effects of suggestive influence. It may be laid down that the aim of the treatment is to remove the patient's resistances and to pass his repressions in review and thus to bring about the most far reaching unification and strengthening of his ego, to enable him to save the mental energy which he is expending upon internal conflicts, to make the best of him that his inherited capacities will allow and so to make him as efficient and as capable of enjoyment as is possible. The removal of the symptoms of the illness is not specifically aimed at, but is achieved as it were, as a by-product if the analysis is properly carried through. The analyst respects the patient's individuality and does not seek to remould him in accordance with his own – that is, according to the physician's – personal ideals; he is glad to avoid giving advice and instead to arouse the patient's power of initiative.

Its Relation to Psychiatry. – Psychiatry is at present essentially a descriptive and classificatory science whose orientation is still towards the somatic rather than the psychological and which is without the possibility of giving explanations of the phenomena which it observes. Psychoanalysis does not, however, stand in opposition to it, as the almost unanimous behaviour of the psychiatrists might lead one to believe. On the contrary, as a *depth-psychology,* a psychology of those processes in mental life which are withdrawn from consciousness, it is called upon to provide psychiatry with an indispensable groundwork and to free it from its present limitations. We can foresee that the future will give birth to a scientific psychiatry, to which psychoanalysis has served as an introduction.

Criticisms and Misunderstandings of Psychoanalysis. – Most of what is brought up against psychoanalysis, even in scientific works, is based upon insufficient information which in its turn seems to be determined by emotional resistances. Thus it is a mistake to accuse psychoanalysis of "pansexualism" and to allege that it derives all mental occurrences from sexuality and traces them all back to it. On the contrary, psychoanalysis has from the very first distinguished the sexual instincts from others which it has provisionally termed "ego instincts." It has never dreamt of trying to explain "everything," and even the neuroses it has traced back not to sexuality alone but to the conflict between the sexual impulses and the ego. In psychoanalysis (unlike the works of C. G. Jung) the term *"libido"* does not mean psychical energy in general but the motive force of the sexual instincts. Some assertions, such as that every dream is the fulfilment of a sexual wish, have never been maintained by it at all. The charge of one-sidedness made against psychoanalysis, which, as *the science of the unconscious mind,* has its own definite and restricted field of work, is as inapplicable as it would be if it were made against chemistry. To believe that psychoanalysis seeks a cure for neurotic disorders by giving a free rein to sexuality is a serious misunderstanding which can only be justified by ignorance. The making conscious of repressed sexual desires in analysis makes it possible, on the contrary, to obtain a mastery over them which the previous repression had been unable to achieve. It can more truly be said that analysis sets the neurotic free from the chains of his sexuality. Moreover, it is quite unscientific to judge analysis by whether it is calculated to undermine religion, authority and morals; for like all sciences, it is entirely nontendentious and has only a single aim – namely to arrive at a consistent view of one portion of reality. Finally, one can only characterize as simple-minded the fear which is sometimes expressed that all the highest goods of humanity, as they are called – research, art, love, ethical and social sense – will lose their value or their dignity because psychoanalysis is in a position to demonstrate their origin in elementary and animal instinctual impulses.

The Non-Medical Applications and Correlations of Psychoanalysis. – Any estimate of psychoanalysis would be incomplete if it failed to make clear that, alone among the medical disciplines, it has the most extensive relations with the mental sciences, and that it is in a position to play a part of the same importance in the studies of religious and cultural history and in the sciences of mythology and literature as it is in psychiatry. This may seem strange when we reflect that originally its only object was the understanding and improvement of neurotic symptoms. But it is easy to indicate the starting point of the bridge that leads over to the mental sciences. The analysis of dreams gave us an insight into the unconscious processes of the mind and showed us that the mechanisms which produce pathological symptoms are also operative in the normal mind. Thus psychoanalysis became a *depth-psychology* and capable as such of being applied to the mental sciences, and it was able to answer a good number of questions with which the academic psychology of consciousness was helpless to deal. At quite an early stage problems of human *phylogenesis* arose. It became clear that pathological function was often nothing more than a *regression* to an earlier stage in the development of normal function. C. G. Jung was the first to draw explicit attention to the striking similarity between the disordered phantasies of sufferers from dementia praecox and the myths of primitive peoples; while the present writer pointed out that the two wishes which combine to form the Oedipus complex coincide precisely with the two principal prohibitions imposed by *totemism* (not to kill the tribal ancestor and not to marry any woman belonging to one's own clan) and drew far-reaching conclusions from this fact. The significance of the Oedipus complex began to grow to gigantic proportions and it looked as though social order, morals, justice and religion had arisen together in the primaeval ages of mankind as reaction-formations against the Oedipus complex. Otto Rank threw a brilliant light upon mythology and the history of literature by the application of psychoanalytical views, as did Theodor Reik upon the history of morals and religions, while Dr. Pfister, of Zurich, aroused the interest of religious and secular teachers and demonstrated the importance of the psychoanalytical standpoint for education. Further discussion of these applications of psychoanalysis would be out of place here, and it is enough to say that the limits of their influence are not yet in sight.

Psychoanalysis an Empirical Science. – Psychoanalysis is not, like philosophies, a system starting out from a few sharply defined basic concepts, seeking to grasp the whole universe with the help of these and, once it is completed, having no room for fresh discoveries or better understanding. On the contrary, it keeps close to the facts in its field of study, seeks to solve the immediate problems of observation, gropes its way forward by the help of experience, is always incomplete and always ready to correct or modify its theories. There is no incongruity (any more than in the case of physics or chemistry) if its most general concepts lack clarity and if its postulates are provisional; it leaves their more precise definition to the results of future work.

Sigmund Freud, *Civilization and its Discontents*

(Source: Sigmund Freud. *Civilization and its Discontents*. Trans. James Strachey. New York: W.W. Norton & Company Inc., 1961, 21-32, 88-91.)

In my *Future of an Illusion* [1927] I was concerned much less with the deepest sources of the religious feeling than with what the common man understands by his religion – with the system of doctrines and promises which on the one hand explains to him the riddles of this world with enviable completeness, and, on the other, assures him that a careful Providence will watch over his life and will compensate him in a future existence for any frustrations he suffers here. The common man cannot imagine this Providence otherwise than in the figure of an enormously exalted father. Only such a being can understand the needs of the children of men and be softened by their prayers and placated by the signs of their remorse. The whole thing is so patently infantile, so foreign to reality, that to anyone with a friendly attitude to humanity it is painful to think that the great majority of mortals will never be able to rise above this view of life. It is still more humiliating to discover how large a number of people living to-day, who cannot but see that this religion is not tenable, nevertheless try to defend it piece by piece in a series of pitiful rearguard actions. One would like to mix among the ranks of the believers in order to meet these philosophers, who think they can rescue the God of religion by replacing him by an impersonal, shadowy and abstract principle, and to address them with the warning words: 'Thou shalt not take the name of the Lord thy God in vain!' And if some of the great men of the past acted in the same way, no appeal can be made to their example: we know why they were obliged to.

....

The question of the purpose of human life has been raised countless times; it has never yet received a satisfactory answer and perhaps does not admit of one. Some of those who have asked it have added that if it should turn out that life has no purpose, it would lose all value for them. But this threat alters nothing. It looks, on the contrary, as though one had a right to dismiss the question, for it seems to derive from the human presumptuousness, many other manifestations of which are already familiar to us. Nobody talks about the purpose of the life of animals, unless, perhaps, it may be supposed to lie in being of service to man. But this view is not tenable either, for there are many animals of which man can make nothing, except to describe, classify and study them; and innumerable species of animals have escaped even this use, since they existed and became extinct before man set eyes on them. Once again, only religion can answer the question of the purpose of life. One can hardly be wrong in concluding that the idea of life having a purpose stands and falls with the religious system.

We will therefore turn to the less ambitious question of what men themselves show by their behaviour to be the purpose and intention of their lives. What do they demand of life and wish to achieve in it? The answer to this can hardly be in doubt. They strive after happiness; they want to become happy and to remain so. This endeavour has two sides, a positive and a negative aim. It aims, on the one hand, at an absence of pain and unpleasure, and, on the other, at the experiencing of strong feelings of pleasure. In its narrower sense the word 'happiness' only relates to the last. In conformity with this dichotomy in his aims, man's activity develops in two directions, according as it seeks to realize – in the main, or even exclusively – the one or the other of these aims.

As we see, what decides the purpose of life is simply the programme of the pleasure principle. This principle dominates the operation of the mental apparatus from the start. There can be no doubt about its efficacy, and yet its programme is at loggerheads with the whole world, with the macrocosm as much as with the microcosm. There is no possibility at all of its being carried through; all the regulations of the universe run counter to it. One feels inclined to say that the intention that man should be 'happy' is not included in the plan of 'Creation'. What we call happiness in the strictest sense comes from the (preferably sudden) satisfaction of needs which have been dammed up to a high degree, and it is from its nature only possible as an episodic phenomenon. When any situation that is desired by the pleasure principle is prolonged, it only produces a feeling of mild contentment. We are so made that we can derive intense enjoyment only from a contrast and very little from a state of things.[1] Thus our possibilities of happiness are already restricted by our constitution. Unhappiness is much less difficult to experience. We are threatened with suffering from three directions: from our own body, which is doomed to decay and dissolution and which cannot even do without pain and anxiety as warning signals; from the external world, which may rage against us with overwhelming and merciless forces of destruction; and finally from our relations to other men. The suffering which comes from this last source is perhaps more painful to us than any other. We tend to regard it as a kind of gratuitous addition, although it cannot be any less fatefully inevitable than the suffering which comes from elsewhere.

It is no wonder if, under the pressure of these possibilities of suffering, men are accustomed to moderate their claims to happiness – just as the pleasure principle itself, indeed, under the influence of the external world, changed into the more modest reality principle –, if a man thinks himself happy merely to have escaped unhappiness or to have survived his suffering, and if in general the task of avoiding suffering pushes that of obtaining pleasure into the

---

1   Goethe, indeed, warns us that "nothing is harder to bear than a succession of fair days."
     [Alles in der Welt lässt sich ertragen,
     Nur nicht eine Reihe von schönen Tagen.
            (Weimar, 1810-12.)]
     But this may be exaggeration.

background. Reflection shows that the accomplishment of this task can be attempted along very different paths; and all these paths have been recommended by the various schools of worldly wisdom and put into practice by men. An unrestricted satisfaction of every need presents itself as the most enticing method of conducting one's life, but it means putting enjoyment before caution, and soon brings its own punishment. The other methods, in which avoidance of unpleasure is the main purpose, are differentiated according to the source of unpleasure to which their attention is chiefly turned. Some of these methods are extreme and some moderate; some are one-sided and some attack the problem simultaneously at several points. Against the suffering which may come upon one from human relationships the readiest safeguard is voluntary isolation, keeping oneself aloof from other people. The happiness which can be achieved along this path is, as we see, the happiness of quietness. Against the dreaded external world one can only defend oneself by some kind of turning away from it, if one intends to solve the task by oneself. There is, indeed, another and better path: that of becoming a member of the human community, and, with the help of a technique guided by science, going over to the attack against nature and subjecting her to the human will. Then one is working with all for the good of all. But the most interesting methods of averting suffering are those which seek to influence our own organism. In the last analysis, all suffering is nothing else than sensation; it only exists in so far as we feel it, and we only feel it in consequence of certain ways in which our organism is regulated.

The crudest, but also the most effective among these methods of influence is the chemical one – intoxication. I do not think that anyone completely understands its mechanism, but it is a fact that there are foreign substances which, when present in the blood or tissues, directly cause us pleasurable sensations; and they also so alter the conditions governing our sensibility that we become incapable of receiving unpleasurable impulses. The two effects not only occur simultaneously, but seem to be intimately bound up with each other. But there must be substances in the chemistry of our own bodies which have similar effects, for we know at least one pathological state, mania, in which a condition similar to intoxication arises without the administration of any intoxicating drug. Besides this, our normal mental life exhibits oscillations between a comparatively easy liberation of pleasure and a comparatively difficult one, parallel with which there goes a diminished or an increased receptivity to unpleasure. It is greatly to be regretted that this toxic side of mental processes has so far escaped scientific examination. The service rendered by intoxicating media in the struggle for happiness and in keeping misery at a distance is so highly prized as a benefit that individuals and peoples alike have given them an established place in the economics of their libido. We owe to such media not merely the immediate yield of pleasure, but also a greatly desired degree of independence from the external world. For one knows that, with the help of this 'drowner of cares' one can at any time withdraw from the pressure of reality and find refuge in a world of one's own with better conditions of sensibility. As is well known, it is precisely this property of intoxicants which also determines their danger and their injuriousness. They are responsible, in certain circumstances, for the useless waste of a large quota of energy which might have been employed for the improvement of the human lot.

The complicated structure of our mental apparatus admits, however, of a whole number of other influences. just as a satisfaction of instinct spells happiness for us, so severe suffering is caused us if the external world lets us starve, if it refuses to sate our needs. One may therfore hope to be freed from a part of one's sufferings by influencing the instinctual impulses. This type of defence against suffering is no longer brought to bear on the sensory apparatus; it seeks to master the internal sources of our needs. The extreme form of this is brought about by killing off the instincts, as is prescribed by the worldly wisdom of the East and practiced by Yoga. If it succeeds, then the subject has, it is true, given up all other activities as well – he has sacrificed his life; and, by another path, he has once more only achieved the happiness of quietness. We follow the same path when our aims are less extreme and we merely attempt to *control* our instinctual life. In that case, the controlling elements are the higher psychical agencies, which have subjected themselves to the reality principle. Here the aim of satisfaction is not by any means relinquished; but a certain amount of protection against suffering is secured, in that non-satisfaction is not so painfully felt in the case of instincts kept in dependence as in the case of uninhibited ones. As against this, there is an undeniable diminution in the potentialities of enjoyment. The feeling of happiness derived from the satisfaction of a wild instinctual impulse untamed by the ego is incomparably more intense than that derived from sating an instinct that has been tamed. The irresistibility of perverse instincts, and perhaps the attraction in general of forbidden things finds an economic explanation here.

Another technique for fending off suffering is the employment of the displacements of libido which our mental apparatus permits of and through which its function gains so much in flexibility. The task here is that of shifting the instinctual aims in such a way that they cannot come up against frustration from the external world. In this, sublimation of the instincts lends its assistance. One gains the most if one can sufficiently heighten the yield of pleasure from the sources of psychical and intellectual work. When that is so, fate can do little against one. A satisfaction of this kind, such as an artist's joy in creating, in giving his phantasies body, or a scientist's in solving problems or discovering truths, has a special quality which we shall certainly one day be able to characterize in metapsychological terms. At present we can only say figuratively that such satisfactions seem 'finer and higher'. But their intensity is mild as compared with that derived from the sating of crude and primary instinctual impulses; it does not convulse our physical being. And the weak point of this method

is that it is not applicable generally: it is accessible to only a few people. It presupposes the possession of special dispositions and gifts which are far from being common to any practical degree. And even to the few who do possess them, this method cannot give complete protection from suffering. It creates no impenetrable armour against the arrows of fortune, and it habitually fails when the source of suffering is a person's own body.[2]

While this procedure already clearly shows an intention of making oneself independent of the external world by seeking satisfaction in internal, psychical processes, the next procedure brings out those features yet more strongly. In it, the connection with reality is still further loosened; satisfaction is obtained from illusions, which are recognized as such without the discrepancy between them and reality being allowed to interfere with enjoyment. The region from which these illusions arise is the life of the imagination; at the time when the development of the sense of reality took place, this region was expressly exempted from the demands of reality-testing and was set apart for the purpose of fulfilling wishes which were difficult to carry out. At the head of these satisfactions through phantasy stands the enjoyment of works of art – an enjoyment which, by the agency of the artist, is made accessible even to those who are not themselves creative.[3] People who are receptive to the influence of art cannot set too high a value on it as a source of pleasure and consolation in life. Nevertheless the mild narcosis induced in us by art can do no more than bring about a transient withdrawal from the pressure of vital needs, and it is

---

2   When there is no special disposition in a person which imperatively prescribes what direction his interests in life shall take, the ordinary professional work that is open to everyone can play the part assigned to it by Voltaire's wise advice [viz., to "cultivate one's garden"]. It is not possible, within the limits of a short survey, to discuss adequately the significance of work for the economics of the libido. No other technique for the conduct of life attaches the individual so firmly to reality as laying emphasis on work; for his work at least gives him a secure place in a portion of reality, in the human community. The possibility it offers of displacing a large amount of libidinal components, whether narcissistic, aggressive or even erotic, on to professional work and on to the human relations connected with it lends it a value by no means second to what it enjoys as something indispensable to the preservation and justification of existence in society. Professional activity is a source of special satisfaction if it is a freely chosen one – if, that is to say, by means of sublimation, it makes possible the use of existing inclinations, of persisting or constitutionally reinforced instinctual impulses. And yet, as a path to happiness, work is not highly prized by men. They do not strive after it as they do after other possibilities of satisfaction. The great majority of people only work under the stress of necessity, and this natural human aversion to work raises most difficult social problems.

3   Cf. 'Formulations on the Two Principles of Mental Functioning' (1911), and lecture XXIII of my *Introductory Lectures* (1916-17).

not strong enough to make us forget real misery.

Another procedure operates more energetically and more thoroughly. It regards reality as the sole enemy and as the source of all suffering, with which it is impossible to live, so that one must break off all relations with it if one is to be in any way happy. The hermit turns his back on the world and will have no truck with it. But one can do more than that; one can try to re-create the world, to build up in its stead another world in which its most unbearable features are eliminated and replaced by others that are in conformity with one's own wishes. But whoever, in desperate defiance, sets out upon this path to happiness will as a rule attain nothing. Reality is too strong for him. He becomes a madman, who for the most part finds no one to help him in carrying through his delusion. It is asserted, however, that each one of us behaves in some one respect like a paranoic, corrects some aspect of the world which is unbearable to him by the construction of a wish and introduces this delusion into reality. A special importance attaches to the case in which this attempt to procure a certainty of happiness and a protection against suffering through a delusional remolding of reality is made by a considerable number of people in common. The religions of mankind must be classed among the mass delusions of this kind. No one, needless to say, who shares a delusion ever recognizes it as such.

I do not think that I have made a complete enumeration of the methods by which men strive to gain happiness and keep suffering away and I know, too, that the material might have been differently arranged. One procedure I have not yet mentioned – not because I have forgotten it but because it will concern us later in another connection. And how could one possibly forget, of all others, this technique in the art of living? It is conspicuous for a most remarkable combination of characteristic features. It, too, aims of course at making the subject independent of Fate (as it is best to call it), and to that end it locates satisfaction in internal mental processes, making use, in so doing, of the displaceability of the libido of which we have already spoken [p. 348-49]. But it does not turn away from the external world; on the contrary, it clings to the objects belonging to that world and obtains happiness from an emotional relationship

to them. Nor is it content to aim at an avoidance of unpleasure – a goal, as we might call it, of weary resignation; it passes this by without heed and holds fast to the original, passionate striving for a positive fulfilment of happiness. And perhaps it does in fact come nearer to this goal than any other method. I am, of course, speaking of the way of life which makes love the centre of everything, which looks for all satisfaction in loving and being loved. A psychical attitude of this sort comes naturally enough to all of us; one of the forms in which love manifests itself – sexual love – has given us our most intense experience of an overwhelming sensation of pleasure and has thus furnished us with a pattern for our search for happiness. What is more natural than that we should persist in looking for happiness along the path on which we first encountered it? The weak side of this technique of living is easy to see; otherwise no human being would have thought of abandoning this path to happiness for any other. It is that we are never so defenceless against suffering as when we love, never so helplessly unhappy as when we have lost our loved object or its love. But this does not dispose of the technique of living based on the value of love as a means to happiness. There is much more to be said about it. ...

We may go on from here to consider the interesting case in which happiness in life is predominantly sought in the enjoyment of beauty, wherever beauty presents itself to our senses and our judgement – the beauty of human forms and gestures, of natural objects and landscapes and of artistic and even scientific creations. This aesthetic attitude to the goal of life offers little protection against the threat of suffering, but it can compensate for a great deal. The enjoyment of beauty has a peculiar, mildly intoxicating quality of feeling. Beauty has no obvious use; nor is there any clear cultural necessity for it. Yet civilization could not do without it. The science of aesthetics investigates the conditions under which things are felt as beautiful, but it has been unable to give any explanation of the nature and origin of beauty, and, as usually happens, lack of success is concealed beneath a flood of resounding and empty words. Psychoanalysis, unfortunately, has scarcely anything to say about beauty either. All that seems certain is its derivation from the field of sexual feeling. The love of beauty seems a perfect example of an impulse inhibited in its aim. 'Beauty' and 'attraction'[4] are originally attributes of the sexual object. It is worth remarking that the genitals themselves, the sight of which is always exciting, are nevertheless hardly ever judged to be beautiful; the quality of beauty seems, instead, to attach to certain secondary sexual characters.

In spite of the incompleteness [of my enumeration (p. 351)], I will venture on a few remarks as a conclusion to our enquiry. The programme of becoming happy, which the pleasure principle imposes on us [p. 348], cannot be fulfilled; yet we must not – indeed, we cannot – give up our efforts to bring it nearer to fulfilment by some means or other. Very different paths may be taken in that direction, and we may give priority either to the positive aspect of the aim, that of gaining pleasure, or to its negative one, that of avoiding unpleasure. By none of these paths can we attain all that we desire. Happiness, in the reduced sense in which we recognize it as possible, is a problem of the economics of the individual's libido. There is no golden rule which applies to everyone: every man must find out for himself in what particular fashion he can be saved.[5] All kinds of different factors will operate to direct his choice. It is a question of how much real satisfaction he can expect to get from the external world, how far he is led to make himself independent of it, and, finally, how much strength he feels he has for altering the world to suit his wishes. In this, his psychical constitution will play a decisive part, irrespectively of the external circumstances. The man who is predominantly erotic will give first preference to his emotional relationships to other people; the narcissistic man, who inclines to be self-sufficient, will seek his main satisfactions in his internal mental processes; the man

of action will never give up the external world on which he can try out his strength.[6] As regards the second of these types, the nature of his talents and the amount of instinctual sublimation open to him will decide where he shall locate his interests. Any choice that is pushed to an extreme will be penalized by exposing the individual to the dangers which arise if a technique of living that has been chosen as an exclusive one should prove inadequate. Just as a cautious business-man avoids tying up all his capital in one concern, so, perhaps, worldly wisdom will advise us not to look for the whole of our satisfaction from a single aspiration. Its success is never certain, for that depends on the convergence of many factors, perhaps on none more than on the capacity of the psychical constitution to adapt its function to the environment and then to exploit that environment for a yield of pleasure. A person who is born with a specially unfavourable instinctual constitution, and who has not properly undergone the transformation and rearrangement of his libidinal components which is indispensable for later achievements, will find it hard to obtain happiness from his external situation, especially if he is faced with tasks of some difficulty. As a last technique of living, which will at least bring him substitutive satisfactions, he is offered that of a flight into neurotic illness – a flight which he usually accomplishes when he is still young. The man who sees his pursuit of happiness come to nothing in later years can still find consolation in the yield of pleasure of chronic intoxication; or he can embark on the desperate attempt at rebellion seen in a psychosis.[7]

Religion restricts this play of choice and adaptation, since it imposes equally on everyone its own path to the acquisition of happiness and protection from suffering. Its technique consists in depressing

---

4   [The German '*Reiz*' means 'stimulus' as well as 'charm' or 'attraction'. Freud had argued on the same lines in the first edition of his *Three Essays (1905), Standard Ed.*, 7, 209, as well as in a footnote added to that work in 1915, ibid., 16.] [Translator's note.]

5   [The allusion is to a saying attributed to Frederick the Great: 'in my State every man can be saved after his own fashion.' Freud had quoted this a short time before, in *Lay Analysis (1926), Standard Ed.*, 20,236.] [Translator's note.]

6   [Freud further develops his ideas on these different types in his paper on 'Libidinal Types' (1931).][Translator's note.]

7   [*Footnote added 1931*:] I feel impelled to point out one at least of the gaps that have been left in the account given above. No discussion of the possibilities of human happiness should omit to take into consideration the relation between narcissism and object libido. We require to know what being essentially self-dependent signifies for the economics of the libido.

the value of life and distorting the picture of the real world in a delusional manner – which presupposes an intimidation of the intelligence. At this price, by forcibly fixing them in a state of psychical infantilism and by drawing them into a mass-delusion, religion succeeds in sparing many people an individual neurosis. But hardly anything more. There are, as we have said, many paths which may lead to such happiness as is attainable by men, but there is none which does so for certain. Even religion cannot keep its promise. If the believer finally sees himself obliged to speak of God's 'inscrutable decrees', he is admitting that all that is left to him as a last possible consolation and source of pleasure in his suffering is an unconditional submission. And if he is prepared for that, he could probably have spared himself the *détour* he has made.

....

Just as a planet revolves around a central body as well as rotating on its own axis, so the human individual takes part in the course of development of mankind at the same time as he pursues his own path in life. But to our dull eyes the play of forces in the heavens seems fixed in a never-changing order; in the field of organic life we can still see how the forces contend with one another, and how the effects of the conflict are continually changing. So, also, the two urges, the one towards personal happiness and the other towards union with other human beings must struggle with each other in every individual; and so, also, the two processes of individual and of cultural development must stand in hostile opposition to each other and mutually dispute the ground. But this struggle between the individual and society is not a derivative of the contradiction – probably an irreconcilable one – between the primal instincts of Eros and death. It is a dispute within the economics of the libido, comparable to the contest concerning the distribution of libido between ego and objects; and it does admit of an eventual accommodation in the individual, as, it may be hoped, it will also do in the future of civilization, however much that civilization may oppress the life of the individual to-day.

The analogy between the process of civilization and the path of individual development may be extended in an important respect. It can be asserted that the community, too, evolves a super-ego under whose influence cultural development proceeds. It would be a tempting task for anyone who has a knowledge of human civilizations to follow out this analogy in detail. I will confine myself to bringing forward a few striking points. The super-ego of an epoch of civilization has an origin similiar to that of an individual. It is based on the impression left behind by the personalities of great leaders – men of overwhelming force of mind or men in whom one of the human impulses has found its strongest and purest, and therefore often its most one-sided, expression. In many instances the analogy goes still further, in that during their lifetime these figures were – often enough, even if not always – mocked and maltreated by others and even despatched in a cruel fashion. In the same way, indeed, the primal father did not attain divinity until long after he had met his death by violence. The most arresting example of this fateful conjunction is to be seen in the figure of Jesus Christ – if, indeed, that figure is not a part of mythology, which called it into being from an obscure memory of that primal event. Another point of agreement between the cultural and the individual super-ego is that the former, just like the latter, sets up strict ideal demands, disobedience to which is visited with 'fear of conscience'.... Here, indeed, we come across the remarkable circumstance that the mental processes concerned are actually more familiar to us and more accessible to consciousness as they are seen in the group than they can be in the individual man. In him, when tension arises, it is only the aggressiveness of the super-ego which, in the form of reproaches, makes itself noisily heard; its actual demands often remain unconscious in the background. If we bring them to conscious knowledge, we find that they coincide with the precepts of the prevailing cultural super-ego. At this point the two processes, that of the cultural development of the group and that of the cultural development of the individual, are, as it were, always interlocked. For that reason some of the manifestations and properties of the super-ego can be more easily detected in its behavior in the cultural community than in the separate individual.

The cultural super-ego has developed its ideals and set up its demands. Among the latter, those which deal with the relations of human beings to one another are comprised under the heading of ethics. People have at all times set the greatest value on ethics, as though they expected that it in particular would produce especially important results. And it does in fact deal with a subject which can easily be recognized as the sorest spot in every civilization. Ethics is thus to be regarded as a therapeutic attempt – as an endeavor to achieve, by means of a command of the super-ego, something which has so far not been achieved by means of any other cultural activities. As we already know, the problem before us is how to get rid of the greatest hindrance to civilization – namely, the constitutional inclination of human beings to be aggressive towards one another; and for that very reason we are especially interested in what is probably the most recent of the cultural commands of the super-ego, the commandment to love one's neighbour as oneself.... In our research into, and therapy of, a neurosis, we are led to make two reproaches against the super-ego of the individual. In the severity of its commands and prohibitions it troubles itself too little about the happiness of the ego, in that it takes insufficient account of the resistances against obeying them – of the instinctual strength of the id [in the first place], and of the difficulties presented by the real external environment [in the second]. Consequently we are very often obliged, for therapeutic purposes, to oppose the super-ego, and we endeavor to lower its demands. Exactly the same objections can be made against the ethical demands of the cultural super-ego. It, too, does not trouble itself enough about the facts of the mental constitution of human beings. It issues a command and does not ask whether it is possible for people to obey it. On the contrary, it assumes that a man's ego is psychologically capable of anything that is required of it, that his ego has unlimited mastery over his id. This is a mistake; and even in what are known as normal people the id cannot he controlled beyond certain limits. If more is demanded of a man, a revolt will be produced in him or a neurosis, or he will he made unhappy. The commandment, 'Love thy neighbour as thyself', is the strongest defence against human aggressiveness and an excellent example of the unpsychological proceedings of the cultural super-ego. The commandment is impossible to fulfil; such an enormous inflation of love can only lower its value, not get rid of the difficulty. Civilization pays no attention to all this; it merely admonishes us that the harder it is to obey the precept the more meritorious it is to do so. But anyone who follows such a precept in present-day civilization only puts himself at a disadvantage *vis-à-vis* the person who disregards it. What a potent obstacle to civilization aggressiveness must be, if the defence against it can cause as much unhappiness as aggressiveness itself! 'Natural' ethics, as it is called, has nothing to offer here except the narcissistic satisfaction of being able to think oneself better than others. At this point the ethics based on religion introduces its promises of a better after-life. But so long as virtue is not rewarded here on earth, ethics will, I fancy, preach in vain. I too think it quite certain that a real change in the relations of human beings to possessions would be of more help in this direction than any ethical commands; but the recognition of this fact among socialists has been obscured and made useless for practical purposes by a fresh idealistic misconception of human nature....

I believe the line of thought which seeks to trace in the phenomena of cultural development the part played by a super-ego promises still further discoveries. I hasten to come to a close. But there is one question which I can hardly evade. If the development of civilization has such a far-reaching similarity to the development of the individual and if it employs the same methods, may we not be justified in reaching the diagnosis that, under the influence of cultural urges, some civilizations, or some epochs of civilization – possibly the whole of mankind – have become 'neurotic'?[8] An analytic dissection of such neuroses might lead to therapeutic recommendations which could lay claim to great practical interest. I would not say that an attempt of this kind to carry psycho-analysis over to the cultural community was absurd or doomed to be fruitless. But we should have to be very cautious and not forget that, after all, we are only dealing with analogies and that it is dangerous, not only with men but also with concepts, to tear them from the sphere in which they have originated and been evolved. Moreover, the diagnosis of communal neuroses is faced with a special difficulty. In an individual neurosis we take as our starting-point

8   Cf. Some remarks in *The Future of an Illusion* (1927).

the contrast that distinguishes the patient from his environment, which is assumed to be 'normal'. For a group all of whose members are affected by one and the same disorder no such background could exist; it would have to be found elsewhere. And as regards the therapeutic application of our knowledge, what would be the use of the most correct analysis of social neuroses, since no one possesses authority to impose such a therapy upon the group? But in spite of all these difficulties, we may expect that one day someone will venture to embark upon a pathology of cultural communities.

Bibliography

Crews, Frederick. "The Revenge of the Repressed," *New York Review of Books*, Nov. 17 and Dec. 1, 1994 (with subsequent discussion Jan. 12, 1995).

Fine, Reuben. *Freud: A Critical Re-Evaluation of His Theories*. New York: David McKay Company, 1962.

Freud, Sigmund. *The Future of an Illusion*. New York: Liveright Corporation, 1953.

Grünbaum, Adolf. *The Foundations of Psychoanalysis: A Philosophical Critique*. Berkeley: University of California Press, 1984.

Nagel, Thomas. "Freud's Permanent Revolution," *New York Review of Books*, May 12, 1994 (with subsequent discussion Aug. 11, 1994).

O'Neill, John, ed. *Freud and the Passions*. University Park, Pennsylvania: Pennsylvania State University Press, 1996.

Rieff, Philip. *Freud: The Mind of the Moralist*. New York: Anchor Books, 1961.

Wollheim, Richard. *Sigmund Freud*, 2nd ed. Cambridge: Cambridge University Press, 1990.

Wollheim, Richard, ed. *Freud: A Collection of Critical Essays*. New York: Anchor Books, 1974.

VIII

BEHAVIORISM AND NON-SELF THEORIES

CHAPTER THIRTY-TWO — DAVID HUME

It will occasion little surprise that selections from a work called *A Treatise of Human Nature* would appear in the present book, particularly when it is added that the work so named is one of the most original and important contributions to philosophy of all time. David Hume (1711-1776), its author, was a Scot: one of several interesting and creative thinkers who made the Scottish Enlightenment the great intellectual endeavour that it was. Perhaps more than in any other area, the achievements of the Scottish Enlightenment are in laying foundations for social science – in some cases going well beyond those foundations. In addition to Hume, we may mention Lord Monboddo, Adam Ferguson, John Millar, and William Robertson, all of whom made significant contributions to the development of cultural anthropology, and Adam Smith, the giant founding figure of economic theory.

Hume aimed to develop a scientific psychology: a naturalist theory of the workings of the human mind. He was particularly interested in the psychology of cognition, the emotions, and moral attitudes. In all cases he sought to trace the origins of our ideas and thought processes to as economical a base as possible, and to explain present activities as reducible to a small stock of kinds of mental states operating according to principles of sense perception and association. His methodology is chiefly introspectionist and phenomenological: that is, it draws on and appeals to what we encounter (or think we encounter) in our inner mental lives and our observations of our experiences of the outer world and of other people.

Much of Hume's philosophical fame comes from ideas and arguments that appear in the course of setting out his psychological theories, especially views that challenge human rationality and the justifiability of our basic beliefs about the world.

David Hume, *A Treatise of Human Nature*

(Source: David Hume. *A Treatise of Human Nature*. Oxford: Clarendon Press, 1888, 251-263, 645-662.)

There are some philosophers, who imagine we are every moment intimately conscious of what we call our SELF; that we feel its existence and its continuance in existence; and are certain, beyond the evidence of a demonstration, both of its perfect identity and simplicity. The strongest sensation, the most violent passion, say they, instead of distracting us from this view, only fix it the more intensely, and make us consider their influence on *self* either by their pain or pleasure. To attempt a farther proof of this were to weaken its evidence; since no proof can be deriv'd from any fact, of which we are so intimately conscious; nor is there any thing, of which we can be certain, if we doubt of this.

Unluckily all these positive assertions are contrary to that very experience, which is pleaded for them, nor have we any idea of *self*, after the manner it is here explain'd. For from what impression cou'd this idea be deriv'd? This question 'tis impossible to answer without a manifest contradiction and absurdity; and yet 'tis a question, which must necessarily be answer'd, if we wou'd have the idea of self pass for clear and intelligible. It must be some one impression, that gives rise to every real idea. But self or person is not any one impression, but that to which our several impressions and ideas are suppos'd to have a reference. If any impression gives rise to the idea of self, that impression must continue invariably the same, thro' the whole course of our lives; since self is suppos'd to exist after that manner. But there is no impression constant and invariable. Pain and pleasure, grief and joy, passions and sensations succeed each other, and never all exist at the same time. It cannot, therefore, be from any of these impressions, or from any other, that the idea of self is deriv'd; and consequently there is no such idea.

But farther, what must become of all our particular perceptions upon this hypothesis ? All these are different, and distinguishable, and separable from each other, and may be separately consider'd, and may exist separately, and have no need of any thing to support their existence. After what manner, therefore, do they belong to self; and how are they connected with it? For my part, when I enter most intimately into what I call *myself*, I always stumble on some particular perception or other, of heat or cold, light or shade, love or hatred, pain or pleasure. I never can catch *myself* at any time without a perception, and never can observe any thing but the perception. When my perceptions are remov'd for any time, as by sound sleep; so long am I insensible of *myself*; and may truly be said not to exist. And were all my perceptions remov'd by death, and cou'd I neither think, nor feel, nor see, nor love, nor hate after the dissolution of my body, I shou'd be entirely annihilated, nor do I conceive what is farther requisite to make me a perfect non-entity. If any one upon serious and unprejudic'd reflexion, thinks he has a different notion of *himself*, I must confess I can reason no longer with him. All I can allow him is, that he may be in the right as well as I, and that we are essentially different in this particular. He may, perhaps, perceive something simple and continu'd, which he calls *himself*; tho' I am certain there is no such principle in me.

But setting aside some metaphysicians of this kind, I may venture to affirm of the rest of mankind, that they are nothing but a bundle or collection of different perceptions, which succeed each other with an inconceivable rapidity, and are in a perpetual flux and movement. Our eyes cannot turn in their sockets without varying our perceptions. Our thought is still more variable than our sight; and all our other senses and faculties contribute to this change, nor is there any single power

of the soul, which remains unalterably the same, perhaps for one moment. The mind is a kind of theatre, where several perceptions successively make their appearance; pass, re-pass, glide away, and mingle in an infinite variety of postures and situations. There is properly no *simplicity* in it at one time, nor *identity* in different; whatever natural propension we may have to imagine that simplicity and identity. The comparison of the theatre must not mislead us. They are the successive perceptions only, that constitute the mind; nor have we the most distant notion of the place, where these scenes are represented, or of the materials, of which it is compos'd.

What then gives us so great a propension to ascribe an identity to these successive perceptions, and to suppose ourselves possest of an invariable and uninterrupted existence thro' the whole course of our lives? In order to answer this question, we must distinguish betwixt personal identity, as it regards our thought or imagination, and as it regards our passions or the concern we take in ourselves. The first is our present subject; and to explain it perfectly we must take the matter pretty deep, and account for that identity, which we attribute to plants and animals; there being a great analogy betwixt it, and the identity of a self or person.

We have a distinct idea of an object, that remains invariable and uninterrupted thro' a suppos'd variation of time; and this idea we call that of *identity* or *sameness*. We have also a distinct idea of several different objects existing in succession, and connected together by a close relation; and this to an accurate view affords as perfect a notion of *diversity,* as if there was no manner of relation among the objects. But tho' these two ideas of identity, and a succession of related objects be in themselves perfectly distinct, and even contrary, yet 'tis certain, that in our common way of thinking they are generally confounded with each other. That action of the imagination, by which we consider the uninterrupted and invariable object, and that by which we reflect on the succession of related objects, are almost the same to the feeling, nor is there much more effort of thought requir'd in the latter case than in the former. The relation facilitates the transition of the mind from one object to another, and renders its passage as smooth as if it contemplated one continu'd object. This resemblance is the cause of the confusion and mistake, and makes us substitute the notion of identity, instead of that of related objects. However at one instant we may consider the related succession as variable or interrupted, we are sure the next to ascribe to it a perfect identity, and regard it as invariable and uninterrupted. Our propensity to this mistake is so great from the resemblance above-mention'd, that we fall into it before we are aware; and tho' we incessantly correct ourselves by reflexion, and return to a more accurate method of thinking, yet we cannot long sustain our philosophy, or take off this biass from the imagination. Our last resource is to yield to it, and boldly assert that these different related objects are in effect the same, however interrupted and variable. In order to justify to ourselves this absurdity, we often feign some new and unintelligible principle, that connects the objects together, and prevents their interruption or variation. Thus we feign the continu'd existence of the perceptions of our senses, to remove the interruption; and run into the notion of a *soul,* and *self,* and *substance,* to disguise the variation. But we may rather observe, that where we do not give rise to such a fiction, our propension to confound identity with relation is so great, that we are apt to imagine[1] something unknown and mysterious, connecting the parts, beside their relation; and this I take to be the case with regard to the identity we ascribe to plants and vegetables. And even when this does not take place, we still feel a propensity to confound these ideas, tho' we are not able fully to satisfy ourselves in that particular, nor find any thing invariable and uninterrupted to justify our notion of identity.

Thus the controversy concerning identity is not merely a despute of words. For when we attribute identity, in an improper sense, to variable or interrupted objects, our mistake is not confin'd to the expression, but is commonly attended with a fiction, either of something invariable and uninterrupted, or of something mysterious and inexplicable, or at least with a propensity to such fictions. What will suffice to prove this hypothesis to the satisfaction of every fair enquirer, is to shew from daily experience and observation, that the objects, which are variable or interrupted, and yet are suppos'd to continue the same, are such only as consist of a succession of parts, connected together by resemblance, contiguity, or causation. For as such a succession answers evidently to our notion of diversity, it can only be by mistake we ascribe to it an identity; and as the relation of parts, which leads us into this mistake, is really nothing but a quality, which produces an association of ideas, and an easy transition of the imagination from one to another, it can only be from the resemblance, which this act of the mind bears to that, by which we contemplate one continu'd object, that the error arises. our chief business, then, must be to prove, that all objects, to which we ascribe identity, without observing their invariableness and uninterruptedness, are such as consist of a succession of related objects.

In order to this, suppose any mass of matter, of which the parts are contiguous and connected, to be plac'd before us; 'tis plain we must attribute a perfect identity to this mass, provided all the parts continue uninterruptedly and invariably the same, whatever motion or change of place we may observe either in the whole or in any of the parts. But supposing some very *small* or *inconsiderable* part to be added to the mass, or subtracted from it; tho' this absolutely destroys the identity of the whole, strictly speaking; yet as we seldom think so accurately, we scruple not to pronounce a mass of matter the same, where we find so trivial an alteration. The passage of the thought from the object before the change to the object after it, is so smooth and easy, that we scarce perceive the transition, and are apt to imagine, that 'tis nothing but a continu'd survey of the same object.

There is a very remarkable circumstance, that attends this experiment; which is, that tho' the change of any considerable part in a mass of matter destroys the identity of the whole, yet we must measure the greatness of the part, not absolutely, but by its *proportion* to the whole. The addition or diminution of a mountain wou'd not be sufficient to produce a diversity in a planet; tho' the change of a very few inches wou'd be able to destroy the

---

1   If the reader is desirous to see how a great genius may be influenc'd by these seemingly trivial principles of the imagination, as well as the mere vulgar, let him read my Lord *Shaftsbury's* reasonings concerning the uniting principle of the universe, and the identity of plants and animals. See his *Moralists: or, Philosophical rhapsody.*

identity of some bodies. 'Twill be impossible to account for this, but by reflecting that objects operate upon the mind, and break or interrupt the continuity of its actions not according to their real greatness, but according to their proportion to each other: And therefore, since this interruption makes an object cease to appear the same, it must be the uninterrupted progress of the thought, which constitutes the imperfect identity.

This may be confirm'd by another phaenomenon. A change in any considerable part of a body destroys its identity; but 'tis remarkable, that where the change is produc'd *gradually* and *insensibly* we are less apt to ascribe to it the same effect. The reason can plainly be no other, than that the mind, in following the successive changes of the body, feels an easy passage from the surveying its condition in one moment to the viewing of it in another, and at no particular time perceives any interruption in its actions. From which continu'd perception, it ascribes a continu'd existence and identity to the object.

But whatever precaution we may use in introducing the changes gradually, and making them proportionable to the whole, 'tis certain, that where the changes are at last observ'd to become considerable, we make a scruple of ascribing identity to such different objects. There is, however, another artifice, by which we may induce the imagination to advance a step farther; and that is, by producing a reference of the parts to each other, and a combination to some *common end* or purpose. A ship, of which a considerable part has been chang'd by frequent reparations, is still consider'd as the same; nor does the difference of the materials hinder us from ascribing an identity to it. The common end, in which the parts conspire, is the same under all their variations, and affords an easy transition of the imagination from one situation of the body to another.

But this is still more remarkable, when we add a *sympathy* of parts to their *common end,* and suppose that they bear to each other, the reciprocal relation of cause and effect in all their actions and operations. This is the case with all animals and vegetables; where not only the several parts have a reference to some general purpose, but also a mutual dependance on, and connexion with each other. The effect of so strong a relation is, that tho' every one must allow, that in a very few years both veg-

etables and animals endure a *total* change, yet we still attribute identity to them, while their form, size, and substance are entirely alter'd. An oak, that grows from a small plant to a large tree, is still the same oak; tho' there be not one particle of matter, or figure of its parts the same. An infant becomes a man, and is sometimes fat, sometimes lean, without any change in his identity.

We may also consider the two following phaenomena, which are remarkable in their kind. The first is, that tho' we commonly be able to distinguish pretty exactly betwixt numerical and specific identity, yet it sometimes happens, that we confound them, and in our thinking and reasoning employ the one for the other. Thus a man, who hears a noise, that is frequently interrupted and renew'd, says, it is still the same noise; tho' 'tis evident the sounds have only a specific identity or resemblance, and there is nothing numerically the same, but the cause, which produc'd them. In like manner it may be said without breach of the propriety of language, that such a church, which was formerly of brick, fell to ruin, and that the parish rebuilt the same church of free-stone, and according to modern architecture. Here neither the form nor materials are the same, nor is there any thing common to the two objects, but their relation to the inhabitants of the parish; and yet this alone is sufficient to make us denominate them the same. But we must observe, that in these cases the first object is in a manner annihilated before the second comes into existence; by which means, we are never presented in any one point of time with the idea of difference and multiplicity; and for that reason are less scrupulous in calling them the same.

Secondly, We may remark, that tho' in a succession of related objects, it be in a manner requisite, that the change of parts be not sudden nor entire, in order to preserve the identity, yet where the objects are in their nature changeable and inconstant, we admit of a more sudden transition, than wou'd otherwise be consistent with that relation. Thus as the nature of a river consists in the motion and change of parts; tho' in less than four and twenty hours these be totally alter'd; this hinders not the river from continuing the same during several ages. What is natural and essential to any thing is, in a manner, expected; and what is expected makes less impression, and appears of less moment, than what is unusual and extraordinary.

A considerable change of the former kind seems really less to the imagination, than the most trivial alteration of the latter; and by breaking less the continuity of the thought, has less influence in destroying the identity.

We now proceed to explain the nature of *personal identity,* which has become so great a question in philosophy, especially of late years in *England,* where all the abstruser sciences are study'd with a peculiar ardour and application. And here 'tis evident, the same method of reasoning must be continu'd, which has so successfully explain'd the identity of plants, and animals, and ships, and houses, and of all the compounded and changeable productions either of art or nature. The identity, which we ascribe to the mind of man, is only a fictitious one, and of a like kind with that which we ascribe to vegetables and animal bodies. It cannot, therefore, have a different origin, but must proceed from a like operation of the imagination upon like objects.

But lest this argument shou'd not convince the reader; tho' in my opinion perfectly decisive; let him weigh the following reasoning, which is still closer and more immediate. 'Tis evident, that the identity, which we attribute to the human mind, however perfect we may imagine it to be, is not able to run the several different perceptions into one, and make them lose their characters of distinction and difference, which are essential to them. 'Tis still true, that every distinct perception, which enters into the composition of the mind, is a distinct existence, and is different, and distinguishable, and separable from every other perception, either contemporary or successive. But, as, notwithstanding this distinction and separability, we suppose the whole train of perceptions to be united by identity, a question naturally arises concerning this relation of identity; whether it be something that really binds our several perceptions together, or only associates their ideas in the imagination. That is, in other words, whether in pronouncing concerning the identity of a person, we observe some real bond among his perceptions, or only feel one among the ideas we form of them. This question we might easily decide, if we wou'd recollect what has been already prov'd at large, that the understanding never observes any real connexion among objects, and that even the union of cause and effect, when strictly examin'd, resolves itself into a customary association of ideas. For from thence it evidently follows, that identity is nothing really belonging to these different perceptions, and uniting them together; but is merely a quality, which we attribute to them, because of the union of their ideas in the imagination, when we reflect upon them. Now the only qualities, which can give ideas an union in the imagination, are these three relations above-mention'd. These are the uniting principles in the ideal world, and without them every distinct object is separable by the mind, and may be separately consider'd, and appears not to have any more connexion with any other object, than if disjoin'd by the greatest difference and remoteness. 'Tis, therefore, on some of these three relations of resemblance, contiguity and causation, that identity depends; and as the very essence of these relations consists in their producing an easy transition of ideas; it follows, that our notions of personal identity, proceed entirely from the smooth and uninterrupted progress of the thought along a train of connected ideas, according to the principles above explain'd.

The only question, therefore, which remains, is, by what relations this uninterrupted progress of our thought is produc'd, when we consider the successive existence of a mind or thinking person. And here 'tis evident we must confine ourselves to resemblance and causation, and must drop contiguity, which has little or no influence in the present case.

To begin with *resemblance;* suppose we cou'd see clearly into the breast of another, and observe that succession of perceptions, which constitutes his mind or thinking principle, and suppose that he always preserves the memory of a considerable part of past perceptions; 'tis evident that nothing cou'd more contribute to the bestowing a relation on this succession amidst all its variations. For what is the memory but a faculty, by which we raise up the images of past perceptions? And as an image necessarily resembles its object, must not the frequent placing of these resembling perceptions in the chain of thought, convey the imagination more easily from one link to another, and make the whole seem like the continuance of one object? In this particular, then, the memory not only discovers the identity, but also contributes to its production, by producing the relation of resemblance among the perceptions. The case is the same whether we consider ourselves or others.

As to *causation;* we may observe, that the true idea of the human mind, is to consider it as a system of different perceptions or different existences, which are link'd together by the relation of cause and effect, and mutually produce, destroy, influence, and modify each other. Our impressions give rise to their correspondent ideas; and these ideas in their turn produce other impressions. One thought chaces another, and draws after it a third, by which it is expell'd in its turn. In this respect, I cannot compare the soul more properly to any thing than to a republic or commonwealth, in which the several members are united by the reciprocal ties of government and subordination, and give rise to other persons, who propagate the same republic in the incessant changes of its parts. And as the same individual republic may not only change its members, but also its laws and constitutions; in like manner the same person may vary his character and disposition, as well as his impressions and ideas, without losing his identity. Whatever changes he endures, his several parts are still connected by the relation of causation. And in this view our identity with regard to the passions serves to corroborate that with regard to the imagination, by the making our distant perceptions influence each other, and by giving us a present concern for our past or future pains or pleasures.

As memory alone acquaints us with the continuance and extent of this succession of perceptions, 'tis to be consider'd, upon that account chiefly, as the source of personal identity. Had we no memory, we never shou'd have any notion of causation, nor consequently of that chain of causes and effects, which constitute our self or person. But having once acquir'd this notion of causation from the memory, we can extend the same chain of causes, and consequently the identity of our persons beyond our memory, and can comprehend times, and circumstances, and actions, which we have entirely forgot, but suppose in general to have existed. For how few of our past actions are there, of which we have any memory ? Who can tell me, for instance, what were his thoughts and actions on the first of *January* 1715, the 11th of *March* 1719, and the 3d of *August* 1733? Or will he affirm, because he has entirely forgot the incidents of these days, that the present self is not the same person with the self of that time; and by that means overturn all the most establish'd notions of personal

identity ? In this view, therefore, memory does not so much *produce* as *discover* personal identity, by shewing us the relation of cause and effect among our different perceptions. 'Twill be incumbent on those, who affirm that memory produces entirely our personal identity, to give a reason why we can thus extend our identity beyond our memory.

The whole of this doctrine leads us to a conclusion, which is of great importance in the present affair, *viz.* that all the nice and subtle questions concerning personal identity can never possibly be decided, and are to be regarded rather as grammatical than as philosophical difficulties. Identity depends on the relations of ideas; and these relations produce identity, by means of that easy transition they occasion. But as the relations, and the easiness of the transition may diminish by insensible degrees, we have no just standard, by which we can decide any dispute concerning the time, when they acquire or lose a title to the name of identity. All the disputes concerning the identity of connected objects are merely verbal, except so far as the relation of parts gives rise to some fiction or imaginary principle of union, as we have already observ'd.

What I have said concerning the first origin and uncertainty of our notion of identity, as apply'd to the human mind, may be extended with little or no variation to that of *simplicity.* An object, whose different co-existent parts are bound together by a close relation, operates upon the imagination after much the same manner as one perfectly simple and indivisible, and requires not a much greater stretch of thought in order to its conception. From this similarity of operation we attribute a simplicity to it, and feign a principle of union as the support of this simplicity, and the center of all the different parts and qualities of the object.

...

Most of the philosophers of antiquity, who treated of human nature, have shewn more of a delicacy of sentiment, a just sense of morals, or a greatness of soul, than a depth of reasoning and reflection. They content themselves with representing the common sense of mankind in the strongest lights, and with the best turn of thought and expression, without following out steadily a chain of propositions, or forming the several truths into a regular science. But 'tis at least worth while to try if the science of *man* will not admit of the same accuracy which several parts of natural philosophy are found susceptible of. There seems to be all the reason in the world to imagine that it may be carried to the greatest degree of exactness. If, in examining several phaenomena, we find that they resolve themselves into one common principle, and can trace this principle into another, we shall at last arrive at those few simple principles, on which all the rest depend. And tho' we can never arrive at the ultimate principles, 'tis satisfaction to go as far as our faculties will allow us.

....

Our author[1] begins with some definitions. He calls a *perception* whatever can be present to the mind, whether we employ our senses, or are actuated with passion, or exercise our thought and reflection. He divides our perceptions into two kinds, *viz. impressions* and *ideas.* When we feel a passion or emotion of any kind, or have the images of external objects conveyed by our senses; the perception of the mind is what he calls an *impression*, which is a word that he employs in a new sense. When we reflect on a passion or an object which is not present, this perception is an *idea. Impressions*, therefore, are our lively and strong perceptions; *ideas* are the fainter and weaker. This distinction is evident; as evident as that betwixt feeling and thinking.

The first proposition he advances, is, that all our ideas, or weak perceptions, are derived from our impressions, or strong perceptions, and that we can never think of any thing which we have not seen without us, or felt in our own minds This proposition seems to be equivalent to that which *Mr. Locke* has taken such pains to establish, viz. *that no ideas are innate.* Only it may be observed, as an inaccuracy of that famous philosopher, that he comprehends all our perceptions under the term of idea, in which sense it is false, that we have no innate ideas. For it is evident our stronger perceptions or impressions are innate, and that natural affection, love of virtue, resentment, and all the other passions, arise immediately from nature. I am perswaded, whoever would take the question in this light, would be

easily able to reconcile all parties. *Father Malebranche* would find himself at a loss to point out any thought of the mind, which did not represent something antecedently felt by it, either internally, or by means of the external senses, and must allow, that however we may compound, and mix, and augment, and diminish our ideas, they are all derived from these sources. *Mr. Locke,* on the other hand, would readily acknowledge, that all our passions are a kind of natural instincts, derived from nothing but the original constitution of the human mind.

Our author thinks, "that no discovery could have been made more happily for deciding all controversies concerning ideas than this, that impressions always take the precedency of them, and that every idea with which the imagination is furnished, first makes its appearance in a correspondent impression. These latter perceptions are all so clear and evident, that they admit of no controversy; tho' many of our ideas are so obscure, that 'tis almost impossible even for the mind, which forms them, to tell exactly their nature and composition." Accordingly, wherever any idea is ambiguous, he has always recourse to the impression, which must render it clear and precise. And when he suspects that any philosophical term has no idea annexed to it (as is too common) he always asks *from what impression that pretended idea is derived* . And if no impression can be produced, he concludes that the term is altogether insignificant. 'Tis after this manner he examines our idea of *substance* and *essence;* and it were to be wished, that this rigorous method were more practised in all philosophical debates.

'Tis evident, that all reasonings concerning *matter of fact* are founded on the relation of cause and effect, and that we can never infer the existence of one object from another, unless they be connected together, either mediately or immediately. In order therefore to understand these reasonings, we must be perfectly acquainted with the idea of a cause; and in order to that, must look about us to find something that is the cause of another.

Here is a billiard-ball lying on the table, and another ball moving towards it with rapidity. They strike; and the ball, which was formerly at rest, now

---

1   Hume is referring to himself. (The selection here is from the 'Abstract' of the *Treatise of Human Nature* that Hume published anonymously, as though written by a reader, in 1740.)

acquires a motion. This is as perfect an instance of the relation of cause and effect as any which we know, either by sensation or reflection. Let us therefore examine it. 'Tis evident, that the two balls touched one another before the motion was communicated, and that there was no interval betwixt the shock and the motion. *Contiguity* in time and place is therefore a requisite circumstance to the operation of all causes. 'Tis evident likewise, that the motion, which was the cause, is prior to the motion, which was the effect. *Priority* in time, is therefore another requisite circumstance in every cause. But this is not all. Let us try any other balls of the same kind in a like situation, and we shall always find, that the impulse of the one produces motion in the other. Here therefore is a *third* circumstance, viz. that of a *constant conjunction* betwixt the cause and effect. Every object like the cause, produces always some object like the effect. Beyond these three circumstances contiguity, priority, and constant conjunction, I can discover nothing in this cause. The first ball is in motion; touches the second; immediately the second is in motion: and when I try the experiment with the same or like balls, in the same or like circumstances, I find, that upon the motion and touch of the one ball, motion always follows in the other. In whatever shape I turn this matter, and however I examine it, I can find nothing farther.

This is the case when both the cause and effect are present to the senses. Let us now see upon what our inference is founded, when we conclude from the one that the other has existed or will exist. Suppose I see a ball moving in a straight line towards another, I immediately conclude, that they will shock, and that the second will be in motion. This is the inference from cause to effect; and of this nature are all our reasonings in the conduct of life: on this is founded all our belief in history: and from hence is derived all philosophy, excepting only geometry and arithmetic. If we can explain the inference from the shock of two balls, we shall be able to account for this operation of the mind in all instances.

Were a man, such as *Adam,* created in the full vigour of understanding, without experience, he would never be able to infer motion in the second ball from the motion and impulse of the first. It is not any thing that reason sees in the cause, which make us *infer* the effect. Such an inference, were it possible, would amount to a demonstration, as being founded merely on the comparison of ideas. But no inference from cause to effect amounts to a demonstration. Of which there is this evident proof. The mind can always *conceive* any effect to follow from any cause, and indeed any event to follow upon another: whatever we *conceive* is possible, at least in a metaphysical sense: but wherever a demonstration takes place, the contrary is impossible, and implies a contradiction. There is no demonstration, therefore, for any conjunction of cause and effect. And this is a principle, which is generally allowed by philosophers.

It would have been necessary, therefore, for *Adam* (if he was not inspired) to have had *experience* of the effect which followed upon the impulse of these two balls. He must have seen, in several instances, that when the one ball struck upon the other, the second always acquired motion If he had seen a sufficient number of instances of this kind, whenever he saw the one ball moving towards the other, he would always conclude without hesitation, that the second would acquire motion. His understanding would anticipate his sight, and form a conclusion suitable to his past experience.

It follows, then, that all reasonings concerning cause and effect, are founded on experience, and that all reasonings from experience are founded on the supposition, that the course of nature will continue uniformly the same. We conclude, that like causes, in like circumstances, will always produce like effects. It may now be worth while to consider, what determines us to form a conclusion of such infinite consequence.

'Tis evident, that *Adam* with all his science, would never have been able to *demonstrate,* that the course of nature must continue uniformly the same, and that the future must be conformable to the past. What is possible can never be demonstrated to be false; and 'tis possible the course of nature may change, since we can conceive such a change. Nay, I will go farther, and assert, that he could not so much as prove by any *probable* arguments, that the future must be conformable to the past. All probable arguments are built on the supposition, that there is this conformity betwixt the future and the past, and therefore can never prove it. This conformity is a *matter of fact,* and if it must be proved, will admit of no proof but from experience. But our experience in the past can be a proof of nothing for the future, but upon a supposition, that there is a resemblance betwixt them. This therefore is a point, which can admit of no proof at all, and which we take for granted without any proof.

We are determined by CUSTOM alone to suppose the future conformable to the past. When I see a billiard-ball moving towards another, my mind is immediately carry'd by habit to the usual effect, and anticipates my sight by conceiving the second ball in motion. There is nothing in these objects, abstractly considered, and independent of experience, which leads me to form any such conclusion: and even after I have had experience of many repeated effects of this kind, there is no argument, which determines me to suppose, that the effect will be conformable to past experience. The powers, by which bodies operate, are entirely unknown. We perceive only their sensible qualities: and what *reason* have we to think, that the same powers will always be conjoined with the same sensible qualities?

'Tis not, therefore, reason, which is the guide of life, but custom. That alone determines the mind, in all instances, to suppose the future conformable to the past. However easy this step may seem, reason would never, to all eternity, be able to make it.

This is a very curious discovery, but leads us to others, that are still more curious. *When I see a billiard-ball moving towards another, my mind is immediately carried by habit to the usual effect, and anticipates my sight by conceiving the second ball in motion.* But is this all? Do I nothing but CONCEIVE the motion of the second ball? No surely. I also BELIEVE that it will move. What then is this *belief*? And how does it differ from the simple conception of any thing? Here is a new question unthought of by philosophers.

When a demonstration convinces me of any proposition, it not only makes me conceive the proposition, but also makes me sensible, that 'tis impossible to conceive any thing contrary. What is demonstratively false implies a contradiction; and what implies a contradiction cannot be conceived. But with regard to any matter of fact, however strong the proof may be from experience, I can always conceive the contrary, tho' I cannot always believe it. The belief, therefore, makes some difference betwixt the conception to which we assent, and that to which we do not assent.

To account for this, there are only two hypotheses. It may be said, that belief joins some new idea to those which we may conceive without assenting to them. But this hypothesis is false. For *first*, no such idea can be produced. When we simply conceive an object, we conceive it in all its parts. We conceive it as it might exist, tho' we do not believe it to exist. Our belief of it would discover no new qualities. We may paint out the entire object in imagination without believing it. We may set it, in a manner, before our eyes, with every circumstance of time and place. 'Tis the very object conceived as it might exist; and when we believe it, we can do no more.

Secondly, The mind has a faculty of joining all ideas together, which involve not a contradiction; and therefore if belief consisted in some idea, which we add to the simple conception, it would be in a man's power, by adding this idea to it, to believe any thing, which he can conceive.

Since therefore belief implies a conception, and yet is something more; and since it adds no new idea to the conception; it follows, that it is a different MANNER of conceiving an object; *something* that is distinguishable to the feeling, and depends not upon our will, as all our ideas do. My mind runs by habit from the visible object of one ball moving towards another, to the usual effect of motion in the second ball. It not only conceives that motion, but *feels* something different in the conception of it from a mere reverie of the imagination. The presence of this visible object, and the constant conjunction of that particular effect, render the idea different to the *feeling* from those loose ideas, which come into the mind without any introduction. This conclusion seems a little surprising; but we are led into it by a chain of propositions, which admit of no doubt. To ease the reader's memory I shall briefly resume them. No matter of fact can be proved but from its cause or its effect. Nothing can be known to be the cause of another but by experience. We can give no reason for extending to the future our experience in the past; but are entirely determined by custom, when we conceive an effect to follow from its usual cause. But we also believe an effect to follow, as well as conceive it. This belief joins no new idea to the conception. It only varies the manner of conceiving, and makes a difference to the feeling or sentiment. Belief, therefore, in all matters of fact arises only from custom, and is an idea conceived in a peculiar *manner*.

Our author proceeds to explain the manner or feeling, which renders belief different from a loose conception. He seems sensible, that 'tis impossible by words to describe this feeling, which every one must be conscious of in his own breast. He calls it sometimes a *stronger* conception, sometimes a more *lively,* a more *vivid,* a *firmer,* or a more *intense* conception. And indeed, whatever name we may give to this feeling, which constitutes belief, our author thinks it evident, that it has a more forcible effect on the mind than fiction and mere conception. This he proves by its influence on the passions and on the imagination; which are only moved by truth or what is taken for such. Poetry, with all its art, can never cause a passion, like one in real life. It fails in the original conception of its objects, which never feel in the same manner as those which command our belief and opinion.

Our author presuming, that he had sufficiently proved, that the ideas we assent to are different to the feeling from the other ideas, and that this feeling is more firm and lively than our common conception, endeavours in the next place to explain the cause of this lively feeling by an analogy with other acts of the mind. His reasoning seems to be curious; but could scarce be rendered intelligible, or at least probable to the reader, without a long detail, which would exceed the compass I have prescribed to myself.

I have likewise omitted many arguments, which he adduces to prove that belief consists merely in a peculiar feeling or sentiment. I shall only mention one. Our past experience is not always uniform. Sometimes one effect follows from a cause, sometimes another: In which case we always believe, that that will exist which is most common. I see a billiard-ball moving towards another. I cannot distinguish whether it moves upon its axis, or was struck so as to skim along the table. In the first case, I know it will not stop after the shock. In the second it may stop. The first is most common, and therefore I lay my account with that effect. But I also conceive the other effect, and conceive it as possible, and as connected with the cause. Were not the one conception different in the feeling or sentiment from the other, there would be no difference betwixt them.

We have confin'd ourselves in this whole reasoning to the relation of cause and effect, as discovered in the motions and operations of matter. But the same reasoning extends to the operations of the mind. Whether we consider the influence of the will in moving our body, or in governing our

thought, it may safely be affirmed, that we could never foretel the effect, merely from the consideration of the cause, without experience. And even after we have experience of these effects, 'tis custom alone, not reason, which determines us to make it the standard of our future judgments. When the cause is presented, the mind, from habit, immediately passes to the conception and belief of the usual effect. This belief is something different from the conception. It does not, however, join any new idea to it. It only makes it be felt differently, and renders it stronger and more lively.

Having dispatcht this material point concerning the nature of the inference from cause and effect, our author returns upon his footsteps, and examines anew the idea of that relation. In the considering of motion communicated from one ball to another, we could find nothing but contiguity, priority in the cause, and constant conjunction. But, beside these circumstances, 'tis commonly suppos'd, that there is a necessary connexion betwixt the cause and effect, and that the cause possesses something, which we call *a power, or force,* or *energy.* The question is, what idea is annex'd to these terms? If all our ideas or thoughts be derived from our impressions, this power must either discover itself to our senses, or to our internal feeling. But so little does any *power* discover itself to the senses in the operations of matter, that the *Cartesians* have made no scruple to assert, that matter is utterly deprived of energy, and that all its operations are perform'd merely by the energy of the supreme Being. But the question still recurs, *What idea have we of energy or power even in the supreme Being?* All our idea of a Deity (according to those who deny innate ideas) is nothing but a composition of those ideas, which we acquire from reflecting on the operations of our own minds. Now our own minds afford us no more notion of energy than matter does. When we consider our will or volition *a priori,* abstracting from experience, we are never able to infer any effect from it. And when we take the assistance of experience, it only shows us objects contiguous, successive, and constantly conjoined. Upon the whole, then, either we have no idea at all of force and energy, and these words are altogether insignificant, or they can mean nothing but that determination of the thought, acquir'd by habit, to pass from the cause to its usual effect. But who-ever would thoroughly understand this must consult the author himself. 'Tis sufficient, if I can make the learned world apprehend, that there is some difficulty in the case, and that who-ever solves the difficulty must say some thing very new and extraordinary; as new as the difficulty itself.

By all that has been said the reader will easily perceive, that the philosophy contain'd in this book is very sceptical, and tends to give us a notion of the imperfections and narrow limits of human understanding. Almost all reasoning is there reduced to experience; and the belief, which attends experience, is explained to be nothing but a peculiar sentiment, or lively conception produced by habit. Nor is this all, when we believe any thing of *external* existence, or suppose an object to exist a moment after it is no longer perceived, this belief is nothing but a sentiment of the same kind. Our author insists upon several other sceptical topics; and upon the whole concludes, that we assent to our faculties, and employ our reason only because we cannot help it. Philosophy wou'd render us entirely *Pyrrhonian,* were not nature too strong for it.

I shall conclude the logics of this author with an account of two opinions, which seem to be peculiar to himself, as indeed are most of his opinions. He asserts, that the soul, as far as we can conceive it, is nothing but a system or train of different perceptions, those of heat and cold, love and anger, thoughts and sensations; all united together, but without any perfect simplicity or identity. *Des Cartes* maintained that thought was the essence of the mind, not this thought or that thought, but thought in general. This seems to be absolutely unintelligible, since every thing, that exists, is particular: And therefore it must be our several particular perceptions, that compose the mind. I say, *compose* the mind, not *belong* to it. The mind is not a substance, in which the perceptions inhere. That notion is as unintelligible as the *Cartesian* that thought or perception in general is the essence of the mind. We have no idea of substance of any kind, since we have no idea but what is derived from some impression, and we have no impression of any substance either material or spiritual. We know nothing but particular qualities and perceptions. As our idea of any body, a peach, for instance, is only that of a particular taste, colour, figure, size, consistence, &c. So our idea of any mind is only that of particular perceptions, without the notion of any thing we call substance, either simple or compound.

The second principle, which I proposed to take notice of, is with regard to Geometry. Having denied the infinite divisibility of extension, our author finds himself obliged to refute those mathematical arguments, which have been adduced for it; and these indeed are the only ones of any weight. This he does by denying Geometry to be a science exact enough to admit of conclusions so subtle as those which regard infinite divisibility. His arguments may be thus explained. All Geometry is founded on the notions of equality and inequality, and therefore according as we have or have not an exact standard of those relations, the science itself will or will not admit of great exactness. Now there is an exact standard of equality, if we suppose that quantity is composed of indivisible points. Two lines are equal when the numbers of the points, that compose them, are equal, and when there is a point in one corresponding to a point in the other. But tho' this standard be exact, 'tis useless; since we can never compute the number of points in any line. It is besides founded on the supposition of finite divisibility, and therefore can never afford any conclusion against it. If we reject this standard of equality we have none that has any pretensions to exactness. I find two that are commonly made use of. Two lines above a yard, for instance, are said to be equal, when they contain any inferior quantity, as an inch, an equal number of times. But this runs in a circle. For the quantity we call an inch in the one is supposed to be *equal* to what we call an inch in the other: And the question still is, by what standard we proceed when we judge them to be equal; or, in other words, what we mean when we say they are equal. If we take still inferior quantities, we go on *in infinitum.* This therefore is no standard of equality. The greatest part of philosophers, when ask'd what they mean by equality, say, that the word admits of no definition, and that it is sufficient to place before us two equal bodies, such as two diameters of a circle, to make us understand that term. Now this is taking the *general appearance* of the objects for the standard of that proportion, and renders our imagination and senses the ultimate judges of it. But such a standard admits of no exactness, and can never afford any conclusion contrary to the imagination and senses. Whether this reasoning be just or not, must be left to the learned world to judge. 'Twere certainly to be wish'd, that some expedient were fallen upon to reconcile philosophy and common sense, which with regard to the question of infinite divisibility have wag'd most cruel wars with each other.

We must now proceed to give some account of the second volume of this work, which treats of the PASSIONS. 'Tis of more easy comprehension than the first; but contains opinions, that are altogether as new and extraordinary. The author begins with *pride* and *humility*. He observes, that the objects which excite these passions, are very numerous, and seemingly very different from each other. Pride or self-esteem may arise from the qualities of the mind; wit, good-sense, learning, courage, integrity: from those of the body; beauty, strength, agility, good mein, address in dancing, riding, fencing: from external advantages; country, family, children, relations, riches, houses, gardens, horses, dogs, cloaths. He afterwards proceeds to find out that common circumstance, in which all these objects agree, and which causes them to operate on the passions. His theory likewise extends to love and hatred, and other affections. As these questions, tho' curious, could not be rendered intelligible without a long discourse, we shall here omit them.

It may perhaps be more acceptable to the reader to be informed of what our author says concerning *free-will*. He has laid the foundation of his doctrine in what he said concerning cause and effect, as above explained. "'Tis universally acknowledged, that the operations of external bodies are necessary, and that in the communication of their motion, in their attraction and mutual cohesion, there are not the least traces of indifference or liberty." – "Whatever therefore is in this respect on the same footing with matter, must be acknowledged to be necessary. That we may know whether this be the case with the actions of the mind, we may examine matter, and consider on what the idea of a necessity in its operations are founded, and why we conclude one body or action to be the infallible cause of another.

"It has been observed already, that in no single instance the ultimate connexion of any object is discoverable either by our senses or reason, and that we can never penetrate so far into the essence and construction of bodies, as to perceive the principle on which their mutual influence is founded. 'Tis their constant union alone, with which we are acquainted; and 'tis from the constant union the necessity arises, when the mind is determined to pass from one object to its usual attendant, and infer the existence of one from that of the other.

Here then are two particulars, which we are to regard as essential to *necessity, viz.* the constant *union* and the *inference* of the mind, and wherever we discover these we must acknowledge a necessity." Now nothing is more evident than the constant union of particular actions with particular motives. If all actions be not constantly united with their proper motives, this uncertainty is no more than what may be observed every day in the actions of matter, where by reason of the mixture and uncertainty of causes, the effect is often variable and uncertain. Thirty grains of opium will kill any man that is not accustomed to it; tho' thirty grains of rhubarb will not always purge him. In like manner the fear of death will always make a man go twenty paces out of his road; tho' it will not always make him do a bad action.

And as there is often a constant conjunction of the actions of the will with their motives, so the inference from the one to the other is often as certain as any reasoning concerning bodies: and there is always an inference proportioned to the constancy of the conjunction. On this is founded our belief in witnesses, our credit in history, and indeed all kinds of moral evidence, and almost the whole conduct of life.

Our author pretends, that this reasoning puts the whole controversy in a new light, by giving a new definition of necessity. And, indeed, the most zealous advocates for free-will must allow this union and inference with regard to human actions. They will only deny, that this makes the whole of necessity. But then they must shew, that we have an idea of something else in the actions of matter; which, according to the foregoing reasoning, is impossible.

Thro' this whole book, there are great pretensions to new discoveries in philosophy; but if any thing can intitle the author to so glorious a name as that of an *inventor*, 'tis the use he makes of the principle of the association of ideas, which enters into most of his philosophy. Our imagination has a great authority over our ideas; and there are no ideas that are different from each other, which it cannot separate, and join, and compose into all the varieties of fiction. But notwithstanding the empire of the imagination, there is a secret tie or union among particular ideas, which causes the mind to conjoin them more frequently together, and makes the one, upon its appearance, introduce the other. Hence arises what we call the *apropos* of discourse:

hence the connection of writing: and hence that thread, or chain of thought, which a man naturally supports even in the loosest *reverie*. These principles of association are reduced to three, *viz.* *Resemblance;* a picture naturally makes us think of the man it was drawn for. *Contiguity;* when *St. Dennis* is mentioned, the idea of Paris naturally occurs. *Causation;* when we think of the son, we are apt to carry our attention to the father. 'Twill be easy to conceive of what vast consequence these principles must be in the science of human nature, if we consider, that so far as regards the mind, these are the only links that bind the parts of the universe together, or connect us with any person or object exterior to ourselves. For as it is by means of thought only that any thing operates upon our passions, and as these are the only ties of our thoughts, they are really *to us* the cement of the universe, and all the operations of the mind must, in a great measure, depend on them.

Bibliography

Árdal, Páll S. *Passion and Value in Hume's Treatise.* Edinburgh: Edinburgh University Press, 1966.

Baier, Annette C. *A Progress of Sentiments: Reflections on Hume's Sentiments.* Cambridge, Mass.: Harvard University Press, 1991.

Capaldi, Nicholas. *David Hume: The Newtonian Philosopher.* Boston: Twayne, 1975.

Chappell, V. C., ed. *Hume.* New York: Doubleday, 1966.

Kemp Smith, Norman. *The Philosophy of David Hume.* London: Macmillan, 1949.

Norton, David Fate, Nicholas Capaldi, and Wade L. Robison, eds. *McGill Hume Studies.* San Diego: Austin Hill Press, 1979.

Penelhum, Terence. *Hume.* London: Macmillan, 1975.

Stroud, Barry. *Hume.* London and New York: Routledge, 1977.

Wright, John P. *The Sceptical Realism of David Hume.* Manchester: Manchester University Press, 1983.

CHAPTER THIRTY-THREE — JULIEN OFFRAY DE LA METTRIE

Julien Offray de La Mettrie (1709-1751) was a French physician who came to a view which we may describe (as he himself does) as extending Descartes's view of non-human animals to human beings, most explicitly in the work from which come the excerpts that follow, but in varying degrees of articulation in several other books.

La Mettrie's ideas were not well received. His first book, *L'histoire naturelle de l'âme* (*The Natural History of the Soul*), was ordered publicly burned when it appeared in 1745. La Mettrie fled to the Netherlands, and eventually sought further refuge, finding it in Prussia under the patronage of Frederick the Great. The Prussian king in fact wrote a praising memoir of La Mettrie at the latter's premature death.

It has taken until the twentieth century for La Mettrie to be viewed as other than the expositor of an essentially frivolous extremist set of provocations, calculated more to shock than to contribute to scientific knowledge of human beings. He is seen now as having articulated in a remarkably focused way the idea of the human being as an aggregate of interlocking physiological systems – a view which has at the present time a sizeable constituency of supporters.

Whether this view in one or other of its formulations – and especially, of course, in La Mettrie's – should be called a *non-self* theory, might be contested. In *Man a Machine*, in fact, La Mettrie *appears*, at least in the earlier stages of the book, to presuppose that humans have rich psychological lives, a unity of personhood, and even what he calls a soul. It is only as the full tale is told – the argument emerges only by degrees – that the reader realizes that some of the terms do not, for La Mettrie, have familiar senses, and that the human machinery has no central pilot.

Is a non-self theory – a theory we can dub *physiological mechanism* – a theory of human nature? In a sense, one may reasonably feel, Yes; and in a sense, No. Such a view as this seems compatible with more than one way of filling in, and "oiling", the machine structures and parts, hence to permit several distinct theories of human nature on its skeletal base. On the other hand, the theory would seem to deny us meaningful freedom, or any possibility of a unity of life or of understanding. We would be found to *be* a certain kind of creature were the theory true, and not able to be what we might otherwise have at least aspired to be.

Julien de la Mattrie, *Man a Machine*

(Source: Julien Offray de La Mettrie. *Man a Machine and Man a Plant*. Trans. Richard A. Watson and Maya Rybalka. Intr. and Notes by Justin Leiber. Indianapolis/Cambridge: Hackett Publishing Company, Inc., 1994, 61-72.)

So there you have far more facts than anybody needs to prove incontestably that every tiny fiber and piece of an organized body moves according to its own principle, and whose actions, unlike voluntary movements, do not depend on the nerves, since these movements take place without the parts in motion having any communication with the circulation. Now if this force is manifested even in cut up pieces of fiber, the heart, which is composed of specially interlaced fibers, must have the same property. I did not need to read Bacon's *Histoire* to be persuaded of this. It is easy enough to figure out both from the perfect analogy in structure between the hearts of man and animals, and from the compactness of man's heart in which this movement is hidden from the eye only because it is smothered in the heart, and last because in cadavers everything is cold and collapsed. If tortured criminals were dissected while their bodies were still warm, one would see the same movements in their hearts that one observes in the muscles of the faces of people whose heads have been cut off.

This motive principle of whole bodies and of cut up parts is such that it produces movements that are not irregular, as formerly believed, but very regular ones just as much in warm, live, whole animals as in those that are cut up and cold. The only recourse remaining for our adversaries, then, is to deny thousands of facts that anyone can easily verify.

Where is the seat of this inborn force in our bodies? Clearly it resides in what the ancients call the *parenchyma,* that is to say, in the very substance of the parts, excluding the veins, arteries, and nerves, in short, the organization of the entire body, and that, consequently, each part contains in itself springs whose forces are proportioned to its needs.

Let us consider the details of these springs of the human machine. Their actions cause all natural, automatic, vital, and animal movements. Does not the body leap back mechanically in terror when one comes upon an unexpected precipice? And do the eyelids not close automatically at the threat of a blow? And as I said before, does not the *pupil* contract automatically in full daylight to protect the retina and enlarge to see in the dark? In the winter, do pores of the skin not close automatically so the cold does not penetrate into the veins? Does the stomach not heave automatically when irritated by poison, a dose of opium, and all emetics? Do the heart, arteries, and muscles not contract automatically when one is asleep, just as when one is awake? Do the lungs not automatically work continually like bellows? Do not the sphincters of the bladder,

rectum, etc. close automatically? Does the heart not contract more strongly than any other muscle, so that the erector muscles raise the rod in man, as they do in animals who beat it on their stomachs, and even in children who have erections if that part is excited? This proves, let me say in passing, that there is in this member an extraordinary spring that is little known and produces effects that have not yet been well explained, despite all the enlightenment of anatomy.

I will not comment further on all the small subordinate springs everyone knows about. But there is another, more subtle and marvelous, that animates everything. It is the source of all our feelings, pleasures, passions, and thoughts, for the brain has its muscles for thinking as do the legs for walking. I mean that impetuous autonomous principle that Hippocrates calls ἑνορμων or the soul. This principle exists and is seated in the brain at the point of origin of the nerves through which it exercises its rule over all the rest of the body. It is the explanatory principle of all that can be explained, including even the surprising effects of the maladies of the imagination.

But to keep from getting bogged down in this ill-understood, teeming swamp, we must limit ourselves to a small number of questions and reflections.

Why does the sight or even the mere thought of a beautiful woman cause such singular movements and desires? Is the behavior of certain organs in this case caused by the nature of these organs? Not at all, but rather by the commerce and sympathy the muscles have with the imagination. There is a first spring excited by what the ancients call the *beneplacitum,* an image of beauty, which excites another spring that is quite dormant until the imagination rouses it. And how is that done, if not by the disordered tumult of the blood and spirits that gallop with extraordinary promptitude to swell the hollow tubes?

Since there are obvious communications between a mother and the child in her womb (at least through the veins, and is it certain there is none through the nerves?); and since it is hard to deny the facts related by Tulpius[1] and other writers who

---

1   Nicolas Tulp (1593-1674) was Praelector of Anatomy of the Surgeons Guild of Amsterdam and he appears as such in Rembrandt's *Anatomy Lesson*. He reported embryonic malformations in *Observationes medicae* (1652). Malebranche gave theoretical expression to the view that the fetus is influenced by maternal emotions in his

deserve our trust (there is no one who deserves it more); I believe that through such connections the foetus experiences the impetuosity of the maternal imagination, just as soft wax receives all kinds of impressions, and that the traces or cravings of the mother can be imprinted on the foetus, without being able to understand how it happens, whatever Blondel and his followers say. Thus, we make amends to Father Malebranche, who was scoffed at far too much for his credulity by authors who have not observed nature closely enough but wanted to subject it to their ideas.

Look at the portrait of the famous Pope, the English Voltaire. The strain, the nerves of his genius are painted on his physiognomy. His face is convoluted, his eyes start out of their sockets, his eyebrows are raised by the muscles of his forehead. Why? Because the origin of the nerves is at work, and because the whole body must be suffering the effects of so difficult a birth. If there were no internal cord pulling the outer ones, from where would these phenomena come? To introduce a *soul* to explain them is to be reduced to depending on the *comings and goings of the Holy Ghost.*

In fact, if what thinks in my brain is not a part of that vital organ, and consequently of the whole body, why does my blood heat up when I am lying tranquilly in bed thinking about my work or reasoning abstractly? Why does the fever of my mind pass into my veins? Ask this of imaginative men, of great poets, of those who are ravished by a well-expressed sentiment, who are transported by an exquisite taste, by the charms of nature, truth, or virtue! It is by their enthusiasm, by the feelings they describe, that you will judge of the cause by the effects. It is by this *harmony* that Borelli, a single anatomist who knew better than all the Leibnizians, confirms the material unity of man.[2] Because, in sum, if the tension of the nerves that causes pain also causes the fever that disturbs the

mind and makes it lose its will power; and if, reciprocally, an excessively exercised mind troubles the body and lights that fire of consumption that took Bayle at such an early age; if such and such a titillation forces me to wish for and desire ardently what I cared not a tittle about a moment before; if, in their turn, certain brain traces excite the same itching desire; why consider as two what is obviously only one?[3] In vain does one protest for the sovereignty of the will. For every order it gives, it submits a hundred times to the yoke. And how marvelously the healthy body is forced by a torrent of blood and spirits to obey the ministers of the will, that invisible legion of fluids quicker than lightning and always ready to serve. But just as this power is exercised through the nerves, through them also is it arrested. The strongest will and the most ardent desires of an exhausted lover, will they restore his lost vigor? No, alas! And the will is the first to be punished, since, given certain circumstances, it is not in its power not to want pleasure. What I have said of paralysis, etc., pertains here.

Jaundice surprises you! Do you not know that the color of bodies depends on that of the glasses through which you look at them! Are you unaware that whatever color the humors have, so do the objects, at least in relation to us vain dupes of a thousand illusions. But let the bile flow through its natural strainer to remove this color from the aqueous humor of the eye, and then through the clear eye, the soul will see yellow no more. Similarly, by couching a cataract and injecting the eustachian canal, one returns sight to the blind and hearing to the deaf. During the centuries of ignorance, how many people who were nothing more than clever charlatans passed for great miracle makers? How lofty and powerful the soul and will, which can act only as far as bodily dispositions permit, and whose tastes change with age and fever! Is it any wonder, then, that philosophers have always

---

Recherche de la vérité. James Blondel criticizes this view in his *The Strength of Imagination in Pregnant Woman Examined: and the Opinion That Marks and Deformities in Children Arise from Thence, Demonstrated to Be a Vulgar Error* (1727).

2   Giovanni Alfonso Borelli (1608-1679), an Italian physicist and anatomist, was an early architect of the Cartesian mechanistic approach to animal physiology. Leibniz proposed a "pre-established harmony" between mind and body, supposing that there is no actual causal interaction between the two. La Mettrie means by the "material unity of man" that the mind simply is the brain.

3   Pierre Bayle died in 1706 at the age of 59, probably of tuberculosis. La Mettrie's suggestion that his death had psychosomatic causes seems unwarranted.

viewed the health of the body as necessary for the health of the soul? Or that Pythagoras carefully prescribed diet and Plato prohibited wine? Sensible physicians always prescribe a regime that is good for the body as a prelude to improving the mind and elevating it to knowledge of truth and virtue, which are nothing but meaningless words when one is suffering the disorders of illness and tumult of the senses! Without the precepts of hygiene, Epictetus, Socrates, Plato, etc., preach in vain. All moral philosophy is unavailing for anyone not endowed with sobriety, which is the source of all virtue, as intemperance is of all vices.

Need I say more (and why should I lose myself in the history of the passions when Hippocrates' ένορμων explains them all) to prove that man is but an animal, or a contraption of springs, each of which activates the next without our being able to tell which one nature used to start the merry-go-round of human society? These springs differ among themselves only in location and strength but never in nature. Thus, the soul is only a principle of movement or sensible, material part of the brain, which one can regard as the machine's principal spring without fear of being mistaken. It has an obvious influence on all the others. It even appears to have been made first so that all the others merely emanate from it, as observations on different embryos illustrate.

This natural oscillation specific to every part of our machine and of which each fiber is endowed, and, so to speak, each fibrous element is like that of a pendulum, but it cannot always take place. As oscillation ceases, it must be renewed: It must be strengthened when it weakens and weakened when disrupted by excess of strength and vigor. True health care consists solely in maintaining this balance.

The body is but a clock, and chyle the clock maker. The first move of nature on entering the bloodstream is to excite a fever, which the chemists, always thinking of furnaces, have taken for a fermentation. It increases the filtration of the animal spirits that automatically animate the muscles and heart, as though sent there by order of the will.

These animal spirits are the life force that maintains the perpetual movement of solids and fluids for a hundred years, as necessary to the one as to the other. Who can say whether solids contribute more to this performance than fluids, or vice versa? This we know: Each is so necessary to the other that the action of the one would be quickly annihilated without the help of the other. The pressure of the fluids on which their circulation depends activates and maintains the elasticity of the veins. Thus, after death, each substance's natural spring remains more or less strong and survives other manifestations of life to expire the last. So although it is true that the force in the springs of animal parts can be maintained and increased by the circulatory force, it does not depend on the circulatory force since it remains even in amputated limbs and vital organs removed from the body, as we have seen!

I am not unaware that not all experts agree with this, and that Stahl in particular strongly disdains it.[4] This great chemist wants to persuade us that the soul is the sole cause of all our movements. But he talks like a fanatic, not a philosopher.

To refute Stahl's hypothesis, one need not go to the lengths of our predecessors. All you need to do is watch a violinist. What suppleness! What agile fingers! They go so fast that they almost seem not to move at all. Now I ask, or rather defy, those Stahlians who know so much about our soul's abilities, to tell me how the soul could possibly command the execution so quickly of so many movements at a distance in so many different places in the body. If this were possible, it would imply that a flute player could execute brilliant trills on an infinity of stops he does not even know and could not even finger.

But, as Mr. Hecquet says, not everyone is allowed to go to Corinth. Were such prodigies possible, would not Stahl himself have been a better man than chemist and physician?[5] But for that, he (fortunate mortal!) would need a soul different from other men, a sovereign soul, which, not content to

---

4   Georg Ernst Stahl (1640-1734), a German chemist and physician, was a vitalist and antimechanist, and the chief opponent of La Mettrie's teacher Boerhaave.
5   Philippe Hecquet (1661-1737) taught medicine at the University of Paris. La Mettrie admired him for his satires on the greed of physicians. The reference is to a line from Horace, "All men may not go to Corinth" (*Epistolae I, xviv,* 36).

reign over the *voluntary* muscles, easily takes the reins of the whole body to control, suspend, calm, or excite its movements at will! If such a despotic mistress held in her hands, so to speak, the beating of the heart and the laws of the circulation of the blood, there would without doubt be no fever, pain, or sickliness, no shameful impotence or embarrassing priapism. The soul wills and the springs stand erect or go limp. So how did the springs of Stahl's machine manage to break down so quickly? Whoever is such a great doctor ought to be immortal.

But Stahl is not the only one who rejects the oscillation principle of organized bodies. Greater intellects than he have failed to employ it when they wished to explain the action of the heart, the erection of the *penis,* etc. All one needs to do is read Boerhaave's *Institutions de medicine* to see what excruciating and seductive systems this great man was forced to give birth to out of the sweat of his powerful genius simply because he refused to admit that the heart has such an impressive force.

Willis and Perrault, lesser intellects but assiduous observers of nature (whose work the famous professor from Leiden knew only from others and almost at second hand), seem to have preferred to my principle the assumption of a soul spread generally throughout the body.[6] According to this hypothesis, held also by Virgil and the Epicureans and, at first sight, supported by the case of the polyp, the movements that survive death or dismemberment come from a *vestigial soul* conserved by parts that contract without being stimulated by the blood and animal spirits. From this one can see that these writers, whose solid works easily eclipse all philosophic fables, were mistaken only the way those are who say matter has the faculty of thinking. I mean they expressed themselves badly in obscure terms that signify nothing. Indeed, what is this *vestigial soul,* if not a poorly labeled Leibnizian motive force, that, nevertheless, Perrault above all really foresaw in his *Traité de la mécanique des animaux.*

Now that it is clearly demonstrated against Cartesians, Stahlians, Malebuncheans, and theologians (who hardly deserve being placed in such company) that matter is self-moved not only, for example, when organized as in a whole heart, but even when such organization is destroyed, human curiosity would like to know how the original endowment of a body with the breath of life in consequence furnishes it with the faculty of feeling and, finally, with the faculty of thinking? God almighty, what efforts certain philosophers have made to find this out! And what gibberish I have had the patience to read on this subject!

Experience teaches us only that as long as the smallest, moribund power of movement subsists in one or several fibers, only a prick is required to revive and animate it. This is shown by the multitude of experiments I have described to overcome the systems. It is an established fact that movement and feeling excite one another in turn, both in whole bodies and in the same bodies when their structure is destroyed, to say nothing of certain plants that show the same phenomena of union of feeling and movement.

Moreover, how many excellent philosophers have demonstrated that thought is only a faculty of feeling, and that the rational soul is merely the sensible soul applied to the contemplation of ideas and reasoning! This is proved by the sole fact that when feeling is extinguished, so is thought, as in apoplexy, lethargy, catalepsy, etc. It is ridiculous to claim, as some have, that the soul continues to think during soporific illnesses but does not remember its thoughts.

It is foolish to waste time looking for the mechanism of this phenomenon. The nature of motion is as unknown to us as that of matter. There is no way to discover how motion is produced in matter unless, like the author of the *Histoire de l'âme,* one resurrects the ancient and unintelligible doctrine of *substantial forms!*[7] I am, therefore, really and truly as content with being ignorant of how inert, simple matter becomes active and compounded into

---

6   Both [Thomas] Willis and Claude Perrault (1613-1688), a French physician and architect, wrote of a soul spread through the body. La Mettrie notes that the polyp, in being divisible into many self-sufficient parts, tells in favor of such a view. While he condemns such vitalism as obscurantist, he presents it as a step in the right direction, not unrelated to the view he himself espouses in *The Natural History of the Soul.*

7   The author of *The Natural History of the Soul* is La Mettrie himself, writing under the name Charp.

organs, as I am with being unable to look at the sun without red glasses. I am equally tranquil about my ignorance of other incomprehensible marvels of nature, such as the production of feeling and thought in a being that, long ago, seemed to our limited view to be nothing more than a glob of mud.

Grant me only that organized matter is endowed with a motive principle, which alone differentiates it from what is not so organized (come on! how could one refuse that most incontestable observation?), and that everything in animals depends on the diversity of this organization, as I have sufficiently proved, and this is enough to solve the riddle of substances and that of man. It is obvious that there is only one substance in the universe and that man is the most perfect animal. Man is to apes and the most intelligent animals what Huygens's planetary pendulum is to a watch of Julien le Roy.[8] If more instruments, wheelwork, and springs are required to show the movements of the planets than to mark and repeat the hours, if Vaucanson needed more art to make his *flute player* than his *duck,* he would need even more to make a *talker,* which can no longer be regarded as impossible, particularly in the hands of a new Prometheus.[9] Similarly, nature had necessarily to employ more art and install more organs to make and maintain a machine that might mark all the throbbings of the heart and mind over an entire century. Because if the pulse does not show the hours, the body is at least the barometer of heat and vivacity by which one can judge the nature of the soul. I am not mistaken. The human body is an immense clock, constructed with so much artifice and skill that if the wheel that marks the seconds stops because of rust or derailment, the minutes wheel continues turning, as does the quarter hour wheel, and all the rest. Because is not the narrowing of a few veins enough to destroy or suspend the force of movement of the heart, as in the mainspring of a machine, since on the contrary, fluids whose volume is diminished, having less distance to cover, cover it that much faster, as by a new current that the force of the heart augments because of the resistance it finds in the extremities of the veins? When a compressed optic nerve prevents the passage of images of objects, this deprivation of sight no more impedes hearing than, when the functions of the *auditory nerve* are curtailed, deprivation of hearing impedes sight.[10] So is it not because of such blockage that one sometimes hears without being able to say that he hears (unless this is caused by disease), and that someone who can hear nothing but whose lingual nerves are freely active in the brain automatically says out loud everything that passes through his head? These phenomena do not surprise well-informed physicians. They know what to expect of the nature of man. And, to remark in passing, of two physicians, the one who merits the most confidence is, in my opinion, always the one most versed in the physics or mechanics of the human body, the one who occupies himself seriously with pure naturalism alone and ignores the soul and all the anxieties this chimera raises in fools and ignoramuses.

So let the so-called Mr. Charp mock philosophers who regard animals as machines.[11] I beg to differ! I think Descartes would have been a respectable man

---

8   Christian Huygens (1629-1695), Dutch physicist, mathematician, and astronomer, designed a mechanical model of the planetary system which, as built by the clockmaker van Ceulen, faithfully indicated the motions of the known planets. Julien Leroy (1686-1759) was a famous French watchmaker who developed a mechanism that automatically adjusted pendulums to temperature changes.

9   Jacques de Vaucanson (1709-1782), a French machine maker, presented his flute player to the French Academy in 1738. He also constructed a mechanical duck and an asp that hissed and darted on a mechanical Cleopatra's breast. La Mettrie was not the only one to suggest that man is a machine that winds its own springs; Descartes was fascinated by mechanical toy men.

10   The portio mollis is the portion of the eighth cranial nerve that leads into the cochlea of the inner ear, subserving hearing.

11   La Mettrie's *The Natural History of the Soul* (1745) is said, on its title page, to be "translated from the English of M. Charp." When La Mettrie published his *Oeuvres philosophiques* (1751), he included *The Natural History of the Soul* as one of his works but changed its title to *Treatise on the Soul,* perhaps to indicate that it was not based on experimental data. Although La Mettrie excuses Descartes for straying from experiment and observation, Descartes in his *The Passions of the Soul* takes an experimentalist and physiological approach; the letters that accompany the

in all respects despite being born in a century he was not able to enlighten – if he had known the value of experiment and observation, and the dangers of straying from them. So it is only just of me to make genuine amends to this great man, to make up for all those petty philosophers, pathetic jokers, and Lockean baboons, who, rather than giving Descartes the horselaugh, would do better to acknowledge that without him the field of philosophy, like science without Newton, would still be fallow ground.

It is true that this celebrated philosopher was often wrong, and no one denies it. Nevertheless, he knew animal nature. He was the first to demonstrate fully that animals are pure machines. After such an important discovery, which implies such great intelligence on his part, only a churl would not forgive him his errors!

In my estimation, this great discovery makes up for all his false notes. Because, even though he harps on the distinction between two substances, it is obvious that this is only a shrewd move, a clever stylistic trick to make theologians swallow a poison hidden behind an analogy that everyone sees but them. This impressive analogy forces all scholars and meticulous investigators to admit that however greatly these proud and vain beings desire to exalt themselves, they are at bottom only animals, perpendicularly crawling machines, more distinguished by their pride than by the name of man. These machines have that marvelous instinct that education makes of all the mind, still seated in the brain. If the brain is absent or ossified, then the mind is seated in the medulla oblongata. But the mind is never in the cerebellum, because the mind continues its functions even when the cerebellum is hardened, as others have found, e.g., as Haller shows in the *Transactions*.[12]

To be a machine, to feel, think, know good from evil like blue from yellow, in a word, to be born with intelligence and a sure instinct for morality, and yet to be only an animal, are things no more contradictory than to be an ape or parrot and know how to find sexual pleasure. And since the occasion presents itself for saying so, who would have ever divined *a priori* that shooting off a gob of sperm during copulation would make one feel such divine pleasure, and that from it would be born a tiny creature who one day, following certain laws, could enjoy the same delights? Thought is so far from being incompatible with organized matter that it seems to me to be just another of its properties, such as electricity, the motive faculty, impenetrability, extension, etc.

Bibliography

Gazzaniga, Michael. *Mind Matters: How the Mind and Brain Interact to Create Our Conscious Lives*. Boston: Houghton Mifflin, 1988.

Hastings, Helen. *Man and Beast in French Thought of the Eighteenth Century*. Baltimore: Johns Hopkins Press, 1936.

Rosenfield, L.C. *From Beast-Machine to Man-Machine: The Theme of Animal Soul in French Letters from Descartes to La Mettrie*. New York: Oxford University Press, 1941.

Vartanian, Aram. *L'Homme machine: A Study in the Origins of an Idea*. Princeton, N.J.: Princeton University Press, 1960.

Wellman, Kathleen. *La Mettrie, Medicine, Philosophy, and Enlightenment*. Durham: Duke University Press, 1992.

Yolton, John W. *Locke and French Materialism*. Oxford: Clarendon Press, 1991.

---

work depict Descartes as hungering for major funding in order to conduct a large scale program of experimental research. Earlier, Descartes had suppressed his *Le Monde,* which contains a hypothetical mechanist account of human bodies. In calling Descartes's dualism a "sleight of hand," La Mettrie further suggests that Descartes was a materialist who believed, as does La Mettrie, that the material body machine is the whole of man. While Descartes most surely believed that the human body is a machine, there is no evidence that he believed that *man* is a machine. Indeed, in the *Passions of the Soul,* he teaches how the mind can control the body. On the other hand, Descartes developed the reflex arc mechanism of stimulus and response that later materialists used to eliminate the mind as unnecessary for explaining body movements.

12   By La Mettrie's time it was realized that "lower parts" of the brain such as the medulla oblongata could carry on automatic motor functions in absence of the cerebrum and cerebellum. Vartanian reports that the Haller reference is to "Observatio de scirrho cerebelli," *Philosophical Transactions,* 43, no. 474: 100-101.

John Broadus Watson – J.B. Watson (1878-1958) – was the founder of behaviorism, once the dominant school of psychology in North America, and still an important influence in later movements in psychology and philosophy of mind. Watson was professor of psychology at Johns Hopkins University (1908-1920); subsequently he left the university and became an advertising executive. He was the author of several books on behaviorism.

It is not uncommon to view some of Watson's behaviorist successors as more scientifically sophisticated than he was, and as more impressive representatives of the school. (B. F. Skinner is at least as famous as Watson, and often seen as typifying models of experiment, key theoretical ideas, and social and philosophical implications or applications of the behaviorist program.) However, none of the later behaviorists set out the fundamentals of this model of human nature as clearly, bravely, and with the same degree of ontological commitment (e.g., to the denial of the reality of consciousness).

John B. Watson, *The Ways of Behaviorism*

(Source: John B. Watson. *The Ways of Behaviorism.* New York and London: Harper and Brothers Publisher, 1928, 1-3, 5-19.)

In the year 1912 "behaviorism" was only a word – a harsh-sounding one at that. The group that understood its tenets and leaned toward it was small.

Would the years to come show behaviorism to be a genuine new and sound development in psychology or just another *ism*? The old line psychologists trained under Wundt freely predicted that it was only a revolt and like most revolts could easily be put down.

But behaviorism was not a revolt or protest. It was a new way of looking at the most important things about human beings – an objective way.

What are the most important things about human beings? When answering let us leave out all speculations about man's origin, his soul, his life hereafter. Aren't the most important things *what he does; how he behaves?* How he works; how he plays? What he does when he is angry, scared, in love? Is he lazy, slovenly, untrustworthy, undependable, a grafter, rude to his inferiors, cringing to the group over him? And don't we as we study him get to the point where we can almost surely *predict* how he is going to act when in a certain situation? Again when we know he can't we arrange situations to get him to act in certain ways? Flattery by a man over him may make him swell up and preen his feathers and accept a project which he had hitherto steadfastly refused to entertain.

Behaviorism is the scientific study of human behavior. Its real goal is to provide the basis for the prediction and control of human beings: Given the situation, to tell what the human being will do; given the man in action, to be able to say why he is reacting in that way.

It is a science based on very simple principles – upon common sense and not speculations. What is man's untutored behavior like? To answer we go to the nursery and study the reactions of the infant where we see reaction patterns forming. Is his behavior inherited or *learned* – and how much is inherited and how much *learned*? Well, go to the laboratory and find out. Why do men and women get married – why divorced – what effect has prohibition had upon human behavior – woman suffrage? Let us study the problem by observing human beings as we would study the effect of continuous light upon the growth of a plant.

Stating our goal in slightly more technical language, we can say that the behaviorists' job is – *given the stimulus, to predict the response – given the response, to predict the stimulus.* A blow on the patellar tendon (stimulus) evokes the knee jerk (response). Stimulating the tongue with vinegar (stimulus) makes the salivary glands pour out their secretions (response). These are life reactions reduced to their simplest terms. But according to the behaviorists, life's most complicated acts are but combinations of these simple stimulus-response patterns of behavior. Even thinking – memory – personality are but easily understandable integrations of stimulus-response behavior.

Behaviorism thus leaves out speculations. You'll find in it no references to the intangibles – the unknown and the unknowable "psychic entities." The behaviorist has nothing to say of "consciousness." How can he? Behaviorism is a natural science. He has neither seen, smelled nor tasted consciousness nor found it taking part in any human reactions. How can he talk about it until he finds it in his path? His way – his method – is to build a psychology without it. He does the same with the subdivisions of consciousness – such as sensations – perceptions – affections – will and the like. In behaviorism you find none of these grand old speculative bugaboos about which so many millions of pages have been so fruitlessly written.

Because of its simplicity and matter-of-factness behaviorism has made rapid progress. Universities now teach it. The public itself demands some knowledge of it....

WHAT IS BEHAVIORISM?
I

A few years ago in psychology we heard only of Freud and of his method, psychoanalysis. With this method his loyal subjects assured us they could solve all psychological problems. To-day when every shop girl will tell you of her dreams and complexes, psychoanalysis is no longer a topic of interest in drawing-room conversations, not because anyone is particularly shocked by the discussion but rather because its novelty has gone.

So it is with all new movements in scientific fields. There was possibly too little science – real science – in Freud's psychology, and hence it held its news value for only a relatively brief span of years.

At this moment there is a new psychological claimant for public interest. During the past ten years it has been threshed out in university circles; now the newspapers are beginning to feed it to the masses, but still in broken doses.

This contestant is behaviorism.

Behaviorism has been an independent study in the larger universities since about 1912. It represents what must be looked upon as a real renaissance in psychology. Up to that time the so-called subjective, or introspective, psychology held complete sway. Subjective psychology was defined as a study of the mind – really of your own mind, since no one else could look in on it and see what was going on there. And when you did look, what did you see? Since you were trained in the system and in the vernacular of James, Angell, Ladd, and Wundt, you said you saw *consciousness*. And then you tried to analyze this consciousness. What was it?... Why, one must describe it by enumerating the units that compose it. Consciousness is made up of sensation units like redness, greenness; sensations of tone, smell, temperature, and the like, and of units of *feeling* tone called "pleasantness" and "unpleasantness." Now when enough of these sensation units are simultaneously present and accompanied by one or another of the two feeling tones, you have what is called a *perception* – e.g., the perception of an orange or an apple.

The matter of consciousness and what constitutes it was made still more complicated when they insisted that when perceptions were absent, that is, when no objects were in front of us, consciousness was made up of representatives of objects called *images*.

All the data of this type of psychology were thus subjective. The only method of studying this data was by introspecting – looking within your own mind. Hence, we call such psychologists subjective psychologists, or introspective psychologists. Verification of findings – really the first objective of every true science – is thus forever denied the introspective student of psychology.

This was the time-honored analysis of mind. It was as thoroughly entrenched as the Bible – as philosophy itself. Surely no one could ever be bold enough or rash enough to question that there is such a thing as mind or that it is made up of conscious units.

And yet this is just what the behaviorist did.

In one sweeping assumption after another, the behaviorist threw out the concepts both of mind and of consciousness, calling them carryovers from the church dogma of the Middle Ages. The behaviorist told the introspectionists that consciousness was just a masquerade for the soul.

Behaviorism's challenge to introspective psychology was: "You say there is such a thing as consciousness, that consciousness goes on in you – then prove it. You say that you have sensations, perceptions, and images – then demonstrate them as other sciences demonstrate their facts."

Naturally, they could not meet this challenge. The only argument open to the introspectionist was that used by every time-honored exhorter since history began, the *argumentum ad hominem,* "no consciousness – no mind! Maybe the behaviorist has no consciousness, no mind, but you and I have."

If the study of mind – the analysis of consciousness – is not what psychology is about, what then is its field and what is its goal?

The behaviorist viewpoint is just common sense grown articulate. Behaviorism is a study of what people *do. What is this man doing now? – any answer to that question made by a trained observer is a psychological fact or happening.* After observing man's behavior long enough, the behaviorist begins to say, "this man or that man will do so and so under such and such conditions." Take a simple case. John Smith will run every time he sees a snake. Every woman in this closed room will scream, stand on a chair or pull her skirts tightly around her if I turn loose ten fierce wild rats. We have begun to make *predictions* about psychological happenings – the first step in any science.

Every science starts this way. It observes in a more or less hit and miss way the happenings round about. It next gets to the point where it can make *predictions, e.g.,* the sun will rise tomorrow – there will be a total eclipse of the sun visible in New York in 2024 – Halley's comet will be seen again in 1986. The next stage in any science is to get "control" of its happenings. Astronomy never can get control. It cannot produce eclipses or prevent them. (Even here possibly we should not be dogmatic!) Chemistry is getting control. Biology is getting control. Can psychology ever get control? Can I make some one who is not afraid of snakes, afraid of them and how? Can I take some one who is afraid of snakes and remove that fear? How?

In other words, the starting point of behaviorism is like that of every other science. Looked at in this way, the old, subjective psychology never had any right to be called a science. To be a science, psychology must use the same material that all other sciences use. Its facts must be capable of verification by other capable investigators everywhere. Its methods must be the methods of science in general.

II

What are the phenomena or happenings that the behaviorist studies in his psychology (human)? He limits his field to the study of man. He makes the field still more circumscribed. He will not attempt to study the physico-chemical make-up of man. He will study only one thing – what man does. Observation shows that he is always doing something – always behaving. He is behaving even when asleep, when in coma, when sitting motionless gazing into the fire.

Suppose I am a stranger scientist just down from some distant planet. I know nothing of human beings as they exist on this earth. Suppose, further, that I am in a balloon so situated above the center of New York that I can watch the city and the surrounding territory. At eight-thirty in the morning I see millions of people hurrying into the city in trains, in automobiles, in subways, on ferries. The movements are rapid, confusing. There seems to be no more system in these movements than in the hurrying, scurrying movements of ants when their nest has been disturbed. With my eye aided by special instruments I follow groups of these individuals. I note that they enter great office buildings, department stores, restaurants. Some begin to wait on customers, some start to work on typewriting machines, others begin to cut and fit clothes, and still others start sewing on power machines. I finally arrive at the conclusion that the people *are going to work.* Just think what a volume I could carry back to Mars on the behavior of New Yorkers if from some central position I could observe their whole twenty-four-hour behavior for a few weeks or months!

Now you are not accustomed to think of accumulation of simple facts of this kind as data of psychology. You have grown up with it. It is part of your everyday life.

Yet when you go to a foreign country it is just these kinds of observations you have to make before you can get along in your foreign environment. From this standpoint you can see that everybody is something of a psychologist.

The people in Mars, after reading my first general report, decide to send me down again for the study of specialized features of human behavior. What are their school and church systems like? What is their social behavior like in the sense of their manners and customs and ethics? What is their sex life like throughout the life cycle? Their home life? What do they read? Do they go to plays and to what kind of plays? What role does the cinema play in their lives?

From these studies I carry back to Mars a tremendous amount of narrow specialized information on the habits and customs of New Yorkers. This also is behavioristic psychology.

After going over my facts and inferences, my colleagues in Mars decide that they are in need of still more specialized data. They tell me to go back and pick out some one individual and bring back a complete report of his behavior. I can carry out these studies only by attaching myself to some individual, say John Smith. By observing him carefully day in and day out I find out his occupation. He is a bricklayer. He can lay two thousand bricks a day when he lets himself out, as, for example, when building his own home or when working by the job on his own contract. I find, though, that on most jobs he is not allowed to work a full day. He must work only a certain number of hours each day. He has to join an organization called a union and, as a member of a union and under the conditions of the union, he rarely lays more than eight hundred bricks per day. For this he receives a certain fixed sum. I find that this man is married, that he has a small home in the suburbs, a Ford car bought on the instalment plan, and a radio bought on the same plan. I find that he drinks a great deal, that he abuses his wife and children, spends a considerable part of his time in the poolroom, that he is given to temper fits, that he is morose and sullen to his companions, that he is not particular in meeting his monetary obligations. He uses only fifteen hundred English words – he practically never writes a letter and he reads only the *Daily Tabloid*. I may wish to make a still more circumscribed study of his behavior, so I invite him into my laboratory and study the rapidity with which he can form new habits. He has never learned to run a machine lathe. How quickly can he learn to do this? He doesn't know any

French. How soon could I teach him to speak the French language moderately well? He has not a system of immaculate personal habits. How soon could I teach him these ? And what methods should I have to use in order to teach him to put on this new behavior?

All business, as well as all social life, is based upon these kinds of observations – and they are psychological observations although not necessarily very articulate ones.

Once again I assemble my data and take them back to my colleagues. After digesting them, they decide that adult human behavior is too complicated to understand without knowing something of the infancy and childhood period of man. We do not understand why one man is a bricklayer, another an artist, another a gambler. We cannot understand why some men are carefree and sober, make good husbands, and others not. We cannot understand why some men never leave home, never get married, and never are seen in women's society. We shall have to have man's early behavior investigated to see if it throws light on later behavior. Are such differences due to inborn differences in behavior – to differences in instincts, or merely to early differences in training?

Again I come back to earth but this time I begin my observations on newborn infants. I note carefully their behavior at birth, what new forms of unlearned behavior appear at definite intervals after birth. I study, too, how early habit formation can begin in these very young infants and note the various factors which make new habits form. In other words, I begin to tease out by my observations what part of man's behavior is inherited and what part is learned. This also is psychology.

You will notice that in all of this description we start from general observations of persons for which no laboratory or special instruments for study are necessary and that we end with the newborn infant in the laboratory, using every bit of instrumentation for the study of our phenomena which has been devised up to the present time. In other words, behaviorism breaks down the distinction between subjective and objective phenomena. All of the phenomena connected with human beings are objective, even the things you now call "memory" and "thinking"! Again, you have been in the habit of calling these more general studies social psychology or sociology, and the more narrow studies where the laboratory is involved psychology proper or experimental psychology. The behaviorist does not believe in these old distinctions. *The whole thing is psychology.* Along with the breaking down of these distinctions comes a threatening note to the whole of philosophy. With the behavioristic point of view now becoming dominant, it is hard to find a place for what has been called philosophy. Philosophy is passing – has all but passed, and unless new issues arise which will give a foundation for a new philosophy, the world has seen its last great philosopher.

So far we have had to take our psychological happenings just as we found them. Have we really gone far enough to be able to predict anything of consequence about individuals? Common sense, rather than scientific psychology, has gone a certain distance in prediction – you can't live with people without making predictions about them. You know in advance what they are going to say and do. That is why most people are so dull. If I fire a revolver behind any ten individuals who are sitting quietly in a room, I can predict without fear of contradiction that at least nine out of ten of these individuals will jump, scream, change rate of respiration and heartbeat. If I throw a hundred unclothed individuals who have never learned to swim into a pool of water, five hundred yards in diameter, all of them will drown unless somebody comes to aid them. If you will think over the problem for a moment, you will see that most of our institutions, banks, churches, great mercantile houses, the institution of marriage itself, are all based on the fundamental supposition that human behavior in general is predictable. Just whisper a word of a gold strike and you can safely predict a stampede. Just whisper a word of scandal about a woman placed high socially, and every tongue in her set will clack. If you wish to make a man preen himself, let some woman notice him when none of his critical friends is around. To make a man swell out his chest, praise and flatter him a bit. To make a woman dress most carefully, tell her her rival is to be present at a given function.

This level of predictability has been reached by the slow accumulation of psychological data through all ages, rather than by the efforts of trained psychologists. The trained investigator must now come in and tell us more accurately about what *this* individual is sure to do in the presence of the life situations he must face; will he work – does he lie – will he steal – will he break under stress?

What about the *control* of psychological phenomena? Can you make an individual display any given bit of behavior by any kind of psychological technic, the way the chemist can make water appear by bringing hydrogen and oxygen together under certain conditions?

We can't go very far in this direction now. But behaviorism has only just been born. Until about thirty years ago biology itself was upon a purely descriptive level. Darwin, in the fifties, was a great observer of facts. Upon the basis of his observations, he built up his theory of *descent*. He never went very much farther. To-day there is an experimental biology. It seeks to control descent by manipulating the chemical and physical environment of plants and animals. It attempts to change and modify species, to control growth and, in general, to alter the course of inheritance.

Psychology is still largely at a descriptive level. Control of psychological phenomena is in a more backward state than is the case with other sciences, partly because it is a newer science, but more largely because psychology wasted its time so long in trying futilely to study mind instead of behavior.

We have made a beginning. Here is a group of moths quiet in a very dim light. Suppose I decide to arouse behavior to make them fly to the right-hand side of the room. How can I control that behavior? I light a candle and put it in the exact position in the room to which I want the moths to fly. In a short time the moths become active and fly toward the source of the light. It may have taken the behaviorists days, weeks, or months to discover this way of controlling the insects. Once found out, it becomes a part of the technic of *every* investigator. The *response* (act, happening) is flying toward the source of the light; the *stimulus* is the lighted candle. In this simple observation you have a part of the mechanics of behavioristic psychology typified in its most elementary form – no response without a stimulus. Every adequate stimulus must produce some response immediately.

No matter how many thousands of reactions a human or animal is capable of performing, there is always some stimulus or object in the environment which will arouse each of these reactions in him. Our search in the laboratory at the present time lies in this direction, to get a better knowledge of the stimuli calling out reactions. With this data well in hand, it is a simple enough matter then to arrange the environment, put the necessary group of stimuli in front of him, to get man or animal to perform any act in his repertoire. Let us go into the human realm. I wish to make a seventy-day-old child blink. What stimulus shall I apply? I can touch its eyeball and produce the blink; I can blow on its eyeball and produce the blink; I can pass a rapid shadow over the eye and produce the blink. In other words, there are three stimuli which will call out this reaction. Suppose I wish to make a baby cry. We will assume that the baby has not as yet put on any habits, learned anything. I can pinch him, cut him, burn him, or apply any other noxious stimuli to make him cry. Suppose I wish to make a twenty-day-old baby smile. I find that the only way is to touch its lips gently, with a feather for example, stroke its skin gently, especially in certain sensitive areas.

But the problem is not always so simple. Many objects will not at first serve as stimuli for calling out a particular form of reaction. Some, indeed, will not at first produce any observable overt reaction. The individual must first be *conditioned* to these stimuli. Environment does the conditioning. The process is quite simple. For example, the first sight of a stick will not cause a youngster to dodge when he sees it. He must be struck (fundamental stimulus) before he dodges. If now I strike his head sharply each time he sees me pick up the stick, he soon dodges the instant he catches *sight* (conditioned stimulus) of it in my hand. I have set up *a conditional visual response*. No "association of ideas" is involved because we can set up similar conditioned responses in our glands over which we have no "control." We can set them up even in the newborn infant; we can establish them in animals – even in the lowly one-cell animals.

Throughout life, objects which have no *kick* (that is, which are not stimuli to certain responses) are constantly borrowing a kick (becoming conditioned stimuli) because they happen to be present when some fundamental stimulus is calling out a reaction from the organism. This is why any object in the world, given the proper history in our past, can arouse a fear reaction. This is why any object or person in the world can be made to call out a love response – even a hunchbacked and disfigured woman of forty evoking such a response in a hand-

some lad of twenty.

To control the individual then – have him behave as society specifies – by confronting him with appropriate stimuli, we must have considerable knowledge not only about native, fundamental stimuli, but also about those which have been *conditioned*. To gain this knowledge, we must go to the laboratory and study the human individual from infancy onward.

John B. Watson, *Behaviorism*

(Source: John B. Watson. *Behaviorism* (rev. ed.) Chicago: University of Chicago Press, 1930, 2-19)

Behaviorism ... holds that the subject matter of human psychology is *the behavior of the human being*. Behaviorism claims that consciousness is neither a definite nor a usable concept. The behaviorist, who has been trained always as an experimentalist, holds, further, that belief in the existence of consciousness goes back to the ancient days of superstition and magic.

The great mass of the people even today has not yet progressed very far away from savagery – it wants to believe in magic. The savage believes that incantations can bring rain, good crops, good hunting, that an unfriendly voodoo doctor can bring disaster to a person or to a whole tribe; that an enemy who has obtained a nail paring or a lock of your hair can cast a harmful spell over you and control your actions. There is always interest and news in magic. Almost every era has its new magic, black or white, and its new magician. Moses had his magic: he smote the rock and water gushed out. Christ had his magic: he turned water into wine and raised the dead to life. Coué had his magic word formula. Mrs. Eddy had a similar one.

Magic lives forever. As time goes on, all of these critically undigested, innumerably told tales get woven into the folk lore of the people. Folk lore in turn gets organized into religions. Religions get caught up into the political and economic network of the country. Then they are used as tools. The public is forced to accept all of the old wives' tales, and it passes them on as gospel to its children's children.

The extent to which most of us are shot through with a savage background is almost unbelievable. Few of us escape it. Not even a college education seems to correct it. If anything, it seems to strengthen it, since the colleges themselves are filled with instructors who have the same background. Some of our greatest biologists, physicists, and chemists, when outside of their laboratories, fall back upon folk lore which has become crystallized into religious concepts. These concepts – these heritages of a timid savage past – have made the emergence and growth of scientific psychology extremely difficult.

AN EXAMPLE OF SUCH CONCEPTS

One example of such a religious concept is that every individual has a *soul* which is separate and distinct from the *body*. This soul is really a part of a supreme being. This ancient view led to the philosophical platform called "dualism." This dogma has been present in human psychology from earliest antiquity. No one has ever touched a soul, or seen one in a test tube, or has in any way come into relationship with it as he has with the other objects of his daily experience. Nevertheless, to doubt its existence is to become a heretic and once might possibly even have led to the loss of one's head. Even today the man holding a public position dare not question it.

With the development of the physical sciences which came with the renaissance, a certain release from this stifling soul cloud was obtained. A man could think of astronomy, of the celestial bodies and their motions, of gravitation and the like, without involving soul. Although the early scientists were as a rule devout Christians, nevertheless they began to leave soul out of their test tubes.

Psychology and philosophy, however, in dealing as they thought with non-material objects, found it difficult to escape the language of the church, and hence the concept of mind or soul as distinct from the body came down almost unchanged in essence to the latter part of the nineteenth century.

Wundt, the real father of experimental psychology, unquestionably wanted in 1879 a scientific psychology. He grew up in the midst of a dualistic philosophy of the most pronounced type. He could not see his way clear to a solution of the mind-body problem. His psychology, which has reigned supreme to the present day, is necessarily a compromise. He substituted the term *consciousness* for the term soul. Consciousness is not quite so unobservable as soul. We observe it by peeking in suddenly and catching it unawares as it were *(introspection)*.

Wundt had an immense following. Just as now it is fashionable to go to Vienna to study psychoanalysis under Freud, just so was it fashionable some 40 years ago to study at Leipzig with Wundt. The men who returned founded the laboratories at Johns Hopkins University, the University of Pennsylvania, Columbia, Clark and Cornell. All were equipped to do battle with the elusive (almost soul-like) thing called consciousness.

To show how unscientific is the main concept behind this great German-American school of psychology, look for a moment at William James' definition of psychology. "Psychology is the description and explanation of states of consciousness as such." Starting with a definition which *assumes* what he starts out to prove, he escapes his difficulty by an *argumentum ad hominem*. Consciousness – Oh, yes, everybody must know what this "consciousness" is. When we have a sensation of red, a perception, a thought, when we *will* to do something, or when we *purpose* to do something, or when we desire to do something, we are being *conscious*.

All other introspectionists are equally illogical. In other words, they do not tell us what consciousness is, but merely begin to put things into it by assumption; and then when they come to analyze consciousness, naturally they find in it just what they put into it. Consequently, in the analyses of consciousness made by certain of the psychologists you find such elements as *sensations* and their ghosts, the *images*. With others you find not only sensations, but so-called *affective elements;* in still others you find such elements as *will* – the so-called *conative element* in consciousness. With some psychologists you find many hundreds of sensations of a certain type; others maintain that only a few of that type exist. And so it goes. Literally hundreds of thousands of printed pages have been published on the minute analysis of this intangible something called "consciousness." And how do we begin work upon it? Not by analyzing it as we would a chemical compound, or the way a plant grows. No, those things are material things. This thing we call consciousness can be analyzed only by *introspection* – a looking in on what takes place inside of us.

As a result of this major assumption that there is

such a thing as consciousness and that we can analyze it by introspection, we find as many analyses as there are individual psychologists. There is no way of experimentally attacking and solving psychological problems and standardizing methods.

THE ADVENT OF THE BEHAVIORISTS

In 1912 the objective psychologists or behaviorists reached the conclusion that they could no longer be content to work with Wundt's formulations. They felt that the 30 odd barren years since the establishment of Wundt's laboratory had proved conclusively that the so-called introspective psychology of Germany was founded upon wrong hypotheses – that no psychology which included the religious mind-body problem could ever arrive at verifiable conclusions. They decided either to give up psychology or else to make it a natural science. They saw their brother-scientists making progress in medicine, in chemistry, in physics. Every new discovery in those fields was of prime importance; every new element isolated in one laboratory could be isolated in some other laboratory; each new element was immediately taken up in the warp and woof of science as a whole. One need only mention wireless, radium, insulin, thyroxin, to verify this. Elements so isolated and methods so formulated immediately began to function in human achievement.

In his first efforts to get uniformity in subject matter and in methods the behaviorist began his own formulation of the problem of psychology by sweeping aside all medieval conceptions. He dropped from his scientific vocabulary all subjective terms such as sensation, perception, image, desire, purpose, and even thinking and emotion as they were subjectively defined.

THE BEHAVIORIST'S PLATFORM

The behaviorist asks: Why don't we make what we can *observe* the real field of psychology? Let us limit ourselves to things that can be observed, and formulate laws concerning only those things. Now what can we observe? We can observe *behavior – what the organism does or says*. And let us point out at once: that *saying* is doing – that is, *behaving*. Speaking overtly or to ourselves (thinking) is just as objective a type of behavior as baseball.

The rule, or measuring rod, which the behaviorist puts in front of him always is: Can I describe this bit of behavior I see in terms of "stimulus and response"? By stimulus we mean any object in the general environment or any change in the tissues themselves due to the physiological condition of the animal, such as the change we get when we keep an animal from sex activity, when we keep it from feeding, when we keep it from building a nest. By response we mean anything the animal does – such as turning toward or away from a light, jumping at a sound, and more highly organized activities such as building a skyscraper, drawing plans, having babies, writing books, and the like.

SOME SPECIFIC PROBLEMS OF THE BEHAVIORISTS

You will find, then, the behaviorist working like any other scientist. His sole object is to gather facts about behavior – verify his data – subject them both to logic and to mathematics (the tools of every scientist). He brings the new-born individual *into his experimental nursery* and begins to set problems: What is the baby doing now? What is the stimulus that makes him behave this way ? He finds that the stimulus of tickling the cheek brings the response of turning the mouth to the side stimulated. The stimulus of the nipple brings out the sucking response. The stimulus of a rod placed on the palm of the hand brings closure of the hand and the suspension of the whole body by that hand and arm if the rod is raised. Stimulating the infant with a rapidly moving shadow across the eye will not produce blinking until the individual is sixty-five days of age. Stimulating the infant with an apple or stick of candy or any other object will not call out attempts at reaching until the baby is around 120 days of age. Stimulating a properly brought up infant at any age with snakes, fish, darkness, burning paper, birds, cats, dogs, monkeys, will not bring out that type of response which we call "fear" (which to be objective we might call reaction "X") which is a catching of the breath, a stiffening of the whole body, a turning away of the body from the source of stimulation, a running or crawling away from it....

On the other hand, there are just two things which will call out a fear response, namely, a loud sound, and loss of support.

Now the behaviorist finds from observing children brought up *outside of his nursery* that hundreds of these objects will call out fear responses. Consequently, the scientific question arises: If at birth only two stimuli will call out fear, how do all these other things ever finally come to call it out? Please note that the question is not a speculative one. It can be answered by experiments, and the experiments can be reproduced and the same findings can be had in every other laboratory if the original observation is sound. Convince yourself of this by making a simple test.

If you will take a snake, mouse or dog and show it to a baby who has never seen these objects or been frightened in other ways, he begins to manipulate it, poking at this, that or the other part. Do this for ten days until you are logically certain that the child will always go toward the dog and never run away from it (positive reaction) and that it does not call out a fear response at any time. In contrast to this, pick up a steel bar and strike upon it loudly behind the infant's head. Immediately the fear response is called forth. Now try this: At the instant you show him the animal and just as he begins to reach for it, strike the steel bar behind his head. Repeat the experiment three or four times. A new and important change is apparent. The animal now calls out the same response as the steel bar, namely a fear response. We call this, in behavioristic psychology, the *conditioned emotional response* – a form of *conditioned reflex*.

Our studies of conditioned reflexes make it easy for us to account for the child's fear of the dog on a thoroughly natural science basis without lugging in consciousness or any other so-called mental process. A dog comes toward the child rapidly, jumps upon him, pushes him down and at the same time barks loudly. Often times one such combined stimulation is all that is necessary to make the baby run away from the dog the moment it comes within his range of vision.

There are many other types of conditioned emotional responses, such as those connected with *love* where the mother by petting the child, rocking, it, stimulating its sex organs in bathing, and the like, calls out the embrace, gurgling and crowing as an unlearned original response. Soon this response becomes conditioned. The mere sight of the mother calls out the same kind of response as actual bodily contacts. In *rage* we get a similar set of facts.

The stimulus of holding the infant's moving members brings out the original unlearned response we call rage. Soon the mere sight of a nurse who handles a child badly throws the child into a fit. Thus we see how relatively simple our emotional responses are in the beginning and how terribly complicated home life soon makes them.

The behaviorist has his problems with the adult as well. What methods shall we use systematically to condition the adult? For example, to teach him business habits, scientific habits? Both manual habits (technique and skill) and laryngeal habits (habits of speech and thought) must be formed and tied together before the task of learning is complete. After these work habits are formed, what system of changing stimuli shall we surround him with in order to keep his level of efficiency high and constantly rising? In addition to vocational habits, there comes the problem of his emotional life. How much of it is carried over from childhood? What part of it interferes with his present adjustment? How can we make him lose this part of it; that is, uncondition him where unconditioning is necessary, and condition him where conditioning is necessary? Indeed we know all too little about the amount and kind of emotional or, better, visceral habits (by this term we mean that our stomach, intestines, breathing, and circulation become conditioned – form habits) that should be formed. We do know that they are formed in large numbers and that they are important.

Probably more adults in this universe of ours suffer vicissitudes in family life and in business activities because of poor and insufficient visceral habits than through the lack of technique and skill in manual and verbal accomplishments. One of the large problems in big organizations today is that of personality adjustments. The young men and young women entering business organizations have plenty of skill to do their work but they fail because they do not know how to get along with other people.

DOES THIS BEHAVIORISTIC APPROACH LEAVE ANYTHING OUT OF PSYCHOLOGY?

After so brief a survey of the behavioristic approach to the problems of psychology, one is inclined to say: "Why, yes, it is worth while to study human behavior in this way, but the study of behavior is not the whole of psychology. It leaves out too much. Don't I have sensations, perceptions, conceptions? Do I not forget things and remember things, imagine things, have visual images and auditory images of things I once have seen and heard? Can I not see and hear things that I have never seen or heard in nature? Can I not be attentive or inattentive? Can I not will to do a thing or will not to do it, as the case may be? Do not certain things arouse pleasure in me, and others displeasure? Behaviorism is trying to rob us of everything we have believed in since earliest childhood."

Having been brought up on introspective psychology, as most of us have, you naturally ask these questions and you will find it hard to put away the old terminology and begin to formulate your psychological life in terms of behaviorism. Behaviorism is new wine and it will not go into old bottles. It is advisable for the time being to allay your natural antagonism and accept the behavioristic platform at least until you get more deeply into it. Later you will find that you have progressed so far with behaviorism that the questions you now raise will answer themselves in a perfectly satisfactory natural science way. Let me hasten to add that if the behaviorist were to ask you what you mean by the subjective terms you have been in the habit of using he could soon make you tongue-tied with contradictions. He could even convince you that you do not know what you mean by them. You have been using them uncritically as a part of your social and literary tradition.

TO UNDERSTAND BEHAVIORISM BEGIN TO OBSERVE PEOPLE

This is the fundamental starting point of behaviorism. You will soon find that instead of self-observation being the easiest and most natural way of studying psychology, it is an impossible one; you can observe in yourselves only the most elementary forms of response. You will find, on the other hand, that when you begin to study what your neighbor is doing, you will rapidly become proficient in giving a reason for his behavior and in setting situations (presenting stimuli) that will make him behave in a predictable manner.

DEFINITION OF BEHAVIORISM

Definitions are not as popular today as they once were. The definition of any one science, physics, for example, would necessarily include the definition of all other sciences. And the same is true of behaviorism. About all that we can do in the way of defining a science at the present time is to mark a ring around that part of the whole of natural science that we claim particularly as our own.

Behaviorism, as you have already grasped from our preliminary discussion, is, then, a natural science that takes the whole field of human adjustments as its own. Its closest scientific companion is physiology. Indeed you may wonder, as we proceed, whether behaviorism can be differentiated from that science. It is different from physiology only in the grouping of its problems, not in fundamentals or in central viewpoint. Physiology is particularly interested in the functioning of parts of the animal – for example, its digestive system, the circulatory system, the nervous system, the excretory systems, the mechanics of neural and muscular response. Behaviorism, on the other hand, while it is intensely interested in all of the functioning of these parts, is intrinsically interested in what the whole animal will do from morning to night and from night to morning.

The interest of the behaviorist in man's doings is more than the interest of the spectator – he wants to control man's reactions as physical scientists want to control and manipulate other natural phenomena. It is the business of behavioristic psychology to be able to predict and to control human activity. To do this it must gather scientific data by experimental methods. Only then can the trained behaviorist predict, given the stimulus, what reaction will take place; or, given the reaction, state what the situation or stimulus is that has caused the reaction.

Let us look for a moment more closely at the two terms – stimulus and response.

WHAT IS A STIMULUS?

If I suddenly flash a strong light in your eye, your pupil will contract rapidly. If I were suddenly to shut off all light in the room in which you are sitting, the pupil would begin to widen. If a pistol shot were suddenly fired behind you you would jump and possibly turn your head around. If hydrogen sulphide were suddenly released in your sitting room you would begin to hold your nose and possibly even seek to leave the room. If I suddenly made the room very warm, you would begin to unbutton your coat and perspire. If I suddenly made it cold, another response would take place.

Again, on the inside of us we have an equally large realm in which stimuli can exert their effect. For example, just before dinner the muscles of your stomach begin to contract and expand rhythmically because of the absence of food. As soon as food is eaten those contractions cease. By swallowing a small balloon and attaching it to a recording instrument we can easily register the response of the stomach to lack of food and note the lack of response when food is present. In the male, at any rate, the pressure of certain fluids (semen) may lead to sex activity. In the case of the female possibly the presence of certain chemical bodies can lead in a similar way to overt sex behavior. The muscles of our arms and legs and trunk are not only subject to stimuli coming from the blood; they are also stimulated by their own responses – that is, the muscle is under constant tension; any increase in that tension, as when a movement is made, gives rise to a stimulus which leads to another response in that same muscle or in one in some distant part of the body; any decrease in that tension, as when the muscle is relaxed, similarly gives rise to a stimulus.

So we see that the organism is constantly assailed by stimuli – which come through the eye, the ear, the nose and the mouth – the so-called objects of our environment; at the same time the inside of our body is likewise assailed at every movement by stimuli arising from changes in the tissues themselves. Don't get the idea, please, that the inside of your body is different from or any more mysterious than the outside of your body.

Through the process of evolution human beings have put on sense organs – specialized areas where special types of stimuli are most effective – such as the eye, the ear, the nose, the tongue, the skin and semi-circular canals. To these must be added the whole muscular system, both the striped muscles (for example, the large red muscles of arms, legs and trunks) and the unstriped muscles (those, for example, which make up the hollow tube-like structures of the stomach and intestines and blood vessels). The muscles are thus not only organs of

response – they are sense organs as well. You will see as we proceed that the last two systems play a tremendous role in the behavior of the human being. Many of our most intimate and personal reactions are due to stimuli set up by tissue changes in our striped muscles and in our viscera.

HOW TRAINING ENLARGES THE RANGE OF STIMULI

One of the problems of behaviorism is what might be called the ever-increasing range of stimuli to which an individual responds. Indeed so marked is this that you might be tempted at first sight to doubt the formulation we gave above, namely, that response can be predicted. If you will watch the growth and development of behavior in the human being, you will find that while a great many stimuli will produce a response in the new-born, many other stimuli will not. At any rate they do not call out the same response they later call out. For example, you don't get very far by showing a new-born infant a crayon, a piece of paper, or the printed score of a Beethoven symphony. In other words, habit formation has to come in before certain stimuli can become effective. Later we shall take up the procedure by means of which we can get stimuli which do not ordinarily call out responses to call them out. The general term we use to describe this is "conditioning"....

It is conditioning from earliest childhood on that makes the problem of the behaviorist in predicting what a given response will be so difficult. The sight of a horse does not ordinarily produce the fear response, and yet among almost every group of thirty to forty people there is one person who will walk a block to avoid coming near a horse. While the study of behaviorism will never enable its students to look at you and predict that such a state of affairs exists, nevertheless if the behaviorist sees that reaction taking place, it is very easy for him to state approximately what the situation was in the early experience of such a one that brought about this unusual type of adult response. In spite of the difficulty of predicting responses in detail we live in general upon the theory that we can predict what our neighbor will do. There is no other basis upon which we can live with our fellow men.

WHAT THE BEHAVIORIST MEANS BY RESPONSE

We have already brought out the fact that from birth to death the organism is being assailed by stimuli on the outside of the body and by stimuli arising in the body itself. Now the organism does something when it is assailed by stimuli. It responds. It moves. The response may be so slight that it can be observed only by the use of instruments. The response may confine itself merely to a change in respiration, or to an increase or decrease in blood pressure. It may call out merely a movement of the eye. The more commonly observed responses, however, are movements of the whole body, movements of the arm, leg, trunk, or combinations of all the moving parts.

Usually the response that the organism makes to a stimulus brings about an adjustment, though not always. By an adjustment we mean merely that the organism by moving so alters its physiological state that the stimulus no longer arouses reaction. This may sound a bit complicated, but examples will clear it up. If I am hungry, stomach contractions begin to drive me ceaselessly to and fro. If, in these restless seeking movements, I spy apples on a tree, I immediately climb the tree and pluck the apples and begin to eat. When surfeited, the stomach contractions cease. Although there are apples still hanging round about me, I no longer pluck and eat them. Again, the cold air stimulates me. I move around about until I am out of the wind. In the open I may even dig a hole. Having escaped the wind, it no longer stimulates me to further action. Under sex excitement the male may go to any length to capture a willing female. Once sex activity has been completed the restless seeking movements disappear. The female no longer stimulates the male to sex activity.

The behaviorist has often been criticized for this emphasis upon response. Some psychologists seem to have the notion that the behaviorist is interested only in the recording of minute muscular responses. Nothing could be further from the truth. Let me emphasize again that the behaviorist is primarily interested in the behavior of the whole man. From morning to night he watches him perform his daily round of duties. If it is brick-laying, he would like to measure the number of bricks he can lay under different conditions, how long he can go without

dropping from fatigue, how long it takes him to learn his trade, whether we can improve his efficiency or get him to do the same amount of work in a less period of time. In other words, the response the behaviorist is interested in is the commonsense answer to the question "what is he doing and why is he doing it?" Surely with this as a general statement, no one can distort the behaviorist's platform to such an extent that it can be claimed that the behaviorist is merely a muscle physiologist.

The behaviorist claims that there is a response to every effective stimulus and that the response is immediate. By effective stimulus we mean that it must be strong enough to overcome the normal resistance to the passage of the sensory impulse from sense organs to muscles. Don't get confused at this point by what the psychologist and the psycho-analyst sometimes tell you. If you read their statements, you are likely to believe that the stimulus can be applied today and produce its effect maybe the next day, maybe within the next few months, or years. The behaviorist doesn't believe in any such mythological conception. It is true that I can give the verbal stimulus to you "Meet me at the Ritz tomorrow for lunch at one o'clock." Your immediate response is "All right, I'll be there." Now what happens after that? We will not cross this difficult bridge now, but may I point out that we have in our verbal habits a mechanism by means of which the stimulus is reapplied from moment to moment until the final reaction occurs, namely going to the Ritz at one o'clock the next day.

GENERAL CLASSIFICATION OF RESPONSE

The two commonsense classifications of response are "external" and "internal" – or possibly the terms "overt" (explicit) and "implicit" are better. By external or overt responses we mean the ordinary doings of the human being: he stoops to pick up a tennis ball, he writes a letter, he enters an automobile and starts driving, he digs a hole in the ground, he sits down to write a lecture, or dances, or flirts with a woman, or makes love to his wife. We do not need instruments to make these observations. On the other hand, responses may be wholly confined to the muscular and glandular systems inside the body. A child or hungry adult may be standing stock still in front of a window filled with pastry. Your first exclamation may be "He isn't doing anything" or "He is just looking at the pastry." An instrument would show that his salivary glands are pouring out secretions, that his stomach is rhythmically contracting and expanding, and that marked changes in blood pressure are taking place – that the endocrine glands are pouring substances into the blood. The internal or implicit responses are difficult to observe, not because they are inherently different from the external or overt responses, but merely because they are hidden from the eye.

Another general classification is that of *learned* and *unlearned* responses. I brought out the fact above that the range of stimuli to which we react is ever increasing. The behaviorist has found by his study that most of the things we see the adult doing are really learned. We used to think that a lot of them were instinctive, that is, "unlearned." But we are now almost at the point of throwing away the word "instinct." Still there are a lot of things we do that we do not have to learn – to perspire, to breathe, to have our heart beat, to have digestion take place, to have our eyes turn toward a source of light, to have our pupils contract, to show a fear response when a loud sound is given. Let us keep as our second classification then "learned responses," and make it include all of our complicated habits and all of our conditioned responses; and "unlearned" responses, and mean by that all of the things that we do in earliest infancy before the processes of conditioning and habit formation get the upper hand.

Another purely logical way to classify responses is to designate them by the sense organ which initiates them. We could thus have a *visual unlearned response* – for example, the turning of the eye of the youngster at birth toward a source of light. Contrast this with a *visual learned response,* the response, for example, to a printed score of music or a word. Again, we could have a *kinaesthetic*[1] *unlearned response* when the infant reacts by crying to a long sustained twisted position of the arm. We could have a *kinaesthetic learned response* when we manipulate a delicate object in the dark or, for example, tread a tortuous maze. Again, we

can have a *visceral unlearned response* as, for example, when stomach contractions due to the absence of food in the 3 day old infant will produce crying. Contrast this with the learned or visceral *conditioned* response where the sight of pastry in a baker's window will cause the mouth of the hungry schoolboy to water.

This discussion of stimulus and response shows what material we have to work with in behavioristic psychology and why behavioristic psychology has as its goal *to be able, given the stimulus, to predict the response* – or, *seeing the reaction take place to state what the stimulus is that has called out the reaction.*

IS BEHAVIORISM MERELY A METHODOLOGICAL APPROACH TO THE STUDY OF PSYCHOLOGICAL PROBLEMS, OR IS IT AN ACTUAL SYSTEM OF PSYCHOLOGY?

If psychology can do without the terms "mind" and "consciousness," indeed if it can find no objective evidence for their existence, what is going to become of philosophy and the so-called social sciences which today are built around the concept of mind and consciousness? Almost every day the behaviorist is asked this question, sometimes in a friendly inquiring way, and sometimes not so kindly. While behaviorism was fighting for its existence it was afraid to answer this question. Its contentions were too new; its field too unworked for it to allow itself even to think that some day it might be able to stand up and to tell philosophy and the social sciences that they, too, must scrutinize anew their own premises. Hence the behaviorist's one answer when approached in this way was to say, "I can't let myself worry about such questions now. Behaviorism is at present a satisfactory way of going at the solution of psychological problems – it is really a methodological approach to psychological problems." Today behaviorism is strongly entrenched. It finds its way of going at the study of psychological problems and its formulation of its results growing more and more adequate.

---

1   By kinaesthetic we mean the muscle sense. Our muscles are supplied with sensory nerve endings. When we move the muscles these sensory nerve endings are stimulated. Thus the stimulus in the kinaesthetic or muscle sense is a *movement of the muscle itself.*

It may never make a pretense of being a *system*. Indeed systems in every scientific field are out of date. We collect our facts from observation. Now and then we select a group of facts and draw certain general conclusions about them. In a few years as new experimental data are gathered by better methods, even these tentative general conclusions have to be modified. Every scientific field, zoology, physiology, chemistry and physics, is more or less in a state of flux. Experimental technique, the accumulation of facts by that technique, occasional tentative consolidation of these facts into a theory or an hypothesis describe our procedure in science. Judged upon this basis, behaviorism is a true natural science.

Bibliography

Broadbent, D.E. *Behaviorism*. London: Methuen, 1961.

Russell, Bertrand. *An Outline of Philosophy*. Cleveland and New York: Meridian Books, 1960. [originally published 1927]

Ryle, Gilbert. *The Concept of Mind*. London: Hutchinson, 1949.

Skinner, B.F. *About Behaviorism*. New York: Vintage, 1974.

Skinner, B.F. *Science and Human Behavior*. New York: Macmillan, 1953.

Tolman, Edward Chace. *Behavior and Psychological Man*. Berkeley and Los Angeles: University of California Press, 1966. [originally published 1951]

It is debatable whether a theory like connectionism properly has a place among theories of human nature. Connectionism purports to provide a theoretical framework, and concrete empirical postulates, for understanding how the human brain works, or more specifically, how it manages to be a thinking machine. No one nowadays – possibly some behaviourists of severely classical type excepted – disputes *that* human mental activity takes place, and no one seriously disputes that it is by means of the physical brain that it does so. It will, as a result, not be contentious that there are *means*, instrumentalities, whereby the brain does what it does. There is a *how*, as well as a that; and there can hardly be an objection in principle to the possibility of human science coming to learn something, or much, of what that *how* is. But, it may be held, specific scientific proposals for what the mechanics of our cerebral engineering is will not, as such, yield a vision of humankind, or, indeed, results which have impact, one way or the other, on any genuine vision of humankind. The how of how we do it should be available to, at any rate compatible with, *any* serious modern understanding of human nature (including views that are strongly non-psychological in orientation).

Connectionism nonetheless finds its place here because it at least appears to imply that something which all other views assume, is an illusion: the idea that there is a single unified self in at least typical human cases. If connectionism were true, then – so it seems – something humans, and human nature theories, broadly suppose is wrong. Human beings would be sophisticated automata, without a central pilot, or seat of subjectivity – for that is (part of) what connectionism evidently affirms. On the other hand some might argue that this way of *putting* things is simply an unfortunate or misleading feature of some current expositions of connectionism, and that the core idea is better grasped as trying to explain what a core self really is and how it is formed, and functions – and not to eliminate it.

At any rate the student of human nature theory deserves to know about connectionism, and to make up his or her mind on its connections to the subject. Here is Margaret A. Boden (b. 1936), a particularly clear proponent of the theory. She is Chairperson of the Department of Philosophy at the University of Sussex. Her areas of specialization are artificial intelligence and the philosophy of mind, and she is the author of several books in these fields.

Margaret A. Boden, *Artificial Intelligence in Psychology*

(Source: Margaret A. Boden. *Artificial Intelligence in Psychology: Interdisciplinary Essays.* Cambridge: MIT Press, 1989. 1-14.)

The Countess of Lovelace was notorious in her lifetime as the daughter of the scandalous Lord Byron, the wife of the progressive Earl of Lovelace, and the champion of the eccentric engineer Charles Babbage. A century later, her fame is due to friend rather than to family. She is remembered primarily as Babbage's amanuensis, as a ghost-writer capable of appreciating the broader implications (if not all the mathematical details [Stein, 1985]) of his work. For Babbage's mid-nineteenth century designs of "Analytical Engines" specified precursors of the machines now being used in computer science [Hyman, 1982].

Psychologists, in particular, recall Ada Lovelace's clear expression of the insight that a machine – of a type essentially comparable to a digital computer – "might act upon other things besides numbers *were objects found whose mutual fundamental relations could be expressed by those of the abstract science of operations, and which should also be susceptible of adaptations to the action of the operating notation and mechanism of the engine.*"

For many theoretical psychologists today believe that the relevant "abstract science of operations" is that branch of computer science known as artificial intelligence (AI), for whose "engines" computer programs provide the "operating notation." And they claim that those "other things" of which the Countess spoke could in principle include not only (as she herself suggested) the composition of "elaborate and scientific pieces of music of any degree of complexity or extent" but also many other – some would say, all other – phenomena generated by the human mind. Accordingly, they believe that AI-concepts can contribute to the substantive content of theories about human (and animal) psychology, and that the coherence and implications of these theories can be rigorously tested if they are expressed as computer programs to be run on functioning machines. Much as Lady Lovelace claimed that Babbage's Analytical Engine *"weaves algebraic patterns just as the Jacquard-loom weaves flowers and leaves,"* so her modern admirers see the mind's rich tapestry as a mass of psychological patterns woven from computational thread.

In short, psychologists inspired by AI-ideas ("computational" psychologists) assume that Ada Lovelace was essentially correct. This assumption underlies the three broad respects in which all such psychologists agree.

They adopt a functionalist approach to the mind, defining mental states in terms of their causal effects (on other mental states and behaviour) and seeking to identify mental processes with specific effective procedures. They see the mind as a representational system, psychology being the study of the various computational processes whereby mental representations are constructed, organized, interpreted, and transformed. And third, they approach neuroscience with computational questions in mind, asking what sorts of logical operations or functional relations are embodied in the brain (rather than which brain-cells do the embodying, and how their physiology makes this embodiment possible).

There are many disagreements, however, about precisely how various psychological phenomena are to be explained in computational terms. Some disputes, occurring against a considerable background of shared theoretical analysis, can be resolved by testing in organisms and/or artefacts; many arguments about the details of low-level vision, or 2D-to-3D mapping, can be so settled. Others involve controversy about the basic theoretical categories appropriate to a certain domain; for instance, theories and computer models of parsing do not all rely on the same underlying grammar. There are "internal" differences, too, over the potential scope of a computational science of the mind: emotions, motivation, belief – and even cryptarithmetic – have each been despaired of by someone of this persuasion (not to mention psychologists of other, non-computational, persuasions). In general, researchers disagree about which particular AI concepts, and which of the various computer-modelling methodologies, are likely to be the most useful from the psychologist's point of view.

Among the things about which computational psychologists – and AI-workers too – differ among themselves is the issue of just how important is the brain's particular way of embodying the mind. Can thought and action be generated only by systems whose basic architecture is brainlike, involving parallel-processing within networks of associated cells? Must the physical properties and organization of any thinking machine, whether in Malibu or on Mars, be fundamentally like the brain? Or could a creature (whether organism or artefact) enjoy comparable psychological powers embodied in an utterly different manner?

Lady Lovelace surmised that some such powers could be attributed not only to biological creatures, but to technological ones too. However, ideas about the potential of technology cannot be demonstrated in practice until the requisite technology exists. Babbage's most ambitious Analytical Engines never left the drawing-board, for even his creative expertise in precision-tooling could not build functional moving-part engines to his own abstract specifications. Likewise, Alan Turing a century later described an abstract machine (a "universal Turing machine") capable of computing any computable function – but he could not (yet) build a useful approximation to it. Such approximations were soon to be built, however (by Turing himself, among others), taking advantage of mid-twentieth century developments in electronics. (Actual machines can at best approximate a universal Turing machine, because this mathematically-defined computational system stores its symbols on an infinite tape.)

Today, the digital computer based on John von Neumann's designs of the 1940's – and fundamentally similar in several ways to Babbage's plans for Analytical Engines (the first of which was drafted over a century earlier) – is a familiar dimension of life in industrialized countries. Artificial intelligence research – indeed, computer science in general – has been done almost without exception on digital computers.

This is true not only of technological projects, but of computer simulations of mental processes too. Virtually all the computer models regarded by psychologists as relevant to mental life are implemented on von Neumann machines. Moreover, many of the theories propounded by computational psychologists show the conceptual influence of this particular technology. For computational concepts drawn from artificial intelligence were developed in the context of research using the von Neumann machine, with its strictly serial processing of precisely-locatable binary symbols. Such concepts and associated theories may be termed formalist, since they assume that *computation* and *representation* necessarily involve symbol-manipulation defined in terms of formal rules.

However, some psychological theories developed within the computationalist persuasion posit mental processes of a type better-suited to "engines" of a very different kind: namely, brains. From the very earliest days of the digital computer, some people used them to simulate machines engaged in the parallel processing of probabilistic, and continuously varying, information. Now, the digital computer is increasingly used in this way, to model brain-like, "connectionist," information-processing systems whose computational properties differ significantly from those of more familiar sorts of programs.

For example, various forms of "parallel distributed processing" (PDP) systems are being investigated in which a pattern, concept, or representa-tion is not stored at any particular (addressable) place in the machine but in an entire network of continually interacting computational units [Rumelhart & McClelland, 1986a]. The units either reinforce or inhibit their neighbours' activity – much as interconnected nerve-cells do. The connections between the units can be (though as yet rarely are) implemented as hardwired links, or they can be programmed (simulated on a von Neumann machine). In either case, the behaviour of the system as a whole emerges from the myriad excitatory and inhibitory connections between its constituent units.

Such a system may be broadly compared with a classroom full of children, each of whom chatters continuously with her neighbours about some detail relevant to the interpretation, or decision, which the class is trying to achieve. A child's current opinion can be directly reinforced or inhibited by the messages she receives from her immediate neighbours. But because her neighbours are communicating directly with children in other desks, who in turn are talking to peers in yet more distant places, her opinion can be indirectly affected by every child in the room who has something relevant to say. Each child repeatedly rnodifies her opinion in the light of what her neighbours say (the desks are arranged so that children holding opinions on the same topic, or on closely relevant topics, are seated near to each other). Eventually, all the children's (confidently-held) opinions come to be mutually consistent. The final interpretation or decision is not made by any one child (there is no "class captain," sitting at an identifiable desk) but by the entire collectivity, being embodied as the overall pattern of mutually-consistent mini-opinions held (with high confidence) within the classroom.

The resultant decision is thus due to the *parallel processing* (all the children chatter simultaneously) of *localized computations* (each child speaks to, and is directly influenced by, only her immediate neighbours), and is *distributed* across the whole system (as an internally consistent set of mini-decisions made by all the children).

This broad analogy can be refined by distinguishing various types of classroom [Boden, 1987, chs. 3 & 7]. For instance, each child may be able to say only "yes" or "no"; or she may be able to differentiate varying degrees of "maybe." Again, each child may always pronounce only opinions consistent with the evidence available to her; or she may sometimes venture an opinion unrelated to the evidence, a sort of random epistemic hiccup. (Nerve cells "hiccup" too: the stochastic nature of neuronal activity has been recognized since the 1950's [Burns, 1968].) The children may have overlapping interests, in that they are sensitive to partially-shared evidence; or they may not. (Many biological cells share evidence: thus retinal cells have overlapping receptive fields.) And the children's individual judgments may be more, or less, finely tuned. (A neurone's range of inputs may be large or small; the receptive fields of retinal cells are not near-approximations to points, but have an appreciable size.)

Diverse classrooms are comparable with connectionist systems having distinct computational properties – some of which may be surprising. Thus a roomful of hiccupping children is in principle (though not in practice) guaranteed to reach the right decision, whereas a class of children who always stick closely to the evidence is not [Hinton & Sejnowski, 1986]. (So stochastic neural activity in the brain may not be "botched" biological engineering, but may convey an evolutionary advantage.) And a decision which involves fine discriminations on several dimensions need not be (though in principle – and sometimes in practice – it can be) carried out by a group of children each of whom is sensitive to only one possible value of only one dimension. Indeed, a complex decision may be more efficiently reached by a smaller classroom containing not very discriminating children (whose interests overlap) than by a much larger classroom of children capable of very finely-tuned individual judgments (each of whom minds only her own business) [Hinton, 1981]. (So the fact that retinal receptors do not respond to stimulus-areas as small as possible may be a strength rather than a weakness.)

Some current investigations of brain-like computational systems are purely abstract or mathematical, as was the later work of Babbage (on Analytical Engines) and the early work of Turing (on universal Turing machines). It is mathematical analysis which proves, for example, that a class of hiccupping children (a "Boltzmann machine") is guaranteed to reach the optimal interpretation eventually. However, "eventually" – as the mathematician understands it – may be a very long, perhaps even an infinite, time. In practice, Boltzmann

machines can be relied on to reach the correct solution only if there is negligible irrelevant information, or noise. Being interested in how finite systems (organisms or computer models) behave in real time, the psychologist needs to know to what extent abstract mathematical analyses of system-competence are practically useful descriptions of actual system-performance. Moreover, an abstract competence-analysis is not always available.

Accordingly, many studies of connectionist computational systems involve empirical explorations of the properties of real "engines." At present, these engines can only be digital computers, programmed to simulate associative networks. But associative hardware of several kinds is now being developed, to serve both technological and theoretical purposes [e.g. Hillis, 1985].

By the turn of the century, the AI-researcher's laboratory will house not only von Neumann computers but various purpose-built parallel machines as well. Some of these, perhaps, may be made not of silicon but of neuroprotein. And their "abstract science of operations" may resemble the equations of thermodynamics (for example) more than the principles of computer science as we know them today. Much as Lady Ada herself could not foresee all the applications of Babbage's visionary ideas, so we cannot know just which mental processes will or will not be modelled when various sorts of associative hardware are routinely available.

Nor do we have an answer with respect to von Neumann architecture, for we cannot specify what computational tasks might actually be effected by such machines. Certainly, digital computers are approximations to universal Turing machines, which can compute any computable function. But a proof that a task could in principle be performed by a certain type of computational system (whether digital computer or Boltzmann machine) does not guarantee that it can be successfully tackled by any such system in practice. With respect both to technological artificial intelligence and to AI-influenced psychology, the potential of digital computers has not yet been exhausted and the exploration of connectionist systems has only just begun.

Nevertheless, AI-workers and psychologists alike can already ask some relevant theoretical questions. Some of these concern the relevance of AI-ideas to specific topics, which are of course innumerable (those discussed below include ethology, education, and equilibration). But of those questions which are more general in nature, five broad classes may be distinguished. These deal respectively with: (1) abstract task-analysis; (2) analysis and (3) testing of various computer-models (perhaps comparing their performance with the behaviour of human – and animal – subjects); (4) the relations between formalist and connectionist approaches within computational psychology; and (5) the nature of *computation* as such, and its relevance to *representation* and *understanding*.

The *first* class of questions concerns the computations which must be performed by any system (brainlike or not) capable of performing a certain task. An answer will be relevant to any psychological theory, or computer model, of the task concerned. Competence-analyses have no necessary connection with computational psychology, and may be produced by researchers not wedded to this approach (Chomsky's grammar was not developed by computer modelling). But because of the quasi-mathematical nature of competence analysis, someone engaged in this pursuit is likely to have some sympathy for the computational approach. Moreover, successful task-analyses will be useful for both traditionalist and "non-von" (parallelist) computer modelling. So insights originally developed and/or incorporated within the formalist tradition are now being applied within the connectionist approach. For example, the notion of gradient space – first formulated within the formalist programme of "scene analysis," whose task was to interpret line-drawings in three-dimensional terms [Mackworth, 1973, 1983] – has been used within parallel-processing theories of low-level vision [Marr, 1982].

A large proportion of work in computational psychology addresses the *second* and *third* types of question, in that it uses both abstract argument and empirical testing of computer models (often backed up by observation of human behaviour) to study the varying computational and representational properties of distinct types of system. For instance, one can investigate various methods of knowledge-representation (semantic nets, scripts, frames, production systems, and so on) in formalist computer models – and in human subjects too. Or one can analyse and explore models, often incorporating similar theoretical ideas, based on diverse forms of connectionism (different sorts of classroom).

The computational advantage of epistemic hiccupping, and the relative efficiency of sets of coarsely-tuned and overlapping discriminators, are examples of surprising abstract results in this area. Surprising empirical results (unexpected computer-performance), likewise, are found in both formalist and connectionist models. One formalist example is a filtering algorithm for economizing on computation, which turned out to be far better at avoiding the combinatorial explosion than its programmer had foreseen [Waltz, 1975; Boden, 1987, pp. 222-226]. A connectionist example is a computer model which learns the past tense of English verbs by "hearing" them, and whose learning-pattern shows temporal changes closely comparable to those observed in infant speech [Rumelhart & McClelland, 1986b]. Although its performance is describable by the rules of English past-tense morphology, these rules are neither programmed into it nor explicitly represented in it as a result of its learning. Rather, it develops associative equilibrium-patterns which cause the system to behave *as though* it were following rules of a type which could be (and often are) made explicit in a von Neumann machine. (What is "surprising" of course depends on one's prior knowledge: someone who understands the general principles of the past-tense learner could predict some, though not all, of the performance-patterns observed.)

As for the relations between formalist and connectionist approaches in artificial intelligence, this *fourth* question can take various forms. One can ask, for instance, whether some specific psychological phenomena, as opposed to others, are better understood (and modelled) in formalist or in connectionist terms. The current consensus is that connectionist theory is better-suited to the understanding of pattern-matching (including analogy) and content-addressable memory. Not only can connectionist systems speedily perform complex pattern-recognition tasks which formalist systems cannot, but their performance shows graceful degradation – it gets gradually worse with increasing noise, as the human's does – where formalist models would give utterly inappropriate responses. (Even so, many of the theoretical insights contributing to connectionist models of pattern-matching originated in a formalist context.) By contrast, formalist models seem better-suited to the understanding of certain sorts of reasoning, such as cryptarithmetic. Indeed, a connectionist pattern-matcher may have to simulate a von Neumann machine in order to do arithmetic [Rumelhart, Smolensky,

McClelland, & Hinton, 1986].

Another way of putting the fourth question is to ask whether connectionism is an example of artificial intelligence, or of computational psychology, at all. Are formalist and connectionist approaches close cousins, enjoying a friendly rivalry in a shared family-game? Or are they fundamentally alien contestants for the prize of understanding the mind?

Some critics of AI's influence on psychology describe recent parallelist models as a potentially "devastating" challenge to conventional computational psychology, and to conventional AI itself [Dreyfus & Dreyfus, in press]. Similarly, connectionist computer-modelers sometimes argue that ideas drawn from AI work on von Neumann machines have fundamentally misled psychologists for the last quarter-century. Indeed, some connectionists describe their approach as "a radical departure from the symbolic paradigm," and assign it to "the sub-symbolic paradigm," instead [Smolensky, 1987, p.101].

However, the "radical departure" of connectionism is not the adoption of a radically incommensurable viewpoint, as would be required for it to constitute a distinct paradigm [Kuhn, 1962]. Rather, it is a change of emphasis with respect to some relatively basic ideas within the general computational approach. Both connectionist and non-connectionist forms of artificial intelligence and of computational psychology owe their origins to the same mid-century ideas about the brain's logical-computational potential [McCulloch & Pitts, 1943]. This seminal work not only led to pioneering connectionist research on neural nets [Rosenblatt, 1958,1962] but also influenced von Neumann in his design of the digital computer. Moreover, many ideas about the computational structure of mental tasks that were originally developed within the von Neumann context have contributed to the design of parallel-processing systems.

It is hardly surprising, in view of these facts, that some leading connectionists insist that "it would be wrong to view distributed representations as an *alternative* to representational schemes like semantic networks or production systems that have been found useful in cognitive psychology and artificial intelligence" [Hinton, McClelland, & Rumelhart, 1986, p. 78; italics in original]. These researchers view PDP-networks rather as "one way of implementing these more abstract schemes in parallel networks," saying that connectionist networks provide powerful pattern-matching operations that can be regarded as "primitives" by psychologists considering higher-level theories implemented (if at all) in more traditional ways.

If computational psychology is a paradigm, then, connectionism should be included as a particular development within it. However, it might be better to avoid the term "paradigm" altogether in this context. A scientific paradigm is largely defined by a sociological criterion, according to which it enjoys the wide, and basically uncritical, acceptance of some entire scientific community. If the relevant community is psychologists at large, then computational psychology does not constitute a paradigm. Many more psychologists ignore, or even oppose, it than profess it (and some of these study those psychological phenomena to which one might expect the computational approach to be relevant, if it is relevant at all). Unless and until this fact changes, the term "paradigm" seems inapplicable purely on sociological grounds.

One might attempt to drive a wedge between the two approaches by reference to the topic of our fifth question: the nature of computation, and of representation. The familiar (formalist) definition of "computation" applies *par excellence* to information-processing in von Neumann machines, which involves the serial application of explicitly stored formal-syntactic rules to explicit, and localizable, symbolic representations. But the information-processes within connectionist models are very different. Are non-sequential, cooperative, and equilibrium-seeking alterations of patterns-of-activity really computations? Are specifications of the progressive self-organization of a network of computational units really *algorithms*? Are information-processing interdependencies that are implicit in the excitatory and inhibitory connections between units really *rules*? Are widely-distributed excitation-patterns really embodiments of *symbols* – or even *representations*? Or does connectionism imply – contrary to the basic assumptions of computational psychology – that there are no representations in the brain (no hardware-independent abstract descriptions), so no question of explaining cognition in terms of representations?

The formalist definition of computation, and of artificial intelligence and computational psychology too, is unnecessarily restrictive. Connectionist systems – like formalist ones – are concerned with information-processing. Formalists sometimes suggest that connectionist theories are concerned with implementation, with "the nervous system's instantiation" of psychological operations [Pylyshyn, 1984, p. 215]. But only if a connectionist system were intended as a neuroscientific model of specific neural circuitry and synaptic interactions would it be a model of implementation, as opposed to information-processing. And connectionist theories satisfy the general criteria of computationalism identified above – albeit in ways which differ from more traditional computer models.

Connectionist systems are not von Neumann machines, in which information-processing rules are explicitly coded within and accessed by the program. But they are designed so as to follow rigorous rules in passing from one state to another, and in seeking an equilibrium. These rules ensure that the patterns of excitation and inhibition in the system vary in a way which reflects significant informational constraints. Such rules are implicit in the system (being implemented as interconnections), and do not enable one to specify precisely "what will happen next" from moment to moment. But their function in determining information-processing justifies their being regarded as a (different) type of algorithm.

Likewise, by means of varying weights and excitation-states, "non-von" machines manipulate symbols – of an unusual kind. In so doing, they may be said to perform computations, for their passage from one symbolic state to another can be mapped onto logical-semantic relations of various kinds. Admittedly, their symbols are implemented very differently from those in a von Neumann computer, and (in an associative machine) are not hardware-independent in the same way. No individual unit implements any identifiable symbol or meaning, for meaningful representations exist only at the level of networks made up of many units. But such (distributed) representations, too, have properties that can be mapped onto abstract relationships of various kinds. And they, too, are able to mediate causal connections with the world, and with other representations and processes internal to the system itself.

The preceding paragraph presupposes a particular sort of answer to the fifth question (concerning the nature of computation). Specifically, it presupposes that meaning, symbolism, representation – and computation too – can be ascribed to a system in virtue of its having certain causal-information

processes going on inside it. Although these processes may be physically implemented, they are not describable in physical terms. Accordingly, the question as to what sort of physical implementation they can have cannot be answered *a priori*. Clearly they can be embodied in the neuroprotein of human and animal brains; possibly, they can be embodied likewise in inorganic materials, such as metal and silicon. The behaviour of the system – above all, its "internal behaviour," describable in information-processing terms – determines whether it computes and understands, and what meanings or semantic contents are represented by it. To compute and to understand are fundamentally similar, which is why computational psychology could give us a science of the mind.

This claim is highly controversial. "Computation" is widely believed (even by many AI-workers and computational psychologists) to exclude semantics. The charge is often made that it therefore cannot possibly explain meaning, representation, or understanding – in a word, intentionality. Since the mind is a source of meanings, and the brain an embodiment of intentionality, theories couched in terms of computation simply cannot (on this view) account for human, or even animal, psychology.

The starting-point for this reasoned rejection of artificial intelligence – and therefore of computational psychology – as a route to the understanding of the mind is the formalist definition of computation (given above), which takes it to be the application of formal-syntactic rules to identifiable symbolic representations. To say that a rule is formal-syntactic is to say that it applies (or not) to the symbol concerned only as a function of the symbol's form. It follows (or so the argument goes) that the symbol's meaning – if indeed it has any – has nothing to do with the application of the rule. A system consisting of such rules, no matter how complex it may be, cannot thereby mean or understand anything: it cannot thereby enjoy intentionality. If it does understand anything, or embody any genuine representation having semantic content, it does so in virtue of some property other than the possession of symbol-manipulating rules. Since a computer program is nothing but a collection of formal-syntactic rules, computer models can never provide an adequate explanation of intentionality.

My response to this charge is that even the simplest computer program has properties which are essential to understanding (though this is not to say that computer programs can "understand" in anything like the familiar sense of the term). Since a program enables a computer to function in specific ways, it is not a mere formal calculus. Rather, it is the basis of a causal nexus of simple, and specifiable, information-processes which are at the same time both sufficiently like and sufficiently unlike the more complex processes involved in genuine understanding to provide an explanation of it [Boden, 1962]. In other words, computer programs provide computers with the beginnings of what in human minds we recognize as intentionality.

Bibliography

Boden, M.A. *Artifical Intelligence and Natural Man.* 2nd ed. expanded. London: MIT Press; New York: Harper and Row (Basic Books), 1987.

Boden, M.A. "The Paradox of Explanation," *Aristotelian Society*, N.S., LXII, 1962, 159-178.

Buris, B.D. *The Uncertain Nervous System.* London: Edward Arnold, 1968.

Dreyfus, S.E., and H.C. Dreyfus. "Towards A Reconciliation of Phenomenology and AI," in D. Partridge and Y.A. Wilks, eds., *Foundational Issues in Artificial Intelligence.* Cambridge: Cambridge University Press, 1990, pp. 471-499.

Hillis, W.D. *The Connection Machine.* Cambridge, Mass.: MIT Press, 1985.

Hinton, G.E. "Shape Representations in Parallel Systems", *Proc. Seventh Int. Joint Conf. Artificial Intelligence*, Vancouver, 1981, 1088-1096.

Hinton, G.E., J.L. McClelland, and D.E. Rumelhart, "Distributed Representations," in D.E. Rumelhart and J.C. McClelland, eds., *Parallel Distributed Processing: Explorations in the Microcontructure of Cognition*, Vol. 1: *Foundations*, Cambridge, Mass.: MIT Press, 1986, pp. 77-109.

Hinton, G.E., and T.J. Sejnoviski. "Learning and Relearning in Boltzmann Machines," in D.E. Rumelhart and J.C. McClelland, eds., *Parallel Distributed Processing: Explorations in the Microcontructure of Cognition*, Vol. 1: *Foundations*, Cambridge, Mass.: MIT Press, 1986, pp. 282-317.

Hyman, A. *Charles Babbage: Pioneer of the Computer.* Oxford: Oxford University Press, 1982.

Kuhn, T.S. *The Structure of Scientific Revolutions.* Chicago: University of Chicago Press, 1962.

Mackworth, A.K. "Interpreting Pictures of Polyhedial Scenes," *Artificial Intelligence*, 4, 1973, 121-138.

Mackworth, A.K. "Constraints, Descriptions, and Domain Mappings in Computational Vision," in O.J. Braddick and A.C. Sleigh, eds., *Physical and Biological Processing of Images.* New York: Springer-Verlag, 1983, pp. 385-392.

Marr, D.C. *Vision: A Computational Investigation into the Human Representation and Processing of Visual Information.* San Francisco: Freeman, 1982.

McCulloch, W.S., and W.H. Pitts, "A Logical Calculus of the Ideas Immanent in Nervous Activity," *Bull. Mathematical Biophysics*, 5, 1943, 115-133.

Pylyshyn, Z.W. *Computation and Cognition: Toward a Foundation for Cognitive Science.* Cambridge, Mass.: MIT Press, 1984.

Rosenblatt, F. *Principles of Neurodynamics.* New York: Spartan, 1962.

Rosenblatt, F. "The Perceptron: A Probabilistic Model for Information Storage and Organization in the Brain," *Psychological Review*, 65, 1958, 386-407.

Rumelhart, D.E., and J.L. McClelland, eds. [1986a] *Parallel Distributed Processing: Exploration in the Microstructure of Cognition*, 2 vols. Cambridge, Mass.: MIT Press, 1986.

Rumelhart, D.E., and J.L. McClelland, eds. [1986b] "On Learning the Past Tenses of English Verbs," in D.E. Rumelhart and J.L. McClelland, eds., *Parallel Distributed Processing: Exploration in th Microstructure of Cognition*, 2 vols. Cambridge, Mass.: MIT Press, 1986, pp. 216-271.

Rumelhart, D.E., P. Smolensky, J.L. McClelland, and G.E. Hinton. "Schemata and Sequential Thought Processes in PDP Models," in D.E. Rumelhart and J.L. McClelland, eds., *Parallel Distributed Processing: Exploration in the Microstructure of Cognition*, Vol. 2: *Psychological and Biological Models.* Cambridge, Mass.: MIT Press, 1986, pp. 7-57.

Smolensky, P. "Connectivist AI, Symbolic AI, and the Brain," *AI Review*, 1, 1987, 95-110.

Stein, D. *Ada: A Life amd a Legacy.* Cambridge, Mass.: MIT Press, 1985.

Waltz, D.C. "Understanding Live Drawings of Scenes with Shadows," in P.H. Winston, ed., *The Psychology of Computer Vision.* New York: McGraw-Hill, 1975, pp. 19-92.

Daniel C. Dennett (b. 1942) is a contemporary philosopher whose work has reached a wide audience. Dennett is prolific and covers a considerable range of topics and themes – centred above all in philosophy of mind. His prose is engaging, and often witty. It is deployed in the service of a naturalist view of humankind, resting upon and alternating between the twin poles of Darwinian theory and what is called (inappropriately, its critics claim) cognitive science. A student of Gilbert Ryle's at Oxford, Dennett shares Ryle's opposition to Cartesian views of selves and consciousness. More explicitly, and eloquently, than perhaps any other philosopher currently at work, Dennett has taken up the philosophical views implicit in (or apparently implicit in) connectionist models of the human mind/brain.

Two metaphysical positions should be identified in reading and reflecting on Dennett's views of human persons. One is *fictionalism*: the thesis that various entities which strictly speaking do not exist at all, as anything, may nonetheless figure prominently, even importantly and (more or less) ineliminably in theories we use and (may) find informative and of descriptive or explanatory value. (This is a thesis originally adumbrated in a systematic way by the German philosopher Hans Vaihinger [1852-1933].) The other is *reductionism*: the thesis that various entities break down into, or are comprised of, constituent parts or elements – possibly in a chain of successively simpler partitions – where the elemental entities are to be regarded as more basic or more real than the complex things they form. (The most important philosophical forerunner of this thesis is Plato, who believed that being [or existence] admits of degrees, such that of the things that there are – all of which truly *are* – some have "more," and more basic, being than others.) These positions obviously have some similarities, and, perhaps, affinities. But they are logically quite distinct, since a *non-existent* thing cannot be reduced to or formed out of existing ones. It is not clear which of these views Dennett is more drawn to, or which will make better sense of his overall stance on human persons. Several of his explicit declarations certainly seem to express the *fictionalist* alternative. Yet a person or self would appear to be the same thing as an *agent*, and Dennett evidently reifies the latter; and in any case – so a number of critics claim – Dennett's actual arguments appear to support a reductionist view at least as strongly as a fictionalist one. Elsewhere in his work Dennett seeks to avoid the whole issue, branding it "essentialist." But what is at stake is whether any of us are real, something, presumably, as basic as anything we could want to know about.

Daniel C. Dennett, *Consciousness Explained*

(Source: Daniel C. Dennett. *Consciousness Explained*. Boston: Little Brown and Company, 1991, 412-430.)

Since the dawn of modern science in the seventeenth century, there has been nearly unanimous agreement that the self, whatever it is, would be invisible under a microscope, and invisible to introspection, too. For some, this has suggested that the self was a nonphysical soul, a ghost in the machine. For others, it has suggested that the self was nothing at all, a figment of metaphysically fevered imaginations. And for still others, it has suggested only that a self was in one way or another a sort of abstraction, something whose existence was not in the slightest impugned by its invisibility. After all, one might say, a center of gravity is just as invisible – and just as real. Is that real enough?

The question of whether there really are selves can be made to look ridiculously easy to answer, in either direction: Do we exist? Of course! The question presupposes its own answer. (After all, who is this I that has looked in vain for a self, according to Hume?) Are there entities, either in our brains, or over and above our brains, that control our bodies, think our thoughts, make our decisions? Of course not! Such an idea is either empirical idiocy (James's "pontifical neuron") or metaphysical claptrap (Ryle's "ghost in the machine"). When a simple question gets two answers, "Obviously yes!" and "Obviously no!", a middle-ground position is worth considering (Dennett, 1991), even though it is bound to be initially counterintuitive to all parties – everyone agrees that it denies one obvious fact or another!

1. HOW HUMAN BEINGS SPIN A SELF

In addition they seemed to spend a great deal of time eating and drinking and going to parties, and Frensic, whose appearance tended to limit his sensual pleasures to putting things into himself rather than into other people, was something of a gourmet.

TOM SHARPE (1977)

The novelist Tom Sharpe suggests, in this funny but unsettling passage, that when you get right down to it, all sensual pleasure consists in playing around with one's own boundary, or someone else's, and he is on to something – if not the whole truth, then part of the truth.

People have selves. Do dogs? Do lobsters? If selves are anything at all, then they exist. *Now* there are selves. There was a time, thousands (or millions, or billions) of years ago, when there were none – at least none on this planet. So there has to be – as a matter of logic – a true story to be told about how there came to be creatures with selves. This story will have to tell – as a matter of logic – about a process (or a series of processes) involving the activities or behaviors of things that do not yet have selves – or are not yet selves – but which eventually yield, as a new product, beings that are, or have, selves.

In chapter 7, we saw how the birth of reasons was also the birth of boundaries, the boundary between "me" and "the rest of the world," a distinction that even the lowliest amoeba must make, in its blind, unknowing way. This minimal proclivity to distinguish self from other in order to protect one*self* is the biological self, and even such a simple self is not a concrete thing but just an abstraction, a principle of organization. Moreover the boundaries of a biological self are porous and indefinite – another instance of Mother Nature tolerating "error" if the cost is right.

Within the walls of human bodies are many, many interlopers, ranging from bacteria and viruses through microscopic mites that live like cliff-dwellers in the ecological niche of our skin and scalp, to larger parasites – horrible tapeworms, for instance. These interlopers are all self-protectors in their own rights, but some of them, such as the bacteria that populate our digestive systems and without which we would die, are just as essential team members in our quest for self-preservation as the antibodies in our immune systems. (If the biologist Lynn Margulis's theory [1970] is correct, the mitochondria that do the work in almost all the cells in our body are the descendants of bacteria with whom "we" joined forces about two billion years ago.) Other interlopers are tolerated parasites – not worth the effort to evict, apparently – and still others are indeed the enemy within, deadly if not rooted out.

This fundamental biological principle of distinguishing self from world, inside from outside, produces some remarkable echoes in the highest vaults of our psychology. The psychologists Paul Rozin and April Fallon (1987) have shown in a fascinating series of experiments on the nature of *disgust* that there is a powerful and unacknowledged undercurrent of blind resistance to certain acts that, rationally considered, should not trouble us. For example, would you please swallow the saliva in your mouth right now? This act does not fill you with revulsion. But suppose I had asked you to get a clean drinking glass, spit into the glass, and then swallow the saliva from the glass. Disgusting! But why? It seems to have to do with our perception that once something is outside of our bodies it is no longer quite part of us anymore – it becomes alien and suspicious – it has renounced its citizenship and becomes something to be rejected.

Border crossings are thus either moments of anxiety, or, as pointed out by Sharpe, something to be especially enjoyed. Many species have developed remarkable constructions for extending their territorial boundaries, either to make the bad kind of crossings more difficult or the good kind easier. Beavers make dams, and spiders spin webs, for instance. When the spider spins its web, it doesn't have to understand what it is doing; Mother Nature has simply provided its tiny brain with the necessary routines for carrying out this biologically essential task of engineering. Experiments with beavers show that even their magnificently efficient engineering practices are at least largely the product of innate drives and proclivities they need not understand to benefit from. Beavers do learn, and may even teach each other, but mainly, they are driven by powerful innate mechanisms controlling what the behaviorist B. F. Skinner called negative reinforcement. A beaver will cast about quite frantically for something – anything – to stop the sound of running water, and in one experiment a beaver found its relief by plastering mud all over the loudspeaker from which the recorded gurgling emerged! (Wilsson, 1974).

The beaver protects its outer boundary with twigs and mud and one of its inner boundaries with fur. The snail gathers calcium in its food and uses it to exude a hard shell; the hermit crab gets its calcium shell ready-made, taking over the discarded shell of another creature, daintily avoiding the ingestion and exudation process. The difference is not fundamental, according to Richard Dawkins, who points out that the result in either case, which he calls *the extended phenotype* (1982), is a part of the fundamental biological equipment of the individuals who are submitted to the selective forces that drive evolution.

The definition of an extended phenotype not only extends beyond the "natural" boundary of individuals to include external equipment such as shells (and internal equipment such as resident bacteria);

it often includes other individuals of the same species. Beavers cannot do it alone, but require teamwork to build a single dam. Termites have to band together by the millions to build their castles.

And consider the astonishing architectural constructions of the Australian bowerbird (Borgia, 1986). The males build elaborate bowers, courtship shrines with grand central naves, richly decorated with brightly colored objects – predominantly deep blue, and including bottle caps, bits of colored glass, and other human artifacts – which are gathered from far afield and carefully arranged in the bower the better to impress the female he is courting. The bowerbird, like the spider, does not really have to understand what he is doing; he simply finds himself hard at work, he knows not why, creating an edifice that is crucial to his success as a bowerbird.

But the strangest and most wonderful constructions in the whole animal world are the amazing, intricate constructions made by the primate, *Homo sapiens*. Each normal individual of this species makes a self. Out of its brain it spins a web of words and deeds, and, like the other creatures, it doesn't have to know what it's doing; it just does it. This web protects it, just like the snail's shell, and provides it a livelihood, just like the spider's web, and advances its prospects for sex, just like the bowerbird's bower. Unlike a spider, an individual human doesn't just *exude* its web; more like a beaver, it works hard to gather the materials out of which it builds its protective fortress. Like a bowerbird, it appropriates many found objects which happen to delight it – or its mate – including many that have been designed by others for other purposes.

This "web of discourses" as Robyn called it at the close of the previous chapter, is as much a biological product as any of the other constructions to be found in the animal world. Stripped of it, an individual human being is as incomplete as a bird without its feathers, a turtle without its shell. (Clothes, too, are part of the extended phenotype of *Homo sapiens* in almost every niche inhabited by that species. An illustrated encyclopedia of zoology should no more picture *Homo sapiens* naked than it should picture *Ursus arctus* – the black bear – wearing a clown suit and riding a bicycle.)

So wonderful is the organization of a termite colony that it seemed to some observers that each termite colony had to have a soul (Marais, 1937).

We now understand that its organization is simply the result of a million semi-independent little agents, each itself an automaton, doing its thing. So wonderful is the organization of a human self that to many observers it has seemed that each human being had a soul, too: a benevolent Dictator ruling from Headquarters.

In every beehive or termite colony there is, to be sure, a queen bee or queen termite, but these individuals are more patient than agent, more like the crown jewels to be protected than the chief of the protective forces – in fact their royal name is more fitting today than in earlier ages, for they are much more like Queen Elizabeth II than Queen Elizabeth I. There is no Margaret Thatcher bee, no George Bush termite, no Oval Office in the anthill.

Do our selves, our nonminimal *selfy* selves, exhibit the same permeability and flexibility of boundaries as the simpler selves of other creatures? Do we expand our personal boundaries – the boundaries of our *selves* – to enclose any of our "stuff"? In general, perhaps, no, but there are certainly times when this seems true, psychologically. For instance, while some people merely own cars and drive them, others are *motorists*; the inveterate motorist prefers *being* a four- wheeled gas consuming agent to being a two-legged food-consuming agent, and his use of the first-person pronoun betrays this identification:

I'm not cornering well on rainy days because my tires are getting bald.

So sometimes we enlarge our boundaries; at other times, in response to perceived challenges real or imaginary, we let our boundaries shrink:

I didn't do that! That wasn't the real me talking. Yes, the words came out of my mouth, but I refuse to recognize them as my own.

I have reminded you of these familiar speeches to draw out the similarities between our selves and the selves of ants and hermit crabs, but the speeches also draw attention to the most important difference: Ants and hermit crabs don't talk. The hermit crab is designed in such a way as to see to it that it acquires a shell. Its organization, we might say, *implies* a shell, and hence, in a very weak sense, tacitly *represents* the crab as having a shell, but the crab does not in any stronger sense *represent itself*

as having a shell. It doesn't go in for self-representation at all. To whom would it so represent itself and why? It doesn't need to remind itself of this aspect of its nature, since its innate design takes care of that problem, and there are no other interested parties in the offing. And the ants and termites, as we have noted, accomplish their communal projects without relying on any explicitly communicated blueprints or edicts.

We, in contrast, are almost constantly engaged in presenting ourselves to others, and to ourselves, and hence *representing* ourselves – in language and gesture, external and internal. The most obvious difference in our environment that would explain this difference in our behavior is the behavior itself. Our human environment contains not just food and shelter, enemies to fight or flee, and conspecifics with whom to mate, but words, words, words. These words are potent elements of our environment that we readily incorporate, ingesting and extruding them, weaving them like spiderwebs into self-protective strings of *narrative*. Indeed, as we saw in chapter 7, when we let in these words, these meme-vehicles, they tend to take over, creating us out of the raw materials they find in our brains.

Our fundamental tactic of self-protection, self-control, and self-definition is not spinning webs or building dams, but telling stories, and more particularly concocting and controlling the story we tell others – and ourselves – about who we are. And just as spiders don't have to think, consciously and deliberately, about how to spin their webs, and just as beavers, unlike professional human engineers, do not consciously and deliberately plan the structures they build, we (unlike *professional* human storytellers) do not consciously and deliberately figure out what narratives to tell and how to tell them. Our tales are spun, but for the most part we don't spin them; they spin us. Our human consciousness, and our narrative selfhood, is their product, not their source.

These strings or streams of narrative issue forth *as if* from a single source – not just in the obvious physical sense of flowing from just one mouth, or one pencil or pen, but in a more subtle sense: their effect on any audience is to encourage them to (try to) posit a unified agent whose words they are, about whom they are: in short, to posit a *center of narrative gravity*. Physicists appreciate the enormous simplification you get when you posit a center of gravity for an object, a single point relative to which all gravitational forces may be calculated. We hetero-phenomenologists appreciate the enormous simplification you get when you posit a center of narrative gravity for a narrative-spinning human body. Like the biological self, this psychological or narrative self is yet another abstraction, not a thing in the brain, but still a remarkably robust and almost tangible attractor of properties, the "owner of record" of whatever items and features are lying about unclaimed. Who owns your car? You do. Who owns your clothes? You do. Then who owns your body? You do! When you say

This is my body

you certainly aren't taken as saying

This body owns itself.

But what can you be saying, then? If what you say is neither a bizarre and pointless tautology (this body is its own owner, or something like that) nor the claim that you are an immaterial soul or ghost puppeteer who owns and operates this body the way you own and operate your car, what else could you mean?

2. HOW MANY SELVES TO A CUSTOMER?

I think we could see more clearly what

This is my body

meant, if we could answer the question: As opposed to what? How about as opposed to this?

No it isn't; it's *mine*, and I don't like sharing it!

If we could see what it would be like for two (or more) selves to vie for control of a single body, we could see better what a single self really is. As scientists of the self, we would like to conduct controlled experiments, in which, by varying the initial conditions, we could see just what has to happen, in what order and requiring what resources, for such a talking self to emerge. Are there conditions under which life goes on but no self emerges? Are there conditions under which more than one self

emerges? We can't ethically conduct such experiments, but, as so often before, we can avail ourselves of the data generated by some of the terrible experiments nature conducts, cautiously drawing conclusions.

Such an experiment is Multiple Personality Disorder (MPD), in which a single human body *seems* to be shared by several selves, each, typically, with a proper name and an autobiography. The idea of MPD strikes many people as too outlandish and metaphysically bizarre to believe – a "paranormal" phenomenon to discard along with ESP, close encounters of the third kind, and witches on broomsticks. I suspect that some of these people have made a simple arithmetical mistake: they have failed to notice that two or three or seventeen selves per body is really no more metaphysically extravagant than one self per body. One is bad enough!

"I just saw a car drive by with five selves in it."
"What?? The mind reels! What kind of metaphysical nonsense is this?"
"Well, there were also five bodies in the car."
"Oh, well, why didn't you say so? Then everything is okay."
" – Or maybe only four bodies, or three – but definitely five selves."
"What??!!"

The normal arrangement is one self per body, but if a body can have one, why not more than one under abnormal conditions?

I don't mean to suggest that there is nothing shocking or deeply puzzling about MPD. It is, in fact, a phenomenon of surpassing strangeness, not, I think, because it challenges our presuppositions about what is *metaphysically* possible, but more because it challenges our presuppositions about what is humanly possible, about the limits of human cruelty and depravity on the one hand, and the limits of human creativity on the other. For the evidence is now voluminous that there are not a handful or a hundred but thousands of cases of MPD diagnosed today, and it almost invariably owes its existence to prolonged early childhood abuse, usually sexual, and of sickening severity. Nicholas Humphrey and I investigated MPD several years ago (Humphrey and Dennett, 1989), and found it to be a complex phenomenon that extends far beyond the individual brains of the sufferers.

These children have often been kept in such extraordinarily terrifying and confusing circumstances that I am more amazed that they survive psychologically at all than I am that they manage to preserve themselves by a desperate redrawing of their boundaries. What they do, when confronted with overwhelming conflict and pain, is this: They "leave." They create a boundary so that the horror doesn't happen to them; it either happens to no one, or to some other self, better able to sustain its organization under such an onslaught – at least that's what they say they did, as best they recall.

How can this be? What kind of account could we give, ultimately at the biological level, of such a process of splitting? Does there have to have been a single, whole self that somehow fissioned, amoeba-like? How could that be if a self is not a proper physical part of an organism or a brain, but, as I have suggested, an abstraction? The response to the trauma seems so creative, moreover, that one is inclined at first to suppose that it must be the work of some kind of a supervisor in there: a supervisory brain program, a central controller, or whatever. But we should remind ourselves of the termite colony, which also seemed, at first, to require a central chief executive to accomplish such clever projects.

We have become accustomed to evolutionary narratives that start from a state in which a certain phenomenon does not yet exist and end with a state in which the phenomenon is definitely present. The innovation of agriculture, of clothing and dwellings and tools, the innovation of language, the innovation of consciousness itself, the earlier innovation of life on earth. All these stories are there to be told. And each of them must traverse what we might call the chasm of absolutism. This chasm is illustrated by the following curious argument (borrowed from Sanford, 1975):

> Every mammal has a mammal for a mother, but there have been only a finite number of mammals, so there must have been a first mammal, which contradicts our first premise, so, contrary to appearances, there are no such things as mammals!

Something has to give. What should it be? The absolutist or essentialist philosopher is attracted to sharp lines, thresholds, "essences" and "criteria." For the absolutist, there must indeed have been a first mammal, a first living thing, a first moment of consciousness, a first moral agent; it was whichever product of saltation, whichever radically new candidate, first met the essential conditions – whatever analysis shows them to be.

It was this taste for sharp species boundaries that was the greatest intellectual obstacle Darwin faced when trying to develop the theory of evolution (Richards, 1987). Opposed to this way of thinking is the sort of anti-essentialism that is comfortable with penumbral cases and the lack of strict dividing lines. Since selves and minds and even consciousness itself are biological products (not elements to be found in the periodic table of chemistry), we should expect that the transitions between them and the phenomena that are not them should be gradual, contentious, gerrymandered. This doesn't mean that everything is always in transition, always gradual; transitions that look gradual from close up usually look like abrupt punctuations between plateaus of equilibrium from a more distant vantage point (Eldredge and Gould, 1972; but see also Dawkins, 1982, pp. 101-109).

The importance of this fact for philosophical theories (and philosophers' predilections) is not widely enough recognized. There have always been – and always will be – a few transitional things, "missing links," quasi-mammals and the like that defy definition, but the fact is that *almost all* real (as opposed to merely possible) things in nature tend to fall into similarity clusters separated in logical space by huge oceans of emptiness. We don't need "essences" or "criteria" to keep the meaning of our words from sliding all over the place; our words will stay put, quite firmly attached as if by gravity to the nearest similarity cluster, even if there has been – must have been – a brief isthmus that once attached it by a series of gradual steps to some neighboring cluster. This idea is uncontroversially applied to many topics. But many people who are quite comfortable taking this pragmatic approach to night and day, living and nonliving, mammal and pre-mammal, get anxious when invited to adopt the same attitude toward having a self and not having a self. They think that here, if nowhere else in nature, it must be All or Nothing and One to a Customer.

The theory of consciousness we have been developing discredits these presumptions, and Multiple Personality Disorder provides a good illustration of the way the theory challenges them. The convictions that there *cannot* be quasi-selves or sort-of selves, and that, moreover there *must* be a whole number of selves associated with one body – and it better be the number one! – are *not* self-evident. That is, they are no longer self-evident, now that we have developed in some detail an alternative to the Cartesian Theater with its Witness or Central Meaner. MPD challenges these presumptions from one side, but we can also imagine a challenge from the other side: two or more bodies sharing a single self! There may actually be such a case, in York, England: the Chaplin twins, Greta and Freda (*Time,* April 6, 1981). These identical twins, now in their forties and living together in a hostel, seem to act as one; they collaborate on the speaking of single speech acts, for instance, finishing each other's sentences with ease or speaking in unison, with one just a split-second behind. For years they have been inseparable, as inseparable as two twins who are not Siamese twins could arrange. Some who have dealt with them suggest that the natural and effective tactic that suggested itself was to consider *them* more of a *her.*

Our view countenances the theoretical possibility not only of MPD but FPD (Fractional Personality Disorder). Could it be? Why not? I'm not for a moment suggesting that these twins were linked by telepathy or ESP or any other sort of occult bonds. I am suggesting that there are plenty of subtle, everyday ways of communicating and coordinating (techniques often highly developed by identical twins, in fact). Since these twins have seen, heard, touched, smelled, and thought about very much the same events throughout their lives, and started, no doubt, with brains quite similarly disposed to react to these stimuli, it might not take enormous channels of communication to keep them homing in on some sort of loose harmony. (And besides, how unified is the most self-possessed among us?) We should hesitate to prescribe the limits of such practiced coordination.

But in any case, wouldn't there also be two clearly defined individual selves, one for each twin, and responsible for maintaining this curious charade? Perhaps, but what if each of these women had become so selfless (as we do say) in her devotion to the joint cause, that she more or less lost herself (as we also say) in the project? As the poet Paul Valéry once said, in a delicious twist of his countryman's dictum: "Sometimes I am, sometimes I think."

In chapter 11 we saw that while consciousness appears to be continuous, in fact it is gappy. A self could be just as gappy, lapsing into nothingness as easily as a candle flame is snuffed, only to be rekindled at some later time, under more auspicious circumstances. Are you the very person whose kindergarten adventures you sketchily recall (sometimes vividly, sometimes dimly)? Are the adventures of that child, whose trajectory through space and time has apparently been continuous with the trajectory of your body, your very own adventures? That child with your name, a child whose scrawled signature on a crayon drawing reminds *you* of the way you used to sign your name – is (was) that child you? The philosopher Derek Parfit (1984) has compared a person to a club, a rather different sort of human construction, which might go out of existence one year, and come to be reconstituted by some of its (former?) members some years later. Would it be the same club? It might be, if, for instance, the club had had a written constitution that provided explicitly for just such lapses of existence. But there might be no telling. We might know all the facts that could conceivably bear on the situation and be able to see that they were inconclusive about the *identity* of the (new?) club. On the view of selves – or persons – emerging here, this is the right analogy; selves are not independently existing soul-pearls, but artifacts of the social processes that create us, and, like other such artifacts, subject to sudden shifts in status. The only "momentum" that accrues to the trajectory of a self, or a club, is the stability imparted to it by the web of beliefs that constitute it, and when those beliefs lapse, it lapses, either permanently or temporarily.

It is important to bear this in mind when considering another favorite among philosophers, the much-discussed phenomenon of split-brain patients. A so-called split brain is the result of *commissurotomy,* an operation that severs the *corpus callosum,* the broad band of fibers directly connecting the left and right hemispheres of the cortex. This leaves the hemispheres still indirectly connected, through a variety of midbrain structures, but it is obviously a drastic procedure, not to be performed unless there are no alternatives. It provides relief in some severe cases of epilepsy that are not otherwise treatable, by preventing the internally generated electrical storms that cause seizures from sweeping across the cortex from an originating "focus" in one hemisphere to the opposite side. Standard philosophical legend has it that split-brain patients may be "split into two selves" but otherwise suffer no serious diminution in powers as a result of the surgery. The most appealing version of this oversimplification is that the original person's two "sides" – uptight, analytic left hemisphere, and laid-back, intuitive, holistic right hemisphere – are postoperatively freed to shine forth with more individuality, now that the normal close teamwork must be replaced by a less intimate *détente*. This is an appealing idea, but it is a wild exaggeration of the empirical findings that inspire it. In fact, in only a tiny fraction of cases are any of the theoretically striking symptoms of multiple serfhood to be observed. (See, e.g., Kinsbourne, 1974; Kinsbourne and Smith, 1974; Levy and Trevarthen, 1976; Gazzaniga and LeDoux, 1978; Gazzaniga, 1985; Oakley, 1985; Dennett, 1985.)

It's not surprising that split-brains patients, like blindsight patients and people with Multiple Personality Disorder, don't live up to their philosophical billing, and it's nobody's fault. It's not that philosophers (and many other interpreters, including the primary researchers) deliberately exaggerate their descriptions of the phenomena. Rather, in their effort to describe the phenomena concisely, they find that the limited resources of everyday language pull them inexorably toward the simplistic Boss of the Body, Ghost in the Machine, Audience in the Cartesian Theater model. Nicholas Humphrey and I, comparing our own careful notes of what happened at various meetings with MPD sufferers, found that we often slipped, in spite of ourselves, into all-too-natural but seriously misleading turns of phrase to describe what we had actually seen. Thomas Nagel (1971), the first philosopher to write about split-brain patients, presented a judicious and accurate account of the phenomena as they were then understood, and, noting the difficulty in providing a coherent account, surmised: "It may be impossible for us to abandon certain ways of conceiving and representing ourselves, no matter how little support they get from scientific research" (1971, p. 397).

It is indeed difficult but not impossible. Nagel's pessimism is itself exaggerated. Haven't we just succeeded, in fact, in shaking ourselves free of the traditional way of thinking? Now some people may

not *want* to abandon the traditional vision. There might even be good reasons – moral reasons – for trying to preserve the myth of selves as brainpearls, particular concrete, countable things rather than abstractions, and for refusing to countenance the possibility of quasi-selves, semi-selves, transitional selves. But that is surely the correct way to understand the phenomena of split-brains. For brief periods during carefully devised experimental procedures, a few of these patients bifurcate in their response to a predicament, temporarily creating a second center of narrative gravity. A few effects of the bifurcation may linger on indefinitely in mutually inaccessible memory traces, but aside from these actually quite primitive traces of the bifurcation, the life of a second rudimentary self lasts a few minutes at most, not much time to accrue the sort of autobiography of which fully fledged selves are made. (This is just as obviously true of most of the dozens of fragmentary selves developed by MPD patients; there simply aren't enough waking hours in the day for most of them to salt away more than a few minutes of exclusive biography per week.)

The distinctness of different narratives is the lifeblood of different selves. As the philosopher Ronald de Sousa (1976) notes:

> When Dr. Jekyll changes into Mr. Hyde, that is a strange and mysterious thing. Are they two people taking turns in one body? But here is something stranger: Dr. Juggle and Dr. Boggle too, take turns in one body. *But they are as like as identical twins!* You balk: why then say that they have changed into one another? Well, why not: if Dr. Jekyl can change into a man as different as Hyde, surely it must be all the *easier* for Juggle to change into Boggle, who is exactly like him.
>
> We need conflict or strong difference to shake our natural assumption that to one body there corresponds at most one agent. [p. 219]

So *what is it like* to be the right hemisphere self in a split-brain patient? This is the most natural question in the world,[1] and it conjures up a mind-boggling – and chilling – image: there you are, trapped

---

1   It is interesting to note that Nagel, in 1971, was already addressing this question explicitly (p. 398), before he turned his attention to bats – a topic we will discuss in the next chapter.

in the right hemisphere of a body whose left side you know intimately (and still control) and whose right side is now as remote as the body of a passing stranger. You would like to tell the world what it is like to be you, but you can't! You're cut off from all verbal communication by the loss of your indirect phone lines to the radio station in the left hemisphere. You do your best to signal your existence to the outside world, tugging your half of the face into lopsided frowns and smiles, and occasionally (if you are a virtuoso right hemisphere self) scrawling a word or two with your left hand.

This exercise of imagination could go on in the obvious ways, but we know it is a fantasy – as much a fantasy as Beatrix Potter's charming stories of Peter Rabbit and his anthropomorphic animal friends. Not because "consciousness is only in the left hemisphere" and not because *it couldn't be* the case that someone found himself or herself in such a pickle, but simply because it *isn't* the case that commissurotomy leaves in its wake organizations both distinct and robust enough to support such a separate self.

It could hardly be a challenge to my theory of the self that it is "logically possible" that there is such a right hemisphere self in a splitbrain patient, for my theory says that there isn't, and says why: the conditions for accumulating the sort of narrative richness (and independence) that constitutes a "fully fledged" self are not present. My theory is similarly impervious to the claim – which I would not dream of denying – that there could be talking bunny rabbits, spiders who write English messages in their webs, and for that matter, melancholy choo-choo trains. There could be, I suppose, but there aren't – so my theory doesn't have to explain them.

3. THE UNBEARABLE LIGHTNESS OF BEING

Whatever happens, where or when, we're prone to wonder who or what's responsible. This leads us to discover explanations that we might not otherwise imagine, and that helps us predict and control not only what happens in the world, but also what happens in our minds. But what if those same tendencies should lead us to imagine things and causes that do not exist? Then we'll invent false gods and superstitions and see their hand in every chance coincidence. Indeed, per-

haps that strange word "I" – as used in "I just had a good idea" – reflects the selfsame tendency. If you're compelled to find some cause that causes everything you do – why, then, that something needs a name. You call it "me." I call it "you."

MARVIN MINSKY (1985), p. 232

A self, according to my theory, is not any old mathematical point, but an abstraction defined by the myriads of attributions and interpretations (including self-attributions and self-interpretations) that have composed the biography of the living body whose Center of Narrative Gravity it is. As such, it plays a singularly important role in the ongoing cognitive economy of that living body, because, of all the things in the environment an active body must make mental models of, none is more crucial than the model the agent has of itself. (See, e.g., Johnson-Laird, 1988; Perlis, 1991.)

To begin with, every agent has to know which thing in the world it is! This may seem at first either trivial or impossible. "I'm me!" is not really informative, and what else could one need to know – or could one discover if one didn't already know it? For simpler organisms, it is true, there is really nothing much to self-knowledge beyond the rudimentary biological wisdom enshrined in such maxims as When Hungry, Don't Eat Yourself! and When There's a Pain, It's Yours! In every organism, including human beings, acknowledgment of these basic biological design principles is simply "wired in" – part of the underlying design of the nervous system, like blinking when something approaches the eye or shivering when cold. A lobster might well eat another lobster's claws, but the prospect of eating one of its own claws is conveniently unthinkable to it. Its options are limited, and when it "thinks of" moving a claw, its "thinker" is directly and appropriately wired to the very claw it thinks of moving. With human beings (and chimpanzees and maybe a few other species), on the other hand, there are more options, and hence more sources of confusion.

Some years ago the authorities in New York Harbor experimented with a shared radar system for small boat owners. A single powerful land-based radar antenna formed a radar image of the harbor, which could then be transmitted as a television signal to boat owners who could save the cost of radar by simply installing small television sets in their boats. What good would this do? If you were lost in the fog, and looked at the television screen, you would know that one of those many moving blips on the screen was you – but which one? Here is a case in which the question "Which thing in the world am I?" is neither trivial nor impossible to answer. The mystery succumbs to a simple trick: Turn your boat quickly in a tight circle; then your blip is the one that traces the little "O" on the screen – unless several boats in the fog try to perform the same test at the same time.

The method is not foolproof, but it works most of the time, and it nicely illustrates a much more general point: In order to control the sorts of sophisticated activities human bodies engage in, the body's control system (housed in the brain) has to be able to recognize a wide variety of different sorts of inputs as informing it about itself, and when quandaries arise or skepticism sets in, the only reliable (but not foolproof) way of sorting out and properly assigning this information is to run little experiments: do something and look to see what moves.[2] A chimpanzee can readily learn to reach through a hole in the wall of its cage for bananas, guiding its arm movements by watching its own arm on a closed circuit television monitor mounted quite some distance from his arm (Menzel et al., 1985). This is a decidedly nontrivial bit of self-recognition, depending as it does on noticing the consonance of the seen arm movements on the screen with the unseen but intended arm movements. What would happen if the experimenters built in a small delay in the videotape? How long do you think it would take you to discover that you were looking at your own arm (without verbal clues from the experimental setup) if a tape delay of, say, twenty seconds were built into the closed circuit?

The need for self-knowledge extends beyond the problems of identifying the external signs of our own bodily movement. We need to know about our own internal states, tendencies, decisions, strengths, and weaknesses, and the basic method of obtaining this knowledge is essentially the same: Do something and "look" to see what "moves." An advanced agent must build up practices for keeping track of both its bodily and "mental" circumstances. In human beings, as we have seen, those practices mainly involve incessant bouts of storytelling and story-checking, some of it factual and some of it fictional. Children practice this aloud (think of Snoopy, saying to himself as he sits on his doghouse roof: "Here's the World War I flying ace ..."). We adults do it more elegantly: silently, tacitly, effortlessly keeping track of the difference between our fantasies and our "serious" rehearsals and reflections. The philosopher Kendall Walton (1973, 1978) and the psychologist Nicholas Humphrey (1986) have shown from different perspectives the importance of drama, storytelling, and the more fundamental phenomenon of make-believe in providing practice for human beings who are novice self-spinners.

Thus do we build up a defining story about ourselves, organized around a sort of basic blip of self-representation (Dennett, 1981). The blip isn't a self, of course; it's a *representation* of a self (and the blip on the radar screen for Ellis island isn't an island – it's a representation of an island). What makes one blip the *me*-blip and another blip just a *he*- or *she*- or *it*-blip is not what it looks like, but what it is used for. it gathers and organizes the information on the topic of me in the same way other structures in my brain keep track of information on Boston, or Reagan, or ice cream.

And where is the thing your self-representation is *about*? It is wherever you are (Dennett, 1978). And *what* is this thing? It's nothing more than, and nothing less than, your center of narrative gravity.

Otto returns:

The trouble with centers of gravity is that they aren't real; they're theorists' fictions.

That's not the trouble with centers of gravity; it's their glory. They are *magnificent* fictions, fictions

---

2   And how do we know that we are doing something? Where do we get the initial bit of self-knowledge we use for this leverage? This has seemed to be an utterly fundamental question to some philosophers (Castañeda, 1967, 1968; Lewis, 1979; Perry, 1979), and has generated a literature of surpassing intricacy. If this is a substantial philosophical problem, there must be something wrong with the "trivial" answer (but I can't see what): We get our basic, original self-knowledge the same way the lobster does; we're just wired that way.

anyone would be proud to have created. And the fictional characters of literature are even more wonderful. Think of Ishmael, in *Moby-Dick*. "Call me Ishmael" is the way the text opens, and we oblige. We don't call the text Ishmael, and we don't call Melville Ishmael. Who or what do we call Ishmael? We call Ishmael Ishmael, the wonderful fictional character to be found in the pages of *Moby-Dick*. "Call me Dan," you hear from my lips, and you oblige, not by calling my lips Dan, or my body Dan, but by calling *me* Dan, the theorists' fiction created by. . . well, not by me but by my brain, acting in concert over the years with my parents and siblings and friends.

That's all very well for you, but *I* am perfectly real. I may have been created by the social process you just alluded to (I must have been, if I didn't exist before my birth), but what the process created is a *real* self, not a mere fictional character!

I think I know what you're getting at. If a self isn't a real thing, what happens to moral responsibility? One of the most important roles of a self in our traditional conceptual scheme is as the place where the buck stops, as Harry Truman's sign announced. If selves aren't real – aren't *really* real – won't the buck just get passed on and on, round and round, forever? If there is no Oval Office in the brain, housing a Highest Authority to whom all decisions can be appealed, we seem to be threatened with a Kafkaesque bureaucracy of homunculi, who always reply, when challenged: "Don't blame me, I just work here." The task of constructing a self that can take responsibility is a major social and educational project, and you are right to be concerned about threats to its integrity. But a brain-pearl, a real, "intrinsically responsible" whatever-it-is, is a pathetic bauble to brandish like a lucky charm in the face of this threat. The only hope, and not at all a forlorn one, is to come to understand, naturalistically, the ways in which brains grow self-representations, thereby equipping the bodies they control with responsible selves when all goes well. Free will and moral responsibility are well worth wanting, and as I try to show in *Elbow Room: The Varieties of Free Will Worth Wanting* (1984), the best defense of them abandons the hopelessly contradiction-riddled myth of the distinct, separate soul.

But don't I exist?

Of course you do. There you are, sitting in the chair, reading my book and raising challenges. And curiously enough, your current embodiment, though a necessary precondition for your creation, is not necessarily a requirement for your existence to be prolonged indefinitely. Now if you were a soul, a pearl of immaterial substance, we could "explain" your potential immortality only by postulating it as an inexplicable property, an ineliminable *virtus dormitiva* of soul-stuff. And if you were a pearl of material substance, some spectacularly special group of atoms in your brain, your mortality would depend on the physical forces holding them together (we might ask the physicists what the "half-life" of a self is). If you think of yourself as a center of narrative gravity, on the other hand, your existence depends on the persistence of that narrative (rather like the Thousand and One Arabian Nights, but all a single tale), which could *theoretically* survive indefinitely many switches of *medium*, be teleported as readily (in principle) as the evening news, and stored indefinitely as sheer information. If what you are is that organization of information that has structured your body's control system (or, to put it in its more usual provocative form, if what you are is the program that runs on your brain's computer), then you could in principle survive the death of your body as intact as a program can survive the destruction of the computer on which it was created and first run. Some thinkers (e.g., Penrose, 1989) find this an appalling and deeply counterintuitive implication of the view I've defended here. But if it is potential immortality you hanker for, the alternatives are simply indefensible.

Bibliography

Borgia, G. "Sexual Selection in Bowerbirds," *Scientific American*, 254, 1986, 92-100.

Castañeda, H.N. "Indicators and Quasi-Indicators," *American Philosophical Quarterly*, 4, 1967, 85-100.

Castañeda, H.N. "On the Logic of Attributions of Self-Knowledge to Others," *Journal of Philosophy*, 65, 1968, 439-456.

Dawkins, R. *The Extended Phenotype*. San Francisco: Freeman, 1982.

Dennett, D.C. "Real Patterns," *Journal of Philosophy*, 89, 1991, 27-51.

Dennett, D.C. "Music of the Hemisphere," a review of M. Gazzaniga, *The Social Brain*, in *New York Times Book Review*, Nov. 17, 1985, 53.

Dennett, D.C. *Elbow Room: The Varieties of Free Will Worth Wanting*. Cambridge, Mass.: MIT Press, 1984.

Dennett, D.C. "Reflections" on "Software," in D.R. Hofstadter and D.C. Dennett, *The Mind's I: Fantasies and Reflections on Self and Soul*. New York: Basic Books, 1981.

Dennett, D.C. "Skinner Skinned," Ch. 4 in D.C. Dennett, *Brainstorms*. Montgomery, Vt.: Bradford Books, 1978.

de Sousa, R. "Rational Homunculi," in Amelie O. Rorty, ed., *The Identity of Persons*. Berkeley: University of California Press, 1976, pp. 217-238.

Eldredge, N., and S.J. Gould. "Punctuated Equilibria: An Alternative to Phyletic Gradualism", in T.J.M. Schopf, ed., *Models in Paleobiology*, San Francisco: Freeman Cooper, 1972, pp. 82-115.

Gazzaniga, M. *The Social Brain: Discovering the Networks of the Mind*. New York: Basic Books, 1985.

Gazzaniga, M., and J. Ledoux. *The Integrated Mind*. New York: Plenum Press, 1978.

Humphrey, N. *The Inner Eye*. London: Faber and Faber, 1986.

Humphrey, N., and D.C. Dennett, "Speaking for Our Selves: An Assessment of Multiple Personality Disorder," *Raritan*, 9, 1989, 68-98.

Johnson-Laird, P. "A Computational Analysis of Consciousness," in A.J. Marcel and E. Bisiach, eds., *Consciousness in Contemporary Science*. Oxford: Clarendon Press, 1988.

Kinsbourne, M. "Lateral Interactions in the Brain," in M. Kinsbourne and W.L. Smith, eds., *Hemisphere Disconnection and Cerebral Function*. Springfield, Ill.: Charles C. Thomas, 1974, pp. 239-259.

Kinsbourne, M., and W.L. Smith, eds. *Hemisphere Disconnection and Cerebral Function*. Springfield, Ill.: Charles C. Thomas, 1974.

Levy, J., and C. Trevarthen. "Metacontrol of Hemispheric Function in Human Split-Brain Patients," *Journal of Experimental Psychology: Human Perception and Performance*, 3, 1976, 299-311.

Lewis, D. "Attitudes *De Dicto* and *De Se*," *Philosophical Review*, 78, 1979, 513-543.

Marais, E.N. *The Soul of the White Ant*. London: Methuen, 1937.

Margulis, L. *The Origin of Eukaryotic Cells*. New Haven: Yale University Press, 1970.

Mengel, E.W., E.S. Savage-Rumbaugh, and J. Lawson. "Chimpanzee (*Pan troglodytes*) Spatial Problem Solving with the Use of Mirrors and Televised Equivalents of Mirrors," *Journal of Comparative Psychology*, 99, 1985, 211-217.

Minsky, M. *The Society of Mind*. New York: Simon and Schuster, 1985.

Nagel, T. "Brain Bisection and the Unity of Consciousness," *Synthèse*, 22, 1971, 396-413.

Oakley, D.A., ed. *Brain and Mind*. London and New York: Methuen, 1985.

Parfit, D. *Reasons and Persons*. Oxford: Clarendon Press, 1984.

Penrose, R. *The Emperor's New Mind*. Oxford: Oxford University Press, 1989.

Perlis, D. "Intentionality and Defaults," in K.M. Ford and P.J. Hayes, eds., *Reasoning Agents in a Dynamic World*. Greenwich, Ct.: JAI Press, 1991.

Perry, J. "The Problem of the Essential Indexical," *Nous*, 13, 1979, 3-21.

Richards, R.J. *Darwin and the Emergence of Evolutionary Theories of Mind and Behavior*. Chicago: University of Chicago Press, 1987.

Rozin, P., and A.E. Fallon. "A Perspective on Disgust," *Psychological Review*, 94, 1987, 23-47.

Sanford, D. "Infinity and Vagueness," *Philosophical Review*, 84, 1975, 520-535.

Sharpe, T. *The Great Pursuit*. London: Secker and Warburg, 1977.

Walton, K. "Fearing Fiction," *Journal of Philosophy*, 75, 1978, 6-27.

Walton, K. "Pictures and Make Believe," *Philosophical Review*, 82, 1973, 283-319.

Wilsson, L. "Observation and Experiments on the Ethology of the European Beaver," *Viltrevy, Swedish Wildlife*, 8, 1974, 115-266.

IX

FEMINISM

CHAPTER THIRTY-SEVEN — MARY WOLLSTONECRAFT

Although distinct parts of feminist analyses and political proposals are identifiable earlier, a fully articulated formulation of feminism, as a set of views about women, men, and their mutual relations, and ideas about social, political, and economic changes concerning women, appears first in the writings of the Marquis de Condorcet (1743-1794) and Mary Wollstonecraft (1759-1797). Although slightly later than Condorcet, Wollstonecraft's work – in the *Vindication of the Rights of Woman* (1792), from which the following selection is taken – is the more extensive and more systematically argued.

In addition to her fundamental role as one of the earliest feminists, Wollstonecraft has a significance also as a clear, and eloquent, proponent of liberalism; and also a critic of Rousseau.

With respect to feminism, Wollstonecraft is not only one of its first advocates. She remains to the present day one of the sharpest, most focused, and searching proponents specifically of *equality feminism*: of the idea that there is little significant *natural* difference between the sexes, such differences as experience affords being due to externally imposed social, cultural, and historical factors.

Mary Wollstonecraft, *A Vindication of the Rights of Woman*

(Source: Mary Wollstonecraft. *A Vindication of the Rights of Woman*. London: J.M. Dent Ltd., 1929, 15-85.)

CHAPTER I
THE RIGHTS AND INVOLVED DUTIES OF MANKIND CONSIDERED

In the present state of society it appears necessary to go back to first principles in search of the most simple truths, and to dispute with some prevailing prejudice every inch of ground. To clear my way, I must be allowed to ask some plain questions, and the answers will probably appear as unequivocal as the axioms on which reasoning is built; though, when entangled with various motives of action, they are formally contradicted, either by the words or conduct of men.

In what does man's pre-eminence over the brute creation consist? The answer is as clear as that a half is less than the whole, in Reason.

What acquirement exalts one being above another? Virtue, we spontaneously reply.

For what purpose were the passions implanted? That man by struggling with them might attain a degree of knowledge denied to the brutes, whispers Experience.

Consequently the perfection of our nature and capability of happiness must be estimated by the degree of reason, virtue, and knowledge, that distinguish the individual, and direct the laws which bind society: and that from the exercise of reason, knowledge and virtue naturally flow, is equally undeniable, if mankind be viewed collectively.

The rights and duties of man thus simplified, it seems almost impertinent to attempt to illustrate truths that appear so incontrovertible; yet such deeply rooted prejudices have clouded reason, and such spurious qualities have assumed the name of virtues, that it is necessary to pursue the course of reason as it has been perplexed and involved in error, by various adventitious circumstances, comparing the simple axiom with casual deviations.

Men, in general, seem to employ their reason to justify prejudices, which they have imbibed, they can scarcely trace how, rather than to root them out. The mind must be strong that resolutely forms its own principles; for a kind of intellectual cowardice prevails which makes many men shrink from the task, or only do it by halves. Yet the imperfect conclusions thus drawn, are frequently very plausible, because they are built on partial experience, on just, though narrow, views.

Going back to first principles, vice skulks, with all its native deformity, from close investigation; but a set of shallow reasoners are always exclaiming that these arguments prove too much, and that a measure rotten at the core may be expedient. Thus expediency is continually contrasted with simple principles, till truth is lost in a mist of words, virtue, in forms, and knowledge rendered a sounding nothing, by the specious prejudices that assume its name.

That the society is formed in the wisest manner, whose constitution is founded on the nature of man, strikes, in the abstract, every thinking being so forcibly, that it looks like presumption to endeavour to bring forward proofs; though proof must be brought, or the strong hold of prescription will never be forced by reason; yet to urge prescription as an argument to justify the depriving men (or women) of their natural rights, is one of the absurd sophisms which daily insult common sense.

The civilisation of the bulk of the people of Europe is very partial; nay, it may be made a question, whether they have acquired any virtues in exchange for innocence, equivalent to the misery produced by the vices that have been plastered over unsightly ignorance, and the freedom which has been bartered for splendid slavery. The desire of dazzling by riches, the most certain pre-eminence that man can obtain, the pleasure of commanding flattering sycophants, and many other complicated low calculations of doting self-love, have all contributed to overwhelm the mass of mankind, and make liberty a convenient handle for mock patriotism. For whilst rank and titles are held of the utmost importance, before which Genius "must hide its diminished head," it is, with a few exceptions, very unfortunate for a nation when a man of abilities, without rank or property, pushes himself forward to notice. Alas ! what unheard-of misery have thousands suffered to purchase a cardinal's hat for an intriguing obscure adventurer, who longed to be ranked with princes, or lord it over them by seizing the triple crown !

Such, indeed, has been the wretchedness that has flowed from hereditary honours, riches, and monarchy, that men of lively sensibility have almost uttered blasphemy in order to justify the dispensations of Providence. Man has been held out as independent of His power who made him, or as a lawless planet darting from its orbit to steal the celestial fire of reason; and the vengeance of Heaven, lurking in the subtle flame, like Pandora's pent-up mischiefs, sufficiently punished his temerity, by introducing evil into the world.

Impressed by this view of the misery and disorder which pervaded society, and fatigued with jostling against artificial fools, Rousseau became enamoured of solitude, and, being at the same time an optimist, he labours with uncommon eloquence to prove that man was naturally a solitary animal. Misled by his respect for the goodness of God, who certainly – for what man of sense and feeling can doubt it! – gave life only to communicate happiness, he considers evil as positive, and the work of man; not aware that he was exalting one attribute at the expense of another, equally necessary to divine perfection.

Reared on a false hypothesis, his arguments in favour of a state of nature are plausible, but unsound. I say unsound; for to assert that a state of nature is preferable to civilisation in all its possible perfection, is, in other words, to arraign supreme wisdom; and the paradoxical exclamation, that God has made all things right, and that error has been introduced by the creature, whom He formed, knowing what He formed, is as unphilosophical as impious.

When that wise Being who created us and placed us here saw the fair idea, He willed, by allowing it to be so, that the passions should unfold our reason, because He could see that present evil would produce future good. Could the helpless creature whom He called from nothing break loose from His providence, and boldly learn to know good by practising evil, without His permission? No. How could that energetic advocate for immortality argue so inconsistently? Had mankind remained for ever in the brutal state of nature, which even his magic pen cannot paint as a state in which a single virtue took root, it would have been clear, though not to the sensitive unreflecting wanderer, that man was born to run the circle of life and death, and adorn God's garden for some purpose which could not easily be reconciled with His attributes.

But if, to crown the whole, there were to be rational creatures produced, allowed to rise in excellence by the exercise of powers implanted for that purpose; if benignity itself thought fit to call into existence a creature above the brutes,[1] who could think and improve himself, why should that inestimable gift, for a gift it was, if man was so created, as to have a capacity to rise above the state in which sensation produced brutal ease, be called, in direct terms, a curse? A curse it might be reckoned, if the whole of our existence were bounded by our continuance in this world; for why should the gracious fountain of life give us passions, and the power of reflecting, only to imbitter our days and inspire us with mistaken notions of dignity? Why should He lead us from love of ourselves to the sublime emotions which the discovery of His wisdom and goodness excites, if these feelings were not set in motion to improve our nature, of which they make a part,[2] and render us capable of enjoying a more godlike portion of happiness? Firmly persuaded that no evil exists in the world that God did not design to take place, I build my belief on the perfection of God.

Rousseau exerts himself to prove that all *was* right originally: a crowd of authors that all *is* now right: and I, that all will *be* right.

But, true to his first position, next to a state of nature, Rousseau celebrates barbarism, and apostrophising the shade of Fabricius, he forgets that, in conquering the world, the Romans never dreamed of establishing their own liberty on a firm basis, or of extending the reign of virtue. Eager to support his system, he stigmatises, as vicious, every effort of genius; and, uttering the apotheosis of savage virtues, he exalts those to demi-gods, who were scarcely human – the brutal Spartans, who, in defiance of justice and gratitude, sacrificed, in cold blood, the slaves who had shown themselves heroes to rescue their oppressors.

Disgusted with artificial manners and virtues, the citizen of Geneva, instead of properly sifting the subject, threw away the wheat with the chaff, without waiting to inquire whether the evils which his ardent soul turned from indignantly, were the consequence of civilisation or the vestiges of barbarism. He saw vice trampling on virtue, and the semblance of goodness taking the place of the reality; he saw talents bent by power to sinister purposes, and never thought of tracing the gigantic mischief up to arbitrary power, up to the hereditary distinctions that clash with the mental superiority that naturally raises a man above his fellows. He did not perceive that regal power, in a few generations, introduces idiotism into the noble stem, and holds out baits to render thousands idle and vicious.

Nothing can set the regal character in a more contemptible point of view, than the various crimes that have elevated men to the supreme dignity. Vile intrigues, unnatural crimes, and every vice that degrades our nature, have been the steps to this distinguished eminence; yet millions of men have supinely allowed the nerveless limbs of the posterity of such rapacious prowlers to rest quietly on their ensanguined thrones.[3]

What but a pestilential vapour can hover over society when its chief director is only instructed in the invention of crimes, or the stupid routine of childish ceremonies? Will men never be wise? – will they never cease to expect corn from tares, and figs from thistles?

It is impossible for any man, when the most favourable circumstances concur, to acquire sufficient knowledge and strength of mind to discharge the duties of a king, entrusted with uncontrolled

---

1 Contrary to the opinion of anatomists, who argue by analogy from the formation of the teeth, stomach, and intestines, Rousseau will not allow a man to be a carnivorous animal. And, carried away from nature by a love of system, he disputes whether man be a gregarious animal, though the long and helpless state of infancy seems to point him out as particularly impelled to pair, the first step towards herding.

2 What would you say to a mechanic whom you had desired to make a watch to point out the hour of the day, if, to show his ingenuity, he added wheels to make it a repeater, etc., that perplexed the simple mechanism; should he urge – to excuse himself – had you not touched a certain spring, you would have known nothing of the matter, and that he should have amused himself by making *an experiment* without doing you any harm, would you not retort fairly upon him, by insisting that if he had not added those needless wheels and springs, the accident could not have happened ?

3 Could there be a greater insult offered to the rights of man than the beds of justice in France, when an infant was made the organ of the detestable Dubois?

power; how then must they be violated when his very elevation is an insuperable bar to the attainment of either wisdom or virtue, when all the feelings of a man are stifled by flattery, and reflection shut out by pleasure! Sure it is madness to make the fate of thousands depend on the caprice of a weak fellow-creature, whose very station sinks him *necessarily* below the meanest of his subjects ! But one power should not be thrown down to exalt another – for all power inebriates weak man; and its abuse proves that the more equality there is established among men, the more virtue and happiness will reign in society. But this and any similar maxim deduced from simple reason, raises an outcry – the Church or the State is in danger, if faith in the wisdom of antiquity is not implicit; and they who, roused by the sight of human calamity, dare to attack human authority, are reviled as despisers of God, and enemies of man. These are bitter calumnies, yet they reached one of the best of men,[4] whose ashes still preach peace, and whose memory demands a respectful pause, when subjects are discussed that lay so near his heart.

After attacking the sacred majesty of kings, I shall scarcely excite surprise by adding my firm persuasion that every profession, in which great subordination of rank constitutes its power, is highly injurious to morality.

A standing army, for instance, is incompatible with freedom; because subordination and rigour are the very sinews of military discipline; and despotism is necessary to give vigour to enterprises that one will directs. A spirit inspired by romantic notions of honour, a kind of morality founded on the fashion of the age, can only be felt by a few officers, whilst the main body must be moved by command, like the waves of the sea; for the strong wind of authority pushes the crowd of subalterns forward, they scarcely know or care why, with headlong fury.

Besides, nothing can be so prejudicial to the morals of the inhabitants of country towns as the occasional residence of a set of idle superficial young men, whose only occupation is gallantry, and whose polished manners render vice more dangerous, by concealing its deformity under gay ornamental drapery. An air of fashion, which is but a badge of slavery, and proves that the soul has not a strong individual character, awes simple country people into an imitation of the vices, when they cannot catch the slippery graces, of politeness. Every corps is a chain of despots, who, submitting and tyrannising without exercising their reason, become dead-weights of vice and folly on the community. A man of rank or fortune, sure of rising by interest, has nothing to do but to pursue some extravagant freak; whilst the needy gentleman, who is to rise, as the phrase turns, by his merit, becomes a servile parasite or vile pander.

Sailors, the naval gentlemen, come under the same description, only their vices assume a different and a grosser cast. They are more positively indolent, when not discharging the ceremonials of their station; whilst the insignificant fluttering of soldiers may be termed active idleness. More confined to the society of men, the former acquire a fondness for humour and mischievous tricks; whilst the latter, mixing frequently with well-bred women, catch a sentimental cant. But mind is equally out of the question, whether they indulge the horse-laugh, or polite simper.

May I be allowed to extend the comparison to a profession where more mind is certainly to be found, – for the clergy have superior opportunities of improvement, though subordination almost equally cramps their faculties? The blind submission imposed at college to forms of belief serves as a novitiate to the curate, who must obsequiously respect the opinion of his rector or patron, if he mean to rise in his profession. Perhaps there cannot be a more forcible contrast than between the servile dependent gait of a poor curate and the courtly mien of a bishop. And the respect and contempt they inspire, render the discharge of their separate functions equally useless.

It is of great importance to observe that the character of every man is, in some degree, formed by his profession. A man of sense may only have a cast of countenance that wears off as you trace his individuality, whilst the weak, common man has scarcely ever any character, but what belongs to the body; at least, all his opinions have been so steeped in the vat consecrated by authority, that the faint spirit which the grape of his own vine yields, can-

---

4   Dr. Price.

not be distinguished.

Society, therefore, as it becomes more enlightened, should be very careful not to establish bodies of men who must necessarily be made foolish or vicious by the very constitution of their profession.

In the infancy of society, when men were just emerging out of barbarism, chiefs and priests, touching the most powerful springs of savage conduct, hope and fear, must have had unbounded sway. An aristocracy, of course, is naturally the first form of government. But, clashing interests soon losing their equipoise, a monarchy and hierarchy break out of the confusion of ambitious struggles, and the foundation of both is secured by feudal tenures. This appears to be the origin of monarchical and priestly power, and the dawn of civilisation. But such combustible materials cannot long be pent up; and, getting vent in foreign wars and intestine insurrections, the people acquire some power in the tumult, which obliges their rulers to gloss over their oppression with a show of right. Thus, as wars, agriculture, commerce, and literature, expand the mind, despots are compelled to make covert corruption hold fast the power which was formerly snatched by open force.[5] And this baneful lurking gangrene is most quickly spread by luxury and superstition, the sure dregs of ambition. The indolent puppet of a court first becomes a luxurious monster, or fastidious sensualist, and then makes the contagion which his unnatural state spread, the instrument of tyranny.

It is the pestiferous purple which renders the progress of civilisation a curse, and warps the understanding, till men of sensibility doubt whether the expansion of intellect produces a greater portion of happiness or misery. But the nature of the poison points out the antidote; and had Rousseau mounted one step higher in his investigation, or could his eye have pierced through the foggy atmosphere, which he almost disdained to breathe, his active mind would have darted forward to contemplate the perfection of man in the establishment of true civilisation, instead of taking his ferocious flight back to the night of sensual ignorance.

CHAPTER II
THE PREVAILING OPINION OF A SEXUAL CHARACTER DISCUSSED

To account for, and excuse the tyranny of man, many ingenious arguments have been brought forward to prove, that the two sexes, in the acquirement of virtue, ought to aim at attaining a very different character; or, to speak explicitly, women are not allowed to have sufficient strength of mind to acquire what really deserves the name of virtue. Yet it should seem, allowing them to have souls, that there is but one way appointed by Providence to lead *mankind* to either virtue or happiness.

If then women are not a swarm of ephemeron triflers, why should they be kept in ignorance under the specious name of innocence? Men complain, and with reason, of the follies and caprices of our sex, when they do not keenly satirise our headstrong passions and grovelling vices. Behold, I should answer, the natural effect of ignorance! The mind will ever be unstable that has only prejudices to rest on, and the current will run with destructive fury when there are no barriers to break its force. Women are told from their infancy, and taught by the example of their mothers, that a little knowledge of human weakness, justly termed cunning, softness of temper, *outward* obedience, and a scrupulous attention to a puerile kind of propriety, will obtain for them the protection of man; and should they be beautiful, everything else is needless, for at least twenty years of their lives.

Thus Milton describes our first frail mother; though when he tells us that women are formed for softness and sweet attractive grace, I cannot comprehend his meaning, unless, in the true Mahometan strain, he meant to deprive us of souls, and insinuate that we were beings only designed by sweet attractive grace, and docile blind obedience, to gratify the senses of man when he can no longer soar on the wing of contemplation.

How grossly do they insult us who thus advise us only to render ourselves gentle, domestic brutes! For instance, the winning softness so warmly and frequently recommended, that governs by obeying. What childish expressions, and how insignificant is

---

5   Men of abilities scatter seeds that grow up and have a great influence on the forming opinion; and when once the public opinion preponderates, through the exertion of reason, the overthrow of arbitrary power is not very distant.

the being – can it be an immortal one? – who will condescend to govern by such sinister methods? "Certainly," says Lord Bacon, "man is of kin to the beasts by his body; and if he be not of kin to God by his spirit, he is a base and ignoble creature!" Men, indeed, appear to me to act in a very unphilosophical manner, when they try to secure the good conduct of women by attempting to keep them always in a state of childhood. Rousseau was more consistent when he wished to stop the progress of reason in both sexes, for if men eat of the tree of knowledge, women will come in for a taste; but, from the imperfect cultivation which their understandings now receive, they only attain a knowledge of evil.

Children, I grant, should be innocent; but when the epithet is applied to men, or women, it is but a civil term for weakness. For if it be allowed that women were destined by Providence to acquire human virtues, and, by the exercise of their understandings, that stability of character which is the firmest ground to rest our future hopes upon, they must be permitted to turn to the fountain of light, and not forced to shape their course by the twinkling of a mere satellite. Milton, I grant, was of a very different opinion; for he only bends to the indefeasible right of beauty, though it would be difficult to render two passages which I now mean to contrast, consistent. But into similar inconsistencies are great men often led by their senses:

To whom thus Eve with *perfect beauty* adorn'd.
My author and disposer, what thou bid'st
Unargued I obey; so God ordains;
God *is thy law, thou mine:* to know no more
Is woman's *happiest* knowledge and her *praise.*

These are exactly the arguments that I have used to children; but I have added, your reason is now gaining strength and, till it arrives at some degree of maturity, you must look up to me for advice, – then you ought to *think,* and only rely on God.

Yet in the following lines Milton seems to coincide with me, when he makes Adam thus expostulate with his Maker:

Hast Thou not made me here Thy substitute,
And these inferior far beneath me set?
Among *unequals* what society
Can sort, what harmony or true delight?

Which must be mutual, in proportion due
Given and received – but in *disparity*
The one intense, the other still remiss
Cannot well suit with either, but soon prove
Tedious alike: of *fellowship* I speak
Such as I seek, fit to participate
All rational delight –

In treating therefore of the manners of women, let us, disregarding sensual arguments, trace what we should endeavour to make them in order to co-operate, if the expression be not too bold, with the Supreme Being.

By individual education, I mean, for the sense of the word is not precisely defined, such an attention to a child as will slowly sharpen the senses, form the temper, regulate the passions as they begin to ferment, and set the understanding to work before the body arrives at maturity; so that the man may only have to proceed, not to begin, the important task of learning to think and reason.

To prevent any misconstruction, I must add, that I do not believe that a private education can work the wonders which some sanguine writers have attributed to it. Men and women must be educated, in a great degree, by the opinions and manners of the society they live in. In every age there has been a stream of popular opinion that has carried all before it, and given a family character, as it were, to the century. It may then fairly be inferred, that, till society be differently constituted, much cannot be expected from education. It is, however, sufficient for my present purpose to assert that, whatever effect circumstances have on the abilities, every being may become virtuous by the exercise of its own reason; for if but one being was created with vicious inclinations, that is positively bad, what can save us from atheism? or if we worship a God, is not that God a devil?

Consequently, the most perfect education, in my opinion, is such an exercise of the understanding as is best calculated to strengthen the body and form the heart. Or, in other words, to enable the individual to attain such habits of virtue as will render it independent. In fact, it is a farce to call any being virtuous whose virtues do not result from the exercise of its own reason. This was Rousseau's opinion respecting men; I extend it to women, and confidently assert that they have been drawn out of their sphere by false refinement, and not by an endeavour to acquire masculine qualities. Still the regal homage which they receive is so intoxicating, that until the manners of the times are changed, and formed on more reasonable principles, it may be impossible to convince them that the illegitimate power which they obtain by degrading themselves is a curse, and that they must return to nature and equality if they wish to secure the placid satisfaction that unsophisticated affections impart. But for this epoch we must wait – wait perhaps till kings and nobles, enlightened by reason, and, preferring the real dignity of man to childish state, throw off their gaudy hereditary trappings; and if then women do not resign the arbitrary power of beauty – they will prove that they have *less* mind than man.

I may be accused of arrogance; still I must declare what I firmly believe, that all the writers who have written on the subject of female education and manners, from Rousseau to Dr. Gregory, have contributed to render women more artificial, weak characters, than they would otherwise have been; and consequently, more useless members of society. I might have expressed this conviction in a lower key, but I am afraid it would have been the whine of affectation, and not the faithful expression of my feelings, of the clear result which experience and reflection have led me to draw. When I come to that division of the subject, I shall advert to the passages that I more particularly disapprove of, in the works of the authors I have just alluded to; but it is first necessary to observe that my objection extends to the whole purport of those books, which tend, in my opinion, to degrade one-half of the human species, and render women pleasing at the expense of every solid virtue.

Though, to reason on Rousseau's ground, if man did attain a degree of perfection of mind when his body arrived at maturity, it might be proper, in order to make a man and his wife *one,* that she should rely entirely on his understanding; and the graceful ivy, clasping the oak that supported it, would form a whole in which strength and beauty would be equally conspicuous. But, alas! husbands, as well as their helpmates, are often only overgrown children, – nay, thanks to early debauchery, scarcely men in their outward form, – and if the blind lead the blind, one need not come from heaven to tell us the consequence.

Many are the causes that, in the present corrupt state of society, contribute to enslave women by cramping their understandings and sharpening their senses. One, perhaps, that silently does more mischief than all the rest, is their disregard of order.

To do everything in an orderly manner is a most important precept, which women, who, generally speaking, receive only a disorderly kind of education, seldom attend to with that degree of exactness that men, who from their infancy are broken into method, observe. This negligent kind of guesswork – for what other epithet can be used to point out the random exertions of a sort of instinctive common sense never brought to the test of reason? – prevents their generalising matters of fact; so they do to-day what they did yesterday, merely because they did it yesterday.

This contempt of the understanding in early life has more baneful consequences than is commonly supposed; for the little knowledge which women of strong minds attain is, from various circumstances, of a more desultory kind than the knowledge of men, and it is acquired more by sheer observations on real life than from comparing what has been individually observed with the results of experience generalised by speculation. Led by their dependent situation and domestic employments more into society, what they learn is rather by snatches; and as learning is with them in general only a secondary thing, they do not pursue any one branch with that persevering ardour necessary to give vigour to the faculties and clearness to the judgment In the present state of society a little learning is required to support the character of a gentleman, and boys are obliged to submit to a few years of discipline. But in the education of women, the cultivation of the understanding is always subordinate to the acquirement of some corporeal accomplishment. Even when enervated by confinement and false notions of modesty, the body is prevented from attaining that grace and beauty which relaxed half-formed limbs never exhibit. Besides, in youth their faculties are not brought forward by emulation; and having no serious scientific study, if they have natural sagacity, it is turned too soon on life and manners. They dwell on effects and modifications, without tracing them back to causes; and complicated rules to adjust behaviour are a weak substitute for simple principles.

As a proof that education gives this appearance of

weakness to females, we may instance the example of military men, who are, like them, sent into the world before their minds have been stored with knowledge, or fortified by principles. The consequences are similar; soldiers acquire a little superficial knowledge, snatched from the muddy current of conversation, and from continually mixing with society, they gain what is termed a knowledge of the world; and this acquaintance with manners and customs has frequently been confounded with a knowledge of the human heart. But can the crude fruit of casual observation, never brought to the test of judgment, formed by comparing speculation and experience, deserve such a distinction? Soldiers, as well as women, practise the minor virtues with punctilious politeness. Where is then the sexual difference, when the education has been the same? All the difference that I can discern arises from the superior advantage of liberty which enables the former to see more of life.

It is wandering from my present subject, perhaps, to make a political remark; but as it was produced naturally by the train of my reflections, I shall not pass it silently over.

Standing armies can never consist of resolute robust men; they may be well-disciplined machines, but they will seldom contain men under the influence of strong passions, or with very vigorous faculties; and as for any depth of understanding, I will venture to affirm that it is as rarely to be found in the army as amongst women. And the cause, I maintain, is the same. It may be further observed that officers are also particularly attentive to their persons, fond of dancing, crowded rooms, adventures, and ridicule.[6] Like the *fair* sex, the business of their lives is gallantry; they were taught to please, and they only live to please. Yet they do not lose their rank in the distinction of sexes, for they are still reckoned superior to women, though in what their superiority consists, beyond what I have just mentioned, it is difficult to discover.

The great misfortune is this, that they both acquire manners before morals, and a knowledge of life before they have from reflection any acquaintance with the grand ideal outline of human nature. The consequence is natural. Satisfied with common nature, they become a prey to prejudices, and taking all their opinions on credit, they blindly submit to authority. So that if they have any sense, it is a kind of instinctive glance that catches proportions, and decides with respect to manners, but fails when arguments are to be pursued below the surface, or opinions analysed.

May not the same remark be applied to women? Nay, the argument may be carried still further, for they are both thrown out of a useful station by the unnatural distinctions established in civilised life. Riches and hereditary honours have made cyphers of women to give consequence to the numerical figure; and idleness has produced a mixture of gallantry and despotism into society, which leads the very men who are the slaves of their mistresses to tyrannise over their sisters, wives, and daughters. This is only keeping them in rank and file, it is true. Strengthen the female mind by enlarging it, and there will be an end to blind obedience; but as blind obedience is ever sought for by power, tyrants and sensualists are in the right when they endeavour to keep woman in the dark, because the former only want slaves, and the latter a plaything. The sensualist, indeed, has been the most dangerous of tyrants, and women have been duped by their lovers, as princes by their ministers, whilst dreaming that they reigned over them.

I now principally allude to Rousseau, for his character of Sophia is undoubtedly a captivating one, though it appears to me grossly unnatural. However, it is not the superstructure but the foundation of her character, the principles on which her education was built, that I mean to attack; nay, warmly as I admire the genius of that able writer, whose opinions I shall often have occasion to cite, indignation always takes place of admiration, and the rigid frown of insulted virtue effaces the smile of complacency which his eloquent periods are wont to raise when I read his voluptuous reveries. Is this the man who, in his ardour for virtue, would banish all the soft arts of peace, and almost carry us back to Spartan discipline? Is this the man who delights to paint the useful struggles of passion, the triumphs of good dispositions, and the heroic flights which carry the glowing soul out of itself? How are these mighty sentiments lowered when he describes the pretty foot and enticing airs of his lit-

---

6   Why should women be censured with petulant acrimony because they seem to have a passion for a scarlet coat? Has not education placed them more on a level with soldiers than any other class of men?

tle favourite ! But for the present I waive the subject, and instead of severely reprehending the transient effusions of overweening sensibility, I shall only observe that whoever has cast a benevolent eye on society must often have been gratified by the sight of humble mutual love not dignified by sentiment, or strengthened by a union in intellectual pursuits. The domestic trifles of the day have afforded matters for cheerful converse, and innocent caresses have softened toils which did not require great exercise of mind or stretch of thought; yet has not the sight of this moderate felicity excited more tenderness than respect? – an emotion similar to what we feel when children are playing or animals sporting[7]; whilst the contemplation of the noble struggles of suffering merit has raised admiration, and carried our thoughts to that world where sensation will give place to reason.

Women are therefore to be considered either as moral beings, or so weak that they must be entirely subjected to the superior faculties of men.

Let us examine this question. Rousseau declares that a woman should never for a moment feel herself independent, that she should be governed by fear to exercise her *natural* cunning, and made a coquettish slave in order to render her a more alluring object of desire, a *sweeter* companion to man, whenever he chooses to relax himself. He carries the arguments, which he pretends to draw from the indications of nature, still further, and insinuates that truth and fortitude, the corner-stones of all human virtue, should be cultivated with certain restrictions, because, with respect to the female character, obedience is the grand lesson which ought to be impressed with unrelenting rigour.

What nonsense! When will a great man arise with sufficient strength of mind to puff away the fumes which pride and sensuality have thus spread over the subject? If women are by nature inferior to men, their virtues must be the same in quality, if not in degree, or virtue is a relative idea; consequently their conduct should be founded on the same principles, and have the same aim.

Connected with man as daughters, wives, and mothers, their moral character may be estimated by their manner of fulfilling those simple duties; but the end, the grand end, of their exertions should be to unfold their own faculties, and acquire the dignity of conscious virtue. They may try to render their road pleasant; but ought never to forget, in common with man, that life yields not the felicity which can satisfy an immortal soul. I do not mean to insinuate that either sex should be so lost in abstract reflections or distant views as to forget the affections and duties that lie before them, and are, in truth, the means appointed to produce the fruit of life; on the contrary, I would warmly recommend them, even while I assert, that they afford most satisfaction when they are considered in their true sober light.

Probably the prevailing opinion that woman was created for man, may have taken its rise from Moses' poetical story; yet as very few, it is presumed, who have bestowed any serious thought on the subject ever supposed that Eve was, literally speaking, one of Adam's ribs, the deduction must be allowed to fall to the ground, or only be so far admitted as it proves that man, from the remotest antiquity, found it convenient to exert his strength to subjugate his companion, and his invention to show that she ought to have her neck bent under the yoke, because the whole creation was only created for his convenience or pleasure.

Let it not be concluded that I wish to invert the order of things. I have already granted that, from the constitution of their bodies, men seemed to be designed by Providence to attain a greater degree of virtue. I speak collectively of the whole sex; but I see not the shadow of a reason to conclude that their virtues should differ in respect to their nature. In fact, how can they, if virtue has only one eternal standard? I must therefore, if I reason consequentially, as strenuously maintain that they have the same simple direction as that there is a God.

It follows then that cunning should not be opposed to wisdom, little cares to great exertions,

---

7   Similar feelings has Milton's pleasing picture of paradisiacal happiness ever raised in my mind; yet, instead of envying the lovely pair, I have with conscious dignity or satanic pride turned to hell for sublimer objects. In the same style, when viewing some noble monument of human art I have traced the emanation of the Deity in the order I admired, till descending from that giddy height, I have caught myself contemplating the grandest of all human sights; for fancy quickly placed in some solitary recess an outcast of fortune, rising superior to passion and discontent.

or insipid softness, varnished over with the name of gentleness, to that fortitude which grand views alone can inspire

I shall be told that woman would then lose many of her peculiar graces, and the opinion of a well-known poet might be quoted to refute my unqualified assertion. For Pope has said, in the name of the whole male sex:

Yet ne'er so sure our passion to create,
As when she touch'd the brink of all we hate.

In what light this sally places men and women I shall leave to the judicious to determine. Meanwhile, I shall content myself with observing, that I cannot discover why unless they are mortal, females should always be degraded by being made subservient to love or lust.

To speak disrespectfully of love is, I know, high treason against sentiment and fine feelings; but I wish to speak the simple language of truth, and rather to address the head than the heart. To endeavour to reason love out of the world would be to out-Quixote Cervantes, and equally offend against common sense; but an endeavour to restrain this tumultuous passion, and to prove that it should not be allowed to dethrone superior powers, or to usurp the sceptre which the understanding should very coolly wield, appears less wild.

Youth is the season for love in both sexes; but in those days of thoughtless enjoyment provision should be made for the more important years of life, when reflection takes place of sensation. But Rousseau, and most of the male writers who have followed his steps, have warmly inculcated that the whole tendency of female education ought to be directed to one point – to render them pleasing.

Let me reason with the supporters of this opinion who have any knowledge of human nature. Do they imagine that marriage can eradicate the habitude of life? The woman who has only been taught to please will soon find that her charms are oblique sunbeams, and that they cannot have much effect on her husband's heart when they are seen every day, when the summer is passed and gone. Will she then have sufficient native energy to look into herself for comfort, and cultivate her dormant faculties? or is it not more rational to expect that she will try to please other men, and, in the emotions raised by the expectation of new conquests,

endeavour to forget the mortification her love or pride has received? When the husband ceases to be a lover, and the time will inevitably come, her desire of pleasing will then grow languid, or become a spring of bitterness; and love, perhaps, the most evanescent of all passions, gives place to jealousy or vanity.

I now speak of women who are restrained by principle or prejudice. Such women, though they would shrink from an intrigue with real abhorrence, yet, nevertheless, wish to be convinced by the homage of gallantry that they are cruelly neglected by their husbands; or, days and weeks are spent in dreaming of the happiness enjoyed by congenial souls, till their health is undermined and their spirits broken by discontent. How then can the great art of pleasing be such a necessary study? It is only useful to a mistress. The chaste wife and serious mother should only consider her power to please as the polish of her virtues, and the affection of her husband as one of the comforts that render her task less difficult, and her life happier. But, whether she be loved or neglected, her first wish should be to make herself respectable, and not to rely for all her happiness on a being subject to like infirmities with herself.

The worthy Dr. Gregory fell into a similar error. I respect his heart, but entirely disapprove of his celebrated *Legacy to his Daughters*.

He advises them to cultivate a fondness for dress, because a fondness for dress, he asserts, is natural to them. I am unable to comprehend what either he or Rousseau mean when they frequently use this indefinite term. If they told us that in a pre-existent state the soul was fond of dress, and brought this inclination with it into a new body, I should listen to them with a half-smile, as I often do when I hear a rant about innate elegance. But if he only meant to say that the exercise of the faculties will produce this fondness, I deny it. It is not natural; but arises, like false ambition in men, from a love of power

Dr. Gregory goes much further; he actually recommends dissimulation, and advises an innocent girl to give the lie to her feelings, and not dance with spirit, when gaiety of heart would make her feet eloquent without making her gestures immodest. In the name of truth and common sense, why should not one woman acknowledge that she can take more exercise than another? or, in other words, that she has a sound constitution; and why, to damp innocent vivacity, is she darkly to be told that men will draw conclusions which she little thinks of? Let the libertine draw what inference he pleases; but I hope, that no sensible mother will restrain the natural frankness of youth by instilling such indecent cautions. Out of the abundance of the heart the mouth speaketh; and a wiser than Solomon hath said that the heart should be made clean, and not trivial ceremonies observed, which it is not very difficult to fulfil with scrupulous exactness when vice reigns in the heart.

Women ought to endeavour to purify their heart; but can they do so when their uncultivated understandings make them entirely dependent on their senses for employment and amusement, when no noble pursuits set them above the little vanities of the day, or enables them to curb the wild emotions that agitate a reed, over which every passing breeze has power? To gain the affections of a virtuous man, is affectation necessary? Nature has given woman a weaker frame than man; but, to ensure her husband's affections, must a wife, who, by the exercise of her mind and body whilst she was discharging the duties of a daughter, wife, and mother, has allowed her constitution to retain its natural strength, and her nerves a healthy tone, – is she, I say, to condescend to use art, and feign a sickly delicacy, in order to secure her husband's affection? Weakness may excite tenderness, and gratify the arrogant pride of man; but the lordly caresses of a protector will not gratify a noble mind that pants for and deserves to be respected. Fondness is a poor substitute for friendship!

In a seraglio, I grant, that all these arts are necessary; the epicure must have his palate tickled, or he will sink into apathy – but have women so little ambition as to be satisfied with such a condition? Can they supinely dream life away in the lap of pleasure, or the languor of weariness, rather than assert their claim to pursue reasonable pleasures, and render themselves conspicuous by practising the virtues which dignify mankind? Surely she has not an immortal soul who can loiter life away merely employed to adorn her person, that she may amuse the languid hours, and soften the cares of a fellow-creature who is willing to be enlivened by her smiles and tricks, when the serious business of life is over.

Besides, the woman who strengthens her body and exercises her mind will, by managing her family and practising various virtues, become the friend, and not the humble dependent of her husband; and if she, by possessing such substantial qualities, merit his regard, she will not find it necessary to conceal her affection, nor to pretend to an unnatural coldness of constitution to excite her husband's passions. In fact, if we revert to history, we shall find that the women who have distinguished themselves have neither been the most beautiful nor the most gentle of their sex.

Nature, or, to speak with strict propriety, God, has made all things right; but man has sought him out many inventions to mar the work. I now allude to that part of Dr. Gregory's treatise, where he advises a wife never to let her husband know the extent of her sensibility or affection. Voluptuous precaution, and as ineffectual as absurd. Love, from its very nature, must be transitory. To seek for a secret that would render it constant, would be as wild a search as for the philosopher's stone, or the grand panacea; and the discovery would be equally useless, or rather pernicious, to mankind. The most holy band of society is friendship. It has been well said, by a shrewd satirist, "that rare as true love is, true friendship is still rarer."

This is an obvious truth, and, the cause not lying deep, will not elude a slight glance of inquiry.

Love, the common passion, in which chance and sensation take place of choice and reason, is, in some degree, felt by the mass of mankind; for it is not necessary to speak, at present, of the emotions that rise above or sink below love. This passion, naturally increased by suspense and difficulties, draws the mind out of its accustomed state, and exalts the affections; but the security of marriage, allowing the fever of love to subside, a healthy temperature is thought insipid only by those who have not sufficient intellect to substitute the calm tenderness of friendship, the confidence of respect, instead of blind admiration, and the sensual emotions of fondness.

This is, must be, the course of nature. Friendship or indifference inevitably succeeds love. And this constitution seems perfectly to harmonise with the system of government which prevails in the moral world. Passions are spurs to action, and open the mind; but they sink into mere appetites, become a personal and momentary gratification when the object is gained and the satisfied mind rests in enjoyment. The man who had some virtue whilst he was struggling for a crown, often becomes a voluptuous tyrant when it graces his brow; and, when the lover is not lost in the husband, the dotard, a prey to childish caprices and fond jealousies, neglects the serious duties of life, and the caresses which should excite confidence in his children are lavished on the overgrown child, his wife.

In order to fulfil the duties of life, and to be able to pursue with vigour the various employments which form the moral character, a master and mistress of a family ought not to continue to love each other with passion. I mean to say that they ought not to indulge those emotions which disturb the order of society, and engross the thoughts that should be otherwise employed. The mind that has never been engrossed by one object wants vigour, – if it can long be so, it is weak.

A mistaken education, a narrow uncultivated mind, and many sexual prejudices, tend to make women more constant than men; but, for the present, I shall not touch on this branch of the subject. I will go still further, and advance, without dreaming of a paradox, that an unhappy marriage is often very advantageous to a family, and that the neglected wife is, in general, the best mother. And this would almost always be the consequence if the female mind were more enlarged; for, it seems to be the common dispensation of Providence, that what we gain in present enjoyment should be deducted from the treasure of life, experience; and that when we are gathering the flowers of the day, and revelling in pleasure, the solid fruit of toil and wisdom should not be caught at the same time The way lies before us, we must turn to the right or left; and he who will pass life away in bounding from one pleasure to another, must not complain if he acquire neither wisdom nor respectability of character.

Supposing, for a moment, that the soul is not immortal, and that man was only created for the present scene, – I think we should have reason to complain that love, infantine fondness, ever grew insipid and palled upon the sense. Let us eat, drink and love, for to-morrow we die, would be, in fact, the language of reason, the morality of life; and who but a fool would part with a reality for a fleeting shadow? But, if awed by observing the improbable powers of the mind, we disdain to confine our wishes or thoughts to such a comparatively mean field of action, that only appears grand and important, as it is connected with a boundless prospect

and sublime hopes, what necessity is there for falsehood in conduct, and why must the sacred majesty of truth be violated to detain a deceitful good that saps the very foundation of virtue? Why must the female mind be tainted by coquettish arts to gratify the sensualist, and prevent love from subsiding into friendship, or compassionate tenderness, when there are not qualities on which friendship can be built? Let the honest heart show itself, and *reason* teach passion to submit to necessity; or, let the dignified pursuit of virtue and knowledge raise the mind above those emotions which rather embitter than sweeten the cup of life, when they are not restrained within due bounds.

I do not mean to allude to the romantic passion, which is the concomitant of genius. Who can clip its wing? But that grand passion not proportioned to the puny enjoyments of life, is only true to the sentiment, and feeds on itself. The passions which have been celebrated for their durability have always been unfortunate. They have acquired strength by absence and constitutional melancholy. The fancy has hovered round a form of beauty dimly seen; but familiarity might have turned admiration into disgust, or, at least, into indifference, and allowed the imagination leisure to start fresh game. With perfect propriety, according to this view of things, does Rousseau make the mistress of his soul, Eloisa, love St. Preux, when life was fading before her; but this is no proof of the immortality of the passion.

Of the same complexion is Dr. Gregory's advice respecting delicacy of sentiment, which he advises a woman not to acquire, if she have determined to marry. This determination, however, perfectly consistent with his former advice, he calls *indelicate,* and earnestly persuades his daughters to conceal it, though it may govern their conduct, as if it were indelicate to have the common appetites of human nature.

Noble morality! and consistent with the cautious prudence of a little soul that cannot extend its views beyond the present minute division of existence. If all the faculties of woman's mind are only to be cultivated as they respect her dependence on man; if, when a husband be obtained, she have arrived at her goal, and meanly proud, rests satisfied with such a paltry crown, let her grovel contentedly, scarcely raised by her employments above the animal kingdom; but, if struggling for the prize of her high calling, she look beyond the present scene, let her cultivate her understanding without stopping to consider what character the husband may have whom she is destined to marry. Let her only determine, without being too anxious about present happiness, to acquire the qualities that ennoble a rational being, and a rough inelegant husband may shock her taste without destroying her peace of mind. She will not model her soul to suit the frailties of her companion, but to bear with them; his character may be a trial, but not an impediment to virtue.

If Dr. Gregory confined his remark to romantic expectations of constant love and congenial feelings, he should have recollected that experience will banish what advice can never make us cease to wish for, when the imagination is kept alive at the expense of reason.

I own it frequently happens, that women who have fostered a romantic unnatural delicacy of feeling, waste their[8] lives in imagining how happy they should have been with a husband who could love them with a fervid increasing affection every day, and all day. But they might as well pine married as single, and would not be a jot more unhappy with a bad husband than longing for a good one. That a proper education, or, to speak with more precision, a well-stored mind, would enable a woman to support a single life with dignity, I grant; but that she should avoid cultivating her taste, lest her husband should occasionally shock it, is quitting a substance for a shadow. To say the truth, I do not know of what use is an improved taste, if the individual be not rendered more independent of the casualties of life; if new sources of enjoyment, only dependent on the solitary operations of the mind, are not opened. People of taste, married or single, without distinction, will ever be disgusted by various things that touch not less observing minds. On this conclusion the argument must not be allowed to hinge; but in the whole sum of enjoyment is taste to be denominated a blessing?

The question is, whether it procures most pain or pleasure? The answer will decide the propriety of Dr. Gregory's advice, and show how absurd and tyrannic it is thus to lay down a system of slavery, or to attempt to educate moral beings by any other rules than those deduced from pure reason, which apply to the whole species.

Gentleness of manners, forbearance and long-suffering, are such amiable Godlike qualities, that in sublime poetic strains the Deity has been invested with them; and, perhaps, no representation of His goodness so strongly fastens on the human affections as those that represent Him abundant in mercy and willing to pardon. Gentleness, considered in this point of view, bears on its front all the characteristics of grandeur, combined with the winning graces of condescension; but what a different aspect it assumes when it is the submissive demeanour of dependence, the support of weakness that loves, because it wants protection; and is forbearing, because it must silently endure injuries; smiling under the lash at which it dare not snarl. Abject as this picture appears, it is the portrait of an accomplished woman, according to the received opinion of female excellence, separated by specious reasoners from human excellence. Or, they[9] kindly restore the rib, and make one moral being of a man and woman; not forgetting to give her all the "submissive charms."

How women are to exist in that state where there is neither to be marrying nor giving in marriage, we are not told. For though moralists have agreed that the tenor of life seems to prove that man is prepared by various circumstances for a future state, they constantly concur in advising *woman* only to provide for the present. Gentleness, docility, and a spaniel-like affection are, on this ground, consistently recommended as the cardinal virtues of the sex; and, disregarding the arbitrary economy of nature, one writer has declared that it is masculine for a woman to be melancholy. She was created to be the toy of man, his rattle, and it must jingle in his ears whenever, dismissing reason, he chooses to be amused.

To recommend gentleness, indeed, on a broad basis is strictly philosophical. A frail being should labour to be gentle. But when forbearance confounds right and wrong, it ceases to be a virtue; and, however convenient it may be found in a companion – that companion will ever be considered as

---

8   For example, the herd of Novelists.
9   *Vide* Rousseau and Swedenborg.

an inferior, and only inspire a vapid tenderness, which easily degenerates into contempt. Still, if advice could really make a being gentle, whose natural disposition admitted not of such a fine polish, something towards the advancement of order would be attained; but if, as might quickly be demonstrated, only affectation be produced by this indiscriminate counsel, which throws a stumbling-block in the way of gradual improvement, and true melioration of temper, the sex is not much benefited by sacrificing solid virtues to the attainment of superficial graces, though for a few years they may procure the individuals regal sway.

As a philosopher, I read with indignation the plausible epithets which men use to soften their insults; and, as a moralist, I ask what is meant by such heterogeneous associations, as fair defects, amiable weaknesses, etc.? If there be but one criterion of morals, but one architype for man, women appear to be suspended by destiny, according to the vulgar tale of Mahomet's coffin; they have neither the unerring instinct of brutes, nor are allowed to fix the eye of reason on a perfect model. They were made to be loved, and must not aim at respect, lest they should be hunted out of society as masculine.

But to view the subject in another point of view. Do passive indolent women make the best wives? Confining our discussion to the present moment of existence, let us see how such weak creatures perform their part? Do the women who, by the attainment of a few superficial accomplishments, have strengthened the prevailing prejudice, merely contribute to the happiness of their husbands? Do they display their charms merely to amuse them? And have women who have early imbibed notions of passive obedience, sufficient character to manage a family or educate children? So far from it, that, after surveying the history of woman, I cannot help agreeing with the severest satirist, considering the sex as the weakest as well as the most oppressed half of the species. What does history disclose but marks of inferiority, and how few women have emancipated themselves from the galling yoke of sovereign man? So few that the exceptions remind me of an ingenious conjecture respecting Newton – that he was probably a being of superior order accidentally caged in a human body. Following the same train of thinking, I have been led to imagine that the few extraordinary women who have rushed in eccentrical directions out of the orbit prescribed to their sex, were male spirits, confined by mistake in female frames. But if it be not philosophical to think of sex when the soul is mentioned, the inferiority must depend on the organs; or the heavenly fire, which is to ferment the clay, is not given in equal portions.

But avoiding, as I have hitherto done, any direct comparison of the two sexes collectively, or frankly acknowledging the inferiority of woman, according to the present appearance of things, I shall only insist that men have increased that inferiority till women are almost sunk below the standard of rational creatures. Let their faculties have room to unfold, and their virtues to gain strength, and then determine where the whole sex must stand in the intellectual scale. Yet let it be remembered, that for a small number of distinguished women I do not ask a place.

It is difficult for us purblind mortals to say to what height human discoveries and improvements may arrive when the gloom of despotism subsides, which makes us stumble at every step; but, when morality shall be settled on a more solid basis, then, without being gifted with a prophetic spirit, I will venture to predict that woman will be either the friend or slave of man. We shall not, as at present, doubt whether she is a moral agent, or the link which unites man with brutes. But should it then appear that like the brutes they were principally created for the use of man, he will let them patiently bite the bridle, and not mock them with empty praise; or, should their rationality be proved, he will not impede their improvement merely to gratify his sensual appetites. He will not, with all the graces of rhetoric, advise them to submit implicitly their understanding to the guidance of man. He will not, when he treats of the education of women, assert that they ought never to have the free use of reason, nor would he recommend cunning and dissimulation to beings who are acquiring, in like manner as himself, the virtues of humanity.

Surely there can be but one rule of right, if morality has an eternal foundation, and whoever sacrifices virtue, strictly so called, to present convenience, or whose duty it is to act in such a manner, lives only for the passing day, and cannot be an accountable creature.

The poet then should have dropped his sneer when he says:

If weak women go astray,
The stars are more in fault than they.

For that they are bound by the adamantine chain of destiny is most certain, if it be proved that they are never to exercise their own reason, never to be independent, never to rise above opinion, or to feel the dignity of a rational will that only bows to God, and often forgets that the universe contains any being but itself and the model of perfection to which its ardent gaze is turned, to adore attributes that, softened into virtues, may be imitated in kind, though the degree overwhelms the enraptured mind.

If, I say, for I would not impress by declamation when Reason offers her sober light, if they be really capable of acting like rational creatures, let them not be treated like slaves; or, like the brutes who are dependent on the reason of man, when they associate with him; but cultivate their minds, give them the salutary sublime curb of principle, and let them attain conscious dignity by feeling themselves only dependent on God. Teach them, in common with man, to submit to necessity, instead of giving, to render them more pleasing, a sex to morals.

Further, should experience prove that they cannot attain the same degree of strength of mind, perseverance, and fortitude, let their virtues be the same in kind, though they may vainly struggle for the same degree; and the superiority of man will be equally clear, if not clearer; and truth, as it is a simple principle, which admits of no modification, would be common to both. Nay the order of society, as it is at present regulated, would not be inverted, for woman would then only have the rank that reason assigned her, and arts could not be practised to bring the balance even, much less to turn it.

These may be termed Utopian dreams. Thanks to that Being who impressed them on my soul, and gave me sufficient strength of mind to dare to exert my own reason, till, becoming dependent only on Him for the support of my virtue, I view, with indignation, the mistaken notions that enslave my sex.

I love man as my fellow; but his sceptre, real or usurped, extends not to me, unless the reason of an individual demands my homage; and even then the submission is to reason, and not to man. In fact, the conduct of an accountable being must be regulated by the operations of its own reason; or on what foundation rests the throne of God?

It appears to me necessary to dwell on these obvious truths, because females have been insulated, as it were; and while they have been stripped of the virtues that should clothe humanity, they have been decked with artificial graces that enable them to exercise a short-lived tyranny. Love, in their bosoms, taking place of every nobler passion, their sole ambition is to be fair, to raise emotion instead of inspiring respect; and this ignoble desire, like the servility in absolute monarchies, destroys all strength of character. Liberty is the mother of virtue, and if women be, by their very constitution, slaves, and not allowed to breathe the sharp invigorating air of freedom, they must ever languish like exotics, and be reckoned beautiful flaws in nature.

As to the argument respecting the subjection in which the sex has ever been held, it retorts on man. The many have always been enthralled by the few; and monsters, who scarcely have shown any discernment of human excellence, have tyrannised over thousands of their fellow-creatures. Why have men of superior endowments submitted to such degradation? For, is it not universally acknowledged that kings, viewed collectively, have ever been inferior, in abilities and virtue, to the same number of men taken from the common mass of mankind – yet have they not, and are they not still treated with a degree of reverence that is an insult to reason? China is not the only country where a living man has been made a God. Men have submitted to superior strength to enjoy with impunity the pleasure of the moment; women have only done the same, and therefore till it is proved that the courtier, who servilely resigns the birthright of a man, is not a moral agent, it cannot be demonstrated that woman is essentially inferior to man because she has always been subjugated.

Brutal force has hitherto governed the world, and that the science of politics is in its infancy, is evident from philosophers scrupling to give the knowledge most useful to man that determinate distinction.

I shall not pursue this argument any further than to establish an obvious inference, that as sound politics diffuse liberty, mankind, including woman, will become more wise and virtuous.

CHAPTER III
THE SAME SUBJECT CONTINUED

....

Women ... sometimes boast of their weakness, cunningly obtaining power by playing on the *weakness* of men; and they may well glory in their illicit sway, for, like Turkish bashaws, they have more real power than their masters; but virtue is sacrificed to temporary gratifications, and the respectability of life to the triumph of an hour.

Women, as well as despots, have now perhaps more power than they would have if the world, divided and subdivided into kingdoms and families, were governed by laws deduced from the exercise of reason; but in obtaining it, to carry on the comparison, their character is degraded, and licentiousness spread through the whole aggregate of society. The many become pedestal to the few. I, therefore, will venture to assert that till women are more rationally educated, the progress of human virtue and improvement in knowledge must receive continual checks. And if it be granted that woman was not created merely to gratify the appetite of man, or to be the upper servant, who provides his meals and takes care of his linen, it must follow that the first care of those mothers or fathers who really attend to the education of females should be, if not to strengthen the body, at least not to destroy the constitution by mistaken notions of beauty and female excellence; nor should girls ever be allowed to imbibe the pernicious notion that a defect can, by any chemical process of reasoning, become an excellence....

Throughout the whole animal kingdom every young creature requires almost continual exercise, and the infancy of children conformable to this intimation, should be passed in harmless gambols that exercise the feet and hands, without requiring very minute direction from the head, or the constant attention of a nurse. In fact, the care necessary for self-preservation is the first natural exercise of the understanding as little inventions to amuse the present moment unfold the imagination. But these wise designs of nature are counteracted by mistaken fondness or blind zeal. The child is not left a moment to its own direction – particularly a girl – and thus rendered dependent. Dependence is called natural.

To preserve personal beauty – woman's glory – the limbs and faculties are cramped with worse than Chinese bands, and the sedentary life which they are condemned to live, whilst boys frolic in the open air, weakens the muscles and relaxes the nerves. As for Rousseau's remarks, which have since been echoed by several writers, that they have naturally, that is from their birth, independent of education, a fondness for dolls, dressing, and talking, they are so puerile as not to merit a serious refutation. That a girl, condemned to sit for hours together listening to the idle chat of weak nurses, or to attend at her mother's toilet, will endeavour to join the conversation, is, indeed, very natural; and that she will imitate her mother or aunts, and amuse herself by adorning her lifeless doll, as they do in dressing her, poor innocent babe! is undoubtedly a most natural consequence. For men of the greatest abilities have seldom had sufficient strength to rise above the surrounding atmosphere; and if the pages of genius have always been blurred by the prejudices of the age, some allowance should be made for a sex, who, like kings, always see things through a false medium.

Purposing these reflections, the fondness for dress, conspicuous in woman, may be easily accounted for, without supposing it the result of a desire to please the sex on which they are dependent. The absurdity, in short, of supposing that a girl is naturally a coquette, and that a desire connected with the impulse of nature to propagate the species, should appear even before an improper education has, by heating the imagination called it forth prematurely, is so unphilosophical that such a sagacious observer as Rousseau would not have adopted it, if he had not been accustomed to make reason give way to his desire of singularity, and truth to a favourite paradox....

...Taught from their infancy that beauty is woman's sceptre, the mind shapes itself to the body, and roaming round its gilt cage, only seeks to adore its prison. Men have various employments and pursuits which engage their attention, and give a character to the opening mind; but women, confined to one, and having their thoughts constantly directed to the most insignificant part of themselves, seldom extend their views beyond the triumph of the hour. But were their understanding once emancipated from the slavery to which the pride and sensuality of man and their short-sighted desire, like that of dominion in tyrants, of present sway, has subjected them, we should probably read of their weaknesses with surprise....

Let not men then in the pride of power, use the same arguments that tyrannic kings and venal ministers have used, and fallaciously assert that woman ought to be subjected because she has always been so. But, when man, governed by reasonable laws, enjoys his natural freedom, let him despise woman, if she do not share it with him; and, till that glorious period arrives, in descanting on the folly of the sex, let him not overlook his own.

Women, it is true, obtaining power by unjust means, by practising or fostering vice, evidently lose the rank which reason would assign them, and they become either abject slaves or capricious tyrants. They lose all simplicity, all dignity of mind, in acquiring power, and act as men are observed to act when they have been exalted by the same means.

It is time to effect a revolution in female manners – time to restore to them their lost dignity – and make them, as a part of the human species, labour by reforming themselves to reform the world. It is time to separate unchangeable morals from local manners. If men be demi-gods, why let us serve them! And if the dignity of the female soul be as disputable as that of animals – if their reason does not afford sufficient light to direct their conduct whilst unerring instinct is denied – they are surely of all creatures the most miserable! and, bent beneath the iron hand of destiny, must submit to be a *fair defect* in creation. But to justify the ways of Providence respecting them, by pointing out some irrefragable reason for thus making such a large portion of mankind accountable and not accountable, would puzzle the subtilest casuist....

Why do men halt between two opinions, and expect impossibilities? Why do they expect virtue from a slave, from a being whom the constitution of civil society has rendered weak, if not vicious?

Still I know that it will require a considerable length of time to eradicate the firmly rooted prejudices which sensualists have planted; it will also require some time to convince women that they act contrary to their real interest on an enlarged scale, when they cherish or affect weakness under the name of delicacy, and to convince the world that the poisoned source of female vices and follies, if it be necessary, in compliance with custom, to use synonymous terms in a lax sense, has been the sensual homage paid to beauty: – to beauty of features; for it has been shrewdly observed by a German writer, that a pretty woman, as an object of desire, is generally allowed to be so by men of all descriptions; whilst a fine woman, who inspires more sublime emotions by displaying intellectual beauty, may be overlooked or observed with indifference, by those men who find their happiness in their gratification of their appetites. I foresee an obvious retort – whilst man remains such an imperfect being as he appears hitherto to have been, he will, more or less, be the slave of his appetites; and those women obtaining most power who gratify a predominant one, the sex is degraded by a physical, if not by a moral necessity....

Besides, if women be educated for dependence, that is, to act according to the will of another fallible being, and submit, right or wrong, to power, where are we to stop? Are they to be considered as viceregents allowed to reign over a small domain, and answerable for their conduct to a higher tribunal, liable to error?

It will not be difficult to prove that such delegates will act like men subjected by fear, and make their children and servants endure their tyrannical oppression. As they submit without reason, they will, having no fixed rules to square their conduct by, be kind, or cruel, just as the whim of the moment directs; and we ought not to wonder if sometimes, galled by their heavy yoke, they take a malignant pleasure in resting it on weaker shoulders....

This is not an overcharged picture; on the contrary, it is a very possible case, and something similar must have fallen under every attentive eye.

I have, however, taken it for granted, that she was well disposed, though experience shows, that the blind may as easily be led into a ditch as along the beaten road. But supposing, no very Improbable conjecture, that a being only taught to please must still find her happiness in pleasing; what an example of folly, not to say vice, will she be to her innocent daughters! The mother will be lost in the coquette, and, instead of making friends of her daughters, view them with eyes askance, for they are rivals – rivals more cruel than any other, because they invite a comparison, and drive her from the throne of beauty who has never thought of a seat on the bench of reason.

It does not require a lively pencil, or the discriminating outline of a caricature, to sketch the domestic miseries and petty vices which such a mistress of a family diffuses. Still she only acts as a woman ought to act, brought up according to Rousseau's system. She can never be reproached for being masculine, or turning out of her sphere; nay, she may observe another of his grand rules, and, cautiously preserving her reputation free from spot, be reckoned a good kind of woman. Yet in what respect can she be termed good? She abstains, it is true, without any great struggle, from committing gross crimes; but how does she fulfil her duties? Duties! in truth she has enough to think of to adorn her body and nurse a weak constitution.

With respect to religion, she never presumed to judge for herself; but conformed, as a dependent creature should, to the ceremonies of the Church which she was brought up in, piously believing that wiser heads than her own have settled that business; and not to doubt is her point of perfection. She therefore pays her tithe of mint and cumin – and thanks her God that she is not as other women are. These are the blessed effects of a good education! These the virtues of man's helpmate![10]

I must relieve myself by drawing a different picture.

Let fancy now present a woman with a tolerable understanding, for I do not wish to leave the line of mediocrity, whose constitution, strengthened by exercise, has allowed her body to acquire its full vigour; her mind, at the same time, gradually expanding itself to comprehend the moral duties of life, and in what human virtue and dignity consist.

Formed thus by the discharge of the relative duties of her station, she marries from affection, without losing sight of prudence, and looking beyond matrimonial felicity, she secures her husband's respect before it is necessary to exert mean arts to please him and feed a dying flame, which nature doomed to expire when the object became familiar, when friendship and forbearance take place of a more ardent affection. This is the natural death of love, and domestic peace is not destroyed by struggles to prevent its extinction. I also suppose the husband to be virtuous; or she is still more in want of independent principles.

Fate, however, breaks this tie. She is left a widow, perhaps, without a sufficient provision; but she is not desolate! The pang of nature is felt; but after time has softened sorrow into melancholy resignation, her heart turns to her children with redoubled fondness, and anxious to provide for them, affection gives a sacred heroic cast to her maternal duties. She thinks that not only the eye sees her virtuous efforts from whom all her comfort now must flow, and whose approbation is life; but her imagination, a little abstracted and exalted by grief, dwells on the fond hope that the eyes which her trembling hand closed, may still see how she subdues every wayward passion to fulfil the double duty of being the father as well as the mother of her children. Raised to heroism by misfortunes, she represses the first faint dawning of a natural inclination, before it ripens into love, and in the bloom of life forgets her sex – forgets the pleasure of an awakening passion, which might again have been inspired and returned. She no longer thinks of pleasing, and conscious dignity prevents her from priding herself on account of the praise which her conduct demands. Her children have her love, and her brightest hopes are beyond the grave, where her imagination often strays.

I think I see her surrounded by her children, reaping the reward of her care. The intelligent eye meets hers, whilst health and innocence smile on their chubby cheeks, and as they grow up the cares of life are lessened by their grateful attention. She lives to see the virtues which she endeavoured to plant on principles, fixed into habits, to see her children attain a strength of character sufficient to enable them to endure adversity without forgetting their mother's example....

In the superior ranks of life how seldom do we meet with a man of superior abilities, or even common acquirements? The reason appears to me clear, the state they are born in was an unnatural one.

---

10 "O how lovely," exclaims Rousseau, speaking of Sophia, "is her ignorance! Happy is he who is destined to instruct her! She will never pretend to be the tutor of her husband, but will be content to be his pupil. Far from attempting to subject him to her taste, she will accommodate herself to his. She will be more estimable to him, than if she was learned, he will have a pleasure in instructing her." – ROUSSEAU'S *Emilius*.
   I shall content myself with simply asking, how friendship can subsist when love expires, between the master and his pupil.

The human character has ever been formed by the employments the individual, or class, pursues; and if the faculties are not sharpened by necessity, they must remain obtuse. The argument may fairly be extended to women; for, seldom occupied by serious business, the pursuit of pleasure gives that insignificancy to their character which renders the society of the *great so* insipid. The same want of firmness, produced by a similar cause, forces them both to fly from themselves to noisy pleasures, and artificial passions, till vanity takes place of every social affection, and the characteristics of humanity can scarcely be discerned. Such are the blessings of civil governments, as they are at present organised, that wealth and female softness equally tend to debase mankind, and are produced by the same cause; but allowing women to be rational creatures, they should be incited to acquire virtues which they may call their own, for how can a rational being be ennobled by anything that is not obtained by its *own* exertions?

CHAPTER IV
OBSERVATIONS ON THE STATE OF DEGRADATION TO WHICH WOMAN IS REDUCED BY VARIOUS CAUSES

That woman is naturally weak, or degraded by a concurrence of circumstances, is, I think, clear. But this position I shall simply contrast with a conclusion, which I have frequently heard fall from sensible men in favour of an aristocracy: that the mass of mankind cannot be anything, or the obsequious slaves, who patiently allow themselves to be driven forward, would feel their own consequence, and spurn their chains. Men, they further observe, submit everywhere to oppression, when they have only to lift up their heads to throw off the yoke; yet, instead of asserting their birthright, they quietly lick the dust, and say, "Let us eat and drink, for to-morrow we die." Women, I argue from analogy, are degraded by the same propensity to enjoy the pre-sent moment, and at last despise the freedom which they have not sufficient virtue to struggle to attain. But I must be more explicit.

With respect to the culture of the heart, it is unanimously allowed that sex is out of the question; but the line of subordination in the mental powers is never to be passed over.[11] Only "absolute in loveliness," the portion of rationality granted to woman is, indeed, very scanty; for denying her genius and judgment, it is scarcely possible to divine what remains to characterise intellect....

Into this error men have, probably, been led by viewing education in a false light; not considering it as the first step to form a being advancing gradually towards perfection;[12] but only as a preparation for life. On this sensual error, for I must call it so, has the false system of female manners been reared which robs the whole sex of its dignity, and classes the brown and fair with the smiling flowers that only adorn the land. This has ever been the language of men, and the fear of departing from a supposed sexual character, has made even women of superior sense adopt the same sentiments.... Thus understanding, strictly speaking, has been denied to woman; and instinct, sublimated into wit and cunning, for the purposes of life, has been substituted in its stead.

The power of generalising ideas, of drawing comprehensive conclusions from individual observations, is the only acquirement, for an immortal being, that really deserves the name of knowledge. Merely to observe, without endeavouring to account for anything, may (in a very incomplete manner) serve as the common sense of life; but where is the store laid up that is to clothe the soul when it leaves the body?

This power has not only been denied to women; but writers have insisted that it is inconsistent, with a few exceptions, with their sexual character. Let men prove this, and I shall grant that woman only exists for man. I must, however, previously remark, that the power of generalising ideas, to any great

---

11 Into what inconsistencies do men fall when they argue without the compass of principles. Women, weak women, are compared with angels; yet, a superior order of beings should be supposed to possess more intellect than man; or, in what does their superiority consist? In the same strain, to drop the sneer, they are allowed to possess more goodness of heart; piety, and benevolence. I doubt the fact, though it be courteously brought forward, unless ignorance be allowed to be the mother of devotion; for I am firmly persuaded that, on an average, the proportion between virtue and knowledge, is more upon a par than is commonly granted.

12 This word is not strictly just, but I cannot find a better.

extent, is not very common amongst men or women. But this exercise is the true cultivation of the understanding; and everything conspires to render the cultivation of the understanding more difficult in the female than the male world.

I am naturally led by this assertion to the main subject of the present chapter, and shall now attempt to point out some of the causes that degrade the sex, and prevent women from generalising their observations.

I shall not go back to the remote annals of antiquity to trace the history of woman; it is sufficient to allow that she has always been either a slave or a despot, and to remark that each of these situations equally retards the progress of reason. The grand source of female folly and vice has ever appeared to me to arise from narrowness of mind; and the very constitution of civil governments has put almost insuperable obstacles in the way to prevent the cultivation of the female understanding; yet virtue can be built on no other foundation. The same obstacles are thrown in the way of the rich, and the same consequences ensue.

Necessity has been proverbially termed the mother of invention; the aphorism may be extended to virtue. It is an acquirement, and an acquirement to which pleasure must be sacrificed; and who sacrifices pleasure when it is within the grasp, whose mind has not been opened and strengthened by adversity, or the pursuit of knowledge goaded on by necessity? Happy is it when people have the cares of life to struggle with, for these struggles prevent their becoming a prey to enervating vices, merely from idleness. But if from their birth men and women be placed in a torrid zone, with the meridian sun of pleasure darting directly upon them, how can they sufficiently brace their minds to discharge the duties of life; or even to relish the affections that carry them out of themselves?

Pleasure is the business of woman's life, according to the present modification of society; and while it continues to be so, little can be expected from such weak beings. Inheriting in a lineal descent from the first fair defect in nature – the sovereignty of beauty – they have, to maintain their power, resigned the natural rights which the exercise of reason might have procured them, and chosen rather to be short-lived queens than labour to obtain the sober pleasures that arise from equality. Exalted by their inferiority (this sounds like a contradiction), they constantly demand homage as women, though experience should teach them that the men who pride themselves upon paying this arbitrary insolent respect to the sex, with the most scrupulous exactness, are most inclined to tyrannise over, and despise the very weakness they cherish....

Women, commonly called ladies, are not to be contradicted in company, are not allowed to exert any manual strength; and from them the negative virtues only are expected, when any virtues are expected – patience, docility, good humour, and flexibility – virtues incompatible with any vigorous exertion of intellect. Besides, by living more with each other, and being seldom absolutely alone, they are more under the influence of sentiments than passions. Solitude and reflection are necessary to give to wishes the force of passions, and to enable the imagination to enlarge the object, and make it the most desirable. The same may be said of the rich; they do not sufficiently deal in general ideas, collected by impassioned thinking or calm investigation, to acquire that strength of character on which great resolves are built....

In the middle rank of life, to continue the comparison, men, in their youth, are prepared for professions, and marriage is not considered as the grand feature in their lives; whilst women, on the contrary, have no other scheme to sharpen their faculties. It is not business, extensive plans, or any of the excursive flights of ambition, that engross their attention; no, their thoughts are not employed in rearing such noble structures. To rise in the world, and have the liberty of running from pleasure to pleasure, they must marry advantageously, and to this object their time is sacrificed, and their persons often legally prostituted. A man when he enters any profession has his eye steadily fixed on some future advantage (and the mind gains great strength by having all its efforts directed to one point), and, full of his business, pleasure is considered as mere relaxation; whilst women seek for pleasure as the main purpose of existence. In fact from the education, which they receive from society, the love of pleasure may be said to govern them all; but does this prove that there is a sex in souls? It would be just as rational to declare that the courtiers in France, when a destructive system of despotism had formed their character, were not men, because liberty, virtue, and humanity, were sacrificed to pleasure and vanity. Fatal passions, which have ever domineered over the *whole* race!

The same love of pleasure, fostered by the whole tendency of their education, gives a trifling turn to the conduct of women in most circumstances; for instance, they are ever anxious about secondary things; and on the watch for adventures instead of being occupied by duties.

A man, when he undertakes a journey, has, in general, the end in view; a woman thinks more of the incidental occurrences, the strange things that may possibly occur on the road; the impression that she may make on her fellow-travellers; and, above all, she is anxiously intent on the care of the finery that she carries with her, which is more than ever a part of herself, when going to figure on a new scene; when, to use an apt French turn of expression, she is going to produce a sensation. Can dignity of mind exist with such trivial cares?

In short, women, in general, as well as the rich of both sexes have acquired all the follies and vices of civilisation, and missed the useful fruit. It is not necessary for me always to premise, that I speak of the condition of the whole sex, leaving exceptions out of the question. Their senses are inflamed, and their understandings neglected, consequently they become the prey of their senses, delicately termed sensibility, and are blown about by every momentary gust of feeling. Civilised women are, therefore, so weakened by false refinement, that, respecting morals, their condition is much below what it would be were they left in a state nearer to nature. Ever restless and anxious, their over-exercised sensibility not only renders them uncomfortable themselves, but troublesome, to use a soft phrase, to others. All their thoughts turn on things calculated to excite emotion and feeling, when they should reason, their conduct is unstable, and their opinions are wavering – not the wavering produced by deliberation or progressive views, but by contradictory emotions. By fits and starts they are warm in many pursuits; yet this warmth, never concentrated into perseverance, soon exhausts itself; exhaled by its own heat, or meeting with some other fleeting passion, to which reason has never given any specific gravity, neutrality ensues....

Fragile in every sense of the word, they are oblig-ed to look up to man for every comfort. In the most trifling danger they cling to their support, with parasitical tenacity, piteously demanding succour; and their *natural* protector extends his arm, or lifts up his voice, to guard the lovely trembler – from what? Perhaps the frown of an old cow, or the jump of a mouse; a rat would be a serious danger. In the name of reason, and even common sense, what can save such beings from contempt; even though they be soft and fair.

These fears, when not affected, may produce some pretty attitudes; but they show a degree of imbecility which degrades a rational creature in a way women are not aware of – for love and esteem are very distinct things.

I am fully persuaded that we should hear of none of these infantine airs, if girls were allowed to take sufficient exercise, and not confined in close rooms till their muscles are relaxed, and their powers of digestion destroyed. To carry the remark still further, if fear in girls, instead of being cherished, perhaps, created, were treated in the same manner as cowardice in boys, we should quickly see women with more dignified aspects. It is true, they could not then with equal propriety be termed the sweet flowers that smile in the walk of man; but they would be more respectable members of society, and discharge the important duties of life by the light of their own reason. "Educate women like men," says Rousseau, "and the more they resemble our sex the less power will they have over us." This is the very point I aim at. I do not wish them to have power over men; but over themselves....

Numberless are the arguments, to take another view of the subject, brought forward with a show of reason, because supposed to be deduced from nature, that men have used morally and physically, to degrade the sex. I must notice a few.

The female understanding has often been spoken of with contempt, as arriving sooner at maturity than the male. I shall not answer this argument by alluding to the early proofs of reason, as well as genius, in Cowley, Milton, and Pope,[13] but only appeal to experience to decide whether young men, who are early introduced into company (and examples now abound), do not acquire the same precocity. So notorious is this fact, that the bare mention-

---

13   Many other names might be added.

ing of it must bring before people, who at all mix in the world, the idea of a number of swaggering apes of men, whose understandings are narrowed by being brought into the society of men when they ought to have been spinning a top or twirling a hoop.

It has also been asserted, by some naturalists, that men do not attain their full growth and strength till thirty; but that women arrive at maturity by twenty. I apprehend that they reason on false ground, led astray by the male prejudice, which deems beauty the perfection of woman – mere beauty of features and complexion, the vulgar acceptation of the word, whilst male beauty is allowed to have some connection with the mind. Strength of body, and that character of countenance which the French term a *physionomie,* women do not acquire before thirty, any more than men. The little artless tricks of children, it is true, are particularly pleasing and attractive; yet, when the pretty freshness of youth is worn off, these artless graces become studied airs, and disgust every person of taste. In the countenance of girls we only look for vivacity and bashful modesty; but, the springtide of life over, we look for soberer sense in the face, and for traces of passion, instead of the dimples of animal spirits; expecting to see individuality of character, the only fastener of the affections.[14] We then wish to converse, not to fondle; to give scope to our imaginations as well as to the sensations of our hearts.

At twenty the beauty of both sexes is equal; but the libertinism of man leads him to make the distinction, and superannuated coquettes are commonly of the same opinion; for when they can no longer inspire love, they pay for the vigour and vivacity of youth. The French, who admit more of mind into their notions of beauty, give the preference to women of thirty. I mean to say that they allow women to be in their most perfect state, when vivacity gives place to reason, and to that majestic seriousness of character, which marks maturity or the resting point. In youth, till twenty, the body shoots out, till thirty, the solids are attaining a degree of density; and the flexible muscles, growing daily more rigid, give character to the countenance; that is, they trace the operations of the mind with

the iron pen of fate, and tell us not only what powers are within, hut how they have been employed....

Friendship is a serious affection; the most sublime of all affections, because it is founded on principle, and cemented by time. The very reverse may be said of love. In a great degree, love and friendship cannot subsist in the same bosom; even when inspired by different objects they weaken or destroy each other, and for the same object can only be felt in succession. The vain fears and fond jealousies, the winds which fan the flame of love, when judiciously or artfully tempered, are both incompatible with the tender confidence and sincere respect of friendship....

Women have seldom sufficient serious employment to silence their feelings; a round of little cares, or vain pursuits frittering away all strength of mind and organs, they become naturally only objects of sense. In short, the whole tenor of female education (the education of society) tends to render the best disposed romantic and inconstant; and the remainder vain and mean. In the present state of society this evil can scarcely be remedied, I am afraid, in the slightest degree; should a more laudable ambition ever gain ground they may be brought nearer to nature and reason, and become more virtuous and useful as they grow more respectable.

But, I will venture to assert that their reason will never acquire sufficient strength to enable it to regulate their conduct whilst the making an appearance in the world is the first wish of the majority of mankind. To this weak wish the natural affections, and the most useful virtues are sacrificed. Girls marry merely to *better themselves,* to borrow a significant vulgar phrase, and have such perfect power over their hearts as not to permit themselves to *fall in love* till a man with a superior fortune offers. On this subject I mean to enlarge in a future chapter; it is only necessary to drop a hint at present, because women are so often degraded by suffering the selfish prudence of age to chill the ardour of youth.

From the same source flows an opinion that young girls ought to dedicate great part of their time to needlework; yet, this employment contracts their faculties more than any other that could have

---

14   The strength of an affection is, generally, in the same proportion as the character of the species in the object beloved, lost in that of the individual.

been chosen for them, by confining their thoughts to their persons. Men order their clothes to be made, and have done with the subject; women make their own clothes, necessary or ornamental, and are continually talking about them; and their thoughts follow their hands. It is not indeed the making of necessaries that weakens the mind; but the frippery of dress. For when a woman in the lower rank of life makes her husband's and children's clothes, she does her duty, this is her part of the family business; but when women work only to dress better than they could otherwise afford, it is worse than sheer loss of time. To render the poor virtuous they must be employed, and women in the middle rank of life, did they not ape the fashions of the nobility, without catching their ease, might employ them, whilst they themselves managed their families, instructed their children, and exercised their own minds. Gardening, experimental philosophy, and literature, would afford them subjects to think of and matter for conversation, that in some degree would exercise their understandings. The conversation of Frenchwomen, who are not so rigidly nailed to their chairs to twist lappets, and knot ribands, is frequently superficial; but, I contend, that it is not half so insipid as that of those Englishwomen whose time is spent in making caps, bonnets, and the whole mischief of trimmings, not to mention shopping, bargain-hunting, etc., etc.; and it is the decent prudent women, who are most degraded by these practices, for their motive is simply vanity. The wanton who exercises her taste to render her passion alluring, has something more in view.

These observations all branch out of a general one, which I have before made, and which cannot be too often insisted upon, for, speaking of men, women, or professions, it will be found that the employment of the thoughts shapes the character both generally and individually. The thoughts of women ever hover round their persons, and is it surprising that their persons are reckoned most valuable? Yet some degree of liberty of mind is necessary even to form the person; and this may be one reason why some gentle wives have so few attractions beside that of sex. Add to this, sedentary employments render the majority of women sickly – and false notions of female excellence make them proud of this delicacy, though it be another fetter, that by calling the attention continually to the body, cramps the activity of the mind.

Women of quality seldom do any of the manual part of their dress, consequently only their taste is exercised, and they acquire, by thinking less of the finery, when the business of their toilet is over, that ease, which seldom appears in the deportment of women, who dress merely for the sake of dressing. In fact, the observation with respect to the middle rank, the one in which talents thrive best, extends not to women; for those of the superior class, by catching, at least, a smattering of literature, and conversing more with men, on general topics, acquire more knowledge than the women who ape their fashions and faults without sharing their advantages. With respect to virtue, to use the word in a comprehensive sense, I have seen most in low life. Many poor women maintain their children by the sweat of their brow, and keep together families that the vices of the fathers would have scattered abroad; but gentlewomen are too indolent to be actively virtuous, and are softened rather than refined by civilisation. Indeed, the good sense which I have met with, among the poor women who have had few advantages of education, and yet have acted heroically, strongly confirmed me in the opinion that trifling employments have rendered woman a trifler. Man, taking her[15] body, the mind is left to rust; so that while physical love enervates man, as being his favourite recreation, he will endeavour to enslave woman: – and, who can tell, how many generations may be necessary to give vigour to the virtue and talents of the freed posterity of abject slaves?[16]

In tracing the causes that, in my opinion, have degraded woman, I have confined my observations to such as universally act upon the morals and manners of the whole sex, and to me it appears clear that they all spring from want of understanding. Whether this arise from a physical or accidental weakness of faculties, time alone can determine;

---

15   "I take her body," says Ranger.

16   "Supposing that women are voluntary slaves – slavery of any kind is unfavourable to human happiness and improvement." – Knox's *Essays*.

for I shall not lay any great stress on the example of a few women[17] who, from having received a masculine education, have acquired courage and resolution; I only contend that the men who have been placed in similar situations, have acquired a similar character – I speak of bodies of men, and that men of genius and talents have started out of a class, in which women have never yet been placed.

Bibliography

Poston, Carol H., ed. *Mary Wollstonecraft: A Vindication of The Rights of Woman*. 2nd ed. New York: W.W. Norton, 1988. [Contains a critical edition of Wollstonecraft's book, together with six authors who provide "Backgrounds" to her work, fourteen contributions to "The Wollstonecraft Debate," and seven essays of "Criticisms." There is also a useful "Selected Bibliography."]

---

17   Sappho, Eloisa, Mrs. Macaulay, The Empress of Russia, Madame d'Eon, etc. These, and many more, may be reckoned exceptions; and are not all heroes, as well as heroines, exceptions to general rules? I wish to see women neither heroines nor brutes; but reasonable creatures.

Simone de Beauvoir (1908-1986) was the student, colleague, and companion and lover of Jean-Paul Sartre, the major French existentialist thinker of the post-World War II period. De Beauvoir was herself an existentialist thinker of stature and was professor of philosophy at the Sorbonne, in Paris, 1941-43. Autobiographer and novelist as well, de Beauvoir's most influential contribution to modern thought, and to modern social and cultural developments broadly, was her book *The Second Sex*, from which the selection that follows is drawn. Published (in French) in 1949, thereafter in English translation in 1953 and in all of the major western languages, this large study of the condition of being female played a signal role in launching contemporary feminism, in its so-called "third-wave." (The first wave was the original formulations of the idea in the writings of Wollstonecraft [and Condorcet], and the second the nineteenth- and early twentieth-century activist struggles for obtaining the franchise, and other changes in the legal condition of women.)

Revolutions famously have a tendency to devour their fathers, and mothers, and de Beauvoir's work was revered, as well as being deeply influential, for a considerable period, and was thereafter viewed often harshly by feminists of the 1970s and 1980s. It is perhaps more usual now to accord it something like the benign museum-like honour that Wollstonecraft also receives, as a major and significant founding mother but with severe limitations and of little direct relevance to today's concerns and issues. De Beauvoir's exploration of the experience and condition of being female may not be – and perhaps did not aspire to be – "demographically correct" (i.e., to fit the actual lives and goals of the great majority of female biological human beings). But it has arguably enduring value in spite of that fact. As an existentialist as well as a feminist, de Beauvoir was concerned with the possibilities of authentic and free existence – serious, inward, self-conscious existence – for women as well as for men, and with the social realities that impede it.

Simone de Beauvoir, *The Second Sex*

(Source: Simone de Beauvoir. *The Second Sex*. Trans. & Ed. H.M. Parshley (1952). Intr. Deirdre Bair. New York: Vintage Books, 1989, 253-263.)

Myth and Reality

The myth of woman plays a considerable part in literature; but what is its importance in daily life? To what extent does it affect the customs and conduct of individuals? In replying to this question it will be necessary to state precisely the relations this myth bears to reality.

There are different kinds of myths. This one, the myth of woman, sublimating an immutable aspect of the human condition – namely, the "division" of humanity into two classes of individuals – is a static myth. It projects into the realm of Platonic ideas a reality that is directly experienced or is conceptualized on a basis of experience; in place of fact, value, significance, knowledge, empirical law, it substitutes a transcendental Idea, timeless, unchangeable, necessary. This idea is indisputable because it is beyond the given: it is endowed with absolute truth. Thus, as against the dispersed, contingent, and multiple existences of actual women, mythical thought opposes the Eternal Feminine, unique and changeless. If the definition provided for this concept is contradicted by the behavior of flesh-and-blood women, it is the latter who are wrong: we are told not that Femininity is a false entity, but that the women concerned are not feminine. The contrary facts of experience are impotent against the myth. In a way, however, its source is in experience. Thus it is quite true that woman is other than man, and this alterity is directly felt in desire, the embrace, love; but the real relation is one of reciprocity; as such it gives rise to authentic drama. Through eroticism, love, friendship, and their alternatives, deception, hate, rivalry, the relation is a struggle between conscious beings each of whom wishes to be essential, it is the mutual recognition of free beings who confirm one another's freedom, it is the vague transition from aversion to participation. To pose Woman is to pose the absolute Other, without reciprocity, denying against all experience that she is a subject, a fellow human being.

In actuality, of course, women appear under various aspects; but each of the myths built up around the subject of woman is intended to sum her up *in toto*; each aspires to be unique. In consequence, a number of incompatible myths exist, and men tarry musing before the strange incoherencies manifested by the idea of Femininity. As every woman has a share in a majority of these archetypes – each of which lays claim to containing the sole Truth of woman – men of today also are moved again in the presence of their female companions to an astonishment like that of the old sophists who failed to understand how man could be blond and dark at the same time! Transition toward the absolute was indicated long ago in social phenomena: relations are easily congealed in classes, functions in types, just as relations, to the childish mentality, are fixed in things. Patriarchal society, for example, being centered upon the conservation of the patrimony, implies necessarily, along with those who own and transmit wealth, the existence of men and women who take property away from its owners and put it into circulation. The men – adventurers, swindlers, thieves, speculators – are generally repudiated by the group; the women, employing their erotic attraction, can induce young men and even fathers of families to scatter their patrimonies without ceasing to be within the law. Some of these women appropriate their victims' fortunes or obtain lega-

cies by using undue influence; this role being regarded as evil, those who play it are called "bad women." But the fact is that quite to the contrary they are able to appear in some other setting – at home with their fathers, brothers, husbands, or lovers – as guardian angels; and the courtesan who "plucks" rich financiers is, for painters and writers, a generous patroness. It is easy to understand in actual experience the ambiguous personality of Aspasia or Mme de Pompadour. But if woman is depicted as the Praying Mantis, the Mandrake, the Demon, then it is most confusing to find in woman also the Muse, the Goddess Mother, Beatrice.

As group symbols and social types are generally defined by means of antonyms in pairs, ambivalence will seem to be an intrinsic quality of the Eternal Feminine. The saintly mother has for correlative the cruel stepmother, the angelic young girl has the perverse virgin: thus it will be said sometimes that Mother equals Life, sometimes that Mother equals Death, that every virgin is pure spirit or flesh dedicated to the devil.

Evidently it is not reality that dictates to society or to individuals their choice between the two opposed basic categories; in every period, in each case, society and the individual decide in accordance with their needs. Very often they project into the myth adopted the institutions and values to which they adhere. Thus the paternalism that claims woman for hearth and home defines her as sentiment, inwardness, immanence. In fact every existent is at once immanence and transcendence; when one offers the existent no aim, or prevents him from attaining any, or robs him of his victory, then his transcendence falls vainly into the past – that is to say, falls back into immanence. This is the lot assigned to woman in the patriarchate; but it is in no way a vocation, any more than slavery is the vocation of the slave. The development of this mythology is to be clearly seen in Auguste Comte. To identify Woman with Altruism is to guarantee to man absolute rights in her devotion, it is to impose on women a categorical imperative.

The myth must not be confused with the recognition of significance; significance is immanent in the object; it is revealed to the mind through a living experience; whereas the myth is a transcendent Idea that escapes the mental grasp entirely. When in *L'Age d'homme* Michel Leiris describes his vision of the feminine organs, he tells us things of significance and elaborates no myth. Wonder at the feminine body, dislike for menstrual blood, come from perceptions of a concrete reality. There is nothing mythical in the experience that reveals the voluptuous qualities of feminine flesh, and it is not an excursion into myth if one attempts to describe them through comparisons with flowers or pebbles. But to say that Woman is Flesh, to say that the Flesh is Night and Death, or that it is the splendor of the Cosmos, is to abandon terrestrial truth and soar into an empty sky. For man also is flesh for woman; and woman is not merely a carnal object; and the flesh is clothed in special significance for each person and in each experience. And likewise it is quite true that woman – like man – is a being rooted in nature; she is more enslaved to the species than is the male, her animality is more manifest; but in her as in him the given traits are taken on through the fact of existence, she belongs also to the human realm. To assimilate her to Nature is simply to act from prejudice.

Few myths have been more advantageous to the ruling caste than the myth of woman: it justifies all privileges and even authorizes their abuse. Men need not bother themselves with alleviating the pains and the burdens that physiologically are women's lot, since these are "intended by Nature"; men use them as a pretext for increasing the misery of the feminine lot still further, for instance by refusing to grant to woman any right to sexual pleasure, by making her work like a beast of burden.[1]

Of all these myths, none is more firmly anchored in masculine hearts than that of the feminine "mystery." It has numerous advantages. And first of all it permits an easy explanation of all that appears inexplicable; the man who "does not understand" a woman is happy to substitute an objective resistance for a subjective deficiency of mind; instead of admitting his ignorance, he perceives the presence of a "mystery" outside himself: an alibi, indeed, that flatters laziness and vanity at once. A heart smitten with love thus avoids many disappointments: if the loved one's behavior is capricious, her

remarks stupid, then the mystery serves to excuse it all. And finally, thanks again to the mystery, that negative relation is perpetuated which seemed to Kierkegaard infinitely preferable to positive possession; in the company of a living enigma man remains alone – alone with his dreams, his hopes, his fears, his love, his vanity. This subjective game, which can go all the way from vice to mystical ecstasy, is for many a more attractive experience than an authentic relation with a human being. What foundations exist for such a profitable illusion?

Surely woman is, in a sense, mysterious, "mysterious as is all the world," according to Maeterlinck. Each is *subject* only for himself; each can grasp in immanence only himself, alone: from this point of view the *other* is always a mystery. To men's eyes the opacity of the self-knowing self, of the *pour-soi*, is denser in the *other* who is feminine; men are unable to penetrate her special experience through any working of sympathy: they are condemned to ignorance of the quality of woman's erotic pleasure, the discomfort of menstruation, and the pains of childbirth. The truth is that there is mystery on both sides: as the *other* who is of masculine sex, every man, also, has within him a presence, an inner self impenetrable to woman; she in turn is in ignorance of the male's erotic feeling. But in accordance with the universal rule I have stated, the categories in which men think of the world are established *from their point of view, as absolute*: they misconceive reciprocity, here as everywhere. A mystery for man, woman is considered to be mysterious in essence.

To tell the truth, her situation makes woman very liable to such a view. Her physiological nature is very complex; she herself submits to it as to some rigmarole from outside; her body does not seem to her to be a clear expression of herself; within it she feels herself a stranger. Indeed, the bond that in every individual connects the physiological life and the psychic life – or better the relation existing between the contingence of an individual and the free spirit that assumes it – is the deepest enigma

---

1   Cf. Balzac: *Physiology of Marriage:* "Pay no attention to her murmurs, her cries, her pains; *nature has made her for our use* and for bearing everything: children, sorrows, blows and pains inflicted by man. Do not accuse yourself of hardness. In all the codes of so-called civilized nations, man has written the laws that ranged woman's destiny under this bloody epigraph: '*Vae victis!* Woe to the weak!'"

implied in the condition of being human, and this enigma is presented in its most disturbing form in woman.

But what is commonly referred to as the mystery is not the subjective solitude of the conscious self, nor the secret organic life. It is on the level of communication that the word has its true meaning: it is not a reduction to pure silence, to darkness, to absence; it implies a stammering presence that fails to make itself manifest and clear. To say that woman is mystery is to say, not that she is silent, but that her language is not understood; she is there, but hidden behind veils; she exists beyond these uncertain appearances. What is she? Angel, demon, one inspired, an actress? It may be supposed either that there are answers to these questions which are impossible to discover, or, rather, that no answer is adequate because a fundamental ambiguity marks the feminine being; and perhaps in her heart she is even for herself quite indefinable: a sphinx.

The fact is that she would be quite embarrassed to decide *what* she *is*; but this not because the hidden truth is too vague to be discerned: it is because in this domain there is no truth. An existent *is* nothing other than what he does; the possible does not extend beyond the real, essence does not precede existence: in pure subjectivity, the human being *is not anything*. He is to be measured by his acts. Of a peasant woman one can say that she is a good or a bad worker, of an actress that she has or does not have talent; but if one considers a woman in her immanent presence, her inward self, one can say absolutely nothing about her, she falls short of having any qualifications. Now, in amorous or conjugal relations, in all relations where the woman is the vassal, the other, she is being dealt with in her immanence. It is noteworthy that the feminine comrade, colleague, and associate are without mystery; on the other hand, if the vassal is male, if, in the eyes of a man or a woman who is older, or richer, a young fellow, for example, plays the role of the inessential object, then he too becomes shrouded in mystery. And this uncovers for us a substructure under the feminine mystery which is economic in nature.

A sentiment cannot be supposed to *be* anything. "In the domain of sentiments," writes Gide, "the real is not distinguished from the imaginary. And if to imagine one loves is enough to be in love, then also to tell oneself that one imagines oneself to be in love when one is in love is enough to make one forthwith love a little less." Discrimination between the imaginary and the real can be made only through behavior. Since man occupies a privileged situation in this world, he is in a position to show his love actively; very often he supports the woman or at least helps her; in marrying her he gives her social standing; he makes her presents; his independent economic and social position allows him to take the initiative and think up contrivances: it was M. de Norpois who, when separated from Mme de Villeparisis, made twenty-four-hour trips to visit her. Very often the man is busy, the woman idle: he *gives* her the time he passes with her; she takes it: is it with pleasure, passionately, or only for amusement? Does she accept these benefits through love or through self-interest? Does she love her husband or her marriage? Of course, even the man's evidence is ambiguous: is such and such a gift granted through love or out of pity? But while normally a woman finds numerous advantages in her relations with a man, his relations with a woman are profitable to a man only in so far as he loves her. And so one can almost judge the degree of his affection by the total picture of his attitude.

But a woman hardly has means for sounding her own heart; according to her moods she will view her own sentiments in different lights, and as she submits to them passively, one interpretation will be no truer than another. In those rare instances in which she holds the position of economic and social privilege, the mystery is reversed, showing that it does not pertain to *one* sex rather than the other, but to the situation. For a great many women the roads to transcendence are blocked: because they *do* nothing, they fail to *make themselves* anything. They wonder indefinitely what they *could have* become, which sets them to asking about what they *are*. It is a vain question. If man fails to discover that secret essence of femininity, it is simply because it does not exist. Kept on the fringe of the world, woman cannot be objectively defined through this world, and her mystery conceals nothing but emptiness.

Furthermore, like all the oppressed, woman deliberately dissembles her objective actuality; the slave, the servant, the indigent, all who depend upon the caprices of a master, have learned to turn toward him a changeless smile or an enigmatic impassivity; their real sentiments, their actual behavior, are carefully hidden. And moreover woman is taught from adolescence to lie to men, to scheme, to be wily. In speaking to them she wears an artificial expression on her face; she is cautious, hypocritical, play-acting.

But the Feminine Mystery as recognized in mythical thought is a more profound matter. In fact, it is immediately implied in the mythology of the absolute Other. If it be admitted that the inessential conscious being, too, is a clear subjectivity, capable of performing the *Cogito*, then it is also admitted that this being is in truth sovereign and returns to being essential; in order that all reciprocity may appear quite impossible, it is necessary for the Other to be for itself an other, for its very subjectivity to be affected by its otherness; this consciousness which would be alienated as a consciousness, in its pure immanent presence, would evidently be Mystery. It would be Mystery in itself from the fact that it would be Mystery for itself; it would be absolute Mystery.

In the same way it is true that, beyond the secrecy created by their dissembling, there is mystery in the Black, the Yellow, in so far as they are considered absolutely as the inessential Other. It should be noted that the American citizen, who profoundly baffles the average European, is not, however, considered as being "mysterious": one states more modestly that one does not understand him. And similarly woman does not always "understand" man; but there is no such thing as a masculine mystery. The point is that rich America, and the male, are on the Master side and that Mystery belongs to the slave.

To be sure, we can only muse in the twilight byways of bad faith upon the positive reality of the Mystery; like certain marginal hallucinations, it dissolves under the attempt to view it fixedly. Literature always fails in attempting to portray "mysterious" women; they can appear only at the beginning of a novel as strange, enigmatic figures; but unless the story remains unfinished they give up their secret in the end and they are then simply consistent and transparent persons. The heroes in Peter Cheyney's books, for example, never cease to be astonished at the unpredictable caprices of women: no one can ever guess how they will act, they upset all calculations. The fact is that once the springs of their action are revealed to the reader, they are seen to be very simple mechanisms: this woman was a spy, that one a thief, however clever the plot, there is always a key; and it could not be otherwise, had the author all the talent and imagination in the world. Mystery is never more than a mirage that vanishes as we draw near to look at it.

We can see now that the myth is in large part explained by its usefulness to man. The myth of woman is a luxury. It can appear only if man escapes from the urgent demands of his needs; the more relationships are concretely lived, the less they are idealized. The fellah of ancient Egypt, the Bedouin peasant, the artisan of the Middle Ages, the worker of today has in the requirements of work and poverty relations with his particular woman companion which are too definite for her to be embellished with an aura either auspicious or inauspicious. The epochs and the social classes that have been marked by the leisure to dream have been the ones to set up the images, black and white, of femininity. But along with luxury there was utility; these dreams were irresistibly guided by interests. Surely most of the myths had roots in the spontaneous attitude of man toward his own existence and toward the world around him. But going beyond experience toward the transcendent Idea was deliberately used by patriarchal society for purposes of self-justification; through the myths this society imposed its laws and customs upon individuals in a picturesque, effective manner; it is under a mythical form that the group-imperative is indoctrinated into each conscience. Through such intermediaries as religions, traditions, language, tales, songs, movies, the myths penetrate even into such existences as are most harshly enslaved to material realities. Here everyone can find sublimation of his drab experiences: deceived by the woman he loves, one declares that she is a Crazy Womb; another, obsessed by his impotence, calls her a Praying Mantis; still another enjoys his wife's company: behold, she is Harmony, Rest, the Good Earth! The taste for eternity at a bargain, for a pocket-sized absolute, which is shared by a majority of men, is satisfied by myths. The smallest emotion, a slight annoyance, becomes the reflection of a timeless Idea – illusion agreeably flattering to the vanity.

The myth is one of those snares of false objectivity into which the man who depends on ready-made valuations rushes headlong. Here again we have to do with the substitution of a set idol for actual experience and the free judgments it requires. For an authentic relation with an autonomous existent, the myth of Woman substitutes the fixed contemplation of a mirage. "Mirage! Mirage!" cries Laforgue. "We should kill them since we cannot comprehend them; or better tranquilize them, instruct them, make them give up their taste for jewels, make them our genuinely equal comrades, our intimate friends, real associates here below, dress them differently, cut their hair short, say anything and everything to them." Man would have nothing to lose, quite the contrary, if he gave up disguising woman as a symbol. When dreams are official community affairs, clichés, they are poor and monotonous indeed beside the living reality; for the true dreamer, for the poet, woman is a more generous fount than is any down-at-heel marvel. The times that have most sincerely treasured women are not the period of feudal chivalry nor yet the gallant nineteenth century. They are the times – like the eighteenth century – when men have regarded women as fellow creatures; then it is that women seem truly romantic, as the reading of *Liaisons dangereuses*, *Le Rouge et le noir*, *Farewell to Arms*, is sufficient to show. The heroines of Laclos, Stendhal, Hemingway are without mystery, and they are not the less engaging for that. To recognize in woman a human being is not to impoverish man's experience: this would lose none of its diversity, its richness, or its intensity if it were to occur between two subjectivities. To discard the myths is not to destroy all dramatic relation between the sexes, it is not to deny the significance authentically revealed to man through feminine reality; it is not to do away with poetry, love, adventure, happiness, dreaming. It is simply to ask that behavior, sentiment, passion be founded upon the truth.[2]

"Woman is lost. Where are the women? The women of today are not women at all!" We have seen what these mysterious slogans mean. In men's eyes – and for the legion of women who see through men's eyes – it is not enough to have a woman's body nor to assume the female function as mistress or mother in order to be a "true woman." In sexuality and maternity woman as subject can claim autonomy; but to be a "true woman" she must accept herself as the Other. The men of today show a certain duplicity of attitude which is painfully lacerating to women; they are willing on the whole to accept woman as a fellow being, an equal; but they still require her to remain the inessential. For her these two destinies are incompatible; she hesitates between one and the other without being exactly adapted to either, and from this comes her lack of equilibrium. With man there is no break between public and private life: the more he confirms his grasp on the world in action and in work, the more virile he seems to be; human and vital values are combined in him. Whereas woman's independent successes are in contradiction with her femininity, since the "true woman" is required to make herself object, to be the Other.

It is quite possible that in this matter man's sensibility and sexuality are being modified. A new aesthetics has already been born. If the fashion of flat chests and narrow hips – the boyish form – has had its brief season, at least the overopulent ideal of past centuries has not returned. The feminine body is asked to be flesh, but with discretion; it is to be slender and not loaded with fat; muscular, supple, strong, it is bound to suggest transcendence; it must not be pale like a too shaded hothouse plant, but preferably tanned like a workman's torso from being bared to the open sun. Woman's dress in becoming practical need not make her appear sexless: on the contrary, short skirts made the most of legs and thighs as never before. There is no reason why working should take away woman's sex appeal. It may be disturbing to contemplate woman as at once a social personage and carnal prey: in a recent series of drawings by Peynet (1948), we see a young man break his engagement because he was seduced by the pretty mayoress who was getting ready to officiate at his marriage. For a woman to hold some "man's position" and be desirable at the same time has long been a subject for more or less ribald joking; but gradually the

---

2   Laforgue goes on to say regarding woman: "Since she has been left in slavery, idleness, without occupation or weapon other than her sex, she has overdeveloped this aspect and has become the Feminine.... We have permitted this hypertrophy; she is here in the world for our benefit.... Well! that is all wrong.... Up to now we have played with woman as if she were a doll. This has lasted altogether too long!..."

impropriety and the irony have become blunted, and it would seem that a new form of eroticism is coming into being – perhaps it will give rise to new myths.

What is certain is that today it is very difficult for women to accept at the same time their status as autonomous individuals and their womanly destiny; this is the source of the blundering and restlessness which sometimes cause them to be considered a "lost sex." And no doubt it is more comfortable to submit to a blind enslavement than to work for liberation: the dead, for that matter, are better adapted to the earth than are the living. In all respects a return to the past is no more possible than it is desirable. What must be hoped for is that the men for their part will unreservedly accept the situation that is coming into existence; only then will women be able to live in that situation without anguish. Then Laforgue's prayer will be answered: "Ah, young women, when will you be our brothers, our brothers in intimacy without ulterior thought of exploitation? When shall we clasp hands truly?" Then Breton's "Mélusine, no longer under the weight of the calamity let loose upon her by man alone, Mélusine set free . . ." will regain "her place in humanity." Then she will be a full human being, "when," to quote a letter of Rimbaud, "the infinite bondage of woman is broken, when she will live in and for herself, man – hitherto detestable – having let her go free."

Bibliography

Cottrell, Robert D. *Simone de Beauvoir*. New York: Ungar, 1975.

Elshtain, Jean Bethke. *Private Man, Public Woman*. Princeton, N.Y.: Princeton University Press, 1993.

Keefe, Terry. *Simone de Beauvoir: A Study of Her Writings*. Totowa, N.J.: Barnes and Noble, 1983.

Tong, Rosemary. *Feminist Thought*. Boulder, Co.: Westview Press, 1989.

Wenzel, Hélène Vivienne, ed., *Simone de Beauvoir: Witness to a Century*. New Haven, Conn.: Yale University Press, 1986.

Whitemarsh, Anne. *Simone de Beauvoir and the Limits of Commitment*. Cambridge: Cambridge University Press, 1981.

CHAPTER THIRTY-NINE — JULIET MITCHELL

Apart from foundational thinkers like Wollstonecraft and Condorcet in the eighteenth century, Mill in the nineteenth, and de Beauvoir in the 1940s, feminism has not produced expositors around whom there is consensus as to their stature and centrality. Certainly, many feminist writers have appeared over the past thirty years whose work has evoked much interested discussion. But along with approbative focus there has also typically appeared dissent. For very many feminists, particular theoretical feminist voices do not manage to capture or express quite the right note, even where much may be thought sound, or on the right track in an important way. Particular constituencies of support have certainly coalesced, perhaps especially around socialist feminist views. But a central consolidated theoretical position has not, at least yet, emerged.

These facts may reflect an ineluctable diversity in women, and women's experiences, or perhaps the fact that feminism has always been at least as much a practical activist movement as a position of theoretical analysis. At any rate it is appropriate to say that Juliet Mitchell (b. 1940), from whose work two selections follow, is just one feminist thinker. The selections seem aptly to express some commonalities of feminist analysis of the human and the female conditions; and also, in the case of one of them, to illustrate both feminist critique of Freudian psychoanalysis and a continuing considerable theoretical interest that many feminists have had in depth psychology of the psychoanalytic type.

Juliet Mitchell, *Psychoanalysis and Feminism*

(Source: Juliet Mitchell. *Psychoanalysis and Feminism*. New York: Pantheon Books, 1974, 364-369; 405-416.)

When Did It All Start?

All questions relating to the position and role of women in society tend, sooner or later, to founder on the bed-rock of 'When did it all start?' Sexual distinction and the consequent oppression of women wanders around in search of its author through the fields of anthropology, biology, psychology, economics, cultural history, religion, sociology and so on. As we read, with partial satisfaction, through accounts of how sexually non-repressive matriarchies gave way to authoritarian private-property patriarchies, or of how man's fear of freedom or love of power made him wish to enslave others physically and psychologically (or variations on these 'alternative' socioeconomic or psychological accounts), we have an uneasy feeling that the answers are somehow more accurate than the questions. In other words, more or less every type of explanation contains some truth. What is wrong, or why can't they be fused to provide a comprehensive picture?

We can see the same dilemma reflected in the practical politics of feminism: women seem to be abused in every sphere, on every level; the attacks must be, in some measure, commensurately random and chaotic. Is it the economic position of women as the worst-paid workers, the social destiny of wife- and motherhood, or the ideological attitudes to women as Adam's rib, baby doll, 'a bit of skirt' that must take precedence as the worst offender – and again which came first?

It seems to me that 'why did it happen?' and 'historically when?' are both false questions. The questions that should, I think, be asked in place of these, are: how does it happen and when does it take place in our society? From this last question we can then go on to ask if, within the terms of our explanation, there are 'universal' features that would enable us to understand the comparable position of women in other cultures and in other historical epochs. In other words, we can start by asking how does it happen, *now*.

It is, I think, ultimately, this search for historical origins that mars what is probably still the most influential work in the field: Engels's *Origins of the Family, the State and Private Property*. Despite its great importance it is his preoccupation with the question of 'when did it start' that makes the inaccuracy of Engels's anthropological sources relevant.

Engels orientated his analysis around the changing nature of work, man's conquest of nature and his sophistication of techniques. The accumulation of wealth and the consequent demand to ensure inheritance are the by now familiar centre points of Engels's theory of the declining status of women. His stress on the respect paid to women in primitive societies where polyandry matched polygamy and jealousy was virtually excluded by being irrelevant, his statement that mothers had the power to choose and reject chiefs in matrilineal societies, and his overall contention that the subjugation of women was no natural subordination, have all been a source of hope for socialist feminism from the date of their first reception.

That woman was the slave of man at the commencement of society is one of the most absurd notions that have come down to us from the period of Enlightenment of the eighteenth century.[1]

Yet, in Engels's account, woman was the first slave – within civilization – and women the first oppressed group. The end of matrilineage was world historical defeat of women; prior to this what he calls the 'natural' division of labour had been nonexploitative. However, there is an aspect of Engels's theses that is usually overlooked by revolutionary optimists, and it is an aspect that allies it far more closely with Freud's apparently opposite hypothesis than anyone cares to contemplate. Monogamous marriage, inheritance and the first class oppression are – for Engels – also coincident with civilization. Patriarchy and written history are

twins. The group marriage that precedes it takes place under conditions of savagery, the pairing family of barbarism. The freedom of women is pre-historic, pre-civilization.

Freud's search for origins lead him to invent the myth of the totem father slain by a gang of jealous brothers who then fairly shared out the women. For Freud this civilization is then, by his own definition, patriarchal. Though he shares with Engels an interest in anthropology, his stress is nevertheless on the history of the different ideologies within culture; so, for example, his task is to explain goddess cults in patriarchal societies. Freud's civilization is not limited to written history and in this he would, therefore, have differed from Engels. For Freud, human society, whatever the level of its culture, is civilization.[2] It certainly seems that all known societies, despite matrilineage, accord the power of the law to men. But Freud too, finds a 'prehistorical' place for matriarchies. A further comparison can be drawn between Freud's and Engels's accounts: in the individual, as Freud depicts it, 'the world historical defeat' of the female takes place with the girl's castration complex and her entry into the resolution of her Oedipus complex – her acceptance of her inferior, feminine place in patriarchal society. As Freud believed ontogeny repeated phylogeny, his reconstruction of the general historical situation would thus match Engels's. The power of women ('the matriarchy') is pre-civilization, pre-Oedipal. Thus even the most seemingly diverse analyses – such as those of Engels and Freud – agree that *civilization* as such is patriarchal, and this gives their accounts an underlying similarity.

However, Freud's stress on ideology rather than social history enables us to interpret his search for origins in a somewhat different light. On the whole it seems fair to say that Freud's work in *Totem and Taboo* must be read as mythology, not anthropology. The myth Freud proposes amounts to an assumption of how mankind 'think' their history. He has deduced this from present-day mental structures on the basis of their 'eternal' nature – but it is

---

1   F. Engels, *The Origin of the Family, the State and Private Property*, 1884, *Selected Works*, Lawrence & Wishart, London, 1958, p. 481.

2   It was fashionable when Freud was first working to distinguish between culture and civilization (for example, this was a favourite theme of Karl Kraus's). Freud rejected this distinction: they were one and the same thing.

also the way in which men *must* believe it happened if they are to live according to the dictates of society. In other words, the story tells us about the present, but, in an important way, in this respect, that is not so very different from the past. The hypothesis of *Totem and Taboo* is complementary to the Oedipus myth – it fills in its lacunae, giving us a myth that had not previously been coherently articulated by the elegant pen of a Sophocles. Just as the story of Oedipus, according to Freud, took its effect from its appeal to fundamental, universal motifs in the human mind, so the great revenge stories (as, for instance, in the major Elizabethan dramas) likewise play on the rivalry, violence and jealousy inherent in the process of assuming one's human-ness. The actual totem meal – a familiar primitive rite – enacts the infantile urge to devour, and fear of being devoured, but the historical narrative Freud elaborated to account for this also enacts it. Infantile phantasy, 'primitive' tribal rites, 'invented' historical accounts, psychoanalytical reconstructions,[3] are all the same thing – each an explanation of the other on a different level.

Although Freud gave his work here, in part, an evolutionist or developmental structure – just as initially his ontogenic observations about individuals were made in terms of 'stages' and ages (the latter usually wrong, and certainly unimportant) – it is quite evident that he viewed the work of psychoanalysis itself as another kind of myth and this suggests that even his anthropology can sustain this interpretation. Thus, for instance, in writing of Schreber's paranoiac delusions, he offered the following rumination:

... I have no motive for avoiding the mention of a similarity which may possibly damage our libido theory in the estimation of many of my readers. Schreber's 'rays of God', which are made up of a condensation of the sun's rays, of nerve-fibres, and of spermatozoa, are in reality nothing else than a concrete representation and projection outwards of libidinal cathexes; and they thus lend his delusions a striking conformity with our theory. His belief that the world must come to an end because his ego was attracting all the rays to itself, his anxious concern at a later period, during the process of reconstruction, lest God should sever His ray-connection with him, these and many other details of Schreber's delusional structure sound almost like endopsychic perceptions of the processes whose existence I have assumed in these pages as the basis of our explanation of paranoia. I can nevertheless call a friend and fellow-specialist to witness that I had developed my theory of paranoia before I became acquainted with the contents of Schreber's book. It remains for the future to decide whether there is more delusion in my theory than I should like to admit, or whether there is more truth in Schreber's delusion than other people are as yet prepared to believe.[4]

This final strange rider serves as a fascinating commentary on Reich's later work: clearly a delusion but not invalid therefore. Reich's theories were private delusions; they did not acquire the status of myth, but no less, and indeed disturbingly comparable to Schreber's, they could be classified as 'endopsychic perceptions' of the libidinal processes. There is truth in both Schreber's and Reich's 'delusions', it is just that the framework is wrong: an advanced society does not offer myths to cover this sort of perception – being private, they became delusions. Except, of course, that psychoanalysis provides the myth for us – reconstitutes the dispersed unconscious elements – and offers us the theory of libido. In a yet more subtle way we have evidence once again of Reich's return to the point from which Freud started. Freud gave credit where it was due to Schreber's analysis of his own paranoia; we could likewise give credit to Reich for his projections – if it were not that they came so much after the event and by custom if not justice, priority counts for something. Reich's metaphors – the bursting bladder of masochism, the character-armour for the insignia within the ego, the cosmic rays of blue genital love – have a pertinence that came too late. It is in this sense, and not with the glibness of dismissal, that we must label Reich's a case of paranoia. Yes, but perceptively so. A private

---

3   Constructions in analysis re-tell man's essential myths.

4   Freud, 'Psychoanalytic Notes on an Autobiographical Account of a Case of Paranoia', op. cit., pp. 78-9. One should also compare this with Freud's comments on hallucinations... .

delusion for a public myth.

It is, of course, for another reason that I introduced Freud's reflections on Schreber here. Psychoanalysis makes conscious the unconscious, not only as a therapeutic technique, but also as the task of its theory. It reconstructs the unperceived, fragmented and incoherent myths and ideas held within the unconscious mind, it makes them coherent and presents them as what they are: myths, representations of ideas, ideology – the word is difficult to find as each has a debased meaning. So the paranoid-psychotic Schreber, the mildly paranoid Reich, the normal man-in-the-street, share a common heritage of past, present and future which can be revealed and made explicit, or can be reconstructed in the whole form to which each suggestion, represented drive, thought or association refers. As has been said, Jung did not need to propose a 'collective unconscious' as the unconscious is already collective.

But if Freud's myth of origins tells us about how we live today, we still have to account for the universal features to which it lays claim. For our purposes here the most crucial of these are the patriarchal structure of society and its two attendant events: the anthropophagic complex (the totem meal) and the Oedipus complex. It seems to be the case that contemporary anthropology supports Freud's contention that human society in many different ways equals patriarchy rather than Engels's notion that patriarchy can be limited to strictly literate civilization. To what extent is this general observation relevant from our point of view?

....

The Cultural Revolution

As we have seen, Freud often longed for a satisfactory biological base on which to rest his psychological theories, and yet the wish was no sooner uttered than forgotten. From the work of Ernest Jones through to that of contemporary feminist analysts such as Mary Jane Sherfy,[5] the biological base of sexual dualism has been sought. Although there is an obvious *use* of the biological base in any social formation, it would seen dubious to stress this. For there seems little evidence of any biological priority. Quite the contrary; we are confronted with a situation that is determinately social. This situation is the initial *transformation* of biology by the exchange system expressed by kinship structures and the *social* taboos on incest that set up the differential conditions for the formation of men and women. This is not, of course, to deny that, as in all mammalian species, there is a difference between the reproductive roles of each sex, but it is to suggest that in *no* human society do these take precedence in an untransformed way. The establishment of human society relegates them to a secondary place, though their ideological reimportation may make them appear dominant.

It is not simply a question of the by-now familiar thesis that mankind, in effecting the move from nature to culture, 'chose' to preserve women within a natural ('animal') role for the sake of the propagation and nurturing of the species, for this suggestion sets up too simple a split between nature and culture and consequently too simple a division between the fate of the sexes. The very inauguration of 'culture' necessitated a different role. It is not that women are confined to a natural function but that they are given a specialized role in the formation of civilization. *It is thus not on account of their 'natural' procreative possibilities but on account of their cultural utilization as exchange-objects (which involves an exploitation of their role as propagators) that women acquire their feminine definition.* The situation, then, into which boys and girls are born is the same, the place to which they are assigned is clearly different. As it stands now, that place is in most important respects the same that it has always been: boys are to take over from fathers, girls are to want to produce babies. Any biological urge to do so is buried beneath the cultural demand that makes the way this wish is acquired coincident with human society itself. The technological conquest of the biological distinction between the sexes that Firestone and others recommend is redundant; in this instance, biology is no longer relevant. In an important sense, on this question, it has not been relevant since the foundation of human society. That foundation itself distinguished between the sexes.

---

5   See Mary Jane Sherfy, 'A Theory on Female Sexuality', in *Sisterhood Is Powerful*, op. cit., pp. 220 ff.

In what way does this emphatic change of terrain affect the tasks of feminism? If we identify patriarchy with human history, the solution to the question of the oppression of women at first seems far less accessible than if we were to explore other theories. It has been suggested that we struggle for an 'ecological revolution' – a *humanized* brave new world of extra-uterine babies – or that in the power games of all men we locate and challenge the enemy. In the first proposition, technology conquers the biological handicap of women – their greater physical weakness and painful ability to give birth. In the second, a sociological analysis matches the perceived actuality of male superiority – men as such *do* have greater economic and political power and thus social equality should right the injustice. One or other, or a combination of both of these technological and sociological answers has held sway in all demands for change and all hopes for equity. Neither socialist practice nor Marxist theory in this field have been exempt from these essentially social-democratic visions.

It is no surprise that in these circumstances the feminist revolution has nowhere come about, and that women, in vastly differing ways and degrees remain 'oppressed'. Even if important details of these theories are correct, the posing of a biological problem and its technological solution or the sociological explanation of *male* domination and its overcoming (by consent or violence) are *both* at base misleading suggestions. It is the specific feature of patriarchy – the law of the hypothesized prehistoric murdered father – that defines the relative places of men and women in human history. This 'father' and his representatives – all fathers – are the crucial expression of patriarchal society. It is *fathers* not *men* who have the determinate power. And it is a question neither of biology nor of a specific society, but of *human* society itself.

Such a proposition possibly seems *more* generalized and its solution *less* available than the biological-technological and sociological theories. But I don't think this need be the case. Patriarchy describes the universal culture – however, each specific economic mode of production must express this in different ideological forms. The universal aspects of patriarchy set in motion by 'the death of the father' are the exchange of women and the cultural taboo on incest, but these are rehearsed diversely in the mind of man in different societies.

It would seem to me that with capitalist society something new has happened to the culture that is patriarchy.

The complexity of capitalist society makes archaic the kinship structures and incest taboos for the majority of the people and yet it preserves them through thick and thin. Freud gave the name of the Oedipus complex to the universal law by which men and women learn their place in the world, but the universal law has specific expression in the capitalist family. (Anthropological arguments that make the Oedipus complex general without demarcating its specificity are inadequate; political suggestions that it is only to be found in capitalist societies are incorrect. What Freud was deciphering was our human heritage – but he deciphered it in a particular time and place.) *The capitalist economy implies that for the masses demands of exogamy and the social taboo on incest are irrelevant; but nevertheless it must preserve both these and the patriarchal structure that they imply.* Furthermore, it would seem that the specifically capitalist ideology of a supposedly natural nuclear family would be in harsh contradiction to the kinship structure as it is articulated in the Oedipus complex, which in this instance is expressed within this nuclear family. It is, I believe, this contradiction, which is already being powerfully felt, that must be analysed and then made use of for the overthrow of patriarchy.

Freud considered that 'discontent' (roughly, the sublimation and repression of desires) was a condition of civilization. It would seem indeed to be a condition, but one that Freud may well have been able to perceive precisely because it had reached a sort of 'ultimate'. Before I elaborate this point, I wish to distinguish it from one to which at first it seems to bear some resemblances. Herbert Marcuse, a Marxist who has consistently used psychoanalysis in the formation of his theories, claims that capitalist society demands a surplus repression – more repression than is needed by society in order to function. Marcuse argues that the reign of actual scarcity is all but over (or could be so), hence liberation from exploitative toil is possible; but capitalism, to retain its own nature (the exploitation of surplus-value), must create new needs, demand new 'performances' and thus institute unnecessary repression of the potentially liberated desires. It seems to me that this argument, although it welds together psychoanalytic and Marxist theory, in fact traps psychoanalysis within Marxist *economics*. In doing so it also casts, like Freud's own presentation of the progress of civilization, too evolutionary a light over the course of human history. Despite appearances and despite its important insights, this theory retains some of the worst aspects of both the sciences that it would use: an economism from Marxism and an evolutionary tinge from psychoanalysis. It is not that civilization has passed beyond the point where it needs its discontents but that there is a *contradiction* between the mode of the immediate expression-repression of these desires and the laws which forbid them as the very basis of culture. The ban on incest and the demand for exogamy howl so loudly in the contemporary Oedipus complex because they are reinforced precisely when they are no longer needed. It is only in this highly specific sense that capitalist society institutes a surplus repression; it is only the concept of *contradiction* (not that of *degree* implied by Marcuse's term 'surplus') that is of use in foreseeing any political transformation.

We can approach this proposition more concretely. Wars in no way change the basic relations of production but they do offer a different political situation and one that foreshadows the future. We can learn certain things from the last world war. Taking Britain as an example, we can see that in the period 1940-45 the family as we present it in our dominant ideologies virtually ceased to exist. In wartime the industrial employment of women was once more predominant and fathers were absent. For the first time there was planned alternative social organization to the family. Compulsory education was extended, pre-school crèches were provided, large-scale evacuation of children was organized, the state took care of food rations and ensured the basic necessary nourishment of small children and provided communal restaurants – all tasks normally left to the nuclear family. After a monumental post-war reaction, a repeat of certain of these trends is becoming visible today. With government plans for pre-school and nursery centres and the continual raising of the school leaving age, the school could rapidly become the main ideological institution into which the child is inserted. Of course such a development happens in an uneven and socially brutal fashion, but it is against such 'massifications' as the vast comprehensive school

and the modern automated factory that romantics of the family and of the intimate and the private hold their own. Like the home-sweet-home songsters of the nineteenth century, they think they are looking back to a pre-capitalist golden age, but in fact they are only humming the descant. Capitalist society establishes the family in the context of its redundancy. The restoration or abolition of the family is not itself important except as a symptom of this redundancy. It is the stress both in reactionary and in revolutionary arguments (such as Reich's) on the family and on its own contradictory nature under capitalism that has obscured the more fundamental contradiction between the specific conditions of the family and the demands of the law of human culture.

With capitalism (in its variant forms: imperialism, fascism, etc.), man reaches the limit of a historical development based throughout on class conflict. In the mass social work that man undertakes for the first time, the conditions of its own dissolution are powerfully present within capitalism. So, too, it would appear, are the conditions needed for a transformation of all previous ideology, the previous conditions of human culture. However, too often, while we acknowledge that the contradictions of capitalism as an economic system will only be resolved and released with its overthrow (and then in no straightforward manner), we forget that something similar holds true for its prevailing ideology. Why do we make this omission?

One important reason, I would suggest, is that we have tended to subject ideological analysis to economic analysis. (Although it seems to be doing the opposite, Marcuse's work is a case in point.) Or perhaps it would be more accurate to propose that the two spheres have become inextricably mingled, and theoretical progress depends not on amalgamation but on specification. However, such a commingling has still more serious consequences. Though, of course, ideology and a given mode of production are interdependent, one cannot be reduced to the other nor can the same laws be found to govern one as govern the other. To put the matter schematically, in analysing contemporary Western society we are (as elsewhere) dealing with two autonomous areas: the economic mode of capitalism and the ideological mode of patriarchy. The interdependence between them is found in the particular expression of patriarchal ideology – in this case the kinship system that defines patriarchy is forced into the straightjacket of the nuclear family. But if we analyse the economic and the ideological situation only at the point of their interpenetration, we shall never see the means to their transformation.

Under capitalism, just as the economic mode of production contains its own contradiction, so too does the ideological mode of reproduction. The social conditions of work under capitalism potentially contain the overthrow of the exploitative conditions into which they are harnessed and it is these *same* social conditions of work that make potentially redundant the laws of patriarchal culture. The working class has the power to take back to itself (for mankind) the products of the labour which are now taken from it; but no simple extension of this position can be taken to apply to patriarchal ideology. The same capitalist conditions of labour (the mass of people working together) create the conditions of change in both spheres, but because of their completely different origins, the change will come about in different ways. It is the working class as a class that has the products of its social labour privately appropriated by the capitalist class; it is women who stand at the heart of the contradiction of patriarchy under capitalism.

The controlled exchange of women that defines human culture is reproduced in the patriarchal ideology of every form of society. It goes alongside and is interlinked with the class conflict, but it is not the same thing. It is not only in the ideology of their roles as mothers and procreators but above all in the very psychology of femininity that women bear witness to the patriarchal definition of human society. But today this patriarchal ideology, while it poses as the ultimate rationalization, is, in fact, in the slow death throes of its own irrationality; in this it is like the capitalist economy itself. But in both cases only a *political* struggle will bring their surcease. Neither can die a natural death; capitalism will, as it is all the time doing, intervene at a political level, to ensure their survival.

It is because it appears as the ultimate rationality, that critics mistake the Oedipus complex for the nuclear family itself. On the contrary, it is the contradiction between the internalized law of patriarchal human order described by Freud as the Oedipus complex, and its embodiment in the nuclear family, that is significant.

The patriarchal law speaks to and through each person in his unconscious; the reproduction of the ideology of human society is thus assured in the acquisition of the law by each individual. The unconscious that Freud analysed could thus be described as the domain of the reproduction of culture or ideology. The contradiction that exists between this law that is now essentially redundant but that of course still continues to speak in the unconscious, and the form of the nuclear family is therefore crucial. The bourgeois family was so to speak created to give that law a last hearing. Naturally enough, it is not very good at its job, so capitalist society offers a stop-go programme of boosting or undermining this family. It is because it is so obviously a point of weakness that so much revolutionary theory and strategy has concentrated on attacking it. But, as we have seen, its importance lies not *within* it so much as *between* it and the patriarchal law it is supposed to express. Of greater importance still is the contradiction between patriarchal law and the social organization of work – a contradiction held in check by the nuclear family.

It is at this moment, when the very structure of patriarchal culture becomes redundant, that with necessary perversity a vogue for man-as-animal comes into its own. Throughout history man has made strenuous intellectual efforts to distinguish himself from the beasts – this was always a dominant feature of his ideology; now, when the basis of his differential culture is in need of transformation, the only possible rearguard action is to consider that that culture was never in any case very significant. In the human zoo the male 'naked-ape' is naturally aggressive and the female naturally nurturative, they must regain their instinctive animal nature and forget what man has made of man. Such absurdities are a symptom of the dilemma of patriarchal human order. A symptom of a *completely different order* is the feminist movements of the nineteenth and twentieth centuries.

Under patriarchal order women are oppressed in their very psychologies of femininity; once this order is retained only in a highly contradictory manner this oppression manifests itself. Women have to organize themselves as a group to effect a change in the basic ideology of human society. To be effective, this can be no righteous challenge to the simple domination of men (though this plays a tactical part), but a struggle based on a theory of the social non-necessity at this stage of development of the laws instituted by patriarchy.

The overthrow of the capitalist economy and the political challenge that effects this, do not in themselves mean a transformation of patriarchal ideology. This is the implication of the fact that the ideological sphere has a certain autonomy. The change to a socialist economy does not by itself suggest that the end of patriarchy comfortably follows suit. A specific struggle against patriarchy – a cultural revolution – is requisite. The battles too must have their own autonomy. It seems to follow that women within revolutionary feminism can be the spearhead of general ideological change as the working class is the agent of the overthrow of the specifically capitalist mode of production. Neither contingent – women nor the working class – can act in such a role without a theory and a political practice. But there need be no order of priority here – it will depend on the conditions in which they have to take place. Because patriarchy is by no means identical with capitalism, the successes and strengths of the two revolutionary movements will not follow along neatly parallel paths. It is perfectly possible for feminism to make more intermediate gains under social democracy than it does in the first years of socialism. Nor, alternatively, because a socialist economy is achieved, does that mean that the struggle against patriarchy must cease. There is no question of either political movement taking precedence, or of either revolutionary group being mutually exclusive or even of each group containing only its own denominational membership. By this I mean that just as when the working class becomes revolutionary, people who do not actually come from the working class can make a political transformation of their own class origins and join it, so *when* the feminist movement has a revolutionary theory and practice, men too (if with difficulty) can give up their patriarchal privileges and become feminists. This is not to say that they can become members of the movement where it operates at the level of feminist consciousness any more than Marxist intellectuals can join the trade union movement which is the equivalent organization of working-class consciousness – they can merely support it in a practical fashion. I am making these comparisons only to help us situate ourselves in current debates on the left about political practice.

When the potentialities of the complexities of capitalism – both economic and ideological – are released by its overthrow, new structures will gradually come to be represented in the unconscious. It is the task of feminism to insist on their birth. Some other expression of the entry into culture than the implications for the unconscious of the exchange of women will have to be found in non-patriarchal society. We should also recognize that no society has yet existed – or existed for a sufficient length of time – for the 'eternal' unconscious to have shed its immortal nature. While matrilineages are certainly to be found, it seems as though matriarchies can be ruled out. Matrilineages only present us with a variation on the theme of the law-of-the-father. Socialist societies have had too little time on earth to have achieved anything as radical as a change in man's unconscious. And a sense of this can be read into a recent conversation between Mao Tse-tung and the late Edgar Snow. In this Mao claimed that despite collective work, egalitarian legislation, social care of children, etc., it was too soon for the Chinese really deeply and irrevocably to have changed their *attitudes* towards women. Or as he had told André Malraux: "'Of course it was necessary to give [women] legal equality to begin with! But from there on everything still remains to be done. The thought, culture, and customs which brought China to where we found her must disappear, and the thought, customs and culture of proletarian China, which does not yet exist, must appear. The Chinese woman doesn't yet exist either, among the masses: but she is beginning to want to exist. And then to liberate women is not to manufacture washing-machines.' It is with understanding how thoughts, customs and culture operate that psychoanalysis is concerned. We have to resist the temptation to neglect the analysis for a dream, for just as pre-Marxist nineteenth-century visions perceived communism as primitive communism, so too there is today a tendency to wish to see a post-patriarchal society in terms of a primitive matriarchy: the reign of nurturing, emotionality and non-repression. Clearly neither vision has much to do with the reality of the past or of the future.

Today, our specific ideology of a natural, biological family (our 'holy family') re-expresses as a repressed Oedipal saga the kinship structure to which it is in contradiction, and the problems of learning differences. Some way of establishing distinctions will always be crucial; that it should be this way is quite another question. However, in the meantime, entering into what would seem to be only a revamped patriarchal society, the little girl has to acquire, and quickly too, her cultural destiny which is made to appear misleadingly coincident with a biological one.

It is not a question of changing (or ending) who has or how one has babies. It is a question of overthrowing patriarchy. As the end of 'eternal' class conflict is visible within the contradictions of capitalism, so too, it would seem, is the swan-song of the 'immortal' nature of patriarchal culture to be heard.

Juliet Mitchell, *Women: The Longest Revolution*

(Source: Juliet Mitchell. *Women: The Longest Revolution: Essays on Feminism, Literature and Psychoanalysis*. London: Virago Press Limited, 1984, 79-91.)

1: What is Feminism?

In an essay entitled 'On the Sexual Theories of Children', Freud wrote:

If we could divest ourselves of our corporeal existence and could view the things of this earth with a fresh eye as purely thinking beings, from another planet for instance, nothing perhaps would strike our attention more forcibly than the fact of the existence of two sexes among human beings, who, though so much alike in other respects, yet mark the difference between them with such obvious external signs.

Feminists are also struck by the numerous human insignia that divide the sexes and they are, I hope, looking at the matter with a fresh eye. Men and women are like each other and are distinct from other animate or inanimate forms, yet whatever constitutes the difference between men and women is socially insisted upon in human societies and always elaborated. It is this social stress on the difference between men and women that is the subject of feminism.

I would suggest that what is important is that feminism in initiating a system of thought, transforms the ideological notion that there is a biological opposition between the sexes which determines social life, and asserts instead that there is a contradiction in the social relations between men and women. This contradiction – which is never static, as a biological opposition would be – shifts, moves and is moved and is therefore one force among others that effects social change and the movement of human history itself.

If we proceed to look at a social relationship between the sexes we can see that this has certain implications for the way we consider the question of the oppression of women, which is, after all, what feminism is about. Even the most progressive thought (both without and within feminism) tends to view women either in isolation from the men of their society or only in relation to the women of other societies. At its crudest, this argument will take the form of a European pointing out that though it is true that women in, say, Italy have a raw deal, women in America enjoy all the wealth-earning power glories of the so-called matriarchy. Somewhat more sophisticated research will engage in the type of cross-cultural argument that shows that Arapesh men are gentler and more feminine than the stereotype of women within advanced capitalist societies. In other words, this type of research tries to show that as there are no absolutes and all values are relative, there is no universal oppression of women.

But as feminists, what we should be talking about is not relativism but a social relationship. What we are therefore concerned with has two aspects: first we are concerned with the particular relationship between men and women within a particular society; and second, we have to draw from that particular relationship any universal features of it that we can. The cross-cultural work that has to be done is to discover the relationship between Arapesh men and women, American men and women, and then to discover what is common not to the men on their own or to the women on their own, or to a man and a woman of different societies, but what is common to the relationship between men and women

Every society makes some distinction between the sexes. This does not mean that every society makes the biological male into a social man, or a biological female into a social woman. Among the Mohave, an American Indian group, for instance, a male in his own behaviour and in the regard of others, can be a social female or vice versa. Nor does it mean that all societies have only two social sexes; among the Navaho there are three gender groups, masculine, feminine and the nadle, an intersex person who may or may not have intersex physiological morphology. Thus, all societies make a distinction between at least two social sexes and a distinction, which, with all the many variations, can be described as a distinction between social men and social women. Some societies mark the difference in extreme ways, others only marginally, but the distinction has always been there.

Across the world, throughout history and, indeed, within prehistory, woman's situation has varied enormously, but relative to the man of her society, woman has always held a very particular place. Since the distinction between the sexes among human beings is a social one (whatever its coincidence with biology), and human beings distinguish themselves from other primates and animals in general by their organisation of society, we can expect the social distinction between the sexes to find expression in ways that are relevant to this organisation.

Reducing the background of my argument about the contradiction in the social relationship between men and women which forms the basic premise of feminism, to its simple essentials, we should argue that mankind transforms nature both by its labour and by its social organisation. It is not that other primates do not have skills or know the use of primitive tools, that animal groups have no systems of communication – clearly they do – but the learned accumulation of both the techniques of labour and the complexities of language is a characteristic peculiar to humans. Humans – male and female – form not groups, but societies.

If then, both labour and social organisation and with it, language, are human characteristics, we would expect to find that the universal social distinction between the sexes takes up its place within these terms. This, indeed, would seem to be the case.

The division of labour by sex is a universal feature of human society. Whatever the degree of overlap, whatever the weight of labour carried by either men or women, a distinction is made between the work predominantly done by men and that predominantly done by women. In this case, it is not a question of which group's labour provides the chief source of a society's subsistence – in some, woman's labour contributes virtually nothing, in others practically the whole – the question is rather what we can find to be a constant characteristic of women's work as it relates to men's. Here it would seem that in all societies, relative to their men, women undertake more childcare. The Nuer man of East Africa may nurture the young more than a man or even an upper-class woman in England, he may cuddle and care for, but a Nuer woman still does that bit more than he does. Even if we exclude her physiological ability to breastfeed, the Nuer woman's social role as nurse is more extensive than that of the man of her tribe.

In a short note written for *The American Anthropologist*, Judith Brown speculated that the contribution women make to the subsistence of their society was determined by the compatibility of the main subsistence activity with child care. She wrote:

> I would like to suggest that the degree to which women contribute to the subsistence of a particular society, can be predicted with considerable accuracy from a knowledge of the major subsistence activity. It is determined by the compatibility of this pursuit with the demands of childcare.... Nowhere in the world is the rearing of children primarily the responsibility of men, and only in a few societies are women exempted from participation in the subsistence activities. If the economic role of women is to be maximised, their responsibilities in child care must be reduced or the economic activity must be such that it can be carried out concurrently with childcare. [6]

Since we are interested in human society, and the social relationship between the sexes, what has to concern us here in the physiological and biological arguments that are bound to be made, is that the females of all species of animals, including humans, give birth, and females of all primates can give primary nourishment to their young. However, what should interest us, in fact, are not the similarities between humans and animals, but the differences. And, in this case, the relevant physiological fact is that the human infant is born prematurely; it is less well-developed at birth, and hence more dependent. This in turn means a reduced capacity for instinctual behaviour and an increased capacity

6   Judith K. Brown, 'A Note on the Division of Labour by Sex,' *The American Anthropologist*, 72, 1970, p. 1075.

for learning. It is not that women do have a 'natural animal instinct' for mother love that matters in this context – they may or may not do so – but that the social organisation of mankind requires women to be the group that provides for the human animal becoming a social being at this primary level. Mother love is a social requisite even where it coincides with a natural urge.

The sexual division of labour with its characteristic of more child care for women would seem to be a significant element in the organisation of human society. It can be either oppressive or non-oppressive. The second universal feature that I want to isolate in the structures of social organisation is the taboo on incest. Just as the universal division of labour according to sex is a universal form with a very various content – in some societies men farm and in others, women – so the taboo on incest is a universal prescription with a very diverse expression – some societies forbid marriage between brothers and sisters, others desire precisely that union for their ruling groups. Again, we have to remember that we're talking about a general social system. The taboo on incest seems to us so natural precisely because it is a key point at which mankind organises its own animal nature into a social nature.

A human kinship system, which is a system within which the taboo on incest is contained, organises human behaviour in a symbolic manner: 'Human kinship is above all a symbolic organisation of behaviour, a cultural construct upon the biological individuals involved.' Kinship involves the socialisation of sexuality into prescribed patterns and the naming of the kinsfolk with whom one may or may not have sexual relations. In other words, it involves both social interchange and language. Whom you call 'mother' may not be your biological mother, but your naming her such tells you your place in a social relationship to her.

The kinship system, like the sexual division of labour, utilises and institutes a social distinction between social men and women. Going back to Freud's quotation, we note that the visitor from outer space was struck (if we looked around us at the literature on the subject we may think that he was indeed struck dumb) by the elaborate effort that the human species has made to distinguish between two sexes which otherwise are so alike. Indeed, we might be right in thinking that this very inordinate desire to thus socially distinguish is one of the marks of human society. Primates such as chimpanzees and baboons, are characterised by a natural biological division between the sexes. As mankind starts to master nature (and we must remember that it is always man's own nature as well as external nature that is bound up in this question of the control of nature, that it is a process that has not only gone on throughout prehistory and all recorded history but is still very much going on and will always go on), it would seem that a natural division between the sexes, such as the primates know, would gradually be overcome. Instead, we find that far from being overcome, it is forcefully redefined in social terms – no primates distinguish between the sexes as assiduously as humans do. In the gap between our hypothetical expectation of mankind's control of its own nature, and hence what we would expect to be a gradual social elimination of natural differences and what, in fact, we do, which is to reinforce sexual differences – lies the question to which we have to address ourselves.

The social behaviour of primates is one of reciprocity: feed and be fed, protect and be protected, produce survival and survive by reproduction. It would also seem that in their most residual elements, the two features of human life that distinguish it from the lives of other primates and, in addition to this, are also universal features of human society – the social divisions of labour by sex and the kinship system – are also reciprocal relationships. In fact, they could be defined as systems set up to ensure reciprocity. The anthropologist Claude Lévi-Strauss suggests that the sexual division of labour is an artificial device where the two sexes, who in their human ability to labour could be so alike, are yet kept distinct and hence, mutually dependent. In proposing this, Lévi-Strauss is extending the work of Marcel Mauss on the significance of the gift. Mauss defines the gift as the first form of social contract – if you give a gift it is expected that you will at some point be given something in return. According to Lévi-Strauss, what else is the kinship system but a complex giving of people to each other in the understanding that one day you will be given someone in return? At first sight, then, it would seem that human kinship and the sexual division of labour reinterpret at a social level the natural reciprocity of primate groups. But do they?

Reciprocal relations are dual relationships – give and take / take and give; but social relations cannot be dual relations because a dual relation is a closed system – a happy or vicious circle. Any social relationship must have as a minimum a third element and a fourth which gives meaning to the third: the gift and the significance of a gift. It is this meaning that transforms a piece of meat exchanged between primates to a shell necklace exchanged between humans – the one is reciprocal survival, the other symbolic of social relations. For two sounds to move from animal communication to become language, a third and fourth term must intervene: the space between the words and the meaning it thus gives to their relationship.

Because of this, it seems that, contrary to most anthropology that has been concerned with explaining the position of women, the key event that marks the humanisation of the primate is kinship and its attendant event language, and that the sexual division of labour is not causal but consequent upon this. In other words, where, for instance, Engels in *The Origin of the Family, Private Property and the State* argues that a natural division of labour becomes a social division of labour which becomes oppressive only with the accumulation of wealth and, hence, property, I think we should see that kinship and language already structure human beings into socially different places before you have any massive accumulation of wealth. Or, to put it schematically, instead of a theory that goes as follows: the natural division of labour among the primates becomes the social-sexual division among humans which becomes organised oppressively by kinship and then by class society, my suggestion goes as follows: the natural division of labour among primates is first transformed by human kinship and language which for its functioning sets up its social human division of labour by sexes. This may seem a pointless quibble – and after all, how can anyone tell whether the egg or chicken came first – but, in fact, it is not an argument about a chronological priority of events, but about the structural place of women's oppression.

Kinship organises sexuality in such a way that it prescribes social relations. To do this it exchanges people from one group to another and sometimes within a group. As a system it doesn't matter who

is exchanged, and, doubtless, a complex anthropology of any given society would find within it that various categories of people are being exchanged. However, what we are looking for within kinship systems, just as it is what we are looking for in class society, is both what is the main social relationship and what is the principal system of organisation? It would seem that whatever other exchanges go on, women are always exchanged between men, thus though it may well be that there are some societies in which some women exchange some men, there are none in which women are not exchanged predominantly by men. Clearly the particular conditions of any kinship group's material base for survival will affect the form of kinship or the form of family organisation, that is to say whether it is agricultural, pastoral, or so on. Later, of course, the form of family will also be determined by class structures. But the other aspect of a material base will also be determinate; that base is the reproduction of human life. Mankind transforms external nature for the production of the needs of life and transforms its own nature, not for the reproduction of the species, but for the reproduction of society. In exchanging women, humans transform the primate ability to continue the species and give a social form to the reproduction of human society. In exchanging women in a way that ensures the reproduction of the society, the sexual division of labour that ties women to child care in a particular social manner is instituted.

Exactly at which point these conditions become oppressive of women is hard to determine. Engels' thesis would suggest that, while labour (as he sees it, the male-dominated sphere) was primitive, it had no more importance than the reproduction of people (the female-dominated sphere), and that hence the sexes occupied equilateral positions. But behind this analysis (and despite its intentions) there seems to me to be a biological determinism – that is to say, that because women give birth they got left behind when labour and production, which determine social change, leaped ahead. At the very least, the exchange of women (itself possibly a determinate system within the various exchanges of kinship) was a precondition for women's oppression. I think it may be more than a precondition. It made their productive labour dependent on their ascribed social functions as mothers, nurses and educators and those functions were already constituted in their 'future': they were subordinate functions.

The question of matrilineal or patrilineal societies – inheritance down the mother's line or down the father's line – is likewise a vexed one. Because of the role of the mother's brother, even where the line of descent is traced through women (matrilineality), women as reproducers are exchanged between men. But in that the exchange is only one exchange among many and in that the role of the mother's brother is only one aspect even of this situation – the husband will probably come to live in the wife's place of residence for instance, he may even be given some gift as recognition of his move of social and geographical location (the male equivalent of bride-price) – then the woman's situation is potentially less oppressive. No more than are class societies uniformly exploitative are kinship systems uniformly oppressive.

What I'm suggesting, however, is that we have a situation which is doubly determined. The internal movement of kinship systems is determined by the nature of the exchange of women. But the relationship *between* the kinship organisation and the economic mode of production of the larger society and the eventual subordination of kinship to class means that class determines the particular form of kinship. There is a contradiction *within* kinship between men and women whose determining moment is the exchange of women, and there is a contradiction *between* kinship systems and the mode of production.

I'm suggesting that the exchange of women always determines the nature of the kinship group from within, but this is not the same as saying that this particular exchange is always dominant. In matrilineal, matrilocal tribes it would not seem to be dominant and this would make the position of women very different from that within patrilineal societies.

The woman who is exchanged is the promise of the next generation – no one wants to receive or, therefore, give, an infertile woman. In the kinship system heterosexuality is assured as the dominant mode and in the exchange of women, women become confined not to the species, as is often argued, but to the social task of reproduction – to mankind's transformation and humanisation of its own nature.

At first sight, there is nothing in itself oppressive about this situation, nor, of course, is it an exclusive one – women do other things than get exchanged. But it is in the interlocking of this determinate aspect of kinship (which in most societies which are, after all, patrilinear ones, is also the dominant one) and the sexual division of labour that I think we have to start asking questions about women's oppression. If in her note in *The American Anthropologist* Judith Brown is correct and we can gauge the degree of women's contribution to the subsistence economy by the extent to which women's work is compatible with child care, then we can see that women's contribution to production is determined by their place in the system of the reproduction of human beings. As the level of production dominates over that of reproduction in society as a whole, we can see that women's ability to produce being dominated by their having to reproduce has very serious consequences. In other words, it is not only, as Engels claims, that as production gets more advanced, class societies come to dominate over kinship groups and women, who are bound to the kinship family, become oppressed. It would seem that in the pre-class intersection of the kinship exchange system and the sexual division of labour (the system which still continues), as the people whose ability to produce is determined by the demand to reproduce social human beings, women must hold a subordinate position to men whose ability to reproduce not themselves but the other material conditions of their society (such as the reproduction of capital), depends on the social demand for them to produce those material goods in the first place.

Thus it is not just a question of class society – the dominance of production over reproduction – coming to dominate over the organisation of the society by kinship (and thus men coming to dominate over women) but rather that within the very system of kinship and its implications for the division of labour the conditions of men's domination over women are instituted.

What implications does this have for feminism? I want to end not by answering this question – because it's too big a question – but by giving two illustrations that might help direct the way in which we should look for answers. The first illustration I've borrowed from an observation I heard an American anthropologist, Norma Diamond, make recently about the Chinese communes. On her visit to the Chinese communes, she noticed that despite egalitarian job possibilities, communal, domestic and child-care facilities and a political policy of sexual equality, women in the communes rarely held positions with as high a status attached to them as did the men. Being a feminist, and a good scholar, she asked two questions: 'Why not?' and 'What particular characteristics did the few women who had managed to get important positions have in common?' To cut a long story short, she found that as a result of the Chinese policy of not only eradicating faults in social practices but also of building on social strengths, many communes were based on old pre-liberation kinship groups. The evil practices, whereby the father of the family was absolute head often with rights of life and death over the rest of the family, whereby the older generation oppress the younger, whereby women were literally chattels without any rights at all, problems of inheritance, and so on, were all absolutely removed, and most of the social reforms that feminists in the west craved for were instituted. But the seemingly harmless residual organisation of kinship was retained. Communes often had old kin names, and the old kin groups had been patrilocal, that is to say, a woman moved to her husband's place of residence on marriage. This practice continued in the communes. Now the women who had high status positions were married women who had, for some reason, stayed in their original commune – their commune of origin. For example, they had married youths who had come out from the cities during the Cultural Revolution. Other women were either unmarried and therefore likely to leave their commune of origin or had come to the commune on marriage. In both cases, they had not the same positions of power – in one case because they were going to leave and in the other case because they had just arrived and had not the well-established influential ties. In other words, an apparently harmless means of social organisation,

invisible unless one looked for it, had quite serious consequences for women.

The more frivolous illustration comes from our own type of society. It exemplifies how kinship still operates even if concealed beneath other complex ideologies and other forms of organisation. The daughter of the Queen of England married a commoner. Her father, who himself was not the king, gave her away to her husband, to whose place of residence she then removed. Princess Anne, as she herself said, is an 'old-fashioned' girl and she embellished the proceedings by promising to honour and obey her husband.

But even without the 'extras' of a patriarchal religious ceremony, the exchange of women and all its consequences still goes on in our society. It has, I think, important implications not only for women's subordination to men in the family but for the unequal sexual division at the place of work. Feminism needs to bring the unseen structures of kinship into the light of day.

Bibliography

Grant, Judith. *Fundamental Feminism*. New York and London: Routledge, 1993.

Grimshaw, Jean. *Philosophy and Feminist Thinking*. Minneapolis: University of Minnesota Press, 1986. [published simultaneously in the U.K. as *Feminist Philosophers*. London: Harvester Wheatsheaf, 1986.]

Jaggar, Alison M. *Feminist Politics and Human Nature*. Totowa, New Jersey: Rowman and Allanheld, 1983.

Tong, Rosemarie. *Feminist Thought*. Boulder and San Francisco: Westview Press, 1989.

Vetterling-Braggin, Mary, Frederick A. Elliston, and Jame English, eds. *Feminism and Philosophy*. Totowa, New Jersey: Rowman and Littlefield Publishers, 1977.

CHAPTER FORTY — CAROL GILLIGAN

It is possible to see in the historical development of feminist theory and analysis (and perhaps more broadly in a great deal of thinking that both women and men have done about women and men) a dialectical progression – or is it a pendular motion? – between notions of sex/gender similarity and sex/gender difference. Particular conceptions have stressed, and celebrated, fundamental human sameness; and others have seen something significantly distinct, and usually morally and ideologically important, in different things that (sometimes for better or worse) the two sexes bring to the human template.

The original feminism of Condorcet and Wollstonecraft, and thereafter of Mill, was egalitarian and liberal, with ideas of a considerable plasticity in sex natures, but equally applicable to both sexes. High Victorian views, held by both feminists and non-feminists, assigned women a special "civilizing mission," needed to smooth down or eliminate some of the rough edges or brutalities that men inflict on women and each other. Parts of this mission included mandates for controlling alcoholic intemperance (substance abuse) and pornography. Women, in this conception, had their own special "culture," which had been neglected by the world to its cost, and suppressed in women themselves by their low self-esteem (imposed on them by men, or by a more impersonally conceived system of control) or by their seeking to emulate male modes.

New instances of this polarity, between equality and difference, have appeared frequently in twentieth-century feminist analysis. There follow two opposing cases.

A "difference" view is advocated by Carol Gilligan (b. 1936), an associate professor of in the Graduate School of Education at Harvard University. An "equality" view is taken by Katha Pollitt (b. 1949), an editor (with a regular column) at *The Nation* and regular contributor to the *New Yorker*, and poet.

Carol Gilligan, *In a Different Voice*

(Source: Carol Gilligan. *In a Different Voice: Psychological Theory and Women's Development.* Cambridge, Mass., and London: Harvard University Press, 1982, 151-176.)

6 Visions of Maturity

Attachment and separation anchor the cycle of human life, describing the biology of human reproduction and the psychology of human development. The concepts of attachment and separation that depict the nature and sequence of infant development appear in adolescence as identity and intimacy and then in adulthood as love and work. This reiterative counterpoint in human experience, however, when molded into a developmental ordering, tends to disappear in the course of its linear reduction into the equation of development with separation. This disappearance can be traced in part to the focus on child and adolescent development, where progress can readily be charted by measuring the distance between mother and child. The limitation of this rendition is most apparent in the absence of women from accounts of adult development.

Choosing like Virgil to "sing of arms and the man," psychologists describing adulthood have focused on the development of self and work. While the apogee of separation in adolescence is presumed to be followed in adulthood by the return of attachment and care, recent depictions of adult development, in their seamless emergence from studies of men, provide scanty illumination of a life spent in intimate and generative relationships. Daniel Levinson (1978), despite his evident distress about the exclusion of women from his necessarily small sample, sets out on the basis of an all male study "to create an overarching conception of development that could encompass the diverse biological, psychological and social changes occurring in adult life" (p. 8).

Levinson's conception is informed by the idea of "the Dream," which orders the seasons of a man's life in the same way that Jupiter's prophecy of a glorious destiny steers the course of Aeneas' journey. The Dream about which Levinson writes is also a vision of glorious achievement whose realization or modification will shape the character and life of the man. In the salient relationships in Levinson's analysis, the "mentor" facilitates the realization of the Dream, while the "special woman" is the helpmate who encourages the hero to shape and live out his vision: "As the novice adult tries to separate from his family and pre-adult world, and to enter an adult world, he must form significant relationships with other adults who will facilitate his work on the Dream. Two of the most important figures in this drama are the 'mentor' and the 'special woman'" (p. 93).

The significant relationships of early adulthood are thus construed as the means to an end of individual achievement, and these "transitional figures" must be cast off or reconstructed following the realization of success. If in the process, however, they become, like Dido, an impediment to the fulfillment of the Dream, then the relationship must be renounced, "to allow the developmental process" to continue. This process is defined by Levinson explicitly as one of individuation: "throughout the life cycle, but especially in the key transition periods ... the developmental process of *individuation* is going on." The process refers "to the changes in a person's relationships to himself and to the external world," the relationships that constitute his "Life Structure" (p. 195).

If in the course of "Becoming One's Own Man," this structure is discovered to be flawed and threatens the great expectations of the Dream, then in order to avert "serious Failure or Decline," the man must "break out" to salvage his Dream. This act of breaking out is consummated by a "marker event" of separation, such as "leaving his wife, quitting his job, or moving to another region" (p. 206). Thus the road to mid-life salvation runs through either achievement or separation.

From the array of human experience, Levinson's choice is the same as Virgil's, charting the progress of adult development as an arduous struggle toward a glorious destiny. Like pious Aeneas on his way to found Rome, the men in Levinson's study steady their lives by their devotion to realizing their dream, measuring their progress in terms of their distance from the shores of its promised success. Thus in the stories that Levinson recounts, relationships, whatever their particular intensity, play a relatively subordinate role in the individual drama of adult development.

The focus on work is also apparent in George Vaillant's (1977) account of adaptation to life. The variables that correlate with adult adjustment, like the interview that generates the data, bear predominantly on occupation and call for an expansion of Erikson's stages. Filling in what he sees as "an uncharted period of development" which Erikson left "between the decades of the twenties and forties," Vaillant describes the years of the thirties as the era of "Career Consolidation," the time when the men in his sample sought, "like Shakespeare's soldier, 'the bauble Reputation'" (p. 202). With this analogy to Shakespeare's Rome, the continuity of intimacy and generativity is interrupted to make room for a stage of further individuation and achievement, realized by work and consummated by a success that brings societal recognition.

Erikson's (1950) notion of generativity, however, is changed in the process of this recasting. Conceiving generativity as "the concern in establishing and guiding the next generation," Erikson takes the "*productivity* and *creativity*" of parenthood in its literal or symbolic realization to be a metaphor for an adulthood centered on relationships and devoted to the activity of taking care (p. 267). In Erikson's account, generativity is the central stage of adult development, encompassing "man's relationship to his production as well as to his progeny" (p. 268). In Vaillant's data, this relationship is relegated instead to mid-life.

Asserting that generativity is "not just a stage for making little things grow," Vaillant argues against Erikson's metaphor of parenthood by cautioning that "the world is filled with irresponsible mothers who are marvellous at bearing and loving children up to the age of two and then despair of taking the process further." Generativity, in order to exclude such women, is uprooted from its earthy redolence and redefined as "responsibility for the growth, leadership, and well-being of one's fellow creatures, not just raising crops or children" (p. 202). Thus, the expanse of Erikson's conception is narrowed to development in mid-adulthood and in the process is made more restrictive in its definition of care.

As a result, Vaillant emphasizes the relation of self to society and minimizes attachment to others. In an interview about work, health, stress, death, and a variety of family relationships, Vaillant says to the men in his study that "the hardest question" he will ask is, "Can you describe your wife?" This prefatory caution presumably arose from his experience with this particular sample of men but points to the limits of their adaptation, or perhaps to its psychological expense.

Thus the "models for a healthy life cycle" are men who seem distant in their relationships, finding it difficult to describe their wives, whose importance in their lives they nevertheless acknowledge. The same sense of distance between self and others is evident in Levinson's conclusion that, "In our interviews, friendship was largely noticeable by its absence. As a tentative generalization we would say that close friendship with a man or a woman is rarely experienced by American men." Caught by this impression, Levinson pauses in his discussion of the three "tasks" of adulthood (Building and Modifying the Life Structure, Working on Single Components of the Life Structure, and Becoming More Individuated), to offer an elaboration: "A man may have a wide social network in which he has amicable, 'friendly' relationships with many men and perhaps a few women. In general, however, most men do not have an intimate male friend of the kind that they recall fondly from boyhood or youth. Many men have had casual dating relationships with women, and perhaps a few complex love-sex relationships, but most men have not had an intimate nonsexual friendship with a woman. We need to understand why friendship is so rare, and what consequences this deprivation has for adult life" (p. 335).

Thus, there are studies, on the one hand, that convey a view of adulthood where relationships are subordinated to the ongoing process of individua-

tion and achievement, whose progress, however, is predicated on prior attachments and thought to enhance the capacity for intimacy. On the other hand, there is the observation that among those men whose lives have served as the model for adult development, the capacity for relationships is in some sense diminished and the men are constricted in their emotional expression. Relationships often are cast in the language of achievement, characterized by their success or failure, and impoverished in their affective range:

At forty-five, Lucky, enjoyed one of the best marriages in the Study, but probably not as perfect as he implied when he wrote, "You may not believe me when I say we've never had a disagreement, large or small."

The biography of Dr. Carson illustrates his halting passage from identity to intimacy, through career consolidation, and, finally, into the capacity to *care* in its fullest sense ... he had gone through divorce, remarriage, and a shift from research to private practice. His personal metamorphosis had continued. The mousy researcher had become a charming clinician ... suave, untroubled, kindly and in control ...

The vibrant energy that had characterized his adolescence had returned ... now his depression was clearly an *affect;* and he was anything but fatigued. In the next breath he confessed, "I'm very highly sexed and that's a problem, too."
He then provided me with an exciting narrative as he told me not only of recent romantic entanglements but also of his warm fatherly concern for patients (Vaillant, 1977, 129, 203-206).

The notion that separation leads to attachment and that individuation eventuates in mutuality, while reiterated by both Vaillant and Levinson, is belied by the lives they put forth as support. Similarly, in Erikson's studies of Luther and Gandhi, while the relationship between self and society is achieved in magnificent articulation, both men are compromised in their capacity for intimacy and live at great personal distance from others. Thus Luther in his devotion to Faith, like Gandhi in his devotion to Truth, ignore the people most closely around them while working instead toward the glory of God. These men resemble in remarkable detail pious Aeneas in Virgil's epic, who also overcame the bonds of attachment that impeded the progress of his journey to Rome. In all these accounts the women are silent, except for the sorrowful voice of Dido who, imploring and threatening Aeneas in vain, in the end silences herself upon his sword. Thus there seems to be a line of development missing from current depictions of adult development, a failure to describe the progression of relationships toward a maturity of interdependence. Though the truth of separation is recognized in most developmental texts, the reality of continuing connection is lost or relegated to the background where the figures of women appear. In this way, the emerging conception of adult development casts a familiar shadow on women's lives, pointing again toward the incompleteness of their separation, depicting them as mired in relationships. For women, the developmental markers of separation and attachment, allocated sequentially to adolescence and adulthood, seem in some sense to be fused. However, while this fusion leaves women at risk in a society that rewards separation, it also points to a more general truth currently obscured in psychological texts.

In young adulthood, when identity and intimacy converge in dilemmas of conflicting commitment, the relationship between self and other is exposed. That this relationship differs in the experience of men and women is a steady theme in the literature on human development and a finding of my research. From the different dynamics of separation and attachment in their gender identity formation through the divergence of identity and intimacy that marks their experience in the adolescent years, male and female voices typically speak of the importance of different truths, the former of the role of separation as it defines and empowers the self, the latter of the ongoing process of attachment that creates and sustains the human community.

Since this dialogue contains the dialectic that creates the tension of human development, the silence of women in the narrative of adult development distorts the conception of its stages and sequence. Thus, I want to restore in part the missing text of women's development, as they describe their conceptions of self and morality in the early adult years. In focusing primarily on the differences between the accounts of women and men, my aim is to enlarge developmental understanding by including the perspectives of both of the sexes. While the judgments considered come from a small and highly educated sample, they elucidate a contrast and make it possible to recognize not only what is missing in women's development but also what is there.

This problem of recognition was illustrated in a literature class at a women's college where the students were discussing the moral dilemma described in the novels of Mary McCarthy and James Joyce:

I felt caught in a dilemma that was new to me then but which since has become horribly familiar: the trap of adult life, in which you are held, wriggling, powerless to act because you can see both sides. On that occasion, as generally in the future, I compromised. (*Memories of a Catholic Girlhood*)

I will not serve that in which I no longer believe, whether it calls itself my home, my fatherland or my church: and I will try to express myself in some mode of life or art as freely as I can and as wholly as I can, using for my defense the only arms I allow myself to use – silence, exile and cunning. (*A Portrait of the Artist as a Young Man*)

Comparing the clarity of Stephen's *non serviam* with Mary McCarthy's "zigzag course," the women were unanimous in their decision that Stephen's was the better choice. Stephen was powerful in his certainty of belief and armed with strategies to avoid confrontation; the shape of his identity was clear and tied to a compelling justification. He had, in any case, taken a stand.

Wishing that they could be more like Stephen, in his clarity of decision and certainty of desire, the women saw themselves instead like Mary McCarthy, helpless, powerless, and constantly compromised. The contrasting images of helplessness and power in their explicit tie to attachment and separation caught the dilemma of the women's development, the conflict between integrity and care. In Stephen's simpler construction, separation seemed the empowering condition of free and full self-expression, while attachment appeared a paralyzing entrapment and caring an inevitable prelude to compromise. To the students, Mary McCarthy's portrayal confirmed their own endorsement of this account.

In the novels, however, contrasting descriptions of the road to adult life appear. For Stephen, leaving childhood means renouncing relationships in order to protect his freedom of self-expression. For Mary, "farewell to childhood" means relinquishing the freedom of self-expression in order to protect others and preserve relationships: "A sense of power and Caesarlike magnanimity filled me. I was going to equivocate, not for selfish reasons but in the interests of the community, like a grown-up responsible person" (p. 162). These divergent constructions of identity, in self-expression or in self-sacrifice, create different problems for further development – the former a problem of human connection, and the latter a problem of truth. These seemingly disparate problems, however, are intimately related, since the shrinking from truth creates distance in relationship, and separation removes part of the truth. In the college student study which spanned the years of early adulthood, the men's return from exile and silence parallels the women's return from equivocation, until intimacy and truth converge in the discovery of the connection between integrity and care. Then only a difference in tone reveals what men and women know from the beginning and what they only later discover through experience. The instant choice of self-deprecation in the preference for Stephen by the women in the English class is matched by a childlike readiness for apology in the women in the college student study. The participants in this study were an unequal number of men and women, representing the distribution of males and females in the class on moral and political choice. At age twenty-seven, the five women in the study all were actively pursuing careers – two in medicine, one in law, one in graduate study, and one as an organizer of labor unions. In the five years following their graduation from college, three had married and one had a child. When they were asked at age twenty-seven, "How would you describe yourself to yourself?" one of the women refused to reply, but the other four gave as their responses to the interviewer's question:

This sounds sort of strange, but I think maternal, with all its connotations. I see myself in a nurturing role, maybe not right now, but whenever that might be, as a physician, as a mother … It's hard for me to think of myself without thinking about other people around me that I'm giving to.(Claire)

I am fairly hard-working and fairly thorough and fairly responsible, and in terms of weaknesses, I am sometimes hesitant about making decisions and unsure of myself and afraid of doing things and taking responsibility, and I think maybe that is one of the biggest conflicts I have had … The other very important aspect of my life is my husband and trying to make his life easier and trying to help him out. (Leslie)

I am a hysteric. I am intense. I am warm. I am very smart about people … I have a lot more soft feelings than hard feelings. I am a lot easier to get to be kind than to get mad. If I had to say one word, and to me it incorporates a lot, *adopted*.(Erica)

I have sort of changed a lot. At the point of the last interview [age twenty-two] I felt like I was the kind of person who was interested in growth and trying hard, and it seems to me that the last couple of years, the not trying is someone who is not growing, and I think that is the thing that bothers me the most, the thing that I keep thinking about, that I am not growing. It's not true, I am, but what seems to be a failure partially is the way that Tom and I broke up. The thing with Tom feels to me like I am not growing … The thing I am running into lately is that the way I describe myself, my behavior doesn't sometimes come out that way. Like I hurt Tom a lot, and that bothers me. So I am thinking of myself as somebody who tried not to hurt people, but I ended up hurting him a lot, and so that is something that weighs on me, that I am somebody who unintentionally hurts people. Or a feeling, lately, that it is simple to sit down and say what your principles are, what your values are, and what I think about myself, but the way it sort of works out in actuality is sometimes very different. You can say you try not to hurt people, but you might because of things about yourself, or you can say this is my principle, but when the situation comes up, you don't really behave the way you would like … So I consider myself contradictory and confused. (Nan)

The fusion of identity and intimacy, noted repeatedly in women's development, is perhaps nowhere more clearly articulated than in these self-descriptions. In response to the request to describe themselves, all of the women describe a relationship, depicting their identity in the connection of future mother, present wife, adopted child, or past lover. Similarly, the standard of moral judgment that informs their assessment of self is a standard of relationship, an ethic of nurturance, responsibility, and care. Measuring their strength in the activity of attachment ("giving to," "helping out," "being kind," "not hurting"), these highly successful and achieving women do not mention their academic and professional distinction in the context of describing themselves. If anything, they regard their professional activities as jeopardizing their own sense of themselves, and the conflict they encounter between achievement and care leaves them either divided in judgment or feeling betrayed. Nan explains:

When I first applied to medical school, my feeling was that I was a person who was concerned with other people and being able to care for them in some way or another, and I was running into problems the last few years as far as my being able to give of myself, my time, and what I am doing to other people. And medicine, even though it seems that profession is set up to do exactly that, seems to more or less interfere with your doing it. To me it felt like I wasn't really growing, that I was just treading water, trying to cope with what I was doing that made me very angry in some ways because it wasn't the way that I wanted things to go.

Thus in all of the women's descriptions, identity is defined in a context of relationship and judged by a standard of responsibility and care. Similarly, morality is seen by these women as arising from the experience of connection and conceived as a problem of inclusion rather than one of balancing claims. The underlying assumption that morality stems from attachment is explicitly stated by Claire in her response to Heinz's dilemma of whether or not to steal an overpriced drug in order to save his wife. Explaining why Heinz should steal, she elaborates the view of social reality on which her judgment is based:

By yourself, there is little sense to things. It is like the sound of one hand clapping, the sound of one man or one woman, there is something lacking. It is the collective that is important to me, and that collective is based on certain guiding principles, one of which is that everybody belongs to it and that you all come from it. You have to love someone else, because while you may not like them, you are inseparable from them. In a way, it is like loving your right hand. *They are part of you*; that other person is part of that giant collection of people that you are connected to.

To this aspiring maternal physician, the sound of one hand clapping does not seem a miraculous transcendence but rather a human absurdity, the illusion of a person standing alone in a reality of interconnection.

For the men, the tone of identity is different, clearer, more direct, more distinct and sharp-edged. Even when disparaging the concept itself, they radiate the confidence of certain truth. Although the world of the self that men describe at times includes "people" and "deep attachments," no particular person or relationship is mentioned, nor is the activity of relationship portrayed in the context of self-description. Replacing the women's verbs of attachment are adjectives of separation – "intelligent," "logical," "imaginative," "honest," sometimes even "arrogant" and "cocky." Thus the male "I" is defined in separation, although the men speak of having "real contacts" and "deep emotions" or otherwise wishing for them. In a randomly selected half of the sample, men who were situated similarly to the women in occupational and marital position give as their initial responses to the request for self-description:

Logical, compromising, outwardly calm. If it seems like my statements are short and abrupt, it is because of my background and training. Architectural statements have to be very concise and short. Accepting. Those are all on an emotional level. I consider myself educated, reasonably intelligent.

I would describe myself as an enthusiastic, passionate person who is slightly arrogant. Concerned, committed, very tired right now because I didn't get much sleep last night.

I would describe myself as a person who is well developed intellectually and emotionally. Relatively narrow circle of friends, acquaintances, persons with whom I have real contacts as opposed to professional contacts or community contacts. And relatively proud of the intellectual skills and development, content with the emotional development as such, as a not very actively pursued goal. Desiring to broaden that one, the emotional aspect.

Intelligent, perceptive – I am being brutally honest now – still somewhat reserved, unrealistic about a number of social situations which involve other people, particularly authorities. Improving, looser, less tense and hung up than I used to be. Somewhat lazy, although it is hard to say how much of that is tied up with other conflicts. Imaginative, sometimes too much so. A little dilletantish, interested in a lot of things without necessarily going into them in depth, although I am moving toward correcting that.

I would tend to describe myself first by recounting a personal history, where I was born, grew up, and that kind of thing, but I am dissatisfied with that, having done it thousands of times. It doesn't seem to capture the essence of what I am, I would probably decide after another futile attempt, because there is no such thing as the essence of what I am, and be very bored by the whole thing ... I don't think that there is any such thing as myself. There is myself sitting here, there is myself tomorrow, and so on.

Evolving and honest.

I guess on the surface I seem a little easy-going and laid back, but I think I am probably a bit more wound up than that. I tend to get wound up very easily. Kind of smart aleck, a little bit, or cocky maybe. Not as thorough as I should be. A little bit hard-ass, I guess, and a guy that is not swayed by emotions and feelings. I have deep emotions, but I am not a person who has a lot of different people. I have attachments to a few people, very deep attachments. Or attachments to a lot of things, at least in the demon-

strable sense.

I guess I think I am kind of creative and also a little bit schizophrenic ... A lot of it is a result of how I grew up. There is a kind of longing for the pastoral life and, at the same time, a desire for the flash, prestige, and recognition that you get by going out and hustling.

Two of the men begin more tentatively by talking about people in general, but they return in the end to great ideas or a need for distinctive achievement:

I think I am basically a decent person. I think I like people a lot and I like liking people. I like doing things with pleasure from just people, from their existence, almost. Even people I don't know well. When I said I was a decent person, I think that is almost the thing that makes me a decent person, that is a decent quality, a good quality. I think I am very bright. I think I am a little lost, not acting quite like I am inspired – whether it is just a question of lack of inspiration, I don't know – but not accomplishing things, not achieving things, and not knowing where I want to go or what I'm doing. I think most people especially doctors, have some idea of what they are going to be doing in four years. I [an intern] really have a blank ... I have great ideas ... but I can't imagine me in them.

I guess the things that I like to think are important to me are I am aware of what is going on around me, other people's needs around me, and the fact that I enjoy doing things for other people and I feel good about it. I suppose it's nice in my situation, but I am not sure that is true for everybody. I think some people do things for other people and it doesn't make them feel good. Once in awhile that is true of me too, for instance working around the house, and I am always doing the same old things that everyone else is doing and eventually I build up some resentment toward that.

In these men's descriptions of self, involvement with others is tied to a qualification of identity rather than to its realization. Instead of attachment, individual achievement rivets the male imagination, and great ideas or distinctive activity defines the standard of self-assessment and success.

Thus the sequential ordering of identity and intimacy in the transition from adolescence to adulthood better fits the development of men than it does the development of women. Power and separation secure the man in an identity achieved through work, but they leave him at a distance from others, who seem in some sense out of his sight. Cranly, urging Stephen Daedalus to perform his Easter duty for his mother's sake, reminds him:

Your mother must have gone through a good deal of suffering ... would you not try to save her from suffering more even if – or would you?

If I could, Stephen said, that would cost me very little.

Given this distance, intimacy becomes the critical experience that brings the self back into connection with others, making it possible to see both sides – to discover the effects of actions on others as well as their cost to the self. The experience of relationship brings an end to isolation, which otherwise hardens into indifference, an absence of active concern for others, though perhaps a willingness to respect their rights. For this reason, intimacy is the transformative experience for men through which adolescent identity turns into the generativity of adult love and work. In the process, as Erikson (1964) observes, the knowledge gained through intimacy changes the ideological morality of adolescence into the adult ethic of taking care.

Since women, however, define their identity through relationships of intimacy and care, the moral problems that they encounter pertain to issues of a different sort. When relationships are secured by masking desire and conflict is avoided by equivocation, then confusion arises about the locus of responsibility and truth. McCarthy, describing her "representations" to her grandparents, explains:

Whatever I told them was usually so blurred and glossed, in the effort to meet their approval (for, aside from anything else, I was fond of them and tried to accommodate myself to their perspective), that except when answering a direct question, I hardly knew whether what I was saying was true or false. I really tried, or so I thought, to avoid lying, but it seemed to me that they forced it on me by the difference in their vision of things, so that I was always transposing reality for them into terms they could understand. To keep matters straight with my conscience, I shrank, whenever possible, from the lie absolute, just as, from a sense of precaution, I shrank from the plain truth.

The critical experience then becomes not intimacy but choice, creating an encounter with self that clarifies the understanding of responsibility and truth.

Thus in the transition from adolescence to adulthood, the dilemma itself is the same for both sexes, a conflict between integrity and care. But approached from different perspectives, this dilemma generates the recognition of opposite truths. These different perspectives are reflected in two different moral ideologies, since separation is justified by an ethic of rights while attachment is supported by an ethic of care.

... [T]he vision of maturity can be seen to shift when adulthood is portrayed by women rather than men. When women construct the adult domain, the world of relationships emerges and becomes the focus of attention and concern. McClelland (1975), noting this shift in women's fantasies of power, observes that "women are more concerned than men with both sides of an interdependent relationship" and are "quicker to recognize their own interdependence" (pp. 85-86). This focus on interdependence is manifest in fantasies that equate power with giving and care. McClelland reports that while men represent powerful activity as assertion and aggression, women in contrast portray acts of nurturance as acts of strength. Considering his research on power to deal "in particular with the characteristics of maturity," he suggests that mature women and men may relate to the world in a different style.

That women differ in their orientation to power is also the theme of Jean Baker Miller's analysis. Focusing on relationships of dominance and subordination, she finds women's situation in these relationships to provide "a crucial key to understanding the psychological order." This order arises from the relationships of difference, between man and woman and parent and child, that create "the milieu – the family – in which the human mind as we know it has been formed" (1976, p.1). Because these relationships of difference contain, in most instances, a factor of inequality, they assume a moral dimension pertaining to the way in which power is used. On this basis, Miller distinguishes between relationships of temporary and permanent inequality, the former representing the context of human development, the latter, the condition of oppression. In relationships of temporary inequality, such as parent and child or teacher and student, power ideally is used to foster the development that removes the initial disparity. In relationships of permanent inequality, power cements dominance and subordination, and oppression is rationalized by theories that "explain" the need for its continuation.

Miller, focusing in this way on the dimension of inequality in human life, identifies the distinctive psychology of women as arising from the combination of their positions in relationships of temporary and permanent inequality. Dominant in temporary relationships of nurturance that dissolve with the dissolution of inequality, women are subservient in relationships of permanently unequal social status and power. In addition, though subordinate in social position to men, women are at the same time centrally entwined with them in the intimate and intense relationships of adult sexuality and family life. Thus women's psychology reflects both sides of relationships of interdependence and the range of moral possibilities to which such relationships give rise. Women, therefore, are ideally situated to observe the potential in human connection both for care and for oppression.

... Miller calls for "a new psychology of women" that recognizes the different starting point for women's development, the fact that "women stay with, build on, and develop in a context of attachment and affiliation with others," that "women's sense of self becomes very much organized around being able to make, and then to maintain, affiliations and relationships," and that "eventually, for many women, the threat of disruption of an affiliation is perceived not just as a loss of a relationship but as something closer to a total loss of self." Although this psychic structuring is by now familiar from descriptions of women's psychopathology, it has not been recognized that "this psychic starting point contains the possibilities for an entirely different (and more advanced) approach to living

and functioning ... [in which] affiliation is valued as highly as, or more highly than, self-enhancement" (p.83). Thus, Miller points to a psychology of adulthood which recognizes that development does not displace the value of ongoing attachment and the continuing importance of care relationships....

Like the stories that delineate women's fantasies of power, women's descriptions of adulthood convey a different sense of its social reality. In their portrayal of relationships, women replace the bias of men toward separation with a representation of the interdependence of self and other, both in love and in work. By changing the lens of developmental observation from individual achievement to relationships of care, women depict ongoing attachment as the path that leads to maturity. Thus the parameters of development shift toward marking the progress of affiliative relationship....

In view of the evidence that women perceive and construe social reality differently from men and that these differences center around experiences of attachment and separation, life transitions that invariably engage these experiences can be expected to involve women in a distinctive way. And because women's sense of integrity appears to be entwined with an ethic of care, so that to see themselves as women is to see themselves in a relationship of connection, the major transitions in women's lives would seem to involve changes in the understanding and activities of care. Certainly the shift from childhood to adulthood witnesses a major redefinition of care. When the distinction between helping and pleasing frees the activity of taking care from the wish for approval by others, the ethic of responsibility can become a self-chosen anchor of personal integrity and strength....

Among the most pressing items on the agenda for research on adult development is the need to delineate *in women's own terms* the experience of their adult life. My own work in that direction indicates that the inclusion of women's experience brings to developmental understanding a new perspective on relationships that changes the basic constructs of interpretation. The concept of identity expands to include the experience of interconnection. The moral domain is similarly enlarged by the inclusion of responsibility and care in relationships. And the underlying epistemology correspondingly shifts from the Greek ideal of knowledge as a correspondence between mind and form to the Biblical conception of knowing as a process of human relationship.

Given the evidence of different perspectives in the representation of adulthood by women and men, there is a need for research that elucidates the effects of these differences in marriage, family, and work relationships. My research suggests that men and women may speak different languages that they assume are the same, using similar words to encode disparate experiences of self and social relationships. Because these languages share an overlapping moral vocabulary, they contain a propensity for systematic mistranslation, creating misunderstandings which impede communication and limit the potential for cooperation and care in relationships. At the same time, however, these languages articulate with one another in critical ways. Just as the language of responsibilities provides a weblike imagery of relationships to replace a hierarchical ordering that dissolves with the coming of equality, so the language of rights underlines the importance of including in the network of care not only the other but also the self.

As we have listened for centuries to the voices of men and the theories of development that their experience informs, so we have come more recently to notice not only the silence of women but the difficulty in hearing what they say when they speak. Yet in the different voice of women lies the truth of an ethic of care, the tie between relationship and responsibility, and the origins of aggression in the failure of connection. The failure to see the different reality of women's lives and to hear the differences in their voices stems in part from the assumption that there is a single mode of social experience and interpretation. By positing instead two different modes, we arrive at a more complex rendition of human experience which sees the truth of separation and attachment in the lives of women and men and recognizes how these truths are carried by different modes of language and thought.

Bibliography

Code, Lorraine, Sheila Mullett, and Christine Overall, eds. *Feminist Perspectives*. Toronto: University of Toronto Press, 1988.

Erickson, Erik H. *Childhood and Society*. New York: W.W. Norton, 1950.

Erickson, Erik H. *Young Man Luther*. New York: W.W. Norton, 1958.

Erickson, Erik H. *Gandhi's Truth*. New York: W.W. Norton, 1969.

Joyce, James. *A Portrait of the Artist as a Young Man* (1916). New York: The Viking Press, 1956.

Levinson, Daniel J. *The Seasons of a Man's Life*. New York: Alfred A. Knopf, 1978.

McCarthy, Mary. *Memories of a Catholic Girlhood*. New York: Harcourt Brace Jovanovich, 1946.

McClelland, David C. *Power: The Inner Experience*. New York: Irvington, 1975.

Miller, Jean Baker. *Toward a New Psychology of Women*. Boston: Beacon Press, 1976.

Vaillant, George E. *Adaptation to Life*. Boston: Little, Brown, 1977.

CHAPTER FORTY-ONE — KATHA POLLITT

Katha Pollitt, *"Marooned on Gilligan's Island: Are Women Morally Superior to Men?"*

(Source: Katha Pollitt. *Reasonable Creatures: Essays on Women and Feminism.* New York: Alfred A. Knopf, 1994, 42-62.)

Some years ago, I was invited by the wife of a well-known writer to sign a women's peace petition. It made the points such documents usually make: that women, as mothers, caregivers and nurturers, have a special awareness of the precariousness of human life, see through jingoism and Cold War rhetoric and would prefer nations to work out their difficulties peacefully so that the military budget could be diverted to schools and hospitals and housing. It had the literary tone such documents usually have, as well – at once superior and plaintive, as if the authors didn't know whether they were bragging or begging. We are wiser than you poor deluded menfolk, was the subtext, so will you please-please-please listen to your moms?

To sign or not to sign? Of course, I was all for peace. But was I for peace *as a woman*? I wasn't a mother then – I wasn't even an aunt. Did my lack of nurturing credentials make my grasp of the horrors of war and the folly of the arms race only theoretical, like a white person's understanding of racism? Were mothers the natural leaders of the peace movement, to whose judgment nonmothers, male and female, must defer, because after all we couldn't *know*, couldn't *feel* that tenderness toward fragile human life that a woman who had borne and raised children had experienced? On the other hand, I was indeed a woman. Was motherhood with its special wisdom somehow deep inside me, to be called upon when needed, like my uterus?

Complicating matters in a way relevant to this essay was my response to the famous writer's wife herself. Here was a woman in her fifties, her child-raising long behind her. Was motherhood the only banner under which she could gain a foothold on civic life? Perhaps so. Her only other public identity was that of a wife, and wifehood, even to a famous man, isn't much to claim credit for these days. ("To think I spent all those years ironing his underpants!" she once burst out to a mutual friend.) Motherhood was what she had in the work-and-accomplishment department, so it was understandable that she try to maximize its moral status. But I was not in her situation: I was a writer, a single woman. By sending me a petition from which I was excluded even as I was invited to add my name, perhaps she was telling me that by leading a nondomestic life I had abandoned the moral high ground, was "acting like a man," but could redeem myself by acknowledging the moral preeminence of the class of women I refused to join.

The ascription of particular virtues – compassion, patience, common sense, nonviolence – to mothers, and the tendency to conflate "mothers" with "women," has a long history in the peace movement, but it goes way beyond issues of war and peace. At present it permeates discussions of just about every field, from management training to theology. Indeed, although the media like to caricature feminism as denying the existence of sexual differences, for the women's movement and its opponents alike "difference" is where the action is. Thus, business writers wonder if women's nurturing, intuitive qualities will make them better executives. Educators suggest that female students suffer in classrooms that emphasize competition over cooperation. Women politicians tout their playground-honed negotiating skills, their egoless devotion to public service, their gender-based commitment to fairness and caring. A variety of political causes – environmentalism, animal rights, even vegetarianism – are promoted as logical extensions of women's putative peacefulness, closeness to nature, horror of aggression and concern for others' health. (Indeed, to some extent these causes are arenas in which women fight one another over definitions of femininity, which is why debates over disposable diapers and over the wearing of fur – both rather minor sources of harm, even if their opponents are right – loom so large and are so acrimonious.) In the arts, we hear a lot about what women's "real" subjects, methods and materials ought to be. Painting is male. Rhyme is male. Plot is male. Perhaps, say the Lacanian feminists, even logic and language are male. What is female? Nature. Blood. Milk. Communal gatherings. The moon. Quilts.

Haven't we been here before? Indeed we have. Woman as sharer and carer, woman as earth mother, woman as guardian of all the small rituals that knit together a family and a community, woman as beneath, above or beyond such manly concerns as law, reason, abstract ideas – these images are as old as time. Open defenders of male supremacy have always used them to declare women flatly inferior to men; covert ones use them to place women on a pedestal as too good for this naughty world. Thus, in the *Eumenides,* Aeschylus celebrated law as the defeat by males of primitive female principles of bloodguilt and vengeance, while the Ayatollah Khomeini thought women should be barred from judgeships because they were too tenderhearted. Different rationale, same outcome: Women, because of their indifference to an impersonal moral order, cannot be full participants in civic life.

There exists an equally ancient line of thought, however, that uses femininity to posit a subversive challenge to the social order: Think of Sophocles' Antigone, who resists tyranny out of love and piety, or Aristophanes' Lysistrata, the original women's-strike-for-peace-nik, or Shakespeare's unworldly, loving innocents: Desdemona, Cordelia. For reasons of power, money and persistent social structures, the vision of the morally superior woman can never overcome the dominant ethos in reality but exists alongside it as a kind of permanent wish or hope: If only powerful and powerless could change places, and the meek inherit the earth! Thus, it is perpetually being rediscovered, dressed in fashionable clothes and presented, despite its antiquity, as a radical new idea.

In the 1950s, which we think of as the glory days of traditional roles, the anthropologist Ashley Montagu argued in "The Natural Superiority of Women" that females had it all over males in every way that counted, including the possession of X chromosomes that made them stabler, saner and healthier than men, with their X and Y. Montagu's essay, originally published in *The Saturday Review* and later expanded into a book, is witty and high-spirited and, interestingly, anticipates current feminist challenge to male-defined categories. (He

notes, for example, that while men are stronger than women in the furniture-moving sense, women are stronger than men when faced with extreme physical hardship and tests of endurance; so when we say that men are stronger than women, we are equating strength with what men have.) But the fundamental thrust of Montagu's essay was to confirm traditional gender roles while revising the way we value them. Having proved to his own satisfaction that women could scale the artistic and intellectual heights, he argued that most would (that is, should) refrain, because women's true genius was "humanness," and their real mission was to "humanize" men before men blew up the world. And that, he left no doubt, was a full-time job.

Contemporary proponents of "difference feminism" advance a variation on the same argument, without Montagu's puckish humor. Instead of his whimsical chromosomal explanation, we get, for example, the psychoanalytic one proposed by Nancy Chodorow in *The Reproduction of Mothering:* Daughters define themselves by relating to their mothers, the primary love object of all children, and are therefore empathic, relationship-oriented, nonhierarchical and interested in forging consensus; sons must separate from their mothers, and are therefore individualistic, competitive, resistant to connection with others and focused on abstract rules and rights. Chodorow's theory has become a kind of mantra of difference feminism, endlessly cited as if it explained phenomena we all agree are universal, though this is far from the case. The central question Chodorow poses – Why are women the primary caregivers of children? – could not even be asked before the advent of modern birth control, and can be answered without resorting to psychology. Historically, women have taken care of children because high fertility and lack of other options left most of them no choice. Those rich enough to avoid personally raising their children often did, as Rousseau observed to his horror.

Popularizers of Chodorow water down and sentimentalize her thesis. They embrace her proposition that traditional mothering produces "relational" women and "autonomous" men but forget her less congenial argument that it also results in sexual inequality, misogyny and hostility between mothers and daughters, who, like sons, desire independence but have a much harder time achieving it. Unlike her followers, Chodorow does not romanticize mothering: "Exclusive single parenting is bad for mother and child alike," she concludes; in a tragic paradox, female "caring," "intimacy" and "nurturance" do not soften but *produce* aggressive, competitive, hypermasculine men.

The relational woman and autonomous man described in psychoanalytic terms by Chodorow have become stock figures in other areas of social science as well. Thus, in her immensely influential book, *In a Different Voice,* the educational psychologist Carol Gilligan argues that the sexes make moral decisions according to separate criteria: Women employ an "ethic of care," men an "ethic of rights." The sociolinguist Deborah Tannen, in the best-selling *You Just Don't Understand,* analyzes male-female conversation as "cross-cultural communication" by people from different backgrounds: the single-sex world of children's play in which girls cooperate and boys compete. While these two writers differ in important ways – Tannen, writing at a more popular level, is by far the clearer thinker and the one more interested in analyzing actual human interactions in daily life, about which she is often quite shrewd – they share important liabilities, too. Both largely confine their observations to the white middle class – especially Gilligan, much of whose elaborate theory of gendered ethics rests on interviews with a handful of Harvard-Radcliffe undergraduates – and seem unaware that this limits the applicability of their data. (In their 1992 book, *Meeting at the Crossroads,* Gilligan and her co-author, Lyn Mikel Brown, make a similar mistake. Their whole theory of "loss of relationship" as the central trauma of female adolescence rests on interviews with students at one posh single-sex private school.) Both massage their findings to fit their theories: Gilligan's male and female responses are actually quite similar to each other, as experimenters have subsequently shown by removing the names and asking subjects to try to sort the answers by gender; Tannen is quick to attribute blatant rudeness or sexism in male speech to anxiety, helplessness, fear of loss of face – to anything, indeed, but rudeness and sexism. Both look only at what people say, not what they do. For Tannen this isn't a decisive objection because speech is her subject, although it limits the extent to which her findings can be applied to other areas of behavior; for Gilligan, it is a major obstacle, unless you believe, as she apparent-

ly does, that the way people say they would resolve farfetched hypothetical dilemmas – Should a poor man steal drugs to save his dying wife? – tells us how they reason in real-life situations or, more important, how they act.

But the biggest problem with all these accounts of gender difference is that they credit the differences they find to universal features of male and female development rather than to the economic and social positions men and women hold, or to the actual power differences between individual men and women. In *The Mismeasure of Woman,* her trenchant and witty attack on contemporary theories of gender difference, Carol Tavris points out that much of what can be said about women applies as well to poor people, who also tend to focus more on family and relationships and less on work and self-advancement; to behave deferentially with those more socially powerful; and to appear to others more emotional and "intuitive" than rational and logical in their thinking. Then, too, there is the question of whether the difference theorists are measuring anything beyond their own willingness to think in stereotypes. If Chodorow is right, relational women and autonomous men should be the norm, but are they? Or is it just that women and men use different language, have different social styles, offer different explanations for similar behavior? Certainly, it is easy to find in one's own acquaintance, as well as in the world at large, men and women who don't fit the models. Difference feminists like to attribute ruthlessness, coldness and hyperrationality in successful women – Margaret Thatcher is the standard example – to the fact that men control the networks of power and permit only women like themselves to rise. But I've met plenty of rigid, insensitive, aggressive women who are stay-at-home mothers and secretaries and nurses. And I know plenty of sweet, unambitious men whose main satisfactions lie in their social, domestic and romantic lives, although not all of them would admit this to an inquiring social scientist. We tend to tell strangers what we think will make us sound good. I myself, to my utter amazement, informed a telephone pollster that I exercised regularly, a barefaced lie. How much more difficult to describe truthfully one's oral and ethical values – even if one knew what they were, which, as Socrates demonstrated at length, almost no one does.

So why are Gilligan and Tannen the toasts of feminist social science, endlessly cited and discussed in academia, and out of it too, in gender-sensitivity sessions in the business world and even, following the Anita Hill-Clarence Thomas hearings, in Congress? The success of the difference theorists proves yet again that social science is one part science and nine parts social. They say what people want to hear: Women really are different, in just the ways we always thought. Women embrace Gilligan and Tannen because they offer flattering accounts of traits for which they have historically been castigated. Men like them because, while they urge understanding and respect for "female" values and behaviors, they also let men off the hook: Men have power, wealth and control of social resources because women don't really want them. The pernicious tendencies of difference feminism are perfectly illustrated by the Sears sex discrimination case, in which Rosalind Rosenberg, a professor of women's history at Barnard College, testified for Sears that female employees held lower paying salaried jobs while men worked selling big-ticket items commission because women preferred low-risk, noncompetitive positions that did not interfere with family responsibilities. Sears won its case.

While early-childhood development is the point of departure for most of the difference feminists, it is possible to construct a theory of gendered ethics on other grounds. The most interesting attempt I've seen is by the pacifist philosopher Sara Ruddick. Although not widely known outside academic circles, her *Maternal Thinking* makes an argument that can be found in such mainstream sources as the columns of Anna Quindlen in *The New York Times*. For Ruddick it is not psychosexual development that produces the Gilliganian virtues but intimate involvement in child-raising, the hands-on work of mothering. Men too can be mothers if they do the work that women do. (And women can be Fathers – a word Ruddick uses, complete with arrogant capital letter, for distant, uninvolved authority-figure parents.) Mothers are patient, peace-loving, attentive to emotional context and so on, because those are the qualities you need to get the job done, the way accountants are precise, lawyers argumentative, writers self-centered. Thus mothers constitute a logical constituency for pacifist and antiwar politics, and, by extension, a "car-

ing" domestic agenda.

But what is the job of mothering? Ruddick defines "maternal practice" as meeting three demands: preservation, growth and social acceptability. She acknowledges the enormously varying manifestations of these demands, but she doesn't incorporate into her theory the qualifications, limits and contradictions she notes – perhaps because to do so would reveal these demands as so flexible as to be practically empty terms.

Almost anything mothers do can be explained under one of these rubrics, however cruel, dangerous, unfair or authoritarian – the genital mutilation of African and Arab girls, the foot-binding of prerevolutionary Chinese ones, the sacrifice of some children to increase the resources available for others, as in the killing or malnourishing of female infants in India and China today. In this country, many mothers who commit what is legally child abuse *think* they are merely disciplining their kids in the good old-fashioned way. As long as the practices are culturally acceptable (and sometimes even when they're not), the mothers who perform them think of themselves as good parents. But if all these behaviors count as mothering, how can mothering have a necessary connection with any single belief about anything, let alone how to stop war, or any single set of personality traits, let alone nonviolent ones?

We should not be surprised that motherhood does not produce uniform beliefs and behaviors: It is, after all, not a job; it has no standard of admission, and almost nobody gets fired. Motherhood is open to any woman who can have a baby or adopt one. *Not* to be a mother is a decision; becoming one requires merely that a woman accede, perhaps only for as long as it takes to get pregnant, to thousands of years of cumulative social pressure. After that, she's on her own; she can soothe her child's nightmares or let him cry in the dark. Nothing intrinsic to child-raising will tell her what is the better choice for her child (each has been the favored practice at different times). Although Ruddick starts off by looking closely at maternal practice, when that practice contradicts her own ideas about good mothering it is filed away as an exception, a distortion imposed by Fathers or poverty or some other outside force. But if you add up all the exceptions, you are left with a rather small group of people – women like Ruddick herself, enlightened, up-to-date, educated, upper-middle-class liberals.

And not even all of them. Consider the issue of physical punishment. Ruddick argues that experience teaches mothers that violence is useless; it only creates anger, deception and more violence. Negotiation is the mother's way of resolving disputes and encouraging good behavior. As Ann Crittenden put it in *The Nation* during the Gulf War: "One learns, in theory and in practice, to try to resolve conflict in ways that do not involve the sheer imposition of will or brute force. One learns that violence just doesn't work." Crittenden would have a hard time explaining all those moms in uniform who participated in Operation Desert Storm – but then she'd have a hard time explaining all those mothers screaming at their kids in the supermarket, too.

As it happens, I agree that violence is a bad way to teach, and I made a decision never, no matter what, to spank my daughter. But mothers who do not hit their children, or permit their husbands to do so, are as rare as conscientious objectors in wartime. According to one survey, 78 percent approve of an occasional "good, hard spanking" – because they think violence is an effective way of teaching, because they think that hitting children isn't really violence, because they just lose it. Even *Parenting* found that more than a third of its readers hit their kids. And *Parenting*'s audience is not only far more educated, affluent and liberal than the general population, it consists entirely of people who care what experts think about child development – and contemporary experts revile corporal punishment. Interestingly, the moms who hit tended to be the ones who fretted the most about raising their children well. Mothers who think too much?

Like old-style socialists finding "proletarian virtue" in the working class, Ruddick claims to be describing what mothers do, but all too often she is really prescribing what she thinks they ought to do. "When their children flourish, almost all mothers have a sense of well-being." Hasn't she ever heard of postpartum depression? Of mothers who belittle their children's accomplishments and resent their growing independence? "What mother wouldn't want the power to keep her children healthy ... to create hospitals, schools, jobs, day care, and work schedules that serve her maternal work?" Notice how neatly the modest and commonsensical wish for a healthy child balloons into the hotly contested and by no means universal wish of mothers for day care and flextime. Notice, too, how Ruddick moves from a mother's desire for social institutions that serve *her* children to an assumption that this desire translates into wanting comparable care for *all* children. But mothers feature prominently in local struggles against busing, mergers of rich and poor schools and the opening in their neighborhoods of group homes for foster children, boarder babies and the retarded. Why? The true reasons may be property values and racism, but what these mothers often say is that they are simply protecting their kids. Ruddick seems to think Maternal Thinking leads naturally to Sweden; in the United States it is equally likely to lead to Fortress Suburbia.

As Gilligan does with all women, Ruddick scrutinizes mothers for what she expects to find, and sure enough, there it is. But why look to mothers for her peaceful constituency in the first place? Why not health professionals, who spend their lives saving lives? Or historians, who know how rarely war yields a benefit remotely commensurate with its cost in human misery? Or, I don't know, gardeners, blamelessly tending their innocent flowers? You can read almost any kind of work as affirming life and conferring wisdom. Ruddick chooses mothering because she's already decided that women possess the Gilliganian virtues and she wants a non-essentialist peg to hang them on, so that men can acquire them, too. A disinterested observer scouring the world for labor that encourages humane values would never pick child-raising: It's too quirky, too embedded in repellent cultural norms, too hot.

Despite its intellectual flabbiness, difference feminism is deeply appealing to many women. Why? For one thing, it seems to explain some important phenomena: that women – and this is a cross-cultural truth – commit very little criminal violence compared with men; that women fill the ranks of the so-called caring professions; that women are much less likely than men to abandon their children. Difference feminists want to give women credit for these good behaviors by raising them from the level of instinct or passivity – the Camille Paglia vision of femininity – to the level of moral choice and principled decision. Who can blame women for embracing theories that tell them the sacrifices they make on behalf of domesticity and children are legitimate, moral, even noble? By stressing the mentality of nurturance – the *ethic* of caring, maternal *thinking* – Gilligan and Ruddick challenge the ancient division of humanity into rational males and irrational females. They offer women a way to argue that their views have equal status with those of men and to resist the customary marginalization of their voices in public debate. Doubtless many women have felt emboldened by Gilliganian accounts of moral difference: Speaking in a different voice is, after all, a big step up from silence.

The vision of women as sharers and carers is tempting in another way, too. Despite much media blather about the popularity of the victim position, most people want to believe they act out of free will and choice. The uncomfortable truth that women have all too little of either is a difficult hurdle for feminists. Acknowledging the systematic oppression of women seems to deprive them of existential freedom, to turn them into puppets, slaves and Stepford wives. Deny it, and you can't make change. By arguing that the traditional qualities, tasks and ways of life of women are as important, valuable and serious as those of men (if not more so), Gilligan and others let women feel that nothing needs to change except the social valuation accorded to what they are already doing. It's a rationale for the status quo, which is why men like it, and a burst of grateful applause, which is why women like it. Men keep the power, but since power is bad, so much the worse for them.

Another rather curious appeal of difference feminism is that it offers a way for women to define themselves as independent of men. In a culture that sees women almost entirely in relation to men, this is no small achievement. Sex, for example – the enormous amount of female energy, money and time spent on beauty and fashion and romance, on attracting men and keeping them, on placating male power, strategizing ways around it or making it serve one's own ends – plays a minute role in these theories. You would never guess from Gilligan or Ruddick that men, individually and collectively, are signal beneficiaries of female nurturance, much less that this goes far to explain why society encourages nurturance in women. No, it is always children whom women are described as fos-

tering and sacrificing for, or the community, or even other women – not husbands or lovers. It's as though wives cook dinner only for their kids, leaving the husband to raid the fridge on his own. And no doubt many a woman, quietly smoldering at her mate's refusal to share domestic labor, persuades herself that she is serving only her children, or her own preferences, rather than confront the inequality of her marriage.

The peaceful mother and the relational woman are a kinder, gentler, leftish version of "family values," and both are modern versions of the separate-spheres ideology of the Victorians. In the nineteenth century, too, some women tried to turn the ideology of sexual difference on its head and expand the moral claims of motherhood to include the public realm. Middle-class women became social reformers, abolitionists, temperance advocates, settlement workers and even took paying jobs in the "helping professions" – nursing, social work, teaching – which were perceived as extensions of women's domestic role although practiced mostly by single women. These women did not deny that their sex fitted them for the home, but argued that domesticity did not end at the front door of the house, or confine itself to dusting (or telling the housemaid to dust). Even the vote could be cast as an extension of domesticity: Women, being more moral than men, would purify the government of vice and corruption, end war and make America safe for family life. (The persistence of this metaphor came home to me when I attended a Women's Action Coalition demonstration during the 1992 Democratic National Convention. There – along with WAC's funny and ferocious all-in-black drum corps and contingents of hip downtown artists brandishing Barbara Kruger posters and shouting slogans like "We're Women! We're Angry! We're Not Going Shopping!" – was a trio of street performers with housecoats and kerchiefs over black catsuits and spiky hair, pushing brooms: Women will clean up government!)

The separate-spheres ideology had obvious advantages for middle-class women in an era when they were formally barred from higher education, political power and most jobs that paid a living wage. But its defects are equally obvious. It defined all women by a single standard, and one developed by a sexist society. It offered women no way to enter jobs that could not be defined as extensions of their domestic roles – you could be a math teacher but not a mathematician, a secretary but not a sea captain – and no way to challenge any but the grossest abuses of male privilege. Difference feminists are making a similar bid for power on behalf of women today, and are caught in similar contradictions. Once again, women are defined by their family roles. Child-raising is seen as woman's glory and joy and opportunity for self-transcendence, while Dad naps on the couch. Women who do not fit the stereotype are castigated as unfeminine – nurses nurture, doctors do not – and domestic labor is romanticized and sold to women as a badge of moral worth.

For all the many current explanations of perceived moral difference between the sexes, one hears remarkably little about the material basis of the family. Yet the motherhood and womanhood being valorized cannot be considered apart from questions of power, privilege and money. There is a reason a nonearning woman can proudly call herself a "wife and mother" and a non-earning man is just unemployed: The traditional male role, with its attendant real or imagined traits and values, implies a male income. Middle-class women go to great heights to separate themselves from this uncomfortable fact. One often hears married mothers defend their decision to stay at home by heaping scorn on paid employment – caricatured as making widgets or pushing papers or dressing for success – and the difference feminists, too, like to distinguish between altruistic, poorly paid female jobs and the nasty, profitable ones performed by men. In *Prisoners of Men's Dreams*, Suzanne Gordon comes close to blaming the modest status of jobs like nursing and flight attending on women's entry into jobs like medicine and piloting, as if before the women's movement those female-dominated occupations were respected and rewarded. (Nurses should be glad the field no longer has a huge captive labor pool of women: The nursing shortage has led to dramatic improvements in pay, benefits and responsibility. Now nurses earn a man-size income, and men are applying to nursing school in record numbers – exactly what Gordon wants.) It's all very well for some women to condemn others for "acting like men" – i.e., being ambitious, assertive, interested in money and position. But if their husbands did not "act like men,"

where would they be? Jean Bethke Elshtain, who strenuously resists the notion of gendered ethics, nevertheless bemoans the loss to their communities when women leave volunteering and informal mutual support networks for paid employment. But money must come from somewhere; if women leave to men the job of earning the family income (an option fewer and fewer families can afford), they will be economically dependent on their husbands, a situation that, besides carrying obvious risks in an age of frequent divorce, weakens their bargaining position in the family and insures that men will largely control major decisions affecting family life.

Difference theorists would like to separate out the aspects of traditional womanhood that they approve of and speak only of those. But the parts they like (caring, nurturing, intimacy) are inseparable from the parts they don't like (economic dependence and the subordination of women within the family). The difference theorists try to get around this by positing a world that contains two cultures – a female world of love and ritual and a male world of getting and spending and killing – which mysteriously share a single planet. That vision is expressed neatly in a recent pop-psychology title, *Men Are From Mars, Women Are From Venus*. It would be truer to say men are from Illinois and women are from Indiana – different, sure, but not in ways that have much ethical consequence.

The truth is, there is only one culture, and it shapes each sex in distinct but mutually dependent ways in order to reproduce itself. To the extent that the stereotypes are true, women have the "relational" domestic qualities *because* men have the "autonomous" qualities required to survive and prosper in modern capitalism. She needs a wage earner (even if she has a job, thanks to job discrimination), and he needs someone to mind his children, hold his hand and have his emotions for him. This – not, as Gordon imagines, some treason to her sex – explains why women who move into male sectors act very much like men: If they didn't, they'd find themselves back home in a jiffy. The same necessities and pressures affect them as affect the men who hold those jobs. Because we are in a transition period, in which many women were raised with modest expectations and much emphasis on the need to please others, social scientists who look for it can find traces of empathy, caring and so on in some women who have risen in the world of work and power. But when they tell us that women doctors will transform American medicine, or women executives will transform the corporate world, they are looking backward, not forward. If women really do enter the workforce on equal terms with men – if they become 50 percent of all lawyers, politicians, car dealers and prison guards – they may be less sexist (although the example of Soviet doctors, a majority of them female, is not inspiring to those who know about the brutal gynecological customs prevailing in the former U.S.S.R.). And they may bring with them a distinct set of manners, a separate social style. But they won't be, in some general way, more honest, kind, egalitarian, empathic or indifferent to profit. To argue otherwise is to believe that the reason factory owners bust unions, doctors refuse Medicaid patients and New York City school custodians don't mop the floors is because they are men.

The ultimate paradox of difference feminism is that it has come to the fore at a moment when the lives of the sexes are becoming less distinct than they ever have been in the West. Look at the decline of single-sex education (researchers may tout the benefits of all-female schools and colleges, but girls overwhelmingly choose coeducation); the growth of female athletics; the virtual abolition of virginity as a requirement for girls; the equalization of college-attendance rates of males and females; the explosion of employment for married women and mothers even of small children; the crossing of workplace gender lines by both females and males; the cultural pressure on men to be warm and active fathers, to do at least some housework, to choose mates who are their equals in education and income potential.

It's fashionable these days to talk about the backlash against equality feminism – I talk this way myself when I'm feeling blue – but equality feminism has scored amazing successes. It has transformed women's expectations in every area of their lives. However, it has not yet transformed society to meet those expectations. The workplace still discriminates. On the home front few men practice egalitarianism, although many preach it; single mothers – and given the high divorce rate, every mother is potentially a single mother – lead incredibly difficult lives.

In this social context, difference feminism is essentially a way for women both to take advantage of equality feminism's success and to accommodate themselves to its limits. It appeals to particular kinds of women – those in the "helping professions" or the home, for example, rather than those who want to be bomber pilots or neurosurgeons or electricians. At the popular level, it encourages women who feel disadvantaged or demeaned by equality to direct their anger against women who have benefited from it by thinking of them as gender traitors and of themselves as suffering for their virtue – thus the hostility of some nurses toward female doctors, and of some stay-at-home mothers toward employed mothers.

For its academic proponents, the appeal lies elsewhere: Difference feminism is a way to carve out a safe space in the face of academia's resistance to female advancement. It works much like multiculturalism, making an end run around a static and discriminatory employment structure by creating an intellectual niche that can be filled only by members of the discriminated-against group. And like other forms of multiculturalism, it looks everywhere for its explanatory force – biology, psychology, sociology, cultural identity – except economics. The difference feminists cannot say that the differences between men and women are the result of their relative economic positions, because to say that would be to move the whole discussion out of the realm of psychology and feel-good cultural pride and into the realm of a tough political struggle over the distribution of resources and justice and money.

Although it is couched in the language of praise, difference feminism is demeaning to women. It asks that women be admitted into public life and public discourse not because they have a right to be there but because they will improve them. Even if this were true, and not the wishful thinking I believe it to be, why should the task of moral and social transformation be laid on women's doorstep and not on everyone's – or, for that matter, on men's, by the you-broke-it-you-fix-it principle? Peace, the environment, a more humane workplace, economic justice, social support for children – these are issues that affect us all and are everyone's responsibility. By promising to assume that responsibility, difference feminists lay the groundwork for excluding women again, as soon as it becomes clear that the promise cannot be kept.

No one asks that other oppressed groups win their freedom by claiming to be extra-good. And no other oppressed group thinks it must make such a claim in order to be accommodated fully and across the board by society. For blacks and other racial minorities, it is enough to want to earn a living, exercise one's talents, get a fair hearing in the public forum. Only for women is simple justice an insufficient argument. It is as though women don't really believe they are entitled to full citizenship unless they can make a special claim to virtue. Why isn't being human enough?

In the end, I didn't sign that peace petition, although I was sorry to disappoint a woman I liked, and although I am very much for peace. I decided to wait for a petition that welcomed my signature as a person, an American, a citizen implicated, against my will, in war and the war economy. I still think I did the right thing.

Bibliography

Bock, Gisela, and Susan James, eds. *Beyond Equality and Difference*. London and New York: Routledge, 1992.

Grant, Judith. *Fundamental Feminism*. New York and London: Routledge, 1993.

Tong, Rosemarie. *Feminist Thought*. Boulder and San Francisco: Westview Press, 1989.

X

SOME CONTRARY VOICES

From one point of view Jean-Paul Sartre (1905-1980) might be held to have no place in the present book, since this volume means to collect significant and influential theories of human nature, and Sartre denied that there is any such thing as human nature. But this is just to say then that he is here as a very fundamental instance of critic of the entire enterprise of seeking to articulate deep truths – *the* truth, if possible – about human beings, and human behaviour. In this role Sartre's may be an extremely important voice to hear.

Sartre is just one of a series of thinkers and schools who have argued that "man makes himself" – that humanity is self-creating, through action and choice, and the crafting thereby of values. For such views something like this is implicit in the very idea of freedom. Hegel is the first to make this idea and its supposed consequences fully explicit.

Nor is Sartre the first existentialist. That distinction belongs to Kierkegaard, the brilliant Danish junior contemporary (and severe critic) of Hegel. For Kierkegaard our condition is one not only of radical freedom, but of radical solitude. Contending with our freedom and an ultimate and only imperfectly bridgeable loneliness is the plight that we characteristically seek to evade, but know, inwardly, that we cannot. Kierkegaard was a Christian for whom authenticity is to be found in religious commitment. Sartre was an atheist, for whom existential loneliness is all the more daunting by virtue of our cosmic solitude.

Sartre became a Marxist in the later phase of his career. Some see deep inconsistency in this development. The radical freedom Sartrean existentialism claims appears closer to something like Ayn Rand's view of our condition and its attendant responsibilities than to Marxian historical materialism, which seems to impose a cocoon of historical circumstance around all of us, hard to see as permitting genuine freedom. Others, on the other hand, see Marxian liberation as a collective affirmation of freedom, and bootstrapping self-creation through action that is essentially rediscovery of what we always have been.

All such views as these must contend with – but rarely do – what to say and think about other animals than human ones, especially given what Darwin and his successors have taught us.

Jean-Paul Sartre, *Existentialism and Humanism*

(Source: Jean-Paul Sartre. *Existentialism and Humanism*. Trans. and Intr. Philip Mairet. London: Eyre Methuen Ltd., 1948, 1973, 26-30.)

.... [T]here are two kinds of existentialists. There are, on the one hand, the Christians, amongst whom I shall name Jaspers and Gabriel Marcel, both professed Catholics; and on the other the existential atheists, amongst whom we must place Heidegger as well as the French existentialists and myself. What they have in common is simply the fact that they believe that *existence* comes before *essence* – or, if you will, that we must begin from the subjective. What exactly do we mean by that?

If one considers an article of manufacture – as, for example, a book or a paper-knife – one sees that it has been made by an artisan who had a conception of it; and he has paid attention, equally, to the conception of a paper-knife and to the pre-existent technique of production which is a part of that conception and is, at bottom, a formula. Thus the paper-knife is at the same time an article producible in a certain manner and one which, on the other hand, serves a definite purpose, for one cannot suppose that a man would produce a paper-knife without knowing what it was for. Let us say, then, of the paper-knife that its essence – that is to say the sum of the formulae and the qualities which made its production and its definition possible – precedes its existence. The presence of such-and-such a paper-knife or book is thus determined before my eyes. Here, then, we are viewing the world from a technical standpoint, and we can say that production precedes existence.

When we think of God as the creator, we are thinking of him, most of the time, as a supernal artisan. Whatever doctrine we may be considering, whether it be a doctrine like that of Descartes, or of Leibnitz himself, we always imply that the will follows, more or less, from the understanding or at least accompanies it, so that when God creates he knows precisely what he is creating. Thus, the conception of man in the mind of God is comparable to that of the paper-knife in the mind of the artisan: God makes man according to a procedure and a conception, exactly as the artisan manufactures a paper-knife, following a definition and a formula. Thus each individual man is the realisation of a certain conception which dwells in the divine understanding. In the philosophic atheism of the eighteenth century, the notion of God is suppressed, but not, for all that, the idea that essence is prior to existence; something of that idea we still find everywhere, in Diderot, in Voltaire and even in Kant. Man possesses a human nature; that "human nature," which is the conception of human being, is found in every man; which means that each man is a particular example of an universal conception, the conception of Man. In Kant, this universality goes so far that the wild man of the woods, man in the state of nature and the bourgeois are all contained in the same definition and have the same fundamental qualities. Here again, the essence of man precedes that historic existence which we confront in experience.

Atheistic existentialism, of which I am a representative, declares with greater consistency that if God does not exist there is at least one being whose existence comes before its essence, a being which exists before it can be defined by any conception of it. That being is man or, as Heidegger has it, the human reality. What do we mean by saying that existence precedes essence? We mean that man first of all exists, encounters himself, surges up in the world – and defines himself afterwards. If man as the existentialist sees him is not definable, it is because to begin with he is nothing. He will not be anything until later, and then he will be what he makes of himself. Thus, there is no human nature, because there is no God to have a conception of it. Man simply is. Not that he is simply what he conceives himself to be, but he is what he wills, and as he conceives himself after already existing – as he wills to be after that leap towards existence. Man is nothing else but that which he makes of himself. That is the first principle of existentialism. And this is what people call its "subjectivity," using the word as a reproach against us. But what do we mean to say by this, but that man is of a greater dignity than a stone or a table? For we mean to say that man primarily exists – that man is, before all else, something which propels itself towards a future and is aware that it is doing so. Man is, indeed, a project which possesses a subjective life, instead of being a kind of moss, or a fungus or a cauliflower. Before that projection of the self nothing exists; not even in the heaven of intelligence: man will only attain existence when he is what he purposes to be. Not, however, what he may wish to be. For what we usually understand by wishing or willing is a conscious decision taken – much more often than not – after we have made ourselves what we are. I may wish to join a party, to write a book or to marry – but in such a case what is usually called my will is probably a manifestation of a prior and more spontaneous decision. If, however, it is true that existence is prior to essence, man is responsible for what he is. Thus, the first effect of existentialism is that it puts every man in possession of himself as he is, and places the entire responsibility for his existence squarely upon his own shoulders. And, when we say that man is responsible for himself, we do not mean that he is responsible only for his own individuality, but that he is responsible for all men. The word "subjectivism" is to be understood in two senses, and our adversaries play upon only one of them. Subjectivism means, on the one hand, the freedom of the individual subject and, on the other, that man cannot pass beyond human subjectivity. It is the latter which is the deeper meaning of existentialism. When we say that man chooses himself, we do mean that every one of us must choose himself; but by that we also mean that in choosing for himself he chooses for all men. For in effect, of all the actions a man may take in order to create himself as he wills to be, there is not one which is not creative, at the same time, of an image of man such as he believes he ought to be. To choose between this or that is at the same time to affirm the value of that which is chosen; for we are unable ever to choose the worse. What we choose is always the better; and nothing can be better for us unless it is better for all. If, moreover, existence precedes essence and we will to exist at the same time as we fashion our image, that image is valid for all and for the entire epoch in which we find ourselves. Our responsibility is thus much greater than we had supposed, for it concerns mankind as a whole. If I am a worker, for instance, I may choose to join a Christian rather than a Communist trade union. And if, by that membership, I choose to signify that resignation is, after all, the attitude that best becomes a man, that man's kingdom is not upon this earth, I do not commit myself alone to that view. Resignation is my will for everyone, and my action is, in consequence, a commitment on behalf of all mankind. Or if, to take a more personal case, I decide to marry and to have children, even though this decision proceeds simply from my situation, from my passion or my desire, I am thereby committing not only myself, but humanity as a whole, to the practice of monogamy. I am thus responsible for myself and for all men, and I am creating a certain image of man as I would have him to be. In fashioning myself I fashion man.

Bibliography

Caws, P. *Sartre*. London: Routledge and Kegan Paul, 1979.

Howells, C., ed. *The Cambridge Companion to Sartre*. Cambridge: Cambridge University Press, 1992.

Jeanson, F. *Sartre and the Problem of Morality*. Bloomington: Indiana University Press, 1980.

Warnock, Mary, ed. *Sartre: A Collection of Critical Essays*. New York: Anchor Books, 1971.

Camille Paglia (b. 1947) is a contemporary voice for the ideas, above all, of Nietzsche and Freud. Another significant figure in the background of her analyses, whom she acknowledges, is the Marquis de Sade (1740-1814). Passionate, hyperbolic, wide-ranging, she has achieved special attention, sometimes notoriety, as an "anti-feminist feminist" – a critic of central features of much contemporary feminism, at the same as she sets out her own special variety of feminist affirmation. Paglia's background is in the study of literature, and art; she is a professor of humanities at the University of the Arts, in Philadelphia. She has also had a considerable presence in the mass media; this partly, at least, reflects her conviction that contemporary electronic popular culture needs to be taken very seriously, and incorporated into the synoptic theoretical understanding of the artistic impulse, and its products, from the Neolithic age to the present.

Paglia's philosophy affirms the ultimately invincible power of nature, including universals of human nature, with specifics of sexual differentiation. The selections that follow, from Paglia's large cultural study of "art and decadence," *Sexual Personae*, show her debts to Nietzsche and Freudian thought; in relation to the latter in particular, Paglia is clearly drawn to "object relations theory," the psychoanalytic account of gender formation developed by Freud's followers Abraham and Klein, and revived in modified form by many contemporary psychoanalytic feminists. In Paglia's conception of it, however, these patterns of formation of sexual identity are, as with Freud himself, rooted in human biology and not seriously modifiable.

Paglia has significance also for the theories of the present volume as a critic of liberalism, of Marxism, and above all, of Rousseau, in many ways a primary originative fount of several of the views of human nature of the nineteenth and twentieth centuries. Positively, Paglia is an advocate of the possibilities of liberating individual creative achievement, through the hard-won nurturing frame of sociality, culture, and law.

Camille Paglia, *Sexual Personae*

(Source: Camille Paglia. *Sexual Personae: Art and Decadence from Nefertiti to Emily Dickinson*. New York: Vintage Books, 1991, 1-39, 230-235, 246-247.)

Sex and Violence, or Nature and Art

In the beginning was nature. The background from which and against which our ideas of God were formed, nature remains the supreme moral problem. We cannot hope to understand sex and gender until we clarify our attitude toward nature. Sex is a subset to nature. Sex is the natural in man.

Society is an artificial construction, a defense against nature's power. Without society, we would be storm-tossed on the barbarous sea that is nature. Society is a system of inherited forms reducing our humiliating passivity to nature. We may alter these forms, slowly or suddenly, but no change in society will change nature. Human beings are not nature's favorites. We are merely one of a multitude of species upon which nature indiscriminately exerts its force. Nature has a master agenda we can only dimly know.

Human life began in flight and fear. Religion rose from rituals of propitiation, spells to lull the punishing elements. To this day, communities are few in regions scorched by heat or shackled by ice. Civilized man conceals from himself the extent of his subordination to nature. The grandeur of culture, the consolation of religion absorb his attention and win his faith. But let nature shrug, and all is in ruin. Fire, flood, lightning, tornado, hurricane, volcano, earthquake – anywhere at any time. Disaster falls upon the good and bad. Civilized life requires a state of illusion. The idea of the ultimate benevolence of nature and God is the most potent of man's survival mechanisms. Without it, culture would revert to fear and despair.

Sexuality and eroticism are the intricate intersection of nature and culture. Feminists grossly oversimplify the problem of sex when they reduce it to a matter of social convention: readjust society, eliminate sexual inequality, purify sex roles, and happiness and harmony will reign. Here feminism, like all liberal movements of the past two hundred years, is heir to Rousseau. *The Social Contract* (1762) begins: "Man is born free, and everywhere he is in chains." Pitting benign Romantic nature against corrupt society, Rousseau produced the progressivist strain in nineteenth-century culture, for which social reform was the means to achieve paradise on earth. The bubble of these hopes was burst by the catastrophes of two world wars. But Rousseauism was reborn in the postwar generation of the Sixties, from which contemporary feminism developed.

Rousseau rejects original sin, Christianity's pessimistic view of man born unclean, with a propensity for evil. Rousseau's idea, derived from Locke, of man's innate goodness led to social environmentalism, now the dominant ethic of American human services, penal codes, and behaviorist therapies. It assumes that aggression, violence, and crime come from social deprivation – a poor neighborhood, a bad home. Thus feminism blames rape on pornography and, by a smug circularity of reasoning, interprets outbreaks of sadism as a backlash to itself. But rape and sadism have been evident throughout history and, at some moment, in all cultures.

This book takes the point of view of Sade, the most unread major writer in western literature. Sade's work is a comprehensive satiric critique of Rousseau, written in the decade after the first failed Rousseauist experiment, the French Revolution, which ended not in political paradise but in the hell of the Reign of Terror. Sade follows Hobbes rather than Locke. Aggression comes from nature; it is

what Nietzsche is to call the will-to-power. For Sade, getting back to nature (the Romantic imperative that still permeates our culture from sex counseling to cereal commercials) would be to give free rein to violence and lust. I agree. Society is not the criminal but the force which keeps crime in check. When social controls weaken, man's innate cruelty bursts forth. The rapist is created not by bad social influences but by a failure of social conditioning. Feminists, seeking to drive power relations out of sex, have set themselves against nature. Sex *is* power. Identity is power. In western culture, there are no nonexploitative relationships. Everyone has killed in order to live. Nature's universal law of creation from destruction operates in mind as in matter. As Freud, Nietzsche's heir, asserts, identity is conflict. Each generation drives its plow over the bones of the dead.

Modern liberalism suffers unresolved contradictions. It exalts individualism and freedom and, on its radical wing, condemns social orders as oppressive. On the other hand, it expects government to provide materially for all, a feat manageable only by an expansion of authority and a swollen bureaucracy. In other words, liberalism defines government as tyrant father but demands it behave as nurturant mother. Feminism has inherited these contradictions. It sees every hierarchy as repressive, a social fiction; every negative about woman is a male lie designed to keep her in her place. Feminism has exceeded its proper mission of seeking political equality for women and has ended by rejecting contingency, that is, human limitation by nature or fate.

Sexual freedom, sexual liberation. A modern delusion. We are hierarchical animals. Sweep one hierarchy away, and another will take its place, perhaps less palatable than the first. There are hierarchies in nature and alternate hierarchies in society. In nature, brute force is the law, a survival of the fittest. In society, there are protections for the weak. Society is our frail barrier against nature. When the prestige of state and religion is low, men are free, but they find freedom intolerable and seek new ways to enslave themselves, through drugs or depression. My theory is that whenever sexual freedom is sought or achieved, sadomasochism will not be far behind. Romanticism always turns into decadence. Nature is a hard taskmaster. It is the hammer and the anvil, crushing individuality. Perfect freedom would be to die by earth, air, water, and fire.

Sex is a far darker power than feminism has admitted. Behaviorist sex therapies believe guilt-less, no-fault sex is possible. But sex has always been girt round with taboo, irrespective of culture. Sex is the point of contact between man and nature, where morality and good intentions fall to primitive urges. I called it an intersection. This intersection is the uncanny crossroads of Hecate, where all things return in the night. Eroticism is a realm stalked by ghosts. It is the place beyond the pale, both cursed and enchanted.

This book shows how much in culture goes against our best wishes. Integration of man's body and mind is a profound problem that is not about to be solved by recreational sex or an expansion of women's civil rights. Incarnation, the limitation of mind by matter, is an outrage to imagination. Equally outrageous is gender, which we have not chosen but which nature has imposed upon us. Our physicality is torment, our body the tree of nature on which Blake sees us crucified.

Sex is daemonic. This term, current in Romantic studies of the past twenty-five years, derives from the Greek *daimon,* meaning a spirit of lower divin-ity than the Olympian gods (hence my pronuncia-tion "daimonic"). The outcast Oedipus becomes a daemon at Colonus. The word came to mean a man's guardian shadow. Christianity turned the daemonic into the demonic. The Greek daemons were not evil – or rather they were both good and evil, like nature itself, in which they dwelled. Freud's unconscious is a daemonic realm. In the day we are social creatures, but at night we descend to the dream world where nature reigns, where there is no law but sex, cruelty, and metamorphosis. Day itself is invaded by daemonic night. Moment by moment, night flickers in the imagination, in eroticism, subverting our strivings for virtue and order, giving an uncanny aura to objects and per-sons, revealed to us through the eyes of the artist.

The ghost-ridden character of sex is implicit in Freud's brilliant theory of "family romance." We each have an incestuous constellation of sexual per-sonae that we carry from childhood to the grave and that determines whom and how we love or hate. Every encounter with friend or foe, every clash with or submission to authority bears the per-verse traces of family romance. Love is a crowded theater, for as Harold Bloom remarks, "We can never embrace (sexually or otherwise) a single per-son, but embrace the whole of her or his family romance."[1] We still know next to nothing of the mystery of cathexis, the investment of libido in cer-tain people or things. The element of free will in sex and emotion is slight. As poets know, falling in love is irrational.

Like art, sex is fraught with symbols. Family romance means that adult sex is always representa-tion, ritualistic acting out of vanished realities. A perfectly humane eroticism may be impossible. Somewhere in every family romance is hostility and aggression, the homicidal wishes of the uncon-scious. Children are monsters of unbridled egotism and will, for they spring directly from nature, hos-tile intimations of immorality. We carry that dae-monic will within us forever. Most people conceal it with acquired ethical precepts and meet it only in their dreams, which they hastily forget upon wak-ing. The will-to-power is innate, but the sexual scripts of family romance are learned. Human beings are the only creatures in whom conscious-ness is so entangled with animal instinct. In west-ern culture, there can never be a purely physical or anxiety-free sexual encounter. Every attraction, every pattern of touch, every orgasm is shaped by psychic shadows.

The search for freedom through sex is doomed to failure. In sex, compulsion and ancient Necessity rule. The sexual personae of family romance are obliterated by the tidal force of regression, the backwards movement toward primeval dissolution, which Ferenczi identifies with ocean. An orgasm is a domination, a surrender, or a breaking through. Nature is no respecter of human identity. This is why so many men turn away or flee after sex, for they have sensed the annihilation of the daemonic. Western love is a displacement of cosmic realities. It is a defense mechanism rationalizing forces ungoverned and ungovernable. Like early religion, it is a device enabling us to control our primal fear.

Sex cannot be understood because nature cannot be understood. Science is a method of logical

---

1   *The Anxiety of Influence: A Theory of Poetry* (New York, 1973), 94.

analysis of nature's operations. It has lessened human anxiety about the cosmos by demonstrating the materiality of nature's forces, and their frequent predictability. But science is always playing catch-up ball. Nature breaks its own rules whenever it wants. Science cannot avert a single thunderbolt. Western science is a product of the Apollonian mind: its hope is that by naming and classification, by the cold light of intellect, archaic night can be pushed back and defeated.

Name and person are part of the west's quest for form. The west insists on the discrete identity of objects. To name is to know; to know is to control. I will demonstrate that the west's greatness arises from this delusional certitude. Far Eastern culture has never striven against nature in this way. Compliance, not confrontation is its rule. Buddhist meditation seeks the unity and harmony of reality. Twentieth-century physics, going full circle back to Heracleitus, postulates that all matter is in motion. In other words, there is no thing, only energy. But this perception has not been imaginatively absorbed, for it cancels the west's intellectual and moral assumptions.

The westerner knows by seeing. Perceptual relations are at the heart of our culture, and they have produced our titanic contributions to art. Walking in nature, we see, identify, name, *recognize*. This recognition is our apotropaion, that is, our warding off of fear. Recognition is ritual cognition, a repetition-compulsion. We say that nature is beautiful. But this aesthetic judgment, which not all peoples have shared, is another defense formation, woefully inadequate for encompassing nature's totality. What is pretty in nature is confined to the thin skin of the globe upon which we huddle. Scratch that skin, and nature's daemonic ugliness will erupt.

Our focus on the pretty is an Apollonian strategy. The leaves and flowers, the birds, the hills are a patchwork pattern by which we map the known. What the west represses in its view of nature is the chthonian, which means "of the earth" – but earth's bowels, not its surface. Jane Harrison uses the term for pre-Olympian Greek religion, and I adopt it as a substitute for Dionysian, which has become contaminated with vulgar pleasantries. The Dionysian is no picnic. It is the chthonian realities which Apollo evades, the blind grinding of subterranean force, the long slow suck, the murk and ooze. It is the dehumanizing brutality of biol-

ogy and geology, the Darwinian waste and bloodshed, the squalor and rot we must block from consciousness to retain our Apollonian integrity as persons. Western science and aesthetics are attempts to revise this horror into imaginatively palatable form.

The daemonism of chthonian nature is the west's dirty secret. Modern humanists made the "tragic sense of life" the touchstone of mature understanding. They defined man's mortality and the transience of time as literature's supreme subjects. In this I again see evasion and even sentimentality. The tragic sense of life is a partial response to experience. It is a reflex of the west's resistance to and misapprehension of nature, compounded by the errors of liberalism, which in its Romantic nature-philosophy has followed the Rousseauist Wordsworth rather than the daemonic Coleridge.

Tragedy is the most western literary genre. It did not appear in Japan until the late nineteenth century. The western will, setting itself up against nature, dramatized its own inevitable fall as a human universal, which it is not. An irony of literary history is the birth of tragedy in the cult of Dionysus. The protagonist's destruction recalls the slaughter of animals and, even earlier, of real human beings in archaic ritual. It is no accident that tragedy as we know it dates from the Apollonian fifth century of Athens' greatness, whose cardinal work is Aeschylus' *Oresteia*, a celebration of the defeat of chthonian power. Drama, a Dionysian mode, turned against Dionysus in making the passage from ritual to mimesis, that is, from action to representation. Aristotle's "pity and fear" is a broken promise, a plea for vision without horror.

Few Greek tragedies fully conform to the humanist commentary on them. Their barbaric residue will not come unglued. Even in the fifth century, as we shall see, a satiric response to Apollonianized theater came in Euripides' decadent plays. Problems in accurate assessment of Greek tragedy include not only the loss of three-quarters of the original body of work but the lack of survival of any complete satyr-play. This was the finale to the classic trilogy, an obscene comic burlesque. In Greek tragedy, comedy always had the last word. Modern criticism has projected a Victorian and, I feel, Protestant high seriousness upon pagan culture that still blankets teaching of the humanities.

Paradoxically, assent to savage chthonian realities leads not to gloom but to humor. Hence Sade's strange laughter, his wit amid the most fantastic cruelties. For life is not a tragedy but a comedy. Comedy is born of the clash between Apollo and Dionysus. Nature is always pulling the rug out from under our pompous ideals.

Female tragic protagonists are rare. Tragedy is a male paradigm of rise and fall, a graph in which dramatic and sexual climax are in shadowy analogy. Climax is another western invention. Traditional eastern stories are picaresque, horizontal chains of incident. There is little suspense or sense of an ending. The sharp vertical peaking of western narrative, as later of orchestral music, is exemplified by Sophocles' *Oedipus Rex,* whose moment of maximum intensity Aristotle calls *peripeteia,* reversal. Western dramatic climax was produced by the agon of male will. Through action to identity. Action is the route of escape from nature, but all action circles back to origins, the womb-tomb of nature. Oedipus, trying to escape his mother, runs straight into her arms. Western narrative is a mystery story, a process of detection. But since what is detected is unbearable, every revelation leads to another repression.

The major women of tragedy – Euripides' Medea and Phaedra, Shakespeare's Cleopatra and Lady Macbeth, Racine's Phèdre – skew the genre by their disruptive relation to male action. Tragic woman is less moral than man. Her will-to-power is naked. Her actions are under a chthonian cloud. They are a conduit of the irrational, opening the genre to intrusions of the barbaric force that drama shut out at its birth. Tragedy is a western vehicle for testing and purification of the male will. The difficulty in grafting female protagonists onto it is a result not of male prejudice but of instinctive sexual strategies. Woman introduces untransformed cruelty into tragedy because she is the problem that the genre is trying to correct.

Tragedy plays a male game, a game it invented to snatch victory from the jaws of defeat. It is not flawed choice, flawed action, or even death itself which is the ultimate human dilemma. The gravest challenge to our hopes and dreams is the messy biological business-as-usual that is going on within us and without us at every hour of every day. Consciousness is a pitiful hostage of its flesh-envelope, whose surges, circuits, and secret murmurings

it cannot stay or speed. This is the chthonian drama that has no climax but only an endless round, cycle upon cycle. Microcosm mirrors macrocosm. Free will is stillborn in the red cells of our body, for there is no free will in nature. Our choices come to us prepackaged and special delivery, molded by hands not our own.

Tragedy's inhospitality to woman springs from nature's inhospitality to man. The identification of woman with nature was universal in prehistory. In hunting or agrarian societies dependent upon nature, femaleness was honored as an immanent principle of fertility. As culture progressed, crafts and commerce supplied a concentration of resources freeing men from the caprices of weather or the handicap of geography. With nature at one remove, femaleness receded in importance.

Buddhist cultures retained the ancient meanings of femaleness long after the west renounced them. Male and female, the Chinese yang and yin, are balanced and interpenetrating powers in man and nature, to which society is subordinate. This code of passive acceptance has its roots in India, a land of sudden extremes where a monsoon can wipe out 50,000 people overnight. The femaleness of fertility religions is always double-edged. The Indian nature-goddess Kali is creator and destroyer, granting boons with one set of arms while cutting throats with the other. She is the lady ringed with skulls. The moral ambivalence of the great mother goddesses has been conveniently forgotten by those American feminists who have resurrected them. We cannot grasp nature's bare blade without shedding our own blood.

Western culture from the start has swerved from femaleness. The last major western society to worship female powers was Minoan Crete. And significantly, that fell and did not rise again. The immediate cause of its collapse – quake, plague, or invasion – is beside the point. The lesson is that cultic femaleness is no guarantee of cultural strength or viability. What did survive, what did vanquish circumstance and stamp its mind-set on Europe was Mycenaean warrior culture, descending to us through Homer. The male will-to-power: Mycenaeans from the south and Dorians from the north would fuse to form Apollonian Athens, from which came the Greco-Roman line of western history.

Both the Apollonian and Judeo-Christian traditions are transcendental. That is, they seek to surmount or transcend nature. Despite Greek culture's contrary Dionysian element, which I will discuss, high classicism was an Apollonian achievement. Judaism, Christianity's parent sect, is the most powerful of protests against nature. The Old Testament asserts that a father god made nature and that differentiation into objects and gender was after the fact of his maleness. Judeo-Christianity, like Greek worship of the Olympian gods, is a sky-cult. It is an advanced stage in the history of religion, which everywhere began as earth-cult, veneration of fruitful nature.

The evolution from earth-cult to sky-cult shifts woman into the nether realm. Her mysterious procreative powers and the resemblance of her rounded breasts, belly, and hips to earth's contours put her at the center of early symbolism. She was the model for the Great Mother figures who crowded the birth of religion worldwide. But the mother cults did not mean social freedom for women. On the contrary, as I will show in a discussion of Hollywood in the sequel to this book, cult objects are prisoners of their own symbolic inflation. Every totem lives in taboo.

Woman was an idol of belly-magic. She seemed to swell and give birth by her own law. From the beginning of time, woman has seemed an uncanny being. Man honored but feared her. She was the black maw that had spat him forth and would devour him anew. Men, bonding together, invented culture as a defense against female nature. Sky-cult was the most sophisticated step in this process, for its switch of the creative locus from earth to sky is a shift from belly-magic to head magic. And from this defensive head-magic has come the spectacular glory of male civilization, which has lifted woman with it. The very language and logic modern woman uses to assail patriarchal culture were the invention of men.

Hence the sexes are caught in a comedy of historical indebtedness. Man, repelled by his debt to a physical mother, created an alternate reality, a heterocosm to give him the illusion of freedom. Woman, at first content to accept man's protections but now inflamed with desire for her own illusory freedom, invades man's systems and suppresses her indebtedness to him as she steals them. By head-magic she will deny there ever was a problem of sex and nature. She has inherited the anxiety of

influence.

The identification of woman with nature is the most troubled and troubling term in this historical argument. Was it ever true? Can it still be true? Most feminist readers will disagree, but I think this identification not myth but reality. All the genres of philosophy, science, high art, athletics, and politics were invented by men. But by the Promethean law of conflict and capture, woman has a right to seize what she will and to vie with man on his own terms. Yet there is a limit to what she can alter in herself and in man's relation to her. Every human being must wrestle with nature. But nature's burden falls more heavily on one sex. With luck, this will not limit woman's achievement, that is, her action in male-created social space. But it must limit eroticism, that is, our imaginative lives in sexual space, which may overlap social space but is not identical with it.

Nature's cycles are woman's cycles. Biologic femaleness is a sequence of circular returns, beginning and ending at the same point. Woman's centrality gives her a stability of identity. She does not have to become but only to be. Her centrality is a great obstacle to man, whose quest for identity she blocks. He must transform himself into an independent being, that is, a being free of her. If he does not, he will simply fall back into her. Reunion with the mother is a siren call haunting our imagination. Once there was bliss, and now there is struggle. Dim memories of life before the traumatic separation of birth may be the source of Arcadian fantasies of a lost golden age. The western idea of history as a propulsive movement into the future, a progressive or Providential design climaxing in the revelation of a Second Coming, is a male formulation. No woman, I submit, could have coined such an idea, since it is a strategy of evasion of woman's own cyclic nature, in which man dreads being caught. Evolutionary or apocalyptic history is a male wish list with a happy ending, a phallic peak.

Woman does not dream of transcendental or historical escape from natural cycle, since she *is* that cycle. Her sexual maturity means marriage to the moon, waxing and waning in lunar phases. Moon, month, menses: same word, same world. The ancients knew that woman is bound to nature's calendar, an appointment she cannot refuse. The Greek pattern of free will to hybris to tragedy is a male drama, since woman has never been deluded (until recently) by the mirage of free will. She knows there is no free will, since she is not free. She has no choice but acceptance. Whether she desires motherhood or not, nature yokes her into the brute inflexible rhythm of procreative law. Menstrual cycle is an alarming clock that cannot be stopped until nature wills it.

Woman's reproductive apparatus is vastly more complicated than man's, and still ill-understood. All kinds of things can go wrong or cause distress in going right. Western woman is in an agonistic relation to her own body: for her, biologic normalcy is suffering, and health an illness. Dysmenorrhea, it is argued, is a disease of civilization, since women in tribal cultures have few menstrual complaints. But in tribal life, woman has an extended or collective identity; tribal religion honors nature and subordinates itself to it. It is precisely in advanced western society, which attempts to improve or surpass nature and which holds up individualism and self-realization as a model, that the stark facts of woman's condition emerge with painful clarity. The more woman aims for personal identity and autonomy, the more she develops her imagination, the fiercer will be her struggle with nature – that is, with the intractable physical laws of her own body. And the more nature will punish her: do not dare to be free! for your body does not belong to you.

The female body is a chthonian machine, indifferent to the spirit who inhabits it. Organically, it has one mission, pregnancy, which we may spend a lifetime staving off. Nature cares only for species, never individuals: the humiliating dimensions of this biologic fact are most directly experienced by women, who probably have a greater realism and wisdom than men because of it. Woman's body is a sea acted upon by the month's lunar wave-motion. Sluggish and dormant, her fatty tissues are gorged with water, then suddenly cleansed at hormonal high tide. Edema is our mammalian relapse into the vegetable. Pregnancy demonstrates the deterministic character of woman's sexuality. Every pregnant woman has body and self taken over by a chthonian force beyond her control. In the welcome pregnancy, this is a happy sacrifice. But in the unwanted one, initiated by rape or misadventure, it is a

horror. Such unfortunate women look directly into nature's heart of darkness. For a fetus is a benign tumor, a vampire who steals in order to live. The so-called miracle of birth is nature getting her own way.

Every month for women is a new defeat of the will. Menstruation was once called "the curse," a reference to the expulsion from the Garden, when woman was condemned to labor pains because of Eve's sin. Most early cultures hemmed in menstruating women by ritual taboos. Orthodox Jewish women still purify themselves from menstrual uncleanness in the *mikveh,* a ritual bath. Women have borne the symbolic burden of man's imperfections, his grounding in nature. Menstrual blood is the stain, the birthmark of original sin, the filth that transcendental religion must wash from man. Is this identification merely phobic, merely misogynistic? Or is it possible there *is* something uncanny about menstrual blood, justifying its attachment to taboo? I will argue that it is not menstrual blood per se which disturbs the imagination – unstanchable as that red flood may be – but rather the albumen in the blood, the uterine shreds, placental jellyfish of the female sea. This is the chthonian matrix from which we rose. We have an evolutionary revulsion from slime, our site of biologic origins. Every month, it is woman's fate to face the abyss of time and being, the abyss which is herself.

The Bible has come under fire for making woman the fall guy in man's cosmic drama. But in casting a male conspirator, the serpent, as God's enemy, Genesis hedges and does not take its misogyny far enough. The Bible defensively swerves from God's true opponent, chthonian nature. The serpent is not outside Eve but in her. She is the garden and the serpent. Anthony Storr says of witches, "At a very primitive level, all mothers are phallic."[2] The Devil is a woman. Modern emancipation movements, discarding stereotypes impeding woman's social advance, refuse to acknowledge procreation's daemonism. Nature is serpentine, a bed of tangled vines, creepers and crawlers, probing dumb fingers of fetid organic life which Wordsworth taught us to call pretty. Biologists speak of man's reptilian brain, the oldest part of our upper nervous system, killer survivor of the archaic era. I contend that the

---

2   *Sexual Deviation* (Harmondsworth, Middlesex, 1964), 63.

premenstrual woman incited to snappishness or rage is hearing signals from the reptilian brain. In her, man's latent perversity is manifest. All hell breaks loose, the hell of chthonian nature that modern humanism denies and represses. In every premenstrual woman struggling to govern her temper, sky-cult wars again with earth-cult.

Mythology's identification of woman with nature is correct. The male contribution to procreation is momentary and transient. Conception is a pinpoint of time, another of our phallic peaks of action, from which the male slides back uselessly. The pregnant woman is daemonically, devilishly complete. As an ontological entity, she needs nothing and no one. I shall maintain that the pregnant woman, brooding for nine months upon her own creation, is the pattern of all solipsism, that the historical attribution of narcissism to women is another true myth. Male bonding and patriarchy were the recourse to which man was forced by his terrible sense of woman's power, her imperviousness, her archetypal confederacy with chthonian nature. Woman's body is a labyrinth in which man is lost. It is a walled garden, the medieval *hortus conclusus,* in which nature works its daemonic sorcery. Woman is the primeval fabricator, the real First Mover. She turns a gob of refuse into a spreading web of sentient being, floating on the snaky umbilical by which she leashes every man.

Feminism has been simplistic in arguing that female archetypes were politically motivated falsehoods by men. The historical repugnance to woman has a rational basis: disgust is reason's proper response to the grossness of procreative nature. Reason and logic are the anxiety-inspired domain of Apollo, premiere god of sky-cult. The Apollonian is harsh and phobic, coldly cutting itself off from nature by its superhuman purity. I shall argue that western personality and western achievement are, for better or worse, largely Apollonian. Apollo's great opponent Dionysus is ruler of the chthonian whose law is procreative femaleness. As we shall see, the Dionysian is liquid nature, a miasmic swamp whose prototype is the still pond of the womb.

We must ask whether the equivalence of male and female in Far Eastern symbolism was as culturally efficacious as the hierarchization of male over female has been in the west. Which system has ultimately benefited women more? Western science

and industry have freed women from drudgery and danger. Machines do housework. The pill neutralizes fertility. Giving birth is no longer fatal. And the Apollonian line of western rationality has produced the modern aggressive woman who can think like a man and write obnoxious books. The tension and antagonism in western metaphysics developed human higher critical powers to great heights. Most of western culture is a distortion of reality. But reality *should* be distorted; that is, imaginatively amended. The Buddhist acquiescence to nature is neither accurate about nature nor just to human potential. The Apollonian has taken us to the stars.

Daemonic archetypes of woman, filling world mythology, represent the uncontrollable nearness of nature. Their tradition passes nearly unbroken from prehistoric idols through literature and art to modern movies. The primary image is the femme fatale, the woman fatal to man. The more nature is beaten back in the west, the more the femme fatale reappears, as a return of the repressed. She is the spectre of the west's bad conscience about nature. She is the moral ambiguity of nature, a malevolent moon that keeps breaking through our fog of hopeful sentiment.

Feminism dismisses the femme fatale as a cartoon and libel. If she ever existed, she was simply a victim of society, resorting to destructive womanly wiles because of her lack of access to political power. The femme fatale was a career woman *manquée,* her energies neurotically diverted into the boudoir. By such techniques of demystification, feminism has painted itself into a corner. Sexuality is a murky realm of contradiction and ambivalence. It cannot always be understood by social models, which feminism, as an heir of nineteenth-century utilitarianism, insists on imposing on it. Mystification will always remain the disorderly companion of love and art. Eroticism *is* mystique; that is, the aura of emotion and imagination around sex. It cannot be "fixed" by codes of social or moral convenience, whether from the political left or right. For nature's fascism is greater than that of any society. There is a daemonic instability in sexual relations that we may have to accept.

The femme fatale is one of the most mesmerizing of sexual personae. She is not a fiction but an extrapolation of biologic realities in women that remain constant. The North American Indian myth of the toothed vagina (*vagina dentata*) is a gruesomely direct transcription of female power and male fear. Metaphorically, every vagina has secret teeth, for the male exits as less than when he entered. The basic mechanics of conception require action in the male but nothing more than passive receptivity in the female. Sex as a natural rather than social transaction, therefore, really is a kind of drain of male energy by female fullness. Physical and spiritual castration is the danger every man runs in intercourse with a woman. Love is the spell by which he puts his sexual fear to sleep. Woman's latent vampirism is not a social aberration but a development of her maternal function, for which nature has equipped her with tiresome thoroughness. For the male, every act of intercourse is a return to the mother and a capitulation to her. For men, sex is a struggle for identity. In sex, the male is consumed and released again by the toothed power that bore him, the female dragon of nature.

The femme fatale was produced by the mystique of connection between mother and child. A modern assumption is that sex and procreation are medically, scientifically, intellectually "manageable." If we keep tinkering with the social mechanism long enough, every difficulty will disappear. Meanwhile, the divorce rate soars. Conventional marriage, despite its inequities, kept the chaos of libido in check. When the prestige of marriage is low, all the nasty daemonism of sexual instinct pops out. Individualism, the self unconstrained by society, leads to the coarser servitude of constraint by nature. Every road from Rousseau leads to Sade. The mystique of our birth from human mothers is one of the daemonic clouds we cannot dispel by tiny declarations of independence. Apollo can swerve from nature, but he cannot obliterate it. As emotional and sexual beings we go full circle. Old age is a second childhood in which earliest memories revive. Chillingly, comatose patients of any age automatically drift toward the fetal position, from which they have to be pried by nurses. We are tied to our birth by unshakable apparitions of sense-memory.

Rousseauist psychologies like feminism assert the ultimate benevolence of human emotion. In such a system, the femme fatale logically has no place. I follow Freud, Nietzsche, and Sade in my view of the amorality of the instinctual life. At some level, all love is combat, a wrestling with ghosts. We are

only *for* something by being *against* something else. People who believe they are having pleasant, casual, uncomplex sexual encounters, whether with friend, spouse, or stranger, are blocking from consciousness the tangle of psychodynamics at work, just as they block the hostile clashings of their dream life. Family romance operates at all times. The femme fatale is one of the refinements of female narcissism, of the ambivalent self-directedness that is completed by the birth of a child or by the conversion of spouse or lover into child.

Mothers can be fatal to their sons. It is against the mother that men have erected their towering edifice of politics and sky-cult. She is Medusa, in whom Freud sees the castrating and castrated female pubes. But Medusa's snaky hair is also the writhing vegetable growth of nature. Her hideous grimace is men's fear of the laughter of women. She that gives life also blocks the way to freedom. Therefore I agree with Sade that we have the right to thwart nature's procreative compulsions, through sodomy or abortion. Male homosexuality may be the most valorous of attempts to evade the femme fatale and to defeat nature. By turning away from the Medusan mother, whether in honor or detestation of her, the male homosexual is one of the great forgers of absolutist western identity. But of course nature has won, as she always does, by making disease the price of promiscuous sex.

The permanence of the femme fatale as a sexual persona is part of the weary weight of eroticism, beneath which both ethics and religion founder. Eroticism is society's soft point, through which it is invaded by chthonian nature. The femme fatale can appear as Medusan mother or as frigid nymph, masquing in the brilliant luminosity of Apollonian high glamour. Her cool unreachability beckons, fascinates, and destroys. She is not a neurotic but, if anything, a psychopath. That is, she has an amoral affectlessness, a serene indifference to the suffering of others, which she invites and dispassionately observes as tests of her power. The mystique of the femme fatale cannot be perfectly translated into male terms. I will speak at length of the beautiful boy, one of the west's most stunning sexual personae. However, the danger of the *homme fatal*, as embodied in today's boyish male hustler, is that he will leave, disappearing to other loves, other lands. He is a rambler, a cowboy and sailor. But the danger of the femme fatale is that *she will stay,* still, placid, and paralyzing. Her remaining is a daemonic burden, the ubiquity of Walter Pater's *Mona Lisa,* who smothers history. She is a thorny symbol of the perversity of sex. She will stick.

We are moving in this chapter toward a theory of beauty. I believe that the aesthetic sense, like everything else thus far, is a swerve from the chthonian. It is a displacement from one area of reality to another, analogous to the shift from earth-cult to sky-cult. Ferenczi speaks of the replacement of animal nose by human eye, because of our upright stance. The eye is peremptory in its judgments. It decides what to see and why. Each of our glances is as much exclusion as inclusion. We select, editorialize, and enhance. Our idea of the pretty is a limited notion that cannot possibly apply to earth's metamorphic underworld, a cataclysmic realm of chthonian violence. We choose not to see this violence on our daily strolls. Every time we say nature is beautiful, we are saying a prayer, fingering our worry beads.

The cool beauty of the femme fatale is another transformation of chthonian ugliness. Female animals are usually less beautiful than males. The mother bird's dull feathers are camouflage, protecting the nest from predators. Male birds are creatures of spectacular display, of both plumage and parade, partly to impress females and conquer rivals and partly to divert enemies from the nest. Among humans, male ritual display is just as extreme, but for the first time the female becomes a lavishly beautiful object. Why? The female is adorned not simply to increase her property value, as Marxism would demystifyingly have it, but to assure her desirability. Consciousness has made cowards of us all. Animals do not feel sexual fear, because they are not rational beings. They operate under a pure biologic imperative. Mind, which has enabled humanity to adapt and flourish as a species, has also infinitely complicated our functioning as physical beings. We see too much, and so have to stringently limit our seeing. Desire is besieged on all sides by anxiety and doubt. Beauty, an ecstasy of the eye, drugs us and allows us to act. Beauty is our Apollonian revision of the chthonian.

Nature is a Darwinian spectacle of the eaters and the eaten. All phases of procreation are ruled by appetite: sexual intercourse, from kissing to penetration, consists of movements of barely controlled cruelty and consumption. The long pregnancy of the human female and the protracted childhood of her infant, who is not self-sustaining for seven years or more, have produced the agon of psychological dependency that burdens the male for a lifetime. Man justifiably fears being devoured by woman, who is nature's proxy.

Repression is an evolutionary adaptation permitting us to function under the burden of our expanded consciousness. For what we are conscious of could drive us mad. Crude male slang speaks of female genitalia as "slash" or "gash." Freud notes that Medusa turns men to stone because, at first sight, a boy thinks female genitals a wound, from which the penis has been cut. They are indeed a wound, but it is the infant who has been cut away, by violence: the umbilical is a hawser sawed through by a social rescue party. Sexual necessity drives man back to that bloody scene, but he cannot approach it without tremors of apprehension. These he conceals by euphemisms of love and beauty. However, the less well-bred he is – that is, the less socialized – the sharper his sense of the animality of sex and the grosser his language. The foulmouthed roughneck is produced not by society's sexism but by society's absence. For nature is the most foulmouthed of us all.

Woman's current advance in society is not a voyage from myth to truth but from myth to new myth. The rise of rational, technological woman may demand the repression of unpleasant archetypal realities. Ferenczi remarks, "The periodic pulsations in feminine sexuality (puberty, the menses, pregnancies and parturitions, the climacterium) require a much more powerful repression on the woman's part than is necessary for the man."[3] In its argument with male society, feminism must suppress the monthly evidence of woman's domination by chthonian nature. Menstruation and childbirth are an affront to beauty and form. In aesthetic terms, they are spectacles of frightful squalor. Modern life, with its hospitals and paper products, has distanced and sanitized these primitive mysteries, just as it has done with death, which used to be a gruelling at-home affair. An awful lot is being

---

3   "The Analytic Conception of the Psycho-Neuroses" (1908), in *Further Contributions to the Theory and Technique of Psycho-analysis,* ed. John Rickman, trans. Jane Isabel Suttie et al. (New York, 1926), 25.

swept under the rug: the awe and terror that is our lot.

The woundlike rawness of female genitals is a symbol of the unredeemability of chthonian nature. In aesthetic terms, female genitals are lurid in color, vagrant in contour, and architecturally incoherent. Male genitals, on the other hand, though they risk ludicrousness by their rubbery indecisiveness (a Sylvia Plath heroine memorably thinks of "turkey neck and turkey gizzards"), have a rational mathematical design, a syntax. This is no absolute virtue, however, since it may tend to confirm the male in his abundant misperceptions of reality. Aesthetics stop where sex begins. G. Wilson Knight declares, "All physical love is, in its way, a victory over physical secrecies and physical repulsions."[4] Sex is sloppy and untidy, a return to what Freud calls the infant's polymorphous perversity, a zestful rolling around in every body fluid. St. Augustine says, "We are born between feces and urine." This misogynistic view of the infant's sin-stained emergence from the birth canal is close to the chthonian truth. But excretion, through which nature for once acts upon the sexes equally, can be saved by comedy, as we see in Aristophanes, Rabelais, Pope, and Joyce. Excretion has found a place in high culture. Menstruation and childbirth are too barbaric for comedy. Their ugliness has produced the giant displacement of women's historical status as sex object, whose beauty is endlessly discussed and modified. Woman's beauty is a compromise with her dangerous archetypal allure. It gives the eye the comforting illusion of intellectual control over nature.

My explanation for the male domination of art, science, and politics, an indisputable fact of history, is based on an analogy between sexual physiology and aesthetics. I will argue that all cultural achievement is a projection, a swerve into Apollonian transcendance, and that men are anatomically destined to be projectors. But as with Oedipus, destiny may be a curse.

How we know the world and how it knows us are underlain by shadow patterns of sexual biography and sexual geography. What breaks into consciousness is shaped in advance by the daemonism of the senses. Mind is a captive of the body. Perfect objectivity does not exist. Every thought bears some emotional burden. Had we time or energy to pursue it, each random choice, from the color of a toothbrush to a decision over a menu, could be made to yield its secret meaning in the inner drama of our lives. But in exhaustion, we shut out this psychic supersaturation. The realm of number, the crystalline mathematic of Apollonian purity, was invented early on by western man as a refuge from the soggy emotionalism and bristling disorder of woman and nature. Women who excel in mathematics do so in a system devised by men for the mastery of nature. Number is the most imposing and least creaturely of pacifiers, man's yearning hope for objectivity. It is to number that he – and now she – withdraws to escape from the chthonian mire of love, hate, and family romance.

Even now, it is usually men rather than women who claim logic's superiority to emotion. This they comically tend to do at moments of maximum emotional chaos, which they may have incited and are helpless to stem. Male artists and actors have a cultural function in keeping the line of emotion open from the female to male realms. Every man harbors an inner female territory ruled by his mother, from whom he can never entirely break free. Since Romanticism, art and the study of art have become vehicles for exploring the west's repressed emotional life, though one would never know it from half the deadening scholarship that has sprung up around them. Poetry is the connecting link between body and mind. Every idea in poetry is grounded in emotion. Every word is a palpation of the body. The multiplicity of interpretation surrounding a poem mirrors the stormy uncontrollability of emotion, where nature works her will. Emotion is chaos. Every benign emotion has a flip side of negativity. Thus the flight from emotion to number is another crucial strategy of the Apollonian west in its long struggle with Dionysus.

Emotion is passion, a continuum of eroticism and aggression. Love and hate are not opposites: there is only more passion and less passion, a difference of quantity and not of kind. To live in love and peace is one of the outstanding contradictions that Christianity has imposed on its followers, an ideal impossible and unnatural. Since Romanticism,

4   *Lord Byron's Marriage* (London, 1957), 261.

artists and intellectuals have complained about the church's sex rules, but these are just one small part of the Christian war with pagan nature. Only a saint could sustain the Christian code of love. And saints are ruthless in their exclusions: they must shut out an enormous amount of reality, the reality of sexual personae and the reality of nature. Love for all means coldness to something or someone. Even Jesus, let us recall, was unnecessarily rude to his mother at Cana.

The chthonian superflux of emotion is a male problem. A man must do battle with that enormity, which resides in woman and nature. He can attain selfhood only by beating back the daemonic cloud that would swallow him up: mother-love, which we may just as well call mother-hate. Mother-love, mother-hate, for her or from her, one huge conglomerate of natural power. Political equality for women will make very little difference in this emotional turmoil that is going on above and below politics, outside the scheme of social life. Not until all babies are born from glass jars will the combat cease between mother and son. But in a totalitarian future that has removed procreation from woman's hands, there will also be no affect and no art. Men will be machines, without pain but also without pleasure. Imagination has a price, which we are paying every day. There is no escape from the biologic chains that bind us.

What has nature given man to defend himself against woman? Here we come to the source of man's cultural achievements, which follow so directly from his singular anatomy. Our lives as physical beings give rise to basic metaphors of apprehension, which vary greatly between the sexes. Here there can be no equality. Man is sexually compartmentalized. Genitally, he is condemned to a perpetual pattern of linearity, focus, aim, directedness. He must learn to aim. Without aim, urination and ejaculation end in infantile soiling of self or surroundings. Woman's eroticism is diffused throughout her body. Her desire for foreplay remains a notorious area of miscommunication between the sexes. Man's genital concentration is a reduction but also an intensification. He is a victim of unruly ups and downs. Male sexuality is inherently manic-depressive. Estrogen tranquilizes, but androgen agitates. Men are in a constant state of sexual anxiety, living on the pins and needles of their hormones. In sex as in life they are driven *beyond* – beyond the self, beyond the body. Even in the womb this rule applies. Every fetus becomes female unless it is steeped in male hormone, produced by a signal from the testes. Before birth, therefore, a male is already beyond the female. But to be beyond is to be exiled from the center of life. Men know they are sexual exiles. They wander the earth seeking satisfaction, craving and despising, never content. There is nothing in that anguished motion for women to envy.

The male genital metaphor is concentration and projection. Nature gives concentration to man to help him overcome his fear. Man approaches woman in bursts of spasmodic concentration. This gives him the delusion of temporary control of the archetypal mysteries that brought him forth. It gives him the courage to return. Sex is metaphysical for men, as it is not for women. Women have no problem to solve by sex. Physically and psychologically, they are serenely self-contained. They may choose to achieve, but they do not need it. They are not thrust into the beyond by their own fractious bodies. But men are out of balance. They must quest, pursue, court, or seize. Pigeons on the grass, alas: in such parkside rituals we may savor the comic pathos of sex. How often one spots a male pigeon making desperate, self-inflating sallies toward the female, as again and again she turns her back on him and nonchalantly marches away. But by concentration and insistence he may carry the day. Nature has blessed him with obliviousness to his own absurdity. His purposiveness is both a gift and a burden. In human beings, sexual concentration is the male's instrument for gathering together and forcibly fixing the dangerous chthonian superflux of emotion and energy that I identify with woman and nature. In sex, man is driven into the very abyss which he flees. He makes a voyage to nonbeing and back.

Through concentration to projection into the beyond. The male projection of erection and ejaculation is the paradigm for all cultural projection and conceptualization – from art and philosophy to fantasy, hallucination, and obsession. Women have conceptualized less in history not because men have kept them from doing so but because women do not need to conceptualize in order to exist. I leave open the question of brain differences. Conceptualization and sexual mania may issue from the same part of the male brain. Fetishism, for instance, a practice which like most of the sex perversions is confined to men, is clearly a conceptualizing or symbol-making activity. Man's vastly greater commercial patronage of pornography is analogous.

An erection is a *thought* and the orgasm an act of imagination. The male has to will his sexual authority before the woman who is a shadow of his mother and of all women. Failure and humiliation constantly wait in the wings. No woman has to prove herself a woman in the grim way a man has to prove himself a man. He must perform, or the show does not go on. Social convention is irrelevant. A flop is a flop. Ironically, sexual success always ends in sagging fortunes anyhow. Every male projection is transient and must be anxiously, endlessly renewed. Men enter in triumph but withdraw in decrepitude. The sex act cruelly mimics history's decline and fall. Male bonding is a self-preservation society, collegial reaffirmation through larger, fabricated frames of reference. Culture is man's iron reinforcement of his ever-imperiled private projections.

Concentration and projection are remarkably demonstrated by urination, one of male anatomy's most efficient compartmentalizations. Freud thinks primitive man preened himself on his ability to put out a fire with a stream of urine. A strange thing to be proud of but certainly beyond the scope of woman, who would scorch her hams in the process. Male urination really is a kind of accomplishment, an arc of transcendance. A woman merely waters the ground she stands on. Male urination is a form of commentary. It can be friendly when shared but is often aggressive, as in the defacement of public monuments by Sixties rock stars. To piss on is to criticize. John Wayne urinated on the shoes of a grouchy director in full view of cast and crew. This is one genre of self-expression women will never master. A male dog marking every bush on the block is a graffiti artist, leaving his rude signature with each lift of the leg. Women, like female dogs, are earthbound squatters. There is no projection beyond the boundaries of the self. Space is claimed by being sat on, squatter's rights.

The cumbersome, solipsistic character of female physiology is tediously evident at sports events and rock concerts, where fifty women wait in line for admission to the sequestered cells of the toilet. Meanwhile, their male friends zip in and out (in every sense) and stand around looking at their watches and rolling their eyes. Freud's notion of penis envy proves too true when the pubcrawling male cheerily relieves himself in midnight alleyways, to the vexation of his bursting female companions. This compartmentalization or isolation of male genitality has its dark side, however. It can lead to a dissociation of sex and emotion, to temptation, promiscuity, and disease. The modern male homosexual, for example, has sought ecstasy in the squalor of public toilets, for women perhaps the least erotic place on earth.

Man's metaphors of concentration and projection are echoes of both body and mind. Without them, he would be helpless before woman's power. Without them, woman would long ago have absorbed all of creation into herself. There would be no culture, no system, no pyramiding of one hierarchy upon another. Earth-cult must lose to sky-cult, if mind is ever to break free from matter. Ironically, the more modern woman thinks with Apollonian clarity, the more she participates in the historical negation of her sex. Political equality for women, desirable and necessary as it is, is not going to remedy the radical disjunction between the sexes that begins and ends in the body. The sexes will always be jolted by violent shocks of attraction and repulsion.

Androgyny, which some feminists promote as a pacifist blueprint for sexual utopia, belongs to the contemplative rather than active life. It is the ancient prerogative of priests, shamans, and artists. Feminists have politicized it as a weapon against the masculine principle. Redefined, it now means men must be like women and women can be whatever they like. Androgyny is a cancellation of male concentration and projection. Prescriptions for the future by bourgeois academics and writers carry their own bias. The reform of a college English department cuts no ice down at the corner garage. Male concentration and projection are visible everywhere in the aggressive energy of the streets. Fortunately, male homosexuals of every social class have preserved the cult of the masculine, which will therefore never lose its aesthetic legitimacy. Major peaks of western culture have been accompanied by a high incidence of male homosexuality – in classical Athens and Renaissance Florence and London. Male concentration and projection are self-enhancing, leading to supreme achievements of

Apollonian conceptualization.

If sexual physiology provides the pattern for our experience of the world, what is woman's basic metaphor? It is mystery, *the hidden*. Karen Horney speaks of a girl's inability to see her genitals and a boy's ability to see his as the source of "the greater subjectivity of women as compared with the greater objectivity of men."[5] To rephrase this with my different emphasis: men's delusional certitude that objectivity is possible is based on the visibility of their genitals. Second, this certitude is a defensive swerve from the anxiety-inducing invisibility of the womb. Women tend to be more realistic and less obsessional because of their toleration for ambiguity, which they learn from their inability to learn about their own bodies. Women accept limited knowledge as their natural condition, a great human truth that a man may take a lifetime to reach.

The female body's unbearable hiddenness applies to all aspects of men's dealings with women. What does it look like in there? Did she have an orgasm? Is it really my child? Who was my real father? Mystery shrouds woman's sexuality. This mystery is the main reason for the imprisonment man has imposed on women. Only by confining his wife in a locked harem guarded by eunuchs could he be certain that her son was also his. Man's genital visibility is a source of his scientific desire for external testing, validation, proof. By this method he hopes to solve the ultimate mystery story, his chthonian birth. Woman is veiled. Violent tearing of this veil may be a motive in gang-rapes and rape-murders, particularly ritualistic disembowellings of the Jack the Ripper kind. The Ripper's public nailing up of his victim's uterus is exactly paralleled in tribal ritual of South African Bushmen. Sex crimes are always male, never female, because such crimes are conceptualizing assaults on the unreachable omnipotence of woman and nature. Every woman's body contains a cell of archaic night, where all knowing must stop. This is the profound meaning behind striptease, a sacred dance of pagan origins which, like prostitution, Christianity has never been able to stamp out. Erotic dancing by males cannot be comparable, for a nude woman carries off the stage a final concealment, that

chthonian darkness from which we come.

Woman's body is a secret, sacred space. It is a *temenos* or ritual precinct, a Greek word I adopt for the discussion of art. In the marked-off space of woman's body, nature operates at its darkest and most mechanical. Every woman is a priestess guarding the temenos of daemonic mysteries. Virginity is categorically different for the sexes. A boy becoming a man quests for experience. The penis is like eye or hand, an extension of self reaching outward. But a girl is a sealed vessel that must be broken into by force. The female body is the prototype of all sacred spaces from cave shrine to temple and church. The womb is the veiled Holy of Holies, a great problem, as we shall see, for sexual polemicists like William Blake who seek to abolish guilt and covertness in sex. The taboo on woman's body is the taboo that always hovers over the place of magic. Woman is literally the occult, which means "the hidden." These uncanny meanings cannot be changed, only suppressed, until they break into cultural consciousness again. Political equality will succeed only in political terms. It is helpless against the archetypal. Kill the imagination, lobotomize the brain, castrate and operate: then the sexes will be the same. Until then, we must live and dream in the daemonic turbulence of nature.

Everything sacred and inviolable provokes profanation and violation. Every crime that *can* be committed *will* be. Rape is a mode of natural aggression that can be controlled only by the social contract. Modern feminism's most naive formulation is its assertion that rape is a crime of violence but not of sex, that it is merely power masquerading as sex. But sex *is* power, and all power is inherently aggressive. Rape is male power fighting female power. It is no more to be excused than is murder or any other assault on another's civil rights. Society is woman's protection against rape, not, as some feminists absurdly maintain, the cause of rape. Rape is the sexual expression of the will-to-power, which nature plants in all of us and which civilization rose to contain. Therefore the rapist is a man with too little socialization rather than too much. Worldwide evidence is overwhelming that whenever social controls are weakened, as in war or mob rule, even civilized men behave in uncivilized ways,

---

5 "On the Genesis of the Castration Complex in Women," *International Journal of Psychoanalysis* 5 (1924):53.

among which is the barbarity of rape.

The latent metaphors of the body guarantee the survival of rape, which is a development in degree of intensity alone of the basic movements of sex. A girl's loss of virginity is always in some sense a violation of sanctity, an invasion of her integrity and identity. Defloration is destruction. But nature creates by violence and destruction. The commonest violence in the world is childbirth, with its appalling pain and gore. Nature gives males infusions of hormones for dominance in order to hurl them against the paralyzing mystery of woman, from whom they would otherwise shrink. Her power as mistress of birth is already too extreme. Lust and aggression are fused in male hormones. Anyone who doubts this has probably never spent much time around horses. Stallions are so dangerous they must be caged in barred stalls; once gelded, they are docile enough to serve as children's mounts. The hormonal disparity in humans is not so gross, but it is grosser than Rousseauists like to think. The more testosterone, the more elevated the libido. The more dominant the male, the more frequent his contributions to the genetic pool. Even on the microscopic level, male fertility is a function not only of number of sperm but of their motility, that is, their restless movement, which increases the chance of conception. Sperm are miniature assault troops, and the ovum is a solitary citadel that must be breached. Weak or passive sperm just sit there like dead ducks. Nature rewards energy and aggression.

Profanation and violation are part of the perversity of sex, which never will conform to liberal theories of benevolence. Every model of morally or politically correct sexual behavior *will be subverted,* by nature's daemonic law. Every hour of every day, some horror is being committed somewhere. Feminism, arguing from the milder woman's view, completely misses the blood-lust in rape, the joy of violation and destruction. An aesthetics and erotics of profanation – evil for the sake of evil, the sharpening of the senses by cruelty and torture – have been documented in Sade, Baudelaire, and Huysmans. Women may be less prone to such fantasies because they physically lack the equipment for sexual violence. They do not know the temptation of forcibly invading the sanctuary of another body.

Our knowledge of these fantasies is expanded by pornography, which is why pornography should be tolerated, though its public display may reasonably be restricted. The imagination cannot and must not be policed. Pornography shows us nature's daemonic heart, those eternal forces at work beneath and beyond social convention. Pornography cannot be separated from art; the two interpenetrate each other, far more than humanistic criticism has admitted. Geoffrey Hartman rightly says, "Great art is always flanked by its dark sisters, blasphemy and pornography."[6] *Hamlet* itself, the cardinal western work, is full of lewdness. Criminals through history, from Nero and Caligula to Gilles de Rais and the Nazi commandants, have never needed pornography to stimulate their exquisite, gruesome inventiveness. The diabolic human mind is quite enough.

Happy are those periods when marriage and religion are strong. System and order shelter us against sex and nature. Unfortunately, we live in a time when the chaos of sex has broken into the open. G. Wilson Knight remarks, "Christianity came originally as a tearing down of taboos in the name of a sacred humanity; but the Church it gave rise to has never yet succeeded in Christianizing the pagan evil magic of sex."[7] Historiography's most glaring error has been its assertion that Judeo-Christianity defeated paganism. Paganism has survived in the thousand forms of sex, art, and now the modern media. Christianity has made adjustment after adjustment, ingeniously absorbing its opposition (as during the Italian Renaissance) and diluting its dogma to change with changing times. But a critical point has been reached. With the rebirth of the gods in the massive idolatries of popular culture, with the eruption of sex and violence into every corner of the ubiquitous mass media, Judeo-Christianity is facing its most serious challenge since Europe's confrontation with Islam in the Middle Ages. The latent paganism of western culture has burst forth again in all its daemonic vitality.

---

6   *Beyond Formalism: Literary Essays 1958-1970* (New Haven, 1970), 23.
7   *Atlantic Crossing* (London, 1936), 111.

Paganism never was the unbridled sexual licentiousness portrayed by missionaries of the young, embattled Christianity. Singling out as typical of paganism the orgies of bored late Roman aristocrats would be as unfair as singling out as typical of Christianity the sins of renegade priests or the Vatican revels of Pope Alexander VI. True orgy was a ceremony of the chthonian mother-cults in which there were both sex and bloodshed. Paganism recognized, honored, and feared nature's daemonism, and it limited sexual expression by ritual formulae. Christianity was a development of Dionysian mystery religion which paradoxically tried to suppress nature in favor of a transcendental other world. The sole contact with nature that Christianity permitted its followers was sex sanctified by marriage. Chthonian nature, embodied in great goddess figures, was Christianity's most formidable opponent. Christianity works best when revered institutions like monasticism or universal marriage channel sexual energy in positive directions. Western civilization has profited enormously from the sublimation Christianity forced on sex. Christianity works least when sex is constantly stimulated from other directions, as it is now. No transcendental religion can compete with the spectacular pagan nearness and concreteness of the carnal-red media. Our eyes and ears are drowned in a sensual torrent.

The pagan ritual identity of sex and violence is mass media's chief check to the complacent Rousseauism of modern humanists. The commercial media, responding directly to popular patronage, sidestep the liberal censors who have enjoyed such long control over book culture. In film, popular music, and commercials, we contemplate all the daemonic myths and sexual stereotypes of paganism that reform movements from Christianity to feminism have never been able to eradicate. The sexes are eternally at war. There is an element of attack, of search-and-destroy in male sex, in which there will always be a potential for rape. There is an element of entrapment in female sex, a subliminal manipulation leading to physical and emotional infantilization of the male. Freud notes, apropos of his theory of the primal scene, that a child overhearing his parents having sex thinks male is wounding female and that the woman's cries of pleasure are cries of pain. Most men merely grunt, at best. But woman's strange sexual cries come

directly from the chthonian. She is a Maenad about to rend her victim. Sex is an uncanny moment of ritual and incantation, in which we hear woman's barbaric ululation of triumph of the will. One domination dissolves into another. The dominated becomes the dominator.

Every menstruating or childbearing woman is a pagan and primitive cast back to those distant ocean shores from which we have never fully evolved. On the streets of every city, prostitutes, the world's oldest profession, stand as a rebuke to sexual morality. They are the daemonic face of nature, initiates of pagan mysteries. Prostitution is not just a service industry, mopping up the overflow of male demand, which always exceeds female supply. Prostitution testifies to the amoral power struggle of sex, which religion has never been able to stop. Prostitutes, pornographers, and their patrons are marauders in the forest of archaic night.

That nature acts upon the sexes differently is proved by the test case of modern male and female homosexuality, illustrating how the sexes function separately outside social convention. The result, according to statistics of sexual frequency: male satyriasis and female nesting. The male homosexual has sex more often than his heterosexual counterpart; the female homosexual less often than hers, a radical polarization of the sexes along a single continuum of shared sexual nonconformity. Male aggression and lust are the energizing factors in culture. They are men's tools of survival in the pagan vastness of female nature.

The old "double standard" gave men a sexual liberty denied to women. Marxist feminists reduce the historical cult of woman's virginity to her property value, her worth on the male marriage market. I would argue instead that there was and is a biologic basis to the double standard. The first medical reports on the disease killing male homosexuals indicated men most at risk were those with a thousand partners over their lifetime. Incredulity. Who could such people be? Why, it turned out, everyone knew. Serious, kind, literate men, not bums or thugs. What an abyss divides the sexes! Let us abandon the pretense of sexual sameness and admit the terrible duality of gender.

Male sex is quest romance, exploration and speculation. Promiscuity in men may cheapen love but sharpen thought. Promiscuity in women is illness, a leakage of identity. The promiscuous woman is self-contaminated and incapable of clear ideas. She has ruptured the ritual integrity of her body. It is in nature's best interests to goad dominant males into indiscriminate spreading of their seed. But nature also profits from female purity. Even in the liberated or lesbian woman there is some biologic restraint whispering: keep the birth canal clean. In judiciously withholding herself, woman protects an invisible fetus. Perhaps this is the reason for the archetypal horror (rather than socialized fear) that many otherwise bold women have of spiders and other rapidly crawling insects. Women hold themselves in reserve because the female body is a reservoir, a virgin patch of still, pooled water where the fetus comes to term. Male chase and female flight are not just a social game. The double standard may be one of nature's organic laws.

The quest romance of male sex is a war between identity and annihilation. An erection is a hope for objectivity, for power to act as a free agent. But at the climax of his success, woman is pulling the male back to her bosom, drinking and quelling his energy. Freud says, "Man fears that his strength will be taken from him by woman, dreads becoming infected with her femininity and then proving himself a weakling."[8] Masculinity must fight off effeminacy day by day. Woman and nature stand ever ready to reduce the male to boy and infant.

The operations of sex are convulsive, from intercourse through menstruation and childbirth: tension and distention, spasm, contraction, expulsion, relief. The body is wrenched in serpentine swelling and sloughing. Sex is not the pleasure principle but the Dionysian bondage of pleasure-pain. So much is a matter of overcoming resistance, in the body or the beloved, that rape will always be a present danger. Male sex is repetition-compulsion: whatever a man writes in the commentary of his phallic projections must be rewritten again and again. Sexual man is the magician sawing the lady in half, yet the serpent head and tail always live and rejoin. Projection is a male curse: forever to need something or someone to make oneself complete. This is one of the sources of art and the secret of its historical domination by males. The artist is the closest man has come to imitating woman's superb self-containment. But the artist needs his art, his pro-

jection. The blocked artist, like Leonardo, suffers tortures of the damned. The most famous painting in the world, the *Mona Lisa,* records woman's self-satisfied apartness, her ambiguous mocking smile at the vanity and despair of her many sons.

Everything great in western culture has come from the quarrel with nature. The west and not the east has seen the frightful brutality of natural process, the insult to mind in the heavy blind rolling and milling of matter. In loss of self we would find not love or God but primeval squalor. This revelation has historically fallen upon the western male, who is pulled by tidal rhythms back to the oceanic mother. It is to his resentment of this daemonic undertow that we owe the grand constructions of our culture. Apollonianism, cold and absolute, is the west's sublime refusal. The Apollonian is a male line drawn against the dehumanizing magnitude of female nature.

Everything is melting in nature. We think we see objects, but our eyes are slow and partial. Nature is blooming and withering in long puffy respirations, rising and falling in oceanic wave-motion. A mind that opened itself fully to nature without sentimental preconception would be glutted by nature's coarse materialism, its relentless superfluity. An apple tree laden with fruit: how peaceful, how picturesque. But remove the rosy filter of humanism from our gaze and look again. See nature spurning and frothing, its mad spermatic bubbles endlessly spilling out and smashing in that inhuman round of waste, rot, and carnage. From the jammed glassy cells of sea roe to the feathery spores poured into the air from bursting green pods, nature is a festering hornet's nest of aggression and overkill. This is the chthonian black magic with which we are infected as sexual beings; this is the daemonic identity that Christianity so inadequately defines as original sin and thinks it can cleanse us of. Procreative woman is the most troublesome obstacle to Christianity's claim to catholicity, testified by its wishful doctrines of Immaculate Conception and Virgin Birth. The procreativeness of chthonian nature is an obstacle to all of western metaphysics and to each man in his quest for identity against his mother. Nature is the seething excess of being.

The most effective weapon against the flux of

---

8   *Sexuality and the Psychology of Love,* ed. Philip Rieff (New York, 1963), 76.

nature is art. Religion, ritual, and art began as one, and a religious or metaphysical element is still present in all art. Art, no matter how minimalist, is never simply design. It is always a ritualistic reordering of reality. The enterprise of art, in a stable collective era or an unsettled individualistic one, is inspired by anxiety. Every subject localized and honored by art is endangered by its opposite. Art is a *shutting in* in order to *shut out*. Art is a ritualistic binding of the perpetual motion machine that is nature. The first artist was a tribal priest casting a spell, fixing nature's daemonic energy in a moment of perceptual stillness. Fixation is at the heart of art, fixation as stasis and fixation as obsession. The modern artist who merely draws a line across a page is still trying to tame some uncontrollable aspect of reality. Art is spellbinding. Art fixes the audience in its seat, stops the feet before a painting, fixes a book in the hand. Contemplation is a magic act.

Art is order. But order is not necessarily just, kind, or beautiful. Order may be arbitrary, harsh, and cruel. Art has nothing to do with morality. Moral themes may be present, but they are incidental, simply grounding an art work in a particular time and place. Before the Enlightenment, religious art was hieratic and ceremonial. After the Enlightenment, art had to create its own world, in which a new ritual of artistic formalism replaced religious universals. Eighteenth-century Augustan literature demonstrates it is the order in morality rather than the morality in order that attracts the artist. Only utopian liberals could be surprised that the Nazis were art connoisseurs. Particularly in modern times, when high art has been shoved to the periphery of culture, is it evident that art is aggressive and compulsive. The artist makes art not to save humankind but to save himself. Every benevolent remark by an artist is a fog to cover his tracks, the bloody trail of his assault against reality and others.

Art is a temenos, a sacred place. It is ritually clean, a swept floor, the threshing floor that was the first site of theater. Whatever enters this space is transformed. From the bison of cave painting to Hollywood movie stars, represented beings enter a cultic other life from which they may never emerge.

They are spellbound. Art is sacrificial, turning its inherent aggression against both artist and representation. Nietzsche says, "Almost everything we call 'higher culture' is based on the spiritualization of *cruelty*."[9] Literature's endless murders and disasters are there for contemplative pleasure, not moral lesson. Their status as fiction, removed into a sacred precinct, intensifies our pleasure by guaranteeing that contemplation cannot turn into action. No lunge by a compassionate spectator can avert the cool inevitability of that hieratic ceremony, ritually replayed through time. The blood that is shed will always be shed. Ritual in church or theater is amoral fixation, dispelling anxiety by formalizing and freezing emotion. The ritual of art is the cruel law of pain made pleasure.

Art makes *things*. There are, I said, no objects in nature, only the gruelling erosion of natural force, flecking, dilapidating, grinding down, reducing all matter to fluid, the thick primal soup from which new forms bob, gasping for life. Dionysus was identified with liquids – blood, sap, milk, wine. The Dionysian is nature's chthonian fluidity. Apollo, on the other hand, gives form and shape, marking off one being from another. All artifacts are Apollonian. Melting and union are Dionysian; separation and individuation, Apollonian. Every boy who leaves his mother to become a man is turning the Apollonian against the Dionysian. Every artist who is compelled toward art, who needs to make words or pictures as others need to breathe, is using the Apollonian to defeat chthonian nature. In sex, men must mediate between Apollo and Dionysus. Sexually, woman can remain oblique, opaque, taking pleasure without tumult or conflict. Woman is a temenos of her own dark mysteries. Genitally, man has a little thing that he must keep dipping in Dionysian dissolution – a risky business! Thing-making, thing-preserving is central to male experience. Man is a fetishist. Without his fetish, woman will just gobble him up again.

Hence the male domination of art and science. Man's focus, directedness, concentration, and projection, which I identified with urination and ejaculation, are his tools of sexual survival, but they have never given him a final victory. The anxiety in sexual experience remains as strong as ever.

9   *Beyond Good and Evil*, trans. Walter Kaufmann (New York, 1966), 158.

This man attempts to correct by the cult of female beauty. He is erotically fixated on woman's "shapeliness," those spongy maternal fat deposits of breast, hip, and buttock which are ironically the wateriest and least stable parts of her anatomy. Woman's billowy body reflects the surging sea of chthonian nature. By focusing on the shapely, by making woman a sex-object, man has struggled to fix and stabilize nature's dreadful flux. Objectification is conceptualization, the highest human faculty. Turning people into sex objects is one of the specialties of our species. It will never disappear, since it is intertwined with the art impulse and may be identical to it. A sex-object is ritual form imposed on nature. It is a totem of our perverse imagination.

Apollonian thing-making is the main line of western civilization, extending from ancient Egypt to the present. Every attempt to repress this aspect of our culture has ultimately been defeated. First Judaism, then Christianity turned against pagan idol-making. But Christianity with wider impact than Judaism, became the most art-laden, art-dominated religion in the world. Imagination always remedies the defects of religion. The hardest object of Apollonian thing-making is western personality, the glamourous, striving, separatist ego that entered literature in the *Iliad* but, I will show, first appeared in art in Old Kingdom Egypt.

....

The Apollonian *things* of western sex and art reach their economic glorification in capitalism. In the past fifteen years, Marxist approaches to literature have enjoyed increasing vogue. To be conscious of the social context of art seems automatically to entail a leftist orientation. But a theory is possible that is both avant-garde *and* capitalist. Marxism was one of Rousseau's nineteenth-century progeny, energized by faith in the perfectibility of man. Its belief that economic forces are the primary dynamic in history is Romantic naturism in disguise. That is, it sketches a surging wave-motion in the material context of human life but tries to deny the perverse daemonism of that context. Marxism is the bleakest of anxiety-formations against the power of chthonian mothers. Its influence on modern historiography has been excessive. The "great man" theory of history was not as simplistic as claimed;

we have barely recovered from a world war in which this theory was proved evilly true. One man *can* change the course of history, for good or ill. Marxism is a flight from the magic of person and the mystique of hierarchy. It distorts the character of western culture, which is based on charismatic power of person. Marxism can work only in preindustrial societies of homogeneous populations. Raise the standard of living, and the rainbow riot of individualism will break out. Personality and art, which Marxism fears and censors, rebound from every effort to repress them.

Capitalism, gaudy and greedy, has been inherent in western aesthetics from ancient Egypt on. It is the mysticism and glamour of *things,* which take on a personality of their own. As an economic system, it is in the Darwinian line of Sade, not Rousseau. The capitalist survival of the fittest is already present in the *Iliad.* Western sexual personae clash by day and by night. Homer's gleaming bronze-clad warriors are the Apollonian soup cans that crowd the sunny temples of our supermarkets and compete for our attention on television. The west objectifies persons and personalizes objects. The teeming multiplicity of capitalist products is an Apollonian correction of nature. Brand names are territorial cells of western identity. Our shiny chrome automobiles, like our armies of grocery boxes and cans, are extrapolations of hard, impermeable western personality.

Capitalist products are another version of the art works flooding western culture. The portable framed painting appeared at the birth of modern commerce in the early Renaissance. Capitalism and art have challenged and nourished each other ever since. Capitalist and artist are parallel types: the artist is just as amoral and acquisitive as the capitalist, and just as hostile to competitors. That in the age of the merchant-prince art works are hawked and sold like hot dogs supports my argument but is not central to it. Western culture is animated by a visionary materialism. Apollonian formalism has stolen from nature to make a romance of *things,* hard, shiny, crass, and willful.

The capitalist distribution network, a complex chain of factory, transport, warehouse, and retail outlet, is one of the greatest male accomplishments in the history of culture. It is a lightning-quick Apollonian circuit of male bonding. One of feminism's irritating reflexes is its fashionable disdain for "patriarchal society," to which nothing good is ever attributed. But it is patriarchal society that has freed me as a woman. It is capitalism that has given me the leisure to sit at this desk writing this book. Let us stop being small-minded about men and freely acknowledge what treasures their obsessiveness has poured into culture.

We could make an epic catalog of male achievements, from paved roads, indoor plumbing, and washing machines to eyeglasses, antibiotics, and disposable diapers. We enjoy fresh, safe milk and meat, and vegetables and tropical fruits heaped in snowbound cities. When I cross the George Washington Bridge or any of America's great bridges, I think: *men* have done this. Construction is a sublime male poetry. When I see a giant crane passing on a flatbed truck, I pause in awe and reverence, as one would for a church procession. What power of conception, what grandiosity: these cranes tie us to ancient Egypt, where monumental architecture was first imagined and achieved. If civilization had been left in female hands, we would still be living in grass huts. A contemporary woman clapping on a hard hat merely enters a conceptual system invented by men. Capitalism is an art form, an Apollonian fabrication to rival nature. It is hypocritical for feminists and intellectuals to enjoy the pleasures and conveniences of capitalism while sneering at it. Even Thoreau's Walden was just a two-year experiment. Everyone born into capitalism has incurred a debt to it. Give Caesar his due.

The pagan dialectic of Apollonian and Dionysian was sweepingly comprehensive and accurate about mind and nature. Christian love is so lacking its emotional polarity that the Devil had to be invented to focus natural human hatred and hostility. Rousseauism's Christianized psychology has led to the tendency of liberals toward glumness or depression in the face of the political tensions, wars, and atrocities that daily contradict their assumptions. Perhaps the more we are sensitized by reading and education, the more we must repress the facts of chthonian nature. But the insupportable feminist dichotomy between sex and power must go. Just as the hatreds of divorce court expose the dark face beneath the mask of love, so is the truth about nature revealed during crisis. Victims of tornado and hurricane instinctively speak of "the fury of Mother Nature" – how often we hear that phrase as the television camera follows dazed survivors picking through the wreckage of homes and towns. In the unconscious, everyone knows that Jehovah has never gained control of the savage elements. Nature is Pandemonium, an All Devils' Day.

There are no accidents, only nature throwing her weight around. Even the bomb merely releases energy that nature has put there. Nuclear war would be just a spark in the grandeur of space. Nor can radiation "alter" nature: she will absorb it all. After the bomb, nature will pick up the cards we have spilled, shuffle them, and begin her game again. Nature is forever playing solitaire with herself.

Western love has been ambivalent from the start. As early as Sappho (600 B.C.) or even earlier in the epic legend of Helen of Troy, art records the push and pull of attraction and hostility in that perverse fascination we call love. There is a magnetics of eroticism in the west, due to the hardness of western personality: eroticism is an electric forcefield between masks. The modern pursuit of self-realization has not led to sexual happiness, because assertions of selfhood merely release the amoral chaos of libido. Freedom is the most overrated modern idea, originating in the Romantic rebellion against bourgeois society. But only *in* society can one *be* an individual. Nature is waiting at society's gates to dissolve us in her chthonian bosom. Out with stereotypes, feminism proclaims. But stereotypes are the west's stunning sexual personae, the vehicles of art's assault against nature. The moment there is imagination, there is myth. We may have to accept an ethical cleavage between imagination and reality, tolerating horrors, rapes, and mutilations in art that we would not tolerate in society. For art is our message from the beyond, telling us what nature is up to. Not sex but cruelty is the great neglected or suppressed item on the modern humanistic agenda. We must honor the chthonian but not necessarily yield to it. In *The Rape of the Lock,* Pope counsels good humor as the only solution to sex war. So with our enslavement by chthonian nature. We must accept our pain, change what we can, and laugh at the rest. But let us see art for what it is and nature for what it is. From remotest antiquity, western art has been a parade of sexual personae, emanations of absolutist western mind. Western art is a cinema of sex and dreaming. Art is form struggling to wake from the nightmare of nature.

....

Return of the Great Mother: Rousseau vs. Sade

Romanticism is the forge of modern gender. Two Renaissance principles reemerge: flamboyant androgynous sex roles and the idea of divinely inspired artistic genius. The Renaissance, we saw, revived the Apollonian element in Greco-Roman paganism. In Renaissance art, even Dionysian beings, like Shakespeare's Cleopatra, are subordinated to social and moral order. Romanticism swings toward Apollo's rival, Dionysus, who appears in a great wave of the chthonian. The Enlightenment, developing Renaissance innovations in science and technology, was ruled by the Apollonian mind. Not since Greek high classicism had clarity and logic been so promoted as intellectual and moral values, determining the mathematical form of poetry, art, architecture, and music. "ORDER is Heav'n's first law," says Pope, from the cold beauty of Descartes and Newton's mechanical universe (*Essay on Man*, IV.49). The Enlightenment, as Peter Gay asserts, used pagan scientism to free European culture from Judeo-Christian theology.[10] Reason, not faith created the modern world. But overstress of any faculty causes a rebound to the other extreme. The Apollonian Enlightenment produced the counterreaction of irrationalism and daemonism which is Romanticism.

Romanticism makes a regression to the primeval, the archaic nightworld defeated and repressed by Aeschylus' *Oresteia*. It brings a return of the Great Mother, the dark nature-goddess whom St. Augustine condemns as the most formidable enemy of Christianity. Turning from society toward nature, Rousseau creates the Romantic world-view. Though he allows authority to the state for public good, his most enduring bequest is the flamingly antiestablishment stance of radicals from Blake and Marx to the Rolling Stones. Rousseau makes freedom a western watchword. Like the Renaissance, the Enlightenment glamourized hierarchy, the great chain of being swept away by

Romanticism. For Rousseau, the Swiss Protestant reformer, no hierarchy comes from nature. Politics can be reshaped by human will, for human benefit. Romanticism regards hierarchy as a repressive social fiction. But man is biologically a hierarchical animal. When one hierarchy is removed, another automatically springs up to take its place. The great irony of Romanticism is that a movement predicated on freedom will compulsively reenslave itself to imaginative orders even more fixed.

Nature, hailed by Rousseau and Wordsworth as a benevolent mother, is a dangerous guest. The ancient cult-followers of Dionysus knew that subordination to nature is a crucifixion and dismemberment. Human identity is obliterated in the Dionysian conversion of matter to energy, a theme of Euripides' *Bacchae*. Romanticism, like the Rousseauist Swinging Sixties, misunderstands the Dionysian as the pleasure principle, when it is in fact the gross continuum of pleasure-pain. Worshipping nature and seeking political and sexual freedom, Romanticism ends in imaginative entrammelment of every kind. Perfect freedom is intolerable and therefore impossible.

Romanticism's overexpanded superself immediately subjects itself to artificial restraints as a chastening *ascesis,* a discipline and punishment. First of all, Romantic poetry invents an archaic ritual form, implicitly pagan. Second, it steeps itself in sadomasochistic eroticism, never fully acknowledged by scholars. The sadomasochism becomes blatant in Decadent Late Romanticism, which defies Rousseau and Wordsworth by rejecting chthonian nature for Apollonian aestheticism. I view nineteenth-century Decadence as a Mannerist convolution of High Romanticism and date it unusually early – 1830. The themes I find in High and Late Romanticism – cruelty, sexual ambiguity, narcissism, fascination, obsession, vampirism, seduction, violation – are all the still-uncharted psychodynamics of erotic, artistic, and theatrical cathexis. I define American Romanticism as Decadent Late Romanticism, in the French manner. Decadence is a counterreaction within Romanticism, correcting its tilt toward Dionysus. This ambivalent pattern is there from the start. Rousseau is savagely answered

---

10   *The Enlightenment: An Interpretation* (New York, 1966). The first volume is called "The Rise of Modern Paganism." Gay seems to use "pagan" as a synonym for what I call Apollonian, only half of my theory of paganism.

by the decadent Marquis de Sade, who stands half in the Enlightenment, half in Romanticism. Blake, Sade's British brother, answers himself, his voices of experience devouring his voices of innocence. And Wordsworth is secretly answered and undermined by his colleague Coleridge, who through Byron and Poe turns Romanticism into Decadence in English, American, and French literature and art.

Rousseau and Wordsworth, loving female nature, open the door of a closet St. Augustine locked. Out pop vampires and spirits of the night, who still stalk our time. We remain in the Romantic cycle initiated by Rousseau: liberal idealism cancelled by violence, barbarism, disillusion, cynicism. The French Revolution, degenerating into the bloody Reign of Terror and ending in the restoration of monarchy in imperial Napoleon, was the first failed Rousseauist experiment. Rousseau believes man naturally good. Evil springs from negative environmental conditioning. Rousseau's saintly child, marred by society, is opposed by Freud's aggressive, egomaniacal infant – whom I hear and see everywhere. But Rousseauism flourishes among today's social workers and childcare experts, whose smooth, sunny voices too often exude piety and paternalism.

In *The Confessions*, modelled on Augustine's, Rousseau says a childhood incident formed his adult sexual tastes. He is eight, beaten and inadvertently aroused by a woman of thirty. Since then, his desires have been masochistic: "To fall on my knees before a masterful mistress, to obey her commands, to have to beg for her forgiveness, have been to me the most delicate of pleasures." In love, he is passive; women must make the first move.[11] Rousseau ends the sexual scheme of the great chain of being, where male was sovereign over female. In Romanticism, unlike the Renaissance, Amazons retain their power. Rousseau wants it both ways. Idolizing woman is natural and right, a cosmic law. On the other hand, male recessiveness is blamed on female coercion. Either way, sadomasochistic dominance and submission are inherent in Rousseauism from the start.

Rousseau feminizes the European male persona. The late eighteenth century, the Age of Sensibility, gives the ideal man a womanlike sensitivity. He is Castiglione's courtier without athleticism or social savvy. He looks to nature and beauty with misty emotion. Rousseau makes sensibility a prelude to Romanticism. The Petrarchan lover fancied himself deliciously powerless vis-à-vis one charismatic ice-queen. The man of feminized sensibility lacks an erotic focus. He is sufficient unto himself, savoring his own thoughts and feelings. His narcissism evolves into Romantic solipsism, doubt about the reality of things outside the self.

For Rousseau and the Romantics, the female principle is absolute. Man is a satellite in woman's sexual orbit. Rousseau calls his first patron, Madame de Warens, "Mamma," and she calls him "Little one." Stendhal's heroes will replay Rousseau's erotics of maternalism. Rousseau says of his sexual initiation by De Warens, "I felt as if I had committed incest." She later "compels" him to put on her dressing gown: he is transvestite priest to a goddess. Rousseau attends the Venetian carnival as a masked lady, then adopts Armenian robes as daily dress and busies himself making laces: "I took my cushion round with me on visits, or worked at my door, like the women."[12] Rousseau absorbs femininity from women, but they cannot reciprocate. They must remain female. He is repulsed by the flat chest of intellectual Madame d'Epinay. But the voluptuous female figure is enhanced by transvestism: Madame d'Houdetot, model for his *Nouvelle Héloise*, conquers Rousseau when she arrives on horseback in men's clothes.

Rousseau's nature-theory is grounded in sex. Worshipping nature means worshipping woman. She is a mysterious superior force. Late in life, Rousseau likes to let his boat drift in a Swiss lake (a scene paralleled in Wordsworth's *Prelude*): "Sometimes I cried out with emotion: 'O Nature! O my mother! I am here under your sole protection. Here there is no cunning and rascally man to thrust himself between Us'."[13] The son-lover of the Great Mother spurns his sibling rivals. For all his talk of tenderness and fraternity, Rousseau was notoriously quarrelsome, finding conspiracy and persecution everywhere. He constantly fought with male friends, including his benefactor, British

---

11 *Confessions*, trans. J.M. Cohen (Baltimore, 1954), 25-28.
12 Ibid., 106, 189, 229, 555.
13 Ibid., 594.

philosopher David Hume. Rousseau's flights from city to nature were pilgrimages purifying him of masculine contamination. He started a fashion. Once Rousseau lauded the Alps, Van den Berg says, people's desire to see Switzerland spread through Europe "like an epidemic": "It was then that the Alps became a tourist attraction."[14]

Through power of imaginative projection, Rousseau imprinted European culture with his peculiar constellation of sexual personae. The man who created modern autobiography made political science autobiographical. He was the first to claim what we call a sexual identity. Before the late eighteenth century, identity was determined internally by moral consciousness and externally by family and social class. Rousseau anticipates Freud in inserting sex into the childhood drama of character development. How striking a departure this was is clear when we compare Rousseau to his self-analytic French precursors. In his *Essays* (1580), Montaigne lists his sexual habits as casually as his menus or bowel movements. Sex for Montaigne is office schedule and flow chart: how often and at what times of day does he lie with his wife? The sex act is rhetorically equivalent to his taste in wines or reluctance to use silverware (an effete Italian import). Montaigne's identity is not shaped by sex. He is discursive intellect musing on social custom. Pascal's *Pensées* (1670) strip away Montaigne's cheerful intimacies. Pascal says Montaigne talks too much of himself. In the transition from Renaissance to seventeenth century, identity has become barer and more anxious. Pascal never reflects upon his sexual identity. The supreme question is the soul's relation to God, or, more fearfully, the soul's relation to a universe without God. Sex is merely part of the earthliness impeding man's spiritual struggles.

Rousseau makes sex a master principle of western character. Psychic fluidity and ambiguity, themes of Shakespeare's transvestite comedies, enter the mainstream of thought and behavior. Autobiography becomes apologia. *The Confessions* are a romance of self. Rousseau is the first to trace adult perversity to childhood trauma. The Christian quest for salvation is recast in erotic terms. Rousseau's guiding female spirits are appari-

tions, angels, and demons. He is a pagan Moses, climbing the Alps to meet his god. Adrift in the lake, he floats in the womb of liquid nature. The sexual revolution he wrought is evident in the emergence of homosexuality as a formal category. From antiquity, there were homosexual acts, honorable or dissolute depending on culture and time. Since the late nineteenth century, there is homosexuality, a condition of being entered after searching or "questioning," a Rousseauist identity crisis. Modern psychology, following Rousseau, pessimistically roots sex deeper than does Judeo-Christianity, which subordinates sex to moral will. Our sexual "freedom" is a new enslavement to ancient Necessity.

Rousseau's philosophizing of sex originates in the failure of social and moral hierarchies in the late eighteenth century. Before the Enlightenment, rigid class stratification, however stultifying, provided a sense of community. Now identity, suddenly expanding, must find other means of definition. But sex is no substitute for metaphysics. Pascal says, "The tendency should be towards the general, and the bias towards self is the beginning of all disorder, in war, politics, economics, in man's individual body."[15] Sex was central to ancient mystery religions, but they had a coherent view of omnipotent nature, both violent and benign. Rousseau, the first fabricator of sexual identity, seeks freedom by banishing social hierarchies and worshipping a uniformly benevolent nature. My theory: when political and religious authority weakens. hierarchy reasserts itself in sex, as the archaizing phenomenon of sadomasochism. Freedom makes new prisons. We cannot escape our life in these fascist bodies. Rousseau's masochistic subordination to women comes from his overidealization of nature and emotion. Making honey, he stings himself.

....

.... Sade alternately celebrates and reviles woman. He gives his intellectual female libertines another male prerogative, in defiance of reality: the passion for sexual atrocities. Anyone can see, just by reading the newspaper, that men commit sex-crimes and women do not. The feminist idea that sexual violence is caused by the social denigration of

---

14 *The Changing Nature of Man*, 233.
15 *Pensées*, trans. A.J. Krailsheimer (Baltimore, 1966), 154.

women is disproved by the many cases of homosexual torture and rape-murder of boys by the
dozen. Sex-crimes arise less from environmental
conditioning than from a failure of socialization.
Mutilating crimes by women are extremely rare.
There are the Papin sisters, whose massacre of their
employers inspired Genet's *The Maids*. After that
we are at a loss, driven as far back as ax-wielding
Lizzie Borden, who may have gotten a raw deal. As
for what Sade calls "lust-murder" or "venereal
murder" – homicide that stimulates orgasm or is a
substitute for it – I beg for female nominees. One of
history's most intriguing women Hungarian
Countess Erzsebet Bathory (1560-1614), the prototypical lesbian vampire of horror films, may have
been sexually aroused in her torture and murder of
610 maidens, but rumor reports only that she
bathed in their blood to preserve her youth. As

Freud says, "Women show little need to degrade the
sexual object."[16]

Serial or sex murder, like fetishism, is a perversion
of male intelligence. It is a criminal abstraction,
masculine in its deranged egotism and orderliness.
It is the asocial equivalent of philosophy, mathematics and music. There is no female Mozart
because there is no female Jack the Ripper. Sade
has spectacularly enlarged female character. The
barbarism of Madame de Clairwil, orgasmically
rending her victims limb from limb, is the sign of
her greater *conceptual* power. Sade's female sex-
criminals are Belles Dames Sans Merci of early
Romanticism. The Romantic femmes fatales will be
silent, nocturnal, lit by their own daemonic animal
eye. But Sade's women, inveterate talkers, retain the
clear Apollonian solar eye of western intellect....

---

16   *Sexuality*, 65.

XI

TWENTIETH-CENTURY VIEWS IN SOCIOLOGY AND ANTHROPOLOGY

Theories, like other commodities, are seen as having more importance or utility, or less, as time goes by. Often a theory, or the individual who originated it, returns to favour, or interest, after a period of eclipse. Once towering giants, whose place in the theoretical pantheon had seemed assured, fall under shadow. How much this is a matter merely of fashion or taste, or what the social economy or the cultural materiality of such things may be, would require considerable probing and argument.

Of a number of thinkers about human nature whose views once enjoyed higher stature than they currently have, the sociologist and social philosopher (and significant Hobbes scholar) Ferdinand Tönnies (1855-1936) may be more than most deserving of reconsideration. Tönnies had a single central idea, of a fundamental distinction between two kinds of societies, approximately traditionary and contractual ones. He characterizes them as ideal types, that actual human societies approximate to in varying degrees. Details will be found in the pages that follow, and need not be anticipated here. There are substantial Hegelian affinities (and some constrasts) in Tönnies' polarity. It is important to remark as well both how influential these models were in the actual development of sociological theory in the course of the earlier twentieth century (especially in the work of Weber and Durkheim), and how arresting and fertile they remain as conceptions against which to place and assess real-world social structures and the people within them. For Tönnies' notions of *Gemeinschaft* and *Gesellschaft* arguably capture individual psychic as well as social typology, and offer interesting prospects of correlation with, or housing within, historical or cultural materialist views.

Ferdinand Tönnies, *Community and Society*

(Source: Ferdinand Tönnies. *Fundamental Concepts of Sociology (Gemeinschaft und Gesellschaft)*. Trans. and Supp. Charles P. Loomis. New York: American Book Company, 1940, 3-29.)

GEMEINSCHAFT UND GESELLSCHAFT
I. KNOWLEDGE AND NONKNOWLEDGE

Sociology is the study of man, not of his bodily nor of his psychical, but of his social nature. His bodily and psychical being are considered only in so far as they condition his social nature. It is our purpose to study the sentiments and motives which draw people to each other, keep them together, and induce them to joint action. We wish especially to investigate the products of human thought which, resulting therefrom, make possible and sustain a common existence. They find their consummation in such important forms as community, state, and church, which are often felt to be realities or even supernatural beings.

"*Nosce te ipsum*" (know yourself); if you want to understand others, look into your own heart. Every one of us has manifold relationships, direct and indirect, with other people. Every one of us knows many people, but only few in proportion to their total number. Thus the question arises, how do I know other people?

We shall first study the distinction between all people and those we know, without regard to the question as to how we come to know people. This distinction will head a list of four dichotomies dealing with one's relation to one's fellow beings. This distinction is:

1. Acquaintanceship and Strangeness.

It is not necessary to do more than simply to indicate the great importance of this distinction. In a strange city one may by chance meet in a crowd of strangers an acquaintance, perhaps even a familiar acquaintance or at least an acquaintance of long standing. This is usually a pleasant experience. One is likely to strike up a conversation with him at once, something one is seldom inclined to do with a complete stranger. Often what little inclination one has to converse with strangers is impeded by a foreign language. If the individual is only a casual acquaintance, it may be the first (and possibly the last) time that one shakes hands with him. Such a casual acquaintance may be a stranger except for the fact that he is known in some special capacity such as that of being engaged in the same profession or line of work; or it may be that the two persons have met once before and exchanged a few words. A casual acquaintance of mine may be a citizen of another country and have a different mother tongue, but he is known to me and is an acquaintance even if we had and still have difficulty in understanding each other. In the German language there is a subtle distinction between an acquaintance and a person whom one only "knows." An acquaintance, my acquaintance, knows me, too; someone whom I only know does not, in all probability, know me or, at least, will not necessarily know me. An individual occupying a high position is seen and known by many whom he himself overlooks, whom he does not know and very often does not wish to know. The person whom I know may not remember me or, even if he should, may not wish to take notice of me. I may not mean anything to him, or he may not like me. In contradistinction, an acquaintance is considered by many as being among their "friends." This may often be a sign of a superficial intellectual attitude or manner of speech, although, of course, acquaintanceship implies a slight tendency toward mutual approval just as strangeness implies a tendency toward mutual negation. This is, to be sure, only a tendency, but tendencies are important.

2. Sympathy and Antipathy.

The fact that one knows a person or is acquainted with him does not necessarily imply that one likes him or is fond of him or (a rarer occurrence) loves him. There is, of course, tremendous difference between those who are congenial to us, and those whom we regard with antipathy. Sympathy and antipathy are feelings; they are often defined as instincts, that is, as something subhuman. In reality, they are frequently connected with thought and knowledge and thus with higher and nobler feelings which distinguish the human being. Indeed, they often spring from such feelings and from our thoughts and knowledge. A certain relationship of some significance exists, as has already been pointed out, between acquaintance and sympathy on the one hand and between strangeness and antipathy on the other. The more sympathy and antipathy are instinctive, the more they are related to outward appearance, especially where women are concerned. This holds true, above all, for the feelings resulting from the impression made upon them by the man. Such impression may be produced by his figure, his face and expression, his dress, his behavior, his manners, his way of speech, even the sound of his voice. Men, too, often fall in love with women at first sight. For some a beautiful figure, for others a lovely face, is the decisive factor; for some it is the expression of the eyes alone or the polished way of speaking, for still others the elegant dress or the smart hat. Immediate and instinctive sympathy or antipathy may, however, be counteracted in actual experience, by a more intimate knowledge of the hitherto strange person. One finds, for instance, that someone who gave one an unfavorable impression at first turns out to be quite a nice person, perhaps interesting or positively charming. It even happens that women and girls may develop a passionate affection for a man who, in the beginning, was as repulsive to them as was Richard the Third to the widowed queen. It is another question whether a steadfast faithful love can spring from such a root. In many cases experience may prove the first impression to have been correct; but the reverse is also well-known and practically a daily occurrence. An excellent impression may so bias one in favor of an individual that after more intimate acquaintance one may reproach oneself for having been taken in by a brilliant outward appearance.

But our souls, our feelings, are indifferent to the great mass of people, not only to those who are unknown to us, the strangers, but also even to those whom we know reasonably well. This indifference is, however, not immovably fixed; there may easily develop a tendency fluctuating between antipathy and sympathy. Sympathies and antipathies can be of many different degrees, especially if we take into consideration the above-mentioned intelligent sympathy and antipathy which are rooted in our thinking consciousness. We shall usually have a certain degree of sympathy, even though this may be small, for those who side with us, whether we have known them before or came to know them only as fellow fighters, comrades, countrymen, or even home folks, or as colleagues, or as persons of the same faith, same political party, same profession. Sympathy may also be engendered by the fact that individuals belong to the same estate, as in the case of the nobility, or the same class, as in the case of the proletariat or the properted class. In the same way there exists, on the other hand, some antipathy toward all those who are in the opposite camp. Such antipathy often increases to the point of hatred, especially if a real conflict exists between the opposing sides. In other instances such antipathy manifests itself only in, and is reduced to, greater indifference, so that it can easily, as a result of close acquaintance or other motives, be transformed into real sympathy. However, the same or similar interests are sufficient to arouse sympathy to the extent that such similarities are in the consciousness of those involved, and by the same token contrary interests will evoke antipathy. For example, at times the masses have and are conscious of common interests as consumers. At such times they will feel a slight sympathy for one another. Their interests are opposed to those of producers and merchants, toward whom their antipathy is directed, and such antipathy is stronger than their mutual sympathy

3. Confidence and Mistrust.

The third difference to which I wish to draw attention is that of confidence or mistrust toward other people. An individual whom we know will inspire in us a certain confidence, however slight; a stranger, on the other hand, is likely to create in us a certain feeling, often quite strong, of mistrust. Furthermore, sympathy may easily and rather quickly lead to a feeling of confidence which is often just as quickly regretted, whereas antipathy

may arouse, strengthen, and further a mistrust which sometimes proves to be unwarranted. But here again, how many gradations exist! Only in a chosen few do we have such great and abiding confidence that we rely on their absolute sincerity, affection, and faithfulness towards ourselves and our nearest, and feel we can build upon their devotion. As is well known, these chosen few are not always our "equals." When not, they have no claim to that sympathy which is characteristic of those of the same class, the same estate. The faithful servant, the faithful maid, are not only figures of sagas and fiction, although they are more frequent under simpler and more rural than under modern conditions. Confidence betrayed – this is indeed a terrible, embittering experience which often leads to despair. But even mistrust can change into confidence, just as abused confidence, apart from arousing indignation, anger, and embitterment, will immediately turn into mistrust directed toward those formerly honored with confidence. Not only one's own but also other people's experience may lead one either to confidence in or mistrust of a person, thus investing him with either a reliable or a dubious reputation.

On the other hand, confidence has become highly impersonalized through modern trade. Personality has come to be of little or no importance. Only the "wealth" of a person counts, for it is assumed, and usually on valid grounds, that self-interest will induce even the personally less reliable businessman to pay his debts as long as he is able to do so. Personal reliability fades as it is transformed into reliability as debtor. As a rule, it is the business or manufacturing firm (irrespective of the moral qualities of its owner or manager), which has financial credit and is sound, or at least is supposed to be sound. In fact, as a result of this kind of confidence in the financial standing of the firm, the moral quality of its head may still be considered intact even though there may exist good reasons for a contrary judgment. Thus, confidence in the financial credit of the person or firm, like confidence in personal qualities, is often betrayed.

Moreover, without being conscious of it, we often trust many people on the strength of very slight knowledge concerning the persons involved. Sometimes we do not even know them or anything about them except that they are at their posts. This, too, is impersonalized confidence. Personal confidence is essentially conditioned by the personalities of those who confide; that is, by their intelligence, their knowledge of human nature, and their experience, on which the latter is based. Thus in the case of personal confidence, simple-minded and inexperienced people are in general inclined to be trustful, whereas the intelligent and experienced persons are inclined to doubt. However, this difference all but disappears where rationalized confidence is concerned. We do not know the engineer who runs our train or the captain and the pilots who direct the course of our ship; in many cases we do not know the doctor whom we ask for advice, to whom we even entrust body and life for a surgical operation. Very often we do not know the lawyer whom we request to take our case, still less do we know the judge who will decide the case for or against us, and who, we hope and expect, will restore our rights and our honor and do justice to our claims. In all these cases we rely (a) on skill (or knowledge), or (b) on volition. As far as that skill (or knowledge) is concerned, we are justified in trusting an individual because (1) skill (or knowledge) is bound up with his profession. How could he dare call himself a doctor, a lawyer, or a judge, if he were not such? The shoemaker, the locksmith, and the tailor also know their trades, their arts. The greater the importance of a matter, the more we rely on (2) examinations, (3) experience, (4) reputation, and (5) the personal advice or recommendation which opened the door for a man or woman to this activity or this office. In many cases, however, as, for instance, in that of the engineer or pilot, only the qualifications (2) and (3) are required.

As far as volition is concerned, we put our trust in (a) certain normal moral qualities and the assumption that the individual in whose care we entrust ourselves could not possibly follow this profession if he did not possess at least a modicum of such qualities. Closely connected therewith is (b) his own self-interest, either material or nonmaterial, both of which usually merge into each other.

But it can easily be seen that something else besides these reasons underlies our peace of mind, our feeling of security. Our confidence in that which is regular and safe, although we are rarely aware of it, rests upon the three great systems of social will which I define as order, law, and morality. The two functions last mentioned, the legal and the moral orders or systems, are the fully developed types of the first one.

4. Interdependence.

And now I come to the fourth difference, which is closely related to and partly contained in the first three. This is the difference between my condition in case I am "bound" in some way to other people and my condition in case I am completely independent and free from them. The condition of being bound to others is the exact opposite of freedom, the former implying a moral obligation, a moral imperative, or a prohibition. There exist a great variety of such "ties," which involve an individual through different types of relationships. These ties may also be called types of social entities *(soziale Wesenheiten)* or forms which link him to his fellow beings. He is bound in these social entities if he is conscious of being linked to them. His consciousness of the tie is either predominantly emotional or predominantly intellectual. From this consciousness there results a feeling or a realization of moral obligation, moral imperative, or prohibition, and a righteous aversion to the consequences of incorrect, illegal, and unlawful, as well as of immoral and indecent conduct and action.

To talk of such relationships as "bonds" implies, of course, a figurative use of the term, just as no social ties or associations are to be interpreted in terms of the literal meaning of the words. That a human being is tied to another human being can indicate a state of complete dependence. This, however, is a figurative expression indicating that one of the two beings involved does not or cannot have a will of his own, but depends for whatever he may desire on the volition of the other one. Thus the dependence of the infant, and, in a diminishing degree, of the small child, on his mother or any other person who takes care of him, is an obvious fact. Of similar character are those types of dependence in which the well-being of a person is determined less by his own will than by the will of others. Such dependence is most typically exemplified by servitude, slavery, and the like. It finds its most visible and thus most forceful expression in such physical constraint as was used with slaves and is still practiced in transporting hardened criminals. Referring to an inability to act on one's own will which may result from a completely weak will, we also speak of hypnotized persons, sexual slavery, and the like.

5. Social Relationship or Bond; Connection.

Social relationship or bond implies interdependence, and it means that the will of the one person influences that of the other, either furthering or impeding, or both. If the volition of the one meets and combines with the volition of the other, there results a common volition which may be interpreted as unified because it is mutual. This common volition postulates or requires, and thus controls, the volition of A in accordance with the volition of B as well as the volition of B in accordance with the volition of A. This is the simplest case of the social will of two individuals, whom I prefer to call persons when referring to volition and action of each toward the other. In the same way as a person can be linked with another person, he can be united with many persons, and these again can be connected with one another; thus the will of each single person who belongs to a group is part of and at the same time conditioned by the group's collective will, which is to say he is dependent on it. Such collective will can take various forms, determined by the number of persons involved, its own character, and the mode of its existence, that is, the way in which it is expressed. Also, the individuals become conscious of it in many different ways. The collective will can remain the same for an indefinite period, but it can also from time to time undergo change by renewed acts. It can affect the persons involved either directly or indirectly in that a more comprehensive collective will may influence a smaller group and this, in turn, exert its influence upon the smallest unit. Every collective will can represent itself in a single natural person or in a number of those whose common will is conceived as the representative of a higher collective will.

Every collective will can be given a special name, but it can also bear the name of a thinking agent which designates the united multitude. What this name stands for is then conceived and thought of by the persons of this group as a person like themselves. That is to say, a collective person is one on whom either other collective persons or, in the simplest case, natural persons ultimately depend. They all know of their dependence on one another and thereby on the collective will which, in the simplest case, represents their own interrelationship or unity, and it is through this very knowledge that they are connected with one another. All following discussions in which such names are used must be interpreted in this sense. These names are taken from everyday language, where they were given a fixed meaning long ago, although very often without the proper insight into their real character. No clear and conscious distinction was made between a meaning that points only to the external form or significance as a group, a crowd, a band, and so on, and a meaning which is given to them by a scientific system of concepts, in which they are to be conceived as personalities and agents of a collective or social will; in other words, as social entities or phenomena.

That all these social entities have both similarities and differences in meaning and form can easily be deduced. Similarity exists in so far as they contain a social will which determines the co-operating individual wills by giving them rights as well as imposing duties on them and by defining the right of one person as the duty of another and vice versa. The difference among them lies in the fact that each finds its most perfect form as an imaginary (artificial) social person. Such a collective person consists of single persons, first individuals or, possibly, other subordinated collective persons. Even in the simplest possible case for every person concerned there is imposed a moral imperative by the collective (joint) will as well as by his own will.

2. BARTER AND EXCHANGE AS SIMPLEST TYPE OF SOCIAL RELATION OR BOND

We shall most easily understand the diverse *modus operandi* of social relationships or bonds if we relate all the varieties to the simplest type, which is also the most rational one. Here we are thinking of the case of simple barter or mutual promissory obligations, which may be conceived of as prolonged barter. Barter presents a typical and clear case because, in its simplest form, it involves two separate objects which are related in no other way than that each is a means with respect to the other, which is considered an end; each of them is useful and thus of value as a means to obtain the other.

If we agree to conceive all acts of mutual aid and assistance as barter or exchange, it will be evident that all living together is a continuous exchange of such aid and assistance and that the degree of its intimacy depends upon its frequency. However, the character of these relationships is determined by the underlying motives involved, which motives will manifest definite differences. In the simple case where only two persons are considered, the essential motive on the part of those involved can be characterized as follows: from one side there may be expectation of and desire for assistance, from the other there may be expectation, desire, and restraint. This condition resembles the expectation and demands of a collective entity which binds the individual; that is to say, so connects him to others and constrains him that this entity may take the place of and represent these others. In distinct contrast is the case in which one's motives to satisfy one's volition and desires take the form of satisfying those of another individual, others, or whole groups, even though one's own volition and desire may apparently be fostered by the similar volition and desires of the other or others. Such volition and desire necessarily result in a different attitude toward the other individual or individuals. It is essentially unconditional, like the love of the mother for her infant, from whom she does not expect or require anything as long as he has not reached the age of reason. Love alone does not bind. Thus definite liking and benevolence, even though it be love, becomes atrophied when one party fails to return it. Such love may be allowed to continue its pitiful existence on the basis of the faintest hope or mere knowledge of the presence of the other loved one because one party may make the welfare of the other his own will, as is true especially in the case of sexual love. However, such love can also turn to hate (the more passionate, the earlier) which then becomes an inverted love, just as self-love frequently leads to self-destruction.

The derived and higher type of social bond always contains that element which we may designate, on the one hand, as containing mutual advantage, assistance, or amicable activity, and, on the other, as always containing an element of binding social will which works on and controls the individual will. Always the obligation and reciprocity makes itself felt and is thereby recognizable in that an inadequate and opposing action of a partner (participant or fellow member) calls forth a counteraction of one or the other and consequently of the whole if this latter continues to exist, which will be the more likely the less this whole's continuity depends upon the action of one person. Thus, for example, a friendship of two and frequently a marriage, even though this latter is conditioned by an existing social will of a higher type, is dependent upon the behavior of both partners and may be broken. On the other hand, in an association the individual cannot as a rule accomplish this, and only the action of a group strengthens or endangers its existence. The opposition between a majority and a minority makes itself felt in such a group and thus it may differ from the condition in which two individuals are involved. This difference is apparent if the majority wishes to retain or change the whole and if it is strong enough, as opposed to the minority, to make its will prevail over the whole. One must conceive as a normal case the condition in which individuals or parts, such as a minority, which act against the social will call forth the indignation of the majority, and the latter is in possession of sufficient power to react accordingly and, in so far as this is the case, will objectively represent the will of the whole even when the will of an important minority is opposed. Sociologically more important, however, is the case in which the principle prevails, perhaps having been recorded in expressed form, that the will of the majority or, at least, an especially large majority, shall prevail as the will of the whole corporation, social organization, or commission, so that after a resolution is passed the opposition is dissolved, at least for the time being.

3

1. Social Entities (Wesenheiten).

Sociology as a special science has as its subject the "things" which result from social life, and only from social life. They are products of human thinking and exist only for such thinking; that is, primarily for individuals themselves who are bound together and who think of their collective existence as dominating them and as a something which is represented as a person capable of volition and action, to which they give a name. The existence of such a something, a social person, can be recognized and acknowledged by outsiders, who may themselves be single or associated individuals, or by a social entity formed by such persons. Such recognition, if mutual, may create a new, essentially similar entity, in the most perfect case, a new social person, which again is existent immediately for its founders but can also be observed, recognized, and acknowledged by outsiders. The manner of existence of this social thing or person is not unlike that of the gods, which, being imagined and thought of by men who are bound together, are also created in order to be glorified, whether the form be that of an animal, a human being, or mixed being. There is, however, an obvious difference in that the gods disappear for the people to whom they belong when their existence is no longer believed in, even though they remain as subjects of the theoretical, historical, and sociological thinking. In contradistinction, social "entities," as we call them, do not require such belief or delusion. They can be thought of as subjects of common volition and operation in clear perception of their imaginary nature. Of course, it is also possible, indeed not an infrequent occurrence, that to the social entities, just as in the case of the gods, a supernatural, or, better stated, a metaphysical nature will be ascribed. The fanciful mythological thinking to which man has always been inclined constantly prevails in this sense and will, therefore, often confuse the inventions and phantasies of one or the other type; the social entities, especially the collective persons, are superior, powerful, and exalted, and so are the gods. Thus in the social entity there exists at least some of the godlike characteristics. They stand under the special protection of the gods, especially when to such an entity a supernatural origin is ascribed, as in the case of the church.

When the god is himself represented as a powerful and feared or as a benevolent and kind ruler, he is ruler over the earthly ruler, giving the latter his consecration, confirming and befriending him, establishing his right, especially the right of hereditary succession, as a god-given right. By the grace of God the earthly ruler reigns, enjoying a godlike veneration. All kinds of veneration, as they spring from natural feeling as childish adoration or as awe of the weak for the strong, who may be hated and detested, are interwoven one with another and with the gods in whom they find their consummation and shine forth as religion. As obedient servants of the gods, powerful men are agents and interpreters of the will of God and thereby increase their own power.

Even though this mere creature of thought does not live in the clouds or on Olympus but has ascribed to it an existence such as that which is perhaps embodied in the assembly of an armed force or other meeting of the people, it will not easily avoid that condition in which its existence is brought into relationship with that of the gods. The belief in the gods can support the belief in the republic just as the belief in the church and the veneration of the priesthood are directly related. The scientific critical attitude destroys all of these illusions. It recognizes that only human thought and human will are contained in all of these imaginary realms, that they are based upon human hopes and fears, requirements and needs, and that in their exalted forms they are comparable to poetical works of art on which the spirit of the ages has worked.

Thus we return to the simple problem and thought: what, why, and how do thinking human beings will and want? The simple and most general answer is: they want to attain an end and seek the most appropriate means of attaining it. They strive toward a goal and seek the correct way leading thereto. This is the action, the behavior, which in the affairs of practical life, of daily work, of struggle, of trade, has through the ages been directed and made easier by pleasure and devotion, by hope and fear, by practice and habit, by model and precept.

2. Human Volition.

The general human volition, which we may conceive as natural and original, is fulfilled through knowledge and ability and is also fundamentally conditioned through reciprocal interaction with them. The whole intellect, even in the plainest man, expresses itself in his knowledge and correspondingly in his volition. Not only what he has learned but also the inherited mode of thought and perception of the forefathers influences his sentiment, his mind and heart, his conscience. Consequently I name the will thought of in this latter sense natural will (*Wesenwille*), contrasting it with the type of rational will (*Kürwille*)[1] in which the thinking has gained predominance and come to be the directing

---

1   "Natural will" does not adequately portray Tönnies' concept of *Wesenwille*, which might also have been translated " integral will." Neither does "rational will" convey the entire meaning of *Kürwille,* as used by Tönnies. Only

agent. The rational will is to be differentiated from intellectual will. Intellectual will gets along well with subconscious motives which lie deep in man's nature and at the base of his natural will, whereas rational will eliminates such disturbing elements and is as clearly conscious as possible.

Deliberation, the thought form of ends and means, can separate the two, one from the other. From this results the inference that the means are not fundamentally connected to the end; that is to say, the means and end are not allied, interwoven, or identical. The means may rather be completely isolated and therefore possibly even stand in strong opposition to the ends. In this case the end under consideration requires that the means be as suitable to it as possible, that no means or segment thereof be used which is not conditioned by the end, but that the means most suitable for the attainment of a given end be chosen and used. This implies a definite divorce and differentiation of end and means which, therefore, permits no consideration of means other than that of their perfect suitability for the attaining of the end. The principle of the rationalization of the means develops everywhere as a necessary consequence the more thought, in accordance with the desire and intention, is intensively focused on the end or the goal. This signifies, therefore, an attitude of indifference to the means with respect to every consideration other than their greatest effectiveness in attaining the end. This indifference is frequently attained only by overcoming resistance resulting from motives other than the consideration of the end, which motives may hinder, dissuade, or frighten one from the application of this means. Thus action which adjusts the means

to the end desired may be viewed with definite reluctance, also with fear and anxiety, or, more characteristically, with aversion and, what is akin thereto, with feelings of opposition such as come with remorse. With some exaggeration, Goethe says the acting man is always "without conscience." In reality, the acting person often finds it necessary, if he "unscrupulously" follows his goal, to repress or overcome his conscientiousness. On account of this necessity, many consider themselves justified in despising or disowning such feelings, and sometimes they even find their satisfaction in bravado and arrogance, making themselves free from all such considerations.

This means, therefore, that on the one hand there is the simple emotional (impulsive) and, therefore, irrational volition and action, whereas on the other there is the simple rational volition and action in which the means are arranged, a condition which often stands in conflict with the feelings. Between these two extremes all real volition and action takes place. The consideration that most volition and action resembles or is inclined toward either one or the other makes it possible to establish the concepts of natural will and rational will, which concepts are rightly applied only in this sense. I call them normal concepts. What they represent are ideal types, and they should serve as standards by which reality may be recognized and described.

3. Gemeinschaft and Gesellschaft.[2]

It is not a question of contrasting the rational will with the nonrational will, because intellect and reason belong to natural will as well as to rational will.

---

the use of the terms in the context of the Introduction and the Second Book will portray to the reader what the author has in mind. However, Tönnies' usage of the two terms *Kürwille* and *Wesenwille* does not preclude the use of the terms rational will and natural will as the following passages will indicate: "Ich habe diesen Typus den Kür-Willen genannt. Er ist der am meisten ausgebildete rationale Wille und alles menschliche Wollen ist durch vernünftiges Denken charakterisiert und, so angesehen, immer rational ... Der Wesenwille – wie ich den anderen Typus benenne – , ist die ältere einfachere und in einem leicht zu verstehenden Sinne, die natürlichere Gestalt des denkenden menschlichen Willens." Tönnies, *Einführung in die Soziologie*, Stuttgart, 1931, pp. 154, 155. See also Tönnies' discussion of the general subject of will which was made earlier: " Das Wesen der Soziologie," in *Neue Zeit- und Streitfragen*, IV. Band, 1907, p. 12.

2   Translator's note: The two German words *Gemeinschaft* and *Gesellschaft* have frequently been translated, respectively, as "community" and "society." However, since the English words do not carry the connotations peculiar to the German concepts as used by Tönnies, and since sociologists are familiar with Tönnies' use of them, it has been deemed advisable to retain the German words in all except First Book, Subject, 1 (pp. 37-39). This procedure is in accordance with Pareto's contention that such concepts might be represented by any two different symbols. As the

Indeed, intellect in natural will attains its fruition in the creative, formative, and artistic ability and works and in the spirit of the genius. This is true even though in its elementary forms natural will means nothing more than a direct, naive, and therefore emotional volition and action, whereas, on the other hand, rational will is most frequently characterized by consciousness. To the latter belongs manufacturing as contrasted with creation; therefore, we speak of mechanical work (as expressed in the German and other languages) referring to forging plans, machinations, weaving intrigues, or fabrications which are directed to the objective of bringing forth the means, the exclusive determination of which is that of producing the outward effects necessary to attain our desired ends.

When these concepts are applied to associations, it should not be understood that we are thinking only of the regular motives leading to the entrance into an association, creating of a confederation, or organizing of a union or special interest group, or even the founding of a commonwealth. It is, however, of importance to recognize what motives lie at the basis of and explain the existence of all kinds of association or cause their persistence, and while we are here interested only in positive bases, this holds also for negative motives upon which persistence may be based. In this connection it is not to be understood that the bases belong fundamentally and persistently either to the one or the other category, that is, of natural will or rational will. On the contrary a dynamic condition or process is assumed which corresponds to the changeable elements of human feeling and thinking. The motives fluctuate so that they are now of one category, then of the other. However, wherever such development takes place a certain regularity or even "law," in the sense of a tendency toward abstract rational forms, may be observed.

I call all kinds of association in which natural will predominates Gemeinschaft, all those which are formed and fundamentally conditioned by rational will, Gesellschaft. Thus these concepts signify the model qualities of the essence and the tendencies of being bound together. Thus both names are in the present context stripped of their connotation as designating social entities or groups, or even collective or artificial persons; the essence of both Gemeinschaft and Gesellschaft is found interwoven in all kinds of associations, as will be shown.

4

1. Relationships, Collectives, Social Organizations.

As social entities or forms, I differentiate: (1) Social relationships *(Verhältnisse)*, (2) Collectives *(Samtschaften)*, (3) Social organizations or corporate bodies *(Körperschaften)*, (leagues, fellowships, associations, or special-interest groups).

The third form is always thought of as a kind of human person capable of creating a definite unified will which, as the will of the natural or artificial persons belonging to it, binds and constrains them to act in conformity with such will, which may be directed inwardly or outwardly. In the social relationship it is not the relationship itself which is so considered, even though it be designated by a special name. However, it is essential that its subjects or bearers, who may be considered as "members" of the relationship, are conscious of it as a relationship which they will affirmatively and thus establish as an existing reality. This manner of establishing a social relationship represents in embryonic or emergent form what is evolved to perfection in the establishment of a social organization or corporation capable of willing and acting.

The collective lies between the social relationship and the social organization. It is thought of as a plurality which, like the social organization, includes a multitude of persons so held together that there result common intentions, desires, incli-

reader will note, the English substantives "community" and "society" and the English adjectives "communal" and "social" appear frequently in the text. In most cases "community" and "society" are respectively the translation of such German terms as *Gemeinde* and *Sozietät*. When the substantive or adjective forms of *Gemeinschaft* and *Gesellschaft* are translated into English words they were used in the original in an empirical sense; however, when they were used as ideal types the German forms are retained. The various meanings of *Gemeinschaft* and *Gesellschaft* as developed in German sociology are explained by Theodor Geiger in *Handwörterbuch der Soziologie*, published by Ferdinand Enke Verlag, Stuttgart, 1931; *Gemeinschaft* on pp. 173-180, and *Gesellschaft* on pp. 201-211.

nations, disinclinations – in short, common feelings and ways of thinking. However, the collective is not capable of real volition. It can reach no decision as long as it does not "organize" itself into a committee, special-interest group, or council.

2. The Social Relationship.

The social relationship is the most general and simplest social entity or form. It also has the deepest foundation, because it rests partly upon the original, natural, and actual conditions as the causes of connections, of mutual dependence, and of attachment among men, and because it rests partly on the most fundamental, most universal, and most necessary requirements of human beings. The one basis, like the other, is raised to consciousness with different effects. If a natural relationship exists, as for example between my brother and me, on one hand, or between my brother-in-law, my stepbrother, adopted or foster brother and me, on the other, I have the feeling that we are intimate, that we affirm each other's existence, that ties exist between us, that we know each other and to a certain extent are sympathetic toward each other, trusting and wishing each other well. This is true although in the latter case, involving persons who are not blood brothers, the relationship is not so natural as in the first where I know the same mother gave birth to both my brother and me. From this it follows that we have certain values in common, whether it be that we are obliged to manage an estate together, or that we divide possessions as inheritances between us, or that the matter of intellectual goods or ideals is involved. At any rate, out of each such relationship, even between two, there results the recognition and acknowledgment of the social relationship as such on the part of each and therefore the knowledge of each that definite mutual action must regularly result therefrom. This action is expected and demanded of each by the other, and each expects and demands of himself that it be carried out in relation to the other. In this lies the embryo of "rights" which each claims for himself but also concedes to the other, as well as "duties" to which one feels obligated but which one puts upon oneself knowing that the other party wills that he be and considers that he is so obligated.

However, when I become conscious of my most urgent needs and find that I can neither satisfy them out of my own volition nor out of a natural relation, this means that I must do something to satisfy my need; that is, engage in free activity which is bound only by the requirement or possibly conditioned by the need but not by consideration for other people. Soon I perceive that I must work on other people in order to influence them to deliver or give something to me which I need. Possibly in restricted individual cases my mere requests will be granted, as, for example, in the case of a piece of bread or a glass of water. However, as a rule when one is not receiving something in a Gemeinschaft-like relationship, such as from within the family, one must earn or buy it by labor, service, or money which has been earned previously as payment for labor or service.

I now enter or have already entered into a social relationship, but it is of a different kind. Its prototype is barter or exchange, including the more highly developed form of exchange, the sale and purchase of things or services, which are the same as things and are therefore thought of as capable of being exchanged for things or for other services. All action which is of an intellectual nature and consequently oriented by reason is of this type because comparison and thinking are necessary to it and furnish a basis for it. Social relationships which result from such barter or exchange are primarily momentary in that they involve a momentary common volition. However, they come to have duration partly through repetition resulting in regularity of the exchange act and partly through the lengthening of the individual act by the postponement of fulfillment on the part of one or both sides. In this latter case there results a relationship, the distinguishing characteristic of which is a one-sided or mutual "promise." It is a real social relationship of obligation or mutual dependence resulting first of all from mutual promises, even though they may be expressly stated by one side and only tacitly understood by the other as such an eventual promise.

Also, the relationships which come to us from nature are in their essence mutual, are fulfilled in mutual performance. The relations produce this mutuality and demand, require, or make it necessary. Having these characteristics, they resemble the exchange relationship However, the natural relationship is, by its very essence, of earlier origin than its subjects or members. In such natural relationships it is self-evident that action will take place and be willed in accordance with the relationship, whether it be what is contained on the one hand in the simplest relationships resulting from desire and inclination, from love or habit, or on the other hand from reason or intellect contained in the feeling of duty. These latter types of natural will change into one another, and each can be the basis of Gemeinschaft.

On the other hand, in the purest and most abstract contract relationship the contracting parties are thought of as separate, hitherto and otherwise independent, as strangers to each other, and perhaps even as hitherto and in other respects inimical persons. *Do, ut des* (I give, so that you will give) is the only principle of such a relationship. What I do for you, I do only as a means to effect your simultaneous, previous, or later service for me. Actually and really I want and desire only this. To get something from you is my end; my service is the means thereto, which I naturally contribute unwillingly. Only the aforesaid and anticipated result is the cause which determines my volition. This is the simplest form of rational will.

Relationships of the first type are to be classified under the concept Gemeinschaft, those of the other type under the concept of Gesellschaft, thus differentiating Gemeinschaft-like and Gesellschaft-like relationships. Gemeinschaft-like relationships differ to the extent that there is assumed, on the one hand, a real, even if not complete, equality in knowledge or volition, in power and in authority on the part of the participants, and on the other hand, an essential inequality in these respects. This also holds for the relations of Gesellschaft. In accordance with this distinction we shall differentiate between the fellowship type and the authoritative type of social relationship. Let us now consider this difference.

A. In Gemeinschaft-like Relationships. (a) The Fellowship Type. The simplest fellowship type is represented by a pair who live together in a brotherly, comradely, and friendly manner, and it is most likely to exist when those involved are of the same age, sex, and sentiment, are engaged in the same activity or have the same intentions, or when they are united by one idea.

In legend and history such pairs occur frequently. The Greeks used to honor such friendships as those of Achilles and Patroclus, Orestes and Pylades, Epaminondas and Pelopidas, to the extent that to Aristotle is ascribed the paradox: He who has friends has no friend. In the German language and literature it is customary to designate such sentiments, the nature of which the Greeks glorified as mutual happiness and sorrow, as a brotherly relationship. This characterization is based more on the thought of the ideal than on actual observation but it is correct in so far as brothers actually make the most natural as well as the most probable pairs of friends, more because of their origin than because of a motive.

(b) Authoritative Type. The relationship of father to child, as observations in everyday life will prove, is to be found in all the strata of society in all stages of culture. The weaker the child and the more it is in need of help, the greater the extent to which the relationship is represented by protection. Protection of necessity always carries with it authority as a condition, because protection regularly can be carried out only when the protected party follows the directions and even the commands of the protector. Although all authority has a tendency to change into the use of force, in the case of the father as well as the mother relationship such a tendency is arrested by love and tenderness. These sentiments, being of animal and vegetative origin, are more likely to be regularly accorded to a child born to a parent than to any other possessed and protected person. The general character of the father relationship can be easily extended to include similar relationships involving protection, examples of which are the stepfather, foster father, the general house father, and the guardian, even though these, as representatives of the father, do not necessarily legally stand in Gemeinschaft-like relation to the ward. The authority of the father is the prototype of all Gemeinschaft-like authority. It is especially true in the case of the priesthood, even though the basis may be different. This rests primarily upon mythological conceptions which place the father in Olympus or in heaven and perhaps ascribe to the father of the gods and men numberless children. Or in a less sensual, more refined form, the father may be represented by an only son whom the struggle against polytheism tends almost to identify with the father. Little wonder that the title Pope (*Papa,* literally "father") in the original church of all bishops was raised to the pinnacle of spiritual dignity in the Roman Church and that in the Oriental Church the especially high priests are called fathers (*Popen*) in the language of the common people. Also, world and political authority, which is often mixed with and may not be less sanctified than the spiritual, easily takes on the character of the well-wishing father, as is most plainly expressed in the term "father" of a country. The fatherly authority, however, is the special case of authority of age, and the prestige-giving quality of age expresses itself most perfectly in the authority of the father. This easily explains the eminence which is attributed to the senator in the worldly and the presbyter in the spiritual commonwealth.

(c) Mixed Relationships. In many Gemeinschaft-like relationships the essence of authority and that of fellowship are mixed. This is the case in the most important of the relationships of Gemeinschaft, the lasting relation between man and woman which is conditioned through sexual needs and reproduction, whether or not the relationship is called marriage.

B. In Gesellschaft-like Relationships. The difference between the fellowship and authoritative types is also to be found in the Gesellschaft-like relationships. It can, however, be derived only from the fact that the authority is based upon a free contract whether between individuals, as service contracts, or by agreement of many to recognize and place a master or head over them and to obey him conditionally or unconditionally. This may be a natural person or a collective person which results directly from individuals uniting in a society, social organization, or corporate body which is capable of volition and action and can be represented through its own totality. The Gesellschaft-like authority attains its consummation in the modern state, a consummation which many predecessors strove to attain until the democratic republic came into existence and allowed for development beyond the Gesellschaft-like foundation. The actual authority results, however, in the simple Gesellschaft-like relationship, from the difference in the power of two parties, as in the labor contract. Such authority results from contracts made between the individual "employer" and individual "employee," and also from the condition out of which come "peace treaties" between victor and conquered. Apparently it is a contract, but in actuality it is coercion and abuse.

3. The Collective.

The second concept of social entity or form is that of the collective. I make distinctions between natural, psychical, and social collectives. Our concept concerns only social collectives, but these rest partly on natural and partly on psychical collectives, partly on both. This is because the essence of a social collective is to be found in the natural and psychological relationships forming the basis of the collective and are consciously affirmed and willed. This phenomenon appears everywhere in the life of a people and in many forms of mutualities, as, for example, in forms of life and customs, superstitions and religion. It is especially in evidence in the distinguishing characteristic through which a segment of a people, that is, certain classes, are given prominence, nobility, and authority. A distinguishing characteristic which has this function is partly an objective phenomenon and partly something positive in the people's consciousness. The consciousness of belonging to a controlling estate makes its appearance in a distinct manner as pride and haughtiness – feelings which in turn are coupled with the submission and modesty of those "lower" classes over which authority is exercised so long as the controlling estates, as such, are honored, and so long as their excellence, or even their divinity, is believed in.

In the case of the collective the concepts of Gemeinschaft and Gesellschaft should also be applied. The social collective has the characteristics of Gemeinschaft in so far as the members think of such a grouping as a gift of nature or created by a supernatural will, as is expressed in the simplest and most naive manner in the Indian caste system. Here, to be fixed to a given calling is just as necessary and natural as being born, and the professional estate or group has the same significance as a large family for which the pursuit and means of making a livelihood, even if this should be accomplished by thievery, is represented as something inherited which it is a duty to retain and nurture. In all systems of ranks or estates, traces of this condition are to be found because (and to the extent that) a complete emancipation from the social relationships established at birth seldom occurred and was often impossible. Thus man as a rule submits to the social status in which parents and forebears, or, as it is wont to be expressed, "God", has placed him as if it were his lot to bear, even though it be felt as a burden, which, however, is habit and is lightened by the recognition that it cannot be changed. Indeed, within these limits there can exist an intellectual self-consciousness which affirms this estate (rank) even though it be recognized as one of the less significant. This intellectual basis manifests itself partly as the group extols itself for certain superiorities or virtues, the lack of which in the dominating estate is noticed and complained about. Also, the intellectual basis is to be found partly in the consciousness of special knowledge and skill of the group, as, for example, its art, craftsmanship, and skill, which are thought of as being at least the equivalent of the other honored or ruling estates.

Consciousness of a social collective has different results when directed toward the attainment of definite and important ends which it knows to be and claims are its own characteristics. This happens in a pronounced way in the political and intellectual struggle in which the social strata of a people stand against each other as classes. The more the consciousness of authority as a feeling of superiority results in putting one class in such a position of power as to force the lower class to stay in its place, the more this latter will strive toward the attainment of equality and therefore the more indignant it becomes concerning oppression and arrogance on the part of the controlling class, which it attempts to restrict and displace.

Whether this process is called class struggle (*Klassenkampf*) or struggle of estates (*Ständekampf*) is not important. The struggle among the estates usually takes place earlier, is less radical, and can be allayed. The lower estates strive only for the opportunity to participate in the satisfactions of life and fundamentals of authority, allowing the controlling estate to remain in power. This latter remains in power by proclaiming its own fitness and disparaging that of the lower estates and by exerting effort to reduce these lower strata to submission.

The class struggle is more unconditional. It recognizes no estates, no natural masters. In the foreground of the consciousness of the whole class which feels that it is propertyless and therefore oppressed, stands the ideal of the Gemeinschaft of property in field and soil and all the implements of labor. These latter have been acquired through the art of trade or as inherited property belonging by "law" to the small minority which, as the propertied class, is set off against the propertyless class. Therefore, the class struggle becomes more conscious and general than the struggle among the estates. However, even though there be no definite form of struggle there is a corresponding consciousness which makes itself felt in many ways. The great propertyless masses prefer to think of themselves as the people (*Volk*), and the narrow class which is in control of property and its use thinks of itself as society, even though each expression is all inclusive. "The" people *(Volk)*, as in the case of the estate, resembles the Gemeinschaft; "the" society, like the class, has, in the sense in which it is here used, the basic characteristic of Gesellschaft.[3]

4. The Social Organization.

The third and most important category of pure or theoretical sociology is the social organization or corporate body, a social body or union known by many other names. It is never anything natural, neither can it be understood as a mere psychical phenomenon. It is completely and essentially a social phenomenon and must be considered as composed of several individuals. Capacity for unified volition and action, a capacity which is demonstrated most clearly as competency to pass resolutions, characterizes it. Just as the thinking individual is capable of making decisions, so is a group of several individuals when they continuously agree or agree to the extent that there prevails and is recognized a definite will as the will of all or sufficient consensus to be the will of the social organization or corporate body. Thus the volition of such a group can be represented by the will of a natural person behind whom the will of the whole social organization or corporate body stands. Continuing our discussion of social organizations or corporate bodies, we may make the following observations:

(1) A social organization or corporate body can originate from natural relationships provided these

---

3   See Tönnies' article "Stände und Klassen," in *Handwörterbuch der Soziologie*, Ferdinand Enke Verlag, Stuttgart, 1931.

are social relationships. In this connection, kinship, the most universal and natural bond which embraces human beings, comes to our attention. The most important social organization or corporate body which originates therefrom and which among all known peoples occurs as the original form of a common life is the kinship group, the gens, clan, or whatever name is applied to designate this ancient union or unity.

Whether or not the totality of adult persons includes the women, whether their council ends in agreement which is sanctioned by a supposed will of God, or whether they rejoice in and willingly accept the decisions of a leader and head, it is under these conditions that there is formed the embryo of a consciousness which matures into something beyond a mere feeling of belonging together, and there is established and affirmed an enduring self or ego in the totality.

(2) A common relation to the soil tends to associate people who may be kinsfolk or believe themselves to be such. Neighborhood, the fact that they live together, is the basis of their union; it leads to counciling and through deliberations to resolutions. Here again the two principles of fellowship and authority will be involved. The outstanding example of an association of this type is the rural village community, which attains its consummation in the cultivation of the soil practiced in common and the possession of common property in village fields or land held in common by the village, and in the Mark-community which comes to represent the unity of several neighboring village communities which originally may have formed one unit.

The rural village community is frequently identical with a great family or clan but the more alien elements are taken in the more it loses its kinship characteristics. The bond of field and soil and living together first takes its place along with and later more and more supplants the bond of common ancestry. Especially when an alien tribe and its leaders become the conquerors of a territory and establish themselves in the seats of control without extirpating or driving out all the former residents and owners does this tendency manifest itself, molding a new people (*Volk*) from the two groups, even though the one was subjected to new masters. The existence of the village community as a social organization or corporate body ordinarily continues in the form of a fellowship. Such a village com-

munity, however, may be modified by the power and rights of feudal lords.

(3) In the more intimate and close living together in the town, the fellowship and co-operative quality attains a new level. Living together tends to depend less on common nature. People not related by blood tend to assemble in the towns since these originally were walled-in villages or strongholds whose inhabitants were forced to co-operate for defense and for the maintenance of peace and order among themselves and thereby to form a political community, either under the rule of a lord or as citizens of equal rights. This was the great mission and service of the town (*Stadt*) community, the "*Polis*" which grew to be that commonwealth which later in Europe and elsewhere up to our time has bequeathed its character and name to the state (*Staat*), the mightiest of all corporate bodies. That assembly of the sovereign people, the religious association (*Ekklesia*), the other great commonwealth of the Roman and post-Roman period, loaned its name to the Church and spread its glory throughout the world in a similar manner.

These social bodies and communities retain their common root in that original state of belonging together which according to our concept is the Gemeinschaft. Indeed, although the original state of common being, living, and working is changed, it retains and is able to renew its mental and political form and its co-operative functions. Thus a people (*Volk*) which feels itself bound together by a common language, when held together within a national association or even when only striving to become a nation, will desire to be represented in a unity or *Volksgemeinschaft*, which may become intensified by national consciousness and pride, but may also thereby lose its original genuineness.

5. Capitalistic, Middle-class, or Bourgeois Society (*bürgerliche Gesellschaft*).

During this development, the original qualities of Gemeinschaft may be lost because there takes place a continued change in the original basis upon which living together rests. This change reaches its consummation in what is frequently designated as individualism. Through this development social life in and of itself is not diminished, but social life of the Gemeinschaft is impaired and a new phenomenon develops out of the needs, interests, desires, and decisions of persons who previously worked co-operatively together and are acting and dealing one with another. This new phenomenon, the "capitalistic society," increases in power and gradually attains the ascendancy. Tending as it does to be cosmopolitan and unlimited in size, it is the most distinct form of the many phenomena represented by the sociological concept of the Gesellschaft.

A great transformation takes place. Whereas previously the whole of life was nurtured and arose from the profoundness of the people (*Volk*), the capitalistic society through a long process spreads itself over the totality of this people, indeed over the whole of mankind. As a totality of individuals and families it is essentially a collective of economic character composed primarily of those who partake in that wealth which, as land and capital, represents the necessary means to the production of goods of all kinds. Within narrow or far-flung borders which are determined by actual or supposed kinship bonds, of the existence of which the language group is the most valuable sign, it constructs its state, that is to say, a kind of unity resembling a town community which is capable of willing and acting. It develops as the capitalistic middle-class republic and apparently finally attains its perfection in the social republic. It considers the state a means of attaining its ends, of which not the least important is protecting its person and property as well as the intellectual attitude which gives status and honor to its supporters.

However, since this capitalistic middle-class society cannot, without betraying itself, admit its uniqueness as a collective of Gesellschaft in contradistinction to the people (*Volk*) or, so to speak, herald this difference by raising its own flag, it can only assert its existence through claiming to be identical with, as well as representative and advocate of, the whole people to which it furnishes guidance. This process, which does not stop with conferring equal political rights on all citizens, to a certain extent closes the always widening hiatus between the wealth monopoly of the narrow and real Gesellschaft and the poverty of the people but it cannot change the essential character of the hiatus. Indeed it deepens it, spreading and strengthening the consciousness of the "social question."

By means of political and other intellectual organization promoted by town and, to a greater extent, by city life, the consciousness of the Gesellschaft gradually becomes the consciousness of an increasing mass of the people. The people come more and more to think of the state as a means and tool to be used in bettering their condition, destroying the monopoly of wealth of the few, winning a share in the products. Thus the laborer would be allowed a share in proper proportion to his reasonable needs and the leaders in production their share of certain goods which are to be divided for consumption, and those things suitable for continued common utilization would be retained as common property of the Gesellschaft, which is to say of the people or their organized association, the state.

Bibliography

Cahnman, Werner J., ed. *Ferdinand Tönnies. A new evaluation. Essays and documents.* Leiden: Brill, 1973.

Heberle, Rudolf. "The Sociology of Ferdinand Tönnies," *American Sociological Review*, Vol. 2, No. 1 (1937).

CHAPTER FORTY-FIVE — MARVIN HARRIS

The enterprise of a science of human nature, launched soon after the inception of a science of inanimate nature with Newton's *Principia* (1687), has continued uninterruptedly since the Enlightenment. New models and blueprints, in diverse areas of social and biological science, and in philosophy, continue to offer themselves to our assent, with a variety of kinds of claim of evidence or comprehensiveness.

One prominent contribution of recent decades from cultural anthropology has been the *cultural materialism* of Marvin Harris (b. 1927). After some years at Columbia University, since 1981 Harris has been graduate research professor of anthropology at the University of Florida in Gainesville. He did extensive field research in Brazil, Mozambique, Ecuador, India, and East Harlem (in New York City), and has served as chair of the General Anthropology Division of the American Anthropological Association. Harris is the author of a textbook in cultural anthropology, a significant work of intellectual history covering much of the human nature enterprise since 1700 (and many of the theories of the present volume) – *The Rise of Anthropological Theory* – theoretical volumes on the principles of cultural materialism, and several semi-popular books of applications of cultural materialist theory to cultural and behavioral patterns in both third-world societies and the United States.

Harris's theory has clear affinities to Marx, to Darwin, and to "functionalist" anthropology, but is also uniquely itself. One might have thought that *anthropology* – etymologically, "the study of humans" – would be a particularly rich and fertile home of theorizing about people. This has not historically been very strikingly the case. With a primary focus on investigations of small-scale societies, especially ones dramatically unlike those of their investigators, twentieth-century anthropology has mostly avoided, and even sometimes had marked hostility to, general theory, and perhaps especially materialist, empiricist, or naturalist theory. Harris is therefore a signal and important exception to this pattern.

Marvin Harris, *Cultural Materialism*

(Source: Marvin Harris. *Cultural Materialism: The Struggle for a Science of Culture*. New York: Vintage Books, 1980, 31-36, 46-75.)

Mental and Behavioral Fields

The scientific study of human social life must concern itself equally with two radically different kinds of phenomena. On the one hand, there are the activities that constitute the human behavior stream – all the body motions and environmental effects produced by such motions, large and small, of all the human beings who have ever lived. On the other hand, there are all the thoughts and feelings that we human beings experience within our minds. The fact that distinctive operations must be used to make scientifically credible statements about each realm guarantees the distinctiveness of each realm. To describe the universe of human mental experiences, one must employ operations capable of discovering what people are thinking about. But to describe body motions and the external effects produced by body motions, one does not have to find out what is going on inside people's heads – at least this is not necessary if one adopts the epistemological stance of cultural materialism.

The distinction between mental and behavioral events moves us only halfway toward the solution of Marx and Engels' quandary. There remains the fact that the thoughts and behavior of the participants can be viewed from two different perspectives: from the perspective of the participants themselves, and from the perspective of the observers. In both instances scientific – that is, objective – accounts of the mental and behavioral fields are possible. But in the first instance, the observers employ concepts and distinctions meaningful and appropriate to the participants; while in the second instance, they employ concepts and distinctions meaningful and appropriate to the observers. If the criteria of empirical replicability and testability are met, either perspective may lead to a knowledge of "real," nonimaginary mental and behavioral events, although the accounts rendered may be divergent.

Emics and Etics

Since both the observer's point of view and the participants' point of view can be presented objectively or subjectively, depending on the adequacy of the empirical operations employed by the observer we cannot use the words "objective" and "subjective" to denote the option in question without creating a great deal of confusion. To avoid this confusion, many anthropologists have begun to use the terms "emic" and "etic," which were first introduced by the anthropological linguist Kenneth Pike in his book *Language in Relation to a Unified Theory of the Structure of Human Behavior.*

Emic operations have as their hallmark the elevation of the native informant to the status of ultimate judge of the adequacy of the observer's descriptions and analyses. The test of the adequacy of emic analyses is their ability to generate statements the native accepts as real, meaningful, or appropriate. In carrying out research in the emic mode, the observer attempts to acquire a knowledge of the categories and rules one must know in order to think and act as a native. One attempts to learn, for example, what rule lies behind the use of the same kin term for mother and mother's sister among the Bathonga; or one attempts to learn when it is appropriate to shame one's guests among the Kwakiutl.

Etic operations have as their hallmark the eleva-

tion of observers to the status of ultimate judges of the categories and concepts used in descriptions and analyses. The test of the adequacy of etic accounts is simply their ability to generate scientifically productive theories about the causes of sociocultural differences and similarities. Rather than employ concepts that are necessarily real, meaningful, and appropriate from the native point of view, the observer is free to use alien categories and rules derived from the data language of science. Frequently, etic operations involve the measurement and juxtaposition of activities and events that native informants may find inappropriate or meaningless.

I think the following example demonstrates the consummate importance of the difference between emic and etic knowledge. In the Trivandwan district of the state of Kerala, in southern India, I interviewed farmers about the cause of death of their domestic cattle. Every farmer insisted that he would never deliberately shorten the life of one of his animals, that he would never kill it or starve it to death. Every farmer ardently affirmed the legitimacy of the standard Hindu prohibition against the slaughter of domestic bovines. Yet it soon became obvious from the animal reproductive histories I was collecting that the mortality rate of male calves tended to be almost twice as high as the mortality rate of female calves. In fact, male cattle from zero to one years old are outnumbered by female cattle of the same age group in a ratio of 67 to 100. The farmers themselves are aware that male calves are more likely to die than female calves, but they attribute the difference to the relative "weakness" of the males. "The males get sick more often," they say. When I asked farmers to explain why male calves got sick more often, several suggested that the males ate less than the females. One or two suggested that the male calves ate less because they were not permitted to stay at the mother's teats for more than a few seconds. But no one would say that since there is little demand for traction animals in Kerala, males are culled and females reared.

The emics of the situation are that no one knowingly or willingly would shorten the life of a calf. Again and again I was told that every calf has the right to life regardless of its sex. But the etics of the situation are that cattle sex ratios are systematically adjusted to the needs of the local ecology and economy through preferential male "bovicide." Although the unwanted calves are not slaughtered, they are more or less rapidly starved to death. Emically, the systemic relationship between Kerala's cattle sex ratios and local ecological and economic conditions simply does not exist. Yet the consummate importance of this systemic relationship can be seen from the fact that in other parts of India, where different ecological and economic conditions prevail, preferential etic bovicide is practiced against female rather than male cattle, resulting in an adult cattle sex ratio of over 200 oxen for every 100 cows in the state of Uttar Pradesh.

A while back I mentioned the burden of unoperationalized terms, which prevents social scientists from solving puzzles or even communicating effectively about their research. The first simple step toward operationalizing such concepts as status, role, class, caste, tribe, state, aggression, exploitation, family, kinship, and the rest is to specify whether the knowledge one professes to have about these entities has been gained by means of emic or etic operations. All notions of replicability and testability fly up the chimney when the world as seen by the observed is capriciously muddled with the world as seen by the observer. As I hope to show later on, research strategies that fail to distinguish between mental and behavior stream events and between emic and etic operations cannot develop coherent networks of theories embracing the causes of sociocultural differences and similarities. And a priori, one can say that those research strategies that confine themselves exclusively to emics or exclusively to etics do not meet the general criteria for an aim-oriented social science as effectively as those which embrace both points of view.

Etics, Emics, and Objectivity

Kenneth Pike formed the words "etic" and "emic" from the suffixes of the words phon*etic* and phon*emic*. Phonetic accounts of the sounds of a language are based upon a taxonomy of the body parts active in the production of speech utterances and their characteristic environmental effects in the form of acoustic waves. Linguists discriminate eti-

cally between voiced and unvoiced sounds, depending on the activity of the vocal cords; between aspirated and nonaspirated sounds, depending on the activity of the glottis; between labials and dentals, depending on the activity of the tongue and teeth. The native speaker does not make these discriminations. On the other hand, emic accounts of the sounds of a language are based on the implicit or unconscious system of sound contrasts that native speakers have inside their heads and that they employ to identify meaningful utterances in their language.

The importance of Pike's distinction is that it leads to a clarification of the meaning of subjectivity and objectivity in the human sciences. To be objective is not to adopt an etic view; nor is it subjective to adopt an emic view. To be objective is to adopt the epistemological criteria ... by which science is demarcated from other ways of knowing. It is clearly possible to be objective – i.e., scientific – about either emic or etic phenomena.[1] Similarly, it is equally possible to be subjective about either emic or etic phenomena. Objectivity is the epistemological status that distinguishes the community of observers from communities that are observed. While it is possible for those who are observed to be objective, this can only mean that they have temporarily or permanently joined the community of observers by relying on an operationalized scientific epistemology. Objectivity is not merely intersubjectivity. It is a special form of intersubjectivity established by the distinctive logical and empirical discipline to which members of the scientific community agree to submit.

Pike's Emic Bias

Much controversy has arisen concerning the appropriation by cultural materialists of Pike's emic/etic distinction. In large measure this controversy stems from the fact that Pike is a cultural idealist who believes that the aim of social science is to describe and analyze emic systems.

What Pike tried to do was to apply the principles by which linguists discover phonemes and other emic units of language (such as *morphemes)* to the discovery of emic units – which he called "behav-

---

1   Despite my reiteration of this point, Fisher and Werner (1978) have me equating science and ethics.

ioremes" – in the behavior stream. By identifying behavioremes, Pike hoped to extend the research strategy that had proved effective in the analysis of languages to the study of the behavior stream. Pike never considered the possibility of studying the behavior stream etically. He rejected virtually without discussion the possibility that an etic approach to the behavior stream might yield more interesting "structures" than an emic approach. To the extent that one could even talk about the existence of etic units, they were for Pike necessary evils, mere steppingstones to higher emic realms. Observers necessarily begin their analysis of social life with etic categories, but the whole thrust of their analytical task ought to be the replacement of such categories with the emic units that constitute structured systems within the minds of the social actors. In Pike's words (1967:38-39): "etic data provide access into the system – the starting point of analysis." "The initial etic description gradually is refined, and is ultimately – in principle, but probably never in practice – replaced by one which is totally emic."

This position clashes head on with the epistemological assumptions of cultural materialism. In the cultural materialist research strategy, etic analysis is not a steppingstone to the discovery of emic structures, but to the discovery of etic structures. The intent is neither to convert etics to emics nor emics to etics, but rather to describe both and if possible to explain one in terms of the other.

....

Theoretical Principles of Cultural Materialism

One cannot pass directly from a description of the ways of knowing about a field to the principles useful for building networks of interrelated theories. First, I have to say something about what's in the field – its major components or sectors. So far I've referred only to the etics and emics of human thought and behavior. But other components remain to be identified before the strategic principles of cultural materialism can be described.

The limitations of alternative research strategies are very much a consequence of how they conceptualize the nature of human societies and cultures. Idealist strategies approach the definition of social and cultural phenomena exclusively from an emic perspective: society exists to the extent that participants view themselves as members of social groups, sharing common values and purposes; social action is a special kind of behavior identified by the social intentions of the participants; and culture consists exclusively of the shared emics of thought and behavior. In extreme versions, such as those associated with cognitivism ...., even the emics of behavior are dropped and culture is restricted to rules allegedly guiding behavior without any investigation of the behavior itself.

On the other hand, cultural materialists approach the definition of social and cultural phenomena initially but not exclusively from an etic perspective. The social nature of human groups is inferred from the density of interaction among human beings found in a particular spatial and temporal locus. Cultural materialists do not have to know whether the members of a particular human population think of themselves as a "people" or a group in order to identify them as a social group. Nor does the interaction among the members of such a group have to be primarily supportive and cooperative in order for it to be considered social. The starting point of all sociocultural analysis for cultural materialists is simply the existence of an etic human population located in etic time and space. A society for us is a maximal social group consisting of both sexes and all ages and exhibiting a wide range of interactive behavior. Culture, on the other hand, refers to the learned repertory of thoughts and actions exhibited by the members of social groups – repertories transmissible independently of genetic heredity from one generation to the next. ... The cultural repertories of particular societies contribute to the continuity of the population and its social life. Hence the need arises for speaking of sociocultural systems, denoting the conjunction of a population, a society, and a culture, and constituting a bounded arrangement of people, thoughts, and activities. The systemic nature of such conjunctions and arrangements is not something to be taken for granted. Rather, it is a strategic assumption that can be justified only by showing how it leads to efficacious and testable theories.

The Universal Pattern

Cultural materialist theoretical principles are concerned with the problem of understanding the relationship among the parts of sociocultural systems and with the evolution of such relationships, parts, and systems. Alternative strategies construe these parts in radically different ways, and many inadequacies of substantive theories are already foreshadowed in general models of the structure of sociocultural systems. Consider, for example, the recurrent cognitive and behavioral components anthropologist Clark Wissler (1926) called the "universal pattern" – components allegedly present in all human societies:

Speech	Knowledge	Property
Material traits	Religion	Government
Art	Society	War

Both epistemological and theoretical problems abound in Wissler's scheme. Note, for example, that the separately listed "material traits" – by which he meant such things as tools, buildings, clothing, and containers – are logically present in at least art, religion, property, government, and war; that "knowledge" must occur in all the other rubrics; that there are such glaring omissions as "economy," "subsistence," "ecology," "demography"; and finally, that it is dubious that "war" and "religion" are universal traits. These defects flow from Wissler's failure to specify the epistemological status of the rubrics in terms of taxonomic principles that would justify the contraction or expansion of the list by reference to systemic structural relationships among its components.

Murdock's Categories

The rubrics under which entries in George Peter Murdock's *World Ethnographic Atlas (1967)* are arranged share the same defects. In the computer punch card version of the atlas, these are the components of sociocultural systems:

Subsistence economy	Type and intensity of
Mode of Marriage	agriculture
Family organization	Settlement Pattern
Marital residence	Mean size of local communities
Communitiy organizations	
Patrilineal kin groups and	Juridictional hierarchy
exogamy	High gods
Matrilineal kin groups and	Types of Games
exogamy	Postpartum sex taboos
Cognatic kin groups	Male genital mutilations
Cousin marriage	Segregation of adolescent boys

Kinship terminology for first	Metal Working
cousins	Weaving
Leather working	Succession to office of local
Pottery	headman
Boat building	Inheritance of real property
House construction	Inheritance of movable property
Gathering	Norm of premarital sex
Hunting	behavior of girls
Fishing	Ground plan of dwelling
Animal husbandry	Floor Level
Agriculture	Wall material
Type of animal husbandry	Shape of roof
Descent	Roofing material
Class stratification	Political integration
Caste stratification	Political succession
Slavery	Environment

Part of the explanation for the peculiar "laundry list" variations in the coverage and focus of these categories (from slavery to shape of roof) is that they reflect the content of ethnographic monographs and are intended to facilitate the tabulation of what is available for tabulation. But that is only part of the story. Note also the neglect of the emic/etic distinction. This neglect adversely affects cross-cultural correlation studies that involve such categories as community organization, mode of marriage, family organization, marital residence, exogamy, jurisdictional hierarchy, clan stratification, and caste stratification – all of which exhibit emphatic emic/etic contrasts. Of course, here, too, the categorizations reflect the fuzzy epistemologies of the anthropologists who have contributed to ethnographic knowledge. But this weakness has been compounded in the coding operations Murdock and his associates employ. For example, the code for postmarital residence refers to "normal residence" without distinguishing between normal in the sense of on-the-ground etic averages or normal in the sense of "normative" – i.e., emically agreed to as the proper or ideal form by a majority of those interviewed.

.... [I]t is no accident that cross-cultural survey *theories* also look like open-ended laundry lists. Murdock and his followers have operated under an eclectic research strategy whose characteristic substantive theoretical products are fragmentary, isolated, and mutually opposed generalizations of limited scope. The laundry list of categories out of which such generalizations are constructed both condition and reflect the chaotic nature of the theoretical products of most cross-cultural surveys.

Parsonian Rubrics

In 1950 a group of five anthropologists and sociologists who subscribed to the research strategy of structural-functionalism associated with the work of Harvard sociologist Talcott Parsons ... drew up a list of universal components based on the identification of the "functional prerequisites of a society" (Aberle et al., 1950). The authors specified nine categories as "the generalized conditions necessary for the maintenance of the system":

1. Provision for adequate relationship to the environment and for sexual recruitment
2. Role differentiation and role assignment
3. Communication
4. Shared cognitive orientations
5. Shared articulated set of goals
6. Normative regulation of means
7. Regulation of affective expression
8. Socialization
9. Effective control of disruptive forms of behavior

The logic behind this list is that each item is supposedly necessary to avoid certain conditions which would terminate the existence of any society – namely, the biological extinction or dispersion of its members, the apathy of its members, "the war of all against all," or the absorption of a society by another one. As the proponents of this scheme themselves insisted, their notions about functional prerequisites were integrally linked to their acceptance of Parsons's structural-functionalist research strategy. Structural-functionalism, the most influential strategy in the social sciences in the United States and Great Britain during the period 1940 to 1965, is a variety of cultural idealism, much criticized for its inability to deal with social evolution and political-economic conflict. Its strategic biases are implicit in the preponderance among the alleged functional prerequisites listed above of emic and mental items such as cognitive orientations, shared goals, normative regulation, and affective expressions.

The commitment to the emics of mental life actually extends to the remaining five items as well, however, since in Talcott Parsons's theory of action, every aspect of social life must be approached from the standpoint of the actor's mental goals, thoughts, feelings, and values. The idealist bias here is also painfully evident in the proposal that *shared* cognitive orientations and *shared* articulated sets of goals are functional prerequisites for social survival, when as a matter of fact there is overwhelming evidence to the contrary, not only from complex state societies divided by bitter class, ethnic, and regional conflict, but in very simple societies as well, where sex and age antagonisms bespeak of fundamentally opposed value orientations. Note also the lack of concern with production, reproduction, exchange, and consumption – demographic and economic categories that cannot easily be crammed into "adequate relationship to the environment and sexual recruitment." Production, exchange, and consumption are not merely relationships with the environment; they denote relationships among people as well. Moreover, from retrospective comments made by Parsons (1970), the absence of "economy" in this scheme can only be understood as a visceral rejection of any form of Marxist determinism.

Universal Pattern in Cultural Materialist Strategy

The universal structure of sociocultural systems posited by cultural materialism rests on the biological and psychological constants of human nature, and on the distinction between thought and behavior and emics and etics. To begin with, each society must cope with the problems of production – behaviorally satisfying minimal requirements for subsistence; hence there must be an *etic behavioral mode of production*. Second, each society must behaviorally cope with the problem of reproduction – avoiding destructive increases or decreases in population size; hence there must be an *etic behavioral mode of reproduction*. Third, each society must cope with the necessity of maintaining secure and orderly behavioral relationships among its constituent groups and with other societies. In conformity with mundane and practical considerations, cultural materialists see the threat of disorder arising primarily from the economic processes which allocate labor and the material products of labor to individuals and groups. Hence, depending on whether the focus of organization is on domestic groups or the internal and external relationships of the whole society, one may infer the universal existence of *etic behavioral domestic economies* and *etic behavioral political economies*. Finally, given the prominence of human speech acts and the importance of symbolic processes for the human psyche, one can infer the universal recurrence of productive behavior that leads to etic, recreational, sportive, and aesthetic products and services. *Behavioral superstructure* is a convenient label for this universally recurrent etic sector.

In sum, the major etic behavioral categories together with some examples of sociocultural phenomena that fall within each domain are:

Mode of Production: The technology and the practices employed for expanding or limiting basic subsistence production, especially the production of food and other forms of energy, given the restrictions and opportunities provided by a specific technology interacting with a specific habitat.

Technology of subsistence
Techno-environmental relationships
Ecosystems
Work patterns

Mode of Reproduction: The technology and the practices employed for expanding, limiting, and maintaining population size.

Demography
Mating patterns
Fertility, natality, mortality
Nurturance of infants
Medical control of demographic patterns
Contraception, abortion, infanticide

Domestic Economy: The organization of reproduction and basic production, exchange, and consumption within camps, houses, apartments, or other domestic settings.

Family structure
Domestic division of labor
Domestic socialization, enculturation, education
Age and sex roles
Domestic discipline, hierarchies, sanctions

Political Economy: The organization of reproduction, production, exchange, and consumption

within and between bands, villages, chiefdoms, states, and empires.

Political organization, factions, clubs, associations, corporations
Division of labor, taxation, tribute
Political socialization, enculturation, education
Class, caste, urban, rural hierarchies
Discipline, police/military control
War

Behavioral Superstructure:

Art, music, dance, literature, advertising
Rituals
Sports, games, hobbies
Science

I can simplify the above by lumping the modes of production and reproduction together under the rubric *infrastructure;* and by lumping domestic and political economy under the rubric *structure.* This yields a tripartite scheme:

Infrastructure
Structure
Superstructure

However, these rubrics embrace only the etic behavioral components of sociocultural systems. What about the mental components? Running roughly parallel to the etic behavioral components are a set of mental components whose conventional designations are as follows:

Etic Behavioral Components	Mental and Emic Components
Infrastructure	Ethnobotany, ethnozoology, subsistence lore, magic, religion, taboos
Structure	Kinship, political ideology, ethnic and national ideologies, magic, religion, taboos
Etic superstructure	Symbols, myths, aesthetic standards and philosophies, epistemologies, ideologies, magic, religion, taboos

Rather than distinguish the mental and emic components according to the strength of their relationship to specific etic behavioral components, I shall lump them together and designate them in their entirety as the *mental and emic superstructure*, meaning the conscious and unconscious cognitive goals, categories, rules, plans, values, philosophies, and beliefs about behavior elicited from the participants or inferred by the observer. Four major universal components of sociocultural systems are now before us: the etic behavioral infrastructure, structure, and superstructure, and the mental and emic superstructure.

. . . .

We are now finally in a position to state the theoretical principles of cultural materialism.

The Major Principles of Cultural Materialism

The kernel of the principles that guide the development of interrelated sets of theories in the strategy of cultural materialism was anticipated by Marx (1970 [1859]:21) in the following words: "The mode of production in material life determines the general character of the social, political, and spiritual processes of life. It is not the consciousness of men that determines their existence, but on the contrary, their social existence determines their consciousness." As stated, this principle was a great advance in human knowledge, surely equivalent in its time to the formulation of the principle of natural selection by Alfred Wallace and Charles Darwin. However, in the context of modern anthropological research, the epistemological ambiguities inherent in the phrase "the mode of production," the neglect of "the mode of reproduction," and the failure to distinguish emics from etics and behavioral from mental impose the need for reformulation.

The cultural materialist version of Marx's great principle is as follows: The etic behavioral modes of production and reproduction probabilistically determine the etic behavioral domestic and political economy, which in turn probabilistically determine the behavioral and mental emic superstructures. For brevity's sake, this principle can be referred to as the principle of infrastructural determinism.

The strategic significance of the principle of infrastructural determinism is that it provides a set of priorities for the formulation and testing of theories and hypotheses about the causes of sociocultural phenomena. Cultural materialists give highest priority to the effort to formulate and test theories in which infrastructural variables are the primary causal factors. Failure to identify such factors in the infrastructure warrants the formulation of theories in which structural variables are tested for causal primacy. Cultural materialists give still less priority to exploring the possibility that the solution to sociocultural puzzles lies primarily within the behavioral superstructure; and finally, theories that bestow causal primacy upon the mental and emic superstructure are to be formulated and tested only as an ultimate recourse when no testable etic behavioral theories can be formulated or when all that have been formulated have been decisively discredited. In other words, cultural materialism asserts the strategic priority of etic and behavioral conditions and processes over emic and mental conditions and processes, and of infrastructural over structural and superstructural conditions and processes; but it does not deny the possibility that emic, mental, superstructural, and structural components may achieve a degree of autonomy from the etic behavioral infrastructure. Rather, it merely postpones and delays that possibility in order to guarantee the fullest exploration of the determining influences exerted by the etic behavioral infrastructure.

Why Infrastructure?

The strategic priority given to etic and behavioral production and reproduction by cultural materialism represents an attempt to build theories about culture that incorporate lawful regularities occurring in nature. Like all bioforms, human beings must expend energy to obtain energy (and other life-sustaining products). And like all bioforms, our ability to produce children is greater than our ability to obtain energy for them. The strategic priority of the infrastructure rests upon the fact that human beings can never change these laws. We can only seek to strike a balance between reproduction and the production and consumption of energy. True, through technology we have achieved a considerable capacity to raise and lower productive and reproductive rates. But technology in turn confronts a series of physical, chemical, biological, and ecological laws that likewise cannot be altered and that necessarily limit the rate and direction of technological change and hence the degree of control which can be achieved over production and reproduction by technological intervention in a specific environmental context. Moreover, all such interventions are limited by the level of technological evolution – a level that cannot be altered by an instantaneous act of will – and by the capacity of particular habitats to absorb various types and intensities of techno-economies without undergoing irreversible changes.

Infrastructure, in other words, is the principal interface between culture and nature, the boundary across which the ecological, chemical, and physical restraints to which human action is subject interact with the principal sociocultural practices aimed at overcoming or modifying those restraints. The order of cultural materialist priorities from infrastructure to the remaining behavioral components and finally to the mental superstructure reflects the increasing remoteness of these components from the culture/nature interface. Since the aim of cultural materialism, in keeping with the orientation of science in general, is the discovery of the maximum amount of order in its field of inquiry, priority for theory building logically settles upon those sectors under the greatest direct restraints from the givens of nature. To endow the mental superstructure with strategic priority, as the cultural idealists advocate, is a bad bet. Nature is indifferent to whether God is a loving father or a bloodthirsty cannibal. But nature is not indifferent to whether the fallow period in a swidden field is one year or ten. We know that powerful restraints exist on the infrastructural level; hence it is a good bet that these restraints are passed on to the structural and superstructural components.

To be sure, much attention is now being paid to pan-human neuropsychological "structural" restraints that allegedly oblige human beings to think in predetermined patterns. Later on I shall examine these structuralist claims rather carefully. In the meantime, what needs to be said is that if, as Levi-Strauss claims, the human mind only thinks thoughts that "are good to think," the menu allows for an extraordinary diversity of tastes. No doubt human beings have species-specific patterns of thought – just as we have species-specific patterns of locomotion and body-heat disposal. But how shall we use this fact to account for the tremendous variation in world views, religions, and philosophies, all of which are indisputably equally "good to think"? Structuralists and other varieties of idealists are no more capable of answering this question than they are capable of explaining why human beings, who are naturally terrestrial bipeds, sometimes ride horses and sometimes fly through the air, or why, given a species-specific endowment of sweat glands, some people cool off by sitting in front of air conditioners while others sip hot tea.

The strategic advantage of infrastructural determinism as opposed to structuralism and sociobiology is that the recurrent limiting factors are variables that can be shown to exert their influence in measurably variable ways. This enables cultural materialism to construct theories that account for both differences and similarities. For example, the need to eat is a constant, but the quantities and kinds of foods that can be eaten vary in conformity with technology and habitat. Sex drives are universal, but their reproductive consequences vary in conformity with the technology of contraception, perinatal care, and the treatment of infants.

Unlike ideas, patterns of production and reproduction cannot be made to appear and disappear by a mere act of will. Since they are grounded in nature they can only be changed by altering the balance between culture and nature, and this can only be done by the expenditure of energy. Thought changes nothing outside of the head unless it is accompanied by the movements of the body or its parts. It seems reasonable, therefore, to search for the beginnings of the causal chains affecting sociocultural evolution in the complex of energy-expending body activities that affect the balance between the size of each human population, the amount of energy devoted to production, and the supply of life-sustaining resources. Cultural materialists contend that this balance is so vital to the survival and well-being of the individuals and groups who are its beneficiaries that all other culturally patterned thoughts and activities in which these individuals and groups engage are probably directly or indirectly determined by its specific character. But we do not contend this out of any final conviction that we know what the world is really like; we contend it merely to make the best possible theories about what the world is probably like.

Thought and Behavior

Much of the resistance to cultural materialism stems from what seems to be the self-evident truth that behavior is governed by thought – that human social life is rule-governed.... What puzzles many people is how it can be maintained that behavior determines thought when their own behavior intuitively appears to be an acting out of mental goals and moral precepts. Take the case of technological change, which is so vital to the evolution of culture. In order for cultures to develop stone tools, bows and arrows, digging sticks, plows, ceramics, and machinery, didn't somebody first have to think about how to make such things?

Cultural materialism does not view inventors or any other human beings as zombielike automata whose activities are never under conscious control. In asserting the primacy of the behavioral infrastructure over the mental and emic superstructure, cultural materialism is not addressing the question of how technological inventions and other kinds of creative innovations originate in individuals but rather how such innovations come to assume a material social existence and how they come to exert an influence on social production and social reproduction. Thoughts in the minds of geniuses like Hero of Alexandria, who invented the steam turbine in the third century, or Leonardo da Vinci, who invented the helicopter in the sixteenth century, cannot assume a material social existence unless appropriate material conditions for their social acceptance and use are also present. Furthermore, the recurrence of such inventions as ceramics and metallurgy independently in different parts of the world under similar infrastructural conditions suggests that not even the most original ideas happen only once. Indeed, from the uncanny way in which the invention of the steamship, telephone, airplane, photography, automobile, and hundreds of other patentable devices have been subjected to conflicting claims of priority by independent individuals and laboratories (cf. Kroeber, 1948), the conclusion seems inescapable that when the infrastructural conditions are ripe, the appropriate thoughts will occur, not once but again and again. Furthermore, there is ample evidence to indicate that some of the greatest inventions ever made – for example, agriculture – were known in thought for thousands of years before they began to play a significant role in the infrastructures of prehistoric societies....

The intuition that thought determines behavior arises from the limited temporal and cultural perspective of ordinary experience. Conscious thoughts in the form of plans and itineraries certainly help individuals and groups to find a path through the daily complexities of social life. But these plans and itineraries merely chart the selection of preexisting behavioral "mazeways." Even in the most permissive societies and the richest in alternative roles, the planned actions – lunch, a lovers' tryst, an evening at the theater – are never conjured up out of thin air but are drawn from the inventory of recurrent scenes characteristic of that particular culture. The issue of behavioral versus mental determinism is not a matter of whether the mind guides action, but whether the mind determines the selection of the inventory of culturally actionable thoughts. As Schopenhauer said, "We want what we will, but we don't will what we want." Thus the human intuition concerning the priority of thought over behavior is worth just about as much as our human intuition that the earth is flat. To insist on the priority of mind in culture is to align one's understanding of sociocultural phenomena with the anthropological equivalent of pre-Darwinian biology or pre-Newtonian physics. It is to believe in what Freud called "the omnipotence of thought." Such a belief is a form of intellectual infantilism that dishonors our species-given powers of thought.

Individual Versus Group Selection

It is essential to the task of constructing cultural materialist theories that one be able to establish a link between the behavioral choices made by definite individuals and the aggregate responses of sociocultural systems. One must be able to show why one kind of behavioral option is more likely than another not in terms of abstract pushes, pulls, pressures, and other metaphysical "forces," but in terms of concrete bio-psychological principles pertinent to the behavior of the individuals participating in the system.

Another way to phrase this imperative is to assert that the selection processes responsible for the divergent and convergent evolutionary trajectories of sociocultural systems operate mainly on the individual level; individuals follow one rather than another course of action, and as a result the aggregate pattern changes. But I don't mean to dismiss the possibility that many sociocultural traits are selected for by the differential survival of whole sociocultural systems – that is, by group selection. Because intense intergroup competition was probably present among early human populations, provision must be made for the extinction of systems that were bio-psychologically satisfying to the individuals concerned, but vulnerable to more predatory neighbors, with a consequent loss of certain cultural inventories and the preservation and propagation of others.

However, such group selection is merely a catastrophic consequence of selection operating on or through individuals. Cultural evolution, like biological evolution, has (up to now at least) taken place through opportunistic changes that increase benefits and lower costs to individuals. Just as a species does not "struggle to survive" as a collective entity, but survives or not as a consequence of the adaptive changes of individual organisms, so too do sociocultural systems survive or not as a consequence of the adaptive changes in the thought and activities of individual men and women who respond opportunistically to cost-benefit options. If the sociocultural system survives as a result of patterns of thought and behavior selected for on the individual level, it is not because the group as such was successful but because some or all of the individuals in it were successful. Thus a group that is annihilated in warfare can be said to have been selected for as a group, but if we want to understand why it was annihilated, we must examine the cost-benefit options exercised by its individual members relative to the options exercised by its victorious neighbors. The fact that some people sincerely act in order to help others and to protect the group does not alter this situation. Saints and heroes sacrifice their lives for the "good" of others. But the question of whether the others accept or reject that "good" remains a matter of the balance of individual costs and benefits. Society does not live by saints alone. Altruism, to be successful, must confer adaptive advantages on those who give as well as on those who take.

This is not to say that the direction of cultural change in the short run can be predicted by summing up what is the greatest good for the greatest number of people. Obviously there are many innovations which are bio-psychologically more satisfying to some members of a society than to others. Purdah, the veiling of women in Moslem societies, facilitates domestic and political control by men over women. Presumably the bio-psychological rewards of purdah are greater for men than for women – indeed, one might say that for the women there are severe penalties. But the men have the power to make their own well-being weigh more heavily in the balance of advantages and disadvantages than the well-being of women. The more hierarchical the society with respect to sex, age, class, caste, and ethnic criteria, the greater the degree of exploitation of one group by another and the less likely it is that the trajectory of sociocultural evolution can be calculated from the average bio-psychological utility of traits. This leads to many puzzling situations in which it appears that large sectors of a society are acting in ways that diminish their practical well-being instead of enhancing it. In India, for example, members of impoverished menial castes avidly uphold the rule of caste endogamy and insist that marriages be legitimized by expensive dowries. Abstractly, it would appear that the members of such impoverished castes would be materially better off if they practiced exogamy and stopped insisting on big marriage payments. But the victims of the caste system cannot base their behavior on long-term abstract calculations. Access to such menial jobs as construction worker, toddy-wine maker, coir maker, and so forth depends on caste identity validated by obedience to caste rules In the lower castes if one fails to maintain membership in good standing one loses the opportunity to obtain work even of the most menial kind, and plunges still further into misery. To throw off the weight of the accumulated privileges of the upper castes lies entirely beyond the practical capacity of those who are at the bottom of the heap; hence, perverse as it may seem, those who benefit least from the system ardently support it in daily life.

Bio-Psychological Constants

The danger in postulating pan-human bio-psychological drives and predispositions is that one is tempted to reduce all sociocultural similarities to an imaginary genetic "biogram" ...., whereas most similarities as well as differences are due to sociocultural evolutionary processes ... [T]he most important observation that one can make about the human biogram is that it is relatively free from species-specific bio-psychological drives and predispositions. As a species we have been selected for our ability to acquire elaborate repertoires of socially learned responses, rather than for species-specific drives and instincts. Nonetheless, without postulating the existence of selective principles operating at the bio-psychological level, one cannot explain how infrastructure mediates between culture and nature.

It is better to begin with a minimal set of human bio-psychological selective principles than with one that tries to render a complete account of what it is to be human. Hence I shall list only four:

1. People need to eat and will generally opt for diets that offer more rather than fewer calories and proteins and other nutrients.
2. People cannot be totally inactive, but when confronted with a given task, they prefer to carry it out by expending less rather than more energy.
3. People are highly sexed and generally find reinforcing pleasure from sexual intercourse – more often from heterosexual intercourse.
4. People need love and affection in order to feel secure and happy, and other things being equal, they will act to increase the love and affection which others give them.

My justification for this list is that its generality is guaranteed by the existence of similar bio-psychological predispositions among most members of the primate order. You may wish to postulate that human beings also naturally seek to create music and art, to dichotomize, to rationalize, to believe in God, to be aggressive, to laugh, to play, to be bored, to be free, and so forth. By succumbing to the temptation to open this list to all nominations, you will rapidly succeed in reducing every recurrent cultural trait to the status of a biological given. But the adequacy of the list must be judged by the adequacy of the theories it helps to generate. The more parsimonious we are about granting the existence of bio-psychological constants, the more powerful and elegant will be the network of theories emanating from sociocultural strategies. Our object is to explain much by little.

Despite the parsimony of my list, everyone can immediately think of antithetical behaviors and thoughts. For the first, there is obesity, voluntary starvation, vegetarianism, and self-inflicted dietary pathology. For the second, there is the intensive expenditure of energy in sports and artistic performance. For the third, there is abstinence, homosexuality, masturbation. And for the fourth, there is infanticide, domestic strife, and exploitation. However, the existence of these apparently contradictory patterns is not necessarily fatal to the scheme as proposed. Nothing in the statement of pan-specific bio-psychological principles indicates that selection acting through the preferences of individuals will in the long term contribute to the maximization of anticipated results. On the contrary, the selection of maximizing traits recurrently leads to ecological depletions. Thus the pursuit of more proteins frequently ends up with people getting fewer proteins; the adoption of labor-saving devices ends up with people working harder; the escalation of male sexual activity leads to a systemic shortage of women; and greater affective bonding transmuted by politics leads to greater exploitation of one class by another. These paradoxes do not invalidate the list of universals nor falsify the principles of cultural materialism; they merely expose the puzzles that cultural materialism proposes to solve more effectively than rival strategies.

Mode of Production and Relations of Production

No general agreement exists as to what Marx meant by infrastructure or the mode of production (Legros, 1979). While he distinguished between the relations and the forces of production, both of these concepts involve fatal ambiguities ... Marx left the problem of objectivity unresolved. Lacking the concepts of emic and etic operations and indiscriminately mixing mental and behavioral phenomena, he bequeathed a heritage of Hegelian dialectical double talk now being pushed to extremes by new-wave Marxists. .... I do not believe it is possible to divine what Marx really meant by the mode of production, nor what components he intended to put into it or take out of it.

As a cultural materialist, I hold that infrastructure should consist of those aspects of a sociocultural system which enable one to predict a maximum number of additional components up to the behavior of the entire system if possible. I have therefore removed certain key aspects of what many Marxists mean by "relations of production" from infrastructure to structure and superstructure. The classic Marxist concept of "ownership of the means of production," for example, denotes differential access to the technology employed in subsistence production and hence is an organizational feature of structure rather than a part of infrastructure. The strategic significance of this departure is that I think it is possible to explain the evolution of the ownership of means of production as a dependent variable in relation to the evolution of demography, technology, ecology, and subsistence economy. It would seem futile to object to the removal of ownership from infrastructure until it can be shown that such an explanation cannot be achieved.

Similarly, I view patterns of exchange – e.g., reciprocity, redistribution, trade, markets, employment, money transactions – not as infrastructure but partly as etic structural components – aspects of domestic and political economy – and partly as emic and mental superstructural components. Once again, the justification for this decision lies in the hope that patterns of exchange can be predicted from a conjunction of more basic variables.

Clearly, some aspects of ownership and exchange will never be predicted simply from a knowledge of the demographic, technological, economic, and environmental components. There are whole universes of phenomena concerning ownership and exchange in price-market settings, for example, which must be approached by means of the categories and models by which economists describe and predict monetary inputs and outputs, capital investments, wages and prices, and so forth. Let me emphatically renounce any pretension that all economic events and processes can be understood as mere reflexes of the modes of production and reproduction. Remember that cultural materialism asserts the strategic priority of etic and behavioral conditions and processes over emic and mental conditions and processes, and of infrastructural over structural and superstructural conditions and processes, but it does not deny the possibility that emic, superstructural, and structural components may achieve a degree of autonomy from the etic infrastructure. Rather, it merely postpones and delays that possibility in order to guarantee the fullest exploration of the determining influences exerted by the infrastructure. To regard price values, capital, wages, and commodity markets as

structure and superstructure rather than infrastructure and to accord them a *degree* of autonomy in determining the evolution of contemporary sociocultural systems is not to reverse or abandon the strategic priorities of cultural materialism. The principles of cultural materialism remain applicable. These principles direct attention to the predominance of the behavioral etics of exchange over the mental emics of exchange, and to the role of the etic behavioral infrastructure in determining the conditions under which price-making markets and money economies have come into existence. Indeed, cultural materialism cannot be reconciled with classical Marxist interpretations of the inner dynamics of capitalism precisely because Marx accorded the essentially emic mental categories of capital and profits a predominant role in the further evolution of modern industrial society, whereas from the cultural materialist perspective the key to the future of capitalism lies in the conjunction of its etic behavioral components and especially in the feedback between political economy and the infrastructure. ....

The Modes of Reproduction and Production

Cultural materialist principles also depart radically from classical Marxism in regarding the production of children as part of the infrastructure. I believe that this departure is necessary in order to explain why modes of production undergo changes that result in systemic transformations and divergent and convergent evolution. Marx attempted to explain the change from one mode of production to another by relying on the Hegelian idea that social formations during the course of their existence develop internal contradictions that are at once the cause of their own destruction and the basis for the emergence of new social formations.

According to Marx, modes of production evolve through the development of contradictions between the means of production and the relations of production. "At a certain stage of their development the material forces of production in society come in conflict with the existing relation of production." That is, the relations of production (as, for example, private ownership and the profit motive) hold back the provision of material satisfactions; they become "fetters" on the production process. They are destroyed and replaced by "higher" relations of production (for example, communal ownership) that permit a more ample expression of the potential of the means of production (an economy of abundance instead of scarcity).

In Marx's dialectic of history no less than in Hegel's, each epoch or social formation is urged onward toward its inevitable negation by an uncanny teleological thrust. For Hegel, it was the growth of the idea of freedom; for Marx, the development of the forces of production. In order for Marx's contradiction between forces and relations to provide the motive force of a sociocultural evolution faithful to Hegel's vision of a spiritualized cosmos dialectically negating itself into a heavenly utopia, the mode of production must tend toward maximum realization of its power over nature. As Marx put it: "No social order ever disappears before all the productive forces for which there is room in it have been developed" (1970 [1859]: 21). Why should one expect this to be true?

I believe that demographic factors help to explain the historic expansion of productive forces. Hence, the necessity arises for speaking of a "mode of reproduction" whose effect upon social structures and ideology is no less important than that of the mode of production.

Anthropologists have long recognized that in broadest perspective cultural evolution has had three main characteristics: escalating energy budgets, increased productivity, and accelerating population growth. (1) Over the long haul the amount of energy per capita and per local system has tended to increase. Cultures at the band level of development used less than 100,000 kilocalories per day; cultures at the level of tropical forest slash-and-burn farming villages, used about a million per day; neolithic mixed dry-farming villages, about 2 million per day; the early irrigation states of Mesopotamia, China, India, Peru, and Mesoamerica about 25 billion per day and modern industrial superstates over 50 trillion per day. (2) Production efficiency, measured as energy output per unit of human labor has also increased, rising, for example, from about 10 to 1 among hunters and gatherers to 20 to 1 among swidden farmers to 50 to 1 among irrigation agriculturalists. (3) And human population has increased. There was a global density of less than 1 person per square mile in 10,000 B.C. Today there are over 65 persons per square mile. Settlements grew from 25 to 50 persons per band; 150 to 200 per slash-and-burn vil-

lage; 500 to 1,500 per neolithic mixed farming village. By 200 B.C. there were more people living in the great preindustrial oriental empires than in all the world ten thousand years earlier.

Why should all three of these factors have increased in unison? Marx never really confronted this question because like Malthus he implicitly assumed that population growth was inevitable. Modern anthropological and archaeological findings, however, don't support this assumption. During as many as two or three million years, hominid populations probably remained stationary or fluctuated within rather narrow limits. Why should population ever have begun to increase? It cannot be argued that it increased as a result of technological progress and rising standards of living. Two additional major evolutionary trends negate such an interpretation. First, despite the increase in technological efficiency, numbers of hours per capita devoted to subsistence increased rather than decreased, reaching a peak with the industrial wage labor system of nineteenth-century capitalism. Second, substantial decrements in quality of life measured in terms of nutritional intake, health, and longevity can be linked to population growth.

In other words, cultures have not generally applied the increments in techno-environmental efficiency brought about by the invention and application of "labor-saving devices" to saving labor but to increasing the energy throughput, which in turn has not been used to improve living standards but to produce additional children. This paradox cannot be explained by the development of class stratification and exploitation, since it was also characteristic of classless societies and was if anything a cause rather than a consequence of the evolution of the state. ....

The solution to the problem of why new and more effficient modes of production produced people rather than reduced labor and/or increased per capita consumption lies in the methods employed by premodern societies to limit population growth. Malthus correctly perceived that the mode of reproduction throughout the preindustrial epoch was dominated by malign population-regulating techniques involving severe forms of psycho-biological violence and deprivation. It is true that relatively benign techniques were also available, principally homosexuality, coitus interruptus, delayed marriage, postpartum sexual abstinence, masturbation, and prolonged lactation. But these measures alone or in combination in historically or ethnographically ascertainable frequencies cannot account for the remarkably slow (.0007 percent to .0015 percent per annum) rate of increase prior to the neolithic, nor for the less than .056 percent rate between the neolithic and the emergence of the first states (Carneiro and Hilse, 1966; Coale, 1974; Kolata, 1974; Van Ginneken, 1974). Additional means of regulation must be invoked to account for the small size of the human global population prior to 3,000 B.C. in view of the inherent capacity of healthy human populations to double their numbers in less than twenty-five years (Hassan, 1973). I believe that these additional measures involved assault against mother and fetus with whole body-trauma abortifacients, infanticide (especially female infanticide), and systematic selective nutritional neglect of infants, especially of female infants and of preadolescent girls (Divale and Harris, 1976; Polgar et al., 1972; Birdsell, 1968; Devereux, 1967). With mode of production held constant, and an average of only four births per woman, almost 50 percent of the females born must be prevented from reaching reproductive age if a population initially in reasonably good health is not to suffer severe cutbacks in the quality of life in a very short time. This exigency constitutes a great determining force of prehistory.

Before the development of the state, infanticide, body-trauma abortion, and other malign forms of population control predisposed cultures which were in other respects adjusted to their habitats to increase production in order to reduce the wastage of infants, girls, and mothers. In other words, because prehistoric cultures kept their numbers in line with what they could afford by killing or neglecting their own children, they were vulnerable to the lure of innovations that seemed likely to allow more children to live. Thus Malthus was correct in his surmise that population pressure exerted an enormous influence on the structure of pre-state societies (cf. Dally, 1971).

It has lately been established that pre-state populations generally stop growing when they reach as little as one-third of the maximum carrying capacity of their techno-environmental situation (Lee and Devore, 1968; Casteel, 1972). As we shall see, this has been interpreted by structural Marxists and others as a refutation of the importance of Malthusian forces. Yet no such interpretation is warranted until the nature of the restraints on population growth has been clarified. As I have just said, the evidence indicated that slow rates of population growth were achieved only at great psycho-biological costs through infanticide, abuse, and neglect. This means that even societies with constant or declining populations may be experiencing severe population pressure – or better said, severe reproductive pressure.

The payment of Malthusian costs may account for many specific features of pre-state societies. The most important of these is warfare. Malthus correctly identified warfare as one of the most important checks on population, but he misunderstood the conditions under which paleotechnic warfare occurred and how it functioned to control population growth. He also overestimated the influence of combat deaths upon the rate of growth of modern societies. Pre-state warfare probably does not regulate population through combat deaths but through its effect on the sex ratio, encouraging people to rear maximum numbers of males and minimum numbers of females. Thus pre-state warfare occurs not simply as an aberration caused by the failure of the mode of production to provide adequate subsistence – a view Marx (1973 [1857-58]:607-608) surprisingly enough shared with Malthus. Warfare also occurs as a systemic means of slowing population growth, conserving resources, and maintaining high per capita levels of subsistence. (As for state-level warfare, it is not a check on population but an incentive for rapid population increase and resource depletion. ....)

The inadequacy of Marx's treatment of what I have called the mode of reproduction resulted from his contemptuous dismissal (1857-58; 1973:606) of the works of the "baboon"[2] Malthus. Marx's rejection of Malthus was motivated by Malthus's contention that no change in political economy could eliminate poverty (cf. Meek, 1971). But one can recognize the importance of the mode of reproduction in determining the course of sociocultural evolu-

2   Among the other characterizations reserved for Malthus: "plagiarist by profession," "shameless sycophant," "a bought advocate."

tion without endorsing Malthus's reactionary view of history. By rejecting the totality of Malthus's work Marx cut his followers off from collaborating in the development of a theory of human demography and ecology without which the divergent and convergent transformations of modes of production and their corresponding superstructures cannot be understood. There is no more important aspect of production than reproduction – the production of human beings. While there are structural and superstructural aspects to the modes of population control, the central issue has always been the challenge the biology of sexual reproduction presents to culturally imposed restraints. In this sphere, as in subsistence production, technological advances are of the greatest import, the only difference being that for production it is the means of increase that is decisive, while for reproduction, it is the means of decrease that is decisive. The failure to accord the development of the technology of population control a central role in the evolution of culture does great damage to the credibility of both classical and new-wave Marxist principles and theories.

If it is objected that much of what I have been saying about the relationship between production and reproduction is speculative and in need of further empirical tests, I surely agree. But the fact that an important original and coherent set of testable theories ... can be formulated by including the mode of reproduction in the infrastructure is a cogent reason for doing so, even though the theories themselves need to be tested by further research.

The Role of Structure and Superstructure

One common criticism of cultural materialism is that it reduces structure and superstructure to mechanical epiphenomena that play only a passive role in the determination of history. From this, critics infer that cultural materialism is a doctrine of political and ideological apathy and inaction. One might very well wish to question the value of a research strategy which holds that political and ideological struggle are futile because the outcome is determined exclusively by the infrastructure. However, the strategy of cultural materialism is incompatible with any such conclusion. Then what precisely is the role of structure and superstructure in the causal determinations anticipated by cultural materialist strategy?

As I have said in previous sections, infrastructure, structure, and superstructure constitute a sociocultural system. A change in any one of the system's components usually leads to a change in the others. In this regard, cultural materialism is compatible with all those varieties of functionalism employing an organismic analogy to convey an appreciation of the interdependencies among the "cells" and "organs" of the social "body."

The conceptualization of the interrelationships in question can be improved by introducing a distinction between system-maintaining and system-destroying interdependencies. The most likely outcome of any innovation – whether it arises in the infrastructure, structure, or superstructure – is system-maintaining negative feedback, the dampening of deviation resulting either in the extinction of the innovation or in slight compensatory changes in the other sectors, changes which preserve the fundamental characteristics of the whole system. (For example, the introduction of progressive federal income taxes in the United States was followed by a series of privileged exemptions and "shelters" that effectively dampened the movement toward eliminating extremes of wealth and poverty.) However, certain kinds of infrastructural changes (for example, those which increase the energy flow per capita and/or reduce reproductive wastage) are likely to be propagated and amplified, resulting in positive feedback throughout the structural and superstructural sectors, with a consequent alteration of the system's fundamental characteristics. Cultural materialism denies that there is any similar class of structural or superstructural components whose variation leads as regularly to deviation amplification rather than to negative feedback.

The causal priority of infrastructure is a matter of the relative probability that systemic stasis or change will follow upon innovations in the infrastructural, structural or superstructural sectors. Cultural materialism, unlike classical structural-functionalism, holds that changes initiated in the etic and behavioral modes of production and reproduction are more likely to produce deviation amplifications throughout the domestic, political, and ideological sectors than vice versa. Innovations initiated in the etic and behavioral structural sectors are less likely to produce system-destroying changes; and innovations arising in the emic super-structures are still less likely to change the entire system (due to their progressively remote functional relationships with the crucial infrastructural components). To take a familiar example: during the late 1960s many young people believed that industrial capitalism could be destroyed by a "cultural revolution." New modes of singing, praying, dressing, and thinking were introduced in the name of a "counterculture." These innovations predictably had absolutely no effect upon the structure and infrastructure of U.S. capitalism, and even their survival and propagation within the super-structure now seems doubtful except insofar as they enhance the profitability of corporations that sell records and clothes.

Nothing in this formulation of the probabilistic outcome of infrastructural changes warrants the inference that structure or superstructure are insignificant, epiphenomenal reflexes of infrastructural factors. On the contrary, structure and super-structure clearly play vital system-maintaining roles in the negative feedback processes responsible for the conservation of the system. Productive and reproductive processes are functionally dependent on etic domestic and political organization, and the entire etic conjunction is functionally dependent on ideological commitments to values and goals that enhance cooperation and/or minimize the costs of maintaining order and an efficient level of productive and reproductive inputs. It follows from this that ideologies and political movements which lessen the resistance to an infrastructural change increase the likelihood that a new infrastructure will be propagated and amplified instead of dampened and extinguished. Furthermore, the more direct and emphatic the structural and superstructural support of the infrastructural changes, the swifter and the more pervasive the transformation of the whole system.

In other words, although I maintain that the probability is high that certain kinds of changes in the modes of production and reproduction will change the system, I also maintain that functionally related changes initiated simultaneously in all three sectors will increase the probability of systemic change. Indeed, it would be irrational to assert that ideological or political struggle could not enhance or diminish the probability of systemic changes involving all three sectors. But the crucial question that separates cultural materialism from its rivals is this: to what extent can fundamental changes be propagated and amplified by ideologies and political movements when the modes of production and reproduction stand opposed to them? Cultural materialism holds that innovations are unlikely to be propagated and amplified if they are functionally incompatible with the existing modes of production and reproduction – more unlikely than in the reverse situation (that is, when there is an initial political and ideological resistance but none in the modes of production and reproduction). This is what cultural materialists mean when they say that in the long run and in the largest number of cases, etic behavioral infrastructure determines the nature of structure and superstructure.

To illustrate, let us consider the relationship between procreative ideologies, domestic organization, and the mode of production in the United States. When there was an agrarian homesteading, frontier infrastructure, families were large and women's roles as mother and unpaid domestic laborer were emphasized. With urbanization and the increasing cost of reproduction relative to benefits expected from children, women began to "raise their consciousness," demanding entrance to the general employment market on an equal basis with males. Clearly the consciousness-raising process has been an important instrument for liberating women from the role of domestic drudge. But one cannot argue that political-ideological struggle by women was responsible for the vast shifts in technology, production, demand for cheap labor, rise of cities, and increased costs of rearing children, and so forth – all of which provide the functional infrastructural conditions upon which the propagation and amplification of modern feminist political-ideological struggle is premised. In order to grasp the asymmetrical nature of the causal relationships between superstructure and infrastructure, let us suppose that somewhere isolated groups of men are beginning to engage in ideological and political struggle aimed at the revival of nineteenth-century sex roles. Can one assert that the decisive factor in their success or failure will be their commitment to their goal – their degree of political-ideological struggle? Scarcely, because in effect their viewpoint is not likely to be propagated or amplified as long as the present urban industrial infrastructure holds sway.

On the other hand, cultural materialism does not propose that goals will be achieved regardless of whether people struggle consciously to achieve them. Conscious political-ideological struggle is clearly capable of sustaining, accelerating, decelerating, and deflecting the direction and pace of the transformational processes initiated within the infrastructure.

The fear that infrastructural determinism deprives people of the will to engage in conscious struggle is based on an entirely false understanding of the status of politically and ideologically relevant cultural materialist theories. Infrastructure is not some simple, transparent, single-factor "prime mover"; rather, it is a vast conjunction of demographic, technological, economic, and environmental variables. Its description and analysis require enormous amounts of research whose results can only be presented as tentative and probabilistic theories and hypotheses. While some alternative political-ideological courses of action can be dismissed as virtually impossible, several alternative courses of action may appear to be supported by theories and hypotheses to which decisively different degrees of certainty cannot be assigned. Where equally probable alternative cultural materialist theories hold sway – as is often the case – the outcome of political ideological struggle will appear to be decisively influenced by the degree of commitment of the opposing factions and parties....

To sum up: cultural materialist theories may invoke different degrees of infrastructural causation ranging from virtual certainty to virtual indeterminacy. Along this entire range, structural and superstructural commitments appear to shape the final outcome through negative and positive feedback processes, in inverse relationship to the ability of existing theories to identify the infrastructural determinants.

Some people assert that by upholding the primacy of the infrastructure, cultural materialism contributes to the "dehumanization" of the social sciences. To this I would reply that failure to attempt an objective analysis of the relationship between infrastructure and a particular set of political-ideological goals serves only those who benefit from the wanton waste of other people's lives and possessions. Self-deception and subjectivity are not the measures of being human. I do not accept the moral authority of obscurantists and mystics. They cannot take away the humanity of people who want to understand the world as well as to change it....

Marvin Harris, *Our Kind*

(Source: Marvin Harris. *Our Kind: Who We Are, Where We Came From, Where We Are Going.* New York: Harper and Row, 1989, 126-128, 180-183, 190-191, 194-196, 216-221, 224-227, 230-233.)

When natural selection had brought the body, brain, and behavior of our ancestors to cultural takeoff, culture itself began to evolve, according to its own principles of selection and with its own patterns of order and disorder, chance and necessity. During the ensuing 35,000 years, natural selection continued to shape and adapt the human body to levels of solar radiation, heat, cold, altitude, and nutritional stress encountered in different habitats. But these changes cannot possibly account for the immense differences between the cultural repertories of modern industrial societies and those of prehistoric times. To understand the relationship between Marshack's Paleolithic serpentine punch marks and the key strokes of a personal computer, theories based on natural selection are useless and fundamentally misleading. We who build and use computers are inherently no smarter than the Ice Age observers who possibly watched and recorded the phases of the moon. Nothing in our genes tells our brains to use floppy disks rather than burins and stone plaques. Nor is there anything in our genes that tells us to live in a high-rise apartment rather than in the mouth of a cave or to get our meat from herds of Black Angus cattle rather than from herds of wild horses. We have floppy disks and domesticated animals because there was cultural selection for these items, not because there was natural selection for them.

Let me try to clarify the distinction. Natural selection acts upon changes in the hereditary program contained within the molecules of DNA located inside the nucleus of the body's cells. If the changes in the program and the physical and behavioral traits that they control result in a higher net rate of reproduction for the individuals in whom they appear, then the changes will be favored in succeeding generations and will become part of a population's genetic program.

How does cultural selection take place? As a result of natural selection, our bodies possess a number of specific urges, needs, instincts, limits of tolerance, vulnerabilities, and patterns of growth and decay, which, in sum, roughly define what one means by human nature. Human cultures are organized systems of socially learned behavior and thought that satisfy or attend to the demands and potentialities of human nature. Cultural selection is human nature's servant. It works by preserving and propagating behavior and thoughts that more effectively satisfy the biological and psychological demands and potentials of individuals in a given group or subgroup. During the course of social life, there is a continuous stream of variations in the way individuals think and behave, and these variations are continuously tested for their ability to increase or decrease well-being. This testing or screening may proceed with or without a conscious weighing of costs and benefits by individuals. The important point is that some variations turn out to be more beneficial than others and are preserved and propagated within the group (or subgroup) and across generations, while other variations that turn out to be less beneficial are not preserved or propagated.

Once cultural takeoff has occurred and cultural selection is operating at full force, differential reproductive success ceases to be the means by which variations in behavior and thought are selected for or propagated. In order for calendars, domesticated cattle, or floppy disks to be favored by cultural selection, there does not have to be any increase in the rate of reproductive success of the individuals who invent and propagate these traits. Some great cultural inventions, in fact, increase well-being, satisfy human nature, and are selected for precisely because they reduce rates of reproductive success – contraceptives, for example. Reproductive success does not serve as drive or appetite for cultural selection because such a drive or appetite is not part of human nature (a point that I'll discuss at greater length later on). Of course, if cultural selection results in a continuously falling rate of reproduction, it will eventually lead to the extinction of the population whose well-being it is serving. But this outcome has no bearing on the question of whether cultural selection must, like natural selection, always operate to *increase* rates of reproductive success. As I will

emphasize later on, human reproductive behavior during the past 300 years becomes utterly unintelligible if one subscribes to the currently fashionable sociobiological axiom that our kind always strives to maximize the number of children and close relatives in succeeding generations. In a post-takeoff human population, rates of reproductive success may rise or fall depending on whether high or low rates satisfy the urges, needs, instincts, limits of tolerance, vulnerabilities, and other known biopsychological components of human nature. When people do strive to maximize their reproductive success, it is not because they are driven by irresistible longings for numerous progeny but because under certain circumstances having numerous progeny leads to having more sex, leisure, food, wealth, allies, support in old age, or other benefits that enhance the quality of life.

My next step, then, will be to identify the components of human nature that test and screen for particular patterns of behavior and thought. Despite vaunted powers of speech and consciousness, our kind's great cultural adventures remain tethered to the mundane conditions imposed by our specific humanity. If somewhere in the universe there are intelligent armor-plated asexual social creatures made of silicon who are energized by photovoltaic receptors and reproduce by fission, I am sure that they are given neither to painting reindeer on cave walls nor to pushing carts up and down the aisles of supermarkets.

....

Natural selection has designed a simple but extravagant method for getting human sperm and egg together on the three days that count. It has endowed us with sexual needs and appetites so strong that people are predisposed to tolerate, if not to crave, sex every day of the month, every day of the year over a span of many years. This takes the guesswork out of the reproductive shell game: To find out where the prize is hidden, we turn over all the shells. Need I add that this doesn't mean that men automatically have erections as soon as they encounter women nor that women will be receptive to any man who solicits sexual intercourse. As we all know, both men and women possess a considerable degree of latitude in regard to whom they solicit and whom they reject or accept as well as when, where, and how often. But the essential point is that for both men and women, sex is an intensely pleasurable experience and there are no physiological or hormonal barriers to having it one or more times a day every day of the year, at least from adolescence to middle age. And it is this astonishing shotgun approach to hitting a three-day target that humans, even more than pygmy chimpanzees, use as a substitute for the precisely aimed rifle fire of species that copulate primarily only when the ovum is there to be hit.

Despite a voluminous ejaculate, human sperm counts are smaller than those of many other primate species, and the percentage of motile sperm is also unusually low. But this is a murky and somewhat alarming subject because studies show that human sperm and motility counts have sharply declined since 1950, possibly as a result of chemical pollution of air, food, and water. In all other respects, humans are one of the sexiest species in the animal kingdom. The human penis is longer and thicker than that of any other primate, and the testes are heavier than in a gorilla or orang. Our kind spends more time in precopulatory courtship, and copulatory sessions last longer than among other primates. The capacity for female orgasm, while not unique to humans as once thought, is highly developed. Copulatory frequency is not as high as among chimpanzees, but then again humans confront the greatest amount of socially imposed restrictions on sexuality. These restrictions lead to peculiarly human nocturnal emissions among males – wet dreams – and to rates of masturbation among both human males and females that are matched only in primates kept in zoos or laboratories. The human male's psychological preoccupation with sex has no parallel in other species. American adolescents aged twelve to nineteen report thinking about sex on average every five minutes during their waking hours, and even at age fifty, American males think about sex several times a day. How did this peculiar pattern of sexuality originate?

Since we have no direct knowledge of the reproductive cycles and mating patterns of afarensis or habilis, this question has to be approached by looking for possible antecedents or "models" in the behavior of pygmy chimps. The relentless economizing of natural selection makes it unlikely that the pygmy chimp's sexual extravagances are merely there to add zest to life. There must be some repro-

ductive payoff that compensates them for their wasteful approach to hitting the ovulatory target. Could it be that this payoff consists of a more intense form of social cooperation between males and females? And could this in turn lead to a more intensely cooperative social group, a more secure milieu for rearing infants, and hence a higher degree of reproductive success for sexier males and females?

Certain contrasts between the social organization of the common chimpanzees and the pygmy chimps support this interpretation. As I said a while back, chimpanzee sexual swellings are associated with promiscuous mating and heightened male tolerance of females and infants. Among common chimpanzees, these mating patterns are further associated with loose, shifting coalitions of adult males who receive visits from sexually receptive females and their infants. About a third of the time, common chimps can be found in these multimale groups temporarily accompanied by females and infants. Another third of the time they live in smaller groups consisting only of adults of both sexes. And during the rest of the time they either live in groups that contain only females and infants or only males. In contrast, the pygmy chimpanzees have a far more integrated form of social organization. They spend three-quarters of the time in groups containing adults of both sexes, juveniles, and infants and can seldom be found in all-male groups or in female-and-infant groups without adult males. In sum, several adult males and their progeny remain close to each other most of the time, traveling, eating, grooming, copulating, and resting together.

I believe that it is plausible to conclude that the intense sexuality of pygmy chimps was selected for because it intensified the solidary bonds among males and females and their progeny. Common chimps have also moved in this direction by their promiscuous matings and their substitution of sperm competition for direct aggression. But since their copulatory behavior is regulated by the tumescence and detumescence of their sexual swellings, mothers (and young) were frequently separated from fathers and from the help that fathers might render in feeding and in protecting mothers and infants. Pygmy chimp females, with their virtually permanent sexual swellings and their continuous sexual receptivity, are in a much better position to receive male support for themselves and their infants.

My theoretical expectation is borne out by another remarkable feature of pygmy chimp social life. Males do in fact regularly share food with females and with young. This applies both to the small animals that they occasionally capture and to certain large fruits that are handed back and forth. Sueshi Karoda of the Laboratory of Physical Anthropology of Kyoto University reports that there is a clear tendency for dominant pygmy males to share food more frequently than dominant common chimpanzee males. Females often approach dominant males to take or beg food. Juveniles also frequently take or beg food from dominant males. Subordinate males tend to be less generous. If they come into possession of a prized fruit such as a pineapple, they try to climb up to a secluded spot. But dominant males are often surrounded by beggars and compelled to share food. Among common chimpanzees, females seldom share food with anyone except their infants; in contrast, among pygmy chimps, females frequently share food with adult members of their group as well as with infants. While both common and pygmy chimp females obtain prized food by begging with their outstretched arm, pygmy females do something seldom observed among any other species, except humans. They precede their begging, or dispense with it entirely, by copulating with the individual who possesses the desired food. Karoda gives these examples: "A young female approached a male, who was eating sugar cane. They copulated in short order, whereupon she took one of the two canes held by him and left. In another case a young female persistently presented to a male possessor, who ignored her at first, but then copulated with her and shared his sugar cane." And females do not restrict themselves to exchanging sex for food with males. Females precede nearly half of all food-sharing incidents with other females with a bout of genitogenital rubbing initiated by the supplicant.

All this new information about pygmy chimpanzees has revolutionary implications for our understanding of the probable forms of social life adopted by the earliest hominids....

....

Giving and taking, or exchange, is the glue that holds human societies together. The primordial form of exchange is the giving and taking of services as embodied in copulation: sex for sex. Primates also take turns carefully picking parasites and dirt from each other's hair and skin, another example of the exchange of a service for a service. But beyond the transfer of milk from mother to infants, or of ejaculate to vagina, the exchange of service for *goods* seldom occurs. The pygmy chimps are the big exception, for, as I emphasized a while back, female pygmy chimps exchange sex for food. And this has momentous implications, for it suggests how afarensis and habilis could have achieved unprecedented levels of social cooperation that prepared them for group life on the perilous savannas. With more regular exchanges of sex for food, females would have been able to obtain a significant part of their food supply from male consorts. Moreover, as females competed for the attention of productive and generous males, they would inevitably discover the well-known path that lies through a male's stomach, and fed him with a choice morsel of their own – ants and termites or a big tuber, perhaps (regrettably, I can't say that it was an apple).

The bonding effects of the exchange of goods for goods increase if each party gives the other something the other wants but doesn't have. Since we already have seen that, among common chimps, males obtain meat more often than females, but females obtain insects more often than males, there is every likelihood that afarensis and habilis males and females engaged in similar kinds of exchanges – probably insects and plant foods obtained by females for morsels of scavenged or hunted meats obtained by males. An inevitable effect of increasing the volume and types of exchange would be the establishment of partnerships among subsets of male and female givers and takers. Individuals could afford to give sexual services indiscriminately to everyone in the troop – they had more than enough of that to give – but they could not afford to give food indiscriminately, since food was far more limited than sex. Partnerships that concentrated food exchanges in two or three groups smaller than the troop as a whole, would have constituted the protocultural beginnings of families. Yet to prevent the permanent dissolution of the troop, some degree of exchange between these protofamilies had to be maintained. Within and between protofamilies, givers had to have confidence that the flow would be reversed, not necessarily with an equal return, nor immediately, but to some degree, from time to time. Otherwise they would stop giving.

Let me point out that none of the steps in the process of building social complexity through exchange relationships presupposes close genetic control over give-and-take response. Our ancestors were no more born to "truck and barter," as Adam Smith and other classical economists believed, than they were born to make hand axes and digging sticks. The expansion of the sphere of exchange beyond the prototypical give-and-take of copulation and mutual grooming required that a simple behavioral relationship be generalized: Afarensis and habilis had merely to learn that if they gave to those from whom they took, they could take again. But generalizing this rule to satisfy more needs and drives to encompass more individuals and longer delays between taking and giving, all the while keeping track of the balance in each "account," does presuppose major advances in memory, attention, and general intelligence. Truly complex exchanges and institutions would have had to await the evolution of language, with its capacity to formalize long-term rights and obligations implicit in each individual's history of giving and taking goods and services.

But once cultural takeoff had been passed, exchange relationships could evolve rapidly into different kinds of economic transactions: gift exchange, barter, trade, redistribution, taxation, and eventually buying and selling, salaries, and wages. And to this day it is exchange that binds people into friendships and marriages, creates families, communities, and higher order political and corporate bodies. By iterations and recursions, by permutating and combining different rewards appropriate to different drives and needs, by spinning fantastically complex webs connecting individuals to individuals, institutions to institutions, and groups to groups, exchange was destined to make our kind not merely the most intensely sexual creatures on earth, but the most intensely social as well.

....

I *would like* to be able to say more about what kind of mating system and family organization prevailed during the formative phases of hominid social life. Over the entire span of four or five million years that separate us from the first afarensis, there is not a simple piece of hard evidence bearing on this question. And the record is equally blank when it comes to post-takeoff Stone Age sapiens hunter-gatherers. This lack of evidence has not deterred various scholars from attempting to identify the form of mating to which all hominids are supposedly innately predisposed. Much popular support can always be found for those who insist the first humans were monogamous and that they lived in troops or bands composed of several nuclear families, each in turn consisting of a mated pair and their children. The logic behind this view is that human sexuality with its personalized, eye-to-eye, frontal orientation naturally leads to strong bonds between one man and one woman. Such pair-bonds supposedly provide the best assurance that human infants will be fed and nurtured during their long period of dependency. Some anthropologists like to round out this scenario by postulating a connection between monogamy and the existence of a home base. Wife and child supposedly stay near the home base while husband/father goes off to hunt at a greater distance, returning at night to share the catch.

While I agree that exchanges of food and sex would lead to the development of stronger bonds between some males and some females, I do not know why these would have to be exclusive pair-bonds. What about contemporary mating patterns? Do they not show that alternative modes of mating and family organization are perfectly well suited to the task of satisfying human sexual needs and rearing human children? Polygyny is an ideal in more societies than is monogamy. And it occurs among foraging societies as well as among state-level societies. Moreover, as a result of the high frequency of divorce, of keeping mistresses and concubines, and having "affairs," most ideologically monogamous societies are behaviorally polygamous. Let's be realistic. One of the fastest growing forms of family in the world today is the single parent family headed by a woman. Sexual practices that go along with this family often correspond to a form of polyandry (one female, several males). In U.S. central cities and throughout much of South America, the Caribbean islands, and urbanizing parts of Africa and India, women have temporary or visiting mates who father the woman's children and contribute marginally to their support.

In view of the frequent occurrence of modern

domestic groups that do not consist of, or contain, an exclusive pair-bonded father and mother, I cannot see why anyone should insist that our ancestors were reared in monogamous nuclear families and that pair-bonding is more natural than other arrangements.

I am equally skeptical about the part of the pair-bond theory that postulates a primordial home base tended by homebody females whose males roamed widely in search of meat. It seems to me much more likely that afarensis and habilis males, females, and infants moved together across the land as a troop and that females who were not nursing took an active part in dispersing scavengers, combating predators, and in pursuing prey animals. My evidence? Women marathon runners. Competing against men in grueling twenty-six-mile races, they are steadily closing the gap between male and female winners. In the Boston Marathon, the women's record of 2:22:43 is only 9 percent off the men's record. This is scarcely the kind of performance of a sex whose ancestors stayed home minding the babies for two million years.

What I have just been saying should not be taken to mean that our presapiens forebears never formed monogamous pair-bonds. The point is simply that they were no more likely than modern-day humans to have mated and reared children according to a single plan. Given an ability to mediate potentially disruptive social arrangements by exchanging services for goods, goods for goods, and goods for services, our presapiens ancestors could have adopted mating and childrearing systems as diverse as the systems that exist today or that existed in the recent past.

We know that modern-day mating and childrearing systems are constantly adjusting to levels of technological competence, population density, deployment of males and females in production, and local environmental conditions. Polygyny prevails, for example where there is an abundance of land and a shortage of labor so that men can become prosperous by adding additional wives and children to their households. These conditions often occur in newly occupied lands, as among the Mormons of Utah, for whom polygyny was a means of establishing control over a vast and sparsely settled region in the American West. At the opposite extreme, polyandry represents an adjustment to extreme scarcity of resources. It occurs in Tibet, where agricultural land is so scarce that two

or three brothers are willing to share one wife in order to limit the number of heirs to their jointly owned farmland. Monogamy seems to prevail at intermediate levels of population pressure and land scarcity. Many other factors may be relevant in particular cases. Ecclesiastical and political policies, themselves rooted in particular conditions, may enjoin one or another mating system ... [O]ne need merely consider the changes taking place in marriage and childrearing in industrial societies to realize that it is cultural selection and not closely controlling genetic predispositions that accounts for today's high rates of divorce, declining fertility rates, and an increase in people living alone. Nor does it account for the strange new high-tech forms of making babies by uniting ovum and sperm in a laboratory dish and planting the conspectus in a biological or surrogate mother's uterus.

In sum, each of these variations is as "natural" as the other, since each represents a socially constructed pattern of mating dictated by prevailing social and natural conditions, rather than by specific genetic instructions. It is certainly human nature to have a powerful sex drive and appetite, and it is certainly human nature to be able to find diverse ways of satisfying these species-given needs and appetites. But it is not human nature to be exclusively promiscuous or polyandrous or monogamous or polygynous.

....

Modern-day industrial-age parents have forgotten just how useful children can be around the house. But in other times and cultures, adults knew that if they didn't manage to rear a certain number of children, life would be extremely harsh. Despite the situation that prevails in industrial societies, children have almost always been expected to "earn their keep" in a material sense ...

In preindustrial farm families, children start to do household chores when they are still toddlers. By age six, they help gather firewood and carry water for cooking and washing; take care of younger siblings; plant, weed, and harvest crops; grind and pound grains; peel and scrape tubers; take food to adults in the fields; sweep floors; and run errands. By puberty, they are ready to cook meals, work full-time in the fields, make pots, containers, mats, and nets, and hunt, herd, fish, or do almost anything that adults do, although somewhat less efficiently. Studies carried out among Javanese peasant families by anthropologist Benjamin White show that boys of twelve to fourteen years of age contribute thirty-three hours of economically valuable work per week and that girls nine to eleven contribute about thirty-eight hours. Altogether, children perform about half of all work done by household members. White also found that Javanese children themselves do most of the work needed to rear and maintain their siblings, freeing adult women to engage in income-producing tasks. Meade Cain, a researcher for the Population Council, came to similar conclusions about the benefits of child labor in rural Bangladesh. Male children begin to produce more than they consume by age twelve. By age fifteen they have already made up for all the years during which they were not self-supporting.

In past eras, children became more valuable as parents grew older and lost the physical strength to support themselves by hunting, foraging, or farming. Aging parents in Third World countries cannot rely on company pension funds, social security payments, welfare allotments, food stamps, or bank accounts; they can rely only on their children.

The faster children pass from consuming more than they produce to producing more than they consume, the greater the number of children parents will strive to bring up. But in seeking to take full advantage of their offspring's potential contribution to parental well-being, couples must allow for the fact that even if they make a total commitment to rearing each child born, some will unavoidably fall victim to injuries and diseases at an early age. Consequently, couples commonly "overshoot" the targeted ideal and increase the number of births in proportion to the rates of infant and child mortality. In rural India, for example, studies have shown that many couples consider three children to be optimal, but knowing that more than one out of three children born will die before reaching adulthood, they will not use contraceptives or other means of separating sex from reproduction until after they have had four or five children. This is why one need not fear that efforts to reduce infant and child mortality will lead to a worsening of the population problem. Healthier babies generally mean fewer babies per couple. But one cannot expect that lowering infant and child mortality rates will actually lower the rate of population growth since, if nothing else changes, couples will still aim at having the same number of living children.

Third World parents also take into account the different kinds of costs and benefits that can be expected from rearing male children versus female children. Where men make a more critical contribution to agricultural production than women, Third World couples prefer to rear boy babies rather than girl babies ... [B]rute strength frequently accounts for the preference. Although men are only marginally stronger than women, marginal differences in productivity can mean life or death. The preference for boys is especially strong where hard-packed soils must be prepared with a hand-held plow and a pair of reluctant yoked animals. This is true of wheat-growing north India, where peasant couples set their sights on rearing at least two boys to maturity and are quite happy not to have any daughters at all. But to ensure survival of at least two males, they must "overshoot" for three. And since in all probability some births will be female, they can easily go through five or six births before they achieve their target of three survivable sons. In southern India and most of Southeast Asia and Indonesia, the principal crop is not wheat but rice. Plowing rice paddies takes second place to "puddling" – walking animals around in the mud – while the most critical operations are transplanting and weeding, both of which tasks women can perform as well as men. In these regions parents are not biased against female children and rear as many girls as boys ...

Any reduction of the value of child labor in agriculture can be expected to depress the rate of childrearing. If, at the same time, the expected economic returns from parental investment in children can be increased by sending them to school and training them to get white-collar jobs, birth rates may fall very rapidly. Parents, in effect, substitute a strategy of rearing only a few well-educated but potentially well-paid and influential children for a strategy of raising a lot of poorly educated farm hands. Numerous case studies support this conclusion, but I'll give one key example. In the 1960s, Harvard University researchers selected a village called Manupur, located in the state of Punjab in northwest India, as the site of a project that aimed at reducing reproduction rates by providing contraceptives and vasectomies. In a follow-up study, Mahmood Mamdani reported that the villagers had no trouble accepting the idea of family planning, but they accepted sterilization and contraceptives only after they had reached their target of two survivable males. "Why pay 2,500 rupees to an extra [hired] hand?" they wanted to know. "Why not have a son?" Fifteen years later, researchers returning to Manupur were astonished to find that women were using contraceptives to achieve substantial reductions in birth rates and that the number of sons desired per couple had fallen considerably. The underlying reason for this shift was that after the first study had been completed, the villagers became involved in a number of technological and economic changes that made the Punjab one of India's most developed states. The increased use of tractors, irrigation wells, chemical weedkillers, and kerosene cooking stoves had greatly reduced the value of children as farm hands. Children were no longer needed to take the cattle to pasture, weed the crops, or collect cattle dung to provide cooking fuel. At the same time, Manupur villagers were becoming aware of opportunities for employment in commercial and governmental firms and offices. They needed to acquire new literacy and mathematical skills just to run their mechanized and bank-financed farm operations. Many parents now want to keep their children in school rather than have them contribute manual labor. As a result, high school enrollment rose from 63 percent to 81 percent for boys and from 29 percent to 63 percent for girls. And Manupur's parents now want at least one son to have a white-collar job so that the family will not be entirely in agriculture; many even plan to send sons and daughters to college.

There is an interesting resemblance between rates of reproduction among disadvantaged ethnic and racial minorities and those of Third World countries. In both cases, it appears as if people are being driven to have more children than they can afford to rear, and at the expense of parental well-being. But I doubt if this is what is really going on. In the United States, for example, it seems as if inner-city women get pregnant over and over again in reckless disregard for their own futures. Yet I think that the key to this situation is not that they cannot control their sexuality but that by getting pregnant they become entitled to welfare subventions that substantially raise the net benefits of rearing children over the net benefits that nonwelfare women of their class can expect from their pregnancies. In

New York City, having a child entitles a welfare mother to monthly support payment, housing subsidies, free medical care, and educational benefits. Ghetto mothers also receive support from a wide network of kin and temporary husbands. And ghetto children, unlike middle-class children, begin to pay for their keep in their teens with incomes derived from part-time jobs, petty theft, and drug sales. Furthermore, inner-city welfare women want sons almost as badly as Indian families want them. Studies conducted by Jagna Sharff in the Lower East Side of Manhattan show that mothers need sons for protection against thieves, muggers, and hostile neighbors. And with homicide the principal cause of death among young ghetto males, ghetto mothers, like Indian farmers, must "overshoot" their target if they want this protection. Given the generally dismal prospects that ill-educated ghetto women confront when they try to compete with educated middle-class women for jobs and status, they are probably no worse off having three or four children than having one or two. Certainly they are better off, on the average, having one or two children than having none, in the circumstances in which they find themselves.

Of course, the life to which these children are condemned guarantees the perpetuation of an underclass at great expense and moral shame to the rest of society. But the irrationality of the system does not lie at the level of the individual ghetto mother. It is not she who created the ineffectual educational system, the lack of good jobs, or the cancer of racial discrimination. It is not her fault that she is paid more to have children than not to have them. The examples I have been discussing show that parents adjust their investment in childrearing to bring about improvements in the net contribution that children make to their well-being. Therefore, one can predict whether reproductive rates will go up or down without taking into consideration the effect that a particular adjustment will have on the overall rate of reproductive success. All one has to know is whether the parents' biopsychological needs, drives, and appetites under the particular circumstances are better served by having more or fewer children. Yet the possibility remains that natural selection has somehow been able to ensure that any adjustments up or down in rearing children that humans may make in conformity with principles of cultural selection will also always maximise overall reproductive success in conformity with principles of natural selection. What is needed to break this impasse is evidence that downward changes in numbers of children reared per woman often unambiguously lower rather than raise the overall rates of reproductive success. This evidence lies close at hand.

....

Recent demographic events in modernizing parts of the Third World such as the Punjab strongly resemble the great changes in reproduction rates that marked transitions from agrarian to industrial societies in the nineteenth and twentieth centuries. As in Manupur, shifting costs and benefits associated with childrearing account for the lowered reproduction rates that have come to prevail in advanced industrial societies east and west. Why? Because industrialization raised the cost of rearing children. Skills essential for earning a living took longer to acquire. So parents had to wait longer before they could receive any economic benefits from their offspring. At the same time, the whole pattern of how people earned their living changed. No longer did family members work on the family farm or in the family shop. Instead, they earned wages as individuals in factories and offices. The return flow of benefits from rearing children came to depend on their willingness to help out in the medical and financial crises that beset parents in old age. But longer life spans and spiraling medical costs now make it increasingly unrealistic for parents to expect such help from their children. Industrial nations have no choice but to substitute old-age and medical insurance and retirement homes for the preindustrial system in which children took care of their aged parents. No wonder that in many industrial nations the fertility rate has fallen below the 2.1 children per woman needed to prevent a population from shrinking. Further transformation of industrial economies from the production of goods to service-and-information production is exacerbating this trend. Since modern middle-class couples will not rear children unless both husband and wife have incomes, marriages are being postponed. Late-marrying couples are aiming at only one child, and more and more young people are refusing to invest in the traditional forms of familial and sexual togetherness.

Over the entire course of this transition from large to small families, high rates to low rates of rearing children, and high rates to low rates of population growth, the standard of living of the working and middle classes has steadily improved. With the exception of certain ethnic and racial minorities, more people today enjoy access to more of the basic necessities of life, such as food and shelter, and to a wider variety of luxuries, such as entertainment and travel, than people did 200 years ago. It is therefore surely incorrect to insist that the postponement of marriage, the delay in having children, and the decline in birthing from over four per mother or more early in the last century to two per mother or less today is nature's way of assuring that reproduction is maximized. When young people in the full flush of fecundity invest in college and graduate school rather than in nurseries, buy stereo televisions, gourmet meals, and $20,000 sports cars rather than bassinets, baby food, and $20 strollers, and don't have children until they reach their thirties, one can safely conclude that they are responding to something other than a naturally selected tendency to rear as many children as they possibly can.

It looks as if those who can have the most children are having the fewest. To test for this inverse relationship, the demographer Daniel Vining compared the number of children fathered by white men listed in *Who's Who* with the average number of children of same-age white women in the population as a whole. Starting with the cohort born from 1875 to 1879, Vining found that the average number of children born to the nation's most educated and successful males has generally been substantially lower than the average per woman. When white women born in 1875 were having 3.50 children, the *Who's Who* male was having only 2.23 children. For the cohort born from 1935 to 1939, the ratio was 2.92 to 2.30. Vining obtained a similar result for men listed in the Japanese *Who's Who*. Over a span of almost one century, Japan's most educated and esteemed men had only about 70 percent of the number of children that the average woman in the same cohort had.

Today's service-and-information middle classes are scarcely the first humans to exhibit a preference for children that is inversely related to the resources available for rearing them. In nineteenth century India, for example, the most lopsided ratios of young males to young females occurred among the

Rajputs and other highranking military and land-owning castes. As reported by British officials, the rajahs of Mynpoorie, the crème de la crème of Rajput aristocracy, systematically killed off every one of their female heirs: "Here when a son, a nephew, a grandson was born to the reigning chief, the event was announced to the neighboring city by the large discharge of wall-pieces and matchlocks; but centuries had passed away and no infant daughter had been known to smile within those walls."

Sociobiologists have attempted to deal with the puzzle of female infanticide among elite castes by arguing that wealthy and powerful parents actually have more offspring even if they rear only males. The logic is that each elite male can have sex with scores of women and father scores of children, while daughters are limited to no more than a dozen or so pregnancies no matter how many men they have sex with. So by rearing sons instead of daughters, elite parents are maximizing their reproductive success. But if the reproductive behavior of the rajahs of Mynpoorie had really been selected for its contribution to reproductive success, children born to daughters would have been a welcome addition to those born to sons, because being the crème de la crème, the rajahs could easily afford to provide the necessities of life for daughters as well as sons.

Cultural selection, not natural selection, accounts best for the practice of elite female infanticide. The root of it is the struggle on the part of elite men to keep their lands and other sources of wealth and power from being divided among too many heirs. It was not reproductive success that governed their behavior, but a refusal to give up the luxurious style of life to which they had grown accustomed. Having lots of children with concubines, mistresses, and courtiers did not pose a threat to the Rajputs because these children could not back up a claim to a share of the estate with a threat of force. But sisters and their male children did pose such a threat because their husbands would have been high-caste Rajputs themselves, capable of demanding a portion of the estate. By destroying their daughters and sisters, the Rajput elites were employing one extreme of a continuum of strategies all of which aimed at preventing the dispersal of wealth and power among females and their descendants. The most common solution was to preempt a woman's claim to landed wealth by having her husband accept a payment in jewels, gold, silk, or cash, known as a dowry, in lieu of any future claims on the estate. To this day in northern India, reluctance to pay dowry for daughters or sisters results in high rates of indirect female infanticide and lopsided ratios of boys to girls. The Rajputs simply took the next step, eliminating the need to pay any dowry by refusing to have any female infants....

I do not see how we can avoid concluding that our kind is by nature just as likely to act in ways that reduce rates of reproductive success as to act in ways that increase it. When having more children increases their biopsychological well-being, people will have more children; when having fewer children increases their biopsychological well-being, people will have fewer children. Let us not be confused by the fact that throughout most of history and prehistory, modes of production were such as to be more likely to reward those who rear large numbers of children. With industrialization, this likelihood was reversed. Large numbers of children became an obstacle to maximizing parental biopsychological well-being. And so people generally chose to have fewer children. To insist that having few or even no children is actually a strategy that leads to greater reproductive success at some future date is to render inexplicable one of the most fundamental features of modern life. There are a billion people in the world today who crave a second income, a second car, and a second house more than they crave a second child. Cultural selection not natural selection, has brought us to this point, and cultural and natural selection will get us to another, whatever it may be.

....

If rates of making babies depended exclusively on their contribution to satisfying parental needs for air, water, food, sex, bodily comfort, and security, fertility rates in Japan and the industrialized West would have dropped to zero by now. On a strictly dollars-and-cents basis, modern-day parents have virtually no hope of recouping their expenditures for day schools and kindergartens, baby sitters and pediatricians, stereos and designer jeans, summer camps and orthodontists, music lessons and encyclopedias, tricycles, bicycles, and cars, and college tuition. Not to mention room and board for eighteen years. Add it all up and you have a bill that's over $200,000. And that does not include the cash value of the services parents render while nursing, bathing, diapering, and burping their little one or the bills for sleepless nights and jangled nerves the next day. Here again, one might be tempted to see the selfish gene at work, compelling people to reproduce like salmon leaping upstream, no matter what the cost to themselves. But biological parents are not the only ones who are prone to rearing children at great expense. How are we to explain the heavy demands placed on adoption agencies and the thriving black market where desperate couples pay cash for babies? Why should adopted children, who have no genetic relationship to their foster parents, be raised with the same extravagant care that parents lavish on "their own flesh and blood"?

I see no way to answer these questions other than to postulate the existence of another biopsychological component of human nature. Children fulfill exceptionally well not a parental need to reproduce, but a need for close, affectionate, emotional relationships with supportive, concerned, trustworthy, and approving beings. In short, we need children because we need to be loved. A long series of studies initiated by Harry Harlow and associates in the 1950s provided experimental evidence that primates brought up in isolation, but otherwise well cared for, quickly turn into the equivalent of human nervous wrecks. Fortunately, no one has tried raising human babies in solitary confinement to see how they react to a lack of companionship and emotional support, but plenty of evidence from clinical psychology shows that people who have been deprived of parental affection during their early years have difficulty functioning as adults. Up until the late 1980s, the standard policy with regard to premature infants placed in incubators was to touch them as little as possible. Through the work of psychologist Tiffany Field, it was found that premature infants who received a gentle massage for fifteen minutes three times a day gained weight 47 percent faster and were ready to leave the hospital six days earlier than infants who were not massaged. After eight months massaged infants were still heavier than the others and outperformed their unmassaged agemates on tests of mental and motor ability. But love is not selfless; it requires an exchange just like every other human bond. And in the support parents lavish on children

there is a culturally instructed expectation that a balance will be struck with the love and affection that children can be so good at giving in return....

I cannot see how the crazy emotions and hormonal juices that flow after a child is born can explain why reproductive rates have not dropped closer to zero. It is the decision taken nine or more months before the child is born, to remove carefully maintained barriers against conception, that needs to be explained. Faced with twenty years of economic hara-kiri and not so much as a zygote to stir the hormonal brew, the aspiring parents could only be committing themselves to parenthood because they have been nudged culturally to believe that children will help them to solve their need for love.

And let me not forget to point out that in a society whose interpersonal relations are dominated by laissez-faire individualism and ruthless competition for wealth and status, whose hostile streets are filled with crime and neighbors who are afraid to say hello, and where next of kin and best friends are scattered over the face of the earth, the hunger for affection runs very strong. Since couples also suffer from the isolation and alienating effects of consumerism and an impersonal bureaucratic workplace, let me add as an additional inducement for becoming a parent the anticipation that a baby will help us give each other the love we crave.

Why the bleary-eyed and besotted couple submit to their baby's insatiable demands seems evident. Committed to building a temple of love in an indifferent and unloving world, it does not take more than a crumb or two for us to renew our faith in the love to come. Even in their least giving mood, babies respond with warm, wet sucking and mouthing; they grasp your fingers and try to put their arms around you. Already you can anticipate the ardent hugs and kisses of early childhood, the tot who clings to your neck, the four-year-old tucked in bed, whispering "I love you," the six-year old breathless at the door or running down the path as you come home from work. And with a little more imagination you can see all the way to a grateful son or daughter, dressed in cap and gown, saying, "Thanks, Mom and Dad. I owe it all to you."

The fact that many rewards of parenthood are delayed does not mean that dreams rule the economy of love. As in every other kind of exchange, mere expectation of a return flow will not sustain the bonds indefinitely. The family sanctuary is a fragile temple. People will not forever marry and have children no matter how far the actual experience departs from expectation. Contemporary society has much to fear from growing numbers of couples who argue over rather than delight in their progeny, and from children, themselves corrupted by the social conditions that make the need for love so strong, who metamorphose into monsters with a single mission, to take all and give nothing, not even a belch or a fleeting instant of eye contact. Rising divorce rates suggest that these cruel disappointments are spreading. If so, prepare for the state to intervene. Society needs children even if sexually active adults do not. I wonder how far away we are from corporations chartered to rent the wombs of surrogate mothers to fill targets set by a Bureau of Procreation. Will there also be a choice of surrogate children for those who cannot or will not get a license to raise real human babies? Already any number of pet owners will be glad to tell you that they get as much love from their cats or dogs as others get from people and at less monetary and emotional expense as well.

Bibliography

Aberle, D.F., A.K. Cohen, A.K. Davis, M.J. Levy, Jr., and F.X. Sutton. "The Functional Prerequisites of a Society." *Ethics* 60, 1950, 100-111.

Adams, Richard N. "Natural Selection, Energetics, and 'Cultural Materialism,'" *Current Anthropology*, 22, no. 6, 1981, (with comments by Donald T. Campbell, et al. and Adams' replies).

Birdsell, Joseph. "Some Predictions for the Pleistocene Based on the Equilibrium Systems among Recent Hunter-gathers." In R. Lee and I. DeVore, eds., *Man the Hunter*. Chicago: Aldine, 1968, 229-249.

Carneiro, Robert, and D. Hilse. "On Determining the Probable Rate of Population Growth during the Neolithic." *American Anthropologist* 68, 1966, 177-181.

Casteel, Richard. "Two Static Maximum Population Density Models for Hunter-Gatherers: A First Approximation." *World Archaeology* 4(1), 1972, 19-40.

Coale, Ansley. "The History of the Human Population." *Scientific American* 231(3), 1974, 41-51.

Dally, Herman. "A Marxian Malthusian View of Poverty and Development." *Population Studies* 25, 1971, 25-38.

Devereux, George. "A Typological Study of Abortion in 350 Primitive, Ancient, and Pre-Industrial Societies." In H. Rosen, ed., *Abortion in America*. Boston: Beacon Press, 1967, 95-152.

Divale, W., and M. Harris. "Population, Warfare, and the Male Supremacist Complex." *American Anthropologist* 78, 1976, 521-538.

Fisher, Lawrence, and O. Werner. "Explaining Explanation: Tension in American Anthropology." *Journal of Anthropological Research* 34, 1978, 194-218.

Hassan, Ferki. "On Mechanisms of Population Growth During the Neolithic." *Current Anthropology* 14, 1973, 535-542.

Kolata, Gina. "!Kung Hunter-Gatherers: Feminism, Diet and Birth Control." *Science* 185, 1974, 932-934.

Kroeber, Alfred. *Anthropology*. New York: Harcourt Brace Jovanovich, 1948.

Lee, Richard, and Irwin DeVore, eds. *Man and the Hunter*. Chicago: Aldine, 1968.

Lee, Richard, and Irwin DeVore, eds. *Kalahari Hunter-Gatherers: Studies of the Kung San and Their Neighbors*. Cambridge: Harvard University Press, 1976.

Legros, Dominique. "Chance, Necessity, and Mode of Production: A Marxist Critique of Cultural Evolutionism." In James Silverberg, ed., *Mode of Production*. New York: Queens College Press, 1979.

Magnarella, P. J. "Cultural Materialism and the Problem of Probabilities," *American Anthropologist*, 84 (1982).

Marx, Karl. *A Contribution of the Critique of Political-Economy*. New York: International Publishers, 1970.

Marx, Karl. *Grundrisse: Foundations of the Critique of Political Economy*. Martin Nicolaus, trans. New York: Vintage, 1973.

Meek, Ronald. *Marx and Engels on the Population Bomb*. Berkeley: Ramparts Press, 1971.

Murdock, George. *Ethnographic Atlas*. Pittsburgh: University of Pittsburgh Press, 1967.

Murphy, Martin F., and Maxine L. Margolis, eds.

Science, Materialism, and the Study of Culture. Gainesville: University Press of Florida, 1995.

Parsons, Talcott. "On Building Social Systems Theory: A Personal History." *Daedalus* 99, 1970, 826-881.

Pike, K.L. *Language in Relation to a Unified Theory of the Structure of Human Behavior*, 2nd ed. The Hague: Mouton, 1967.

Polgar, Steven, et. al. "Population History and Population Policies from an Anthropological Perspective." *Current Anthropology* 13, 1972, 202-215.

Van Ginneken, J.K. "Prolonged Breastfeeding as a Birth-Spacing Method." *Studies in Family Planning* 5, 1974, 201-208.

Western, Drew. "Cultural Materialism: Food for Thought or Bum Steer?" *Current Anthropology* 25 (1984).

Whorf, Benjamin. *Language, Thought, and Reality.* New York: Wiley, 1956.

Wissler, Clark. *The Relation of Nature to Man in Aboriginal America.* New York: Oxford University Press, 1926.

ACKNOWLEDGEMENTS

Part One

from *Nicomachean Ethics*, Aristotle, trans. Terence Irwin, 1985. Reprinted by permission of Hackett Publishing Co., Inc.

Part Two

from *Selected Writings of St. Thomas Aquinas*, Robert P. Goodwin, 1983. Reprinted by permission of Prentice-Hall, Inc., Upper Saddle River, NJ.

from *On Free Choice of Will: Augustine*, trans. Anna S. Benjamin, 1964. Reprinted by permission of Prentice-Hall, Inc., Upper Saddle River, NJ.

from *Religion Within the Limits of Reason Alone*, Immanuel Kant, trans. Theodore M. Greene and Hoyt H. Hudson, 1934. Reprinted by permission of Open Court Publishing Company, a division of Carus Publishing.

from *A Testament To Freedom: The Essential Writings of Dietrich Bonhoeffer*, ed. Geffrey B. Kelly and F. Burton Nelson, 1995. Reprinted by permission of HarperCollins Publishers, Inc.

Part Three

from *Sketch for a Historical Picture of the Progress of the Human Mind*, Antoine-Nicolas de Condorcet, trans. June Barraclough, 1955 Weidenfeld and Nicolson. Reprinted by permission of Weidenfeld and Nicolson.

from *The Limits of State Action*, Wilhelm von Humbolt, trans. J.W. Burrow 1969 by Cambridge University Press. Reprinted by permission of Cambridge University Press.

from *Political Liberalism*, John Rawls, 1993 by Columbia University Press. Reprinted by permission of Columbia University Press.

Part Four

from *For the New Intellectual*, Ayn Rand, 1961 by Ayn Rand. Reprinted by permission of Dutton Signet, a division of Penguin Books USA, Inc.

from *Rationalism in Politics*, Michael Oakeshott, 1962 by Methuen and Company. Reprinted by permission of Prof. William Letwin.

Part Five

from *Discourse on the Origins of Inequality (Second Discourse). Polemics and Political Economy*, Jean-Jacues Rousseau, 1992 by the Trustees of Dartmouth College. Reprinted by permission of the University Press of New England.

from *Philosophy of Right*, G.W.F Hegel, trans. T.M. Knox. 1942 Oxford University Press. Reprinted by permission of Oxford University Press.

from *On the Genealogy of Morals and Ecce Homo*, Nietzsche, trans. Walter Kaufmann & R.J. Hollingdale, 1967 Random House, Inc. Reprinted by permission of Random House, Inc.

Part Six

from *Sociobiology: The New Synthesis*, Edward O. Wilson, 1975 by the Presidents and Fellows of Harvard College. Reprinted by permission of Harvard University Press.

Part Seven

from *Civilization and its Discontents*, Sigmund Freud, Sigmund Freud Copyrights, The Institute of Psycho-Analysis and The Hogarth Press for permission to quote from *The Standard Edition of the Complete Psychological Works of Sigmund Freud*, translated and edited by James Strachey. "Two Encyclopeaedia Articles," Sigmund Freud, Sigmund Freud Copyrights, The Institute of

Psycho-Analysis and The Hogarth Press for permission to quote from *The Standard Edition of the Complete Psychological Works of Sigmund Freud*, translated and edited by James Strachey.

Part Eight

from *Man a Machine and Man a Plant*, Julien Offray de La Mettrie, trans. Richard Watson and Maya Rybalica, 1994. Reprinted by permission of Hackett Publishing Co., Inc.

from *Behaviorism*, John B. Watson, 1924, 1925 by the People's Institute Publishing Company. 1930 by W.W. Norton & Company, Inc., renewed 1952, 1953, 1958 by John B. Watson. Reprinted by permission of W.W. Norton & Company, Inc.

from *The Ways of Behaviorism*, John B. Watson, 1928, Harper and Brothers, renewed 1956 by John B. Watson. Reprinted by permission of HarperCollins Publishers, Inc.

from *Artificial Intelligence in Psychology: Interdisciplinary Essays*, Margaret A. Boden, 1989 by Margaret A. Boden. Reprinted by permission of The MIT Press.

from *Consciousness Explained*, Daniel C. Dennett, 1991 by Daniel C. Dennett. Reprinted by permission of the author and Little, Brown and Company.

Part Nine

from *The Second Sex*, Simone De Beauviour, trans. by H.M. Parshley, 1952 and renewed 1980 by Alfred A. Knopf Inc. Reprinted by permission of Alfred A. Knopf.

from *The Second Sex* by Simone De Beauviour, trans. by H.M. Parshley, 1952 . Reprinted by permission of the Estate of Simone de Beauviour and Jonathan Cape.

from *Psychoanalysis and Feminism*, Juliet Mitchell, 1974 by Juliet Mitchell. Reprinted by permission of Pantheon Books, a division of Random House, Inc.

from *The Longest Revolution: Essays on Feminism, Literature Psychoanalysis*, by Juliet Mitchell, 1984. Reprinted by permission of Juliet Mitchell and Rogers, Coleridge and White Ltd.

from *In a Different Voice*, Carol Gilligan, 1982 by Carol Gilligan. Reprinted by permission of Harvard University Press.

from *Reasonable Creatures*, Katha Pollitt, 1994 by Katha Pollitt. Reprinted by permission of Alfred A. Knopf, Inc.

Part Ten

from *Existentialism and Humanism*, Jean-Paul Sartre, translation and introduction by Philip Mairet, 1973. Reprinted with permission of Routledge, Ltd.

from *Sexual Personae*, Camille Paglia, 1991 by Yale University Press. Reprinted by permission of Yale University Press.

Part Eleven

from *Cultural Materialism*, Marvin Harris, 1979 by Marvin Harris. Reprinted by permission of Random House.

The Editor would also like to acknowledge the University of Saskatchewan for generous support for the production of this volume.